Achievements of the Left Han
Essays on the Prose of John M

Michael Lieb and
John T. Shawcross, Editors

This first and only collection of essays
concerned exclusively with Milton's
prose brings together the ideas of scholars
of Milton and the seventeenth century,
crowning the canon of Milton scholarship
with a much-needed consideration of this
facet of his writing.

The original essays include "The Theo-
logical Context of Milton's *Christian
Doctrine*" (William B. Hunter, Jr.);
"The Images of Poet and Poetry in Milton's *The Reason of Church-Government*" (John F. Huntley); "The Higher
Wisdom of *The Tenure of Kings and
Magistrates*" (John T. Shawcross); and
"Logic and the Epic Muse: Reflections
on Noetic Structures in Milton's Milieu"
(Walter J. Ong, S.J.). Other contributors
are Joseph Anthony Wittreich, Jr., Michael
Lieb, Edward S. Le Comte, Florence Sandler, Austin Woolrych, and Harry Smallenburg. A substantial appendix, "A Survey
of Milton's Prose Works," makes available information, much of it new, on
texts, dates of composition, and influences.

Achievements of the
Left Hand

Achievements of the Left Hand: Essays on the Prose of John Milton

Edited by Michael Lieb
and John T. Shawcross

The University of Massachusetts Press

Amherst

Library of Congress Catalog Card Number 73-79506
ISBN Number 0-87023-125-1
Printed in the United States of America
University of Massachusetts Press
Amherst, Massachusetts 01002
Publication of this book has been financially assisted
by the American Council of Learned Societies under
a grant from the Andrew W. Mellon Foundation.

Contents

Preface   vii

JOSEPH ANTHONY WITTREICH, JR.
"The Crown of Eloquence": The Figure of the Orator in Milton's
Prose Works   3

MICHAEL LIEB
Milton's *Of Reformation* and the Dynamics of Controversy   55

JOHN F. HUNTLEY
The Images of Poet and Poetry in Milton's *The Reason of Church-
Government*   83

EDWARD S. LE COMTE
Areopagitica as a Scenario for *Paradise Lost*   121

JOHN T. SHAWCROSS
The Higher Wisdom of *The Tenure of Kings and Magistrates*   142

FLORENCE SANDLER
Icon and Iconoclast   160

AUSTIN WOOLRYCH
Milton and Cromwell: "A Short But Scandalous Night of
Interruption"?   185

HARRY SMALLENBURG
Government of the Spirit: Style, Structure and Theme in *Treatise
of Civil Power*   219

vi Contents

WALTER J. ONG, S.J.
Logic and the Epic Muse: Reflections on Noetic Structures in Milton's Milieu   239

WILLIAM B. HUNTER, JR.
The Theological Context of Milton's *Christian Doctrine*   269

Appendix

JOHN T. SHAWCROSS
A Survey of Milton's Prose Works   291

Selected Bibliography   393

Contributors   395

Preface

A collection of original essays, this volume brings together the work of outstanding scholars invited to write at some length about Milton's prose. Our editorial policy has been to achieve within the limited space available both breadth and depth. To do that, we proceeded with an awareness of what general areas we wanted covered, but we were careful to be as flexible as possible in communicating that awareness to our contributors. We wanted them to respond to their own interests as well as to the interests of the volume as a whole. The results, we think, are admirable.

In breadth, the volume spans practically Milton's entire career as a writer of prose. The essays range in their concerns from Milton's antiprelatical tracts to his tracts about the affairs of state, with individual attention to his treatises on logic and on Christian doctrine. Of necessity, some areas have not received exclusive treatment, not because those areas are in themselves unimportant but because we felt it wiser to devote extended coverage to certain areas rather than superficial coverage to the complete body of Milton's prose. We were more interested in a work of scholarship than in a work of stamina.

As a work of scholarship, *Achievements of the Left Hand* explores in depth a number of topics that bear upon Milton's prose. In doing so, it provides new perspectives through which we can better understand Milton's unique achievements as a prose writer. The way in which Milton viewed his role as orator, a role inherited from classical and biblical precedents, is the main concern of Joseph A. Wittreich, Jr. Likewise interested in Milton's response to a particular vocation, Florence Sandler considers Milton's commitment to the role of iconoclast as an implicit comment upon his behavior as a polemicist. In practice, that behavior is analyzed by Austin Woolrych, who treats the historical ironies and complexities of Milton's role in the Cromwellian regime. From the literary point of view, Milton's polemical behavior is the subject of Michael Lieb's study of how Milton utilized the techniques that were available to him as a writer of tracts. Similarly, Harry Smallenburg treats Milton's stylistic, structural, and thematic practices in his prose as they condition a reader's response. William B. Hunter, Jr., and John T. Shawcross are also interested in Milton's readers. Professor Hunter establishes the theological context of *Christian Doctrine,* taking into account the kind of audience envisioned by Milton's treatise, while Professor Shawcross stresses the universal bearing of Milton's prose as it presupposes an audience responsive to values that transcend immediate polemical concerns.

But Milton's response to his role as orator and iconoclast, his position in matters of debate, his techniques as a prose writer, and his relationship with his audience are not the only perspectives offered by the volume. John F. Huntley, Edward S. Le Comte, and Walter J. Ong, S.J., provide additional insights as they approach the prose with Milton's poetic outlook in mind. If Professor Huntley devotes himself to Milton's views of the poet and his craft within the polemical context that gave rise to these views, then Father Ong complements that approach in his study of the *Logic* by showing how successfully Milton was able to fulfill, as well as to reconcile, the demands imposed upon him by his vocations as prose writer and as poet. The essential relationship between those vocations is made quite evident by Professor Le Comte's essay, which reveals how the imagery of *Areopagitica* anticipates comparable patterns in *Paradise Lost.*

All the foregoing essays, in turn, reinforce the underlying assumption of Professor Shawcross's prose survey: if much has been written about Milton's prose, a great deal more has still to be written. Covering Milton's entire canon as a prose writer, Professor Shawcross's final essay is valuable not only for the information (much of it new) that it makes available about Milton's texts, dates of composition, and influence; it is valuable likewise for the insights and incentives it provides for additional research. With this essay, the volume concludes as a tribute to Milton's achievements in the field of prose and as a sign of the recognition that his achievements have inspired.

M. L.

Achievements of the
Left Hand

'The Crown of Eloquence':
The Figure of the Orator
in Milton's Prose Works

JOSEPH ANTHONY WITTREICH, JR.

University of Wisconsin, Madison

Certainly there is no true orator who is not a hero. His attitude on the rostrum, or the platform, requires that he counterbalance his auditory. He is challenger, and must answer all comers. The orator must ever stand with forward foot, in the attitude of advancing. His speech must be just ahead of the assembly, ahead of the whole human race, or it is superfluous. His speech is not to be distinguished from action.

Ralph Waldo Emerson

With the exceptions of a few scattered notes in the Yale *Milton*[1] and an illuminating essay by O. B. Hardison, Jr.,[2] little attention has been given to the figure of the orator in Milton's prose works, and even less to the relationship Milton defines between himself and the audience he addresses. Predicated on the belief that Milton's accomplishments of the "left hand" are most fully comprehended and best judged within the context of oratorical tradition—classical and Christian—and ranging freely over the prose works from the early prolusions to *Defensio secunda,* this essay gathers into focus the figure of the orator and his conception of his audience. It begins with an examination of oratorical tradition and proceeds toward a consideration of the ways in which Milton fulfilled but also extended that tradition: he harmonizes the three styles, while shaping them into a symbol that supports and reflects his themes; he integrates the five divisions of the classical oration, but overlays them with complementary—and sometimes contending—structures that reveal his rage for order and, on occasion, mirror the siege of contraries that Milton found in all aspects of fallen life. This essay takes into account the ideal orator who existed in the imagination of Cicero and Quintilian and in the person of Christ; and it illustrates how, by mastering style, and form, by marshaling the various kinds of proof available to the orator, and by fulfilling the multiple functions assigned to the orator by tradition, Milton realizes the classical ideal; it also illustrates how, by combining classical tradition and Christian models, Milton radically transforms the classical oratorical form into one that is distinctively his own.

The oration is a convenient place to begin a study of Milton's use of literary form. Critics writing before Milton had detailed and elaborated the unrealized potentiality of the genre. This is true of no other "kind." Customarily the critic was content with surveying the existing examples within a genre and with drawing both definitions and models of perfection from them. Such surveys were made of existing orations, but the results proved less fruitful. Instead of finding perfection, the critic discovered and recorded insufficiencies. Within this context, we see Milton reaching for the kind of perfection described by critical tradition, but we also see him grasping for a higher perfection through which he can create a new literary tradition that his successors may use with the same liberties and to the same advantage that Milton used the traditions that he was heir to.

I

Cicero in *Orator* and *De Oratore* and Quintilian in *Institutio Oratoria* present complementary portraits of the ideal orator.[3] For both, the orator and the poet are closely allied, with the orator receiving the higher rank because he is the source of "the virtues" the poet must seek (*Orator* XIX.67). Though all the great orators, from Cicero's point of view, have displayed perfection of character, none has attained the ideal of being equally successful in all three oratorical styles (plain, intermediate, and grand); nor has anyone achieved absolute mastery of oratorical form. To the extent that any orator approaches perfection in either respect, Demosthenes exemplifies mastery of the three styles and Isocrates exhibits mastery of form. The latter fixes the pattern for an oration (exordium, narration, confirmation, refutation, peroration), while the former correlates the three styles with the three functions of the orator (to please, to prove, to persuade) and the three divisions of an oration (exordium, proof [narration, confirmation, refutation], peroration). However, since the end of rhetoric is to persuade and since that end is most closely identified with the grand style, the ideal orator, mastering it, will reveal himself as a man who has attained "the highest power in the state," says Cicero; "I mean the kind of eloquence which rushes along with the roar of a mighty stream. . . . This eloquence has power to sway men's minds and move them in every possible way. Now it storms the feelings, now it creeps in; it implants new ideas and uproots the old" (*Orator* XXVIII.97). It is in terms of style and form, then, that Cicero portrays the ideal orator—the orator (he is quick to tell Brutus) whom "we are seeking" in imagination since the world does not yet possess him (*Orator* XXVIII.100).

In *Institutio Oratoria*, after explaining that his aim is to educate the perfect orator, Quintilian confesses that, like Cicero, he is "not describing any orator who actually exists or has existed" but has instead in his "mind's eye an ideal orator, perfect down to the smallest detail" (I.x.4). No orator, says Quintilian, has achieved perfection (not Isocrates, Demosthenes, or Cicero) because none has been sufficiently familiar with the hidden secrets of oratory, none has recognized that these qualities are beyond imitation.[4] To disregard the rules of oratory may be to alienate the audience and to lose the power to persuade; but even so there are moments when the integrity of the speaker and the rules of speech are at variance. "Whenever this occurs," says Quintilian, the rules of oratory must yield to personal integrity: "Who does not realize that nothing would have contributed more to secure the acquittal of Socrates than if he had employed the ordinary forensic methods of defence and had conciliated the minds of his judges by adopting a submissive tone . . . ? But such a course would have been unworthy of his character" (XI.i.9-10). What the example of Socrates shows is that "there are occasions when to persuade would be a blot upon" a man's honor (XI.i.11). This discussion suggests an emphasis in Quintilian different from the accents of Cicero.

Cicero understood that the orator must be a virtuous man if he is "to discuss good and evil, things to be preferred and things to be shunned, fair repute and infamy . . . besides moral perfection" (*De Oratore* II.xvi.67); and he understood, too, that the orator, if he is to attain to "a knowledge of all important subjects and arts" (I.vi.20), must possess "the subtlety of the logician, the thoughts of the philosopher, a diction almost poetic, a lawyer's memory, a tragedian's voice, and the bearing almost of the consummate actor" (I.xxviii.128). However, Cicero chose to stress the technical aspects of style and form.

Quintilian, on the other hand, recognized that a single style is

not suited to every audience, speaker, or occasion; nor is each
style equally appropriate to each part of a single oration. Like
Cicero, he conceded that, when one style had to be chosen over
the others, the grand style, "by far the strongest and the best
adapted to the most important cases" (XII.x.63), was the one to
select: "It . . . will bring down the Gods to form part of his [the
orator's] audience or even to speak with him" (XII.x.62). Quintilian also counsels the perfect orator to cultivate the three styles
with special regard for their relation to the three parts of an
oration: the orator should eschew metaphor in his exordium
and colloquial language in his peroration, since "all ornament
derives its effects not from its own qualities so much as from
the circumstances in which it is applied" (XI.i.7). At the same
time that the orator is fitting the various styles to the different
parts of an oration, he should suit them to the diverse elements of
society represented in his audience; for if an orator is to transform
the thinking of an entire nation he will have to cultivate one
style for the erudite and quite another for the populace. Thus
Quintilian concludes:

> . . . in one and the same speech he will use one style for stirring
> the emotions, and another to conciliate his hearers. . . . He will
> not maintain the same tone throughout his *exordium, statement
> of fact, arguments, digression* and *peroration.* He will speak
> gravely, severely, sharply, with vehemence, energy, fullness,
> bitterness, or geniality, quietly, simply, flatteringly, gently,
> sweetly, briefly or wittily; he will not always be like himself,
> but he will never be unworthy of himself. Thus the purpose
> for which oratory was above all designed will be secured, that
> is to say, he will speak with profit and with power to effect his
> aim, while he will also win the praise not merely of the learned,
> but of the multitude as well. (XII.x.71-72)

Quintilian points to the same matters of style and form as did
Cicero—and, indeed, he says more about these matters than did
his predecessor. But his accents are differently placed. Quintilian,
less convinced than Cicero of the moral excellence of past orators,
places primary stress on his belief that "above all" the perfect
orator must be "a good man": he "must . . . devote his attention
to the formation of moral character and must acquire a complete
knowledge of all that is just and honourable" (XII.ii.1). While
acknowledging the excellence of Cicero and Demosthenes, Quintilian observes that, lacking "the perfection of virtue," neither
attained to "that which is the highest perfection of man's nature"

(XII.i.18). This is the challenge that "above all" Milton attempts
to meet.

The ideal pattern, described by Cicero and Quintilian, is one
with which Milton's own training would have made him familiar.
"Curriculum and texts," we know, "had become practically uniform"[5] by the middle of the sixteenth century; and Isocrates,
Demosthenes, Cicero, and Quintilian were invariably on the reading lists. Milton's frequent references to these authors—and the
contexts in which these references occur—make clear that he was
intent upon realizing the perfection they describe, and more. In
their respective formulations Cicero and Quintilian diverge importantly, but they also show significant points of coincidence.
Both celebrate eloquence as a "mighty and glorious" achievement,
the aim of which is "to gather scattered humanity" together and
"to lead it out of its brutish existence in the wilderness" into a
state of civilization (*De Oratore* I.25, 29, 31). Both contrast the
true and false orators, emphasizing the binding and elevating
effects of the one and the divisive and demeaning effects of the
other, the interest of the one in widening human freedoms and
of the other in curtailing them.

The tradition represented by the ancient rhetoricians held great
sway in shaping Milton's ideas of *orator* and *oratoria*. Not only
does Milton gather together his polemical efforts under the master-theme of liberty; he also makes a concerted effort to project
the image of an orator who, having taken all of human knowledge
for his province, is ready to impart that knowledge to a nation
and thereby prepare it for apocalypse, for the moment when the
Prince comes forth from his "Royall Chambers," puts on "the
visible roabes of . . . imperiall Majesty," takes up "that unlimited
Scepter," and ushers into Eternity all those who "sigh to bee
renew'd" (*Anima.* I.707).[6] Yet Milton's attitude toward the tradition represented by Cicero and Quntilian reveals an ambivalence
that has, for the most part, gone unobserved. The references to
the classical oratorical tradition in Milton's prose pull oppositely,
revealing, on the one hand, a desire to identify his polemical
efforts with this tradition and, on the other, a desire to transcend
that tradition—a desire implied in virtually every one of Milton's
prose works but most clearly articulated in *Reason of Church-
Government* and *Defensio secunda*.

In the antiprelatical tract, Milton celebrates mental warfare
as the "approved" warfare prescribed by Scripture: "*warfare,
not carnall, but mighty through God*" (I.848). In this tract Milton
is taking up the tradition of the Athenian orators who made

their country's "small deeds great and renowned" in contrast
to England's unskillful orators who have "made small" the
"noble atchievments" of their nation (I.812). Milton claims to
surpass in subject and theme his classical predecessors and in
skill his contemporaries. The first part of the claim is boldly reiterated in *Defensio secunda.* Again Milton alludes to the idea of
the orator as mental warrior, this time placing his own form of
warfare above that of the ordinary soldier. In physical warfare,
the soldier uses his "lower powers"; in mental warfare Milton
exercises those that are "higher and stronger." "If God wished
those men to achieve such noble deeds," writes Milton, "He
also wished that there be other men by whom these deeds, once
done, might be worthily praised and extolled, and that truth defended by arms be also defended by reason—the only defence
truly appropriate to man" (IV.i.553).[7] Once having asserted the
superiority of "Mental Fight" Milton continues by asserting his
superiority over the classical orators: "in the degree that the distinguished orators of ancient times undoubtedly surpass me, both
in their eloquence and in their style . . . in that same degree shall
I outstrip all the orators of every age in the grandeur of my subject and my theme" (IV.i.554).

Milton takes precisely the same stance in relation to the classical oratorical tradition that he was later to take in relation to the
classical epic tradition. When in *Paradise Lost* he asks to achieve
an "answerable style" and announces his argument to be "Not
less but more Heroic then the wrauth/Of stern *Achilles*" (IX.
14-15, 20), he at once pays tribute to his predecessors and
promises that his Christian themes will supersede in importance
those of Homer and Virgil. Correspondingly, Milton links his
prose works with the orations of Demosthenes, Isocrates, and
Cicero, thereby paying homage to the form which they utilized
and which he is bringing to perfection, then recreating in order
to give appropriate shape to his nobler ideals and perfected
values. The ideology Milton associates with oratorical form
finds its most perfect embodiment in Milton's Christian heritage.

When Cicero and Quintilian contemplated the ideal orator they
looked to the future, to a time when a skillful orator, who was
also a perfect man, would assimilate their rhetorical principles
and achieve oratorical perfection. However, when Milton considered the ideal orator, he looked to the past, not only (and perhaps not even principally) to the theoretical treatises of antiquity
but to Christ, the perfect poet-orator, who had already translated
the ideal of Cicero and Quintilian into reality. Milton understood

that all types are destroyed by Christ's coming, even the types
of the orator. If antiquity had only imperfect types, like Demosthenes and Isocrates, for its models, Christianity had a perfect
pattern for the orator in Christ and still another nearly perfect
pattern in St. Paul. Augustine knew this when, turning the second
part of his *De doctrina christiana* into "a Christian *Ars Rhetorica*
. . . a Christian *De Oratore,*" he insisted that the orator was able
to "find what models he needs in Scripture and in Christian
authors" and could, therefore, "ignore the technical treatises in
rhetorical theory and learn, so to speak, by immersion in the
text."[8] Milton knew it, too, as his prose works testify; he did not,
of course, "ignore" the classical treatises but, turning to the
"revolutionary doctrine" of Augustine, attempted instead to accommodate classical theory and Christian practice.

Milton's references to the classical orators are incidental when
compared to the grand analogies he draws between Christ and
himself and the repeated references to St. Paul as both authority
and model. In *An Apology Against a Pamphlet,* after attributing
to Christ mastery over the three styles, Milton suggests that He
alone has subsumed the oratorical virtues and graces divided
among the many teachers of the church (I.899-900). Christ is
the moral authority for Milton's satiric voice, having been Himself "the fountaine of meeknesse" but also having "found acrimony anough to be . . . galling and vexing"; Christ is the model
for Milton's prophetic voice, which speaks *"to rip up the wounds
of* Idolatry and Superstition" (I.900, 903). He is the perfect ruler,
who presides over the spiritual life of man; He is the perfect mental warrior, who strikes with scorn, and the perfect poet, who
teaches through metaphor. Hence Scripture contains the perfect
pattern of the ideal orator; but it also contains, as Milton's contemporaries were fast to point out, "the most excellent and sub-
limest eloquence."[9]

By the time Milton writes the divorce tracts he has so completely embraced the oratorical tradition represented by Christ
and Paul that he can cite them as his authority for requiring mental gymnastics from his reader:

> . . . there is scarce any saying in the Gospel, but must be read
> with limitations and distinctions, to be rightly understood; for
> Christ gives no full comments or continu'd discourses, but . . .
> as *Demetrius* the Rhetorician phrases it, speaks oft in Mono-
> syllables, like a maister, scattering the heavenly grain of his
> doctrin like pearle heer and there, which requires a skilfull and
> laborious gatherer; who must compare the words he finds, with

other precepts, with the end of every ordinance, and with the
general *analogy* of Evangelick doctrine. . . . (*Divorce.*II.338)

Like Augustine, Milton believed that the obscurity of Scripture
was part of God's design: through it, He exercised the mind, leading it from the realities of this world to those of the next. At the
same time that God is "exercising" Milton's mind and the minds
of his great protagonists (Adam, Christ, and Samson) Milton is
forcing difficult mental exertions upon his audience, hoping
through those exertions to cleanse the doors of perception and
thereby move his audience from discourse to vision. Christ and
Paul also provide Milton with a precedent for the revolutionary
posture he assumes in the prose tracts. They rebuked custom,
flew in the face of tradition, associating both with error, and
thereby took their place at the head of the tradition of dissent,
religious and political, which Milton embraces most directly in
The Judgement of Martin Bucer. [10] Bucer, the most recent hero
of radicalism, is presented as an "excellent pattern" for the nation
to follow; yet he is but a type of the true liberator who "by his
birth, his slavery, and his suffering under tyranny . . . won for us
all proper freedom" (*1 Def.,*IV.i.374). It was Christ who put on
the form of the slave without relinquishing the heart of the liberator and who perfected the ideology that Milton embraces as a
vital part of oratorical form.

By the examples of Christ and Paul from which Augustine ex-
trapolated his rhetorical theory, Milton was reminded that although rhetoric and Christianity may come into conflict "there
[is] a sense in which Christianity can be called a rhetorical religion."[11] The Christian orator may, indeed, use the devices—
stylistic and structural—of classical oratory; but if he is to follow
the examples of Christ and Paul his ends will be different: he will
value eloquence not as an end in itself but as a vehicle for truth;
he will be a defender of liberty but also of faith; he will not ignore secular matters but will make them subordinate to religious
ones; he will combine with the qualities of poet and philosopher
those of the theologian; and in doing so he will emerge both as
legislator in the secular world and as interpreter in the spiritual
realm. It is fitting that Milton, who confronted all problems of
state and celebrated all forms of liberty under the aspect of religion, should allow his talents to culminate simultaneously, it
seems, in the writing of a Christian epic and in the composition
of *De doctrina christiana.*

It was long ago acknowledged that "without treading often in
the footsteps of his guides" Milton "pressed forward after them

in the same track."[12] This statement acquires validity from Milton's own claims and spells out the direction that any study of Milton in relation to tradition must take. It is not enough to observe merely that "the sum of his many references to rhetoric and eloquence indicates that he followed contemporary usage in applying the terms to prose and poetry alike."[13] Any study of Milton and tradition must become an essay on tradition and the individual talent, and in such a study the accent will fall unequivocally on *the individual talent.* Milton takes the oratorical form used by his predecessors and brings it to perfection, first by pursuing the unrealized potentiality of the form, then by stripping it of the specious values it customarily embodied and inculcating it with a perfected ideology. Milton's constant transformation of forms is a revolutionary element in his art. It requires attention that we may best give it by considering the matters of style and form, which Milton's *Defensio secunda* feigns not to have mastered, while asking what these matters indicate about the orator and the relationship he defines with his audience.

II

Milton repeatedly invokes representatives of the classical oratorical tradition for the purpose of calling attention not to that tradition alone but to the technical perfection he has achieved within its context. Milton's own statement in *Defensio secunda* to the effect that the ancient orators surpass him in their eloquence and in their style would seem to indicate that we should look for neither stylistic accomplishment nor innovation in the prose tracts. However, the passage comes within Milton's exordium, and the modesty is as false here as it was in "Lycidas." There Milton prefaces what Tennyson and others have regarded as technically the most perfect poem in the English language with an apology for its artlessness. But the "forc't fingers rude" that strike the jarring discords in the early verse paragraphs also fashion the larger harmonies to which those discords contribute. Milton has employed the modesty *topos*, but once his accomplishment is comprehended the ironic thrust of the *topos* is understood: what seemed initially to be a perfunctory nod to tradition becomes a playful violation of it. The same principle operates in *Defensio secunda*.

In the early pages of this defense Milton underplays his stylistic achievement—a considerable one when we recall that he is writing in Latin rather than in English just as he had done in *Pro Populo Anglicano Defensio,* which, whatever its deficiencies, shows astonishing stylistic virtuosity. In the words of its most recent translator, "At times it is senatorial rhetoric. . . . At times it is Plautine comedy. . . . At times the dominant tone is the satirist's *saeva indignatio.*"[14] Milton's audience, presumably familiar with this earlier achievement, would doubtless recall its stylistic accomplishment—the mastery Milton displays in his use of the three styles; and even if his audience were led to take Milton's statement at face value it would soon have to alter its thinking, since Milton's achievement in style here surpasses what he had attained in his first defense.

Milton's artistic triumph is all the more considerable when we recall that "historically the trail of the three styles has been baneful"[15] and that, however frustrating the demand for absolute mastery of them may have been to his predecessors, Milton, now a polemicist of stature, having already displayed extraordinary virtuosity in his native language, matches the earlier achievements of the Seventh Prolusion, *Of Reformation, Reason of Church-Government,* and *Areopagitica* in *Defensio secunda.* Hence, after eclipsing his classical predecessors by mastering the three styles in English, Milton shifts to Latin and scores a more impressive victory because it is a more difficult one. Moreover, unhappy with merely meeting the expectations of antiquity Milton pushes significantly beyond them, creating a symbolic style whose dialectics mirror a central theme and major structural principle in the prose works—the theme of truth triumphing over falsehood organized around the opposition between the true and false orator. If these stylistic matters cannot be fully explored in this essay, they can at least be pursued to the point that further inquiry can proceed from them and to the point that they may shed important light on the figure of the orator and the relationship he assumes with his audience.

Classical, Medieval, and Renaissance theorists relate the hierarchy of styles to social and poetical categories. In the case of oratory, they go still further and relate the three styles (plain, intermediate, grand) to the three parts of an oration (exordium, proof, peroration) and to the three functions of the orator (to please, to prove, to persuade). The scheme can be extended *ad infinitum*:

Society	*Locale*	*Genre*	*Style*
soldier (aristocracy)	court	epic	GRAND
farmer (middle class)	field	didactic	INTERMEDIATE
shepherd (lower class)	pasture	pastoral	PLAIN

What is important is that when Milton speaks of the three styles in *Of Education* (II.401),[16] he reveals his familiarity with this system of classification and especially with the way in which style must be suited to both subject matter and audience. The preponderance of the sublime style in Milton's prose is doubly significant: the "grand, impetuous, and fiery style" is the one that Cicero associates with the person who has attained "the highest power in the state" and the one he identifies with revolutionary purpose (*Orator* XXVIII.97, 99). In the "lofty" style Milton finds a correlative for his exalted themes and through it defines his oratorical stance, both as a speaker who has achieved eminence and as one who wants to cast "the morning beam of *Reformation*" (*Anima.*I.705).[17] But the prominence of the sublime style in Milton's prose should not be allowed to obscure the mixture of styles cultivated for the various segments of society to which the orations are being fitted. Milton's concern with audience manifests itself first and most conspicuously in his oratorical efforts.

Responding to the dictum that the perfect orator should display mastery of the three styles and should through them instruct, delight, and persuade, Milton mixes styles in the separate orations, according to the counsel of Cicero, not as "a surface varnish" but so as to "permeat[e] their arterial system" (*De Oratore* III.li.199). This stylistic complexity represents an effort on Milton's part to transform the thinking of a large part of his audience: Milton understood that the ends of oratory are more easily achieved before "a wise deliberative body" than before the multitudes who, if they are to be convinced, require "the full employment of powerful and weighty oratory" (*De Oratore* II.lxxxii.333-334). But with that understanding Milton elected the more difficult task, perceiving that reformation is instigated by the multitudes, this perception obliging him to attend to the people in order to educate and thereby ennoble them.

Two images of the orator, both commonly used during the Renaissance, convey the kind of ideal relationship between orator and audience that Milton sought. Hercules is typically portrayed as "a lustie old man with a long chayne tyed by one end at his tong, by the other end at the peoples eares." As George Puttenham explains, the people, standing "farre of" seem "to be drawn to him by the force [sic] of that chayne fastned to his tong, as . . . by force of his perswasions."[18] The second image is used ironically by Milton in the Sixth Prolusion, where he says that "Orpheus and Amphion used to attract an audience consisting only of rocks and wild beasts and trees" (I.269).[19] Quintilian points to the accepted allegorization of that part of the Orpheus

myth to which Milton refers. Orpheus, he explains, represents
the union of the roles of musician, poet, and philosopher; and
drawing after him the wild beasts, rocks, and trees suggests the
"concord of discordant elements" (I.x.9-12). A more elaborate
interpretation of this aspect of the Orpheus myth is provided
by Alexander Ross: Orpheus represents a type of the minister-
orator; his instrument is "the Harp of Gods Word." "By *Orpheus*
charming of stones, trees, birds and beasts with his musick, is
meant," says Ross, that governors and orators "by their wisdom
and eloquence did bring rude and ignorant people . . . to Civility,
and Religion."[20] In his role as poet-priest-orator, Orpheus is a
type of the ideal orator for Milton and, in his relations with
the natural world, implies the ideal relationship between orator
and audience that Milton achieves through the artful joining
of the three styles.

Significantly, as Milton acquires greater mastery of style and
form his postulated audience enlarges. Though the Prolusions
take an academic assembly as their audience, Milton's audience
is widened greatly when we come to the antiprelatical tracts. In
the peroration of *Reason of Church-Government*, Milton addresses
directly the "worthy Peeres and Commons" of the English Parliament but then insinuates an audience composed of King, Parliament, Prince, People—wealthy men and learned men (I.860-861).
An observation offered by J. Max Patrick on *Of Prelatical Episcopacy* pertains here as well. Explaining that the tract is a reply to
Hall, Ussher, and "Peloni Almoni," Patrick observes that Milton
"was attempting to address a wider public than the erudite
theologians and scholars to whom Ussher's pamphlet would have
appealed."[21] As Milton's major statement against prelacy, *Reason
of Church-Government* is directed not to one or the other of these
audiences but to both. Reform, if it is to come, will be generated
by the discontents of the people; but its implementation will depend first on garnering the support of respected churchmen and
then on altering thinking in Parliament. In the divorce tracts (except for *Colasterion*) and in *Areopagitica*, Parliament is singled
out on the title page and addressed directly within the oration,
a device that has misled readers into thinking Milton wrote for a
highly restricted audience composed of those who were his
nation's lawmakers.

This common misconception veils an important aspect of Milton's prose—the strategy he employs in tract after tract. Milton's
apostrophes to Parliament in the divorce tracts and in *Areopagitica*

have considerable political significance and rhetorical force; they
reveal his audacity and his political acumen as an orator. As a
"revolutionary force" in the state, Parliament symbolizes the
radical political elements in English society. To these elements
Milton's appeals are openly addressed. But for Milton Parliament
is also a metaphor for the people, so that his prose tracts, like
Scripture, call to instruction "not only the *wise*, and *learned*, but
the *simple*, the *poor*, the *babes*" (*Ref*.I.566). And the analogy
may be extended. If Milton's orations are like Scripture, Milton
is like the teachers in Scripture, a prophet, a discerner, insisting
that he will "make a knowing people, a Nation of Prophets, of
Sages, and of Worthies" (*Areo*.II.554) and wondering why he
should "tugge for a Barony to sit and vote in Parliament" when
he, though not a member, can be its "teacher" and "perswader."
From Milton's point of view, his own power is greater than
Parliament's: "the perswasive power in man to win others to
goodnesse by instruction," he says, "is greater, and more divine"
than the "compulsive power" of Parliament, which "restraine[s]
men from being evil by the terrour of the Law." Parliament is
like "Moses . . . the Lawgiver" and Milton like Christ who "came
downe" to be a "teacher" (*Anima*.I.722). It is not the givers of
law whom Milton finally addresses, but those whom the lawgivers represent.

By infusing his addresses to Parliament with metaphorical
significance, Milton directs oratory away from the aristocracy to
the people, bringing it into accord with the new political reality.
The weight of Milton's metaphor has not been recognized. The
members of Parliament, he says repeatedly, are themselves the
people,[22] theirs is "the power of the people" (*1Def*.IV.i.487).
When given to qualification, Milton concedes that "it is understood that the *Commons* represent the whole people, and are
therefore stronger and more exalted than the nobles" (*1Def*.IV.
i.485; my italics), and when disillusioned he says that the Parliament, chosen by the people from men with "the public good"
in mind, has some members who are also "men of wisdome and
integritie" (*Britain*.X.319 [CM]). As the people become more
and more oppressed their leaders become less and less adequate,
but Parliament continues to be representative of the people, says
Milton, both when "the lofty expectation of their minds [keeps]
them from being a mob" and when their broken expectations reduce them to a vulgar herd (*2Def*.IV.i.552).

The metaphorical character of these apostrophes is emphasized in *The Doctrine and Discipline of Divorce* where Milton addresses Parliament so as to pay tribute to those whose "watchfulnes, couragious and heroick resolutions" were exercised, for the moment at least, to liberate the people from the tyranny of church government and whose sympathies Milton hopes to elicit in behalf of domestic freedoms (II.233). But Milton makes clear, too, that this tract is for all his countrymen—the erudite and the multitudes—and in doing so offers his best general description of the audience for whom he writes: "Let the statutes of God be turn'd over, be scann'd a new," he says, not by "the narrow intellectuals of quotationists and common placers" but by men "of eminent spirit and breeding joyn'd with a diffuse and various knowledge of divine and human things; able to ballance and define good and evill, right and wrong, throughout every state of life; able to shew us the waies of the Lord . . . with divine insight and benignity measur'd out to the proportion of each mind and spirit, each temper and disposition" (II.230).

However disappointed Milton may have become in the multitudes (in *Defensie secunda* he expresses regret for having written *The Doctrine and Discipline of Divorce* "in the vernacular" for it "met with vernacular readers, who are usually ignorant of their own good, and laugh at the misfortunes of others" [IV.i.610]), that disappointment does not show here. Nor is it very conspicuous in *Defensio secunda* where, alongside remarks like this one, Milton celebrates the citizens who with "a nobility and steadfastness surpassing all the glory of their ancestors, invoked the Lord, followed his manifest guidance, and after accomplishing the most heroic and exemplary achievements since the foundation of the world, freed the state from grievous tyranny and the church from unworthy servitude" (IV.i.548-549). In his description of the "fit" audience Milton makes clear that insofar as he distinguishes between levels of audience that distinction is made in terms of morality, not class.[23] His hope is that through the strokings of conscience at all levels of society he will "wipe away ten thousand teares out of the life of man" (*Divorce* II.245). Like Christ, Milton speaks "*to the regenerat*," but without abandoning the vulgar (*Divorce* II.344). Because of widespread misunderstanding about Milton's attitude toward his audience, some further comment is desirable.

It has already been observed that Milton's faith in the multitudes is significantly qualified between the writing of *The Doctrine and Discipline of Divorce* and the later Defenses, and it has also been observed that despite a waning faith in the populace

Milton does not disregard it, understanding as he does that its failing vision is the result of the tyranny it has tried unsuccessfully to overthrow. In this regard, William Grace has said that in the first of his defenses "Milton temporarily identifies himself with what Salmasius calls 'the plebian scum,'" but Grace also insists that Milton later takes "a more conservative position," concluding that Salmasius' description may fairly represent "the dregs of the populace." Grace's views are shared by Don Wolfe. Commenting on Milton's apostrophe to the people in *Defensio secunda* ("You, therefore, who wish to remain free, either be wise at the outset or recover your senses as soon as possible" [IV.i.684]), Wolfe suggests that passages like this one reveal Milton's contempt for men "generally found among the lower classes."[24]

The Defenses celebrate not the deeds of a "minority" as Grace would have us believe,[25] but rather the heroic deeds of Cromwell's army (a group of plebians) over the King's army (a group of courtiers)—triumphs accomplished only through the help of "a great part of the citizenry." Together the Army and the people ("a great part" of them) performed deeds more "excellent" and more "worthy" than those of "the most heroic days of old" (*1Def*.IV.i.330). Those deeds, Milton insists, were performed by a people "wise, learned, and noble enough to know what should be done with its own tyrant"—by a people "wise, learned, and noble enough," we may conjecture, to serve as a type of the "fit" audience to whom Milton addresses his orations. Milton deliberately, not unwittingly, identifies himself with the very elements in the social order that Salmasius ridicules, insisting always that Salmasius' "plebian scum" is not a fair representation of the large part of the "people."

Milton's fit audience represents a "majority" which is "the sound part," "the regenerate," "the spiritual elite," of his country and the continent. The people whom he celebrates and those whom he addresses either "drove the nobles out of Parliament" or are endowed both with the intelligence to ascertain tyranny when it exists and the will to remove its "unbearable yoke." There were, of course, members of Parliament who preferred "enslavement and putting the commonwealth up for sale" (*1Def*.IV.i. 457), and there were people in the state who "despite a pledge of complete loyalty" deserted the libertarians "in the midst of their undertaking," they too preferring "slavery with inaction and comfort" over "a secure and sincere peace" (*1Def*.IV.i.518). Though this retrograde element in the government and in the citizenry is not "the sound part," though it does not represent an ideal audience to which Milton may appeal, it is not wholly discounted either. Both in *The History of Britain* and in *The Readie & Easie Way* Milton reveals a profound sense of disillusionment. The "Christian multitude" of *Animadversions* becomes the "rude multitude" of *The History*. The "people" of *Areopagitica* who more "then at other times" are wholly taken up with "the study of highest and most important matters to be reform'd" (II.557) are by oppression unfitted "to receave or to digest libertie at all" (*Britain* X.324 [CM]). At this point, Milton's audience becomes more, not less, demanding on his talents; for if he is to be "doctrinal and exemplary to a Nation" (*Reason* I.815), if empire is really to follow art, he must educate the "misguided" rulers of his nation and its "abused" multitude, who together have led England to the "precipice of destruction" (*Way* VI.149 [CM]). Milton knew in the early 1640s that "if the multitude be rude," or become rude, their teacher "must give knowledge" (*Reason* I.829). His greater task, requiring from him a deed above heroic, is now to impart wisdom and to instill justice in men who must be made "more then vulgar" by being "bred up . . . in the knowledge of Antient and illustrious deeds" (*Britain* X.325 [CM]).

Milton's technique, initiated in *The Doctrine and Discipline of Divorce,* of openly addressing Parliament and then marking off a much wider audience, continues through most of the divorce tracts and is used in *Areopagitica* as well. Until this point Milton has been addressing only his countrymen through the figure of Parliament; now he suggests a larger ambition, insinuating that like Isocrates he hopes to win the minds of men not only in "Cities and Siniories" but those of men "in other Lands" as well (II.489).[26] The audience hinted at here is boldly claimed as *Pro Populo Anglicano Defensio* gets underway. Responding to Salmasius' *Defensio Regia,* Milton directs his counter-statement to a continental audience. Wishing "to treat worthily all those great events," Milton composes "a memorial" for "every nation and every age" (IV.i.305). Here Milton ridicules Salmasius for trying "to snatch all the prizes for eloquence from Cicero or Demosthenes" and for taking "the whole world as audience" (IV.i.324). But Milton himself attempts to do both in *Defensio secunda,* where he claims superiority to his classical models and to his audience. Not "surrounded by one people alone, whether Roman or Athenian," Milton holds "virtually all of Europe attentive," his audience being composed of "the entire assembly and council of all the most influential men, cities, and nations everywhere"

(IV.i.554). Now "the focal point of the world's struggle for freedom,"[27] Milton is surrounded by "great throngs, from the pillars of Hercules [Gibraltar, the westermost boundary of Europe] all the way to the farthest boundaries of Father Liber [the farthest boundaries of India]" (IV.i.555). Not allowing the point to be missed, Milton proclaims several pages later that he speaks "under the protection of God" not for one people "but rather for *the entire human race* . . . amid the common and well-frequented assembly (so to speak) of all nations" and of all time (IV.i.557-558; my italics).

There is no small irony in Milton's addressing Parliament and flattering its members with praise. By establishing Parliament as his "fictive" audience, Milton observes a fundamental principle of rhetoric: to address the legislative body of a nation, not to say of all nations, is to reveal oneself as an orator of highest stature and accomplishment. "The greatest public good," according to Plato, is "the ability to persuade with speeches judges . . . or statesmen . . . or the commons . . . on public affairs (*Gorgias* 279). The real rhetorical point made through these apostrophes is that Milton, an orator of highest standing and of wide-ranging influence, is the true liberator of his people and should be distinguished from Parliament, a body of lawgivers, an oppressor of the people. Parliament will restrain the will of the people; Milton will restore to it freedom. Parliament as lawgiver Milton scorns; Parliament as the "people" he speaks to. The first is his fictive audience, the second his real one.

One ironclad rule of rhetoric, worth recalling here, is the insistence that the orator enthusiastically commend his audience and bring it to a hatred of his adversary. The rule is difficult to observe when the orator's audience is also his antagonist. By creating a fictive audience Milton is able to resolve the problem, turning what was a potential problem to his advantage. In the prolusions an academic audience is fictively addressed; in the divorce tracts, then in *Areopagitica,* Parliament is fictively addressed. Through this device, Milton, on the one hand, is able to insinuate his enormous stature as an orator; and, on the other hand, by opposing his will to that of academicians and politicians, associating both directly or obliquely with the reactionary forces in society, he is able, paradoxically, to elicit the sympathies of his real audience composed of readers drawn from all segments of society and presumably, like Milton, interested in reforming the social and political and religious orders.

The desire to reach all segments of society encouraged Milton to master all three styles, but those styles are not always equally prominent in each oration. Sometimes the three styles are synchronized, as they are in the Seventh Prolusion, *Of Reformation, Reason of Church-Government, Areopagitica,* and *Defensio secunda;* but this is not true of the attacks on Hall or Salmasius. Milton, it seems, chose not only to make the various parts of different orations appeal to various elements in his audience; but even more importantly he chose to pitch different tracts to different elements in society and, when doing so, elected a method and a style appropriate to the segment of society he wished to reach. *Of Reformation* and *Reason of Church-Government* provide instances of this. The first tract is directed toward the multitude, the other—more refined in both argument and style—toward the learned. In the first instance, Milton is fighting "the people's battle," in the second, the intellectual's battle. But in neither tract does he disregard any segment of his potential audience. Instead he weights his arguments toward one group or another. In *Of Reformation* there are markedly different styles ranging from the extremes of rhetorical ornament to artless simplicity. In one moment Milton is talking about "God vomiting"; in the next he soars upon extended wing. Amidst the more erudite arguments and involved aesthetics of *Reason of Church-Government,* Milton, having admitted to writing poetry, thus impressing the learned, disparages it, unwilling to withhold a gesture from the Puritan multitude. *Areopagitica,* as I have suggested elsewhere, is Milton's crowning achievement in style: the three styles are perfectly harmonized, but Milton also, and more importantly, creates a dialectic of styles through which he separates himself (the true orator) from Isocrates (the false orator).[28]

The formation of a symbolic style is an early development in Milton's art. When he wrote "Lycidas," the dialectic of styles had already been perfected. In the elegy for Edward King, Milton encompasses the extremes of style—one artlessly simple, the other richly adorned—and through them mirrors the contrary states of the speaker's mind and the opposing worlds of the poem. However, the first occasion on which Milton makes symbolic use of contrary styles is the Sixth Prolusion, which is an extended and highly imaginative portrayal of the "idle vacancies given both to schools and Universities . . . forcing the empty wits of children to compose . . . Orations" (*Edu.* II.371-372). In its two prose sections, written in Latin, Milton runs the range of style from crude satire to playful irony. In the poem, written in English, he adopts the grand style. The opposition of styles within the prose

sections and the fiercer opposition between those sections and
At a Vacation Exercise establish a bold contrast between the
"empty conformities" of oratorical performance and the nobler
activity of writing poetry, between the vapidity of Milton's audience and his own gravity of mind.

To see in the Sixth Prolusion only "attempts at humor [that]
are downright vulgar" and "vulgar phraseology" that "paves the
way for an understanding of the type of language Milton was
sometimes later to employ in his scurrilous attacks upon personal
adversaries like Salmasius" is quite to miss the mark.[29] The crude
jokes, the vulgar braying, the conspicuous sniping—all expose
what Milton believes to be the intellectual level and interests
of his audience; the pointed ironies and later the grand style of
the poem reveal the larger capacities of a speaker who, having
observed the "custom" of performing for a large, unruly, and
dim-witted audience, is ready to forget the meaningless ceremonies of the University and to commit his talents to "some graver
subject"—one that will enable his mind to "soare/ Above the
wheeling poles, and at Heav'n's dore / Look in" (ll.30, 33-35).
Through the dialectic of styles, Milton has distinguished himself
as "true orator" from the host of academic rhetoricians he addresses. This contest of styles, this opposition between speaker
and audience, points to a central theme in all Milton's prose and
a major structural device in the blistering attacks on Hall, Salmasius, and More. In these satires, Milton sets in fierce opposition
the true and false orators—an opposition created and brilliantly
sustained by the abusive rhetoric that dominates the *refutatio*
and the sublime style of the personal digressions and perorations.

It has not been sufficiently recognized that Milton's revolutionary stance as an orator-poet places particular stress upon ethical
proof, though Milton's understanding of the importance of
ethical proof is clear enough. Not without significance, he places
the autobiographical "digressions" at the very center of both
Reason of Church-Government and *Areopagitica* and allows them
to pervade the three Defenses. The various divisions of an oration
—exordium, narration, confirmation, refutation, and peroration—
are variously suited to ethical, logical, and pathetic proof. In the
exordium there is the opportunity for the orator to establish his
virtue; in the confirmation and refutation the orator presents
arguments with logic and coherence; in the peroration he makes
his stirring emotional appeal. But Milton (and this point I shall
elaborate later) distorts the formal proportions of the classical
oration not only as a gesture of rebellion but in order to enable

the oration to carry the heavy weight of the ethical proof he offers. This realization brings us to an understanding of a basic difference between Milton and his classical predecessors, epic poets
and orators alike. They write poems and deliver orations in order
to codify the reigning values of their culture; Milton, on the
other hand, is intent upon uprooting the old and replacing it
with a new scheme of values. Epic poets and orators who allow
their audience to generate the values they celebrate may depend
almost exclusively upon logical and pathetic proof; but the orator-
poet who presumes to generate new values for his culture must
rely heavily upon ethical proof. If he expects to inspire his audience to burst the fetters of tradition he must first establish his
own moral authority. This Milton does not only in his exordia
(not even primarily there) but in the parenthetical asides and
long digressions wherein he projects the image of a true orator—
"a spirit of the greatest size, and divinest mettle. And certainly
no lesse a mind" (*Ref.*I.571).

The abusive rhetoric of tracts like *An Apology Against a Pamphlet* and *Pro Populo Anglicano Defensio* is part of this larger
design. Through ridicule and invective Milton establishes an
image of the false orator, his adversary, and then uses that image
to highlight his self-portrait, the image of the true orator. Behind
this design is the clear realization that any speech questioning
the morality of someone "must necessarily be based on *ethos*"
and especially "when it is engaged in portraying" the immoral
"character" of an opponent (*Institutio Oratoria* VI.ii.17).

In *An Apology Against a Pamphlet* Milton, for the first time,
makes major use of the contrast between the true and the false
orator—a contrast that is a central structural and rhetorical device both here and in the later tracts mounted on vituperation
and satire. Milton finds precedents for exploiting the opposition
in Cicero and especially in Christ who, as a true orator, a true
prophet, combated and exposed the false prophets (*Apology* I.
900). If Milton's intention was to make the Lord's people into
prophets, his responsibility, like that of the "Prophets of old,"
was to teach the people to *"discern and beware of false Prophets"*
(*Apology* I.931). In *An Apology Against a Pamphlet,* through
abusive rhetoric adopted from *A Modest Confutation*, Milton exposes the misguided arguments and foul character of his opponent; through the personal digressions he lends credibility to his
own arguments and reveals his own virtue. The *refutatio* projects
an image of the false orator, which, in turn, accentuates the
image of the true orator emerging from the autobiographical
statements.

Significantly, it is in the prose tracts whose rhetoric has been judged most offensive that Milton says the most about himself and about his functions as an orator. We know only by insinuation that Milton is fulfilling the technical demands placed upon the ideal orator by Cicero and Quintilian; but we know by countless statements that Milton regards the moral demands formulated by Quintilian as the highest obligation of the orator. Quintilian binds the twelve books of *Institutio Oratoria* with reminders that the orator must show himself to be a virtuous man if he is to teach virtue to others. If Milton is less given to redaction than Quintilian, he is no less insistent upon the moral character of the orator: "how he should be truly eloquent who is not withall a good man, I see not," says Milton (*Apology* I.874). And later he remarks,

> . . . he who would not be frustrate of his hope to write well hereafter in laudable things, ought him selfe to bee a true Poem, that is, a composition, and patterne of the best and honourablest things; not presuming to sing high praises of heroick men, or famous Cities, unlesse he have in himselfe the experience and the practice of all that which is praise-worthy. (*Apology* I. 890; cf. *Letters* XII.93, 95 [CM])

To insure that the rhetoric of abuse does not tarnish his own image Milton makes clear that he is conforming to the rules of rhetoric that require him to answer his opponent in kind. Milton, in other words, acknowledges a decorum for vituperation different from the decorum for praise.[30] In refutation (and this is essentially what *An Apology Against a Pamphlet* is) the orator's style is not determined by him but is dictated by the one his opponent used. "The rules of best rhetoricians, and the famousest examples of the Greek and Roman Orations" provide Milton with his precedents (*Apology* I.899). But he recognizes, too, that the issue here is not an aesthetic but a moral one; and this perception causes Milton to introduce a *persona* into his prose. Vituperation and satire, he knows, are foreign to moral character; hence he adopts a *persona* that matches the character of his opponent, reminding us that "the author is ever distinguisht from the person he introduces" (*Apology* I.880).

In this technique, Milton is no different from Christ the satirist who heaped "scorn upon an object that merits it" (*Apology* I. 899), or from Christ the artist who used a mixture of styles, or from Christ the moralist who wore all masks but who understood, in doing so, that in times of tyranny and corruption moderation is not enough. "Zeale whose substance is etherial" is required. In this context, Milton speaks illuminatingly of the "fiery Chariot drawn with two blazing Meteors figur'd like beasts . . . the one visag'd like a Lion to expresse power, high autority and indignation, the other of count'nance like a man to cast derision and scorne upon perverse and fraudulent seducers" (*Apology* I.900). Both images are appropriate to the orator-poet; the one is a figure of wrathful indignation, the other a figure of the true discerner. The one, to adopt language from Blake, is the voice of the roaring Rintrah, the other the voice of the poet-prophet. Milton recognizes in satire, in "tart rhetorick" (*Apology* I.901), an incidental value for the erudite who are by it reminded of the true nature of Christlike indignation and a value of major import for the multitudes who depend upon mockery for having "the false Prophets" exposed to them (*Apology* I.903). That exposure is accomplished only by a "competent discerner," a true prophet, a faithful teacher, a virtuous orator. In his discussion of satire Milton acknowledges the didactic force of grim laughter and scornful indignation, but he also acknowledges the limitation of the genre—an acknowledgment through which he can distinguish himself from Bishop Hall. Milton's adversary never reaches beyond the confines of satire or of the style associated with it, but Milton is continually pushing beyond it and in the process shows his mastery of the different "kinds" and of the various styles, and mixture of styles, appropriate to them.

The concerns of *An Apology Against a Pamphlet* are renewed in Milton's defenses of the English people and of himself. These works constitute an interrelated series of statements that bring to perfection Milton's art of refutation practiced in tracts like *Of Prelatical Episcopacy, Animadversions, An Apology,* and *Eikonoklastes.* They are organized around the contrast between the true and false orator, with the emphasis in *Pro Populo Anglicano Defensio* falling upon the false orator and that in *Pro se Defensio* upon the true orator. *Defensio secunda* holds the two concepts in perfect balance—concepts supported, here as before, by two strains of rhetoric, the one of vilification, the other of patriotic and moral fervor, but also sustained, here for the first time, by a dialectic of forms, satire and panegyric.[31]

In *Pro Populo Anglicano Defensio* Milton twice reiterates his need for a *persona* through which he may portray the false orator (Salmasius) without tarnishing his own image:

> You should know . . . that we should consider not so much
> what the poet says, as who in the poem says it. Various figures,
> some good, some bad, some wise, some foolish, each speaking

not the poet's opinions but what is appropriate for each person. (IV.i.439)

... it is the custom of poets to place their own opinions in the mouths of their great characters. . . . (IV.i.446)

These explanations of the *persona* are accompanied by additional defenses of satire and its low style. Milton twice implies that had Salmasius not compelled him to write in this particular mode and in the style suited to it he would be doing otherwise:

> If, Salmasius, your opinions on the right of kings in general had been advanced without invective against anyone, there would have been, even during the present revolution in England, no reason for any Englishman to become angry with you, for you would have but employed your freedom to write; nor would the assertion of your beliefs have been the less effective. (IV.i.474)

> So long as the nature of my *Defence* had to be suited to them [Milton's adversaries], I thought that I ought to aim, not always at what would have been more decorous, but at what they deserved. (IV.i.574)

Milton uses the long "preface" to *Pro Populo Anglicano Defensio* to establish a contrast between the true and false orators (Milton and Salmasius), and in the formal parts of the oration reinforces his portrait of the false orator by underscoring Salmasius' rhetorical insufficiencies. Only the preface need detain us here. Employing the modesty *topos* (with unusual modesty) Milton associates himself with "light, truth, reason, and the hopes and teachings of all the great ages of mankind," and simultaneously he identifies Salmasius with "deception, lies, ignorance and savagery" (IV.i. 307). As the true orator takes on the posture of humility, the false one, like Satan in *Paradise Lost*, "swells with haughty pride" and, like Moloch in the same poem, "lurks behind the ranks" in fear. The true orator, observing the venerable laws of oratorical tradition, elicits the sympathies of his audience whereas the false orator not only fails to elicit the goodwill of his listeners but, worse, arouses them to laughter by his "manifold improprieties" (IV.i.310). The true orator, writing for all men and for all time, protests that the false orator's *Defensio Regia* will be "seize[d] and hurl[ed] to oblivion" and that if the book should retain any life at all it will be by virtue of Milton's reply to it (IV.i.324). Having represented himself as a noble man endowed with virtue and learning, as an orator knowledgeable in theory and skilled in practice, Milton allows a tissue of epithets to keep the false

orator in view throughout his oration: "barbarous rhetorician
. . . prattling orator . . . weakly-raging eloquence . . . flowery
rhetoric . . . shopworn, oratorical coloring . . . mounted grammarian . . . raving sophist." These appellations, and many more,
testify to the oratorical incompetence of Milton's adversary.

In *Defensio secunda* Milton pursues the same contrast, this
time establishing a delicate balance between his portraits of the
true and false orator. The image of the former is projected in the
exordium, the long personal digression, and the peroration; that
of the latter in the short *narratio* and in the extended *refutatio*.
Here the true orator takes a less humble stance, first identifying
"the glorious achievements of his country as his own" (IV.i.550),
then transferring the "purity of life" and "blameless character"
of the people to himself (IV.i.552). Salmasius continues as the
object of occasional parenthetical insults, each of them underscoring the "manifest improprieties" of the false orator; but here
the real object of Milton's satire changes.

Now the thrust of Milton's "tart rhetorick" is levelled at Alexander More, with the pointed reminder that Morus in Greek
means "fool" (IV.i.565). The importance of that reminder has
been curiously ignored. Through it Milton translates his "name-
less" antagonist, not into an individual as most readers have assumed,
but into a type. It is the "meaning, not the Name" that Milton
calls (*PL* VII. 5). That the thrust of Milton's attack is directed
against a type rather than an individual is reinforced by his introduction of Salmasius and also the publisher Vlacq, then by his
identification of the collective villain as an actor. The implication
is clear: the false orator is uncommitted and unprincipled, the
perpetrator of vain conceits and specious rhetoric; the true orator
is dedicated to his purpose and accomplishes it by "persuasion
which lies in truth itself" (IV.i.604).

Drunk with "intellectual vision" (IV.i.589), clothed in "the
light of the divine countenance" (IV.i.590), the true orator
emerges as the hero of political radicalism and of religious dissent,
as the new Moses delivering another Chosen People from the
yoke of oppression into the Promised Land. Having "erected
a monument that will not soon pass away," having celebrated
"deeds that were illustrious, that were glorious, that were almost
beyond praise," the true orator emerges in the peroration as
"him selfe . . . a true Poem." Fully defined and greatly accomplished, the orator as prophet, king, and priest embraces, appropriately, the role of epic poet. Having celebrated "one heroic
achievement of [his] countrymen," Milton lays down the crown

of the orator and takes up the garland of the poet as he prepares
to celebrate both the tragic defeat and spiritual triumph of all
mankind in the garden and to tell of "deeds/Above Heroic, though
in secret done" (PR I. 14-15).

III

Distinguishing between the conservative and revolutionary artist,
Northrop Frye suggests that the one (like Pope and Byron) becomes an "indwelling spirit" within the forms he uses, bringing
those forms to perfection, while the other (like Blake and Milton)
shatters and then reconstructs literary forms so as to express his
own talent rather than that of his predecessors.[32] Milton's revolutionary stance is nowhere more conspicuous than in his polemical
works, chiefly because here the radical character of his thought
is undisguised. What has been ignored is the equally revolutionary character he displays in his handling of literary form. Not
only does Milton distort the proportions of the classical oration,
but he continually turns on end the small forms of exordium and
peroration that the large form embraces. In the process, a rigidly
fixed form becomes elastic and thus capable of accommodating
itself to Milton's diverse aims and emphases. The effect of this
"experiment" is not only to blur the usual divisions of the classical oration but to entangle the various tracts in such a way as to
present a large unified vision to which each of the individual
prose works contributes.

Though the analogy between God and the poet as creators and
the related one between God's creation and the poet's is most
conspicuous in Milton's poetry, especially in "Lycidas" and
Paradise Lost, it is implied in the prose works as well. Just as
the Father impressed upon the mind of the Son a pattern that
the Son executed, so a pattern, a form, conceived in Eternity and
impressed upon the mind of the orator-poet, is executed by him.
Moreover, the analogy between God and the poet implies a
similar one between the orator-poet and his audience, and yet
another between the orator-poet and his canon. God awakens
the spirit of imagination in the orator who, in turn, must awaken
the same spirit in his audience; the orator also extends to his
audience a perfect pattern of virtue and a perfect plan for reformation, which his audience is expected to adopt and to execute.
Still further, just as the diverse elements in God's creation par-

ticipate in a larger unity, so the orator-poet must subdue his various statements to a comparable unity. This Milton does by continually echoing or referring to one prose tract in another and by gathering them all together, as he suggests in *Defensio secunda,* under the master-theme of liberty—religious, domestic, and civil (IV.i.pp. 623ff).

The important matter is not whether this principle of unity was an afterthought or part of an original conception but that such a principle is articulated at all. Through it, the orator fulfills his priestly function, which, according to Milton, involves "making a kind of creation like to Gods" (*Anima*.I.721). In this duplicate act of creation, discords and enmities, the agony and strife of contraries, are resolved in unity. Imitating God, the orator-poet attempts to bring "the due likeness and harmonies of his workes together" (*Divorce* II.272). Words spoken by Milton in another context pertain here. Commenting on building the "Temple of the Lord," Milton says that "when every stone is laid artfully together, it cannot be united into a continuity, it can but be contiguous in this world; neither can every peece of the building be of one form; nay rather the perfection consists in this, that out of many moderat varieties and brotherly dissimilitudes that are not vastly disproportionall arises the goodly and the graceful symmetry that commends the whole pile and structure" (*Areo*.II.555). The passage appropriately subordinates the "unity" of the poet to that of God. Fully cognizant of the classical oratorical form and exceedingly facile in his use of it, Milton is also, and more importantly, intent upon effecting a radical transformation of the form, first by defying the "rules" long associated with it, then by allowing imagistic and thematic structures to override the formal divisions of the classical oration, and finally by entwining individual prose works within a larger design and more encompassing statement.

Milton's prose works are, therefore, a dramatic revelation of his belief that form is part of effect and must sometimes be "frustrated by its end" (*Logic* XI.55 [CM]). But before turning to specific tracts for explanation, it may be helpful to look at Milton's attitude toward the "rules" and toward literary form (so far as his philosophy of literary form may be put together from inference and from parenthetical aside). The Sixth Prolusion provides an interesting gloss on both. The ironic thrust of the entire first section called "The Oration" is gathered into focus when, in the peroration, Milton announces that he is about to take off "the fetters of rhetoric" and shake loose from the "usual custom" of adhering to "the strict rules of modesty" (I.

276-277). The fact is that Milton defies the rules of rhetoric
and the modesty *topos* throughout "The Oration." At the very
moment that he seems to be imitating classical form he is busily
undermining it. Usual proportions are distorted; the exordium,
expected to be brief, extends over seven paragraphs ("The Oration" is only fourteen paragraphs long). As Milton says elsewhere,
he is refusing to submit to "a rigid externall formality" or to be
saddled by "a grosse conforming stupidity" (*Areo.*II.564). In
line with this assertion is Milton's flouting of the modesty *topos*.
If Junius Brutus could "disguise his almost *godlike mind* and
wonderful natural talents under the semblance of idiocy, there
is assuredly no reason," says Milton, "why I should be ashamed
to play the wise fool for a while" (I.267; my italics). Then adopting the modesty *topos* momentarily, Milton explodes it: "let no
one wonder that I triumph . . . at finding so many men eminent
for their learning . . . ; for I can scarce believe that a greater
number flocked of old to Athens to hear those two supreme
orators, Demosthenes and Aeschines, contending for the crown
of eloquence"; and Milton continues:

> I cannot help flattering myself a little that I am . . . far more
> fortunate than Orpheus or Amphion, for they did but supply
> the trained and skilful touch to make the strings give forth
> their sweet harmony. . . . But if I win any praise here to-day,
> it will be entirely and truly my own, and the more glorious
> in proportion as the creations of the intellect are superior to
> manual skill. Besides, Orpheus and Amphion used to attract
> an audience consisting only of rocks and wild beasts and trees,
> and if human beings came, they were at best but rude and
> rustic folk; but *I* find the most learned men altogether en-
> grossed in listening to my words and hanging on my lips. (I.
> 268-269)

The most revealing gloss on Milton's passage is one from John
Rainolds' *Oratio in Laudem Artis Poeticae:*

> Do not think, therefore, that . . . Orpheus by his tuneful play-
> ing on the lyre moved mountains, held rivers, softened rocks,
> charmed deserts, tamed savage beasts, and made trees follow
> him; but believe that by the sweetness of the poet's song he
> soothed men more wrathful than mountains, restrained men
> more changeable than rivers, softened men harder than stone,
> civilized men ruder than forests, mastered men fiercer than
> wild beasts, and delighted men more senseless than blocks of
> wood.[33]

The context for Rainolds' comment is illuminating. Rainolds is discussing the cryptic nature of allegory, explaining that it entices good men to solve riddles and, by its obscurity, prevents evil men from penetrating them. "Gross ignorance," says Rainolds, will interpret allegory literally, while truly learned men, comprehending subtlety, will discern its deeper meaning. This is precisely the point Milton is making in the oratorical section of the Sixth Prolusion: the "fool" comprehends the allegory, while his "learned" audience accepts the literal interpretation he sportively offers it. The jest—the irony—lies in the fact that Milton, assuming the posture of "idiocy," imposes a literal interpretation on a received allegory and invites his audience of "learned" men to accept it. Through this irony, Milton accomplishes two things: he reveals himself to be other than fool and implies that his audience is less than learned; and in doing so he paves the way for the direct assault on his audience with which Section II, "The Prolusion," begins, where his audience is represented as "the commonwealth of fools" and he as its "Dictator" (I.277).

The Orpheus passage in the Sixth Prolusion is doubly significant. The passage relates importantly to the figure of the orator and to the audience he addresses. Puttenham cites Amphion and Orpheus as two poets of the first age, as "the first Priests and ministers of the holy misteries," the one building cities through "eloquent persuasion," the other subduing savage people through magnificent harmonies.[34] In the Orpheus passage, Milton presents an appropriate image for himself as orator; and he also projects an image of his audience. This is one dimension of meaning conveyed by the Orpheus myth in the Sixth Prolusion. The other relates directly to the matter at hand. By using the Orpheus myth ironically and thereby delivering a veiled insult to his fictive audience, by using it in a way that inflates the speaker and deflates those whom he addresses, Milton displays a willingness, indeed an eagerness, to flout the rules governing literary form and takes a firm stand against the "tyrant custom."

Milton's interest in literary form is manifested in virtually everything he writes, and it is pointed to by Milton himself when he lays down a plan for educational reform and, even earlier, when he maps out his poetical career.[35] In *Of Education,* Milton refers to Aristotle, Horace, and certain Italian critics as the teachers of "what the laws are" of epic, dramatic, and lyric poetry and of "what decorum is, which is the grand master peece to observe" (II.404-405). The context is important, for Milton is not merely encouraging the study of genre but is saying that from such study will come a knowledge of the inadequacies of the "kinds" as they exist and, thus, a perception of "what Religious, what glorious and magnificent use might be made of Poetry both in divine and humane things" (II.405-406). The yield of such study, in other words, will be an understanding not only of the "laws" that govern the various kinds but a sense of how those forms may be modified by a *new* decorum emerging from the effort to make "secular" forms serve "spiritual" ends.[36]

The importance Milton attaches to form in *Of Education* is punctuated in *Artis Logicae* where he says, "To form the first place is to be conceded, since end is nothing other than a sort of product of form" (XI.57, 59 [CM]), and in *Reason of Church-Government* where he provides a short history of literary form and thereby encourages us to give special attention to it. In the latter work, Milton wonders whether in writing epic poetry (diffuse or brief) "the rules of *Aristotle* . . . are strictly to be kept, or nature to be follow'd, which in them that know art, and use judgement is no transgression, but an inriching of art." Still further, Milton wonders "in whom to lay the pattern of a Christian *Heroe*" and whether "the instinct of nature," producing the "imboldning of art," should be "trusted" (I.813-814). The key word in both quotations is *nature;* and in each instance the term appears within the context of interrogation rather than declaration. This note of caution should cause us to question any authoritative statement about Milton's attitude toward the "rules," "decorum," or "form" based on this remark alone. The simple fact is that Milton is questioning whether one ought to observe strict classical patterning; he is not making a final determination one way or the other.[37]

The problem with most interpretations of this passage is that they ignore the distinction Milton is making—and ignore it because of widespread misinterpretation of the meaning Milton assigns to *nature.* Milton's meaning is spelled out in both quotations. He is not saying that rules "are strictly to be kept *and* nature to be follow'd" but instead is distinguishing the "rules" from "nature." Milton's *nature* refers not to imitation of nature in the Aristotelian sense but to nature as individual genius. The forms the poet wonders whether to imitate are not to be found in the external world; they exist in the imagination and are passed on to the poet from Eternity. If the question confronted by Milton is unresolved here, it is quickly answered by turning to his theory and practice.

Writing that "One Central Form composed of all other Forms

being Granted, it does not therefore follow that all other Forms
are Deformity. All Forms are Perfect in the Poet's Mind, but
these are not Abstracted nor Compounded from Nature, but
are from Imagination," Blake epitomizes Milton's thinking on
the subject of literary form.[38] "Single things . . . have form
single and proper to themselves," says Milton; "they differ
among themselves in forms, but not in common forms"—a statement that Milton explains by saying that "the rational soul is
the form of man generally; the soul of Socrates is the proper
form of Socrates" (*Logic* XI.59 [CM]). Milton, like Blake, preserves the identity of a form but also allows it to assume its individual shape so as to achieve its own particular end.

Milton understood that literary forms are (1) modes of reaction
(they produce particular effects by which one form is differentiated from another, epic from lyric, tragedy from comedy), (2)
principles of structure (they provide a rough scaffolding for ordering a succession of insights into a unique discovery), (3) vehicles
with their own ideologies (they project an attitude toward
human existence that all the examples of the genre share and
that differentiates these examples from those belonging to another kind). If epic is the form in which great deeds of men and
nations are commemorated and celebrated, the oration should
be the form which effects such accomplishments and the orator
the instrument by which individuals are delivered into freedom
and nations released from tyranny. Epic poetry provokes high
thoughts, and the oration inspires noble deeds. Epic poetry presents a vision of the ideal, and the oration translates the misery,
fever, and fret of human existence into the ideal.[39] Diversity of
form is, therefore, an important element of meaning; it is what
differentiates the "effect" of one oration or epic poem from another (*Logic* XI.245 [CM]). Form is, in Milton's words, "the
cause through which a thing is what it is"; it is the "peculiar essence of the thing . . . [the] essential distinction . . . the source
of every difference" (*Logic* XI.59, 61 [CM]). "*Form is produced,*"
says Milton, "*in the thing simultaneously with the thing itself.
Therefore the maxim is altogether true: When the form is given,
the thing itself is given; when the form is taken away, the thing is
taken away*" (*Logic* XI.61 [CM]). Thus, the ultimate objective
of any study of forms is "to know the internal form" which is
difficult, Milton concedes, since "external" form, expressed "to
the senses, is more easily observed" (*Logic* XI.63 [CM]).

Like Blake after him and like Euripides long before him, Milton
sought beauty "throughout all the shapes and forms of things"
and understood that "many are the shapes of things divine"

(*Letters* I.326). For this reason Milton looks disparagingly on *"the expediency of set forms,"* on "the compelling of set formes" (*Apology* I.936, 938), observing that while he is not "utterly untrain'd" in the rules of rhetoric or "unacquainted with those examples which the prime authors of eloquence have written" true eloquence is none other than "the serious and hearty love of truth" (*Apology* I.949).

Milton's entire discussion of liturgy (insofar as it is a statement on tradition, ceremony, and custom) may be regarded as a comment on literary form. It has been suggested, and quite correctly, that despite all the hostility Milton registered against the liturgy it is a significant element of meaning in his poetry.[40] What Milton objects to is not the liturgy *per se* but the unimaginative uses to which it is put. So committed were the Anglicans to fixing the liturgy that they resisted any deviations from it; they stilled invention. Milton's position is that no liturgy, and by extension no literary form, is to be slavishly imitated; instead it should each time be modified so as to become a new particular form that matches perfectly the special experience it records. "This very word of patterning or imitating," says Milton, "betraies it to be a mere childe of ceremony" (*Reason* I.765). This is the attitude toward literary form that informs Milton's oratorical efforts and that is reflected by them, beginning with the academic exercises.

Milton's prolusions are more of a piece than is generally acknowledged. Concerned with reforming education by ridicule and thus dealing with what Milton was later to describe as "one of the greatest and noblest designes, that can be thought on, and for the want whereof this nation perishes" (*Edu.* II.363), the prolusions are not only integrated with one another; but they are also an integral part of the larger vision to which the prose works individually contribute. In these seven orations, Milton announces the master-theme sounded insistently throughout the later polemics—the triumph of truth and learning over false-hood and ignorance. Appropriately, the arena for the contest is the University, providing Milton with an opportunity to dramatize the atrophied state of education that he ridicules but seeks to reform in *Of Education.* The harsh strains of Milton's indictment (an indictment that he insists is not "toothless" [I. 285]) emerge in the first two prolusions where oratorical form itself becomes a symbol of the oppression within the University and where Milton's violation of the rules becomes a figure for the war he wages against ceremony, custom, and error in behalf of truth. The Third Prolusion levels a severe mental blow at scholastic philosophy, which the next two prolusions continue.

The Sixth Prolusion widens Milton's indictment to embrace the
entire academic community, which, by following ceremony and
custom, has been transmuted into a "commonwealth of fools."
Placing this unhappy reality in perspective, Milton commits himself in poetry to higher matters nobly celebrated in the Seventh
Prolusion.

"Ignorance," says Milton, has "found her champion" in the
University and so the "defence of Learning" devolves on him (I.
290). Drawing from the past an analogy for the present, Milton
looks back to a time when "all the noble arts had perished and
the Muses had deserted all the universities," to a time when
"blind illiteracy had penetrated and entrenched itself everywhere"
(I.293). That the analogy is fittingly used, the earlier prolusions
testify. The last prolusion issues yet another warning but also en-
visions the time when Ignorance, driven from the "porticos and
walks," will be seen in "her final efforts and her dying struggle"
(I.301, 306). The first six prolusions, through the technique of
gradual exposure, portray what is and the last offers a vision of
what ought to be. This thematic integration is a part of Milton's
larger experiment in form. But the prolusions also point to formal-
istic devices that persist in the later prose works.

Through tenaciously repeated allusions, Milton places himself
and these early oratorical efforts within the context of the tradition represented by Orpheus and Amphion, Plato, Demosthenes,
and Cicero. Beside these pointed references Milton sets the
commonplaces of rhetoric which these representatives of the
classical oratorical tradition either formulated or were used to
exemplify. In the First Prolusion Milton alludes to the three kinds
of oration—demonstrative, deliberative, and judicial—and to the
demand that the speaker begin his oration by eliciting the good-
will of his audience (I.218); in the peroration of the same prolusion he speaks of the power of eloquence (I.232). If somewhat
hidden here, the principle is reiterated by Milton in the Third
Prolusion where he expresses his concern with the "threefold
function of a speaker" whose "fundamental duties . . . are first
to instruct, secondly to delight, and thirdly to persuade" (I.240).
Then again he spells out the power of eloquence, which "capti-
vates the minds of men and draws them after it so gently en-
chained that it has the power now of moving them to pity, now
of inciting them to hatred, now of arousing them to warlike valour,
now of inspiring them beyond the fear of death" (I.244). Moreover, Milton draws a correlation between "eloquent speech and
noble action" (I.246). So insistent is he upon having these com-

monplaces fixed in the reader's mind that he reasserts them in
the Seventh Prolusion. First, he recalls that the orator, through
"the power of eloquence" (I.290), may lead "a whole state to
righteousness" (I.292), then that by "expanding [the mind]
through constant meditation on things divine" (I.295) he may
establish "a kingdom" within "far more glorious than any earthly dominion" (I.297). Throughout the prolusions Milton remains
aware of the fact that the goal he hopes to achieve may be spoiled
by "the speaker's fault" (I.221).

This last admission, coming as accompaniment to Milton's conspicuous obsession with the tradition and the rules of classical
rhetoric, leads into the irony that pervades the seven prolusions.
Milton has deliberately recalled a tradition that he violates and
a set of rules that he defies. On the surface of things, Milton is
assiduously observing the classical pattern for deliberative oratory
fixed by Isocrates—a pattern which he executes most perfectly in
the Seventh Prolusion. Three paragraphs are devoted to the exordium, three to narration, eight to confirmation, ten to refutation, and one to the peroration. But even here the principle of
imbalance is evident, though not to the extent that it is in the
biting satire of the oratorical section of the Sixth Prolusion.
There (the point is worth repeating) the exordium occupies seven
of the oration's fourteen paragraphs, with two paragraphs each
being given to narration, confirmation, and refutation, and one
paragraph to the peroration. In the other five prolusions proportions continue to be upset or simply disregarded.

Besides over-elaborating some divisions of the oration and thereby disturbing the balance of the classical oration, Milton omits
the *refutatio* from the Third Prolusion and in the Second Prolusion blurs the divisions between confirmation and refutation.
These devices, which signify a gesture of rebellion in the prolusions, recur in the later prose works and there provide a way of
defining the "particular" form of each oration. *Animadversions*
and *An Apology Against a Pamphlet,* like the three Defenses, are
essentially refutations of charges levelled against Milton or his
"party" by opponents. To the extent that these and other satires
contain a confirmation it is postponed until the personal digression, which, in turn, is transformed into an integral part of Milton's argument. With Milton's exordia being used for posturing,
the "digressions" become the reservoirs of ethical proof. In
Areopagitica the divisions between confirmation and refutation
are obscured, allowing Milton to dispose of opposing arguments
at relevant points in his oration. Indeed, here the divisions are so

completely blurred and the arguments of refutation so generally confined to the early portions of the essay that Milton may be said to have inverted the proof sections of the oration.[41] Pursuing yet another modification of the usual pattern in *The Tenure of Kings and Magistrates* and in *Eikonoklates,* Milton divides the proof sections between the two orations, the first gathering together his confirming arguments, the second disposing of those presented by his opponents. *Defensio secunda* presents a further complication. Here Milton allows his oration to take its primary form not from deliberative rhetoric but from panegyric and diatribe,[42] but even so the fivefold pattern continues to provide a rough scaffolding on which to erect a more coherent structure. Thus Milton introduces a contest of forms, supported by the contest of styles, both of them mirroring the opposition between the true and false orator; but Milton also complicates his structure by harmonizing two formal patterns, the one derived from demonstrative rhetoric, the other from deliberative rhetoric. The effect is to create an oration of various structures rather than one of a single structure.

Besides allowing different oratorical forms to contribute to the work's structure (as he does in *Defensio secunda*) and letting poetical and rhetorical structures complement one another (as he does in *Areopagitica*), Milton introduces still another principle of structure, incidental to *Areopagitica,* but still important, and central to the three Defenses.[43] Both Cicero and Quintilian counselled the orator on the rhetorical advantage to be achieved from taking the form of an exordium or a peroration from one's opponent and making it serve new ends. In this regard, Quintilian says that "a most attractive form of *exordium* is that which draws its material from the speech of our opponent" (IV.i.54), and later he observes that "the most attractive form of peroration is that which we may use when we have an opportunity of drawing some argument from our opponent's speech" (VI.i.4). Milton simply extends this principle so as to allow the entire oration to assume the form of the treatise to which he alludes and which he proceeds to answer.

Milton's *Areopagitica,* which of all the prose tracts most assiduously follows the fivefold structure of the classical oration, is, according to Milton, written "on the model of a *genuine* speech" (*2Def.* IV.i.625; my italics)—*genuine* here referring not only to the *regular* pattern of the classical oration fixed by Isocrates but to a specific speech, Isocrates' *Areopagitic Discourse,* where Isocrates argues, unlike Milton, that liberties be restricted rather than relaxed.[44] The Defenses take their various structures from *Defensio Regia, Regii Sanguinis Clamor,* and *Fides Publica* respectively. In each instance Milton observes the rhetorical pattern established by the work he is refuting, arguing point-by-point against his opponent, exposing contradictions and pressing proofs offered by his adversary into his own service.[45] Through these subtle modifications of oratorical form, we see Milton taking the initial steps toward establishing himself as a revolutionary artist. In the bolder advances he makes against the small forms of exordium and peroration, his revolutionary stance becomes fully forged.

Ernst Curtius has observed that *topoi* are "the cellars—and foundations!—of European literature."[46] As the "expressional constants of European literature," they are also part of and symbol of "an immense historical process" that is a kind of "countermovement" against the intellectual revolution which in its two aspects we call the Renaissance and the Reformation.[47] In this context, Milton's handling of *topoi* takes on special significance. By turning *topoi* on end (many of which had acquired the status of "rule"), Milton assumes his revolutionary stance; but using those *topoi* seriously on occasion, he reveals a readiness to gather the best of the past into a new cultural moment. Milton's achievement is to use imaginatively what too often was used unimaginatively and to demonstrate that the small forms, and the large form that embraces them, are capable of impressive renewal. Moving beyond the level of historical parallel and stylistic ornament, Milton creates out of past and present experience "a kind of simultaneous order"[48] and invites his successors to do the same.[49]

Milton's Commonplace Book shows his familiarity with the tradition of *topoi*, and Ruth Mohl has demonstrated the importance of these commonplaces to Milton's prose works.[50] It is useful, nevertheless, to distinguish immediately between two kinds of *topoi*: (1) those gleaned from one's reading and then subsumed by his confirming and confuting arguments; (2) those appropriate to the fixed forms of exordium and peroration and used over and over again whatever the orator's subject. The distinction is admirably presented through the chapter headings used by Thomas Blount. The first type of *topoi* he subsumes under the heading of "Formulae Majores, or, Common Places," the second under the rubric of "Formulae Minores, or, Little Forms."[51] In either case, Milton makes uncommon use of *topoi*. In the first instance, he employs the commonplaces of argu-

mentation not to support but to overturn customary beliefs. In
the second instance, he invokes the "little forms" only to flaunt
them. In one instance, the effect is the disintegration of the
established structure of belief; in the other, the effect is the
demolition of traditional forms. Through his handling of *topoi*
in the prose works, then, Milton creates an image of the orator
as a revolutionary artist—an artist who generates new and more
perfect values by which his culture may live. The paradox at the
center of *Paradise Lost* pertains here: an act of destruction is
causally, not casually, related to one of creation; without the
one, the other cannot take place. Milton's orator-poet *here*
imitates God *there*. The orator's creative act occurs within the
context of a destructive one. The old forms and the erroneous
values they customarily embodied are shaken apart and new ones
set in their place. The values emerging from Milton's political
radicalism and religious dissent are, thus, embodied in literary
forms radically different from what they were before Milton
appropriated them. In this act of transforming tradition, coincidence is achieved between the revolutionary stance of Milton
as thinker and artist, each stance supporting and reflecting the
other.

Aristotle defines the analogy between epic poem and exordium
that Cicero and Quintilian extend and augment. He also describes
the purposes of the exordium and peroration that subsequent
theorists adopt. The exordium, says Aristotle, projects an image
of the speaker, testifies to the importance of his subject, and
defines the relationship between the orator, his audience, and
his adversary. Like the exordium, the peroration should make
the audience favorably inclined to the orator by putting the
listeners in an emotional frame of mind; its special functions are
amplification of arguments and deprecation of adversaries
(*Rhetoric* III.xiv, xix). Of special interest here is the fact that
both Cicero and Quintilian seek to relax many "rules" that had
become codified by practice, and yet both agree that "the rules"
governing the exordium "ought to be observed in *all* speeches"
(*De Oratore* II.xix.81; my italics). Nothing, says Cicero, "is more
important than to win for the orator the favour of his hearer"
(II.lxii.178), something best accomplished by exploiting ethical
proof within the exordium. "Conciliation of the audience," however, should not be confined to the exordium but rather should
"permeate the whole of the speech, and especially the peroration"
(II.lxxix.322).

Quintilian makes the same points, and more. "The sole purpose of the *exordium*," he says, "is to prepare our audience in such a way that they will be disposed to lend a ready ear to the rest of our speech" (IV.i.5). This is most easily effected, according to Quintilian, by observing the rules he lays down: no meanness of intent, no abuse except for the adversary, no excesses except in praise of audience. Most importantly, however, there should not be the slightest tinge of arrogance or even a "hint" of displeasure with the audience or judge. Finally, just as there are two kinds of exordia, one direct and the other by insinuation, there are two kinds of perorations, those that recapitulate the facts and those that stir the emotions. The peroration is the place to "let loose the whole torrent of our eloquence" (VI.i.51), but no "buffoonery" is appropriate to it (VI.i.46-47). Besides observing these rules, both exordia and perorations should exhibit "shrewd design and well-concealed artifice" (II.v.7). Nor are these views confined to ancient rhetoricians. One Renaissance theorist fairly represents the thinking of his contemporaries: "a true *decorum*" must be maintained; the orator, "having regard unto the Auditor," must insure that "nothing be uttered but what is honourable and gracious" in the "portall" of his speech; the orator should also insure that the peroration is "the utmost bounde of every speeche."[52] In brief, these are the rules governing the "little forms," and within their context Milton's practices are best assessed.

By forbidding arrogance in the oration, Cicero and Quintilian codify the modesty *topos* that Curtius brilliantly elucidates. The most inflexible rule of rhetoric is that modesty should be "affected" in order to put the reader in a "favorable, attentive, and tractable state of mind." Since the orator must obtrusively call attention to his modesty, explains Curtius, it is "affected" modesty; and the affectation is best achieved by humbling oneself before an audience, while simultaneously praising it. Thus submission and humility should stand side by side in both the exordium and the peroration.[53]

In the prolusions, Milton flagrantly defies what he calls "the first and chief duty of the orator" (I.219): conciliation of his audience. The First Prolusion begins with an open acknowledgment that "the speaker must begin by winning the good-will of his audience" without which "he cannot make any impression upon them, nor succeed as he would wish in his cause" (I.218). This acknowledgment, however, is followed first by an oblique, then by a direct, attack on the audience. Milton says, "I care not if 'Polydamas and the women of Troy prefer Labeo to me;—a trifle this'" (II.219-220). Labeo, a notoriously bad translator of

Homer, is here a type of the bad orator; Polydamas, a mindless critic, is a type of the audience Milton addresses. Tillyard comments appropriately: Milton cares not "if a bad critic and a worthless audience prefer a rotten poet to him"; the allusion is "as obvious as it is uncomplimentary to his audience."[54] Milton follows this criticism of his audience with a more direct one: "The approval" of a "few" is more important to him, he says, than "that of the countless hosts of the ignorant," who comprise his audience and who lack "all intelligence, reasoning power, and sound judgment" (I.200). Submission and humility are thus replaced by asperity and arrogance.

The exordia of the next two prolusions assiduously observe the modesty *topos*. In the Second Prolusion, Milton describes himself as "an insignificant person" and hopes that his "small powers" will not bore the academics who have already heard "so many eminent speakers" (I.234). The peroration is equally modest, its abruptness explained by Milton's wish not to offend anyone by his "confused and unmelodious style" (I.239). Again in the Third Prolusion Milton sets his "poor abilities" in contrast with the greater ones possessed by the "erudite" men in his audience (I. 240). But here Milton uses his peroration to withdraw the modesty and the accompanying flattery feigned in the exordium. Milton's audience, well versed "in every branch of learning" (I.240), is presented with an attack on scholastic philosophy; but in the peroration Milton invokes Aristotle, the founder of scholasticism, as the chief supporter of his position. When the irony tumbles forth it is clear that, by inviting his audience to accept Aristotle as an authority for arguments he cannot possibly support, Milton exposes his audience to playful ridicule. The entire oration becomes a comment on the ineffectuality of eloquence within an academic community that values authority more than truth. The prolusions that follow are all calculated to explode the *topoi* customarily associated with the exordium.

The orator is charged by tradition with the responsibility of defining the importance of his subject and of presenting his arguments lucidly. The orator, therefore, is expected "to clear away ambiguities" and "to unravel perplexities" (*Institutio Oratoria* XII.ii.10). In the Fourth Prolusion, while never sacrificing accuracy, Milton does exactly the opposite: he represents his subject as one of "the most trifling importance" (I.251). By forcing his audience to follow him through metaphysical bramblebushes and calculated ambiguities, Milton inspires boredom rather than interest—so much of it that the orator himself is "bored . . . to

extinction" (I.254) and can do no more than "beat a retreat" in
his peroration (I.256). The Fifth Prolusion is yet another example
of the dullness Milton associates with scholastic philosophy; and
the Sixth Prolusion (as indicated earlier) is a succession of jests
that exposes Milton to the charge of arrogance. In the words of
Kathryn McEuen, the most recent translator of the prolusions,
if Milton "was given to this kind of arrogant utterance, his unpopularity at the university is by no means inexplicable."[55] Nor
does Milton cast off Selfhood in the more serious Seventh Prolusion, which causes Tillyard to couch his praise of it in an apology
for its "arrogance" and its "rhetoric."[56]

At the same time that Milton is openly violating the rules, he is
willing to discredit his opponents for ignoring the authority of
tradition. Salmasius is charged with committing "manifold improprieties" in his exordium—improprieties so infelicitous that
his audience is roused to laughter rather than sympathy (*1Def.*
IV.i.310). Another adversary is chastised for breaking "everyone's
expectations" in his exordium (*3Def.* IV.ii.775). Yet Milton also
resolves the apparent contradiction between his own practice and
his criticism of others by explaining that the kind of exordium
suggested by Aristotle and codified by Cicero and Quintilian is
often denied him:

> I must descend, unwillingly and reluctantly, from relating
> matters great and glorious to those which are darksome, to
> seek out the lurking places of nameless men and the dens
> and shames of the basest adversary. Though this may seem
> to be not very honorable to one making an exordium and
> less suitable to rendering the mind of readers more attentive,
> still . . . my situation, being not without its parallel, has its
> consolations. (*3Def.* IV.ii.699).

Milton is finally distinguishing between those who violate the
rules mindfully and those who violate them mindlessly. By defying the rules of rhetoric, Milton accomplishes two things. First,
having set out to eclipse the classical orators who had fallen
short of the Ciceronian and Quintilian ideals, Milton is able to
exhibit a mind whose grasp of subtlety and of the hidden secrets
of oratory surpasses the collective mind of the classical rhetoricians. Second, he is able to establish an organic relationship between form and matter. The violations of the rules identify
Milton's mode as satire and underscore the figure of irony that
pervades it. Irony involves saying one thing and meaning another, verbal elements being inverted when the irony is perceived.

The figure of irony in Milton's prose is underscored and supported
by the inversion of the "little forms." Nowhere is this more in evidence than in the oratorical triumph of Milton's *Areopagitica.*
There, gestures of rebellion are transformed into elements of
meaning that reveal in full complexity the orator's mind and that
exhibit in equal complexity the vast profundities of his theme.

IV

Arthur Barker has written that "a full and exact understanding
of Milton's prose is essential to a complete understanding of his
great poems."[57] The statement is true and in a wider sense than
is usually acknowledged. Milton's literary achievement cannot be
fully understood nor can it be fairly judged by taking account
of his poetry alone. Neither can it be understood or judged by
studying his prose exclusively for its "content" and ignoring its
"art." To the extent that passages gleaned from the prose gloss
lines in the poetry, study of Milton's prose content has been
judged "productive." But to the extent that it exposes contradictions between Milton's polemics and poetry, seeming to justify
the eighteenth-century opposition between Milton the poet and
Milton the polemicist, the prose has been underplayed and often
ignored. The apparent division between polemicist and poet has
been used by Miltonoclasts to symbolize the divided mind of a
poet who allows rifts to open in the initial books of *Paradise Lost*
—rifts, we are told, that become a chasm in Book IX. The center
of the poem cannot hold, and so we are invited to behold (not
necessarily to read) a poem that is grand in its ruins.[58] Invariably,
such interpretations are pinned to the authority of Blake who,
proclaiming that Milton "was a true Poet and of the Devil's party
without knowing it,"[59] allegedly points to a conflict between
conscious and unconscious meanings in *Paradise Lost.* Thus Milton's admirers (Stanley Fish is a notable exception) have avoided
their living antagonists and, retreating into the past, have directed
their hostility toward Blake.
  The fact is that Blake's famous passage supports neither "party"
of Miltonists and largely because, wrenched from an illuminating
context, it has been misread—embarrassingly so. *The Marriage of
Heaven and Hell* is a satire, in the manner of Milton, pointed in
its ironies, often brutal in its wit. Moreover, the poet who wrote
it was probably closer to Milton in his sympathies than many of

his admirers believe; well-versed in Milton's prose, Blake possessed
a highly developed historical sense. The wit of his remark has
been lost on witless critics whose historical sense has gone dull.
Blake probably did not forget that Milton's opponent in *Regii
Sanguinis Clamor* spoke of him as one who prefers "hell," as one
who is "influenced by hell," associating Milton's voice with the
voice of the devil and the whole group of Puritan revolutionaries
with the diabolical party.[60] At one level, Blake is translating this
scorn for Milton into praise. But Blake's famous phrase has another related dimension of meaning to it: Blake well understood
that "the devil's party" was a clichéd appellation associated, during the eighteenth century, with the Jacobins and later with the
religious dissenters. The major thrust of his comment is toward
identifying Milton as a poet, radical in his religion and politics
and revolutionary in his artistry. Blake thus perceived a continuity
between polemicist and poet that has for a long time been ignored.

In one sense, Milton is Blake's harpist, who sings and in his singing moves us to the perception that "the man who never alters
his opinion is like standing water, & breeds reptiles of the mind."[61]
Much of what Milton says in his prose is consistent with his poetry,
but there are some moments of contradiction. More often, however, ideas and themes brought to refinement in the prose tracts
are later adjusted to Milton's epic vision. This is also true of the
figure of the orator and his conception of audience that emerge
from the prose works.

Milton's experiments in prose—the mixture of styles developed
in fine gradations and used to appeal to a full spectrum of society,
the subsequent dialectic of styles employed to support themes
and to differentiate characters, the violation of rhetorical rules in
order to achieve minute particularization of form, the depression
of rhetorical patterning for the purpose of creating interlocking
structures, the playing off of one genre against another, the blurring of the formal divisions of an oration, first to achieve greater
coherence within a work, then to achieve a unity of many works
—all these experiments testify to Milton's brilliance as an orator
and to his belief that "Mechanical Excellence is the Only Vehicle
of Genius."[62] Moreover, these interrelated experiments with
style, form, and genre are by no means confined to Milton's polemical efforts. In "L'Allegro" and "Il Penseroso" Milton combines poetical and rhetorical devices which structure his poems
and drive their themes. In the "Nativity Ode" the poet draws
upon various "kinds"—the ode, the dream-vision, the incidental
genre of the nativity poem—to accomplish similar ends. "Lycidas"

combines many of these techniques. The dialectic of styles supports a contest of forms that, in turn, provides a variety of structures through which the poet articulates his vision.

These devices, many of them perfected in the early poems as well as in the prose, most of them deriving from Milton's advances upon rhetorical tradition, persist in the epics. In *Paradise Lost* and *Paradise Regained* Milton brings into the service of "song" and "argument" every technique that he had earlier mastered; and he maintains the stance of the orator-poet as revolutionary, along with the complex relationship between speaker and audience that his prose works define. When in the final pages of *Defensio secunda* the figures of the orator and epic poet merge, so, too, do the forms of oration and epic. If Milton had initially distinguished between them—the one effecting great deeds, the other commemorating and celebrating them—that distinction blurs as the epic poet takes on the task of both praising deeds above heroic and precipitating them. It is no coincidence that *Defensio secunda* concludes by figuring the orator as a new and greater Moses who delivers a second Chosen People from the yoke of tyranny and custom and that *Paradise Lost* commences with the epic poet's assuming the same role and the same relationship to his audience.

O. B. Hardison, Jr., has argued that Milton "illustrates both the ideal [of the Renaissance orator] and the reason for its ultimate failure." "Mesmerized by his vision of the future" and unable to bring society into accord with it, says Hardison, Milton in *Paradise Lost* separates the poet from the orator, making the poet into "a blind prophet who turns away from the visible world" and transforming the orator from "hero" into "demon."[63] Hardison properly calls our attention to two passages on oratory, one from each of the epics, but draws wrong conclusions from them. As the temptation of Eve is about to begin, Satan appears,

> As when of old som Orator renound
> In *Athens* or free *Rome*, where Eloquence
> Flourishd since mute, to som great cause addrest,
> Stood in himself collected, while each part,
> Motion, each act won audience ere the tongue,
> Sometimes in highth began, as no delay
> Of Preface brooking through the Zeal of Right.
> So standing, moving, or to the highth upgrown
> The tempter all impassiond thus began.
>
> (IX.670-678)

According to Hardison, the condemnation of oratory, handled
here by insinuation, becomes overt in Milton's brief epic. Satan
offers to Christ the power of eloquence, and Christ rejects it (IV.
97-102, 353-364). Whether one approves of his "words" or not,
says Hardison, "they constitute a decisive rejection not only of
the temptation but of the ideal of social reform itself. They thus
strike at the heart of the humanistic belief that the orator and
the poet have complementary roles."[64]

Christ's "words" at this point are worth quoting:

> Thir Orators thou then extoll'st, as those
> The top of Eloquence, Statists indeed,
> And lovers of thir Country, as may seem:
> But herein to our prophets far beneath,
> As men divinely taught, and better teaching
> The solid rules of Civil Government
> In thir majestic unaffected stile
> Then all the Oratory of *Greece* and *Rome.*
> In them is plainest taught, and easiest learnt,
> What makes a Nation happy, and keeps it so,
> What ruins Kingdoms, and lays Cittes flat;
> These only with our Law best form a King.
> (IV.353-364)

What Christ says here and what Milton says of Satan in *Paradise
Lost* are perfectly compatible with what the orator says about
oratory in the prose works. The poet who invites us to follow
him through his "great Argument," who structures his poem
rhetorically and pursues the analogy between an oratorical exordium and an epic poem, cannot seriously ask for us to think that
the fusion between the orator and poet is "simply false." Hardison's conclusion does not mesh with the facts of either poem:

> The orator and the poet are not cousins—they are not even of
> the same race. Their functions, in fact, are antithetical. . . .
> The error of the humanists was to put poetry in the same
> category—to treat it as a higher eloquence, a more persuasive
> goad to action.[65]

Milton's entire literary career was devoted to his design of
eclipsing the classical orators and poets and then forging a new
literary tradition just as Christ had eclipsed his types and superseded their teachings with his own. Throughout Milton's prose
works he invokes the classical orators and theorists but only to
distinguish himself from them. Milton, in other words, obtains

to the ideal that Cicero and Quinilian articulated by mastering style and form, but he also supersedes Cicero and Quintilian by deriving a new standard of eloquence from the models of Christ and St. Paul.[66] When Milton invokes the tradition of Isocrates, Demosthenes, and Cicero it is to make differentiations; when he invokes Christ and St. Paul it is to establish "the knit of identity." Milton and Milton's Christ may cast a dubious eye on specious rhetoric but not without also embracing the "loudest Oratorie" of which Milton was the Renaissance's greatest master.

In his prose works Milton was intent upon establishing a sharp opposition between the true and false orator. This is what he does in the Defenses, opposing himself to Salmasius, More, and company; it is also what he does in *Paradise Lost* by contrasting Satan and the epic narrator.[67] The key phrase in the quotation from *Paradise Lost* cited by Hardison is "No delay / Of Preface," which recalls Moloch's bold entry into the infernal debate but also Milton's belief, formulated in *Pro Populo Anglicano Defensio*, that "not even in the treatment of an ordinary subject should one be so hasty" as to forgo some appropriate "introduction" (IV.i.302). The phrase is one of many by which Milton opposes himself (the true orator) to Satan (the false orator). Milton knew about "the devil's rhetoric" (*3Def.* IV.ii.823), and thus he opposes it with his own. Satan may have "fashioned his Tongue to the Dialect of Angels" but not so well that Milton could not discern him and expose his "ordinary practice of Deceit."[68] So doing, he presents his audience with credentials sufficient, he hoped, that "all Creatures [who] sigh to bee renew'd" would accept him as their moral guide (*Anima.* I.709).

Milton the epic poet persists in the belief that "the *Poet* is the neerest Borderer upon the Orator, and expresseth all his vertues."[69] Indeed, from Milton's point of view, the epic poet derives his moral character from the orator and through that character achieves superiority over his audience. The Renaissance epic began with *Orlando Furioso*. Whether or not it is an epic poem is unimportant here. What matters is that as a poem it makes an important statement about epic poetry and formulates certain premises about the poet and his audience that dominated the period. Ariosto invokes the epic tradition and subjects it to ridicule, not because the form is irrelevant but because its traditional values are. *Orlando Furioso* proclaims the viability of epic form and begs for future poets to accommodate it to Renaissance culture. An accommodation is made by Milton, but on somewhat different terms from those Ariosto proposed.

Like Ariosto, Milton promises to pursue "Things unattempted yet in Prose or Rhime" (*PL* I.16); but unlike him, Milton pursues them not into an ironic vision but into what Blake would call the "Divine Vision." In both *Orlando Furioso* and *Paradise Lost* there is "ironic disparagement operating," but in the two poems it operates differently.[70] Ariosto's irony seeks to replace what was with what is; Milton's seeks to replace what was *and what is* with a vision mounted on "original" Christianity, which, during the Middle Ages and in his own time, was perverted into an image of what it most deplored. Whereas Ariosto urged the poet to adjust his epic statement to the values of Renaissance culture, Milton asks his audience (a total culture) to reorient the reigning values and when necessary, to discard them, so as to bring them in line with his own moral vision. Herein lies the difference between the figure of the epic poet in *Paradise Lost* and in *Paradise Regained* and the figure of him in previous epics, and from this difference emerges Milton's complicated relationship with his audience.[71]

Milton not only draws his moral character from the orator; he derives from him his epic stance as well. Epic, more than any other literary mode, is bound to cultural history and class divisions. The oral epic belonged to the "people" and was sung to them. The Renaissance literary epic, however, recognized class divisions and was addressed to an aristocracy defined along economic lines. The poet, therefore, addresses an aristocracy; and though he assumes, like Ariosto, an artistic superiority, he proceeds to draw his values from those whom he addresses and from the culture he celebrates. In Milton, there remains a strong sense of elitism—and a continuing interest in audience. This is true from the First Prolusion, where Milton chastises his audience for its ignorance, to *Paradise Regained,* where through Christ he says that his audience should bring to books "A spirit and judgment equal or superior" to those qualities possessed by their authors (IV.324). In *Paradise Lost* Milton hopes "fit audience [to] find, though few" (VII.31). What distinguishes Milton from his epic predecessors is the fact that his "fit" audience is finally a moral rather than a social category of readers. Moreover, though Milton knows that the full comprehension of his art is restricted to this "elite" he also knows that the moral vision he articulates must be made accessible to all. The Greek quotations and formal title page of *Areopagitica* alongside its translations and subtitle, also the highly specialized theological and legalistic vocabulary of Book III of *Paradise Lost* alongside lucidly formulated con-

clusions, reveal Milton's continuing concern for all who can read
and comprehend. The artistry of the epics is a gift to the fit
readers, their moral vision a gift to all. Through it Milton hopes
to expand the consciousness of all readers and bring them into
an ever-widening group of the morally elect. Neither Milton's
prose works nor his epics were written *only* for the "fit audience
. . . though few." In both media Milton adopted a revolutionary
stance, overthrowing specious orthodoxies and replacing them
with perfected values; through both media Milton sought to be
"doctrinal and exemplary to a Nation" by opening the doors of
perception and thereby transforming the Lord's people into
prophets. When he saw that Empire would not follow him, he
ceased trying to build Jerusalem in England's green and pleasant
land and started instead to build mansions in Eternity.

It has been said that Ramus was "superficially revolutionary
but at root highly derivative."[72] The opposite is true of Milton.
Continually invoking traditions—poetical and intellectual—Milton
is simultaneously distinguishing himself from them. In a letter
to Benedetto Buonmattei, Milton expresses great respect for the
orator, the poet, the critic, "who tries to fix by precepts and rules
the order and pattern of writing received from a good age of the
nation, and in a sense enclose it in a wall; indeed in order that no
one may overstep it, it ought to be secured by a law all but
Romulean" (*Letters* I.329). A seemingly reactionary formulation
becomes less so when we recognize that the rule Milton devoted
his life and art to "fixing" was the first rule of revolutionary art:
approach literary forms (and by extension intellectual traditions)
"analytically and externally, tearing them to pieces and putting
them together again"[73] in a way that expresses individual genius.
Milton grasped that revolution in the arts and in society is "perpetual"—"all things . . . never remaine the same."[74] It is no wonder that, when experimentation with literary forms resumed at
the end of the eighteenth century, the Romantic poets turned
instinctively to Milton whom they took as their model for sonnet,
lyric, ode, and epic and celebrated as "the Awakener" of the
nation. Milton, these poets insisted, charged atrophied forms
with life and used those forms to discharge the lightning that
rolled the dark clouds of ignorance into the distance.[75]

Notes

This essay was researched and written during my tenure as a Research Fellow at the Folger Shakespeare Library. I owe a large debt to the Trustees of Amherst College, who awarded the grant, and to the Librarians, who provided valuable assistance and many kindnesses.

1. Whenever possible I have taken my quotations of Milton's prose from *Complete Prose Works of John Milton,* ed. Don M. Wolfe et al. (New Haven: Yale University Press, and London: Oxford University Press, 1949-1966). Works quoted in this paper but not yet available in the Yale *Milton* are cited from *The Works of John Milton,* ed. Frank Allen Patterson (New York: Columbia University Press, 1931-1938). References to both editions are given parenthetically within the text of this paper. I have used the symbol [CM] to indicate those citations referring to the Columbia *Milton.*

2. "The Orator and the Poet: The Dilemma of Humanist Literature," *Medieval and Renaissance Studies,* 1 (1971), 33-44. My own note, "Milton's Idea of the Orator," *Milton Quarterly,* 6 (1972), 38-40, provides an introduction to the concerns of this paper; it also suggests the direction that a counter-statement to Hardison's essay must take.

3. Quotations of classical authors, unless otherwise indicated, are taken from the translations in the Loeb Classical Library, and citations are given parenthetically within the text of the paper.

4. Quintilian insists that he is concerned with not only presenting the rules of oratory but also bringing "to light the secret principles of this art" and revealing "the inmost recesses of the subject" (VI.ii.25).

5. Sister Miriam Joseph, *Shakespeare's Use of the Arts of Language* (New York: Columbia University Press, 1947), p. 8.

6. Milton's prose works with the widest circulation today are those that project the image of a philosophical libertarian, but equally important to Milton's image are tracts like *Artis Logicæ, Tetrachordon, The History of Britain,* and *De doctrina christiana* that project the images of rhetorician-logician, biblical exegete, historian, and theologian respectively. It is not without significance that Milton's oratorical efforts culminate in the writing of a theological treatise, especially when we recall Augustine's belief that "The Christian orator is . . . 'divinarum Scripturarum tractator et doctor,' the commentator and teacher of the Sacred Scriptures"; for an illuminating discussion of this "guiding principle" of Christian oratory, see Dennis Quinn, "Donne's Christian Eloquence," *ELH,* 27 (1960), 276-297.

7. In *Pro se Defensio,* Milton again speaks of the mental warfare to which he is committed, explaining that the time has come for eloquence to serve the state: "imaginary eloquence" and "exercise-shafts" must be cast aside as the orator ventures "into the sun, and dust, and field of battle, now to exert real brawn, brandish real arms, seek a real enemy" (IV.ii.795).

8. I quote from M. L. Clarke, *Rhetoric at Rome: A Historical Survey* (London: Cohen and West, 1953), p. 151, and from Joseph Anthony Mazzeo, *Renaissance and Seventeenth-Century Studies* (New York: Columbia University Press, and London: Routledge and Kegan Paul, 1964), pp. 4-5. But for other insightful discussions of the Christian oratorical tradition that derives from Augustine,

see Richard McKeon, "Rhetoric in the Middle Ages," *Speculum*, 17 (1942), 1-32; Erich Auerbach, *Literary Language and Its Public in Late Latin Antiquity and in the Middle Ages,* trans. Ralph Manheim, Bollingen Series, No. 74 (New York: Pantheon Books, 1965), especially pp. 27-66. In *Areopagitica*, Milton himself observes that the Middle Ages cultivated "a new Christian grammar" (Yale *Milton*, II, 509); and Milton's own oratorical practices reveal his interest in creating an even more perfect Christian rhetoric than Augustine had presented, first by reconciling classical theory with the practices of his Scriptural models, then by bridging the "clear distinction," which persisted into the Renaissance, "between secular and divine oratory" (Quinn, p. 280, but see also p. 282). If it can be said that the Renaissance establishes "the aims, rules, and types of classical oratory as the basis of Christian oratory" (p. 280), it can also be said that, working off the tradition of Christian eloquence, Milton creates a still more perfect Christian rhetoric as revolutionary in the context of the Renaissance as Augustine's was in the context of the Middle Ages.

9. John Smith, *The Mysterie of Rhetorique Unveil'd* (London, 1665), sig. [A5] What Quinn concludes about John Donne ("His eloquence—style, structure, imagery . . . —proceeds from that great source [Scripture]" [p. 297]) is equally true of Milton.

10. See Wolfe, "Introduction," Yale *Milton*, IV, i, 111.

11. Clarke, p. 149.

12. T. Holt White, "Prefatory Remarks," *Areopagitica* (London, 1819), p. xxxvii.

13. John M. Major, "Milton's View of Rhetoric," *Studies in Philology*, 64 (1967), 686.

14. Donald C. MacKenzie, "Translator's Note," Yale *Milton*, IV, i, 296.

15. Charles Sears Baldwin, *Ancient Rhetoric and Poetic Interpreted from Representative Works* (New York: Macmillan Co., 1924), p. 57

16. It is also important to observe with Irene Samuel that this statement does not in any sense reveal all of Milton's thinking on the subject of style; see Milton on Style," *Cornell Library Journal,* 9 (1969), 39-58. Milton's prose works are as much a search for an "ultimate style" (the phrase is Samuel's) as they are a search for the ultimate oratorical form.

17. Two comments by Longinus are pertinent: "Sublimity . . . reveals, at a stroke and in its entirety, the power of the orator"; it is "the note which rings from a great mind" (*On the Sublime,* trans. A. O. Prickard [Oxford: Clarendon Press, 1906], pp. 2-3, 14). It should be observed, however, that there is an ironic inversion of styles in *Paradise Lost*, where the lofty style is associated with Satan and the plain style with God. The same inversion of styles persists in *Paradise Regained*, and in both instances the inversion of styles finds its justification in the evolving biblical aesthetic that is Milton's ultimate source for "decorum."

18. *The Arte of English Poesie* (1589; rpt. London, 1811), p. 118.

19. For elaboration of this point, see my note, "Another 'Jest' in Milton's 'Sportive Exercises,'" *Milton Quarterly*, 7(1973), 5-8.

20. *Mystagogus Poeticus, or the Muses Interpreter,* 5th ed. (London, 1672), pp. 337-338.

21. "Preface," Yale *Milton*, I, 619.

22. See *Defensio secunda*, IV, i, 635.

23. Significantly, in "Preface to *Theatrum Poetarum*," Edward Phillips observes that those "commonly call'd the vulgar or Multitude" constitute a moral rather than a class category of

readers; see *Critical Essays of the Seventeenth Century*, ed. J. E. Spingarn, II (Oxford: Clarendon Press, 1908), 257.

24. See Grace's note and Wolfe's "Introduction," in Yale *Milton*, IV, i, 339, 264 respectively.

25. See Grace's note, Yale *Milton*, IV, i, 423.

26. It should be noted that Milton's famous exemption of "Popery, and open superstition" from toleration (Yale *Milton*, II, 565) is generally interpreted as an imposition of limits on toleration and as part of a strategy that discounts extremes of opinion on either side of the political spectrum. The passage is, of course, an important part of Milton's strategy, but it operates differently from what commentators, like Ernest Sirluck, have supposed (see "Introduction," Yale *Milton*, II, 178-181). Sirluck's discussion of Milton's strategy in *Areopagitica* reinforces my observations above, but in this one particular we are at odds: instead of excluding the far left and the far right from his rhetorical strategy, Milton's exemption involves an appeal to both extremes. By exempting Popery from toleration, Milton appeals to the reactionary forces in Parliament—those incapable of digesting the libertarian principles expounded in the course of his formal argument. By invoking Paul's speech, by seeming to violate scholarly principles in his interpretation of it, and by finally presenting Paul (and by analogy himself) in the posture of self-criticism, Milton underscores for his fit audience that what he says here is part of a political strategy rather than an ideology. For an interpretive context that illuminates these assertions, see my essay, "Milton's *Areopagitica*: Its Isocratean and Ironic Contexts," *Milton Studies*, 4 (1972), 101-115, n. 20. The interpretation I suggest in this note and elaborate in my essay is

in line with the reminder provided by Milton's anonymous biographer that the poet "was not blindly prejudiced" (XVIII, 375 [CM]); it is in line with Leo van Aizema's manuscript report of Milton's activities relating to the "Socinian Racovian Catechism" (XVIII. 369 [CM]).

27. See Donald Roberts' note, Yale *Milton*, IV, i, 555.

28. See my essay cited in n. 26.

29. See Kathryn McEuen's headnote to the Sixth Prolusion, Yale *Milton*, I, 265.

30. See Roberts' "Preface," Yale *Milton*, IV, i, 538-544.

31. Ibid:, but see also the "Translator's Note" by Helen North, p. 545.

32. *The Return of Eden: Five Essays on Milton's Epics* (Toronto: University of Toronto Press, and London: Routledge and Kegan Paul, 1965), pp. 90-93.

33. Ed. William Ringler and trans. Walter Allen, Jr. (Princeton: Princeton University Press, 1940), p. 45. Though written about 1572, Rainolds' *Oratio* was not published until 1614. It was reprinted twice, once in 1619, again in 1628.

34. *The Arte of English Poesie*, p. 4.

35. It cannot be overemphasized that the oration is the place to begin the study of Milton's use of literary form. The unrealized potentiality of the form is carefully detailed by Cicero and Quintilian; so are the rules that govern the form. This critical tradition, hardened into orthodoxy by the Renaissance, provides the kind of critical context for assessing Milton's oratorical art that simply does not exist for any of the poetical forms he used. It should also be recalled that the oration is typically distinguished from poetical forms: oratory is a mode of imitation and invention rather than, like poetry, one of

mental creation. In his use of oratorical form, Milton exhibits the licenses more typical of the poet, handling traditions here as freely as he did when writing pastorals and epics.

36. In "The Style and Genre of *Paradise Lost*," John Shawcross comments incisively: "Milton created his own decorum" (p. 17). Shawcross is, of course, talking about Milton's epic; but even so, many of his remarks there relate to many of mine here (see *New Essays on Paradise Lost*, ed. Thomas Kranidas [Berkeley and Los Angeles: University of California Press, 1969], pp. 15-33).

37. However, the general thrust of these comments, especially the first one, is in the direction of relaxing rather than observing the "rules." This autobiographical digression is too often wrenched from an illuminating context. Milton is arguing against prelacy and especially against the codification of liturgy: what he says about *liturgical form* coincides with (may be used as a gloss on) his attitude toward *literary forms*.

38. *The Complete Writings of William Blake with Variant Readings*, ed. Geoffrey Keynes (New York, Toronto, and London: Oxford University Press, 1966), p. 459.

39. See Roberts' note, Yale *Milton*, IV, i, 548, where he observes that Milton "considered the defence of liberty and the denunciation of tyrants the special province of orators."

40. See, e.g., Thomas Bradley Stroup, *Religious Rite and Ceremony in Poetry* (Lexington: University of Kentucky Press, 1968). It is, however, the brilliance of interpretations suggested by A. B. Chambers in his forthcoming book that convinces me of the value of this approach.

41. G. K. Hunter remarks, "Confirma-

tion and refutation here reverse the usual order"; see "The Structure of Milton's *Areopagitica*," *English Studies*, 39 (1958), 118.

42. See Roberts' "Preface," Yale *Milton*, IV, i, 540.

43. At the same time that Milton takes the form of a speech from his opponent he is apt to overlay it with the form of a speech taken from a sympathizer. In *Tetrachordon*, for instance, he allows his commentary to assume the form of those written by David Pareus (see Arnold Williams' "Preface," Yale *Milton*, II, 572); in *Areopagitica*, he alludes not only to Isocrates' *Areopagitic Discourse* but also to St. Paul's speech before the Areopagus.

44. See my essay cited in n. 26; but see also White's "Prefatory Remarks," especially his reference to Isocrates' *Areopagitic Discourse* as the "immediate copy" for Milton's *Areopagitica* (p. xxiii) and his headnote, pp. [cxlvii] - cxlix.

45. See Wolfe's "Introduction," Yale *Milton*, IV, i, 110, for remarks that pertain here.

46. *European Literature and the Latin Middle Ages*, trans. Willard R. Trask (1953; paper ed. New York and Evanston: Harper and Row, 1963), p. 79.

47. Ibid., pp. 114, 228.

48. See Kester Svendsen's note, Yale *Milton*, IV, ii, 699.

49. Curtius observes that oratory had become atrophied during the Middle Ages, but "in England from the eighteenth century onwards, eloquence has been the expression of political forces, the concern of the nation" (p. 63). This phenomenon—the rebirth of a genre—was made possible largely through the accomplishment of Milton. *Areopagitica* and *Defensio secunda* are to later examples of oratory what *Paradise Lost* and *Paradise Regained* are to Mil-

ton and *Jerusalem, The Prelude, Prometheus Unbound* and Keats's Hyperion poems.

50. See Mohl's "Preface," Yale *Milton*, I, 344-359, but see also (and more importantly) her study, *John Milton and His Commonplace Book* (New York: Frederick Ungar, 1969).

51. *The Academy of Eloquence: Containing a Compleat English Rhetorique Exemplified* (London, 1656), pp. 49, 119.

52. Daniel Tuvill, *The Dove and the Serpent* (London, 1614), pp. 70-71, 79.

53. Curtius, pp. 83-91.

54. *Milton: Private Correspondence and Academic Exercises* (Cambridge: Cambridge University Press, 1932), p. 135.

55. See McEuen's note, Yale *Milton*, I, 220.

56. *Milton: Private Correspondence*, p. xxxix.

57. *Milton and the Puritan Dilemma* (Toronto: University of Toronto Press, and London: Oxford University Press, 1942), p. xi.

58. See, e.g., A. J. A. Waldock, *Paradise Lost and Its Critics* (New York and Cambridge: Cambridge University Press, 1947).

59. Keynes, p. 150.

60. See Roberts' note, Yale *Milton*, IV, i, 575.

61. Keynes, p. 156.

62. I adopt language from Blake; see ibid., p. 453.

63. Hardison, pp. 38, 40.

64. Ibid., pp. 41-42.

65. Ibid., pp. 43-44.

66. See n. 8.

67. See, e.g., William G. Riggs, "The Poet and Satan in *Paradise Lost*," *Milton Studies*, 2 (1970), 59-82.

68. Tuvill, pp. 7, 71. Milton's concept of the true and false orator is irrevocably involved with his concept of the true and false prophet, and David Pareus provides him with a precedent for associating both the false orator and the false prophet with Satan. Commenting upon Rev. 19.20, Pareus explains that the false prophet, associated with the Beast, is "the individual *Achates* and Orator of the *Beast*." Thus the false prophet, the Beast, and "the other Beast with two hornes" (Rev. 13.11) are related to, not distinct from, one another. The false prophet, Pareus explains, simply makes apparent "the *Character of the Beast*" and is an "Image" of him; the Beast is a type of all the false prophets and false orators, the most notable of whom are Satan and the other devils. See *A Commentary Upon the Divine Revelation of the Apostle and Evangelist John*, trans. Elias Arnold (Amsterdam, 1644), pp. 494-495.

69. In *Timber*, Ben Jonson quotes Cicero to this effect; see Spingarn, I, 55.

70. The phrase is T. J. B. Spencer's; see "*Paradise Lost*: The Anti-Epic," in *Approaches to Paradise Lost*, ed. C. A. Patrides (London: Edward Arnold, 1968), p. 87. Milton's use of epic irony may be further distinguished from Ariosto's by observing that whereas Ariosto wants to put new wine in old bottles Milton seeks a radically new form for the vision he presents. This is the point of his belittling epic conventions—and with a vengeance that has caused Spencer to conclude that *Paradise Lost* is an "anti-epic" (p. 98). Spencer's conclusion, however, is misleading. *Paradise Lost*, rather than destroying the epic tradition (as Spencer and others would have us believe), brings about its purification. Having purged the tradition of its atrophied machinery—of all that obstructs

"vision"—Milton creates from the "ruines" of the classical epic a new kind of epic exemplified by *Paradise Regained*. This poem, not *Paradise Lost*, constitutes the truly revolutionary moment in the history of epic poetry. Significantly, Blake, too, uses epic irony in *Milton* and in the manner of Milton; see Brian Wilkie, "Epic Irony in Milton," in *Blake's Visionary Forms Dramatic*, ed. David V. Erdman and John E. Grant (Princeton: Princeton University Press, 1970), pp. 359-372. Wishing to bring into focus the Miltonic vision, which epic paraphernalia in *Paradise Lost* obscured, Blake takes the form, structure, and theme of *Milton* from *Paradise Regained*, replacing Milton's Christ with Milton himself. The difference between the way Ariosto uses epic irony and the way Milton and Blake use it is important to observe. The ironic perspective (twofold vision) dominates *Orlando Furioso*; it is but one of several perspectives in Milton's epics and Blake's, where vision fourfold, or the "divine vision," predominates. Ariosto is a poet of "experience," Milton and Blake, poets of "higher innocence."

71. My remarks should be considered within the context of those made by Robert M. Durling, *The Figure of the Poet in the Renaissance Epic* (Cambridge, Mass.: Harvard University Press, 1965), especially pp. 91-237.

72. Walter J. Ong, *Ramus: Method, and the Decay of Dialogue* (Cambridge, Mass.: Harvard University Press, 1958), p. ix.

73. Frye, p. 91; but see also pp. 90, 92-93.

74. I quote from the concluding paragraph of Samuel Daniel's *A Defence of Ryme*, in *Elizabethan Critical Essays*, ed. G. Gregory Smith (Oxford: Clarendon Press, 1904), II, 384.

75. Since completing this essay, I have had the opportunity to read Angus Fletcher's *The Transcendental Masque: An Essay on Milton's Comus* (Ithaca, N.Y.: Cornell University Press, 1971). This book is the most sophisticated statement to date on Milton's conception of literary form, and thus I am pleased to discover that Fletcher's conclusions corroborate my own.

Milton's *Of Reformation* and the Dynamics of Controversy

MICHAEL LIEB

University of Illinois, Chicago Circle

I

Reminded of Milton's assumption that the writing of tracts represented a lower order of endeavor than the writing of poetry, we might well hesitate to subject a tract such as *Of Reformation* to the kind of analysis we would ordinarily devote to a poem like *Paradise Lost*.[1] Tract writing, after all, was a task Milton had undertaken with his "left hand," a task that did not lend itself to "all the curious touches of art, even to the perfection of a faultlesse picture," since "in this argument the not deferring is of great moment to the good speeding, that if solidity have leisure to doe her office, art cannot have much" (I, 807-808). These statements would seem to corroborate prevailing negative responses to the artistry of Milton's prose. In *Essays on Milton*, for example, E. N. S. Thompson points to "the absence in the tracts of that high artistry that is noticeable in all his [Milton's] poems,"[2] and, commenting on the apparent lack of organization in Milton's prose, Don M. Wolfe objects to "Milton's topical arrangement of ideas, which is so often disorganized as to defy logical analysis. Almost never in Milton's prose does one find the logical organization and thematic unity of his verse paragraphs. Compared to the prose of Bacon, Dryden and Jeremy Taylor, or even that of Sidney and Raleigh, Milton's prose is singularly chaotic and capricious in organization."[3] *Of Reformation* is hardly free of such critical strictures. According to Everett Emerson, Milton's tract "bears signs of hasty composition, particularly in its organization."[4]

In light of these remarks, an analysis of Milton's first antiprelatical tract necessitates some kind of justification. That justification resides in a number of particulars, the most obvious being that an understanding of the issues raised in *Of Reformation* will provide significant insight into Milton's place in the whole antiprelatical controversy.[5] But of most immediate importance is the insight that a study of *Of Reformation* will offer in comprehending the nature of Milton's polemical strategies. If we can come to terms with those strategies, perhaps we shall more readily discern what principles govern the execution of a tract such as *Of Reformation*. For that purpose, I shall consider Milton's tract thematically and structurally as a way of determining the fundamental issues underlying polemical discourse. Thematically, I shall explore the historical account embodied in *Of Reformation* in order to suggest the character of Milton's revelatory approach. Structurally, I shall analyze Milton's accommodation of traditional rhetorical techniques to his own radical vision of what polemical discourse is supposed to do. In both cases, I shall attempt to show how Milton drew upon prevailing modes of discourse in order to transcend them. Since the historical account embodied in *Of Reformation* is of such pressing importance, a consideration of that aspect of his polemics should represent a fitting point of departure.

David Masson's classification of *Of Reformation* as "an original historical essay"[6] is not unfounded: a large portion of Milton's tract is cast in the form of an historical narrative. In that way, his tract fulfills its professed aim, as indicated by the title, of describing "the Causes that hitherto have hindered" the fulfilling of the Reformation in England, "initiated," as William Haller says, "three centuries earlier by Wyclif."[7] Historically, then, Milton provides us with an account of the various corruptions of the English church, extending through Henry VIII, Edward VI, and Elizabeth and culminating in the lapses of the present. Biographically, his treatment is interesting because it reveals the way in which he embodied in polemical form his earlier impulse to write an Arthuriad,[8] an impulse that was to be given expression throughout his career, manifesting itself, among other places, in his account of the history of licensing in *Areopagitica*, in his full-scale treatments of Britain and Muscovia, and poetically in his narrative of Biblical history in *Paradise Lost*.[9]

Recalling the historical account in *A Postscript* appended to the Smectymnuan *Answer*,[10] *Of Reformation* reveals Milton's intimate acquaintance with historians like Holinshed, Camden, Speed, and Stow (historians to whom Milton had repeatedly referred in his Commonplace Book),[11] and his disposition to engage in what Haller calls the "apocalyptic fervour" of Foxe, Jewel, and Aylmer.[12] According to Don M. Wolfe, this historical section was "new and vital material in the pamphlet literature of 1641. William Prynne's *Antipathie of the English Lordly Prelacie* (July 5) was the only contemporary pamphlet to trace in full the historical process Milton reviews in brief."[13] This may be true in part, but one cannot forget the fact that as early as 1628 Alexander Leighton, in *An Appeal to the Parliament; or Sions Plea against Prelacie,* gave an historical account (much in the manner of Milton's *Of Reformation*) of prelatical corruption beginning in the seventh century and ending in his own day. This leads us to suspect, therefore, that Milton's incorporation of the historical element into polemical discourse is not so innovative (or "original," to use Masson's term) as we might assume. Rather, the safer assumption is that it accords with standard polemical practices.

Certainly, Milton's treatment of ecclesiastical history between the time of Christ and Constantine (as well as the corruptions that ensued after Constantine) reflects one of the most pressing issues of the entire prelatical dispute, that concerning the prelates' claim to *jure divino*, derived from apostolic appointment, within the hierarchical structure of the church. (See, for example, Joseph Hall's *Episcopacie by Divine Right. Asserted* [1640], which purports to trace the divine origins of episcopacy through what Wolfe calls "the practices of the primitive church and the testimony of the fathers"[14] and thereby to establish episcopacy as " 'an eminent order of sacred function, appointed by the Holy Ghost, in the Evangelicall Church, for the governing and overseeing thereof; and for that purpose indued with . . . perpetuity of Jurisdiction'."[15])

Basic to such sixteenth-century disputes as those between Whitgift and Cartwright, the issue of prelatical authority pervaded the entire debate between Hall and the Smectymnuans and subsequently left its mark on Milton. It is of main concern, for example, in *Of Prelatical Episcopacy*, which argues that we should resort not to "the offalls, and sweepings of antiquity" (as have the prelates) but to the Bible in order to see that episcopacy is of human constitution rather than of divine (I, 651). It argues, that is, that we

> doe injuriously in thinking to tast better the pure Euangelick Manna, by seasoning our mouths with the tainted scraps, and fragments of an unknown table; and searching among the verminous, and polluted rags dropt overworn from the toyling shoulders of Time, with these deformedly to quilt, and interlace the intire, the spotlesse, and undecaying robe of Truth, the daughter not of Time, but of Heaven, only bred up heer below in Christian hearts, between two grave & holy nurses the Doctrine, and Discipline of the Gospel. (I, 639)

This approach had earlier dictated Milton's attitude toward antiquity in *Of Reformation*. There, he calls upon the very patristic sources of antiquity (commonly invoked by the prelates to support their claim to authority) in order to prove that the sources themselves warn against a trust in antiquity. Thus, we find that Lactantius argued against "the vaine trust in Antiquity," that Ignatius "exhorted" the church "to adhere close to the written doctrine of the Apostles" rather than trust in tradition, that Cyprian questioned *"whence is this tradition? is it fetcht from the authority of Christ in the Gospel, or of the Apostles in their Epistles . . . what obstinancie, what presumption is this to preferre human Tradition before divine ordinance?"* (I, 561-563)

Milton's recourse to ecclesiastical history thereby performs the ironic function of revealing the unreliability of human testimony. Implicitly, Milton demonstrates that history based solely upon human testimony negates itself as a means of arriving at truth. Drawing upon the testimony of the fathers in order to counter its very assumptions, Milton causes that form of argumentation to expose itself and thus to expose what he considers to be the prelatical dependence upon custom and tradition.[16] Used in this way, history becomes revelatory, a "laying open," to cite Milton, of "the faults and blemishes of *Fathers, Martyrs*," and "Christian *Emperors*" (I, 535). As Milton's statement indicates, his exposé goes even beyond the fathers of the church: all-inclusive and uncompromisingly radical, it embraces those whom the church had commonly designated martyrs and ideal Christian emperors.

Significantly, in those he chose as targets for his assaults, Milton departed from views shared not only by the Anglican church but by many of his Nonconformist brethren as well. Established martyrs of the church (memorialized by Foxe in *The Actes and Monuments* [1576]), Cranmer, Latimer, and Ridley, for example, do not escape Milton's condemnation (I, 531-533). Anticipating the criticism of those who would call these men martyrs, Milton says:

> What then? Though every true Christian will be a *Martyr* when he is called to it; not presently does it follow that every one suffering for Religion, is without exception. Saint *Paul* writes that *A man may give his Body to be burnt*, (meaning for Religion) *and yet not have Charitie*: He is not therfore above all possibility of erring, because hee burnes for some Points of Truth. (I, 333)[17]

Milton's treatment of Constantine is likewise in direct opposition to the very Smectymnuans he supported. While the Smectymnuans looked upon Constantine as "'that great promover and patron of peace of the Christian church'," "Milton . . . traces back to the emperor the two great banes of the church, the corruption of the clergy by riches and worldliness, and the confusion of the secular and religious spheres. . . . Through his introduction of ceremonies, fasts, and feasts, his building of stately churches, and his giving 'great riches and promotion' to bishops, Constantine becomes a symbol of the degeneration of Christianity and particularly of the ministry."[18]

Precisely how Milton justified his revelatory approach in his historical treatment of religious subjects may be seen in his statement that God provides the incentive: Milton thereby "invokes" none other than "the Immortall DEITIE," the "*Reveler*" of "Secrets" (I, 535), whose divine testimony is embodied in the Gospel. For this reason, Milton urges us to "hold" the Gospel ever in our faces "like a mirror of Diamond, till it dazle, and pierce" our "misty ey balls, maintaining it the honour of its absolute sufficiency, and supremacy inviolable" (I, 569-570). As Milton's assertion suggests, divine testimony is not only revelatory but purgative: it lays bare in order to purify. With his dependence upon divine testimony rather than upon human (a distinction Milton makes in *The Art of Logic* [I.xxxii-xxxiii]), Milton similarly causes his account to assume a purgative role, a clearing away of the mists engendered by the prelates. That role is essential to the attaining of truth, the nature of which Milton describes in the following terms:

> The very essence of Truth is plainnesse, and brightnes; the darknes and crookednesse is our own. The *Wisdome* of *God* created *understanding*, fit and proportionable to Truth the object, and end of it, as the eye to the thing visible. If our *understanding* have a film of *ignorance* over it, or be blear with gazing on other false glisterings, what is that to Truth? If we will but purge with sovrain eyesalve that intellectual ray which *God* hath planted in us, then we would beleeve the Scriptures protesting their own plainnes, and perspicuity. . . . (I, 566)

According to Don M. Wolfe, "this primary principle in Milton, which he was to restate hundreds of times in later works, in reality encompassed the explosive, revolutionary quality of Protestant dynamics, the right of each man to follow the social or personal truth he found in Scriptures and work for it in his daily life."[19] It sanctioned Milton's radical root and branch attitude in *Of Reformation*, as expressed by the uncompromising assertion of the London Petition (December 11, 1640) that episcopacy "with all its dependancies, rootes and branches . . . bee abolished, and all lawes in their behalfe made voide."[20] Such an attitude extends back at least as far as the fiery 1572 *Admonition to the Parlia-*

ment, "the first open manifesto of the Puritan party," which states,

> You may not do as heretofore you have done, patch and piece, nay rather go backward, and never labour or contend to perfection. But altogether remove whole Antichrist, both head, body, and branch, and perfectly plant that purity of the word, that simplicity . . . and severity of discipline, which Christ hath commanded to his church.[21]

These radical sentiments were ones precisely shared by Milton in his desire that the Reformation be "sudden & swift," "speedy and vehement," that the reformers ought to "hie" themselves "from evill like a torrent," and "rid" themselves of "corrupt Discipline," as they would "shake fire" out of their "bosomes" (I, 602). In this, Milton was like Robert Browne, who would have *Reformation without Tarrying for Anie* (1582). As Arthur Barker states, Milton "thought of reform as a transformation of the whole church rather than a change in the ministerial body. It seemed to him, as to Henry Vane, that the church was undergoing a kind of regeneration, not the purification merely of its form of government, but the renewal of its primitive simplicity."[22]

If this is the point of view to which Milton's radicalism led him in his first antiprelatical tract, it might be worthwhile to explore in greater detail what strategies Milton adopted in order to express his point of view. After all, we cannot with Masson call *Of Reformation* an "historical essay" and have done with it, since the historical element is only one part of the overall design, a part that is subsumed by the larger whole. In order to be aware of what that whole is, we must concern ourselves even further with Milton's conception of polemical discourse, especially as it becomes an integral expression of his educational grounding in the use of rhetoric for matters of debate.

We might well expect to find in *Of Reformation* the fruits of Milton's rigorous rhetorical training. Little need be said about his acquaintance not only with the rhetorical theories of Plato, Aristotle, Cicero, Quintilian and others but with the incorporation of those theories into Renaissance manuals.[23] As E. M. W. Tillyard points out, the rhetorical training so fundamental to a Renaissance education involved both theory and practice, both a thorough inculcation of principles and an habitual attendance at public debates.[24] In the university, "everything was supposed to lead up to the *Disputation*, a medieval legacy which took the place of the modern examination. To qualify for a degree, every student had from time to time to maintain or attack a given thesis before an audience."[25]

Out of those disputations arose Milton's own Prolusions, structured for the most part upon classical rhetorical paradigms (*exordium, narratio, confirmatio, refutatio, peroratio*).[26] These rhetorical principles were, of course, at hand when Milton engaged himself in writing tracts for national causes. We have commonly (and correctly) associated such principles with *Areopagitica*, a tract based, as Milton himself states, "on the model of a genuine speech" (*Second Defence*, IV, 625). But they are likewise present in tracts so diverse as *Of Prelatical Episcopacy*, in which Milton "utilized almost all the rhetorical skills and devices of classical oratory,"[27] and *The Tenure of Kings and Magistrates*, which accords closely with the oratorical form of the Prolusions.[28] I hope to show that their presence in *Of Reformation* indicates not only how consciously Milton applied his rhetorical training to the writing of prose tracts at the outset of his polemical career, but how we might better understand at least one aspect of his polemical practices through a consideration of rhetorical *topoi*.

Although the epistolary division of *Of Reformation* into two books seems gratuitous, Wilbur E. Gilman feels that the tract, as an example of deliberative oratory, accords generally with classical form,[29] and it is quite evident that Milton makes use of specific rhetorical devices despite the fact that *Of Reformation* is not based upon a preconceived classical model. Thus, according to Gilman, both books move from an *exordium* to a *narratio*, then on to elaborate proofs of the antiprelatical assertions, these, in turn, bolstered by the *refutatio*,[30] and the second book culminates in what Everett Emerson sees as "a powerful peroration, a prayer, and a curse."[31]

To cite specific examples from Book I, the *exordium* introduces the nature of episcopal corruption in very graphic terms and contrasts that corruption with the original purity of the church (I, 519-524). The following sections provide a statement (*narratio*) of the causes hindering *"true Discipline"* (I, 528), the various proofs of that statement through the historical rendering we have discussed (I, 528-534), and the refutation of possible objections that might be brought against the proofs. (Among other places, *refutatio* comes into play in what we have seen as Milton's rebuttal of those who would defend Cranmer, Latimer, and Ridley as martyrs to the Reformation [I, 533]; it later comes into play in Milton's rebuttal of those who might contend that the Scriptures do not provide enough light for their own understanding [I, 565-570].)

An even further indication that Milton looked upon his tract in oratorical terms may be seen from a statement he makes in Book II: "Sir, you have now at length this question for the time, and as my memory would best serve me in such a copious, and vast theme, fully handl'd. . . ." (I, 598). Milton's reference to his "memory" is quite relevant in this context, for it suggests that he views himself oratorically as attempting to fulfill, in the exposition of his "copious, and vast theme," one of the five "parts" of rhetoric (that of *memoria*) envisioned by Cicero.³² But these are not the only reasons for seeing in Milton's tract a disposition to invoke fundamental rhetorical principles in order to conduct a polemical argument.

What is likewise striking about the performance is the elaborate series of divisions and subdivisions that its argument neatly embodies. Critical observations to the contrary, this approach would tend to support Milton's own contention in *Of Reformation* that his argument is "orderly" (I, 528). Significantly, Milton himself implies that "orderly proceeding" is founded upon the idea of "division" (*divisio*), an organizational concept decidedly influenced by the Ramistic tendency to dichotomize one's argument into classes and subclasses. According to Wilbur Howell, "Ramus' habit of dividing a subject . . . led to the assumption that for him the natural method is essentially the method of dichotomies—of proceeding always to separate a logical class into . . . subclasses . . . and to separate the subclasses and the sub-subclasses in the same way."³³

That technique formed an integral part of Puritan polemic. In tracts so widely diverse as Robert Greville, Lord Brooke's restrained and philosophical *Discourse Opening the Nature of that Episcopacy, which is Exercised in England* (1642) and Alexander Leighton's impassioned *Appeal to the Parliament* (1628), we discover an elaborate logical superstructure impelling the course of the argument. Abundantly clear in both tracts, the manner of proceeding provides the necessary perspective for viewing the idea of division in Milton's tract. The argument of Leighton's *Appeal*, for example, is divided into sections and subsections and these further divided into various statements of positions and proofs of these statements, expressed in major and minor propositions. Similarly, the argument of Lord Brooke's *Discourse* is divided into sections, these divided into chapters, and these divided into proofs of the subject.

Indeed, Lord Brooke's entire first chapter involves a qualifying statement of the "*Subject*" to be treated by the discourse as a whole and an exposition of the "*Method propounded for the first Section*" (pp. 1-3). That method is clearly one of division. Defining his "*Ad-*

versary" as "One monstrously compounded, of different, yea opposite Offices," he divides those offices into *"Ecclesiastical and Civill."* His purpose is to show how the prelate is in "no way fit" for his offices by drawing upon arguments "which may bee brought from *Scripture, Church-Antiquity, State-Policy."* Treating state policy in section one, he will consider the bishop "as a private man, *before his Office,"* and "as a Lord over Church and State, *in his Office."* This treatment of the causes of corruption (what Lord Brooke terms the *"Antecedents"* and *"Concomitants,"* respectively) will then yield the effect or the "necessary *Consequents to his* [the bishop's] *Office"* (pp. 2-3). (Appropriately, the antecedents are divided into the bishop's *"Birth, Education, Election, Ordination"*; the concomitants into his *"Judicial"* and *"Delegative"* power; the consequents into his *"Relations" "Upward"* with God and *"Downward"* with man.)

As such an analysis makes clear, Lord Brooke's principal concern in his *Discourse* is with cause (and its inevitable effect), a concern that is integral to our discussion of the Ramistic tendency to dichotomize one's argument, for it reveals an additional aspect of Ramistic procedure, that is, according to Franklin Irwin, the all-important stress upon "cause" (*causa*).[34] If that stress is discernible in Lord Brooke, it is no less apparent in Alexander Leighton, whose primary purpose in his *Appeal* is to make the Parliament "sensible" to the "provokinge cause" (elsewhere, the "principall" and "chiefe cause," even the *"Conjunct* or immediate working cause") of "all the evill" that is upon them (sigs. B 1^r-B 1^v). It is no accident, therefore, that in structuring his tract Milton based the conduct of his argument, as the title states, upon "the Causes that have hindered" "Church-Discipline in England" (I, 517). Nor is it an accident that his discussion of causes (and their inevitable effects) is founded upon the concept of division. A brief structural analysis of the first book of *Of Reformation* should serve to suggest the importance of Ramistic procedure to Milton's polemical methods.

In his analysis of causes, Milton divides his "inquirie into our *Fore-Fathers dayes,* and into *our Times"* (I, 528). The discussion of "our *Fore-Fathers dayes"* is then divided into what we have seen as the historical treatment of the reigns of Henry VIII, Edward VI, and Elizabeth, while the discussion of *"our Times"* is divided into a treatment of antiquarians, libertines and politicians. (Critics are, of course, correct in pointing out that the space devoted to each of these three classes is hardly proportional: except for the brief concluding treatment of libertines, the remainder of Book I concerns antiquarians, and Book II is principally concerned with politicians.) Proceeding further, the argument against the antiquarians is supported by three contentions: (a) that to return the bishops to the habits of purer times would be to deprive them of their present riches; (b) that these so-called purer times were really corrupt; (c) that, as we have discussed, even the writers of the purer times disclaimed their own works and advised going directly to the Scriptures (I, 541). The working out of these contentions, finally, involves even further subdivisions. (The second contention, for example, is subdivided into three causes of corruption: the spreading infection of the times; the tainting of the men of the times; and the adulterating of the writings of those men [I, 549].) Without going into a discussion of the second book, suffice it to say that it too proceeds through a complex series of divisions and subdivisions as a means of supporting its arguments. All this should indicate, I think, not only the importance of classical *topoi* to Milton at the outset of his polemical career but a significant aspect of Milton's habits of mind in the structuring of his tracts. It suggests at least that he was not a capricious worker in prose, even when his prose might seem most chaotic to us.

As important as an appreciation of the classical *topoi* in *Of Reformation* might be, however, a full appreciation may not rest content merely with that aspect of Milton's rhetorical art. Milton's tract is too flexible, even unpredictable, to subscribe itself to some predetermined polemical framework. It is for this reason that William Haller observes in Milton's antiprelatical tracts a constant vacillation from one mode of discourse to another.[35] The validity of such an assertion may be seen by the fact that unexpectedly, in the midst of the second book of *Of Reformation*, Milton informs us that he is "put . . . into the mood" to tell us a "tale" before he "proceeds further" (I, 583). What results is an allegorical digression freely adapting the popular fable of the Belly and the bodily Members found in Livy's *Historiarum . . . Libri* (II.xxxii) and elsewhere.[36]

This somewhat surprising intrusion deserves our attention. We cannot pass it off as a standard rhetorical device allowable in oratorical discourse,[37] although it might be argued that, based upon classical precedence, prevailing rhetorical theory allowed for digressions. (In his *Arte of Rhetorique* [1560], for example, Thomas Wilson states: "We swarue sometimes from the matter, vpon iust considerations, making the same to serue for our purpose, as well as if we had kept the matter still."[38]) The mode of digression Milton engages in, on the other hand, is much less formal, a great deal more whimsical than what Wilson had in mind.[39]

Milton's digression represents the characteristic unpredictability that is so often discernible in the prose tracts of the period. In the

midst of William Prynne's *A Looking-Glasse for all Lordly Prelates*
(1636), for example, we suddenly discover an epistle from "Lucifer
Prince of darknesse, writing to the persecuting Prelates of the Popish
Clergie" (sigs. B 1^r-B 4^v). Similarly, in Milton's own *Pro se Defensio*,
we find testimonials and letters used for the purposes of self-vindi-
cation (IV, 707-717). This unpredictability as to precisely what
we shall find in a pamphlet underlies Joan Webber's observation
that "any given tract may include four or five or more different
exhibits. A private letter written in 1638 is included in a tract
dated about 1645. . . . Warrants, petitions, letters, pleas, speeches
are imbedded in the tracts wherever relevant."[40] What is especially
significant about Professor Webber's statement is that, while it
stresses the unpredictability of Puritan polemics, it also stresses
the relevance of that unpredictability to the polemicist's total conception. This fact is certainly true of Milton: although decidedly
unexpected and apparently out of place given the method of his
argumentation, his digression is quite functional, first as an expression of his antiprelatical views and second as an expression of
his polemical practices.

As an expression of his antiprelatical views, the digression justifies
its presence by embodying succinctly the thrust of the political
argument presented in Book II. In order to see how the digression
does this, it might be well to review briefly the way in which Milton adapted to his own polemical purposes the fable of the Belly
and the bodily Members as the Renaissance understood it. In the
version appearing in North's *Plutarch*, for instance, the Belly is
called upon to placate the mutinous bodily Members, which
charge "that it [the Belly] only remained in the midst of the body,
without doing anything."[41] The Belly defends its usefulness by
saying: "It is true, I first receive all meats that nourish man's body;
but afterwards I send it again to the nourishment of other parts
the same." The moral, as Menenius Agrippa applies it, is that the
senate (the Belly of the fable) benefits the commonwealth (the
bodily Members) by being the "cause of the common commodity
that commeth unto every one of them."[42]

In Milton, on the other hand, the Wen (that is, the Belly become
episcopal encumbrance) is shown to be not only completely use-
less but destructive, despite its protestations to the contrary that
the Wen's "Office" was the Body's "glory," for "so oft as the
soule would retire out of the head from over the steaming vapours
of the lower parts to Divine Contemplation," with the Wen "shee
found the purest, and quietest retreat, as being most remote from
soile, and disturbance" (I, 584). The response of the "wise and

learned Philosopher," directed by the Members "to examine and discusse the claime and Petition of right put in by the Wen," is that "all the faculties of the Soule are confin'd of old to their severall vessels, and *ventricles* from which they cannot part without dissolution of the whole Body" (I, 584). That is, the Body is a self-sustaining entity, complete unto itself.

The distinction is one Milton expressed early in Book II. There, he distinguishes between the functions of the church and state in this manner:

> Seeing that the Churchmans office is only to teach men the Christian Faith, to exhort all, to incourage the good, to admonish the bad, privately the lesse offender, publickly the scandalous and stubborn; to censure, and separate from the communion of *Christs* flock, the contagious, and incorrigible, to receive with joy, and fatherly compassion the penitent, all this must be done, and more than this is beyond any Church autority. What is all this either here, or there to the temporal regiment of the Wealpublick . . .? Where doth it intrench upon the temporal governor, where does it come in his walk? where does it make inrode upon his jurisdiction? (I, 575-576)

Having violated the church-state relationship, the prelates have become corrupt through what Milton earlier discussed as the effect of Constantine upon the church. With their desire for wealth and power, with their ostentatious ceremonies and courts, with their "Idolatrous erection of Temples beautified exquisitely to out-vie the Papists," with their "costly and deare-bought Scandals, and snares of Images, Pictures, rich Coaps, gorgeous Altar-clothes" (I, 590), they "have weaken'd and withdrawne the externall Accomplishments of Kingly prosperity, the love of the People, their multitude, their valour, their wealth; mining, and sapping the outworks, and redoubts of *Monarchy*" (I, 592).

As a result, the Philosopher of Milton's *Tale* accuses the Wen of being nothing to the Head but "a foul disfigurement and burden," good for nothing but to be severed (I, 584), or, as Milton later says, "if we will now resolve to settle affairs either according to pure Religion, or sound policy, we must first of all begin roundly to cashier, and cut away from the publick body the noysom, and diseased tumor of Prelacie" (I, 598). In this manner, Milton ironically inverts the popular fable of the Belly and the bodily Members to suit his own needs. Customarily used to placate those who criticize policy, the fable, as Milton conceives it, serves to bolster that criticism.

Such is the effect that his *Tale* has as an expression of his anti-prelatical views. As an expression of his polemical practices, the *Tale* represents an additional aspect of the genre we are exploring. Like Prynne's epistle from "Lucifer" to the "Popish Clergie" in *A Looking-Glasse*, Milton's *Tale*, with its sense of directness and colloquial immediacy, reveals Milton's ability to assume dramatic stances, to cast himself in implicitly comic roles. Compared to the account we find in Livy, for example, Milton's account is quite forceful and dramatic. Whereas in Livy there is no sense of the dramatic (no one in the fable gestures or speaks), in Milton we are provided with what we have seen to be that cast of imposing comic characters which includes the Head, the Wen, and the "wise and learned Philosopher" "summon'd" by the Body "to meet in the Guild for the common good" (I, 583). Dramatically conceived, Milton's characters move and speak: the Head "by right takes the first seat," the "unweildy" Wen "with much adoe gets up and be-speaks the Assembly," the Philosopher deliberates and accuses in decidedly abusive and colloquial terms ("Lourdan, quoth he . . .") (I, 583-584).

Exploiting fully the dramatic potentialities of the fable, Milton thereby causes his *Tale* to take on elements of a little self-contained drama. Indeed, his adaptation of the fable for dramatic effect re-calls Shakespeare's earlier rendering of the fable in *Coriolanus.* Dramatizing the account as he found it in North's *Plutarch,* Shake-speare has Menenius Agrippa allow the Belly of the fable to engage in direct discourse with the bodily Members: " 'True is it, my in-corporate friends,' quoth he. . . ."[43] Shakespeare's intentions as a dramatist are, of course, far different from Milton's as a polemicist, but the comparison allows us to see how willing Milton was to in-corporate the dramatic element into polemical discourse. In order to come to terms with this aspect of Milton's practices, we might do well to consider the dramatic element within a broader context, for through an analysis of that element, we shall be better equipped to understand the nature of polemical controversy.

II

Those forces that gave rise to the dramatic element implicit in tracts like *Of Reformation* depended, to a great extent, upon the contro-versial milieu in which tracts were written. Unlike poems, which were most often composed for their own sake, tracts were composed either to provoke replies or to act as replies to earlier tracts. Although commonplace, this fact bears repetition, for it reminds us of the need to concern ourselves with the milieu from which tracts emerged. That idea is true, whether we are considering the participation of Whitgift and Cartwright in the Admonition controversy, Bridges, Cooper, and their adversaries in the Marprelate controversy, or Hall and the Presbyterian divines (along with Milton) in the Smectymnuan controversy. For this reason, it is not at all surprising to find so many tracts, including Milton's written in the form of a point-by-point refutation of what someone else has written in another tract. As George Wesley Whiting points out, the second book of *Of Reformation* (I, 601 ff.) contains an implicit but detailed rebuttal of the arguments against the London Petition found in George Digby's "The third speech . . . to the House of Commons" (1640).[44]

Examples of this kind thus serve to indicate what comprises the essentially controversial nature of polemical literature. I refer to the sense of dialogue created by the fact that the audience of that literature was not only the public at large but the specific person (or group of people) at whom the polemic was directed. To embark upon any of the controversies of the time is to get the singular feeling that one is in the midst of many voices, each voice uttered in response to what another voice has said. As in the Smectymnuan controversy, one voice utters a humble remonstrance, another voice answers it; the first voice defends what it originally said, the second voice vindicates its answer to the original remonstrance, and so on. Now, in executing one's attack or counterattack, a polemicist has the option of making full use of the dramatic resources inherent in such a controversial atmosphere. Unlike the Smectymnuan divines, whose tracts represent staid and sober point-by-point rebuttals of Hall's contentions, Milton did not hesitate to exploit the dramatic possibilities.

Presenting us with a dialogue between two characters, the Remonstrant and the Answerer, *Animadversions Upon the Remonstrants Defence against Smectymnuus* represents a case in point. What the Remonstrant says embodies the argument of Hall's 1641 *Defence of the Humble Remonstrance*; what the Answerer says signifies Milton's own rebuttals of that argument. What results is not only heated debate (with the Answerer, of course, undermining each of the Remonstrant's assertions) but quite often something that resembles comic drama characterized by a decidedly colloquial air. We might consider, for example, a brief interchange between the Remonstrant and Answerer concerning the corruptions of the church. The Remonstrant is arguing that the church has effected beneficial changes:

Remon.	Could yee see no Colleges, no Hospitals built?
Answ.	At that *priméro* of piety the Pope and Cardinals are better gamesters, and will cogge a Die into heav'n before you.
Remon.	No Churches re-edified?
Answ.	Yes, more Churches then soules.

. . . .

Remon.	No seduced persons reclaim'd?
Answ.	More reclaimed persons seduced.
Remon.	No hospitality kept?
Answ.	Bacchanalia's good store in every Bishops family, and good gleeking.

. . . .

Remon.	No holiness in living?
Answ.	No.
Remon.	Truely brethren I can say no more; but that the fault is in your eyes.
Answ.	If you can say no more than this, you were a proper Remonstrant to stand up for the whole tribe.
Remon.	Wipe them, and looke better.
Answ.	Wipe your fat corpulencies out of our light.

(I, 731-732)

Referring to the *"late and hot bickerings between the* Prelates *and* Smectymnuans," the writer of *A Modest Confutation* (1642) responded to what Milton was doing in *Animadversions* in decidedly theatrical terms: *"To make up the breaches of whose solemn Scenes, (it were too ominous to say Tragicall) there is thrust forth upon the Stage, as also to take the eare of the lesse intelligent, a scurrilous* Mime, *a personated, and (as himself thinks) a grim, lowring, bitter fool."*[45] In *An Apology*, Milton, in turn, admonished the writer of *A Modest Confutation* for "likening those grave controversies to a piece of Stagery, or Scenework where his owne Remonstrant whether in Buskin or Sock must of all right be counted the chiefe Player" (I, 879). Rather, Milton would have preferred to associate tracts like *Animadversions* with the "Dialogues of *Plato*," since "there is scarce one of them, especially wherein some notable Sophister lies sweating and turmoyling under the inevitable, and mercilesse dilemma's of Socrates" (I, 880). Despite Milton's objections, however, the writer of *A Modest Confutation* put his finger on a very important aspect of the polemical milieu, an aspect of which Milton himself was aware, as is demonstrated by his early theatrical references to oratory in the Sixth Prolusion. There, he views himself as an actor entreating, in the manner of Plautus, the laughter and applause of the audience (I, 277).[46] Again, as late as the Second Defence, we find Milton envisioning the circumstances surrounding his argument with Salmasius in decidedly theatrical terms:

> . . . for Vlacq is not the only one concerned in the presentation of the tragedy, as it were, of the King's Cry against us. Observe then, at the beginning, as is customary, the cast of characters: the "Cry," as prologue; Vlacq, the buffoon (or if you prefer, Salmasius disguised in the mask and cloak of Vlacq the buffoon); two poetasters, tipsy with stale beer; More the adulterer and seducer. What splendid actors for a tragedy! (IV, 573-574)

Thus, Milton dispenses with what he derisively calls "a troupe of actors" (IV, 574).

One might well expect that attitude to have a pervasive influence upon the controversial nature of Milton's prose. It is certainly an attitude that Francis Bacon censured in *An Advertisement Touching the Controversies of the Church of England* (1641): "it is more than time that there were an end and surcease made of this immodest and deformed manner of writing lately entertained, whereby matter of religion is handled in the style of the stage."[47] As we have seen, Bacon's assumptions are not unfounded: the theatricality he complains of is discernible especially in those tracts veritably fashioned in the form of dramatic performances. One might invoke such works as Anthony Gilby's *A Pleasaunt Dialogue, Between a Soldier of Barwicke, and an English Chaplaine* (1581), in which the soldier Miles Monopodious undercuts the hypocrisy of the priest Sir Bernard Blinkard;[48] as John Lilburne's *The Triall of . . . John Lilburne* (1653), in which "the names of the participants are printed, as in a playbill";[49] and as [Richard Overton's] *The Araignement of Mr. Persecution* (1645), in which Mr. Long-Sufferance, Mr. Reward-of-Tyranny, and Sir Simon Synod, among other characters, participate in a trial.[50] (The allegorical temper of *A Pleasaunt Dialogue* and *The Araignement*, incidentally, suggests how easily the modes of allegory and drama were combined in religious controversy, a fact that bears upon Milton's own allegorical account of the Wen and the bodily Members in *Of Reformation*.[51])

Significantly, the title page of *The Araignement* attributes the tract to "Yongue Martin Mar-Priest, Son to old Martin the Metrapolitane." The attribution is most important not only because it suggests the influence of the Marprelate tracts upon seventeenth-century polemics but because it attests implicitly to the nature of that influence. I refer to what John S. Coolidge, among others, sees as the theatrical bearing of the Marprelate tracts.[52] Indeed, the dramatic element that we have been discussing may in large part be traced to the Marprelate controversy, in which Martin consciously adopts a *decorum personae* in order to suit the character of the persons whose arguments he is attempting to undermine. The effect of Martin's act of taking upon himself a dramatic role for satiric purposes was that of altering the course of polemical discourse from that time on. As William Holden observes, "the Martin Marprelate tracts had most seriously complicated the discussion of the religious issues. Theological dialectic in a 400-page book, with arguments ordered and supporting references to Holy Writ in the margins, would no longer be the surest way of converting the English people to an ecclesiastical position. In the future the force of logic would be only one persuasion beside the force of satire."[53]

The Marprelate tracts caused appropriate reactions on the parts of their enemies. First, in plays suppressed for their grossness, Martin's enemies portrayed Martin Marprelate as an ass upon the stage (1588-1589).[54] Second, such writers as Thomas Nashe and John Lyly composed tracts directly aimed at undermining the comedy of Martin's satiric poses.[55] What results are tracts that are wittily conceived but which rarely speak to the issues. The thrust of their arguments is usually directed at Martin himself: one insult follows the next, with constant attempts at verbal ingenuity. In *Pappe with a hatchet . . .* (1589), for example, Lyly, addressing Martin, sounds like a comedian pulling jokes out of the air.[56] The Martin Marprelate tracts, on the other hand, are quite seriously conceived and do speak to the issues.

For all their seriousness, however, their scurrility is such that it won them the condemnation of those who felt that the treating of religious subjects in a debased manner represented a serious breach of decorum. This kind of criticism extended back as far as Whitgift's censuring of Cartwright's "vein of gibing and jesting" in the Admonition controversy: The "jest . . . ought not to be in serious matters; and therefore I leave it to them that are disposed to laugh, when they should rather weep."[57] It likewise was reiterated even more elaborately in Bacon's *Advertisement*:

> To leave all reverent and religious compassion towards evils, or indignation towards faults, and to turn religion into a comedy or satire; to search and rip up wounds with a laughing countenance; to intermix Scripture and scurrility, sometimes in one

sentence, is a thing far from the devout reverence of a Christian, and scant beseeming the honest regard of a sober man. 'Non est major confuso, quam serii est joci.' There is no greater confusion than the confounding of jest and earnest. The majesty of religion, and the contempt and deformity of things ridiculous, are things as distant as things may be.[58]

Bacon's condemnation reveals an acute sensitivity to (and dislike of) the polemical assumptions that motivated tracts such as those produced by Martin Marprelate and, later, by John Milton. Indeed, Bacon's attitude provides an essential background against which we are able to view more clearly what Milton was doing in those tracts that are characterized by extreme scurrility.

Of Reformation represents a case in point, for there Milton unleashes upon the prelates vilification of the most uncompromising sort. Envisioning what he calls the "obscene," "canary-sucking" (I, 548) prelates as objects of reproach, he maintains that the disgust they engender ("belching the soure Crudities of yesterdayes *Poperie*" [I, 520] and "the new-vomited Paganisme of sensuall Idolatry" [I, 520]) is such that it "gives a Vomit to God himselfe" (I, 537); allegorically depicted as the Wen in the *Tale* we have been discussing, the prelates are likewise exposed by the "wise and learned Philosopher" to be nothing but "a bottle of vitious and harden'd excrements" (I, 583-584). Through this invective, Milton's language thereby descends to the level of what Don M. Wolfe calls "the wharfmen and dung-hill women."[59] Indeed, at its extreme in *Animadversions,* it assumes the form of nonverbal outbursts: "Ha, ha, ha" (I, 726).

In that respect, Milton was firmly in line with the radical Puritans of his time. His compeers were writers like Bastwick, whose *Letany* (1637) anticipated in its virulence Milton's own invective. The following example from the *Letany* should indicate something of the milieu in which Milton wrote: "One would think that hell were broke loose and that the devils, in surplices, in hoods, in copses, in rochets, and in foursquare cowturds upon their heads, were come among us and had beshit us all—foo, how they stink!"[60] Like Bastwick (and Prynne and Burton too), Milton had an ear for the kind of writing that would unsettle the most composed, that resorted to blatant subliterary tactics in order to undermine his enemies. Like them, he viewed his tracts as weapons to be used in combat, his language as a club to be used in striking down the adversary.[61] Such an approach is a far cry from the techniques employed by the Smectymnuan divines, as well as other men Milton admired like Lord Brooke. Significantly, as William Haller

makes clear, Milton realized that his approach was "best observed
by men with whom he had otherwise least in common and deplored by some of those with whom he had most."[62] If we are not
to rest content with Tillyard's condemnation of Milton as one who
behaved deplorably and inexcusably in controversial writing,[63]
we would do well to attend to the rationale governing Milton's
vituperative practices.

The most obvious point of departure would be to examine the
classical precedent upon which that rationale is based. In his *Pro se
Defensio* (IV, 744-745), Milton himself directs us to the rhetoricians
whose principles form the cornerstones of his own strategies.[64]
Aristotle, Cicero, and Quintilian, among others, taught Milton the
use of pathetic proof (*affectus*), characterized by "sarcasm, invective, and scurrility," in order to sway the emotions.[65] In his *Rhetoric*
(III), Aristotle advocates the use of invective to "confound the opponent"; in his *De Oratore* (II), Cicero likewise supports the use of
invective, when appropriate, to "repulse" an opponent and to "relieve dullness"; finally, in his *Institutes of Oratory* (VI), Quintilian
outlines elaborate techniques by which an orator might cast odium
upon his adversary.[66] More specifically, Quintilian suggests that
the orator move the affections through *visiones*: "images by which
the representations of absent objects are so distinctly represented
to the mind, that we seem to see them with our eyes, and to have
them before us. Whoever shall best conceive such images, will have
the greatest power in moving the feelings."[67] The graphic nature
of Milton's own depictions is thereby given rhetorical sanction.[68]

These ideas were basic to Renaissance rhetorical theory. In his
earlier years, Milton was undoubtedly exposed to them through
"the grammar school exercises taught according to the formularies
of Aphthonius."[69] In his *Progymnasmata*, Aphthonius introduces
vituperation (like encomium) as an essential aspect of demonstrative rhetoric.[70] Furthermore, the ideas concerning vituperation
formulated by the classical rhetoricians were available in so fundamental a Renaissance manual as Wilson's *The Arte of Rhetorique*.
In his introduction to his observations on laughter, Wilson justifies
the rhetorical effectiveness of invective by saying:

> Now when we would abashe a man, for some wordes he hath
> spoken . . . we either doult him at the first, and make hym
> beleeue, that he is no wiser then a Goose; or els we confute
> wholy his sayings with some pleasaunt ieste, or els we extenuate
> and diminish his doings by some pretie meanes, or els we cast
> the like in his dish, and with some other deuise, dash him out
> of countenance: or, last of al, we laugh him to scorne out right,

and sometimes speake almoste neuer a worde, but onely in continuaunce, shew our selues pleasaunt.[71]

Wilson's statements provide a fitting analogue for Martin Marprelate's defense of his style in *Hay Any Worke for Cooper* (1589):

Aye for jesting is lawful by circumstances even in the greatest matters. . . . I never profaned the word in any jest. Other mirth I used as a covert wherein I would bring the truth into light. The Lord being the authour both of mirth and gravitie, is it not lawful in it selfe for the trueth to use eyther of these wayes when the circumstances do make it lawful?[72]

Directly in line with Martin's defense is Milton's own justification of his language in the preface to *Animadversions*:

And although in the serious uncasing of a grand imposture (for to deale plainly with you Readers, Prelatry is no better) there be mixt here and there such a grim laughter, as may appeare at the same time in an austere visage, it cannot be taxt of levity or insolence: for even this veine of laughing (as I could produce out of grave Authors) hath oft-times a strong and sinewy force in teaching and confuting; nor can there be a more proper object of indignation and scorne together then a false Prophet taken in the greatest dearest and most dangerous cheat, the cheat of soules: in the disclosing whereof if it be harmfull to be angry, and withall to cast a lowring smile, when the properest object calls for both, it will be long enough ere any be able to say why those two most rationall faculties of humane intellect anger and laughter were first seated in the brest of man. (I, 663-664)

It is clear from this passage that Milton placed himself squarely in the tradition that had its basis in classical and Renaissance rhetorical theory and that manifested itself in Puritan polemic. Like Martin Marprelate, Milton was hardly adverse to exploiting the potentialities of polemic to their fullest when that mode of discourse was called for in the undermining of one's adversary. His concept of polemical decorum embraced the extremes of oratory by which the austere orator could defend the holiest of causes in the most abusive of terms. This is an attitude that Milton was to embrace throughout his polemical career. As early as his entry on "Reproof" in the Commonplace Book, Milton cited Luther as one who "refrained neither from harshness nor from jests that were now and then even a little shameful" (I, 390).[73] And as late as *Pro se Defensio*, he reaffirmed his refusal to confine his concept of decorum within narrow and strict limits but vowed to speak plainly after "the example of gravest authors" who "have always thought that words unchaste and plain thrust out with indignation signify not obscenity, but the vehemence of gravest censure" (IV, 744).[74]

Among the "gravest authors" Milton invokes, we encounter such Biblical figures as Moses, Jacob, and Solomon. Appropriately, it is within this Biblical spectrum that Milton found his most compelling source for the use of invective. Even more than the classical precedents, the Bible gave him the authority he needed to justify his polemical point of view. There, he found a God whose attitude (as Milton discovered in his translation of "Psalm 2") could provide the rationale for his own: "he who in Heav'n doth dwell / Shall laugh, the Lord shall scoff them, then severe speak to them in his wrath" (11. 8-10).[75] Upon this foundation, Milton justified his radical concept of decorum in the antiprelatical tracts. In *An Apology*, for example, he defended his use of "tart rhetoric," after the fashion of Martin Marprelate, by maintaining that the "spirit of God, who is purity it selfe" will resort to obscenities "as fittest in that vehement character wherein" God sometimes speaks (I, 901-905). Thus Christ, "speaking of unsavory traditions, scruples not to name the Dunghill and the Jakes" (I, 895).[76] Milton thereby maintains that his own approach has precise Biblical precedence: what he says in his tracts is inspired by God's frankness in the Bible.

It is important to realize at the outset, however, that Milton's recourse to Biblical precedence for his own polemical stance has not merely rhetorical significance. As his statements in *The Reason of Church-Government* reveal, Milton looked upon himself as one of "those ancient profets" who felt compelled by the dictates of their conscience "to take the trumpet, and blow a dolorous or a jarring blast" when called upon by God to do so (I, 803). His was not necessarily a pleasant task; rather, like the prophets, he felt that "the irksomeness of that truth which he brought was so unpleasant" to him that he did not hesitate to "call it a burden" (I, 803).

This uniquely Puritan characteristic suggests something still further about the nature of the polemics at which Milton was so adept. The idea of viewing oneself as a zealous prophet whose writings are trumpet blasts goes far to explain the essentially homiletic overtones that Milton's tracts assumed. In that way, they accord with William Perkins' view, as expressed in *The Arte of Prophecying, or a Treatise Concerning the Sacred and Onely True Manner and Methode of Preaching* (1631), that prophecy, comprised of preaching and praying, is "a publicke and solemne speech . . . pertaining

to the worship of God, and to the salvation of our neighbour."[77]
This would tend to corroborate the idea that for the Puritan mind
tract writing and sermon writing were based fundamentally upon the
same principles.[78] Indeed, W. Fraser Mitchell suggests that the sermon was commonly looked upon as "an oration adapted to suit
religious purposes": "the *rhetoricae sacrae* . . . were not far removed
from the *artes concionandi* with their manifest intention of instruct-
ing men how to preach effectively."[79] Arousing the emotions in
one's sermons through rigorous speech, reproaches, and exhortations
had been sanctioned by Augustine,[80] and one came to expect in
Puritan sermons especially what Perry Miller terms "holy violence."[81]
As John Downame states in *A Treatise of Anger* (1609): "when God
is dishonoured, his name blasphemed, his whole worship and sermon
contemned," one must engage in "sanctified anger,"[82] the kind of
anger one confronts in such homiletic discourses as John Lilburne's
A Worke of the Beast (1638) and John Goodwin's *Anti-Cavalierisme*
(1642). Emerging from that milieu, we confront Milton's concept of
the polemicist as God's vicar blowing dolorous and jarring blasts
upon his trumpet in a time of trouble.

If Milton was church-outed by the prelates, his tracts provided
the outlet for the apocalyptic exhortation he would have otherwise thundered from the pulpit. That is the impression one receives
from reading the prayer that culminates *Of Reformation.* Combining
a tone of celebration and denunciation, the prayer serves to praise
as well as to blame:

> Then amidst the *Hymns,* and *Halleluiahs* of *Saints* some one may
> perhaps bee heard offering at high *strains* in new and lofty *Measures*
> to sing and celebrate thy *divine Mercies,* and marvelous *Judgements*
> in this land throughout all Ages. . . . But they contrary that by
> the impairing and diminution of the true *Faith,* the distresses and
> servitude of their *Countrey* aspire to high *Dignity, Rule* and
> *Promotion* here, after a shamefull end in this *Life* . . . shall be
> thrown down eternally into the *darkest* and *deepest Gulfe* of
> HELL. . . . (I, 616-617)

The pride Milton took in these prayers and the role he viewed himself as performing in them are discernible in *An Apology.* There, he
defends himself against the accusation made in the *Modest Confutation* that his prayers are "long, tedius, theatricall, big-mouthed" and
"astounding."[83] His defense is founded upon a contrast between
his own "hymnes in prose" and those prayers that are "to be sung in
an antick Coape upon the Stage of a High Altar" (I, 930). The importance of the contrast resides in the fact that Milton clearly saw

himself in his prayers fulfilling through secular means a role ordinarily attributed to the clergy.

Such an idea accords well with the multi-faceted nature of polemical discourse that has emerged in our analysis of *Of Reformation*. This additional aspect of Milton's practices suggests once again the richness and complexity to which tract-writing could (and in Milton's case, did) lend itself. In Milton's case particularly, it suggests that poetry was not the only form of expression that would provide an outlet for one's creative powers. Although by its nature far different from that of poetry, the writing of tracts had its own artistic demands, its own expressive criteria. In accommodating those demands, those criteria, to his particular needs as a polemicist, Milton was in this, as in all else, a radical.

Notes

1. All parenthetical references to Milton's prose in my text are to the Yale *Complete Prose Works*, gen. ed. Don M. Wolfe, 6 vols. to date (New Haven, Conn., 1953-). I would like to take this opportunity to thank the Folger Shakespeare Library for the grant that aided me in the completion of this study.

2. (New Haven, Conn., 1914), p. 62.

3. "Introduction," *Complete Prose Works*, I, 109.

4. "Foreword," *The Prose of John Milton*, gen. ed. J. Max Patrick (New York, 1967), p. 36. See, however, David Masson, *The Life of John Milton* (London, 1871), II, 239: "He [Milton] was not a fast writer, and there was every reason why into this, his first, pamphlet he should throw as much of himself as he could."

5. For analyses of this aspect, see Don M. Wolfe, "Introduction," *Complete Prose Works*, I, 108-115; Don M. Wolfe, *Milton in the Puritan Revolution* (New York, 1941), esp. pp. 41-66; Arthur Barker, *Milton and the Puritan Dilemma* (Toronto, 1942), esp.

pp. 15-59; Robert Duvall, "Time, Place, Persons: The Background for Milton's *Of Reformation*," *SEL*, 7 (1966), 107-118; William Riley Parker, *Milton: A Biography* (Oxford, 1968), I, 197-201; Will Taliaferro Hale, "Introduction," *Of Reformation* (New Haven and London, 1916).

6. *The Life*, II, 239.

7. *Foxe's Book of Martyrs and the Elect Nation* (London, 1963), p. 239.

8. Ibid., pp. 239-240.

9. See J. Milton French, "Milton as a Historian," *PMLA*, 50 (1935), 469-479; French Fogle, "Introduction," *Complete Prose Works*, vol. V, part 1, pp. xix-xlix.

10. For evidence of Milton's authorship of *A Postscript*, see Don M. Wolfe's "Preface" to *A Postscript*, *Complete Prose Works*, I, 961-965, and John T. Shawcross' "The Authorship of 'A Postscript,' *N & Q*, 13 (1966), 378-379.

11. Wolfe, "Introduction," *Complete Prose Works*, I, 962-963; Hale, "Introduction," *Of Reformation*, p. lxxii.

12. *Foxe's Book of Martyrs*, p. 240.

13. "Introduction," *Complete Prose Works*, I, 109-110. In the "Epistle Dedicatory," Prynne refers to his work as a *"bare Historicall discovery* of their [the prelates'] *Trecheries* and *villanies* in all ages." He informs us in "The Prologue" that he plans to begin his account with "the *Arch-Prelates* of Canterbury," then to move to *"the Archbishops* of York" and to conclude with a castigation of present prelatical corruptions.

14. "Introduction," *Complete Prose Works*, I, 53.

15. *Episcopacie by Divine Right*, Part II, p: 4, cited by Wolfe, *Complete Prose Works*, I, 53.

16. Don M. Wolfe is correct, of course, in asserting that in actual practice Milton likewise drew upon custom and tradition when it suited his argumentative needs. Thus, says Wolfe ("Introduction," *Complete Prose Works*, I, 111), "Much as he [Milton] hated the use of church fathers as the basis of theological guidance, he was forced by the exigencies of controversy to draw arguments from tradition as well as Scriptures."

17. For his assaults on Cranmer and Ridley, Milton did receive the censure of Thomas Fuller, who said in *The Holy State* (1642): "Thus the prices of Martyrs ashes rise and fall in Smithfield market" (cited in *Complete Prose Works*, I, 532, n. 56).

18. Barker, pp. 33-34.

19. "Introduction," *Complete Prose Works*, I, 111.

20. Reprinted in *Complete Prose Works*, I, 977.

21. Reprinted in *Complaint and Reform in England*, ed. William H. Dunham, Jr., and Stanley Pargellis (New York, 1938), pp. 242-243.

22. Barker, pp. 32-33.

23. Aside from Milton's own statements in *Of Education*, see Donald L. Clark, *John Milton at St. Paul's School* (New York, 1948), and Harris F. Fletcher, *The Intellectual Development of John Milton*, 2 vols. (Urbana, Ill., 1956-1962), among others.

24. "Introduction," *Milton: Private Correspondence and Academic Exercises* (Cambridge, 1932), p. xviii. See also Wilbur Howell, *Logic and Rhetoric in the Renaissance, 1500-1700* (Princeton, N. J., 1956).

25. Tillyard, p. xvii.

26. Kathryn A. McEuen, "Preface" to the *Prolusions, Complete Prose Works*, I, 217. According to Walter J. Ong, S. J., "Tudor Writings on Rhetoric," *Studies in the Renaissance*, 15 (1968), 40-43, these divisions varied from two to seven. See also John M. Major, "Milton's View of Rhetoric," *SP*, 64 (1967), 685-711.

27. J. Max Patrick, "Preface" to *Of Prelatical Episcopacy, Complete Prose Works*, I, 619.

28. John T. Shawcross, "Foreword" to *The Tenure, The Prose of John Milton*, p. 341.

29. *Milton's Rhetoric: Studies in His Defense of Liberty*, The University of Missouri Studies, XIV (Columbia, Missouri, 1939), pp. 66-67.

30. Gilman, pp. 66-67.

31. "Foreword" to *Of Reformation, The Prose of John Milton*, p. 38.

32. See Ong, "Tudor Writings," p. 44. The other four "parts" are *inventio, disposito, elocutio*, and *pronuntiatio*.

33. *Logic and Rhetoric*, pp. 162-163. See also Leon Howard, " 'The Invention' of Milton's 'Great Argument': A Study of the Logic of 'God's Ways to Men,' " *HLQ*, 9 (1946), 149-173; Walter J. Ong, S. J., *Ramus: Method and the Decay of Dialogue* (Cambridge, Mass., 1958).

34. "Ramistic Logic in Milton's Prose

Works" (Ph.D. diss., Princeton Univ., 1941), p. 10. According to Irwin, in Ramistic thinking "*Cause* is given precedence over all other logical forms." See Milton's *Art of Logic* (I.ii).

35. *Liberty and Reformation in the Puritan Revolution* (New York, 1955), p. 57.

36. I, 583, n. 39. According to E. K. Chambers ("Appendix B," *The Tragedy of Coriolanus* [Boston, n.d.], p. 195), the tale is over three thousand years old and may be found, among other places, in Egyptian, Buddhist, Brahman, and Magian literature. Indeed, Chambers suggests that "St. Paul probably had it [the tale] in mind when he wrote 1 Cor. XII: 12-26." Its popularity in the Renaissance may be attested to by its presence in Sidney's *Apologie for Poetrie* and in Shakespeare's *Coriolanus*, as well as in North's *Plutarch* and Camden's *Remaines*. It is also "familiar to modern Europe from the so-called *Fables of Aesop*, a fifteenth-century compilation based principally upon the Greek *Fables of Phaedrus*" (Chambers, p. 95). For the bodily implications of this "tale," see my essay "Milton and the Organicist Polemic," *Milton Studies*, IV (1972), pp. 79-99.

37. Ralph Haug, "Preface" to *The Reason of Church-Government, The Complete Prose Works*, I, 740, notes that Cicero in *De Oratore* permitted digressions in orations.

38. Ed. G. H. Mair (Oxford, 1909), p. 181. Cf. the examples of digressions Wilson gives (p. 181): "As in making an inuectiue against Rebelles, and largely setting out the filth of their offences, I might declare by the way of digression, what a noble countrey England is, how great commodities it hath, what traffique here is vsed, and how much more neede other Realmes haue of vs, then we haue of them. Or when I shall giue euidence, or rather declame against an hainous murtherer, I may digresse from the offence done, and enter in praise of the dead man, declaring his vertues in most ample wise, that the offence done may be thought so much the greater, the more honest he was, that hath thus bene slaine." Wilson warns (p. 182), however: "Notwithstanding, thir would bee learned, that (when we make any such digression) the same may well agree to the purpose, and bee so set out that it confounde not the cause, or darken the sense of the matter deuised."

39. It is more nearly characteristic of the "merry tale" *topos* employed by, among others, Sir Thomas More in his tracts. The *topos* has its precedence in the humorous anecdotes of the medieval *exempla*. See Rainer Pineas, "Thomas More's Use of Humor as a Weapon of Religious Controversy," *SP*, 58 (1961), 97-114. See also Rainer Pineas, "More Versus Tyndale: A Study of Controversial Technique," *MLQ*, 24 (1963), 144-150.

40. *The Eloquent "I": Style and Self in Seventeenth-Century Prose* (Madison, Wisconsin, 1968), p. 73.

41. In "The Life of Martius Coriolanus," *Shakespeare's Plutarch*, ed. T. J. B. Spencer (Baltimore, Maryland, 1964), p. 303.

42. Ibid. Similarly, in *Caxton's Aesop*, ed. R. T. Lenaghan (Cambridge, Mass., 1967), p. 117, the fable has it that the Belly is absolutely essential to the bodily Members. The moral: "a seruant ought to serue wel his mayster" and not rebel against him.

43. *Coriolanus* (I.i.129 ff.), *The Works of Shakespeare*, ed. W. J. Craig and R. H. Case (London, 1922).

44. *Milton's Literary Milieu* (Chapel

Hill, 1939), pp. 282-292.

45. "To the Reader," *A Modest Confutation* (sig. A 3^r), reprinted in William Riley Parker's *Milton's Contemporary Reputation* (Columbus, Ohio, 1940).

46. See also *Complete Prose Works*, I, 275, n. 37; 276, 277, n. 39.

47. *The Works of Francis Bacon, Lord Chancellor of England*, ed. Basil Montagu (Philadelphia, 1841), II, 413.

48. Reprinted in Everett Emerson's *English Puritanism from John Hooper to John Milton* (Durham, North Carolina, 1968), pp. 96-101.

49. Webber, p. 66.

50. Reprinted in *Tracts on Liberty in the Puritan Revolution, 1638-1647* (New York, 1934), vol. III. This form of tract writing held true not only for the Puritans but for Anglican and Catholic apologists as well. In *Anti-Puritan Satire, 1592-1642* (New Haven, Conn., 1954), p. 70, William Holden takes note of an anonymous Anglican tract entitled *Dialogue Betwixt Three Travelers, as Accidentally They Did Meet on the Highway* (1641), in which Crucy Cringe, the Papist; Accepted Weighall, the Anglican; and Factious Wrestwrit, a Brownist, discuss matters of religion. From the Catholic point of view, we have such tracts as Sir Thomas More's *The Dialogue Concerning Tyndale* (1528) and *A Dialogue of Comfort against Tribulation* (1557). According to Rainer Pineas, "Thomas More's Use of the Dialogue Form as a Weapon of Religious Controversy," *Studies in the Renaissance*, 7 (1960), 193, dialogue as a weapon had been used for many centuries by Catholic apologists, among them, St. Augustine. As More employed the dialogue form, he was at once "the author, casting agent, and director of his drama" (p. 199).

51. For a study of the popular ramifications of the idea, see Helen White's *Social Criticism in Popular Religious Literature of the Sixteenth Century* (New York, 1944), esp. pp. 9-12.

52. "Martin Marprelate, Marvell, and Decorum Personae as a Satirical Theme," *PMLA*, 74 (1959), 526-532. See, however, Raymond A. Anselment, "Rhetoric and the Dramatic Satire of Martin Marprelate," *SEL*, 10 (1970), 103-119.

53. *Anti-Puritan Satire*, p. 51.

54. William Pierce, *An Historical Introduction to the Marprelate Tracts* (New York, 1909), p. 120. These plays unfortunately have not survived.

55. These tracts are conveniently included in *The Works of Thomas Nashe*, 5 vols., ed. Ronald B. McKerrow, (Adelphi, London, 1910), and *The Complete Works of John Lyly*, 3 vols., ed. R. Warwick Bond (Oxford, 1902), respectively.

56. According to Bond (III, 392), Gabriel Harvey referred to this tract as "alehouse and tinkerly stuff" not "worthy a scholar or a civil gentleman."

57. Cited by Donald J. McGinn, *The Admonition Controversy* (New Brunswick, N. J., 1949), pp. 76-77.

58. *Works of Bacon*, II, 413.

59. "Introduction," *Complete Prose Works*, I, 524.

60. In Emerson's *English Puritanism*, p. 256.

61. See Webber, p. 69; Fred Emil Ekfelt, "The Graphic Diction of Milton's English Prose," *PQ*, 25 (1946), 66.

62. *The Rise of Puritanism* (New York, 1938), p. 360.

63. *Milton* (London, 1956), p. 129. See also Hale, "Introduction," *Of Reformation*, p. lxviii.

64. See also *An Apology* (I, 899).

65. John R. Mulder, *The Temple of the*

Mind: Education and Literary Taste in Seventeenth-Century England (New York, 1969), p. 39.

66. *The "Art" of Rhetoric*, trans. John Henry Freese (London, 1926), p. 467; *De Oratore*, trans. E. W. Sutton and H. Rackham (Cambridge, Mass., 1942), II, 373; *Institutes of Oratory*, trans. Rev. John Selby Watson (London, 1856), I, 420-429.

67. *Institutes*, p. 427.

68. See also the *Rhetorica Ad Herennium*, trans. Harry Caplan (Cambridge, Mass., 1954), p. 349.

69. Clark, p. 242.

70. Ibid., p. 14.

71. Wilson's *Arte of Rhetorique*, p. 136.

72. In *The Marprelate Tracts, 1588, 1589*, ed. William Pierce (London, 1911), p. 239. Ironically, as Donald J. McGinn states (p. 126), this defense was aimed not at the Anglicans but at those Puritans whose cause Martin supported and who had condemned his use of satirical invective. Compare Martin's statement in *The Epitome:* "The Puritans are angry with me; I mean the Puritan preachers. And why? Because I am too open; because I jest. I jested because I dealt against a worshipful jester, Dr. Bridges, whose writings and sermons tend to no other end than to make men laugh. I did think that Martin should not have been blamed of the Puritans for telling the truth openly. For may I not say that John of Canterbury is a petty pope, seeing he is so? You must then bear with my ingramness [sic]. I am plain; I must needs call a spade a spade; a pope a pope" (p. 118). In this same tradition of self-defense, incidentally, we find both Nashe and Lyly justifying their vituperative styles. In *The First Parte of Pasquils Apologie* (1590), for example, Nashe says: "Contention is a coale, the more it is blowne by disputation, the more it kindleth: I must spit in theyr faces to put it out" (*Works of Nashe*, I, 110). Even more to the point, Lyly states in *Pappe with a hatchet. Alias A figge for my God sonne* . . . (1589): "I was loath so to write as I have done, but that I learnde, that he that drinkes with cutters, must be not without his ale dagger; now hee that buckles with *Martin*, without his lavish termes," and "I seldome use to write . . . that in speech might seeme undecent, or in sense unhonest; if here I have used bad tearmes: for whatsoever shall seeme lavish in this Pamphlet, let it be thought borrowed of *Martins* language" (*Works of Lyly*, III, 395, 396). According to William Holden (pp. 52, 58), the Anglican pamphlet began as serious polemic but then became "dominantly satirical," arriving ultimately at a parody of the Puritan tract. Its lowest form was that of obscene humor in the popular poetry and ballads. One thinks, for example, of the scurrilous works of John Taylor.

73. Milton, of course, had even earlier demonstrated his willingness in the Sixth Prolusion to engage in low humor when the occasion demanded it. His Prolusion contains an elaborate defense of low humor, drawing upon Homer, Socrates, Cicero, and Erasmus, among others, for support (I, 265-286).

74. For a full study of Milton's concept of decorum, see Thomas Kranidas, *The Fierce Equation* (The Hague, 1965).

75. *The Complete Poetry of John Milton*, ed. John T. Shawcross (New York, 1971).

76. For further studies of Milton's use of invective, see Kester Svendsen, *Milton and Science* (Cambridge, Mass., 1956), pp. 182-190; J. Milton French, "Milton as Satirist," *PMLA*, 51 (1936), 414-429; Allan H. Gilbert, "Milton's Defense of Bawdry," *SAMLA Studies*

in Milton, ed. J. Max Patrick (Gainesville, Florida, 1953), 54–71; Edward
Le Comte, "Milton as Satirist and Wit,"
Th'Upright Heart and Pure, ed. Amadeus Fiore, O. F. M. (Pittsburgh, 1967),
pp. 45–69.

77. In *The Works of . . . William
Perkins* (1631), II, 646.

78. See Lawrence A. Sasek, *The Literary Temper of the English Puritans*
(Baton Rouge, Louisiana, 1961), p. 41:
Sermon and treatise were both looked
upon as "a kind of preaching."

79. *English Pulput Oratory from
Andrewes to Tillotson* (New York,
1962), p. 397.

80. Mitchell, p. 93.

81. *The New England Mind: The
Seventeenth Century* (Cambridge,
Mass., 1954), p. 301.

82. In *Four Treatises* (1609), p. 12.

83. In Parker's *Milton's Contemporary
Reputation*, p. 22. The writer is referring
specifically to the passage in *Animadversions* addressed to the "Prince of
all kings of the earth" (I, 707).

The Images of Poet & Poetry in Milton's *The Reason of Church-Government*

JOHN F. HUNTLEY
University of Iowa

In the early months of 1642 Milton was thirty-three and civil war hung over England like a threatening pestilence. Five months after Strafford's execution (May 12, 1641), news of spreading insurrection in Ireland slowly reached London infecting her people with fears of a calculated Protestant massacre. Amid endemic civil disruption that fall, Pym and his slender majority stalked the sovereignty of England. Rumor preceded and verbiage obscured every move. Thick clouds of language issued from the press, the chambers of Parliament, from street corner and pulpit—rumors, warnings, positions, exhortations, accusations, animadversions, reclarifications. Charles returned to his capital from an ominous excursion to Edinburgh on November 25, his purposes frustrated, but his power and his intentions still unknown for the most part. Within a week he summarily rejected the Grand Remonstrance in which Pym had detailed 204 grievances. Throughout Christmas week, crowds milled around Whitehall rioting at the sight of bishop, lord, or king's officer. "No Bishops." "No Popish Lords." "Hang up the Popish Lords and redcoats." On December 30, riding the crest of popular feeling, Commons impeached the twelve remaining bishops and lodged them in the Tower with Archbishop Laud. Responding to the rumored impeachment of his Queen, Charles attempted the arrest of five Parliamentary leaders on January 3. Failing in fact and in posture, Charles slipped out of London to send Henrietta Maria to France. By March of 1642, he was moving up from Dover, avoiding London in hopes of establishing himself among friends in the North for a final thrust against the leaders of Parliament and mobs of London. He "raised the royal standard," as historians say, on August 22, 1642, in Nottingham, and declared for open war. "God save King Charles and hang up the Roundheads."

In the midst of other personal business, Milton took this tense and confused occasion to portray himself as a man of extraordinary public conscience and rare poetic gift, obligating himself publicly for a major, serious poem "so written to aftertimes, as they should not willingly let it die." He made this promise in the preface to the second book of *The Reason of Church-Government Urg'd against Prelaty* which he wrote between August and late December of 1641, and published in January or February of 1642.[1] Its sixty-five pages are organized into an opening first preface, seven chapters of Book 1, the famous second Preface on poetry, three chapters of Book 2, and a Conclusion.

Quite apart from their inauspicious occasion, the observations on poetry puzzle students of Milton for several other reasons. First, one continually expects that the most revolutionary, scholarly, and self-conscious poet of the seventeenth century would declare a profoundly new view of poetry's nature and function.[2] But Milton's literary comments for the most part are scattered, occasional, and fragmentary. The digressing second preface in *Church-Government* is no exception, even though it is the fullest statement on poetry that Milton wrote until he offered a summary explanation of tragedy in 1671 for *Samson Agonistes*, and his publisher elicited a justification of the verse for *Paradise Lost* in 1668.[3] Buried in the middle of a complex topical argument about ecclesiastical administration, what does a discussion of poetic forms and public promises mean? And written twenty-five years before the appearance of *Paradise Lost*, how does it really bear on the design of the long-expected epic? Is the critical reader authorized, for example, in constructing a useful context of poetic theory and intention for the late epic out of materials provided in the early pamphlet?

Secondly, *Church-Government* is the fourth of Milton's antiprelatical pamphlets, but the first to which he put his name. One expects that all his rhetorical training and the full power of his art would be displayed. But the blatant discord between confessing one's literary ambition and urging patterns of church government continues to feed some latent doubts about the focus of Milton's personality. Does bursting self-confidence warp the larger design of his argument? Do his promises of great poetry and scorn of "hoars disputes" reveal a vanity that mangles art and a naiveté which hobbles the intellectual's attempt to play at politics? Does his "left hand" not know what the right hand is doing? Some attempts to "cut Milton down to size," initiated by the Satanic school of interpretation and entertained by Professor Tillyard, find gratuitous support in these speculations.[4]

The following consideration of *The Reason of Church-Government* and its context will urge that the organization of Milton's pamphlet was acutely and subtly conceived, and that its "digression" served as keystone in Milton's rhetorical and argumentative strategy. The pamphlet reflects in highly characteristic form the architectonic impulse which readers acknowledge in Milton's poetry. The discussion will also show that Milton's remarks on poetry reflect a coherent poetic theory, but a theory rooted in the rhetoric of propaganda and aimed at social change. Stripped of its Christian dress and autobiography, Milton's poetic in 1641 is the dominant theory of poetry derived from the classical rhetoricians and traditionally augmented by fanciful descriptions of the force of pulpit oratory and the nearly irresistible power of poetic ornament and style as implanters of thought. In the evolution of Milton's literary thinking, these opinions mark a shift from the Orphic visions, the magical Christianity, and romantic Ovidianism of his youth, but they bear little direct relation to the concept of poetry which finally gave "strength and structure" to *Paradise Lost*. In fact, the *Paradise Lost* that we know is inconceivable from the mind revealed in *Church-Government*. Yet the poetic Milton embraced in 1642, as Arthur Barker suggests, might have been a necessary stage in the journey toward making the thing "unattempted yet in Prose or Rhyme."[5]

What is the rhetorical purpose of the preface to Book 2? A first reading of *Church-Government* shows that Milton did not try to disguise the apparent irrelevance of his poetic thoughts. Rather, he emphasized the point.

> For although a Poet . . . might without apology speak more of himself then I mean to do, yet . . . [and he goes on for four pages].

> Time servs not now, and perhaps I might seem too profuse to give any certain account of what the mind . . . hath liberty to propose to her self, . . . [yet, and he goes on for three pages].[6]

When he is finished, Milton returns to his argument in Book 2 on a similar note: "After this digression it would remain . . ." (2.1; 823). These phrases and the very personal tone of the digression suggest that it serves as an "ethical proof" for the main argument: because the author is trustworthy in other respects (being cultivated, poetical, and above petty vanity), his comments on ecclesiastical administration must also be significant.[7]

These qualities of tone and the unusual prominence of the middle preface also suggest that the voice we hear in *Church-Government* is not entirely artless, but the voice of a spokesman whose attributes and interests Milton artfully shapes from the beginning. In the raw, these qualities are Milton's own, we can be sure. And perhaps, as Professor Parker avers, the very close if not envious relation that Mil-

ton draws between poetry and pulpit oratory might even be traced
to personal frustration at losing his long-expected place in the church.[8]
But in the pamphlet the voice is framed for a specific purpose with
as much care as Milton shapes the private citizen who speaks against
censorship before the "High Court of Parliament," or the blind bard
who sees and tells of "things invisible to . . . sight."[9]

Although the image and voice of Milton's speaker appear most
sharply in the second preface, that preface is not the singular agent
of Milton's claim to respectful attention, but part of a more coherent
strategy for developing the speaker's "ethos" and matching it with
the reader's. At the outset Milton offers his speaker as a young man
("green yeers" upon his head, Milton later says) whose reasonable perceptions, if not his experience and renown, deserve a hearing. "For
my yeares, be they few or many, what imports it? so they bring
reason, let that be lookt on" (1p; 749). Besides, he will trust "the
supreme inlightning assistance" to guide him where Plato and Moses
have already trod, not to arbitrary prescriptions, but toward rational,
perhaps inspired, explanation of what things ought to be.

Early in the second preface, the speaker becomes a man whose
motives and goals, as well as rationality and knowledge, lift him beyond the level of the partisan pamphleteer heard so often in London
that winter. He has not chosen this path for "some self-pleasing
humor of vain-glory," but by "the enforcement of conscience only"
(2p; 806). He neglects his own fame and welfare in order to assist
"in so dear a concernment as the Churches good" (804). Even stronger
than free volition, Milton hints that a divine compulsion, willingly
embraced, literally forces some men to speak on occasion:

> When God commands to take the trumpet and blow a dolorous
> or a jarring blast, it lies not in mans will what he shall say, or what
> he shall conceal. (803)

But he is more than rational youth or selfless man. Milton augments
the image of himself by suggesting kinship with the prophets Tiresias
and Jeremiah. Like them, he must resolve the natural conflict between
an impulse to convenience and a commitment to destiny. Like them,
he is naturally and temperamentally reluctant to barter for souls
against "the great Marchants of this world" (802) at times and in
ways not of his own pleasing. But the words he would utter are
"certain pretious truths of such an orient lustre as no diamond can
equall" (801). They are not his own, but God's.

In the closing chapters of *Church-Government*, Milton gives this
speaker his anticipated, full, prophetic voice, moving the image from
young, reasonable man in the first preface, through eloquent, self-

less, fearless activist in the second preface, to prophetic dispenser
of judgments in the conclusion. In his closing disdain of evil and
certitude of righteousness this spokesman assumes the style of
Jeremiah's passion as well as kinship with his circumstances.

> This is the sum of [the prelate's] . . . loyal service to Kings; yet
> these are the men that stil cry, the King, the King, the Lords
> Anointed. We grant it, and wonder how they came to light
> upon any thing so true; and wonder more, if Kings be the
> Lords Anointed, how they dare thus oyle over and besmeare
> so holy an unction with the corrupt and putrid oyntment of
> their base flatteries; which while they smooth the skin, strike
> inward and envenom the life blood.[10]

The character of Milton's orator becomes more distinct as his argument proceeds. So do the roles which reflect the developing identity
of Milton's readers. The question at issue, Milton says at the beginning, is "needfull to be known . . . by every meaner capacity," but
Scripture's answers to the problem of church government "easily
imply themselves" to those "that [heed] attentively the drift and
scope of Christian profession" (1p; 749-50). Thus Milton elicits
his first response from those thoughtful, active Christians who would
be willing to teach the commons what they themselves have learned
from Scripture and the inference of faith. Milton asks the reader
either to teach or to tolerate common Englishmen. Consider them
friends of decency, malleable to our good influences, the speaker
urges. They are "no rabble sir Priest, but a unanimous multitude of
good Protestants [who] will then joyne to the Church, which now
because of [the prelates] stand separated" (1.6; 787-88). "The
Englishman," Milton adds, "of many other nations is least atheisticall,
and bears a naturall disposition of much reverence and awe towards
the Deity; but in his weaknesse and want of better instruction, . . .
he may fall . . . as any other land man into an uncouth opinion"
(1.7; 796-97).

> Sects and errors it seems God suffers to be for the glory of good
> men, that the world may know and reverence their true fortitude
> and undaunted constancy in the truth. (1.7; 795)

At midpoint, Milton elevates the reader, thus elevated already, by
asking him to leave behind the prelates, their hopeless dupes, and
those "of no Empyreall conceit." He begs leave to be heard for a
while only by "the elegant & learned reader," the "gentler sort"
who sympathizes with poetry and poetic persons. It may seem
foolish to reveal more of myself, Milton says, inviting the next level

of intimacy, "yet since it will be such a folly, as wisest men going about to commit, have only confest and so committed, I may trust with more reason, because with more folly to have courteous pardon" (2p; 808).

In the Conclusion, turning to address "the Lords and Commons" of the realm, Milton invites his reader to consider not only his role as educated Christian and sensitive friend, but to assume the sober responsibilities of England's destiny, or else to invite total destruction.

> No: they will not, Lords and Commons, [the prelate] . . . will not favour ye so much. What will they do then in the name of God and Saints, what will these man-haters yet with more despight and mischiefe do? Ile tell ye, or at least remember ye, for most of ye know it already. That they may want nothing to make them true merchants of Babylon, as they have done to your souls, they will sell your bodies, your wives, your children, your liberties, your Parliaments, all these things. . . . (C; 851)

By the time Milton reaches his Conclusion, the heightened fervor of the speaker and the elevated role of his auditory are closely matched.

In terms of rhetorical strategy, at least, the beginning, middle, and end of *Church-Government* round out a cogent, artistic whole. The preface to Book 2, although advertised as a digression, functions in the systematic elevation of roles and responsibilities which relate speaker to audience. Specifically, it helps to build the image of Milton's speaker, a rhetorical personality who claims the right to discuss his countryman's most practical *and* most ultimate welfare by offering untaintable honesty, inexhaustible energy, extravagant skill in this or any other form of speech, and inspiration. But Milton also conceived the unity of *Church-Government* in logical and symbolic terms, and in each of these dimensions, the apparent digression on poetry performs an integral function.

The logical substance of *Church-Government* is deployed into two books. But the twofold argument is only hinted at the beginning in the reiterated distinctions between "doctrine and discipline," "manner and order," and the implied balance between theoretical knowledge and practical action. Milton does not provide a technical *partition* like that which anticipates the development of *Areopagitica*. Approaching this thesis more obscurely, Milton takes the word "Reason" from his title in a double sense and moves the argument from a general theory of church government in Book 1 (reason as the source of authority and material arrangement of government) to its specific operation in Book 2 (reason as the form and end of church government which benefits men both as Christians and as citizens). In Book 1, Milton raises two questions and gives two answers. Where does church government come from? What is it made of? It is commanded in the Gospel, Milton answers, and is composed of presbyters. The transition is made at the beginning of 1.3:

> We may returne now from this interposing difficulty thus remov'd, to affirme, that since Church-government is so strictly commanded in Gods Word, the first and greatest reason why we should submit thereto, is because God hath so commanded. But whether of these two, Prelaty or Presbytery can prove it selfe to be supported by this first and greatest reason, must be the next dispute. (761-62)

Book 2 poses two more questions and offers two further answers. At what does church government aim? How does it work? It aims at a spiritual state for man revealed by the gospel, and it works by personal admonition and social pressure, not by legalistic jurisdiction and corporal punishment. The idea of final purpose introduces Book 2:

> And this is the great mistery of the Gospel made good in Christ himself, who as he testifies came not to be minister'd to, but to minister; and must be fulfil'd in all his ministers till his second coming. (2.1; 824)

Both the end and the appropriate means are particularized in the three remaining chapters.

Thus, the concept of church government is delimited by declaring its four Aristotelian causes or "reasons." And, as we might expect from Milton's peculiar reading of the *Metaphysics*, the efficient and material causes coalesce, as do the formal and final causes.[11] It is interesting to anticipate poetry's relation to this definition as a quintessence insofar as it participates in the same "causes" even more perfectly than a government for the visible church. Poetry moves from God (an "inspired guift . . . rarely bestow'd, but yet to some"). It draws matter out of man's "passions" and "thoughts" and "the whole book of sanctity and vertu." It works specific transformations (having "power . . . to imbreed . . . , to allay"). And it exists for the sake of a rectified society and salvation. Apparently some kinds of poetry working upon some kinds of men engender an internal government or self-discipline even more successfully than church government does.

To return to Milton's argument. In Book 1, the "reasons" for these major reasons of church government are drawn first from general considerations of philosophy (Plato's example and the nature of universal discipline in 1p and 1.1). Milton next draws on Scripture in chapters 2 through 5. In 2, he cites relevant passages in sequence from the Pentateuch, the histories, and Ezekiel; then from Acts, the Epistles of Paul and Peter, and finally from Revelation interpreted by "the drift and scope of Christian profession." In the next three chapters Milton answers "trivial" theological arguments from Bishops Andrewes and Ussher by applying the fundamental distinction between the law and the gospel which the sequence of his citations has implied typologically. He argues that the Jewish law (ch. 3), the Jewish priesthood (ch. 4), and Jewish kings (ch. 5) are imperfect and grossly inappropriate types on which to ground a Christian ministry. Milton turns to the writings of his adversaries again in chapter 6 and 7 to raise a question of sociology (God's use of sects and schisms) and then a final question of politics (the problem of Ireland). Thus in Book 1, he arranges his authorities by logic (from universal to particular), by chronology (from early to late), by dignity (from religious to secular), and by significance (from essential to derivative). In the second book, Milton draws his supporting arguments from the nature of a religious society (the ends of this society and the ordering of means are treated in chapters 1 through 3), and finally from the constitution of a specifically English religious society (in the Conclusion to Book 2). Thus the discourse moves with oscillatory sweeps, incremental repetitions, and mirrored oppositions from general to specific reasons, and from spiritually essential to naturally manifest reasons.

Against Professor Wolfe's claim that Milton virtually ignores Biblical evidence for Presbyterianism, Professor Haug cites the all-pervading character of Biblical allusion in Milton's prose.[12] It appears to be the pattern of ideas relating the old dispensation to the new, and a process of spiritual maturation implied by the motion from Genesis to Revelation which constitutes the "drift . . . of Christian profession" or the "argument of faith" as others called it, rather than specific citations within the patterned whole. When Milton urges that truly authoritative reasons for presbyterial government will "easily imply themselves" (1p; 750), being sometimes "for the plainnesse thereof a matter of eye sight, rather then of disquisition" (1.5; 775) to one who attends Scripture, he suggests that the reader must also attend the interconnection of his arguments, the organizing principles of Scripture, and the rich texture of his prose, particularly, for example, the underlying metaphor of the temple in 1.2:

It cannot be wonder'd if that elegant and artfull symmetry of
the promised new temple in *Ezechiel*, and all those sumptuous
things under the Law were made to signifie the inward beauty
and splendor of the Christian Church thus govern'd. (758)

I add only the observation that when Milton moves systematically
through the direct testimony of the Bible and other sources of
argument, he moves in approximately the same order observed in
Of Education from "the morall works" of Plato et al. to "the
determinat sentence of . . . Scriptures," to politics and law, thence
to "highest matters of Theology, and Church History ancient and
modern." In the curriculum, these studies are antecedent to those
capping stones of art, "heroic poems, and Attic tragedies of statliest,
and most regal argument." In the tract, the discussion of poetry
balances the argument at midpoint.

We must look more closely at the twice bisected and then tri-
sected parts of this argument, however, to focus the fine structure
of Milton's thought and to locate other reasons for his joining policy
with poetry. The complex argument of Book 1 is designed to answer,
one by one, three false "reasons" for episcopal government put forward by the hypothetical prelates of Milton's dialectic. First, they
assert, not the government of the church, but only the doctrine
of Christianity, is "platform'd in the Bible"; therefore church
discipline "is left to the discretion of men" (1.1; 750). This was
Hooker's thesis, nearly fifty years old, although Milton barely
identifies it and quickly dismisses the reason and authority behind
it.[13] Rather, he answers that their "inconsequent opinion" is unsound and untrue. It is unsound because discipline is an essential
feature of all goal-seeking human endeavor, according to chapter 1.
It is untrue, in chapter 2, because in the Old Testament a pattern
of church policy is promulgated by Moses, its administration is
described in the books of history, and its future is projected by
Ezekiel in typical, shadowy figures "as sorted best to the apprehension of those times." In strictly parallel passages, the Gospel records
the promulgation, Acts and the Epistles describe the administration,
and Revelation projects the future of a new social relationship
among the faithful. Observation of these parallels, as through the
image of the temple, Milton argues, leads to the conclusion that
God has revealed the discipline as well as the doctrine of his church.

Fancying that the hypothetical prelate has been stung by the
first rebuttal, Milton makes him shift ground for the second point.
We grant that Scripture reveals the basis of a church government,
the prelate mutters, but God's plan is found partly in the Old Testament's institution of priests and Levites and "partly from the imita-

tion therof brought in by the Apostles" (1.3; 763). Milton lowers
his guns to fire three salvoes at slippery compromise. The first is
theological: the Levitical and evangelical priesthoods must be distinguished as the law is radically distinguished from the gospel
(ch. 3). The second is historical: the person and office of priest
were established in the character and work of Christ (ch. 4). The
third is behavioral: the Christian priest is concerned with the inner
man and his next life, not the outward, political man and his present,
national life (ch. 5)

Blasted by these reasons, the straw prelate retreats to lower
ground for a final, futile stand. We now concede that a democratic
or presbyterial government was established in the gospel, he says
abjectly, but the need to suppress schism and rebellion in the generations after Saint Paul required modification toward a prelatical
hierarchy of bishops and archbishops. Milton answers that historical
pragmatism, like the first opinion, confesses its own weakness by
confessing the human sources of prelaty. But specifically, schism
(ch. 6) and rebellion (ch. 7) are subdued by plentiful preaching,
evangelical discipline, and democratic, synodical councils, all of
which Presbyterianism promotes and prelaty opposes.

The general conclusion secured by the arguments of Book 1 is
brief and clear: prelaty is of man, presbyterial government is of
God. Although it is widely recognized that Milton makes almost
trivial use of the materials in *Certain Briefe Treatises, Written by
Diverse Learned Men, Concerning the Ancient and Moderne Government of the Church*, the ostensible occasion for *Church-Government*,
it is apparent that he does considerably more than cite Ussher and
Andrewes and then forget the point-by-point method of refutation
indulged in *Animadversions*. Milton offers to systematize the sum
and essence of prelaty rather than parry each of its spokesmen. He
methodically exposes the illogical logic of the position from the
first audacious premise that God would neglect discipline to the
plethora of meretricious conclusions. And in passing he suggests
that the prelate is more magician than man (casting "a mist of
names" before our eyes, 1.6; 788), more a child of Antichrist than
son of God ("for Lucifer . . . was the first prelat Angel," 1.3; 762),
and kin to the first corrupters of the Christian church ("faire pre-
tenders even of the next ages" who with "ventrous boldnesse of innovation" would immediately change God's immutable decrees,
1.2; 760).

In Book 2 Milton raises a more practical set of questions than
the logical reduction of Book 1, but treats them on a more elevated
level of discourse. "I must confesse to be half in doubt whether I

should bring . . . forth or no" my reasons for thinking prelaty a
church tyranny rather than government, Milton opens,

> it being so contrary to the eye of the world, and the world so
> potent in most mens hearts, that I shall endanger either not to
> be regarded, or not to be understood. For who is ther almost
> that measures wisdom by simplicity, strength by suffering, dig-
> nity by lowlinesse, who is there that counts it first, to be last,
> something to be nothing, and reckons himself of great command
> in that he is a servant? (2.1; 824)

The transition has been accomplished in part by the analysis of his
own motives and his appeal to more "empyreall conceits" in the intervening preface. Both speaker and reader stand among those who
measure command by service, and strength by clarity of vision. Thus
in Book 2, Milton talks in terms of the spirit, not of the world, of
the inward effects, not the outward forms, and of the heavenly
destiny, not the social ramifications of church discipline. Milton
also shifts his stance from a defense in Book 1 to an attack in Book
2.

His basic argument is again twofold. Three arguments support the
first proposition that prelaty subverts the evangelical goals of Christian religion. By its carnal government of the visible church, prelaty
destroys Christ's intention. Not the hierarchic form of a tyranny,
but the lateral form of a democracy was the social order proclaimed
in the gospel (2.1). More essentially, prelaty destroys the doctrine
of faith by its carnal pollutions (2.2). Finally, by its legalistic and
jurisdictional attitude toward the individual believer, prelaty destroys the embryonic image of God in man (2.3). Persuasion and
social pressure, not force usurped from the magistrate, describe
the intended relation between the religious society and its members.
In three steps Milton moves from the prior intention to the present
work of grace and from the circumstantial hindrances to the essential, abortive horror of prelaty. The second concern of Book 2,
embodied in the Conclusion, moves from the pernicious visible
effects to the hidden, vicious motives of the prelates and returns
the reader from the spiritual future to his temporal present. The
prelate opposes "the reason and end of the Gospel" in order to
usurp the pomp and power of the secular state, subvert the magistrate, destroy the parliament, and replace the king. From the first
general reason of church government, namely God's command and
Christ's example, Milton now educes in his peroration the particular
and derivative welfares of "religion, . . . civil government, . . . King
or Parliament, . . . Prince or people, . . . law, liberty, wealth, [and]

learning" (C; 861). All reasons move the conclusion that prelaty derives from slavish men who would be God-Kings, and the presbyterial design is for kingly men who would come to God. Milton has replaced an antithetical structure of false assumptions and consequences with an inverse structure of fundamental authority and practical effect.

For regaining perspective on this highly wrought web of propositions, images, and stylistic insinuations, it helps to ask where Milton might be going on the whole with his discourse. Insofar as his professed goals are argumentative he seeks a negative judgment against prelaty. But the judicial form of his rhetoric is weak in a way that Milton's later critics delighted to ridicule.

> It is all windy foppery from the beginning to the end, written to the elevation of that Rabble and meant to cheat the Ignorant. . . . You fight alwayes with the flat of your hand like a Rhetorician, and never Contract the Logicall fist. . . . You trade altogether in universals the Region of Deceits and falacie, but never come so near particulars, as to let us know which among diverse things of the same kind you would be at. . . . Beside this, as all your politiques reach but the outside and circumstances of things and never touch at realities, so you are very solicitous about weeds [or "words," as the following thought suggests] as if they were charmes, or had more in them then what they signifie: For no Conjurer's Devill is more concerned in a spell, then you are in a meer word, but never regard the things which it serves to express.[14]

Socrates points out to the evasive Euthryphro, in the dialogue of that name, that no one seriously argues whether murder is good or bad. The debatable question is whether or not this man's act is murder and therefore universally condemned. Perhaps too reluctant to leave the "calme and pleasing solitarynes" of his mind, Milton does not argue that these acts committed by those churchmen are "prelatical." After sixty-five pages, his reader must be willing to confess that prelaty is bad, but scarcely knows whose deeds, committed before what witnesses, and recorded in what documents are provable instances of the detested type. Apart from the documented words of Andrewes and Armagh, Milton's most literal image is also the fleeting and offhanded:

> That the Prelates have no sure foundation in the Gospell, their own guiltinesse doth manifest: they would not else run questing up as high as *Adam* to fetch their originall, as tis said one

of them lately did in publick. To which assertion, had I heard
it, because I see they are so insatiable of antiquity, I should
have gladly assented, and confest them yet more ancient. (1.3;
762)

And besides, by imprisoning the bishops on December 30, Commons
had secured in fact the sort of judgment which Milton was urging
in words, at least in "fleshly supportment" if not in spiritual essence.
Content with general categories and verbal bombast, rather than a
specific indictment, Milton is true to the letter, but not to the spirit
of his argumentative intention. As promised, his discourse does "incite, and in a manner, charme the multitude into the love of that
which is really good" (1p; 746). But it charms them into the easy
belief that prelaty, like murder, rape, and arson, is horrible. Judged
by Socrates' more stringent standards of judicial discourse, however,
Milton's arguments do not present the evidence, nor invite the voluntary judgment which would cause free men to embrace that which is
really good "not of custome and awe, which most men do, but of
choice and purpose, with true and constant delight" (1p; 746).

But Milton's argument seeks a second, more positive goal in the
hastening of overt reformation. Let the gospel be preached abundantly (Book 1), and right discipline begin its work (Book 2) so
that Englishmen may demonstrate their readiness before God to
receive his promises. To sympathize with Milton's fervency one
must grant his interpretation of reformed reformation and his
millenarian faith that his day would behold the "materialization
of the Kingdom of Glory":

> The basis for Milton's optimism was not any sort of faith in an
> ideal system of government, but rather in the capabilities men
> enjoyed of being ennobled by their education and regenerated
> by their religion. . . . It is more useful, therefore, to regard
> Milton at this phase not as characteristically utopian or im-
> practical, but as one for whom piety meant an ideology, an
> instrumental conviction that the Church, under the guidance
> of the Spirit, must be allowed to do its work in the world. . . .[15]

Milton is clear about his general priorities for securing the imminent
end: a change of essence precedes a significant change in outward
accidents:

> Tis not rebellion [in Ireland] that ought to be the hindrance of
> reformation, but it is the want of this which is the cause of that.
> (1.7; 798)

The timeliest prevention of schisme is to preach the Gospell

abundantly and powerfully throughout all the land, to inštruct
the youth religiously, to endeavour how the Scriptures may be
easiest understood by all men. (1.6; 791)

But the absence of a specific program belies the spirit of Milton's
understanding of Matthew 25, namely that active human endeavor
must answer God's enabling grace, or, abstractly stated, that a shift
in accidents invites a change in essence:

> The doore of grace turnes upon smooth hinges wide opening to
> send out, but soon shutting to recall the precious offers of mercy
> to a nation: which unlesse Watchfulnesse and Zeale . . . be there
> in our behalfe to receave, we loose: and . . . the ofter we loose,
> the straiter the doore opens, and the lesse is offer'd. (1.7; 797)

Watchfulness and Zeal offer no concrete program for the hastening
of reformation. Toward his own salvation Milton offers only the
demonstration that he has labored in prose toward the cause: "For
me I have determin'd to lay up as the best treasure, and solace of a
good old age . . . the honest liberty of free speech . . . in so dear a
concernment as the Churches good" (2p; 804). And in other pamphlets, Milton represents himself as ready to celebrate with new
songs the arrival of the end:

> Then amidst the *Hymns*, and *Halleluiabs* of *Saints* some one may
> perhaps bee heard offering at high *strains* in new and lofty
> *Measures*. . . . (*Of Reformation*, Yale *Prose*, I, 616)

> Then perhaps [I] may take up a Harp, and sing thee an elaborate
> Song to Generations. (*Animadversions*, I, 706)

But what are others to do? Milton calls on Parliament and the spiritual
elite to do something mighty. But what in particular? when? and how?
remain unanswered in this tract. The pamphlet lacks imaginative, concrete detail, even the utopian detailing of The Grand Remonstrance
which Woodhouse sees as typical of the active, reforming spirit of
Puritanism.[16]

Insofar as Milton sought these judicial ends, the pamphlet must be
considered, I believe, a seventeenth-century instance of what politicians
today call "jawboning." It is a general exhortation to become more
virtuous in every way which fails to specify the political, social, or
economic realities which hinder change, or to name the mechanisms
to bring it about. Perhaps the best that can be said on Milton's behalf has been said by Arthur Barker. No one could perceive in 1641,
much less untangle, the latent contradictions in the Puritan attempt
to secure both reformation and liberty. Until these threaded but

opposing goals were defined in action over the next six years, one
beholds Lilburne enthusiastically distributing Prynne's pamphlets,
and Milton writing for the Smectymnuans while echoing Baillie's
phrases.[17]

But consonant with Milton's emphasis on the soul of reformation
rather than its carnal husks and rinds, the pamphlet's dominant
thrust seems to be expository rather than argumentative. Milton
seeks to expose a concept rather than enforce commitment to a
moral proposition or political act. Two forensic goals are discernible.
Foremost, Milton desires his reader's understanding of the nature
and operation of church discipline or "ecclesial jurisdiction": why
and what it is, how it works, what it reflects of faith or doctrine,
what it seeks for the church as well as for each believer, and what
it aims to achieve for the state as well as for the individual citizen
(2.3; 831). Each man must yield his body to the one discipline,
but his soul to the other. Although Milton verbally affirms the
unity of the whole man, as he does with more thorough conviction
in *Christian Doctrine*, his world in 1641 is still divided by Calvin's
theology and segregated into the realm of spirit and the realm of
nature.[18] What Milton seeks to implant is an understanding that
the best of nature can only be achieved under the direction of
spirit.

Out of this understanding emerges the second goal of Milton's
exposition, a kind of unprogrammed, self-generated behavior by
which Englishmen can prepare their hearts, the rational temple,
God's true church, for the interior reformation which is half-ac-
complished. Chapter 3 of Book 2 shows what this discipline should
be like. The process of discipline is better called "censure" than
"jurisdiction," Milton says. It is a "saving medicine" rather than a
violent punishment. It aims at the inward, rather than the outward
man. And it consists of "admonition," "reproof," and "excommunication."

> This is the approved way which the Gospell prescribes, these are
> the *spirituall weapons of holy censure,* and ministeriall *warfare,*
> *not carnall, but mighty through God to the pulling downe of*
> *strong holds, . . . imaginations, and every high thing that exalteth*
> *it selfe against the knowledge of God. . . .* (2.3; 848, quoting
> from 2 Cor.)

Were these actions put in use as "the Apostles warrant us to do,"
then "would the congregation of the Lord soone recover the true
likenesse and visage of what she is indeed, a holy generation, a
royall Priesthood, a Saintly communion, the household and City

of God" (2.3; 844). And to build the city of God in England,
Milton adds, "I hold to be another considerable reason why the
functions of Church-government ought to be free and open to any
Christian man, though never so laick, if his capacity, his faith, and
prudent demeanour commend him" (2.3; 844).

Inventing a discourse to achieve these multiple goals opened for
Milton an issue so fundamental to his aspirations as a spokesman
for, and perhaps within, the New Jerusalem, that the rhetorical
stratagems and ideational substance of *Church-Government* are
better conceived as manifestations and mere symptoms of his more
radical concern. Or perhaps the concept he used for analyzing
church government became itself the real subject of Milton's discussion. The root problem stems from the concept of *bene dicendi*
or effectively communciating—finding a mode of speech which
will not only beget understanding, but will move to free and positive action. "Ye hear and do not do," Jesus lamented, and St. Paul,
as Milton describes him, found a solution first in preaching and then
in establishing an "evangelick discipline" which would translate
word to deed and diffuse both "knowledge and charity" throughout the church (1.2; 758).

As Milton considered it in *Church-Government*, the problem of
good speaking in this broadest sense, speaking in a manner both
"doctrinal" and "exemplary," will arise for anyone who would
effectively serve the truth. "How and in what manner" should the
prophet "dispose and employ those summes of knowledge and
illumination, which God hath sent him into this world to trade
with?" (2p; 801) In God's prime intention and their own they are
"selected heralds of peace, and dispensers of treasure . . . to them
that have no pence" (802). The question is not what to say, for
that is given, but how to say it. How should a spokesman for God
frame "those sharp, but saving words," which bear a message
of "gladnes and contentment . . . to all mankind," but for speaking which he knows he will be accused of "stomach, virulence
and ill nature," and then scornfully dismissed? (2p; 803-804)
With sobering irony Milton observes that the more effectively the
prophet discharges his "great commission," the more certainly he
must know that worldly scorn and vituperation will be his lot.

In each of his major roles, as poet, polemicist, teacher, grammarian,
logician, and theologian, Milton confronted a different aspect of this
basic question. His thinking about it permeates the arguments of
Church-Government. It colors not only Milton's description of St.
Paul, but his definition of the priest's twofold office "which is

preaching & administering" (1.4; 768).

> Doctrine indeed is the measure, or at least the reason of the measure, . . . but unlesse the measure be apply'd . . . how can it actually doe its proper worke. (1.2; 761)

And earlier:

> Publick preaching indeed is the gift of the Spirit working as best seemes to his secret will, but discipline is the practick work of preaching directed and apply'd as is most requisite to particular duty; without which it were all one to the benefit of souls. . . . (1.1; 755-56)

In Milton's thinking, a man becomes what he does, not what he knows. Or, as he put it more sharply in *Of Christian Doctrine*, the psychological force that moves the process of renovation is a reciprocal relation between insight and action which generates more perfect insight (faith), and then more perfect action (the works of charity).[19] The point is made for readers of *Paradise Lost* in the brilliantly simple line, "Light after light well us'd they shall attain." As the priest is fulfilled in becoming like Christ, so the individual Christian is fulfilled in submitting to church discipline, not merely in listening to church doctrine from the pulpit. In one vivid medical image, Milton emphasizes the point. How could we expect the cure of bodies any more than of souls, he asks,

> if all the Physitians in London should get into the severall Pulpits of the City, and assembling all the diseased in every parish should begin a learned Lecture of Pleurisies, Palsies, Lethargies, . . . and so without so much as feeling one puls, or giving the least order to any . . . Apothecary, should dismisse 'em . . . with this only charge to look well to themselves, and do as they heare. (1.1; 756)

Bridging the two halves of *Church-Government*, the Preface to Book 2 reflects within itself the fundamental relation between essentially knowing and spontaneously doing God's new law which articulates the concept of effective speech. Milton opens the preface in general terms: what the prophet knows and what he must do with his knowledge (2p; 801-802). Narrowing the focus by means of analogies with Jeremiah, St. John, and Tiresias (802-803), Milton turns to what his own speaker (or himself) also knows about himself (804-12), and consequently what he must do (813-23). He must not only write this tract which says what he knows about communicating God's word, but in time to come must create the act itself, a poem "doctrinal and exemplary to a Nation" (813-20)—

to which he now pledges himself (820-21), this tract being part of that pledge (821-23), that pledged self-discipline being part of his present authority to speak (823). Collapsing the priest's dual office and elevating his roles in the single image of the poet, Milton focuses his discussion of knowing and doing on a kind of poetic speech that would at once show what virtue is ("the whole book of sanctity and vertu") and, with the help of other supports, make men virtuous ("the paths of honesty and good life . . . would then appear to all men both easy and pleasant though they were rugged and difficult indeed," 2p; 817-18).

Thus, the preface to Book 2, which is offhandedly offered as a digression, is deeply intermeshed with the underlying principles of Milton's analysis. And poetry itself, as Milton presents it, draws into a single symbol the essential point of his larger argument. Milton's promise to write a poem which perfectly answers "the sacred office of speaking" would seem as ambitious as the claim that such poetry exists might appear audacious had not Milton charged the language of his tract from the outset with anticipations of the symbol.

Both the beginning and end of Milton's tract establish foundations for his epitomizing discussion of poetry. The introductory preface reminds us that before the magistrate can hope to influence the behavior of a free people he must offer some explanation of the laws he would enforce.

> Seeing that persuasion . . . is a more winning . . . way to keepe men in obedience then feare, . . . there should be us'd as an induction, some well temper'd discourse, shewing how good . . . it must needs be to live according to honesty and justice. . . . (1p; 746)

The style of such an induction is just as important as its substance. It should be

> utter'd with those native colours and graces of speech, as true eloquence the daughter of vertue can best bestow upon her mothers praises. . . .

Armed with such a style and substance, the lawgiver seeks to

> incite, and in a manner, charme the multitude into the love of that which is really good as to imbrace it ever after, not of custome and awe, which most men do, but of choice and purpose, with true and constant delight.

Plato was wise in knowing this much. Moses was wiser still in supplying a narrative prologue for the following four books of his law.

> *Moses* therefore the only Lawgiver . . . visibly taught of God . . . began from the book of Genesis, as a prologue to his lawes . . . that the . . . Jewes, reading therein the universall goodnesse of God to all creatures . . . and his peculiar favour to them . . . might be mov'd to obey sincerely by knowing so good a reason of their obedience. (1p; 747)

Milton imitates his wiser teacher. He anticipates the second book of *Church-Government,* which describes what the laws of church censure actually are to which a Christian must submit, with the first book, which offers the general reasons in logical and chronological order for having a church government at all.

At the end of the tract, Milton lays the other footing in his analysis of relationships among the faculties of fallen human nature. The implications of his allegory explain the practical wisdom of Plato and Moses. They also authorize the persuasive strategy which Milton adopts in prose and would try to perfect in poetry. The figure likens Reason to a queen isolated in her presence chamber.[20] "The severall Affections and Desires" mediate between Queen Reason and the limits of her domain. They "keep the ports and passages between her and the object" under their own self-serving control. Truth appears at the gates of sensation in the likeness of an ambassador seeking audience with the queen, hoping to present herself to Reason for "triall and inspection."

> Being to passe through many little wards and limits of the severall Affections and Desires, [Truth] cannot shift it, but must put on such colours and attire, as those Pathetick handmaids of the soul please to lead her in to their Queen. And if [Truth] find so much favour with them, they let her passe in her own likenesse; if not, they bring her into the presence habited and colourd like a notorious Falshood. (2.3; 830)

Either Truth must seduce the powerful handmaids with pleasing disguises, or they will disguise and cripple her before she speaks to Reason. Only a temporizing or innocuous Truth pleases the handmaids by her native dress and is ushered directly into Reason's chamber. When Falsehood presents herself, however, the servants of Reason gain their pleasure with another deception.

> If they like the errand [Falsehood] brings, they are . . . artfull to counterfeit the very shape and visage of Truth. . . . (p. 831)

Reason or understanding, in nominal command of the micro-kingdom, is virtually dependent on her handmaids.

> Not being able to discern the fucus which these inchantresses with such cunning have laid upon the feature sometimes of Truth, sometimes of Falshood interchangeably, [Reason] sentences for the most part one for the other at the first blush, according to the suttle imposture of these sensual mistresses. (p. 831)

Because of the near autonomy of passion and virtual dependence of reason, evangelic discipline works. Gently administered by the local presbytery, it proceeds by tolerant persuasion, patient explanation, and gently applied social pressure. For the same reasons, the coercive system of prelatical discipline does not ultimately work. But reality is a double-edged sword. The same analysis of fallen man explains why prelaty seems to work in the short term, and why evangelicism seems not to.

Milton scores this point heavily for it applies not only to priests, magistrates, and orators, but to poets as well and to each of their opposites. Every feature of the universe embraced in Milton's discussion finds its real identity and its dangerous parody in the spectrum between Christ and Antichrist. Opposing the true poet are the "libidinous and ignorant Poetasters" from whose "writings and interludes" the nation daily sucks in "corruption and bane," lapping up "vitious principles in sweet pils" (2p; 818). Opposite the true pastor, Milton sets the false prelate. Milton exposes not only his carnal doctrine and tyrannical discipline, but also his greedy, materialist motives, and especially the mischievous methods by which he aims to seduce the pathetic handmaidens of the soul. Their argument about schism

> hath the outside of a specious reason, & specious things we know are aptest to worke with humane lightnesse and fraility, even against the solidest truth, that sounds not plausibly. . . . (1.6; 779)

Their description of the English people as dangerous sectists is another

> quiver of slander, wherein lyes your best archery. And whom ye could not move by sophisticall arguing, them you thinke to confute by scandalous misnaming. Thereby inciting the blinder sort of people to mislike and deride sound doctrine and good christianity under two or three vile and hatefull terms . . . , a mist of names cast before their eyes. (1.6; 788)

Their ominous warnings about the Irish rebellion are

> meere fictions and false alarmes . . . thereby to cast amazements

and panick terrors into the hearts of weaker Christians. . . . (1.7; 794)

In Book 2, the prelates display a pastoral corruption to match their political mischief:

> But our Prelats instead of expressing the spirituall power of their ministery by warring against this chief bulwark and strong hold of the flesh, have enter'd into fast league with the principall enemy against whom they were sent, and turn'd the strength of fleshly pride and wisdom against the pure simplicity of saving truth. (2.2; 826-27)

In the transitional preface to Book 2, *how* the prelate speaks becomes even more central to Milton's characterization than *what* or *why* he speaks:

> The great Marchants of this world fearing that this [honest] cours [of the prophets] would soon discover, and disgrace the fals glitter of their deceitfull wares wherewith they abuse the people, like poor Indians with beads and glasses, practize by all means how they may suppresse the venting of such rarities. . . . Therefore by gratifying the corrupt desires of men in fleshly doctrines, they stirre them up to persecute with hatred and contempt all those that seek to bear themselves uprightly in this their spiritual factory. . . . (2p; 802)

Thus, the conceptualizing pattern emerges which underwrites Milton's discussion of poetry. In his last chapter, Milton anatomizes the raw, human matter from which the true Christian must be formed. In his opening chapters, he dwells on discipline, the "line and levell" of a man's soul "which is his rationall temple" (1.2; 758).

> The state . . . of the blessed in Paradise, though never so perfect, is not . . . left without discipline, whose golden survaying reed marks out and measures every quarter . . . of new Jerusalem. . . . Our happinesse [too] may orbe it selfe into a thousand vagancies of glory and delight, and with a kinde of eccentricall equation be as it were an invariable Planet of joy and felicity. . . . (1.1; 752)

The argument which seemed to concern the government of the material church resolves into an exposition of the framing of the inward temple. By means of his prophets, God seeks to "forme and regenerate in us the lovely shapes of vertues, and graces, the sooner to edifie and accomplish that immortall stature of Christs body which is his Church" (1.2; 758). The unspecifiable disciplines of charity supply the true formal cause of this inward structure. At

midpoint, in the preface to Book 2, Milton joins the two causes
by describing a world in which carnal doctrines of the great mal-
forming merchants compete with the saving words of God's prophets (2p; 801-04). A related set of self-reflecting, self-engendering
terms jointly describes the efficient cause which reforms human
matter more and more perfectly for the sake of the kingdom to
come: man and his chief work, his chief work best perceived as
knowing and doing, and his doing best seen in spokesman and
speech, preacher and disciplinarian, poet and poem, and the entire chain epitomized in the idea of a poem.

These, I take it, are the ramifications of Milton's "urgent reason"
(820) for divulging, as though in a digression, his views on poetry.
And these are some of the determinants which affect Milton's discussion of his plans. The conceptual relationships may not be so
intriguing or delightful as the inversions of *Paradise Lost*. But the
same habit of mind is discovered in the pamphlet which the poem
manifests in its "mazes intricate,/Eccentric, intervolv'd, yet regu-
lar/Then most, when most irregular they seem."

Having come to the artistic center, let us focus what Milton actually says about the future ideal poem. Like a sermon, poetry can do
the evangelical work of transforming even those who must, by
nature, "resist and oppose their own true happinesse" (2p; 803).
And the right kind of poetry, Milton affirms, might be preliminary
to, parallel with, or in some cases better than the traditional instruments of preaching and censure applied by the priest (816).
Milton's explanation of the right kind of poetry fulfills the specifications established by its context.

In the character of his prophetic speaker, Milton first describes
three early signs which led to his life-shaping decision. The praise
of his early teachers, the response of the Italians, and "an inward
prompting which now grew daily upon me" led him to conclude
"that . . . labor and intense study, . . . joyn'd with the strong
propensity of nature" might enable him to "leave something so
written to aftertimes, as they should not willingly let it die" (2p;
810).

This resolution determined a rough choice of means and ends.
Abjuring "verbal curiosities" and a vain attempt to compete with
the world's great poets, he chose "the adorning of my native tongue"
for a tri-fold end: to memorialize England's "noble atchievments,"
for "the honour and instruction of my country," and in the service
of "Gods glory" (2p; 810-12).

Milton next elaborates the chosen alternative in more specific detail. The means will be a poem, either in the epic, dramatic, or lyric form.[21] Epic, which seems to be favored, is anatomized by Form (either "brief" or "diffuse" following the Book of Job or the examples of Homer, Vergil, or Tasso), by Rule (either the prescriptions of Aristotle or the instincts of the poet's genius), and by Subject (some King or "Knight before the conquest" in whom "the pattern of a Christian *Heroe*" might be laid) (2p; 813-14).

Interestingly enough, a specific subject is not essential to the ideal poem. Its substance, following Tasso's bold and generous example, might be left to a public opinion poll of some sort. If the poet will be trusted and the circumstances are propitious, "it haply would be no rashnesse from an equal diligence and inclination, to present the like offer in our own ancient stories" (2p; 814). Whatever story the magistrate or public desires—expressing, naturally, the desires of their souls' greedy handmaids—the poet offers to transform popular story into a conveyer of unpopular moral truth.

The moral subject or theme, however, is not left to public choice, but is discovered in "the whole book of sanctity and vertu." Coming down from God as inspiration, or arising from experience as an acute insight into the moral law, the theme of the poem is as stable as the pastor's doctrine or the prophet's "eye-brightning electuary"; it is the "guift of God rarely bestow'd, but yet to some . . . in every Nation" (2p; 816).

Clearly the thematic element is not found in a collection of moral precepts nor in any man's "marginal stuffings." It flows from an inspired vision of some aspect of the disciplines of charity which the poet then manifests in story and language by means of his craft. And just as clearly, although Plutarch's definition of the good orator as a good man lies behind Milton's thinking, Milton has completely reconceived and rerationalized in Christian terms the "good man" of classical rhetoric. Given the nature and source of poetic truth, there is little Milton can do but define the poet by spiritual rather than craftsmanly or even intellectual qualities. Just as the framer of civil discipline must be "a true knower of himselfe" and combine within himself

> contemplation and practice, wit, prudence, fortitude, and eloquence . . . both to comprehend the hidden causes of things, and span in his thoughts all the various effects that passion or complexion can worke in mans nature (1.1; 753),

so the poet prepares for his vision of the "eccentricall equation"

by devout prayer to that eternall Spirit who can enrich with all

utterance and knowledge, and sends out his Seraphim with the
hallow'd fire of his Altar to touch and purify the lips of whom
he pleases: to this must be added industrious and select reading,
steddy observation, [and] insight into all seemly and generous
arts and affaires. (2p; 821)

After epic, two other kinds of poetry are summarily explained
and justified. Both the classics and Scripture provide possible models
for "Dramatick constitutions" or—"if occasion shall lead"—for lyric
forms. We notice again that neither the authorizing source, the generic form (or "frame" as Milton calls it), the material subject (the
"matter" wherein some classical odes are faulty), nor the verbal
texture ("the very critical art of composition") are sufficient determiners of the true poem. These material embodiments and con-
veyers are not totally indifferent to the essential "divine argument,"
I presume, although Milton allows the possibility that they might
be. They are qualities to be negotiated against the local handmaidens'
appetites. What the poet's great and rare ability comes to is a certain
skill at effectively disguising truth in passion-pleasing dress made
out of language, story, and generic form. By this act he serves the
handmaids; by his theme, he speaks to the rational soul of his
reader. Such a poet is ready to engage the great merchants at their
own game and to seduce the handmaidens of understanding for
their own, and their Queen's, good. I hear the distant, but distinct
echo of Cicero, in a claim that was not seriously questioned until
Coleridge—poetry is a more intense form of rhetoric, the force of
poetry and rhetoric lies in ornament, and the substance ornamented
is a rational argument which derives its authority from supra-verbal
disciplines. More than any other kind of preacher-prophet or
spiritual "disciplinarian," a poet knows and exploits the ambassa-
dorial arts for penetrating to the presence chamber of Queen Reason.

Noting briefly that the ability to create poetry of such power is a
"guift of God," Milton turns from the nature of poetry in its several
kinds to the work of each kind and the effect of right poetry in
general. "Beside the office of a pulpit," poetry can accomplish
five specific operations along a spectrum of effects. Epic in particular can "imbreed and cherish in a great people the seeds of vertu,
and publick civility." Drama, and especially tragedy which traditionally purged the pathos while epic shaped the ethos, can "allay the
perturbations of the mind, and set the affections in right tune."
"Lyrick poesy" embraces "those magnifick Odes and Hymns wherein Pindarus and Callimachus are in most things worthy," and also
those "frequent songs throughout the law and prophets." Lyric seeks
"to celebrate in glorious and lofty Hymns the throne and equipage

of Gods Almightinesse, and what he works, and what he suffers to be wrought with high providence in his Church." If that is the proper work of "hymns," then "odes" are designed "to sing the victorious agonies of Martyrs and Saints, the deeds and triumphs of just and pious Nations doing valiantly through faith against the enemies of Christ." Finally, poetry also serves "to deplore the general relapses of Kingdoms and States from justice and Gods true worship." Perhaps this function belongs to satire, a form presumably beneath Milton's dignity to mention in this context.[22] One notices that the priority of genres is directly keyed to the nobility of the end they accomplish: epic works for the positive, personal, and public; tragedy, the negative and personal; lyric, the positive and impersonal (hymns dealing with God and the church; odes, with martyrs and nations); and satire seeks the negative and impersonal.

Milton now summarizes the means-ends argument by generalizing the subject, method, and effect of right poetry as he conceives it. In general, poetry's abstract subject or doctrinal content is "whatsoever in religion is holy and sublime, in vertu amiable, or grave, whatsoever hath passion or admiration in all the changes of that which is call'd fortune from without, or the wily suttleties and refluxes of mans thoughts from within." The poet's prime responsibility before God is apparently to make persuasive connections between the transitory and the permanent, lifting nature into the vision of spirit. The poet "with a solid and treatable smoothnesse" must "paint out and describe" the accidents of experience which appear to obscure, but under a proper vision can be made to betray, and ultimately to manifest the essence of experience. This he does with a story suitable to the times and in language appropriately ornamented.

The effect of this work on men of grave temperament is not specified.[23] Not needing the beguilement of their feelings in order to consider the desirability of truth, they are ready for doctrine and discipline as it comes undiluted from Scripture and learned commentary. But on soft tempers, true poetry works the charm that Plato had sought. The poet teaches

> through all the instances of example with such delight to those especially of soft and delicious temper who will not so much as look upon Truth herselfe, unlesse they see her elegantly drest, that whereas the paths of honesty and good life appear now rugged and difficult, though they be indeed easy and pleasant, they would then appear to all men both easy and pleasant though they were rugged and difficult indeed.

How are these benefits to be realized in the state? Milton concludes this phase of the discussion with the most practical suggestion to be found in the tract. In the reformed community now coming into existence by English effort answering special grace, he would enlarge the magistrate's responsibility. Milton patterns the spiritual dimensions of this new community after the early Christian cells established by Paul and Clement in the first two generations after Christ. Republican Rome provides a model for its secular dimensions (2.3; 831-32). Like those spiritual and secular magistrates of old, Milton urges, our new leaders should concern themselves not only with law and litigation, but with the sports and pastimes of the people.

In their fallen condition men need recreation, and the pathetic handmaids need their play as well as reason her work. In this tract, Milton respects natural need by inserting the preface to Book 2, itself a "recreating intermission of labour, and serious things" which leads the reader from matters serious enough in Book 1 to the greater "mistery of the Gospel made good in Christ" which opens Book 2. The wise magistrate should also respect the natural passions and appetites of the common people, but he should satisfy legitimate needs with a view to developing, not corrupting, the soul. Milton suggests several ways. In the place of Sunday sports under the smiling prelate's eye, offer the people "martial exercises" to harden the body. Also, "civilize, adorn and make discreet our minds" by establishing academies and procuring "wise and artfull recitations sweetned with eloquent and gracefull inticements to the love and practice of justice." This last might be done, Milton says, not only "in Pulpits," but after "another persuasive method, at set and solemn Paneguries, in Theaters, porches, or what other place, or way may win most upon the people to receiv at once both recreation, & instruction" (820).

What Milton apparently intends are the poetic recitations of ancient Athens, the stimulating academies he recently experienced in Italy, and national theater groups sponsored by the state on behalf of the church. These performances of poetry and drama throw legitimate sops to the Cerberean mistresses of the soul, but aim at the inward man and his spiritual welfare. Take religion back to the people, Milton cries, in terms they understand, for the health they truly but ineffectively desire. It seems outrageous to suggest, but I suppose by this temper Milton would have to approve at least one feature of modern society, "pop" prayer, religious jazz, beat poetry and drama performed in churches, or church services performed in off-Broadway theaters.

To fulfill the great "covenant" for which "I am now indebted,"

Milton says, I will do my part with God's help, my own endeavor, and a permitting social environment ("that there by nothing advers in our climat, or the fate of this age," 2p; 814). The first two enablements, Milton can guarantee with considerable certainty. But for the last he depends on those around him. With this logic he justifies his involvement in politics and the use of his "left hand" to prepare a fitting place for the poetic product of his right hand.

Two questions remain to be asked. Had "the fate of this age" allowed Milton to fulfill his promise immediately, what kind of poem would he have written? Does the extrapolation match *Paradise Lost*, or adequately describe features of the poetry published after 1667?

The specifications in *Church-Government* form a fairly clear picture of the type of poem Milton thought fit to promote and celebrate the spiritual maturity of his people in 1642. The subjects he considered in "Manso," "Damon's Epitaph," and the pages of the Trinity manuscript, as well as his comments on poetry in the "Commonplace Book" substantiate the projection. It would be allegoric, moral, and propagandistic, aimed at disciplining man's weakness, not exercising his strength. It would be written with local circumstances in mind to charm or seduce the errant passions with benign intent in order to lodge with reason the undoubted truths of Calvinist doctrine, Presbyterian discipline, and Roundhead policy. The poem would be a conveyer of truths out of its own domain rather than a substance conveyed for its own sake. It would hold some affinity with a versified sermon, allegorized theology, or sententious history. Following the classical, rhetorical prescription, the poetry Milton envisioned in 1642 seems more on the order of *Comus* or "On the Fifth of November."[24] He appears to be moving toward poetic structures like Joseph Beaumont's *Psyche, or Love's Mysterie* (1648), Davenent's *Gondibert* (1651), Edward Benlowes' *Theophilia, or Love's Sacrifice* (1652), Cowley's *Davideis* (1656), or William Chamberlayne's *Pharonnida* (1659), although doubtlessly clothed in language more noble.[25] Professor Haller observes that Milton's plans

> reflect the hope that in the regenerated commonwealth . . . poets might have opportunity to match the sermons of preachers with poetic dramas *ad populum*. . . . The audience in his theater would have witnessed the same texts dealt with on the stage which it had often heard expounded in church. It would have brought to the consideration of what it saw and heard a familiarity not

simply with the Biblical story but also, thanks largely to the pulpit, with a code of meaning and store of association which the
modern reader knows little of.[26]

Professor Fixler speculates that

had Milton sketched an Arthuriad, like Spenser's *Faerie Queene*
and probably more markedly, it almost certainly would have
dealt in some fashion with the contemporary view of national
election and the nation's providential destiny in the course of
Reformation.[27]

Whether Milton had found a tractable subject in fable, history, or
Scripture, Fixler argues that "the themes and preferences of the
early work" indicate "the basically ambivalent attitude Milton felt
towards the public function and direction of his art." On the one
hand,

the esoteric nature of [Milton's] vision . . . appealed markedly to
the particularism of the Puritan saint, a particularism which
found its counterpart later in an overt prejudice compounded
of an aristocratic bias and theocratic beliefs. His most spontaneous artistic inclinations had been toward what Bacon called
"Poesy Parabolical," an art tending "to retire and obscure . . .
the secrets and mysteries of religion, policy, or philosophy."

On the other hand, "Milton could scarcely forget that the end of
all human activity was regeneration."

Moreover, the moral and spiritual authority, and through these
the political authority the Puritans claimed in the name of religion, imposed upon them the obligation to endeavour by all
means the regeneration of the greatest number possible.

There are, of course, Miltonic qualities reflected in both the anti-
prelatic prose and late poetry which survive Milton's withdrawal
from Presbyterianism, the fading of his millenarian vision, the
alliance with Independency, his radical conversion to Arminian
theology, his blindness, the meticulous detailing of his Christian
belief, and the political restoration. The central personage of the
inspired poet remains, as do the reciprocities between speaker and
speech, the exfoliating-involuting plays of relationship, the thought-
reflecting images, the passion-saturated ideas, and always the sheer
force of Milton's language.

But differences between the poetry projected in 1642 and the
poems published after 1667 seem to me more important. I will
conclude with a list of differentiae, acknowledging the impossibility

of distinguishing phases of a process without overstating the polarities. Properly qualified and fitted together, with due regard for rational coherence and (if ever possible) a sound chronology, each of these points might find a place in that yet-to-be-written study of Milton's mature poetic.[28]

Because his three major poems are so radically different from other long, Christian poems written in the mid- and late seventeenth century, it would be interesting to know what unique vision of poetry guided Milton into the final drafts of *Paradise Lost, Paradise Regained,* and *Samson Agonistes.* The seeds for these poems are discovered in the late 1630s. Probably some of the writing occurred in the 1640s and '50s at first, no doubt, under the aegis of a poetic theory whose character, sources, and intents are displayed in *Church-Government* but whose hold on Milton's ever-evolving mind was less than compulsive. It is difficult to tell when and how separate elements of this theory slipped out of place, changed, and found new equilibrium with other altered concepts. And it is impossible to say whether evolving perceptions of poetry's nature and function left a traceable mark on redrafted passages of poetry in progress. But somewhere along the line, a drama conceived for the stage became stageless; an epic conceived in ten books and perhaps five dramatic parts set forth in rhymed verse became rhymeless blank verse organized in twelve books; and an allegoric presentation of "Baptistes" and "Christus patiens" became the brief epic vision of a poetic narrator telling the never-before-knowable story of *Paradise Regained.* Little of the evolutionary process appears until the end products are published between 1667 and 1674. And even then, the poetic data stand alone with very little critical explanation, no prefatory epistles "to the learned reader," nor annotated guides to arcane references which are standard apparatus for Benlowes, Cowley et al. Hence it would be interesting to know, and barring knowledge, it is certainly useful to speculate about the rationalizations Milton might have given his readers. How did he view "the main consistence of a true poem" (2p; 818) in the 1660s and '70s. What was poetry's origin, nature, and function, its relation to the real world, the authority of its fiction, the force of its several parts, its dependency on literary traditions and trustworthy history, and its actual value in the light of God's hope for man's endeavor? In a number of ways and for many reasons, it seems to me, the answers Milton gave in 1642 would be very different from those he might have given in 1674.

First, the quality and number of Milton's intended audience

changes from those many of the world who are "either weakly,
or falsly principl'd, . . . through ignorance, and . . . through custom
of license" (2.3; 831) to the "fit audience . . . though few" of
Paradise Lost 7.31. At the same time, the quality and number of
the potentially saved also changes in Milton's mind from the
elected few, or expectant many, of his Presbyterian commitment
to mankind universally in *Christian Doctrine*.[29] According to
Christian Doctrine, renovation springs from within as a natural
impulse of the will and is uniquely described by each man's experience.[30] Saving truth is no longer held to be a condition in-
fused from above by special grace. Nor is truth inserted from
without by preachers or poets sufficiently skilled to "assay those
wily Arbitresses who in most men have . . . the sole ushering of
Truth and Falshood between the sense, and the soul" (1.3; 831).
If this is the case by 1660, for whom and why did Milton conceive his poems?

Second, the function of rhyme and ornament change. In 1642
"eloquence" is the element responsible for charming and inciting
the multitude. But by 1667 Milton abandons rhyme (as he had in
the narrative parts of "Arcades" and *A Masque*) for the sake of
"true musical delight" and on-rushing sense. He explains why
in 1668:

> This neglect then of Rime so little is to be taken for a defect,
> though it may seem so perhaps to vulgar Readers, that it
> rather is to be esteem'd an example set, the first in *English*,
> of ancient liberty recover'd to Heroic Poem from the . . .
> bondage of riming.

In 1671 he published a tragedy never intended for the stage whereas
in 1642 he had sought the most popular, most compulsive form of
poetry. If Professor Barker is correct, he obscured a five-act dramatic
structure in recasting *Paradise Lost* as a twelve-book epic.[31] Milton
seems to have abandoned the handmaid/reason concept of human
nature as well as the husk/kernel idea of poetry as he modified his
original notion of the wellsprings of saving truth. And in consequence
he seems to relinquish what might be called the "illegitimate" or
"seductive" enforcers of poetic speech, either the spectacular element of drama or the extrinsic verbal ornaments of verse.

Third, the relation between relatively indifferent story material
and essential meaning also changes. Milton did not conduct a con-
sumer survey, but by "long choosing, and beginning late" apparently
found the story that could uniquely embody the patterns of "Patience
and Heroic Martyrdom." His radically dichotomized concept of

poetry, one part sensuous and "exemplary," the other part divine and "doctrinal," is replaced by a concept more uniform and harmonious even as the segregated cosmos of nature and grace is replaced in *Christian Doctrine* by a monistic cosmos. These changes are all consonant with the essentializing, inward-tending character of Milton's intellectual development and bear on the poetry published in his later years.

Yet, to suggest a fourth point of difference, although each of Milton's subjects is Biblical and his language echoes Scripture at every turn, each poem preserves its fictive character and makes no extra-literary claim for authority. These poems do not appear to be instances of a versified sermon (whose truth claim rests on "logic" as then understood), or allegorized morality (whose truth derives from orthodox theology), or narrated history (whose authenticity derives from the chronicle parts of Scripture). Each of these categories seems to be a plausible actualization for poetry projected in the Trinity papers and *Church-Government*. But the credibility of the three late poems arises from intrinsic qualities of probability, necessity, and intense interrelatedness rather than extrinsic forces. Any claim concerning Milton's reliance on Scriptural authority for the "truth" of his Christian tragedy must account for the fact that the day on which Milton's Samson awakens into death by confronting, among others, a non-Scriptural Harapha, is marked in Judges only by the destruction of the Philistines. The action of *Paradise Regained* was known to the angels, but witnessed by no man and unknown until now (1. 16-17, 128-72). The episodes of *Paradise Lost* are manifestly products of Milton's imagination working from Biblical details with "the traditions of men." In the case of the two epics, Milton's bardic voice claims special vision as his authority, a claim to latter-day knowledge of matters "above the air and below the earth" that no philosopher could make since Socrates' day and no Christian would make since Simon Magus. Nor does Milton ask his reader to equate belief in poetic fiction with the illegitimate act of belief he condemns in popery: "a Religion taken up and believ'd from the traditions of men and additions to the word of God . . . [is heresy]. Of all known Sects or pretended Religions . . . Popery is the only or the greatest Heresie."[32] What is the relation between the total and sufficient revelation of God, the recorded memories of men, the traditions of human art, and poetic fiction? What sort of contract with reality does a man make when he commits his "belief" to each set of terms?

Fifth, the role of religious teacher changes during this twenty-five year span in Milton's thinking. In the early 1640s, he is a man particularly gifted and rigorously trained, a member of a spiritual and intellectual elite. In 1659, Milton abandons the trappings of formal preparation and draws a simpler picture of the pastor. Or rather, the pastoral function is served by an exchange of views among small gatherings of the faithful like-minded which stimulates in each a more individualized and differentiated vision of truth.[33] In the preface to *Christian Doctrine* Milton sets it down that religious truth, far from being doctrine impelled upon reason through sense, is that rational harmony of propositions discovered by an individual in meditative analysis upon experience and offered to others for criticism.[34] What happens in the two epic poems to the role of teacher? A bardic voice stands behind each poem, fully developed in *Paradise Lost* as Anne Ferry has shown, existing more subtly but just as fully in *Paradise Regained.*[35] In *Paradise Lost* this person undergoes the experience of the poem in the very act of delivering it. With considerable danger to himself, he participates in the descents and flights of his vision. When we apprehend this personage early in the poem, he is very much rapt above the clouds, "his garland and singing robes about him" (2p; 808). But as the poem approaches the world we know, he becomes more recognizably like ourselves. In Book 9, he speaks most mundanely and technically about his craft and about certain practical decisions which shaped the work of his hands. After that, the image fades, as have the ironic observations and moral applications which characterize the first five books. In Books 10, 11, and 12 we are left with the story itself almost forgetting the mediator who brought it before our eyes. It is curious to observe the contradictory process of this image: as it incarnates, it evaporates. Is this a fault in Milton's design, or does it reflect his considered understanding of the teacher's role? What is the relation between poet and reader, and to whom and for what are the teacher and taught responsible?

Sixth, if it is only speech which binds men together as seekers for truth, the poetic speech of the last three poems does not appear to depend on "the secondary law of fallen nature" to as great a degree as appeared in 1642. There, both good and bad poetry comes into existence in response to man's psychic dissociation. Milton had consulted the "lofty Fables and Romances" and the whole "Laureat fraternity of Poets," and had set them aside.[36] He was looking for the "new song" of Revelation 14:3 or "the unexpressive nuptial song" of "Lycidas." One can only speculate about the verbal texture and structural character of the "new and lofty *Measures*" or the "elaborate Song to Generations" which he might have sung had the savior arrived.[37] But in *Paradise Lost*, poetry stems from another

law. It is more natural in paradise than in our world whose characteristic sounds are the "barbarous dissonance" of Thrace or "Sea-mews
clang." One recalls the unanimous and unpremeditated prayers of
Adam and Eve. They are elaborate and artful in a manner diametrically opposed to George Herbert's conception of the totally pure and
natural poem, "My God, My King."[38] One recalls, also, Raphael
assuming the role of epic bard with a narrative poem which makes
no pretense about its fictive and artful character. What were Milton's ground for legitimizing vicarious, imaginary experience and
the attractive powers of poetry?

   And lastly, if poetry in this world is more fit for the regenerate
than for the lost, what happens to the evangelic function of poetic
speech? Stanley Fish outlines a way of participating in *Paradise
Lost* by which the reader finds his sin and hence his salvation.[39]
But Milton makes no mention of poetry in *Christian Doctrine* as
being a renovative agent either sufficient, necessary, or incidental.
And manifestly, Adam and Eve fall despite experiencing what can
only be construed as a representation of the best of epics told by
the most capable of bards in pursuit of the clearest of missions.
One bearing on the question can be found in an idea that continued
to grow from the time of *Areopagitica* to *True Religion.* "A man
may be a heretick in the truth" (Yale *Prose*, II, 543). In his last
pamphlet Milton writes that heresy is an "implicit faith." The man
"wise unto salvation" gives an explicit account of his beliefs. The
key is not what a man knows, but how he knows and how he acts
on it. In this light, the poetry Milton considered in 1642 would
appear destined to incite or charm a reader into heresy. Perhaps
the poetry of Milton's final years was designed to provoke a few
readers to explicate the latent relationships of their own faith
more fully and persistently than the accidents of natural experience might call for. But we are left with a haunting question which
twentieth-century criticism does not seem ready to cope with.
What is the reader's responsibility to Milton's poem and to his
own "salvation" as Milton defined the process? If one of the "fit
. . . though few" were permitted to read only *The Christian Doctrine* or *Paradise Lost*, which book would Milton hand him? and
why?

Notes

1. Ralph A. Haug, "Preface and Notes," *The Complete Prose Works of John Milton,* ed. Don M. Wolfe (New Haven: Yale University Press, 1953-), I, 737-38, surveys the evidence for dating.

2. For some critics the expectation has been fulfilled: In his remarks on poetry "Milton may be said to have broken new ground, . . . especially in his conception of its nature and function." J. W. H. Atkins, *English Literary Criticism: The Renascence* (London: Methuen & Co., 1947), p. 337.

3. "Although Milton wrote treatises on education and the art of logic, he left no formal criticism as such . . . ; mainly what we possess is . . . by way of lordly apologetic . . . or consists of quasi-biographical utterances that appear with fervid abruptness in the course of arguments against episcopacy." Edward W. Tayler, *Literary Criticism of Seventeenth-Century England* (New York: Alfred A. Knopf, 1967), p. 184. "Thus, in . . . the first tract to which he signed his name, Milton identified himself as a poet, and spoke ingenuously of his high ambitions. Literary enthusiasm, political optimism, and pride in this particular pamphlet combined to inspire an autobiographical digression which is still startling in its revealing irrelevance." William R. Parker, *Milton: A Biography,* 2 vols. (Oxford: The Clarendon Press, 1968), I, 210.

4. E. M. W. Tillyard, "*Paradise Lost:* the Unconscious Meaning," in *Milton* (London: Chatto and Windus, 1930), pp. 276-94.

5. Milton "entered the controversial arena on the side of Puritanism because the reformation of the church seemed to promise the long-sought fulfillment of his powers; but the view of reformation he adopted was modified by his high view of his poetical function." In *Church-Government* "he is demanding something more than the mere reorganization of the national church government. He is thinking less of reformation than of a national regeneration. . . . [His definition of the liberty to which the saints are called] will serve to express his sense of particular calling as a Christian poet; and that fact will make his interpretation of the doctrine the measure of his divergence" both from orthodox Puritanism and the Separatists. *Milton and the Puritan Dilemma, 1641-1660* (Toronto: University of Toronto Press, 1942), pp. 36, 42.

6. 2p; 808, 812. References to *Church-Government* will be made by book and chapter, 1st or 2nd prologue, or conclusion in the pamphlet, and by page number to Ralph Haug's edition in volume I of the Yale *Complete Prose.*

7. Both Michael Fixler, *Milton and the Kingdoms of God* (Evanston: Northwestern University Press, 1964), p. 103, and John Diekhoff, "The Function of the Prologues in *Paradise Lost,*" *PMLA,* 58 (1942), 697-704, speak of the "ethical proof" as it functions in this pamphlet and in Milton's poetic work. Haug (p. 823, n. 1), however, points out that the formal "digression," which ought to precede the "peroration," comes a little early according to Cicero's standards. It should also be noticed that it comes rather late for establishing the speaker's character, since that function should occur at the very beginning according to both Cicero (*De Oratore,* I, 143) and Milton (First Prolusion, Yale *Prose,* I, 218: "It is a frequent maxim of the most eminent masters of rhetoric . . . that in every style of oration, whether demonstrative, deliberative, or

judicial, the speaker must begin by winning the good-will of his audience; without it he cannot make any impression upon them, nor succeed as he would wish in his cause.")

8. *Milton: A Biography*, I, 113, 211, and II, 776, n. 95.

9. As he says of the speaker who answers Bishop Hall's *Modest Confutation* in Milton's *An Apology Against a Pamphlet*: "I conceav'd my selfe to be now not as mine own person, but as a member incorporate into that truth whereof I was perswaded." (Yale *Prose*, I, 871).

10. C; 859-60. H. J. C. Grierson, in *Milton & Wordsworth: Poets and Prophets* (New York: Macmillan, 1937), pp. 33-35, hears the 63rd chapter of Isaiah in Milton's "prophetic, or rather apocalyptic, strain."

11. *The Art of Logic*, 1.7 in *The Works of John Milton*, 18 vols., ed. Frank Patterson (New York: Columbia University Press, 1931-38), XI, 55.

12. "One searches in vain for Milton's New Testament sources that trace the full range of Presbyterian hierarchy. His only source is I Peter 5, a chapter of vague generalizations, . . . in comparison to hundreds of citations of Biblical sources by Andrewes, Ussher, Rainolds, and Mason." Yale *Prose*, I, 199, and cf. Haug's comments, pp. 739-40.

13. Hooker outlined Cartwright's claims for the divine authority of Presbyterianism in Book 3 of the *Ecclesiastical Polity*, and argued "with equal consistency from a belief in the ability and the right of the human reason, assisted by God and guided by the general principles set forth in Scripture, to evolve a system capable of fulfilling the divine purpose while meeting the requirements of chang-ing human societies." Barker, pp. 21-22. In 1.2 (pp. 759-60 and n. 25), Milton merely challenges Hooker's interpretation of a referent in the concluding injunction of 1 Tim. 5:14-15.

14. *The Censure of the Rota . . .* (London, 1660), p. 13, reprinted in W. R. Parker, *Milton's Contemporary Reputation* (Columbus: Ohio State University Press, 1940). For authorship, see P. B. Anderson, "Anonymous Critic of Milton: Richard Leigh? or Samuel Butler?" *SP*, 44 (1947), 504-18.

15. Fixler, p. 97.

16. A. S. P. Woodhouse, *Puritanism and Liberty* (2nd ed.; Chicago: University of Chicago Press, 1951), pp. [44]-[48].

17. Barker, pp. 19, 24-27.

18. "The Magistrat hath only to deale with the outward part, I mean not of the body alone, but of the mind in all her outward acts, which in Scripture is call'd the outward man" (2.3; 835). Compare Milton's mature view in *Christian Doctrine*, 1.7: "Man is a living being, intrinsically and properly one and individual, not compound or separable, not, according to the common opinion, made up and framed of two distinct and different natures, as of soul and body, but that the whole man is soul, and the soul man, that is to say, a . . . substance" (Columbia *Works*, XV, 41). See Woodhouse, *Puritanism and Liberty*, pp. [59]-[60] and [84]-[86] on the "segregation" of the two realms.

19. "Works are the end and fulfilling of precepts," but precepts are merely the externals of "faith" which is the true form of "works"; "whence it follows that conformity not with the written, but with the unwritten law, that is, with the law of the Spirit given by the Father to lead us into all truth, is to be accounted the true essential

form of good works." Because the works of believers are works of the spirit itself, they can never contradict the love of God and neighbor "which is the sum of the law," but they may "deviate from the letter even of the gospel precepts" (*CD* 2.1; Columbia *Works*, XVII, 9).

20. Milton's figure derives in part from "Bacon's use of it in his essay 'Of Truth,' [and] was frequent in Puritan controversy," Merritt Hughes observes in *John Milton: Complete Poems and Major Prose* (New York: Odyssey Press, 1957), p. 675, n. 203. The justification of eloquent language from the needs and capabilities of man's deranged faculties was a dominant strain in Italian criticism as it sought the qualities of poetry "through the study of its effects upon an audience rather than within itself" (Bernard Weinberg, *A History of Literary Criticism in the Italian Renaissance,* 2 vols. [Chicago: University of Chicago Press, 1961], II, 805). It derives ultimately from Roman rhetorical theory which found room for poetry in a consideration of ornament (Donald L. Clark, *Rhetoric and Poetry in the Renaissance* [New York: Columbia University Press, 1922], pp. 47-55), and it was extensively applied in medieval sermon theory (Harry Caplan, *Of Eloquence* [Ithaca: Cornell University Press, 1970], pp. 130-31).

21. Students of Milton are indebted to Barbara Lewalski for recovering the literary genres and many of the specific poems Milton referred to as brief epics and scriptural dramas. See *Milton's Brief Epic* (Providence: Brown University Press, 1966), pp. 3-129, and "*Samson Agonistes* and the 'Tragedy' of the Apocalypse," *PMLA*, 85 (1970), 1050-62.

22. A few months later Milton observed "that many of the Martyrs . . . were not sparing to deride and scoffe their superstitious persecutors. Now may the confutatnt advise againe with Sir *Francis Bacon* whether *Eliah* and the Martyrs did well to turne religion into a Comedy, or Satir; to *rip up the wounds* of Idolatry and Superstition *with a laughing countenance*." (*An Apology,* Yale *Prose*, I, 903).

23. In *An Apology* (Yale *Prose*, I, 891), consonant with passages in *Areopagitica* (II, 511-12) and *Paradise Regained* (4. 321-64), Milton suggests that the graver his temper, the more capable a man becomes in finding instruction even in the works of "libidinous and ignorant Poetasters" whose power over most men is to make them swallow "vitious principles in sweet pils" and ever after "make the tast of vertuous documents" seem "harsh and sowr" (2p; 818).

24. "Milton's two sketches of a drama on 'Paradise Lost' show that he was still close to the mood of *Comus.* He greatly admired the drama of the Greeks, but his projected play hovers somewhere between Jacobean masque and Italian neo-classical tragedy." Parker, I, 192.

25. Authorial explanations for these poems echo most of Milton's sentiments, suggesting that the thing "unattempted yet in Prose or Rhyme" had been very frequently attempted, at least in a superficial sense. Chamberlayne (in his "Epistle to the Reader"): "Poesy . . . being so attractive a beauty . . . doth rather, like an Orphean harmony, draw that emblem of a beast, the unpolished clown, to a listening civility, than, like Circe's enchantments, change the more happily educated to a swinish and sordid lethargy." Benlowes (in his "Preface"): "Divine Poesy is the internal triumph of the

mind, rapt with St. Paul into the third heaven, where she contemplates ineffables; 'tis the sacred oracles of faith put into melodious anthems that make music ravishing, no earthly jubilation being comparable to it."

26. William Haller, *Liberty and Reformation in the Puritan Revolution* (New York: Columbia University Press, 1955), p. 60.

27. *Milton and the Kingdoms of God,* p. 66, and subsequent quotations from pp. 73-74.

28. This is not the place to discuss fully, nor do I have any new information to add to, the controversy over a correct dating of Milton's major poetry. On one side are Professors Parker, Allan Gilbert, and J. T. Shawcross arguing for an "early" *Samson Agonistes* and *Paradise Regained*. On the other side are Professors E. Sirluck and Ants Oras arguing both negatively and positively for the "traditional" *Paradise Lost, Paradise Regained*, and *Samson Agonistes* sequence. The arguments were quantified in Oras' "Milton's Blank Verse and the Chronology of his Major Poems," *SAMLA Studies in Milton* (Gainesville, Fla., 1953); the data were used to support different conclusions by Shawcross in "The Chronology of Milton's Major Poems," *PMLA*, 56 (1961), 345-58; Oras used slightly modified data to reassert his earlier conclusions in *Blank Verse and Chronology in Milton,* Univ. of Florida Monographs No. 20 (Gainesville, Fla.: Univ. of Florida Press, 1966). It appears to me that both arguments propose conclusions based on too many independent variables; that nothing can be shown to be a function of anything else; that quantifiable elements of style can develop in a linear pattern as Shawcross asserts; and that they can also develop in a rising-falling pattern, as

Oras asserts, or in any other pattern; but that data without a theoretically sound assertion of interdependency do not admit of clear interpretation. I hear my own reservations about the attempt of either argument to settle the issues echoed in three major reviews by Professors Karina Williamson, *Studia Neophilogica*, 39 (1967), 184-5; Purvis E. Boyette, *South Atlantic Bulletin*, 32 (May, 1967), 11-12; and J. Max Patrick, *SCN*, 25 (Summer, 1967), 27-28. For purposes of the present argument, in which I want to assert neither too much nor too little, I assume that whatever might have been the actual history of composition, we can speak with profit about poems that could have been written, altered, and rewritten at any time up to 1667, 1671, or 1674, but not thereafter.

29. *CD* 1.4; XIV, 147 of the Columbia *Works*.

30. *CD* 1.17 and 20; XV, 347, 361, and 407.

31. "Structural Pattern in *Paradise Lost,*" *PQ*, 28 (1949), 16-30.

32. *Of True Religion, Heresie, Schism and Toleration*, Columbia *Works*, VI, 167.

33. *Considerations Touching the Likeliest Means to Remove Hirelings out of the Church* (Columbia *Works*, VI, 77-78): "If it be objected that this itinerarie preaching will not serve to plant the gospel . . . , I answer, that if they stay there a year or two, which was the longest time usually staid by the apostles in one place, it may suffice to teach them, who will attend and learn, all the points of religion necessary to salvation; then sorting them into several congregations . . . , out of the ablest and zealousest among them to create elders, who, exercising and requiring from themselves what they have learned (for no learning is retaind without con-

stant and methodical repetition) may
teach and govern the rest: and so exhorted to continue faithful and sted-
fast, they may securely be committed
to the providence of God and the
guidance of his holy spirit. . . ."

34. Columbia *Works*, XIV, 5-9: "It
is only to the individual faith of each
that the Deity has opened the way of
eternal salvation, and as he requires
that he who would be saved should
have a personal belief of his own, I
resolved not to repose on the faith or
judgment of others in matters relating
to God. . . ." "If I communicate the
result of my inquiries to the world at
large . . . I hope to meet with a candid
reception . . . since we are ordered 'to
prove all things,' and since the daily
progress of the light of truth is productive far less of disturbance to the
Church, than of illumination and edifi-
cation." And in *True Religion*, Columbia *Works*, VI, 176, Milton complains
bitterly of the dependency of learners
upon teachers which perpetuates a
people "ever learning and never
taught."

35. *Milton's Epic Voice: The Narrator
in Paradise Lost* (Cambridge, Mass.:
Harvard University Press, 1963). Roger
H. Sundell, "The Narrator as Interpreter in *Paradise Regained*," in *Milton
Studies II,* ed. J. D. Simmonds (Pittsburgh: University of Pittsburgh Press
1970).

36. *An Apology,* Yale *Prose,* I, 891.

37. *Of Reformation* and *Animadversions,* Yale *Prose,* I, 616, 706.

38. "Jordan" I: "Who says that fic-
tions onely and false hair / Become a
verse?" Herbert, in turn, professes the
rhetorical doctrine of poetry which
Milton deployed in *Church-Government* in the couplet, "A verse may
finde him, who a sermon flies, / And
turn delight into a sacrifice."

39. *Surprised by Sin: the Reader in
Paradise Lost* (London: Macmillan,
1967).

Areopagitica as a Scenario for *Paradise Lost*

EDWARD S. LE COMTE
State University of New York at Albany

Modern commentators have done much to bring Milton's prose closer to his verse. Tillyard and Grierson and Hutchinson, taking a hint from Milton himself, declared that the *Defensio secunda* has some qualities of an epic.[1] Haller saw *Comus* as the Puritan sermon that its author never mounted a pulpit to deliver.[2] Lines 108-31 of "Lycidas" must be counted, obviously, as the first Antiprelatical Tract. Barker makes a literally picturesque connection: "Episcopacy assumed in his eyes the lineaments of Comus; it was the public manifestation of the perversions of carnal sensuality against which he had striven in favor of high seriousness. The reformed discipline of the Puritan church similarly assumed the aspect of the virgin Lady, possessed of transcendent spiritual powers."[3] Backing this observation stands G. Wilson Knight's, published the same year: "A great poet rarely modifies his primary impressionisms, but, using them as constants, gears them to the ever-changing world of his experience."[4] The Yale editors of *Of Reformation* point out in their first footnote that that prose debut is one extended metaphor.[5] As part of his argument that *Samson Agonistes* was a composition of Milton's second period, Parker gave seven pages of exact verbal parallels with the 1640s prose.[6]

Areopagitica is not polemics, like the 1641-42 episcopal assaults. It is not a tractate. As oratory it is one of the "organic arts" that Milton had linked with poetry a few months before.[7] "According to the theory of poetry that Milton accepted, the poet and the orator share the desire to move men to virtuous action. Persuasion, the chief end of oratory, is also part of the function of poetry."[8] The outstanding authorities have, of course, noticed the change from the preceding tracts. Haller finds "Milton wrote not a pamphlet but a poem."[9] Wolfe sees "a broad humanism fresh as the spirit of Plato's praise of music or Sidney's paeans for poetry."[10] Barker is reminded of the "Nativity Ode."[11]

It seems, then, a question of just what poetry Milton had in mind. The present essay aims to provide detail to Tillyard's statement: *"Areopagitica* looked back to the once planned Arthuriad; it also contained hints of *Paradise Lost."*[12] Tillyard is very brief in his discussion of *Areopagitica*, perhaps feeling that it had been gone over too much already. In fact the remark just quoted occurs in his chapter on *Defensio secunda*. Also, it is still possible to contribute some fresh annotations to the relevant passages.

Of course both *Areopagitica* and *Paradise Lost* deal with the limits of freedom, which was always Milton's subject. Both works portray temptation.

Areopagitica is not lacking in the personages of *Paradise Lost.* It has, more than once, Adam (514, 527) and by implication, or association, Eve.[13] It has "an Angel" (519) or two. It has Lucifer (570). There is even a snake (557). And there is the snake's favorite vegetable, fennel (*Paradise Lost* ix, 581), in the form of "the ferular" (531), which is the giant fennel. There are "limbo's,"[14] "hells," and "damned" (506).

Knowing that Milton had behind him four outlines for a tragedy on the *Paradise Lost* theme, knowing that he had already written ten lines of what became Book IV of the epic,[15] we have some license to make the experiment of describing the future poem in phrases taken entirely from *Areopagitica*. There is, first, the poet who, though "stark blind" (550) and facing up to the possibility of being "the worst for two and fifty degrees of northern latitude" (490; cf. the "cold / Climate" of ix, 44-45), but "with hope," "with confidence" "at the beginning of no meane endeavour" (486), and not unmindful of the prospect of "lasting fame" (531; same phrase as at iii, 449), receives "the dictat of a divine Spirit" (534). He "justifies the high Providence of God" (527) "to that haples race of men" (535). Lucifer, "fall'n from the Starres" (570), is still the "suttlest enemy to our faith" (508). "He of the bottom-less pit . . . broke prison" (504); it is not given even to the angels to "barre him down" (504); he has passed "dores which cannot be shut" (537; cf. ii. 883-84), "custody" of "all the locks and keyes" (544; "the fatal Key," ii, 725, 871) not having been faith-fully kept. Rather futilely, Gabriel is assigned to guard Paradise, "to walk the round and counter-round with his fellow inspectors, fearing lest any of his flock be seduc't" (547).

As "the triall of vertue" (528; "Matter of glorious trial," ix, 1177) "a dangerous and suspicious fruit" (507), indeed "the rinde of one apple tasted" (514), proves too much for the first couple,

largely on account of Eve's insistence that she "may walk abroad
without a keeper" (536). Unwarily they underrated the difficulty
of obeying God, "whose command perhaps made all things seem
easie and unlaborious to them" (530; cf. Adam's first speech to
Eve: "this easy charge . . . let us not think hard / One easy prohibition," iv, 421, 432-33). " 'Tis . . . alleg'd we must not expose our
selves to temptations without necessity" (521). Raphael teaches
that we "not imploy our time in vain things" (521). But the Fall
has taken place, the way is open from Hell "to scout into the
regions of sin" (517), and nothing is left now but to await and
prophesy "the end of mortall things" (564-65: "mortal things,"
i, 693), while noting that there are times when "God . . . raises
to his own work men of rare abilities" (566).

"Lasting fame" and "mortal things" are but two of the phrases
in *Areopagitica* to be found in *Paradise Lost*. "The bottomless
pit" is Revelation (ch. IX, 1, 2, 11; XI, 7; XVII, 8; XX, 1, 3); it
is also *Paradise Lost*, vi, 866. "*Beatific* vision" (549) becomes
"vision beatific" (i, 684). T. Holt White in 1819[16] observed that
the words in the opening sentence, "not a little alter'd and mov'd
inwardly in their mindes" (486) with the mention of "passion" in
the next sentence come out twenty odd years later as "works in
the mind no change" and "unmov'd" (viii, 525, 532)—the effect of
the regular pleasures of Paradise in contrast to Adam's "passion"
(viii, 529) for Eve, as confessed to Raphael. From the passion of
oratory to the passion of copulation, "Transported touch" (viii,
530)—it is a singular but verbally recognizable connection. Moreover, to mention what has not been noticed, Milton in the same
places associates "joy and gratulation" (487): "the Earth / Gave
sign of gratulation, and each Hill; / Joyous the Birds" (viii, 513-
15). And the futility of "this cautelous enterprise of licencing" is
apparently to be compared with the crafty conspiracy of Lucifer in
Heaven, "vain and impossible attempts" (520), "vain attempt" (i, 44).[17]

A most interesting resemblance in this class was noticed by
Tillyard,[18] who saw the statement that "God . . . gives us minds
that can wander beyond all limit and satiety" (527-28) as anticipatory of Belial's argument against annihilation, "for who would
lose . . . Those thoughts that wander through Eternity" (ii, 146,
148).[19] God's bounty in the prose sentence includes what the
rebellious angels have just lost: "powrs out before us ev'n to a pro-
fusenes all desirable things" (the old spelling suggesting a pun,
powers). Belial, the intellectual, clings to his mind as all that he
has left. He fancies *it* has not been made captive. There is irony,

if not poignance, here.[20] In actuality the formerly angelic mind
has lost its intuitive power and can no longer be sure of the truth,
"in wand'ring mazes lost" (ii, 561). "Wander beyond all limit"—
"found no end, in wand'ring mazes": there is a parallel, too (to
wander is to err), reflecting the author's impatience with scholastic
abstractions. He is such a "materialist" that, as we have seen, his
own metaphors become literal or mythic. But his message will
continue to be that Truth is a hard quest.

Postponing consideration of another central message, "reason
is but choosing" (527)—"Reason also is choice" (iii, 108), we need
to give some attention to the exordium of *Areopagitica* as it compares to the proem to *Paradise Lost.* The *furor poeticus* of the
exordium, with its disjointed syntax, its inserted qualifications
—it begins with an anacoluthon and the reader has to keep sharp
eye out for the antecedent of a "which" or an "it," or the subject
of "likely might"—is highly characteristic. The orator, as he de-
picts his own attitudes, is endeavoring to wind his audience into
a receptive frame of mind. He does not feel unworthy but he must
not sound proud. It is necessary to compliment Parliament but not
to be taken for a flatterer.[21] It is a difficult course to steer, and
the ship rocks before it steadies. There is just enough uneasiness
to conjure up someone else whose "appeal is a skilful union of
logical machinery . . . and rhetorical insinuation." So a recent
critic characterizes the speech of—Belial.[22]

But it is St. Paul whose shoes Milton, as teacher or preacher,
is filling in going "unto Areopagus" (Acts XVII, 19), even as he
associated himself with Moses at the beginning of his epic. The
commentators, concentrating on Isocrates, have overlooked the
certainty that the other orator on Ares' Hill would have been not
only in Milton's mind[23] but the obvious first thought of his readers.
All these knew the Bible better than any other book and only some
of them knew the Greek rhetorician whom, in fact, *Areopagitica*
never names, as it does name, more than once, St. Paul. (Indeed,
Milton was indulging his usual tendency to be "rather too academic
and isolated to catch the public ear."[24]) The title page has nothing
of Isocrates: rather, a quotation from Euripides. There is no particular resemblance between Isocrates' oration and Milton's. The
feminine form of Milton's title, whether considered as an adjective,
which it properly is, or a noun, does not fit Isocrates' *Logos
Areiopagitikos.* It looks as if the English arguer is much more concerned with drawing an analogy between the "High Court of Parlament" (so his opening words designate it, 486, and his title page
reads "To the Parlament of England") and the high court of Athens,

a court that functioned for centuries and that Paul addressed[25] and
Isocrates did not. We need only grasp the implications of the facts,
as stated by R. C. Jebb:[26] "The *Areopagiticas* of Isokrates (355
B.C.) is a speech, supposed to be made in the ekklesia, *about* the
Areiopagos—urging the restoration of its old powers. The *Areopagi-
tica* of Milton is a speech *to* the English Areiopagos." The Title
Areopagitica; A Speech translates into Latin as *Areopagitica Oratio.*
The author, in two Latin references, using his title as a noun, is
still careful to keep the other noun nearby: "Areopagitica, sive de
libertate Typographiae Oratio;" ". . . ad justae orationis modum
Areopagiticam scripei."[27]

He "who from his private house wrote that discourse to the
Parlament of Athens" (489, referring to the ekklesia, not the
Areiopagos) does not get alluded to until page three, and then
never again—just the one sentence. Besides, he is just the first example of "a privat Orator" (489), Dion Prusaeus being another.
But "Moses, Daniel & Paul" are joined, six pages further on, as
"skilfull in . . . learning" (507), and "Paul especially" (508) singled
out, not without a reference to that very chapter in Acts XVII that
relates how "Paul stood in the midst of Mars' hill, and said, Ye men
of Athens, I perceive that in all things ye are too superstitious"
(22). This is the accusation that Milton, with such tact as he can
manage, is directing at an English Parliament that has gone
papistical in its restraint of the press. The word "superstition"
is significantly planted on his very first page (487).

How much Milton felt like St. Paul, whom he quoted more than a
dozen times in *Areopagitica,*[28] ranks among more difficult questions—
along with to what extent he identified with Jesus in *Paradise Regained.* He had, like Dante, a habit of grouping himself with the
best: when blind, with the great blind. If Isocrates was a poor
orator for physical reasons, so Paul admitted it was said of himself that "his bodily presence is weak and his speech contemptible"
(II Corinthians X, 10). Milton, still obscure and having won nothing
but attack lately, had the complex of imagining the breaking through
from obscurity to "sudden blaze."[29] This becomes one part of his
affinity with Moses as the poet mounts again, Horeb and Sinai, for
it is to be remembered that the author of the Pentateuch was
"slow of speech" (Ex. IV, 10) until kindled by the Lord, even as
the author of *Paradise Lost* was "long choosing, and beginning late"
(ix, 26). Parker is the latest of Milton's biographers to comment,
"it was his destiny to be slow in development."[30]

Whatever sort of speaker Milton was—about which we have no
information—he does show in *Defensio secunda*[31] some defensive-

ness in regard to his very middling height, which may have been one of the reasons he was called "Lady" at Christ's College. The Anonymous Biographer reported he "was of a moderate Stature," but Aubrey indicated he was less than that.[32] *Areopagitica* thrusts forward an interesting but rather gratuitous comparison with Truth as at first "unsightly and unplausible" (Milton with his innovative doctrines?) "ev'n as the person is of many a great man slight and contemptible to see to" (565-66). "Contemptible" returns us to the St. Paul quotation, but to what degree, if any, is Milton thinking of himself? There is the verbal parallel with "a certain Shepherd Lad" in *Comus*, 619-20. "Of small regard to see to, yet well skill'd," who Hanford argued was Milton.[33] "Person . . . of many a great man slight" comes back in *Defensio secunda* when Milton is defending himself against the personal abuse of the *Regii Sanguinis Clamor*: "sed quid si parva, qua & summi saepe tum pace tum bello viri fuere? quanquam parva cur dicitur, quae ad virtutem satis magna est?"[34] The author's motto, twice chosen for an autograph album, was the Pauline "My strength is made perfect in weakness."[35]

Leaving venturesome biographical conjecture, we come next to a passage that weirdly looks forward to Sin's tale to Satan of, first, Death's birth and, next, Death's incestuous rape that produced the hell-hounds that continuously ravage her:

> . . . the Councell of Trent, and the Spanish inquisition engendring together brought forth, or perfeted those Catalogues, and expurging[36] Indexes that rake through the entralls of many an old good Author, with a violation wors then any could be offer'd to his tomb. (502-3)

> Thine own begotten, breaking violent way
> Tore through my entrails. . .
> . . . .
> Forth issue'd. . .
> . . . .
> Ingend'ring with me, of that rape begot
> These yelling Monsters. . . .
>
> (ii, 782-83, 786, 794-95)

Considering how different the context, it is astounding how much the phrasing is the same: "engendring"—"Ingend'ring": "brought forth"—"Forth issu'd": "rake through the entralls"—"Tore through my entrails": "violation"—"violent." Needless to say, to violate a tomb is not to violate a womb, and *entrails* has a different reference

in the prose, suggesting the priest-augur poring over intestines for
signs and also the hangman "drawing," disembowelling, his victim.
But, after all, it is the author, rather than his tomb, that is being
violated, and "entralls" is as close as Milton can get to womb, consistent with his experience that authors are invariably male—as close
as he can get in one sentence, that is. The paragraph becomes
hermaphroditic:

> Till then Books were ever as freely admitted into the World as
> any other birth; the issue of the brain was no more stifl'd then
> the issue of the womb: no envious *Juno* sate cros-leg'd over
> the nativity of any mans intellectual off spring; but if it prov'd
> a Monster, who denies, but that it was justly burnt, or sunk
> into the Sea. (505; cf. "the birth . . . of books," 530)

To quote Blake's *Jerusalem* (76), "these are the Female Males."
Furthermore, despairing Adam, when he longs for death, makes
a womb-tomb equation, "how glad would lay me down / As in my
Mother's lap" (x, 777-78). St. Sigmund will go wild here, and the
latest critic will contend that "mould" (x, 744) is a pun.[37]

As for entrails-womb, a bit of unnatural natural history makes a
connection. *Of Reformation* alluded to this: "let not the obstinacy
of our halfe Obedience and will-Worship bring forth that *Viper
of Sedition*, that for these Fourescore Yeares hath been breeding
to eat through the entrals of our *Peace*; but let her cast her Abortive
Spawne without the danger of this travailling & throbbing *Kingdom*"
(Yale I, 614-15). The editors are silent, but Sir Thomas Browne
explains: "That the young Vipers force their way through the
bowels of their Dam, or that the female Viper in the act of generation
bites off the head of the male, in revenge whereof the young ones
eat through the womb and belly of the female, is a very ancient
tradition." Thus, as again the editors do not tell us, in tearing through
his Dam's entrails at birth Death was being viperous, and his offspring
still are: "hourly conceiv'd / And hourly born, with sorrow infinite
/ To me, for when they list, into the womb / That bred them thy
return, and howl and gnaw / My Bowels, thir repast" (ii, 796-800;
cf. 656-69).[38]

The word "Monster" in the "*June* . . . cros-leg'd" sentence renews
the whole "engendering" parallel. The late Kester Svendsen[39] remarked, "The motifs of miscegenation, hermaphroditism, and dis-
natured conception occur in the prose and have their counterpart
in the epic." One recalls that "loathed Melancholy" was "Of *Cerberus*
and blackest midnight born" ("L'Allegro," 1-2)—a promising start
for a hideous series. Is it inquiring too curiously to ask who, in the

union of the Council of Trent and the Spanish Inquisition, is the female? Presumably, the latter, on the basis of a prior phrase that also sounds hell-whelpish: "this project of licencing crept out of the Inquisition" (493). And was not the copulation monstrous and bound to produce monstrous offspring, for two reasons: on account of incest and on account of a generation gap? Certainly it is Milton's point that the Council of Trent and the Spanish Inquisition are closely related. But the former was born in 1545, while the latter dates from 1478,[40] when Ferdinand and Isabella obtained Papal approval for it. Thus the female is sixty-seven years older than her lover, a disgusting and eugenically unpromising situation, as, indeed, incest has always been thought to be. Michael Lieb comments on the *Paradise Lost* passage, "With the stress upon inbreeding and offspring among the three diabolic figures, we are presented with the primitive idea that inbreeding is related to deformed, unhealthy, indeed, monstrous offspring."[41] The monstrous offspring in *Areopagitica*, Catalogues of Forbidden Books and Indexes of Censored Books, tear and torment entrails-wombs with the pertinacity of Sin's hell-hounds.

They are *expurging* Indexes, a more emphatic form of purging. No good will issue from that operation, from those entrails. It is creation in reverse—and how well the unflinching Dante would have understood it. Nor does Milton dodge the implication, in this same paragraph: "I feare their next designe will be to get into their custody the licencing of that which they say Claudius intended, but went not through with" (504). Milton's marginal note gives, in the decency of Latin, a reference to flatulence. All this, too, looks forward (or backward) to what Lieb in his provocative book, *The Dialectics of Creation: Patterns of Birth and Regeneration in Paradise Lost,* analyzes as the anality of Hell. We have, before we ever reach the unholy Trinity, the "fuell'd entrails" "Of thund'ring Aetna" (i, 233 ff.), on which Lieb expatiates, "The hill is torn forcibly because of a 'subterranean wind,' and Etna erupts because its 'combustible' and 'fewel'd entrails' undergo a process of pregnancy and birth: the 'entrails,' whose normal function is excretory, now perform a generative function in their conceiving of fire. The combustible birth is certainly of an anal nature, for the eruption of the entrails 'leave[s] a singed bottom all involv'd /With stench and smoak.'"[42] Embarrassingly plain is the *analogy* of the infernal cannon, "whose roar / Embowell'd with outrageous noise the Air, / And all her entrails tore, disgorging foul / Thir devilish glut" (vi, 586-89). "Tore through my entrails" (ii, 783)— "And all her entrails tore" (vi, 588): birth has been connected with the digestive system, as in folklore and in psychoanalysis and in *Areopagitica* (always remembering that the word proceeds from the mouth).

In his *Animadversions,* 1641, Milton had already grumbled over "Monkish prohibitions, and expurgatorious indexes" (Yale I, 669). The date for the birth of the monstrous progeny of his 1644 sentence can be given as 1559, when the Index Librorum Prohibitorum and the Index Expurgatorius were approved by the Council of Trent (that is, recognized by the father). Some further historical remarks are worth making. The next sentence in *Areopagitica* reads: "Nor did they stay in matters Hereticall, but any subject that was not to their palat, they either condemn'd in a prohibition, or had it strait into the new Purgatory of an Index" (503). One of Milton's favorite authors was thus banned, as Jebb did not know when he recorded the following: "The first Italian index, containing about 70 books, was printed by Giovanni della Casa, an intimate friend of [Cardinal] Caraffa, at Venice. More complete catalogues appeared in 1552 at Forence and in 1554 at Milan. In 1559 a catalogue was printed at Rome [Caraffa Laviu, having become Pope Paul IV] in the form which long remained the model: it included the writings of Cardinals, and Casa's own poems."[43] In December 1629 Milton bought (for ten-pence) a copy of the 1563 Venice edition of della Casa's poems,[44] which survives, and which greatly influenced his own English and Italian sonnets.[45] Thus particular annoyance over the condemnation of "an old good Author" much to his "palat" may have sharpened his reference. Della Casa had died three years before, in 1556; to be put on the Index was "a violation wors then any could be offer'd to his tomb."

Yet there is the irony that the Italian poet had cooperated in printing a Catalogue of Prohibited Books, even as Milton served briefly as a licenser of a newsletter under the Commonwealth.[46] The key sentence of 1644 happens to be prophetic of a good deal of Milton's future besides *Paradise Lost.* Books of his suffered the purgatory—"the fire and the executioner" (569)—of being publicly burned by the common executioner in France before the Restoration and in England after.[47] Indeed, Herbert Palmer in a sermon before Parliament had already singled out *The Doctrine and Discipline of Divorce* as "deserving to be burnt."[48] On November 23, 1694, as if timed for the exact fiftieth anniversary of *Areopagitica*, Milton's Letters of State were put on the Roman Catholic Index Librorum Prohibitorum. Paolo Rolli's translation of *Paradise Lost* followed in 1732.[49] As for "violation . . . to his tomb," that came to him, too, not so soon as to Cromwell, Bradshaw, and Ireton, but in

1790. A contemporary narrative of that act of desecration by morbid curiosity-seekers and mercenary souvenir-hunters echoes Milton's key word in referring to "the sole atonement, which can now be made, to the violated rights of the dead."[50]

The two Adam passages in *Areopagitica* have often been quoted, but little commented on. The first has this author's characteristic mix of Christian and pagan story:

> Good and evill we know in the field of this world grow up together almost inseparably; and the knowledge of good is so involv'd and interwoven with the knowledge of evill, and in so many cunning resemblances hardly to be discern'd, that those confused seeds which were impos'd on *Psyche* as an incessant labour to cull out, and sort asunder, were not more intermixt. It was from out the rinde of one apple tasted, that the knowledge of good and evill as two twins cleaving together leapt forth into the World. And perhaps this is that doom which *Adam* fell into of knowing good and evill, that is to say of knowing good by evill. (514)

The student of Milton's imagery notes, "He is fond of the metaphor of twine, which he uses eight times, although it seems to have no special psychological significance."[51] It is probably not in the same class with his monster imagery, which may be seen as part of what John Carey decides is "the uneasiness Milton feels on the subject of fecundity."[52] Carey's earlier chapter on the prose infers: "The images draw on organic processes almost exclusively for the purpose of conveying disgust. There is no complementary strain of healthful bodily functions."[53] Those twins are not both good, and a reference in *The Reason of Church-Government* to "a certain monstrous haste of pregnancy" (Yale I, 781) is a reminder—we have been looking at others—that there are cells that should not multiply.

Editors should put beside the last sentence in the quoted paragraph the same statement in *De doctrina christiana*: "It was called the tree of knowledge of good and evil from the event; for since Adam tasted it, we not only know evil, but we know good only by means of evil"; ". . . sed ne bonum quidem nisi per malum"[54]—a pun, since "malum" is also Latin for apple. The Adam of *Paradise Lost* breaks out with greater pessimism: "since our Eyes / Op'n'd we find indeed, and find we know / Both Good and Evil, Good lost, and Evil got, / Bad Fruit of Knowledge" (ix, 1070-73).

The *Areopagitica* sentence that mentions the apple dangles before us a twofold meaning. First, we are put in mind of Eve by the very absence of mention of her. The apple has been divided in "two,"

split into two hemispheres for the loss of one world: Eve ate the
first half. The couple—"cleaving" has simultaneously the opposite
meanings of separate and together—are under "doom." The second
meaning is that the apple has a worm in it, evil. Satan is the serpent
called "Worm" in *Paradise Lost* (ix, 1068). We ought, then, to remember the early appearance of "rinde" in the poem, involving the
Devil as Leviathan, whom "The Pilot of some small night-founder'd
Skiff, / Deeming some Island, oft, as Seamen tell, / With fixed Anchor
in his scaly rind / Moors by his side" (i, 204-07).

Finally, to move up to the first sentence, "Good and evill we know
in the field of this World grow up together almost inseparably," we
seem to have an echo of a statement by St. Ambrose that God "has
likewise planted within us a seedplot of the knowledge of good and
evil."[55] Following Philo Judaeus, Ambrose allegorized Eden as "in
our highest part, thick set with the growth of many opinions." "In
our highest part"—i.e., the soul: this would have set Milton off to
thinking of *Psyche*! He has his Apuleian fairy tale, and he has his
psychomachy.

The other Adam passage also has to do with the Tree of Knowledge:

> many there be that complain of divin Providence for suffering
> *Adam* to transgresse, foolish tongues! when God gave him reason,
> he gave him freedom to choose, for reason is but choosing; he
> had bin else a meer artificiall *Adam*, such an *Adam* as he is in
> the motions. We our selves esteem not of that obedience, or love,
> or gift, which is of force: God therefore left him free, set before
> him a provoking object, ever almost in his eyes; herein consisted
> his merit, herein the right of his reward, the praise of his abstinence.
> (527)

"Many there be that complain"—Milton has foreseen William Empson
and a myriad other of his and God's critics. The contemptuous allusion to "motions" may inform us that the poet has given up any
thought of doing a medieval mystery. As Merritt Hughes says in
his Introduction to *Paradise Lost*, "In puppet shows or 'motions'
that drama still survived in Milton's youth, and a capital criticism
of its main weakness is implied in Milton's sneer in *Areopagitica* at
its failure to make Adam anything but a pawn in a game between
God and the Devil."[56]

The *De doctrina christiana* betrays what trouble this Christian had
making a clean-cut decision with reference to the Tree of Knowledge.
Was it just a symbol of obedience, or did it possess, as strongly
suggested by the original story (or stories), some magic power? As
justifier of God's ways, Milton gives the first interpretation early in

his Chapter X (Book I): "It was necessary that something should be forbidden or commanded as a test of fidelity, and that an act in its own nature indifferent, in order that man's obedience might be thereby manifested."[57] Thus, as *Areopagitica* so vividly has it, there was "set before him a provoking object." It is to be understood that "The tree of knowledge of good and evil was not a sacrament, as it is generally called; for a sacrament is a thing to be used, not abstained from: but a pledge, as it were, and memorial of obedience."[58] But such insistence is at odds with the allusion in Chapter XI to "the penalty incurred by the violation of things sacred (and such was the tree of knowledge of good and evil)."[59] Grierson uses *this* passage against Milton. "It is a little strange to hear Milton speaking of the tree as a holy thing, in view of his general refusal to recognise holiness in things at all. Is he not here confounding the holiness of principles, of justice, etc. and the sacredness of tabus, the breach of which entails mischief on good and bad alike?"[60] (Basil Willey also spoke of taboos.[61]) A fuller and fairer account would not pass over Chapter X and *Areopagitica*. But Milton, who liked to have his cake and eat it too, ultimately fudged it, gave a taste of both interpretations by turning the apple into an intoxicant, as if it were, at the least, hard cider.

This may remind us that Eve has again returned as a provoking object herself, holding forth the fruit that her spouse, "Against his better knowledge, not deceiv'd, / But fondly overcome with Female charm" (ix, 998-99), chooses not to resist.

Adam knew what he was doing, as Eve did not. "Reason is but choosing"—"Reason also is choice" (iii, 108) as God explained at length (iii, 95-128). Aristotle had a word for it that *Of Education* had employed: "By this time, yeers and good generall precepts will have furnisht them more distinctly with that act of reason which in *Ethics* is call'd *Proairesis*: that they may with some judgement contemplat upon morall good and evill" (396). Eve would not have been a seemly mention in *Areopagitica*, since Milton wants to keep his discussion on the highest level of right reason, which the Chain of Being showed was male, even as books are male births and none of the Lords and Commons is a woman. (Also, he was smarting from Palmer's attack before Parliament on his "wicked book" on divorce.[62]) Eve comes revengefully back by presenting her husband with the arguments of *Areopagitica* (which the Serpent will also use to her). The prose had been: "If every action which is good, or evill in man at ripe years, were to be under pittance, and prescription, and compulsion, what were vertue but a name?"

(527). The verse is, "And what is Faith, Love, Vertue unassay'd?" (ix, 335).

The all-too-common assertion that Milton has ceased to believe what he once preached receives its prime answer in the difference in situation between fallen and unfallen man. But another answer is to point out that the *Speech . . . for the Liberty of Unlicenc'd Printing* does have boundaries, as, indeed, the phrase "at ripe years" suggests. There is the idea of tutelage, of what Warner Rice[63] calls "a judicious censorship" which is part of Milton's concession that some books in some hands may work mischief. "The rest, as children and childish men, . . . well may be exhorted to forbear, but hinder'd forcibly they cannot be. . . ." (521) When Eve, though still sinless, began to reason like a child,[64] Adam sought to impose a judicious censorship on her, but, consistent with *Areopagitica*, he did not tie her up. Still, she should not have bound *him*: "her Gifts / Were such as under Government well seem'd, / Unseemly to bear rule, which was thy part" (x, 153-55). Reason did not govern choice or will. "Understanding rul'd not" (ix, 1127).[65]

The two Adam passages prove that Milton had the fall of man on his mind. But then, so do his four Outlines for a Tragedy. However, what was uniformly missing from the planned *sacre rappresentazione* was the central scene of *Paradise Lost*—the seduction of Adam and Eve. There was, for the play, the problem of nudity or costume (even as Dryden's *The State of Innocence* was never produced). There was the problem of the speaking Serpent. But the fall of man reverberates through *Areopagitica* as it will through *Paradise Lost*. It is a fair guess that, with the theaters closed, Milton had turned his thoughts towards transforming his drama into an epic.

In what way did *Areopagitica* look back on the once planned Arthuriad, last heard of in "Epitaphium Damonis" (circa 1639)? Tillyard quotes the latter portion of the pamphlet that bursts with patriotic fervor, "Lord and Commons of England, consider what Nation it is wherof ye are, and whereof ye are the governours . . . (551)."[66] And "Methinks I see in my mind a noble and puissant Nation rousing herself like a strong man after sleep, and shaking her invincible locks. . . ." (557-58). But the latter analogy is with Samson and had, indeed, been used in *The Reason of Church-Government* (Yale I, 858-59). An Arthuriad would be a national epic that his country would have to deserve. The poet's destiny was tied to that of England.[67] "There be pens and heads there, sitting by their studious lamps, musing, searching, revolving new notions and idea's wherewith to present, as with their homage and their fealty the approaching Reformation" (554). He would eventually sever the patriotic bond in disillusionment and produce a more universal poem. As Tillyard comments, already "in *Areopagitica* beneath the excitement of hope there can be detected the whisper of doubt."[68]

Tillyard's only other citation is more specific, but also more doubtful. "I cannot praise a fugitive and clositer'd vertue, unexercis'd & unbreath'd, that never sallies out and sees her adversary, but slinks out of the race, where that immortall garland is to be run for, not without dust and heat" (515). For Tillyard this was more aggressive because, using the Bohn edition, he read "sees her adversary" as "seeks her adversary."[69] However, despite the immediately prior reference to "true wayfaring Christian" corrected to "true warfaring Christian," we seem to have in this sentence, rather than knightly warfare, a race, classical, after the fashion of the Olympic games or Homer and Virgil. (At ix, 31 ff. there is the same sequence of "Battles" followed by "Races and Games.") The only dubious expression is "sallies out." Unless we have mixed metaphors,[70] it means "ventures forth" (from the cloister), with perhaps some of the athletic "leap" residue of *salio*. Indeed, in the famous footrace in *Aeneid* V, 321 ff., there is the competitor who happens to be named Salius: Nisus cuts Salius out of the race by blocking him, enabling Euryalus to win. For battle we can do better with William Walwyn, even, who is not suspected of an Arthuriad: "that so errour may discover its foulnesse, and truth become more glorious by a victorious conquest after a fight in open field: they shun the battell that doubt their strength."[71] Surely the Civil War was enough to inspire martial language.

It is surprising that Tillyard did not rather quote:

> When a man hath bin labouring the hardest labour in the deep mines of knowledge, hath furnisht out his findings in all their equipage, drawn forth his reasons as it were a battell raung'd, scatter'd and defeated all objections in his way, calls out his adversary into the plain, offers him the advantage of wind and sun, if he please; only that he may try the matter by dint of argument, for his opponents then to sculk, to lay ambushments, to keep a narrow bridge of licencing where the challenger should passe, though it be valour anough in shouldiership, is but weaknes and cowardise in the wars of Truth. (562)

"Pale trembling coward, there I throw my gage!" (*Richard II*, I, i, 69) The rhetoric is torn between two worlds—the modern one of "shouldiership," of sneaky and unfair tactics, Prince Rupert's

ambushes and King Charles's clever retreats—and the bygone
chivalry of open, forthright, individual challenge and combat,
the honorable test of strength. Cromwell had begun to look like
a knight, while Essex and Manchester acted as if they were definitely
trying to avoid victory.

The next year the publisher of Milton's minor poems was to
link him and Spenser, and Tillyard's later essay on "Milton and
the Epic" sees *The Faerie Queene* as an inevitable influence on
any Arthuriad,[72] though not for allegory. Thus any Spenserian,
or possibly Spenserian, allusion is suspect, beginning with the naming of him, that "better teacher then *Scotus* or *Aquinas*" (516),
and Sir Guyon. We look, then, at "the champions of Truth" (548)
and think of Book I, Una and the Red Cross Knight[73] and the more
effective Prince Arthur. We wonder if a missing episode is being
longed for in, "Let her and Falshood grapple; who ever knew
Truth put to the wors, in a free and open encounter" (561). Are
we to picture Una and Duessa wrestling?[74] Duessa, who presumes
to call herself Fidessa? Is this in part another swipe at the Roman
Catholic Church, the superstitious dragon that this champion of
Truth is always ready for another hack at, right up to *Of True
Religion*, 1673? "I mean not tolerated Popery, and open superstition" (565). Granted that in general and outside allegory,
"Milton has as little sympathy for the woman-warrior—the *donna
guerriera* and the *femme forte*—as for female sovereignty. Both
violate the order of nature and female decorum."[75] It was through
Spenser that we saw "simple Truth subdue avenging wrong"—in
the episode of Una's lion (I, iii, VI, 5). Milton has so many figurative
excursions, one-sentence allegories. But female knights are rare
enough, except in *The Faerie Queene*. Even here, though, Hughes[76]
would have us see the epic of salvation: "All the faith in Truth's
power to crush Falsehood in any open encounter that Milton
poured into *Areopagitica* is symbolized in the all-seeing eyes of
the victorious Son's chariot."[77]

It does not add up to much, that inchoate never-born Arthuriad,
compared to those hooked atoms (as the author of *The Road to
Xanadu* would have called them) that eventually became manifest
in *Paradise Lost*.

Notes

1. E. M. W. Tillyard, *Milton* (New York, 1967), pp. 163 ff.; Sir H. J. C. Grierson, *Milton and Wordsworth* (Cambridge, 1937), pp. 71-72; F. E. Hutchinson, *Milton and the English Mind* (London, 1946), p. 84. Cf. Lawrence A. Sasek, "Milton's Patriotic Epic," *HLQ*, 20 (1956), 1-14.

2. William Haller, *The Rise of Puritanism* (New York, 1938), p. 318.

3. Arthur Barker, *Milton and the Puritan Dilemma* (Toronto, 1942), p. 15.

4. *Chariot of Wrath* (London, 1942), pp. 97-98.

5. Don M. Wolfe and William Alfred, p. 519 of *Complete Prose Works of John Milton,* I (New Haven, 1953).

6. William Riley Parker, *Milton: A Biography* (Oxford, 1968), II, 911-17. Verbal parallels were the subject of my *Yet Once More: Verbal and Psychological Pattern in Milton* (New York, 1953; rptd., 1969), to which the present essay is a sequel.

7. *Of Education,* Yale *Complete Prose,* II (New Haven, 1959), p. 401

8. John S. Diekhoff, *Milton's "Paradise Lost": A Commentary on the Argument* (New York, rptd., 1958), p. 1.

9. Haller, ed., *Tracts on Liberty in the Puritan Revolution, 1638-1647* (New York, 1934), I, 75. Compare the same author's *Liberty and Reformation in the Puritan Revolution* (New York, 1955), p. 184: "a poet's expression of the excitement of a people." Similar remarks can be found, early and late: e.g., "Milton's *Areopagitica* is prose, but it is the prose of a poet, gorgeous in imagery, and full of noble music." W. E. A. Axon in *Milton Memorial Lectures,* ed. Percy W. Ames (London,

1909), p. 45. "Rightly and inevitably we consider Milton's prose as a poetic performance." Michael S. Davis, ed., *Areopagitica and Of Education* (New York, 1963), p. 12.

10. Don M. Wolfe, *Milton in the Puritan Revolution* (New York, 1941), p. 124.

11. Barker, p. 85.

12. Tillyard, *Milton,* p. 167; cf. pp. 133-34, 136-37.

13. I give page numbers for *Areopagitica* in Yale II, ed. Ernest Sirluck. I quote the poetry from *Complete Poems and Major Prose,* ed. Merritt Y. Hughes (New York, 1957), using small Roman numerals to refer to the books of *Paradise Lost.*

14. See Joseph Horrell, "Milton, Limbo, and Suicide," *RES,* 18 (1942), 413-27.

15. Edward Phillips in Helen Darbishire, ed., *The Early Lives of Milton* (London, 1932), pp. 72-73.

16. White, ed., *Areopagitica* (London, 1819), p. 2.

17. "The bottomless pit" is also in *Of Reformation,* Yale I, 614, as is "beatific vision," 616. "Mortal things" makes a reappearance in *Paradise Regained,* iv, 318.

18. *Milton,* p. 137.

19. First expressed in the Third Prolusion: "sed nec iisdem, quibus orbis, limitibus contineri et circumscribi se patiatur vestra mens, sed . . . divagetur." Columbia edition of *Works,* XII, 170.

20. Isabel MacCaffrey, *Paradise Lost as "Myth"* (Cambridge, Mass., 1959), finds the word *wander* a key word in the epic, p. 188, having "almost always a pejorative, or melancholy connotation," but Stanley Fish well

argues against that view as exaggerated, *Surprised by Sin: The Reader in Paradise Lost* (London, 1967), pp. 130 ff.

21. He fails for some commentators. "One obvious rhetorical device he employed was none too subtle flattery." J. Max Patrick, ed., *The Prose of John Milton* (New York, 1967), p. 251. "His specious flattery." Rose Macauley, *Milton* (London, 1957), p. 90. ". . . [H]e humbles himself to management and the reasonings of flattery." Sir Walter Raleigh, *Milton* (London, 1900), p. 56.

22. Fish, p. 15.

23. Wilbur E. Gilman must be given credit for at least mentioning this, in a three-line footnote, p. 23 of *Milton's Rhetoric: Studies in his Defense of Liberty* (Columbia, Missouri, 1939), followed twenty years later by seven lines in the first footnote by the Yale editor. Since 1929 a much-used textbook has said noncommittally, "For another famous address in connection with the Areopagus (Mars' Hill), see St. Paul's speech, Acts 17." Robert P. T. Coffin and Alexander M. Witherspoon, *A Book of Seventeenth-Century Prose* (New York), p. 408; same footnote in the latest revision by Witherspoon and Frank J. Warnke, *Seventeenth-Century Prose and Poetry* (New York, 1963), p. 395.

24. Douglas Bush, *English Literature in the Earlier Seventeenth Century*, Ed. 1 (Oxford, 1945), p. 330.

25. According to the marginal note in the King James Bible. *The Oxford Dictionary of the Christian Church*, ed. F. L. Cross (London, 1958), p. 80, s. v. "Areopagus," summarizes: "It is not entirely clear whether, when St. Paul was brought to the Areopagus to explain his 'new teaching' (Acts 17. 19), it was before the official court or whether the place was merely chosen

as convenient for a meeting. The language of Acts suggests the latter view, though a marginal note in some MSS indicates the other alternative, which was that adopted by St. Chrysostom."

26. Jebb, ed., *Areopagitica* (Cambridge, 1918), p. xxiii.

27. Presentation to Rous, Columbia *Works*, XVIII, 270; *Defensio secunda*, VIII, 134.

28. For references and citations see pp. 507, 508, 512, 515, 549, 554, 561, 563, 564, 565, 566. Note especially "this Christian liberty which *Paul* so often boasts of" (563).

29. The application of this phrase, appearing five times in his poetry, degenerates like Lucifer: "Arcades," 2; "Lycidas," 74; *Paradise Lost*, i, 665; iv, 818; x, 453.

30. *Milton*, I, 145.

31. Columbia *Works*, VIII, 60. But he has courage and is adept with the sword, like King Edgar, who well knew how to answer the insult, "such a little dapper man." *History of Britain* in Yale *Prose*, V, 325.

32. In Darbishire, pp. 32, 3.

33. *TLS*, Nov. 3, 1932, p. 815; James Holly Hanford, *John Milton, Englishman* (New York, 1949), p. 65; and in some editions of Hanford's *A Milton Handbook* (New York), e.g. 1939, p. 160, but the subject has been dropped in the latest (fifth) edition done with James G. Taaffe, 1970.

34. Columbia *Works*, VIII, 60.

35. From II Corinthians, xii, 9. Parker, *Milton*, I, 389.

36. Patrick, in his edition, mistakenly has "expurgating," p. 279.

37. Apropos of Mother and Mother Earth, Ch. XI of *Eikonoklastes* has a sentence beginning, "And if it hath bin anciently interpreted the presaging signe of a future Tyrant, . . . to dream of copulation

with his Mother." *Complete Prose,*
III, ed. Merritt Y. Hughes (New Haven,
1962), p. 467. "Robert Allott, *Wits
Theater of the Little World* (1599) supplies an explanation of the cryptic allusion: 'Caesar dreamed, that hee lay
with his mother, which the Sooth-
sayers interpreting, the earth to bee
his mother, sayde, That hee should
bee conquerour of the world.'" Kester
Svendsen, *Milton and Science* (Cambridge, Mass., 1956), p. 189. Relevant
is Arnold Toynbee's distillation of
Frazer: "the image of the seed that
dies and is buried in the womb of
Mother Earth and then rises again in
next year's crop or in the next generation of a human family. The image
went into action in the worship of the
sorrowing mother or wife and her suffering son or husband who has met a violent death and achieved a glorious resurrection. This religion radiated out of
the Land of Sumer to the ends of the
Earth. The Sumerian goddess Inanna
(better known under her Akkadian
name Ishtar) and her consort Tammuz
reappear in Egypt as Isis and Osiris, in
Canaan as Astarte and Adonis, in the
Hittite World as Cybele and Attis, and
in distant Scandinavia as Nana and
Belder—the goddess here still bearing
her original Sumerian name, while the
god, in Scandinavia as in Canaan, becomes an anonymous 'Our Lord.'"
Hellenism (New York, 1959), p. 12.
So the Isis and Osiris paragraph
(*Areopagitica,* 549) is another augury
of things to come.

38. The "thousand yong ones" of
Spenser's Error return "Into her
mouth" (*The Faerie Queene,* I, i, XV),
as Browne maintained was observable
of vipers: "For the young one supposed to break through the belly of
the Dam, will upon any fright for
protection run into it; for then the
old one receives them in at her mouth,
which way the fright being past, they
will return again, which is a peculiar
way of refuge; and although it seem
strange is avowed by frequent experience and undeniable testimony." Milton, thinking more of Scylla, details a
still more "peculiar way of refuge."
Both quotations from Browne come,
needless to say, from the *Pseudodoxia
Epidemica* (Third Book, Ch. XVI;
Works, ed. G. Keynes [London, 1928],
II, 237, 238).

39. *Milton and Science,* p. 188.

40. Sirluck, p. 493, footnote 26,
wrongly states, "in 1478, Torquemade
was appointed first Grand Inquisitor."
That was not to be until 1483.

41. *The Dialectics of Creation: Pat-
terns of Birth and Regeneration in
Paradise Lost* (Amherst: Univ. of
Massachusetts Press, 1970), pp. 161-62.

42. Ibid., pp. 30-31. Cf. "the first
broadside," anti-papal cartoon by
Martin Luther and Lucas Cranach,
Birth of the Papacy, woodcut, 1545,
reproduced in *Art News,* 70 (1972),
p. 51.

43. Jebb, ed., *Areopagitica,* p. 76.

44. Parker, *Milton,* I, 61; II, 749-50.

45. The latest discussion is in *A
Variorum Commentary on the Poems
of John Milton,* I, Italian Poems ed.
J. E. Shaw and A. Bartlett Giamatti
(New York, 1970), pp. 371 ff.

46. *Mercurius Politicus;* Parker,
Milton, I, 394.

47. Parker, I, 387-88; 574; cf. 661.

48. Ibid., I, 263.

49. Ibid., II, 1185.

50. [Philip Neve], *A Narrative of the
Disinterment of Milton's Coffin in the
Parish-Church of St. Giles, Cripplegate,
on Wednesday, 4th of August, 1790;
and of the Treatment of the Corpse
During that, and the following day*
(London, 1790), pp. 32-33. See, further,

J. Milton French, ed., *The Life Records of John Milton*, V (New Brunswick, 1958), 136; Allen W. Read, "The Disinterment of Milton's Remains," *PMLA*, 45 (1930), 1050-68; James G. Nelson, *The Sublime Puritan* (Madison, 1963), pp. 4-5. Happily the strands of hair that occasioned poems from Leigh Hunt and Keats were not those exhumed on this occasion but came from Milton's youngest daughter Deborah to Addison; see French, V, 135.

51. Theodore H. Banks, *Milton's Imagery* (New York, 1950), p. 69.

52. *Milton* (London, 1969), p. 105.

53. Ibid., pp. 68-69. Are, then, the twins monstrous? So White, p. 62, found them and compared xii, 83-85, and *Eikonoklastes*, Ch. XXI (Yale, III, 542).

54. Columbia *Works*, XV, 114.

55. *Epistolae*, xlv, quoted (not in this connection) by J. M. Evans, *Paradise Lost and the Genesis Tradition* (Oxford, 1968), p. 74. I would guess that Ambrose's inspiration may have been the parable of the wheat and the tares, also referred to in *Areopagitica* (564), Matthew XIII, 24-30; interpreted 36-43 (note especially 38): "The field is the world; the good seed are the children of the kingdom; but the tares are the children of the wicked one." Denis Saurat, *Milton Man and Thinker* (New York, 1925), p. 292, quoted the *Zohar*: "Had not the Holy one (Blessed be He) created the spirit of good and the spirit of evil, man could have had neither merit nor demerit; that is the reason why God created him a mixture of the two spirits."

Apropos of Milton's optimism, note, since his title page quotes Euripides' *The Suppliants*, Theseus' dictum: "For there are who say, there is more bad than good in human nature, to the which I hold a contrary view, that good o'er bad predominates in man, for if it were not so, we should not exist." Translation by E. P. Coleridge, p. 925 of *The Complete Greek Drama*, ed. W. J. Oates and Eugene O'Neill, Jr. (New York, 1938), Vol. I. (Incidentally, if Milton had continued his quotation from the play, 442 ff., he would have proclaimed himself an anti-monarchist: "Again, where the people are absolute rulers of the land, they rejoice in having a reserve of youthful citizens, while a king counts this a hostile element, and strives to slay the leading men, all such as he deems discreet, for he feareth for his power." Ibid., p. 931.)

56. Hughes, p. 175.

57. Columbia *Works*, XV, 113-15.

58. Ibid., p. 115.

59. Ibid., p. 185. The rationale seems to be that Milton wanted to add "sacrilege" to the heap of crimes Adam and Eve were guilty of, pp. 181-83.

60. *Milton and Wordsworth*, pp. 96-97.

61. *The Seventeenth Century Background* (London, 1934), pp. 250-51.

62. Compare Harold J. Laski's comment, "the *Areopagitica* is the sublimation of a Milton who resents the criticism of his marriage-theories." P. 171 in Herman Ould, ed., *Freedom of Expression* (London, 1945).

63. "A Note on *Areopagitica*," *JEGP*, 40 (1941), 478. Compare the footnote in Hanford-Taaffe, *Handbook*, p. 81: "In *The Reason of Church-Government* [Yale, I, 818-19] . . . Milton did argue that the magistrates exercise their power to prevent young men from being influenced by 'libidinous and ignorant Poetasters.'"

64. ". . . we are told that Eve has

suddenly taken it into her head to go and do her pruning by herself. Adam makes a long speech, in impeccable blank verse, pointing out that, as they are about to be assailed by a clever and ruthless enemy, it might be better for them to stay together and not separate. Eve says that that is very true, and that she would like to go off and prune by herself. Adam makes another long speech, in equally impeccable blank verse, making the same point with elaborations. Eve says that all that is very true, and that she will now go off and prune by herself." Northrop Frye, *The Return of Eden* (Toronto, 1965), p. 67.

65. On the theological background, see A. B. Chambers, "The Falls of Adam and Eve in *Paradise Lost*," pp. 118-30 in Thomas Kranidas, ed., *New Essays on Paradise Lost* (Berkeley, 1969).

66. Tillyard, pp. 134-35.

67. Joan Webber, *The Eloquent "I": Style and Self in Seventeenth-Century Prose* (Madison, 1968), pp. 188 ff.

68. Tillyard, p. 135.

69. Elsewhere I have argued that this may have been the reading Milton intended. *Yet Once More*, p. 149. Stefan Grotz, in "Milton: A Study of Psychological Tension" (Master's Essay, University of California at Berkeley, 1963), has pointed to the parallel with Elegia VII, 57: "Haec ego non fugi spectacula grata severus."

70. "Milton normally favors a simple metaphor or simile." Alan F. Price, "Incidental Imagery in *Areopagitica*," *MP*, 49 (1952), 222. Whether "wayfaring" be cast out or not, it should be noticed that *Areopagitica* has, besides "wars of Truth" (562), "waies of Truth" (557).

71. Quoted in the Introduction to Yale II, p. 87, from *The Compassionate Samaritane* (London, 1644), pp. 55-56. This plea for religious toleration had come out in June or July.

72. "I conclude that Milton meant to use Spenser as Tasso had used Ariosto. He would adopt the total historical and patriotic material of Spenser and recast it in the neoclassic form of Tasso." *The Miltonic Setting* (London, 1938), p. 192. For the "narrow bridge" passage, John W. Hales, ed., *Areopagitica* (Oxford, 1904), p. 146, quotes *The Faerie Queene*, V, ii, IV. On Milton's attitude in his three long poems, see George Williamson, "Milton the Anti-Romantic," *Milton and Others* (Chicago, 1970), pp. 11-25. We have the paradox of "an heroic poet who denounced the central values of ancient heroic poetry." J. H. Summers, "Milton and the Cult of Conformity" (1956), reprinted in *Milton: Modern Judgements*, ed. A. Rudrum (London, 1968), p. 32.

73. For a different association, see Mother M. Christopher Pecheux, "Spenser's Red Cross and Milton's Adam," *ELN*, 6 (1969), 246-51.

74. A skill that is part of being a good warrior, as *Of Education* made explicit: "They must be also practiz'd in all the locks and gripes of wrastling, wherein English men were wont to excell, as need may often be in fight to tugge, to grapple, and to close" (409).

75. John M. Steadman, *Milton and the Renaissance Hero* (Oxford, 1967), p. 126. Boadicea is a case in point. See my "Milton's Attitude Towards Women in the *History of Britain*," *PMLA*, 62 (1947), 977-83.

76. Hughes, p. 178.

77. Compare "kills reason it selfe, kills the Image of God, as it were in the eye" (492) with "One Spirit in them

rul'd, and every eye / Glar'd lightning"
(vi, 848-49). Four years after
Areopagitica Richard Crashaw published "In the Glorious Epiphanie
of Our Lord God, A Hymn. Sung as
by the Three Kings," of which lines
13-14 read: "The EAST is come /
To seek her self in thy sweet Eyes."
Complete Poetry, ed. G. W. Williams
(New York, 1970), p. 40. "Grapple"
enters Milton's poetry in a significant
parallel at the end of *Paradise Regained* IV, 567. See the annotations
in *Poems*, ed. John Carey and Alastair
Fowler (London, 1968), p. 1164.
Pascal is supremely relevant: "La
Vérité subsiste éternellement, et
triomphe, enfin de ses ennemis, parce
qu'elle est éternelle et puissante
comme Dieu même." *Provinciales*,
Lettre 12, cited by E. de Guerle,
Milton, Sa Vie et Ses Oeuvres
(Paris, 1868), pp. 230-31.

The Higher Wisdom of
The Tenure of Kings & Magistrates

JOHN T. SHAWCROSS
Staten Island Community College

Some while ago E. M. W. Tillyard[1] argued that Milton achieved in
his prose writings the high hopes expressed in *The Reason of Church-
Government*, among other places, for fame and for a furtherance of
God's kingdom on earth.[2] Certainly the statement in *Defensio secunda*
(p. 90)[3] suggests that at least hindsight yielded a pattern to the prose
works which strove for religious liberty (in the antiprelatical tracts),
for domestic liberty (in the divorce tracts as well as *Areopagitica*
and *Of Education*), for political liberty (in *The Tenure of Kings
and Magistrates* and *Pro Populo Anglicano Defensio*).[4] The divisions
are similar to those of Aristotle for all knowledge. If we accept the
underlying thought of the statement in *Reason*, written within about
seven months of his first prose venture, as one that dominated most,
if not all, of his prose and poetry, we shall see the prose work as
something more than a reaction to stimuli and current events.
Milton knew and meant a further meaning in the word "defense"
used for three tracts, a point made clear in his use of the word in
Sonnet 22: by his work to maintain and spread liberty he was *preventing* its opposites from asserting themselves over man—both
servitude to things ecclesiastical, "domestic," and civil and licence
whether in the worlds of the church, the home, or the law.[5] This
constitutes "Gods prime intention" for "those that seek to bear
themselves uprightly in this their spiritual factory," "to inbreed
and cherish in a great people the seeds of vertu, and publick civility,
to allay the perturbations of the mind, and set the affections in right
tune, . . . to deplore the general relapses of Kingdoms and States
from justice and Gods true worship" (*Reason*, pp. 34, 39). Despite
the frequent commentary on *Sonnets 7, 19,* and *22*, the rationale
for Milton's very being which they expose is little observed behind the prose. Since most of the writings arose out of temporal
concerns, the prose works are viewed with that limited sense of

"relevance" which has in the last few years been short-changing our evaluation of literature and art. True, there is the overply of debate, of contemporary issues and men, of rebuttal of specific statements and actions—and in these things Milton's effect was short-lived and gnat-like. But there is more: there is philosophic and enduring significance.

Milton is amazingly modern in his views: the driving forces behind his work clearly agree with the so-called radical views of the youth of our last decade, though he would never even approach the license (both public and personal) which some have practised. His emphasis on God as co-worker of the achievements of man through inspiration and guidance echoes at least the contemporary rise of a *religioso* world, well short, however, of Jesus-freaks. The hope that a paradise within can be attained to control each man's life and thus all men's lives without the false imposition of laws and punishments and enforcement institutions is tantamount to the cult of love today. No other prose work of Milton's, it seems to me, argues these thoughts more cogently, more lucidly than does *The Tenure of Kings and Magistrates.*

His first statement in the pamphlet is a ringing declamation against the Idols of the Tribe and Cave: "If Men within themselves would be govern'd by reason, and not generally give up their understanding to a double tyrannie, of custome from without, and blind affections within, they would discerne better what it is to favour and uphold the Tyrant of a Nation" (p. 1). Reason cannot operate, that is, if one pursues a course or belief, first, only because it is normal, customary, traditional, whatever, for him to do so: some of Milton's fellow Englishmen simply could not conceive of their land without a monarch any more than, say, some people can conceive of a classroom without a teacher (in all the old senses of that word) or the United States government without either a Republican or a Democratic male white president. Can one weigh the worth of any course of action, can one evaluate any person or thing, Milton is really asking, if one's objectivity is blinded by custom and the past? But more pernicious, as his second sentence indicates, are the self-serving interests of man: man looking only to his own position in his little world does not offend the tyrant. One doesn't make waves; one follows through the "logic of domination." Only good men can love freedom heartily, Milton writes; the bad cannot accept freedom, for it is a danger to their positions, or concepts of position, and so they are servile, afraid to speak out or to do or, really, to think. Curiously as one achieves freedom— which is clearly that state in which repression through human outside forces of the past or present does not exist—one imposes self-discipline to become an individual in a world of individuals, with none exerting dominance over another. But as one abides in the repressed state of servitude to his phantoms, he moves through indulgences to total license—a license which harms self and, perhaps more unconscionably, so many others. "The rest love not freedom, but license," Milton writes here, just as in *Sonnet 11* he lamented, "License they mean when they cry Liberty."

Although the Royalists exhibit these vain loves of custom and self, Milton is talking of those who have alleged a deep-seated antipathy to the Tyrant, those who have seemingly opposed him. The Tyrant—that is, anyone who exerts his will over another without restraint, without relief, and without consultation with the governed—owes his position to custom and to self-centered hope. Men deceive themselves by words—mere words—like *Loyalty* and *Obedience*, but their end is gain for themselves in a *known* world. Men fear tyrants because of their hopes for themselves, for as Satan was to say later, where there is no hope, there is no fear.[6] Reason only, God's viceroy, as Donne called it, can judge, but custom and blind affections incapacitate Reason, so much so that men turn against those "endu'd with fortitude and Heroick vertue" to act as Reason directs. In a page and a half Milton has set up the recurrent opposites of this world: the followers or noncommitted and the true doers or truly committed, the forces of the past and the forces of the future. But the world is not a dichotomized simplicity of bad and good, for the followers, the noncommitted, the forces of the past lie among those who have fostered the removal of the Tyrant. As Milton wrote—or is it always?—the "good Patriots" had the upper hand throughout the land despite the drift of that faction then asserting itself through trial and condemnation of the adjudged Tyrant, "to remove, not onely the calamities and thraldomes of a people, but the roots and causes whence they spring" (p. 2). The "good Patriots," who cursed the king and bore arms against him, partake as much of custom and servile selfhood as those they have opposed. What does one ever do with henchmen?

Milton wrote *The Tenure of Kings and Magistrates* not to argue against adherents of the king but against those who align themselves with reform yet draw back as consequent acts, dictated by reason, arise. It was obvious at the end of 1648 and during January 1649 when trial was in progress that past critics of Charles in the spheres of parliament and legislation (particularly financial) and of religion were resisting what Milton saw as reasonable future action: removal of king and replacement of monarchy by a more

representative government. While concerned with the contemporary situation, Milton clearly sees that the problem is not ever one
of the here and now. It persists through all times, for Man is always victim of himself. The resistance to reasonable outcomes
indicates the falseness of some of the actions which have led to
this point of decision, on the part of some. Such abetters belie
principle, truth, and liberty, and evidence-rutted reliance on the
past, fear of the future or of change, and the hopes of self-advance-
ment. Theirs is the position of Belial (*Paradise Lost* II, 119–225),
who argued "with words cloath'd in reasons garb" that the fallen
angels should accept their known world, Hell.[7] Milton knows that
"most men are apt anough to civill Wars and commotions as a
noveltie, and for a flash, hot and active" (p. 2)—shades of our
recent upsets!—but like Belial who "Counsel'd ignoble ease, and
peaceful sloth" they betray their cause by "contesting for Privileges,
customes, formes, and that old intanglement of iniquitie, thir
gibrish Lawes" or by pleading for their Prince ("in a new garbe
of Allegiance"), pitying him, extolling him, protesting "against
those that talke of bringing him to the tryall of Justice" (p. 3).
And today as well, the "liberal majority" that beset Ibsen's
Dr. Stockmann have been most vocal in the recent years of tumult,
and, unfortunately, their voice has also seemed to prevail.

The decline in reformative action would have been discerned
amid the violence and heated argument on our campuses and
in our beleaguered ghettos and in our marches for peace if only
one had really looked. The persistent and finally prevailing voice
has been that remarking the storms weathered in the past, the
institution not damaged but only chipped, the "wisdom" of
uniting what is meaningful in the criticism levelled with the achievements of the past. The liberal majority always seem to see the other
man's point—largely because it is to their advantage to do so—but
draw back in time to make sure that nothing really changes. Indeed,
the most subversive of all political groups is that which outwardly
agrees but essentially—perhaps unconsciously—rejects the basic
philosophy of the group of which it somehow has become a part.
But the adherents of reformative action are so gratified to have
support for their ideas—particularly from those who might otherwise not be thought of as swelling their numbers—that they do not
look into the essential ideology of this "liberal majority" and thus
do not recognize that the impending withdrawal of support will go
far to subvert the action deemed necessary. Milton's unsuccessful
task was to try to persuade those who professed agreement with
the antimonarchic group to support the acts that group deemed

necessary for true liberty to exist. Possibly his audience should
have been the antimonarchic group only and his purpose to persuade them not to seek the help of these "conspirators" when it
meant compromise and a persistence of history.

Yet another group may be discerned among the recently anti-
Charles party, those fellow travellers who are impressed by an act
attributable to nobleness of being or popular courage—the under-
dog syndrome, we might say. Appeals to emotion, "honest" con-
fessions, and promises of change delude the ignorant, and they
forget principle and proved tyranny. While "the Common wealth
nigh perishes for want of deeds in substance," the impressionable
revise their view of things so that no deed in substance will be done.
"He who but erstwhile in the Pulpits was a cursed tyrant, an enemie
to God and Saints, laden with all the innocent blood spilt in three
Kingdomes, and so to bee fought against, is now though nothing
penitent or alter'd from his first principles, a lawfull Magistrate,
a Sovrane Lord, the Lords Annointed, not to bee touch'd, though
by themselves imprison'd" (p. 6). But obedience, Milton urges,
is not the preservation of "the meere uselesse bulke of his person."
Milton's purpose is not to set forth the Tyrant's "particular charge,"
which he leaves "to the uprighter sort" of the Magistrates and to
the people, "though in number lesse by many, in whom faction
least hath prevaild above the Law of nature and right reason, to
judge as they finde cause" (p. 7). His purpose is to assure those who
have hesitated for whatever reason in reaching a decisive deed in
substance that tyrants "may bee as lawfully deposed and punished,
as they were at first elected" (p. 7).

Milton's audience in *Tenure* is not the Royalists; they are neither
persuadable nor in a position to act at this time. It is only hopefully those of the first sort who have resisted Charles only to balk
at reasonable outcomes of their prior actions because of custom
and self-interest; they are neither sincere nor honest with themselves. Rather his audience consists of those who "begin to swerve
and almost shiver" through false argument and emotional tugs
upon them. His aim is not to argue for deposition, specifically, or
execution, even more specifically, but to demonstrate that such
acts "after due conviction" are not only lawful but incumbent.

The fact that *Tenure* is so much a result of Charles' trial and so
interwoven with the events of November 1648-January 1649 has
obscured the significance of Milton's fundamental analysis of the
political animal which is common man. In any struggle of controls
(religious, domestic, governmental) there is a polarization of opposing views: the views of the past and custom and institutions like
law fostered to maintain those views of the past and custom, and

the views of the future and change and liberty from all kinds of repressive force. But all things become confounded and split, though
with much less polarization, yet nevertheless split. The view that
may seem to look to the future is far from being a solid one.
The paths to the future may encompass known paths and compromise, but Milton is not concerned with that issue here since circumstances had developed too far for viability in compromise. He sees
men supposedly encouraging change to be victims of their own
brand of compromise, of inaction, a result of allegiance to tradition and of hopes of personal gain; or victims of show and false
argument. Indeed, wherever we look in man's multitude of struggles—
whether it be in educational philosophy or sexual orientation or
ethnic mobility or whatever—there are those speakers for the "cause"
who harm the cause by drawing back to compromise, who by taking
the best from all possible courses only propound a chaotic mess
through fear of the new and change. The answer for Milton, and
those who believe like him in whatever sphere of action contention
lies, is to break with the past, cut the roots, as it were, and begin
anew with the wisdom that the past has afforded. Radical? Yes, the
proposal was radical in that it rejected the past simply because it
was the past and in that it looked forward to a new form of governmental structure, hopefully at opposites with all the points of
tyranny in the past.

Surely among the sources of defeat for any reformative action is
the corruption of the new power, first; the unchangeability of the
new power, the *status quo* of which is maintained through time
rather than its being insured of development and sensitivity to new
conditions, second; and the incompleteness of reform, due to compromise, to strange bedfellows, to the need for sheer numbers of
backers, to a lack of bold thought and courage, an important third.
Are we talking of seventeenth-century England or twentieth-century
welfare states? education? women's lib? political doctrines? This
significant analysis of the political man and the institutions he
generates has been lost for too long for too many people.

In the exordium to his tract (pp. 1-8) Milton has defined his
audience, stated his aim and procedure succinctly, and made some
telling categorizations of common man, the would-be political
mover. It was not until some years later that he realized that fit
audience is always few; and perhaps he never really learned that
in the realm of government idealism not only is ineffectual but
generally unrecognized. For it has seemed to me that Milton's contribution (or perhaps noncontribution) to political theory has
usually gone unnoticed. One must be instead a Robert Filmer urging some kind of tangible structure, even though it be traditional,

or a Thomas Hobbes establishing covenants and hierarchies, even though they be based on defeat, or a Henry Vane—practical and pragmatic. The ways in which modern ideas have been submerged by obvious stupidities and the venalities of man simply iterate the lesson Milton never really learned: idealism and logic are little recognized and even less seldom effective. Yet in its idealism Milton's argument is peculiarly modern.

The previous remarks assume that the tract is rhetorically deliberative: it aims at persuading and it is concerned with future action. It does not accuse or defend, although some discussions of it would lead one to think it does, nor does it praise or blame. The narration (the second division of the prolusion-tract) sets forth "facts" which may suggest accusation and blame, but these evidence background for the need for change. The strategy is to expose how kings became kings, thus negating a concept of divine appointment; what their responsibilities are, which are predicated upon the reason for their existence; how a king may become a tyrant and what dereliction of responsibilities constitutes tyranny; and the duty of the people to depose and punish the king legally. Milton knew that the people viewed kingship as divine, and indeed Charles was identified with David the King (as type of the second mediatorial office of Christ). Persuasion had first to give the lie to such a view. Milton readily realized the analogy between king and people as one between master and servant. He does not conclude the unavoidable thesis that what has passed as a standard economic relationship (and thence social relationship) should undergo comparable change, but as he moves into the narration he does stress the basis underlying that thesis. "No man who knows right, can be so stupid to deny that all men naturally were borne free . . . and were by privilege above all the creatures, borne to command and not to obey" (p. 8). Kings and magistrates were not advanced by the people "to be thir Lords and Maisters . . . but, to be thir Deputies and Commissioners" (p. 8). Milton knew that people are often won over by "Testimonials" and so he cited authority often (see, for example, pp. 26-28, a part of the *refutatio*). He erroneously thought that man was also influenced by logic, and that syllogistic (and Ramistic) logic led to inevitable conclusions. But of course that's not correct; man does not feel compelled to accept the logical conclusion. Not, certainly, when it disagrees with his previous beliefs, his position in life, his concept of himself.

The narration (pp. 8-17) is built on Ramistic lines: we are given four statements which should have made the reader conclude that "the title and just right of reigning or deposing in reference to God, is found in Scripture to be all one; visible onely in the people, and depending meerly upon justice and demerit" (p. 17). The schematization alone is Ramistic. The four points consider that

1) man was originally free and through common consent had chosen one or more as deputy to expedite the businesses of life, with conditions and oaths. Idealistically Milton states the conclusion to be drawn: "It being thus manifest that the power of Kings and Magistrates is nothing else, but what is onely derivative, transferred and committed to them in trust from the people to the Common good of them all, in whom the power yet remaines fundamentally, and cannot be tak'n from them, without a violation of thir natural birthright, . . . it follows from necessary causes that the titles of Sovran Lord, naturall Lord, and the like, are either arrogancies, or flatteries . . ." (p. 10).
2) kingship is supposedly hereditary and irrevocable. But this implies man as all "one body inferior to him single, which were a kinde of treason against the dignity of mankind to affirm" (p. 11).
3) the king is accountable only to God. But kings "have writt'n and decreed themselves accountable to Law" (p. 13).
4) the people hold the authority to retain or depose the king, tyrant or not.

There may be those who would deny or qualify some of Milton's "facts" along the way, but in large part Milton, I believe, would have received nods of agreement until his conclusion, and I see this tragicomedy enacted over and over again. Controversies like those over abortion, the release of secret governmental files, the penal system, *de facto* segregation, come immediately to mind.

We say, for example, the penal system serves a function, being a product of man's mind to make life safe for others; we say that we can alter the judicial system as wisdom dictates, for it serves us, not we it; and we say that it must be accountable to the people, not some Attorney-General or Governor only. But let it be proposed on good evidence and logic that, say, jail sentences for "social crimes" be outlawed, and a hue and cry is raised. We cannot, for some reason, tamper with "the law," tradition, our way of life. Of course, eventually such a change (or something like it) will probably be effected, just as most of the English sided with the removal of James II in 1688 and just as the dissidents in the Colonies finally broke ties with the motherland. And there will be cogent arguments advanced against such a proposal, but at base

is not the reaction one of abhorrence for the move against authority of the past (our precious precedents)? or against the classification of what has been criminal in the past? or against the uncertainty of the future which such an action predicates? The tragicomedy of life is that people are never won over by logic and
evidence. (One wonders whether the argument about the date of
Samson Agonistes is not pertinent.)

It should be clear that the narration points to future action. More
must be said, however, in proof of the preceding statements, whereby the harmfulness in the existing governmental administration will
be more thoroughly exposed. The *confirmatio* (pp. 17-25) tries to
"determin what a Tyrant is, and what the people may doe against
him" (p. 17). Though any "man of cleare judgement" should be able
to recognize tyranny, Milton knows that "the vulgar folly of men"
is "to desert thir owne reason, and shutting thir eyes to think they
see best with other mens." He thus proceeds to back up his four
previous points by example and authority. Again there is an assumption that men will recognize a logic behind the analogies; the "it
can't happen here" delusion and the "but it doesn't apply to me"
blindness do not receive specific attention. Milton's error in judgment in so many of his prose works—like the error of some modern-
day theorists—was to believe that one could argue tellingly, whereas
other, more "practical" men have known that the best argument
"to persuade" involves tangible "rewards." Rather than lead his
reader through scriptural discussions of master-servant relationships
(e. g., "*Mark* 10.42. *They that seem to rule*, saith he, either slighting or accounting them no lawful rulers, *but yee shall not be so,
but the greatest among you shall be your servant*" [p. 22]) and
citations or action or remarks against tyranny by important personages of the past (e. g., "*Ludovicus Pius*, himself an Emperor, . . .
being made Judge . . . between *Milegast* King of *Vultzes* and his
subjects who had depos'd him, gave his verdit for the subjects, and
for him whom they had chos'n in his room" [pp. 22-23]), Milton
might have been more effective by charging Charles head-on. But
Milton's sights were higher; his aims, more generalized and philosophic; his concerns, the future which only the hoped-for present
action could effect. His level of discussion—observable in most of
the other tracts—was well above the level of the two groups he
discerned as being on the side of the Parliamentarians in the immediate past and now backing down from the necessary subsequent
deed in substance. He was not presenting a blueprint for removal
of the king and monarchy, or for a new government. But his ideas
should have underlain the principles of that new government,

though the difficulties of 1653 and then 1658 made clear that they did not. I doubt that Milton was so unaware of the failures of the government during 1649-53 as some people seem to think.

The confirmation slides smoothly into the *refutatio* (pp. 25-28). "Yet because that some lately with the tongues and arguments of Malignant backsliders have writt'n that the proceedings now in Parlament against the King, are without president [i. e., precedent] from any Protestant State or Kingdom, the examples which follow shall be all Protestant and chiefly Presbyterian" (pp. 25-28). Such tongues as he refutes belong to the first category or "good Patriots" observed at the outset of the tract. Yet once more Milton assumes that historical example is meaningful to his reader. As our own various controversies have illustrated precedent is meaningful to "the people" only when it serves their prejudged beliefs—beliefs which are so often tied to custom and self-interest. Milton seems to be trying to counter the Idols of the Market-Place with what is at least potentially part of the Idols of the Theater. After all, which precedent does one use? and if the "oldest" is the answer, why should that be valid? We should do well to observe with science that nothing is valid unless it is judged valid currently. We have very frequently been required to unlearn the axioms of the past. Milton's refutation (a series of historical examples) does counter statements that precedents did not exist for the trial and the awaited sentence of the king; it does vindicate the expedient action. But it achieves little in persuading those of different mind.

Thus far in *Tenure* Milton has written that the power of kings and magistrates has been conferred upon them by the people in covenant for common peace and benefit; and that when such power is abused, it is the people's right and duty to reassume that power. The implications are a removal of the king, an establishment of a more democratic government (although we must note the theocratic proportions of that government), and an instrument of government which would ensure 1) the deterrence of a development of new tyranny, 2) the people's right and duty to reassume the reins of government as determined through proper legal action, and 3) the natural rights of man to free conscience and justice. The first and second implications became realities, but not because of *Tenure* which appeared too late (ca. February 13, 1649) for such effects. The instrument of government which Milton called for did not come into existence and his disappointment may have even verged on disillusionment at times, except that he did compromise by doing what he could to try to make the new government work (most specifically through *Pro Populo Anglicano Defensio*).

The theocratic form of government would, at this time, seem to offer some positive virtues for Milton. The interwoven strands of religion and politics made at least a kind of theocracy viable. Milton fell into the trap he himself had already pointed out: conclusion based on custom and existing order of things. We do not find a bold proposal that totally separated church and state. Only later did he urge the kind of separation that many today, with hindsight, the national experiments since the eighteenth century, and modern views, seem to take for granted as being necessary. On the other hand none of his work to date (1649) had been directly concerned with this matter, and even *Tenure* is not directed toward principles of constitutionalism. Second, Milton was always and strongly a believer in God's immanence, and that which right reason proposed as generated by the true God must of necessity be good. Third, the chiliastic movements of the period, with rumor of 1657 as significant year, must have persuaded many, Milton included, that the reign of Charles II must end, as of an Antichrist, to prepare for a government of God on Earth so that the millennium might proceed. Again Milton was self-victim—if indeed he gave any credence to such rumor—of a way of thought which he had seen as potentially false: decision dependent on hope. Personally, I feel that Milton recognized that one has to do something to make what he wants actually come about (the meaning of "deed in substance"), and this was positive achievement despite the pitfalls that thought would have reared up to stymie any kind of movement.

Where many historians fault Milton, I suppose, is in his lack of proposal of definite structures and principles which would advance the emerging English constitution. That Milton was not involved in this subject in *Tenure* may only be excuse, and that he does not show himself to be free from traditional thought patterns may not be condonable in one so otherwise astute. For had definite proposals for the institution of more truly democratic worlds of politics, economics, and society sprung into Milton's consciousness, they would have certainly taken verbal form. Yet we can see a contribution, I think, a contribution which underlies all of his poetic and prose attempts of engendering lasting liberty in the minds and hearts of all the people.

The last section of the tract, the peroration (pp. 29-42), restates what has gone before and asserts his audience's part in the action now leading to deposition, thus negating the effect which the word *rebellion* has in deterring further action by them. (This point has recently loomed up again with the reminder to American citizens that they owe their nation to Revolution and that other people—

even some groups of Americans among them—are not necessarily "bad" because they are struggling in a revolution to replace a tyranny with what purports to be a more democratic institution.) To these premises Milton adds that God, "as we have cause to trust," will oversee Parliament's deeds, and approve and aid the "reformed Common-wealth," and is thus able to conclude: "Let men cease therfore out of faction and hypocrisie to make outcrys and horrid things of things so just and honorable" (p. 38).

Milton can now discharge some of his idealism of the future, the ringing end to his peroration. Parliament "henceforth may learn a better fortitude to dare execute higher Justice on them that shall by force of Armes endeavour the oppressing and bereaving of Religion and thir liberty at home; that no unbridl'd Potentate or Tyrant, but to his sorrow for the future, may presume such high and irresponsible licence over mankind to havock and turn upside-down whole Kingdoms of men as though they were no more in respect of his perverse will than a Nation of Pismires" (pp. 38-39). And he knows that there will be those who, for their own ends, will try to recoup their losses and get revenge, charging the perpetrators of the new government with all manner of ill. Some, agents of "an old and perfet enemy," Satan *qua* Charles, will try to bind others' consciences, and among these agents will be the seemingly agreeable groups Milton delineated at the start of the tract. He pleads with them "not to fall off from thir first principles; nor to affect rigor and superiority over men not under them; not to compell unforcible things in Religion especially, . . ." (p. 39). Part of the problem that the future holds is thus not the organizational and legal questions of government but the subversiveness of compatriots. Milton's appeal is to the individual, to his mind and his wisdom. He does not even for a second consider enforcing men to perform acts of liberty with the proffered end of liberty for all. But he does know that some action may have to be taken to ensure Justice for all. Idealistically— a word that is, for me, constantly attached to Milton—he asks men not to "oppose thir best friends and associats who molest them not at all, infringe not the least of thir liberties" (p. 39). Unlike some of today's advocates of "do your own thing" who, by following that byword, infringe upon others' doing their own thing, Milton recognizes self-discipline, a way of thought and life achieved only by a proper regard of self and of each of one's fellow men.

But one group remains to be admonished: the divines, who had fought against certain religious injustices but who now appeared to be united against the political actions of the Parliament and Army. If such divines be ministers of Mammon instead of Christ, "aspiring also to sit the closest and the heaviest of all Tyrants, upon the conscience" (p. 42), they will be visited with the curse put on Meroz: "Curse ye Meroz, said the angel of the Lord, curse ye bitterly the inhabitants thereof; because they came not to the help of the Lord, to the help of the Lord against the mighty" (Judges v.23).

The future that Milton sees therefore is one in need of "deeds in substance" from all who believe in justice for man. Surely one of the greatest of sins is sloth, and of the slothful the worst is he who observes the need to do but who does nothing. Too easily will there be those who will sit by doing nothing, or who will be persuaded (through false reason, greed, pride, and such) to berate the new leaders (the deliverers from the bondage of tyranny), some to the point of working for defeat of the new government, internally or from forces without. Sadly Milton was right on all counts. But the failures of the Commonwealth in truth encouraged and gave momentum to its two-stage fall to Protectorate and thence Restoration.

The world and its architects and their customers are not much different today. Unfortunately, too few recognize that "power to the people" simply cannot mean all the people. The lesson learned in recent years is that democratic vote (taken after fact-finding and debate and logic and auspicious planning) doesn't always end with the logical decision. Milton's answer to this is the idealistic one of developing a paradise within each person so that each person will work in justice with every other, all being individuals, and none being dominant over another. The thought is not far from the ideal attributed to Gerrard Winstanley, the Digger. Only by *preventing* evil from existing within each person (the aim of Milton's scheme of education which was to repair the ruins of our first parents) could a full state of freedom be attained, and the most oppressive of internal forces is self-pride. Self-pride takes on illogic, personal gratifications, acceptance of the known and fears of the unknown, prejudice, and, through the dominance of self over all others' selves, license. For freedom cannot be freedom unless it exists for everyone, and it cannot "exist" for more than a few if thought and action are not disciplined to foster freedom for everyone equally at all times.[8] *Tenure* hopes to influence some people—seemingly they are good prospects —to reach the thought and action which will make reasonable an extended power to a more numerous group of people. (Milton's

last tract, *Of True Religion, Hæresie, Schism, Toleration,* makes
a similar point in extending toleration to all but the Roman
Catholics, whose religious beliefs, he felt, denied the supremacy
of the political in affairs of man's world and who followed too
frequently without question the dictates of the Papacy. His aim
is really to divert the growing Catholic drift of Charles II.)

Elitist though some of these ideas are, Milton foresaw the need
to educate the masses to understand and accept the "truth" of
the few, a problem that modern radicals seem not to have attended to. Like Milton, they have usually thought that expression
of their "truth" would be so overwhelmingly evident, and would
so logically proceed, that nonbelievers would be won over. And
indeed as "power to the people" agitators have learned, their
worst enemies are members of their own factions, like Milton's
"good Patriots."

Milton's contribution to political theory appears in points of
counsel which underpin the overt discussion of kingship:

1. educate man to judge more objectively, without the false
   thinking of custom or self-interest,
2. educate man in discrimination of ideas and action and in self-
   discipline,
3. protect the natural rights of all men,
4. develop a proper regard of each man for every other,
5. ensure action by a wide spectrum of men,
6. develop a reliance on the future, though unknown, through
   such assurances as an instrument of government,
7. remove the fears of the future by developing a proper regard
   for self in each man,
8. aim for the ideal state; though it may not be attainable, such
   belief will eventually achieve more.

In this, it seems to me, Milton is in agreement with modern political
theorists like Jacques Ellul who saw the answer to the world's
political dilemma in a re-formation of the democratic citizen, not
of institutions. The attitude is the direct opposite of Hobbes':[9]
"the use of Lawes . . . is not to bind the People from all Voluntary
actions; but to direct and keep them in such a motion, as not to
hurt themselves by their own impetuous desires, rashnesse, or in-
discretion, as Hedges are set, not to stop Travellers, but to keep
them in the way."[10] Bertrand de Jouvenal has noted that "The vision
of man seen by Hobbes is in essence the modern view";[11] and unfortunately that has been so, except for the nonprevailing Miltonic
view held by our so-called radicals. Milton's contribution is funda-

mental to an improved political world rather than tangible structures, laws, and principles.

Tenure fails in achieving what is really desired on any kind of broad scale in its own time; and so does every other prose work of Milton's that argues to the same kind of effect in its own time. Perhaps part of the failure is unavoidable in a pamphlet that confounds the immediate context with futural action, while not sufficiently distinguishing either as the ethos of the tract. Fundamental ideas are only seldom explicitly stated. And this I find common to such major philosophical statements as *Of Reformation* and *A Treatise of Civil Power.* But it is Milton's idealism, his lack of attention to the inadequacies of his audience, and his firm presupposition that man confronted with fact or argument and logic will accept or at least weigh the evidence and conclusions. For Milton the means to achieve fame and further God's kingdom on earth has been his talent to argue against ignorance, to educate his readers, to inculcate virtue and advance right reason— and this he attempts in the prose. But only with the creation of *Paradise Lost* was he finally truly successful for the generations that have followed.

While *Tenure* has an optimistic air of future achievement should the "good Patriots" and those who "begin to swerve, and almost shiver" continue their approval of the Good Old Cause and its results, there is also an air of uncertainty. Milton discerned in such pamphlets as *A Serious and Faithful Representation of Ministers of the Gospel within the province of London* (1649) the lack of backing being given the men who "for the deliverance of their Countrie, endu'd with fortitude and Heroick vertue, . . . would goe on to remove, not onely the calamities and thraldomes of a people, but the roots and causes whence they spring." The figure of Samson immediately jumps to mind, and if William R. Parker is indeed correct that the tragedy was composed first in 1646-48, this important concern of *Tenure* would seem to evolve out of the kind of disillusion that produced *Samson Agonistes*. In a recent article I have proposed that the real tragedy behind the poem is the hope that people under rigor show in being delivered from their bondage.[12] But hope means nothing without action by the oppressed: man must be one of the true doers, one of the truly committed. Without such action by the people, Milton foresaw the failure of the English people to break from the tyranny of monarchy just as the people of Dan remained in bondage of the Philistines despite Samson's final act "endu'd with fortitude and Heroick vertue."

The higher wisdom that *The Tenure of Kings and Magistrates* has offered generations of readers has been little heeded and unhappily lost on too many. The preceding reading of the tract shows that it conforms patently to Milton's early hopes for his talents in *The Reason of Church-Government*:

> How happy were it for this frail, and as it may be truly call'd mortall life of man . . . if knowledge yet which is the best and lightsomest possession of the mind, were as the common saying, no burden, . . . For not to speak of that knowledge that rests in the contemplation of naturall causes and dimensions, which must needs be a lower wisdom, as the object is low, certain it is that he who hath obtain'd in more then the scantest measure to know any thing distinctly of God, and of his true worship, and what is infallibly good and happy in the state of mans life, what in it selfe evil and miserable, though vulgarly not so esteem'd, he that hath obtain'd to know this, the only high valuable wisdom in deed, remembring also that God even to a strictnesse requires the improvment of these his entrusted gifts, cannot but sustain a sorer burden of mind, and more pressing then any supportable toil, or waight, which the body can labour under. . . .   (p. 33)

What makes it modern? Its truth—its idealism—its burden of this our life.

Notes

1. *Milton* (London, 1930), pp. 94–99.

2. See *Reason*, pp. 33–41.

3. "Since, then, I observed that there are, in all, three varieties of liberty without which civilized life is scarcely possible, namely ecclesiatical liberty, domestic or personal liberty, and civil liberty, and since I had already written about the first, while I saw that the magistrates were vigorously attending to the third, I took as my province the remaining one, the second or domestic kind," trans. Helen North, Yale *Prose*, IV, i, 624.

4. To these would later be added *Of True Religion* and *De doctrina christiana* for religious liberty, and *Defensio secunda*, *A Treatise of Civil Power*, *Considerations touching the likeliest* means to remove Hirelings, *A Letter to a Friend*, "Proposalls of certaine expedients," *The Readie & Easie Way*, *The Present Means*, and *Brief Notes* for political liberty. Although *Accedence Commenc't Grammar* and *Artis Logicæ* would fall under an "œconomicus" classification, and *Observations upon the Articles of Peace*, *Eikonoklastes*, *Pro se Defensio*, *The History of Britain*, *A Declaration*, *Character of the Long Parliament*, and *Moscovia* under a "politicus" label, yet they are not firmly related to Milton's point in *Defensio secunda*.

5. Compare the following from the Preface to *Reason* (p. 1): "In the publishing of humane lawes, which for the most part aime not beyond

the good of civill society, to set them barely forth to the people without reason or Preface . . . in the judgement of *Plato* was thought to be done neither generously nor wisely. His advice was, seeing that persuasion certainly is a more winning, and more manlike way to keepe men in obedience then feare, that to such lawes as were of principall moment, there should be us'd as an induction, some well temper'd discourse, shewing how good, how gainfull, how happy it must needs be to live according to honesty and justice, which being utter'd with those native colours and graces of speech, as true eloquence the daughter of vertue can best bestow upon her mothers praises, would so incite, and in a manner, charme the multitude into the love of that which is really good as to imbrace it ever after, not of custome and awe, which most men do, but of choice and purpose, with true and constant delight."

6. "So farwell Hope, and with Hope farewell Fear" (*PL* IV, 108).

7. The contextual differences are, of course, manifest: Charles has been a tyrant and is not a David, but God is just and loving (in Milton's view).

8. It will be obvious to many that I view Milton approaching a principle of love, well short of license, such as Herbert Marcuse elaborated in *Eros and Civilization* (Boston, 1966), but Milton is not bothered by Promethean figures; rather he praises them. (Compare *On the inventor of Gunpowder*: "Antiquity in blindness praised the son of Iapetus [Prometheus], who brought down celestial fire from the chariot of the sun, but to me he will be greater who is believed to have stolen the ghastly weapons and threeforked thunder-

bolt from Jove.") Some of Marcuse's remarks do not conflict with what we see as basic concepts in Milton: "The images of Orpheus and Narcissus reconcile Eros and Thanatos. They recall the experience of a world that is not to be mastered and controlled but to be liberated—a freedom that will release the powers of Eros now bound in the repressed and petrified forms of man and nature. These powers are conceived not as destruction but as peace, not as terror but as beauty" (p. 164), and "If Prometheus is the culture-hero of toil, productivity, and progress through repression, then the symbols of another reality principle must be sought at the opposite pole. Orpheus and Narcissus . . . stand for a very different reality. . . . theirs is the image of joy and fulfillment; the voice which does not command but sings; the gesture which offers and receives; the deed which is peace and ends the labor of conquest; the liberation from time which unites man with god, man with nature" (pp. 161-62).

9. John Aubrey reported that Milton's "widowe assured me that Mr Hobbs was not one of his acquaintance: y^t her husband did not like him at all: but he would acknowledge (grant) him to be a man of great parts, & a learned man. Their Interests & tenets were diametrically / did run Counter to each other" (f. 63v; *The Early Lives of Milton*, ed. Helen Darbishire [London, 1932], p. 7). However, we should note that Abednego Seller, in *The History of Passive Obedience Since the Reformation* (Amsterdam, 1689), p. 18, likens Milton and Hobbes by saying that Hobbes' authority and reasons had been derived from Mil-

ton and both Milton's and Hobbes'
from Doleman (i.e., Robert Parsons,
the Jesuit): "That Power is originally
in the Body of the People, that the
Foundation of all Government is
laid in compact, and that the breach
of Conditions by one Party dispenses
with the Duty of the other, tho confirmed by Sacraments, Oaths, and
reiterated Promises; that a Prince
may be opposed in his Politick, tho
not in his personal Capacity, that
when Religion is part of our Property
it may be defended." It is thus even
more noteworthy that their divergence from each other is so extreme.

10. *Leviathan*, ed. A. D. Lindsay
(New York, 1950), Part II, Chapter
XXX.

11. *Soveriegnty*, trans. J. F. Huntington (Chicago, 1963), p. 234.

12. "Irony as Tragic Effect: *Samson
Agonistes* and the Tragedy of Hope,"
in *Calm of Mind,* ed. Joseph A. Wittreich, Jr. (Cleveland, 1971).

Icon & Iconoclast

FLORENCE SANDLER
University of Puget Sound

In the evolution of Milton's polemical position there is a certain logical progression that in retrospect is apt to obscure the ambiguity of the decision that confronted him at any one time. In particular, since the poet-prophet is also, according to the Biblical tradition, an iconoclast, one appreciates the logic that brought Milton within ten years from breaking the "idol" of prelacy to breaking the "idol" of kingship. It was the same logic by which King James on the other side of the quarrel had insisted that "no bishop" meant "no king." In the years between, Milton had been engaged in smashing his own household idol, the solemnization of matrimony, which was idolatrous, he had proclaimed, where the partners were unfit and the ends of marriage not accomplished.

Confronting the bishops, Milton had been one among a host of Presbyterian prophets, for whom the consummation of the Reformation in England meant the abolition of everything that smacked of Popish practice, and who regarded the Laudian prelates as "popish" on the two counts of authoritarianism and superstition. When Laud replaced the communion-table in the body of the church with a railed altar in the sanctuary, it was clear that he was attaching a special sanctity to a thing and a place, thereby falling into the superstition of thinking in material or "carnal" terms of God who is Spirit. Thus the Laudians, like the Papists, incurred the anathemas which the Hebrew prophets had delivered against the worshippers of the graven images of Baal.

The very title of the *Eikon Basilike* gave Milton the opportunity to bring the same batteries against King Charles, and the heartfelt reception of the book in England fell into line as another manifestation of the popish corruption which consisted in the veneration of the shrines and relics of saints. As for the "Image of the King," it contained "little els but the common grounds of tyranny

and popery, drest up, the better to deceiv, in a new Protestant guise."[1]
The "image" or "icon" consisted, of course, not merely in the engraving which showed Charles spurning the crown of the world's
vanity, taking up the crown of thorns and affliction, and attaining
eventually the martyr's crown of glory. That was "Protestant"
enough, for the Reformation had always exempted engraven images
from the strictures upon graven ones; and the engraving in the
King's Book, though more emblematic in style, served the same purpose as the woodcuts in the *Acts and Monuments*, illustrating and
offering a visual schema for the text itself wherein, as with Dürer's
Erasmus, "the better image is shown." Nor did the King, according
to his image in the text itself, constitute only a "weak and puny
adversary," though Milton said so, employing his customary technique of belittling the adversary's strength.

In 1649, Milton was no longer one of a host of prophets, but
more like Elijah, confronting singly the worshippers of Baal and
denouncing the bewildered majority for continuing to halt between
two opinions. Since the majority were themselves sons of the
Reformation and inheritors of the tradition of Foxe and Bale,
and since many of them had done more fighting against King
Charles than Milton himself, it may be worthwhile to examine
the causes of their reluctance to accept Milton's argument that
the King's execution and the smashing of this particular "image"
were the necessary conclusion of their enterprise.

In the first place, the word "image," Janus-like, faces two ways,
and the Latin word merely continues the ambiguity which is to
be found also in the Hebrew of the Old Testament and the Greek
of the New. The Hebrew uses the same word, *tselem*, for God's
command (e.g., in Numbers 33:52) to destroy all the molten
images of the Canaanites and for his undertaking in the first chapter of Genesis to make man in His own image. Likewise, the Greek
eikon is used to describe both the image of the Beast in the Book
of Revelation and "Christ, who is the image of God" (2 Corinthians
4:4). Already, however, these texts held the solution of the dilemma.
If both Truth and Falsehood, Christ and the Beast, had their images,
then the difference lay in the fact that one was a "living," internal-
ized image, and the other an external simulacrum. As distinct from
those who worshipped the mere form (the *eidolon*), the worshipper
of the true God discovered the Image of God within himself when
he was transformed into the living image of Christ who was Himself the living image of the Father.

It would be difficult to overestimate the importance for the
Reformation of the Pauline idea of the conversion of the whole

man as distinct from the observance of outward ceremonies. It became for Bale and Foxe the difference between the True Church and the False, the Protestant and the Papist. The martyrs of the Primitive Church and now of the Reformation had—as the word "martyr" suggests—borne the ultimate witness of their conversion into the image of Christ. On the title page of the *Acts and Monuments,* Foxe had shown the Image of the Two Churches, where on the one side the Protestant martyrs rejoiced as they burned at the stake, filling out in their bodies the sufferings of Christ because they were already at one with Him and shared His Glory; while on the other side, the Romish priests bowed down before the Mass, the empty form, the "idol," of Christ's Sacrifice.[2] It was true that Antichrist was able to feign a remarkably close resemblance to Christ, and that he even had his "martyrs" (among which the Protestants were apt to place the Jesuits and the Anabaptists). *Causa facit martyrum.* Nevertheless, the conversion of one's life and body to Christ through a sacrificial death was telling evidence that here was a true image of Christ.

The difficulty for Milton in 1649 was that the King appeared to have a monopoly on martyrdom. Milton's irritation at the "Protestant guise" of the *Eikon* betrays the effectiveness of the book's implied claim that Charles' death represented the culmination of Foxe's tradition of martyrs. For, while William Haller has pointed out the impact of Foxe upon the left wing of Protestantism in the 1640s, it is to be remembered that Foxe was the common property of all Protestant Englishmen and was read as assiduously by the community at Little Gidding as by the divines of the Westminster Assembly and the Independent weavers. In an important sense, the Foxe tradition in England had been all along represented by the monarchy. Foxe himself had remained a strong supporter of Elizabeth's Church Settlement against the disruptions of Cartwright, and he had made the tale of the Queen's own persecution in childhood and her survival to inherit the throne and set up a Protestant bulwark against Rome the last of his martyr-histories and, in a sense, the vindication of the others. James I, who had written his own Paraphrase upon Revelation, in the manner of Foxe and Bale, proving the Roman Church to be Antichrist, had also in his years of public pamphleteering made the most of his position as the Protestant bulwark, and the chief intended victim of the Jesuits with their Gunpowder Plots. However ancient the origin of the Divine Right of Kings for which James made himself the spokesman, the form in which the doctrine was revived in the sixteenth and seventeenth centuries, as John Neville Figgis has demonstrated, was directly connected with the Reformation and with the need on the part of the new nationalist states to assert a sanction for their leadership that would effectively oppose the sanctions claimed by the Pope in Rome.[3] Those medieval apologists (Marsilio of Padua, Dante, William of Occam and others) who had, as it were, anticipated James' doctrine by claiming for the Emperor against the Pope his own quasi-spiritual power to wield the Temporal Sword, were enrolled by Foxe among the members of the True Church which had continued through the Dark Ages of Popery.

It was evident to James, however, that the danger to the monarchy and the Reformation came no longer from only one side, and he spent his years exposing the errors of Papists and "Puritan-papists" who had borrowed from each other a doctrine of tyrannicide which both groups might be irresponsible enough to apply to himself, a good Christian king. In retrospect, James' own position is full of irony. He was the son of one "royal martyr" and the father of another, but he himself was not of the stuff of which martyrs are made. He used the doctrine of Divine Right as the best safeguard against invasion and assassination, but was canny enough not to lose his head over it; while his son, who appears to have taken the sacral kingship seriously, went to the block. Meanwhile, the argument for the interdependence of the monarchy and the Reformation in England represented the position of most Englishmen in the 1640s, including those who took up pen and sword to prove to the King that the Reformation Church in England could no longer be episcopal. One is not surprised that the Presbyterian majority in the country were stunned and dismayed when the intractability of the King on the one side and the Army on the other led to the King's execution, and when they themselves appeared to have delivered the King over to those few men on the left who espoused the disreputable doctrine of tyrannicide. A Protestant reader might well feel that he had caught sight of the cloven hoof when he came to the point in *Eikonoklastes* where Milton derives a right of jurisdiction for subjects over their king from the ancient jurisdiction over the Emperor claimed by the (Popish) Church and from Saint Ambrose's excommunication of Theodosius.[4] As Buchanan in the *De Jure Regni* had freely admitted, this was an argument borrowed from the Papalists. It was not a true Protestant argument at all.

Nor was Milton's argument from Biblical exegesis decisive, for here there were at least two schools of interpretation. If kings were only tyrants by another name, and if God's people in their true selves were republican, then it was of course necessary to show that kingship first began with Nimrod, to exalt the exploits

of the uncrowned and unanointed leaders of Israel in the Book
of Judges, and to deplore the Israelites' petition to Samuel that
God would give them a king "after the manner of the heathen."
In praising David, one would point out that his virtues were independent of his being a king and that he had spared the life of
Saul, the Lord's Anointed, not because he thought the person
of the king sacred but because he would not use his advantage
to prosecute a private quarrel. Kingship had reached its natural
conclusion in Rehoboam who had threatened to whip his subjects with scorpions; God had not merely permitted but actively
approved the rebellion of Jeroboam against Rehoboam and the
House of David, and that rebellion was to be dissociated from
the later establishment in the North of the cult of the Golden
Calf.

But if, on the other hand, the king was "the breath of our
nostrils," and God's people were at their best monarchical, then
kingship had probably begun with Adam and only its perversion,
tyranny, was seen in Nimrod. The covenant that Israel in her
primitive republican days had reached with God through Moses
was not complete until it had been extended to include the kingship of the House of David (and therefore the Messianic promise).
The good kings of that line, such as Josiah and Hezekiah, were indeed offset by some vicious kings, such as Rehoboam, but the
latter were to be accepted as the scourge that God had sent
upon his ungrateful people until they should again deserve a
good king. At the institution of kingship Samuel had warned the
Israelites to this effect in God's name, and God had also clearly
disapproved of Jeroboam's rebellion, seeing that rebellion had
been straightway coupled with the idolatry of the Golden Calf.[5]

The Old Testament, being by no means monolithic, certainly
allowed for both readings, and one could say that the schools of
interpretation in seventeenth-century England were no more at
variance on the main issue than successive editors of the Book
of Judges in ancient Israel. On the whole, however, the latter part
of the Old Testament material, having been edited by the
Deuteronomic historians, proved to be partial to kingship and the
legitimate line of David, except when the Davidic kings so far forgot themselves as to share in Ephraim's sin of idolatry, allowing
the *Baalim* to stand in the temple and the *Ashtaroth* and High
Places to flourish. From the time of the original alliance between
the Davidic kings and the Yahwistic prophets, the Biblical tradition had joined inextricably the two issues of "idolatry" and
"tyranny." They were still interdependent issues in seventeenth-
century England, where Charles was brought to trial on a charge

of tyranny and accused in the Independent pamphlets of superstition and idolatry, while his apologists were equally sure that
he was both a good Christian and a good king.

From the perspective of Higher Criticism there is an additional
irony which was not available in the seventeenth century, but
would surely have amused such a man as John Selden. The form
of worship employed at Dan and Bethel by the Northern Kingdom
after the secession appears to have been as legitimate as the worship
at Jerusalem—indeed, it was the Southern Kingdom which for its
own political purposes had introduced the novelty of the Deuteronomic Reform, insisting that sacrifice could be offered at Jerusalem
only. Likewise the golden bull or calf, the notorious "idol" at
Bethel against which the Southerners inveighed, was probably as
old a throne and symbol of God's presence as the ark-throne with
the cherubim at Jerusalem, and Solomon's brazen sea. Only the
overthrow of the more powerful Northern Kingdom had left the
Southerners free to claim without challenge that God had all the
while been offended by the "idolatrous" cult, and to proffer
their own version of the Exodus material into which had been
written, as an anticipation of the later offence, an account of
Moses discovering and anathematizing a cult of the Golden Calf
which had distracted the people from the reception of the Law
and the Covenant.[6] In short, in the Old Testament period also
there had been rival Israels, as there were rival Protestant groups
in seventeenth-century England, each sure that it represented the
true "new Israel," the Church, and each in the course of proving
its own claim brought to accuse its rivals of nothing less than
idolatry.

Whereas the Independents preferred to argue from the period
of Gideon and Samson, the royalists felt themselves to be on
stronger ground in the New Testament material, for here, in the
specifically Christian writings, the pattern of kingship was the
Christos, Messiah, Anointed One, in whom the line of David had
been restored and fulfilled. It could be argued that all Christians
participated with Christ in his kingly office, and that, as all the
Lord's people might be prophets and priests, so they might also
be kings. Only the Christian antinomians had carried the doctrine
to its fullest extent. Paul himself, having a healthy respect for
Roman law and order and a mistrust of the apocalyptic tradition
of his own people, had avoided that conclusion, and had on the
contrary, in his famous Thirteenth Chapter in Romans, counselled
obedience to the "Powers that be" which are "ordained of God."
The mistake of the antinomians was to fail to understand that

Christ's kingship had in this world been spiritual only, confusing
the spheres of civil and spiritual liberty which Luther, and even to
some extent Calvin, had kept apart. Milton, the protagonist of the
power of a Christian people, is cautious at this point of the argument, admitting by his syntax that that does not follow from the
quality of Christ's own kingship:

> Christ . . . declares professedly his judicature to be spiritual, ab-
> stract from Civil managements, and therefore leaves all Nations
> to thir own particular Lawes, and way of Goverment. Yet be-
> cause the Church hath a kind of Jurisdiction within her own
> bounds, . . . it will be firm and valid enough against him, if sub-
> jects, by the Laws of Church also, be *invested with a power of
> judicature* both without and against their King.[7]

Where Milton admits a *non sequitur,* and proceeds with his
"papalist" argument, the royalists could draw a direct inference.
Sharing in Christ's kingship meant following the example of One
who had not worn an earthly crown, although he was the heir of
David, and had not approved of the attempts of the zealots to
overthrow the civil power even in order to establish a theocracy.
Christ, on the contrary, had recognized the civil power and submitted to its jurisdiction even to the point of death. The Primitive
Christians had likewise submitted to the rule of Nero and Diocle-
tian, obeying them in all things short of their injunction to practice
idolatry; and even in this apparent disobedience they had followed
Christ's example of "passive obedience" in submitting to the civil
penalties. (Only a man as crass as the regicide John Cook would
argue that the Primitive Christians had been "patient" because
God had not yet sent them an Army.[8]) But if on earth Christ had
submitted, in Heaven he sat enthroned, and it was in Heaven,
and only there, that crowns awaited those Christian saints and
martyrs who followed him thither. At the end of time, Christ
would indeed return with the saints to reign visibly upon earth;
the error of the chiliasts was to project that reign prematurely,
confusing the eras of the First Coming and the Second.

Meanwhile, God had so far alleviated the sufferings of his people
as to replace the heathen emperors by Christian kings who took
their title from Constantine, and were stewards unto God for the
good order of the Church in their realms. Such indeed was King
James' understanding of his Christian "calling" as a king. There
was a certain aptness in a Stuart king's enunciation of a doctrine
of stewardship. The Christian king, he said, has a "duetie to his
Subiects . . . clearly set down in many places of the Scriptures,"

and openly confessed in his Coronation Oath by which, at least in Britain, he promises to maintain "the Religion presently professed, all the lowable and good Lawes made by . . . predecessours," and the "ancient Priuiledges and Liberties" of the country. Moreover, he must "maintaine concord, wealth and ciuilitie among [his subjects], as a louing Father, and careful watchman, caring for them more then for himselfe, knowing himselfe to be ordained for them, and not they for him and therefore countable"—not, as Milton insisted, to his subjects, but—"to that great God, who placed him as his lieutenant ouer them, vpon the perill of his soule. . . . And this oath in the Coronation is the clearest, civill, and fundamental Law, whereby the Kings office is properly defined."[9]

For either side, then, the argument about Christ's kingship finally pointed back to whatever was the fundamental law of the Christian realm, "leaving all Nations to thir own particular Lawes, and way of Goverment," as Milton had said. And here was the major weakness of Milton's apologetic for the regicide since, the cases of Edward II and Richard II notwithstanding, there had been no precedent in England for the trial and execution of the King in the name of a sovereign power vested in the people.

Either the king is the source of the law, or the people are, says Milton, assuming since he addresses the "people" that his audience will choose the latter option. Either the king may do his will and pleasure, or else parliament by itself is sufficient to make legislation without the king's "negative voice." The strategy is calculated to persuade that there is no middle ground, but only a choice of polarized alternatives. Most of Milton's contemporaries, however, occupied the very middle ground that he denied. For in England, they held, there was a "mixed monarchy," which combined the merits of Aristotle's three separate types of government: Monarchy, Aristocracy and Democracy. Against Bodin, they maintained that sovereignty was divisible—at least in England where the sovereign was the *King in Parliament*. The mixed constitution had indeed been threatened, in 1640, by the incursions of the royal prerogative; in 1649, however, the threat was no longer from the king but from the Commons which in the intervening years had "devoured" the other constituents of Parliament, the Lords Spiritual and Temporal, and now the monarchy itself.

Moreover, since 1642, Charles had himself become the spokesman for the mixed monarchy. Under the guidance of the moderates who surrounded him at that time, Falkland, Colepepper and Hyde, he had returned his Answer to the Nineteen Propositions by refusing to make over the executive power to Parliament, and declaring his adherence to the traditional mixed monarchy. He had in fact conceded more than tradition required, for, whereas the king was habitually described as standing over and above the Three Estates of Parliament (the Lords Spiritual and Temporal and the Commons), Charles described Three Estates of government which were to be correlated with Monarchy, Aristocracy and Democracy respectively, and thus came to include the king as one of those three, along with the Lords as a group and the Commons.[10] If it was (as some believed) a violation of the fundamental law of the land that the King had ruled for eleven years without Parliament, there was no doubt that the Commons were violating the constitution in purporting now to rule without the Lords and the King. Along with their appropriation of the sole executive and legislative power in the land, the Commons had also, in the case of the King's trial, assumed a judicial power—and such a jurisdiction, as the King rightly claimed, had never been seen in England before.

Milton's position in *Eikonoklastes* is thus to be defined not against the supporters of a royal absolutism (who were always negligible in number) but against the broad group of reasonable men who appreciated the interdependency of the various components of government and were now distressed by the usurpation of one element at the expense of the others. These for practical purposes constituted the "royalists" in 1649. But Milton was separated even from that smaller group which adhered to the novel doctrine of the sovereignty of Parliament—a position which his later reputation as the "grand Whig" has tended to obscure. In 1649, those who valued the integrity of Commons were alarmed by the Army's use of force to bend the House to its will: Colonel Pride's seclusion of the Presbyterian members from their seats must have appeared more offensive than the King's attempt some years before to arrest the five members on the floor of the House. When Milton therefore justifies the regicide court as acting with the authority of the people, he offends the good parliamentarian by refusing to recognize the distinction between a free House of Commons and a Rump sitting at the behest of the Army, and he aligns himself with the small group of extremists who are prepared to force the actual forms of the law and the constitution to fit their own arbitrary version of the "fundamental law." The King had had justification for claiming at his trial that it was he, rather than the regicides, who stood for the fundamental laws and liberties of the people against an arbitrary tyranny. To appreciate the extremity of Milton's position, one might remember that he was prepared to justify the regicide which horrified even Fairfax, the leader of the Army; and that he asserted the "legality" of the regicide court from

which the ablest judges and lawyers of the parliamentary opposition
—men such as Rolle, St. John, Selden, Whitelocke and Widdrington—
specifically dissociated themselves, despite Cromwell's pressure upon
them.

One should also admit that the *Eikon Basilike* had not won its audience without literary merit. It will not do to dismiss the *Eikon* as "a
masterpiece of calculated sentimentality, a pathetic and pietistic collection of prayers and meditations," and to attribute Milton's failure
to diminish the book's effect as due to the impossibility of answering
"a sentimental and vulgar appeal" with reason.[11] That is simply to
take Milton's partisan disparagement of the book at face value. The
Eikon is neither a great book nor a contemptible one; some may prefer it for its lucidity and reasonableness to Donne's *Devotions* in the
same genre. Milton's attack on the literary quality of the book turns
on the point that its style is "prelatical," especially when "wee come
to the devout of it, model'd into the form of a privat Psalter. Which
they who so much admire, either for the matter or the manner, may
as well admire . . . many other as good *Manuals*, and *Handmaids of
Devotion*, the lip-work of every Prelatical Liturgist, clapt together . . .
out of Scripture phrase, with . . . much ease, and . . . little need of
Christian diligence, or judgement."[12] But his opinion may be balanced
by that of Burnet, for whom the prelatical style was in itself no demerit, and for whom there was in this particular book exactly the
quality which Milton denied: "a nobleness and justness of thought
with a greatness of style." Burnet was puzzled when confronted with
evidence for Gauden's authorship, since "*Gawden* never writ anything
with that force, his other writings being such, that no man from a likeness of style would think him capable of writing so extraordinary a
book as that is."[13]

The later scandal about the authorship of the *Eikon* has drawn away
attention from Milton's original motive in questioning whether Charles
had written the work himself. By way of discrediting the sincerity
of the "image," it was an obvious tactic to imply that some other
party had a mercenary interest in sponsoring it. The more important
consideration, however, no matter what the authorship, was the one
to which Milton then proceeded, namely, whether the image was a
true delineation of Charles; and, if so, whether the character delineated
was that of a hypocrite or a true Christian. The difficulty here was
that the portrait presented by the *Eikon* did indeed fit the lineaments
of the King as he had appeared at his trial and execution: his penitence
for the betrayal of Strafford, his rebukes of the "tumult" of Parliament and the Army against the natural order and law of the realm,
and finally his dignified acceptance of humiliation and death.

At his trial and execution, Charles had been impressive in his confidence. He had at the trial proved more than a match for Bradshaw, with an eloquence unexpected in one known throughout his life as a poor speaker, and with a skill in argument all the more remarkable in that he had had no legal counsel throughout the proceedings and no knowledge in advance of how the court would proceed against him. His calm bearing on the scaffold, which his enemies felt obliged to explain away as stoicism or sheer hypocrisy, reminded most Englishmen instead of the affirmation in the twenty-third psalm that "though I walk through the Valley of the Shadow of Death, I will not fear, for Thou art with me." As he had dressed on the morning of the execution, he had said to his attendant, "This is my second marriage day; I would be as trim today as may be, for tonight I hope to be espoused to my blessed Jesus,"[14] and on the scaffold itself, when Bishop Juxon who had prayed with the King in the last months of his life assured him that the axe would carry him "from Earth to Heaven; and there you shall find, to your great joy, the prize you hasten to, a Crown of Glory," the King had replied, "I go from a corruptible to an incorruptible Crown, where no disturbance can be, no disturbance in the world."[15]

In retrospect, there can be little doubt that Charles derived his strength at the last from having been reduced to a situation where he stood finally for simple certainty. From the time of the Treaty of Uxbridge, the issues between himself and Parliament had narrowed down to the two things on which, in Charles' view, he could not compromise, since he held them in stewardship, namely, the power of the sword and the order of the Church. He was no longer distracted by the administrative problems that he had always found uninteresting and difficult; he was no longer obliged to fight a war; and at the end he was no longer deluded by the hope of escape. The one last act that God apparently required of him was that he should die as a witness for monarchy and Christianity, and to that act Charles brought his two best resources, his courage and his piety. More than anybody else, it was Charles himself who insisted upon martyrdom.

Even now, when the story of the authorship has been untangled,[16] it is impossible to separate in the *Eikon* Gauden's image of the King and his position from the King's image of himself. I am inclined to put in a word for Gauden whose reputation suffered from both royalists and regicides. He was not necessarily mercenary-minded. Like Milton, he had begun as an advocate of the presbytery, without thinking of himself as an enemy of the King. The experience of reading the King's private papers captured at Naseby had apparently confirmed his sympathy for Charles, and he had proceeded not only to copy the papers but to edit and rewrite them. By 1648 he was appalled at the prospect of the regicide, against which he protested—ineffectively—in his own name.[17] The way to arouse men to a realization of the enormity of the deed was to have them see the situation from the King's point of view and to get inside the King's soul as Gauden had done! One does not know how much Gauden revised Charles' material, or Charles Gauden's. But it seems that they were at one in their image of what the royal Christian martyr must be, and Charles had taken the image seriously in his preparation for death.

The particular kind of Anglican piety that Charles knew had consistently emphasized the mortality of the world and the flesh, and the necessity of "dying daily" in the body for the sake of liberating the immortal soul. The great exemplar of Jacobean Anglican piety, John Donne, had dedicated to Charles his *Devotions upon Emergent Occasions* ("this image of my humiliation"), and had preached before him his famous sermon "Deaths Duell," "being his last sermon, and called by His Majesty's Household, the Doctor's own funeral sermon."[18] The Dean's example of holy dying had been reinforced by George Herbert, whose book of poems had become a favorite with the King. *The Temple*, by its very schema, makes it clear that the experience of Affliction which recurs in the life of the Body of the Church is related to the Crucifixion, which is placed at the entrance to the Church; and that to "die daily" by a sacrificial mode of life is to participate in the "one, perfect and sufficient Sacrifice" of Christ upon the Cross. Such piety was thus inclined to dwell upon the suffering (i.e., patience) and pathos of Christian life in the world; to take the Crucifixion as the event which characterizes this present life and to reserve the Resurrection as an assurance of the life hereafter. It is to be distinguished from certain other strains of Protestant piety in which the Crucifixion was chiefly relevant to the original experience of the conviction of Sin; that conviction having been since succeeded by the conviction of Salvation, the pattern of the life of the Christian saints thereafter was derived rather from the Resurrection. In seventeenth-century England, there appears to be a rough correlation between these two types of piety and the opposing views on the subject of the world's decay. It is at least clear that Donne, in his Anniversary Poems, had been the spokesman for both the world's decay and the immortality of the soul, whereas Milton, who in his student years had written the Latin poem *Naturam non pati senium* to support Hakewill's argument against the world's decay, was to show eventually a strong inclination to mortalism. Meanwhile, he had, in the "Nativity Ode" and his abortive Passiontide poem, encountered a difficulty in associating God with pathos, preferring his manifestations of Power; and he had shown impatience with humility and resignation, whether "Christian" or otherwise.

But in the present instance, the pathos and the sacrificial overtones of the *Eikon Basilike* which so exasperated Milton were to most Englishmen, whether episcopal or presbyterian, the mark of authenticity upon Charles' witness. The portrait was that of a Christian soul, penitent for his sins but resolute in his faith, undergoing in imprisonment a self-examination more rigorous than his public trial, and finding, in the face of death, atonement and reconciliation with God. In the cadences of the penitential psalms, the King prays for the "inward grace which Thou [God] alone breathest into humble hearts."

> O make me such, and Thou wilt teach me, Thou wilt hear me, Thou wilt help me. The broken and contrite heart, I know, Thou wilt not despise.
>
> Thou, O Lord, canst at once make me Thy temple, Thy priest, Thy sacrifice, and Thine altar; while from an humble heart I (alone) daily offer up in holy meditations, fervent prayers, and unfeigned tears myself to Thee.[19]

While the recitation and paraphrase of the psalms had always held a special place in Christian (not just "prelatical") devotion, there was a special significance in the use of psalms in the *Eikon*. There the "psalmistry," as Milton called it, brought two royal penitents, Charles and David, to speak as it were with one voice. Indeed, they were linked by a third king, Christ, who at his Crucifixion had recited the psalms of his ancestor, David. And while every martyrdom was a kind of reenactment of the Passion of Christ, the martyrdom of Charles produced some remarkably close parallels with the Crucifixion which did not fail to have their effect upon the seventeenth-century mind, accustomed to regard historical parallels as proofs, and prepared to see the Christian *mythos* as the basic pattern of life. It is my contention that these parallels affected not only Charles himself, who accepted and affirmed them, but also John Milton who rejected them.

To the end Charles kept with him his father's writings. James' *Collected Works* of 1616 open upon the engraving which shows the King in later life, crowned, seated upon his lion-throne and holding his sceptre, while beside him there repose the Book "Verbum Dei" and the Sword "Iustitia." About him, the legends and mottoes proclaim the qualities upon which he prided himself as a king—his irenicism (*"Beati pacifici"*) and his wisdom (for God had given to him as to Solomon a "wise and understanding heart"). But the *Collected Works* in their final form include the two additions of 1619, and thus the volume that opens upon the engraving of James as the very image of a king closes with his strange meditation upon part of the Passiontide narrative, where in the scene of the soldiers mocking Christ he found the clue to the "Paterne for a Kings Inauguration." Even the circumstances of the meditation must have been peculiarly affecting to Charles. The old king had been so taken by the aptness of the passage, he said, "that my heart hammered upon it divers times after, and specially the Crowne of thornes went never out of my mind, remembering the thorny cares, which a King (if he have a care of his office) must be subiet unto, as (God knowes) I daily and nightly feele in mine own person." He had shared his thoughts with Buckingham who had volunteered to take them down at his dictation to spare the "slownesse, ilnesse, and uncorrectnes of my hand." James' first manual of kingship, the *Basilikon Doron,* had been his gift to Prince Henry, now "with God"; *A Paterne for a Kings Inauguration* was written for Charles alone, and the scribe had been the same Steenie whom Charles had first disliked, but who had later become his dearest friend and had been assassinated for his unpopularity in Charles' service.

In his affliction unto death, James explains, Christ had provided the pattern for every Christian man, but also a particular pattern for the Christian king, and it is to this that he will address himself "as properly belonging to my calling." Then, in words which anticipate the image of Christian kingship that Charles would eventually present to the world in his own "King's Book," the father commends to the son, as to a man dying daily, self-examination, the reception of the Sacrament, and the confidence that *"via virtutis est ardua."* "And for my part I will pray the Lord of heauen and earth so to blesse you (that are the sonne and heire of a King) with the paterne of the inauguration of a King written by a King; as you may in the owne time be worthy of a heauenly and permanent Kingdome."[20]

In the scene of the mockery James finds, as the gospel writers had intended, that God's truth is apparent even through the soldiers' falsehood, for when they deck their Messiah in the purple robe, putting upon his head a crown of thorns and in his hand the reed for a sceptre, they acknowledge better than they know the true kingship of Christ; as Pilate will do later when he allows Christ's kingly title to stand above the Cross. James does not miss the opportunity to point out that Christ's humiliation here and on the Cross is the supreme instance of his passive obedience to temporal authority. But he proceeds to a discussion of the significance of the regalia of Christ and of Christian kings: the dignity of the purple Throne-robe (the purple also admitting a "metaphoricall allusion to the blood of Christ that was shed for us"), the responsibility of the Sceptre (that "pastorall rod"), and the cares of the Crown.[21] For Charles in 1648, waiting for the soldiers to summon him to his trial at Westminster Hall, there must have been some pungency in James' dwelling on the fact that the scene took place in the "*Praetorium*, which was the common *Hall*, like our *Westminster* Hall, and serued for administration of Iustice, as the place of greatest resort,"[22] and that it was at the hands of the soldiers that Christ's kingship was most vilely mocked (and yet at the same time most truly asserted on Christ's own part). Likewise, he would have endorsed the King's sour remark that the soldiers who bowed the knee before Christ in mockery at least knew better than "our foolish superstitious *Puritanes*" who were ignorant of the civility of the knee before God or King. (At Charles' own trial they would neither bow nor doff their hats.)

Lest King James be too easily dismissed as the amiable dunce, it is worthwhile to point out that his insistence that it is in the Passiontide narrative that Christ's kingly attributes are chiefly vindicated is neither eccentric nor unduly partisan. Not James, but the author of *Paradise Regained* is the innovator here. Even aside from the weight of traditional exegesis, there is the evidence of the gospels themselves which constantly allude in the Passiontide narrative to the oracles about the Suffering Servant/Shepherd/ King concentrated in Zechariah, Deutero-Isaiah and the Davidic (i.e., royal) Psalms. Indeed, it would be difficult to account otherwise for the sequence of events from Palm Sunday (when the people cried, "Hosanna to the Son of David") through the Passion and into the Resurrection on Easter Sunday of the King who had conquered Death. Moreover, even without the benefit of *The Golden Bough* and the Babylonian kingship rituals, it would have been possible for the seventeenth century, knowing of Oedipus and Pentheus, to appreciate that the *agon* and passion of the King was a mystery to which the Gentiles also had been given access. In the

Biblical tradition, however, with its strong emphasis on genealogy, the kingship of the sacred victim is grounded in the principle of legitimacy, in a manner altogether reassuring to the Stuart apologist. Christ is the cosmic king in his spiritual and divine nature, but he is the King of the Jews in his physical and human nature because he is the legitimate heir of David, as Herod the usurper is not. In view of the Messianic oracles, especially those of the Suffering Servant, Christ's humility and legitimacy are interdependent proofs, as James explains. But Christ had not always been so humiliated— he had "ever admixed glances of glory, in the midst of the greatest humilitie," and when the scourge lay in his own hands he had proved that he could wield it against the moneychangers who defiled the temple.

One supposes that these recognitions, which made King James' head hammer, would prove equally striking to King Charles when, following his father's example, he in turn came to meditate upon the texts. He had many months, while preparing the *Eikon Basilike* and his own heart, to ponder the coincidences between his own trial and Christ's. Not the least coincidence was that he too would stand before the judges, the soldiers and the people, as the legitimate and humiliated king who, having used his royal prerogative in an abortive attempt to cleanse the Church of what he saw as Puritan defilements and punish the mercenary sequestrators of Church property, was now arraigned by those same groups which he had offended. Having hazarded the security of his kingdoms and his life upon the issue of Church order, Charles is likely to have found consolation in the New Testament assertion that Christ's humiliation and death were the means found in God's economy to effect the true cleansing of the temple; for the sacrificial blood of Christ had become the foundation of the Church.

The execution of Charles was attended by "providences" that were as astonishing to the royalists as the "providences" attending Oliver Cromwell's career were to the New Model Army. Through no one's plan (unless it was God's!) there was business to despatch in Parliament that held up the execution, and so it was not until three o'clock in the afternoon—the ninth hour—that Charles on the scaffold gave up the ghost. Moreover, since Charles could not recognize the jurisdiction of the regicide court, he had not entered his plea against the charges, and thus, like Jesus at his trial and like Isaiah's Suffering Servant, he had "opened not his mouth, as a lamb to the slaughter, and as a sheep before her shearers is dumb."

The effect of such providences, however, rested upon a more comprehensive analogy that was apparent in the 1640s between the salvation-history of England and of Israel. In that decade, England, distressed by Civil War, appeared to be as alienated from God as ancient Israel had been in the days when Ephraim was at war with Judah. At that time the Yahwistic prophets had inevitably proclaimed that the way to reconciliation was to put away the idols and to make a sacrifice unto God. In England in the 1640s, there was profound disagreement as to what constituted the idols, for each side was in a position of accusing the other of substituting Diana of Ephesus for the True Church, whether from misdevotion or a greed for Church lands. Still there was a consensus that unless the idolatry were rooted out and the sacrifice offered, God would continue in his wrath. But the notion of sacrifice in the Old Testament was superseded by the New Testament thesis that only Christ had been able to offer the full sacrifice of reconciliation, by sacrificing himself; and that Israel, incorrigible to the last, had killed the One whom God had sent to save her.

Consider a sermon preached on the Fast-day in December 1642, by one John Shawe,[23] who identifies himself as a pastor of Rotterham and a "Roundhead," and his Yorkshire congregation as partisans of Parliament hot to turn the militia against the "malignant party." His texts are those which urge repentance, e.g., "But to this man will I looke, even to him that is poore and of a contrite spirit, and trembleth at my Word" (Is. 66:2), and he preaches to such effect that "the watery eyes, attentive eares and tongues of many" beg him to publish his sermon to the nation. Shawe's analysis of England's woes brings him of course to the sins she must repent, and particularly the sin of idolatry for, as he notes, "Never was misery upon the *Jewes* but idolatry was one or the onely Cause; or as the *Jewes* spake in every calamity there was something of the golden Calfe." Shawe himself upholds the tradition of Foxe and the Marian martyrs and he is anxious now lest the Reformation be undone through hardness of heart. "In the beginning of this Parliament how did the beautiful *Zerah* of mercy and reformation, *Gen.* 38. 28,29,30. Breake out with a pretious hand, full of blessings." But now there is civil war, division and bloodshed, attributable chiefly to "Grievous Idolatry, a dividing sinne." "What caused God to divide the Kingdome of *Israel* into two Kingdomes twixt *Solomon* his Sonne and servant, but because *Solomon* divided Gods worship twixt God and idolls? See 1 *Kings* 11. 6,7,8,11. Oh that we should suffer those *Canaanites* and *Perizzites*, of whom God hath so by fire and water warned us, still to prick in our sides, and themselves to be snares to us. Iudge. 2. 3." From Shawe's point of view the Canaanites and Perizzites who were to be purged were presumably the Laudians, yet he was still so far from thinking of Charles himself as a snare to Israel that he cites as an indication of the gravity of England's situation that even "his sacred Majesties person is in danger, the breath of our nostrills &c. Lam. 4. 20."[24] Let the nation repent and offer unto God the Grand Sacrifice of a Broken Heart!

A similar thesis, but with the opposite application, is to be found in a sermon preached before the members of the Royalist House of Commons at Oxford by the Bishop of Downe,[25] who took as his text the verse from Luke 19:41-42: "And when he was come neere, he beheld the City and wept over it, Saying: if thou hadst knowne, even thou, at least in this thy day the things which belong unto thy peace." The things which belong unto peace include, again, national self-examination for sins, among which the Bishop is puritanical enough to include "sabbath-breaking," masques and stage-plays. In all her sins, England surpasses ancient Israel, but particularly, in her reenactment and aggravation of Jeroboam's rebellion and idolatry. "We have a new Rebellion, such as was not knowne unto Gods people, and cannot be parallel'd amongst the heathen: we have got a new Covenant to strengthen that Rebellion; two new Idols set up, like *Jeroboams* Calues to draw away the people from the house of *David*, but that the one is inconsistent with the other; the Presbytery of *Geneva*, and the independence of *New England*; and we haue almost as many new Religions as there were gods amongst the heathen." The Bishop too calls upon England to put away her idols and to offer the sacrifice which will restore the defiled land and the temple as in the days of Judas Maccabeus; but now it must be the sacrifice of a broken and contrite heart which God will not despise. Nevertheless, he says, "I know there is a sacrifice intended; but it is such as will make no atonement. Many divelish politicians would now make a sacrifice of the Church; they call it a Reformation of Religion, but it will prove the destruction of it." Against such reformers he quotes their own Cartwright: *"Whilest they beare us speake against Bishops and Cathedrall Churches* (saith the author of the *Ecclesiasticall discipline*) *it tickleth their eares, looking for the prey they had before of Monasteries; Yea, they have in their hearts devoured already the Churches inheritance. . . . They could be content to crucifie Christ, so they might have his garments."*[26] The Bishop's fears were to be realized beyond his worst imaginings when, in 1649, the idolaters, not content to devour the Church would, according to his terms, turn to devour the king also, "so they might have his garments" and his sovereignty.

The most elaborate series of parallels and proofs was drawn up by the Bishop of Rochester in a sermon given on Quinquagesima Sunday within a few days of Charles' death.[27] He chose his text from the gospel appointed for that Sunday which, by a coincidence men did not fail to remark, was a portion of the Passiontide narrative. In the circumstances, one can understand why the Bishop at times sounds overwrought. Interestingly, he describes what has taken place in England as a "complete tragedy," comprising three Acts: the Betrayal, the Mocking and the Killing of the King. What he has in mind goes beyond Marvell's reference to Charles as the "Royal Actor" adorning his "Tragick Scaffold," for the Bishop assumes that the original of this tragedy is the Passion and Crucifixion of the *Christos*. In view of what is known about the ritual derivation of drama in ancient Greece and in the Christian Middle Ages, his instinct appears to be sound.

The protagonist of the Passion Play is one "*Ch:*", the rightful king of Israel/England whom his ungrateful subjects condemn to death. He is confronted by an unholy alliance of the Elders of the Jews, the lawyers, the scribes and Pharisees, and the occupying military power. These are readily recognizable in their English counterparts: the Elders (*Presbyteroi* in the Greek text) being the Presbyterians with their Sanhedrin, the Westminster Assembly; the lawyers being that group represented by John Bradshaw and John Cook; and the scribes and Pharisees, the engineers of the regicide, being the pamphleteering Independents. As for this last group, the Bishop points out that the Hebrew word "pharisee" translates very nearly into the English "sectary"; and that the Independents had inherited the peculiar vices of the Pharisees in that they pretended "to perfect understanding and frequent use of the Scriptures" only to pervert them to ungodly uses, and "they held, and made the world believe, that themselves and such as they, were the onely Saints to be saved." In the Bishop's Passion Play there is no doubt but that John Milton is cast among the scribes and Pharisees, especially as he remarks that it was among the Pharisees that Jesus encountered a notoriously easy doctrine of divorce.

There is even a parallel for the English Papists, though here the Bishop's anxiety to do justice to an abused group overwhelms the New Testament parallel: the Samaritans, he says, "were to the Jews as Papists to Protestants, and branded by the Jewes as inhumane and bloudy men: and though *Ch:* the King did all he possible could for the Jewes, and nothing at all for the Samaritans more than to pity them, and not suffer them to be destroyed, when some of his Disciples (like fiery zealots) desired it: yet these would not joyne in the bloudy act with the more seeming holy Professors, but shall at last rise up and condemne them"[28]

The original Betrayal, for the Bishop, was the Solemn League and Covenant; in Parliament's demand for control of the King's militia ("the reed for a sceptre") and in its resolution of "No more addresses" he saw the Mockery. Now it had come to the Killing. As the Jews on Palm Sunday had sung "Hosanna" and on Good Friday, "Crucify him," so Charles' subjects had cried at first, "God Save the King," and now, "Justice," meaning "Blood." The *Presbyteroi* of the Parliament had begun the conspiracy. They "were deep in the first plotting & carrying on this Treason; and were as chief instrumentall meanes in bringing *Ch:* the King to his end; though towards the end, or last act of the Tragedy (his condemnation and execution) for feare or policy they appeared not."[29] As the Sanhedrin had been swayed by the Pharisaical faction and had invoked the military power of Rome, so the Presbyterians had been unnerved by the Independents and had given the business over to the Army.

As for the charges brought against "*Ch:* the King," he was accused of blasphemy and violation of the Law of Moses, whereas in fact he had come "not to destroy but to fulfil the Law," and his accusers were themselves the chief offenders. The parallel was not lost upon those who sympathized with the legal antiquarianism of Charles' and Laud's methods in their attempt to restore the ancient Church and found the new jurisdiction of the Commons, on the other hand, repugnant to the law. More specifically, "*Ch:* the King" had been accused of sabbath-breaking, and this charge suggested a certain identity of those who were offended by Jesus' disciples eating in the cornfield and by the Stuarts' authorization of the Book of Sports.[30]

But the Bishop gets his best effect from the Stuart legitimacy. He invokes the parable of the Vineyard which had long been recognized as the symbol for Israel and the Church. In the parable, the conspirators, having killed the Lord's servants, are carried by their logic to the decision to kill the Heir also, for then, they hope, there will be no one to avenge the robbery and no bar to their possession of the Vineyard, "which rather than *Ch:* the King would surrender up unto them, it being his rightful inheritance, and committed to his trust by God himselfe, he would rather suffer this ignominious death." And though the Heir was "tender and meek" and "forgave and prayed even for his Murderers; yet the guilt of their hate, malice and murder against him was so deep a staine that they could not, that they would not believe either; and therefore as their elder Brother *Cain*, they crying out, *Our sinnes are greater than he can forgive us*: can find no other way to save or secure

themselves but by his death." In this comment one can recognize
the unsympathetic interpretation of the argument used by Milton
and the regicides that if the leaders of the Army did not use their
present ascendancy to bring the King to trial and put the blood-
guilt for the war upon him, he would eventually find occasion
for putting it upon them. What the Jews cannot forgive in Jesus,
continues the Bishop, is that "he calls himself king," and they
complain that "he that is so, can be no friend to Caesar." Caesar
in the present instance presumably stands for the vaunted sovereignty of Parliament, which they say they honor. Such men, he
says, who reject their king as king, "will never serve and obey any
but either a Conquerour who holds them to it by dint of Sword,
or some tame Creature who will serve their turnes, and obey their
wills."[31]

Indeed, there are more dire consequences. As a judgment upon
Jerusalem for having killed the Lord's prophets and His Son, the
city was later conquered and razed by Titus the Roman. England
presumably could look to a similar fate, unless God were gracious.
Meanwhile, like Christ Himself, Charles the Martyr *"shall ascend,
and for an earthly ignominious Crowne, he shall receive an heavenly glorious one,"* and the tale of his Passion shall spread throughout the world.[32]

It would be a mistake, I think, to assume that the extravagances
of the interpretation invalidate the central thesis. The ordinary
Englishman would take both the Bishop and Milton with a grain
of salt, and conclude that Charles personally had been neither
Christ nor an idol, but simply an obstinate, pious, personally
virtuous and politically untalented king. On the political level it
was difficult to distinguish whether Charles or the opposition were
the more culpable for the continuation and the extremity of the
Civil War. The final death of Charles had, however, not only a
political but a heavily symbolic significance; and here, I suspect,
the Bishop had the better part of the argument over Milton. For
the regicides admitted that they saw Charles' death as a sacrifice
and appeared to approve the reasoning of Caiaphas that it was expedient that one man (in this case Charles Stuart) should die for
the people. But the development in the Biblical material of the
theme of sacrifice had shown that particular notion of sacrifice
to be primitive and "Judaic." Through the psalms and the prophetic
oracles the idea of the sacrifice of a human being—even an enemy
and a foreigner—had been transformed into the sacrifice of the
humble and contrite heart, as being the only sacrifice acceptable
to God. Finally, in the New Testament, it was the enemies of

Christ, the scribes and Pharisees, who maintained that primitive notion. The Christian, following Christ, sacrificed not someone or something else, but himself. Charles, it appeared, had understood this, and prepared himself sacrificially for death. By contrast, the regicides showed a singular crassness in citing the Old Testament parallels, which could turn against themselves. Thus, John Cook, the Solicitor for the Commonwealth at the trial, who published his self-justifying pamphlet of 1651 with the title: *Monarchy no Creature of Gods making: Wherein is proved . . . that the Execution of the late King was one of the fattest sacrifices that ever Queen Iustice had*, was fond of citing the famous deed of Joshua who had hanged thirty-one kings of the Canaanites in a day, as if he, John Cook, would have relished having thirty more kings to hang himself. He followed this with a question as to whether "those thirty one Kings which *Joshua* hanged up . . . were they not innocent, nay Saints in comparison of this man? Those that crucified Christ did it ignorantly, For had they known him, they had not crucified the Lord of Glory."[33] Many of his readers would have regarded this last as a thoroughly self-incriminating statement. Milton runs the same risk as Cook with his more cautious reference to the execution as a "most gratefull and well-pleasing Sacrifice."[34]

The deep gloom which, according to common testimony, settled over England at the time of the execution may be an indication of an inarticulate horror at having participated in a kind of reenactment of the Crucifixion. Horror is written through the confessionary verse of General Fairfax who, even though he had withdrawn from the trial, was implicated more than most:

> Oh let that day from time be blotted quite,
> And let belief of't in next age be waived.
> In deepest silence th'act concealed might,
> So that the Kingdom's credit might be saved.
> But if the Power Divine permitted this,
> His Will's the law and ours must acquiesce.[35]

To acquiesce in being placed alongside Pilate and the scribes and Pharisees would be, however, little consolation.

To arouse England to the misguidedness of her despair, Milton had various strategies of argument. He could "Canaanize" and heathenize the king and the *Eikon Basilike*, using the ethos of the Book of Judges which counted the destruction of the heathen enemy to the glory of God. Charles, the Christian king of England, was thus removed into the category of Nebuchadnezzar and the "brats of Babylon" who were to be thrown against the wall and for whom only a waverer in the faith would feel pity. This was the corollary of the political argument he had employed in the *Tenure* that the English king who was a tyrant had forfeited all obligation and loyalty on the part of his subjects since he had become as a foreigner: "no better then a Turk, a Sarasin, a Heathen."[36] He could also, for his Presbyterian audience, question the efficacy of a sacrificial death on the part of a man who had shown himself to be an unrepentant enemy of the presbytery, and therefore a foe of the Reformation and of Christ. Even on that point, however, the Presbyterians were apparently not altogether convinced.

Against the powerful persuasion of Charles' sacrifice, Milton had already, in *Areopagitica*, armed himself with his own myth of the strong and puissant nation rousing itself to action, overcoming all tyrannical and superstitious obstacles to the fulfillment of its purpose. While the royalist myth was tied to the Crucifixion, Milton's was as clearly tied to the Resurrection and the apocalyptic triumph of the saints. Visionary England and Milton, as the apologist for the regicide, were gathering up further pieces of the scattered Body of Truth/Osiris to bring it to its Epiphany. It was exasperating, then, that actual England, and even the Presbyterians of the Parliament, should perceive the act of beheading the King as a further rending of the Body of Truth and an enactment of another passion of Osiris. Let them mourn for their Thammuz or Osiris, says Milton. But he leaves unanswered the question as to the relationship between the passion of the heathen fertility god and the Passion of Christ. Only Christ's Resurrection was to the point. Later, however, after his experience of the Protectorate and the Restoration, the prophet-iconoclast would find it more difficult to affirm that Resurrection in England, being obliged to fall back from visual evidence to faith alone.

With the Restoration, the burden of carrying the pathos of the witness of Christ passed from the royalists back again to the sectaries. Even then, Milton refused to accept the authenticity of the pattern of the imitation of Christ in affliction unto death. The true "martyrdom" (i.e., witness) is that of Abdiel, the just one among many unjust, who rebukes the Devil to his face and returns to God to have his reward in "Well done, thou good and faithful servant." Israel's true judge and champion is the mighty iconoclast Samson, to whom the counsel of "patience" is for the most part a distraction. Since the Temple of the Established Church which Samson pulled down was indeed the Temple of Dagon, the house of idolatry, and not, as the Anglicans insisted, the Temple of the true God on Mount Zion,

woe unto the Israelites that they had since allowed the Temple to
be rebuilt!

In *Paradise Regained* Milton returned to the issue of defining
Christ's kingship in such a way as to leave no possibility of its being
identified in any way with the kingship and martyrdom of Charles
Stuart. Already in *Paradise Lost*, he had presented Christ as the
Victor in Heaven (whose victory follows not His Passion but his
mere absence from the stage until the Third Day); while in Michael's
prophecy of the history of God's world, the Crucifixion is presented
in a passage of mere legalistic exposition. In Milton's later poem, his
human Christ is one whose suffering consists chiefly of endurance;
when the storms of affliction wash over his head, the opportunity
for the sacrificial pathos of the *Eikon Basilike* is turned down with
the flat scorn of "Mee worse then wet thou find'st not." As Milton's
eighteenth-century commentators noted,[37] Milton had Paradise regained with minimal reference to the Crucifixion, the event which
in traditional exegesis had carried all the weight of the Atonement.
It was as if Milton's career as the iconoclast and the enemy of
sacramentalism had brought him to the point of rejecting not only
the *Eikon Basilike* but the Gospel of John.

Notes

1. The writer wishes to express her
gratitude to the Huntington Library
for a research grant in 1971 that enabled her to prepare this article. *Complete Prose Works,* ed. Don M. Wolfe
(New Haven and London, 1953-   ),
III, 339.

2. For Foxe's statement on the
papists' "idolatrous abuse" of the
Sacrament, see his summary "Of
Sacraments" in the section entitled
"The Primitive Church of Rome Com-
pared with the Latter Church of
Rome." The importance for Bale and
Foxe of the "Image of Both Churches"
(the title of Bale's Commentary on the
Book of Revelation) is described by
William Haller in *The Elect Nation:
The Meaning and Relevance of Foxe's
Book of Martyrs* (New York and

Evanston, 1963).

3. John Neville Figgis, *The Divine
Right of Kings,* Harper Torchbook
edition (New York and London, 1965).
First published 1896.

4. *Complete Prose,* III, 587.

5. For an illustration of "monarchical"
exegesis, see King James' *The Trew
Law of Free Monarchies* in the *Collected Works* (London, 1616), especially p. 196 where James quotes and comments on Samuel's warning in the
passage from 1 Samuel 8.

6. See, for example, Theophile James
Meek, *Hebrew Origins,* Harper Torchbook edition (New York and Evanston,
1960), p. 136 ff.

7. *Complete Prose,* III, 587.

8. John Cook, *Monarchy no Creature
of Gods making* (Waterford, Ireland,

Printed by Peter de Pienne, 1651), especially pp. 73 and 108. The summary given above of a "republican" exegesis fits Cook's thesis in this book as well as it does Milton's in the *Tenure*.

9. *The Trew Law of Free Monarchies* in *Collected Works*, pp. 194-95. James' subtitle is: "The Reciprocall and mutuall duetie betwixt a free King and his naturall Subiects."

10. Corinne Comstock Weston, "The Theory of Mixed Monarchy under Charles I and After," *English Historical Review*, 75, No. 296 (1960), 426-43.

11. William Riley Parker, *Milton: A Biography*(Oxford, 1968), I, 360-61.

12. *Complete Prose*, III, 360.

13. Bishop Burnet, *History of His Own Time* (London, 1724), I, 50-51.

14. C. V. Wedgwood, *A Coffin for King Charles* (New York, 1964), p. 208.

15. Ibid., p. 222.

16. See Francis F. Madan, "A New Bibliography of the *Eikon Basilike*," Publications of the Oxford Bibliographical Society, New Series, III (Oxford, 1950), pp. 126-63. Also Philip A. Knachel, Introduction to *Eikon Basilike* (Ithaca, N.Y., 1966).

17. John Gauden, *The Religious and Loyal Protestation* (London, 1648/49).

18. John Donne, *Devotions, Together with Death's Duel* (Ann Arbor, 1959), pp. 3 and 161.

19. *Eikon Basilike*, ed. Philip A. Knachel, in Folger Documents of Tudor and Stuart Civilization (Ithaca, N.Y., 1966), pp. 147-48.

20. *A Paterne for a Kings Inauguration*, dedicatory epistle, *Collected Works*, pp. 602-05.

21. Ibid., pp. 607-14.

22. Ibid., p. 609.

23. John Shawe, *A Broken Heart, or the Grand Sacrifice*, As it was laid out in a sermon preached at St. Maries in Beverley. . . . See, among many similar sermons, John Conant, *The Woe and Weale of Gods People*, Displayed in a Sermon preached before the Honourable House of Commons at their late solemn Humiliation (London, 1643).

24. *A Broken Heart*, pp. 28-31.

25. [Bishop Bramhall of Downe], *Sermon at S. Mary's Oxford* (Oxford, Printed by Leonard Lichfield, 1643/44). See also William Stampe, *Sermon Preached before His Maiestie at Christchurch in Oxford* (Oxford, 1643).

26. *Sermon at S. Mary's Oxford*, pp. 27-32.

27. [Bishop John Warner of Rochester], *The Devilish Conspiracy, Hellish Treason, Heathenish Condemnation, and Damnable Murder, Committed and executed by the Iewes, against the Anointed of the Lord, Christ their King. . . .*(London, 1648/49).

28. *The Devilish Conspiracy*, pp. 1-10, and, for the reference to the Divorcers among the Pharisees, p. 19.

29. Ibid., p. 9.

30. Ibid., p. 18.

31. Ibid., pp. 21-23.

32. Ibid., p. 34.

33. John Cook, *King Charles His Case* (London, printed by Peter Cole for Giles Calvert, 1649), "To the Reader." The reference to Joshua's hanging the kings appears also in *Monarchy no Creature of Gods making*, p. 18.

34. Quoted by Wedgwood, p. 226.

35. *Complete Prose*, III, 596.

36. *Complete Prose*, III, 215.

37. See the article by Joseph Wittreich, Jr., "William Blake: Illustrator-Interpreter of *Paradise Regained*" in his *Calm of Mind* (Cleveland, Ohio, 1971), pp. 93-132.

Milton & Cromwell: 'A Short but Scandalous Night of Interruption'?

AUSTIN WOOLRYCH
University of Lancaster

Short of imagining Shakespeare as Queen Elizabeth's secretary of state, it is hard to conceive of a more striking conjunction of giants than that of Milton and Cromwell in the service of the English Commonwealth. What the Lord Protector thought about his Secretary for Foreign Tongues is not on record. He probably saw little of him, and he must have been quite unaware of the stature of his genius. But Milton wrote memorably about Cromwell, and his judgement underwent a drastic change over the years. From the sonnet of 1652 and the lofty panegyric in the *Second Defence of the English People* two years later, he moved to the complete rejection of the Protectorate that we find in the tracts of 1659-1660. He never criticized Cromwell in his lifetime or censured him by name after his death, but in the course of 1659 he identified himself completely with the Protector's republican enemies and endorsed their condemnation of rule by any single person whatsoever as an evil that every servant of the state should be required to abjure. He came in fact to regard Cromwell's assumption of the headship of the state as an aberration from which the Commonwealth needed to make a painful recovery. This essay will seek the clues to such an apparent change of allegiance, for it has an interest that transcends personalities. As well as raising basic questions concerning Milton's consistency, it bears upon his whole conception of civil and spiritual liberty.

Our examination of his attitude towards Cromwell can best begin with three closely interwoven events: his writing of *The Tenure of Kings and Magistrates* in January 1649, to justify the trial of Charles I; the establishment of the Commonwealth that inevitably ensued upon the king's execution; and Milton's appointment as Secretary for Foreign Tongues on March 13 following. Milton does not mention Cromwell either in *The Tenure* or in his next large prose work, *Eikonoklastes*; their subject matter and purpose give him no particular pretext for doing so. In *The Tenure*, however, his political convictions become more explicit than in his previous tracts. As several commentators have remarked,[1] it was inspired more by animus against the Presbyterians than by personal commitment to the governors and government of the nascent Commonwealth. Yet he did commit himself to them, in his vindication of "those Worthies which are the soule of that enterprize"[2] (*i.e.* the proceedings against the king), and in his exhortation to waverers to continue "adhering with all thir strength & assistance to the present Parlament & Army, in the glorious way wherin Justice and Victory hath set them; the only warrants through all ages, next under immediat Revelation, to exercise supream power."[3] His main argument, however, is about the justice of deposing tyrants rather than the iniquity of monarchy as such. He avoids any doctrinaire engagement to republican institutions, and in contending for the right of the people to choose and remove their governors he does not prescribe what form of government they should establish. Nevertheless he clearly affirms the superiority of republics, notably in the passage where he trusts that God will incline the people "to heark'n rather with erected minds to the voice of our Supreme Magistracy, calling us to liberty and the flourishing deeds of a reformed Common-wealth."[4] He hopes too that England's example will inspire other nations, where hereditary monarchy, *"though not illegal, or intolerable,* hangs over them as a Lordly scourge, not as a free government; and therefore to be abrogated."[5]

This is a qualified condemnation, applied here strictly to hereditary monarchy; it will not involve Milton in any real inconsistency when he comes to support Cromwell's Protectorate. He already has to accommodate the principle of popular sovereignty to the fact of rule by a minority, which he does by allowing that the people may be represented by those, "though in number less by many, in whom faction least hath prevailed above the Law of nature and right reason."[6] But monarchy, or any form of one-man rule, must have seemed a remote prospect early in 1649. Later in the same year he would declare that "It were a Nation miserable indeed, not worth the name of a Nation, but a race of Idiots, whose happiness and welfare depended upon one man."[7] After Pride's Purge had removed the members who persisted in negotiating with Charles I, Milton could assume that Parliament and army were in close accord. Both seemed pledged to a republican settlement; the officers' quarrel with the Rump lay far ahead, and Cromwell's elevation to the headship of the state farther still.

Here it is worth clarifying what Cromwell's place in the Commonwealth really was from 1649 to 1653, for it is commonly exaggerated. He was of course a member of Parliament, one out of well over 200 who retained their seats after Pride's Purge and sat in the House at one time or another under the Commonwealth, though the core of really active members was much smaller.[8] He served throughout on the Council of State, but that body was elected annually by the Parliament and strictly subordinated to it. It had forty other members besides Cromwell. He was lieutenant-general of the army, and still second in command to Fairfax. When Milton, at the climax of the Second Civil War in 1648, was moved to write a sonnet to England's deliverer from the new royalist threat, it was to Fairfax that he addressed it, even though that deliverance hung more critically on Cromwell's encounter with the Scottish army than on Fairfax's conclusion of the siege of Colchester. Only when Fairfax insisted on resigning his commission in June 1650, did Cromwell succeed him as commander-in-chief. It is sometimes assumed that because the Rump's authority depended upon the army, the army's most dynamic commander dominated the state. The Rump saw to it that this was not so. Cromwell in any case was away on campaign for most of the time from his departure for Ireland in August 1649, until after his final victory at Worcester in September 1651. During the first three critical years of the Commonwealth's existence his personal influence on politics was exceeded by that of men who sat at Westminster week in, week out, especially Sir Arthur Haslerig, Thomas Scot and Sir Henry Vane the younger. Even after Worcester he cannot be said to have dominated either Parliament or Council. Major issues were decided against his wishes: the long postponement of the Rump's dissolution, the Dutch war, the confiscation of royalists' estates—these are only examples.

If it is easy to exaggerate Cromwell's political role before 1653, it is easier still to exaggerate Milton's. Masson and others after him have certainly overstated it, but William Riley Parker has taken a just measure of it in his recent biography.[9] Milton gained his appointment and earned his salary mainly by his literary and polemical skill in defending the Commonwealth against the pens of its enemies, and to a government execrated abroad and widely hated at home, *The Tenure, Eikonoklastes* and the two great *Defences* were no mean services. His other duties were mainly occasional: casting formal state letters into elegant Latin, translating incoming diplomatic documents into English, acting as interpreter to foreign envoys at audiences and conferences, examining the papers of subversive pamphleteers and other suspects, and later licensing certain works (including the official newspaper) for the press. Some of these duties required him to attend meetings of the Council of State or its Committee for Foreign Affairs, but he did not share in their decision-making. Very possibly, the only occasions on which he sat in the same room with Cromwell were some Council meetings between his own appointment and the lieutenant-general's departure en route for Ireland four months later,[10] and again during the brief intermission between Cromwell's Irish and Scottish campaigns. By the time that Cromwell finally returned from the field in the autumn of 1651, Milton was all but totally blind, and his official tasks had thinned to a trickle.[11] Valuable as his services were, they were not those of a working politician, nor were they of a kind to confer much insight into the higher reaches of statecraft.

The earliest mention of Cromwell in Milton's writings occurs in the first pamphlet that he wrote to the order of the Council of State. It was commissioned only a fortnight after he was appointed, and his task was to expose the iniquity (in Parliament's eyes) of the articles of peace recently signed between the Marquis of Ormond, the king's Lord Lieutenant of Ireland, and the Roman Catholic Confederacy that then ruled that kingdom. Answering a contemptuous reference to Cromwell by Ormond, Milton affirms

> that *Cromwell* whom he couples with a name of scorne, hath done in a few yeares more eminent and remarkable Deeds whereon to *found* Nobility in his house, though it were wanting, and per-petuall Renown to posterity, then *Ormond* and all his Auncestors put together can shew from any record of thir *Irish* exploits, the widest scene of their glory.[12]

This was of course written before the butcheries at Drogheda and Wexford, but judging by his searing condemnation of the Irish rebels elsewhere in this tract Milton probably shared the common view that slaughtering such "a mixt Rabble, part Papists, part Fugitives, and part Savages"[13] was proper work for God's Englishmen. This is borne out by the one passing reference to Cromwell in *A Defence of the People of England*, written not long after the victorious general's return from Ireland, where Milton tells Salmasius

> I am well pleased that your people hate Cromwell, the brave leader of our army, for undertaking in the company of a joyful host of friends, followed by the good wishes of the people, and the prayers of all good men, the war in Ireland in full accordance with the will of God.[14]

Thus by February 1651, when *A Defence* was published, Milton had made two brief laudatory references to Cromwell—neither more nor less than the context demanded in the two officially commissioned pieces of polemics in which they occur. But in May 1652, he committed himself far more personally in Sonnet XVI, which addressed Cromwell as "our cheif of men." The opening octave pays him splendid homage for pursuing in all his victories the work of God, but as so often the essential message comes in the last six lines:

> yet much remaines
> To conquer still; peace hath her victories
> No less renownd then warr, new foes arise
> Threatning to bind our soules with secular chaines:
> Helpe us to save free Conscience from the paw
> Of hireling wolves whose Gospell is their maw.

This abhorrence of a "hireling" clergy runs through Milton's works from "Lycidas" onwards, and the threat "to bind our soules with secular chaines" had animated his diatribe against the Presbyterians in *The Tenure*. Now that threat had arisen again in different form, as he made clear in the extended title that he originally gave to this sonnet, and then deleted: "On the proposalls of certaine ministers at the Committee for Propagation of the Gospell." This committee of the Rump was busy over the vexed question of an ecclesiastical settlement to replace the abortive Presbyterian establishment of the late 1640s, and the group of ministers to whom Milton refers had sought to define certain fundamentals of the Christian faith, which they hoped that Parliament would accept as the criterion of what should or should not be tolerated.[15] But to Milton it was obnoxious that any agency of the state should either uphold an established clergy or set bounds to the faith that a man might derive from his own sincere searching of the Scriptures. Only last January he had been called to account for licensing the notorious Racovian Catechism, a Socinian manifesto which was impounded by the Council of State and publicly burnt by order of Parliament. Milton was examined both by the Council and by a parliamentary committee, and although the government did not further harass its triumphant defender against Salmasius it employed him no more as a licenser.[16]

The sonnet to Cromwell needs to be read with its twin, which Milton addressed to Sir Henry Vane the younger a few weeks later. Of all the politicians of the Rump, Vane was most to be counted upon to resist any encroachment by the state upon the realm of free conscience. This Milton acknowledges in the lines

> besides to know
> Both spirituall powre and civill, what each meanes
> What severs each thou'hast learnt, which few have don.

> The bounds of either sword to thee wee ow.

Here is an adumbration of *A Treatise of Civil Power*, just as the close of the Cromwell sonnet looks forward to its companion-tract, *The Likeliest Means*. Both sonnets express the same concern, and both mark Milton's growing misgivings as he finds his masters seriously divided over those questions of ecclesiastical policy that always lay closest to his heart. Through them he appeals to the two most eminent champions of religious liberty among England's governors to exert themselves against the new forcers of conscience that are raising their heads under the Commonwealth. He could not yet know that Cromwell's conception of "the bounds of either sword" would be very different from his own and Vane's, nor that the final rupture between his two heroes lay less than a year ahead.

We do not know how he reacted at the time to the final stages of the quarrel between army and Parliament, which culminated in Cromwell's expulsion of the Rump on April 20, 1653, or to the ensuing brief experiment of the Nominated or Barebone's Parliament. But he lost no time in committing himself publicly and ardently to Cromwell's Protectorate. His *Second Defence of the English People* was published towards the end of May 1654, a mere five months after the Lord General had become Lord Protector. Its great eulogy of Cromwell is cast largely in narrative form, and it rides boldly over the steps that had brought him to the headship of the State. But the brevity with which it treats the breaking of the Rump may suggest a passing touch of doubt:

> Daily you toiled in Parliament, that the treaty made with the enemy might be honored, or that decrees in the interest of the State might at once be passed. When you saw delays being contrived and every man more attentive to his private interest than to that of the state, when you saw the people complaining that they had been deluded of their hopes and circumvented by the power of the few, you put an end to the domination of these few men, since they, although so often warned, had refused to do so.[17]

Milton's dismissal of Barebone's Parliament is even briefer, and incidentally even less accurate.[18] He does not mention that that assembly finally broke over issues about which he felt deeply, namely the retention of an established church and a publicly maintained ministry, nor that those who sought like him to abolish both were frustrated by the conservative majority's carefully planned resignation of authority into Cromwell's hands. One might indeed have expected him to side with the losers, if spiritual liberty in his own special sense was all that he cared about. But it was not, and nearly six years later he would condemn that "pretending to a fifth monarchie of the saints" which had been the aim of the extremist minority in Barebone's Parliament.[19] He probably shared the general dismay at the disrepute that their excesses were bringing upon the Commonwealth.

One must remember the purpose for which *A Second Defence* was written. It was not primarily an attempt to justify the new Protectoral constitution to the people of England. That task had been committed to Marchamont Needham, whose *True State of the Case of the Commonwealth,* published in the previous February,[20] had gone fully into the reasons for the ejection of the Rump and the failure of Barebone's Parliament. Milton was writing not so much for home consumption as for a European audience, as when he had replied to Salmasius. He was rebutting the charges against the Commonwealth and himself in *Regii Sanguinis Clamor ad Coelum,* a violently royalist tract by an Anglican clergyman called Peter du Moulin, though Milton unfortunately attributed it to Alexander More, who had merely arranged its publication at the Hague.[21] He was defending the regicide regime once more against its international enemies, and it was not an occasion for washing its dirty linen in public.

Obviously the recent change of government, no less than du Moulin's flood of personal abuse, demanded a special vindication of Cromwell. "For it is to the interest not only of the state," writes Milton, "but of myself as well (since I have been so deeply involved in the same slanderous accusations) to show to all peoples and all ages, so far as I can, how supremely excellent he is, how worthy of all praise."[22] And through fifteen pages of the Latin first edition the praise flows unstinted, pausing only to give Fairfax his share of the glory for Parliament's victories in the Civil Wars. It is a tremendous panegyric, and it leaves no room to doubt that Milton strongly and sincerely admired Cromwell at this time. Nor did he balk at justifying rule by a single person:

Cromwell, we are deserted! You alone remain. On you has fallen the whole burden of our affairs. On you alone they depend. In unison we acknowledge your unexcelled virtue. No one protests save such as seek equal honours, though inferior themselves, or begrudge the honors assigned to one more worthy, or do not understand that there is nothing in human society more pleasing to God, or more agreeable to reason, nothing in the state more just, nothing more expedient, than the rule of the man most fit to rule. All know you to be that man, Cromwell![23]

Other apologists such as Needham—and indeed Cromwell himself—
would stress the checks and balances whereby the Instrument of
Government, the new written constitution, restrained the Protector's
personal authority. But not Milton; his only hint at limitations
comes where he praises Cromwell for spurning the name of king
and taking a title "very like that of father of your country."[24]

Yet for all its eloquence this whole eulogy has an air of imperson-
ality. Milton truly admires Cromwell, but from a certain distance.
He is saluting the saviour and upholder of an ideal cause rather than
an individualized human being, and the cause is what mainly concerns him, for he proceeds to define it with some care. The virtues
he ascribes to Cromwell are the conventional republican and Puritan
virtues; what he gives us is a literary celebration of an archetypal
hero rather than a spontaneous tribute to a man known and loved.
So far from portraying him warts and all he leaves him somewhat
faceless. This is perhaps what we should expect, bearing in mind
that *A Second Defence* is an exercise, at the highest level, in public
rhetoric. Yet it is also more than that, and nothing inhibits Milton
from including warmly personal touches in some of the other tributes
that he pays in this work: to Bradshaw, for instance, who "at home
. . . is hospitable and generous according to his means, the most
faithful of friends and the most worthy of trust in every kind of
fortune";[25] or Fleetwood, "whom I know to have shown the same
civility, gentleness, and courtesy from your earliest days in the army
even to those military commands which you now hold";[26] and most
strikingly Overton, "who for many years [has] been linked to me
with a more than fraternal harmony, by reason of the likeness of
our tastes and the sweetness of your disposition."[27] There is, as we
have seen, every reason to suppose that Milton did not know Cromwell nearly as personally as he knew Bradshaw and Overton. Thus
when he would come to repudiate the Protectorate he would not
be casting aside a fallen idol; his breach would be with the policies
of a government rather than with the memory of a man, though
inevitably that memory would suffer too.

A Second Defence contains two strong clues that he felt certain
reservations in committing himself to the Protectoral regime, even
from its inception. One is in the men whom he singles out for praise
in company with Cromwell, the other in the long exhortation that
he addresses to the Protector himself.

The names that he chose to celebrate alongside Cromwell's have
interested and puzzled a number of scholars.[28] The most significant
is that of John Bradshaw. Since Milton had to justify the proceedings against the king once more and Bradshaw had presided over the

High Court of Justice, there was good rhetorical reason for emphasizing his probity, dignity and humanity, especially as du Moulin had called him "an utterly unknown and insolent rascal." But that does not sufficiently explain the warmth and length of Milton's tribute —three glowing pages of print in the first edition, far more than he accorded to anyone else except Cromwell.[29] He cannot have been unaware that Bradshaw had been an opponent of Cromwell's ever since the expulsion of the Rump, if not earlier. After clearing the House, Cromwell had gone to the Council of State that same afternoon and told it that its authority too was at an end. "Sir," Bradshaw had boldly answered, "we have heard what you did at the House in the morning, and before many hours all England will hear it: but, Sir, you are mistaken to think that the Parliament is dissolved; for no power under heaven can dissolve them but themselves; therefore take you notice of that."[30] Milton was clearly not prepared to jettison all his old heroes, however ill they stood with the new government. Vane, however, he did omit; Cromwell's denunciation of him before the House in that famous last session had been so notorious, and Vane's subsequent disaffection so marked, that to have praised him openly would have aligned Milton with the opponents of the government, to an extent no doubt beyond his own wishes and his masters' tolerance. But he did rather curiously name Bulstrode Whitelocke, who had always been a monarchist in principle and had also come under Cromwell's lash at the breaking of the Rump,[31] though he would remain in the service of the Protectorate throughout its duration.

The other significant figure in this gallery of heroes is Colonel Robert Overton. He had never been as close to Cromwell or to the centre of politics as the others whom Milton names, and one senses something more than the poet's obviously warm personal friendship behind the special prominence and enthusiasm with which he is saluted. He was indeed under a cloud when *A Second Defence* appeared. His case was different from Bradshaw's, however, for whereas Bradshaw had finally broken with Cromwell over the expulsion of the Rump, Overton had warmly applauded that deed. He was a Fifth Monarchist, and his misgivings arose only when Cromwell parted company with the saints in Barebone's Parliament and set up as Protector. Cromwell eventually saw him and questioned him about his fidelity. Overton then promised to let Cromwell know when he could serve him no longer, "adding, that when I perceived his lordship did only design to set up himself, and not the good of those nations, I would not set one foot before another to serve him; to which he replied, thou wert a knave if thou wouldst."[32] We know from Marvell's letter to Milton on June 2, 1654, that this interview, or at any rate its outcome, was still pending when *A Second Defence* was published.[33] Whether Milton wrote his encomium to his old friend knowing that his future was about to be decided we can only guess, but Masson was probably right in surmising that he conspicuously honoured both Bradshaw and Overton as a hint to Cromwell that these were men to be reconciled if humanly possible.[34] Overton was in fact not yet irreconcilable, and he shortly returned to Scotland to resume his command. It was only in the following December that he was arrested on the discovery of a serious army plot in Scotland. He had probably done no worse than countenance some officers who were more disaffected than himself, but Cromwell with quite untypical severity kept him imprisoned without trial throughout his Protectorate.[35]

This harshness to a friend and hero doubtless influenced Milton's judgement of the regime, yet the famous pages of advice and exhortation to Cromwell are full of indications that his disillusion would stem mainly from less personal grounds. In these he seems to forget his royalist adversary; it is almost as if he is defining the criteria whereby the Protector's trusteeship will be judged. His first charge is to cherish liberty—to preserve that of others lest Cromwell himself should become a slave. Yet no revolutionary government escapes its burden of political prisoners, and the Protectorate was to be no exception. They would not be very many, but Vane as well as Overton would be among them. Milton, after praising Cromwell for spurning the royal title, adjures him "to flee from the pomp of wealth and power."[36] Yet Cromwell would hesitate long before refusing the crown that Parliament pressed upon him in 1657, and his Court would assume many of the trappings of monarchy. Next, Milton urges him to admit "those men whom you first cherished as comrades in your toils and dangers to the first share in your counsels."[37] Yet Bradshaw, Vane, and nearly all the republican leadership that Milton had known in the Council of State before his blindness would remain in opposition, while among Cromwell's old comrades-in-arms Harrison, Okey, Alured, Saunders, Overton, Ludlow, Lambert and Packer were all to lose their commissions for displaying various degrees of disaffection. Milton would observe sourly the large estates accumulated by the new "grandees" and courtiers; he would find the Protectorate departing always a little further from the plain republican virtues that these pages extol. Disliking a House of Lords as he did,[38] he would not welcome the establishment in 1657 of an "Other House" whose members would assume the style as well as some of the political functions of lords, nor would he think the better of

Cromwell for conferring a couple of hereditary peerages in addition to far more numerous baronetcies and knighthoods.[39]

There were other matters that he urged in *A Second Defence* which would not lack Cromwell's good will, limited though the actual achievement would be: the simplification and liberalization of the laws, for example, and better provision for educating the young whose talents and industry merited support at the public expense. But he would fail in his plea, reiterated from *Areopagitica,* for the right of "those who wish to engage in free inquiry to publish their findings without the private inspection of any petty magistrate."[40] In August 1655 three commissioners would be appointed to regulate printing, and from the following month Thurloe's permission would be required for the publishing of all news items.[41] From then until after the fall of the Protectorate only the two official newspapers would be allowed to appear. It is clear from Thomason's great pamphlet collection that the censorship was neither rigid nor inescapable, but to Milton it must have seemed a retrograde step.

The advice, however, to which he attached the greatest weight concerned the right relation between the civil and ecclesiastical powers. The issue of spiritual liberty had inspired his first published writings in English and prose and would prompt his last,[42] as well as filling many sections of his largest work of all, *De doctrina christiana.* In 1659 he would break a long silence as a polemical writer to publish *A Treatise of Civil Power* and *The Likeliest Means to Remove Hirelings*, in which he would amplify the points made so briefly in *A Second Defence*. There his counsel is concentrated into three sentences:

> Next, I would have you leave the church to the church and shrewdly relieve yourself and the government of half your burden (one that is at the same time completely alien to you), and not permit two powers, utterly diverse, the civil and the ecclesiastical, to make harlots of each other and while appearing to strengthen, by their mingled and spurious riches, actually to undermine and at length destroy each other. I would have you remove all power from the church (but power will never be absent so long as money, the poison of the church, the quinsy of truth, extorted by force even from those who are unwilling, remains the price of preaching the Gospel). I would have you drive from the temple the money-changers, who buy and sell, not doves, but the Dove, the Holy Spirit Himself.[43]

Here is where the Protectorate's policy was to cross his own most acutely, and where Cromwell would most disappoint him. The two men were in basic agreement over liberty of conscience for all who, as true Protestants, sought their faith in the Scriptures. Apart from papists and "prelatists," whose proscription Milton approved, the only religious groups that came under the Protectorate's restraint were Fifth Monarchists who aimed at the physical overthrow of the government to make way for a rule of the saints, Quakers who interrupted the worship of others or refused the customary respect to magistrates, a few eccentric sects whose antinomian beliefs led them to "practise licentiousness," and a handful of individuals who, like John Biddle and James Nayler, perpetrated what contemporaries regarded as outrageous blasphemies or heresies. Even towards such as these, Cromwell's attitude was notably more tolerant than that of his Parliaments or of most of the county magistrates.

But Milton was not content with toleration outside the established church; he wanted to abolish the established church itself. He wished the state to renounce virtually all authority over institutional religion, especially over the enforced maintenance of the clergy, and to leave each congregation to support its own pastor purely by voluntary offerings. Cromwell, however, while protecting the peaceable sects in the exercise of their faith, believed that a Christian commonwealth bore a sacred responsibility to ensure that each parish had a zealous preaching minister, so that none of its subjects need fail to hear the Word for lack of opportunity. This was a view strongly shared by the Independent divines like Thomas Goodwin, John Owen and Hugh Peter who stood closest to him. Consequently, a loose but effective establishment was erected during 1654 by ordinances of the Protector and Council. The first was passed in March, well before *A Second Defence* appeared; it empowered a central body of "commissioners for approbation of ministers," commonly called the Triers, to adjudge the fitness of candidates for livings who were presented by patrons or called by their parishioners. Another ordinance in August set up further bodies of commissioners in the counties, known as the Ejectors, to get rid of unfit or "scandalous" incumbents.[44] As for the established clergy's maintenance, the Instrument of Government envisaged a source more equitable and less taxing to tender consciences than tithes, but from September 1654, the legislative power passed from the Protector and Council to Parliament, and no alternative scheme was forthcoming. Cromwell was probably disappointed, but he stood firmly committed to the principle that the state should guarantee a settled income to the parochial clergy. "For my part," he told Parliament in 1656, "I should think I were very treacherous if I should take away tithes, till I see the Legislative power to settle maintenance to them another way.''[45] But Milton had denounced "the ignoble Hucsterage of pidling *Tithes*" in his first prose tract of all, back in 1641,[46] and he continued to regard any form of state-enforced stipend as corrupting to the clergy and intolerable to nonconformists, who had to contribute to ministrations that they could not in conscience accept.

For both men the issue was of course far broader than tithes. Cromwell stood closer to the main Protestant and Puritan tradition, which had always looked to a close partnership between a godly magistracy and a Gospel ministry to make each church a holy community and England an elect nation. He renounced the magistrate's coercive power over church discipline and conformity, but he clung to the early reformers' ideal of the state as nursing father to the churches. Milton, however, believed that the magistrate could do only harm to religion if he went beyond his proper concern, which was solely with the outward man; he went most of the way with the sectarian position, classically defined in Roger Williams's *Bloudy Tenent of Persecution* (1644), which wholly segregated secular authority from spiritual. Cromwell was also a traditional Protestant in believing that the clergy should have a guaranteed stipend, in order to possess the tools of learning and to practise charity, hospitality and an exemplary family life. Like Milton, he abhorred any kind of priestly pretensions and condemned the divisive distinction between clergy and laity,[47] but he did not draw Milton's conclusion that none who preached the Gospel should take any other reward than the apostles had done.

During the 1650s, after the failure of the unpurged Long Parliament's attempt to establish a single, exclusive, broadly Presbyterian national church, the main line of religious controversy shifted. It no longer lay primarily between Presbyterians and Independents. On the one side, moderate Puritans who shared a common doctrinal orthodoxy were drawing together under the Protectorate in defence of a publicly maintained clergy, whether they were nominally Presbyterians, Independents, non-separating congregationalists, or "meer Catholicks" like Richard Baxter. On the other stood the separatists and voluntaryists who like Milton opposed the state's claim to enforce any clerical maintenance or any "public profession" of the Christian faith.[48] Cromwell was more tolerant than most of the orthodox clergy, but basically he was on one side of this divide and Milton on the other.

From *A Second Defence* until after Cromwell's death on September 3, 1658, Milton gave scarcely any indications of what he thought of the Protector and his government. He made two passing references

to Cromwell, both of them neutral, in the only new prose writing
that he published during these years, the *Defence of Himself* of
August 1655;[49] but that unhappy work was concerned with other
things. He continued to draw his salary and to perform a few tasks
for the Council of State, but the gaps between the occasional state
letters that he composed were often months long, and he withdrew
his interests more and more from state affairs. In December 1657,
when a young foreign friend asked his help in securing employment
under George Downing, England's new minister in the Netherlands,
Milton excused himself, "partly because of my very few intimacies
with the men in favour, since I stay at home most of the time, and
by choice."[50] It would be rash to read into this withdrawal any
active discontent with the Protectorate, which he continued to serve
when needed. The fact is that he had other work in mind—work that
would tax his powers to the utmost. Soon after publishing *A Second
Defence*, he had written that "this unexpected contest with the
enemies of liberty snatched me away against my will when I was
intent on far different and much pleasanter studies."[51] Thereafter
the Cromwellian state was secure enough not to need his pen to defend it further. For a while he resumed work on his *History of Britain*,
but he soon became immersed in a vaster project, the great Latin
treatise *De doctrina christiana*. It was a colossal labor for a blind
man, especially if Parker's conjecture is right that it was completed
in draft between May 1655 and May 1658.[52] And as he toiled at it,
he must have been increasingly meditating the supreme exercise of
his genius, for by 1658 he was almost certainly at work on *Paradise
Lost*.

   Clearly one does not have to seek far for reasons why the fulfillment of his highest vocations took increasing precedence over his
now very modest official duties and his involvement in the state's
concerns. Yet he probably disliked what from his relative seclusion
he saw of the later trends of Cromwell's government. It was not
merely the rejection of his cherished ecclesiastical or rather anti-
ecclesiastical ideals, nor the further return towards old forms that
the Humble Petition and Advice effected in 1657, nor the gradual
approximation of the Protectorate to a limited monarchy in all but
name. In Cromwell's later years the political scene was dominated
by two contending factions: the military grandees headed by Lambert, Fleetwood and Desborough, through whom the Lord General
had been raised to Lord Protector, and a group of conservative
civilians who included men of royalist background like Lord Broghil
and Sir Charles Wolseley, together with such great lawyer-officials
as Bulstrode Whitelocke, John Glyn, John Lisle, Nathaniel Fiennes,

and the Long Parliament's trimming Speaker, William Lenthall.
These men opposed the regime of the major-generals, promoted the
offer of the crown, and stood generally for a revival of the old political nation's "natural" authority against military encroachment,
sectarian excesses and any lingering threats of social revolution.
Neither faction was to Milton's taste. He would show in his tracts
of 1659-60 that his allegiance increasingly reverted to the republican
leaders of the Rump, who led the opposition to the Protectorate in
both Cromwell's Parliaments during the brief spells when they were
allowed to take their seats. He probably sympathized with Sir Henry
Vane's attempt in *A Healing Question* (1656) to build a common
platform on which commonwealthsmen and sectaries could unite
in reasserting the "good old cause" against the usurping interest of
grandees and courtiers. He must have deplored Vane's consequent
imprisonment for over three months in Carisbrooke Castle.

He kept his peace (and his salary) when Richard Cromwell succeeded
to the Protectorate in September 1658 but there are indications that
his discontent deepened. There were obvious reasons why it should.
Oliver, however disenchanting his later years, had been a hero worthy
of his celebration, but what could he hope from this affable, easy-
going, not very intelligent young squire who had spent most of his
time sharing the traditional country sports and pastimes with his
royalist gentry neighbors and was a total stranger to the arduous
Puritan aspirations of the revolution's more heroic years? On the ecclesiastical front the orthodox Independent ministers gathered in con-
ference at the Savoy late in September, and swiftly produced a declaration of faith. Was this intended to be the confession that the Humble
Petition and Advice had announced, with various implications restrictive to religious radicals like Milton? In the political arena the old
rivalry remained between the military faction and the conservative
civilians, though now without Oliver's strong hand to restrain it and
with Richard's personal preferences strongly favoring the conservatives.
When a new Parliament was called in January 1659 the scene was set
for a major challenge by the old republicans, though the majority of
members were neither republicans nor Cromwellian "courtiers" but
unattached country gentry with markedly conservative and anti-
militarist leanings.

It was to this Parliament that he addressed in February *A Treatise
of Civil Power in Ecclesiastical Causes*. He dedicated it "to the Parlament of the Commonwealth of England," which he greeted as
"supream Councel,"[53] which may or may not have implied some
derogation of the Protector's authority. He went on to identify himself rather more explicitly with the republican opposition by recall-

ing how he had heard some of the members rightly distinguishing
the spheres of civil and ecclesiastic power "at a councel next in
autoritie to your own,"[54] by which he clearly meant the Council
of State of the Commonwealth, in the years before Cromwell became Protector. The preface as a whole is an appeal to Parliament
to reverse the ecclesiastical policies of the Protectorate.

If Milton really hoped that this Parliament would follow his advice, he was to be disappointed on two scores. In the first place the
republicans were outvoted on almost every issue, and in the second
they were divided among themselves on this particular one. Vane,
who largely shared Milton's desire to segregate spiritual from secular
authority, had a smaller following than Sir Arthur Haslerig, who
spoke in favor of "a moderate Presbytery."[55] The conservative
majority of the House must have dismayed him still more, if he
heard what they were proposing. They voted that the old peers who
had been faithful to Parliament should sit in the Other House, and a
few of them spoke openly in favor of monarchy.[56] They gave little
of their time to religious matters, but enough to show that their intentions were very far from Milton's wishes. Parliament, for instance,
published a declaration for a fast day throughout the three nations
on the grounds that God was venting his wrath upon Britain for the
many blasphemies and heresies that were rife, and for the failure of
the civil magistrate to punish them.[57] Shortly afterwards the Grand
Committee for Religion ordered that the confession of faith formulated by the Presbyterian-dominated Westminster Assembly in 1647-
48 should, except for its sections on church discipline, be "held forth
as the public profession of the nation."[58] These were only two of
several indications that so far from abdicating the temporal power's
control over religion, this Parliament intended to strengthen it.

Milton undoubtedly sympathized with much of the agitation against
both Parliament and Protectorate in the name "of the good old cause"
that mounted in press and pulpit between January and April 1659.
He can have felt no regret when the army commanders finally forced
Richard to dissolve Parliament on April 22, and he openly applauded,
as we shall see, when the broad mass of junior officers in turn forced
the commanders to restore the Rump on May 7 to the supreme
authority that it had enjoyed before its ejection six years earlier.[59]
That spelled the end of the Protectorate, and he never mourned it;
on the contrary, his last political writings would confirm that he
came to regard it as a grave aberration in the Commonwealth's development. His dissatisfaction had been increasing lately. At some
time in the spring he wrote a letter to Moses Wall which is only
known from Wall's reply.[60] Wall admits he had been uncertain

whether Milton's relation to the Court—"though I think a Commonwealth was more friendly to you than a Court"—had not clouded
his former light, but *A Treatise of Civil Power* has set his doubts
at rest. "You complaine," he continues, "of the Non-progresency
of the nation, and of its retrograde Motion of late, in Liberty and
Spiritual Truths." He urges Milton to fulfill his promise in *Of Civil
Power* and write a companion-treatise on the evil of hire in the
church.

That is what Milton next did. He did not publish *Considerations
Touching the Likeliest Means to Remove Hirelings* until August
1659 but there are signs that he dictated parts of it, perhaps considerable parts, not later than June.[61] His prefatory address reminds
the Rump of his defence of its actions against Salmasius in 1650,
though not of course of his strictures upon it in *A Second Defence*
four years later. Nevertheless he silently repudiates here the position
he had taken in 1654 and warmly reaffirms his allegiance to the
Commonwealth's first rulers. He hails the Rumpers as "authors,
assertors and now recoverers of our libertie,"[62] and as

> next under God, the authors and best patrons of religious and
> civil libertie, that ever these Ilands brought forth. The care and
> tuition of whose peace and safety, after a short but scandalous
> night of interruption, is now again by a new dawning of Gods
> miraculous providence among us, revolvd upon your shoulders.[63]

That "short but scandalous night of interruption" is a staggering
phrase, and it has troubled many commentators. Can Milton really
have meant to describe the Rump's six-year lapse of power as short?
Still more, could he condemn so harshly and abruptly the regime
that he had served throughout, whose wages he had taken, and
whose right to rule he had once defended so resplendently in the
universal language of learning? Could he cast such a slur on Cromwell's memory, and on the reputations of men still living whose names
he had celebrated as Cromwell's loyal counsellors? Masson thought it
"utterly impossible," and took the words to refer to the two weeks
between the army's forcible breaking of Richard's Parliament and
the restoration of regular government with the return of the Rump.[64]
It is a reading attractive to all who care for Milton's consistency and
integrity, and the present writer was for long inclined to accept it.
Yet it presents considerable difficulties. Milton had not previously
regarded the military violation of a Parliament as a thing scandalous
in itself, either when Colonel Pride shut out the working majority
of the House in December 1648 or when Cromwell expelled the rest
in 1653. Moreover the same army that broke Richard's Parliament

restored the Rump, for which he later that year expressly commended it.[65] How could he applaud the one act and impugn the other, its necessary precursor? For these and other reasons most later scholars, including Smart, Wolfe, Lewalski and Fixler, have taken the offensive phrase as describing the whole span of the Protectorate.[66]

Even more recently, William B. Hunter, Jr., has proposed a third interpretation which would shift Milton's opprobrium from the Protectorate as a whole to Richard's eight-month tenure of the Protector's office.[67] This bears so closely on Milton's retrospective opinion of Oliver and on his whole consistency as a political writer that it is worth examining in some detail. Hunter's interesting hypothesis, which he presents with due caution, can be summarized as follows. Soon after the Humble Petition and Advice empowered him to name his own successor, Cromwell nominated his son-in-law Fleetwood in a paper which he sealed and kept to himself, divulging its contents to no one. When he sent for this paper from his deathbed, however, it could not be found, and through certain machinations which we must examine further, Richard became the unwitting usurper of the Protector's office. Milton somehow came to know of this, probably from Fleetwood himself, and his dark words in *The Likeliest Means* express his condemnation of an act of usurpation. Hunter rests his case to a considerable extent on a closely argued article by E. Malcolm Hause which reopened the whole question of Richard's nomination and concluded that Fleetwood was defrauded of the Protectorship by the Secretary of State, John Thurloe, and others.[68]

Hause's and Hunter's contributions together raise a series of questions which we must consider in turn. How trustworthy is the evidence that Cromwell at one time designated Fleetwood as his successor? Is it likely that Fleetwood remained his choice to the end, or did he indeed nominate Richard on his deathbed? Did the secret in that lost paper leak out, or were at least rumours current in 1658-59 that Fleetwood had been fraudulently ousted? How close was Milton to the deepest secrets of state, and how intimate was he with Fleetwood? Finally, did his dissatisfaction with the Protectorate date from Richard's accession or did it extend further back into Oliver's rule?

We can begin by agreeing with Hause that there are grave dubieties and discrepancies in the evidence concerning Richard's nomination. Some of them are recognized in the standard histories by Firth and Godfrey Davies,[69] though neither probe them as closely as Hause. We can accept too that Cromwell had left a sealed paper concerning his successor at Whitehall, for this rests on the strictly contemporary testimony of Thurloe himself.[70] But was Thurloe truthful in saying that it could not be found, and that its contents were known only to Cromwell?

The first suggestion that it contained Fleetwood's name was published in 1663 by George Bate, a physician who attended Cromwell in his last illness. Bate does not claim to know what was in the lost paper, and he describes quite circumstantially how Cromwell, when asked by his privy councillors if he named Richard as his successor, assented with a nod.[71] Some pages later, however, after describing Cromwell's funeral on November 23, he says that certain *"Democratici"* repaired to Fleetwood's house and hinted that the office of Protector belonged by right to Fleetwood, he having been designated in Cromwell's last will, made when he was *compos mentis*; but that Richard had been surreptitiously substituted by the craft of some of the Council, when his father had lost his senses.[72] Bate pronounces no judgement on these allegations, and his story is incredible if *"Democratici"* means the republican politicians who led the opposition in Richard's Parliament of January-April 1659 as his translator of 1685 suggests.[73] Far from courting Fleetwood as alternative leader to Richard, as Bate goes on to say they did, the republicans wanted no truck with any "single person" as head of state, and when the army leaders attempted a *rapprochement* with them towards the end of March 1659 their leaders (Ludlow excepted) declined even to meet them at Wallingford House, Fleetwood's London residence.[74]

The next version to be published of an alleged nomination of Fleetwood differs very widely from Bate's. This first appeared in 1665, in the continuation of Sir Richard Baker's *Chronicle of the Kings of England* by Milton's nephew Edward Phillips. The one point of agreement is that Cromwell really did nominate Richard, though Phillips says he did so twice: first on Tuesday, August 31, to Thurloe and Thomas Goodwin, and again on Thursday, September 2, in the further presence of Fiennes, Whalley and Goffe. An hour after Cromwell died on the 3rd, so Phillips goes on, certain privy councillors who had been leading promoters of the Humble Petition and Advice met together and received Thurloe's account of these two declarations. Thurloe then told them that "long before his death" Cromwell had designated Fleetwood as his successor, in a document that could not be found. Thereupon two of them went at once to Fleetwood and Desborough, told them frankly of this paper as well as the verbal nominations of Richard, and obtained Fleetwood's solemn promise to abide by Richard's succession even if the paper naming himself should be found. Only after this did the full Privy Council meet and accept the testimony of the five witnesses to Cromwell's last wishes.[75]

This is all very circumstantial, but it bristles with difficulties. Postponing for the moment that earlier nomination on the Tuesday, for which Phillips is the sole source, the main stumbling block is his state-

ment, again supported by no other evidence, that Thurloe told a group
of privy councillors that the lost paper contained Fleetwood's name.
Five days earlier he had written to Henry Cromwell that its contents
were known only to Oliver himself.[76] Why should he tell different
stories to Henry and to these councillors, who as the closest supporters
of the house of Cromwell were unlikely to keep anything from the
new Protector's brother? The question most relevant to Hunter's
thesis, however, is whether an earlier nomination of Fleetwood was
known about or believed in when Milton wrote *The Likeliest Means.*
The indications are that it was not. The Privy Council became bitterly
divided during Richard's brief rule between his own adherents and
the Wallingford House or pro-military faction, and it is scarcely
credible that Fleetwood, in company with about ten others,[77] knew
he had once been Protector-designate without a single rumor leaking
into the abundant records of the years 1658-59 until well after the
Restoration, when bogus "state secrets" about the late troubles
sprouted like mushrooms. It is true, as Hause recounts,[78] that the
republicans cast doubts on Richard's nomination in Parliament during February 1659 but they were then exploiting every possible pretext for assailing the Protectoral constitution, and they had quite
sufficient grounds for this particular tactic in the absence of a written
instrument, the paucity of witnesses, and the state of Cromwell's
consciousness in his last days. They never suggested that Cromwell
had named anyone else, and Ludlow, who was one of them, records
only a general uncertainty over the whole affair.[79] Phillips, of course,
always needs to be used with great caution. His main informant was
Monck's brother-in-law Thomas Clarges, who had some standing as
agent for the Irish and Scottish armies, though his modest place in
the corridors of power was more likely to enable him to know who
came and went during and after Cromwell's last days than what was
spoken in their secret counsels. We can really discount any notion
that Phillips learned his "secrets" from his uncle. It is strange how
assumptions that Milton remained in close contact with the men
at the center of power persist, in the face of his own denials[80] and
the silence of the state papers.

The only other source of the Fleetwood story with any element
of contemporary authority is a memoir of Roger Boyle, Earl of
Orrery, written by his chaplain Thomas Morrice at a date not earlier
than 1691.[81] This is very late and Morrice is a far from inspiring
chronicler, but Orrery as Lord Broghil had been a close adviser of
both Oliver and Richard, though never a privy councillor. Morrice's
tidbit is that one of Oliver's daughters purloined the document
nominating Fleetwood and burned it.[82]

And yet dubious though the evidence is, it is not inherently implausible that Cromwell contemplated Fleetwood as his successor in 1657. He had a warm personal affection for the man, who stood next to himself in the army hierarchy and had married his daughter Bridget. There had been a report in 1656 that he was thinking of making Fleetwood general in his stead,[83] and when the French ambassador Bordeaux reported on the succession prospects in October 1657 he wrote of Fleetwood as "nearest the first place whether one considers his age, his employment, his service and the inclination of the militia, especially of the Anabaptists, of whose doctrine he professes to approve."[84] Cromwell may well have reckoned that the man who could best control the army would stand the fairest chance of surviving, for it was in fact the sectarian junior officers who eventually played the main part in overthrowing his son. If Fleetwood was his original choice, it would explain why he was so slow to give Richard any employments that would prepare him for the tight-rope of the Protector's office.

Yet if he did first favor Fleetwood, he probably changed his mind over the ensuing months. The famous occasion when he called Fleetwood a milksop for demurring at his dissolution of Parliament on February 4, 1658, was probably only the culmination of growing doubts about his competence, and he was having enough trouble then with some "godly" officers (especially Packer, Fleetwood's recent deputy as major-general) to heighten his exasperation.[85] Henry Cromwell's formal supersession of Fleetwood as Lord Deputy of Ireland on November 16, 1657, may mark a stage, for Henry's letters had been revealing for some time how weak his brother-in-law's political judgement had been, and how excessive his partiality towards the sectaries. Cromwell did, as Hause relates,[86] rebuke Henry for regarding Fleetwood as an enemy, but that does not mean that the stream of evidence from Ireland left him unaffected. Richard's appointment to the Privy Council on December 31, 1657, and to the command of a cavalry regiment soon afterwards, may well reflect Cromwell's recognition that a hereditary successor might after all be the least contentious solution. If that sealed paper did contain Fleetwood's name, perhaps he sent for it in order to destroy it, or perhaps as Bate suggests he had burnt it himself[87] but could not be sure, as sickness darkened his memory, whether he had done so.

Here we are inevitably driven into a realm of conjecture. Hause's conjectures are that Thurloe found the paper, read Fleetwood's name in it and destroyed it, that he failed to get a nomination of Richard from the dying man, and that Richard unwittingly succeeded through "a conspiracy among a cabal of Protectorians."[88] This really raises more objections than it answers. For one thing, Cromwell was visited by Fleetwood towards evening on August 31, when a respite from his paroxisms had cleared his mind.[89] He had his chance then to repair the loss of that sealed paper and broach the succession. That he evidently did not do so, and that Fleetwood so promptly accepted Richard's nomination as valid, are futher evidence against the theory that Fleetwood remained Cromwell's choice to the last. Hause also has to reject the testimony of Dr. Bate, who was at the deathbed, and who, writing a thoroughly hostile book when he was physician to Charles II and a fellow of the new Royal Society, had no motive for covering up a conspiracy by Cromwellians. Hause's thesis would also make Dr. Thomas Goodwin the compounder of a fraud. Goodwin was not Cromwell's physician, as Hause states,[90] but the senior of his chaplains and his chief spiritual comforter as he lay dying. The fearless integrity of the man's whole life makes it hard to believe that he would perjure himself in so solemn a matter.

In any case we are asked to believe that not just one or two men but at least five conspired to cheat the dying Protector, his intended successor, the Privy Council and the nation at large. This strains credulity very hard. In the Privy Council as it met on September 3, just after Cromwell's death, the eleven members present were nicely balanced between the pro-military and "Protectorian" factions—a body, one would think, that would neither succumb easily to such a deception nor, if they penetrated it, agree to foist it upon the country. Yet without "any doubtful dispute"[91] they resolved unanimously that Richard had succeeded his father according to the Humble Petition and Advice, "being fully enformed," says the Council Register, "as well by writeing as by word of mouth, by certaine members of the Counsell, and others who were called in, That his late Highness did, in his life tyme, appoynt and declare the Lord Richard to succeed him."[92] Whether the actual witnesses were Thurloe, Goodwin, Fiennes, Whalley and Goffe, as Phillips states,[93] or whether Fauconberg was right that Cromwell named Richard "in presence of 4 or 5 of the councell,"[94] is not a discrepancy that need give us much trouble.[95] The fact is that the Privy Council, including Fleetwood and Desborough, was convinced. If Thurloe's letters with their curious contradictions did not survive, the balance of the evidence that Cromwell did assent to Richard's succession on the last evening of his life would surely be decisive, whether or not he had already done so more informally two or three days earlier.

Yet Hause had reason to probe those contradictions, and we must see whether they can be explained. To recapitulate them briefly, Thurloe wrote to Henry on Monday, August 30, that "truely I believe he [Cromwell] hath not yet" named his successor, though "This day he hath had some discourse about it, but his illness disenabled hym to conclude it fully." Yet in his letter to Henry on September 4 Thurloe states baldly "He did it upon munday." Fauconberg wrote to Henry on August 31 (Tuesday) "a successor there is none named, that I can learn," and on September 7 that Cromwell nominated Richard "the preceding night [before his death], and not before."[96] Now one factor in the situation that historians have largely ignored is that until his very last days Cromwell had a conviction that he would recover. Bate describes contemptuously how one night before he left Hampton Court his chaplains dispersed to several parts of the palace to keep vigil and pray, and how they came back with the unanimous assurance that he would get well again.[97] Thomas Goodwin's rash pledges to this effect became notorious after the Restoration.[98] Thurloe wrote of Cromwell on August 30 "that the Lord, as in some former occasions, hath given to himselfe a perticuler assurance, that he shall yet live to serve him, and to carry on the worke he hath put into his hands."[99] Fleetwood, after seeing him the next day, reported that "his highnes himselfe hath hade great assurances of his recovery, which, I doe think, hath much in it."[100]

If he really believed he would recover, Cromwell had obvious political reasons for *not* openly declaring his successor, for his choice could not please everybody and would probably open wider the existing divisions in his Council. The confidence that he expressed was enough in itself to make Thurloe, who did not share it, approach the task of bringing him to a declaration very gingerly. Cromwell may nevertheless have indicated his wishes more positively on the Monday than Thurloe dared at the time to disclose even to Henry; the injunction to secrecy at the end of the letter, which Hause finds so suspicious, may only echo Cromwell's strict instructions to his Secretary. Thurloe would certainly not tell Fauconberg of these most delicate discussions; Fauconberg would believe that the nomination on the Thursday was the only one. Thurloe's letter to Henry on the Saturday remains a problem, but we must remember that he must have been tired out by the strains of the past week and the complex arrangements for Richard's public proclamation. Is it not possible, too, that his usual lucidity was clouded by genuine personal grief? "I am not able to speake or write," he told Henry,[101] and the broken expressions that follow are not necessarily hypocritical. He may have momentarily forgotten that the Thursday nomination, which was common knowledge now at Whitehall, would not yet be known to Henry, and he may have wished to convey to him that Cromwell spoke his mind earlier, when it was clearer. Phillips's story of a declaration to Thurloe and Goodwin on the Tuesday may refer to the same occasion, misdated by one day. At any rate, Thurloe's apparent self-contradiction was a very clumsy slip if he was the kind of plotter that Hause suggests.

What then remains of the thesis that Milton in the preface to *The Likeliest Means* was condemning a usurpation? The answers proposed so far are that there was no usurpation; that the evidences for Cromwell's having earlier nominated Fleetwood are late, dubious, inconsistent and few; and that the indications are against any such rumor having been current in 1658-59. Even supposing that Fleetwood then believed he had been unjustly ousted from the Protectorship, was Milton likely to have been aware of it? It is most improbable. Evidence is totally lacking that he was close enough to the Court to have inside knowledge of any secrets regarding the succession, and Hunter does not succeed in establishing any probability that he was intimate with Fleetwood himself at this time.[102] He certainly admired Fleetwood's character and his record as a soldier when he wrote *A Second Defence*, but his four or five lines of tribute there do not necessarily indicate a closer personal acquaintance than he could have gained when Fleetwood sat on the Council of State in 1651.[103] What he says of Fleetwood's civility, gentleness and courtesy from the beginnings of his military career (*ab ipsis tyrociniis*) could have been learned from others or from common fame; he himself obviously had no direct experience of Fleetwood's demeanor in the military context to which he here refers. His ranking of Fleetwood "next only to the first" (better "highest") is a literal statement of fact, for Fleetwood's promotion in 1650 to lieutenant-general, a unique appointment, placed him next to Cromwell in command. All the other relevant evidence of a more personal relationship dates from well after the Restoration, when common adversity drew many of the proscribed sons of the revolution closer together.[104] It is moreover misleading to argue "that Milton sided with Fleetwood, the Army, and their Parliamentary agent, the Restored Rump."[105] Milton certainly sided with the restored Rump, but Fleetwood and his Wallingford House colleagues had been virtually coerced into recalling it by their more radical subordinates, and they tried in vain to save some semblance of authority, if only honorific, for Richard. The Rump certainly did not regard itself as the "Parliamentary agent" of the army grandees, whom it soon proceeded to cut down to size. Allegiance to the Rump and allegiance to Fleetwood were quite different things in the summer of 1659, and when the already developing quarrel between army and Parliament came to an open breach in October, Milton (as we shall see) was to condemn the great officers in the roundest terms.

So we are left to decide whether his "short but scandalous night of interruption" meant the whole of the Protectorate or merely the army's brief usurpation of civil authority in April-May 1659. Some light on that vexing word "short" is cast by an anonymous pamphlet which Thomason acquired on May 18, 1659. It is entitled *A Publick Plea, Opposed to a Private Proposal, or, Eight Necessary Queries Presented to the Parliament and Armies Consideration, in this Morning of Freedom, after a Short, but a Sharp Night of Tyranny and Oppression.*[106] Although this writer referred to "a new Tyranny (become hereditary)" as a particular evil, there is no doubt that *his* "short night" covered the whole of the Protectorate. He urged that Cromwell's name should be publicly disgraced, and called upon the Rump to employ those men in the state and the army who had refused to act under him, or had been ousted from their commands. His tract, like *The Likeliest Means*, was printed for Livewell Chapman. Can Milton have had a copy of it, and may the title have stuck in his memory? It certainly reinforces Wolfe's arguments that Milton too was condemning the whole of the Protectorate, though one may still wonder with Wolfe "if he purposely left the passage capable of either interpretation."[107]

Earlier in this essay, in discussing *A Second Defence*, we suggested reasons for believing that Milton's dissatisfaction in 1659 was not a recent growth, but had arisen by degrees from the whole ethos of the Protectorate as its policies developed and its basis of support gradually changed. It remains to see what confirmation of this view can be found in his last political writings, from October 1659 to April 1660.

In *A Letter to a Friend*, dated October 20, 1659, and hence written a week after the army's second interruption of the Rump, Milton confesses that hitherto he has not given close consideration to state affairs, "resigning my self to the Wisdom and Care of those who had the Government; and not finding that either God, or the Publick requir'd more of me, than my Prayers for them that govern."[108] But now that he is aroused to the Commonwealth's imminent danger of disintegration he completely reverses the position that he had taken up in 1654, when he justified the first expulsion of the Rump. He was overjoyed last May, he says, when the army was brought by God's holy spirit "to confess in publick thir backsliding from the good Old Cause" and to restore "the old famous Parliament, which they had without just Authority dissolved."[109] He is careful to qualify his praise of the Rump,[110] but this time he denounces as "most illegal and scandalous, I fear me barbarous, or rather scarce to be

exampl'd among any Barbarians, that a paid Army should, for no
other cause, thus subdue the Supream Power that set them up."[111]
The only hope for the Commonwealth lies in the establishment of
a Senate, secure from military interruption. He would clearly prefer
that the Rump should be recalled to fill this role, though he allows
that it may "be thought well dissolv'd" because it has not fully
granted liberty of conscience or abolished the forced maintenance
of ministers—his obsession with these issues persists. But whatever
kind of Senate is established, "The Terms to be stood on are,
Liberty of Conscience to all professing Scripture to be the Rule
of thir Faith and Worship; *and the Abjuration of a single Person.*"[112]

The tracts that follow all reinforce these "fundamentals," and it
would be tedious to enumerate every repetition. Only once does
he depart a shade from his now fixed aversion to a single man as
head of state, which runs through the *Proposalls of Certaine Expedients* of November 1659 and *The Present Means and Brief Delineation of a Free Commonwealth* of March 1660, as well as both
editions of *The Readie & Easie Way.* The partial exception comes
in a reply that he wrote to a royalist sermon early in April 1660
when the Restoration appeared all but inevitable. If, he says, we are
too degenerate to rise to the virtues and responsibilities of a free
commonwealth, and if the people are absolutely intent on the
thraldom of monarchy, "yet chusing out of our own number
one who hath best aided the people, and best merited against
tyrannie, the space of a raign or two we may chance to live happily
anough, or tolerably."[113] He can have had only General Monck in
mind at that stage; from Milton's viewpoint a King George would
at least have been better than a King Charles. Yet what a counsel
of despair he makes this appear, and how far this whole passage
is in spirit from the uninhibited justification of Cromwell's right
to rule in *A Second Defence*!

There is no compromise with one-man rule in the second and much
enlarged edition of *The Readie & Easie Way*, which he probably
finished revising at about the same time.[114] This work combines
the outward function of a tract for the times, in that it offers
hopeless expedients for turning back the now irresistible tide of
royalism, with something of the character of a political testament.
Faced with that tide and knowing its power, Milton is taking advantage of "a little Shroving-time first, wherin to speak freely, and
take our leaves of Libertie."[115] He nowhere mentions Cromwell,
but the achievements that he celebrates are those of the Long Parliament and the Commonwealth, not of the Protectorate. He almost
certainly alludes to the latter where he writes of "our liberty and

religion thus prosperously fought for, gaind and many years possessd, *except in those unhappie interruptions, which God hath remov'd.*"[116] He probably does so again where he refers to "just and religious deeds, though don by som to covetous and ambitious ends," and castigates the folly of betraying "a just and noble cause for the mixture of bad men who have ill manag'd and abus'd it."[117] Not that the promoters of the Protectorate were the only bad or ambitious men who had sullied the cause—the digression on the Long Parliament as it was before Pride's Purge that he inserted in his *History of Britain* is evidence enough of that[118]—but in the context they can be taken as included in his condemnation.

The most memorable parts of the work are those where he contrasts the moral virtues of a free commonwealth with the corruptions and servitudes that monarchy inevitably entails. "Certainly then that people must needs be madd or strangely infatuated, that build the chief hope of thir common happiness or safetie on a single person";[119] and that a crowned king is not the only kind of single person that he condemns can be seen where he compares England with the Netherlands and hopes "that our liberty shall not be hampered or hovered over by any ingagement to such a potent family as the house of *Nassaw* of whom to stand in perpetural doubt and suspicion."[120] How close an analogy did he see in the house of Cromwell, when it too threatened to become hereditary? "'Tis true indeed," he sighs, "when monarchie was dissolvd, the form of a Commonwealth should have forthwith bin fram'd . . . this care of timely setling a new government instead of ye old, too much neglected, hath bin our mischief. Yet the cause therof may be ascrib'd with most reason to the frequent disturbances, interruptions and dissolutions which the Parlament hath had partly from the impatient or disaffected people, partly from som ambitious leaders in the Armie."[121] He is careful not to ascribe all England's ills to that one act of force against the Rump in 1653, but the implication is very plain that by that deed and by Cromwell's subsequent assumption of power the Commonwealth had been gravely deflected from its true line of development.

In conclusion, perhaps it is worth suggesting to those who would save Milton's consistency at all costs that fixity of opinions and judgements is not necessarily a virtue in a constantly developing revolutionary situation. Like Cromwell, Milton was not "wedded and glued to forms of government";[122] in constitutional matters they were fellow-empirics. Consequences are notoriously hard to forecast when constitutional foundations are shifting, and Milton was not the only idealist who hailed Cromwell for saving the Commonwealth from collapse and lived to become disillusioned with him. We do not have to believe, as Hunter puts it, "that Milton betrayed his faith in his old leader Oliver as soon as the man was dead."[123] He reacted against a whole regime rather than a single personality; better than some modern historians, he recognized the collective character of Cromwellian rule. We may believe that his assessment of the Protectorate was wrong, and that his sense of political realities was much weaker than Cromwell's. He had little idea of the compromises that were necessary if the revolution was to survive, and the extreme ecclesiastical policies which were his touchstone of political virtue were so obnoxious to the majority of Englishmen that they would have been fatal to any government that adopted them. He showed little awareness that in a hierarchical society, where status, landed property and political influence went roughly together, the social foundations of political power were supremely important. After the abolition of the monarchy, the Protectorate was the only regime that made any progress towards reconciling the traditional political nation, and in applauding its overthrow Milton was unwittingly promoting the doom of all that he valued in church and state. It is hard to think of a more unacceptable and impracticable solution to the political problems of 1659-60 than the perpetual Senate that he advocated with increasing insistency. Yet beneath the inescapable inconsistencies of his political writings from 1649 to 1660 the essentials remain firm: the vision of a regenerate nation, the ideal of an aristocracy of virtue, the constant vindication of intellectual and religious liberty. When he brought out the second edition of *The Readie & Easie Way* with the Restoration only a very few weeks ahead, he risked his life, his liberty and his unfinished poetic masterpiece to assert these essentials once more to all posterity.

Notes

1. See especially Merritt Y. Hughes' introduction to *Complete Prose Works of John Milton*, 6 vols. to date (New Haven: Yale University Press, 1953-   ; hereafter cited as *Complete Prose*), III, 101-109.

2. *Complete Prose*, III, 192.

3. Ibid., p. 194.

4. Ibid., p. 236.

5. Ibid., p. 237; my italics.

6. Ibid., p. 197.

7. *Eikonoklastes: Complete Prose*, III, 542.

8. David Underdown, *Pride's Purge: Politics in the Puritan Revolution* (Oxford: Clarendon Press, 1971), ch. VIII.

9. William R. Parker, *Milton: A Biography*, 2 vols. (Oxford: Clarendon Press, 1968), esp. pp. 352-55.

10. For one such occasion see *Complete Prose*, IV, 3.

11. Parker, *Biography*, pp. 389, 393-94. No credence can be given to Anthony Wood's statement in *Athenae Oxonienses*, quoted in J. Milton French, *Life Records of John Milton*, 5 vols. (New Brunswick: Rutgers University Press, 1949-58), IV, 172, that Milton was 'very intimate and conversant with' Cromwell at the time that Andrew Marvell was appointed as his assistant in 1657. Wood was in no position to know, and the contemporary evidence strongly suggests the contrary.

12. *Observations upon the Articles of Peace* (1649): *Complete Prose*, III, 312.

13. Ibid., p. 315.

14. *Complete Prose*, IV, 458.

15. William A. Shaw, *A History of the English Church . . . 1640-1660*, 2 vols. (London, 1900), II, 79-85; Wilbur K. Jordan, *The Development of Religious Toleration in England*, 4 vols. (Cambridge, Mass., 1932-40), III, 140-43; *Complete Prose*, IV, 169-77.

16. Parker, *Biography*, pp. 394-95.

17. *Complete Prose*, IV, 671. Milton was here retailing the allegations by Cromwell and the Council of Officers in their declaration of April 22, but convincing evidence that the Rump did *not* refuse to make way for a new Parliament is advanced by Blair Worden, "The Bill for a New Representative: the dissolution of the Long Parliament, April 1653," *English Historical Review*, 86 (1971), 473-96.

18. Unless "the suffrage granted only to those who deserved it" meant that only the Council of Officers deserved it; see Austin Woolrych, "The Calling of Barebone's Parliament," *English Historical Review*, 80 (1965), 492-513.

19. *The Readie & Easie Way*, 1st edition, in *The Works of John Milton*,

18 vols. (New York: Columbia University Press, 1931-38; hereafter cited as Columbia), VI, 366.

20. British Museum, Thomason Collection E728(5), *sub* February 8, 1654; published anonymously, though Sir Charles Firth's ascription to Needham in *The Last Years of the Protectorate*, 2 vols. (London, 1909), I, 156, is almost certainly correct.

21. *Complete Prose*, IV, 252-58, 542-43.

22. *Second Defence: Complete Prose*, IV, 666.

23. Ibid., pp. 671-72.

24. Ibid., p. 672. This passage does not seem to me to support the remark of the annotator here that "Milton's anxiety about Cromwell's new title . . . grows more than it abates."

25. Ibid., p. 638.

26. Ibid., p. 675.

27. Ibid., p. 676.

28. See particularly David Masson, *The Life of John Milton*, 7 vols. (Cambridge, 1875-94), IV, 605-08; Don M. Wolfe in *Complete Prose*, IV, 261-64; Parker, *Biography*, pp. 440-45.

29. *Complete Prose*, IV, 637-39.

30. *The Memoirs of Edmund Ludlow*, ed. C. H. Firth, 2 vols. (Oxford, 1894), I, 357.

31. See DNB. Whitelocke's political stance departed even further from Milton's with the years, but his inclusion may be linked with Milton's tribute to Queen Christina (*Complete Prose*, IV, 603-606), since Whitelocke was currently ambassador to Sweden.

32. *State Papers of John Thurloe*, ed. T. Birch, 7 vols. (London, 1742), III, 110.

33. Marvell had just presented Bradshaw with a copy of *A Second Defence*, which Thomason acquired on

May 30. He writes "I have an affectionate Curiosity to know what becomes of Colonell Overtons businesse" (French, *Life Records*, III, 386). Overton signed a letter from Hull, where he was governor, on May 11 (*Calendar of State Papers, Domestic, 1654*, p. 489), so he probably came to London to see Cromwell very close to the time when *A Second Defence* was published.

34. Masson, *The Life*, IV, 607.

35. No particular significance attaches to the remaining names cited by Milton, all but one of which belonged to members of Cromwell's Council of State. He omitted six other councillors, but although one could suggest possible objections that he had to them, the simpler explanation is that he did not know them. Even those he named were, he said, "known to me either through friendship *or by report*" (*Complete Prose*, IV, 676; my italics).

36. Ibid., pp. 672, 674.

37. Ibid., p. 674.

38. In the first *Defence* he justifies the abolition of the House of Lords, but explains to Salmasius that nobles may still sit in Parliament as elected representatives (*Complete Prose*, IV, 470-71). In *Proposalls of Certaine Expedients* (1659) he would have the Parliament and army unite in abjuring a House of Lords as well as a single person (Columbia, XVIII, 4). In *The Readie & Easie Way* (1660) he maintains his strong objection to the House of Lords as a political institution (Columbia, VI, 124-25, 133, 135). He envisages the continuance of a nobility (ibid., p. 144), but would have "all distinctions of lords and commoners, that may any way divide or sever the publick interest, remov'd" (p. 146).

39. Wilbur C. Abbott, *Writings and Speeches of Oliver Cromwell*, 4 vols. (Cambridge, Mass., 1937-47), IV, 952-53.

40. *Complete Prose*, IV, 679.

41. Christopher Hill, *God's Englishman: Oliver Cromwell and the English Revolution* (London: Weidenfeld & Nicolson, 1970), pp. 149-50.

42. *Of True Religion, Haeresie, Schism, Toleration* (1673).

43. *Complete Prose*, IV, 678.

44. For fuller accounts of the Cromwellian ecclesiastical settlement see S. R. Gardiner, *History of the Commonwealth and Protectorate*, 3 vols. (London, 1897-1901), II, 318-25; Shaw, *English Church*, II, 247-48, 284-86; Jordan, *Religious Toleration*, III, 152-60. Milton clearly had the Triers in mind in his hostile references to "examinant committies" and "committees of examination" in *The Likeliest Means*: Columbia, VI, 83, 96.

45. Abbott, *Cromwell*, IV, 272. This speech on September 17, 1656, is Cromwell's fullest exposition of his views on toleration and the magistrates' responsibility towards religion.

46. *Of Reformation: Complete Prose*, I, 613.

47. Milton could easily have been led into believing that Cromwell was close to his own mind by the latter's declaration to the people of Ireland, and particularly to the Irish Catholic clergy, early in 1650. "I wonder not," wrote Cromwell, "at discontents and divisions, where so Antichristian and dividing a term as Clergy and Laity is given and received: a term unknown to any save to the Antichristian Church. . . . It was your pride that begat this expression, and it is for filthy lucre's sake that you keep it up. . . !" Abbott, II, 197; quoted and commented on in Hill, *God's Englishman*, pp. 126-27.

48. The term "public profession" occurs in both the Instrument of Government of 1653 and the Humble Petition and Advice which redefined the constitution in 1657, though the latter drew tighter the terms on which toleration was to be extended to those who dissented from the public profession. See S. R. Gardiner, *Constitutional Documents of the Puritan Revolution* (3rd ed., Oxford, 1906), pp. 416, 454-55.

49. *Complete Prose*, IV, 703, 720.

50. French, *Life Records*, IV, 190. There may be a faintly pejorative ring in the word *gratiosis* which Milton uses for the men in favor at Court.

51. Milton to Henry Oldenburg, July 6, 1654, in French, *Life Records*, III, 410.

52. Parker, *Biography*, p. 1052. The most authoritative discussion of its dates is by Maurice Kelley in *This Great Argument* (Princeton, 1941), and we await Kelley's latest opinion in his forthcoming new edition in *Complete Prose* [recently published—editors' note].

53. Columbia, VI, 1.

54. Ibid., p. 2.

55. *Diary of Thomas Burton,* 4 vols., ed. J. T. Rutt, (London, 1828), IV, 336.

56. Burton, III, 125-28, 158, 181, 403.

57. *Parliamentary or Constitutional History of England*, 24 vols. (London, 1751-66), XXI, 321-24; Burton, IV, 300, 329-33, 335-45.

58. Burton, IV, 402.

59. For these events and their background see Godfrey Davies, *The Restoration of Charles II* (San Marino: Huntington Library, 1955), ch. V and VI; Austin Woolrych, "The Good Old Cause and the Fall of the Protectorate," *Cambridge Historical Journal*, 13 (1957), 133-61, and ch. IV of the introduction to *Complete Prose*, VII.

60. Wall's letter is reprinted in French, *Life Records*, IV, 267-69 and is dated May 26, but this date presents difficulties. Wall bewails the bad times at length, but makes no mention of the restoration of the Rump on May 7, which had changed the whole political situation. He writes as though a military tyranny were still in force, and the nation still enslaved to a supreme magistrate. It seems incredible that this avowed commonwealthsman should not refer to such a momentous change of government if it had taken place. His letter survives only in an eighteenth-century copy, and I wonder whether the copyist may not have misread as May some abbreviation of March, or whether Wall's own date was a slip of the pen. The precise dating does not of course affect the value of this evidence of Milton's discontent with the course of Richard's Protectorate.

61. The evidence is discussed in *Complete Prose*, VII, Introduction, ch. V.

62. Columbia, VI, 45.

63. Ibid., p. 43.

64. Masson, *The Life*, V, 606-607.

65. *A Letter to a Friend* (October 20, 1659), Columbia, VI, 101-102.

66. John S. Smart, *The Sonnets of Milton* (Glasgow, 1921); Don M. Wolfe, *Milton in the Puritan Revolution* (New York, 1941), pp. 289-90; Barbara K. Lewalski, "Milton: Political Beliefs and Polemical Methods," *PMLA*, 74 (1959), 192-93; Michael Fixler, *Milton and the Kingdoms of God* (London: Faber & Faber, 1964), pp. 189-99. Parker in his biography strangely ignores the whole question.

67. Wm. B. Hunter, Jr., "Milton and Richard Cromwell," *English Language Notes*, 3 (1966), 252-59.

68. E. Malcolm Hause, "The Nomination of Richard Cromwell," *The Historian* 27 (1965), 185-209.

69. Firth, *Last Years*, II, 302-307; Davies, *Restoration*, pp. 3-4. Both accept the essential validity of Cromwell's nomination of Richard.

70. *Thurloe S.P.*, VII, 364.

71. George Bate, *Elenchi motuum nuperorum in Anglia. Pars secunda* (1663), pp. 416-17. The English version of 1685 misleadingly translates "Annuit ille" as "he answered, *Yes.*" Hause ascribes the Latin original to 1661, but this appears to be an error shared by several bibliographers, including Wing and Godfrey Davies. The first edition of the *Pars secunda* seems to have always been bound up with a new edition of the *Pars prima* which is indeed dated 1661, but the title page of the *Pars secunda* itself has "Aerae Christianae Anno 1662" after Bate's name and credentials, and "1663" after the names of the printer (J. Flesher) and bookseller (R. Royston). I have used the copy in the John Rylands Library, Manchester, which Wing dates 1661, but the British Museum copy of the same edition of the two works is correctly catalogued as "1661, 63." Flesher and Royston issued another edition in 1663 with different pagination and with "editio nova emendata" on the title page. It is verbally identical with the first edition in all that bears upon Richard's nomination and Fleetwood's alleged claim.

72. Bate, *Elenchi, Pars secunda* (1st ed., 1663), pp. 426-27.

73. Bate, *Elenchus motuum . . .* (English version, 1685), pp. 241-42.

74. Ludlow, *Memoirs*, II, 63-64; *Cambridge Historical Journal*, 13 (1957), 146-48.

75. Sir Richard Baker, *A Chronicle of the Kings of England* (London,

1670), pp. 652-53. (The 1670 edition, cited for its greater accessibility, does not differ significantly from the 1665 at any relevant point.)

76. *Thurloe S.P.*, VII, 364. Phillips presumably did not know of this letter.

77. Thurloe, Goodwin, Fiennes, Whalley, Goffe, Desborough, and those other privy councillors who according to Phillips met Thurloe an hour after Cromwell died.

78. "Nomination of Cromwell," 206-207.

79. Ludlow, *Memoirs*, II, 44-45, 55.

80. Above, p. 198 and below, p. 209. One has to ask who of the possible sharers in a guilty secret about the succession might have divulged it to Milton. I can imagine none. A possible link with Henry Lawrence, President of the Council, through Milton's friendship with Lawrence's son Edward, had been weakened by Edward's death in 1657.

81. Thomas Morrice, ed., *A Collection of the State Letters of . . . Roger Boyle*, 2 vols. (Dublin, 1743), memoir prefixed to vol. I, 53-54. Morrice records the death of one of Orrery's sons in 1691.

82. The brief reference to Fleetwood's nomination in the royalist Sir Philip Warwick's *Memoirs of the Reign of King Charles I* (London, 1702), pp. 389-90, is later still, and probably derives from Bate and Phillips. The work by Jesse cited by Hause is a nineteenth-century compilation of no independent value.

83. *Calendar of State Papers, Venetian, 1655-56*, p. 227.

84. Quoted in C. H. Firth, "Cromwell and the Crown," *English Historical Review*, 17 (1902), 434.

85. See David Underdown, "Cromwell and the Officers, February 1658," *English Historical Review*, 83 (1968),

101-107. Cromwell may also have had some evidence that Fleetwood was keeping in sympathetic contact with Lambert after the latter's dismissal: see Ivan Roots, *The Great Rebellion 1642-1660* (London: Batsford, 1966), p. 229.

86. "Nomination of Cromwell," 196.

87. Bate, *Elenchi, Pars secunda* (1663), p. 417.

88. "Nomination of Cromwell," 207 and passim.

89. Fleetwood to Henry Cromwell, August 31, in *Thurloe S.P.*, VII, 367; partly quoted by Hause, p. 190.

90. "Nomination of Cromwell," 191. Hause is strictly correct (p. 203) that Phillips is the sole authority for Goodwin's presence at Cromwell's alleged nominations of Richard, but that Goodwin attended him in his last illness is confirmed by Ludlow in *Memoirs*, II, 43, and Gilbert Burnet, *History of My Own Time*, ed. Osmund Airy, 2 vols. (Oxford, 1898), I, 148. Burnet had it from Tillotson, who attended a fast in the Cromwell household a week after the Protector's death. Nothing is more probable in Phillips's account than that this much trusted divine remained in Cromwell's presence to hear him determine a matter that so deeply touched his conscience as the succession.

91. Fauconberg to Henry Cromwell, September 7, in *Thurloe S.P.*, VIII, 375; Hause asks (p. 193) "Why the protest?" But it was surely most natural for Fauconberg to reassure Henry that the length of the Council's meeting was caused by the care needed in drafting the proclamation of Richard and not by any dispute over his title.

92. Quoted in Davies, *Restoration*, p. 4, where the councillors present are also named.

93. Baker, *Chronicle* (1670), pp. 652-53. It is very possible that Phillips had sound contemporary testimony, probably from Clarges, as to who was present, but tried to marry it with post-Restoration gossip about the sealed paper.

94. *Thurloe, S.P.*, VII, 375.

95. Although only Fiennes and Thurloe were privy councillors among the five named by Phillips, Thurloe, Fiennes, Whalley and Goffe were all members of a committee of nine that had been set up in June to prepare business for the Parliament that Cromwell had then intended to call. Cromwell had come to consult it privately on other high matters of state: see *Thurloe S.P.*, VII, 192, and Baker, *Chronicle*, p. 652. Fauconberg, who was not a councillor, may have described these men loosely as "of the councell," or he may not yet have been accurately informed, but the Council Register's mention of "others who were called in" proves that the witnesses included non-councillors. Bordeaux's statement that the Council was informed by five of its own number may derive from Fauconberg, like his earlier news of Cromwell's death: see F.P.G. Guizot, *History of Oliver Cromwell and the English Commonwealth*, 2 vols. (London, 1854), II, 598-600.

96. *Thurloe S.P.*, VII, 364, 365, 372, 375.

97. Bate, *Elenchi* (1663), pp. 413-15.

98. Ludlow, *Memoirs*, II, 43; Burnet, *Own Time*, I, 148; Warwick, *Memoires*, p. 388. Warwick claimed to know this through his intimate acquaintance with one of Cromwell's physicians; was he Bate?

99. *Thurloe S.P.*, VII, 364.

100. Ibid., p. 367.

101. *Thurloe S.P.*, VII, 372.

102. The evidences that he offers

are in "Milton and Cromwell," 257-58, esp. n.13, to which n.104 below refers.

103. Fleetwood of course sat on the Protectoral Council of State, but that was long after Milton ceased to attend.

104. Masson's supposition of a boyhood friendship seems to be a hangover from that misreading of *ab ipsis tyrociniis* which Hunter notes. Parker in *Biography*, p. 837, admits there is no evidence, though on p. 250 he assumes that a friendship did develop in the 1640s, apparently on the sole evidence of *A Second Defence*. It may or may not have. Nothing can be built on the proximity of Milton's and Fleetwood's former homes in the teeming city of London, which rose from about a quarter to half a million inhabitants in Milton's lifetime—especially as an age gap of about ten years separated the two young men. Nor can anything be deduced concerning their relationship in 1658-59 from Milton's renting of the Chalfont cottage from a not very close relation of Fleetwood's in 1665, or from the marriage of Milton's nephew to Fleetwood's niece as far ahead as 1672.

105. Hunter, "Milton and Cromwell," p. 258. The description on p. 259 of the republicans as the army's pawns is even wider of the mark. See Davies, *Restoration,* ch. VI and VII, and ch. IV of my introduction to *Complete Prose,* VII.

106. British Museum, E983(18).

107. Wolfe, *Puritan Revolution,* p. 289.

108. Columbia, VI, 101.

109. Ibid., pp. 101-102.

110. "I call it the famous Parliament, tho not the harmles, since none well-affected, but will confes, they have deserved much more of these Nations, than they have undeserved." Ibid., p. 102.

111. Ibid., p. 102. "For no other cause" refers to the Rump's recent cashiering of Lambert and eight other senior officers. It had also terminated Fleetwood's appointment as commander-in-chief and put the command of the armies in commission.

112. Ibid., p. 104; my italics.

113. *Brief Notes upon a Late Sermon,* Columbia, VI, 160.

114. The argument for a completion date close to the beginning of April will appear in *Complete Prose,* VII.

115. Columbia, VI, 111.

116. Ibid., p. 116; my italics. "Interruptions" in the plural doubtless includes that other military usurpation, the rule of the Committee of Safety from October to December 1659.

117. Ibid., p. 117.

118. Columbia, X, 317-25.

119. Columbia, VI, 121.

120. Ibid., p. 134.

121. Ibid., pp. 124-25.

122. Words spoken by Cromwell at the Putney Debates, October 28, 1647: A.S.P. Woodhouse, ed., *Puritanism and Liberty* (London, 1938), p. 36.

123. "Milton and Cromwell," 259.

Government of the Spirit:
Style, Structure and Theme in
Treatise of Civil Power

HARRY SMALLENBURG
Wayne State University

Critics have generally noted a difference in style between Milton's earlier and later tracts. Kenneth Muir, for instance, calls the later prose "plain and direct"—"there are no 'lushious metaphors,' no elaborate rhetorical artifice, no obscurity." He attributes the plainness primarily to the general shift in prose style during the course of the century and relates Milton's intentions to the stylistic program of the Royal Society.[1] Tillyard and Saurat, who also discuss the apparent differences in the later prose, see behind them a personal disillusionment with the revolution and disappointment with life that have dispelled the enthusiasm implicit in the stylistic variety of the early tracts.[2]

Using the *Treatise of Civil Power,* however, it is possible to discuss the style and its effects in much more specific and precise terms, and to locate the reason for its "plainness" in the political division, strife, grievances, and violence to which it responds in 1659. As early as 1642, in *Reason of Church-Government,* Milton had described the civil and spiritual disorder created by monarchy in terms similar to those of Clarendon and modern historians:

> That government which ye hold, we confesse prevents much, hinders much, removes much; but what? the schisms and grievances of the Church? no, but all the peace and unity, all the welfare not of the Church alone, but of the whole kingdome. And if it be still permitted ye to hold, will cause the most sad I know not whether separation be anough to say, but such a wide gulph of distraction in this land as will never close her dismall gap, untill ye be forc't (for of your selvs ye wil never do as that Roman *Curtius* nobly did) for the Churches peace & your countries, to leap into the midst, and be not more seen.[3]

His awareness and concern for the general conditions are evident still in 1659. In December he received this letter from Henry Oldenburg:

> Would . . . that [the English troubles] would settle down, and that
> the cultivation of peace and justice would take the place of all
> wars and evil! Men treat men too, too extravagantly. There is too
> much of the old cause of war and waging wars, too deep a desire
> of power and riches.

Milton's answer suggests the purpose he had in writing *Treatise of Civil Power*:

> I am far from preparing the history of our commotions, which you
> seem to encourage; for they are more deserving of silence than of
> celebration; *nor is the need with us for someone who can prepare
> a history of our commotions, but for someone who can happily
> settle the commotions themselves*; for I fear with you lest among
> these civil discords of ours, or rather madnesses, we may seem too
> exposed to the new recently associated enemies of liberty and
> religion; but they will not have inflicted a severer wound on
> religion than we ourselves have long been doing by our crimes.[4]

Further, in *The Readie & Easie Way*, Milton acknowledges that the
commonwealth has not realized its ideals, and prescribes in general
how the establishment of the new government should have been
handled:

> . . . when monarchie was dissolved, the form of a Commonwealth
> should have forthwith bin fram'd; and the practice therof im-
> mediatly begun; that the people might have soon bin satisfi'd and
> delighted with the decent order, ease and benefit therof: we had
> bin then by this time firmly rooted past fear of commotions or
> mutations, & now flourishing: this care of timely settling a new
> government instead of ye old, too much neglected, hath been
> our mischief.[5]

Milton senses the danger of the republic, and writes in 1659 to
prevent the return of monarchy. The republican government
seemed to bring only violence and disunity. In the *Treatise* Milton
uses stylistic and structural devices rhetorically, to renew his
audience's confidence in parliamentary rule. The style identifies
the republic as the only form of government that can restore "decent order, ease and benefit" to the Commonwealth. After the
years of disruption in the state, the pamphlet itself is low-keyed
and rational. Descriptions of the civil order under each form of
government dramatize by their formulation the way that monarchy
by nature perpetuates tension, disunion and disruption, while

parliamentary rule naturally encourages and perpetuates unity
and stability. Milton shows the way toward establishing in actuality
what he believes to be the only true order by moving the reader
to an understanding of and preference for that order. In the final,
natural resolution of conflicts, the outer, civil order will be transformed to correspond to the sense of inner, spiritual reality which
the reader has developed. This, in turn, reflects and draws upon

> the righteous and all wise judgements and statutes of God . . .
> [which] are most constant and most harmonious each to other.[6]

This strategy is reflected in the introduction, which establishes
relationships and implications that will appear more overtly in the
structure and syntactical figures of the actual tract. The collocation
of words in the first sentence, for example, unobtrusively makes
the reader aware of the resolution that can follow conflict. Though
the content does not explicitly concern civil order and disorder,
a necessary and basic pattern of responses begins:

> I have prepared, supreme council, against the much expected time
> of your sitting, this treatise.[7]

Our first sense is that of action performed in the past—"I have prepared"—by a single person in anticipation of a future occurrence.
The address, "supreme council," suspends the forward movement
of the statement, so that we retain the sense of "having looked
forward to." The grammatical suspension continues into the next
clause, however, with an apparent shift as our sense of anticipation
from the clause "I have prepared" is reversed by the word "against."
"Against," initially suggesting opposition, seems to clash with "I
have prepared" from the other side of the address. This tension,
however, along with that implicit in "the much expected time,"
dissolves with the reader's virtually instantaneous recognition of
the normal locution "to prepare against." Instead of sensing a new
conflict between the anticipatory nature of "the much expected
time" and the oppositional "against," we read the phrase as naturally and simply following the locution. "Sitting," a verbal noun describing continued action without definite temporal occurrence,
continues and extends the sense of resolution. What we have felt
as incompatibilities of meaning are conclusively resolved by the
straightforward "this treatise," a direct object grammatically, and
a phrase that simply refers to a specific object without lending itself to the examination of its suggestions in relation to other words.
In the clause as a whole, our true apprehension of a created order
has put to rest the incompatibilities of meaning that otherwise would

have made the clause meaningless. It is apparent, moreover, that conflict is a consequence of superficial and incomplete understanding.
The general point beginning to develop is clear: the political chaos
can be resolved only where civil and ecclesiastical governments are
in their true independent relationship.

In the next part of the sentence, Milton becomes more overt and
finally explicit as he approaches the *distributio* governing the companion tracts (*Treatise* and *Readie & Easie Way*):

> which, though to all Christian magistrates equally belonging, and
> therefore to have been written in the common language of Christen-
> dom, natural duty and affection hath confined, and dedicated first
> to my own nation:

"Which" continues the solid, straightforward nature of the phrase
preceding: the reference is directly and securely back to "treatise."
Instead of continuing straightforwardly with "natural duty and
affection," however, Milton again suspends the grammatical completion of the sentence with the initial part of what will be a formulation related to the *distributio*. "Though" has adversative force, the
direction of the sentence shifts, and we get the broad "all Christian
magistrates." The sentence becomes contrary to fact as we come to
"equally belonging" and realize that we are being informed of a
choice not made, though entirely plausible and in a way even required since the subject belongs equally to all. The second half of
the statement introduces the coordinate concepts, "natural duty
and affection," that govern the choice between an address to all
and the confinement to his own nation.

The meaning of this short passage is in the fact of related pairs of
concepts—one of which I will call a "disparate," the other a "coordinate." The disparate pair is "all Christian magistrates" and "my
own nation." They are disparate because they represent conflicting
demands and commitments. The subject is inherently relevant to the
broader audience and a certain propriety demands that it be written
in Latin and addressed to all of Europe. That has not been done,
however. Yet we sense no conflict between the more generalized
and the limited address. Rather, the potential tension is resolved
both syntactically and affectively by the coordinate concepts that
govern the choice: "natural duty and affection." These enable us
to recognize the proper order in a hierarchy—natural duty and affection are demands from within and must be honored before the external and less immediate demand that the treatise be written to all of
Europe. As in the clause preceding, a potential incompatibility has
been resolved, with the further implication that the impulses of the

spirit within are to have greater sway than a conventional, external propriety. For this reason, the civil magistrate must not attempt to force an individual against his "inward perswasion."

"Natural duty and affection" as coordinate concepts lead us to further sets of terms. By the nature of their relationships, these terms can have a beneficial effect if realized in the actual political world. The syntax and grammar suggest the political order that is to come: unlike the earlier, adversative "though" clause, phrases and clauses now extend continually forward:

> and in a season wherein the timely reading therof, to the easier accomplishment of your great work, may save you much labor and interruption . . .

We feel immediately the differences between this and the preceding sequence of clauses, where "though" noticeably altered the direction of the meaning. Here, the feeling is one of continuity, beginning with the coordinate conjunction "and," extended by the modifying phrase "to the easier accomplishment . . ." and completed naturally in the last section of the clause. Instead of sensing hindrance, we sense an ease with which statements fall into their syntactical places.

The rhythm of the statements, further, brings to our attention more combinations of terms. These are thrown into affective relationships that, significantly, repeat patterns we have already observed. "Timely reading," "easier accomplishment," and "labor and interruption" coordinate with other terms not merely to *tell* what the advantages are of the political reform advocated, but, as before, to give a feeling that will suggest the quality or nature of existence when true political relationships are effected. "Easy" by itself would suggest absence of effort or trouble, or of something like the hindrance and reversal undergone by implication in the "though" clause. "Easier," the comparative adjective, intensifies this feeling in preparation for "accomplishment." By itself "accomplishment" indicates effect achieved after activity and implies a discernible break between the actual performance of the effort and its completion and cessation, with the concrete fact of the completed task. The suggestions of effort are reduced, however, by the word "easier," while accomplishment remains and persists in fact. The implications are: accomplishment and well-being, the satisfaction and fulfillment that persist after the completion of effort, but with the effort itself reduced.

Essentially the same pattern of responses, only more overt, occurs in the completion of the clause—"may save you much labor and interruption." Here the rhythm emphasizes "labor and interruption," which make explicit concepts suggested by "accomplishment" and thereby should intensify what we have already felt. In fact, the words dramatize the necessary steps leading to "accomplishment"; "interruption," moreover, burdens "labor" by adding a sense of frustration at hindrance to the easy realization of accomplishment, toward which effort is directed. If "easier" reduced the implications of labor in "accomplishment," here "save" *eliminates* the intensified ("much") sense of labor and frustration before it even occurs. Further, "save" eliminates labor and interruption positively—the emphasis is, paradoxically, on the accumulation and conservation of nonexpenditure. The syntactical arrangement reinforces these implications: "save you labor and interruption" brings the sentence grammatically to rest, as the actuality brings people to rest and conserve in their administration of the country.

Milton reserves explicit distribution of the subject and of his audience for the last part of the sentence:

> of two parts usually proposed, civil and ecclesiastical, recommending civil only to your proper care, ecclesiastical to them only from whom it takes that name and nature.

The language preceding, however, has foreshadowed both the division of power set up and the effects of this division. We have seen repeated a pattern in which momentary or potential tensions are resolved. The resolution first involves our own true perception of a created syntactical order; in the second instance, resolution derives from a choice based upon acknowledgment of and willingness to act in accord with true inner impulses as opposed to an external propriety. These may be seen as the preliminary steps of true understanding and then right action based on intuitions. Finally, we have instances naturally and inevitably following these preliminary steps, in which there is relief from an unpleasantness and then elimination of it altogether. Only an untroubled, conserving state remains, which corresponds to the desirable state described in succeeding passages. We come to recognize the proper distribution of powers within the state as the condition which makes possible this ideal existence.

From this point distribution and related patterns (i.e., those which variously relate concepts and sets of concepts, though not necessarily actual distribution) recur. The very next sentence begins by adding a second cause to what has preceded; this cause itself breaks down into two parts:

> Yet not for this cause only do I require or trust to find acceptance, but in a two-fold respect besides. . . .(1)

Within the explanation of the "twofold respect" the coordinate terms "scripture and protestant maxims" appear. Later, a comparison appears: "so to regard other men's consciences, as you would your own should be regarded in the power of others." Complicating the effect are the repetitions and playings-off of terms against each other.

We have seen that the formulation even of introductory statements initiates the reader into a mode of consideration that quickly becomes explicit and recurrent. True perception of order and proprieties offers possibilities of resolution, and pairs of terms suggest beneficial relationships in actual civil society. The body of the tract further enacts and extends these introductory implications. In the following passage, for instance, Milton argues that the magistrate must be excluded from settlement of religious affairs—"as a magistrate he hath no right." In the style of the argument, the truly-functioning polity is felt to be not only easing and fulfilling, but one in which distinctions and suppositions that we as fallen humans tend to expect dissolve away, along with the civil strife. Words and syntactical patterns become symbolic of individual and group interrelationships.

> Christ hath a government of his own, sufficient of it self to all his ends and purposes in governing his church; but much different from that of the civil magistrate; and the difference in this verie thing principally consists, that it governs not by outward force, and that for two reasons. First because it deals only with the inward man and his actions, which are all spiritual and to outward force not lyable: secondly to shew us the worldly force to subdue all the powers and kingdoms of this world, which are upheld by outward force only. That the inward man is nothing els but the inward part of man, his understanding and his will, and that his actions thence proceeding, yet not simply thence but from the work of divine grace upon them, are the whole matter of religion under the gospel, will appeer planely by considering what that religion is; whence we shall perceive yet more planely that it cannot be forc'd. What evangelic religion is, is told in two words, faith and charitie; or beleef and practise. That both these flow either the one from the understanding, the other from the will, or both jointly from both, once indeed naturally, but now only as they are regenerat and wrought on by divine grace, is in part evident to common sense and principles unquestioned, the rest

by scripture. . . . If then both our beleef and practise, of the inward man, free and unconstrainable of themselves by nature,
and our practise not only from faculties endu'd with freedom,
but from love and charitie besides, incapable of force, and all
these things by transgression lost, but renewd and regenerated
in us by the power and gift of God alone, How can such religion
as this admit of force from man, or force be any way appli'd to
such religion, especially under the free offer of grace in the gospel,
but it must forthwith frustrate and make of no effect both the
religion and the gospel? (20-21)

The separateness of civil and religious government is fundamental.
The order and resolution implicit in subsequent separations naturally
follow. If England will institute a sound political and religious order,
a true spiritual order can follow. Milton suggests this by initially
separating concepts and breaking problems down into coordinate
parts. Shortly after, the language begins to merge and unify the
apparently distinct and separate. The characterization of religion
as governing not by outward force, for instance, implies an antithesis, the positive half of which is taken up in the next sentence
as one of two reasons (another breaking-down, dividing device).
That is, "outward force" implies something "inward" as its opposite:
religious government "deals only with the inward man and his actions"; the distinction is essentially repeated (accumulatio) "which
are all spiritual and to outward force not lyable." The second reason,
"to shew us the worldly force to subdue all the powers and kingdoms
of this world, which are upheld by outward force only," implies a
basic paradox that will become explicit later—spiritual battles must
be won by weakness and humility rather than by repressive force.
Paradox itself, in which two concepts are ostensibly incompatible,
becomes involved in the complex of two-way conceptual relations.
Like the formulations analyzed earlier, the incompatibility of the
members is resolved in a true understanding of the terms themselves, and in the real world by making the stated conditions prevail. We understand that humility and weakness of spirit are true
strength, and of more power ultimately than worldly force.

Having separated civil from spiritual government, the outer from
the inner man, Milton develops his argument in terms which define
and clarify the spiritual part of the original distributio. The stylistic
process reflects the inward resolution and freedom consequent upon
orderly separation. We now get complementary terms—for faculties,
forces or concepts that function coordinately and smoothly. The
"inward man," for instance, Milton defines as "the inward part of

man, his understanding and his will." Appositives replace separated, antithetical relationships; words now further reveal the nature of initial, tentative formulations instead of posing conflicting ideas. As in the introduction, we have moved from the separate and incompatible to a realm of resolution, smoothness and coordination. In a *correctio,*Milton conjoins "the work of divine grace" with "the inward part of man" as the coordinate forces from which men's actions issue. Again, the "yet not" of the *correctio* seems to introduce an adversative direction which turns, with "simply thence," to an additive formulation. The new, more complex (not "simply") and transcendent force of God is coordinated with the inward man: man's actions proceed from his will and understanding, but in conjunction with the work of divine grace upon them. The feeling of coordination in the figure is carried out in the syntax as well, for the terms are established in parallel dependent, suspended clauses, connected by the coordinate conjunction "and."

The syntactical resolution of the dependent clause resolves the coordinate "dependencies" into a larger whole: "are the whole matter of religion under the gospels." Milton's conceptual system resolves coordinates into more and more comprehensive entities, which themselves break down into other sets of coordinate concepts. Spiritual growth perpetuates itself. "What evangelic religion is, is told in two words, faith and charity; or beleef and practise." When the reader reaches what may be called a transcendent realm of spiritual generality (all of "evangelic religion"), terms begin to leave behind even their coordinate existence and the reader feels fusion of meaning as distinctions or attempts to distinguish cease. The next sentence is constructed as a *distributio* of coordinates: both faith and charity flow "either the one from the understanding, the other from the will"; but the introductory "either" implies an "or," and when it occurs it essentially resolves the initial division of functions into a "sameness"—"or both jointly from both." The "which way?" implied by the "either . . . or" construction becomes irrelevant as such distinctions cease to exist.

The following two clauses exhibit a combination of the modes of development we have already seen. The truly governed state not only evolves from point to point in time, it builds upon what has preceded and includes it in present development. "Once indeed naturally free, but now only" sets up a major distinction between man's prelapsarian state and his present state and suggests some such statement as "but now enslaved by sin." But this suggested distinction, a potentially irresolvable disparity between unfallen past and fallen present, is not made. The sentence moves us instead into resolution. Man was once naturally free; despite the fall, he is now *also* free nonetheless. The disparity between fallen and unfallen painfully exists, but it is resolved both syntactically and in actuality by regeneration and divine grace. The terms in turn fuse in meaning; "regeneration" refers to the change within and "divine grace" to the external agent, yet the conjunction "and" implies their simultaneous operation: neither can be distinguished as either preceding or causing the other. This linguistic pattern of disparity-resolution-union derives from and in turn suggests a basic and crucial rhythm of human existence. The reader, as he becomes attuned to this pattern, begins to make it part of his "inner spirit"; he feels it as the natural and inevitable set of assumptions by which he should understand and act in the political crisis. Moreover, since the "inner light" is for the protestant the most trustworthy guide to divine moral and spiritual order, not to realize politically and spiritually the continually affirmed pattern is to live in perpetual violation of God's intended order, and thereby to miss the way of ultimate spiritual union with God and immediate harmony within the polity.

Succeeding combinations of terms have varied but related effects. "Common sense and principles unquestion'd," for instance, are syntactically and rhythmically parallel but different in meaning. "Evident to common sense" means that the argument is valid because the conclusion is consistent with our experience of the actual world. To say "evident to principles unquestion'd," on the other hand, means evident in the light of principles inherently known—natural reason ("those unwritten lawes and Ideas which nature hath engraven in us"[8]). The syntactic coordination of the two terms implies again the ideal unity of the inner and the outer.

"Free and unconstrainable" similarly registers as a set of coordinate internal-external concepts. Here, however, we also feel the second term as a further clarification of the first—it exists in a double relationship. The terms further operate within a larger distributive syntactical framework which continues with the second part—"and our practice," which in turn is broken down: "not only from faculties endu'd with freedom, but from love and charity besides." The effect of even further branching in "love and charity" relates back to the fusion of "both jointly from both," for either term could indicate the internal spiritual state or its manifestation in action. (There are acts of "love" or "charity," for instance, or we say he is full of "love," or "charity.")

The following two clauses repeat the effect of "once indeed naturally free, but now only. . . ." "And all these by trangression lost" abruptly (and with a misleading conjunction) takes away the accumulated sense of faculties working in perfect spiritual coordination with each other and in conjunction with God's divine power. As above, however, and in imitation of the pattern of human experience, what was lost is doubly restored in the very next phrase, "but renewed and regenerated." The alliteration and coordination complete the double fusion of meaning—each term indicates action performed upon us from without as well as the process of the action within.

"Power and gift" characterize the means by which God effects regeneration. The terms exemplify again an affective pattern that we have seen. "Power" distances God by suggesting force, superiority, and the absence of any necessity to yield or to meet a subject on his level. "Gift," on the other hand, carries the very different connotations of "giving to" rather than "exercising over," of humility and the desire to please and meet another at his own level. The terms enforce us with an understanding of the qualities of God's relationship to man, and the order of their occurrence in the reader's apprehension is significant. The qualities are different, seemingly irreconcilable; we feel an almost instantaneous "softening" or state of sympathy replace the initial feeling of harshness and separation. The progression parallels patterns we have seen before and suggests the movement away from harshness, tension and separation toward the unity and harmony of a polity which properly separates powers within itself. In this way the ideal course for the state parallels God's own worldly manifestations of himself: the Hebrews of the Old Testament knew his power; the believers in Christ, his merciful giving. But the coordination of the terms also *resolves* the tension between them; the polity need not give up one for the other when the two can be combined and coordinated. God's power is exercised in giving as is the polity's in allowing freedom of belief.

After repeated coordinations which branch off into other coordinations, and potential conflicts which are resolved by yet further coordinations, the syntactical resolution of this sentence returns us to the problem of forcing the conscience. The final clause emphasizes the nature of true civil government under the gospel by contrasting with previous formulations sets of coordinated terms that create an unresolvable situation. Force must forthwith "frustrate and make of no effect both the religion and the gospel." From these coordinated terms Milton turns to *antithesis*: "to compel outward profession is to compel hypocrisy, not to advance religion." As the previous figures first established the sense of true government and then showed the spiritual state attainable, so Milton here first establishes the false, irresolvable conditions, and then characterizes the nature of false government in antithesis. The reader senses forces opposed to one another; the impulses of the inner spirit no longer flow outward to create a continually evolving, harmonious, and self-refining order. External force blocks the free manifestation of the internal spirit, and, further, as also suggested by the antithesis, causes disparity between the inner nature and outer appearance of the individual— hypocrisy.

The distributions, antitheses, coordinate sets of terms, disparities and so on, create a feeling for the essential qualities of two basic conditions: one in which the church and state are in their proper relationship to each other, the other in which they are not. True, spiritual religious government, allowing free movement to the individual conscience, eases and fulfills its participants: it is one in which possible tensions exist, paradoxically, in a state of resolution; ostensible losses are more than restored, and there is a continual unfolding and branching out of untroubling interrelationships. Civil government remains on its own side, so to speak, of the formulation "civil and religious." Though inherently separate, in this proper relation to religion, the civil magistrate makes up part of the totally coordinated, smoothly and freely functioning state. Interference from the civil magistrate, on the other hand, is disruptive. Instead of internal resolution and unity, one senses strain and contradiction. The figures separate, frustrate, and divide rather than make cohesive. Concepts remain disjunct, and the attempt to unify or regain is frustrated rather than furthered.

If these patterns pervade the tract in its syntactical figures and in verbal relationships, the essential nature of the truly free Christian commonwealth is revealed as well in the general structure of the tract. The experience and meaning of the organization differ from but complement the verbal and syntactic patterns. Milton calls our attention to structure in the final paragraph:

> On these four scriptural reasons as on a firm square this truth, the right of Christian and evangelic liberty, will stand immoveable against all those pretended consequences of license and confusion which for the most part men most licentious and confused themselves, or such as whose severities would be wiser than divine wisdom, are even aptest to object against the waies of God. . . . (39)

The natural inference from the demonstrative pronoun is that four clearly identifiable reasons have been given, and that each has had clear scriptural support. On looking back to clarify in our minds the organization of the tract, however, we do not find any such simple structuring. Before the final paragraph, the nearest indication of a major break is the paragraph on page thirty-two, which begins "A fourth reason why the magistrate ought not to use force in religion. . . ." Milton begins the whole discussion with a statement that would seem to correspond to this:

> That for beleef or practise in religion according to this conscientious perswasion no man ought to be punished or molested by any outward force on earth whatsoever, I distrust not, through Gods implor'd assistance, to make plane by these following arguments.
>
> First it cannot be deni'd, being the main foundation of our protestant religion that we of these ages . . . can have no other ground in matters of religion but only from the scriptures. (5-6)

Between this "first" and the "fourth reason," however, the reader loses his sense of a clearly-ordered numerical structure. The four major paragraph breaks mark definite changes in subject, but they do not reflect the complexities, subtleties, and shades by which the argument develops within the paragraphs. Milton does not give four simple and distinct proofs, and he elsewhere omits parts and divisions whose presence he has implied. Enunciation of the "second" and "third" gives way to local enumerations, responses to objections, and "lastly's."

Why, then, does Milton specifically refer to the square and its four sides? The answer lies in the sense of order to which the strongly affirmative "as on a firm square" returns us after a continually "de-structured" reading experience. The writer of the tract yielded to the inner impulses of "natural duty and affection" over the demands of an external, conventional, and secondary propriety. The tract, in turn, reorients the reader. Resolution, wholeness, consistency and freedom from tension and division can only result, Milton implies, when the reader relinquishes his commitment to the established conventional order of things, to the external rule of worldly Custom and Error.

To transform men from creatures of custom to creatures of God's spirit, Milton suggests initially an organizational structure that, if followed carefully, would have the directive, controlling feeling of worldly logic and argumentation. The reader's attention is immediately drawn, however, to the pressing problems of moment-to-moment reading and conflicting structures. He experiences, in the diverse motions of the prose, the continual unfolding that the spirit can achieve in the perfect freedom of God's service. When the reader finally returns to a basic scriptural order, it is with the understanding that proper separation of government frees men to "re-form"—to act upon the immediate promptings of the spirit, but still in conjunction with and according to God's divine purpose.

The "First it cannot be deni'd" sentence initiates the process of reform, for the complex syntax necessitates a concentration on immediate linguistic events. The sentence provides information in a manner different from the too easily and externally apparent order of an enumerated series of points:

> First it cannot be deni'd, being the main foundation of our protestant religion, that we of these ages, having no other divine rule or autoritie from without us warrantable to one another as a common ground but the holy scripture, and no other within us but the illumination of the Holy Spirit so interpreting that scripture as warrantable only to our selves and to such whose consciences we can so perswade, can have no other ground in matters of religion but only from the scriptures. (6)

Structurally, the sentence consists of a main clause broken up at two points by dependent clauses which suspend completion. The dependent clauses increase in length from first to last, and the second two form the *distributio* pattern we have seen before, differentiating between inner and outer grounds for religious belief. The effect of the sentence, however, is not exactly "progressive," as we expect meaning to be. We have essentially an enthymeme-like statement in which the first premise is also the conclusion: the only external authority is holy scripture; the only internal authority is our interpretation (illuminated by the Holy Spirit) of holy scripture; therefore the only ground of belief is holy scripture. The sentence involves us, very literally, so that we lose our sense of what the beginning was and emerge with a sense only of the clear resolution of the syntactical structure: "can have no other ground in matters of religion but only from the scriptures." In the tautology of the statement, the individuation of each member becomes subordinate to its existence as part of the whole from which the conclusion gathers and seems to draw us away and finally spring us free.

The succeeding sentence has somewhat the same effect:

> And these being not possible to be understood without this divine illumination, which no man can know at all times to be in himself, much less to be at any time for certain in any other, it follows clearly, that no man or body of men in these times can be the infallible judges or determiners in matters of religion to any other mens consciences but thir own. (6)

Effects of sound in the first half of the sentence (the rhyme and repetition of "these being not possible to be" and "no man can know at all times to be . . .") and the difficult series of phrases ("to be at any time for certain in any other . . .") combine with the dependency of the clauses to withhold the anxious reader from resolution. The comparatively straightforward nature of the second half gives a feeling of relieved stability when reached, and the reader again emerges from the sentence primarily (if not entirely) with the memory of what he has most recently encountered: "no man or body of men in these times can be the infallible judges or determiners in matters of religion to any other mens consciences but thir own." Even in this second half one feels continual extensions and qualifications until the sentence is tied down with "but thir own."

Like the sentences, the argument itself seems to evolve and move in random, momentarily important directions rather than to conform to any strictly laid out organizational plan. After "first it cannot be deni'd," for instance, there is what may be called an "incremental" development. That is, the argument advances slightly as each sentence explores an aspect of the subject—the subject is "filled in" in our apprehension. The first sentence, as we have seen, is premises and conclusion in itself—only scripture can be the basis for belief. The second sentence, another such self-contained unit, adds to the first that no man can judge any man's conscience but his own. The two are related grammatically by "these" but not logically. The second sentence follows the first but does not necessarily follow from it. In the form of explanation, the third, "And therefore . . . , " offers both example and proof for the preceding premises; the fourth performs the same function in a slightly different way.

These statements have a relatively close relationship to one another. The fourth sentence, however, shifts unexpectedly from a statement of principle to a *contrarium* comparing Catholic and Protestant. The statement follows from what had preceded, as indicated by the "if then," but like the statements above, it does not follow necessarily. Each sentence allows for a variety of statements that could follow from it, though none is necessarily implied. We can see by hindsight where we have been, though we can not predict where we are going. Thus the fifth sentence, also, "With good cause therfore . . . ," follows logically, as indicated by "therfore," but not predictably from the fourth. Here, in fact, the discussion has circled back to essentially a restatement of the earlier proposition: "neither traditions, councels nor canons of any visible church, much less edicts of any magistrate or civil session, but the scripture only can be the final judge or rule in matters of religion, and that only in the conscience of every Christian to himself." (7)

This restatement, like the first sentence, collects and includes material from statements in-between. Milton goes on to a parenthetical subject, the origin of the name Protestant, and then restates the essential doctrine again:

> And with that name hath ever bin received this doctrine, which prefers the scripture before the church, and acknowledges none but the Scripture sole interpreter of itself to the conscience. (7)

Following this restatement and again growing out of previous material, the explanation as to why conscience must be the supreme judge in all things introduces another slight advance. Later, the supremacy of conscience is again proposed:

> Seeing then that in matters of religion, as hath been prov'd, none can judge or determin here on earth, no not church-governors themselves against the consciences of other beleevers, my inference is, that in these matters they neither can command nor use constraint; lest they run rashly on a pernicious consequence, forwarnd in that parable *Matthew* 13. . . . (9)

Here again, however, more material has been assimilated into the argument gradually, so that the subject has expanded to include the concept of Christ as the only true judge in things spiritual and the impossibility of constraint from any nonspiritual force. The argument collects and assimilates, keeping basic doctrines always in view; it rounds itself out as it fills itself in, and without explicit indications of shifts in subject, it advances within large paragraphed sections almost imperceptibly. We are aware of advance only by comparing where we are with where we started. The argument might be said to have a kind of continually assimilative movement, within the "firm square" Milton mentions explicitly.[9]

But if the sense of enumeration is soon abandoned as integral to the overall structure of the tract, there are nonetheless local passages where it does exist and is carried out. In the second major paragraph of the Columbia edition (beginning "From the riddance of these objections . . ."), for instance, Milton sets up the following order:

> . . . the difference in this verie thing principally consists, that it governs not by outward force, and that for two reasons. First because it deals only with the inward man and his actions, which are all spiritual and to outward force not lyable: secondly to shew us the divine excellence of his spiritual kingdom, able without worldly force to subdue all the powers and kingdoms of this world, which are upheld by outward force only. (20)

After a short discussion of the "first" section, he introduces the second part in language identical to the outline:

> The other reason why Christ rejects outward force in the govern-
> ment of his church, is, as I said before, to shew us the divine excel-
> lence of his spiritual kingdom, able without worldly force to subdue
> all the powers and kingdoms of this world, which are upheld by out-
> ward force only. . . . (22)

Yet even here, as is evident from the analysis above of the intervening material, the reader is tremendously involved in the immediate movement of the prose. "The other reason" comes almost as a surprise and one looks back to recall that there was a "first." Again, on pages twenty-five and twenty-six Milton returns "a three-fold answer," the parts of which follow in relatively close succession.

Given the presence of this completed pattern, it is possible to suspect Milton of simple inconsistency. Why, it might be asked, if he effective-ly unstructures the tract as a whole, does he allow structuring devices at all? Presumably, that is, he admits the effect here that he is trying to avoid elsewhere. The answer leads us to the meaning implicit in all the stylistic phenomena we have observed.

In both of these instances we may think of coordinate members of a single answer to a problem. It is significant that the completed pat-terns occur when Milton is explaining the government of Christ's church and building a response to the opposition. That is, consistent with other examples of coordination and proper distribution we have noticed, these coordinations occur on Milton's side rather than on the opponents'. Further, they occur as a consequence of how the argument moves—its "process." The reader feels the validity of yield-ing to the spirit. The argument happens into these lesser structures as part of its onward development, finds it convenient to sustain them for the moment, and then moves on through other forms to the end. The tract as a whole is left to accumulate its points (both in the sense we saw in the above analysis, and the sense of repeated *accumulatio's*) free from the controls of a directing structure. Our apprehension of the argument is that we read and simply forget, in our attention to immediate complexities, that there was an initial "first" and the hint of a controlling structure until we get to "A fourth reason . . . ," which reminds us that there was a first. Even by this time, however, as we look back, the argument has shifted. The "fourth" is a final reason why the magistrates "ought not to use force in religion," while the "First it cannot be deni'd" (6) set forth basic principles of protes-tant religion.

In fact, the major transition to which "A fourth reason . . . " seems to relate occurs about two-thirds through the tract. The transition again implies a structure that makes enumeration irrelevant:

> I have shewn that the civil power hath neither right nor can do right by forcing religious things: I will now shew the wrong it doth; by violating the fundamental privilege of the gospel, the new-birth-right of everie true beleever, Christian libertie. (28)

From "no right" to "wrong" seems an equivocal advance in the argument, another barely perceptible shift. Like the development from clause to clause and from statement to statement, this new section seems to emerge inevitably, to have been implicit in the old section; it is a natural and coordinate growth from it, and the explicitness of the transition asks us to consider *this* the important mode of development in comparison to the vague numerical scheme.

We are not, therefore, to apprehend the tract as having a clear, directing overall structure, the product of forethought and outline. The effects of the freely-moving argument suggest rather an abstract concept, which Milton defines explicitly:

> It will be sufficient in this place to say no more of Christian liberty, than that it sets us free not only from the bondage of those circumstances, place and time in the worship of God: which though by him commanded in the old law, yet in respect of that veritie and freedom which is evangelical, S. Paul comprehends both kindes alike, that is to say, both ceremonie and circumstance, under one and the same contemtuous name of *weak and beggarly* rudiments. . . . (29)

The gift of the gospel is Christian liberty, and the spiritual freedom now natural to man is part of the subject implicit in the style of the tract. The abandoned numerical schemes within the *Treatise* become symbolic of the human forms that may confine and restrict the spirit; as man has spiritually left behind the bondage of the Old Testament, so the tract, as we have seen, subordinates one organizational form for a mode of development that affectively creates in us an understanding of the true and necessary evolution of the spirit. Its natural existence is to explore freely, to move into unanticipated understandings grounded in the basic principles of Christian protestant faith, which are in turn grounded in scripture. The "first" exists to be departed from. The reader is made to concentrate on an immediate and developing present, which forms the basis for an unpredictable future; he is aware primarily of the most immediate past as that from which the present has developed. The style of the tract brings the reader to a sense of his own spiritual potential, one of maturity, greater wisdom, and freedom to participate in the ideal states Milton presents, and to further their fulfillment in the polity itself. Restoration of the scriptural framework is a resolution present from the beginning, but forgotten. In a new fullness of spiritual experience, the reader finally combines within himself a sense of the "foursquare" framework and the moment-to-moment accumulative development. He becomes in spirit like the phalanx that allows for infinite inclusiveness.

Given the political situation outlined in the introduction, one can extend the stylistic implications of the *Treatise*. Milton hopes to effect reformation by creating in his audience, specifically Cromwell's summoned council, but also the public at large, a sense of the difference between a government functioning as it should and a government functioning as it has. Beginning with the first sentence, as we have seen, the government operating in accord with God's New Testament is one in which contrarieties and antitheses can be instantaneously resolved. The true and proper separation of functions allows, paradoxically, for unity and harmony, an extension into the civil realm of that unity and harmony of spirit in the Christian regenerate in God. The ideally performing polity, the reader must come to feel, is one in which elements are properly distributed, each to its own realm; momentary problems or potential conflicts are resolved by sensitive and careful attention to the true nature of their elements and the order created for them. Once this harmonious coexistence of disparate elements is established, it perpetuates itself; spirit and state are the reciprocal beneficiaries of freedom—the freedom allowed the spirit by the state manifests and reinvests itself in the polity. Inner and outer existence are fused, so that paradox, for instance, is no longer felt as paradox but as further harmony. As the inseparability of the various linguistic configurations from the onward movement of the argument in which they arise implies, Christian liberty and the harmonious existence of disparate but unified elements are inextricable and mutually supportive. For the civil magistrate to exceed the limits defined for him by the natural and proper order signified in the distribution is to create the England between 1640 and 1660, a state in which internal contradiction, antithesis and conflict prevail. The absence of tropes suggests a general unwillingness to associate the ideal government with the often harsh but moving, exciting, and emotionally stimulating world of, say, *Areopagitica* and the antiprelatical tracts. The mood of the *Treatise* is unity and harmony, easy conjunction of elements that have been in conflict. The style of the tract answers to the decorum of the entities represented; they in turn have been created in response to a need in the polity. The reader must take the way that literally "feels best."

Notes

1. *John Milton* (London, 1955), pp. 99-100.

2. E. M. W. Tillyard, *Milton* (London, 1930), p. 212; Denis Saurat, *Milton, Man and Thinker* (New York, 1925), pp. 26-27.

3. *Reason of Church-Government*, in *Complete Prose Works of John Milton*, ed. D. M. Wolfe, 6 vols. to date (New Haven, 1953-   ), I, 792. I will refer after this to *Complete Prose*.

4. Both letters are in *Life Records of John Milton*, ed. J. M. French (New York, 1966), IV, 285-88; my italics.

5. *The Works of John Milton*, ed. Frank Allen Patterson, 18 vols. in 21 (New York, 1931-38), VI, 105-25. Unless otherwise specified, succeeding references are to this edition and volume.

6. *Doctrine and Discipline of Divorce, Complete Prose*, III, 321.

7. This whole passage is on page 1, Vol. VI, Columbia ed.

8. *Complete Prose*, I, 764.

9. The reading experience suggests the image of true church government in *Reason of Church-Government*, where each "parochiall Consistory is a right homogeneous and constituting part beginning in it self as it were a little Synod, and towards a general assembly moving on her own basis in an even and firme progression, as those smaller squares in battell unite in one great cube, the main phalanx, an embleme of truth and stedfast-nesse" (*Complete Prose* I, 789).

Stanley Fish, in *Self-Consuming Artifacts: Studies in Seventeenth-Century Prose and Poetry* (Berkeley, 1972), pp. 265-302, emphasizes the importance of this image to the structure of the tract; Michael Lieb, in *The Dialectics of Creation* (Amherst, 1970), n. 1, p. 108, observes that "the angelic phalanx . . . in its sublimity of movement [in *Paradise Lost*] enacts symbolically the very spiritualizing that man might undergo if he remains obedient."

Logic & the Epic Muse:
Reflections on Noetic Structures
in Milton's Milieu

WALTER J. ONG, S.J.
Saint Louis University

1. The Age of Logic

In John Milton we have a rare if not unique phenomenon, a major poet who produced a textbook treatise on logic. No one has quite known what to make of this poet as logician. Particularly since the onset of the romantic age, much criticism has looked with suspicion at any attempt to couple formal logic with poetry. Yet, knowing Milton's poetry and its milieu, we are haunted by the thought that perhaps Milton really did undertake just such a coupling, particularly in his great exercise in theodicy, *Paradise Lost.* "To justifie the wayes of God to men" certainly implies some kind of logical procedure.

We have had some studies, and some very good ones, of certain relationships between Milton's *Artis logicæ plenior institutio ad Petri Rami methodum concinnata* and his other writings, particularly his poetry.[1] For, paradoxically, in Milton's poetry logic appears perhaps more assertive than in his prose, which commonly runs more to rhetoric than to straightforward reasoning. These studies commonly follow a valid enough procedure: we work through Milton's poetry, and perhaps some prose as well, for structures identified in his logic; we find that there are some inevitable enough to have occurred even had he not studied logic at all, but that many others evince the programming of a self-conscious logician; we thereby assure ourselves that logic, even conscious logic, can be at work in forceful poetry; and finally with virtuous expostulation we downgrade much latter-day antilogical poetic and perhaps become crusaders for logic in poetry.

The lesson this kind of exercise teaches may be a good one to learn. But the studies which have conveyed it to us have also opened the way to larger questions which might be worth examination. What produced a poet-logician at this particular juncture of history? How does Milton's logic fit into the history of logic as a whole? Looking to how it does, could we say something more about the relationship of his logic to his poetry, and particularly to *Paradise Lost*? For both logic and epic do have a history. There was a time when they were not, they came into being under specific circumstances, and the relationship of each of them to the human lifeworld is a changing one.

Milton lived toward the end of what we may call the age of logic, in a culture which had assumed, quite explicitly for over four hundred years and before that less intently for some 1500 years, that the study of formal logic was central to liberal education, to each individual man's full realization of his potential as man. The age of logic continued through and beyond the Renaissance until the romantic movement realigned cultural and psychic structures. Of course, in profound ways logic has an abiding effect on us still. Indeed, it has an intensified effect, for formal logic (or, as it is often styled, logistic or mathematical logic or symbolic logic) makes possible our computer culture and puts men on the moon. But since the romantic and technological revolutions—or revolution, because the two coincide in time and share common roots[2]—the position of logic in the curriculum and in consciousness has shifted. Logic is now taken to be specialized equipment, the possession either of bemused intellectual boondogglers or of direct users, perhaps equally bemused but nonetheless often important and powerful users, involved in major decision making with the support of computerized information. These specialists, however, are relatively few in number, and they are the only ones directly concerned with formal logic, which is simply not a part of the noetic equipment of every well-informed man.

The "age of logic" can be used as a cultural denominator together with a correlative term, the "age of rhetoric."[3] Even the most recent histories of logic, however, do not use such denominators. Bochenski's invaluable work, for example, treats formal logic in well-programmed and quite legitimate isolation, eschewing any "psychologism" or other divagations whereby logic might be related to anything in the human lifeworld outside itself.[4] William and Martha Kneale's history is more culturally oriented but does not go into any of the deeper structures of culture.[5] Bochenski, however, does point out that formal logic grew out of discussion or dispute,[6] and thus suggests its connection with rhetoric. The "age of rhetoric" and the "age of logic" in fact take on meaning not from standard histories or rhetoric or logic but from studies such as those of Neumann and Havelock and Durand,[7] although such "ages" are not fully worked out by any of these scholars either. Most other

historians of thought have not even begun to assimilate or interior-
ize the grounds for such concepts—which is regrettable, since without awareness of the relationship of rhetoric and logic to psychic
evolution, historical thinking exhibits a certain externalism which
is less and less satisfying to an age attracted to history in psychological and existential depth.

2. The Rhetorical Roots of Logic

In the West what we are here calling the age of logic grew up within,
and eventually out of, a vastly longer preceding age, which we can
style the age of rhetoric. Until the first scripts, some 6000 years ago
(around 3500 B.C.), for hundreds of thousands of years of human
existence verbal knowledge storage and hence thought itself was
dependent upon oral skills. Verbalized knowledge could not be
"looked" up; it had to be re-*called*, brought back orally. In the absence of writing, oral cultures around the globe have placed a value
on speech which strikes those in literate, technologized cultures now
as at best quaint and at worst hollow and pretentious: savages appear
to us childlike in their fascination with the skilled verbalizer, by
whom it seems, they somehow want to be bamboozled. At the
opening of the age of logic we find Socrates and Plato reproaching
poets and rhetoricians and their audiences precisely for courting
deception of the sort facilitated by orality as manifest in poetry
for, as Havelock has shown, Socrates and Plato were opting for an
economy of thought and expression made possible by writing and
quite different from the oral economy inherited from Homer's
day and earlier.[8] Plato's exclusion of poets from his Republic was
neither whimsical nor incidental, but absolutely *de rigueur*, for
the poets at that stage of cultural development were, with orators,
standard-bearers for the old oral or rhetorical order of things.
  Oral speech, of which the epic poets and orators were such masters
and which the Sophists, paradoxically, with the help of writing, had
brought to new stages of perfection, differed in a primary oral culture, or preliterate culture, from oral speech in our highly literate
cultures today. In primary oral or oral-aural culture speech had a
built-in mnemonic function and a corresponding texture, woven
of proverbs, apothegms, epithets, and other mnemonic equipment,
almost entirely missing from our literate oral speech today. This
kind of speech, with the thought patterns it registers and supports—
repetitious, balanced, fulsome, hyperbolic, unstinted in *copia* or

flow, when at its best punctuated by epigram and aphorism, highly polarized or partisan, characterized in short by the features still associated today with highly "oratorical" style—was itself a major accomplishment. It had not been come by easily and was of course never thoroughly mastered by a majority of the members of any oral-aural society. In such societies expert oral performance was, and still is, held in high esteem precisely because it is something which everyone in an oral culture desperately needs but which only the few really achieve.

In Athens around the fourth century before Christ, oral perfor-mance was reduced to a reflective science or "art" (*techne*) of rhetoric. Writing had made possible such "arts," unknown and quite simply unthinkable in purely oral cultures. The new medium of writing, which would be brought to a peak with print, thus be-gan by reinforcing the oral, although it also transformed it—for the scientific or "linear" thinking made possible by writing would now be available in written documents but also would feed back into oral performance and, ultimately, alter the entire oral economy described above: today old-style oratory has vanished from tech-nologized cultures. But it was long in disappearing and continued effectively to dominate academic and intellectual life through the Renaissance until the rise of romanticism.[9] Milton came along when the force of oral performance was very much alive but giving out, as we shall see.

The development of rhetoric as an "art" or organized field of knowledge is a major stage in the history of consciousness. For rhetoric moves the mind from the polysemous sign language of symbols into more explicit consciousness, to the point where more and more signs have "proper meaning."[10] Symbols, psychologically rooted below the level of articulation, operate from deep within the unconscious, whence they work their way more or less into conscious light. As it makes its way out of the preconceptual, rhetoric "euphemizes" actuality through its typical devices of hyperbole and antithesis and its typical tonality of hope.[11] (Today as in the past, the oppressed are deeply devoted to, and moved by, rhetoric.)

Out of the rhetorical world grew formal logic, as already noted, developed by the ancient Greeks from the methodology of discussion or dispute. Recognition of formal logical structures arose from at-tempts to deal with the problem: *Why* does what this man says de-molish what that man says? The transit from a totally rhetorical culture to a culture knowing formal logic is another major stage in the history of consciousness. The transit is not a direct progression but an antithetical movement: logic is rooted in rhetoric, but it also contrasts with rhetoric. It works the mind still further out of the subconscious (though never entirely so—the persuasion that it does or can do is an illusion from which some logicians, notably Ramists, or other philosophers often suffer[12]). Rhetoric, too, had related antithetically to the state which preceded it. But logic is even more antithetical, being so not only in its relationship to the antecedent rhetorical stage, but in its very being: logic is polarized in one way toward negativity and violent destruction. It moves toward greater and greater explicitation, typified especially by stress on definition. But, since definition (*de-finire*, to mark off the limits) manifests what a thing is by making clear what it is not, logic proceeds by setting up greater and greater antitheses, typified by stress on division and distinctions—in the case of Ramist logic dichotomies, the most divisive of divisions, modeled on the difference between yes and no, and featured today in the binary structures of computer operations. The term "logic chopper" expresses a deep awareness of what formalized thought does, of the price man has to pay for clarity and distinctness: he has to segment actuality, tearing it to pieces, setting one part against another. All logic is diaeretic. The development of consciousness exacts an awful price.

It has been pointed out that formal logic has shown no evenly continuous evolution in its two millennia and more of existence: a century of rapid development is followed by a decline, and when new beginnings are made once more, often the search must begin anew, the older achievements having been lost except for a few fragments.[13] Nevertheless, if we look at the history of logic in the very long perspectives of the total history of mankind, we can readily discern an overall pattern of growth.

With only minimal adumbrations in earlier thinkers, formal logic was actually invented by Aristotle (384-322 B.C.), as he himself accurately claimed. It languished somewhat after Boethius (A.D. 480?-524?). The scholastic philosophers revived it in the twelfth century, and starting in the latter half of the same century constructed a new logic unknown to antiquity, formulated metalogically with an extremely sophisticated semiotics (Latin based, of course).[14] Many of the developments of medieval scholastic logic, unexamined since the early 1500s, still remain to be explored. It is certain that this logic is not only a major intrinsic advance in the science but also a development of incalculable psychological and cultural importance. Scholastic logic, with the scholastic philosophy accompanying it, is, for example, inseparable from the appearance of the medieval European universities and thus ultimately of all universities anywhere in the world today, which, without exception, trace essentially if not in every detail directly or indirectly to the universities of medieval Europe. This fact itself shows something about what can happen when consciousness "rises": once risen, it somehow implements its own spread through prolific and productive institutions.

The Renaissance marks a temporary regression in the interior development of logic, but by no means the total disappearance of interest in the subject, for the medieval curricular emphasis which had made logic central to the entire educational enterprise continues through the Renaissance to a great extent unimpaired. The humanists were more concerned with man's lifeworld than with formal structures, but despite their protests against logical formalism, logic remained with very few exceptions absolutely integral to the common Renaissance curriculum, although it shrank to a residual science—with the result that there are no great Renaissance logicians comparable to the great logicians of antiquity or the Middle Ages.[15] Besides retaining logic within the curriculum, the Renaissance expressed its continuing interest in the subject by producing the first histories of formal logic, the earliest of them by Peter Ramus.[16] They were not very good histories and were at points disablingly hostile, but they showed that even at the center of humanism logic could not be ruled out of the intellectual tradition. Indeed, humanist rhetoric, which was calculated to dislodge logic, in some ways effectively preserved it: compared to rhetoric as this is taught today, humanist rhetoric is strikingly close to formal logic in its vaunting of formal structures.[17]

Nevertheless, humanism did set logic back, condemning many scholastic discoveries to temporary oblivion. Modern logic, or "mathematical logic" (also called "symbolic logic" or "logistic"), which had its indecisive beginnings more or less with Leibnitz (1646-1716) but took its effective rise from the work of George Boole starting in 1847, branched out first from the object-language of ancient logic supplemented by its own rich use of variables, but only after 1930 picked up again the medieval interest in semantics which the humanists had discarded.[18]

This brief overview of the history of the logic can serve to situate Milton in some general way. In logic Milton was a follower of Peter Ramus (1515-1572) in the very patent sense that his *Artis logicæ plenior institutio*, published first in 1672 but almost certainly written around 1648,[19] is an edition, with commentary worked in, of Ramus' *Dialectic* or *Logic*. Milton's complete Latin title can be rendered, *A Fuller Course in the Art of Logic Conformed to the*

Method of Peter Ramus. Developed by Ramus out of preliminary works of his which had begun to appear in 1543, Ramus' *Dialectic* had been given its first definitive form in 1555 and its final form in 1572, just before its author's tragic death.[20] Ramus' position in the history of logic has been detailed by Risse[21] and Bochenski, and more perfunctorily by William and Martha Kneale, and need not be rehearsed here. We know that Ramist logic signals no real development in the internal history of the science, for Ramus was not a speculative or structural innovator. The syllogism with singular terms, sometimes cited as one innovation of Ramus', is to be found treated over two centuries earlier in Ockham.[22] Ramus' logic is essentially a residual form of earlier logic minus the significant medieval developments, simplified for pedagogical purposes with the help of Ramist "method," which itself was part of logic. "Method" maximized visualist assimilation and recall, in accord with noetic developments encouraged by the invention of print.[23]

Ramus' own brand of humanism was a hybrid: it combined a standard humanist revulsion for the scholastic curriculum in which he had been educated, an interest in the human lifeworld which was really subhumanist in its lack of the poetic vision of a Petrarch or the wit of an Erasmus or the warmth of a More, a fund of real learning which was humanistic in its historical grounding, a drive toward practicality or achievement which strongly recommended him to upwardly mobile Calvinist bourgeois, and an overwhelming concern with classification which identifies him as the most scholastic of scholastics in one way while in another way the nonspeculative, rule-of-thumb quality of his classifications reveal a mind which is basically not effectively philosophical. It is ironic—and Ramist logical method did not at all prepare the soul for irony— that this antischolastic, humanistic reformer of the curriculum should be known chiefly for the most omnivorous logic the world has ever seen.

3. Ramist Logic: Its "Practical" Bent

The structure and content of Ramist logic is well known and need only be sketched here. Ramist logic is divided into two "parts." The first part was called *inventio*, the finding or discovery of "arguments" or middle terms, ways of proving or disproving a statement—for in the disputatious climate of both the age of rhetoric and the age of logic, all utterance was more or less paradigmatically taken to be position-taking, a form of commitment opposed to some other position, and thus demanding proof. Ramus' headings for arguments—cause, effect, related things, etc.—are what other writers from classical antiquity had styled *loci*, places (or *loci communes*, commonplaces), but Ramists usually avoid these terms, simply referring collectively to "arguments."

The second part of Ramist logic was called *dispositio*, arrangement, or *iudicium*, judgment. (Ramus had earlier used the first of these terms and later changed to the second; Milton uses the first and explains why.) Arrangement or judgment treats how to dispose arguments first "axiomatically" into statements and secondly "dianoetically" into combinations of statements, which are in turn divided into syllogisms and "method." All of logic that Ramus treats is organized in binary subdividisions and subsubdivisions of his initial two "parts."

Ramus' procrustean organization of the material of logic into prefabricated dichotomies would have been agony to a more insightful and speculative mind. It recommended itself to Ramus because his mind was nonspeculative and "practical." He wanted to get through the material—the "course"—expeditiously, to "cover" the matter. It is this impatiently or bluntly pragmatic quality of Ramist thought that is important here. Ramus' mind was not a speculative mind. His hostility to metaphysics is well known, vaunted by Ramus himself in his captious commentary on Aristotle's *Metaphysics* and elsewhere, and further advertised by his many followers.[24] Ramus' own insistence on *usus* or exercise earned him the name of *usuarius* or usufructuary.[25] All studies were to feature *usus* or exercise, and in the case of logic this meant particularly that logic was to be put to use immediately in analyzing texts and in the student's own writing and speech making. By implication logic enabled one to gain the upper hand not only over other men but also over the physical environment. Logic governed not only thought but action. It is from Ramism that we today inherit the idea of "acting logically," which seldom has much to do with formally cognized structures.

Ramus' stress on *usus* or exercise derived from the humanist concept of education as basically rhetorical, preparing the boy and young man to express himself in the life of the citizen, to lead an active life of affairs. At the core of much humanism, as typified for example in Lorenzo Valla, we find an utter scorn of philosophy in the sense of knowledge for the sake of knowing, and a belief that the only knowledge worthy of man is that ordered to action.[26] Because it was thought of as governing human action and interaction rather than as concerned with purely formal mental structures, Ramist logic has been styled a rhetorical logic, as in this sense indeed it was,

although paradoxically again, it was basic to Ramus' reform to separate rhetoric as an art absolutely from logic.[27] It should be pointed
out that Ramus was to a notable degree concerned with formal
logical structures and to this extent truly a logician.[28]

Many of the particulars treated in Ramist logic (including Milton's)
hardly appear very usable for practical purposes, it is true. What immediate tactical advantage would there be in knowing, for example,
that in the argument of distribution and the argument of definition
there is "a relation of reciprocity, one of all parts with the whole in
the first and one of definitions with what is defined in the second?"[29]
This is typical of the "rules" in Ramus' logic which are reproduced
in Milton's. But the age of logic had developed precisely the mentality
which could believe that such "rules" enabled one to cope with
actuality. And indeed if such rules were as often as not trivia for
practical purposes, in their conglomerate impact they did in a way
enable one to cope. Such rules symbolized and fostered the aggressive,
no-quarter-given, intently analytic habits of mind which are at the
base of modern science and technology and which have roots of course
reaching back beyond Ramus through medieval scholasticism and,
more remotely, to the ancient Greeks.

4. Ramist "Method" and Memory

The Ramist tendency to reduce logic to an elaborate memory system
is allied to the Ramist sense of practicality, for as a memory system
logic implements an essentially practical operation, the storage and
retrieval of knowledge. All logic has to do with storage and retrieval
of knowledge at least in the sense that it reports on the formal structures within which the mind more or less organizes its holdings.
But Ramist logic specialized in storage and retrieval functions more
than most. This was so because of its stress on "method," which
was the most, if not the only, distinctive feature of Ramist logic.

"Method" was a subpart of dialectic or logic, but it also governed
the way in which logic itself, as well as everything else, was organized
and taught. "Method" prescribed how to organize all assemblages
of statements longer than or other than a syllogism. "Method,"
Ramus explains, proceeds ideally always from the general to the
more and more particular, although at times, by concession, because
of ignorance or recalcitrancy or other defect in the audience, "cryptic
method" must be used, proceeding from the particular to the general.
"Method" governs the organization of even itself, for it governs the

organization of all logic, of which it is a subdivision. Thus "method" shows up as a "part" of logic in a dichotomized outline of logic which is itself the result of "method."

These celebrated dichotomized charts or outlines, into which one can purportedly break down or "analyze" any well-organized discourse to display the "method" by which it necessarily proceeds (if it is any good at all) are in fact, we now recognize, exactly the same in design as flow charts used to program computers today for information storage and retrieval.[30] One of them is reproduced here. The storage-and-retrieval function of such charts has simply become much more evident in our computer age. They are hardly an aid to understanding at all, but rather a way of racking up information so that it can be retrieved in bits as required. Bracketed outlines were not invented by Ramus, of course, for they occur at times in manuscripts. But elaborate charts are much more difficult to copy exactly in manuscript than is straight text, and their widespread currency had to wait until print, since once they are set up in a form, they are as easy to print as text or anything else. Moreover, most charts other than Ramist divide materials into any number of parts, as each subject matter requires. What is characteristic of Ramism is the insistence on division of everything by twos, in the same procrustean binary fashion enforced by computerization.

In many Ramist works or works influenced by Ramists, the same dichotomized outlines serve as analytic tables of "contents," and thus advertise their storage-and-retrieval function. For until typography was pretty fully interiorized so that words in books were thought of as fixed in space, localized and locatable, and the notion that books had "contents" effectively replaced the older notion that books "said" something, tables of contents were commonly skimpy or primitive things, where they were found at all. The Ramist dichotomized charts also serve as models for analytic indexes (later replaced by alphabetic indexes), which are exceedingly rare in manuscript cultures (each copy of a work would normally demand a separate index) and exceedingly common in print cultures, though they take some time to develop there. These charts are arrangements of classes of "places" (*loci*) or "commonplaces" (*loci communes*)— which, as has been seen, Ramus by synecdoche styled simply "arguments." Thus the term "index" as we use it today is shorthand for the original *index locorum* or *index locorum communium* (index of places or index of commonplaces). This term again refers to knowledge storage and retrieval; one went to the "places" to find arguments metaphorically stored there.

5. Ramist Logic as Knowledge Storage and Retrieval

The significance of Ramist logic as a knowledge storage and retrieval device has been made eminently clear by Frances Yates, who has related Ramism circumstantially to the most massive knowledge storage and retrieval systems ever developed apart from writing and print themselves. These were the arts of memory, which flourished in the West from classical antiquity. Although the arts of memory have their roots in oral culture, they continue to compete with writing and print until they pretty well die out as significant phenomena in the period immediately following the appearance of *Paradise Lost* in 1667,[31] when the effects of writing and print are maximized with tables of contents and indexes responding to a sense of localization of knowledge on the page, as suggested above.

To those living in a computer age, the storage system in the Ciceronian or traditional, non-Ramist arts of memory appears essentially "poetic" because of its iconographic procedures. Miss Yates has shown that the principal basis of most arts of memory is the imaginative organization of imagery in space. It should be noted that the arts of memory which she treats are not simply mnemonic verses or formulas, conditioning of the auditory imagination to run through a set routine, but massive structures which implement storage in the imagination and subsequent recall of hundreds and thousands of items. Mnemonic verses are not "arts" of memory since each refers to some specific material. A true art of memory is a generalized system which works for any material at all.

We say an art of memory is "generalized" rather than "abstract," for in a sense most arts of memory are surprisingly concrete. In a typical art of memory, one is taught to fix in the imagination a memory "theater," the interior of some building (at best, a real building to structure the imagination permanently), with its exact sequence of pillars, pilasters, alcoves, panels, or whatever, along one side after the other. To each of these component parts is assigned a highly charged iconographic figure—Leda and the swan, the pillars of Hercules, Jove with his thunderbolts, Hercules and his club, Perseus holding Medusa's head. Ideally, one chooses a building or buildings—for many memory adepts carried a whole acropolis in their heads—which actually house at least some such statuary or paintings, but one generally has to add in the imagination a good deal of supplementary iconographic equipment so that every part of the building, or memory "room," has its own piece. These memory "rooms" remain fixed forever in the imagination of the user, frozen in their sequence by the architecture in which they are situated really and/or imaginatively.

Ramist "method" applied to dialectic or logic, showing what the "parts" of the art are. The binary arrangement here is like that of a computer flow chart today.

According to Ramist doctrine, all communication on any subject ideally proceeds the way in which the subject of dialectic or logic is organized on this chart, that is, from "generals" to "specials" (particulars). Variations from this order can be tolerated only where a particular audience makes special demands, by its recalcitrancy, ignorance, or other ineptitude.

Note that "method," which prescribes this order, is itself a part of dialectic, which in this sense as in other senses is a closed system. "Method" appears (in the ablative case, methodo) at the bottom of the chart.

From an edition of Ramus' "arts" entitled Professio regia executed by Johannes Thomas Freige (Basileae, 1576). Freige or Freigius is the author of the Latin Life of Peter Ramus (Petri Rami vita), which Milton abridges as an appendix to his Logic (Artis logicæ plenior institutio ad Petri Rami methodum concinnata).

65

P. RAMI DIALECTICA.
TABVLA GENERALIS.

Logicæ partes duæ sunt:

INVENTIO argumentorum. Est autem argumentü aut
- Artificiale
  - Primum
    - Simplex
      - Cõsentaneum
        - Absolutè — Causa / Effectus
        - Modo quodam — Subiectum / Adiunctum
      - Dissentaneum
        - Diuersa — Disparata
        - Opposita — Contraria — Affirmata (Relata / Aduersa) / Negata (Priuantia / Contradicentia)
    - Compáratum
      - Quãtitatis — Paria / Imparia (Maiora / Minora)
      - Qualitatis — Similia / Dissimilia
  - A primo ortum
    - 1. Nomen — Coniugata / Notatio
    - 2. Distributio (Partitio / Diuisio) / Definitio
- Inartificiale, ut Testimonium.

IVDICIVM, quod est aut
- Axiomaticum in Enunciato: in quo consider.
  - 1. Partes — Antecedens / Consequens
  - 2.
    - Affectiones
      - 1. Affirmatio / Negatio → Hinc contradictio.
      - 2. Verum — Contingens, cuius iudicium Opinio. / Necessarium, cuius iudicium Scientia. Falsum. Imposibile oppositum necessario.
    - Species
      - Simplex — Generale / Speciale (Infinitum seu particulare / Proprium)
      - Compositü — Cõgregatiuum (Copulatum / Connexum) / Segregatiuum (Discretum / Diiunctum)
- Dianoëti cum in
  - Syllogismo:
    - 1. Partes — Antecedens (Propositio / Assumptio) / Consequens
    - 2. Affectio, quã vrget — Species — Simplex (Contractus / Explicatus) / Compositus (Connexus / Diiunctus)
  - Methodo — Perfecta / Imperfecta, κρυπτ ‹ινᾶ›.

DE INVEN.

Reprinted, by permission of the Harvard College Library, from Petrus Ramus, *Professio regia*, ed. Johannes Thomas Freigius (Basileae: Sebastianus Henricpetri, 1576).

To store knowledge and recall it, one associated it bit by bit with the items in their fixed sequence. Thus—to use an example of my own construction—if one were memorizing a list of the kings of England, one assigned them successively to the successive "rooms" with their respective icons in one's "theater." The heavy symbolic load each icon carried enabled the trained imagination to associate with any individual icon anything that happened to fall with it. For example, if in the sequence of the kings of England King Alfred happened to fall in the position of the pillars of Hercules (pictured as two upright stone pillars), one could think of King Alfred's cakes being cooked on a grid suspended by the pillars; if it was King Stephen who happened to fall there, one could picture his patron Stephen the martyr being stoned to death (*stone* pillars); if Henry VIII, he was a bigamist and worse (*two* pillars with room for more); if James I, he had two numbers (VI of Scotland, I of England) and so on. Other symbols worked in comparable fashion. A good mnemotechnician with a "theater" in his head could learn a list of a hundred names in a quarter of an hour or less, and could repeat the list backwards or forwards equally well, or give every third name or seventh name, or follow other varied patterns of retrieval as real need or pure virtuosity demanded. A recent experimental psychological study has shown how thoroughly efficient this ancient art of memory actually is.[32]

Miss Yates has shown how Ramist logic supplanted this ancient iconographic art by a new noniconographic charting system, which ranged only alphabetized words in an exceedingly simple, abstract diagrammatic order—corresponding exactly, as we have seen, to flow charts for a digital computer and dependent, as I had undertaken to show earlier, upon the feeling for knowledge fostered by the invention of movable alphabetic type.[33] Miss Yates has beautifully characterized the Ramist operation as "a kind of inner iconoclasm,"[34] corresponding to the outer iconoclasm, or actual physical image-breaking tendencies of the Calvinists, to whom Ramism chiefly appealed—and appealed for unstated psychological reasons rather than on doctrinal grounds: the Calvinist mind was print-bound, and found iconographic images dysfunctional.

Ramus knew that his logic served memorization, but his concern with memory is incidental rather than direct. He did not regard memory as "part" of logic or rhetoric or any other art, but instead dropped memory from the curriculum entirely. Memory had traditionally been one of the five parts of rhetoric, the counterpart of the two parts of logic. These five parts of rhetoric, inherited through

Cicero, were: invention, disposition, style, memory, and delivery.
In the Ciceronian tradition dialectic or logic had been constituted
in two parts, invention and disposition. Ramus simply accepted
the two parts of logic, assimilated the first two parts of rhetoric
to these corresponding parts of logic, and assigned style and delivery alone to rhetoric, dropping memory entirely. The reason given
by Ramus for elimination of memory as part of an art was that
memory required no special attention if one always thought (recalled) in terms of the "natural" order of things, which was identical
with the "methodical" order, running from the more "general" to
the more "specific." Such analysis brought forth knowledge in
automatic recall patterns, since one followed the way things themselves "naturally" were—which meant, in fact, the way they were
arranged after being analyzed by Ramist logic into binary flow charts.
charts.

Ramus took this arrangement to be self-evident and self-enforcing,
though it seldom was either. Few persons other than Ramists thought
it self-evident that logic or dialectic was divided into invention and
judgment, judgment into axiomatic and dianoetic, and so on, through
scores of descending dichotomies. But if such divisions of a given
subject were not self-evident, once the subject had been pictured
in a dichotomized chart or its imaginative equivalent, it was rendered
quite susceptible to systematic recall. In place of a memory "theater"
equipped with heavy iconographic figures, Ramus proposed an arrangement of words in a simple dichotomized branching outline.
This was indeed "inner iconoclasm." The images were annihilated
and the visualism of the age was redirected to a text, to visualizable
words.

In ways somewhat suggesting the epic, which incorporates the lifeworld of an entire culture, memory theaters were cosmological in
their sweep. They related to both the microcosm and the macrocosm,
since their symbols were drawn from and referred to both the world
of man, the microcosm or "little world," and the universe exterior
to man, the macrocosm or "great world." Standing in imagination
(or sometimes in reality) in the middle of a "theater" of mnemonic
icons, the mnemotechnician could readily feel himself a "little
world" with which the "great world" (the entire universe around
him) was aligned, point for point, through the mediation of the
symbols along the walls standing between him and it.[35]

Overcome in their imaginations and subconscious by a sense of
this kind of alignment, experts such as Giordano Bruno (1548-1600)
proposed esoteric keys to the "true" interrelation of the iconographic
symbols in the belief that proper selection and arrangements of the

symbols with relation to one another would implement a super-
science explaining all reality at a glance or at least facilitating discourse about any conceivable subject. In the generation before
Bruno, Giulio Camillo Delminio (ca. 1480-1544) had earlier talked
one French king and one Spanish Governor of Milan (who had been
Ariosto's patron) into subsidizing his never completed attempt to
erect an actual physical memory theater of wood with all the symbols
in proper alignment.[36]

Enlarging on some of Miss Yates's suggestions, one can see how
Ramism utilizes this projective cosmology antithetically. The Ramist
could feel himself a noniconographic, logical "little world" aligned
with an equally noniconographic and logical "great world" through
the mediation of the rack of dichotomies which in the various arts
show how things "really" are. The Ramist projection is the wave of
the future, more in accord with a feeling for pure Newtonian space
and computized conceptualizing than were the obsolescent icono-
static theaters.

The plausibility of ventures such as Camillo's and Bruno's was in
great part due to the mnemonic serviceability of iconography from
the time of earliest human beginnings. For early man iconography
was not something decorative, added to already apprehended
actuality for convenience or decoration. Iconography was a way
of life. One reason is that it was essential to knowledge storage and
retrieval.

We know what we can recall. If a person was aware of something
once but can never retrieve it again, we do not and cannot say that
he knows it. To know something is not at all necessarily to have
it in actual consciousness, "in mind," here and now. To know
geometry is not to think of every geometrical theorem here and
now—an impossible feat—but to be able to recall here and now
what one wants to recall. (The old distinction between knowledge
as *actus*, an act, and knowledge as *habitus*, a possession, is in play
here. "Knowledge" normally refers to a *habitus*, not an act.) Since
only if we can recall something do we know it, anything conceived
of in a fashion not implementing recall is to all intents and purposes simply never conceived of.

In a culture with writing and print and electronic storage, we
have a variety of ways of setting knowledge aside for retention
immediately upon its conception. In an oral or a residually oral
culture man was in more difficult straits: he could not think of
something in nonmnemonic fashion and then devise a way to remember it. Since he had no script, unless the thought itself was
mnemonically structured somehow, there was no way to retain

the thought or its equivalent while he put himself to devising a mnemonic scheme for it. By the time he got the memory scheme worked out, he could not remember what he worked it out for: the thought he was concerned with memorizing would have vanished. Under such conditions, what was crucial was not iconographic decoration but iconographic apprehension. One could not think first and add the memory devices later. Insofar as iconography was a memory device, and a major one, one conceived thought iconographically to start with. If knowledge came into being loaded with associations, non-abstract, the hold on it was stronger and it was preconditioned not to get away. Thus for an oral culture images and mythologies are neither decorative luxuries nor primitive crudities: they are indispensable and sophisticated ways of laying hold of actuality and of making thought feasible.

Writing sets up new kinds of visual structures unimaginable in an oral storage and retrieval economy, and print improves the structures, locking words in the same position on the page in thousands upon thousands of identical copies and advertising tables of contents and indexes, to a degree unknown in manuscript cultures, as access routes to what is known. Iconographic thinking is no longer needed and is indeed dysfunctional, for highly charged images clog analytic procedures now implemented by abstract indexed space. The Ramist chart of printed words, without images, the product of Miss Yates's "interior iconoclasm," is a welcome substitute. The knowledge-storing and knowledge-retrieving drives in Ramist logic—and in the age of logic as a whole, which Ramism in its way brings to a climax and even caricatures—reach their apogee in the Enlightenment with the *Encyclopédie* of Diderot and d'Alembert. Indeed, encyclopedism, from Johann Heinrich Alsted (Alstedius, 1588-1638) on, grows out of Ramist logic and in particular out of Ramist "method," which provided a universal paradigm for treating any subject whatsoever by proceeding from the "general" to the "particular." This paradigm in large part replaced the old paradigm for discourse, the oration, which from classical antiquity had been virtually the only literary genre ever taught in the schools (letter writing was taught, but letters themselves were commonly regarded as variants of orations and organized accordingly).[37] The *Encyclopédie*, complete with its fold-out chart or *système figuré*, which in modified Ramist fashion arranged all knowledge in a spatial display, marks the completion of the transit from orality to print and the full development of the feeling for knowledge storage which print makes possible: knowledge is now locked in space and "looked" up there through indexes. The *Encyclopédie* thus culminates the age of logic and the cult of clarity and distinctness which this age had fostered.

The next stage of noetic development begins immediately: romanticism takes its start at the very time when the *Encyclopédie* is appearing (1751-1772). Indeed, the Enlightenment and the romantic age represent opposite reactions to the same situation.[38] In an oral culture knowledge is in short supply and constantly in danger of slipping away: oral cultures are thus necessarily conservative in their emphases. But now finally, after hundreds of thousands of years of human existence, with the aid first of writing and then of print, a vast amount of knowledge had been stored permanently and in immediately accessible form. The Encyclopédistes react by bumptious self-congratulation such as one finds in the "Discours préliminaire" of *Encyclopédie*. The romantics react by allowing themselves the luxury of obscurantism —in earlier cultures not unknown, but altogether too much a luxury to have general currency and to constitute a "movement," such as romanticism became after the mid-eighteenth century. We live today in the encyclopedic-romantic age. In some sense, as we have seen, logic is more operative today than ever before. But its centrality is gone. The age of logic is caught up in the age of romanticism, which, despite the rationalism of technological culture, appears to be our lot for the entire foreseeable future.

6. Epic as Knowledge Storage and Retrieval

The same iconographic economy of thinking which connects on the one hand with the Ramist organization of logic accounts on the other hand for much in the history and fate of the epic, for the epic was intimately related originally with the knowledge storage and retrieval economy of an oral culture. This can be seen through some extrapolations on the work of Eric A. Havelock in his *Preface to Plato*. Here Havelock has shown how the characteristics of epic style—formulaic expressions, heavily weighted characters (heroes and gods) free of any character "development," episodic structure —are due to the "psychodynamics of the memorizing process"[39] which in the totally oral culture of Homeric Greece underlay the production (that is, the performance) of an epic. However, this memorizing process was not peculiar to the epic poet: to send a message from Samos to Athens a tribal official would have to cast it up in mnemonic formulas or it would not be fixed in the messenger's mind. And he would not be able to recall it himself to repeat it the second time to the messenger who had not got it the first time. But casting the message in mnemonic form was not difficult

for a competent person in the culture: competent thinking was
normally done in mnemonic patterns,[40] so the message occurred
to the sender's mind mnemonically processed. (Of course, there
were degrees of mnemonic processing. Some thoughts were more
memorable than others: these became *ipso facto* important thoughts.)

Havelock has further shown how what a later literate culture would
be able to conceptualize in abstract categories had for the most part
to be otherwise conceived by oral-aural man. Unable to manage explicitly without writing anything more than very elementary categories,[41] persons in an oral culture have to assimilate everything to
the human lifeworld. "Phenomena other than persons can be described, but only as they are imagined to be behaving as persons
would. The environment becomes a great society and the phenomena
are represented as members of this society who interact upon each
other as they play their assigned roles."[42] Knowledge which literate
and typographical cultures would store in lists or descriptions to
be "looked" up as occasion demands would have to be conserved,
if it was to be retained at all, in narrative depicting the interactions
of men. Hence the nearly three hundred lines listing the Greek
ships and leaders in the second book of the *Iliad*—there is no effective place for an oral culture to store its demographic accounts
other than in a story about a war—or the description in the *Odyssey*
of routine activity such as shipbuilding, which an oral culture would
have virtually no occasion to articulate outside an epic *agōnia*.

The oral epic poet in a culture without writing was thus far more
than a poet in the present-day sense of this word. He was an indispensable information dispository, like a city directory, among
other things. Moreover, his "poetic" operations were continuous
with the nonpoetic. The devices he used—formulas, weighted or
typed characters, highly rhythmic verbalization, iconographic conceptualization, episodic expression[43]—are not typical of epic but
of verbalization generally in primary oral cultures. Such devices are
not merely poetic devices but conceptualizing devices which keep
knowledge in shape even today for ready use in the day-to-day life
of oral cultures—Havelock reports, for example, from T. E. Lawrence, the improvised verses accompanying the line-up of modern
Arab warriors.[44] But the good epic poet could elaborate these
widespread devices beautifully and work magic with them as others
could not. His achievement lay not in inventing devices which later
ages, unable to construe a human lifeworld outside their literate
frames of reference, would identify as peculiar to epic poetry.
His achievement lay rather in maximizing—with of course a few
twists of his own—the modes of conceptualization and expression
which his culture enforced on all its members.

7. Logic and Milton's Epic

Looking at the epic and logic conjointly as knowledge storage and
retrieval devices has the value of opening larger perspectives for
Milton's work. For Milton, knowledge demands to be logically
packaged. He organizes the *De doctrina christiana* in accordance
with Ramist method,[45] and he is often quite ostentatiously logical
in other writings, referring by name to various logical procedures
in prose and poetry in the very act of employing them.[46] In setting
up the study course for his nephews John and Edward Phillips,
Milton clearly uses Ramist method, proceeding from the general
to the special or particular. Thus he prescribes reading Latin or
Greek texts on meteorology, mineralogy, botany, biology, and
anatomy, in that order.[47] Meteorology and mineralogy are more
general, since they refer to a wider sweep of being (minerals are
of themselves nonliving, but they enter into living beings, too)
whereas the life sciences of botany, biology, and anatomy are restricted to a narrower band of material existence. Everyone, Milton
thought, should observe method. In his *Animadversions upon the
Remonstrant's Defence against Smectymnuus* (1641), Milton ad-
monishes Bishop Hall that the latter fails to note the "Law of
Method" where it is at work, reminding Hall that this law "bears
chief sway in the art of teaching."[48]

But what does Milton's addiction to Ramist logic and "logical
method" ultimately signify? What does Milton's use of logic even
in poetry mean beyond the fact that he uses a pretty formal logic
in poetry and thereby contrasts with at least the conscious aims
of, let us say, the Symbolists of a later day? It can mean much
more than this, I believe, if we look with the perspectives just
elaborated here at certain long-range developments in intellectual,
literary, and cultural history.

Many such developments are being interpreted now in psychological depths never before achieved. Havelock has made the
point that Plato proscribed the poets in his *Republic* for very
specific reasons. They stood for the psychological structures
of the primitive oral cultures of mankind (by far the oldest
cultures, for script was developed only some 6,000 years ago).
In primitive or primary oral cultures knowledge was organized
around the *agōnia* of human beings, so that it could not be stored
"objectively," but only as involved with the lifeworld of heroes
and other narrative characters as well as with the lifeworld of the
knower. Education consisted less of learning to "think" than of
learning to get "with" it. Boys were made to memorize the *Iliad*

and the *Odyssey*, perhaps rocking back and forth in the way
common among memorizers in highly oral cultures still today.
In proscribing poets, Plato equivalently was protesting, "This is
not education." He advocated instead objective study demanding
fully mature abstractions, his "ideas." Havelock shows, in consummate detail, how the shift to Plato's mode of thinking was
brought about by the interiorization of the alphabet—taken up by
the Greeks some three hundred years earlier but until Plato's
time left largely to hired professional scribes and not affecting
the feeling for knowledge generally. The abstract, philosophical
approach to knowledge, which in the hands of Aristotle generated
logic, was brought about by writing.

In so far as writing was the precondition for scientific thought,
it also marked the obsolescence of the epic. The epic was long in
dying, but once writing set in the epic took radically new forms. And
it had to. Lord's work with the Yugoslavian epic singers shows that
illiteracy is a prerequisite for the oral epic singer.[49] If he can read and
write, he cannot sing an epic which works the way those of illiterates
do. Little wonder that the Yugoslavian epic singers in Lord's massive
samplings in many ways sound more like Homer than does Virgil,
whose epic was almost two thousand years closer to Homer than
those of Lord's illiterate epic poets. Virgil wrote his.

In Milton, two divergent traditions are crossing one another to
mark the end of one age and the beginning of another. The long-
drawn-out demise of the epic is destined soon to be over. The old
heroes were dead—for the reason, among others, that they were no
longer serviceable as figures around which to organize knowledge.
The ancient epic had been of a piece with oral culture, constructed
out of knowledge storage and retrieval devices found through the
entire culture, far beyond the epic tradition itself. The epic was of
course much more than a knowledge storage and retrieval device.
It could be a great work of creative art, the greatest of all such works,
many believed in Milton's day. But its thought processes and modes
of expression were those with which an oral culture manages its own
noetic economy.

The literary epic retains or seeks to retain the momentousness of
the oral epic without being able to share its urgency. With our knowledge of the psychology of oral as compared to chirographic and typo-
graphic cultures, we can feel that the death of the epic was predict-
able, by hindsight only, of course. Virgil is the most eminent early
figure in the long line of epic poets whose productions would be
progressively less and less like the original. On the eve of print, when
the medieval addiction to the written word, far greater than that of

antiquity, had drastically transformed modes of knowledge storage and with them the psyche itself, Boiardo (1434-1494) and Ariosto (1474-1533) had already found the epic unmanageable in any entirely serious fashion. Spenser's post-typographical attempt to take the genre in full seriousness resulted in a poem unlike anything before or since. In a paper at the Modern Language Association meeting of December 1968 Professor Robert Kellogg brilliantly reviewed the discrepancies between the stated epic aims of Renaissance poets and their actual performance. The poets—and there were hundreds upon hundreds of poets turning out epics, mostly Latin, in the sixteenth and seventeenth centuries—found it impossible in practice, despite their best efforts, to produce anything like the epics they so admired. Despite the most assiduous imitation, the relation of the poem to their lifeworld differed from that of Homer's or even Virgil's poem to his. Even though the epithets and other forms were copied verbatim, the voice differed. By the eighteenth century the mock epic was the only kind of epic any first-rate serious writer could produce.

Paradise Lost appears on the eve of this eighteenth-century crisis. Milton succeeded in giving his poem a momentousness beyond that of any of the epics attempted for centuries before or since. Neither Orlando—Boiardo's or Ariosto's—nor the Red Cross Knight nor King Arthur nor (if we may reach far back into the 1100s to even more ambiguously epic forms) even el Cid Campeador bears so heavy a cultural load as Milton's Adam or Eve or Christ have to bear. Besides epic tradition itself, all of Christian theology and the ancillary classical and other mythology accumulated through Western and some Eastern cultures and fed out through Milton's vast reading are borne by the poem's characters into the epic *agōnia*.

Milton had once projected an epic with old-style heroes in his well-known earlier sketches for an Arthuriad. His reasons for abandoning this plan are not all clear, but they doubtless included the feeling that old-style epic heroes were not working very well any more. As much is intimated in Milton's persuasion that nothing less than the biblical story of the first man can serve his epic purpose. But to opt for the biblical is to opt against ancient heroism to a significant degree. It is true that Milton appears to state otherwise when he writes that the subject of his epic is

> Not less but more Heroic then the wrauth
> Of stern *Achilles* on his Foe pursu'd
> Thrice Fugitive about *Troy* Wall, or rage
> Of *Turnus* for *Lavinia* disespous'd,

Or *Neptun's* ire or *Juno's*, that so long
Perplexed the *Greek* and *Cytherea's* Son.

(IX, 14-19)

But Milton was aware that "more Heroic" meant to some degree anti-heroic. With the astuteness which Kierkegaard would be better able to articulate in his contention that no heroic machinery can ever work to portray the existential situation of the "knight of faith" in personal relationship with Christ and His Father, Milton knew that many of the old heroic virtues were in fact incompatible with the person and the role of Christ, and by the same token incompatible with the role of Adam, who is the "hero" of *Paradise Lost* and whose role is ultimately defined in relation to Christ. Hence Milton unloads on to Satan, who is clearly not meant to be a hero, some major heroic characteristics (pride, wrathfulness, addiction to war as a way to glory) which he finds unassimilable to Christian virtue.

Redistributed this way, the old epic load no longer possesses the unifying center of gravity it once had.[50] As early as Blake, it was quite plausible to think of Satan as the hero of the poem, and this plausibility is still urged today. Moreover, the drama had had its effects on the feeling for literary form. Milton's resort to dramatic techniques has been much commented on. Paradoxically, the drama was the first major genre to be controlled completely by writing; for, though oral in production, the drama was actually composed in writing from ancient Greece on, and was the first form—and until print virtually the only form—of literature presenting action with a tightly structured plot and developing characters. In *Paradise Lost* Adam and Eve and even Satan develop in character. Epic loads sit uneasily on the backs of characters who are not types, such as Achilles and Odysseus and their associates are in the *Iliad* and the *Odyssey*.

To compensate for the unavoidable disturbance in the heroic economy of narrative, Milton had to introduce a more rationalized mode of organization. Isabel MacCaffrey has shown that, although Milton's work is truly mythical in its imagery, the images, even the dark and mystifying images of evil, are subject to rational control—they do not live their own, rather wandering and rationally vague, life.[51] In *Paradise Lost* Milton's characters speak either with consummate logic, as God the Father in Book X, 34-84, or with contrived sophistry, illogically, as Satan in Book IX.[52] Compared to the speeches of Homer's characters, those of Milton's are classroom lectures. *Paradise Lost* is "to justifie the wayes of God to men." The phrase suggests an operation at least in some degree conspicuously logical. Milton refers to the poem as "this great Argument" (I, 24).

The term "argument" is used often for plot or for plot summaries, such as those Milton added at the head of each book of *Paradise Lost* in the second (1674) edition. But the term even in this sense retains strong logical implications: not only is it a crucial operative term for all of Ramist logic, but it more than suggests the Ramist doctrine that any poem, like any other example of discourse, could be reduced by "logical analysis" to a summary which was at root or in effect a syllogism.[53] Ramus' own lectures on poetry were often unsuccessful or even ludicrous, apparently because of his espousal of this principle.[54] It is doubtful whether Milton would have subscribed to the principle in all its Ramist vigor, but it held some place in his thinking as in that of many others in his age and earlier.

In the Ramist "method," which he considered part of logic, Milton had a rational apparatus comparable in its sweep to the sweep of the epic. The lines just quoted from *Paradise Lost,* IX, 14-19, as well as the Trinity manuscript and much else often reviewed in Milton's writings make it clear how sweeping or inclusive of all actuality in its deeply human roots Milton intended his epic to be. But Ramist method, if you believed in it in a general way even though neither you nor any other living person could ever make it work, gave one a feeling that reason was also inclusive of all actuality in the sense that it encompassed or controlled all. We recall, as noted above, that Milton clearly and demonstrably undertook to organize all of Christian teaching in the *De doctrina christiana* in strict accordance with Ramist dichotomized method, proceeding from the general to the particular. *Paradise Lost* is quite obviously not so straightforwardly methodized, for it uses epic digressions, flashbacks, and all the rest of the conventional epic equipment. If this is method, there is crypsis in it.[55] But *Paradise Lost* also incorporates some tight reasoning in places and is obviously thought of by Milton as on the whole "logical" in one of the vaguely adulatory senses of this term fostered by Ramism and still quite current in speech today. ("You are not acting logically." "It was the logical thing to do." The sense of "logic" in such expressions, as has been suggested above, makes a strict logician wince.)

The logical or rational economy of *Paradise Lost* is perhaps best caught by noting that, as opposed to the biblical account which it purports to sustain, it opts for the closure of existence itself. Eric Voegelin has recently discussed this quality of the poem and has shown how it helped set the fashion later typified in romanticism and Symbolism and still being generally followed today.[56] After the fall, Adam is reassured by the angel Michael:

> then wilt thou not be loath
> To leave this Paradise, but shalt possess
> A Paradise within thee, happier farr.
>
> (XII, 585-587)

Paradise is to be found somehow in this life, and when it is not, something specific in this life—the Catholic horror, or episcopacy, or kingship, or some other villainy—is directly accountable. The biblical and Christian view, less rationally contrived, is one of open existence: man's day-to-day life is accepted as essentially incapable of fulfilling the aspirations it arouses in man. It always opens on a "beyond," suggesting something other than itself, so that no scapegoat can be found within day-to-day life to carry off to the wilderness our burden of unhappiness.

It appears to me that Professor Voegelin too readily assimilates to Eden the "beyond" of Christian eschatological existence, which is fulfilled at the end of time, not at its beginning, for he suggests (p. 29) that Eden is something to be "regained . . . through grace in death," whereas in Christian teaching it is not really regained at all but becomes a point of departure permanently transcended in the eschatological life established through Christ's death and resurrection. But be that as it may, Eden in the Bible does represent a state of existence different from the day-to-day life of man now, and it indicates that man's day-to-day life is open to a different kind of life than itself, a "beyond" whose frontier since Eden is death and since Christ death-and-resurrection. Milton's Paradise turns out to have been different from this Eden of the Bible. It becomes an immanentist Eden, not something beyond natural life at all, but natural life at its best, "pure" natural life, for which one can substitute if need be "a Paradise within," an Eden constituted within this world even though always plagued by some specific thing in this same world that makes it go wrong. Voegelin notes, as others in various ways have noted, that the quest for an immanent Eden or Paradise marks much of modern literature and art from Blake through Henry James and on to Kafka and Musil and Sartre and the vast literature about the American Adam. Inevitably, any immanentist or closed-life Eden is portrayed as breaking up (or down), only to be replaced by a new prospective immanentist Eden (which will, inevitably, also break down). The Commonwealth went under with the Restoration.

Whether or not we agree with Professor Voegelin's argument in its totality—and it is a great argument—his immanentist Miltonic Paradise accords with much in the growing rationalism of Milton's milieu and with Milton's espousal of Ramist logic. For Ramism, and particularly Ramist logic, certainly proposed a closure of existence. The term and concept "system," and the sense of closure which this term and its cognates express perhaps more forcefully than any other in Western European languages, first became widely operative in philosophy in the post-Copernican Ramist milieu of the early 1600s. So far as I can ascertain, the first effective propagators of the concept of a philosophical "system" and of other noetic "systems" were the semi-Ramists Johann Heinrich Alsted (Alstedius—1588-1638), mentioned above as one of the inventors of the modern encyclopedia, and Bartholomew Keckermann (Keckermannus—1571-1608). Both published series of textbooks, in Latin of course, featuring the term: *Systema astronomiae, Systema ethicae, Systema logicae*, and so on.[57] The next two centuries produced an incalculable number of "system" titles, together with other titles advertising a feeling for closed noetic space. One of the favorites was the "key" (*Clavis artis Lullianae*, etc.), another "method," another "idea."[58] Antiquity and the Middle Ages conspicuously lack such closure concepts in their approach to knowledge: *summa* (high points) or *via* (way) are the typical medieval expressions which most nearly approximate "system," and they do not approximate it closely at all.

Closure marks Ramist thought conspicuously. Ramist "arts" are totalities, purportedly embracing all there is of their subjects, and doing so in a way which admits readily of being diagrammed. This sense of closure—which can be identified more or less with the rationalism maturing in the Enlightenment—certainly plagued Milton in his effort to pack the reality of Christian revelation into *Paradise Lost*, if indeed it was the reality and not a theoretical construct that he actually dealt with.

Milton's place in the long-range development of the epic and of logic can thus be described rather neatly, if not with full inclusiveness, in terms of open and closed existence. The epic, which came into being as (among other things) a massive knowledge-storage creation of the prephilosophic world, projected an open cosmology, one in which explanation is at best partial and incompleteness is a permanent quality of mortal life. Epic was based on *agōnia*, struggle, typically between persons, which is never-ending, but continues generation after generation. This *agōnia*, as Havelock has shown, functions to hold together even knowledge which a later philosophic age would regard as purely "objective." The original epic universe, physical and moral and intellectual, is one of human interaction, struggling toward a completeness which patently it can never itself achieve. It is faced outside itself, implying some other, some beyond. The sophisticated cyclic theories of time which from antiquity attempt to impose closure on the cosmos mean little to epic *agōnia* or human struggle generally: they smell of the lamp, not of the arena.

Logic, on the other hand, the paradigmatic knowledge-storage device of the post-philosophical of rationalist world, symbolizes closed existence: the logical universe, certainly as conceived by Ramus and Milton's age generally, purports to carry within itself a full explanation of itself. It does not suggest, much less face, an outside or beyond. So great a thinker as Immanuel Kant, ingenuously and with an ignorance all the more devastating because virtually universal in his time, could believe that since Aristotle logic had been "unable to advance a step, and thus to all appearance has reached its completion."[59] Views such as this of Kant's can be plausible because logic as pure form—which it never entirely is, for logical form always carries with it a residue of "problems"—knows no *agōnia*, contest, struggle, only "work." Its issues are not interpersonal, or appear not to be. *Labor omnia vincit* is the motto on one of the most frequently reprinted portraits of Ramus.[60] The logical world would be more fetching if only a total logic of everything could be set forth completely and exhaustively. Ramist "method" purportedly made it possible to do just that. But method was really not "logic" in any formal sense at all. It had been grafted on to logic from rhetoric in the 1540s by Johann Sturm, Philip Melanchthon, and Ramus himself.[61] "Method" could even be used to destroy logic by implementing an exercise in digressions, as Robert Burton used it in his *Anatomy of Melancholy.*[62] But Milton's Ramist theory did not allow for this, although in actuality Milton's commitment to a closed system of existence was less than total. No man can live or write by method alone. But the rational didactic aim in *Paradise Lost*—"to justifie the wayes of God to men"—and his attraction to Ramist logic (which led him in his own *Logic* to suggest that the divine Trinity was illogical), with much else in his writings and career, suggest how strongly Milton was attracted to ultimate closure. In this he was part of his age and the immediately succeeding ages, up to our own.

Notes

1. See, for example, Dan S. Collins, *Rhetoric and Logic in Milton's English Poems,* North Carolina, 1960 (microfilm; Ann Arbor, Mich.: University Microfilms, 1961); John S. Diekhoff, "The Function of the Prologues in *Paradise Lost,*" *PMLA,* 57 (1942), 697-704; P. Albert Duhamel, "Milton's Alleged Ramism," *PMLA,* 67 (1952), 1035-1053; Harry Lee Frissell, *Milton's Art of Logic and Ramist Logic in the Major Poems,* Vanderbilt, 1951 (microfilm: Ann Arbor, Mich.: University Microfilms, 1952); Leon

Howard, " 'The Invention' of Milton's 'Great Argument': A Study of the Logic of 'God's Ways to Men,'" *HLQ*, 9 (1945-46), 149-173; Theodore Long Huguelet, *Milton's Hermeneutics: A Study of Scriptural Interpretation in the Divorce Tracts and in De Doctrina Christiana,* North Carolina, 1959 (microfilm: Ann Arbor, Mich.: University Microfilms, 1959); Franklin Irwin, *Ramistic Logic in Milton's Prose Works,* Princeton, 1941 (microfilm: Ann Arbor: University Microfilms, 1941); Richard Lewis, "Milton's Use of Rhetoric and Logic in *Paradise Lost* to Develop the Character of Satan" (Stanford, 1949); Isabel Mac-Caffrey, *Paradise Lost as "Myth"* (Cambridge, Mass.: Harvard University Press, 1959); John M. Steadman, *Milton's Epic Characters: Image and Idol* (Chapel Hill: University of North Carolina Press, 1968).

2. See Walter J. Ong, *Rhetoric, Romance, and Technology* (Ithaca and London: Cornell University Press, 1971), pp. 278-280, 294-295.

3. Ibid., pp. 1-19, and passim (Ch. 1, "Rhetoric and the Origins of Consciousness").

4. *A History of Formal Logic,* trans. and ed. by Ivo Thomas (Notre Dame, Ind.: University of Notre Dame Press, 1961).

5. *The Development of Logic* (Oxford: Clarendon Press, 1962).

6. *A History of Formal Logic,* pp. 10-18, 26-39 (esp. 31-39), 417.

7. Erich Neumann, *The Origins and History of Consciousness,* with a Foreword by C. G. Jung, trans. from the German by R. F. C. Hull, Bollingen Series, XLII (New York: Pantheon Books, 1954); Eric A. Havelock, *Preface to Plato* (Cambridge, Mass.: Belknap Press of Harvard University Press, 1963); Gilbert Durand, *Les Structures anthropologiques de l'imaginaire* (Paris: Presses Universitaires, 1960).

8. See Havelock, *Preface to Plato,* pp. 28, 47, and passim.

9. Ong, *Rhetoric,* pp. 255-303; cf. Walter J. Ong, *The Presence of the Word* (New Haven and London: Yale University Press, 1967), pp. 17-110.

10. Durand, p. 451; cf. pp. 453-459.

11. Ibid., pp. 452, 455.

12. See Michael Polanyi, *Personal Knowledge: Toward a Post-Critical Philosophy* (Chicago: University of Chicago Press, 1958).

13. Bochenski, p. 12.

14. Ibid., pp. 12-13, etc.

15. Ibid., pp. 4-9, 254-264. Since he is concerned only with formal logic and, as has been noted earlier here, abhors "psychologism" in treating logical matters, Father Bochenski rightly gives the Renaissance period very short shrift.

16. Ibid., p. 4.

17. See Ong, *Rhetoric,* pp. 48-103 (Ch. 3, "Tudor Writings on Rhetoric, Poetic, and Literary Theory").

18. Bochenski, pp. 267-270 ff.

19. See William Riley Parker, *Milton: A Biography,* 2 vols. (Oxford: Clarendon Press, 1968), pp. 259, 325, 615, 620-622, 862, 905, 938, 1139 (the two volumes are continuously paginated). The late Professor Parker urges very good reasons for the period 1640-48 and especially for the year 1648 itself, reasons which can be supplemented by still further, if somewhat roundabout, arguments. These I am detailing in the Introduction to the forthcoming edition in English translation of the *Artis logicæ plenior institutio,* the work of Charles Ermatinger and the present author, to appear in the *Complete Prose Works of John Milton,* general editor Don M. Wolfe (New

Haven and London: Yale University Press, 1953-).

20.Walter J. Ong, *Ramus and Talon Inventory* (Cambridge, Mass.; Harvard University Press, 1958), pp. 178-185.

21.Wilhelm Risse, *Die Logik der Neuzeit*, 1 Band, *1500-1640* (Stuttgart-Bad Canstatt: Friedrich Frommann, 1964), pp. 122-200.

22.Bochenski, p. 232.

23.Walter J. Ong, *Ramus, Method, and the Decay of Dialogue* (Cambridge, Mass.: Harvard University Press, 1958), pp. 314-318, 225-269; Frances A. Yates, *The Art of Memory* (Chicago: University of Chicago Press, 1966), pp. 231-242, etc.

24.Ong, *Decay of Dialogue,* p. 32; *Ramus,* pp. 355-356.

25.Ong, *Decay of Dialogue*, pp. 6-7, 178, 190-193, 321-322.

26.See Jerrold E. Seigel, *Rhetoric and Philosophy in Renaissance Humanism: The Union of Eloquence and Wisdom, Petrarch to Valla* (Princeton, N.J.: Princeton University Press, 1968), pp. 142-143 and passim.

27.Ong, *Decay of Dialogue,* p. 290.

28.Bochenski, p. 4.

29.John Milton, *Artis logicæ plenior institutio*, Book I, chap. xxv—translation from the forthcoming edition prepared by Charles J. Ermatinger and Walter J. Ong, S. J., in the forthcoming vol. VIII of the *Complete Prose Works.*

30.See the reproductions of some of these charts in Ong, *Decay of Dialogue,* pp. 202, 300, 301, 317.

31.For an interesting late survival see [J. Millar] *The New Art of Memory: founded upon the principles taught by M. Gregor von Feinaigle . . .* (London: Sherwood, Neely, and Jones, 1812), a full-fledged iconographic "art" with fold-out memory "rooms." A "third edition, corrected and enlarged" was issued by the same publishers in 1813.

Copies of both these editions are in Pius XII Memorial Library, St. Louis University.

32.Gordon H. Bower, "Analysis of a Mnemonic Device," *American Scientist* 58 (1970), 496-510. Bower finds that everything in the memory procedures Miss Yates outlines is highly effective with the exception of the use of bizarre imagery, which is a feature of some arts of memory and which thus far has tested as inconsequential. But it may be that such imagery is only a variant of high definition concrete imagery and that it may, in subsequent testing, prove as effective as the other features of the memory arts: this is perhaps suggested by what Bower has to say about "imaginal associations and their properties" (on p. 503).

33.Ong, *Decay of Dialogue*, pp. 79, 310-318.

34.Yates, pp. 231-242, esp. 234-235.

35.Ong, *Rhetoric*, pp. 104-112, commenting on Yates, *Memory.*

36.Yates, *Memory*, pp. 129-134, 199-230.

37.Ong, *Decay of Dialogue*, pp. 299-300; Ong, *The Presence of the Word*, pp. 243-245.

38.Ong, *Rhetoric,* pp. 278, 323-326.

39.Havelock, *Preface to Plato*, p. 169.

40.Ong, *The Presence of the Word*, pp. 27-28, citing Havelock.

41.Complex kinship or similar categories may be present *implicitly* in oral cultures, just as complex grammatical categories may be, but primitive oral peoples cannot make them reflectively explicit; only a Lévi-Strauss or other twentieth-century structuralist can work them out explicitly. Similarly, only a grammarian (who knows how to write —*technē grammatikē*, the art of grammar, means at root the "art of letters") can describe explicitly the bewilderingly complex rules which oral language users employ without being able to state.

42. Havelock, *Preface to Plato*, p. 168.

43. Without the aid of writing, there is no way to organize lengthy narrative in a nonepisodic, tight plot. The first tightly plotted genre in the West, the Greek drama, is a written composition, though designed for oral production. There is almost no comparably tight-plotted narrative until well after print with the development of the short story and novel.

44. *Preface to Plato*, p. 139.

45. Irwin, *Ramistic Logic in Milton's Prose Works*, pp. 66-85; see especially the two-page table between pp. 68 and 69.

46. Ibid., passim; Steadman, *Milton's Epic Characters*, pp. 139-173, and passim.

47. Parker, p. 209.

48. Ibid., pp. 208-109, quotes and comments on Milton's remarks here.

49. Albert B. Lord, *The Singer of Tales*, Harvard Studies in Comparative Literature, 24 (Cambridge, Mass.: Harvard University Press, 1960).

50. See Appendix I, "Renaissance Definitions of the Hero," in Steadman, *Milton's Epic Characters*, pp. 319-323.

51. MacCaffrey, *Paradise Lost as "Myth,"* passim.

52. Steadman reviews and knowledgeably assesses the literature on Satan's fraudulence, in *Milton's Epic Characters*, pp. 227-240.

53. See Ong, *Decay of Dialogue*, pp. 265-266. The relation of this syllogism to method Ramus never successfully explained. In principle, all protracted discourse, including an epic poem, was a movement from general to particular. A syllogism could of course be considered as such a descent, since the conclusion must always "follow the weaker side" of the premises: if one premise is uni-versal and the other particular, the conclusion must be particular. All men are mortal; Peter is a man; therefore Peter is mortal. The difficulty is that in his explanation of method Ramus instances not syllogisms but "rules" of an "art" (generally grammar).

54. See Ong, *Decay of Dialogue*, p. 33.

55. Ramus' teaching on crypsis or cryptic method was that, if the audience was ignorant, or recalcitrant, or otherwise ill disposed—and it was one of the unlovely features of Ramist logical teaching that poetry was written for just such less-than-ideal audiences—one could reverse the normal general-to-special (particular) procedure of method and move from the special (or particular) to the general. See Ong, *Decay of Dialogue*, pp. 252-254.

56. "Postscript: On Paradise and Revolution," *The Southern Review*, 7, New Series (1971), 28-36. This "Postscript" is the second half of a collection, "The Turn of the Screw," by Eric Voegelin [et al.], ibid., 1-48.

57. See Ong, *Decay of Dialogue*, pp. 298-307, and *The Barbarian Within* (New York: Macmillan, 1962), pp. 81-82.

58. See Ong, *Decay of Dialogue*, pp. 314-318.

59. Bochenski, pp. 5-9, quotes Kant and others with like views. Medieval logic had of course made massive advances beyond Aristotle, as we are now well aware, and from the time of George Boole's *The Mathematical Analysis of Logic* to the present, logic has achieved vast new growth.

60. Ong, *Decay of Dialogue*, frontispiece.

61. Ibid., pp. 230-239.

62. David Renaker, "Robert Burton and Ramist Method," *Renaissance Quarterly*, 24 (1971), 210-220.

The Theological Context of
Milton's *Christian Doctrine*

WILLIAM B. HUNTER, JR.
University of New Hampshire

Every writer intends for his work to be read by some particular
audience. The character of that real or imagined audience directly
affects both the style and the content of his composition. Though
it did not appear in print until a century and a half after its
author's death, the *Christian Doctrine* is no exception to this general principle. Identification of the readers for whom Milton composed this treatise should accordingly illuminate both its style
and its contents.

Such an attempt requires first an approximation of the date of
its composition. Hanford argued half a century ago that Milton
worked on the book from about 1655 to 1660,[1] a conclusion that
is still convincing. A brief review of the evidence will be useful. The
fact that the manuscript is entirely in the handwriting of amanuenses
suggests that it received its present form after Milton's final loss of
vision early in 1652. Further evidence is the citation of a "recent"
edition of the Bible in England, which Fletcher proved to be
Walton's Polyglot of 1657.[2] No other internal evidence seems to
require a date later than this, though the reference to Walton's book
does at least prove that Milton was occupied with this part of the
treatise after 1657. How much later cannot be demonstrated from
internal evidence, nor does it prove when he first began work on it.

External evidence is more helpful, supporting a date between
about 1655 and a short time after 1660, the period when the
anonymous biographer reports that Milton was "framing a *Body of
Divinity* out of the Bible: All which, notwithstanding the several
Calamities befalling him in his fortunes, he finish'd after the Restoration."[3] But this activity seems to be the formal culmination of a
lifetime of reflection on the Bible. Edward Phillips reports that in
the early 1640s Milton's students were busy "writing from his own
dictation, some part, from time to time, of a Tractate which he

thought fit to collect from the ablest of Divines, who had written of that Subject; *Amesius, Wollebius,* &c. *viz.* A perfect System of Divinity."[4] Milton himself testifies that even earlier as a youth he had carefully read the Old and New Testaments in the light of "a few of the shorter systems of divines"—presumably such dogmatists as Ames and Wolleb—so as to extract textual proofs to be incorporated under various doctrinal headings (XIV, 5). A regular practice of Reformed dogmatists was such a compilation of proof texts for disputed points.[5] Milton's subject headings probably derived from the "shorter systems" which he was studying, but the proof texts would mostly be his own collection, agreeing to a greater or lesser degree with those of the dogmatists. The results of such reading, which he seems to have carried on throughout most of his life, survive in the extensive collections of proof texts which fill the pages of the *Christian Doctrine.* Insertions in the manuscript of new proof texts by various hands show that he continued to consider them as long as he worked on the treatise. Wherever he cites clusters of proof texts without any analysis of them in the treatise, it appears that they have simply been added to his main running text, which reads meaningfully without any interruption if they are omitted.[6] Such proof texts, that is, seem to have been inserted from a separate compilation after or during the composition of the running text.

It seems likely then that in his youth, guided by well-known Reformed dogmatists, Milton began an attempt to organize disparate biblical texts into some kind of theological outline, that throughout much of his adult life he continued to work on it, and that in the latter part of the 1650s he developed it from an outline collection of texts into its present state with the title, *De doctrina christiana.* If so, who were the readers of about 1655 to 1660 whom he wished to favor with a work which he considered to be his "best and richest possession" (XIV, 9)? Obviously, they had to be people of profound religious conviction, but even a cursory reading shows that it was not addressed to Catholics, Lutherans, or Anglicans. Rather, its imagined audience must have been men trained in the kind of theological analysis which the *Christian Doctrine* itself represents—members of the various branches of the Reformed or Calvinistic churches. In England their most obvious representatives were the Presbyterians, who had controlled England from 1642 until Cromwell's purge of them from Parliament in 1648 and who were not a negligible group a decade later.

While still in power in 1647, these Presbyterians had published what has become the most important statement of Calvinist belief

which that church has made, the *Westminster Confession of Faith.*
That Milton was not intimately familiar with it is inconceivable,
but the *Christian Doctrine* makes no mention of it whatsoever,[7] a
fact which cannot be accidental. The reason, of course, is not far to
seek in his total disenchantment with the Presbyterians, brought on
in great part by their hostile reception of his divorce pamphlets.
Indeed, he must have felt that the *Confession* itself contained a
personal attack upon him in its assertion that "the corruption of
man [is] such as is apt to study arguments, unduly to put asunder
those whom God hath joined together in marriage" (XXIV, 6). In
England in 1647 everyone would understand the meaning to be
"the corruption of John Milton is such as to study these arguments."
In response, Milton resolutely deprecated or ignored the Presbyterians
for the rest of his life. The *Christian Doctrine* is certainly not addressed to them though, as will be seen, their *Confession* influenced
it in several significant respects.

Other religious groups in England during the later 1650s were
either relatively powerless, like the Church of England, or lacking
in an interest in formal theological dogma, like many of the Independents (though the *Christian Doctrine* may in a sense be Milton's
attempt to provide a statement for some of the latter group). Thus
for a suitable audience he had to turn to the continent. The fact that
the treatise was written in Latin is in itself a strong argument that he
was addressing readers there, for with the possible exception of his
Logic all of his Latin prose written after he left Cambridge is addressed to readers abroad. In this respect the *Christian Doctrine*
parallels the three Latin *Defenses* published earlier in the decade.

In France and especially Holland, not to mention Switzerland,
the Reformed Church was thriving, even though it was far from
being a unified movement. Milton appears to have addressed his
study to all of the Calvinistic groups abroad ("To all the churches
of Christ," he begins the work) in a sincere attempt to bring them
into harmony with one another and with his own branch of Independency. Such a goal helps to explain somewhat the eclectic
nature of the book and even some of its heterodox arguments.

On the continent in the later 1650s three major interpretations
of the Reformed tradition should be recognized. First are the
Calvinists proper, the traditionalists, who are also called conservative dogmatists or Reformed scholastics. The canons of the Synod
of Dort (1618-19), directed against the Remonstrant Arminians,
represent their view, which generally parallels that of the English
Presbyterians as expressed in their *Westminster Confession* and
which was reaffirmed in the Helvetic Consensus of 1676. Generally

synonymous with the Reformed Establishment, safeguarders of Calvinist orthodoxy, this group actually is closer to the theology of Theodore Beza (1519-1605) than to that of Calvin.[8] Among its leaders whom Milton actually cites in the *Christian Doctrine* are William Ames (1576-1633), Francis Gomarus (1563-1641), Wolfgang Musculus (1497-1563), David Pareus (1548-1622), Amandus Polanus (1561-1610), Zachary Ursinus (1534-1583), and Jerome Zanchy (1516-1590). Because he names them as authorities, there can be no question that he knew their writings and was intimately familiar with the Calvinist tradition which they represent. John Wolleb (1586-1629) must certainly be added to this list, as will be seen. Like these scholastics, Milton refers time and again to Beza's biblical text and to his interpretations of it, but Calvin himself receives only one passing mention (XVII, 183), the same relatively negligible treatment accorded him on the whole by the Reformed dogmatists. At mid-century the important theologians active in this tradition included Peter du Moulin, father of Milton's antagonist in the *Defenses,* Frederick Spanheim, whom Milton praised in a letter to his son Ezekiel (XII, 75-77), and Andrew Rivet, whom he had cited favorably in the divorce tracts and had quoted in his Commonplace Book.

The school of Saumur in France may be recognized as a second major group. Founded in 1604 by du Plessis-Mornay, by 1650 it had become the largest and most influential of Reformed seminaries on the continent, led by three famous scholars, Louis Cappel (1585-1658) and Joshua de la Place (1596-1655), both of whom are cited as authorities in the *Christian Doctrine*, and Moise Amyraut (1596-1664).[9] Much of the intellectual thrust at Saumur dated from the appearance there in the 1620s of a Scot, John Cameron, whom Milton assumes to be known to the readers of his treatise (XVI, 147). In opposition to the Reformed dogmatists, these men argued against a rigid conception of predestination and reasserted the views of Calvin against those of Beza. As a result of their arguments they came perilously close to condemnation as Arminians, though they were exonerated of the charge at the French national synods of Alençon (1637) and Charenton (1645). Finally in 1676 the super-orthodoxy of the Helvetic Consensus judged their position to be indeed Arminian.[10]

The last continental group are the Arminians themselves, lineal descendants of the Reformed church if at times its bitter antagonists. They originate with James Arminius, who had died in 1609, leaving his followers to remonstrate against the Calvinist scholastics and be damned for their pains by the Synod of Dort. After a decade of

persecution they were permitted to establish a theological school
in Amsterdam, led by Simon Episcopius (1583-1643), author of
an Arminian *Confession* of the 1620s and until his death probably
the foremost theologian of the group. The first volume of his *Opera*,
containing the important *Institutio Theologicarum,* appeared in
1650. Within the movement were a number of outstanding leaders,
the most famous being Hugo Grotius; but for the *Christian Doctrine*
the writings of Episcopius seem to be most pertinent, supplemented
perhaps by those of Etienne de Courcelles (1586-1659) and of
Conrad Vorst (1569-1622), especially his *Tractatus Theologicus de
Deo,* a work which horrified the orthodox when it appeared in 1610
and aroused such wrath in King James that diplomatic relations
between England and Holland were threatened for a time.

The audience of the *Christian Doctrine* thus seems to include in
one way or another all three groups: the Reformed scholastics on
the continent, with their unmentionable brethren in Scotland and
England, the school of Saumur, and the Arminians. Representative
opinions from all three are cited, and authorities from the former
two are named. Milton, however, does not commit himself to identification with any single point of view. Although at first glance it
would seem to be impossible to come any closer to an understanding
of Milton's relations with these three subdivisions of Calvinism,
two aspects of his method permit a somewhat more specific indenti-
fication.

Milton's indebtedness to the Remonstrant position upon predestination, condemned by the Synod of Dort and by all orthodox
Calvinists, has long been recognized.[11] The followers of Arminius
had argued that Christ's sacrifice was made for all mankind, not
merely for the elect. God foreknows who will believe and who will
not, but though grace and redemption are intended for all, some
(the damned) will resist and yet others will fail to persevere and
so will fall away. Man's own will, in other words, becomes part of
the system of his redemption; Christ in a sense "wasted" his sacrifice
by making it for those who willfully refuse it. Even though Milton
does not name any Arminians in the *Christian Doctrine,* he certainly
adopts these views there (especially XV, 315ff., and XVI, 87ff.)
despite their rejection at Dort and their condemnation in the *Westminster Confession* (III, XIII, and X).

The audience of the *Christian Doctrine* thus seems to include in
one way or another all three groups: the Reformed scholastics on
the continent, with their unmentionable brethren in Scotland and
England, the school of Saumur, and the Arminians. Representative
opinions from all three are cited, and authorities from the former
two are named. Milton, however, does not commit himself to identification with any single point of view. Although at first glance it
would seem to be impossible to come any closer to an understanding
of Milton's relations with these three subdivisions of Calvinism,
two aspects of his method permit a somewhat more specific indenti-
fication.

In the first place, the ordering of the chapters of the *Christian
Doctrine* aligns the work with that of the group who have been
called the Reformed scholastics rather than with either of the other
two. Highly methodical in the arrangement of their arguments, they
usually divided their analysis of Christianity into two parts, the former

concerned with "faith" and the latter with "works." Such, for example, is the arrangement of Ames's *Marrow*, of Wolleb's *Compendium*, and of Polanus' *Substance*.[12] Occasionally the first part appears alone, as in Zanchy's *Confession*[13] and in the *Westminster Confession*. In general, the Arminians and the Salmurians do not arrange their arguments in this way, not being so governed by scholastic method. Milton, however, does so and thereby reveals his profound indebtedness to this Calvinist school even as he disagrees with many of its conclusions. Thus the *Christian Doctrine* consists of 50 chapters, divided into the customary two books, of 33 and 17 chapters respectively. Ames's *Marrow* has 63 chapters divided into 41 and 22; Wolleb's *Compendium* has 50 (the same as Milton's total), divided into 36 and 14; Polanus' *Substance* has 72, divided into 63 and 9. As for the equivalents to Milton's first part alone, Zanchy's *Confession* has 30 chapters and the *Westminster Confession* exactly the same number, 33. Generally speaking, each of these works is concerned with the same subjects as all the others, but the chapters appear in differing order, the positioning of that on "Predestination" being perhaps most significant. Like the Reformed scholastics, Milton placed his main discussion of this subject immediately following that of the divine decrees rather than after his discussion of Christ's redemption of mankind. Predestination, that is, derives in this arrangement from an antecedent decree of the Father rather than from the Passion and Resurrection of the Son, the same position that it occupies in Aquinas (*Summa Theologica*, I, 23), in Beza, and in the *Westminster Confession* (III, 3, 4) but at sharp variance from Calvin, who considered it only *after* his discussion of Christ's sacrifice.[14]

Whether the correspondence as to number of chapters between the *Christian Doctrine* and the *Westminster Confession* has any significance seems impossible to say. There is some similarity in the ordering of subjects from "Of God" to "The Last Judgment," but the arrangement of the *Christian Doctrine* appears to be closer to that of the 36 chapters of Wolleb's *Compendium*, which Milton certainly followed closely as to both order and contents in his second book.[15] The important conclusion to be drawn is that he chose for the framework of his argument the same method of organization as that practiced by the Reformed scholastics. He must, then, have anticipated readers from such centers of Calvinistic orthodoxy as Leyden and Geneva.

A second clue as to his audience can be found in the proof texts for various matters of dogma against which Milton disputed. Because the Bible rather than church tradition was their authority, Calvinists cited innumerable quotations from it in support of their arguments, different groups stressing different texts. Accordingly, these proof texts reveal traditions within themselves which help to identify the unnamed authorities with whom Milton disagreed in his treatise. Two examples from the many available will demonstrate how these proof texts help to identify these anonymous opponents whom Milton is trying to convert to his own point of view. In Chapter X he argues in support of polygamy. Having completed his affirmative statement, he answers "those who deny its lawfulness," analyzing at some length the proof texts by which "they" have supported their position. The following table presents the proof texts in order as Milton answers them, together with the proof texts actually cited by a representative sampling of the Calvinist scholastics on this subject:[16]

Christ.Doc.	Polanus	Ames	Wolleb	Westminster
Gen 2.24	*Gen 2.24*	Gen 2.22	*Gen 2.18ff*	*Gen 2.24*
Matt 19.5	*Mal 2.14-5*	Mal 2.15	*Matt 19.5*	*Matt 19.5*
Lev 18.18	*Matt 19.5*	Matt 19.4-5	Gen 4.9	Prov 2.17
Deut 17.17	*1 Cor 7.2-3*	1 Cor 7.2	Gen 30	
Mal 2.15	*1 Tim 3.2*	*Lev 18.18*	1 Sam 1.4-6	
1 Cor 7.2-4	Titus 1.6		*Lev 18.18*	

The italicized texts correspond with those which Milton enumerated. It is evident at once that although all have certain citations in common only Ames is identical so far as he goes, with Milton's citation of Deut 17.17 alone coming from some other source. Arminian and Salmurian discussions of the subject are not at all comparable.

For a second example, Milton argued against the strongly held Calvinist dogma that children rather than adults should be baptized. The tabulation of proof texts follows:[17]

Christ.Doc.	Polanus	Ames	Wolleb	Westminster
Matt 19.14	Gen 17.14	Rom. 4.11	*Matt 19.14*	*Gen 17.7-9*
1 Cor 10.2	Ex 4.24-26	Gal 3.7-9	*Gen 17.7*	Gal 3.9, 14
Gen 17.7	Matt 11.28	*Col 2.11-12*	Acts 2.39	*Col 2.11-12*
Acts 2.39	18.14		"Circumcision"	Acts 2.38-9
Col 2.11	*19.13*		(=Col 2.11)	Rom 4.11-12
"Whole fam-	Mark 10.14		"Whole fam-	1 Cor 7.14
ilies"	Luke 18.15		ilies"	Matt 28.19
	John 3.5			Mark 10.13-16
	Acts 2.39			Luke 18.15
	[and many others]			

Inspection readily shows that for this subject Milton's response is to Wolleb rather than to any of the others, with only 1 Cor 10.2

deriving from some other source. Again, Arminian and Salmurian analyses of the subject are quite different.

These two examples reveal the context of Milton's replies to be the Calvinist scholastics, but they also show that he did not limit his responses to a single work, like either the *Medulla* or the *Compendium*. They also demonstrate rather forcefully how he minimized the *Westminster* position in favor of continental authorities.

Inspection of proof texts is thus a useful means to identify Milton's audience. Sometimes, indeed, it reveals that the context of his reply goes beyond the Reformed scholastics. One of the most interesting sets of texts occurs in the crucial chapter on the Son of God, following Milton's argument to prove his subordination to the Father. Probably because of the centrality of the issue to Milton's complete theology, the opposing texts which he cites are rather numerous. He divides the New Testament texts into two groups, a major and a minor, which are matched with those of the Calvinists in the following table:[18]

Christ.Doc.	Polanus	Ames 1623	Ames 1627	Wolleb	Westminster
John 1.1	John 1.14	Rev 1.11	*John 1.1*	*John 1.1*	1 John 5.7
John 20.28	1.18	*1 John 5.20*	*Rom 9.5*	John 17.3	Matt 3.16
Heb 1.8	1.34	*Titus 2.13*	*1 Tim 3.16*	John 20.31	Matt 28.19
———	3.16	*Jude 4*	*Rev 17.14*	*Acts 20.28*	2 Cor 13.14
Matt 1.23	Matt 3.17	*Rom 9.5*		*Romans 9.5*	John 1.14
Acts 16.31	2 Cor 1.19	*Rev 19.6*		*Titus 2.13*	1.18
16.34	Luke 1.31	*Rev 17.14*			———
20.28	Rom 1.4				*John 1.1*
Rom 9.5					1.14
1 Tim 3.16					*1 John 5.20*
Titus 2.13					*Phil 2.6*
1 John 3.16					Gal 4.4
5.20					
Phil 2.6					
Jude 4					

In his analysis of this famous issue Milton seems to have been somewhat more eclectic in his response to proof texts, again most clearly answering Wolleb. *Westminster*, however, appears to figure in this argument, and the appearance of Jude 4, cited only in Ames's edition of 1623, suggests that Milton may have consulted this printing; at least, I have not found it elsewhere.

A surprising entry is the inclusion of Hebrews 1.8 as one of the three "principal texts" to be discussed inasmuch as none of these representative Reformed scholastics employs it. The explanation may lie in yet a different tradition of proof texts for this subject, in particular that of Saumur. There the argument included

> *John 1.1*
> *John 20.28*
> *1 Tim 3.16*
> *Acts 20.28*
> *Heb 1.8*
> *Titus 2.13*
> *Rom 9.5*
> *1 John 5.20,*

a list in remarkable agreement with Milton's, though it is not so extensive, and employing Hebrews 1.8.[19] One may conclude from the kind of evidence that has been presented here that Milton was trying to respond to the different Calvinistic traditions on the continent, though it would be pressing the argument too far to hold that on any issue he was addressing a single dogmatist or perhaps even a single group.

If, then, he was attempting to convert both the Reformed scholastics and the Salmurians to his own conception of the subordination of the Son to the Father, what of the third group, the Arminians? As has been observed, there is no question as to his familiarity with and acceptance of their position upon predestination. It would, therefore, be surprising if he had not known other details of their theology. Arminius himself had argued a conservative Christology, quite unlike Milton's,[20] but his theological successors, especially Episcopius,[21] developed a radical conception of the subordination of the Son to the Father which is remarkably similar to Milton's well-known views that the Son is neither equal with the Father nor coeternal with him.

Accepting the divinity of Father, Son, and Holy Spirit, Episcopius proceeds to assert that they are not equal persons: "divinity and divine perfections are attributed to these three persons not collaterally or coordinately, but subordinately, so that the Father derives from himself or from no other his divinity and his divine perfections, whereas the Son and Holy Spirit possess them from the Father. . . . The words *Son* and *Holy Spirit* in their original meaning signify subordination by generation or by being breathed forth."[22] Episcopius accordingly concludes that the Father alone possesses full divinity and thus "is first, as he is highest, in order, in dignity, in power."[23] He goes on to point out that even the Calvinist scholastic Zanchy had admitted that the Son is in some senses inferior to the Father.[24]

The basis of this subordination of Son to Father lies for Episcopius in the generation of the former. As Logos in John 1.1, he was generated "in the beginning," a phrase which Episcopius interprets as did Milton to mean not from all eternity but "from the beginning of all things," the same beginning which Moses describes in Genesis 1.1, "the beginning of that time in which everything began to be made that was made."[25] He refuses, however, to speculate about how the Son was generated, and, unlike Milton, he professes ignorance as to whether he derived from the divine substance and whether the begetting was voluntary or not.[26]

The reason which Episcopius offers for his willingness to accept such subordinationism is that the Bible requires only the belief that Jesus is the Son of God: "apostles and evangelists did not judge it necessary for salvation that it be believed that Jesus was eternally begotten from the essence of his Father."[27] Further proof for his position, as it was also for Milton, is the fact that church fathers did not require belief in the "orthodox" Trinity, the Apostles' Creed is silent about the matter, and this same argument appears in the Dialogue with Trypho written by the earliest Christian Apologist, Justin Martyr.[28] Accordingly, Episcopius and Milton arrive at identical conclusions: as the Father and Son differ in person, they must also differ in essence: "it is asserted in vain by those who assert the Son of God to be of one numerical essence with God his Father, since it cannot be denied that God gave the Son his glory. For the Son, qua Son, is not of himself but of the Father; and since the Son is not God except inasmuch as he is Son, he cannot have his divine essence or nature unless it is given and communicated to him by his Father. You argue, it is one thing to give the Son his essence, another to communicate it by generation. I reply, to generate, to communicate, to give (which comes to the same thing) are synonyms."[29] On the authority of 1 John 5.7 (which has given trouble to all subordinationist Christologies), he agrees that the Trinity are indeed one in number, but he insists that they are not one in essence.[30]

In thus distinguishing their essences, Episcopius is following his conception of what constitutes individuality; like Milton he concludes that where there are two individuals there are two persons, each possessed of its own essence. The argument may in part be indebted to the Racovian Catechism, which asserts that "the essence of God is one, not in kind but in number. Wherefore it cannot, in any way, contain a plurality of persons, since a person is nothing else than an individual intelligent essence. Wherever, then, there exist three numerical persons, there must necessarily, in like manner, be reckoned three individual essences."[31] Vorst had unsuccessfully tried to escape from the difficulty by distinguishing between an essence *common* to more than one being and one *proper* to an individual and hence not communicable,[32] but he was damned as a Socinian anyhow. As Heidanus complained, "The Remonstrants talk about the incomprehensible generation of the Son, but not of his eternal generation from the Father's essence."[33]

Statements made by Etienne de Courcelles reinforce the argument favoring the subordination of the Son to the Father, strongly suggesting that Episcopius' position was not the aberration of one man but a belief which may be identified with the entire school in Amsterdam.[34] Thus he begins his discussion of the relationship of Father to Son by arguing that "although the Son and the Holy Spirit far excell all creatures, yet they are subordinate to the Father, by whom they receive their existence and divinity; for in the Father alone is perceived the highest degree of divinity . . . in that he is from himself, or receives his divine nature from no other being but rather is the source of all divinity."[35] Going on to question, as did Milton, the authenticity of the text of 1 John 5.7, he proceeds to define the Arian position as having arisen from its two assertions that the Son was made from nothing and that there was a time when he was not. Taking up the latter point first, he observes that "there have always been many famous theologians and philosophers (like the contemporary Cartesians) who believe that time began with the world and that everything which antedated this creation is eternal"[36]—a conception which in this respect would define Arianism within orthodoxy in that it agreed with the Christian tradition that the Logos or Son of John 1.1 had created the universe and so must antedate it. On the other hand, de Courcelles goes on to argue that *creating* and *generating* in the context of the begetting of the Son mean the same thing and thus he does not believe, as did Milton, that the Son originated from the Father's substance.[37] He is moving, that is, beyond the positions of Episcopius and of Milton in the direction of true Arianism.

Considering the known indebtedness of Milton to the Arminian conception of man's freedom and the part which man must play in his own salvation, it is difficult not to see in the arguments originating in Amsterdam a major parallel to Milton's Christology. Some aspects of Arminian theology had in fact long been influential in the Church of England; especially through the support of Laud it became identified with the King's cause, whereas Parliament was generally Calvinist, with the notable exception of John Goodwin who, however, was not a subordinationist like Milton.[38] The Dutch Arminians, on the other hand, would have attacked the English

sacramentarianism, just as Milton did. At the Restoration this
English form returned to ecclesiastical power. It is not, then, surprising to find Episcopius' ideas to be central to the theology of
some of Milton's Church of England contemporaries, the Cambridge
Platonists.[39] The kinship of Milton's subordination to that of Cudworth is easily recognizable. It seems probable that both are indebted to the seminary in Amsterdam in testimony to its influence
in Cambridge. The entire movement ultimately derives from neo-
platonism, which exerted an extraordinary influence upon the
thought of the earliest fathers of the Christian Church, where its
subordinationism permanently established itself, to reappear
throughout ecclesiastical history because of the authority which
the primitive church has always held. Thus it is not accidental
that de Courcelles claims as authorities for his beliefs the same
church fathers whom Cudworth cited, all neoplatonists: Justin
Martyr, Irenaeus, Clement of Alexandria, Origen, Tertullian,
Novatian, Lactantius, and so on.[40]

One major aspect of Christology is the relationship of Son to
Father which has been discussed here. The other is the historical
union of the Son with mankind which took place at the Incarnation.
In the *Christian Doctrine* Milton argues that two persons rather
than two natures were then joined, a heresy long associated with
the name of Nestorius.[41] Upon this issue Episcopius is more conventional, holding that "there would be two Sons of God and two
persons . . . if the Son of man had ever subsisted in himself, apart
from union with the divine person of the Son of God. But since
the one never existed apart from the other, only a single Son of
God is necessarily supposed."[42] This Nestorian position, however,
appears in statements by other Remonstrants. Thus Episcopius'
own *Remonstrant Confession* had asserted that Christ was a true
man as well as the Son of God, with a truly human body and
rational soul,[43] exactly Milton's belief, though not expressly Nestorian. Vorst had interpreted the union to mean that when the two
natures joined in Christ there was "a certain *influx* of divine virtue
into the human nature," a concept quickly challenged by "Four
Professors of Leyden," Reformed scholastics all, as being the
"heresy which was condemned long ago in Nestorius by the ancient
church."[44] The trouble lay in the employment of the concept of
influx, implying as it does the addition of an entity subsequent to
the origin of the human individual with the result that two persons,
divine and human, would be within the body of Christ.[45] Episcopius
could only answer rather lamely that the hapless Vorst did not really
agree with Nestorius in this heresy.[46] But his follower de Courcelles

welcomes the concept of *influx* and the implications that go with it. Like Milton he believes that the humanity of Jesus existed in the maternal uterus before being united to the divine,[47] though (also like Milton) he does not know how the union was achieved: "It seems," he says, "that the divine Spirit of Christ flowed into (*influxisse*) his human nature in a unique way."[48] Some individuals at least among the schismatics of Amsterdam appear to have been open to the charge of Nestorianism, as was Milton.

In all of the elements of his Christology, including its relationships with the divine decrees, predestination, and the process of man's redemption, Milton thus seems to have agreed with the Arminian tradition. He holds a similar conception of God's grace. The danger which the Remonstrants (and Milton) obviously had to face was the accusation of Pelagianism, the heterodox belief that man was a completely free agent who by his own free choice could save himself without divine assistance. The Arminian emphasis upon man's free will in the process of redemption seems superficially to lead to this Pelagian position. Such an interpretation, with which the Arminians have been accused, overlooks, however, a central fact in their system: that God *first* must extend his grace to all. Such grace, *prevenient grace* as they called it, was accordingly developed as a basic element in the Arminian system, and Milton gladly adopted the idea (*Paradise Lost* XI, 3). It is, indeed, the point of departure in God's scheme of salvation for mankind:

> Man shall not quite be lost, but sav'd who will,
> Yet not of will in him, but grace in me
> Freely voutsaf't.
>
> (III, 173-75)

This decree is that of prevenient grace, the fundamental difference between the Arminian and the Pelagian. From this conception of an inward-working grace available to everyone derives one interpretation of the Christian conscience. It is not a very important concern for the Reformed scholastics, who believed that only the foreseen elect may possess it. True Calvinists accordingly placed their trust in an external compulsion exercised upon the depraved by the Godly Elect through the instrument of their established churches. Arminians —and Milton—on the other hand, believed in the power of the inner conscience, available to all even though it might be resisted. God observes in *Paradise Lost* that he has placed within mankind as a guide his "Umpire conscience" (III, 195), an idea which is prominent throughout Milton's mature writings. As Andrew Marvell evaluated these Dutch schismatics,

> Hence *Amsterdam, Turk-Christian-Pagan-Jew,*
> Staple of Sects and Minto of Schisme grew;
> That *Bank of Conscience,* where not one so strange
> Opinion but finds Credit, and Exchange.
> In vain for *Catholicks* our selves we bear;
> The *universal Church* is onely there.
> *(The Character of Holland,* ll. 71-76)

But many details of Milton's systematic theology must have originated in some source other than these Arminians, for he frequently disagrees with them. Thus, though Episcopius recognized as did Milton that the Hebrew word in Genesis 1.1, translated κτιζειν or *creare* or *create*, does not mean to create from nothing, yet he resolutely accepted the traditional view that the universe originated *ex nihilo,* whereas for Milton it originated *ex deo.*[49] Unlike Milton, the Dutch group did not favor polygamy.[50] In his interpretations of many details of Christian dogma the differences are so great between Milton and any other single group that one can only conclude that the *Christian Doctrine* presents the highly eclectic system of a man who has read widely but who has refused to be dominated by any single school. Addressing himself to traditional Calvinists like those in Leyden or Geneva, to moderates like those in Saumur, and to the radicals in Amsterdam, he probably would have pleased none entirely and indeed would have won no followers for his systematic theology had it been published. But in its attempt to bring together these separate sects on a common Christian ground, it remains one of the most important individual projects of any seventeenth-century religious thinker.

Notes

1. J. H. Hanford, "The Date of Milton's *De Doctrina Christiana,*" *SP,* 17 (1920), 309-19.

2. *The Works of John Milton* (New York, 1931-38), XIV, 261; Harris Fletcher, "Milton and Walton's *Biblia Sacra Polyglotta,*" *MLN,* 42 (1927), 84-87.

3. Helen Darbishire, *The Early Lives of Milton* (London, 1932), p. 29; see also p. 46, where Wood repeats substantially the same information.

4. Ibid., p. 61.

5. An example is by Amandus Polanus, *Enchiridii Locorum Communium Theologicorum* (Basil, 1600). It is arranged in alphabetical order.

6. A helpful fact which shortened *The Student's Milton* (New York, 1933) by many, many pages. I do not believe that the collection of proof texts assumed here was the same as the lost *Index Theologicus* referred to in the *Commonplace Book,* for the surviving

subject entries of the *Index* are in no case those that are found in such systematic compilations as those of Ames or Wolleb—or in the *Christian Doctrine*, for that matter.

7. Near the end of his chapter on the Son of God, Milton observes that his interpretation accords with that of "the celebrated confession of faith (illius fidei celebrata confessio)" (XIV, 352, 353), but this cannot be the *Westminster* statement, with which it is in flat disagreement. More probably he means the "Nicene" Creed of 381. See my argument in W. B. Hunter, C. A. Patrides, and J. A. Adamson, *Bright Essence* (Salt Lake City: Univ. of Utah Press, 1971), pp. 50ff.

8. See John W. Beardslee's Introduction to *Reformed Dogmatics* (New York, 1965), p. 19, and Brian G. Armstrong, *Calvinism and the Amyraut Heresy* (Madison, Wisc., 1969), pp. 37ff. The term *scholastics* is used deliberately to suggest the influence on them of St. Thomas, especially in their ordering of arguments and their dependence upon Aristotle, dependence which helps to account for Milton's reliance upon his authority which I have noted in "Milton's Power of Matter," *JHI*, 13 (1952), 551-62, and *Bright Essence*, pp. 19ff. See Armstrong, pp. 127ff., who observes, however (p. 173), that, somewhat unlike Milton, the Reformed scholastics do not generally employ the principle of accommodation—as others, the Salmurians for instance, do.

9. Amyraut strongly supported King Charles and in 1650 wrote a book attacking those who had executed him. His religious views were adopted by Milton's antagonist, Alexander More, who had consequent difficulties in scholastic Geneva. See Armstrong, pp. 108, 112n., and 115.

10. Following Cameron, Amyraut had argued for a "universal salvation" offered through the sacrifice of Christ to everyone. This is indeed Arminian, but Amyraut immediately qualified the universality of such salvation so as to make it apply only to those whom God had already chosen as believers: to the foreseen elect. See Thomas M. Lindsay, "Amyraldism," in the *Encyclopedia of Religion and Ethics;* Philip Schaff, *Bibliotheca symbolica ecclesiae universalis: The Creeds of Christendom* (New York, 1919), I, 478ff.; and Armstrong, passim. These views were advanced in the Westminster Assembly on October 22, 1645, by Mr. Calamy, later supported by Mr. Vines. Mr. Gillespie (the "Galasp" of Milton's Sonnet XII) objected, arguing that John 3.16 ("God so loved the world that he gave his only begotten Son") meant that "God so loved the *elect*," the strict Calvinist position. Milton mentions this interpretation of the verse, only to disprove it (XV, 321). I believe that he himself would have seen Amyraut's position as essentially Arminian like his own, as will be seen.

11. See Maurice Kelley, "The Theological Dogma of *Paradise Lost,* III, 173-202," *PMLA*, 52 (1937), 75-79.

12. Ames is conveniently available in the translation by J. D. Eusden, *The Marrow of Theology* (Boston, 1968); Wolleb's treatise is translated in Beardslee. Polanus' work is *The Substance of Christian Religion* (London, 1608). The same division is made in his outline, *Partitionum Theologicarum Logica Methodo* (Basil, 1600).

13. H. Zanchius, *His Confession of Christian Religion* (Cambridge, 1599).

14. *Institutes,* III, 21; see Beardslee,

pp. 16ff., and Eusden, p. 26. Ames
follows Calvin here rather than Beza.
The doctrinal ordering of *Paradise
Lost* III, 80ff., is the same as that of
the *Christian Doctrine*.

15. See Maurice Kelley, "Milton's
Debt to Wolleb's *Compendium Theologiae Christianae*," *PMLA*, 50 (1935),
156-65.

16. *Christian Doctrine*, XV, 123-37;
Polanus, *Enchiridion*, *s.v.* Polygamy;
Ames, *Marrow*, p. 318; Wolleb, *Compendium*, in Beardslee, p. 242; *Westminster Confession*, XXIV, 1.

17. *Christian Doctrine*, XVI, 171-
83; Polanus, *s.v.* Baptism; Ames, p.
211; Wolleb, pp. 130-31; *Westminster*,
XXVIII, 4.

18. *Christian Doctrine*, XIV, 253-75;
Polanus, *Substance*, p. 43 (the citations in his *Enchiridion*, pp. 92-97, are
too lengthy to enter here); Ames
(1623) Disputation Six; Ames (1627
et seq.), Disputation Five and in
Eusden's translation (from the 1629
edition), p. 89; Wolleb, p. 43; *Westminster*, II, 3; VIII, 2. Similar proof
texts, though not so close to Milton's
as Wolleb's, appear in such authorities
as Zacharias Ursinus, *The Summe of
Christian Religion* (London, 1645),
Question 18 of his *Catechism*; Wolfgang Musculus, *Loci Communes Theologiae Sacrae* (Basil, n.d.), Chapter II;
and Johannes Polyandrus et al.,
Synopsis Purioris Theologiae (the so-
called "Leyden Synopsis") (Leyden,
1652), pp. 89ff. The two citations
from Ames indicate the changes which
he made in this Disputation between
1623 and subsequent editions.

19. *Syntagma Thesium Theologicarum
in Academia Salmuriensi* (Saumur,
1655), Part I, p. 161. This book is a
joint collection of essays by La Place,
Amyraut, and Cappell, the last of
whom wrote this thesis. Milton cited

his *Specilegium* on 1 Cor 11.4 (XVII,
93).

20. See, for instance, his "On the
Person of the Father and the Son,"
in *Twenty-Five Disputations*, conveniently available in *The Works of
James Arminius*, trans. James Nichols
(Auburn and Buffalo, 1853), I, 390ff.
The argument is not similar to Milton's even though Arminius cites
the church fathers' metaphors of
fountain-stream and luminary-light.
Milton (and the fathers) meant them
in a subordinationist sense. See my
argument in *Bright Essence*, pp. 149ff.
Also unlike Milton's conclusions,
Arminius' statements about the Incarnation are entirely orthodox.

21. See the *Institutio Theologicarum*
in his *Opera*, I (Amsterdam, 1650). It
is not clear just why this development
should take place in the emerging
Arminianism of the seventeenth century, though a possibility is that it
represents the impact of Socinianism
upon the movement and particularly
of its *Racovian Catechism* of 1605ff.
See H. John McLachlan, *Socinianism
in Seventeenth-Century England* (Oxford, 1951), especially p. 21.

22. ". . . personis his tribus divinitatem divinasque perfectiones tribui,
non collateraliter aut coordinatè, sed
subordinatè: ita ut Pater solus naturam
istam divinam & perfectiones istas
divinas à se habeat, sive à nulla alio,
Filius autem & Spiritus sanctus à
patre . . . ; voces Filii & Spiritus
sancti . . . subordinationem à gener-
ante & spirante important in primo
conceptu suo," *Institutio*, IV, ii, 32,
in *Opera*, I, 333.

23. "unde consequitur, Patrem sic
esse primum, ut etiam summus sit,
tum ordine, tum dignitate, tum
potestate," p. 334.

24. Episcopius quotes from a letter

of Zanchy, "Imò ut filius quoque minor Patre non incongrue dici potest, quia plus est esse à nullo quam esse ab alio, & generare quam generari. Et hoc sensu multi Patres locum illum, Pater major me est, interpretantur," p. 334.

25. "... per ... αρχην intelligi principium temporis istius, quo omnia ista fieri coeperunt quae facta sunt," p. 335.

26. "Hisce sic demonstratis, quaerat aliquis, quae & qualis haec sit generatio, sive quomodo ea facta sit. An videlicet Pater produxerit Filium de substantia sua. Si sic, an produxerit cum de substantia sua tanquam ex materia, ut vult Durandus: an tanquam ex principio consubstantiali & formali, ut sentit Thomas & alii?. . . Denique an generatio haec facta sit per intellectum, an per voluntatem. . . . Resp[ondeo:] Fateor lubens me haec ignorare & non capere," p. 337.

27. "Apostolos & Evangelistas non judicasse ad salutem scitu necessarium esse, ut credatur, Jesum ex essentia Patris sui ante secula genitum esse; . . . concludo ergo, eos judicasse, sufficere ad salutem, ut credatur, Jesum esse Filium Dei," p. 338.

28. Pp. 339-40. See my argument from the Apologists in *Bright Essence*, pp. 38ff. Here also appears a full statement of Milton's subordinationist position.

29. "Dico id frustra afferri ab iis, qui Filium Dei unius numero essentiae esse afferunt cum Deo Patre suo; quia ne sic quidem negari potest, Deum Filio dedisse gloriam suam. Filius enim, qua Filius, non est à se, sed à Patre; & quia Filius non est Deus, nisi quà & quia Filius est, divinam etiam essentiam sive naturam suam non potest habere nisi datam & communicatam sibi à Patre suo. Dices: Aliud est,

datam esse Filio essentiam, aliud communicatam per generationem. Respondeo: Generare, communicare, dare (quod attinet ad hanc rem) synonyma sunt," p. 343.

30. ". . . dato enim jam, versum illum qui ex Joannis Epistola citatur, canonicae ac certae aut indubiae autoritatis esse, imo verba ista, *Et hi tres unum sunt,* idem praecisè significare, quod, hi tres una numero essentia sunt, atque ita etiam exponi verba Matthaei, baptizantes eos in nomen Patriae, Filii, & Spiritus S. qui tres videlicet unum sunt essentia; quid inde? Ergo, quia Marcus dicit, Qui crediderit, & baptizatus fuerit in tres istos, servabitur, qui non crediderit condemnabitur, etiam necessarium ad salutem esse esserit id credere, quod isti tres ita unum sint? quis non miretur talem consequentiam?" p. 340. Milton questions the authenticity of the text of the epistle and interprets it to mean that the three are one only in "unity of agreement and testimony," XIV, 215.

31. *The Racovian Catechism,* trans. Thomas Rees (London, 1818), p. 33. This is not to argue that Milton and the whole Arminian movement are full-fledged Socinians—only that they agree in their definitions of individuality and essence. See further *Bright Essence*, pp. 19ff.

32. ". . . quum singulae personae vera ac realia Entia sint . . . omne vero ens suam quandam peculiarem essentiam habeat . . . omnino hinc consequi, singular personas suam quandam *propriam* essentiam habere. . . . Sic v.g. *Pater,* quà pater, suam quandam *propriam* habet essentiam, puta quae non modò ipsam divinitatem, absolutè sumtam, sed & peculiarem hujus in Patre subsistentiam, sive cum propriâ Patris praerogativâ consider-

atam, includat," *Apologetica Exegesis,* appended to his *Tractatus Theologicus de Deo* (Steinfurt, 1610), pp. 38ff. See *Bright Essence,* pp. 19ff.

33. *"Remonstrantes* loquuntur quidem de incomprehensibili generatione Filii, sed non loquuntur de aeterna generatione Filii ex essentia Patris," quoted in Adrian Cattenburgh, *Specimen Controversiarum inter Remonstrantes et Socinum,* p. 70, bound following his *Bibliotheca Scriptorum Remonstrantium* (Amsterdam, 1728).

34. De Courcelles was Episcopius' successor and edited his *Opera* of 1650. De Courcelles' own statements appear in his *Religionis Christianae Institutio,* first printed posthumously in his *Opera Theologica* (Amsterdam, 1675). See also in the same volume, his *Dissertatio Theologica de vocibus Trinitatis.* It is not demonstrable that Milton read his arguments in manuscript; what is important here is the fact of his agreement with Episcopius so as to indicate a continuing theological tradition.

35. "Sed quamvis Filius & Spiritus S. longe supra omnes creaturas excellant, Patri tamen sunt subordinati, à quo existentiam & divinitatem suam acceperunt in Patre enim solo reperitur istud summum Deitatis fastigium . . . , quod ex se ipso sit Deus, seu naturam suam divinam à nulla acceperit, sed contra omnis Divinitatis sit fons," *Institutio,* p. 72.

36. "Et multi sunt fueruntque semper celeberrimi Theologi & Philosophi, ut hodie Cartesiani, qui tempus cum mundo incepisse, & omnia quae ejus creationem antecesserunt, aeterna esse voluerunt," p. 75.

37. Others have held the Father "generavisse Filium per decisionem

particulae alicujus ex sua essentia, ac proinde Dei essentiam esse divisibilem & corruptibilem. Neque etiam docebat eos contendere, praesertim tanta cum vehementia, ut fecerunt, de re captum humanum exsuperante; qualis erat ista, quodnam apud Deum discrimen sit inter generare & creare seu facere. Nam quod respondent Deum generare, cum Filium ex sua substantia producit; quaere vero quoties aliquid, sive ex nihilo, sive ex praeexistente materia efficit; nullius est momenti: cum jam ostenderimus talem generationem, quae fiat per decisionem substantiae, in Deum non quadrare; nec usquam legamus in S. Literis Deum ex substantia sua Filium genuisse; sed contra certum sit ipsum longe alio modo sibi filios procreare solere," p. 75.

38. Samuel Dunn, *Christian Theology by John Goodwin* (London, 1836), p. 45.

39. See Rosalie L. Colie, *Light and Enlightenment* (Cambridge, 1957). Unhappily, the book only partially achieves the promise of its subtitle: *A Study of the Cambridge Platonists and the Dutch Arminians.* I have discussed the similarity of their Christology and Milton's in *Bright Essence,* pp. 44ff.

40. *Institutio,* pp. 79-81.

41. I have argued the issue at some length in *Bright Essence,* pp. 133ff.

42. "Sic erunt duo Filii Dei & duae personae; una quae subsistit antequam nasceretur altera. Resp [ondeo:] Id sequeretur quidem, si Filius hominis substitisset unquam per se, extra unionem cum divina persona Filii Dei. Sed vero, quia ea extra illam nunquam per se substitit, hic unus dumtaxat Filius Dei statuatur necesse est," p. 338. Milton, on the other hand, argued (against Zanchy) that the human being (the Son of man) existed prior to its

union with the divine Son (XV, 267ff.).
See *Bright Essence*, pp. 133ff.

43. "Factus autem est homo non
mody verus, sive quoad substantiam
integer, ac perfectus, corpore scilicet
vere humano, & anima rationali con-
stans," *Confessio sive Declaratio Sententiae Pastorum, qui in foederato
Belgio Remonstrantes vocantur*, reprinted in Episcopius, *Opera*, II (Rotterdam, 1665), Part 2, p. 82.

44. Their attack is reprinted in
Episcopius' *Apologia . . . contra Censuram
Quatuour Professorum Leydensium* in
Opera, II, 156: "Videntur . . . sedulo
cavisse autores, ne ita se exprimerent,
ut subterfugium omne tolleretur Vorstio,
qui unionem duarum in Christo naturarum constituebat in influxu quodam
divinae virtutis in naturam Christí
humanam, vel in aliqua divinitatis
operatione. . . . Quae haeresis in Nestorio à veteri Ecclesia olim damnata fuit."

45. In his *Apologetica Exegesis* Vorst
interpreted John 1.14 ("And the Word
was made flesh") as referring to the
personal union, "per quam scilicet
humanam naturam ita sibi appropriat,
& quasi ad se attrahit, ut illapsu
(sicut loquuntur) sive influxu suae
personalitatis eam sustentet," p. 88.

46. "Vorstium non constituisse cum
Nestorio unionem duarum naturam
in Christo in divinae virtutis influxu,
nedum in solo divinae virtutis influxu,"
Opera, II, 156.

47. *Institutio*, p. 222.

48. "Modum unionis duarum
istarum naturarum nemo facile
dixerit; nec etiam scire nobis
necesse est . . . ; videtur Spiritus
Christi divinus in humanam ejus
naturam peculiariter influxisse,"
p. 229. Milton does not appear to
have employed the term *influx* in
this disputed sense.

49. See *Opera*, I, 345; *Remonstrant

Confession, Chapter V; Arminius, II,
54ff. For Milton's view see J. A.
Adamson's study in *Bright Essence*
pp. 81ff.

50. Episcopius, *Opera*, I, 119, but
also note his views on divorce, I,
118ff. He does not stress infant
baptism, I, 260.

Appendix

A Survey of Milton's Prose Works

JOHN T. SHAWCROSS

This survey of Milton's prose attempts to pull together all known information about editions, dates of composition, public reaction to and knowledge of the works, and general scholarly discussions of them. Not all of the material has been previously recorded, and what has been noted or discussed in the past has, for the most part, lain scattered and unfocussed. The three main sources today of such information present difficulties for the student of Milton's prose: the textual and general introductions to the editions in the Yale Prose are at best incomplete, frequently inaccurate, and generally limited;[1] the notices in *The Life Records of John Milton*, ed. J. Milton French,[2] are, of course, scattered over five volumes, but also incomplete in certain ways or not always exact or clear; and the discussions in *Milton: A Biography* by William R. Parker[3] are usually relegated to the notes for the kind of material cited here, which procedure makes handy reference impossible, and they are limited or incomplete because of the nature of the presentation.

The amount of investigation and time necessary to produce this survey justifies the effort. Corrections and new material here are seldom indicated. The works are discussed chronologically by publication date. However, editions of the works in selected form and in multiple or "complete" collections are mentioned at the end of this survey, along with some general criticism.

The first acknowledged prose work published by John Milton[4] was *Of Reformation Touching Church-Discipline in England: And the Causes that hitherto have hindered it*, a tract in two books "Written to a Friend," according to the title page.[5] It appeared in May 1641, having been printed for the bookseller Thomas Underhill. Underhill was also the publisher of Milton's next two tracts and the register of *Of Education* on June 4, 1644 (Stationers' Register, I, 117). The printing has been assigned—I believe in error—to both Richard Oulton and Gregory Dexter, who produced the next two pamphlets.[6] There are a few errata, and some changes in spelling and punctuation were made while the tract was being printed.[7]

The question of the printer or printers has not been raised since Parker's article noted before. Parker himself in *Milton: A Biography*, II, 847, says that "The unnamed printers have been identified" citing his article as evidence. But the article does not explicitly argue for their joint printing of this tract. Oulton and Dexter began their association early in 1641, but there are also books dated 1641 produced by Oulton alone. The only reason for assigning them both to *Of Reformation*, it seems, is that they printed *Of Prelatical Episcopacy* and *Animadversions* together. However, the nature of their collaboration in these two pamphlets is not in evidence in the first tract. An examination of the first tract indicates that the only place at which the manuscript might have been divided between them is between Books I and II, pp. 41 and 42, sigs. G_1r and G_1v respectively. It is inconceivable that sig. G_1v would have been set as the beginning of Book II and sig. G_1r left blank. Rather, copy would have been struck off so that pp. 1-40 (Book I) would be expected to fill sigs. B-F and pp. 41-88 (Book II) to fill sigs. G-M. When the printer came close to p. 40 and found that the less than half a page of material that now constitutes p. 41 would be in excess of his limit, he would have adjusted by using reduced type, increasing type per line and squeezing or increasing lines per page. (This additional page for Book I necessitated an additional leaf, sig. N_1, both sides of which were used, the total pages equalling ninety; that is, Book II is printed on pp. 42-90.) Besides, p. 41 is signed and has the proper catchword "OF." It is unlikely that the two printers would have divided the work and then not composed it simultaneously. My examination of the spelling of the first book and of the second book also does not show differences as in the next two tracts; the spelling seems to be a mixture of Milton's practices and common practices not assignable, or at least not generally assignable, to Milton. The possibility raised by Donald MacKenzie for the eighteenth century, that copy might be set by more than one printer working on random signatures,[8] does not seem valid for this tract.

The date has been variously assigned, but its limits are determined by a reference to *The Petition of the University of Oxford* requesting the continuation of episcopacy, presented to the House of Commons on May 12, and by an allusion to Milton's tract in the anonymous *A Compendious Discourse Proving Episcopacy To Be of Apostolicall and Consequently of Divine Institution*, the preface of which is dated

May 31. Attempts to push the tract's composition backward a month
or two are unconvincing or in error through misinterpretation of
Milton's remarks. Although William London advertised the work
for sale on September 25, 1658,[9] the only other separate edition of
this tract has been that by Will T. Hale. Aside from the annotated
editions, with introductions, by Hale, by Don M. Wolfe and William
Alfred (Yale *Prose*, I, 514-617), and by Everett H. Emerson,[10] *Of
Reformation* has drawn comment on its date of publication, its
style and imagery, and its place in the antiprelatical controversy.[11]
A Japanese translation by Jun Harada appeared in 1972.

Milton's vision of a self-reforming commonwealth[12] elicited
antagonistic reference from an anonymous author, calling himself
Peloni Almoni, Cosmopolites (that is, "anonymous"[13]), in *A Compendious Discourse* (May 1641), p. [3]; from Thomas Fuller in
The Holy State (1642) in his "Life of Bishop Ridley," Book IV,
Chapter 11, pp. 291-92; and from John Bramhall in *The Serpent
Salve, Or, A Remedie for the Biting of an Aspe* (1643), pp. 211-12.
Only the author of *A Light Shining Out of Darkness* (1659), identified as Henry Stubbe, calls Milton an excellent author for *Of Reformation*, pp. 174-75; he copies out Milton's translation from Dante. It
is interesting to note, however, that Thomas Jefferson, in his commonplace book, summarized and quoted from this pamphlet along with
Reason of Church-Government.[14] Obviously Milton's democratic
views and his awareness that a great cultural gap in societal, economic,
political, and religious life had evolved were not recognized and little
appreciated in his own times. But perhaps the main deterrent to such
recognition was the close relationship of the pamphlet with contemporary events and people rather than a sense of the universal,
which is certainly not stressed, as Everett Emerson has remarked.[15]

*Of Prelatical Episcopacy, and Whether it may be deduc'd from the
Apostical times,* Milton's second tract, was printed by R[ichard]
O[ulton] and G[regory] D[exter] for Thomas Underhill in June
or July 1641.[16] The text shows variations in punctuation and spelling.[17]
A short work of only twenty-four pages, it directly answers Joseph
Hall's *Episcopacie by Divine Right Asserted* (entered February 10,
1640), James Ussher's *The Iudgement of Doctor Rainoldes touching
the Originall of Episcopacy* (entered May 21, 1641), and the afore-
mentioned *A Compendious Discourse* (ca. May 31, 1641). Ussher's
work is referred to on the title page as a view of episcopacy that
Milton was refuting. J. Max Patrick has shown the insubstantiality
of the attempts to place composition before June.[18] The only external piece of evidence for dating is George Thomason's purchase

of a copy in July. Although also advertised by London in 1658, no
other separate edition has been published. The only annotated edition
(with introduction) is Patrick's in the Yale *Prose*, I, 618-52. Scholarship on the tract has generally been similar to that on *Of Reformation*,
though in much less quantity: the date, style, and imagery, and antiprelatical contexts. The only direct evidence we may have of its influence
are the alleged paraphrases by Robert Greville, Lord Brooke, in *A Discourse Opening the Nature of that Episcopacie* (ca. November 1641).[19]

The third antiprelatical tract is a section-by-section lampoon of arguments raised by Bishop Joseph Hall in *Defence of the Humble
Remonstrance against the frivolous and false exceptions of Smectymnuus*, which was registered on April 12, 1641, and which enjoyed
two editions in 1641. It appeared in July (?) 1641 as *Animadversions
upon the Remonstrants Defence, Against Smectymnuus*, and was
printed by Richard Oulton and Gregory Dexter for Thomas Underhill.[20] The division of labor was that Oulton set sigs. B-G, pp. [1-48],
and Dexter, sigs. H-K$_2$, pp. 49-68.[21] There are textual variants and
signatures; A$_1$ was printed as K$_3$, and K$_3$ as K$_4$. A cancel occurs
for G$_3$-G$_4$, pp. 45-48, which would have corresponded to Sections
6-12 of Hall's *Defence*.[22] The reason for the cancel is not clear; no
uncancelled copy is known. Interestingly and without explanation,
a cancel appears at this same position in *A Complete Collection*
(1698), I, 155-58, sigs. X$_2$-X$_3$.[23]

The tract appeared anonymously and soon evoked a full reply:
*A Modest Confutation of a Slanderous and Scurrilous Libell,
entitvld, Animadversions vpon the Remonstrants Defence against
Smectymnuus*, published after March 25, 1642. The authorship
is uncertain, although Hall or sometimes he and his son Robert have
been suggested as authors. This pamphlet is reprinted in facsimile
by Parker in *Milton's Contemporary Reputation. Animadversions*
was cited in *The Transproser Rehears'd* (1673), and an extract
appears in *An Old Looking-Glass* (Philadelphia, 1770; New Haven,
1774), pp. 45-50. A separate edition appeared in 1919 from the
press of Norman McLean, Cambridge. The only annotated edition
is that by Rudolf Kirk in the Yale *Prose*. Most scholarship has
treated its position in the antiprelatical controversy.

The fourth of Milton's antiprelatical tracts was *The Reason of
Church-Governement Urg'd against Prelaty By Mr. John Milton.
In two Books* (London, 1641). It was printed by Edward Griffin
the Younger[24] for John Rothwell, and it appeared probably at
the end of January 1642. With this edition Milton's name, in full,

first appeared on a title page. A three-line listing of errata is included, and there are press variants. The suggested date of composition has ranged from August 1641 through January 1642, although the shorter period of December–January (given by Parker) seems more likely.[25] The work made no impact, as far as we know, and it was reissued in 1654 without even its original title page being cancelled. The volume in which this reissue appears includes a preceding reissue of *An Apology* with a new title page; see later. The 1654 issue was advertised twice by Rothwell and by London; see later. In succeeding years the tract seems to have continued its lack of significance for the reading public, for no separate editions occur, almost no allusions are made, and, except for rather recent discussions encompassing many of the antiprelatical works and their milieu, little scholarly attention has been paid the work. Jefferson, however, did read it approvingly, for he summarized and quoted from it in his Commonplace Book, pp. 384–85 (see note 14). Of importance for Milton scholars has been the biographical "digression" beginning Book II. The only annotated edition is Haug's in the Yale *Prose.*

An Apology Against a Pamphlet Call'd A Modest Confutation of the Animadversions upon the Remonstrant against Smectymnuus, as the title page of the first edition has it, was printed by Edward Griffin, the Younger, for John Rothwell, soon after April 8, 1642. There is one erratum on p. 59, and the tract has variant states. It aimed at countering the slander directed against Milton as author of *Animadversions* in *A Modest Confutation* (ca. late March), and therefore to present himself without misunderstanding. The significance of the tract is its personal statements and raw material for an analysis of the idealist, the hopeful literary artist, and (in Freudian terms) the anal personality, both expulsive and retentive. Attention has been paid the pamphlet as the last of Milton's antiprelatical tracts and as a statement concerning the source for the first two of the foregoing matters. But a study of Milton the late bloomer, the servant constantly preparing himself for service but waiting for command, the contemplative whose self-regard and high ambition finally discharge his burden of thought and emotion might wisely start with this volume.

The first edition caused no reactions and apparently did not sell well, for leftover copies were reissued in 1654 by Rothwell, along with *Reason* and a new title page.[26] The next year it was advertised by Rothwell in *A Catalogue of the Most Approved Divinity-Books . . . Continued down to this present Year, 1655, Mensis Martis 26*;

two years later he again advertised it in *A Catalogue of the Most Approved Divinity-Books . . . Continued down to this present Year, 1657, Mensis Junii 13*; and the following year it was on London's list. Besides its republication in collected volumes of the prose, an excerpt from *An Apology* was included in the American 1770 edition of *Hirelings* (rptd. 1774), pp. 71-74. It was given a facsimile and annotated edition by Milford C. Jochums in 1950 as well as an annotated edition in the Yale *Prose* by Frederick L. Taft.

Milton's first divorce tract and the main source of antagonism toward him for his views on the subject was *The Doctrine and Discipline of Divorce,* published on August 1, 1643, according to Thomason's note. It was printed by Thomas Paine and Matthew Simmons; there is a long erratum. Claud A. Thompson suggests that Paine set sigs. B and C, and Simmons sigs. D-H on the basis of orthography.[27] Although printed reactions to this first edition are not in evidence, the volume apparently sold out rapidly enough because on February 2, 1644, appeared the greatly expanded second edition: *Now the second time revis'd and much augmented. In two Books: To the Parlament of England with the Assembly. The Author J. M.* The printer or printers are not recorded, but there is no reason to believe they were not Paine and Simmons. At least the printing house was Simmons' as Parker had suggested; see Thompson's discussion (pp. 92-93) of a hand-carved wood block factotum employed in Ed. 2 on sigs. B_1 and E_4 and in Simmons' *The Troubles of Jerusalems Restauration* (London, 1646), sig. B_1. Thompson (pp. 22-26) distinguishes two compositors working in what seems random fashion, and though the more careful may be Simmons, the work of the less careful compositor does not show a consistency with the work of the compositor of sigs. B and C in Ed. 1 (that is, apparently, Paine); see p. 130. A cancel of G_2 occurs with the stub occasionally showing either horizontally (with correct pagination) or vertically. A few errata are given; manuscript corrections made in the print shop are found, except that the corrector frequently made errors in doing his work. Various signatures are in various states, all known copies being composites of corrected and uncorrected states.[28] The alterations of text often involve spelling changes generally moving toward Miltonic practice. This revised, second edition is so different from the 1643 version that it almost constitutes a second volume on divorce.

Within the year a further edition was required even though the run of the second edition seems to have been large for the times. This next edition attempted to follow the second edition closely so as to appear to be simply another issue, but it is a complete resetting with numerous differences from the second edition. The title page within a ruled border gives "The author I. M." and is dated 1645. The errata are repeated and there are two states.[29] The orthography of this edition has seemed to be often closer to Miltonic practice than that of edition two,[30] but the full analysis of edition two by Thompson has shown that edition three was often drawn from "corrected" states in edition two and that those instances where edition three had seemed to alter the Miltonic practice of edition two sometimes derived from "uncorrected" states.[31] Again, the printing house was Simmons', for the factotum noted before appears on sig. B_1. The third edition seems to be the work of two compositors (Thompson, pp. 96-97), but the signatures produced are again random. Evidence is provided by skeletons, fonts, and orthography. One of the compositors may have been the more careful compositor of the second edition (Simmons?); whether the other compositor of Ed. 3 was the less careful compositor of Ed. 2 is not really discernible. A fourth edition also appeared in 1645; it is a generally poor job of printing and frequently differs from Ed. 3, its copy source, though it attempts to be a duplicate.[32] It would thus seem to be a pirated edition, produced because of the controversy which ensued upon the second edition and the apparent demand for copies. The title page, which does not have a ruled border, gives "The author J. M." and shows other differences. There are no errata although all corrections were not made. Pages 42-47 are incorrectly numbered and pp. 69-72 are repeated in pagination.

The first reaction to the tract recorded occurred in a sermon which was printed a few months later. Herbert Palmer's *The Glasse of Gods Providence towards his Faithfull ones. Held forth in a Sermon preached to the two Houses of Parliament, at Margarets, Westminster, Aug. 13, 1644* (London, 1644) was registered on November 7, 1644 (I, 136); the citation appears on p. 57. The Journal of the House of Commons for August 24-26, 1644 (III, 605-6), indicates that a petition against this book on divorce was introduced. On September 16, 1644, appeared William Prynne's *Twelve Considerable Serious Questions touching Church Government* with reference on p. 7; and on November 19, 1644, a full-scale anonymous attack was published, having been registered on October 31, 1644 (I, 135), and licensed on November 14. This was *An Answere to a Book, Intituled, The Doctrine and Discipline of Divorce. Printed by G[eorge] M[oule] for William Lee, 1644.* Further allusions occur in often reprinted books by Daniel Featley, Ephraim Pagitt, and Robert Baillie: Featley's *The Dippers Dipt* alludes to Milton in the dedicatory epistle dated January 10, 1645, on p. [B₂v]; Thomason dated his copy February 7, and there were several editions through the next few decades. Pagitt's *Heresiography*, registered on March 5, 1645, was dated May 8 by Thomason; an allusion appears on p. [A₃v]. Ed. 2 (1645) adds another allusion on p. 142; this occurs in Ed. 3 (1647) on p. 87 and in Ed. 4 (1647) on pp. 86-87. A further citation is found in this last edition on pp. 145-46. Baillie's *A Dissvasive from the Errours of the Time*, dated November 24, 1645, by Thomason, alludes to Milton or quotes from *Doctrine and Discipline of Divorce* on pp. [xvii], 116, 144-45; there were several editions or issues in the ensuing years. Reference is also found in a letter written by Baillie and dated November 15, 1645; see *Letters and Journals, Written by the Deceased Mr Robert Baillie, Principal of the University of Glasgow. Carefully Transcribed by Robert Aiken* (Edinburgh: for W. Gray, J. Buckland, and G. Keith, 1775), II, 168.

Further antagonism, directed largely against this first divorce tract, although by this time the other divorce works may have contributed to the adverse reaction, appeared in the following four years. John Bachiler, the licenser of John Goodwin's *Twelve Considerable Cautions*, dated February 17, 1646, by Thomason, referred to Milton's tract on p. [A₁v]; Thomas Edwards cited it in *Gangræna*, dated February 26, 1646, on p. 34. This volume went through various editions. It may have appeared earlier according to a letter by Robert Baillie (*Letters and Journals*, II, 177). *The Second Part of Gangræna*, dated May 28, 1646, also alludes to the divorce tract on pp. 10-11. Milton's anger and then wry humor in "I did but prompt the age," "On the Forcers of Conscience," and "A book was writ" can be easily understood when one examines these reactions. Further comments appeared by John Wilkins in the second edition of *Ecclesiastes* (1647), p. 87 (rptd. 1651 and 1656, p. 119); by Edward Hyde (later Earl of Clarendon) in a letter to Sir Edward Nicholas, dated April 7, 1647 (*State Papers Collected by Edward, Earl of Clarendon* [London, 1773], II, 363); by the anonymous author of *A Testimony to the Truth of Jesus Christ, and to Our Solemn League and Covenant . . . Subscribed by the Ministers of Christ within the Province of London, Decemb. 14 &c. 1647* (1648), p. 19 (dated January 18, 1648, by Thomason); by T. C. in *A Glasse for the Times* (1648), p. 6 (dated July 29, 1648, by Thomason); by the anonymous author of *A True and Perfect Picture of our Present Reformation* (1648), p. 16 (a statement taken almost verbatim from *Gangræna*); and by Joseph Hall in *Resolutions and Decisions of Divers Practicall Cases of Conscience in continuall Use amongst men* (1649), pp. 389-91 (dated April 9, 1649, by Thomason, and reprinted in 1650 and 1654). The one positive view of Milton as divorcer came from I. H. (Iohn Hackluyt?) in *The Metropolitan Nuncio*, No. 3, From Wednesday June 6 to Wednesday June 13, 1649 (i. e., June 11), last page.

The infamy attached to Milton the divorcer did not disappear in the next quarter of a century before his death. Allusions from the 1650s will be found in John Hacket's *Scrinia Reserta: a Memorial Offer'd to the Great Deservings of John Williams* (1693), Part II, pp. 161-62 (but written around 1652); in Sir John Birkenhead's (?) *Paul's Church-yard. Libri Theologici, Politici, Historici, Nundinis Paulinus (unà cum Templo) prostant venales* (ca. 1652), pp. A$_2$v-A$_3$ (there were further editions); in Henry Hammond's *A Letter of Resolution to six Quaeres, Of Present Use in the Church of England* (1653), p. 122 (however, dated November 1, 1652, by Thomason; it was reprinted once); in Alexander Ross's *Pansebeia: or, A View of All Religions in the World* (1653), pp. 400, 413 (dated June 7, 1653, by Thomason; there were several other editions in the century); and in James Howell's *Epistolæ Ho-Elianæ* (Ed. 3, 1655), vol. IV, no. 7, p. 19 (dated June 11, 1655, by Thomason; frequently reprinted).

Allusions from the 1660s include remarks in *A Free-Parliament-Letany* (1660), an uncertain reference (dated March 17, 1660, by Thomason); in George Starkey's (?) *Britain's Triumph, for her Imparallel's Deliverance* (1660), p. 15 (dated May 14, 1660); in Thomas Forde's letter to "Mr. T. P." in *Fœnestra in Pectore, or, Familiar Letters* (1660), pp. 103-6 (dated ca. October 15, 1660; reissued later); in letters from Hermann Conring to Joannes Christianus de Boineberg, dated October 14, 1662, from Boineberg to Conring, dated October 16, 1662, and from Boineberg to Conring, dated November 3, 1662 (see Iohann D. Gruber, *Commercii Epistolici Leibnitiani* [Hannover-Göttingen, 1745], pp. 951, 947-48, 963-64). In the seventies John Eachard commented on Milton the divorcer in *The Grounds & Occasions of the Contempt of the Clergy and Religion* (London, 1670), pp. A$_4$v-A$_5$ (there were numerous further editions), and Andrew Marvell's antagonist Richard Leigh (?), in *The Transproser Rehears'd* (London, 1673), pp. 135-37 (published before May 6). Marvell replied in *The Rehearsal Transpros'd, The Second Part* (London, 1673), p. 379 (published in early May).

The eighteenth century was aware of Milton's infamous reputation as an adherent of divorce. We might note a few interesting examples. Jonathan Swift voiced the usual cause for Milton's sallies into divorcing: "when Milton writ his book of divorces, it was presently rejected as an occasional treatise; because every body knew, he had a shrew for his wife" in *Remarks upon a Book In-*

tituled 'The Rights of the Christian Church, &c' (London, 1708).
A reviewer for *Acta Eruditorum. Anno MDCCX Publicata* (Lipsiæ:
Christiani Goezl, apud Joh. Grossii, Joh. Frid. Gleditsch et fil., et
Frid. Groschuf, 1710), remarked on Milton's views in his summary
of Andrew Adam's *Hochstettori Collegium Pufendorfianum,* p. 175.
In a letter to Samuel Richardson, dated July 28, 1752, Lady Brad-
shaigh wrote: "I never read Milton's Treatise upon Divorce, but
have heard it much condemned, as a thing calculated to serve his
own private ends."[33] And most noteworthy of all as to Milton's
reputation is the allusion in Lady Mary Walker's novel entitled
Munster Village (1778) when Mrs. Lee leaves her husband alleging
Milton's *Doctrine and Discipline of Divorce* as her rationale.

The *Doctrine and Discipline of Divorce* has not been so popular
or well read as during Milton's lifetime. Although Lieuwe van
Aitzema alluded to having had the tract translated into Dutch, no
such translation is known. See a letter to Milton, dated January 29,
1655 (BM Add. MS 5016*, f. 8). In a bookseller's catalogue found
in the anonymous English translation of William Chappell's *The
Preachery, or the Art and Method of Preaching* (London, 1656),
a title is listed as "The Works of Mr. John Milton, concearning
Divorce, digested into one Volume" published by Edward Farnham. No such edition is known. The tract was also advertised in
1658 by London, which fact suggests that the book had not sold
so well in 1645 and after as the two editions in that year would
suggest, unless London was marketing "new" but second-hand
books. A collection of the divorce tracts was published in 1820
"With a Preface Referring to Events of Deep and Powerful Interest
at the Present Crisis; Inscribed to the Earl of Liverpool. By a Civilian"
(London: Sherwood). The only other separate editions recorded are
a German translation by Franz von Holtzendorff in 1855
(Berlin)[34] and a Japanese translation by Tetsusaburo Nishiyama
in 1961 (Tokyo). The only annotated editions are by Lowell
Coolidge in the Yale *Prose*, giving a composite text of the first
and second editions, and by Arthur Axelrad in *The Prose of
John Milton* giving the text of the first edition.

Lester D. Moody and K. G. Hamilton have presented rhetorical
analyses of the work in, respectively, "John Milton's Pamphlets
on Divorce" (Ph.D. diss., University of Washington, 1956), and
"The Structure of Milton's Prose," in *Language and Style in
Milton*, ed. Ronald David Emma and John T. Shawcross (New
York: Frederick Ungar, 1967), pp. 304-32. Kester Svendsen
studied natural scientific imagery in the tract in "Science and
Structure in Milton's *Doctrine of Divorce*,"*PMLA*, 67 (1952),

435-45. A dissertation by Axelrad (1962)[35] and an investigation
of *Milton and the Idea of Matrimony: A Study of the Divorce
Tracts and Paradise Lost* (New Haven: Yale University Press, 1970)
by John Halkett examine the philosophic concepts and their background. We should also note two older statements concerning this
tract. C. B. Wheeler, finding Milton's work on divorce a major contribution to the removal of man from bondage, recounted the
argument of the tract approvingly and indicated the relationship
with *Tetrachordon*;[36] and Chilton Latham Powell, summarizing
the problem of the date of composition, concluded that Milton
did not need a personal experience to lead him to this important
subject.[37]

Registered to Thomas Underhill on June 4, 1644 (I, 117), *Of Education* was apparently received by Thomason on the next day. There
is no title page or printing legend; it is headed simply: *Of Education.
To Master Samuel Hartlib.* We do not know its printer, and it does
not show printing peculiarities. Not really favorable references to it
appear in correspondence of Hartlib and his friends (e. g., John
Dury to Hartlib, dated July 11, 1644; Sir Cheney Culpepper to
Hartlib, dated November 12, 1645; John Hall to Hartlib, dated December 21, [1646]; and Peter Smith to John Beale (?), dated
April 11, 1650). Hartlib, an advocate of educational reform and
friend to John Comenius, the Bohemian educator, requested, it is
supposed, Milton's views on education, perhaps because he was
aware of the private tutoring that Milton had been engaged in since
1639. According to A. W. Pollard, the tractate was advertised by
Humphrey Moseley in 1653, but where is not known.[38] A negative
allusion occurs in print in John Eachard's *The Grounds and Occasions* (1670), sigs. A_4v-A_5; there were many further editions.
    The second edition of the work is included in the second edition
of the minor poems: *Poems, &c. Upon Several Occasions. By Mr.
John Milton: Both English and Latin, &c. Composed at several times.
With a small Tractate of Education To Mr. Hartlib. London, Printed
for Tho. Dring at the White Lion next Chancery Lane End, in Fleet-
street. 1673.* This is issue 1: the second reads: "Printed for Tho.
Dring at the Blew Anchor next Mitre Court over against Fetter Lane
in Fleet-street. 1673." The printer was probably "W. R." (as attached to the Latin poems), but none of the various suggested identi-
fications is certain. It is listed in *A Catalogue of Books*, No. 15
(Term Catalogues, I, 151), licensed on November 24, 1673, and in
Robert Clavel's *General Catalogue of Books* (London, 1675), p. 102.
    During the succeeding centuries the tractate became one of the

most popular and well-discussed of Milton's works. In the eighteenth century it was readily available in editions of *Paradise Regain'd*, *Samson Agonistes,* and the minor poems. Separate editions in England were: in a translation of Tannequi Lefevre's *A Compendious Way of Teaching Ancient and Modern Languages* (London: J. Downing, 1723), pp. 99-116;[39] a previously unnoticed edition "To which are added, Four Papers, On the same Subject, From the Spectator" (Glasgow: R. Urie, 1746); *An Essay on Education* (London: Charles Corbett, 1751);[40] in R. Wynne, *Essays on Education by Milton, Locke, and the Authors of the Spectator, &c. To which are added observations on the Ancient and Modern Languages* (London: J. and R. Tonson, 1761), pp. 1-22; in [Francis Blackburne], *Remarks on Johnson's Life of Milton. To which are added, Milton's Tractate of Education and Areopagitica* (London, 1780), pp. 161-201. The following, rather typical, show varied awareness and use of the work. John Dennis alluded to and quoted from it in *Iphigenia. A Tragedy, Acted at the Theatre in Little Lincoln-Inn-Fields* (London: for Richard Parker, 1700), Preface, p. [vi], as did Charles Gildon in *The Complete Art of Poetry. In Six Parts* (London: for Charles Rivington, 1718), I, [xiv-xv]. Note also the possible influence on John Jebb's *Remarks Upon the Present Mode of Education in the University of Cambridge: To which is added, A Proposal for Its Improvement* (Cambridge, 1773), which employs a quotation from *Of Education* as epigraph, p. [iv]; there were four editions within two years. Sir John Hawkins quoted from the pamphlet twice in *A General History of the Science and Practice of Music* (London: for T. Payne and Son, 1776), I, ix-xi, and in "Orthopaedia: or, Thoughts on Publick Education," published in *Prose on Several Occasions; Accompanied with some Pieces in Verse* (London: for T. Cadel, 1787), George Colman quoted from and discussed it.

Translations include Pieter le Clercq's found in a Dutch translation of George Savile's *New Year's Gift* (no date),[41] and "Lettre de Milton où il propose une nouvelle manière d'élever la jeunesse d'Angleterre," in Claude de Nonney de Fontenai, *Lettres sur l'éducation des princes* (Edinbourg, 1746), trans. J. B. Le Blanc.[42] Daniel Morhof alluded to *Of Education* in 1682,[43] and it was important to Jean-Jacques Rousseau's *Emilius and Sophia: Or, A New System of Education* as an allusion in Book V shows (see, e.g., the London edition of 1763, IV, 161-62).

Significant editions during the nineteenth and twentieth centuries are the following:

1) *Milton's Treatise on Education. To Master Samuel Hartlib* (Boston: Directors of the Old South Work, [1800]).

2) *Milton's Plan of Education, in His Letter to Hartlib (Now Very Scarce), with the Plan of the Edinburgh Institution Founded Thereon* (Edinburgh: W. Laing, 1819), by William Scott; rptd., *Pamphleteer* (London), 17 (1820), [121]-56.

3) Henry Barnard, "Milton's Views on Education," *Barnard's American Journal of Education*, 2 (1856), 61-85, with complete tractate; rptd., 4 (1864), 159-90; and (text only), 22 (1871), 181 ff., and 23 (1872), 151 ff.

4) J. Zelle, "Remarks on and Translation of Milton's Treatise *Of Education*," in *Beilage zum Programm des Königl. und Stadt-Gymnasium zu Cöslin* (1858), English preface and German text.

5) Barnard's *English Pedagogy* (Philadelphia, 1862), pp. 145-88, with annotations; rptd., 1876.

6) "Über Erziehung," in *Neue Jahrbücher für Philologie und Pädagogik*, 2 (1890), 81-105, trans. Hermann Ullrich.

7) "John Milton's Essay *Of Education*. Englischer Text und deutsche Übersetzung mit Einleitung und erklärenden Erläuterungen," in *Beilage zum Programm der Löheren weiblichen Bildungs- anstalt zu Aschaffenburg* (1892), trans. Joseph Reber; rptd., 1893.

8) *John Milton's Treatise on Education. Edited with Preface by Paul Chauvet* (Paris, 1909).

9) *De educación, traducido por Natalia Corsio* (Madrid: Acabo, 1916).

10) *The Tractate of Education with Supplementary Extracts from Other Writings from Milton* (New Haven, 1928), ed. Oliver M. Ainsworth.

11) Yale *Prose*, II (1959), edited and annotated by Donald C. Dorian.

12) A translation into Japanese by Jun Harada was published in 1972.

Interesting discussions of the work are Vicesimus Knox's in "Remarks on the Tendency of Certain Clauses in a Bill now Pending in Parliament to Degrade Grammar Schools," *Pamphleteer* (London), 19 (1821), which gives a digest of the tract; reprinted in Knox's *Works* (London, 1824), Vol. 4; E. N. S. Thompson's "Milton's *Of Education*," *SP*, 15 (1918), 159-75; V. J. Petersen's "Milton—Akademiet. Et Bland af Paedagogiske Syners Historie," *Edda*, 37 (1937), 35-43; Herbert Kreter's "Bildungs- und Erziehungsideale bei Milton," *Studien zur englischen Philologie*, 93 (Halle: Niemeyer, 1938); and William R. Parker's "Education: Milton's Ideas and Ours," *College English*, 24 (1962), 1-14. Most discussions of the tractate either use it to argue reform or analyze its aims and rationale.

To counter adverse criticism of his views of divorce, Milton chose to present important passages, from the respected German divine Martin Bucer, which advanced like concepts. The pamphlet, with preface and postscript, translated or summarized Chapters 15-47 of Book II of *De Regno Christi ad Edwardo VI.* It was registered on July 15, 1644 (I, 122), and appeared on August 6, 1644, as: *The Ivdgement of Martin Bucer, Concerning Divorce. Writt'n to Edward the sixt, in his second Book of the Kingdom of Christ. And now Englisht. Wherin a late Book restoring the Doctrine and Discipline of Divorce is heer confirm'd and justify'd by the authoritie of Martin Bucer. To the Parlament of England.* It was printed by Matthew Simmons. Parker suggests that the two-page postscript was written shortly before publication. The work was condemned by Herbert Palmer on August 13 before both Houses of Parliament; soon afterward this opinion appeared in print in Palmer's *The Glasse of Gods Providence*, p. 57. But since then the pamphlet has attracted little comment or study. It was included in the 1820 collection of divorce tracts noted before, but otherwise there have been no further separate editions and only one annotated edition, that by Arnold Williams in the Yale *Prose.*

Areopagitica; a Speech of Mr. John Milton for the Liberty of Vnlicens'd Printing, To the Parlament of England. London, Printed in the Yeare, 1644 was published on November 23, 1644. (Thomason had dated his copy November 24, which has been frequently repeated.) The printer is unknown. The suggestion that it was Matthew Simmons seems to arise only from the fact that he had done *Doctrine and Discipline of Divorce* in 1643 and apparently again in 1644 and 1645, *Bucer* in 1644, and *Tetrachordon* and *Colasterion* in 1645. However, the printer of *Of Education* is also unknown and would not have been Simmons when Thomas Underhill registered it. The font used in *Areopagitica* is old and battered and not distinctive, and the ornaments, though commonplace, are entirely different from the kinds of ornaments, devices, etc., given in other tracts printed by Simmons for Milton. Is there a possibility that Milton returned to Augustine Mathewes for such a dangerous job as this tract presented? Mathewes apparently printed *Comus* in 1637 (i. e., 1638) after having lost his license because of the act of July 11, 1637,[44] and *Epitaphium Damonis* in 1640 (?) while still unlicensed.[45] The type and ornaments are like those used by Mathewes; the problem is that the type is so poor that broken types and the like do not allow for any certain identification. Because of his operating without license during this period he is not listed as printer of works of this period in the Wing catalogue. There is a significant manuscript correction on p. 12 in many copies, which was probably made in the print shop; "wayfaring" is changed to "warfaring."[46]

Allusions or references to the tract are very few; today we like to think that it was immediately significant and telling, because people must have recognized its worth, but evidence does not support this. In resigning his office as licenser Gilbert Mabbott in May 1649 seems to have used Milton's arguments but without citing any source. There seems to be an allusion in J[ohn] H[all]'s *An Humble Motion to the Parliament of England Concerning the Advancement of Learning and Reformation of the Universities* (London, 1649), pp. 28-29, with possible influence passim. Samuel Hartlib alluded to Milton's tract in his diary ("Ephemerides") for 1650,[47] as did Christopher Arnold in a letter dated August 7 (July 26), 1651;[48] and Richard Watson cited the tract specifically in *The Panegyrike and the Storme . . . by Ed. Waller . . . Answered* (London, 1659), sig. A4r. Later, first Richard Leigh (?) referred to the work in his criticism of Milton as friend of his opponent Andrew Marvell in *The Transproser Rehearsed* (London, 1673), p. 131, and then Samuel Parker did the same in *A Reproof to the Rehearsal Transprosed* (London, 1673), p. 191.

But like other tracts by Milton, *Areopagitica* became important in the hands of opponents of governmental controls during the last quarter of the century. First, Charles Blount adapted the tract in *A Just Vindication of Learning: Or, An Humble Address to the High Court of Parliament in Behalf of the Liberty of the Press. By Philopatris* (London, 1679); it is only eighteen pages long, and Milton is discussed in the proem.[49] This was reprinted in the *Harleian Miscellany* (London: for T. Osborne, 1744-46), vol. 6 (1745), pp. 71-79; (London: for Robert Dutton, 1808-11), vol. 8 (1810), pp. 290-300; and (London: for John White, John Murray, and John Hardy, 1808-13), vol. 6 (1810), pp. 77-86. There are notes in the latter by Thomas Park on p. 79 concerning Milton but without awareness of the relationship of this work with *Areopagitica*. Second, William Dunton also adapted it in *Jus Caesaris et Ecclesiæ vere dictæ. Or a Treatise of Independency, Presbytery, the Power of Kings, and of the Church* (London: John Kersey and Henry Faythorn, 1681), given as "An Apology for the Liberty of the Press," added pages 1-[12]. Third, Blount again drew on the work for idea and language in *Reasons Humbly Offered for the Liberty of Unlicens'd Printing* (London, 1693).[50]

The eighteenth century saw a new edition with a preface (anonymous) by the poet James Thomson in 1738; the tract and the preface were reprinted in Blackburne's *Remarks* (1780), pp. 203-369.[51]

There were editions in 1772 (London), in 1791, ed. James Losh (London), in 1792 (Blamire), and in 1793, ed. Robert Hall (London: Robinsons). Gabriel Honoré Riquetti, Count Mirabeau, translated it as *Sur la liberté de la presse, imité de l'Anglois, de Milton. Par le Comte de Mirabeau* (Londres [i.e., Paris], 1788); rptd., 1789 (twice), 1792 (called the second edition; Paris: Le Jay), and 1826 as *De la Liberté de la presse et de la censure, traduit de Milton* (Paris). There are not many direct and important references to *Areopagitica*, other than in biographical accounts and major discussions of Milton. Daniel Defoe was undoubtedly influenced in his *Vindication of the Press: or, an Essay on the Usefulness of Writing, on Criticism, and the Qualifications of Authors* (London: for T. Warner, 1718), which has an allusion on p. 12. Interestingly the "Plan of the Undertaking" for *The American Magazine or a Monthly View of the Political State of the British Colonies* (Philadelphia: Andrew Bradford, 1741), p. viii, employs Milton's translation from Euripides prefixed to *Areopagitica* as epitomizing its credo. Jonathan Mayhew drew from the work in "The Right and Duty of Puritan Judgment Asserted" (Sermon III) in *Seven Sermons upon the Following Subjects* (Boston: Rogers and Fowle, 1749), pp. 41-64.[52] In *A Modest Plea for the Property of Copy Right* (Bath: R. Cruttwell, for Edward and Charles Dilly, 1774), Catharine Macauley [Graham] discussed Milton's ideas on pp. vii, 18, and 22-26.

A most often reprinted work, separately, in selection, and with other Miltonic pieces, *Areopagitica* received the following noteworthy editions in the nineteenth and twentieth centuries:

1) *Areopagitica. With Prefatory Remarks, Copius Notes and Excursive Illustrations by T. Holt White. To which is Subjoined a Tract Sur la Liberté de la Presse, imité de l'Anglois de Milton par le Comte de Mirabeau* (London: R. Hunter, 1819).
2) *Areopagitica. Übersetzt von Dr. Richard Koeppell* (Berlin, 1851).
3) *Miltons Rede über Pressfreiheit* (Berlin, 1852).
4) *Milton's Prophecy of Essays and Reviews, and His Judgment on Prosecution of Them. Extracted from the "'Areopagitica' ..." By John Milton. To which is added An Extract from the Charge Delivered to his Clergy in 1861, by Walter Kerr, Bishop of Salisbury, on "Unity with the Bishop of Rome"* (London: Charles Westerton, 1861), pp. 5-46, with a few notes from White.
5) *Milton's Areopagitica: Edited with Introduction and Notes by J. W. Hales* (Oxford: Clarendon Press, 1866); rptd., 1874; revised, 1882; rptd., 1886, 1898, 1917, 1932, 1939.

6) *John Milton. Areopagitica, 24 November 1644. Preceded by Illustrative Documents. Carefully edited by Edward Arber* (London, 1868); rptd., 1869, 1895, 1903.
7) *Areopagitica . . . Ansgewählt und mit Anmerkungen versehen von R. Ritter* (1925).
8) *Areopagitica. The Noel Douglas Replicas* (London: Noel Douglas, 1927).
9) *John Milton. Areopagitica. Traduzione e prefacione di S. Breglia* (Bari: Laterza, 1933).
10) *John Milton. Om Trykkafrihed. Areopagitica* (Copenhagen: Berlìngske Forlag, 1936), trans. A. C. Krebs.
11) *John Milton. Areopagitica, traducción y prólogo de José Carner* (Mexico City: Fondo de cultura economica, 1941).
12) *Genron-to-Jijū* (Tokyo: Shingetsusha, 1948), trans. Kenji Ishida, Shungo Yoshida, and Seichi Ueno.
13) Yale *Prose*, II, ed. with introduction and annotations by Ernest Sirluck.
14) *John Milton. Areopagitica* (Calcutta: Jignasa, 1963), trans. into Bengali by Šašibhushan Dasgupta.
15) *John Milton. Areopagitica* (New Delhi: Sahitya Akademi, 1965), trans. into Hindi by Balakrishna Rao.
16) *Areopagitica*, ed. J. Max Patrick with introduction and notes, in *The Prose of John Milton.*
17) *For the Liberty of Unlicensed Printing, Areopagitica / Pour la Liberté de la presse sans autorisation ni censure, Areopagitica* (Paris: Aubier-Flammarion, 1969), ed. with an introduction by Olivier Lutaud, bilingual facing edition; revision of 1956 edition.
18) A translation into Japanese by Jun Harada was published in 1972.

While most discussions of *Areopagitica* have stressed the cry in the wilderness against censorship and the infractions on man's freedom of speech which it imposes, they have also misrepresented Milton's beliefs in certain ways. A good review of the place of the tract in the struggle against censorship is F. S. Siebert's "The Control of the Press During the Puritan Revolution," in *Freedom of the Press in England* (Urbana, 1952), pp. 165-236. We should remember, however, that Milton "licensed" *Mercurius Politicus* from No. 33 (January 23, 1651) through No. 85 (January 22, 1652), when he ran afoul of the government because, guided by his own philosophy, he had let a Socinian manifesto known as the Racovian Catechism be published. But though Milton objected to licensing (that is, pre-publication censorship), he did not believe in total lack of censoring or in

a lack of punishment for abusers of their freedoms. This is clear
from a careful reading of Milton's text, such as John Illo, in "The
Misreading of Milton," *Columbia University Forum*, vol. 8, no. 2
(1965), 38-42, and Willmore Kendall, in "How to Read Milton's
Areopagitica," *Journal of Politics*, 22 (1960), 439-73, have given it.

Reacting to criticism of his divorce views in *The Doctrine and Discipline of Divorce*, Milton decided to justify his position by recourse
to scripture and its interpretation. The passages explicated at length
are Genesis i.27-28; Deuteronomy xxiv.1-2; Matthew v.31-32; and
1 Corinthians vii.10-16. The work was printed on March 4, 1645
(Thomason's dating) as *Tetrachordon: Expositions upon The foure
chief places in Scripture, which treat of Mariage, or nullities in
Mariage . . . Wherin the Doctrine and Discipline of Divorce, as was
lately publish'd, is confirm'd by explanation of Scripture, by Testimony of ancient Fathers, of civill lawes in the Primitive Church, of
famousest Reformed Divines, And lastly, by an intended Act of the
Parlament and Church of England in the last yeare of Edward the
sixth. By the former Author J. M.* The two printers were Thomas
Paine and Matthew Simmons.[53] Sigs. G_1-G_2 were mispaged 37-40
rather than 41-44, and the error is continued through the end.
There are two states, press corrections, and two lines of errata.
Paine apparently set sigs. A, G-O, pp. [iii-viii], 37-98, and Simmons,
sigs. B-F, pp. 1-40.[54] The tract is mentioned by John Wilkins in
Ecclesiastes, 1647 (the second edition), p. 87, as well as in 1651
and 1656, p. 119 in both. This work supplies the source for the
comment of the anonymous author of *The Censure of the Rota*
(March 30, 1660) that Milton "achieved the honour to be styled
the founder of a sect." It was advertised in *A Catalogue of Books
Printed for John Starkey Bookseller, at the Mitre in Fleetstreet
near Temple Bar*, found in various volumes dated 1671-80. At
least part of the advertisement seems to have been made up around
May 1670, although the whole should not have been because
Paradise Regain'd is included in the listing. Still, curiously, *Regain'd* was licensed on July 2, 1670 and registered on September 10,
1670, and a catalogue advertising it was licensed on November 22,
1670. (Cf. French, V, 17, 29, 32-33.) *Tetrachordon* was included
in the 1820 collection of the divorce tracts. The only annotated
edition is in the Yale *Prose* by Arnold Williams. Two sonnets ("I
did but prompt" and "A book was writ") related Milton's reaction
to his public.

The catalyst for Milton's final divorce tract was the anonymous

An Answer to a Book, Intituled, The Doctrine and Discipline of Divorce, or, A Plea for Ladies and Gentlewomen, and all other Maried Women against Divorce (G[eorge] M[oule] for William Lee, 1644). It was registered on October 31, licensed on November 14, and apparently published on November 19 (Thomason's date). Milton's "scourge," *Colasterion,* was published on March 4, 1645, along with *Tetrachordon* (Thomason's dating, Masson and others erroneously taking his old style 1644 as the correct year), and Milton refers to this fact in his sonnet "I did but prompt" in the allusion to the birth of Apollo and Diana (Latona's twin-born progeny). The sonnet was originally titled "On the detraction wch follow'd upon my writing certain treatises," the plural indicating that both works were meant. *Colasterion* is thus equated with Diana, the moon, the lesser of the two lights provided to guide men, being but cold and reflected light shining in the darkness (as rebuttal against the ignorance of an antagonist who did not have the courage of identifying himself). The metaphor implies that the moon does not so much give light (knowledge) as it guides the misled traveller from his false and erring path should he have followed this *ignis fatuus.*

The work appeared as: *Colasterion: A Reply to a Nameles Answer Against the Doctrine and Discipline of Divorce. Wherein the trivial Author of that Answer is discover'd, the Licencer conferr'd with, and the Opinion which they traduce defended. By the former Author, J. M.* Its printer seems to have been Matthew Simmons, one of the two printers of *Tetrachordon,* who, because he had frequently worked on Milton's pamphlets, offered here a text which was generally close to Milton's orthographic practices.[55] The volume is mentioned by Wilkins as *"Vindication."* An abridgment is given in the 1820 collection of the divorce tracts. No further separate edition appeared; it was annotated in the Yale *Prose* by Lowell Coolidge.

One of Milton's most significant prose works appeared at the beginning of 1649, returning him to contemporary controversy after almost four years of "nonpublic" concerns and writing, and helping to bring him to the attention of the government then being formed. *The Tenure of Kings and Magistrates: Proving, that it is Lawfull, and hath been held so through all Ages, for any, who have the Power, to call to account a Tyrant, or wicked King, and after due conviction, to depose, and put him to death; if the ordinary Magistrate have neglected, or deny'd to doe it. And that they, who of late, so much blame Deposing, are the Men that did it themselves.*

The Author, J. M. has frequently been misrepresented both as to intent and content and as to its publication. The first edition was "Printed by *Matthew Simmons,* at the Gilded / Lyon in Aldersgate Street, 1649." It appeared by February 13, 1649, the date inscribed by Thomason; but its date of composition by internal evidence seems to be between January 15 and January 29.[56] The condemnation of the king was made on January 26-27 and signed on January 29; he was executed January 30. The reference to putting the king to death on the title page, of course, does not require that he have been executed prior to Milton's writing, and reference to this tract in *Defensio secunda* (pp. 92-93) has been, I believe, misinterpreted, primarily through faulty translation.[57] This edition exists in two slightly different states; its text runs forty-two pages.

Milton argues that the power of kings and magistrates has been conferred upon them by the people in covenant for common peace and benefit; when this power is abused, it is the people's right and duty to reassume that power or to alter it in whatever way is most conducive to public good. It is not specifically concerned with judging or sentencing Charles; Milton is not a "regicide" in the sense that the later seventeenth century and the eighteenth meant by that epithet. Rather he sets down a philosophic argument which leads to the conclusion that deposition and punishment of a tyrant is legal by delineating how kings came into being, their responsibilities toward the people, the nature of tyranny, and the duty of the people when tyranny exists. Of necessity he had to refute many of the arguments of pro-Royalist pamphlets (for example, *A Serious and Faithful Representation of the Judgements of Ministers of the Gospel within the Province of London,* presented to Commons on January 20, 1649, which protested *A Remonstrance of His Excellency Thomas Lord Fairfax, Lord Generall of the Parliaments Forces, and of the Generall Councell of Officers,* passed by Commons on November 20, 1648), and to try to remove the king from a sacrosanct position as the "Lord's Anointed," a David who had been divinely called to his office.

The first edition received some published reference, although Parker says it "attracted very little attention in print" (I, 373); for example, by John Goodwin in *The Obstructours of Justice,* May 30, 1649 (with numerous quotations); by John Canne or John Hall in *The Discoverer,* Part II, July 13, 1649; and by Clement Walker in *Anarchia Anglicana, Second Part,* August 20, 1649. Besides, John Canne's *The Golden Rule, or, Justice Advanced,* February 16, 1649, has often been cited as deriving ideas and argument from *The Tenure.* It did not receive a full-scale rebuttal, but this may be so because it is not really directed against Charles so much as it is a reasoned, lucid discussion of a philosophic problem, as we have already said. Indeed the references to the pamphlet throughout the century make clear that it was often read in this way, despite the charge against Milton of "regicide."

The second edition, a full resetting of the first edition, appears in three issues. The title page of issue one reads: "Printed by *Matthew Simmons,* at the Gilded Ly- / on in Aldersgate Street, 1649." Parker (II, 969) reports that the copy in the library of Emmanuel College, Cambridge, reads "at the Gilded / Lyon." If so, this may indicate another issue, or it may simply be a second state of the title page. (Probably, however, Parker's correspondent erred.) There are two states of text in issue one: the Alexander Turnbull Library copy has state one of the text; the University of Illinois copy 821 M64 / N9 / 1649^2 has both states of text. The title page of issue two reads: "Printed by *Matthew Simmons,* nextdoore to the Gil- / Lyon in Aldersgate Street, 1649." The title page of issue three reads: "Printed by *Matthew Simmons,* nextdoore to the Gil- / Lyon in Aldersgate Street, 1650." Issues two and three have the second state of the text. Thomason dated his copy of this third issue February 15, 1649; the date of the first two issues may thus be Old Style, or, it is more probable, the second edition actually was first published in 1649. Parker (II, 969) reports that Simmons changed the designation of the location of his printing house in October 1649. This suggests that issue one came out before October 1649 and that all previous datings of the second edition are in error; that the second issue came out after October 1649 and before February 15, 1650; and that the third issue came out around February 15, 1650. In any case the three issues and two states of text point to a demand for the pamphlet. If the first issue of edition two is actually before October 1649, then Parker's comment that the first edition "attracted very little attention in print" is certainly misleading as to the general awareness of readers.

The second edition seems to have used a copy of the first edition, corrected and supplemented, with accidentals altered both in the direction of what seem to be Milton's practices and in a contrary direction. This suggests (1) that the corrector used original copy to alter the first edition or that he was aware of Milton's practices (perhaps because trained by him as student and/or amanuensis) and (2) that the compositor altered the text from which he set in the process of composing. Neither text, if this is valid, can therefore be employed as complete and absolute guide to Milton's spelling and punctuation practices.

Parker writes (I, 337), "A second edition of *The Tenure of Kings* was needed—not as a result of any replies, but simply because of afterthoughts." This is a generally uncritical interpretation of a statement on the title page: "Published now the second time with some additions, and many Testimonies also added out of the best & learnedest among Protestant Divines asserting the position of this book." There were no full-length replies, but a few notices did appear, as we have seen. The second edition does seem to reflect such reactions, and thus to call its differences from the first "afterthoughts" is to misrepresent them. There are only slight additions (ten or so), some changes in wording, and the supplementary testimonies along with further scriptural argument (about thirteen and a half pages). The second edition is sixty pages in length. The additions and alterations clarify a thought or issue rather than present afterthoughts, and the testimonies are quite different from what would be so labelled. Hughes (p. 102) called the addition of these testimonies a "neglected promise of the first edition"; but this is a misreading of Milton's statement (pp. 7-8): "This I shall doe by autorities and reasons, not learnt in corners among Schismes and Herisies, as our doubling Divines are ready to calumniate, but fetch't out of the midst of choicest and most authentic learning, and no prohibited Authors, nor many Heathen, but Mosaical, Christian, Orthodoxal, and which must needs be more convincing to our Adversaries, Presbyterial." This Milton does throughout the first edition (note specifically pp. 21-28). The long final addition of edition two suggests that Milton was attempting to counter such adverse criticism of his views as Clement Walker's. It is not an afterthought, and it was not promised in edition one. Besides, the addition breaks the structure of the prolusion on which the tract is built. The reason for the second edition of *The Tenure* seems to be that the supply had run out; the alterations and slight additions seem to have been made in an attempt to clarify; and the testimonies seem to have been added to forestall such comments as Walker's that Milton would "be tied to no obligation to God or man." The first edition, incidentally, was used for the 1698 complete prose edition, although that of 1697 used the second edition.

A number of references to *The Tenure* appear after 1650 although it received no sustained reaction, either positive or negative. For example, an author whose initials were J. P. and who may have been John Price adapted a quotation from the tract in *Tyrants and Protectors. Set forth In their Colours* (London: for H. Cripps and L. Lloyd), p. 8. It is dated June 5, 1654. Sir Roger L'Estrange condemned *The Tenure* as treason in *Considerations and Proposals In order to the Regulations Of the Press,* p. 19; it is dated June 3, 1663.

The anonymous author of *A Treatise of the Execution of Justice, Wherein is clearly proved, that the Execution of Judgement and Justice, is as well the Peoples as the Magistrates Duty; And that if Magistrates pervert Judgement, the People are bound by the Law of God to execute Judgement without them, and upon them* probably used Milton's tract as the full title would indicate. This thirty-two page pamphlet was probably printed in London, perhaps by John Twyn, sometime during the 1660s (1663?). Later, Edward Pelling alluded to Milton's work in *A Sermon Preached on the Thirteenth of January 1678/9. Being the Anniversary of the Martyrdom of King Charles the First* (1679), p. 4, and in *The Good Old Way* (1680), pp. 114-15 (including a quotation).

In the midst of the succession controversy after the Bloodless Revolution of 1688, some one altered the first edition of Milton's tract to argue for William III's election to kingship: *Pro Populo Adversus Tyranno: Or the Sovereign Right and Power of the People Over Tyrants, Clearly Stated, and Plainly Proved. With Som Reflections on the Late Posture of Affairs. By a True Protestant Englishman, and Well-Wisher to Posterity* (1689).[58] The bookseller was Randal Taylor; Parker suggests that James Tyrrell may have been the editor. For some reason the book was entered in the Term Catalogues under the Easter Term, 1691 (see II, 361) as "The Sovereign Right and power of the People over Tyrants clearly stated. The Author, John Milton." The tract was again employed for a contemporary issue in 1784 in Dublin: *The Tenure of Kings and Magistrates . . . Originally Written by the Celebrated John Milton. Now Corrected, and re-published with Additional Notes and Observations; and Particularly Recommended, at this time, to the Perusal of the Men of Ireland.* The text is slightly abbreviated, though primarily through the omission of the testimonials and quotations. The notes are few, but directed to the contemporary Irish audience. Agitation for independence had been emboldened by the recent American and French revolutions, and thus Milton seems to have contributed in this way to political activity which led to the rebellion of 1798 under the leadership of the Society of United Irishmen.

There have been a number of annotated editions: William Talbot Allison's in 1911, Merritt Y. Hughes' in 1947 (*Prose Selections*), in 1957 (*Complete Poems and Major Prose*), and in 1962 (Yale *Prose*, III), and the present writer's in 1967 (*The Prose of John Milton*). It was also included, with the 1650 additions in quotation marks, in Francis Maseres' brief collection entitled only *The History of Britain* (London: R. Wilks, 1818). Jun Harada produced the first Japanese translation of the tract in 1972. The tract has been extensively discussed in studies like Arthur Barker's *Milton and the Puritan Dilemma* and Michael Fixler's *Milton and the Kingdoms of God.* The best single article on this pamphlet is Hughes' "Milton's Treatment of Reformation History in *The Tenure of Kings and Magistrates,*" in *The Seventeenth Century: Studies in the History of English Thought and Literature from Bacon to Pope,* ed. R. F. Jones (Stanford, 1951), pp. 247-63. The style of the tract has been described by Wilbur Gilman in *Milton's Rhetoric: Studies in His Defense of Liberty,* University of Missouri Studies, No. 14 (1939), and by Hughes in the Yale *Prose,* III, 120-46.

Milton's first official tract was a discussion of the agreements between Charles I and his agent James Butler, Earl of Ormond, and the Irish who had been wooed to fight for the Royalists against the Parliamentarians. The government decided to publish these agreements (made on January 17, 1649) to help turn the people from their idolatrous attitude toward the king as martyr, by giving evidence of his duplicity. At the same time, the government moved to block a coalition of the Irish against English rule (declared on February 15), a coalition which could now serve as a Royalist springboard against the Commonwealth. Accordingly, Milton was ordered by the Council of State on March 28, 1649 "to make some observations vpon the Complicaõn of interest wch is now amongst the severall designers against the peace of the Coõnonwealth." The work was published on May 16, 1649, with Milton's "Observations" appended: *Articles of Peace, Made and Concluded with the Irish Rebels, and Papists, by James Earle of Ormond, For and in behalfe of the late King, and by vertue of his Autoritie. Also a Letter sent by Ormond to Col. Jones, Governour of Dublin. With his Answer thereunto. And A Representation of the Scotch Presbytery at Belfast in Ireland. Upon all which are added Observations.* The printer was Matthew Simmons, now official printer to the Council of State. Milton's remarks were given a special heading, "Observations Upon the Articles of Peace with the Irish Rebels, on the Letter of Ormond to Col. Jones, and the Representation of the Presbytery at Belfast," and printed on pp. 45-65. Authorship is not indicated, and it was assigned to Milton in the early lives only by Edward Phillips (1694). It was published in the 1697 and 1698 collections of his prose. The tract has not been printed separately again, and the only annotated edition is Merritt Y. Hughes' in the Yale *Prose,* III. It has attracted little comment, except for Hughes' major discussion, "The Historical Setting of Milton's *Observations on the Articles of Peace,*" *PMLA,* 64 (1949), 1049-73.

In terms both of egregious errors and of Milton's spelling, the tract is poorly printed, despite the fact that it was turned out by Simmons, who had done work for Milton in the past. The results suggest that an apprentice may have been assigned the work—for Simmons was surely extremely busy in his new capacity—and this has some corroboration in the fact that Milton's next work, *Eikonoklastes*, also came from Simmons' shop (as did the second edition of *Tenure*), but that its second edition was produced by Thomas Newcomb. The foregoing remarks on the text imply that some of the texts of Milton's prose furnish much better evidence of his spelling, punctuation, etc., practices than others, and that some provide misleading evidence.

Eikon Basilike, purportedly Charles I's meditations in prison during his trial and while awaiting sentence, was published soon after his execution, January 30, 1649, and by February 9, George Thomason's date of purchase. Charles was buried on February 8 and the publication may have been made to coincide. It was written largely by John Gauden, the king's chaplain, but the matter of authorship was a major controversy during the century.[59] Milton became secretary to the Council of State for foreign tongues around March 15. At some time thereafter he was ordered to answer the king's book. "I take it on me as a work assign'd," he wrote in *Eikonoklastes,* pp. [vi–vii], "rather, then by one chos'n or affected." Perhaps he was working on it by June 11 when *The Metropolitan Nuncio,* No. 3, reported that an answer was being prepared; the allusion may be to Milton as author of *The Doctrine and Discipline of Divorce,* but it could also be to John Selden as author of *Uxor Ebraica* (1646). Selden had apparently been asked to answer the king's book and refused. There is also the slightest outside possibility that Andrew Marvell contributed to the writing of the tract (or the *Defensio prima*); Anne Sadleir, aunt of Cyriack Skinner, Milton's pupil, friend, amanuensis, and biographer, and through whom Milton seems to have met Marvell, suggests this in a letter to Roger Williams, dated 1653. The Cokes, Skinner's mother's family, were friends of the Marvells. Other works both in favor of and opposed to the king also appeared: *The Princely Pellican. Royal Resolves presented in sundry choice Observations, extracted from His Majesties Divine Meditations,* defending Charles' authorship, was published around July 2, 1649,[60] and an anonymous refutation entitled *Eikon Alethine, The Pourtraicture of Truths most sacred Majesty* appeared by August 16, 1649. This latter volume, a chapter-by-chapter refutation, contains a dedicatory epistle to the Council of State. It is nonetheless not a forceful answer; it does question Charles' authorship. *The Constant Man's Character* (1650) also considered *Eikon Basilike* a fraud, pp. 53-62.

Milton's tract seems to have been published on October 6, the date given by Thomason, but this may be an error because *A Briefe Relation of Some Affairs*, No. 9 (November 13-20, 1649), p. 96, published by Matthew Simmons as was *Eikonoklastes*, notes that the tract was "published the last weeke." There are two states. The text of this edition was that reprinted after 1650 and until 1756. The accidentals of the first edition seem not to be very accurate, for a second edition, slightly augmented, has numerous changes, some in the direction of what seem to be Milton's own spelling and punctuation practices, some altering what seem to be his practices. The second edition of 1650 was printed by Thomas Newcomb and sold by Thomas Brewster and George Moule. There are two different title pages, and press variants occur. Its date lies after June 19, 1650, since news of the murder of Cromwell's envoy, Anthony Ascham, in Madrid, alluded to on p. 208, reached London on that date.

The book and Milton were both praised and attacked on the basis of prejudice for or against the king, for or against the Cromwellian government, or (on the continent) for or against Catholicism or Protestantism. Contemporary allusions are fairly numerous and need not be enumerated. The tract's organization is similar to that of *Eikon Alethine*; it was so successful in its way that Milton's reputation during the seventeenth and eighteenth centuries suffered, even alongside the praise directed toward *Paradise Lost*, because it and the *Defensio prima* classified Milton as a regicide in the popular mind. The aim of the volume, of course, was to counter the sympathy for Charles which *Eikon Basilike*, his "martyrdom," and his equation with Christ evoked even among the non-Royalists. To do this, Milton had to write as if Charles were the author and to discredit his honesty and sincerity in *Eikon Basilike*. It had damaging effects, but nothing could quite overcome the sentimentality of the king's book or the infallibility of a king in the people's eyes. As the monarchy returned, all things and people connected with the antimonarchists were held in disrepute; Milton, because of his poetry, eventually faired much better than most.

One of the earliest proclamations of Charles II, dated August 13, 1660, suppressed *Eikonoklastes* and the *Defensio prima*. Notice of the burning of these books appeared in *Mercurius Publicus*, No. 37 (September 6-13, 1660, p. 578), and *The Parliamentary Intelligencer*, No. 37 (September 3-10, p. 589). Almost a quarter of a century later both volumes were again suppressed at Oxford; see *The Judgment and Decree of the University of Oxford Past in Their Convocation*

July 21. 1683. Against Certain Pernicious Books and Damnable Doctrines Destructive to the Sacred Persons of Princes, Their State and Government, and of All Humane Society ([Oxford], 1683).

The first edition was the source for an anonymous transcription of extracts in British Museum, Stowe MS 305, ff. 89b-137b. It was reprinted in 1690 in London (although the title page reads Amsterdam), with a twelve-page preface discussing the controversy over the authorship of *Eikon Basilike*. Like *The Tenure* it was reprinted to advance argument in the succession settlement. Its position against the royal tyranny that Charles I represented justified the succession of William III as co-monarch with Mary. The second edition was the source for a French translation by John Dury, published in London in 1652 (by November); there are two states, and its text has slight differences from the original. It was advertised in [François Raguenet's] *Histoire d'Olivier Cromwel* (Paris: Claude Barbin, 1691), p. *6^V, in the midst of a controversy over *Eikon Basilike*; Morisot's *Carolus I* (see later) was also advertised on the same page.[61] Apparently Lewis Du Moulin, younger brother of Milton's future antagonist, Peter Du Moulin, produced a Latin translation of Chapter One; perhaps it was printed but no edition or even manuscript has been found.[62] *Eikonoklastes* was among the books advertised for sale by William London in 1658. In 1756 Richard Baron reprinted the second edition; a preface discusses "The Transcendent Excellency of Milton's Prose Works"; a second edition of this volume appeared in 1770. In addition an extract from the Preface was published as *The Immortal Milton's Opinion of the Bishops* [London ?, 1820 ?]. The only annotated edition is Merritt Y. Hughes' in the Yale *Prose*, III, with an extensive introduction and stylistic analysis.

A major printed reaction to *Eikonoklastes* was Joseph Jane's *Eikon Aklastos. The Image Unbroaken. A Perspective of the Impudence, Falshood, Vanitie, and Prophannes, Published in a Libell Entitled Eikonoklastes against Eikon Basilike or the Pourtraicture of His Sacred Majestie in His Solitudes and Sufferings* ([London], 1651), reissued in 1660 as *Salmasius His Dissection* to help bolster sales. It seems to have been written before December 4, 1650, the date of a letter from Jane's brother-in-law Sir Edward Nicholas to Lord Hatton.[63] Another argument against *Eikonoklastes* was Claude Barthelemy Morisot's Latin defense of Charles, entitled *Carolus I., Britanniarum Rex. A Securi et Calamo Miltonii Vindicatus*; it was published in Dublin in 1652. Simon Patrick adopted some sentences from pp. 206-7 of the second edition of *Eikonoklastes* in his *A Continuation of a Friendly Debate* (1669), pp. 127-29. (See Kathleen A. Coleridge's discussion in *The Turnbull Library Record* [May 1972], pp. 28-31.)

The two major controversies which *Eikon Basilike* and *Eikono-klastes* raised, however, were the question of authorship in the former and the problem Milton pointed out concerning Pamela's prayer from Sidney's *Arcadia*, which had been printed as one of Charles' meditations. The two controversies are generally inter-twined. In argument with *Eikon Alethine* over the authorship was the anonymous *Eikon Episte. Or, The Faithfull Pourtraicture of a Loyall Subject, in Vindication of Eikon Basilike. In Answer to an Insolent Book, Intituled Eikon Alethine* (September 11, 1649). Other tracts between 1650 and 1690 also defended Charles and assume his authorship.[64] But the main phase of the argument arose with the reprinting of Milton's tract in 1690. Some copies contained an advertisement of a memorandum penned by Arthur Annesley, Earl of Anglesey (found by Edward Millington when he auctioned off Annesley's books in 1686), stating that Gauden had written the king's book (see French, II, 22-26, and V. 409).[65] Immediately fol-lowed Richard Hollingworth's *A Second Defense of Charles I* (London, 1690) and *Vindiciæ Carolinæ: or, A Defence of Eikon Basilike, the Portraicture of His Sacred Majesty in His Solitudes and Sufferings. In Reply to a Book Intituled Eikonoklastes, Written By Mr. Milton, and Lately Re-Printed at Amsterdam* (London, 1692), which de-fended Charles and his authorship and helped set in motion a re-examination of both books. The latter vindication has been assigned to both Hollingworth and John Wilson. Anglesey's memorandum was reprinted in *Restitution to the Royal Author or a Vindication of King Charles the Martyr's most Excellent Book; Intituled Eikon Basilike From the False, Scandalous, and Malicious Reflections lately Published against it. Licensed, May 10. 1691: Z. Isham* (London, for Samuel Keble, 1691), p. 3. This volume also discussed the prayer on pp. 7-8. Anthony Walker's *A True Account of the Author of a Book entituled Eikon Basilike* (London, 1692), identified Gauden as author of *Eikon Basilike* and Dr. Brian Duppa, Bishop of Salisbury and later of Winchester, as a contributor; and Thomas Long's *Dr. Walker's True, Modest, and Faithful Account of the Author of Eikon Basilike* (London, 1693) attempted to rebut this. Edmund Lud-low (pseudonym) employed *Eikonoklastes* in *A Letter from General Ludlow to Dr. Hollingworth, Their Majesties Chaplain at St. Botolph-Aldgate* (Amsterdam, 1692), pp. 31-49, to praise Milton and to off-set Hollingworth's defences; and Joseph Wilson (pseudonym?)[66] in *Ludow no Lyar* (Amsterdam, 1692), argued against Hollingworth's *Second Defense,* iterated Walker's contentions, and employed *Eikono-dlastes* in doing so, especially in the prefatory letter. This latter volume brought reaction from Hollingworth in *The Character of*

*King Charles I. From the Declaration of Mr. Alexander Henderson
... To which is Annex'd Some Short Remarks upon a Vile Book,
call'd Ludlow no Lyar: With a Defence of the King from the Irish
Rebellion* (London: R. Taylor, 1692). (It was licensed on July 28,
1692.) He further debated Walker and the attribution to Gauden
in the Epistle Dedicatory to *The Death of King Charles I. Proved
a Down-right Murder, With the Aggravations of it. In a Sermon at
St. Botolph Aldgate, London, January 30. 1692/3* (London: R.
Norton for Walter Kettilby, 1693).

A further phase occurred with the publication in *A Letter from
Major General Ludlow to Sir E*[dward] *S*[eymour] (Amsterdam,
1691) of a "Postscript," pp. 29-30, giving Charles' alleged prayer
and Pamela's prayer in parallel columns. Thomas Wagstaffe contended in *Vindication of King Charles the Martyr* (London, 1693)
that Milton had forged Pamela's prayer into the king's book, while
he (Wagstaffe) otherwise defended Charles' authorship. This book
was reprinted in 1697 with further evidence for the charge derived
from the former Parliamentarian printer Henry Hills (pp. 50-51),
and again in 1711 (with some ancillary material). "Ludlow" commented on Pamela's prayer in *Truth Brought To Light: Or the
Gross Forgeries of Dr. Hollingworth* (London, 1693), p. 34, and
published the substance of Gauden's letter to Clarendon, p. 37.
John Toland's *Life,* published in *A Complete Collection* (1698),
I, 5-47, reprinted separately in the next year, aroused antagonism
associated with this question, such as Offspring Blackall's *Remarks
on the Life of Mr. Milton, As Publish'd by J. T. With a Character
of the Author and His Party* (London, 1699).[67] Toland's answer,
Amyntor: or, A Defence of Milton's Life (London, 1699), was
particularly concerned with the controversy as his subtitle shows:
*Containing ... A Complete History of the Book, Entitul'd Icon
Basilike, Proving Dr. Gauden, and not King Charles the First, to be
the Author of it: With an Answer to All the Facts Alleg'd by
Mr. Wagstaf to the Contrary.* Toland referred to Gauden's letters
(there were six related ones in all) and Hyde's replies in both his
Life and *Amyntor.* In answer Blackall published *Mr. Blackall's
Reasons for Not Replying to a Book Lately Published, Entituled,
Amyntor* (London, 1699), and Wagstaffe, *A Defence of the Vindi-
cation of King Charles the Martyr ... In Answer to a Late Pamphlet, Intituled, Amyntor* (London, 1699). Toland defended him-
self in his preface to his edition of *The Oceana of James Harring-
ton* (London, 1700), frequently reprinted, and in *Vindicius
Liberius: Or, M. Toland's Defence of Himself, Against the Late
Lower House of Convocation* (London, 1702), pp. 19-22.

Biographical dictionaries in succeeding years recite this phase of argument under various entries (e. g., Wagstaffe). The controversy was frequently reprised during the eighteenth century, for example by Thomas Birch in the first edition of the prose works in 1738, but in Richard Baron's revision of this edition in 1753 Milton's "forgery" is rejected. Or see John Burton's discussions and quotation from Wagstaffe in *The Genuineness of Ld Clarendon's History of the Rebellion Printed at Oxford Vindicated* (Oxford, 1744), pp. 114-19, 149-73, which attempted to reaffirm Charles' authorship. William Lauder, trying to recoup his damaged reputation as forger, revived the matter in *King Charles I. Vindicated from the Charge of Plagiarism Brought Against Him by Milton, and Milton Himself Convicted of Forgery, and a Gross Imposition on the Publick* (London, 1754). William Harris' *An Historical and Critical Account of the Life and Writings of Charles I. King of Great Britain* (London: for W. Strahan et al., 1772) quotes and discusses many of the foregoing items. See quotations from *Eikonoklastes* on pp. 43-44, 97-98, 102-4 (on Pamela's prayer), 115-16 (on the authorship of *Eikon Basilike*), 121, 315-17, 328-29, 337, 345-46, 348, 359-60, 397, and 420-21; from Wagstaffe's *Vindication* and Toland's *Amyntor* on pp. 104-6; from Perrinchief's *The Royal Martyr*, pp. 106-8 and 110-11 (both on the authorship); and from *Truth Brought to Light*, pp. 110-11 (on the authorship).[68] And there is Samuel Johnson's credulous reference to the forgery in his attempt to downgrade Milton's reputation (*Life*, I, 157-58, ed. 1781). In 1824 Christopher Wordsworth reconsidered the question in *"Who Wrote Eikon Basilike?" Considered and Answered. In Two Letters, Addressed To His Grace the Archbishop of Canterbury*, arguing for Charles as author. This was followed by *Documentary Supplement to "Who Wrote Eikon Basilike?"* in 1825, after disagreement from Henry John Todd in *A Letter To His Grace the Archbishop of Canterbury Concerning the Authorship of Eikon Basilike* (1825). Further opposition came from William Grant Broughton in *A Letter to a Friend touching the Question, "Who was the Author of Eikon Basilike?"* (1826) and Sir James Mackintosh in the *Edinburgh Review*, No. 87. Others who discounted Charles as author were Lingard in *History of England*, vol. VI; William Godwin in *The History of the Commonwealth*; and Henry Hallam in *The Constitutional History of England*. Against all of these Wordsworth wrote *King Charles the First, the Author of the Icon Basilike further proved* in 1828, which in turn brought reactions from Todd (*Bishop Gauden the Author of Icon Basilike* [1829]) and Broughton (*Additional Reasons In Confirmation of the Opinion that Dr. Gauden, and Not*

King Charles the First was the author of Eikon Basilike [1829]).
The controversy emerged once in a while further in the nineteenth century and was revived in the twentieth century by antagonists to Milton in their attempt to discredit him: S. B. Liljegren, Paul Phelps-Morand, and William Empson. Most telling in all this, however, are the ignorance and scholarly amateurishness as well as vindicative hostility which people like Johnson and Empson manifest in themselves in their dishonest approach to Milton. Let them dislike him as person and author, and express that dislike, but not through such reprehensible means. Their ignorance of contrary materials easily at hand indicates their incompetency as scholars. The charges have been refuted frequently in this century, by John S. Smart, R. W. Chambers, F. F. Madan, Merritt Y. Hughes, and various correspondents in argument with Empson. One hopes the refutation is final.

In actual fact the manuscript of *Eikon Basilike* was ready around December 24, 1648, and contained none of the king's alleged prayers; on February 23, 1649, John Playford was licensed to print the prayers; and around March 15 William Dugard brought out an edition with the prayers included within the text, based on another, slightly amplified manuscript delivered by Edward Simmons, a former servant of the king. (In other words Pamela's prayer did not appear in the earliest editions of the king's book.) Dugard was arrested on March 16 and released because of the license for the prayers; but James Cranford who had licensed them was removed from office, and Matthew Simmons entered *Eikon Basilike* as a blocking tactic. In 1694 Thomas Gill and Francis Bernard, physicians to Charles, reported a story told by the printer Henry Hill, referred to before, which became the basis for Wagstaffe's 1697 accusation. A letter from Gill, dated May 1, 1694, and a testimonial statement from Bernard, dated May 10, 1694, were printed by Wagstaffe.

Eikonklastes, aside from its relationship with other works favoring or disfavoring the king and aside from the questions of authorship and the alleged forgery in *Eikon Basilike*, has elicited articles only on its sources. Some of the former discussions incidentally examine the work for its literary and philosophic value, but Hughes' excellent analysis of Milton's style and method of presentation in *Eikonoklastes* (see Yale *Prose*, III, 126-46, 161-67) is the only adequate discussion of these important subjects.

A work of which Milton was justifiedly proud was next published, after about a year of work and eventually at the expense of his eyesight. *Joannis MiltonI Angli Pro Populo Anglicano Defensio contra Claudii Anonymi, aliàs Salmasii, Defensionem Regiam. Londini, Typis*

Du-Gardianis. Anno Domini 1651 was ordered by the Council of State on January 8, 1650, as an answer to *Defensio Regia pro Carolo I ad Serenissimum Magnæ Britanniæ regem Carolum II. Filium natu majorem, Heredem & Successorem legitimum. Sumptibus Regiis.* Anno MDCXLIX, by Claude de Saumaise (Salmasius). It had appeared in England by May 11, 1649. The official order for printing Milton's work came on December 23, 1650; it was registered on December 31 (I, 357), and came out on February 24, 1650.[69] There were ten or eleven editions in 1651 (one issue of which was dated 1650), which are described by F. F. Madan,[70] with three variant issues recorded for the first and two for the fourth. But there are numerous variations among different copies of the same edition or issue;[71] whether these are only states of text or constitute reissues has not been determined, for no complete analysis has as yet been undertaken. Some editions also print an index. At least three of the editions were in England ("authorized"), and at least six in the United Provinces. The editions come from various presses (e. g., Elzevir's, Jansson's) in various places (e. g., Gouda, Utrecht, Antwerp). Madan No. 2, a folio printed by Dugard, advertises itself as "Editio emendatior." The Durham University copy of this edition does not have a variant title page, as Parker reports. Among these eleven (Madan No. 11) is a Dutch translation: *Joannis Miltons Engelmans Verdedignigh, des gemeene Volcks van Engelandt, tegens Claudius sonder Naem, alias Salmasius Konincklijcke Verdedigingh. Wt het Latijn overgeset, Na de Copy gedruckt tot Londen, by Du Gardianis* [Gouda: G. de Hoere,] *1651.* Salmasius' and Milton's defenses were also reissued ca. June-May 1651 in one volume in Paris: *Claudii Salmasii Defensio Regia, Pro Carolo I. Rege Angliæ &c. et Joannis Miltoni Defensio, Pro Populo Anglicano, Contrà Clavdii Anonymi, aliàs Salmasii Defensionem Regiam. Accesserunt huic editioni Indices locupletissimi. Parisiis, Apud viduam Mathvrini dv Pvis, Viâ Iacobæa, sub signo Coronæ. M.DC.LI. Cvm Permissione.* Milton's work is a reissue of Madan No. 3 and there is a preface to the volume, pp. [iii–xvi]. Some copies read 1650. *Defensio prima* had two further editions in the next year, both in the Lowlands. In October 1658 an altered edition with an important personal postscript appeared, "Editio correctior et auctior, ab autore denuo recognita," from the press of Thomas Newcomb. The work was finally translated into English by Joseph Washington in 1692 as *A Defence of the People of England, by John Milton . . . In Answer to Salmasius's Defence of the King* [London?], with a preface by the translator; it may have been published by Nathaniel Rolls. It was reissued in 1695; there are two different title pages, one of which lists Rolls. *A Complete Collection* (1698) and Birch's edition (1738, 1753) reprinted both the Latin and Washington's translation. There is a poem by Nahum Tate called "In Memory of Joseph Washington," which alludes to this translation, in *State Poems; Continued from the Time of O. Cromwel, To this Present Year 1697* ([London], 1697), p. 225; the collection was variously reprinted. Milton's tract was placed on the Spanish provincial Index of Prohibited Books although this has not previously been observed; see *Novissimus Librorum Prohibitorum et Expurgandorum Index pro Catholicis Hispaniarum Regnis, Philippi V. Reg. Cath.* ([n.p.], 1707), I, 660, and *Index Librorum Prohibitorum, ac Expurgandorum Novissimus. Pro Universis Hispaniarum Regnis Serenissimi Ferdinandi VI. Regis Catholici, hac Ultima Editione* (Matriti: Emmanuelis Fernandez, 1747), II, 686.

Auguste Geffroy (*Étude sur les pamphlets politiques et religieux de Milton*, p. 253) said that the original manuscript was owned by Sir Francis Egerton, probably through some kind of misunderstanding. There are copies in the Bodleian, Rawlinson MS Misc. 230, pp. 1024, with an index on ff. 124-29, and in the Royal Library, Copenhagen, Old Royal, 8vo, 3579. The tract was advertised in such items as London's catalogue (1658); *Mercurius Politicus*, 18-25 November 1658, No. 443, p. 29 (the 1658 edition); Elzevir's catalogue (1674), p. 121; *Catalogus Librorum ex Variis Europæ Partibus Advectorum. Per Robertvm Scott Bibliopolam Londinensem. Londini, Venales Prostant, apud dictum Robertum Scott, 1674*, p. 129; and *Catalogus Librorum Bibliothecæ Juris utriusque, tam Civilis quam Canonici, Publici quam Privati, Feudalis quam variorum Regnorum* (Edinburgh: Georgii Morman, 1692), with a preface by George Mackenzie, p. 140.

Reactions were immediate, numerous, and harsh. There are many references, generally negative, in letters and in print through the next quarter of a century. In France the work was condemned and burned in Toulouse under an order dated June 7 (17), 1651, and in Paris under orders dated June 26 (July 6) and July 1 (11). There was also a proclamation at Ratisbon, Germany, in December 1653 that *all* books by Milton were to be searched out. A weak, anonymous answer came forth as *Pro Rege et Populo Anglicano Apologia contra Johannis Polypragmatici, (Alias Miltoni Angli) Defensionem Destructivam Regis & Populi Anglicani. Antverpiæ, Apud Hieronymam Verdussen, M. DC. LI*; it was written by John Rowland though at first it was thought to be by Bishop John Bramhall. Another edition was called for in 1651; another (often cited as the second) in 1652; and still another (often cited as the third) again in 1652.[72] A Dutch translation by the same printer was available in 1651 as well: *Verdediging voor den Konnig, Ende het Volck van Engeland, Tegens*

Johannes Moey-al (alias Milton). Other reactions were Claude Morisot's *Carolus I* (Dublin, 1652), already mentioned under *Eikonoklastes*, and Sir Robert Filmer's *Observations Concerning the Originall of Government, Upon Mr. Hobs Leviathan. Mr Milton against Salmasius. H. Grotius De jure belli. Mr. Huntons Treatise of Monarchy* (London: for R. Royston, 1652), pp. 12-22. This latter item is dated February 18; it was reprinted in Filmer's *Reflections Concerning the Original of Government* (London, 1679), pp. 17-32, and *The Free-Holders Ground Inquest, Touching Our Sovereign Lord the King and His Parliament. To which are added Observations Upon Forms of Government* (London, 1679), reissue of 1652,[73] and in Parker's *Milton's Contemporary Reputation*. An allusion occurs also in John Lilburne's *As You Were or The Lord General Cromwel and the Grand Officers of the Armie Their Remembrancer . . . May 1652* (London, 1652), pp. 15-16.[74] And a work that has not been cited before is Peter Negesch's *Comparatio Inter Clavdivm Tiberivm Principem, et Olivarivm Cromwellivm Protectorem. Instituta à Petro Negeschio. Excusa Typis Anno M.DC.LVII*; it has a number of snide references to Milton.[75]

Surely a "first," however, is the contemporary treatment of Milton and the *Defensio prima* in German academic dissertations in 1652-57. Milton is not specifically cited by Caspar Ziegler in *Circa Regicidivm Anglorum Exercitationes, Literis Lanckisianis. Ex Scribebat Christoph. Cellarius, Anno 1651*; this was apparently delivered in 1651 and discussed before an academic audience in September 1652. But it was reprinted with a dissertation by James Schaller under the title: *Caspari Ziegler Lipsiensis Circa Regicidivm Anglorum Exercitationes. Accedit Jacobii Schalleri Dissertatio ad Loca Quædam Miltoni. Lugd. Batavorum* [Leyden], *Apud Johannes à Sambix, MDCLIII*. Erhard Kieffer defended Schaller's thesis on November 13, 1652 (although it was supposed to have been delivered at the end of September), and this was published as *Dissertationis ad Quædam Loca Miltoni Pars Prior; Quam Annuente Deo, Præside, Dn. Iacobo Schallero, S. S. Theolog. Doct. et Philosoph. Pract. Professore. Solenniter Defendere Conabitur die mensis Septembris Erhardus Kieffer. Argentorati* [Strassbourg], *Apud Friderici Spoor MDCLII*. Another defense of Schaller's thesis was given on September 17, 1657, by Christopher Güntzer and was soon published: *Dissertationis ad Quædam Loca Miltoni Pars Posterior, Quam Adspirante Deo Præside Dn. Iacobo Schallero, SS. Theol. Doct. & Philos. Pract. Prof. Ord. h. t. Facult. Phil. Decano. Solenniter Defendet die 17 Mens. September. Christophorus Güntzer, Argentorat. Argentorati, Apud Friderici Spoor, MDCLVII*. Soon afterward Spoor reprinted the work of all three in one volume: *Dissertationis ad*

Quædam Loca Miltoni Pars Prior et Posterior, Quas Adspirante Deo Præside Dn. Iacobo Schallero, SS. Theol. Doct. & Philos. Pract. Prof. Ord. h. t. Facult. Phil. Decano. Solenniter Defenderunt Erhardus Kieffer et Christophorus Güntzer. (The preceding is given in some detail because of the confusion in French's and in Parker's accounts.) In each of these dissertations, the regicides and Milton's defense of the actions of the Parliamentarians are condemned, generally on pseudo-religious and traditional monarchic grounds.

Much more significant than Rowland's work was the rebuttal by Pierre (Peter) Du Moulin: *Regii Sanguinis Clamor Ad Cœlum Adversus Parricidas Anglicanos. Hagæ-Comitvm, Ex Typographia Adriani Vlac* [q]. *M.DC.LII.* The author was thought to be Alexander More, who did contribute the epistle to the king and who delivered the manuscript to Vlacq. However, it was Vlacq who signed the epistle, and Salmasius who had relayed the manuscript from Du Moulin to More. Various letters and a note in *Mercurius Politicus,* September 20 (30), 1652, misinformed Milton that More was the author. The work probably appeared in August, at least before September 17 (27). There seem to have been three editions in 1652, except that Thomason dated his copy of the third March 22, 1653.[76] The "second edition" (so advertised on the title page) was printed by Vlacq ("Ulac") (?) in 1661. Du Moulin confessed his authorship in *Petri Molinæi P. F. Parerga Poematum Libelli Tres* (Canterbury: John Hayes for John Creed, 1670), Book III, pp. 141-42,[77] as well as in *A Replie to a Person of Honour* (1675), p. 40. Expected, however, was a reply to *Defensio prima* by Salmasius, who died in 1653. An answer did not appear until 1660, reputedly by Salmasius, with a preface by his son. Whether this indeed was by Milton's antagonist is uncertain. *Ad Ioannem Miltonvm Responsio, Opus Posthvmvm Clavdii Salmasii. Divione* [Dijon], *Typis Philiberti Chavance, . . . M.DC.LX* was published around September 15, 1660; in England it appeared as *Claudii Salmasii ad Johannem Miltonum Responsio, Opus Posthumum. Londini, Typis Tho. Roycroft; Impensis Jo. Martin, Ja. Allestry, & Tho. Dicas . . . MDCLX* in December, having been registered on September 19 (II, 278).

We have already remarked under the discussion of *Eikonoklastes* that one of Charles II's first proclamations was the confiscation and burning of the *Defensio* in August 1660 and notices of it in the news journals at that time. This act is recalled by later commentators often enough; see, for example, Daniel Neal's *The History of the Puritans* (London, 1733), II, 369-70. Probably Milton's imprisonment during October-December 15, 1660, is due in large part to this tract and its effects. Likewise it was condemned anew at Ox-

ford in 1683. And the controversy with Salmasius attracted notice
in a number of letters and books through the last part of the century,
among them the following: Robert South, *A Sermon Preach'd on
the Anniversary-Fast for the Martyrdom of King Charles I* on January 30, 1663;[78] Georg Matthias König, *Bibliotheca Vetus et Nova*
(Altdorofi: Henrici Meyeri, 1678), p. 541; *Danielis Georgii Morhofii
Polyhistor, Sive de Notitia Auctorem et Rerum Commentarii*
(Lübecæ: Petri Boeckmanni, 1688), I, 301-2 (there were a number
of reprints); Johannis Alberti Fabricius, *Decas Decadem sive Plagiari-
orum & Pseudonymorum Centuria, Accessit Exercitatio de Lexicus
Græcis, eodum auctore* (Lipsiæ: Frid. Lanckischii, 1689), pp. [H4;
i.e., 63-64], under "LII. Claudius Salmasius." The *Defensio* was em-
ployed twice in 1682 in argument concerning the "Christian's" relationship with his king, which depends on whether one considers
him divinely appointed or not. In *Julian the Apostate: Being a Short
Account of his Life* (London: for Langley Curtis, 1682), Samuel
Johnson used Milton's tract in "The Preface to the Reader," pp. iii-
xxix, and in *Mr. Hunt's Argument for The Bishops Right: With the
Postscript* (London, 1682), Thomas Hunt derived much of "The
Postscript" from the same work. These debts were first pointed out
by Thomas Long in *A Vindication of the Primitive Christians, In
Point of Obedience to their Prince, against the Calumnies of a Book
intituled The Life of Julian* (London: J. C. and Freeman Collins,
1683). See "The Epistle Dedicatory," pp. [xv-xix]; "To the Reader,"
p. [xxvi]; "Reflections on the Behaviour of Those Christians," pp.
180-86, 191-94, 196-97, with quotations from the *Defensio*; and
"An Appendix, Containing a more full and particular Answer to
Mr. Hunt's Preface and Postscript," pp. 291-347.

From the eighteenth through the twentieth centuries attention
given the *Defensio prima* has been generally slight, except in larger
biographical and contextual discussions. Partially, at least, this is
so because the work attacked monarchy, and thus seldom have
Milton's basic concepts been examined without the digressive
matter of controversy. Edward Ward gave a summary of the argument of the tract in *The History of the Grand Rebellion* (London,
1713), II, 794,[79] and Jonathan Mayhew derived much of the substance of *A Discourse Concerning Unlimited Submission and Non-
resistance to the Higher Powers* (Boston: D. Fowle and D. Gookin,
1750) from it. A poem by Bonnel Thornton, "City Latin," employs as an epigraph lines from Milton's poem on Salmasius; see
*New Foundling Hospital for Wit . . . A New Edition, Corrected,
and Considerably Enlarged* (London: for J. Debrett, 1784), III,
119. The Salmasius-Milton dispute continued to be noticed in the

eighteenth century also; see Zacharias Conrad von Uffenbach, *Merkwürdige Reisen durch niedersachsen Holland und Engelland* (Ulm und Memningen: Johann Friederich Gaums, 1753-54), III (Ulm, 1754), 585; and [Pierre Jean Grosley], *Londres* (Lausanne, 1770), I, 344; II, 233-34; III, 339-40 n. In *An Essay on the Life and Genius of Samuel Johnson, LL.D.* (London: for T. Longman et al., 1792), Arthur Murphy discussed Milton's republicanism, gave an apology for Johnson's censures, and quoted from Washington's translation on pp. 179–86.

There were no separate editions of the work in English in these centuries. In French translation are *Théorie de la royauté d'après la doctrine de Milton* ([Paris], 1789), adapted by J. B. Salaville, with Comte Mirabeau's "Sur Milton et ses ouvrages," and a second edition in the same year; a third edition was produced in 1791; and a fourth in 1792 without the essay by Mirabeau, under the title, *Défense du peuple anglais, sur le jugement et la condamnation de Charles Premier, Roi d'Angleterre. Par Milton* (Valence: P. Aurel). An abbreviated German translation in "Die Schutzrede von Johann Milton für das englische Volk," in *Fürst und Volk nach Buchanans und Miltons Lehre* (Aurau, 1821), pp. 81-141, trans. I. P. V. Troxler. The only annotated edition is that in the Yale *Prose*, IV, i, by William J. Grace, in a translation by Donald MacKenzie.

In answer to *Regii Sanguinis Clamor*, which we remember he took to have been written by Alexander More, Milton produced another major prose work with a long biographical section, the source of much important information: *Joannis MiltonI Angli Pro Populo Anglicano Defensio Secunda. Contra infamem libellum anonymum cui titulus, Regii sanguinis clamor ad cœlum adversus parricidas Anglicanos* (Londini: Typis Neucomianis, 1654). It is an octavo; there are errata; and it was dated May 30 by Thomason. Robert W. Ayers' bibliographic description of the volume in the Yale *Prose*, IV, ii, 1144-45, needs a few emendations: a comma is omitted with the catchword "domi" on p. 163; breath and stress marks are different on the Greek catchword on p. 43 from those on the word on p. 44; there is a trace of a period in the head on p. 49, after "Secunda"; and it should be mentioned that two different thetas are used in the Greek catchword on p. 47 and the word on p. 48. Notice of publication appeared in *Mercurius Politicus,* June 1-8, 1654, No. 208, p. 3540. Friends of More, it would seem, tried to dissuade Milton from publishing the work according to a letter from the Dutch ambassador Willem Nieuport to More, dated

June 23 (July 3), 1654, and published in More's *Fides Publica,*
pp. 19-21.

As Parker points out (II, 1033-34) and no other textual discussion
of the tract does, a pirated edition appeared supposedly from the
press of Thomas Newcomb in London (like the authorized edition).
It is a duodecimo in 128 pages, but with a collation of [ ]^1, A-E^{12},
F^5. The material in sig. F is in larger type than the rest. Apparently
F was a half gathering with F$_6$ serving as the preliminary sheet. The
fact that the text uses 128 pages suggests that the printer was Adrian
Vlacq and the place of publication The Hague (see the ensuing discussion), and the fact that it tries to pass as a London edition, that
it does not contain Vlacq's address to the reader, and that sig. F is
treated as it is suggests that this edition preceded the next ones to
be discussed. Perhaps it should be dated around late June on the
basis of an unsigned letter dated July 24, 1654, which implies
that a Hague edition was out by that time.[80] More's attempted
suppression of the work may better apply to this edition than to
the next to be cited.

Three additional pirated editions followed not long after by the
Dutch printer Adrian Vlacq, the second and third of which differ
textually from the first.[81] The first of these is: *Joannis Miltoni
Angli Defensio Secunda Pro Populo Anglicano: Contra infamem
libellum anonymum cui titullus, Regii sanguinis clamor ad cœlum
adversus parricidas Anglicanos. Editio secunda auctior & emendatior.
Hagæ-Comitvm, Ex typographia Adriani Vlacq. M. DC. LIV.* It contains a Preface to the Reader by Vlacq, with a basic text of 128 pages.
Ayers, unaware of the previously mentioned pirated edition, suggested
this edition as the one which More tried to suppress, having heard of
its impending publication from John Dury, the translator of *Eikonoklastes* and correspondent of Samuel Hartlib.[82] The second of these
further pirated editions reads: *Joannis Miltoni Defensio Secunda
Pro Populo Anglicano . . . Accessit Alexandri Mori Ecclesiastæ,
Sacrarumque litterarum Professoris Fides Publica, Contra calumnias
Ioannis MiltonI Scurræ. Hagæ-Comitvm, Ex typographia Adriani
Vlacq. M. DC. LIV.* It has a foreword by "Georgius Crantzius" and
Vlacq's statement now titled, "Typographvs Pro Se-Ipso." There are
press variants. Milton's *Defensio* on sigs. A-E is a reissue of the first
Vlacq edition without change; the preliminary material, because it
is augmented, is reset, and sig. F, pp. 121-28, is partially reset to
allow for the addition of *Fides Publica.* That is, the outer forme is
reset, but the inner forme was reprinted without change. The third
of these editions attempts to be a duplicate of the second, but *Defensio secunda* has been entirely reset and thus has innumerable

differences from the former edition. Vlacq reissued the parts set for his second edition (that is, sigs. *, F, and *Fides Publica*) and reset the rest (that is, sigs A-E). These editions appeared, perhaps, in October and in later 1654 (see Masson, V, 150-51). Both the London and Hague editions are advertised in *Catalogus Librorum Qui In Bibliopolio Danielis Elsevirii venales extant* (Amsterdam, 1674), p. 121.

In reaction to the charges which Milton brought against him, More wrote *Fides Publica* in 1654 and a *Supplementum* in 1655. The former was published as: *Alexandri More Ecclesiastæ & Sacrorum Litterarum Professoris Fides Publica, Contra calumnias Ioannis Miltoni. Hagæ-Comitvm, Ex typographia Adriani Vlacq, M. DC. LIV.* Included is a statement by Vlacq to the reader. But this work seems to have been issued *only* in the volume that Vlacq produced containing the *Defensio secunda*; it has a separate title page (as given here), separate signatures, and separate pagination. The copies which exist of *Fides Publica* by itself seem to have been created by separation of the tract from the full volume. It has been assumed that the same thing occurred with More's addition in 1655, for the 1654 volume without a title page or date change was reissued with continuous pagination for the addition of *Alexandri Mori Ecclesiastæ & Sacrarum Litterarum Professoris Supplementum Fidei Publicæ, Contra calumnias Ioannis Miltoni. Hagæ-Comitvm, Ex typographia Adriani Vlacq, M. DC. LV,* that being the separate title page. The pagination is 133-238 plus two blank pages. However, it was issued separately under the aforesaid title, pagination being: [ii] + 1-104. The separate issue should logically have preceded the volume combining the *Defensio secunda, Fides Publica,* and the *Supplementum* with its continuous pagination. The *Supplementum* should perhaps be dated in April 1655. Milton's reply to both volumes by More was, of course, *Defensio pro Se,* published in August.

Defensio secunda figured in much of the contemporary or near-contemporary talk concerning Milton and his advocacy of the Parliamentarian government; for example, Eli Bouhereau's letter to Marquis Turon de Beyrie, dated November 12 (22), 1672, praises and quotes the work.[83] It has frequently been excerpted, particularly the biographical sections, over the years; we might note two eighteenth-century occurrences. In his *Memoirs of the Life and Actions of Oliver Cromwell: As Delivered in Three Panegyrics of Him, Written in Latin . . . With an English Version of Each . . .* (London, 1740), Francis Peck presented as Panegyric III a selection from *Defensio secunda,* with a separate Latin title page, in Latin on pp. 33-47 and, with another separate English title page, in English on pp. 115-29.

John Banks added to his *A Short Critical Review of the Political Life of Oliver Cromwell . . . By a Gentleman of the Middle-Temple*, first published in 1739, a short excerpt in a note on pp. 100-1 of the third edition (London, 1747). Further issues of this *Life* appear through the century. *Defensio secunda* was translated into English by Francis Wrangham and published in vol. III, pp. 1-199, of his *Sermons Practical and Occasional; Dissertations, Translations, Including New Versions of Virgil's Bucolics and of Milton's Defensio Secunda; Seaton Poems . . .* (London: Baldwin, Craddock & Joy, 1816). It was reprinted in the same year in *Scraps* (London: C. Baldwin, 1816), pp. 1-199; the volume contains other non-Miltonic pieces. The first fully annotated edition of the work is Donald A. Roberts' in the Yale *Prose*, IV, i, with a translation by Helen North.

Modern scholarship has paid attention to either the contemporary arguments which the *Defensio* and the attacks upon it helped develop or its biographical import.

Much has also been written about the historical context of Milton's third defense in surveys of the controversies in which he became embroiled in the 1650s: *Joannis MiltonI Angli pro se Defensio contra Alexandrum Morum Ecclesiasten, Libelli famosi, cui titulos, Regii sanguinis clamor ad cœlum adversus Parricidas Anglicanos, authorem rectè dictum.* Written in answer to More's *Fides Publica* (October 1654) and his *Supplementum* (April 1655), both of which Vlacq had published with *Defensio secunda* in 1655,[84] the third *Defensio* appeared on August 8, 1655 (according to Thomason's dating), from the press of Thomas Newcomb. The edition is in variant states. The date of composition may have been earlier in the year, with the remarks on the *Supplementum* added after the main attack. The work was immediately reprinted as *Ioannis Miltoni Angli Pro se Defensio* by Vlacq at The Hague. Notice of publication appears in *Nouvelles Ordinaires de Londres*, No. 298 (February 17-24, 1656, new style), p. 1194. Both editions were offered for sale in Elzevir's catalogue (1674), p. 121. Kester Svendsen edited the text with introduction and annotations in the Yale *Prose*; the introduction and notes summarize Svendsen's prior work on More, his reputation, and Milton's use of the stories which reached him. The humor and style of the tract are also ably discussed in this edition.

One of the curiosities of Milton bibliography is his edition of *The Cabinet-Council: Containing the Cheif Arts of Empire, And Mysteries of State; Discabineted In Political and Polemical Aphorisms, Grounded on Authority, and Experience; And illustrated with the choicest Ex-*

*amples and Historical Observations. By the Ever-renowned Knight,
Sir Walter Raleigh, Published by John Milton Esq.,* which has a two-
page preface by Milton. It was published by Thomas Newcomb for
Thomas Johnson in 1658 from a manuscript which Milton reported
he received from a friend and had refound amongst his papers. It was
entered in the Stationers' Register on May 4, 1658. The author was
not Ralegh. On the basis of manuscripts of the work, Ernest A.
Strathmann has shown that the author was T. B.,[85] but suggestions
of identity have not proved meaningful. There is no information to
lead to an identification of Milton's friend or the date of acquisition,
and we can only accept his reason for having the work published:
he simply thought it worthy of public perusal. The aphorisms frequently enough accord with Milton's views, but not always, and
such differences militate against this being offered for political reasons
at this difficult time for the Protectorate. However, it seems to me
that the number of editions of Ralegh's works around 1658 must
have contributed to the decision: *The Marrow of Historie* appeared
in 1650 and 1662; *The Maxims of State* in 1651; *Observations Touching Trade and Commerce* in 1651; *The Prerogative of Parliaments in
England* in 1657; *The Remains of Sir Walter Raleigh viz. Maxims of
State* in 1657 and 1664, and the editions of 1669, 1675, and 1681
included *Observations* and *The Prerogative.*

But if we do take Milton at his word, we may have another piece
of evidence of what he was doing around 1655-59, after he seems
to have been generally less employed by the government and before
the flurry of writing to hold back the Restoration. In October 1658
another edition of *Defensio prima* added an important postscript,
usually interpreted as indicating Milton's concerted return to *Paradise Lost.*[86] His report about finding the manuscript of *The Cabinet-
Council* seems to agree with the view that during the later 1650s
Milton was reorganizing his life, returning to his personal writing
activities, and simply cleaning out and rearranging the accumulations
of the past. Not only does he seem to return to *Paradise Lost* at this
time, but it is the period when *De doctrina christiana* is considered
to have been developed, possibly as an outgrowth of an earlier
theological compilation, and within the next decade the apparently
early *Artis Logicæ* and *Accedence Commnc't Grammar* appeared.
The implication of William B. Hunter, Jr., that *Considerations
touching the likeliest means to remove Hirelings* was an earlier
tract (written sometime around 1653) revamped for the political
circumstances of 1659[87] may receive some collaboration from the
above.

In 1661 the work was republished as *Aphorisms of State,* again

for Thomas Johnson, but without Milton's name or preface. The
explanation is quite simple: at this time Milton was in general disrepute in the political and governmental world, and sales would undoubtedly be better without his connection with the book being
noted. In 1692, with a regained position both in literary circles
(because of the fourth edition of *Paradise Lost* in 1688) and in
political arenas (because of the Whig ascendency and recent succession controversy), the volume could be reprinted with his name
and preface. It was produced by G. Croom for Joseph Watts, and
was entitled: *The Arts of Empire, and Mysteries of State Discabineted
. . . By the Ever-Renouned Knight Sir Walter Raleigh, Published by
John Milton Esq.* It appeared again in 1697, without printer or
bookseller being noted, as *The Secrets of Government, and Misteries
of State, Plainly laid open, in all the several Forms of Government
in the Christian World. Published by John Milton, Esq.* French,
correctly but vaguely, says that at least some copies lack the preface
(IV, 221) and Parker writes without qualification and in gross error,
"Milton's preface was discarded" (II, 1191). A reissue of 1692, it
appears in two forms: all copies consulted contain the two-page
preface, "To the Reader," except for the Carl H. Pforzheimer copy
which instead of A^4 has [ ]^1, being a title page and blank verso on
different paper from the work itself.[88] The usual copy (e. g., in the
Folger, Yale, Indiana, Huntington, etc.) has: [i], title page; [ii],
blank; [iii]-iv, Milton's "To the Reader"; v-viii, Contents. This
signature gathering, A^4, is on the same paper stock as the rest of
the volume. A cancel appears between sigs. A and B (probably as
a result of its being a reissue of the 1692 printing).

   In 1751 Thomas Birch, who had edited Milton's prose, produced
*The Works of Sir Walter Ralegh, Kt. Political, Commercial, and
Philosophical; Together with his Letters and Poems. The Whole
never before collected together, and some never yet printed. To
which is prefix'd, A new Account of his Life,* two vols., in which
he included "The Cabinet-Council; containing the chief Arts of
Empire and Mysteries of State," I, 39-170. Page 39 is a title page
for the work, again advertising that it was "Published by JOHN
MILTON," and reprinting his preface as p. 40. The edition of Ralegh's
Works in 1829 also prints this item (VIII, 35-150). The only near-
contemporary references to the work (other than editions) which
link Milton with it are in biographies and dictionaries (usually
under *Ralegh*).

As it became obvious that the Protectorate was declining and that
even adherents of the Parliamentarians had become disenchanted

with the government, forces which finally led to the Restoration caused Milton to try to divert or color the settlement of the Restoration with seven items. The first of these was registered on February 16, 1659 (II, 214): *A Treatise of Civil Power in Ecclesiastical causes: Shewing that it is not lawfull for any power on earth to compell in matters of Religion. The author J. M. London, Printed by Tho. Newcomb, Anno 1659.* Parker concludes that Milton would have been working on the tract in December 1658. It was advertised in *The Public Intelligencer*, No. 163, February 7-14, 1659, p. 221; again in No. 174, April 25-May 2, p. 397; and in *Mercurius Politicus*, No. 554, February 10-17, p. 237. Any immediate effect that the tract may have had is not in evidence. However, in the problems of censorship attendant upon the reign of Charles II, William Denton, in his pamphlet which included a paraphrase of part of *Areopagitica* (mentioned before), presented "The Summe of Mr. J. M. His Treatise," pp. 1-3 with further allusions on pp. 3 and 4; see *Jus Cæsaris* (1681).

The tract was "Re-printed for J. Johnson" with a dedication and Milton's name in full in 1790. It appeared in two editions of *Tracts for the People*, No. 1 (London, 1839), which included also part of *Of True Religion* and Sonnets 16 and 17, and again in *Buried Treasures*, Part II (London, 1851). The latter edition is titled: *On the Civil Power in Ecclesiastical Causes. The author J. M. With a Historical Sketch and Notes*; the author of the sketch and notes was C[yrus] R. E[dmonds]. The only annotated edition at present is Barbara Lewalski's in *The Prose of John Milton*. Aside from larger discussions of Milton's ideas and position in contemporary affairs (such as in Barker's *Milton and the Puritan Dilemma*), the reader should consult Lewalski's article "Milton: Political Beliefs and Polemical Methods, 1659-1660," *PMLA*, 74 (1959), 191-202, for the works of this period.

The work on tithes and hirelings promised in *A Treatise* (pp. 1-2) in February appeared in August (according to Thomason): *Considerations touching the likeliest means to remove Hirelings out of the church. Wherein is also discours'd of Tithes, Church-fees, Church-revenues; And whether any maintenance of ministers can be settl'd by law. The author J. M. London, Printed by T[homas] N[ewcomb] for L[ivewell] Chapman at the Crown in Popes-head Alley. 1659.* A friend, Moses Wall, had urged its publication, upon reading *A Treatise*, in a letter dated May 26, 1659, which survives in a transcription by the Reverend Josiah Owen (BM Additional MS 4292, No. 121, ff. 264^V-6^V). The letter was first printed in

Richard Baron's revision of Birch's collected prose in 1753 (I, xlii-xliii) where the correspondent is called "John" Wall. It appeared again in the preface to Baron's edition of *Eikonoklastes* (1756, 1770); the title page advertised it as "an original letter to Milton, never before published." A separate two-page octavo sheet with notes by R[ichard] B[aron], dated June 20, 1756, reprinted it as *A Letter from Mr. Wall to John Milton, Esquire. Printed and Distributed Gratis by the Society for Constitutional Information. London, 1781.* The tract was advertised in *Mercurius Politicus*, No. 585, September 1-8, 1659, p. 713, and No. 591, October 13-20, 1659, p. [809]. Allusions to it occur in the anonymous *The Censure of the Rota*, before March 30, 1660, and in Thomas Long's *A Compendious History of all the Popish & Fanatical Plots* (London, 1684), p. 93.

There have been frequent reprintings, apparently because the subject of tithing and state remuneration of the clergy continued as live issues. It appeared as *A Supplement to Dr. Du Moulin, Treating of the Likeliest Means to Remove Hirelings out of the Church of England . . . With a brief Vindication of Mr. Rich. Baxter. By J. M. London, Printed in the Year M DC LXXX*; known copies show textual variations. It was again reprinted in London in 1717 by S. Barker, in 1723, in 1736,[89] and in 1743. The first publication of a Miltonic work in the Colonies was this tract under the title *An Old-Looking-Glass for the Laity and Clergy . . . Being Considerations touching the likeliest means to Remove Hirelings out of the Church of Christ. By John Milton, author of Paradise Lost. With the Life of Milton: also large extracts from his works, concerning bishops. Philadelphia, for Robert Bell, and to be sold by J. Crukshank and I. Collins, 1770.* The *Life* is Elijah Fenton's and the extracts come from *Animadversions*, pp. 45-50; *Reformation*, pp. 50-70; and *An Apology*, pp. 71-74. This volume was reprinted in New Haven in 1774. There were also four separate editions in the nineteenth century: one in London in 1831, another by J. Cleave in 1834 (though undated), one in Aberdeen by Murdock in 1839, and one in London as part of the *Buried Treasures* series, Part II, pp. 29-68, in 1851. An extract, not previously noticed, was printed as *An Address to the House of Commons, in the Year 1659, in favour of the Removal of Tithes* (London: James Low, 1817). The only annotated edition at this writing is William B. Hunter, Jr.'s in *The Prose of John Milton*.

The date of composition has always been assumed as 1659, but Hunter implies that the tract may have been written before that date, being issued to comply with the promise in *A Treatise*. The latest datable allusion is to William Prynne's *A Gospel Plea . . . for the Lawfulness and Continuance of the Ancient Setled Maintenance and Tenthes of the Ministrys of the Gospel*, published in autumn 1653. The period of 1652-53 was more involved in the questions of tithing and state maintenance of the clergy than was that of 1659, although Milton saw these two issues as being central to the relationship between church and state. In *A Treatise* he is more concerned with political aspects. No one has raised a question over the date of composition of that tract.

One of the items which Milton produced in his flurry of attempts to stay the Restoration was *A Letter to a Friend; concerning the Ruptures of the Commonwealth*, which was "Publish'd from the Manuscript" in *A Complete Collection* (1698), I, 779-81. The friend is unidentified, although Gualter Frost, Philip Meadows, Sir Henry Vane, and Bustrode Whitelocke have been proposed. The date of composition was October 25, 1659, which is given with its transcription in the Columbia MS, pp. 21-23, now owned by Columbia University. The scribal text in this compendium of both Miltonic and non-Miltonic material appends the initials J. M. It was reprinted in Francis Maseres' collection entitled *History of Britain* (London: R. Wilks, 1818).

Another item is "Proposalls of certaine expedients for ye p^{r}venting of a civill war now feard, & ye settling of a firme governm^t.," found only in the Columbia MS, pp. 19-21, and first published in the Columbia Edition, XVIII, 3-7. The scribe assigned it to J. M. There are ten proposals generally similar to ideas in *A Letter to a Friend* (for example, life tenure for army officers and members of the senate, abjuration of a House of Lords, freedom of conscience). It is dated between October 26 and December 26, 1659, when the Committee of Safety, to which it would have been directed, flourished. Parker thus suggests November as composition date.

Important as a statement of Milton's willingness to compromise between belief and practicality is *The Readie & Easie Way To Establish A Free Commonwealth. And The Excellence therof Compar'd with The inconveniences and dangers of readmitting kingship in this nation. The author J. M.* (London, 1660). It was printed by T[homas] N[ewcomb] for Livewell Chapman, appearing on March 3, 1660, according to Thomason, but February according to Wood and White Kennet in *A Register and Chronicle* (London, 1728), p. 73 (probably from Wood). It was advertised in *Mercurius Politicus,*

No. 610, March 1-8, 1660, p. 1151, with errata given (see French, IV, 303). According to the arguments of Evert Mordecai Clark the tract was written between February 4 and 21, 1660, probably before February 15, because the "secluded" members of Parliament were seated on February 21 and thus the original Long Parliament was theoretically restored. The preface, on the other hand, is placed between February 21 and 29.[90] Probably, as the errata seem to indicate, the tract was rushed to press because of the fast movement of events; it is only eighteen pages long. Within a month (probably after April 20) a second, longer edition appeared with the added statement: "The second edition revis'd and augmented. The author J. M. London, Printed for the Author, 1660."

With this, still another tract which aimed at influencing the Restoration settlement had no effect, but it did bring forth reactions. On March 13 came Sir Roger L'Estrange's *Be Merry and Wise; or, A Seasonable Word to the Nation* with a reference on p. 86;[91] on March 17, *The Character of the Rump* with a comment on pp. 2-3; on March 24, William Colline's *The Spirit of the Phanatiques Dissected. And the Solemne League and Covenant solemnly discussed in 30 Queries* with snide remarks on pp. [7-8]; on March 30, *The Censure of the Rota Upon Mr Miltons Book Entituled, The Ready and Easie Way to Establish A Free Commonwealth* (London, Printed by Paul Giddy, Printer to the Rota, 1660);[92] ca. March 31 (date of registry, II, 255), G[eorge] S[tarkey]'s (?) *The Dignity of Kingship Asserted: In Answer to Mr. Milton's Ready and Easie way to Establish A Free Common-wealth* (London, Printed by E. C. for H. Seile and W. Palmer, 1660);[93] and ca. April 20-25, Sir Roger L'Estrange's *No Blind Guides. In Answer to a Seditious Pamphlet of J. Milton's, Intituled Brief Notes upon a Late Sermon* (London, for Henry Brome, 1660).[94]

The second edition of *The Ready and Easy Way* was published separately in 1744 and 1791 (London: for J. Ridgway), and it is included in *History of Britain* by Francis Maseres (London, 1818). It was reprinted in Boston by the Directors of the Old South Work in 1895 and 1896.[95] The first edition was the basis for an annotated edition with collations, introduction, and glossary by E. M. Clark in 1915; and there is an annotated edition of the second edition by Barbara K. Lewalski in *The Prose of John Milton*. A Japanese translation by Jun Harada appeared in 1972.

A sixth item was *The Present Means and brief Delineation of a Free Commonwealth, Easy to be put in Practice, and without Delay. In a Letter to General Monk*, which also was "Published from the

Manuscript," in *A Complete Collection*, I, 799-800. It has also been known as "A Letter to General Monk," but these words were probably added by Toland, who referred to the item along with *A Letter to a Friend* in his *Life*. He says he received it from a worthy friend (unidentified), who had purchased it from Milton's nephew (presumably Edward Phillips). It would seem to date after March 3, 1660, and Don M. Wolfe suggests late March or early April in *Milton in the Puritan Revolution*, p. 461. It was reprinted in Maseres' 1818 collection, and with *A Ready and Easy Way* in 1895 and 1896 by the Directors of the Old South Ward in Boston (see note 95).

More important is *Brief Notes Upon a Late Sermon, Titl'd, The Fear of God and the King; Preachd, and since Publishd, By Matthew Griffith, D. D. And Chaplain to the late King. Wherin many Notorious Wrestings of Scripture, and other Falsities are observ'd by J. M.* (London, 1660). Griffith's sermon at the Mercer's Chapel on March 25, 1660 was based on Proverbs xxiv.21: "My son, fear God and the king, and meddle not with them that be seditious or desirous of change." The prospect of the Restoration apparently provoked Griffith's action, much to the consternation of those who were preparing the coup. As a result he was imprisoned in Newgate by the Council of State. His likening of Charles II to Samson is interesting first in view of the frequency of this allusion in the late 1640s when the Civil Wars were raging and the Royalists were cast in the role of the Philistines, and second in the realization that Griffith did not recognize Samson as a metaphoric figure who stood for change and sedition against the established (albeit evil) state. The sermon was registered for publication on March 31. Milton's pamphlet was written and published between that date and April 20 when Sir Roger L'Estrange finished (?) and gave to his printer Henry Broome *No Blind Guides*, which was out by April 25. This was reprinted in *L'Estrange his Apology*, dated June 6, 1660, and in facsimile in Parker's *Milton's Contemporary Reputation*. Milton denounces Griffith's praise of kings and exhorts readers to praise the Commonwealth; L'Estrange attacks Milton on personal grounds, on interpretation of the Bible, and through his plan for a free commonwealth in *The Readie & Easie Way*. The lack of effect and probably of knowledge of *The Tenure* and its cogent argument is overwhelming: fit audience did not exist. Milton erred not only in thinking that anything could hold back the tide of monarchy but also in thinking that such a windmill as Griffith deserved attention.[96]

When Milton wrote his schoolboy text on grammar is unknown.

The Anonymous Biographer lists it as one of the works finished
after the Restoration, and it seems logical that Milton would have
prepared it during his years of tutoring. An altered view of the
Italian pronunciation of Latin between *Of Education* and the preface of *Accedence Commenc't Grammar* suggests a date after June
1644; accordingly Parker has suggested 1645 (?). The persistence
in the published volume of spelling practices used by Milton points
toward concluding that the manuscript from which the edition
was set was in Milton's holograph, originally at least, and this in
turn would require a date of composition prior to around 1650.[97]

The work was entered in the Term Catalogues on June 28, 1669,
and apparently published shortly thereafter in two issues. The title
page of issue one reads: *Accedence Commenc't Grammar, Supply'd*
with sufficient Rules, For the use of such as, Younger or Elder, are
desirous, without more trouble then needs, to attain the Latin
Tongue; the elder sort especially, with little teaching, and thir
own industry. J. M. London, Printed by S. Simmons, next door
to the Golden Lion in Aldersgate-street, 1669. The title page of
issue two shows a number of variations (including two non-Miltonic
spelling changes, *than* and *their*) and a changed printing legend:
Accedence Commenc't Grammar, Supply'd with sufficient Rules,
For the use of such (Younger or Elder) as are desirous, without more
trouble than needs to attain the LATIN Tongue; the Elder sort es-
pecially, with little Teaching, and their own Industry. By John Mil-
ton. London, Printed for S. S. and are to be sold by John Starkey
at the Miter in Fleet-street, near Temple-bar, 1669. Apparently
the compositor who set up the title page and ran off the new issue
was a worker in Simmons' shop. It is advertised by John Starkey's
Catalogue of Books, perhaps dated May 1670; see previous discussion under *Tetrachordon.* The grammar was alluded to by Richard
Leigh (?) in his attack on Milton in *The Transproser Rehears'd* (1673),
p. 126, and apparently by the anonymous author of *A Common-place*
Book out of the Rehearsal Transprosed (London, 1673), pp. 35-36.

Little attention has been paid to Milton's grammar. It is not entirely original, of course, for of 530 Latin quotations, 330 are directly taken from William Lilly's *A Shorte Introduction of Grammar*
(frequently reprinted), and other grammars were also employed.
But Milton seems to have contributed about 175 quotations from
classical authors which are not found in other grammars. J. Milton
French's excellent analysis is the only one in print and provides us
with an investigation of sources and content.[98]

The early eighteenth century frequently cited Milton as an authority on early British history and on historiography. The work on which this reputation depended appeared around November 1670: *The History of Britain. That Part especially now call'd England. From the first Traditional Beginning, Continu'd to the Norman Conquest. Collected out of the Antientest and Best Authours thereof by John Milton* (London: J[ohn] M[acock] for James Allestry, 1670). This first issue of the first edition, a quarto, contains a portrait by William Faithorne, also dated 1670, errata, and an index; there are 368 pages. A new issue appeared in 1671 apparently because of the death of Allestry on November 3 and the acquisition of rights by Spencer Hickman, cited on the new title page. Not all copies contain the portrait. The first edition exists in various states.[99] The month of publication of the first issue is suggested by its entry in the Term Catalogues at that time (I, 56); see *A Catalogue of Books Printed and Published at London in Michaelmas Term, 1670. Licensed Novemb. 22. 1670. Roger L'Estrange,* No. 3. The Term Catalogues list the bookseller as Hickman, allowing that the first issue might be dated somewhat earlier. October would agree with the book's appearance during Michaelmas Term and make understandable the issuing of a title page with Allestry's name on it, when he died so early in November. Parker argues that it must have been within "a very few months" of December because the portrait lists Milton's age as 62, which he would become on December 9. However, Parker also speculates that the portrait may have been executed for *Paradise Regain'd*, licensed July 2, 1670, and scheduled to appear around September 10, its date of registration (II, 415). Perhaps therefore we can not give much weight to the evidence of the portrait for specific dating of *Britain.* According to Parker the second issue with its 1671 dating probably appeared after the first issue was sold out and probably after March 15, 1671.

Rights were acquired by John Dunmore from Hickman, according to the interpretation of an entry in the Stationers' Register (II, 451) for December 29, 1672, before August 24, 1671. They then passed to Sir Thomas Davies from Dunmore on August 24, 1671, and thereafter to John Martyn on December 29, 1672 (see II, 452). Martyn did not reissue the work or bring out a second edition for over four years. The first edition was advertised by Robert Clavell in *The General Catalogue of Books* in 1675, p. 34.

The second edition in octavo is known in two different issues. The first of these was printed by Macock for John Martyn in 1677; there are 416 pages and errata are changed. It was listed in the Term Catalogues for Easter Term (II, 277). The second issue, which Macock produced for Mark Pardoe in 1678, advertised itself on the title page as "The second Edition." Another edition (usually considered another issue of the preceding) appeared in 1695 by R[ichard?] E[veringham?] for R[obert] Scot[t], R[ichard] Chiswell, R[ichard] Bently, and G[eorge] Sawbridge; it was sold by A[bel] Swall and T[imothy] Child. This issue was registered by Scott on August 21, 1683 (III, 181-85), rights being claimed from Martyn who had died in 1681. Reissue at that time must have been considered unsound financially or unnecessary. In the same year, 1695, a second issue of the third edition (usually considered another issue of the second edition) was produced for Ri[chard] Chiswell and was sold by Nath[aniel] Roles. This issue had been entered in the Term Catalogues for Michaelmas Term, 1694 (II, 531). These reissues and new editions suggest that the second edition did not sell so well as expected, but perhaps the celebrity brought by the 1688 fourth edition of *Paradise Lost* and the 1695 *Poetical Works* by Jacob Tonson made Milton's name a good prospect for sales.

Textual complication exists for *Britain* because of the version printed in *A Complete Collection* (1698), I, 1-137, which has a separate title page with a date of 1694 and which is advertised as "Publish'd from a Copy corrected by the Author himself." This version includes most of the errata changes and various additional revisions.[100] The 1698 version is followed in all further editions except for those of John Hughes, John Mitford, the Columbia Edition, and the Yale *Prose*. Hughes made some but not all of the errata and additional changes. The Hughes edition, generally called White Kennet's edition because he contributed the third volume devoted to more recent history, is *A Complete History of England, With the Lives of All the Kings and Queens Thereof; from the earliest account of time, to the Death of His Late Majesty King William III* (London: Brab. Aylmer [et al.], 1706), three vols. The title page of vol. 1 reads: "Beginning with the History of Britain to William the Conqueror. By Mr John Milton"; it comprises pp. 1-82 and omits the index. The second edition, corrected, was published by R. Bonwick [et al.] in 1719.

Thomas Birch's edition in 1738 (II, 1-126) repeats the 1698 statement "Publish'd from a Copy corrected by the Author himself" but also inserts the digression on the Long Parliament (the 1681 version; see later) on p. 39 after the words "in great undertakings." Birch does not include the index. Baron's edition of Birch in 1753 does not change the text. The index was not repeated until Francis Maseres' 1818 edition of various prose items (London: R. Wilks); even the Columbia Edition prints it by itself in vol. XVIII, and Yale *Prose* omits it. There have been only two separate publications of *Britain* since the editions of 1677-95, excluding Hughes' compendium: in 1870 the firm of A. Murray and Son issued an octavo "Verbatim reprint from Kennet's England, ed. 1719," entitled *Britain under Trojan, Roman, Saxon Rule. By John Milton, with notes correcting Milton,* and in 1878 the firm of Ward, Locke and Co., issued a stereotype reproduction of this edition. An excerpt is given in *Retrospective Review*, 6 (1882), 87-100. An edition with introduction and notes has recently appeared in the Yale *Prose*, V, i, by French Fogle.

Early notices of *Britain* initiate the respect which it was to enjoy. John Aubrey referred to the work authoritatively in his discussion of Wiltshire, which was not published until much later but in which the preface is dated April 28, 1670.[101] Thomas Blount in *Animadversions upon Sr Richard Barker's Chronicle, and it's continuation. Wherein many errors are discover'd, and some truths advanced* (Oxon [Oxford]: H[enry] H[erringman] for Ric. Davis, 1672), cited the work to correct errors on pp. 20, 58, and 98-99. In *Britannia Antiqua Illustrata: or, the Antiquities of Ancient Britain* (London: Tho. Roycroft, 1676), Aylett Sammes referred to Milton for information (pp. 48, 50, 83, 387, 559) and for a paraphrase of Gildas (pp. 476-77). James Tyrrell praised Milton's work although he lamented its omissions of information from Anglo-Saxon documents probably not available to him. See the first volume of *The General History of England, both Ecclesiastical and Civil* (London: W. Rogers, J. Harris, R. Knaplock, A. Bell, and T. Cockerill, 1697), pp. vi, viii, 17, 20, 136; pp. 17 and 116 (second pagination, Book VI), which concludes the history with Milton's admonition of the bad in man which ranges throughout life. This volume was reissued in 1698 with a reset title page, only the date being altered.

Edmund Bohan discussed the work in *The Method and Order of Reading Both Civil and Ecclesiastical Historie . . . By Degory Wheare, . . . With Mr. Dodwell's Invitation to Gentlemen to Acquaint themselves with Antient History. Made English, and Enlarged, by Edmund Bohun, Esq*; (London: for Charles Brome, 1698), p. 172. *The State of Church-Affairs In this Island of Great Britain Under the Government of the Romans, and British Kings* (London: Nat. Thompson for the Author, 1687) draws from *Britain* repeatedly; it erroneously has been attributed to Milton himself and is now often assigned in card catalogues and listings to his brother Sir Christopher. And parts were copied out in manuscripts probably dating from the last part of the century: there are an extract in French in BM MS Sloane 1030, f. 90^v, and notes in BM MS Sloane 1506.

The 1706 edition of *A Complete History of England* was reviewed

(among other places) with most favorable remarks on Milton in
Acta Eruditorum. Anno MDCCIX Publicata (Lipsiæ: Christian Goezl,
apud Joh. Grossii, Joh. Frid. Gleditsch et fil., et Frid. Groschuf,
1709), pp. 289-93. Milton's position as historiographer is certain
from Aaron Thompson's comments in *The British History. Translated into English from the Latin of Jeffrey of Monmouth. With a
Large Preface Concerning the Authority of the History* (London,
for J. Bowyer, H. Clements, and W. and J. Innys, 1718), pp. iii, lii
and n., lxxvi and n., [CC$_2$r], as well as Laurence Echard's in *The
History of England* (London: for Jacob Tonson, 1707-18), three
vols., I, a$_1$r; II, 410, 678; III, 369 (a biographical statement). "The
Third Edition, with Additions" appeared in 1720. Although John
Oldmixon's views of history and historians in *The Critical History
of England, Ecclesiastical and Civil,* 2 vols. (London: for J. Pemberton, 1724-26), was challenged by Zachary Grey, Milton was viewed
by both men as an authority. Oldmixon referred to Milton at I, 31,
of *The Critical History,* and Grey cited him on pp. 2-6 and 56 of
*A Defence of our Antient and Modern Historians, Against the
Frivolous Cavils of a Late Pretender to Critical History* (London:
for Charles Rivington, 1725). Edition 2 appeared in the same year.
In a further statement a few months later Grey again credited Milton's
scholarship; see *An Appendix to the Defence of Our Antient and
Modern Historians* (London: for Charles Rivington, 1725), pp. 2-3,
25. Oldmixon countered with *Clarendon and Whitlock Compar'd. To
which is occasionally Added, A Comparison between The History of
the Rebellion, and Other Histories of the Civil War* (London: for J.
Pemberton, 1727); see pp. xiv-xv for references to Milton. Even the
American poet Richard Lewis in his English translation of Edward
Holdsworth's "Muscipula" (*The Mouse-Trap, or The Battle of the
Cambrians and Mice* [Annapolis: W. Parks for the author, 1728])
cites *Britain* as an authority for some of his material; see the notes
on pp. 46-47.

We might remark just two further and less expected eighteenth-
century laudatory references to Milton's *History of Britain.* The unfortunate prelate William Dodd, whose knowledge of Milton's works
was quite extensive, discussed *Britain* with a quotation in *The Christian's Magazine, or a Treasury of Divine Knowledge* [for December]
(London: for J. Newbery and J. Coote, 1760), pp. 347-49, and the
literary critic Lewis Morris, in a letter dated April 22, 1760, indicated Welsh attitude toward Milton's early history.[102] On the other
hand the nineteenth century saw Milton as a significant historian,
one who cast aside the theories of the past in order to reexamine
the past through his own point of view, but at the same time as

an imperfect historian, one whose attention to the demands of history and to details was at best temporary.[103]

Three important studies of the work are Sir Charles H. Firth's "Milton as an Historian" in *Proceedings of the British Academy,* III (1908), 225-57 (rptd. in *Essays, Historical and Literary* [Oxford, 1938], pp. 61-102); J. Milton French's "Milton as a Historian" in *PMLA,* 50 (1935), 469-79; and Michael Landon's "John Milton's *History of Britain*: Its place in English Historiography," *UMSE,* 6 (1965), 59-76.[104] Important annotations to *Britain* are in Constance Nicholas' *Introduction and Notes to Milton's History of Britain Designed To Be Used with Volume X, Columbia Edition, The Works of Milton* (Urbana: University of Illinois Press, 1957).[105]

The question of the date of composition of *The History of Britain* is generally but not precisely settled. The evidence is this: 1) Milton said in *Defensio secunda* (p. 94) that he had completed four books (of the six) before becoming Secretary to the Council of State, that is, before mid-March 1649; 2) Theodore Haak remarked to Samuel Hartlib in a letter apparently dated in 1648 that Milton was "writing a universal history of England" (French, II, 214-15); 3) the digression of the Long Parliament, deleted from the beginning of the third book, refers to a period when the civil wars seem to be dormant or near an end, in 1648 (see later); and 4) the earliest biography, that by Cyriack Skinner, recorded that it was finished after the Restoration. The foregoing would therefore suggest that books I-II were written before ca. fall 1648, book III during 1648, book IV before mid-March 1649, and books V-VI sometime thereafter. Skinner's remark may mean simply that the history was written before the Restoration but only published after it. The date by which Milton had begun to compile the history seemed to Parker to be 1648 primarily because of Haak's note (II, 939). My investigation of the orthography places books I and II after mid 1644; early 1648 seems quite possible, but slightly earlier dating as reviewed by Fogle seems even more likely according to orthography. Books V and VI employ Sir Roger Twysden's edition of Simeon of Durham's *Historia de Gestis Regum Anglorum* in *Historiæ Anglicanæ Scriptores X* (London, 1652), and thus a date after that time would seem correct. See Columbia Edition, X, 207-8, 270. However, there is also a reference to Simeon in book IV: see Columbia Edition, X, 180-1. In view of Milton's statement in *Defensio secunda* this would seem to be a brief discussion added to book IV after 1652, as Fogle has suggested. Books V and VI were placed in later 1655 by Parker (I, 465-68) because this period seemed to him the first one in which Milton would have had free

time to return to the project. The idea of Milton's picking up
fallow projects and other manuscripts during 1655-59, already
suggested in this survey, is in agreement with this dating. The
orthography of books V and VI is frequently different from that
in the first four books, although it does reflect some Miltonic practices—I suspect because of the training of the amanuensis either as
scribe or as former student rather than by specific attention on
Milton's part at this time. But whether these must be dated around
1655, rather than, say, 1653 when there may have been some free
time to return to *Britain* is open to question.

Undoubtedly an early work, probably associated with his tutoring,
the *Art of Logic* has been an important document in studying Milton's scheme of logic, its bearing on his major poetry and his
theology, and the rhetoric of the prose and poetry.[106] Although
Ramistic logic is influential upon Milton and his works, one should
not assume that Milton accepted all aspects of Ramus's thought
without qualification or that Ramus is the only informing influence
on his own arguments (for example, in *Areopagitica*) or on his
creations (such as Satan in *Paradise Regain'd*). His intention seems
to have been to clarify the system of logic in the *Dialectica*, which
he had studied himself at Christ's College.

   The work appeared as Joannis Miltoni Angli, *Artis Logicæ Plenior
Institutio, ad Petri Rami Methodum concinnata, Adjecta est Praxis
Annalytica & Petri Rama vita. Libris duobus. Londini: Impensis
Spencer Hickman, Societatis Regalis Typographia, ad insigne Rosæ
in Cæmeterio, D. Pauli, 1672.* The month was perhaps May, for it
is listed in the Term Catalogues (I, 105); see *A Catalogue of Books*,
No. 9, licensed 13 May 1672. It was reissued the next year with a
new title page, which listed a new bookseller: *Joannis Miltoni Angli,
Artis Logicæ . . . Impensis S[pencer] H[ickman]. Prostant pro
R[obert] Boulter ad Insigne Capitis Turcæ exadversum Mercatorio
Regali in Vico vulgò Cornhill dicto. 1673.* This issue is listed in the
Term Catalogues (I, 128 [see *A Catalogue of Books,* No. 12, licensed
February 7, 1673]), and twice in Robert Clavel's *General Catalogue
of Books* (1675), pp. 104, 113. A frontispiece is an engraving by
William Dolle, made in 1671 from the engraving by William Faithorne
executed in 1670 for *Britain.* The author's age is altered to agree with
the new publication date. Parker supposes that the Dolle version was
made for a second edition of *Paradise Lost* around 1671, but for
some reason the edition was delayed until 1674. The second edition
of the epic does employ Dolle's engraving.

   There is no evidence of date of composition. The Anonymous

Biographer lists the work as having been finished after the Restoration, and this squares with the widespread belief that it is connected with the period of tutoring. Whether "finished" means anything significant, one cannot say; probably it means only that it was readied for publication rather than substantially written or revised. Parker places it in "early 1648 with no great confidence" (II, 938).

The Term Catalogues (I, 135), No. 13, dated May 6, 1673, lists *Of True Religion, Hæresie, Schism, Toleration, And what best means may be us'd against the Growth of Popery. The Author J. M.*, which must have appeared therefore sometime between that date and February 7, the date of Catalogue No. 12. The bookseller was Thomas Sawbridge. It was advertised on November 2, 1674, in Robert Clavel's *General Catalogue of Books*, p. 47. Other than its inclusion in collected editions, this tract was reprinted in 1809, 1811, and 1826.[107] Despite the significance of the work as a summary of Milton's ideas of the important topics cited in the title and as a statement against Roman Catholicism, only two articles specifically discuss Milton's view of limited toleration: see Nathaniel Henry, "Milton's Last Pamphlet: Theocracy and Intolerance," in *A Tribute to G. C. Taylor* (Chapel Hill: University of North Carolina Press, 1952), pp. 197-210, and Don M. Wolfe, "Limits of Miltonic Toleration," *JEGP*, 60 (1961), 834-46.

We know of forty-one personal letters written by Milton, thirty-seven in Latin and four in English. Thirty-one (all in Latin) were published in May 1674 under the title *Joannis Miltonii Angli, Epistolarum Familiarium Liber Unus: Quibus Accesserunt, Ejusdam, jam olim in Collegio Adolescentis, Prolusiones Quædam Oratoriæ* by Brabazon Aylmer. The other ten are:

> To an Unknown Friend (Thomas Young?), undated, in Trinity MS, two drafts. Dated variously from 1633 to 1637. Both drafts were first printed in *A General Dictionary, Historical and Critical: In which a New and Accurate Translation of that of the Celebrated Mr. Bayle, With the Corrections and Observations Printed in the Late Edition at Paris, is included* (London, 1758), ed. John Peter Bernard, Thomas Birch, and John Lockman, under *Milton*, VII, 576-77 n. In English.
>
> To Hermann Mylius, dated November 7, 1651, ms; given in Columbia Edition. In Latin. A copy also exists in Mylius's Tagebuch.
>
> To Hermann Mylius, dated January 8, 1652, ms; given in Columbia Edition. In Latin.

To Herman Mylius, dated January 20, 1652, ms; given in Columbia
Edition. In Latin.

To Hermann Mylius, dated February 10, 1652, ms; given in Columbia
Edition. In Latin.

To Bulstrode Whitelocke, dated February 12, 1652, ms; given in
Columbia Edition. In English.

To Hermann Myius, dated February 13, 1652, ms; given in Columbia
Edition. In Latin. In hand of Edward Phillips.

To Herman Mylius, dated February 21, 1652, ms; given in Columbia
Edition. In Latin.

To John Bradshaw, dated February 21, 1653, ms; first published by
Todd (1826), I, 162-64. In English.

To Christopher Milton (?), ms; given in Columbia Edition. In English.
Uncertain; may be from Milton to his brother, and if so, it would
probably have been sent in January 1658.

Three letters printed in 1674 have been found in manuscript: those to
Lucas Holstenius (Lukas Holste), dated March 30, 1639, holograph; to
Carlo Dati, dated April 21, 1647, holograph; to Hermann Mylius, dated
December 31, 1651 (endorsed, January 2, 1652).

The edition was listed in the Term Catalogues (I, 172) on May 26,
1674, and entered in the Stationers' Register (II, 481) on July 1. The
licenser was Milton's former antagonist Sir Roger L'Estrange. Parker
speculates that Aylmer may have tried to compensate for his loss of
the publication of the letters of state by this volume. According to
his prefatory remarks, the seven college Latin prolusions which were
added to the letters were acquired from Milton on Aylmer's request
"to counterbalance the paucity of letters, or at least occupy the blank."
In addition an early prolusion in Latin, called "Mane citus lectum
fuge," was discovered on a sheet found with Milton's Commonplace
Book in 1874. It was printed by Alfred Horwood in 1876 in his
edition of the CPB.

The letters were edited in translation by Robert Fellowes (1806,
in Charles Symmons' edition of the prose works, I, i-xliii), John
Hall (1829), Phyllis Tillyard (1932), as well as in the Columbia
Edition (with Latin), French's *Life Records* (with Latin), and the
Yale *Prose* (in progress; translated and annotated by Alberta and
W. Arthur Turner); see also the annotated selection in *The Prose
of John Milton* by the present writer. In addition a translation by
"A. B. E." of the letter to Leonard Philaras, September 28, 1654,
is found in *Monthly Magazine*, 24 (1807), 565-66. The prolusions
were published in translation by Phyllis Tillyard (1932), as well as
in the Columbia Edition (with Latin) and the Yale *Prose* (anno-

tated by Kathryn McEuen). The second prolusion was printed in Latin and an English translation by Francis Peck in *New Memoirs of the Life and Poetical Works of Mr. John Milton* (London, 1740). It was also translated by B. Smith and published in the *Quarterly Journal of Speech*, 14 (1928), 392-95. Most scholarship on the letters and prolusions has dealt with problems of dating; see William R. Parker, "Milton and Thomas Young, 1602-1628," *MLN*, 3 (1938), 399-407; A. S. P. Woodhouse, "Notes on Milton's Early Development," *UTQ*, 13 (1943), 66-101; Eugenia Chifos, "Milton's Letter to Gill, May 20, 1628," *MLN*, 62 (1947), 37-39; Alberta and W. Arthur Turner, Yale *Prose*, I-IV (in progress); John T. Shawcross, "Speculations on the Dating of the Trinity MS. of Milton's Poems," *MLN*, 75 (1960), 11-17; and John T. Shawcross, "The Dating of Certain Poems, Letters, and Prolusions Written by Milton," *ELN*, 2 (1965), 261-66, for letters; and see Woodhouse's article and mine in *ELN* for the prolusions. Cf. Parker's biography for both. The sources, content, and significance of the prolusions are investigated by Thomas R. Hartmann in an unpublished dissertation at New York University (1962); see also his introduction to and annotated translation of the seventh prolusion in *The Prose of John Milton*.

A Declaration, or Letters Patents of the Election of this present King of Poland John the Third, Elected on the 22ᵈ of May last past, Anno Dom. 1674 . . . Now faithfully translated from the Latin Copy (London, 1674) was printed for Brabazon Aylmer, perhaps around July 1674. The Latin version was issued just after June. Milton's name was not attached to the translation, but it was listed as his by Phillips. Why Milton did the translation is not known, but Parker (I, 638) surmises that he could well use whatever payment there was and that the subject matter—the free election of a commoner to kingship—was agreeable. There has been no scholarship expended on the work, and it has been reprinted only in collected editions.

In his capacity as Secretary to the Council of State Milton translated various state papers, primarily letters, into Latin to be communicated to foreign powers. Official orders are recorded from time to time and those that have been noted are reproduced by French in *Life Records*. Letters prepared by Milton were published after his death as: *Literæ Pseudo-Senatûs Anglicani, Cromwellii, Reliquorumque Perduellium nomine ac jussu conscriptæ a Joanne Miltono*. [ornament]. *Impressæ Anno 1676*. The volume appears in two editions, whose order has been established by Bruce Harkness.[108] That with a device of a basket of fruit was the first edition, printed in Amsterdam by Peter and John Blaeu;[109] that with a device of a face was the second edition, printed perhaps in Brussels by E. Fricx.[110] Parker speculated that Daniel Elzevir printed the second edition on the basis of the face ornament; but not only is this not evidential, it is highly questionable in terms of prior attempts by Elzevir to get the papers into print. The date suggested for the first edition is late September or early October because of correspondence in late 1676 and 1677 concerning possible "corrective" publication. Apparently copies or drafts of these official papers in Milton's possession passed to his last amanuensis, Daniel Skinner, at his death. Skinner, attempting to acquire position and preferment, had tried to make arrangement for publication of the papers, among other items, but before such arrangement could be effected, it would seem, the first edition appeared. There is a statement concerning the matter by Skinner, dated October 18, 1676, preserved in the Public Record Office (1). Skinner had informed Samuel Pepys, Secretary to the Admiralty, and Sir Joseph Williamson, Secretary of State, of his intention to have the letters published, but Williamson blocked publication. After the papers were published from a manuscript different from Skinner's and apparently through Moses Pitt, a bookseller with whom Skinner had earlier attempted to bring about publication by Elzevir, Skinner wrote to Williamson suggesting that his more authentic collection be produced. But again Williamson refused and Skinner found himself in difficulties with Trinity College, Cambridge, where he had hoped to obtain a position. (Eventually he did receive an appointment but apparently through recantation of any views to be associated with Milton and perhaps through such gifts as the Trinity MS.) A series of letters, all of which have not been previously brought together in discussion of this matter, comment upon the situation: (2) Williamson to Sir Leoline Jenkins (Plenipotentary at Nimeguen), dated October 31, 1676; (3) Skinner to Pepys, dated November 9 (19), 1676, preserved in the Bodleian; (4) Elzevir to Williamson, dated November 10 (20), 1676, in the Dutch archives; (5) Williamson to a Mr. Chudleigh (Secretary to the Embassy at The Hague), dated November 28, 1676; (6) Williamson to R. Meredith, dated January 19 (29), 1677, in the Dutch archives; (7) Skinner to Pepys, dated January 28 (February 7), 1677, in the Bodleian;[111] (8) [Skinner's father to Elzevir, dated February 2, 1677, in which he apparently thanked Elzevir for sending him the manuscript, which he turned over to Williamson]; (9) Meredith to Williamson, dated February 5, 1677, in the Dutch archives; (10) another, dated

February 9, 1677, in the Dutch archives; (11) Elzevir to Skinner's father, dated February 9 (19), 1677, in the Dutch archives; (12) Meredith to Williamson, dated February 12, 1677, in the Dutch archives; (13) Isaac Barrow (Master of Trinity) to Skinner, dated February 13, 1677; (14) Meredith to Williamson, dated February 26, 1677, in the Dutch archives; (15) W. Perwich (agent for Williamson) to William Bridgeman (Williamson's secretary), dated March 15, 1677; and (16) Elzevir to Skinner, dated March 6 (16), 1677, in the Dutch archives.[112]

The 1676 edition gives 137 papers, dated between April 10, 1649, and May 15, 1659; these at least we can probably accept as Milton's work. However, it should be evident that we have no assurance that the text of 1676 has any better claim to being authentic than others which were in existence (see later), although most Miltonists have treated the edition as unquestionable. In fact, a number of dates are different from those on originals, or are incomplete, and some letters do not have so complete a salutation or close as copies found elsewhere. The significance of these papers lies first in biographical implications of what Milton was or was not doing at specific times as a result of his being Secretary; second, in whether there is any intrinsic importance in them; and third, in their relationship with Milton's other writing in rhetoric, style, or ideas. J. Max Patrick has pursued these latter two points in "Significant Aspects of the Miltonic State Papers," *HLQ*, 33 (1970), 321-30. With three exceptions Edward Phillips translated these papers into English and published them with the life of his uncle as *Letters of State* (London, 1694). The three omissions are a letter to Tuscany, dated May 22, 1651; one to Count de Bordeaux, dated August 1657; and one to the Parliament of Paris, dated September 1658 (?). An earlier anonymous translation had appeared in garbled version as: *Milton's Republican-Letters or A Collection of such as were written by Comand of the Late Commonvvealth of England; from the Year 1648. to the Year 1659. Originally writ by the learned John Milton, Secretary to those times, and now translated into English, by a Wel-wisher of Englands honour. Printed in the Year 1682.* Probably this volume was printed abroad, and, of course, the letters were not originally written by Milton. Another Latin edition appeared on the continent a few years later, with a preface by George Pritius, the apparent editor: *Literæ nomine Senatus Anglicani, Cromvvelli Richardique Ad diversos in Europa Principes & Respublicas exaratæ a Joanno Miltono, quas nunc primum in Germania recudi fecit M. Jo. Georg. Pritius. Lipsiæ & Francofurti, Sumptibus Jo. Caspari Mayeri. Typis*

Christiana Banckmanni. Anno MDCXC. And still another anonymous translation made clear that these letters were not written by Milton, but that he served as translator of materials written by members of the Council of State. It is entitled: *Oliver Cromwell's Letters to Foreign Princes and States, For strengthening and preserving the Protestant Religion and Interest* (London: John Nutt, 1700); it was advertised in the Term Catalogues for Trinity Term, 1700 (III, 200). The appendix (pp. 40-45), which discusses Milton's function, says that he was of *"Romish* stamp" but that he translated "(to give the Devil his due) admirably well." This edition prints only nineteen letters in a different order from that in 1676.

In succeeding years the collection was reprinted in complete editions of the works, often including Phillips' translation. The only separate edition thereafter is H. Fernow's in Hamburg in 1903. The volume was placed on the Roman Catholic Index of Books on November 23, 1694, according to F. Hamel in *The Library,* Third Series, I (1910), 368, and Parker (II, 1185), but December 22, 1700, according to *Appendix ad Indicem Librorum Prohibitorum Vero, & Accurato Alphabetico Ordine Disposita ab anno 1681. Usque ad mensam Junii inclusivè 1704* [Romæ: Cameræ Apostolicæ, 1704], pp. 347 and 361.[113]

Some of the letters had appeared prior to the publication of Milton's collection. The letter to Sweden, dated February 7, 1656, was included in *Literæ Ab Olivario Protectore Angliæ &c. Sacrum Regiam Majestatem Sueciæ Datæ 7 Februarij Anno M. D. CLVI.* Two pamphlets reproduced the letter to the United Provinces, dated August 21, 1656: *Apographum Literarum Serenissimi Protectoris Oliverii Cromwelli Quas scripsit ad Excelsos & Præpotentes D. D. Ordines Generales Fœderati Belgi Die 21/31. Augusti, 1656. Unà cum Responso eorundam Ordinum ad D. Protectorem Dato 22. Septembris 1656. Anno M. DC. LVI.,* and *Verax Prodomus in Delirium* (1656?), pp. 16-18. Samuel Morland's *The History of the Evangelical Churches of the Valleys of Piemont* (London: Henry Hills for Adoniram Byfield, 1658) printed eight items which are found in the 1676 edition. J. Milton French notes also that the letter to France, May 26, 1658, appears in a different version in V. E. P. Chasles' *Olivier Cromwell* (Paris, 1847), pp. 326-29.[114] Further, the letter to Geneva, dated June 7, 1655 (French, IV, 34, and V, 446-47), was noticed and summarized with some quotation by Isaac Spon in *The History of the City and State of Geneva* (London, 1687), p. 180. This was republished by Jacob Spon as *Histoire de Geneva, Par Mr. Spon. Rectifié & considerablement augmentée per d'amples Notes*

(Geneva: Chez Fabri & Barrillot, 1730), II, 588-91. Thurloe (VI, 479) gives a version of the letter to Sweden, dated August 20, 1657, in English.

Some of the Piedmont letters are given by William S. Gilly in *A Narrative of An Excursion to the Mountains of Piedmont, and Researches among the Vaudois, or Waldenses* (London, 1824), discussed on pp. 217-29. These are printed in Latin and English in Appendix 8, pp. cliii-clxxvii (seven items), and Appendix 9, p. clxxviii (two items). Morland's speech is also given within the text itself. Three state letters taken from the originals, it would seem, were published by Paul d'Estrée, "Lettres inedites d'Olivier Cromwell: une *Alliance Anglo-Françaises au XVIIe siècle*," *La Revue des Revues*, 33 (1900), 221-35; these are: to the United Provinces, dated May 25, 1655 (French, IV, 26), received June 5, 1655, pp. 226-27, in French; to France, dated July 31, 1655 (French, IV, 43), pp. 230-31, in French; and to Mazarin, dated May 20, 1658 (French, IV, 224-25), pp. 233-34, in French. Two state letters appear in Theophil Ischer's *Die Gesandtschaft der protestantischen Schweig bei Cromwell und den General-staaten der Niederlande 1652/54* (Bern: Buchdruckerei Gustav Grunau, 1916): one is a letter identical with that to the Swiss Cantons, dated November 28, 1653 (French, III, 348-49), on pp. 104-7, and one is dated January 10, 1654, beginning "Cum nobilis vir Johannes Jacobus Stoharus" [i. e., Stockart, a Swiss agent], on pp. 107-8.[115]

Daniel Skinner's manuscript omits thirteen papers included in the 1676 edition and gives fourteen not found in that edition; these are to Spain, April 27, 1650 (?); France, May 25, 1655; Savoy, 1656 (?); France, January 13, 1656; France, April 14, 1656; Mazarin, April 14, 1656; Passport for Romswinckel, June 13, 1656; Sweden, June 13, 1656; France, July 1, 1658; Mazarin, July 1, 1658; Portugal, April 1659; Tuscany, April 19, 1659; another of the same date; Sweden, April 15, 1659. The letter to France, January 13, 1656, appears in Thurloe's *State Papers*, IV, 415; another, May 25, 1655, is given in an English translation in Morland, pp. 564-65. Hamilton was the first to call attention to this manuscript and to print these fourteen papers. In addition he prints a letter to Hamburg, dated August 2, 1649 (French, II, 240-41), and Sir Samuel Morland's speech (French, IV, 29-30), and employs the manuscript to supply dates for various letters printed in 1676. The fourteen Skinner letters and that to Hamburg are accepted as Milton's; Morland's speech is not, and so is disregarded further in this survey. The speech, of course, is included in Morland's *History*, pp. 568-71.

A number of letters have been discovered in various repositories throughout the world; some are the original letters, some are contemporary copies.[116] Of those published in the first edition 80 originals or copies (including multiples) have been found, and 11 originals or copies (including multiples) of the fourteen additional Skinner items, as well as the original and a copy of that printed by Hamilton. Of the 152 letters noted above, originals or copies have been discovered for 63 individual letters. There are twenty further original or manuscript copies for twelve documents not otherwise given in 1676 or Skinner: translations of two letters from Princess Sophie (to Prince Rupert and to Prince Maurice), dated after April 13, 1649; Spain, January 21, 1651; Safeguard for Henry Oldenburg, February 17, 1652; Geneva, March 27, 1654; Mazarin, June 29, 1654; Geneva, June 7, 1655; Swedish Treaty, April 1656 (?); Bremen, January 16, 1657; Bremen, June 30, 1657; Sweden, June 30, 1659; Denmark, June 30, 1659. All except the two translations and the Safeguard have been considered questionable additions to the canon. The two translations are in the hand of Milton's nephew, John Phillips, and one has corrections by Milton himself. The Safeguard was published by J. J. Winkelmann in *Oldenburgische Friedens- und der benachbarten Oerter Kriegs-Handlungen* (Oldenburg, 1671), pp. 390-91; and in Thurloe, V, 192. The Swedish Treaty was given in outline by Thurloe, IV, 486-87, and printed by Samuel Pufendorf in *De Rebus a Carolo Gustavo* (Norimbergæ, 1696), pp. 221-22, with a date of July 17, 1656, and a reference to Milton on p. 219; in *Receuil de Traitez de Paix* (Amsterdam, 1700), III, 694-96 (No. 343); in *A General Collection of Treatys of Peace and Commerce, Renunciations, Manifestos, and other Published Papers* (London, 1732), III, 162-75 (in English); and in George Chalmers' *A Collection of Treaties Between Great Britain and Other Powers* (London, 1790), I, 29-43 (in English).

Another important manuscript is that in the Columbia University Library which omits three of the letters in the 1676 collection but which gives twenty additions. Of these, ten also appear in Skinner's manuscript: Spain, April 27, 1650 (?); Savoy, 1656; France, April 14, 1656; Mazarin, April 14, 1656; France, July 1, 1658; Mazarin, July 1, 1658; Portugal, April 1659; Tuscany, April 19, 1659; another of the same date; Sweden, April 25, 1659. Whether the remaining ten should be added to the canon is uncertain: they are all in English and four of them are translations of letters from Spain or Denmark.[117] Two items were included by Thurloe: a version of the letter to Algiers (Hamet Basha), dated April 1656, is given on I, 745, and the Instructions to Richard Bradshaw, dated April 1657 (?), appears on VI, 278-79.

Most of the preceding information on the papers themselves has been known and is given by J. Milton French under the dates of the documents. These dates are sometimes different from those attached to the 1676 printings, being altered by evidence of the originals, contemporary copies, Skinner's manuscript, and the like. However, various questions remain concerning dates, and of course there are some questions of attributions.[118] Patrick, in the *HLQ* article cited before, states that Milton's state papers number less than 300; yet the preceding number cited in French, including uncertain ones in the Columbia Edition, total only 174. Patrick's edition of the papers in the Yale *Prose*, V, ii, has recently appeared and here he has printed or noted only 175 items plus 3 miscellaneous papers; some of the 174 counted separately before are grouped together and some of his 175 are multiple items. Patrick omits nine of the preceding: Spain, January 21, 1651 (II, 345); Tuscany, May 22, 1651 (III, 32, duplicate of No. 29 [III, 149-50]); Damages against the Dutch (III, 225-26), see pp. 599-600; Mazarin, June 29, 1654 (III, 402-3); Geneva, June 7, 1655 (IV, 35); Bremen, January 16, 1657 (IV, 132); Bremen, June 30, 1657 (IV, 167-68); Sweden, June 30, 1659 (IV, 272-73), see p. 871; Denmark, June 30, 1659 (V, 454). A number of new manuscript versions are reported, drawn often from the Nalson Papers in the Bodleian, the Marten-Loder Papers in the Brotherton Library (Leeds), the Tanner MSS in the Bodleian, the Baker MSS in Cambridge University Library, and the Calendar of State Papers (Domestic and Venetian) in the Public Record Office.[119] He lists or prints fourteen additional items:[120] 1) Hamburg, April 2, 1649, No. 2; 2) translations of letters from the Dutch Ambassadors, ca. May 18, 1649 (II, 251), No. 4 (unknown); 3) Tetuan, ca January 30, 1650 (II, 292-93), No. 9 (unknown); 4) Anglo-Portuguese negotations, February 10, 1651 ff., No. 26 (Latin versions unknown); 5) Spain, June 1651 (III, 33, 51), No. 27 (English versions given); 6) paper from the Dutch Ambassadors, January 24, 1652 (III, 156), No. 30 (unknown); 7) Dutch Ambassadors, January 30, 1652, No. 31; 8) Dutch Ambassadors, January 30, 1652 (III, 156), No. 32; 9) reply to Dutch Ambassadors' thirty-six articles (III, 207-8), No. 38; 10) paper of demands from Dutch Ambassadors, March 15, 1652 (III, 214, 216-17), No. 39 (unknown); 11) paper from Dutch Ambassadors, April 20, 1652 (III, 214), No. 44 (unknown); 12) the Declaration against the Dutch (III, 232-33), No. 47 (see my discussion of this item later); 13) the Declaration against the Spanish (IV, 48-49), No. 84 (see my discussion of this item later); 14) the final form of No. 149 to Mazarin (IV, 225), given as No. 150. Patrick has also been able to alter or affirm certain dates as given by French: see Nos. 7, 8, 18, 20, 21, 22, 23, 24, 28, 33, 37, 42, 43, 45, 49, 50, 54, 55, 59, 60, 61, 62, 82, 83, 85, 86, 96, 118, 120, 122, 123, 133, 134, 146, 147, 148, 149, 159, 162, 170, Miscellaneous 1. No. 143 also makes a differentiation between the earlier and the later forms in terms of date: March 30, 1658, and April 2, 1658. Nonetheless, questions do exist about the evidence for redating; for example, no reason is given for the month and day attached to No. 45; no reason whatsoever is advanced for the dating of No. 118. Other uncertainties also exist; for example, Patrick does not mention a manuscript copy of No. 93, but French cites Abbott (IV, 137-38) as having found it in the Archives in Paris (if it doesn't exist, Patrick should have corrected Abbott and French); no manuscript copy is noted for No. 160, although French quotes from it. And should the negotiations with the States-General, given in the Nalson Papers, be treated like the Anglo-Portuguese negotiations? See XVIII, Nos. 83 (2), 87, 88, 89; Thurloe included copies of four of these items: I, 179 (2), 181, 183. Patrick does not mention these items which were read before the Council of State on July 2, 1651.

However, none of the work on the letters, including the edition of Cromwell by Abbott, explores certain volumes which include some of the letters, at times with differing dates and expanded or varied salutations and closes. Some of these volumes include letters which, by their presence with accepted Milton pieces, may fall into the area of possible ascription. In 1692 Gregorio Leti published an important, albeit antagonistic, biography of Oliver Cromwell in two volumes in Italian. It was reprinted or translated into Dutch, French, and German in 1692, 1694, 1696, 1703, 1706, 1708, 1710, 1714, 1720, 1728, 1730, 1744, 1745, 1754, 1794-95, and yet it has not been employed by Milton and Cromwell scholars to review such matters as we are discussing here. Perhaps Abbott did not use it as a source for the letters because he considered it "Largely fabulous." Leti includes 49 state letters, all of which appear in *Literæ*; their order is by date, except that errors are made, particularly in new and old styles. The letters are given in Latin in 1692; later editions sometimes translate some letters (even giving two versions) and sometimes omit or summarize others. The second volume of the first edition is: *Historia, e Memorie recondite sopra alla vita di Oliviero Cromvele, Detto il Tiranno senza vizi, il Principle senza virtu. Parte Seconda* (Amsterdam: Pietro e Giovanni Blaev, 1692). The letters with reference to French's *Life Records* and with notes of differences follow:

Portugal (French II, 297-98), pp. 64-65.

Spain (II, 297), 66-67.

Spain (II, 297), 67-68.

Portugal (II, 300), 69-70.

Austria (II, 303), 70-72.

Hamburg (II, 258-59), 78-80.

Hamburg (II, 304-5), 103-4; dated April 2, 1649, in error; signed by John Bradshaw, President of the Council, which is not indicated in any other known copy.

Andalusia (II, 330), 104-5; dated November 7, 1649, in error.

Danzig (II, 348), 105-6.

Portugal (II, 306), 186-88.[121]

Spain (II, 318), 189-90; dated November 28, 1650. French dates June 28, 1650, on the basis of *Literæ*.

Tuscany (III, 149-50), 266-67; dated October 17, 1651. French gives January 20, 1652, from *Literæ*, but note another copy (III, 32), dated May 22, 1651.

Venice (III, 317-18), 273-75; dated February 14, 1652. French gives only February 1652 (from *Literæ*), and Parker (*Life Records*, V, 438) suggests that this was the letter ordered by the Council on February 2. In addition *Literæ* gives only the signature "Concilii Præses," whereas Leti specifies William Masham.

Cardenas (III, 210; V, 435), 275-77; dated March 21, 1652, as is *Literæ*. In addition Leti again specifies the signatory as William Masham.

Swiss Cantons (III, 348-49), 333-36; dated October 29, 1653. *Literæ* has October 1653; Skinner, October 8; the official letter, November 28.

Sweden (III, 414-15), 361-63; dated July 4, 1654 as in *Literæ*. It is August 29 in the original and two manuscript copies; Skinner has July 11.

Haro (III, 416-17), 370-71; dated July 13, 1654, which seems much too early. *Literæ* has September 1654, and Skinner, September 4.

Oldenburg (III, 404), 374-75; dated February 7, 1654. *Literæ* dates June 27, 1654, but the original and copies in Skinner, Columbia, Rawlinson A.261 give June 29, 1654. On the other hand a contemporary copy at Oldenburg is dated as in Leti.

Tarente (IV, 22), 375-76; dated June 26, 1654. French dates April 4, 1655, on the basis of *Literæ* (no day) and Skinner. This letter appears in further eighteenth-century volumes with Leti's specific date.

Transylvania (IV, 33-34), 405-8; dated July 23, 1655. *Literæ* has May 1655 and Rawlinson A.261, May 31.

France (IV, 43), 408-10; dated May 18, 1655, in obvious error since it refers to a letter of May 25. French dates July 29 or 31, 1655.

Denmark (IV, 27-28), 411-12; dated May 23, 1655. *Literæ* and Morland have May 1655, except that the heading for the copy in Morland is May 25.

Savoy (IV, 24-25), 413-16; dated May 26, 1655. *Literæ* has May; Skinner May 10; Morland and a manuscript copy have May 25.

Geneva (IV, 34), 423-25; dated June 8, 1655, as in *Literæ*. The original has June 7.

Swiss Cantons (IV, 60-61), 425-27; dated February 23, 1655. *Literæ* has January 1655.

Denmark (IV, 74), 428-30; dated April 14, 1655. Masson conjectured February 1656, which French gives; but Abbott (III, 692-93), without citing evidence or reasons, dated the letter April 14, 1655, as in Leti. Leti gives an ending (apparently the only version that does): "Majestatis Vestræ Studiosissimus OLIVERIUS Reip. Angliæ, Scotiæ, Hyberniæ, &c. *Protector.*Westmonasterio. April. 14. 1655."

Sweden (IV, 74-75), 430-31; dated April 28, 1655. French dates February 7, 1656, on basis of original and copy in *Literæ Ab Olivario Protectore*; but note that this pamphlet next gives a letter from Emperor Ferdinand dated August 24, 1655.

Venice (IV, 53), 431-32; dated December 16, 1655. Abbott conjectured the same date.

Mazarin (IV, 44), 454; dated December 26, 1656. French dated July 29 or 31, 1655, from *Literæ* and a letter to the king of similar date. This letter also appears in further eighteenth-century volumes, again with specific date.

Russia (IV, 141-42), 461-63; dated April 26, 1656. *Literæ* has April 1657, and a contemporary copy, April 10.

France (IV, 224), 490-91; dated May 24, 1658. See French for discussion of what appear to be a draft and a letter, which he dates May 20, 1658 (?), on the basis of the date of a related document. The Leti copy is in disagreement with the date given by Patrick.

Mazarin (IV, 225), 491-92; dated May 24, 1658. See French for discussion of what appear to be two drafts, which he dates May 20, 1658 (?), on the basis of the date of a related document. The Leti copy is in disagreement with the date given by Patrick.

France (IV, 229), 498-99; dated June 26, 1658. A contemporary copy has June 19, 1658, and this was Abbott's conjecture; Masson had suggested June 16-21.

Mazarin (IV, 229-30), 499-500; dated June 26, 1658. On the basis of the preceding letter, this is also dated June 19, 1659 (?), by French.

France (IV, 226-27), 504-7; dated May 26, 1658. The same date is given by Morland and by Chasles.

Mazarin (IV, 29), 507-9; undated, but apparently out of chronological order at this point. French dates May 25, 1655 on basis
of original letter.

Tuscany (IV, 220), 511-12.

Sweden (IV, 228), 518-19; dated June 29, 1658.[122] *Literæ* has June
1658; the official letter, June 4.

France (IV, 234), 561.

Mazarin (IV, 234-35), 561-62; dated September 5, 1658. *Literæ*
has September 1658 and a contemporary copy, September 6.

Sweden (IV, 239-40), 562-63; dated September 22, 1658. *Literæ*
has October 1658.

Sweden (IV, 240), 563-64; dated October 3, 1658. *Literæ* has
October 1658.

West Friesland (IV, 250), 564-65.

France (IV, 255), 565-66.

Mazarin (IV, 255), 566-67; dated February 23, 1659. French dates
February 19, 1659 (?), on the basis of Phillips, Skinner, and
Columbia; *Literæ* gives February 29.

Portugal (IV, 256), 567-68;[123] dated March 17, 1659. French
gives the date as February 23, 1659, on the basis of *Literæ*.

Mazarin (IV, 256), 569-70; dated March 25, 1659. Dated February 22, 1659, in *Literæ*, Skinner, and Columbia; Phillips has February 25.

Sweden (IV, 264-65), 579-80.

Denmark (IV, 265-66), 580-81.

It is obvious that Leti did not take his citations from the 1676 edition in view of so many differences, supplied dates and endings, and
the like. His dating may be in error at times, but at times it is cor-
roborative of dating in other sources and of conjectures. That he
should include forty-nine authenticated items from a different source
is most significant. Without question Leti's work should have been
consulted in the past to avoid some of the questions over these state
letters that persist in French's *Life Records*. The source of Leti's
copies should be investigated, for what is suggested is that another
manuscript of Milton's state papers had been available before 1692.

Various letters also appear in Johan Christian Lünig's *Literæ
Procerum Europæ, ab Imperatoribus, Electoribus, Principibus,
Statibusque Sacri Imperii Romano-Germanici . . . Ab Anno 1552
Usque ad Annum 1712 . . . Lipsiæ: Apud Jo. Frider, Gleditsch &
Filium. Anno MDCCXII*, three volumes. Leo Miller made this dis-
covery and reported his findings (on which I here depend) in *N&Q*,
17 (1970), 412-14. Interspersed by date throughout the work are

115 letters printed in the Columbia Edition. Among the omissions
in Lünig are letters found in Leti, and among the omissions in the
Skinner and Columbia MSS are letters found in Lünig. Thus these
all come from independent sources. There are also several letters
that have not been assigned to Milton, although correspondence
between Parliament and the Dutch in April and May 1653 (Lünig,
Nos. 168, 169, 170, 171, 176) certainly sounds as if it should be
further investigated. Differences from the texts in *Literæ* exist. The
letter to Russia (IV, 141-42) gives the czar's name, Alexius
Michaelowitch; the letter to Portugal (IV, 231) gives the king's
name, Alfonso VI, and another (IV, 256) says correctly "Alphonso
Portugalliæ Regi." The two letters to Portugal written by Richard
(IV, 256, 258) inaccurately address the former (dead) king, John IV.
(Incidentally, the Columbia Edition and French erroneously talk
of Alfonso V.) Dates are sometimes more explicit than in *Literæ*:
the letter to Sweden (IV, 74-75) is dated February 13, 1656, but
February 7 in the original; the letter to Denmark (IV, 74) is dated
February 1656, which was Masson's conjecture; the letter to
Portugal (III, 412) is dated February 1656, though French uses
July 25, 1654, from Rawlinson A.260; the letter to the United
Provinces (IV, 110-11) is dated August 21, 1656, as in the original;
the letter to Austria (III, 410-11) is dated August 1658, which is
the date in Skinner, but French chooses July 18, 1654, from Rawlinson A.260. The letter to Sweden (IV, 264-65) is given, but instead of the letter to Denmark (IV, 265-66) immediately following,
Lünig has the letter to Sweden (IV, 272-73), dated June 30, 1659,
and found in the archives in Stockholm.[124] The version here shows
variants. The numerous differences from the *Literæ* texts and the
use of courtesy signatures make clear that a different source produced these letters. In addition the way in which the complimentary
closes are set up suggest that the printer set from actual drafts of
the letters, made ready for affixing of the seal and the signature.

Other volumes incidentally giving state papers are the following.
Roger Coke published at least one Milton item in *A Detection of
the Court and State of England* (London, 1694), rptd., 1696, 1697,
1719: Damages against the Dutch, dated June 10, 1652 (French,
III, 225-26), II, 16-17; there are also two letters to the Dutch, to
be dated around April 1, 1652 or 1653. French dates the Damages
"June or July (?)"; had he known of this printing, he would have
been less suspicious that this is not at least part of the answer to the
Dutch envoy Adrian de Pauw, which he notes as "before June 11 (?)."
Coke would seem not to have used *Literæ*. John Oldmixon referred
to and quoted from a number of letters in *The History of England,
During the Reigns of the Royal House of Stuart* (London: for J. Pem-

berton et al., 1730): 1) Portugal (II, 297-98), 378; 2) Austria (II, 303), 378; 3) Hamburg (II, 258), 379; 4) Spain (II, 318), 385; 5) Mazarin (IV, 44), 412, dated December 26, 1656, as in Leti; 6) Savoy (IV, 24-25), 409 of second set of pages (should be p. 413); 7) Tarente (IV, 22), 422-23, dated June 26, 1654, as in Leti; 8) France (IV, 234), 428 of second set; 9) Mazarin (IV, 234-35), 428 of second set; 10) Sweden (IV, 239-40), 428 of second set; 11) Sweden (IV, 240), 428 of second set; 12) West Friesland (IV, 250), 428 of second set; 13) France (IV, 255), 428 of second set. Nos. 5 and 7 indicate that Oldmixon did not draw the letters from *Literæ*; probably he used Leti since all these letters do appear there.

Isaac Kimber's *Life of Oliver Cromwell, Lord Protector of the Common-Wealth of England, Scotland, and Ireland. Impartially Collected from the Best Historians, and Several Original Manuscripts* (London: for J. Brotherton and T. Cox, 1731), "The Third Edition with Additions," refers to Milton as secretary, p. 283, and proceeds to give the letter to the Prince of Tarente, same date as in Leti, on pp. 283-84, and to translate it on pp. 284-85.[125] *A General Collection of Treatys of Peace* (1732) includes a letter to Sweden from Cromwell, dated July 15, 1656, along with the Swedish treaty already cited. This is the date of Cromwell's signature on the treaty. Should the letter be looked at as possibly Milton's? In Daniel Neal's *History of the Puritans or Protestant Non-Conformists* (London: for Richard Hett, 1732-38), IV, there are letters to the Prince of Tarente, dated as in Leti, on p. 126; to Savoy, dated 1655 (French, IV, 24-25), in English, on p. 144; and to Mazarin, dated December 28, 1656 (as in Leti except for a slightly different day), in English on p. 161. Neal's work was frequently reprinted in the eighteenth and nineteenth centuries. Francis Peck included letters to the Portuguese agent (French, II, 334), pp. 3-4, and John IV of Portugal (French, III, 412), p. 10, in *Memoirs of the Life and Actions of Oliver Cromwell* (London, 1740). William Harris in *Historical and Critical Account of the Life of Oliver Cromwell* (London: for A. Millar, 1762), p. 304, quoted the letter to the Spanish ambassador in English concerning attendants at mass (French, III, 311-12); there were further editions. *A Collection of Treaties of Peace, Commerce, and Alliance, between Great-Britain and Other Powers, From the Year 1619 to 1734* (London: for J. Almon and J. Debrett, 1781) cited the treaty with Sweden on pp. 90-91. A different edition, *A Collection of All the Treaties of Peace, Alliance, and Commerce, Between Great-Britain and other Powers, From the Treaty signed at Minister in 1648, to the Treaties signed at Paris in 1783* (London: for J. Debrett, 1785), also gives the Swedish treaty on I, 98-100. Chal-

mers' collection of treaties (1790) also includes with the Swedish
treaty letters dated July 15, 1656.

Among the state papers often alleged to have connection with Milton are two manifestos, one dealing with Holland in 1652 and the
other with Spain in 1655. We cannot admit these to the canon at
this time, and there are those who would reject them totally.
Patrick cites both in the Yale *Prose*, as has already been stated.
But Parker's view that there is "no valid reason" for assigning
such work to Milton or that this authorship is "most unlikely"
strikes me as a curious attitude directed toward all the state papers.
Parker seems to want to dismiss all real consideration of such work
as not representing significant composition on Milton's part, but
rather as mere translation of someone else's work or as graphic
reduction of someone else's ideas. They may be only this, but we
cannot assume that this is so until all such work is examined along
with non-Miltonic state papers of the same period to determine
likenesses and differences. We must determine what is "Miltonic"
(if anything) and assess this as contribution to the political milieu.
What is needed is a full stylistic analysis of these items, a tool which
also may go a long way in ascertaining whether a specific item is admissible to the extended canon.[126] In any case, a biographer should
welcome evidence of the activities of his subject, and these two
specific manifestos are particularly significant in Milton's biography
because of their dates. If they are Milton's, then we must recognize
1) that here is another piece of evidence which shows that in July
1652, after his total blindness of February, the death of his wife
and birth of another daughter in May, and the death of his son in
June, Milton was engaged in governmental service and was not in
the total bereaved retirement that sometimes has been alleged, and
2) that in October 1655, he was also engaged in governmental
service and not so unemployed as has been thought from August 8
(the date of *Pro se Defensio*) through mid-December 1655 (the date
of state letters to the Doge of Venice and Louis XIV of France).[127]
   *A Declaration of the Parliament of the Commonwealth of England,
Relating to the Affairs and Proceedings between this Commonwealth
and the States General of the United Provinces of the Low-Countreys*
was published by John Field apparently on July 9, 1652, after having
been accepted by the Council of State on July 7.[128] The manifesto
contains a narrative of recent Anglo-Dutch diplomatic activities,
letters and speeches by Adrian de Pauw, the Dutch agent in England,
replies to him and votes by the Council of State. There was a separate printing of the *Declaration* in Leith by Evan Tyler soon after.

An order to turn it into Latin, French, and Dutch was given on
July 13, and an order for the printer William Dugard to talk to Milton about printing the manifesto (in such translation) was recorded
on July 20. The Latin translation appeared as *Scriptum Parlamenti
Reipublicæ Angliæ De iis quæ ab hac Repub. cum Potestatibus
Fœderatarum Belgii Provinciarum Generalibus, & quibus progressi-
bus acta sunt* on July 29, 1652, from Dugard's press. (Thomason
dated his copy in August.) The orders of the Council do not require
that Milton was the Latin translator. There may have been two issues
or states (see Columbia, XVIII, 503). Hamilton first suggested Milton's probable authorship;[129] see also Masson, IV, 447, 482. Various
editions of the *Declaration* appeared on the continent in 1652, all
translated from the English according to their title pages: one in
Danish was apparently published in Copenhagen (undated); one
Dutch translation appeared in Amtserdam [*sic*]; a different translation occurs in three editions in the same year; a third translation is
found in two editions from Rotterdam; and a fourth translation,
published in The Hague by I. Iansz, is undated; of two German
editions (different translations), one was published by Caspar Erffens
in Cologne; an Italian translation appeared in Florence; and a French
version entitled *Declaration Dv Parlement de la Repvblique d'Angleterre, sur les differans d'entr'elle & les Etats Generaux des Provinces-
Vnies des Païs bas* was published on November 8, 1652.[130] It was
reprinted in French as "Manifeste des Anglois, au suject de la
même Guerre dont il est parle dans le même," that is, the declaration sent to the "Etats Généraux des Provinces-Unies," in Raguenet's
Histoire d'Olivier Cromwel (1691), pp. 333-42. No date is given, but
August 2, 1652, is recorded for the date of the Dutch reply. The
Dutch two-volume edition gives the "Manifeste" in II, 183-99. It
appears in Latin in *Recueil de Traitez de Paix* (Amsterdam, Chez
Henry et la veuve de T. Boom, a la Haye, Chez Andrian Moetjens
et Henry van Bulderen, 1700), III, 620-22, as "Manifeste du Parle-
ment d'Angleterre contre les Provinces-Unies des Pays-bas, publié
de 31. Juillet, 1652." *The Declaration* was also published as "The
English Parliament's Manifesto against the United Provinces of the
Netherlands, Publish'd July 31, 1652," in *A General Collection of
Treatys of Peace* (1732), III, 36-44; see also the reference in the
introduction, pp. ix-x.

Two issues of the other manifesto are listed from London in
1655; the title pages read:

*A Declaration of the Lord Protector of the Commonwealth of
England, Scotland, Ireland, etc., published by the advice and with
the consent of his Council; in which the cause of the Common-*

wealth against the Spaniards is shown to be just.

A Declaration of His Highness, By the Advice of His Council; Setting forth, On the Behalf of this Commonwealth, the Justice of their Cause against Spain. Friday the 26th of October, 1655.

These were both printed by Henry Hills and John Field around October 16, 1655, the date of an order from the Council for publication. The latter issue was reprinted in Edinburgh by Christopher Higgins, within a day or two of the London publication. A Latin version soon appeared as *Scriptum Dom Protectoris Reipublicæ Angliæ, Scotiæ, Hiberniæ, &c. Ex consensu atque sentantiâ Concilii Sui Editum; In quo hujus Reipublicæ Causa contra Hispanos justa esse demonstratur,* printed also by Henry Hills and John Fields. Masson dated this version November 9, Columbia says about December 9, and Patrick gives November 23. A Spanish version published by the English, otherwise unnoted, is owned by the Newberry Library: *Manifiesto de Protector de Inglaterra, Hecho con accuerdo de su Consejo, declarando à fabor desta Republica, la Iustiçia de su Causa contra España. Traduçido del Ingles en Español. Viernes à 26. de Ottubre 1655, estilo viejo. Se ha ordenado por su Alteça el Señor Protector y Consejo que esta Declaraçion se estampe y publique luego. Firmado. Henrrique Escobel, Secretario del Consejo. Londres, Impreso por Henrrique Hills y Juan Field, Estampadores de su Alteça. 1655.* A Dutch translation is mentioned by Joseph Jane in letters of November 23 and 26, and although French says that such an edition is not recorded, there were two:

> *Declaratie ofte Manifest van syn Hoocheyt door advijs van Synen Raedt, Thoonende . . . de rechtveerdicheyt van haer sake tegens Spaengien. Getranslateert uyt het Engels* [The Hague?], *1655.*

> *Een Manifest, ofte een Declaratie . . . vertoonende in den name van dese Republijcque, de gerechtigheyt van hare saeck tagen Spaengien. Amstelredam, voor J[an] Hendricks en J[an] Rieuwertsz, 1655.*

A German version, perhaps from November or December, was published in 1655 as *Manifest oder Erklärung vorgebracht bey seiner Hochheit dem Protector Olivier Cromvel, von seinem Rathen, In dem Nahmen der Republic, die Gerechtigkeit derselben gegen Spanien betreffend. Aus der Engellandischen in die Hochdeutsche Spraach übersetzt. Im Jahr M. DC. LV.*

The Latin translation was first attributed to Milton by Thomas Birch in his edition of the prose (1738), I, xxxiv, where it is reprinted in Latin and English. In this same year the bookseller Andrew Millar published the document as *A Manifesto of the*

Lord Protector of the Commonwealth of England, Scotland, Ireland, &c. Published by Consent and Advice of his Council. Wherein is shewn the Reasonableness of the Cause of this Republic against the Depredations of the Spaniards. Written in Latin by John Milton, and First Printed in 1655, now translated into English. The ascription to Milton and the implication that this was the first English version, derived from the Latin version, are noteworthy. The original English and the foreign language translations from it, of course, need not owe anything to Milton. Another edition was put out for T. Cooper in 1741, entitled, *A true Copy of Oliver Cromwell's Manifesto Against Spain, Dated October 26, 1655,* in English, with a reference to Milton in the preface, p. [v]. This edition is supposed to be taken from the original manuscript in English, according to the editor. Richard Baron's revision of Birch's edition of the prose in 1753, of course, continued to reproduce both the Latin and English texts. And John Banks, in *A Short Critical Review of the Political Life of Oliver Cromwell* (London, 1739), discussed the document and quoted from its English version on pp. 223 ff. (This volume was frequently reprinted.) It is included in the Columbia Edition as well as the Yale *Prose.*

Two main questions surround the posthumous work published in 1681 for Henry Brome as *Mr John Miltons Character of the Long Parliament, and Assembly of Divines. In MDCXLI. Omitted in his other works, and never before Printed. And very seasonable for these times.* First, why was this passage from Book 3 of *History of Britain* not published in 1670 and by whom was it struck out? and second, how complete and reliable is the text? Certainly, as Masson (VI, 806-12) and Parker (II, 940) indicate the publication is curious, particularly such a relatively short time after 1670, and the passage was as seasonable then as in 1681. Parker suggests that it was Milton himself (Masson even raises the question of authorship) who omitted the passage as a digression into a criticism of events, an inappropriate aside for an objective history.[131] The problem of text exists because of a manuscript in a scribe's hand owned by Harvard University and entitled, "The Digression to com in Lib. 3 page 110 after these words [from one misery to another]" (12 pp.). After "Digression" a different and much later hand has added "in Miltons History of England." The text is somewhat longer than the published form and contains a number of variations. The orthography of the edition is often standardized as comparison with the same words in the manuscript shows.[132] Nonetheless both exhibit spelling both like and unlike Milton's. The tract refers to the confusion of the then Long Parliament toward the end of the civil wars in 1648, largely during the first four months of the year. The spelling which agrees with Milton's practices (in both forms of the work) can be dated after middle 1646, and thus we can conclude that this work was probably originally in Milton's holograph, being written during 1648, perhaps early in the year, and well before work as Secretary to the Council of State limited his time. What the relationship between the manuscript and the printed edition is cannot be determined with certainty, but perhaps it was something like this: Milton's holograph became the source directly of the manuscript and a revised copy, from which the 1681 version was taken, or Milton's holograph became the source for a copy, from which the manuscript and the 1681 text, revised for publication, both derived. The date of the extant manuscript lies after 1670 because of the specification of the page on which the insertion was to be made; the statement is contemporary with the text.

The volume is dated April 1681 since it is listed in the Term Catalogues (I, 443) for Easter Term, 1681, and is briefly summarized and discussed in *Heraclitus Ridens*, No. 10, April 4, 1681.[133] John Moore quoted from it twice in 1698 (see note 67). It was first reinserted in *History of Britain* by Thomas Birch in 1738. It was reprinted three times in the *Harleian Miscellany*, V, 540-43, in 1745; V, 576-79, in 1810, the ten-volume edition published for John White et al., and V, 37-41, in 1810, the twelve-volume edition published for Robert Dutton. Francis Maseres called it "Reflections on the Civil War in England" and published it in *Select Tracts Relating to the Civil Wars in England in the Reign of King Charles the First* (London: R. Wilks, 1815), II, 805-15. It is edited with annotations separately from *Britain* in the Yale *Prose*, V, i, by French Fogle, who records the differences between the 1681 printing and the manuscript, on pp. 458-65.

Among the posthumous works is *A Brief History of Moscovia: and Of other less-known Countries lying eastward of Russia as far as Cathay. Gather'd from the Writings of several Eye-witnesses. By John Milton. London, Printed by M[iles] Flesher, for Brabazon Aylmer at the Three Pigeons against the Royal Exchange. 1682.* Since it is listed in the Term Catalogues (I, 472) under Hilary Term, 1682, it is dated February (?). But Phillips attached "Oct." to his listing but no year date, and Wood, probably confounding the two, gives the same month plus the year. Aside from the question of the date of composition and the sources, the history has attracted comment on the reason for its being written, its methodology, and its artistry.[134] Cawley and Parks view it primarily as travel literature, but a successful compendium of its sources, and Bryant and Gleason pay attention to its historical nature, the latter generally condemning it as inchoate.[135]

Obviously there will be questions of date with posthumous materials. Aylmer's advertisement in the volume, if accurate, and there is no reason to doubt it, tells us that the history was written by the author's own hand before he lost his sight, and that Milton had disposed of it to be printed before his death. The reason for delay in publication might have been a questionable market, but more probably, it would seem from Aylmer's remarks attached to *Epistolarum Familiarium* that its brevity was the cause. In the previous decade various works about Muscovy had appeared—for example, *The Present State of Russia, Written in a Letter to a Friend in London, by Dr. Samuel Collins, who resided at the great Czar's Court of Mosco for the Space of nine years* (London: John Winter, for Dorman Newman, 1671) and Sir R. M.'s *The Russian Impostor, or the History of Moscovy, under the Usurpation of Beris, and the Imposture of Demetrius, late Emperors of Moscovy* (London: J. C., for T. Basset, 1674, Ed. 1; 1677, Ed. 2)—which helped create a market. The date of blindness was February 1652, but Milton seems not to have been writing anything extensive in his own hand after 1649. Because of his governmental duties a *terminus ad quem* may be March 1649. Hanford guessed that it might have been written during the Horton period, I presume only because of Milton's studious retirement at that time. Lloyd E. Berry, finding relationships with Giles Fletcher's work on Moscovy, suggested 1632–38,[136] the years implied by Hanford. Others have assumed a connection between Milton's tutoring and this project: Bryant proposed 1639-41; Mirsky, the early 1640s; Shawcross, 1642-early 1643 or at least middle 1644;[137] Parker (I, 325; II, 938-39), 1648. Parks would date it between October 6, 1649, and January 8, 1650, because of what he argued was the diplomatic occasion for the work. Milton was not reading the kind of material before 1639 that is compiled in *A Brief History*: Hanford's and Berry's assignments of date seem to have no substance. Parks's main argument is tenuous at best, and the date offered is in conflict with Milton's governmental activities and his steadily increasing disability. My dating is based on what seem to be Milton's orthographical practices, some of which are not in evidence from his hand after the middle of 1644. It should be noticed that the most important source for *Moscovia* was Samuel Purchas's *Hakluytus Posthumus or Purchas His Pilgrimes, Contayning a History of the World in Sea Voyage and Lande Travells, by English-*

men and Others(1625), and that Milton's three citations from him in the Commonplace Book are dated 1642-44 (?) by Miss Mohl; see pp. 13 and 57. Parker's reasoning for 1648 depends upon the first apparent "vacant" time before governmental service when Milton might have worked on this history; upon its possible inception along with *The History of Britain*, allegedly begun in 1648; and upon Theodore Haak's comment to Samuel Hartlib recorded in 1648 that Milton was writing a universal history of England as well as an epitome of all Purchas's volumes (identified with *Moscovia*).[138] However, there were other "vacant" times; *Britain* may have been begun quite independently; and as Parker notes, *Moscovia* was apparently already completed by the time Haak informed Hartlib. During 1642-middle 1644, aside from familial matters and tutoring, Milton seems to have been "free" in April 1642-June 1643 (allowing composition of *Doctrine and Discipline of Divorce* in July-August 1643), September 1643-December 1643, and March 1644-May 1644 (allowing composition of the enlarged *Divorce* in January-February 1644 and *Of Education* in June 1644). This is a total of twenty-two "free" months. The date of *A Brief History of Moscovia* can not, therefore, be settled at this time, but in any case the years 1642 through early 1648 seem more certain than any others, and I would urge that the evidence of orthography and citing of Purchas in the Commonplace Book constitute stronger external reasons than any other for a date of 1642-middle 1644.

Jodocus Crull seems to allude to the volume, here and there, for example in I, [xii], in *The Antient and Present State of Muscovy, Containing a Geographical, Historical and Political Account Of all Nations and Territories Under the Jurisdiction of the Present Czar* (London: for A[bel] Roper and A. Bosvile, 1698), and he uses Chapter IV for his Chapter XII.[139]

De doctrina christiana was discovered by Robert Lemon in 1823 among the papers of the Public Record Office; it was published two years later in Latin and in English by Charles R. Sumner: *Joannis Miltoni Angli De Doctrina Christiana Libri Duo Posthumi, Quos Ex Schedis Manuscriptis Deprompsit et Typis Mandari Primus curavit Carolus Richardus Sumner* (Cantabrigiæ: Typis Academicus excudit J. Smith, 1825); and *A Treatise on Christian Doctrine, Compiled from the Holy Scriptures Alone . . . Translated from the Original by C. R. Sumner* (Cambridge: Cambridge University Press, by J. Smith for C. Knight, 1825), with notes on the translation. The translation was immediately reprinted in two volumes by Cummings, Hilliard, and Co., in Boston. The Latin edition was reprinted by E.

Fleischer in Brunswick, Germany, in 1827. The translation has been the basis for editions and studies since that time, despite its inexactness here and there and its confusion of some terms. It was slightly revised by Sumner for John St. John's Bohn edition of the prose in 1853 (there is an added account of other documents found by Lemon) and in the Columbia Edition. A new translation by John Carey has just appeared in the Yale *Prose;* the work was edited by Maurice Kelley.

The manuscript consists of 745 numbered pages, pp. 625-35 being given twice. Of these, 196 were copied by Daniel Skinner presumably from the copy in the hand of Jeremy Picard, the scribe of the remaining pages. Revisions and additions are also in the handwriting of at least five other people. The date at which the treatise may have been begun is uncertain, and even its completion date (that is, if it is as complete as Milton would have wished it) can not be definitely decided. The Anonymous Biographer's comments lend themselves to the belief that it was begun after the three defenses and finished after the Restoration. That it may have been worked on in a different form (for example, as a theological index similar to the extant Commonplace Book) has been suggested, but such a view seems to be most unanalytic; see later. The preface suggests that there were two stages in its composition. The first was apparently around 1645-46, being "A Perfect System of Divinity" noted by Phillips; the second, around 1655-60. At least the manuscript in some form was "completed" around 1658-60, for Picard seems to have been employed by Milton then (and only then as far as we know, although there may be evidence of a connection between them around 1655; see the discussion under the Commonplace Book). Picard's work is a transcription, which suggests 1) that a manuscript recording an earlier stage of the work existed and 2) that the copy in Picard's hand was considered "finished." The revisions and additions in the extant manuscript and the kind of copying that Skinner did do not indicate further development after Picard's work, that is, after 1660. No important points of doctrine are altered. Skinner seems to have worked for Milton in only the very last years of Milton's life. That Milton was working on the treatise in the later part of the 1650s is certain, however, since he employed Brian Walton's Polyglot Bible published in 1657.[140]

Possibly there had been a move to publish the treatise after Milton's death, but if so, it ran afoul of authorities and subsequently the document disappeared for a century and a half. Among the papers which Daniel Skinner was able to divert in 1674 were *De*

doctrina christiana and the state papers; the action against these
papers by the authorities in England and the reluctance of the
Dutch publisher, Daniel Elzevir, relegated the treatise to its long
oblivion even though the state papers were finally published (with
no connection with Skinner, it would seem) in 1676. The publication of the treatise in 1825 and its effect are related by Kelley in
"The Recovery, Printing, and Reception of Milton's *Christian
Doctrine*," *HLQ*, 31 (1967), 35-41.[141] The primary reaction, voiced
by W. Ellery Channing[142] and Henry John Todd,[143] concerned the
anti-Trinitarian beliefs (erroneously called Arian beliefs by many
commentators) which were discerned in the treatise. Such views
did not square with most people's reading of *Paradise Lost*.[144]
Other reviews of the publication generally speculated similarly
or agreed with the author of "Milton on Christian Doctrine,"
North American Review, 22 (1826), 364-73, who found the work
useful as a general survey of scriptural matters but who was highly
critical of Milton for pursuing such unacceptable views. A survey
of the question is found also in *Opinion de Milton sur la Trinité*
(Paris, 1842). The publication of Milton's treatise was also the
stimulus for the popular "life" of Milton by Thomas Babington
Macauley in *Edinburgh Review*, 84 (1825), 304-46, frequently
reprinted as a separate volume.

Maurice Kelley, an adherent of the anti-Trinitarian interpretation,
set off the controversy of the last twenty-five years with his views
in *This Great Argument*--views that were challenged by William B.
Hunter, Jr., in "Milton's Arianism Reconsidered," *HTR*, 52 (1959),
9-35. The scholarship on the question is long and involved; see
Kelley's most recent statement, "Milton and the Trinity," *HLQ*,
33 (1970), 315-20, for references to most of the ensuing discussions.
Bright Essence, a collection of previously published essays by J. H.
Adamson, W. B. Hunter, Jr., and C. A. Patrides on the subject and
arguing against labelling *De doctrina christiana* anti-Trinitarian, has
recently appeared. Related to this problem is the harmony or
conflict between the treatise and *Paradise Lost*. The documents
seem to have been worked on at the same time (1655?-60?), although the poem was finished in 1660-65. The basic examinations
of the treatise and this question are Arthur Sewell's *A Study in
Milton's Christian Doctrine* (London: Oxford University Press,
1939; rptd., Hamden: Shoe String Press, 1967) and Kelley's *This
Great Argument*, which frequently corrects Sewell. Nonetheless
both remain important studies of the *Treatise* and Milton's thought.
See also Patrides' *Milton and the Christian Tradition* (Oxford:
Clarendon Press, 1966). A not very successful analysis of the treatise,

limited by a Roman Catholic bias, is J. Th. Eisenring's *Milton's De Doctrina Christiana: An Historical Introduction and Critical Analysis* (Fribourg: Society of St. Paul, 1946).

A number of selected versions exist: 1) *John Milton's Last Thoughts on the Trinity. Extracted from His Posthumous Work, A Treatise on Christian Doctrine* (London: Printed by Richard Taylor, sold by Rowland Hunter, 1828);[145] 2) another (Boston: William Crosby and H. P. Nicholas, 1847); 3) a reprint, *John Milton's Last Thoughts on the Trinity Extracted from His Posthumous Work Entitled A Treatise on Christian Doctrine New Edition* (London: E. T. Whitfield, 1859); 4) *Milton On the Son of God and the Holy Spirit, from his Treatise on Christian Doctrine* (London: for British and Foreign Unitarian Association, 1908), with an Introduction by Alexander Gordon; rptd., London: P. Green, 1908; and 5) Merritt Y. Hughes' annotated selections in *Prose Selections* (1947) and *Complete Poems, and Major Prose* (1957).

Milton's collection of notes and citations from some of his reading, generally in his own hand, known as the Commonplace Book was found in 1874 at Netherby Hall, Longtown, Cumberland, and published by Alfred Horwood in facsimile in 1876 and in an edition in the same year; a correction of this edition appeared in 1877. It has since been published with translations in the Columbia Edition and in English only in the Yale *Prose,* edited by Ruth Mohl. None of the transcriptions is without fault. The disposition of the manuscript after Milton's death is uncertain; it passed from Daniel Skinner, Milton's last amanuensis, or from Edward Phillips to Sir Richard Graham, Viscount Preston, who made many entries in the volume. Netherby Hall was the ancestral seat of the Grahams.

Mohl's description of the notebook (I, 345 and n. 6) follows Horwood's and is confusing: the notebook consisted of five quires of 25 leaves each plus a covering sheet (or two leaves), that is 127 leaves, or [2] + 250 + [2] pages; two unnumbered pages, pages numbered 1-250, and two unnumbered pages [251-52]. Milton or his amanuensis wrote on 74 pages, including pages with two division titles but no notes, a page (20) with a one-word false heading start, and the index ([251]); Lord Preston wrote on 14 pages not used by Milton; 134 pages still exist in blank form;[146] 30 pages have been cut away (as well as the lower halves of pages 1-14); and the front cover leaf has disappeared. The leaves were divided into natural sections for each of the Aristotelian categories of knowledge employed: the Index Ethicus used two quires, or 100 pages, its title being given on p. 1 and the first subdivision being given on

p. 4; the Index Œconomicus (domestic or social matter) used a quire and a half (thirteen of the leaves, that is), or 76 pages (pp. 101-76), its title being given on p. 101 and the first subdivision on p. 105; and the Index Politicus used a quire and a half (twelve of the leaves, that is), or 74 pages (pp. 177-250), its title being given on p. 177 and the first subdivision being given on the same page. The volume index was kept up for all subheadings in each division.

The name Commonplace Book for Milton's manuscript, a title given to it by Horwood, signifies that it is a collection of *topoi* or topics to be employed as proofs in an argument. The implication in Milton's development of such a collection is that he was planning to employ such topical proof in one or more works—not just as a record of things that interested him as he read. Those few scholars who have discussed the notebook seem to write from the belief, often enough, that Milton was incidentally, even haphazardly, entering items which might somehow serve him in the future. But a total view of the notebook and an analysis of contents does *not* lead me to wonder why certain things or authors are not included (a frequent enough speculation by others); it does lead me to recognize that the schematization of knowledge which Milton was achieving had a definite purpose for the future, one involved in asserting liberty and Christian virtue and in examining the sources of servitude and wrong reason. And this purpose was to be a work or works which would encompass all of man's knowledge and history. Eventually it emerged as *Paradise Lost,* but its path is laid out and paved by the stones of religious, domestic, and political freedoms. If we can dispel the thought that Milton simply recorded material which struck him as potentially interesting as he read without a fairly clear though far-off view, we can realize that the Commonplace Book yields evidence of the preparation of a Milton to "leave something so written to aftertimes, as they should not willingly let it die." I can square this concept of his Commonplace Book only with his decision to become a poet.

We can thus note that "literary" matter was cited for "information" or attitudes, not because of literary subject, techniques, or evaluation, as citations from Chaucer and Boiardo, for example, show. "Literary" entries are few, undoubtedly because their substance (such as material from Shakespeare) did not fit into the schematization that Milton had undertaken. The same would be true of the Bible. There are no entries from Scripture, and this has caused unnecessary uneasiness on the part of some commentators. Not only would Milton know his Bible well, but he was not engaged in setting down the kind of philosophic and metaphoric ideas or history which the Bible would supply. This view of the omission of scriptural citations should be considered in discussing twelve references to a theological index and in speculating upon the origin of what came to be *De doctrina christiana*.

On the basis of handwriting, apparent order of entry, and editions used, the Commonplace Book has been examined for dating by James Holly Hanford,[147] Ruth Mohl,[148] and William R. Parker.[149] Refinement of some representative dates has been suggested by the present author,[150] but no further reexamination has been published. The date when Milton first employed the Commonplace Book has been placed variously from "about 1636" (Hanford, p. 286 or p. 103), from about 1631 (Mohl, pp. 348-49), and "late 1634 or, at least, 1635" (Parker, II, 801).[151] Without any evidence or clear-cut reason offered, the preceding have assumed that Milton's studious retirement (1632-35? at Hammersmith; 1635?-1637/8? at Horton) must have produced the need for this Commonplace Book. But an examination of the entries and their suggested dates and attention to the purpose of the notebook and Milton's activities lead me to a quite different conclusion.

Of the entries made prior to the European trip, Mohl gives the dates 1635?-37? for 20 citations; 1635?-38? for 5 citations; 1635?-39? for 1 citation; and 1637?-38? for 29 citations; that is, all might be dated from 1637 onward, and only 26 are suggested as possibly lying before that date. It is illogical to suggest that so few entries were made before 1637 during the studious retirement, and over a possible two years at that, particularly when 29 seem to have been made in ca. 1637-38 (Milton went to the continent in April 1638) and roughly 200 were made in ca. 1639-41 (he returned somewhere around August 1639). The point makes even more ludicrous Mohl's suggestion of 1631 and Parker's of late 1634.

If my contention that the Commonplace Book was begun because of Milton's decision to become a poet and if my argument that such decision was made ca. September 1637 are correct,[152] then it can be dated as having been started in the fall of 1637. Corroborating that date are the earliest entries which, as we have seen, could all have been written in 1637 according to Hanford and Mohl's listings. Further corroboration may be garnered from Milton's two letters to Charles Diodati (now dated November 1637) in which he discusses his reading program and his plans. The question of the small writing on which Hanford based his differentiation of entries between 1635?-37/8/9? and 1637?-38?, and which Parker makes much of, disappears if my contention that the Trinity MS was also begun around this time be accepted, for one need only compare those Commonplace Book entries with the manuscript copies of the three English odes, the pasted leaf of "Comus," and the drafts of a letter to an unknown friend. At least the handwriting is smaller than usual and similar to that recording the Greek (primarily) in the Commonplace Book. The nature of the two manuscripts may also account for certain differences of handwriting style.

In addition to Milton's holograph entries, the Commonplace Book contains entries by various amanuenses, the latest entries by Milton being dated by Mohl ca. 1647/48. Amanuensis A was John Phillips;[153] Amanuensis B was Edward Phillips (see Hanford); Amanuensis C was Jeremy Picard (see Hanford); and the so-called Machiavelli scribes were apparently only John Phillips.[154] The Phillips's boys' work has been dated 1650?-52?, but identification of John Phillips allows that an earlier date is possible. Picard's work has been cited as 1658?-60?, but we cannot be certain when he began to work for Milton. An audit concerned with the Piedmont Massacre and made for Sir Samuel Morland in the middle of 1655 is in Picard's hand and suggests that Milton's connection with him was through governmental relationships.[155] Amanuensis D (who penned the manuscript of Book I of *Paradise Lost*), Amanuensis E, and Amanuensis F have not been identified. That the Commonplace Book should have continued to have been used much after 1650/1 for only a few scattered items seems odd. But the dating here really depends on the identity of the scribes and what we can learn of their association with Milton. For example, we do not find the hand of the scribe of the Bradshaw letter or the copies of and corrections to sonnets in the Trinity MS, dated around February 1653. Or, a different kind of example, the two entries of Amanuensis D have generally been considered to date close to 1665 when the manuscript of *Paradise Lost* in his hand may have been produced; but interestingly and without explanation Mohl lists 1650-67? for that on p. 197 from Dante's "Purgatorio" although she gives ca. 1665 for that on p. 249 from Nicetas Acominate, which must have been entered after 1647 since this is the date of the edition used. Perhaps our upward limit for the Commonplace Book should be revised.

The question of a theological index is raised by twelve references on pp. 12 (2), 109, 112, 151, 183 (2), 197, 221, 244, 246 (2). It is supposed that Milton must have kept a corresponding index for such matters and that it may have furnished the foundation for *De doctrina christiana*. These references lie after 1639 (on the basis of handwriting), and thus so may any index developed. The references to *De Bonis Ecclesiasticus*, according to the suggested dating of surrounding entries, indicate the index's existence after 1641 and before 1646-48; those to *De Idolatria*, after 1641; that to *De Conciliis,* probably after 1641 and probably before 1647; that to *De Religione non Cogenda,* in Edward Phillips' hand, before the date of the entries from Machiavelli's *Discorsi*; that to *Papa,* after 1641; those to *Ecclesia*, probably after 1644. The references, therefore, suggest that a theological index existed at least by 1647 and possibly as early as 1641. There is no evidence that it existed as a companion index during the first years of existence of the extant Commonplace Book; suggested is that the theological index began later as a kind of afterthought, allowing for more specialized and focussed categories. There is one reference to a page number for the theological index; see p. 221 where *Papa* is cited as being on p. 42 in another index.

The theological index, from what one can infer from the subdivisions listed and from the extant indices, would have stressed matters which otherwise would have fallen under the categories of the Index Ethicus or the Index Politicus. Why such items were not, at least at first, entered into the extant Commonplace Book is curious, yet they could not have been because no such entries are given on the index on p. [251] and entries there were made at the same time that pages were begun in the volume. Perhaps the theological index was begun during the period when Milton was engaged in antiprelatical controversy (from mid-1641 on) or later when he moved into discussion of divorce (from mid-1643 on) or even later still when he may have been working on poetic statements of his ideas of man's fate and of true liberty (from 1646 on). Possibly one reason why entries in the extant Commonplace Book decline after 1644 is that much of the kind of reading and kind of entry recorded fell under a more generally "theological" classification. This may account for the sparseness of entries by amanuenses also. In any case the omission of scriptural citations would probably have continued in the kind of theological index described by the references to it that we have. It thus seems unlikely to me that this theological index was directly a source for *De doctrina christiana.*[156] Rather what seems a more valid possibility is that need for a compendium of scriptural proof became evident to Milton as he worked with this index, or, later, as he examined doctrinal questions through his reading of people like Wolleb and Ames or his early work on *Paradise Lost.* (See also William B. Hunter's discussion of *De doctrina christiana* in the present collection of essays.)

The only extensive study of the Commonplace Book, aside from those dealing with text and date, is Mohl's *John Milton and His Commonplace Book* (New York, 1969). The notes on law in the Columbia MS and printed in the Columbia Edition and the Yale *Prose* show nothing to recommend them as Milton's.

Important collections of Milton's prose, some of which have been noted earlier, are listed below in order to complete this survey of the prose. Most tend to be complete, often giving translations of the Latin works. These, however, are not annotated, although a note may be given here or there, with the notable exception of the Yale *Prose*. Annotations in selected prose collections, e. g., by Hughes and Patrick, cited before, as well as in individual twentieth-century editions of specific items are and have been significant in leading readers to an understanding of the prose.

1) *The Works of Mr. John Milton. Printed in the Year MDCXXVII* [London]. Includes *Doctrine and Discipline of Divorce, Tetrachordon, Colasterion, Bucer, Reformation, Reason, Civil Power, Hirelings, Episcopacy, Animadversions, Apology, Ready and Easy Way, Areopagitica, Tenure* (Ed. 2), *Brief Notes, True Religion, Eikonoklastes, Observations.* Most items have individual simulated "title pages" usually dated 1697. Perhaps produced as rival to the forthcoming 1698 edition, some of the individual title pages of which are dated 1694. There seems to be no connection between this and the registry of rights (Stationers' Register, III, 345) by Awnsham Churchill on January 30, 1689: "Tracts of John Million [*sic*] of Divorce, Colasterion, Tetrachordon, Areopagitica, Notes on Griffith Sermon, True Religion, Heresy &c, Observaçons on Jicsk [*sic*] peace, pro populo Anglicano, et Salmatij Lat & Eng: defensio secundo lat Engl; pro se contra Moram lat; Engl; epistola familiares lat & Eng on Rawleigh' Cabinet counsell Johannis Phillipis Angl responsio. Lat & Engl, Lrē Cromwelianee, Lat & Engl, of Rimerius herelius [*sic*], of civill power." The licenser was Ro[bert] Midgley.

2) *A Complete Collection Of The Historical, Political, and Miscellaneous Works of John Milton, Both English and Latin. With som Papers never before Publish'd. In Three Volumes. To which is Prefix'd The Life of the Author, Containing, Besides the History of his Works, Several Extraordinary Characters of Men and Books, Sects, Parties, and Opinions. Amsterdam* [i. e., London], *Finish'd in the Year M. DC. XC. VIII.* Three vols.: two of English works or translations, one of Latin.[157] Note "Finish'd"; individual title pages are dated 1694-98, indicating publication plans over at least a four to five year period. The

Life, dated September 3, 1698, although one passage dates after that time, is by John Tonson, and thus the publication has erroneously been called Tonson's edition. The *Life* was registered to John Darby, Jr., on December 15, 1698 (III, 485); it was published separately in 1699. Apparently the publishers were more than one, but they are unidentified, unless they should prove to be Awnsham and John Churchill. Some sets are bound in two volumes; the Latin third volume is often found without the other two. Pagination is erratic; it is separate for each volume. Includes the first printing of *A Letter to a Friend* and *The Present Means*; a slightly revised and augmented *Britain* purportedly reflecting changes made in a copy by Milton; John Phillips's *Responsio* as well as Joseph Washington's translation of *A Defence of the People of England*. Omits *Character of the Long Parliament*.

3) *A Complete Collection of the Historical, Political, and Miscellaneous Works of John Milton: Correctly printed from the Original Editions. With an Historical and Critical Account of the Life and Writings of the Author; Containing several Original Papers of His, Never before Published. In Two Volumes. London: Printed for* A[ndrew] *Millar . . . M. DCC. XXXVIII.* The editor was Thomas Birch; the volume was published on March 1; the preliminary remarks make use of the Trinity MS, here first noted in print. Includes *Scriptum dom. Protectoris* (Latin and English), as well as Washington's translation of *Defensio prima* and Phillips' *Responsio*; inserts *Character of the Long Parliament* into *Britain*.

4) *The Works of John Milton, Historical, Political, and Miscellaneous. Now more correctly printed from the Originals, than in any former Edition, and many Passages restored, which have been hitherto omitted. To which is prefixed, An Account of his Life and Writings. London: Printed for A. Millar, in the Strand. M. DCC. LIII.* [Vol. II: for W. Innys et al. and A. Millar.] Revision of (3) by Richard Baron.[158]

5) *The Prose Works of John Milton; with a Life of the Author, Interspersed with Translations and Critical Remarks, by* C[harles] *Symmons*, 7 vols. (London: J. Johnson, 1806). First full English translation of *Defensio secunda* by Robert Fellowes.

6) *The Prose Works of Milton, Containing His Principal Political and Religious Pieces, with New Translations and an Introduction by George Burnett*, 2 vols. (London: Miller, 1809). First English translation of *Pro se Defensio*.

7) *The Prose Works of John Milton; with an Introductory Review*

by R[obert] *Fletcher* (London: [Westley & Davis], 1833). Frequently reprinted; index added to *Britain* in edition published by William Bell, 1838.

8) *Milton. I. Prose Works. II. Poetical Works,* 2 vols. in one, derived from (7) (Paris: A. and W. Galignain, [1836]).

9) *The Prose Works of John Milton, with a Biographical Introduction. Edited by R*[ufus] *W. Griswold,* 2 vols. (Philadelphia: Hooker, 1845). Frequently reissued or reprinted.

10) *The Prose Works of John Milton . . . With a Preface, Preliminary Remarks, and Notes, by J. A. St. John* (London, [1848]-81), "Bohn's Standard Library." Frequently reprinted; vol. IV includes a revised edition of Sumner's translation of *De doctrina christiana.*

11) *The Works of John Milton in Verse and Prose, Printed from the Original Editions with a Life of the Author by the Rev. John Mitford,* 8 vols. (London: William Pickering, 1851); reissued 1863, 1867. Adds some state papers; lacks *De doctrina christiana* and other items.

12) *The Prose Works of John Milton,* 2 vols. (Philadelphia: Caxton Press, 1864).

13) *The Prose Works of John Milton* (New York: Hurst and Co., [1885]).

14) *The Works of John Milton,* gen. ed., Frank A. Patterson, eighteen vols. in twenty-one (New York: Columbia University Press, 1931-38). Only complete edition, with foreign language texts and English translations. First printing of "Proposalls of certaine expedients," certain state papers, and similar items; includes "A Postscript."

15) *Complete Prose Works of John Milton,* gen. ed., Don M. Wolfe, six vols. in eight to date (New Haven: Yale University Press, 1953-   ). Complete except for foreign language texts, which are given in translation only. Fully annotated.

16) *Prose Works, 1641-1650,* 3 vols. (Menston: Scolar Press, 1967-68), in facsimiles of early editions. All prose works within above dates except "A Postscript" and "Observations."

Aside from such biographical studies as Masson's *Life,* Stern's *Milton und Seine Zeit,* and Parker's *Biography,* the following are most helpful for a study of the prose: Auguste Geffroy, *Étude sur les pamphlets politiques et religieux de Milton* (Paris, 1848); Harris F. Fletcher, *The Use of the Bible in Milton's Prose* (Urbana, 1929); Don M. Wolfe, *Milton in the Puritan Revolution* (New York, 1941), rptd., 1963; Arthur Barker, *Milton and the Puritan Dilemma, 1641-1660* (Toronto, 1942); and Helmut Heinrich, *John Miltons Kirchen-*

politik, puritanische Ideen zum Problem Staat und Kirche (Berlin: Junker und Dünnhaupt, 1942), as well as introductions in the Yale *Prose*. In progress is a computerized concordance to the prose, using the text of the Yale *Prose*, under the general editorship of Laurence Sterne.

During the nineteenth and twentieth centuries particularly a number of volumes have presented selections or brief collections, some of which have been noted before. Such volumes are cited in Stevens, Fletcher, or Huckabay, although one wishes that a descriptive list of inclusions had been given for each volume. Here I cite a few noteworthy volumes not mentioned earlier:

1) "Aréopagitique, par Milton, traduit de anglais, 1644; De l'éducation, par Milton, traduit de anglais, 1650," in *Bibliothèque étrangère, par M.* [Etienne] *Aignan* (Paris, 1823), vol. 2. The date for *Education* is not explainable.

2) "John Miltons prosaische Schriften über Kirche," in *Historisches Taschenbuch*, III, Nos. 3 and 4, ed. F. von Raumer (Leipzig, 1852-53). Reprinted in *Geschichte des Reformations-Zeitalters*, ed. Georg Weber (Leipzig, 1874), pp. 398-616.

3) *Autobiography of John Milton; or Milton's Life in His Own Words*, ed. J. J. G. Graham (London, 1872).

4) *John Miltons Politische Hauptschriften. Übersetzt und mit Anmerkungen versehen von Wilhelm Bernhardi*, 3 vols. (Berlin and Leipzig, 1874); rptd., 1876, 1879. These are pamphlets dated 1871-79.

5) *Miltons pädagogische Schriften und Äusserungen*, ed. Jürgen Bona Meyer (Langensalza, 1890), including *Education*, four letters, and parts from *Areopagitica* and the church pamphlets.

6) *Of Education; Areopagitica; The Commonwealth, by John Milton; with Early Biographies of Milton, Introduction, and Notes*, ed. Laura E. Lockwood (Boston, [1911]); rptd., London, 1912.

7) *Milton's Prose Selected and Edited with an Introduction by M. M. Wallace* (Oxford, 1925); frequently reprinted.

8) *The Student's Milton, Being the Complete Poems of John Milton, with the Greater Part of His Prose Works*, ed. Frank A. Patterson (New York, 1930); revised, 1933.

9) *Milton on Himself. Milton's Utterances Upon Himself and His Works*, ed. John S. Diekhoff (New York, 1939); rptd., 1965; London, 1966.

Notes

1. *Complete Prose Works of John Milton*, gen. ed. Don M. Wolfe, 6 vols. to date (New Haven: Yale University Press, 1953-   ).

2. 5 vols. (New Brunswick: Rutgers University Press, 1954-58).

3. 2 vols. (Oxford: Clarendon Press, 1968).

4. It has been argued that "A Postscript" added to *An Answer to a Booke entituled, An Humble Remonstrance,* by Smectymnuus, dated March 1641, since it was entered in the Stationers' Register on March 20 (I, 16), was written by Milton. Masson, Hale, Wolfe, and the present author have advanced reasons for this assignment on the bases of parallels, the nature of the material cited, similarities between the sources and source references of "A Postscript" and citations in Milton's Commonplace Book, style, and spelling. See David Masson, *The Life of John Milton* (London, 1871), II, 238; Will T. Hale, ed., *Of Reformation* (New Haven, 1916), pp. liii-liv; Don M. Wolfe, "A Postscript," Yale *Prose,* I, 961-65; John T. Shawcross, "What We Can Learn from Milton's Spelling," *HLQ,* 26 (1963), 358-59; and "The Authorship of 'A Postscript,'" *N&Q,* 13 (1966), 378-79. Opposed to this assignment have been Whiting and Fixler on the basis of seemingly contradictory statements concerning Milton's reading of Martin Bucer in "A Postscript" and *The Judgement of Martin Bucer.* See George W. Whiting, "Milton and the 'Postscript,'" *MLR,* 30 (1935), 506-8, and Michael Fixler, *Milton and the Kingdoms of God* (Evanston, 1964), p. 112 n. The volume, published by John Rothwell, publisher also of Milton's *Reason of Church-Government* and *An Apology,* is in two states of signatures and pagination, so that "A Postscript" appears on pp. 85-94 (sigs. M-N) and (corrected) pp. 95-104 (sigs. N-O). It was reprinted as *Smectymnuus Redivivus* in 1654 with a preface by Thomas Manton; "A Postscript" appears on pp. 71-78. The volume was reissued in 1660 (twice), 1661, and 1669; again the publisher was John Rothwell. It was registered on August 16, 1660. A sixth edition appeared in Edinburgh in 1708 from the press of John Moncur; "A Postscript" is given on pp. 69-75, sig. K.

5. William Riley Parker and Arthur Barker individually suggested that the friend was Milton's former tutor Thomas Young; see *TLS,* May 16, 1936, p. 420, and "Milton's Schoolmasters," *MLR,* 32 (1937), 517-36, respectively.

6. See William R. Parker, "Contributions Toward a Milton Bibliography," *The Library,* Fourth Series, 16 (1935-36), 425-38.

7. Variant states may particularly be noted by the resetting of two lines on p. 6 through the deletion of "the" before *"lost Truth"* and the inclusion of "Lib. I" in running heads on pp. 2, 3, 6, 7. The Bodleian presentation copy (4^0 F.56.Th.) has holograph corrections.

8. See "Printers of the Mind: Some Notes on Bibliographical Theories and Printing-House Practices," *SB,* 22 (1969), 1-75, and compare the discussion of Ed. 2 of *Doctrine and Discipline of Divorce* later.

9. *A Catalogue of the most vendible Books in England* (London, 1658), sig. p^v. The pertinent listing is reproduced by Parker in *Milton's Contemporary Reputation* (Columbus, 1940), p. 94, and by French, II, 177-78. French erred in dating the catalogue, and the entry should be transferred to II, 237; see French, V, 452. Lon-

don assigned the works in the catalogue specifically to Milton. Further references to materials given under date by French will not be cited unless a special problem is noted.

10. *The Prose of John Milton,* gen. ed. J. Max Patrick (New York: Doubleday Anchor, 1967), pp. 41-92.

11. The reader should consult the analyses of contents and contexts of each of the prose works by William Riley Parker in his important biography of Milton, as well as David Masson's still indispensable *Life;* Arthur Barker's *Milton and the Puritan Dilemma, 1641-1660* (Toronto: University of Toronto Press, 1942; rptd., 1956); and Don M. Wolfe's *Milton in the Puritan Revolution* (New York: Nelson, 1941; rptd., Humanities Press, 1963).

12. See Robert F. Duvall, "Time, Place, Persons: The Background for Milton's *Of Reformation," SEL,* 7 (1967), 107-18.

13. See Leo Miller, "Peloni Almoni, Cosmopolites," *N&Q,* N.S. 7 (1960), 424.

14. See Gilbert Chinard, ed., *The Commonplace Book of Thomas Jefferson, a Repertory of His Ideas on Government,* Johns Hopkins Studies in Romance Literature and Languages, Extra Vol. II (Baltimore, 1926), pp. 384-85. An excerpt appears in the first Miltonic work printed in the Colonies, *Hirelings,* entitled *An Old Looking-Glass* (Philadelphia, 1770; New Haven, 1774), pp. 50-70. Extracts from *Of Reformation, Reason of Church-Government,* and *Areopagitica* are printed in *The Christian Examiner,* 3 (1826), 120-24, 186-89, mentioned here since David H. Stevens' *Reference Guide to Milton* and Harris F. Fletcher's *Contributions to a Milton Bibliography* do not list them.

Indeed, a complete and more exacting bibliography of Milton for the years 1800-1928 is needed, as anyone who has gone beyond general use of these two volumes must know. Other early allusions also exist, such as Henry Burton's *A Vindication of the Churches, Commonly Called Independent,* 1644, three editions, p. 41. which refers to the divorce controversy; not all early editions of others' works are specifically cited here.

15. Emerson, p. 38.

16. Oulton apparently set sig. A (pp. 1-8), and Dexter, sigs. B and C (pp. 9-24). See Parker, "Contributions," and Shawcross, "Milton's Spelling," pp. 357-58.

17. Note particularly the variant "Whither" on the title page and "Ttm." in the margin of p. [2], which is changed to "Tim." Although not previously noticed, there were two issues of this tract, one with a cancel of sigs. [ ]3-4 between pp. [8]-9.

18. See J. Max Patrick, "The Date of Milton's *Of Prelatical Episcopacy," HLQ,* 13 (1950), 303-11.

19. See George W. Whiting, "Milton and Lord Brooke on the Church," *MLN,* 51 (1936), 161-66.

20. Parker, "A Cancel in an Early Milton Tract," *The Library,* Fourth Series, 15 (1934), 243-46.

21. Shawcross, "Milton's Spelling," pp. 356-58.

22. Parker, "A Cancel."

23. Parker pointed this out, and Hugh C. H. Candy, in a letter to *The Library,* Fourth Series, 16 (1935), 118, noted that the 1697 printing of the prose does not indicate such a cancel.

24. See Parker, "Milton, Rothwell, and Simmons," *The Library,* Fourth Series, 18 (1937), 89-103.

25. Ralph Haug, ed., Yale *Prose,* I, 738, offers August 4, 1641-before Janu-

ary 1, 1642; J. George, "Milton's *Reason of Church Government*," *N&Q*, 3 (1956), 157, argues (unconvincingly) that it could not have been written before late November.

26. Parker, "Milton, Rothwell, and Simmons," p. 94, suggested that the printer may have been T. C. who printed *Smectymnuus Redivivus* for Rothwell in the same year; see note 4.

27. See Claud A. Thompson, "Milton's *The Doctrine and Discipline of Divorce*: A Bibliographical Study" (Ph.D. diss., University of Wisconsin, 1971), pp. 14-18.

28. See Thompson, pp. 18-91.

29. The first real distinction that there were four editions of the tract rather than two, the second of which supposedly had two further issues, was made by Parker in *Milton's Contemporary Reputation*, pp. 272-73. The remarks on the text by Lowell Coolidge in the Yale *Prose* are uninformed and the text presented is inadequate and unusable. Besides Thompson's study, see the review article by G. Blakemore Evans, "The State of Milton's Text: The Prose, 1643-1648," *JEGP*, 59 (1960), 497-505.

30. See John T. Shawcross, "One Aspect of Milton's Spelling: Idle Final 'E'," *PMLA*, 78 (1963), 502, n. 4.

31. Thompson, pp. 96-99. The compositors of Ed. 3 frequently changed the spelling of Ed. 2.

32. See Thompson, pp. 111-27, for likenesses to and differences from Ed. 3.

33. *The Correspondence of Samuel Richardson* (London, 1804), VI, 198.

34. *John Miltons Abhandlung über Lehre und Wesen der Ehescheidung mit der Zueignung an das Parlament vom Jahre 1644. Nach der abgekürtzen Form des George Burnett.*

35. "One Gentle Stroking: Milton on Divorce" (Ph.D. diss., New York University, 1962).

36. "Milton's *Doctrine and Discipline of Divorce*," *Nineteenth Century*, 69 (1907), 127-35.

37. "The Date and Occasion of Milton's First Divorce Tract," in *English Domestic Relations* (New York: Columbia University Press, 1917), pp. 225-31.

38. See "Bibliography of Milton," *The Library*, 10 (1909), 17.

39. Frequently reprinted; the fourth edition, printed for W. Meadows (1750), gives the tract on pp. 126-48. The edition of this translation in 1721 does not include Milton's work. An allusion to Milton is found in the anonymous introduction, p. 6.

40. Parker lists an edition in 1753 (no other information), but this I have not discovered; it is not cited by John W. Good in *Studies in the Milton Tradition* (Urbana, 1915) or listed in the British Museum Catalogue.

41. *Nieuwjaaregift aan de Jufferschap . . . Waar agter Gevoegd is een Brief, over de Opvoeding van Jonge Heeren, van den vermaarden Heer John Milton* (n.p., n.d.).

42. According to Good, a German translation was printed in 1752 and 1781 in German editions of the poetry, but I have not found this to be so.

43. *Daniel Georg Morhofens Unterricht von der teutschen Sprache und Poesie* (Kiel, 1682), pp. 568-69; rptd., Lübeck, 1700, II, 4.

44. See Parker, "Contributions," pp. 425-38.

45. See John T. Shawcross, "The Date of the Separate Edition of Milton's *Epitaphium Damonis*," *SB*, 18 (1965), 262-65.

46. Parker (II, 890) simply repeated French's error (II, 114-15) by saying it was the other way around. See the

facsimile edition or Ernest Sirluck's note in the Yale *Prose* (II, 515).

47. See G. H. Turnbull, *Hartlib, Dury and Comenius* (London, 1947), p. 41.

48. See *G. Richteri, JC. Ejusque Familiarum, Epistolæ Selectiores* (Nürnberg, 1662), p. 491.

49. *A General Dictionary, Historical and Critical: In which a new and accurate translation of that of the celebrated Mr. Bayle is included* (London: J. Roberts, 1775), ed. John Peter Bernard, Thomas Birch, and John Lockman, cites Milton in discussing Blount's *Just Vindication* (III, 401 n.).

50. Both adaptations were reprinted in *The Miscellaneous Works of Charles Blount Esq.* ([London], 1695). See the analyses of the debts of all three items by George F. Sensabaugh in *That Grand Whig Milton* (Stanford, 1952).

51. The Preface was also reprinted in *New Foundling Hospital of Wit . . . A New Edition, Corrected, and Considerably Enlarged* (London: for J. Debrett, 1784), IV, 197-205; rptd., 1786 (twice); and in Sidney Humphries' edition of the tract (London, 1911); reissued, 1912; rptd., 1913.

52. For items published in the Colonies or drawn from writers in America, also see George F. Sensabaugh, *Milton in Early America* (Princeton: Princeton University Press, 1964).

53. Parker, "Milton, Rothwell, and Simmons," pp. 99-100.

54. Shawcross, "Spelling," pp. 355-56. Parker notes a difference in paper stock between sigs. A-F and sigs. G-O; but the spelling evidence disagrees with the implication that the compositor of sig. A also set sigs. B-F.

55. Ibid.

56. See my article, "Milton's 'Tenure of Kings and Magistrates': Date of Composition, Editions, and Issues," *PBSA*, 60 (1966), 1-8.

57. See ibid., pp. 2-3.

58. There may also be influence throughout in an anonymous pamphlet entitled *Tyranny no Magistracy, or A modest and Compenious Enquirie into the nature, and boundaries of that Ordinance of Magistracy. With an essay to Demonstrate it's specifick distinction from Tyranny. By an Enemy to Tyranny and lover of true Magistracy . . . Printed in the Year 1687.*

59. Gauden acknowledged his authorship in a letter to Edward Hyde, Earl of Clarendon and Lord Chancellor, on January 21, 1661; see *Clarendon State Papers* (London, 1786), III, Supplement, pp. xxvii-xxx. It was printed in Thomas Wagstaffe's *A Vindication of King Charles* (1697), pp. 20-22.

60. It was reprinted in *Memoirs of the Two last Years of the Reign of that unparallell'd Prince, of ever Blessed Memory, King Charles I* (London: for Robert Clavell, 1702), pp. 241-99.

61. A different edition in two volumes appeared in the same year in Utrecht, printed by Pierre Elzevir; see I, [xiv]. Another (duodecimo) edition, *"Suivant la Copie imprimie A Paris,"* gives the listings on pp. [xi-xii].

62. See the comment reported from White Kennet in Anthony Wood, *Athenæ Oxoniensis*, "Fasti," ed. Philip Bliss (London, 1820), IV, ii, 126 n., and a letter from Gui Patin to André Falcourt, dated July 5/15, 1660, in *L'Esprit de Guy Patin* (Paris, 1710), p. 64.

63. See George F. Warner, ed., *The Nicholas Papers. Correspondence of Sir Edward Nicholas, Secretary of State* (Westminster, 1886), Camden Society, N. S., vol. XL; I, 207.

64. See, for example, Richard Perrinchief's *The Royal Martyr: Or, The Life and Death of King Charles I*

(London, 1676); Milton is alluded to on pp. 209-10.

65. A holograph note in British Museum, Additional MS 4816, f. 35, validates Anglesey's knowledge of the forgery. See also Francis F. Madan, *A New Bibliography of the Eikon Basilike of King Charles the First* (Oxford, 1950), pp. 126-63. Compare the ensuing discussion with Sensabaugh, *That Grand Whig Milton,* esp. pp. 46-49, 142-55. Various volumes during 1660-99 (and onward) tried to discredit Charles the person and king, and others, to counter these arguments; they are not directly pertinent to Milton or *Eikonoklastes* and so are not cited in this survey.

66. Often assigned to Slingsby Bethel.

67. See also Blackall's *A Sermon Preached Before the Honourable House of Commons, at St. Margaret's Westminster, January 30th. 1698/9* (London, 1699), p. 16 and marginal note. This was reprinted in 1708 by Henry Hills; the allusions concerning authorship occur on pp. 11-12. Much of the discussion involving Toland is devoted to an examination of his religious tenets, since he espoused Socinianism, and this is extended unhappily to Milton, as one guilty by association. It is also interesting to note the references to Milton in sermon literature of the last decade or so of the seventeenth century; see, for example, John Moore's *A Sermon Preach'd Before the House of Lords, in the Abby-Church at Westminster, upon Monday, January 31, 1697* (London, 1697 [1698]), which employs two quotations from *Character of the Long Parliament,* p. 27, and one from *Eikonoklastes,* p. 33.

68. This volume also quotes from *Defensio prima* (with translations),

Samson, Paradise Regain'd, Reason, Areopagitica, and Newton's "Life," as well as material pertinent to Milton from Dugdale's *Short View,* Bayle, and Hume's *History.*

69. See French, "The Date of Milton's First *Defense," The Library,* Fifth Series, 3 (1948), 56-58.

70. "A Revised Bibliography of Salmasius' *Defensio Regia* and Milton's *Pro Populo Anglicano Defensio," The Library,* Fifth Series, 9 (1954), 101-21. See French, II, 351, for a summary.

71. See Maurice Kelley, "A Note on Milton's *Pro Populo Anlicano Defensio," The Library,* Fourth Series, 17 (1937), 466-67, and Clarissa O. Lewis, "A Further Note on Milton's *Pro Populo Anglicano Defensio," The Library,* Fourth Series, 23 (1943), 45-47. Robert W. Ayers cites variants "of substantial or stylistic significance and presumably of auctorial origin" in the London editions (Madan Nos. 1, 2, and 14) in Yale *Prose,* IV, ii, 1120-39; this discounts Madan No. 10, which may or may not be a London edition. Bibliographical descriptions are included for these same three editions on pp. 1140-44. However, I find numerous differences from my own collations (e. g., Ayres gives "LONDINI" in each case whereas it should be "*LONDINI*").

72. In answer to Rowland's *Apologia* a chapter-by-chapter refutation was published entitled, *Joannis Philippi Angli Responsio Ad Apologiam Anonymi cujusdam tenebrionis pro Rege & Populo Anglicano infantissimum. Londini, Typis Du-Gardianis. An. Dom. M. DC. LII.* This was the product of Milton's younger nephew John Phillips, but apparently with various kinds of help from Milton. The question of collaboration is reviewed by Robert Ayers in the preface to his edition of the work in the Yale *Prose,* IV, ii, 877-79. This is

the only annotated edition of the work, which has not been separately published since the original editions although it has been included in complete collections of Milton's works, such as that in 1698, Birch, Symmons, Burnett (first English translation), Fletcher, Mitford, and the Columbia Edition. There were four separate editions, one in 1651 and three in 1652; these are described by Ayers in his preface. (See also his article, "The John Phillips-John Milton *Angli Responsio*: Editions and Relations," *PBSA*, 56 [1962], 66-72.) The first apparently appeared during December and had the next year's date (new style) attached to it. For a review of the evidence, see Ayers, "The ·Date of the John Phillips-John Milton *Joannis Philippi Angli Responsio*," *PQ*, 38 (1959), 95-101. Thomason marked his copy "Dec. 24." This edition was the source of the next by Ludovic Elzevir of Amsterdam; the third edition attempted to duplicate the second as a kind of counterfeit. Ayers says in the Yale *Prose* that the printer was Jean Jansson of Amsterdam. The fourth edition (at least that seems to be the order of printing) was printed by Jansson and is textually independent of the third edition. The work received a rebuttal by Rowland: *Polemica sive Supplementum ad Apologiam Anonymam pro Rege et Populo Anglicano adversus Jo: Miltoni Defensionem Populi Anglicani.... Per Io. Rowlandum Pastorem Anglicum.* [London] *M. D. C. LIII.* The particular significance of the latter work is that it identifies the author of the *Apologia*. There were no other printed reactions to the *Responsio*, although the matter of the works and of authorship was alluded to in letters and the like.

73. In *Two Treatises of Government* (London, 1690), often reprinted, John Locke argued against Filmer; some of his remarks react to Filmer's position in *Observations*.

74. The beginning of an anonymous manuscript answer is found in the Royal Library, Copenhagen, Old Royal 4º, 2259, dated sometime before January 1, 1659: "Ambiorigis Ariovisti i.e. Henr. Erastii Annotationes ad Joannis Miltoni Angli Præfationem Libri, quem Scripsit pro Populi Anglicani Defensione Psal. XXXIII. Jehova gentium consilia dissolvit, populorum conatus reddit irritos."

75. The work is listed by Abbott in *The Bibliography of Oliver Cromwell*, No. 901; he notes that it was translated into Dutch as *Vergelyckinge tusschen Claudius Tiberius Kayser van Romen, en Oliver Cromwel, Protector of misschien toekomenden Koninck van Engelant.* I quote and translate the sections alluding to Milton, since the work has been unknown to Miltonists and is not easily available. (I use the copy in the Yale University Library.)

Miseranda fuit Aggrippe cædes, sed hæc, quae in persona Regis (bona cum Miltoni venia ita loquor) est commissa, cum refertur;

> Quis talia fando,
> Temperet à lachrymis? (p. 9)

... sed eligente Cromvvellio, tribunali præfectos Romano Prætori, facta similitudine, opponam, & populum Anglicanum Miltoni, id est, non totam sed minimam & pessimam populi partem insanæ genti Judæorum, ut utri illorum meliores aut turpiores fuerint intelligatur.... In Pontio Pilato melioris notæ virum video, quam in Pontijs Anglicanis; in populo Miltoni eandem levitatem & petulantiam quam in Judæis deprehendo. (p. 16)

Pilatus abhorruit à fœdo Judæorum clamore, qui *Hosianna* suum lætum, quo venientem Christum exceperant, edocti à Sacerdotibus suis verterant in miserabile illud *Crucifige, Crucifige*: Anglicani Pilati applaudebant Miltoni populo, & distributis per illum Discipulis suis, qui, cum olim millies cecinissent, *Vivat Rex, Vivat,* jam clamabant *moriatur Rex! moriatur!* Id est, *ad securim, ad securim.* . . . Anglicanis Pilatis sanctitas illius nominis adeo evilescere cœpit, ut Advocatus illorum Miltonus egregiam laudem illos esse adeptos jactitet, qui præclaro suo facto hanc gentium dissipaverint superstitionem venerandi Reges, . . . (p. 18)

Peracta tota hac Tragœdia, Cromwellius per præcones suos epilogum recitantes populum Miltoni Anglicanium excitavit ad illud, in quo comœdiæ & tragœdie desinere solent, *plaudite.* (p. 20)

& Miltonus, qui ab illo tempore, ex quo adversus Reges scripsit, ocularum cæcus factus tunc quóq; animi cœcus fuisse videtur, cum scripsit Cromvvellium suum triumphare. (p. 28)

A Comparison between Claudius Tiberius, Emperor, and Oliver Cromwell, Protector. Drawn by Peter Negesch. Printed in the Year 1657. "Pitiable was the slaughter of Agrippa, but this, which was perpetrated on the person of a king (with the good grace of Milton it is thus expressed), may rather be reported: What punishment is to be declared / That may restrain our tears?" (p. 9); ". . . but I oppose through analogy to the Roman dictator the deeds done by Cromwell in his election by the officers of the Parliament, as well as Milton's 'English people,' that is, not

all, but the puniest and most evil faction of the people through analogy to the monstrous race of the Jews, so that it is understood which of them was worthier or baser. . . . In Pontius Pilate I see a man of more worthy note than in the English Pontius; in Milton's 'people' I detect the same fickleness and impudence as in the Jews" (p. 16); "Pilate abhorred the detestable cry of the Jews, who, taught by their priests, had turned their joyous hosanna, with which they had received the coming of Christ, into that wretched 'Crucify, Crucify': The English Pilates were applauding Milton's 'people,' and, by that means, their divided disciples, who, although formerly they had sung a thousand times, 'Long live the king, long may he live,' now were crying, 'Let the king die! May he die!' That is, 'To the block, to the block'. . . . To the English Pilates the sanctity of that name even began to become despicable, enabling their advocate Milton to proclaim the illustrious fame to be acquired by them who through their noble achievement may overthrow this superstition of venerating kings of all races" (p. 18); "At this point [the people] totally defeated by tragedy, Cromwell aroused the English people of Milton through his heralds reciting a peroration to them; just as comedies and tragedies used to be concluded, let us applaud" (p. 20); "And Milton, who from that time forth wrote against kings, is seen to have been made blind then of eyes as well as blind of intellect, when he wrote to exult his Cromwell" (p. 28).

76. Paul W. Blackford, translator of parts of *Regii Sanguinis Clamor* in the Yale *Prose*, IV, ii, points out that *Catalogus Impressorum Librorum in Bibliotheca Bodleiana in Academia Oxoniensi* (Oxford, 1853), II, 767,

listed an octavo edition in 1652 from
The Hague. Perhaps the compiler
erred in calling it an octavo; it is not
otherwise known.

77. Internally Book III has a publication date of 1669. The work was
reissued in 1671.

78. See the edition of 1708, p. 12.

79. Reprinted as *The Lord Clarendon's History of the Grand Rebellion
Compleated . . . The Second Edition*
(London: for John Nicholson, 1717),
p. 138; there is also a reference to
"Milton's Answer to Salmasius" on
p. [xiii].

80. See *A Collection of the State
Papers of John Thurloe* (London,
1742), II, 394.

81. See J. Milton French, "An Un-
recorded Edition of Milton's *Defensio
Secunda* (1654)," *PBSA*, 49 (1955),
262-68, which gives the variants between the second and third of these
editions, and Robert W. Ayers, "A
Suppressed Edition of Milton's *Defensio Secunda* (1654)," *PBSA*, 55
(1961), 75-87, which describes the
first of these. In all there were five
editions: the original London edition;
the pirated "Newcomb, London"
edition; Ayers' Vlacq A; Ayers' Vlacq
B or French's A; and Ayers' Vlacq C
or French's B.

82. See also letters in the Thurloe
collection, II, 394, 452, 529.

83. See *Proceedings of the Huguenot
Society of London*, 9 (1909-11), 241-
42. Edmund Elys quoted a few pages
as "Animadversions" in his *Joannis
Miltoni Sententiae Potestati Regiae
Adversus Refutatio. Cui annexes sunt,
Animadversiones in execrabilem
libellum, cui titulus est, "Joannis
Miltoni Angli Defensio Secunda"*
(London, 1699), pp. 11-15. The
sententiae precede on pp. 5-10.

84. See previous citations.

85. See *TLS*, April 13, 1956, p. 228.

86. "I am pursuing after yet greater
things if my strength suffice (nay, it
will if God grant), and for their sake
meanwhile am taking thought, and
studying to make ready" (Columbia
Edition, VII, 559).

87. See the remarks prefacing
Hunter's edition of the tract in *The
Prose of John Milton*, p. 476.

88. Listed by Emma Unger and William Jackson, eds., *The Carl H. Pforzheimer Library English Literature 1475-
1700* (New York: Privately Printed,
1940), III, 843-44. Note also that
Thomas N. Brushfield, in *A Bibliography
of Sir Walter Ralegh Knt. Second Edition with Notes Revised and Enlarged*
(Exeter: James G. Crimmin, 1908),
says "(Probably published without Milton's note, as in a copy *penes* me),"
p. 131. W. Carew Hazlitt in *Second
Series of Bibliographical Collections
and Notes on Early English Literature
1474-1700* (London: Bernard Quaritch,
1882), p. 510, specifically lists the preface as being included.

89. This edition has not been pre-
viously noted; its printing legend is:
"Edinburgh, Reprinted by Alexander
Alison and Sold by Messrs. Davidson
and Trail, at Their Shop in the Parliament-
Closs; and other Booksellers in Town. M
DCC XXXVI. [Price Sixpence.]"

90. See the introduction to Clark's
annotated edition (New Haven: Yale
University Press, 1915).

91. Reprinted in *L'Estrange his
Apology* (London, for Henry Brome,
1660), p. 86.

92. Reprinted with notes in the
Harleian Miscellany in IV, 179-86
(1745); IV, 188-95 (1809); and VII,
115-24 (1810), and in Parker's *Milton's Contemporary Reputation*.

93. *Dignity of Kingship Asserted* was
advertised in *Mercurius Publicus*, No.

20 (London), May 10-17, 1660, p. 31, and No. 28 (London), July 5-12, 1660, p. 457. It was reprinted as *Monarchy Triumphing over Traiterous Republicans or the Transcendent Excellency of that Divine Government fully proved against the Utopian Chimera's of our Ridiculous Common-wealths-men. By G. S.* (London, 1661).

94. Reprinted in *L'Estrange his Apology* and Parker's *Milton's Contemporary Reputation.*

95. *Old South Leaflets,* No. 63, Thirteenth Series, 1895 (not listed in Stevens' *Reference Guide*), and the reprint of the entire series, vol. 3, apparently in 1896. The pamphlet occupies pp. 1-22 and is followed by the *Brief Delineation of a Free Commonwealth* ("A Letter to General Monk," i. e., *The Present Means and Brief Delineation of a Free Commonwealth*), pp. 22-23, and an editorial note, pp. 23-24. (This reprinting of *The Present Means* has not been previously noted.)

96. *Brief Notes* was also included in Maseres' 1818 collection.

97. See my unpublished dissertation, "Milton's Spelling: Its Biographical and Critical Implications" (New York University, 1958), pp. 218-20. No section of the volume shows predominantly non-Miltonic orthography and all sections show orthography in agreement with Milton's practices. Evidence is too slight to narrow the possible date of composition with any assurance, although middle 1646 (?) might best accord with spelling variations. Parker's suggestion of 1645 (?) is not in disagreement with the evidence of spelling.

98. "Notes on Milton's *Accedence Commenc't Grammar,*" *JEGP,* 60 (1961), 641-50; reissued as *Milton Studies in Honor Of Harris Francis Fletcher* (Urbana, 1961), pp. 33-42.

99. See Harris F. Fletcher, "The First Editions of Milton's *History of Britain,*" *JEGP,* 35 (1936), 405-14. Fletcher lists variants in the Columbia Edition, XVIII, 646-47, as well as the errata omitted in Columbia's edition of *Britain,* XVIII, 256-57. French Fogle (Yale *Prose,* V, i) reports the existence of further variants in additional copies examined.

100. These are listed and discussed by Harry Glicksman in "The Editions of Milton's *History of Britain,*" *PMLA,* 35 (1920), 116-22. The Columbia Edition gives these additional revisions separately.

101. See *Wiltshire. The Topographical Collections of John Aubrey,* ed. John Edward Jackson (Devizes: Henry Bull for the Wiltshire Archaeological and Natural History Society, 1862), pp. 66, 74, 258.

102. See "Letters Addressed by Lewis Morris (Llewelyn Ddu) to Edward Richard of Ystradmeurig," *Y Cymmroder,* 1 (1877), 163.

103. See, for example, the remarks of Eugene Lawrence in *The Lives of the British Historians* (New York: Charles Scribner, 1855), pp. 376-80.

104. See also French R. Fogle, "Milton as Historian," in *Two Papers on Seventeenth Century English Historiography* (Los Angeles: William A. Clark Memorial Library, 1965), pp. 1-20.

105. See also Harry Glicksman, "The Sources of Milton's *History of Britain,*" *Wisconsin Studies in Language and Literature,* 11 (1920), 105-44.

106. See particularly G. C. Moore Smith, "A Note on Milton's *Art of Logic,*" *RES,* 13 (1937), 335-40; P. A. Duhamel, "Milton's Alleged Ramism," *PMLA,* 67 (1952), 1035-53; T. S. K. Scott-Craig, "The Crafts-

manship and Theological Signification of Milton's *Art of Logic*," *HLQ*, 17 (1953), 1-15; Wilbur S. Howell, *Logic and Rhetoric in England, 1500-1700* (Princeton: Princeton University Press, 1956), pp. 213-19; and Peter F. Fisher, "Milton's Logic," *JHI*, 23 (1962), 37-60. The most important statement concerning Ramism in the English Renaissance is Walter J. Ong, S. J., *Ramus: Method, and the Decay of Dialogue* (Cambridge, Mass.: Harvard University Press, 1958).

107. *Occasional Essays on Various Subjects, Chiefly Political and Historical* (London: Wilks, 1809), pp. 416-30; *Thoughts on True Religion, Heresy, Schism, and Toleration by John Milton . . . To Which Are Added Remarks on Essentials in Religion, Charitableness and Uncharitableness, Extracted from the Writings of Isaac Watts*, ed. B. Fowler (Harlow: Fowler, 1811); and *Protestant Union. A Treatise of True Religion, Heresy, Schism, and Toleration. To which is affixed a preface on Milton's Religious Principles and Unimpeachable Sincerity. By T. Burgess* (London: F. and C. Rivington, 1826). See also the two editions of *Tracts for the People*, No. 1 (London, 1839), which reprint parts of this pamphlet.

108. "*The Precedence of the 1676 Edition of Milton's Literæ Pseudo-Senatus Anglicani*," *SB*, 7 (1955), 181-85.

109. See Maurice Kelley, "First Editions of Milton's *Literæ*," *TLS*, April 29, 1960, p. 273.

110. Alphonse Willems assigned both editions to Fricx in *Les Elzevirs: Histoire et Annales Typographiques* (Brussels, 1880), p. 562.

111. Parker cites this as "20 (10?) January 1677" (II, 1131), though the manuscript (Rawlinson A.185, ff. 133-34) clearly reads "Jan: 28.th styl. vet."

112. These documents have been printed in Sumner's edition of *De doctrina christiana* (15); Todd's 1826 or 1842 editions of the *Poetical Works* (1, 4, 11, 13); W. Douglas Hamilton, *Original Papers Illustrative of the Life and Writings of John Milton* (London, 1859) (1, 3, 4, 11, 13, 15); Masson's *Life* (2, 5, 7); and M. M. Kleerkooper and W. P. Van Stockum, Jr., *De Boekhandel to Amsterdam voornamelijk in de 17e eeuw* (The Hague: Martinus Nijhoff, 1914), pp. 211-14 (6, 9, 10, 11, 12, 14, 16). Item No. 8 is referred to in No. 11; I am not aware of its existence in manuscript.

113. The specific title page for the index is: *Index Librorum Prohibitorum Innoc. XI. P. M. Jussu Editus Usque Ad Annum 1681. Einem Accedit in Fine Appendix Usque ad Mensem Junij 1704* (Romæ: Cameræ Apostolicæ, 1704). There were two other issues of the 1704 *Index*. The entry is repeated in successive issues during the eighteenth century. It is also listed by Jean-Baptiste Hannot in *Index ou catalogue des principaux livres condamnés & defendus par l'Eglise* (Namur: Pierre Hinne; Liege: Chez Barthelemi Colletti, 1714), p. 155. Hamel says that the book was placed on the Index as a result of a decree of 1694; Parker seems to have added the specific date. He misleadingly gives dates of 1694 and 1732 for the *Index* in his index (II, 1331); editions did not appear in those years. For example, Rolli's translation of *Paradise Lost* was indeed placed on the Index on January 21, 1732, but this is first reported in print in *Appendix Novissimæ Appendici ad Indicem Librorum Prohibitorum a Mense Maii MDCCXVIII. Usque ad totum mensem Julii MDCCXXXIX* (Romæ: Cameræ Apostolicæ, 1739), p. 506.

114. A translation in French follows

on pp. 329-33. Chasles also prints the letter to Mazarin, dated June 29, 1654, found in manuscript and alleged to be by Milton (see later) on pp. 301-2. This is therefore the first printing of this letter.

115. Of course, Masson also printed a number of the papers in his *Life*. There are also editions of Cromwell's letters in the biographical studies by Thomas Carlyle and by Wilbur C. Abbott (*The Writings and Speeches of Oliver Cromwell*, 4 vols. [Cambridge, Mass., 1937-47]. Many of these letters have no connection with Milton.

116. I include here the two brief collections in Bodleian MSS Rawlinson A.260 and A.261. French (V, 412) has a note concerning a letter to Hamburg immediately following that of April 2, 1649 in the Marten-Loder MSS, Third Series, vol. XI, ff. 1-2, which should be another ascription, but which is not counted here. Originals and copies discovered by Maurice Kelley, all fourteen of which are taken into consideration here, were printed in "Additional Texts of Milton's State Papers," *MLN*, 67 (1952), 14-19.

117. These are: Algiers, 1650 (?); three Spanish letters, after November 24-28, 1650; a Danish letter, February 16, 1656; Algiers, April 1656; another of the same date; Sir Thomas Bendish, April 19, 1656; Algiers, June 1656; Instructions for the Agent to Russia, April 1657 (?).

118. Parker (II, 958) notes other state letters in which Milton may have had a hand, although he is generally disinclined to pay much attention to these papers. In 1743 John Nickolls, Jr., published *Original Letters and Papers of State, Addressed to Oliver Cromwell; Concerning the Affairs of Great Britain. From the Year MDCXLTX to MDCLVIII. Found among the Political Collections of Mr. John Milton*. These apparently came by way of Thomas Ellwood and his friend Joseph Wyeth, and are *to* Cromwell (or others of the Council) only.

119. See also Patrick's discussion in "Milton's State Papers in the Commonwealth Period," *SCN*, 18 (1960), 23-26. A review article by Leo Miller in *Notes and Queries* (December 1972), pp. 474-78, indicates many of the inadequacies and omissions of this latest edition.

120. Patrick also cites *Memoriael Ofte Schrift Van Don Stephano De Gamarra . . . Mitgaders een Brief Vom de Heere Protector Cromwell* ([The Hague], 1656), pp. 7-9, for the letter to the United Provinces (French, IV, 110-11), No. 109; and notes a French translation of the letter to Geneva (French, III, 366), Miscellaneous No. 2, in Bernard Gagnebin's "Cromwell to the Republic of Geneva," *Proceedings of the Huguenot Society of London*, 18 (1948), 171-72.

121. The version in *La Vie d'Olivier Cromwel. Par Gregoire Leti* (Amsterdam: Henri Desbordes, 1708), II, 145-46, gives the date as April 20, 1650, in error; the letter is given in French translation only.

122. The version in *Het Leven van Olivier Cromwel* (Amsterdam: Filip Verbeek, 1706), II, 557-59, in Dutch, gives the date as June 26, 1658.

123. Milton is referred to specifically on II, 569, as translator for the Council of State. Note too that there are citations from the Dutch Manifesto and the Articles of Peace.

124. Miller calls it Columbia Edition 136 bis (it should be 135 bis; see XIII, 628-29) and says that the text was found in Copenhagen.

125. Other editions are 1724, 1725, 1755, 1778, and 1840, and the follow-

ing. "The Fourth Edition, with Additions" appeared in Dublin in 1735 and in London in 1741. References in the first are on pp. 272, 273, and 273-75; and in the second on pp. 267, 267-68, and 268-69.

126. Note the use of this principle by J. Max Patrick in his remarks on some of the letters of state in *The Prose of John Milton*, p. 585.

127. Compare, however, my suggested date for Sonnet XIX (October-November 1655) partially on the basis of its indication of inactivity in public life and its heralding of a period to be devoted to important poetic and prose works; "Milton's Sonnet 19: Its Date of Authorship and Its Interpretation," *N&Q*, N. S. 4 (1957), 442-46. But also see note 17 in that article which mentions larger governmental activities of August-October 1655 from which Milton would of necessity have been disengaged.

128. A copy of the July 7 "Declaration of Parliament against the States-General" appears in the Nalson Papers (XVIII, 139); *Manuscripts*, p. 655.

129. See Hamilton, pp. 20-21.

130. This is No. 132 on pp. 1045-56 of an apparent series of treaties and other state papers; I have found only this disbound item without further bibliographic information.

131. Parker is following the lead of Masson and of Charles H. Firth, "Milton as an Historian," p. 30. Phillips had reported that the *History of Britain* was "all compleat so far as he went, some Passages only excepted, which being thought too sharp against the Clergy, could not pass the Hand of the Licenser, were in the Hands of the late Earl of *Angelsey* while he liv'd; where at present is uncertain" (*Life*, p. xxxix). Toland repeated the statement (I,

43), which has been interpreted as referring to the "Digression."

132. See my unpublished dissertation on Milton's spelling, pp. 222-25.

133. The complete run of this paper, edited by Thomas Flatman, was reprinted in 1713 (for Benjamin Tooke) in two volumes.

134. See the introduction by Prince D. S. Mirsky to his edition (London: Blackamore Press, 1929); Robert R. Cawley, *Milton's Literary Craftsmanship: A Study of A Brief History of Moscovia, with an Edition of the Text* (Princeton: Princeton University Press, 1941; rptd., Stapleton, N.Y.: Gordian Press, 1965); George B. Parks, "The Occasion of Milton's *Moscovia*," *SP*, 40 (1943), 399-404; Joseph A. Bryant, Jr., "Milton and The Art of History: A Study of Two Influences in *A Brief History of Moscovia*," *PQ*, 29 (1950), 15-30; Parks, "Milton's *Moscovia* Not History," *PQ*, 31 (1952), 218-21, and Bryant, "A Reply to Milton's *Moscovia* Not History," pp. 221-23; and John B. Gleason, "The Nature of Milton's *Moscovia*," *SP*, 61 (1964), 640-49. Mirsky's and Cawley's are the only later separate editions, except for a Russian translation by Iu. v. Tolstoi, published by the Imperial Society of Russian History and Antiquities at the Moscow University (Moscow, 1875; rptd., 1907).

135. It should be noted that there are biographical errors or questions in Gleason's argument. His main point, however, is worthy of attention: that the volume represents a preparatory stage in a project which was soon abandoned.

136. Lloyd E. Berry, "Giles Fletcher, the Elder, and Milton's *A Brief History of Moscovia*," *RES*, N. S. 11 (1960), 150-56.

137. "Spelling," pp. 360-61.

138. See French, II, 214.

139. See B. Eugene McCarthy, "A Seventeenth-Century Borrowing From Milton's 'A Brief History of Moscovia'," *N&Q*, N. S. 15 (1968), 99-101. Unlikely is the contention of W. H. Mallock in "Early Romances of English Trade with Russia," in *Dublin Review*, 157 (1915), 226-40, that *Moscovia* served as the source for various other items dealing with Russia.

140. See Harris F. Fletcher's "Milton and Walton's *Biblia Sacra Polyglotta* (1657)," *MLN*, 42 (1927), 84-87.

141. See also Kelley's "The Composition of Milton's *De Doctrina Christiana* —The First Stage," in *Th'Upright Heart and Pure*, ed. Amadeus P. Fiore (Pittsburgh: Duquesne University Press, 1967), pp. 35-44.

142. See his review article in *The Christian Examiner*, 3 (1826), 29-77. This was reprinted as "Remarks on the Character and Writings of John Milton" (Boston: I. R. Butts and Co., 1826); again (Boston Printed; and London Re-Printed: for E. Rainsford, 1826), with a second edition in 1828, a third edition in 1828, and another edition in 1830; in *The Pamphleteer* (London), 29 (1828), [507]-47; in Henry Stebbing's edition of *The Complete Poetical Works of John Milton* (London, 1839), with frequent editions and with reprints in other collections or editions of *Paradise Lost*; and in collected editions of Channing's *Works* (Boston: J. Munroe and Co., 1841-43), vol. 1. Not all of these are listed by Stevens.

143. See *The Poetical Works of John Milton . . . The Third Edition* (London: C. and J. Rivington et al., 1826), Section VIII of "Some Account of the Life and Writings of John Milton," I, 291-364; rptd., ed. 4 (1842).

144. See also Augustus Hopkins Strong, *The Great Poets and Their Theology* (Philadelphia: American Baptist Publication Society, 1897), pp. 257-64.

145. Stevens and the British Museum Catalogue inaccurately cite only "R. Hunter."

146. The listing of blank pages by Mohl is curious; it should be: 2-3, 7-11, 21-32, 37-52, 54, 56, 60, 62-66, 68-69, 99-100, 102-4, 107-8, 117-47, 149, 152-59, 161-76, 192, 194, 196, 206, 209-10, 222-24, 229, 235-39, 250, [252].

147. "The Chronology of Milton's Private Studies," *PMLA*, 36 (1921), 251-314; rptd. in *John Milton Poet and Humanist* (Cleveland: The Press of Case Western Reserve University, 1966), 75-125.

148. Yale *Prose*, I, 344-513.

149. See *Milton: A Biography*, II, 801-3 (with corrections of Hanford's interpretation of a pertinent passage from *An Apology*), 803-4, 841-42, 881-84, and "Milton's Commonplace Book: An Index and Notes," *MQ*, 3 (1969), 41-54.

150. See "One Aspect of Milton's Spelling," p. 510; and "Spelling," pp. 359-60.

151. Without explanation, Robert W. Ayers, in a review of Mohl's book on the Commonplace Book in *PQ*, 23 (1970), 489, gives dates of "about 1624 to about 1665"—that is, Milton is amazingly supposed to have begun it even before entering Cambridge. Mohl relates the Commonplace Book procedure to Milton's education at St. Paul's; see pp. 17-18 of *John Milton and His Commonplace Book* (New York: Frederick Ungar, 1969).

152. See "Milton's Decision to Become a Poet," *MLQ*, 24 (1963), 21-30.

153. See my discussion in "Notes on Milton's Amanuenses," *JEGP*, 58

(1959), 29-38.

154. Ibid.

155. See French, IV, 200-11. The audit is in the Public Record Office, SP 46/112, f. 63-63v.

156. This is also the conclusion of Maurice Kelley in "The Composition of Milton's De Doctrina Christiana—The First Stage."

157. Thomas Yalden wrote a poem "On the Reprinting Mr. Milton's Prose Works, with his Poems Written in His *Paradise Lost*," in which, typically for the age, he praised Milton the poet but deplored Milton the controversialist in prose; see Elijah Fenton, ed., *Oxford and Cambridge Miscellany Poems* (London: for Bernard Lintott, [1709]), pp. 177-78.

158. Baron's edition of *Eikonoklastes* (1756, 1770) includes a "Preface Shewing the Transcendent Excellency of Milton's Prose Works." There is an interesting letter from Andrew Eliot to Thomas Hollis, dated December 10, 1767, praising the prose; see *Collections of the Massachusetts Historical Society* (Boston, 1858), IV, 412-13. Samuel Johnson criticized the prose style and Latinate constructions in his *Life* (1779), but compare T. Holt White's *A Review of Johnson's Criticism on the Style of Milton's English Prose; with Strictures on the Introduction of Latin Idiom into the English Language* (London: Rowland Hunter, 1818). The scattered remarks on the prose by Lord Monbaddo (James Burnet) in *Of the Origin and Progress of Language* (Edinburgh, 1774-89), vols. 2-5, offer a strong balance to Johnson.

Selected Bibliography

Allison, William T., ed. *The Tenure of Kings and Magistrates, by John Milton.* New York: Holt, 1911.

Barker, Arthur. *Milton and the Puritan Dilemma, 1641-1660.* Toronto: Univ. of Toronto Press, 1942; reprinted, 1956.

Cawley, Robert R. *Milton's Literary Craftsmanship: A Study of A Brief History of Moscovia, with an Edition of the Text.* Princeton: Princeton Univ. Press, 1941; reprinted, New York: Gordian Press, 1965.

Clark, Evert M., ed. *The Ready and Easy Way to Establish a Free Commonwealth, by John Milton.* New Haven: Yale Univ. Press, 1916.

Evans, John X. "Imagery as Argument in Milton's *Areopagitica,*" *Texas Studies in Language and Literature,* 8 (1966), 189-205.

Fink, Zera S. *The Classical Republicans: An Essay in the Recovery of a Pattern of Thought in Seventeenth Century England.* Evanston: Northwestern Univ. Press, 1945; reprinted, 1962.

Fixler, Michael. *Milton and the Kingdoms of God.* London: Faber and Faber, 1964.

Fletcher, Harris F. *The Use of the Bible in Milton's Prose.* Urbana: Univ. of Illinois Press, 1929.

French, J. Milton, ed. *The Life Records of John Milton.* 5 vols. New Brunswick: Rutgers Univ. Press, 1949-1958.

——. "Some Notes on Milton's *Accedence Commenc't Grammar,*" *Journal of English and Germanic Philology,* 60 (1961), 641-650.

Gilman, W. E. *Milton's Rhetoric: Studies in His Defense of Liberty.* Columbia: Univ. of Missouri Press, 1939.

Hale, Will T., ed. *Of Reformation Touching Church Discipline in England, by John Milton.* New Haven: Yale Univ. Press, 1916.

Haller, William. *The Rise of Puritanism.* New York: Columbia Univ. Press, 1938.

Hamilton, Kenneth G. "The Structure of Milton's Prose," *Language and Style in Milton,* ed. Ronald David Emma and John T. Shawcross. New York: Frederick Ungar, 1967. Pages 304-332.

Henry, Nathaniel H. "Milton's Last Pamphlet: Theocracy and Intolerance," *A Tribute to G. C. Taylor.* Chapel Hill: Univ. of North Carolina Press, 1952. Pages 197-210.

Kelley, Maurice W. *This Great Argument: a Study of Milton's* De doctrina christiana *as a Gloss upon* Paradise Lost. Princeton: Princeton Univ. Press, 1941; reprinted, Gloucester: Peter Smith, 1962.

Kranidas, Thomas. *The Fierce Equation: A Study of Milton's Decorum.* The Hague: Mouton, 1965.

Lewalski, Barbara K. "Milton: Political Beliefs and Polemical Methods, 1659-60," *PMLA*, 74 (1959), 191-202.

——. "Milton on Learning and the Learned-Ministry Controversy," *Huntington Library Quarterly*, 24 (1961), 267-281.

Masson, David. *The Life of John Milton: Narrated in Connexion with the Political, Ecclesiastical, and Literary History of His Time.* 7 vols. New York: Peter Smith, 1946, reprinted.

Nicholas, Constance. *Introduction and Notes to Milton's History of Britain To Be Used with Volume X, Columbia Edition, The Works of Milton.* Urbana: Univ. of Illinois Press, 1957.

Parker, William R., "Education: Milton's Ideas and Ours," *College English*, 24 (1962), 1-14.

——. *Milton: A Biography.* 2 vols. Oxford: Clarendon Press, 1968.

——. *Milton's Contemporary Reputation.* Columbus: Ohio State Univ. Press, 1940.

Patrick, J. Max, gen. ed. *The Prose of John Milton.* New York: Doubleday, 1967.

Patrides, C. A. *Milton and the Christian Tradition.* Oxford: Clarendon Press, 1966.

——. *The Phoenix and Ladder: The Rise and Decline of the Christian View of History.* Berkeley: Univ. of California Press, 1964.

Patterson, Frank A., gen. ed. *The Works of John Milton.* 18 vols. in 21. New York: Columbia Univ. Press, 1931-1938.

Sensabaugh, George. *That Grand Whig, Milton.* Stanford: Stanford Univ. Press, 1952.

Sirluck, Ernest. "Milton's Political Thought: The First Cycle," *Modern Philology*, 61 (1964), 209-224.

Svendsen, Kester. "Science and Structure in Milton's *Doctrine of Divorce*," *PMLA*, 67 (1952), 435-445.

Thompson, E. N. S. "Milton's Prose Style," *Philological Quarterly*, 14 (1935), 1-15.

Tillyard, Phyllis B., trans. *Private Correspondence and Academic Exercises, Translated from the Latin . . . With an Introduction and Commentary by E. M. W. Tillyard.* Cambridge: Cambridge Univ. Press, 1932.

Webber, Joan. *The Eloquent "I" Style and Self in Seventeenth-Century Prose.* Madison: Univ. of Wisconsin Press, 1968.

Wolfe, Don M., gen. ed. *Complete Prose Works of John Milton.* 6 vols. in 8 published to date. New Haven: Yale Univ. Press, 1953-

——. *Milton in the Puritan Revolution.* New York: Thomas Nelson, 1941; reprinted, New York: Humanities Press, 1963.

Zagorin, Perez. *A History of Political Thought in the English Revolution.* London: Routledge, 1954.

Contributors

William B. Hunter, Jr., is Professor of English at the University of New Hampshire. A member of the Executive Council of the Northeast Modern Language Association and secretary of the Milton Society of America, he is author with C. A. Patrides and J. A. Adamson of *Bright Essence: Studies in Milton's Theology* and editor of *The Complete Poetry of Ben Jonson.* Currently, he is working on Milton's Spenserian predecessors.

John F. Huntley is Associate Professor of English at the University of Iowa, where he teaches Renaissance literature and Milton and directs the internship program in college teaching for graduate students. Having published on Milton and Renaissance literature, he is currently working on seventeenth-century scriptural exegesis as the prototype art of literary interpretation.

Edward S. Le Comte is Professor of English at the State University of New York at Albany. Among other works on Milton and Renaissance literature, his writings include *Yet Once More: Verbal and Psychological Pattern in Milton* and *A Milton Dictionary,* as well as biographical studies of Donne and Lady Essex. His latest essay is "Milton Versus Time."

Michael Lieb is Associate Professor of English at the University of Illinois at Chicago Circle, where he teaches courses in Milton and the Renaissance. His works on Milton include *The Dialectics of Creation: Patterns of Birth and Regeneration in Paradise Lost.* He is currently writing a book to be entitled *The Poetics of the "Holy": A Reading of Paradise Lost.*

Walter J. Ong, S. J., is Professor of English at Saint Louis University, as well as Professor of Humanities in Psychiatry in the University's School of Medicine. Known for his works on Ramism, Father Ong has recently published *Rhetoric, Romance and Technology,* which touches on some themes in his earlier work, *The Presence of the Word.* He is a member of the National Council on the Humanities and a Fellow of the American Academy of Arts and Sciences, and has lectured widely in the United States and abroad.

Florence Sandler is Associate Professor of English at the University of Puget Sound. Her interest lies in Biblical traditions in English literature, especially in the periods of the Renaissance and the eighteenth century and in the work of Milton and Blake.

Harry Smallenburg is Assistant Professor of English at Wayne State University. He is currently preparing a book on the stylistic effects in Milton's major prose tracts and has contributed essays to *Language and Style* and the forthcoming *Milton Encyclopedia.*

John T. Shawcross is Professor of English at Staten Island Community College, CUNY. Editor of *The Complete Poetry of John Milton,* he is an editor of the *Milton Encyclopedia.* Other books include *Milton: The Critical Heritage* and *Language and Style in Milton.* At present, he is preparing a bibliography of Milton's works and Miltonic criticism during the seventeenth and eighteenth centuries.

Joseph Anthony Wittreich, Jr., is Associate Professor of English at the University of Wisconsin, Madison. In addition to articles in various journals, his works include *The Romantics on Milton,* of which he is the editor; *Calm of Mind: Tercentenary Essays on Paradise Regained and Samson Agonistes,* of which he is editor and contributor; and *Blake's Sublime Allegory,* of which he is co-editor and contributor.

Austin Woolrych is Professor of History and head of the History Department at the University of Lancaster. Besides articles, he has published *Battles of the English Civil War* and *Oliver Cromwell,* and has written the introduction to vol. VII of the Yale edition of Milton's *Complete Prose.* He is currently working on a monograph on Barebone's Parliament.

Global Health Histories

Series editor:

Sanjoy Bhattacharya, University of York

Global Health Histories aims to publish outstanding and innovative scholarship on the history of public health, medicine and science worldwide. By studying the many ways in which the impact of ideas of health and well-being on society were measured and described in different global, international, regional, national and local contexts, books in the series reconceptualise the nature of empire, the nation state, extra-state actors and different forms of globalization. The series showcases new approaches to writing about the connected histories of health and medicine, humanitarianism, and global economic and social development.

Difference and Disease

Medicine, Race, and the Eighteenth-Century British Empire

Suman Seth

Cornell University, New York

CAMBRIDGE
UNIVERSITY PRESS

CAMBRIDGE
UNIVERSITY PRESS

University Printing House, Cambridge CB2 8BS, United Kingdom

One Liberty Plaza, 20th Floor, New York, NY 10006, USA

477 Williamstown Road, Port Melbourne, VIC 3207, Australia

314–321, 3rd Floor, Plot 3, Splendor Forum, Jasola District Centre,
New Delhi – 110025, India

79 Anson Road, #06-04/06, Singapore 079906

Cambridge University Press is part of the University of Cambridge.

It furthers the University's mission by disseminating knowledge in the pursuit of
education, learning, and research at the highest international levels of excellence.

www.cambridge.org
Information on this title: www.cambridge.org/9781108418300
DOI: 10.1017/9781108289726

First published 2018

Printed in the United Kingdom by Clays, St Ives plc.

A catalogue record for this publication is available from the British Library.

Library of Congress Cataloging-in-Publication Data
Names: Seth, Suman, 1974– author.
Title: Difference and disease : medicine, race, and the eighteenth-century
British empire / Suman Seth.
Description: Cambridge, United Kingdom; New York, NY:
Cambridge University Press, 2018. I Includes bibliographical references.
Identifiers: LCCN 2018002424 I ISBN 9781108418300 (hardback)
Subjects: I MESH: Geography, Medical – history I Travel-Related Illness I
Climate I Colonialism – history I Racism – history I History, 18th Century I
West Indies I United Kingdom
Classification: LCC RA651 I NLM WZ 70 FA1 I DDC 614.4/2–dc23
LC record available at https://lccn.loc.gov/2018002424

ISBN 978-1-108-41830-0 Hardback

"… bad intentions alone do not invalidate knowledge. For that to happen it takes bad epistemology …"

Johannes Fabian, *Time and the Other*

For Ashima

Contents

Acknowledgements   *page* xiii

Introduction: Difference and Disease   1
Difference and the Postcolonial History of Colonial Medicine   6

Part I Locality

1 'The Same Diseases Here as in Europe'? Health and Locality
   Before 1700   25
   1.1 A Hippocratic Revival   30
   1.2 The Flexibility of the Hippocratic Tradition   38
   1.3 Local Knowledge and Medical Expertise   44
        Conclusion   55

2 Changes in the Air: William Hillary and English Medicine in
   the West Indies, 1720–1760   57
   2.1 A Rational and Mechanical Essay   61
   2.2 Weathering Epidemics   65
   2.3 From Bath to Barbados   68
   2.4 Yellow Fever   74
   2.5 Slavery, Nativity, and the Production of Similarity   80
        Conclusion   86

Part II Empire

3 Seasoning Sickness and the Imaginative Geography of the
   British Empire   91
   3.1 Seasoning on the Periphery   94
   3.2 Seasoning an Empire   101
        Conclusion   111

4   Imperial Medicine and the Putrefactive Paradigm, 1720–1800   112

    Introduction   112
    4.1   Tropical Climates in Metropolitan Medicine   119
    4.2   Towards a New Putrescent Medicine   123
    4.3   John Pringle: The Putrefactive Turn   129
    4.4   Putrefaction in the Periphery   136
    4.5   The End of the Putrefactive Paradigm   146
    Conclusion   159

Part III Race

5   Race-Medicine in the Colonies, 1679–1750   167

    Introduction   167
    5.1   Race: The Terms of the Debate in the Early Enlightenment   174
    5.2   Gender, Medicine, and Climate   179
    5.3   Race and Medicine, 1679–1740   188
    5.4   A Little Heterodox: John Atkins, Polygenism, and African Diseases   196

6   Race, Slavery, and Polygenism: Edward Long and
    The History of Jamaica   208

    6.1   Anti-Abolitionism and The Somerset Case   213
    6.2   Slavery and *The History of Jamaica*   220
    6.3   Special Creation and the Problem of Race   228
    6.4   Polygenism, Theology, Materialism   237
    Conclusion   238

7   Pathologies of Blackness: Race-Medicine, Slavery,
    and Abolitionism   241

    7.1   Medicine and Abolitionism   250
    7.2   Race, Climate, Disease   260
    7.3   Racial Pathologies   265
    Conclusion   275

    Conclusion: Place, Race, and Empire   277

    Locality and Expertise   277
    Race and Place   280
    Medicine and the Making of Empire   287

Bibliography   291
Index   319

Acknowledgements

I did not imagine, when I finished my first book, that I would write this one, which has required that I learn the histories of a new discipline, period, and place. Whatever insight I've managed has come through the support and guidance of many friends and colleagues. Robert Travers has taught me much about the eighteenth-century British Empire; Chris Hamlin was unstinting in his generosity in helping me come to some mastery of the history of eighteenth-century medicine, while Steve Stowe and John Waller introduced me to the historiography of medicine during a sabbatical year at Michigan State University; James Delbourgo offered critical and enormously helpful suggestions for ways to engage with social histories of slavery in the Atlantic World; and both Michael Gordin and Mary Fissell turned critical eyes to my introduction and helped make it both more precise and more reflective of the fields with which it engages. The Science and Technology Studies (STS) department at Cornell has provided a mostly supportive and congenial environment in which to teach and research. My colleagues – including Peter Dear, Steve Hilgartner, Ron Kline, Bruce Lewenstein, Mike Lynch, Trevor Pinch, Sara Pritchard, Jessica Ratcliff, Margaret Rossiter, Phoebe Sengers, Rebecca Slayton, and Malte Ziewitz – can be counted on to engage seriously and deeply. Special thanks to Rachel Prentice and to Ann Johnson, who I miss terribly. Much love to my broader Cornell and Ithaca family: Cynthia Brock, Shelley Feldman, Deb van Galder, Trina Garrison, Durba Ghosh, Sara Hatfield, Deirdre and George Hay, Geo Kloppel, Patricia Lia, Hope Mandeville, Vlad Micic, Lucinda Ramberg, Mark and Evan Stevens, Stacey Stone, and Marne, Larry, Maya, and Casey Honigbaum. Ray Craib and Jenny Mann remind me regularly of the kind of scholar and person I'd like to be. Holly Case, Nicole Giannella, Murad Idris, and Theresa Krüggeler left Ithaca a while ago, but they are – and always will be – family.

Various chapters of this book were presented at The Institute for Comparative Modernities and the STS Colloquium Series, Cornell University; the Vanderbilt History Seminar, Vanderbilt University; Universidad Autonoma de Yucatan; Louisiana State University; the Porter Fortune Symposium, University of Mississippi; Halle University; the Science, Technology, and Society Colloquium at the University of Michigan;

the University of California, Los Angeles; History of Science and Technology Colloquium, Johns Hopkins University; the History and Philosophy of Science Colloquium, University of Sydney; the Science and Society Speaker Series, Drexel University; the History Colloquium, Princeton University; the Gallatin School of Individualized Study, New York University; the University of Pennsylvania; and the Politics Department at the University of Virginia. A special thanks to those, like Suzanne Marchand and Nonny de La Peña, who opened their homes to me on my travels. Matt and Janelle Stanley were generous in every possible way. They are, both metaphorically and literally, the people I'd want in my corner in a fight. For invitations, questions, and comments, thanks to Sanjoy Bhattacharya, Richard Blackett, Tom Broman, Debbie Coen, Steffan Igor Ayora Diaz, Tony Grafton, Rana Hogarth, Sarah Igo, Myles Jackson, Bill Jordan, Stephen Kenny, Fabio Lanza, Theresa Leavitt, Natalie Melas, Lisa Messeri, Emmie Miller, Ole Molvig, Sarah Naramore, Deirdre Cooper Owens, Susan Scott Parrish, Kapil Raj, Ruth Rogaski, Richard Rottenburg, Simon Schaffer, Londa Schiebinger, Alistair Sponsel, Helen Tilley, Gabriela Vargas-Cetina, Keith Wailoo, Aaron Windel, and Anya Zilberstein. In terms of the final product, I could not have asked for a more professional, engaged, or fun editor than Lucy Rhymer. The team at Cambridge, including Daniel Brown, Sue Barnes, and Nicola Howcroft, were exceptional. Readers will join me in thanking Janelle Bourgeois for her work on the index.

New projects need the support of old friends. Laura Stark is the epitome of thoughtful, open, and engaged humanistic research and thinking. She is also dear to me beyond measure. Any day in which I see Heidi Voskuhl – H-Dog – is a great one. Mary Terrall, Helen Tilley, and Elaine and Norton Wise remain both mentors and role models. Angela Creager is, quite simply, the best. Seeing and learning from Warwick Anderson, Ofer Gal, Daniela Helbig, and Hans Pols continues to be one of my favourite things about returning to Sydney University. Thanks to Arlan and Carol Smith for many years of love and care. Sharrona Pearl's ideas about my arguments and writing have made this book immeasurably better, just as I am a better person for knowing her. I don't know how her unflagging generosity is possible. I would be lost without friends like Lisa Bailey, Scott Bruce, Johanna Crane, James Cunningham, Katy Hansen, Kevin Lambert, Anne Lester, Dan Magaziner, Valeri Kiesig, Erika Milam, Tania Munz, Anjali Singh, Richard Staley, and Chuck Wooldridge, who comfort the heart and inspire the mind. Patrick McCray is the God of Thunder.

Amber Lia-Kloppel has been tireless in helping me find images for my front cover. She has been equally tireless in making me feel joyful and cared for and grounded. I look forward to repaying favours and incurring new debts to her and Isabella in the years to come. My father has never once doubted in my success, even when my own confidence would break. My siblings, Sanjay and Vanita, are my best and quickest readers, to be counted on to tell me what works and what is dull or unnecessary. Vastly more importantly, they – and Kelly, Raju and Nishad – are to be counted on for love and laughter, food and foolishness.

Mindy Smith has been my best friend and strongest support for the years this work has taken and for many more besides. She has been reader, sounding-board, advisor, and critic. Thanking her for her part in this project would do little justice to all the debts she's owed. Books are written while lives are forged and it's the lives that matter most. Together, we've raised a daughter who is the best thing I will ever produce. It's to our daughter – who has never known a time when I was not working on this project – that this book is dedicated.

Introduction: Difference and Disease

One morning in late December, 1750, two physicians in Kingston, Jamaica fought a duel to the death. After an ever-more contentious debate, in print, over the preceding several months, the two confronted one another in person. Intemperate language led to blows, then to the offer and acceptance of a challenge. Very early on the 29th, Parker Bennet arrived at John Williams' house, armed with sword and pistols, and called his adversary out. Williams, according to a later report, loaded his pistols with 'Goose or Swan shot', affixed his sword to his wrist with a ribband, and opened his door enough to present his pistol, shooting Bennet in the chest. Bennet, by this version of events at least, was considerably more chivalrous and having delivered his own arms to his servant, reeled backwards under the force of the shot to get them. Pursuing him, Williams fired a second time, catching Bennet in the knee. By this point, Bennet had reached his sword, which he now found to be stuck so firmly in its scabbard that he could not draw it. Williams, drawing his own weapon, struck Bennet under the right arm and ran him through, before turning to make his exit from the scene. Bennet, somehow still alive, caught his opponent before he could make his escape. Having finally worked his own sword free, his thrust pierced Williams beneath his right clavicle, severed the jugular vein, and broke off in the body. Williams died almost instantly, while Bennet survived him by roughly four hours (one assumes just long enough to offer a story that reflects considerably better on his honour than his adversary's).[1]

Although the two had known one another for several years and had possibly harboured grudges for some time, the immediate cause of their dispute was a book Williams had published earlier in 1750, *An Essay on the Bilious,*

---

[1] John Williams and Parker Bennet, *Essays on the Bilious Fever: Containing the Different Opinions of Those Eminent Physicians John Williams and Parker Bennet, of Jamaica: Which Was the Cause of a Duel, and Terminated in the Death of Both* (Jamaica and London: T. Waller, 1752). The duel is discussed briefly in Richard B. Sheridan, *Doctors and Slaves: A Medical and Demographic History of Slavery in the British West Indies, 1680–1834* (Cambridge: Cambridge University Press, 1985), 68; and G. M. Findlay, 'John Williams and the Early History of Yellow Fever', *The British Medical Journal* 2, no. 4574 (1948).

or Yellow Fever of Jamaica.[2] On reading, the *Essay* seems insufficient to have produced such an effect, for it is a reasonably innocuous medical work, no more critical of other authors and physicians than most others of its time. What seems to have incensed Bennet, however, was a relatively brief passage in Williams' Preface, which drew a distinction between practitioners who had been in the West Indies for some time – and who hence possessed adequate local knowledge and experience – and those who had arrived more recently, having possibly been trained at an elite medical institution in one of Europe's metropolitan centres. 'It appears to me', wrote Williams, 'that no man, let his genius or stack of learning be what it will, can be a judge of the disorders of this country without faithful observation and experience; yet the passion for novelty is so great amongst us that some persons sacrifice life itself to it'. Williams appended a Latin tag from Virgil's 'Aenied' (*quae tanta insania cives?* 'Oh what great insanity is this, citizens?') before continuing:

A new comer, whose head is filled with theory and darling hypotheses, by some will be trusted before a man who … hath made himself acquainted with the diseases of the country, and prudently follows the vestigial of nature; never sacrificing his patient to any favourite hypothesis.[3]

Bennet was precisely such a 'new comer', having obtained his medical degree in Edinburgh in 1745.[4] And his gloss on Williams remarks, published in *An Enquiry into the Late Essay on the Bilious Fever*, provides an idea of how quickly the discussion would devolve:

The second paragraph in the 4th page is a very extraordinary one, and requires a small paraphrase … *Oh ye men of* Jamaica! *Are ye not a parcel of blockheads? To trust your lives in the hands of a NEW COMER! Of a man who has been at the University! Who has attended the nasty lectures of* Morgagni, Albinus, *or* Monroe, *whose head is filled with the whimsical notions of* Boerhaave! *And who knows no more of diseases than what he has learned by seeing the trifling practice of* European *hospitals! – Come to me! I am your faithful* Hippocrates *of* Jamaica!*[5]

If he was young and new to Jamaica, Bennet nonetheless also claimed relevant experience: 'some of us have been in *Africa*, on board *Guineamen*, and in other islands of the *West-Indies*, as well as he; consequently are equally entitled to write upon and cure the *yellow fever*'.[6] Yet Bennet would draw on relatively little of that experience in making a mockery of Williams' probity, competence, Latin, erudition, and – with repeated references to his opponent

[2] John Williams, *[an] Essay on the Bilious, or Yellow Fever of Jamaica* (Kingston, Jamaica: William Daniell, 1750).
[3] Williams and Bennet, iv.
[4] Brief biographical material on each man is offered in Findlay.
[5] Williams and Bennet, 60–1.
[6] Ibid., 61.

as *Mr.* John Williams – his lack of a degree.[7] Williams replied in print with a poem, describing '*Bennet*, whose trifling writings no point hit:/That fop in learning, and that fool in wit'.[8] Bennet in turn responded with an attack on Williams' 'bad poetry, false measure, and vile logic', referring to the poem as the 'idle nonsense of a conceited dunce' and its author as 'a forward cringing fop'.[9] Why Williams thought it would be helpful to reply at this point is not clear. Perhaps he saw that the alternative to words was a violence the end of which could not be predicted. In any case, reply he did, defending himself against charges that he had prescribed a deadly quantity of opium to some of his unfortunate patients by appending supportive letters from the apothecaries who had filled his prescriptions. He also responded to the central point of Bennet's original indignation.

But you were pleased to take offence at the Preface, I hear; where I say, 'a new comer must be liable to more errors in his practice, than a person who hath had a great share of observation and experience', or words to that purpose. Pray, Sir, is not this Truth? Would doctor Mead deny this? And would not that great man be at a loss himself on his first arrival in a southern climate?[10]

The final document in Williams' *Letter to Doctor Bennet* was dated 27 November 1750. Both men would be dead a little over a month later.

The story of Bennet and Williams is a bizarre one. But it is also revealing, opening a door towards a more general set of questions that this book seeks to examine: what determined the social status of medical practitioners in the metropole and far-flung colonies? Which of several competing epistemologies and ontologies were correct? Was there something that bound the diseases of the tropics together and marked them as distinct to those of more temperate regions of the earth? How might one become habituated to a climate and a range of distempers radically different from that in which one was born? Let me elaborate on these questions before I turn, in the next section, to my historical and historiographical stakes.

At the heart of Bennet and Williams' deadly disagreement, we can see, were concerns over who had the appropriate training, social standing, and experience to speak to medical matters in the colonies. That socio-political question could not be resolved, of course, without simultaneously considering a second set of questions: to what extent were the diseases of the Indies really different to those of Northern Europe? If they were essentially the same, surely one might prefer the ministrations of a physician who had received a degree from

---

[7] E.g. ibid., 75.
[8] Ibid., 33–4.
[9] Ibid., 36, 39.
[10] Ibid., 48.

one of the leading universities in Europe, and who could claim – as Bennet did, practice in European hospitals? If the disease environments were radically different, on the other hand, one might well call in a doctor whose knowledge went beyond the ailments afflicting the inhabitants of London or Edinburgh.

The question sounds strange to our modern ears, for we are familiar with tropical medicine as a particular speciality. As a child in Australia, born to Indian parents, I remember well the trepidation that accompanied excitement at the thought of visits to relatives in Delhi. Foul-tasting quinine tablets and painful shots always diluted my enthusiasm for the journey, as did almost ritualised discussions between adults about the relative likelihood of us contracting cholera, typhoid, or malaria. But tropical medicine was born at the end of the nineteenth century, and in 1750 Bennet and Williams were on the cusp of a new understanding of illness between the tropics.

When, then, and why did Anglophone physicians begin to see the diseases of warm climates as different in kind, not merely degree, from those of cooler locations to the north? Relatedly, when and why did medically significant differences *within* northern Europe – which had been an object of considerable interest for some time – begin to pale in significance relative to a larger difference between Europe and the tropics? A sizeable part of the answers to these questions came in analyses of the disease that was the subject of Williams' first essay: yellow fever. It was an irony utterly lost on the two rancorous combatants that the fever in question gained much of its intellectual interest from the fact that it, like Williams, seemed to distinguish sharply between those who were habituated to the climate of the West Indies, and those who were new to it. The fever was particularly fatal, Williams noted, 'to strangers, *Europeans*, and *North Americans*'. If one survived the first attack, however, one was unlikely to be afflicted again. At the very least, a second bout of the fever would be considerably less violent. Today, when we point to the transmission of the yellow fever virus through the bite of mosquitoes, we invoke the body's production of antibodies to explain our acquired immunity. For eighteenth-century physicians, almost no part of this reasoning would have made sense.

According to Williams, newcomers from the North were particularly vulnerable to the disease because they possessed tense fibres and were 'plethoric', having a comparative surfeit of blood, which was also heated upon arrival in the Indies. The warmth caused the blood to expand and become 'rarefied', pressing upon the rigid vessels that contained it. The rarefied blood travelled more quickly through the body, increasing all secretions 'recrementitious and excrementitious' except those by urine and stool. Yet these last two were the body's means of removing excess bile. '[A] redundance of bile', Williams declared, 'together with that stiffness of the fibres, and richness of the blood, are obvious and sufficient causes of their proneness to this fever'. For Williams, then, the best treatment was to bleed strangers on their arrival, reducing their excess blood, a process to be continued until their bodily fibres relaxed, and their 'juices assimilated to the air of the country'.[11] At that point, in common parlance, they could be said to be 'seasoned' to the climate.

Associated, then, with questions concerning socio-political status, conceptual foundations, and geographical taxonomies, another strand that runs through this book is the history of the idea of seasoning. The term dates back to at least the fifteenth century, when one finds the verb *to season* used in a sense very similar to the most common modern understanding: 'to render (a dish) more palatable by the addition of some savoury ingredient'. The word derives from the Old French *saisonner*, meaning 'to ripen, to render (fruit) palatable by the influence of the seasons'. A second, somewhat different and later English term flows from this original French usage, for one also speaks of seasoned timber, or seasoned metal. In this case, a particular treatment, usually related to the way in which the material will later be used, brings it to a kind of maturity or ripeness. The analogous use of the term for people – to be inured to rough conditions by training and experience – appears already in the early seventeenth century.[12] It seems commonplace to speak of seasoned soldiers, in particular, by the 1680s.

The idea of a 'seasoning sickness', however, meaning an illness that habituates the body to a particular environment or climate – and which, crucially, is only experienced once – seems to be a product of the late seventeenth century.[13] Certainly, eighteenth-century travellers, doctors, soldiers, and sailors all paid a great deal of attention to an illness that seemed to be a disease of *place*. Seasoning affected neither 'natives' nor those who had spent a good deal of time in a specific locale. Only those habituated to one location who ventured to another in which they were strangers fell ill. If they survived their affliction, their bodies were then inured to the novelties of the environments in which they now found themselves. And increasingly through the eighteenth century, yellow fever was seen by many as the seasoning sickness *par excellence*.

Bennet and Williams' dispute, then, turned on a number of the differences alluded to in my title. Both men, however, were silent – perhaps because it was beyond dispute? – on what may have been the most important distinction for social life in the West Indies: that between populations enslaved and free. For much of the eighteenth century, that social and legal distinction mattered more for physicians interested in the diseases of the Islands than did questions of race. Doctors treated black slaves, and noted that they often suffered disproportionately from the same diseases that afflicted whites, and sometimes from

---

[11] Ibid., 30.
[12] *Oxford English Dictionary*, 'season, *v*'. Meanings 1a. 4a. 4c.
[13] The *Oxford English Dictionary* cites Daniel Denton's *A Brief Description of New York* (1670) as the first usage of the word 'seasoning' with this meaning.

diseases that seemed distinctive to them. Yet most put those differences down to factors derived from their patients' position as slaves – poor diet, inadequate clothing and housing – or else to different beliefs about the causes and cures of their afflictions. White and black bodies – neither of which were deemed 'native' to the Indies – responded in similar ways to the climate. Matters would begin to change, however, beginning in the 1760s. In later chapters, then, *Difference and Disease* explores the relationship between the theories of what has become known as 'race-science' – and has been examined, particularly for the eighteenth century, almost exclusively within the European metropole – and the theories of medicine and science within a colonial, racially mixed population. The history of medicine, I hope to show, provides an ideal way of exploring the history of an empire defined as much by its structuring differences as by its putative unity, while the history of empire allows us to tease out the locatedness of medical discourse about specific locations.

Difference and the Postcolonial History of Colonial Medicine

For some time, imperial historians have contested the idea that a sense of being British was first created at home and then diffused to the colonies. As scholars including Linda Colley, Christopher Bayly, and others have argued, the colonies and other far-flung places in which Britons found themselves were among the sites in which Britishness was born.[14] It was, at least in part, in the periphery that the centre as we know it was brought into being. In recent years, historians of eighteenth-century medicine have similarly turned away from a near exclusive attention to the metropole and towards a broader analysis of what might be termed 'medicine in a global context'. Among historians of imperial medicine, Mark Harrison's work has been pre-eminent and my own book draws upon and seeks to complement arguments made in his *Medicine in an Age of Commerce and Empire* (2010).[15] Harrison's study aims to provide a history of medicine within the British Empire as a whole, not merely in select colonies, and to describe the circulations of people, knowledge, and practices within and between the centre and peripheries. The book rightly works to diminish differences long critiqued

---

[14] Linda Colley, *Britons: Forging the Nation, 1707–1837* (New Haven and London: Yale University Press, 2009); C. A. Bayly, *Imperial Meridian: The British Empire and the World, 1780–1830* (London and New York: Routledge, 1989). Catherine Hall, *Civilising Subjects: Colony and Metropole in the English Imagination, 1830–1867* (Chicago: University of Chicago Press, 2002). Kathleen Wilson, *The Island Race: Englishness, Empire and Gender in the Eighteenth Century* (London: Routledge, 2003); (ed.) *A New Imperial History: Culture, Identity, and Modernity in Britain and the Empire, 1660–1840* (Cambridge: Cambridge University Press, 2004). See also Kapil Raj, *Relocating Modern Science: Circulation and the Construction of Knowledge in South Asia and Europe, 1650–1900* (Basingstoke: Palgrave Macmillan, 2007).

[15] Mark Harrison, *Medicine in an Age of Commerce and Empire: Britain and its Tropical Colonies, 1660–1830* (Oxford: Oxford University Press, 2010).

within the secondary literature on the history of colonial science. Medical men in the colonies were not derivative drones following the lead of their colleagues in the metropole, but rather proponents of creative 'dissent' – that word used by Harrison to denote not merely a religious position common to many of the leading physicians in the colonies, but also a willingness to work against long-held traditions. Practitioners working in hospitals in the Indies 'rejected the genteel, text-based medicine of the physician elite for an avowedly empirical form of medicine supported by the twin pillars of bedside observation and post-mortem dissection'. Similar changes were occurring in Britain, but they proceeded at a more rapid pace overseas, where colonial practitioners could take 'advantage of unparalleled opportunities for dissection and the correlation of morbid signs with symptoms in living patients'.[16] Physicians in the 'peripheries', then, were *ahead* of those at the so-called centre. As a result, the rational medicine that emerged at the end of the eighteenth century should be understood as being 'as much a product of the colonies as of the infirmaries of revolutionary Paris; or, for that matter, of the hospitals and anatomy schools of Britain'.[17] The difference between metropole and colony is thus at the heart of Harrison's work, as it was for earlier studies, but the advantage is now given to the latter.[18]

I have considerable sympathy for this inversion, and where Harrison and I overlap topically, I have gratefully made use of his many insights and turned my attention towards those differences – in theories, for example, or social status – that are less relevant to the eventual emergence of so-called 'Paris medicine'. But the dominance of the distinction between practitioners in Europe and those in the colonies tends to lead to the diminution of other forms of difference that I try to stress.[19] The role of eighteenth-century medicine in the construction of race, for example, receives a much fuller treatment here than in any previous work.[20] The book's geographic scope is broad, tracking

---

[16] Ibid., 27.

[17] Ibid., 9.

[18] Pratik Chakrabarti, *Materials and Medicine: Trade, Conquest and Therapeutics in the Eighteenth Century* (Manchester: Manchester University Press, 2011).

[19] In paying so much attention to difference, I am drawing from recent work in the 'new imperial history'. For a discussion, see Kathleen Wilson, 'Introduction: Histories, Empires, Modernities', in *A New Imperial History: Culture, Identity, and Modernity in Britain and the Empire, 1660–1840*, ed. Kathleen Wilson (Cambridge: Cambridge University Press, 2004). See also Linda Colley, 'Britishness and Otherness: An Argument', *Journal of British Studies* 31 (1992). Hall. Wilson, *The Island Race: Englishness, Empire and Gender in the Eighteenth Century*.

[20] In Harrison's book, the discussion of race is largely limited to the period after 1790, in spite of the book spanning the years from 1660 to 1830. An earlier essay is more concerned with the period after 1780 and especially with the early nineteenth century. It is in the 1820s, it is argued there, that 'biological explanations ... began to appear in medical texts'. As one reason for this, Harrison points to the abolition of the slave trade in 1807, which 'may have served to focus medical attention more closely on questions of racial difference'. Mark Harrison, ' "The Tender Frame of Man": Disease, Climate and Racial Difference in India and the West Indies,

materials derived not only from Britain's 'tropical colonies' – largely the East and West Indies – but also from areas maintained by British representatives of the African slave trade as well as North America. I have also chosen to focus on a long-term, diachronic study of Britain's imperial holdings, rather than a shorter-term synchronic account of exchanges between and across empires in a given location, such as the Caribbean.

Perhaps as a result of its wide geographical scope, which includes but goes beyond the 'Atlantic world', relationships between medicine, slavery, and abolitionism are key elements of this study. I have tried, too, to be attentive to the differences between all of these locations. Among the implications of this attention is the fact that I cannot quite agree with those who have argued that military medical texts are the most important sources for understanding medicine outside of the British Isles in the eighteenth century.[21] The claim might be accurate for India, but it does not seem applicable to the West Indies for much of the century. While tracts on the diseases of soldiers and sailors focused on British bodies in locations described broadly as those 'nearer, or under the line' as William Cockburn phrased it in 1696, or in 'hotter Countries' as he put it in *Sea Diseases* a decade later, 'location-specific' works tended to stress the particularity of their location, radically distinguishing between lands located between the tropics. An over-emphasis on military rather than civilian works can thus also over-emphasise the similarities assumed between locations. In addition, medical men treating soldiers and sailors, as J. D. Alsop has noted, had a rather restricted group of patients under their care: for the most part, they ministered to younger, European men.[22] John Hunter was interested in the question of 'race', writing a dissertation on the varieties of human kind in 1775 before being appointed physician to the army and, from 1781 to 1783, superintendent of the military hospitals in Jamaica. However, in the text that he wrote based on his experiences, *Observations on the Diseases of the Army in Jamaica* (1788), he noted that '[t]he diseases of Negroes fell seldom under my

---

1760–1860', *Bulletin of the History of Medicine* 70, no. 1 (1996): 82, 83. Curtin, similarly, emphasises the period after 1780: Philip D. Curtin, ' "The White Man's Grave": Image and Reality, 1780–1850', *Journal of British Studies* 1 (1961); 'Epidemiology and the Slave Trade', *Political Science Quarterly* 83, no. 2 (1968); *The Image of Africa: British Ideas and Action, 1780–1850* (Madison: University of Wisconsin Press, 1964). On relationships between medicine and slavery, I am indebted to the works of Richard B. Sheridan: 'Africa and the Caribbean in the Atlantic Slave Trade', *The American Historical Review* 77, no. 1 (1972); 'The Guinea Surgeons on the Middle Passage: The Provision of Medical Services in the British Slave Trade', *The International Journal of African Historical Studies* 14, no. 4 (1981); *Doctors and Slaves: A Medical and Demographic History of Slavery in the British West Indies, 1680–1834*.

[21] J. D. Alsop, 'Warfare and the Creation of British Imperial Medicine, 1600–1800', in *British Military and Naval Medicine, 1600–1830*, ed. Geoffrey L. Hudson (Amsterdam: Rodopi, 2007), 23. Harrison, *Medicine in an Age of Commerce and Empire: Britain and its Tropical Colonies, 1660–1830*, 14.

[22] Alsop, 37.

observation'.[23] This is to be contrasted to the testimony concerning the slave trade of Dr John Quier and others the same year, in which all three (civilian) physicians noted that they had under their care three to four *thousand* slaves a year as part of their practice.[24] Civilian surgeons and physicians also – unsurprisingly – paid much more attention to the afflictions of women than their military counterparts. One might note, finally, that attention to the many different kinds of patients outside of the metropole makes one rather less sanguine about the 'opportunities' for dissections and other more novel medical practices, for dissections and experimentation were often carried out on the bodies of those – soldiers, perhaps, and often slaves – who could not always easily resist.[25]

At its core, this book is about the mutual shaping of medicine and the eighteenth-century British Empire.[26] As such, I put it forward as an example of the *postcolonial history of colonial medicine.*[27] Such histories were once fairly common,[28] but today historians of science, medicine and colonialism seem loath to engage with postcolonial approaches. Indeed, two recent essays by prominent historians of science and colonialism have been markedly critical of postcolonial methods and their potential utility.[29] Where the issue is antipathy rather than apathy, however, such critiques seem rooted in misunderstandings of the state of postcolonial science studies as it is today. For, in the last few decades, histories of science and colonialism have followed many of the same paths as postcolonial studies. Historians of the colonial past, like postcolonial

---

[23] John Hunter, *Observations on the Diseases of the Army in Jamaica; and on the Best Means of Preserving the Health of Europeans, in That Climate* (London: G. Nicol, 1788), 305.

[24] Assembly. Jamaica., *Two Reports (One Presented the 16th of October, the Other on the 12th of November, 1788) from the Committee of the Honourable House of Assembly of Jamaica, Appointed to Examine into … The Slave-Trade … Published, by Order of the House of Assembly, by Stephen Fuller … Agent for Jamaica.* (London: B. White and Son; J. Sewell; R. Faulder; and J. Debrett, and J. Stockdale, 1789).

[25] Londa Schiebinger, 'Human Experimentation in the Eighteenth Century: Natural Boundaries and Valid Testing', in *The Moral Authority of Nature*, ed. Lorraine Daston and Fernando Vidal (Chicago: University of Chicago Press, 2004); *Secret Cures of Slaves: People, Plants, and Medicine in the Eighteenth-Century Atlantic World* (Stanford: Stanford University Press, 2017).

[26] For a somewhat similar project, from a different perspective, see Alan Bewell, *Romanticism and Colonial Disease* (Baltimore: Johns Hopkins University Press, 1999).

[27] For a fuller discussion of the relationship between postcolonial science studies and the history of science and colonialism, see Suman Seth, 'Colonial History and Postcolonial Science Studies', *Radical History Review* 127 (2017).

[28] See, for example, Megan Vaughan, *Curing Their Ills: Colonial Power and African Illness* (Stanford: Stanford University Press, 1991); David Arnold, *Colonizing the Body: State Medicine and Epidemic Disease in Nineteenth-Century India* (Berkeley: University of California Press, 1993); Gyan Prakash, *Another Reason: Science and the Imagination of Modern India* (Princeton: Princeton University Press, 1999).

[29] Kapil Raj, 'Beyond Postcolonialism … And Postpositivism: Circulation and the Global History of Science', *Isis* 104 (2013); James McClellan III, 'Science & Empire Studies and Postcolonial Studies: A Report from the Contact Zone', in *Entangled Knowledge: Scientific Discourses and Cultural Difference*, eds. Klaus Hock and Gesa Mackenthun (Münster: Waxmann, 2012).

theorists today, are sceptical of the telos and boundaries of the nation state; have called into question the dichotomies and divisions of the colonial age as analytic, rather than actors' categories; have stressed the global setting as a way to understand the flows and movement of sciences and technologies; and are fascinated by hybridity and heterogeneity.

In particular, much of the literature in postcolonial science studies has been concerned with the troubling of binaries and boundaries. 'We have to be sensitive', Warwick Anderson and Vincanne Adams have written in a particularly important formulation, 'to dislocation, transformation, and resistance; to the proliferation of partially purified and hybrid forms and identities; to the contestation and negotiation of boundaries; and to recognizing that practices of science are always multi-sited'.[30] A similar move is common in the history of colonialism and science. Indeed, for scholars like Kapil Raj, this is one of the appeals of a circulatory model of knowledge exchange, since such a model does not reify the categories of knowledge into those of coloniser and colonised.[31] Sujit Sivasundaram has made a similar claim, arguing that a focus on the global may allow us to think beyond such binaries and 'fragment traditions of knowledge on all sides'.[32] An excellent recent collection accepts 'it may make sense to conceptualise encounters between Europeans and other peoples as dualistic and antagonistic', but that there is no reason to assume '*essentially* confrontational relations'.[33] Instead, one may look at the go-betweens in exchanges, those who allowed boundaries to be blurred and exchanges to occur, even as they sometimes maintained and objectified the boundaries they transgressed. The volume is thus concerned with people whose tasks involve the *intra* and the *trans:* 'those tricky and often elusive characters who seemed newly important in networks linking cultures and, as often, confusing their boundaries'.[34] There is a good argument to be made that histories of science, medicine, and colonialism are remarkably methodologically close to being postcolonial studies of medicine and technoscience done in the past, and vice versa. And in that situation, there seems little reason for each field not to borrow from and engage with one another more.

---

[30] Vincenne Adams and Warwick Anderson, 'Pramoedya's Chickens: Postcolonial Studies of Technoscience', in *The Handbook of Science and Technology Studies*, ed. Edward J. Hackett et al. (Cambridge, MA: MIT Press, 2007), 183–4.

[31] Raj, *Relocating Modern Science: Circulation and the Construction of Knowledge in South Asia and Europe, 1650–1900*.

[32] Sujit Sivasundaram, 'Sciences and the Global: On Methods, Questions, and Theory', *Isis* 101 (2010): 154. At times, however, Sivasundaram seems to fall into the trap of seeing globalisation as a force of history in its own right, arguing, for example, that '[g]lobalization enabled the precolonial, the colonial, and the postcolonial to fit together', ibid., 156.

[33] Simon Schaffer et al., eds., *The Brokered World: Go-Betweens and Global Intelligence, 1770–1820* (Sagamore Beach: Science History Publications, 2009), xv.

[34] Ibid., xvii.

There is an alternative, however, to the blurring of extant boundaries and it is a valuable one. It is here, in fact, that the value of historical work that engages with postcolonial writings becomes particularly clear. For there is a danger in so much attention being paid to the (important) fact that conceptualised ways of dividing the world did not always hold in practice. We should not understand the critique of an absolute (such as Said's totalising model of the power of colonial epistemologies over the colonised) as a negation.[35] After all, not everyone was able to slip between and over boundaries. That boundaries could be blurred by those sufficiently fortunate or skilled did not mean that many were not bound, limited, and governed within such boundaries. In our valuable attention to the manoeuvrings of those who were, in the omnipresent metaphor of much of this literature, involved in forms of trade and exchange, we should not lose track of those who, usually against their will, were exchanged and traded. We need, then, to pay attention to the functioning of categorical divisions, without reifying them or regarding them as absolutes. One means of doing so is to investigate not the blurring of extant boundaries, but the socially imbricated, tentative, and complex coming-into-being of the categories and binaries in the first place.

Such a task has been integral to postcolonial studies, from Said's germinal *Orientalism* through more recent studies of time and history by Johannes Fabian and Dipesh Chakrabarty.[36] These works inform the analysis here. This book is built around an exploration of the role played by science and medicine in the emergence of three categories fundamental to colonialism: race, particularly in the form of racialised pathologies; the division of the world into 'tropical' and 'temperate' disease zones; and the medical mapping of empire and, in particular, of zones of familiarity and strangeness according to whether newcomers to a location had to undergo a 'seasoning sickness'. Historians of colonialism and imperialism have come to be very wary of an analytic distinction between centres and peripheries. 'The point', insists a recent overview of work in the history of Atlantic science, 'is to distribute knowledge production, to insist on its contingency, and to break away from the geographies of center and periphery as a framework for classifying both people and knowledge'.[37] The point might, as I have suggested, be taken too far, since boundaries and

---

[35] See, for example, Edward W. Said, *Orientalism* (New York: Vintage, 2003).

[36] Johannes Fabian, *Time and the Other: How Anthropology Makes Its Object* (New York: Columbia University Press, 1983). Dipesh Chakrabarty, *Provincializing Europe: Postcolonial Thought and Historical Difference* (Princeton: Princeton University Press, 2000). For related works within the history of science (sometimes without the postcolonial label) see Helen Tilley, 'Global Histories, Vernacular Science, and African Genealogies: Or, Is the History of Science Ready for the World?', *Isis* 101 (2010). For further discussion, see Seth.

[37] Marcelo Aranda et al., 'The History of Atlantic Science: Collective Reflections from the 2009 Harvard Seminar on Atlantic History', *Atlantic Studies* 7 (2010): 499.

divisions, however porous, serve to limit movements.[38] But beyond this, one should ask how such boundaries were conceived of in the first place? How was the ideational distinction between (imperial) centre and periphery, between the place where 'Britons' were home and where they were 'strangers', produced and maintained? How, more particularly, did science and medicine play a role in this production and maintenance and how did this far-from-monolithic or static division change over time?

Such are at least some of the historiographical questions driving my analysis. Structurally, the material below is divided into three parts, within which chapters are arranged roughly chronologically. Part I, 'Locality' is comprised of Chapters 1 and 2; Chapters 3 and 4 make up Part II, 'Empire'; Part III, spanning Chapters 5 to 7, explores the relationships between 'race-medicine and race-science'. The three themes are fairly distinct, but there is considerable overlap, both temporal and substantial, between each part. The conclusion then seeks to bring all into a common conversation. In the next section, I offer a more detailed summary of the argument of each chapter, while simultaneously aiming to provide some sense of the literatures to which I hope to make contributions.

Before embarking upon such detail, and after having supplied some sense of what this book is (or hopes to be), it would be well to be clear about what it is not. I have already noted that my geographical focus is the British Empire: comparative accounts or inter-imperial exchanges are not at the centre of analysis. Such exchanges almost certainly occurred, although perhaps more often at the level of quotidian practice than in the somewhat more formal published documents that make up the bulk of my sources. British texts about the diseases of warm climates tended to be rather parochial in the figures and works outside European metropoles that they cited and by mid-century, British writings were extensive enough that they could provide a seemingly complete set of references on their own.[39] One sees this via patterns of internal citation, but the most striking evidence might be that from a source outside the British Empire. In a prize-winning essay published in English in 1762, Solomon de Monchy, city physician at Rotterdam, proclaimed the pre-eminence of English writers on the diseases of the West Indies. Somewhat idiosyncratically, given the long history of Dutch colonialism and writings on medicine, de Monchy

---

[38] Breaking down the centre/periphery divide has been an essential element of studies that have taken the Atlantic world as their geographical focus. See, e.g. James Delbourgo, *A Most Amazing Scene of Wonders: Electricity and Enlightenment in Early America* (Cambridge, MA: Harvard University Press, 2006); Susan Scott Parrish, *American Curiosity: Cultures of Natural History in the Colonial British Atlantic World* (Chapel Hill: University of North Carolina Press, 2006).

[39] Schiebinger alludes to a similar phenomenon, suggesting that the 'invisible boundaries of empire' may have 'limit[ed] interisland exchange'. Schiebinger, *Secret Cures of Slaves: People, Plants, and Medicine in the Eighteenth-Century Atlantic World*, 181.

suggested of his compatriots that, if they were not 'totally strangers to navigation', they were 'yet little acquainted with the many changes and effects, which
living at sea, and sailing into different climates, very generally produce in the
human constitution'. As a result, he relied, for his own understanding, on 'the
many observations of the English physicians and Surgeons, who, at present, to
the great benefit of that commercial nation, make the Sea-distempers a considerable object of their study, and have written on them from their own experience'.[40] For British medical authors in the colonies, a significant expansion
in their engagement with texts written by their non-Anglophonic counterparts
appears to have begun only towards the end of the eighteenth century.[41]

I draw gratefully throughout the subsequent pages from work in the last few
decades on the social histories of medicine, colonialism and slavery – particularly within the Caribbean and North America. Mine, however, is fundamentally a work of intellectual history, although I mean to signify by this term not
a context-free history of ideas, but rather a profoundly context-laden *history
of arguments*. And, although I rely on printed sources, which suggests that the
subjects of my analysis were members of a fairly elite class in cultural terms,
it would be wrong to imagine that most were even to be numbered among the
economically secure, let alone the wealthy. Some medical writers in the colonies (for example William Hillary, the principal subject of Chapter 2) made
comfortable livings, were regularly cited throughout the empire, and had books
that underwent multiple editions. But the majority of those outside European
metropolitan centres (and often even within them) were far more obscure figures, struggling – like Bennet and Williams – in a difficult medical market-
place. This is intellectual history, then, with a capacious understanding of what
an 'intellectual' might be, and with an aim to recover not simply the best and
boldest ideas of an age, but the thought-worlds and ideational stakes of medical
practitioners of many kinds.

If my sources encompass a fair diversity in terms of economic status or educational training, it must be acknowledged that they lack in diversity in other
ways. I am attentive to gender as a category of analysis throughout, with a
sustained focus on relationships between gender, sexuality, race, and medicine
in Chapters 5 and 7 in particular. But women enter most of the stories recounted
here as patients rather than practitioners. The voices of non-European medical
practitioners are similarly muted.[42] Some British authors were happy to bolster

[40] Solomon de Monchy, *An Essay on the Causes and Cure of the Usual Diseases in Voyages to
the West Indies* (London: T. Becket and P. A. De Hondt, 1762), ii, lv.

[41] See, e.g. Benjamin Moseley, *A Treatise on Tropical Diseases; And on the Climate of the West-
Indies* (London: T. Cadell, 1787).

[42] The vast majority of those providing medical treatment for the enslaved were themselves slaves.
For classic accounts, see for the West Indies, Sheridan, *Doctors and Slaves: A Medical and
Demographic History of Slavery in the British West Indies, 1680–1834*, and for the antebellum

their own claims to the possession of local knowledge by citing more or less reliable 'native' informants, so that one can, at times, get a sense of competing forms of knowledge within the pages of Anglophonic texts. Yet even such mentions tend to be limited. I should be clear, too, on the fact that the absence of non-European voices is also the result of my own authorial choices. I am less interested here, for example, in the specifics of treatments and therapeutics – where indigenous or slave knowledge might more often be cited – than I am in medical theories, where British men of medicine tended to emphasise their own 'rationalist' expertise and to downplay or ignore the contributions or claims of their non-European counterparts.[43]

Locality

Chapter 1 explores the role of Hippocratic ideas about the relationship between health and location – laid out most clearly in the Hippocratic text *Airs, Waters, and Places* – prior to 1700. Our understanding of this material has been

United States, Todd L. Savitt, *Medicine and Slavery: The Diseases and Health Care of Blacks in Antebellum Virginia* (Champaign: University of Illinois Press, 1978); Ronald Numbers and Todd L. Savitt, eds., *Science and Medicine in the Old South* (Baton Rouge: Louisiana State University Press, 1999); Sharla M. Fett, *Working Cures: Healing, Health, and Power on Southern Slave Plantations* (Chapel Hill and London: University of North Carolina Press, 2002). For superb recent accounts of Afro-Caribbean medical knowledge in the Atlantic world, see Karol Weaver, *Medical Revolutionaries: The Enslaved Healers of Eighteenth-Century Saint Domingue* (Urbana and Chicago: University of Illinois Press, 2006); James H. Sweet, *Domingo Álvares, African Healing, and the Intellectual History of the Atlantic World* (Chapel Hill: University of North Carolina Press, 2011); Pablo F. Gómez, 'Incommensurable Epistemologies?: The Atlantic Geography of Healing in the Early Modern Caribbean', *Small Axe* 18 (2014); *The Experiential Caribbean: Creating Knowledge and Healing in the Early Modern Atlantic* (Chapel Hill: University of North Carolina Press, 2017); 'The Circulation of Bodily Knowledge in the Seventeenth-Century Black Spanish Caribbean', *Social History of Medicine* 26 (2013); Schiebinger, *Secret Cures of Slaves: People, Plants, and Medicine in the Eighteenth-Century Atlantic World.*

43   As Karol Weaver notes: 'Although eighteenth-century physicians, plantation surgeons, and white planters used slave remedies, they downplayed the role of the slave healer by placing the remedy within the traditional European therapeutic framework or by making reference to the healing traditions of esteemed nations', Weaver, 74. Willingness to explicitly cite local informants also appears to have changed across time and space. Londa Schiebinger offers the revealing example of differences in the way that Thomson reported his results and sources in a text intended largely for a West Indian audience (*Treatise on the Diseases of Negroes*, 1820) and the way he presented similar materials to a metropolitan audience in the *Edinburgh Medical and Surgical Journal.* 'In his Jamaican *Treatise*', Schiebinger notes, 'Thomson valued "Negro" knowledge; in his European version, this knowledge often fell from view', Schiebinger, *Secret Cures of Slaves: People, Plants, and Medicine in the Eighteenth-Century Atlantic World*, 179. In writing about botanical knowledge, Miles Ogborn observes that British authors in the early eighteenth century were willing to admit that non-Europeans might know about or experiment with nature. By the 1780s, however, such admissions were becoming much rarer: Ogborn, 'Talking Plants: Botany and Speech in Eighteenth-Century Jamaica'. *History of Science* 51 (2013): 275–6. See also Jorge Cañizares-Esguerra, *How to Write the History of the New World: Histories, Epistemologies, and Identities in the Eighteenth-Century Atlantic World* (Stanford: Stanford University Press, 2001), 60–129.

shaped, to a sizeable extent, by a comment made in 1707 by Hans Sloane, later to become President of the Royal Society. Sloane declared that he had been informed, before travelling to the West Indies, that 'the Diseases of this place were all different from what they are Europe, and to be treated in a differing Method'.[44] Historians, taking Sloane at his word, have thus often characterised the period before the beginning of the eighteenth century as one in which the orthodox position held that substantially different climates produced radically different diseases. I show, to the contrary, that medical men tended to work with similitudes more than differences, most often analogising warmer climates overseas to warmer seasons at home. Insofar as differences existed – and they obviously did – it was because one found more cases of diseases commonly suffered in English summers in Jamaica all year round. *Contra* Sloane, I have found very few examples of any authors arguing that the diseases of warmer countries were utterly unknown in Europe. Yet one does find several examples of medical men advocating for novel *treatments* in different locations and in this claim we locate, I would contend, the stakes of Sloane's statement. Arguing, in Jamaica, with local practitioners who insisted that their local knowledge might trump that of a metropolitan physician, Sloane rejected any claim that his expertise might not be transferable to his new location. In examining the relationship between differences of places and distempers, then, one is forced simultaneously to an analysis of differences in social standing and the locatedness of claims to expertise.

Chapter 2 continues the analysis of Hippocratic thought by focusing on the author of the most influential text on the diseases of the West Indies for the mid-eighteenth century, William Hillary. Hillary serves as guide through a thicket of interrelating ideas relevant to medicine in warm climates from the 1720s to the 1760s, including the roles of the mechanical philosophy and medical meteorology, and debates between those who favoured contagionist rather than climatic theories of disease causation. Focus on the author of *Observations on the Changes of the Air, and the Concomitant Epidemical Diseases in the Island of Barbadoes* also allows the elaboration of two related arguments. The first involves what has become known as the Hippocratic revival in early eighteenth-century British medicine and points to the ways that a study of the colonies can inform our understanding of the history of medicine within the British Isles. As Chapter 1 shows, *Airs, Waters, and Places* had already, prior to 1700, become a model for understanding the illnesses deemed characteristic

---

[44] Hans Sloane, *A Voyage to the Islands Madera, Barbados, Nieves, S. Christophers and Jamaica, with the Natural History of the Herbs and Trees, Four-Footed Beasts, Fishes, Birds, Insects, Reptiles, &C. Of the Last of Those Islands; to Which Is Prefix'd an Introduction, Wherein is an Account of the Inhabitants, Air, Waters, Diseases, Trade, &C. of That Place, with Some Relations Concerning the Neighbouring Continent, and Islands of America.*, 2 vols. (London: printed by B. M. for the author, 1707 & 1725), 1707, xc.

of a given location. The turn to Hippocratism in the metropole thus happened later than that in the colonies. More significantly, it also had a different object. Authors within Britain tended to emphasise epidemic, rather than endemic illnesses, taking as their touchstone the Hippocratic works, *Epidemics I* and *III*. Contrasting the forms of Hippocratic thought in Britain and its imperial holdings, then – and speaking not of Hippocratism but geographically specific *Hippocratisms* – one can come to a more nuanced and specific understanding of precisely what neo-Hippocratism meant and the different kinds of work it might do. And in Hillary's work – as befits a physician who practiced in both the West Indies and Britain – one can also see how different forms of Hippocratism might be fused. The chapter's second argument takes up a question posed by the material in Chapter 1. If one does not find arguments for the distinctiveness of the diseases of tropical countries before 1700, when do such arguments first emerge? In Hillary, we find part of an answer, one that would bring the issue of slavery and the slave trade to the fore. For Hillary, a putative similarity between the warmth of climates in the West Indies and the Guinea Coast was not sufficient to produce a common disease environment: after all, differences abounded. Where one found diseases common to both locations and unfamiliar within Europe, then, one looked to other causes, such as the movement of human cargo. At mid-century, then, one could not so much speak of the diseases of the Tropics as of the diseases of lands connected by the triangular trade in slaves and goods.

Empire

The first two chapters of this book share a common geographical focus, using close readings of texts (mostly) written in and about the West Indies as a means of unpacking assumptions about the relationships between sickness and place more generally. Chapters 3 and 4 aim to widen the scope of analysis, embracing and elaborating upon the notion of an 'imperial medicine'. It seems obvious to note that the metaphorical health of the British Empire rested on the literal health of its subjects, both military and civilian. Yet in many ways, historians of eighteenth-century British imperialism have tended to take the history of medicine for granted. Almost incredible death rates from disease, of course, form the backdrop for any narrative of imperial expansion. And death rates could, at times, reach such levels that they were marshalled by those agitating for political change, or for alterations in the organisation and structure of the armed forces. For many imperial historians, however, *theories* of disease – their causation and treatment – function as an effectively irrelevant superstructure in relation to vastly more significant basal facts of morbidity and mortality. Ideas that appear laughably antiquated to modern eyes merely help explain why tropical service was deadly and to be avoided when possible.

Medical history, when invoked, functions in a supportive role for a more fundamental political, social, or intellectual history of empire and imperialism.

And yet, as I show in Chapter 3, theories of disease and their relationships to place can be used as profoundly illuminating sources for understanding a basic issue: How did Britons conceive of their empire? How did they conceptualise the relationship between centres and peripheries? How did relations of similitude and difference shape reactions to places deemed utterly foreign or suitably home-like? Answers, of course, changed over time. Dividing the century into rough thirds, Linda Colley has argued that the period up to the end of the Seven Years War was one in which the empire could be regarded as largely homogenous.[45] The spectacular expansion in imperial territories after the victories of the war, however, led to a sense that the Empire was suddenly unfamiliar, a feeling that began to dissipate after the loss of the American colonies. Medical discourse allows one to paint a somewhat different narrative, although the turning points remain roughly the same. As is made clear by insistences on 'seasoning' new arrivals to different climes, homogeneity was never a medical assumption about far-flung lands. The Seven Years War marks a turning point in imperial conceptions of self, but this is because before midcentury, the empire could be conveniently bifurcated – split between a metropolitan home, where one was already seasoned to the climate, and a periphery where such seasoning took time and could potentially prove deadly. After the War, one does indeed see an anxiety, as Colley suggests, but it manifested as the sense that even 'home' could prove dangerous: one might well need time to become seasoned even within the British Isles. After the 1770s, such reflexive concerns would dissipate, and one begins to see a kind of medical nationalism, as authors increasingly cast warm climates as profoundly and completely foreign spaces, to be contrasted with the ideal environs of the metropole.

If Chapter 3 is thus concerned with the ways in which understandings of medicine in the periphery informed conceptions of empire, Chapter 4 is concerned with the inverse question. How did an 'imperial sensibility' come to inform British medicine in the eighteenth century? Material about the diseases of warmer climates is fairly rare in medical texts that were not primarily concerned with that topic before around 1700. From the 1720s, however, the periphery comes to take up a (admittedly small) part of many major works, with a larger place in those texts dedicated to medical meteorological analyses. As Harrison has shown, a sea change would occur in the 1750s, after the publication of John Pringle's *Observations of the Diseases of the Army* in 1752.[46] Carrying the logic of medical meteorology to its most extreme conclusion,

---

[45] Colley, *Britons: Forging the Nation, 1707–1837*.
[46] Harrison, *Medicine in an Age of Commerce and Empire: Britain and its Tropical Colonies, 1660–1830*, esp. Chapter 3.

Pringle would argue not only that the state of the air contributed to the production of the illnesses that plagued soldiers, but that it was by far the most important cause, eclipsing either diet or climate. And the most dangerous air was that rendered putrid by a variety of causes. Although putrefaction – in the sense of corruption – had been an important element in theories of disease since antiquity and had been emphasised by Pringle's teacher, the famed Hermann Boerhaave, one may identify in Pringle's text the source of what might be termed a 'putrefactive turn' in imperial medicine. While Pringle had largely been interested in the diseases of soldiers fighting in the low countries during the War of Austrian Succession, the association of putridity with warm weather quickly made his theories central to etiological analyses of the diseases of warm climates. And such analyses made their mark on metropolitan medicine and natural philosophy. The stakes of the debate between the English reverend and chemist, Joseph Priestley and the Edinburgh physician, William Alexander over 'the noxious quality of the effluvia of putrid marshes', I argue, were imperial ones. In questioning the ability of putrid air to cause putrid fevers, Alexander was not only challenging Pringle's logic – ensconced by the time of the debate in the mid-1770s – he was calling into question the logics governing the management of the military in the colonies.

Race

Chapters 5 and 7 take up the history of 'race-medicine', a term I have coined by way of analogy with 'race-science', first introduced by Nancy Stepan in the early 1980s.[47] Turning away from the emphasis, in most of the secondary literature, on questions of morphological structure and hence on racialised *anatomy* (questions shared between natural history and medicine), I ask instead about more specifically medical racial *physiologies* and, particularly, racial *pathologies*.[48] When, I ask most basically, does one find the first instances of diseases conceived of as 1) characteristic of a given race and 2) caused not by the same kinds of environmental factors that produced racial difference in the first place, but rather by racialised physical differences between (for example) black and

---

[47] Nancy Stepan, *The Idea of Race in Science: Great Britain, 1800–1960* (Hamden: Archon, 1982).

[48] Roxann Wheeler, *The Complexion of Race: Categories of Difference in Eighteenth-Century British Culture* (Philadelphia: University of Pennsylvania Press, 2000); Andrew S. Curran, *The Anatomy of Blackness: Science & Slavery in an Age of Enlightenment* (Baltimore: Johns Hopkins University Press, 2011). For a similar approach, in spite of its title, see Rana Asali Hogarth, 'Comparing Anatomies, Constructing Races: Medicine and Slavery in the Atlantic World, 1787–1838'. PhD Thesis (New Haven: Yale University, 2012). Among my inspirations for this turn are Warwick Anderson, *The Cultivation of Whiteness: Science, Health and Racial Destiny in Australia* (New York: Basic Books, 2003) and *Colonial Pathologies: American Tropical Medicine, Race, and Hygiene in the Philippines* (Durham, NC and London: Duke University Press, 2006).

white bodies? Or, to phrase this another way, when does race become a *cause* of illness, rather than (like most diseases of the period) an *effect* of climate, diet, and other environmental factors? The answer given in Chapter 5 is that this does not happen before at least mid-century. In at least partial distinction to sexual difference – which I discuss as a counter-point to and a flexible, mutually constitutive element of discourses concerning racial difference – race was not construed as an essential medical category for most of the eighteenth century. Focusing on the multiple and changing writings of the naval surgeon, John Atkins – perhaps the first author to introduce polygenist ideas (those positing a separate act of creation for different human races) in a medical text – I demonstrate that notions of racial fixity and the theoretical presuppositions of the medicine of warm climates did not mix. Atkins believed that blacks and whites were fundamentally different in their physical structures, and that neither diet nor climate could change this, but he made no arguments suggesting that such racial differences were the cause of the diseases he deemed characteristic of and peculiar to the Guinea Coast. Polygenism and medical environmentalism occupied different parts of the same text and little would change in Atkin's medical explanations when he recanted his unorthodox polygenetic views in the early 1740s.

In common with a number of historians, I date the turn towards hardening conceptions of race as part of a response to the abolitionist movement, beginning roughly in the 1760s.[49] The effect of anti-slavery propaganda was to politicise the very question of natural equality. 'It was one thing to entertain the possibility in the abstract', John Wood Sweet has wryly observed, 'It was quite another to confront it as a political challenge to immensely profitable colonial plantation regimes'.[50] Chapter 6 turns from race-medicine to race-science to explore the racial theories of Edward Long, author of a massive, three-volume *History of Jamaica* (1774), who first publicly espoused his polygenist views in response to the outcome of a court case in 1772 that appeared to support the anti-slavery cause. The chapter's aim is thus to situate debates about the origin of human races concretely in the context of responses to abolitionist critique. It is also, however, to draw attention to the difference that geographical

---

[49] The claim is of very long standing. In 1945, for example, Ashley Montagu argued, in a chapter on 'The Origin of the Concept of "Race"', that '[i]t was only when voices began to make themselves heard against the inhuman traffic in slaves and when these voices assumed the shape of influential men and organizations that, on the defensive, the supporters of slavery were forced to look about them for reasons of a new kind to controvert the dangerous arguments of their opponents'. Ashley Montagu, *Man's Most Dangerous Myth: The Fallacy of Race*, 2nd ed. (New York: Columbia University Press, 1945), 10. See also Seymour Drescher, 'The Ending of the Slave Trade and the Evolution of European Scientific Racism', *Social Science History* 14 (1990).

[50] John Wood Sweet, *Bodies Politic: Negotiating Race in the American North, 1730–1830* (Baltimore: Johns Hopkins University Press, 2003), 276.

specificity makes in the history of race, even when the focus is on anatomy rather than pathology. Race-science during the Enlightenment in the West Indies looks very different to metropolitan race-science in the same period, for reasons very specific to the location of its production. Long's polygenism also appears quite dissimilar to the kinds of rigid racialism with which we are more familiar from nineteenth-century sources. The reason for the differences is twofold. First, although Long was willing to buck biblical orthodoxy, he balked at materialism, a position that gained traction in racial studies following the successes of the phrenological movement in the early nineteenth century. Second, Long presents us with a (relatively rare) case of an eighteenth-century writer on 'race-science' with political sympathies toward a part of the world that was both outside the bounds of the European metropole and contained a majority black population. As a result, one finds a fundamental ambivalence in his writings on race, an ambivalence that stemmed directly from his desire to manage social relations and political systems in a slave society. Metropolitan figures who believed in the fixity of race (regardless of the question of origin) made a cornerstone of their position the essential identity of newly arrived African slaves and their descendants. For Long, however, the difference between 'salt-water' and 'creole' Negroes was to be the solution to the most pressing social problem of the sugar islands: slave insurrection. This understanding of the (potential) political and social differences between generations of slaves required a physical corollary: Long's polygenism presumed less fixity than the monogenism of a figure like Immanuel Kant.

Chapter 7, finally, returns to the history of race-medicine, picking up the thread from Chapter 5, as medicine begins to play a central role in debates about the end of the slave trade. I look first at critiques and defences of slavery that relied on medical experience and expertise, at tracts in which doctors and surgeons invoked their own histories and practices to point to ways that enslavement might be meliorated or – as some contended – that it already had been, in spite of the accusations of those who charged planters with neglect and brutal treatment. The chapter turns next to the questions of 'racialised' pathologies in the last decades of the century. Clear continuities to the earlier period may be traced: fixed physical characteristics were rarely invoked as explanations. And yet climate did not quite function in the same way that it once had. In the majority of earlier accounts, the diseases of non-Europeans had largely been examined as part of studies of the illnesses peculiar to non-European locations. Among the responses to abolitionist critiques, however, was greater attention paid to the illnesses of Afro-Caribbean slaves as explicitly compared to those of Europeans and white Creoles who inhabited the same geographical space. In situations where climate was essentially held in common, one finds increasing emphasis on diet, clothing, housing, and behaviour as explanations for health disparities between whites and blacks. If one does not find 'race' in these – still orthodox – writings, one does find more emphasis on the social and cultural differences that separated Northern Europeans from others. The final section of the chapter turns from the orthodox to the heterodox, looking at polygenist and rigidly racialist accounts in medical texts. Pathological and anatomical claims were to be found in particular abundance, I show, in discourses that asserted an innate capacity for Africans to labour under environmental conditions that putatively made it impossible for Europeans to take their place. And from the 1780s, one can locate precisely those claims that had been marked by their absence in the earlier period discussed in Chapter 5: claims that invoked physical variation as the *cause* of racialised medical differences. By the 1800s, race-medicine was beginning to take shape.

In the conclusion, I try to draw together two of the largest threads of the book, attempting to find common answers to two puzzles that have previously been seen as distinct. The last quarter of the eighteenth century saw the emergence of a growing agreement concerning human races. Where, as Nicholas Hudson has shown, one had previously spoken of near-innumerable 'nations' or 'peoples' in order to divide humanity into meaningful groupings, from the late 1700s, humankind was increasingly divided into a small number of races.[51] Many smaller differences had been elided to produce larger similitudes, to be contrasted with a few, now-large differences. Similarly, medical men had once found near-innumerable points of commonality between various points on the globe, noting, as Hans Sloane did in 1707, that parts of Jamaica were no warmer than Montpelier, and also noting multiple points of difference between even nearby locations, identifying 'micro-climates', in Katherine Johnston's account, as explanations for disease variation on the island of Jamaica.[52] By the 1780s, however, such small-scale differences were disappearing, as one begins to find accounts of 'tropical diseases', that bound the East and West Indies to each other and to locations in Africa. That growing similitude only made sense in the context of a larger difference: the distinction between the diseases of temperate and tropical climes. In discourses of race and discourses concerning the diseases of warm climates, then, one finds – at essentially the same time – a similar set of moves: smaller intra-regional differences ignored and inter-regional differences emphasised. That, I argue, is no mere coincidence. The emergence of modern conceptions of race, and the emergence of a category of tropical diseases were intertwined phenomena, to be explained by a history of medicine, race, slavery, and empire.

---

[51] Nicholas Hudson. 'From "Nation" to "Race": The Origin of Racial Classification in Eighteenth-Century Thought'. Eighteenth-Century Studies 29, no. 3 (1996): 246–64.

[52] Katherine Johnston, 'The Constitution of Empire: Place and Bodily Health in the Eighteenth-Century Atlantic', *Atlantic Studies* 10 (2013).

Part I

Locality

1   'The Same Diseases Here as in Europe'? Health and Locality Before 1700

Toward the end of January, 1686, the London doctor, Hans Sloane wrote to the naturalist John Ray, reporting to him (among other things) the ways that unscrupulous merchants were currently seeking to fool unwary purchasers of the febrifuge known as Jesuit's Bark. '[I]t being so good a drug, that they begin to adulterate it with black cherry and other barks dipped in a tincture of aloes, to make it bitter'. Sloane noted that anyone familiar with the substance might spot the trickery immediately, for 'the bitterness of the adulterated bark appears upon its first touch with the tongue, whereas the other is a pretty while in the mouth before it is tasted'.[1] The letter included news that suggested Sloane might soon have considerable use for the drug himself. 'I have talked a long while', he wrote, 'of going to Jamaica with the Duke of Albemarle as his physician, which, if I do, next to serving his grace and family in my profession, my business is to see what I can meet withal that is extraordinary in nature in those places. I hope to be able to send you some observations from thence, God Almighty granting life and strength to do what I design'.[2]

Although only twenty-six at the time, Sloane had already made a name for himself as a skilful collector of natural historical specimens.[3] Travelling through France while undertaking a medical degree (granted at the University of Orange in 1683), he spent a portion of his time gathering a sizeable collection of flora, which he then sent to Ray to make use of in his three-volume *History of Plants* (1686–1704). Sloane's previous work was on Ray's mind when he responded to the news that the young man might soon be working on an island that had only recently come into English possession. 'Were it not for the danger and hazard of so long a voyage', wrote Ray in April 1687, 'I would heartily wish such a person as yourself might travel to Jamaica, and search out

---

[1] Dr Hans Sloane to Mr Ray, Jan 29, 1686. In John Ray, *The Correspondence of John Ray: Consisting of Selections from the Philosophical Letters Published by Dr. Derham: And Original Letters of John Ray in the Collection of the British Museum / Edited by Edwin Lankester* (London: Printed for the Ray Society, 1848), 190.

[2] Ibid., 189.

[3] James Delbourgo, *Collecting the World: Hans Sloane and the Origins of the British Museum* (Cambridge, MA: Belknap Press, 2017).

and examine thoroughly the natural varieties of that island. Much light might be given to the history of the American plants, by one so well prepared for such an undertaking by a comprehensive knowledge of the European'.[4] In June, Ray got more detailed about the kinds of questions he hoped Sloane could answer. Great things were expected, 'no less than the resolving all our doubts about the names we meet with of plants in that part of America ... You may also please to observe whether there be any species of plants common to America and Europe'.[5] The largest number of specific queries derived from Ray's readings of a recent book by a Jamaican doctor, Thomas Trapham. Trapham's *Discourse of the State of Health in the Island of Jamaica* had appeared in 1679, and contained a number of natural historical observations.[6] Ray wanted the better-trained Sloane to determine the origin of ambergris (was it really the juice of a metal or aloe dropped into the sea?), the nature of the plant known as 'dumbcane', and precisely what Trapham meant when he described the 'shining barks of trees' that he had seen.[7]

Sloane had presumably already read Trapham's text, not least as preparation for the work expected of him as physician to Jamaica's new Governor.[8] Trapham's *Discourse* was the first English book written on the diseases of the West Indies. Indeed, today it is considered by some to be the first English monograph on tropical medicine more generally.[9] Sloane would soon meet Trapham in Jamaica, where the two butted heads over the Duke's medical treatment. The elite metropolitan physician was clearly irritated when Trapham was called in for a consultation as 'one who understood the country diseases having lived there several years'. By his own account, however, Sloane 'declined quarrelling with him. Thought my case hard enough in that I was blamed by some for want of success when his Grace would not take advice'.[10] Neither

---

[4] Mr Ray to Dr Hans Sloane, 1 April 1687. In Ray, 192.

[5] Mr Ray to Dr Hans Sloane (No date, presumably late June 1687). In ibid., 194–5.

[6] Thomas Trapham, *A Discourse of the State of Health in the Island of Jamaica with a Provision Therefore Calculated from the Air, the Place, and the Water, the Customs and Manner of Living &C* (London: Printed for R. Boulter, 1679).

[7] Ray, 195.

[8] The charge was not necessarily a promotion. '[King] James knew that Albemarle was a profligate and irresponsible man who had squandered his fortune in England', writes Dunn. '[H]e sent him to Jamaica to get rid of him. The duke, for his part, was eager to go because he had an interest in Caribbean treasure hunting'. The Duke's eventual death in 1688 was apparently tied to his profoundly immoderate celebrations following the announcement of the birth of the queen's son. Richard S. Dunn, *Sugar and Slaves: The Rise of the Planter Class in the English West Indies, 1624–1713* (Chapel Hill and London: University of North Carolina Press, 2000), 160.

[9] M. T. Ashcroft, 'Tercentenary of the First English Book on Tropical Medicine, by Thomas Trapham of Jamaica', *British Medical Journal* 2 (1979).

[10] This story derives from Estelle Frances Ward, *Christopher Monck, Duke of Albemarle* (London: J. Murray, 1915). Ward refers to the doctor as 'Traphan'. Sheridan notes the exchange in Richard B. Sheridan, 'The Doctor and the Buccaneer: Sir Hans Sloane's Case History of Sir Henry Morgan, Jamaica, 1688', *Journal of the History of Medicine and Allied Sciences* 41 (1986): 84.

doctor would achieve a great deal. The Duke died in October 1688, after which Sloane returned to England, having spent only fifteen months away.

Sloane's interactions with both Ray and Trapham would profoundly shape the most substantial product of his brief sojourn in the West Indies, his two-volume *Voyage to the Islands Madera, Barbados, Nieves, S. Christophers, and Jamaica* (1707 & 1725). Prior to this English-language work, in 1696 (by which time he had been elected secretary of the Royal Society), Sloane had published a Latin catalogue of Jamaican plant life. In writing a 'short account' of the catalogue at Sloane's request, Ray answered a number of the questions he had first posed a decade earlier.[11] Sloane, he noted 'hath informed us that the Dumb-cane so called, which being tasted, inflames the tongue and jaws in that manner, that, for awhile, it takes away the use of speech, is not properly any species of reed or cane, but of arum, or wake-robin'.[12] More generally, 'we are assured by his work that there are some plants common, not only to Europe and America, but even to England and Jamaica, notwithstanding the great distance of place, and difference both of longitude and climate'.[13] The import of this statement appeared in Sloane's *Preface* to the 1707 volume of his *Voyage*. Responding to the potential retort that his discoveries in the West Indies were hardly surprising, since one might imagine that all the plant life in such a foreign clime was novel, Sloane wrote, 'I answer it is not so ... I find a great many plants common to Spain, Portugal, and Jamaica, more common to Jamaica and the East-Indies, and most of all common to Jamaica and Guinea'. The natural history he was offering, he argued, could 'reasonably be suppos'd' to describe not only the botanical world of the Americas, but even of Guinea and the East Indies and thus 'to contribute to the more distinct knowledge of all those parts'.[14]

The argument that related plants in America to those in England was important to Sloane's overall purpose, which was, in part, to encourage a kind of trade of plant life between the Old and New Worlds. If one of Sloane's aims was to teach those who lived in or near Jamaica the uses of plants growing wild or in their gardens, another was to educate those in England about the virtues – particularly the therapeutic virtues – of the materials that he brought back. 'It may be objected', he suggested, 'that 'tis to no purpose to any in these Parts of the World, to look after such [Jamaican] Herbs, &c. because we never see them; I answer, that many of them and their several Parts have been brought over, and are used in Medicines every day, and more may, to the great Advantage of physicians and Patients, were People inquisitive enough to look

[11] Mr Ray to Dr Hans Sloane (no date). In Ray, 464.
[12] 'Preface by Mr Ray to Dr. Hans Sloane's Catalogue of Plants', in ibid., 465–8, on 67.
[13] Ibid., 468.
[14] Sloane, Preface, 12.

after them'.[15] As he made this argument, Sloane could, presumably, count on his readership calling to mind the efficacy of Jesuit's (or Peruvian) Bark.[16] Now medicinal and other plants were thriving throughout Europe: in England and Ireland, Holland, Germany, and Sweden.[17]

An argument about the similarity between Jamaica and Europe was also central to the medical portion of *Voyage*, which made up roughly 40 per cent of the 154-page Introduction to Volume I.[18] Before leaving with the Duke, Sloane narrated, 'I was told that the Diseases of this place were all different from what they are in Europe, and to be treated in a differing Method. This made me very uneasie, lest by ignorance I should kill instead of curing'. Sloane went on to inform the reader that his own experiences had shown that the notion that diseases in Europe and the West Indies were very different was false. '[A]bating some very few Diseases, Symptoms, &c. from the diversity of the Air, Meat, Drink &c. any person who has seen many sick people will find the same Diseases here as in *Europe*, and the same Method of Cure'. In fact, Sloane continued, in an oft-quoted sentence:

For my own part, I never saw a Disease in Jamaica which I had not met with in Europe, and that in People who never had been in either Indies, excepting one or two; and such instances happen to people practicing Physik in England, or anywhere else, that they may meet, amongst great number, with a singular disease, that they had never seen before, nor perhaps meet after with a parallel instance.[19]

Most scholars who have written about this aspect of Sloane's work have tended to take the author's statements at face value, seeing Sloane as an outlier largely because he portrayed himself as one. Thus, Harrison has argued that: 'A few European physicians, such as Sir Hans Sloane (1660–1753), expressed scepticism about the distinctiveness of diseases in the tropics, but such opinions (as Sloane himself noted) were at variance with both lay and professional opinion in the West Indies'.[20] Wendy Churchill, similarly, has read Sloane as offering a 'challenge to the developing notion that illness manifested

---

[15] Ibid., Preface, 11.

[16] On the history of the Peruvian bark, see Matthew Crawford, *The Andean Wonder Drug: Cinchona Bark and Imperial Science in the Spanish Atlantic, 1630–1800* (Pittsburgh: University of Pittsburgh Press, 2016).

[17] Sloane, Preface, 11.

[18] This section would later be translated into German and published as a work in its own right. Hans Sloane and Christoph L. Becker, *Johann Sloane ... von den Krankheiten, Welche er in Jamaika Beobachtet und Behandelt hat: aus dem Englischen Übersetzt und mit Einigen Zusätzen Begleitet* (Augsburg: Klett, 1784).

[19] Sloane, xc.

[20] Harrison, ' "The Tender Frame of Man": Disease, Climate and Racial Difference in India and the West Indies, 1760–1860', 70.

differently in different climates'.[21] It makes some intuitive sense to think of Sloane's as an unorthodox position, for it would seem to run counter to ideas dating back to antiquity that related climates and characteristic diseases. Andrew Wear, for example, has identified an early modern European tradition based on the Hippocratic text, *Airs, Waters, and Places*. That tradition, he has argued, 'contains both the constitution-shaping aspect of place and the belief that particular diseases reside in particular places' and 'acted in Europe as a conscious or unconscious template for views on the relationship between places, health, and disease'.[22] However, although it is clear that a Hippocratic lineage for eighteenth-century texts on diseases and places existed, one must also emphasise the fact that the lineage was neither continuous, straightforward, nor hegemonic.[23]

I argue in this chapter that Sloane's characterisation of medical understandings of the relationships between health and place were, if not wrong, at least rather selective. They served, at least in part, a particular set of social claims about the necessity, or not, for a doctor in Jamaica, to have expert, local knowledge of disease. Before making that case, however, it is necessary to capture the complexity of discourse about diseases and places prior to 1700. Section 2.1 explores the relative absence of references to *Airs, Waters, and Places* until the late sixteenth century, as well as the eventual deployment of the text in works such as Prosper Alpini's *De Medicina Aegyptiorum* (1591) and Jacobus Bontius' *De Medicina Indorum* (1645). Section 2.2 examines the flexibility and nuances of this neo-Hippocratic tradition from the seventeenth century onward, for Hippocrates' text was used as much to draw similarities between far-flung locations with common airs, waters, and places as it was to delineate differences. Far from solely being a resource for rote arguments about the peculiarity of afflictions in foreign locations (although it was this, too) the arguments of *Airs, Waters, and Places* could also be deployed to draw distant lands closer, allowing boosters for colonial settlement to cast new areas as new-found 'relations': sites seemingly designed for British settlement.[24] Different

---

[21] Wendy D. Churchill, 'Bodily Differences?: Gender, Race, and Class in Hans Sloane's Jamaican Medical Practice, 1687–1688', *Journal of the History of Medicine and Allied Sciences* 60, no. 4 (2005): 396.

[22] Andrew Wear, 'Place, Health, and Disease: The Airs, Waters, Places Tradition in Early Modern England and North America', *Journal of Medieval and Early Modern Studies* 38, no. 3 (2008): 445, 43. See also G. Miller, ' "Airs, Waters, and Places" in History', *Journal of the History of Medicine* 17 (1962).

[23] L. J. Jordanova, 'Earth Science and Environmental Medicine: The Synthesis of the Late Environment', in *Images of the Earth: Essays in the History of the Environmental Sciences*, ed. L. J. Jordanova and Roy Porter (London: British Society for the History of Science, 1979).

[24] 'The perfect agreement of English constitutions and American Air', Kupperman notes, 'was even urged as proof that God had intended North America for the English nation'. Karen

climates resulted in different diseases, to be sure. But we should be wary of ascribing our contemporary conceptions of the marked differences between the climates of the West Indies and of Britain (for example) to eighteenth-century actors, who also found many connections between the two sites.

With both the complexity and flexibility of the Hippocratic tradition in mind, then, Section 3.1 turns to the simple fact that it is difficult to find many texts about the West Indies that make the claim that Sloane insisted was the standard. Instead, therefore, of reading Sloane as a single figure rebutting a consensus position, I suggest that we see his claims as having emerged, at least partly, from his disputes with Trapham and other local physicians. As in the deadly dispute between Williams and Bennet, at stake was not, or not merely, the onto-logical question of the nature of diseases in different places, but also the epis-temological question of how one learned to diagnose and treat such diseases, and the social question – related to these others – of whom should be granted the authority and expertise to speak and act on such matters. When could local experience trump putatively generalisable scholarship and learning?

1.1   A Hippocratic Revival

By the early 1700s it was certainly not uncommon for medical works on the diseases of specific locations to invoke Hippocrates as their most illustrious classical forebear. Friedrich Hoffmann's 1705 *Dissertation on Endemial Diseases,* for example, opened by defining 'endemial' as 'an epithet of those Diseases which are peculiar to the Inhabitants of certain Nations, or Countries'. He then offered a long quotation (almost thirty lines) from the beginning of *Airs, Waters, and Places* to support his claim that 'With these diseases and their respective Natures the Physicians ought to well acquainted'.[25] Richard Towne, physician and author of *A Treatise of the Diseases Most Frequent in the West-Indies* (1726), was a world away from the illustrious Hoffmann, both geographically and professionally. The German was a professor at Halle, with an international reputation, while Towne – about whom we know little else – evidently had a medical practice in Barbados. Yet Towne too found it unproblematic to introduce his text by similarly suggesting that the idea that 'human Bodies are greatly influenced by the *Climate, Air, Soil, Diet &c.* of the

---

Kupperman, 'The Puzzle of the American Climate in the Early Colonial Period', *The American Historical Review* 87 (1982): 1283.

[25] Friedrich Hoffmann and Bernardino Ramazzini, *A Dissertation on Endemial Diseases or, Those Disorders Which Arise from Particular Climates, Situations, and Methods of Living; Together with a Treatise on the Diseases of Tradesmen ... The First by the Celebrated Frederick Hoffman ... The Second by Bern. Ramazini ... Newly Translated with a Preface and an Appendix by Dr. James* (London: Printed for Thomas Osborne and J. Hildyard at York, 1746), 1.

Places we inhabit, has been long ago judiciously and fully proved by the divine *Hippocrates* in his Book *de Aere, Aqua & Locis*'.[26]

Hippocrates was indeed a natural referent for those concerned with the relationship between environments and human health. His text admonished the physician to pay attention first to seasonality, then to winds, both hot and cold, distinguishing between those common in all places and those 'peculiar to each locality'. 'Whoever wishes to investigate medicine properly' needed to study the qualities of water – its taste and weight, whether it was marshy, soft or hard, whether it ran down from rocky heights, and if it was brackish and poorly suited for cooking. Was the soil well-watered or dry; locked within valleys or exposed on hilltops? Arriving in a city as a stranger the Hippocratic doctor needed to study its position relative to prevailing winds and the course of the sun. And the good physician must also be, in contemporary terms, something of an anthropologist, for he must consider 'the mode in which the inhabitants live, and what are their pursuits, whether they are fond of drinking and eating to excess, and given to indolence, or are fond of exercise and labour, and not given to excess in eating and drinking'.[27]

Most simply, certain locations gave rise to characteristic constitutions and illnesses. A city exposed to hot winds, but sheltered from cold, northern ones contained inhabitants with flabby bodies, who tended to eat and drink little, avoiding the excessive consumption of wine in particular. Women menstruated excessively, 'are unfruitful from disease, and not from nature', and suffered from frequent miscarriages. Children were prone to convulsions and asthma, men to 'dysentery, diarrhea, hepialus, chronic fevers in winter, of epinyctis, frequently, and of hemorrhoids about the anus'. On the other hand, they were largely spared diseases characteristic of cities with inverted exposure to prevailing winds: pleurisies, peripneumonies, ardent fevers, and acute diseases more generally.[28] Over all, Hippocrates' was a discourse concerned with differences, even small ones. A city that was turned to the rising sun was likely to be healthy, while one turned to the North would be less so, even if both were only a furlong from each other. Diseases in cities that lay to the east would be relatively rare and women would be both fecund and blessed with easy deliveries.[29] Climatic differences had even more profound effects. Asia and Europe, Hippocrates claimed, differed from one another 'in all respects'. Asia was much milder than Europe, its inhabitants concomitantly gentler, and its natural

---

[26] Richard Towne, *A Treatise of the Diseases Most Frequent in the West-Indies, and Herein More Particularly of Those Which Occur in Barbadoes* (London: J. Clarke, 1726), 1.

[27] Hippocrates. 'Airs, Waters, and Places', in *The Genuine Works of Hippocrates*, translated by Francis Adams (London: Printed for the Sydenham Society, 1849), 190.

[28] Ibid., 192.

[29] Ibid., 194–5.

products larger and more beautiful. The various seasons resembled one another in Asia, while in Europe, the year was marked by striking changes.[30] Asiatic equilibrium was not, however, to be envied. '[F]or a climate which is always the same induces indolence, but a changeable climate, laborious exertions both of body and mind; and from rest and indolence cowardice is engendered, and from laborious exertions and pains, courage'. If change – both temporal and spatial – mattered enormously in *Airs, Waters, and Places*, changeability mattered even more, the changes of the seasons being 'the strongest of the natural causes of difference'. Where the seasons changed little, as in Asia, one found comparatively little variation among peoples, so that Europeans, as well as being more warlike and hardier, were also more varied among themselves than their eastern counterparts.[31]

The arguments of *Airs, Waters, and Places* remained well known to both medical and lay audiences in the Islamic Middle Ages.[32] But the same was not true in Europe. Nancy Siraisi suggests that we should regard the text as essentially 'new' to Renaissance audiences until the early sixteenth century.[33] *Airs, Waters, and Places* was not included in printed editions of Hippocratic works until 1515 and it was not until the second half of the sixteenth century that one could begin properly to speak of a Hippocratic revival, one that involved a detailed, dedicated, and direct engagement with more than a few of Hippocrates' works.[34] This is not to suggest, of course, that healers in the Middle Ages or Renaissance were unaware of or unconcerned with the relationship between environments and health. Of the six Galenic 'non-naturals' – those factors over which patients had some control – two (air and diet) depended at least in part on location. What is perhaps more significant about Hippocrates' text was that it examined the relationship between environments and the health of *groups*. Galenic therapeutics, on the other hand, was more concerned with

---

[30] Ibid., 205–7. 'Given the author's preoccupation with a Europe/Asia divide', Denise Eileen McCoskey has written, 'one that insists on the superiority of the Europeans in both climatic and political terms, some have suggested that the text functions in part to help justify the recent Greek defeat of the Persians during the Persian Wars (499–479 BCE)'. Denise Eileen McCoskey, 'On Black Athena, Hippocratic Medicine, and Roman Imperial Edicts: Egyptians and the Problem of Race in Classical Antiquity', in *Race and Ethnicity: Across Time, Space, and Discipline*, ed. Rodney D. Coates (Leiden: Brill, 2004), 320.

[31] Hippocrates. 'Airs, Waters, and Places', 219, 221.

[32] Peter E. Pormann and Emilie Savage-Smith, *Medieval Islamic Medicine* (Washington, DC: Georgetown University Press, 2007), 45.

[33] 'Among the parts of the Hippocratic corpus that were in some sense "new" in the early sixteenth century – that were little or only partially or indirectly known in the Middle Ages, were not commented on by scholastic authors, and were not standard in university curricula – were two works of especial significance for the relation between medicine and history: the *Epidemics* and *Airs, Waters, Places*'. Nancy Siraisi, *History, Medicine, and the Traditions of Renaissance Learning* (Ann Arbor: University of Michigan Press, 2007), 73.

[34] Vivian Nutton, 'Hippocrates in the Renaissance', *Sudhoffs Archiv* 27 (1989). A more precise meaning of neo-Hippocratism in the eighteenth century is taken up in Chapter 2.

the particular history, constitution, diet, and behaviour of a given patient than the characteristic diseases of whole cities or even countries.[35]

If one can thus speak of a Hippocratic revival beginning in the universities in the mid-sixteenth century, it would be some time before tracts on health in foreign climes drew upon *Airs, Waters, and Places* as a resource. One finds, for example, little trace of a 'Hippocratic heritage' in Garcia d'Orta's *Colloquies on the simples and drugs of India* (1563), another text often cited as the first on 'tropical medicine'.[36] Born in Portugal around 1500, d'Orta studied in Spain before returning home in 1523 and receiving his medical qualifications in 1526. In 1530, he was appointed to a lectureship in natural history at the University of Lisbon and four years later sailed to Goa as personal physician to M. A. de Sousa, who would go on to become the Portuguese Viceroy in India. D'Orta remained in Goa until his death in 1568, penning his most famous work after almost thirty years of medical practice in India.

D'Orta's book is structured in the form of a series of dialogues between a character named for the author and a fictitious Spanish doctor named Ruano. Having known one another in their university days, the two meet again in Goa, as the newly arrived Ruano visits d'Orta and expresses his 'great desire to know about the medicinal drugs (such as are called the drugs of pharmacy in Portugal) and other medicines of the country, as well as the fruits and spices'.[37] Ruano continues with a longer list of his interests (and hence a fuller description of the contents of the non-fictitious d'Orta's book):

I further wish to learn of their names in different languages, and the trees or herbs from which they are taken. I also desire to know how the native physicians use them; and to learn what other plants and fruits there are belonging to this land, which are not medicinal; and what customs will be met with; for all such things may be described as having been seen by you or by other persons worthy of credit.[38]

---

[35] On the 'harnessing of the non-naturals to the "airs, waters, and places" approach' in the eighteenth century, see L. J. Jordanova, 'Earth Science and Environmental Medicine: The Synthesis of the Late Enlightenment', in *Images of the Earth: Essays in the History of the Environmental Sciences*, ed. L. J. Jordanova and Roy S. Porter (London: The British Society for the History of Science, 1979), 125.

[36] Harrison, *Medicine in an Age of Commerce and Empire: Britain and its Tropical Colonies, 1660–1830*, 33–4. Harrison notes that 'd'Orta had nothing to say about the effects of climate on European bodies', *Climates & Constitutions: Health, Race, Environment and British Imperialism in India, 1600–1850* (New Delhi and New York: Oxford University Press, 1999), 27.

[37] Garcia de Orta, Francisco Manuel de Melo Ficalho, and Clements R. Markham, *Colloquies on the Simples and Drugs of India* (London: H. Sotheran and Co., 1913), 1. Timothy Walker, 'Acquisition and Circulation of Medical Knowledge within the Early Modern Portuguese Colonial Empire', in *Science in the Spanish and Portuguese Empires, 1500–1800*, ed. Daniela Bleichmar, Paula De Vos, and Kristin Huffine (Stanford: Stanford University Press, 2008), 251–2.

[38] Orta, Ficalho, and Markham, 1–2.

The focus of the *Colloquies*, then – as with later works by Nicolás Monardes and Cristobál Acosta – was less on the distinctiveness of disease environments outside Europe and considerably more on the description of natural historical products that could be put to use in grappling with familiar ailments.[39] D'Orta's book is credited with offering the first Western description of the symptoms of Asiatic cholera, yet D'Orta himself made little of the disease's novelty, noting that it was known in the Latinate world as *Colerica Passio*, although the Indian form 'is more acute than in our country, for it generally kills in twenty-four hours'.[40] He offered no explanation for this difference and his discussion of the disease's aetiology made no mention of climatic differences between Goa and Europe. To Ruano's question: 'What men are most liable to take this disease, and at what time of the year is it most prevalent?', d'Orta's answer was as much moral as medical, pointing to excesses of the flesh:

Those who eat most, and those who consume most food. I knew a young priest here who died of eating cucumbers. Also those who have much intercourse with women. The disease is most prevalent in June and July, which is the winter in this country. As it is brought on by over-eating, the Indians call it MORXI, which means, according to them, a disease caused by much eating.[41]

Among the first physicians to write in what we should probably term a neo-Hippocratic *Airs, Waters, and Places* tradition was Prosper Alpini (1553–1616), who published a work on Egyptian medicine (*De Medicina Aegyptiorum*) in 1591. Alpini completed a medical degree at Padua in 1578. Two years later, after becoming physician to Giorgio Emo, Venetian Consul to Cairo, he accompanied Emo to Egypt, where he stayed for three years before returning to Venice. In 1603 he became Director of the botanical garden at Padua.[42] *De Medicina Aegyptiorum* was written, like D'Orta's book, as a dialogue between the author and a friend; in this case Alpini's master at Padua and a former director of the Botanical Garden, Melchior Guilandino. An introduction detailed Alpini's adventures with Emo on their way to Alexandria. (As a nineteenth-century commentator noted, dryly: 'When a man undertakes a voyage, and afterward writes a book, one may be pretty sure that he meets with a storm in which he is

[39] On Monardes' *Historia medicinal de las cosas que se traen de nuestras Indias Occidentales que sirven en medicina* (1565–74), see Daniela Bleichmar, 'Books, Bodies, and Fields: Sixteenth-Century Transatlantic Encounters with New World Materia Medica', in *Colonial Botany: Science, Commerce, and Politics in the Early Modern World*, ed. Londa Schiebinger and Claudia Swan (Philadelphia: University of Pennsylvania Press, 2005). Cook describes Acosta's (1578) *Trata de las drogas y medicinas de las Indias Orientales* as 'almost entirely derivative of Orta'. Harold J. Cook, *Matters of Exchange: Commerce, Medicine, and Science in the Dutch Golden Age* (New Haven and London: Yale University Press, 2007), 200.
[40] Orta, Ficalho, and Markham, 155.
[41] Ibid., 158.
[42] Jerry Stannard, 'Alpini, Prospero', in *Complete Dictionary of Scientific Biography* (Detroit: Charles Scribner's Sons, 2008).

nearly shipwrecked. Alpinus forms no exception to the general rule.')[43] Of the four books into which the main text was broken, the latter three were largely concerned with a description of Egyptian medical practices. Alpini was, for the most part, a critical witness, believing, for example, that Egyptian physicians bled too much and too often. In the first book, however, he described the climate and characteristic diseases of the country. To Guilandino's question as to whether there were many diseases 'which the Greeks call endemic',[44] Alpini answered that there were, and proceeded to offer a long list, including 'what the Greeks call ophthalmia' (caused by a local 'nitrous dust' that inflamed the eyes); leprosy (explained by an Egyptian diet that involved, he claimed, the consumption of salted and rotten fish); and elephantiasis (another illness the physician ascribed to dietary causes, brought on by the consumption of local fish, by bad water, and by vegetables like yams and cabbages, which Alpini argued generated a thick and viscous phlegm that gravitated to the feet, producing the malady's characteristic tumours.)[45] Among the most oft-referenced parts of Alpini's text was his discussion of the plague, which he claimed had taken half a million lives in Cairo alone in the year he arrived. The physician sought to refute common notions about the disease, which had killed so many in Europe, first in the fourteenth century and intermittently thereafter. It was a very rare occurrence, Alpini argued, for the plague to be produced in Egypt itself. Such an event required unusually large flooding of the Nile. Certainly, the disease was neither produced nor reproduced in the country every seven years, as some had claimed. Instead, it spread contagiously from Greece, Syria, and the Barbary Coast.[46] For European readers with much more than an academic interest in questions of the origin and means of transmission of the plague, Alpini's views remained points of reference and contention well into the nineteenth century.

Alpini's was, of course, a scholarly medical text, filled with learned references to classical sources. But the association between places and diseases was accepted far beyond the university's walls. Travelling through the Middle East in 1596–7, Fynes Moryson encountered an area on the road toward Constantinople where a 'Fenny Plaine lies, and the mountains, though more remote, doe barre the sight of the Sunne, and the boggy earth yielding ill vapours makes Sanderona infamous for the death of Christians'.[47] At roughly

[43] Joseph Ince, 'Prosper Alpinus, de Medicina Aegyptiorum Libri Quatuor. A. D. 1591', *Pharmaceutical Journal and Transactions* II (1860): 368.

[44] Prosper Alpinus and Jacobus Bontius, *Prosperi Alpini, Medicina Aegyptiorum ... Ut Et Jacobi Bontii, Medicina Indorum* (Apud Lugduni Batavorum: Gerardum Potvliet, 1745), 49; Prosper Alpini, *La Médicine Des Egyptiens*, trans. R. de Fenoyl (Paris: Institut français d'archéologie orientale, 1980), 87.

[45] Alpini, *La Médicine Des Egyptiens*, 93, 99.

[46] Ibid., 104–24.

[47] Wear, 445.

the same time, 'G.W'. – identified in the 1915 reproduction of his 1598 text as 'the poet and swashbuckler, George Whetstone' – penned a work on *The Cures of the Diseased in Forraine Attempts of the English Nation*.[48] The dedication, to Queen Elizabeth, mentions Whetstone's 'iniust imprisonment in *Spayne*', the illness he contracted, and his cure 'by an especiall Phisition of that King', from whom he learned 'his methode for the same, and such other Diseases, as have perished your Maiesties people in the *Southerne* parts'. The same disease that had laid him low, Whetstone claimed, was the means by which 'whole Kingdomes in both the *Indias* have been depopulated'.[49] One finds no reference to Hippocrates, Galen, or any other medical writers in the short work, but the force of the *Airs, Waters, and Places* tradition seems clear in afflictions such as the 'Erizipila', 'a Disease very much raigning in those Countries, the rather proceeding of the unwholesome aires and vapours, that hot Climates doo yield, whereof many people doo perish'.[50]

It does seem to me, however, that it requires too much of a stretch to associate all comments that relate health to location with the arguments in *Airs, Waters, and Places*. Where the Hippocratic text was concerned with the relationship between specific afflictions and the locations in which they were found, much of the non-medical discourse – unsurprisingly, since it was often written by explorers, current or prospective settlers, or those more interested in geography than the physician's arts – seems concerned with the more general and rather simpler question of whether particular sites were healthy or not. More specific and widespread references to this specific Hippocratic work would appear to be the product of the mid-seventeenth century onward. We should also be wary of assuming that even such weakly Hippocratic ideas were uncontested. Among early modern sailors seeking to circumnavigate the globe, for example, the insistence on the differences between lands took a back seat to the more profound distinction between the earth's terrestrial and aqueous surfaces. They believed, Chaplin has argued, 'that all humans suffered from being removed from land and that any land was sufficient to recover them; this was an especially strong countercurrent against the airs, waters, places tradition, and at odds with other beliefs that differentiated among human bodies in place-specific ways'.[51]

This maritime counter-narrative lasted until at least the mid-eighteenth century. From that point sailors' beliefs that any land – and only land – could cure

[48] G. W., 'The Cures of the Diseased in Forraine Attempts of the English Nation, London, 1598. Reproduced in Facsimile', ed. Charles Joseph Singer (Oxford: Clarendon Press, 1915), 'Introduction', 5.

[49] Ibid., 10.

[50] Ibid., 17.

[51] Joyce E. Chaplin, 'Earthsickness: Circumnavigation and the Terrestrial Human Body, 1520–1800', *Bulletin of the History of Medicine* 86, no. 4 (2012): 517.

scurvy, that classic naval disease, came under increasing criticism. A belief in 'earthsickness' (a need and longing for the land that paralleled homesickness) seems to have faded quickly in the wake of James Cook's voyages and his much popularised cures for scorbutic illnesses. Considerably before that, of course, the age of exploration had given way to the age of empire, and for the majority of those who concerned themselves with events beyond the bounds of Europe, Hippocrates' text increasingly provided a template for new ways of discussing novel locations for trade and conquest. In 1645, slightly more than fifty years after its first appearance, Alpini's book was republished, bound together with a work on the diseases of the East Indies: Jacob Bontius' *De Medicina Indorum*.[52]

Born in 1591, the son of the first professor of medicine at the University of Leiden, Bontius obtained his medical degree in 1614 and began to try and build a practice. By the mid-1620s, however (as he later noted in a letter to his brother), he had decided that the competition in his native land was too great. 'The profits of physic were small on account of the multitude of medicasters', he wrote, acknowledging the perspicacity of his sibling's counsel to 'make for the fertile plains of Java, where, to speak ingenuously, virtue is held in some higher esteem'.[53] In 1627 he sailed with his family to the East Indies. Bontius was, however, to be no mere physician. He was appointed to oversee all the medical operations of the Dutch East India Company, tasked with running the hospital in Batavia, supervising the medical outfitting of the Company's ships, inspecting the settlement's physicians and surgeons, and providing medical care for the most eminent men in the Company's service.[54]

Apart from these many medical duties, Bontius was also expected to provide a natural history of Holland's oriental holdings. He seems to have revelled in this latter task. As soon as he arrived in the East Indies, he wrote to his brother, 'I applied myself not only to attain a knowledge of the herbs growing here in Java, but likewise to acquire a more perfect idea of the aromatics in which our part of the country is most fruitful'.[55] Illness plagued his family's first few years. He lost his first wife before he reached the Indies, his second in 1630 (less than three years after their marriage), and his eldest son in 1631. Bontius himself had fallen dangerously ill twice, both times while Batavia was being (unsuccessfully) besieged by Sultan Agung, king of the Mataram Sultanate.

[52] Prosper Alpinus and Jacobus Bontius, *P. Alpini, De Medicina Aegyptiorum & Jacobus Bontii, De Medicina Indorum* (Paris: Nicalaus Redelichuysen, 1645).

[53] James Bontius, *An Account of the Diseases, Natural History, and Medicines of the East Indies* (London: John Donaldson, 1776), 169.

[54] Harold J. Cook, 'Global Economies and Local Knowledge in the East Indies: Jacobus Bontius Learns the Facts of Nature', in *Colonial Botany: Science, Commerce, and Politics in the Early Modern World*, ed. Londa Schiebinger and Claudia Swan (Philadelphia: University of Pennsylvania Press, 2005).

[55] Bontius, 167.

Botany apparently occupied his mind even through his afflictions. '[W]ould to God', he wrote in 1629, 'that the disease, by which I have been confined these four months, still permitted me, as for long after I arrived here, to roam thro' the delightful circumambient woods of Java, and attain a more perfect knowledge of the many noble herbs which are to be met with in this country'.[56]

As with earlier writers about the New World, Bontius was very explicit about the connection between his medical and natural historical interests. Where diseases were endemial, he noted, 'there the bountiful hand of nature has profusely planted herbs whose virtues are adapted to counteract them'.[57] These endemial diseases were many; so profuse in fact that Bontius claimed that his discussion was limited only to those maladies whose manifestation or cure was different to that known in Europe. Like Alpini, he placed great stress on certain climates' capacities to promote putrefaction. At pains to refute the notion that the air in this part of the 'torrid zone' was hot and dry, Bontius argued that the island's warm and moist atmosphere was the principal cause of the cholera morbus, a potentially deadly disease, aggravated by locals' excessive consumption of fruit.[58] The airs, waters, and places of the country, that is, had a profound effect on its characteristic illnesses. How strongly indebted Bontius was to a neo-Hippocratic tradition may be seen from the following long discussion of the fever known as 'Tymorenses, peculiar to the Indies'.

This fever arises from various causes, of which the principal are these: the smell of the saunders tree when newly felled; which (on the testimony of the inhabitants of the country) sends out from its bark some vapours of I know not what poisonous quality, and noxious to the brain ... Besides, the constitution of the air is thick, and extremely heavy: for, the dwellings of the inhabitants are on the highest mountains, where on account of the situation, clouds and watery vapours prevail. The cold, likewise, is sometimes as severe as in Holland: all which concur to produce thick humours and turbid spirits. Add to these several causes, the custom, in this country, of eating a great deal of fruits, which as they are for the most part green, and on account of their moisture, obnoxious to putrefaction, generate bad juices in people whose constitutions have been altered by the sea, hard labour, gross diet, and intemperature of the air.[59]

This is a Hippocratic litany: local plants, the patient's geographic and altitudinal situation, the temperature of their surroundings, their diet, and habits.

1.2   The Flexibility of the Hippocratic Tradition

And yet, even in this passage, one also sees the problem in associating Hippocratic ideas with the notion of which Sloane was apparently critical: that

---

[56] Ibid., 24.
[57] Ibid., 27.
[58] Ibid., 52.
[59] Ibid., 66–7.

diseases were all different in different places. For, as often as not, *De Medicina Indorum* sought to draw parallels between European nations and the Indies. One might note above that one of the causes of the Tymorenses was not, in fact, the humid climate for which Java was famed, but rather the cold of its mountains, which was 'sometimes as severe as in Holland'. Indeed, the passage quoted above continued with a longer comparison:

I had almost omitted to subjoin, as another cause, the sudden change of air which our people experience when they descend from the cold mountains to the shore and the ships, where they are scorched with heat ... What are also greatly to be guarded against, are the winds which blow from the mountains after midnight, in Java and the circumadjacent islands: just as in some of the southern parts of France and Italy, especially in the kingdom of Naples, and the territory of the Pope, the cold wind which blows from the hills, and is called the serene, produces pleurisies, peripneumonies, and other acute disorders.[60]

Nor are these invocations of similarity solely to be found in discussion of cold-weather afflictions. The consumption of fruit, Bontius argued, contributed greatly toward the production of dysentery. Were a person incautious, eating the local produce 'without rice, or bread, or a little salt, he scarcely can escape the disorder'. Yet, the same thing happened in France and Spain, 'where people, who eat much grapes without bread, are immediately seized with a Diarrheoea or Dysentery'.[61] The myriad constructions of both similarity and difference in fact follow from the logic of Hippocrates' own text. To be sure, where climates were diametrically opposed, one found radically different diseases. But such oppositional climates were largely abstractions. 'It is not everywhere the same with regard to Asia',[62] Hippocrates acknowledged of Europe's counterpart. Indeed, the opposition between a uniform East and a changeable West might be read as much as pedagogic as literally descriptive, for *Airs, Waters, and Places* concluded by noting that the text had largely concerned itself with extremes: 'Thus it is with regard to the most opposite natures and shapes; drawing conclusions from them, you may judge of the rest without any risk of error'.[63]

This flexible aspect of the Hippocratic tradition in fact proved to be of crucial importance in the discussion of the New World. Few writers in British North America, for example, had an interest as portraying their climate as antithetical, and hence potentially inimical, to that found at home. Colonists

---

[60] Ibid.
[61] Ibid., 15. Harrison suggests that '[t]his mention of France and Spain – both Catholic countries – is perhaps significant, in as much as the Dutch Protestant Bontius may be equating dietary indulgence with the supposed laxity of these nations'. Harrison, *Climates & Constitutions: Health, Race, Environment and British Imperialism in India, 1600–1850*, 49.
[62] Hippocrates. 'Airs, Waters, and Places', 206.
[63] Ibid., 222.

declared America to be England's sister or mother, and emphasised those parts of each country that lay within the same latitudinal bounds. George Peckham, describing America's appearance on Mercator's map, claimed that the 'Counterey dooth (as it were with arme advaunced) above the climats both of Spayne and Fraunce, stretche out it selfe towards England onlie'.[64] For some, America's climate was not only not detrimental, it was positively salutary for the sons and daughters of Albion. For Francis Higginson, in 1630, 'the Temper of the Aire in *New-England* is one speciall thing that commends this place. Experience doth manifest that there is hardly a more healthfull place to be found in the World that agreeth better with our English Bodyes'.[65] A 'sup' of this air, he suggested, 'is better than a whole draft of old England's ale'.[66] *Airs, Waters, and Places* certainly suggested that different diseases were to be found in different climates. But there was considerable disagreement over whether climates in very different geographical locations were, in fact, radically distinct.

One found fewer defenders of the climate in Africa, where discussions turned on the slave trade rather than settlement. If Asia had been Europe's foil for Hippocrates, Africa increasingly took on that role after the discovery of the New World. In the late seventeenth century, Willem Bosman spent more than a dozen years as Chief Factor for the Dutch on the Guinea Coast. In 1704 he wrote a description of that time in the form of a series of letters to a physician friend (now identified as Dr Havart, who had served as a surgeon in the service of the Dutch West India Company).[67] The book was rapidly translated into other European languages: English and French in 1705; German in 1708; Italian in 1752. The book's popularity presumably stemmed from the fact that Bosman was largely correct in declaring that:

[T]he Coast of Guinea, which is part of Africa, is for the most part unknown, not only to the Dutch, but to all Europeans, and no particular description of it is yet come to light; nor indeed any thing, but a few scraps, scattered in books written upon other subjects, most of which are contrary to truth, and afford but a sorry sketch of Guinea.[68]

---

[64] Joyce E. Chaplin, *Subject Matter: Technology, the Body, and Science on the Anglo-American Frontier, 1500–1676* (Cambridge, MA: Harvard University Press, 2001), 134.

[65] Ibid., 154.

[66] Wear, 454.

[67] Willem Bosman, *A New and Accurate Description of the Coast of Guinea, Divided into the Gold, the Slave, and the Ivory Coasts ... Illustrated with Several Cutts. Written Originally in Dutch by William Bosman ... To Which Is Prefix'd, an Exact Map of the Whole Coast of Guinea* (London: Printed for James Knapton, and Dan. Midwinter, 1705). Albert Van Dantzig, 'Willem Bosman's "New and Accurate Description of the Coast of Guinea": How Accurate Is It?', *History in Africa* 1 (1974). I use the English edition in the discussion below, but see: 'English Bosman and Dutch Bosman: A Comparison of Texts', *History in Africa* 2 (1975).

[68] Bosman, Preface, 1.

Few who read the text could envy Bosman his time in the region. With rare exceptions – and most of those in the past – the country was described as unwholesome and deadly. Better care and cultivation might improve it, but at present Guinea bore a 'dreadful mortal name'.[69] The Isle of St Thomé, he claimed, was known in Europe as 'the Dutch Church-Yard', and even the Portuguese, to whom the Dutch had ceded the island, were, 'tho' more used to this scorching Air', dying in huge numbers.[70] The first time Bosman visited the Kingdom of Benin, he noted, 'we lost half our men'.[71] He wrote to Havart during his second voyage there, observing that an equal number of men were now dead, that most of the rest were sick, and that this had 'struck such general terrour into the Sailors, that the oldest of them is afraid of his life'. The problem was the place itself. Sudden changes between the heat of the day and the cold of the night induced diseases in European bodies. Even worse was the 'thick, stinking, and sulphurous' mist which spread through the valleys. '[I]f this odious Mixture of noisome stenches very much affects the state of health here', wrote Bosman, 'it is not to be wondered, since 'tis next to impossibility, not only for new Comers, but those who have long continued here, to preserve themselves intirely from its malign Effects'. The only people to be spared the ravages of the destructive mist were the 'Natives', since they were 'bred up in the Stench' and hence, presumably, were unaffected by it.[72] Yet they had their own diseases, in particular small pox and the worm named for the region. Worst for their health were their moral sensibilities, about which Bosman was vicious. 'The Negroes are all without exception, Crafty, Villanous, and Fraudulent, and very seldom to be trusted', and their 'too early and excessive venery' was given as the reason that, despite otherwise healthy lives, natives 'seldom arrive to a great Age'.[73]

The difference between this early eighteenth-century description of the disease environment of Africa, and those given of the West Indies at the same time is striking. Clearly no sense of a disease environment common to the tropics yet existed. But perhaps nothing makes clearer the relative health of the two parts of the world in European eyes than the changing claims about the origins of a disease that had been associated with the Americas almost since the time of Columbus: syphilis. By the 1530s, the new disease was laid at the feet of America's Indians, a new people who were unfamiliar with the word of Christ and who were portrayed as without any moral restraint. 'They have as many wives as they desire', wrote Amerigo Vespucci, 'they live in promiscuity without regard to blood relations; mothers lie with sons, brothers with sisters;

---

[69] Ibid., 17.
[70] Ibid., 414.
[71] Ibid., 429.
[72] Ibid., 105–6, 108.
[73] Ibid., 117, 10.

they satisfy their desires as they occur to their libidos as beasts do'.[74] Against this orthodoxy, however, Daniel Turner, in a 1717 text on the disease, noted that no less a figure than Thomas Sydenham (soon to become known as the English Hippocrates) denied the New World origin of syphilis.[75] Sydenham acknowledged the (by then) common explanation, which traced the disease from the West Indies to Europe the year after Columbus' discovery: 'But it seems rather to me', he argued, 'to have taken its rise from some Region of the Blacks near *Guinea,* for I have learn'd from many of our People of good Credit, who live in the *Caribbee-Islands,* that the Slaves brought from *Guinea,* even before they land, and also those that live there, have this Disease without impure Copulation'.[76] As we will see in Chapter 2, the idea that it was African slaves who were ultimately responsible for many virulent West Indian diseases, and not the country's own climate, would become a central trope from the mid-eighteenth century onwards.

Like America and unlike Guinea, the West Indies had many settlers who served as boosters and propagandists, unwilling to have the islands dismissed as intrinsically unhealthy. And, perhaps more generally, as Bontius' example shows, writers had become somewhat leery of classical distinctions, particularly those among the frigid (or polar), temperate, and torrid (or tropical) zones. From the late fifteenth century, scholars and explorers had argued that there was clearly a problem in the division between a habitable 'temperate' region below the Polar Circle and above the Tropic of Cancer and the uninhabitable areas that were supposed to bound it.[77] As Tomaso Giunti noted in 1563: '[I]t is clearly able to be understood that this entire earthly globe is marvelously inhabited, nor is there any part of it empty, neither by heat nor by cold deprived of inhabitants'.[78] Increasingly, the areas between the Tropics were portrayed not

---

[74] Anna Foa, 'The New and the Old: The Spread of Syphilis (1494–1530)', in *Sex and Gender in Historical Perspective*, ed. Edward Muir and Guido Ruggiero (Baltimore: Johns Hopkins University Press, 1990), 31–2.

[75] Daniel Turner, *Syphilis. A Practical Dissertation on the Venereal Disease ... In Two Parts* (London: Printed for R. Bonwicke, Tim. Goodwin, J. Walthoe, M. Wotton, S. Manship, Richard Wilkin, Benj. Tooke, R. Smith, and Tho. Ward, 1717).

[76] Sydenham continued: 'It seems therefore probable to me, that the *Spaniards,* that first brought the Disease into *Europe,* were infected with it by the Contagion of the Blacks bought in *Africa,* to some Nation whereof it may be Endemial; for there are many People that border upon *Guinea,* among whom that barbarous Custom of changing Men for Ware prevails'. Thomas Sydenham, *The Whole Works of That Excellent Practical Physician, Dr. Thomas Sydenham Wherein Not Only the History and Cures of Acute Diseases Are Treated Of ... But Also the Shortest and Fastest Way of Curing Most Chronical Diseases*, 9th ed. (London: Printed for J. Darby, A. Bettesworth, and F. Clay, in trust for Richard, James, and Bethel Wellington, 1729), 247–8.

[77] See, in general, Nicolás Wey Gómez, *The Tropics of Empire: Why Columbus Sailed South to the Indies* (Cambridge, MA: MIT Press, 2008).

[78] Quoted in John M. Headley, 'The Sixteenth-Century Venetian Celebration of the Earth's Total Habitability: The Issue of the Fully Habitable World for Renaissance Europe', *Journal of World History* 8, no. 1 (1997): 3.

as searing deserts, but as seasonally constant versions of climates with which Europeans were familiar. The Bermudas were, for the poet Edmund Waller in 1645 (playing on the name of the company that had held the charter for the islands at the time) the 'summer isles'. Switching seasons in the main text, he contrasted the idyllic region – 'so moderate the clime' – with England: 'For the kind Spring which but salutes us here/Inhabits there and courts them all the year'.[79] In 1682, Abraham Cowley lyricised about the 'temprate summer' to be found in the tropics: 'More rich than Autumn and the Spring more fair'.[80] Nor was this merely a poetic trope. In 1679, the Jamaican doctor, Thomas Trapham described Jamaica approvingly as 'a summer country' with a 'whole summer year'.[81]

It should be noted, of course, that although such claims demonstrated a cosmopolitan enthusiasm for places beyond one's home, they were not devoid of Eurocentrism. For their effect was to render England, in particular, a microcosm for the globe. The seasons experienced over the course of a year in Britain were mapped on to the climates of other parts of the world, at all times. The analogy between European seasons and foreign climates had been in Hippocrates. Asia, it was claimed in *Airs, Waters, and Places* 'both as regards its constitution and mildness of the seasons, may be said to bear a close resemblance to the spring'.[82] The point was much more systematically enunciated, however, in the late seventeenth and early eighteenth centuries: indeed, almost precisely at the same time that Sloane published the first volume of his *Voyage*. In 1696, William Cockburn related 'hotter constitutions, hot Countries, or a warmer Season'.[83] A dozen years later, in 1708, John Polus Lecaan published a work purporting to offer advice to aid English forces in southern Europe, and 'all other hot Climates, as our Plantations in the West Indies, &c'. 'If then the difference of Season produces in our Bodies different Effects', he wrote, 'no

---

[79] 'The Battel of the *Summer-Islands*' in Edmund Waller, *The Works of Edmund Waller, Esq., in Verse and Prose: Published by Mr. Fenton* (London: J. and R. Tonton and S. Draper, 1744), 52–4.

[80] Abraham Cowley, *The Poetical Works of Abraham Cowley in Four Volumes* (Edinburgh: Apollo Press, 1784), 203.

[81] Trapham, 3 & 59. 'Drawing upon the early Spanish promotion of the Caribbean', Parrish notes, 'writers promoting the British "Sugar-Isles" painted a world always green and fertile while ignoring the more distempered facts of earthquakes and hurricanes'. Parrish, *American Curiosity*, 32.

[82] Hippocrates. 'Airs, Waters, and Places', 206. In this, Asia was, therefore, also like an East facing city, which 'resembles the spring as to moderation between heat and cold', 194.

[83] W. Cockburn, *An Account of the Nature, Causes, Symptoms, and Cure of the Distempers that are Incident to Seafaring People with Observations on the Diet of the Sea-Men in His Majesty's Navy: Illustrated with Some Remarkable Instances of the Sickness of the Fleet During the Last Summer, Historically Related* (London: Hugh Newman, 1696), 51. Cf. 109–10: 'These, by the bye, are the fatal, but almost perpetual, consequences of a diaphoretical practice in Fevers; especially on young people, in a hot season of the year, or a warm climate'.

doubt but the Difference of Climate, and Change of Diet, will likewise alter our Constitutions'.[84] Earlier, he had made a similar point in more detail:

As in other countries the Differences of Seasons produce different Effects in our Bodies; for by the more or less Heat the Pores of our Bodies are more or less open, the Air more or less pure, Food more or less spirituous; so without doubt great Difference of Climate, or of Heat or Cold, is very prejudicial to all Strangers, and the cause of numerous Distempers, especially to the *English*, who are very Irregular and Careless in their way of Living.[85]

The following year, J. Christie, in his *Abstract of Some Years Observations Concerning such General and Unperceived Occasions of Sickliness in Fleets and Ships of War*, was considerably less prolix, both in title and text: 'as the Season or Climate are varied', he stated simply, 'so do all our Distempers vary to the very same kinds'.[86]

1.3   Local Knowledge and Medical Expertise

The analogy between seasons and climates had a rather clear corollary. If the West Indies were, like other warm climates, just like Europe in a given season, it should follow that the diseases found in such climates should be similar to seasonal distempers in Europe. That is – even as a good Hippocratic – one would not necessarily expect to find that diseases were, as Sloane intimated he had been told, 'all different from what they are in Europe'. Richard Ligon's brief remarks in his *True and Exact History of the Island of Barbadoes* might function as one example, although it is not quite clear whether he regarded the differences between the diseases of England and Barbados as those of degree or kind. '[S]icknesses are there more grievous', he wrote, 'and mortality greater by far, than in *England*, and these diseases many times contagious'. In terms of treatment, Ligon encouraged physicians to learn about the 'simples' to be found in the Caribbean: 'For certainely every Climate produces Simples more proper to cure the diseases that are bred there, than those that are transported

---

[84] John Polus Lecaan, *Advice to the Gentlemen of the Army of Her Majesty's Forces in Spain and Portugal: With a Short Method How to Preserve Their Health; and Some Observations Upon Several Distempers Incident to Those Countries, and All Other Hot Climates, as Our Plantations in the West-Indies, &C. To Which Are Added the Medicinal Virtues of Many Peculiar Plants Growing Naturally in Those Parts, and Not Wild in England.* (London: P. Varenne, 1708), 20.

[85] Ibid., 4.

[86] J. Christie, *An Abstract of Some Years Observations Concerning Such General and Unperceived Occasions of Sickliness in Fleets and Ships of War* (1709), 3. See also Stubbes: 'in hot Countreys, as well as in hot seasons, the rule of *Hippoc.* takes place'. Henry Stubbes, 'An Enlargement of the Observations, Formerly Publisht Numb. 27, Made and Generously Imparted by That Learn'd and Inquisitive Physician, Dr. Stubbes', *Philosophical Transactions* 3 (1668): 709.

from any other part of the world: such care the great Physitian to mankind takes for our convenience'.[87] It is worth noting, however, that Sloane knew of at least one major source (and the number of such sources was small)[88] in large agreement with his own position, namely that the diseases of the West Indies were essentially the same as those familiar to a European physician.[89] The text was Hickeringill's *Jamaica Viewed*, which had appeared first in 1661. A new edition of the work, of which Sloane owned a copy, was published in 1705.[90] The discussion of the disease environment in the West Indies was short, but one suspects that the following passage, rich with analogies to the growth of plants, would have caught Sloane's eye:

That though *Infant-Settlements*, like *Infant-Years*, are usually most fatal; yet their *Blossoms* once set, are not so easily *Blasted*. Happily experimented in *Jamaica*, whose blooming hopes now thrive so well, and their Stocks so well *Rooted*, that they are not easily *Routed*. The Major part of the Inhabitants being old *West-Indians*, who, now *Naturalized* to the Country, grow better by their *Transplantation*, and flourish in Health equivalently comparable to that of their *Mother-Soil*. For which I need not beg Credit, since there is no *Country Disease* (as at *Virginia* and *Surinam*) endemically raging throughout the Isle; nor any new and unheard of Distempers that want a *name*.[91]

Given how few sources were available at the time on diseases in Jamaica, and given that they clearly do not all argue that the diseases there were all different to those found in Europe, it seems likely that Sloane had something rather specific in mind when he sought to counter this claim. Indeed, I would

---

[87] Richard Ligon, *A True and Exact History of the Island of Barbados* (London: Humphrey Moseley, 1657), 117, 18. The idea that cures of local afflictions were to be found nearby was common enough that it was often referenced through a Latin tag: *ubi morbus, ibi remedium.* See James Lind, *A Treatise of the Scurvy. In Three Parts. Containing an Inquiry into the Nature, Causes, and Cure of That Disease. Together with a Critical and Chronological View of What Has Been Published on the Subject* (London: A. Millar, 1753), 263.

[88] It was not merely that the number of *medical* writings about the West Indies was small. '[T]he island colonists', notes Dunn, 'publicized their doings very little. Back in the Elizabethan era, when English sailors knew the Antilles far better than the North American coast, reports from the New World centered on the Caribbean. But after 1607 the focus shifted decisively north ... None of the islands boasted a printing press, nor did the islanders use the London presses. During the entire course of the century eight or ten promotional tracts designed to lure immigrants to the Caribbean colonies were issued in England, whereas the Virginia Company sponsored some twenty propaganda pieces in the period from 1609 to 1612 alone'. Dunn, *Sugar and Slaves: The Rise of the Planter Class in the English West Indies, 1624–1713*, 23–4.

[89] Stubbes does not suggest that there are diseases peculiar to the West Indies in his Henry Stubbes, 'Observations Made by a Curious and Learned Person, Sailing from England, to the Caribe-Islands', *Philosophical Transactions* 2 (1666); 'An Enlargement of the Observations, Formerly Publisht Numb. 27, Made and Generously Imparted by That Learn'd and Inquisitive Physician, Dr. Stubbes'.

[90] Churchill, 398.

[91] Edmund Hickeringill, *Jamaica Viewed with All the Ports, Harbours, and Their Several Soundings, Towns, and Settlements Thereunto Belonging.*, 3rd ed. (London: Printed and sold by B. Bragg, 1705), 41–2. Cf. Churchill, 427–8.

suggest that we do not read Sloane's claims as transparent descriptions of the medical consensus in the late seventeenth century, but rather as a fairly pointed response to another text: Trapham's. For Trapham had made the argument that Sloane opposed very clearly in his *Discourse*. Due to its climate, Trapham claimed, Jamaica was a much more salubrious country than England, being largely free of many of the diseases that plagued the colder country. 'As for diseases usually found here', he suggested:

they are far short of the long beadrowl [beadroll] which infest our native country: No small Pox or very rarely, saving sometimes brought from *Guinny* by Negroes, terrify or remark us; no Scurvy that almost universal contagion of our native country is got here, or continued if brought; no depopulating Plague that ere I have heard of in the West *Indies*; Consumption nothing so frequent, and when, never so piningly tedious. As for Venereal Affects their symptoms are all lessened, and their discharge more easy far than in colder climes[.][92]

And just as local conditions affected the manifestations of diseases, they also affected their treatment.

For that the place alters much the cure of the Disease, I question not; wherefore Holland which is cold and moist requires a double dose generally of that Physick, whereof in France single will well work and serve the turn. And in a confirmed Pox, they generally remove from one to the other place, from heavier phlegmatick low Countries to the more brisk and drier Air of *France*, placing much of cure in the nature of the Region. And ours of Jamaica being so sweatingly warm, and the air from its Nitre piercingly cleansing, assists much our ready cure[.][93]

Reading Sloane against Trapham opens the text to a much more natural interpretation than is commonly accorded it. For Sloane's claim was *not* that climate had no effect on disease. As a protégé of the famed London physician, Thomas Sydenham, such a position would be profoundly odd. Indeed, to determine what Sloane's argument was, it is useful to keep the dicta of Sydenham in mind, as we will see below.

We should, I think, take both seriously and literally Sloane's clear claim that he encountered virtually no *new* diseases in Jamaica. As Churchill has shown, more than a third of the 128 case histories that made up the section of *Voyage* entitled 'Of the Diseases I observed in Jamaica, and the Method by which I used to cure them', are made up of three kinds of illness then all too familiar to the European doctor: twenty-six intermittent fevers, nine cases of 'bellyach', and eleven of venereal afflictions.[94] One reads of 'tertians', 'dropsies',

---

[92] A beadroll was, originally, 'a list of persons to be specially prayed for', and hence, later, 'a list or string of names'. The OED gives the first usage with this latter meaning in 1529. Trapham, 68–9.

[93] Ibid., 122–3.

[94] Churchill, 407.

and lethargy; of miscarriages and attempted abortions; of 'hectics' and 'fluxes' and the effects of excessive alcohol consumption. Sloane includes only one disease seemingly peculiar to 'Blacks' on the Island, a flesh-eating illness that appeared to be governed by the phases of the moon:

The virulency of the Humour was such, as that after it had eaten into the Bone, the joints of the fingers and toes would drop off, and they die, as I have been assur'd by those who have lost several Negros of this Disease, I was assur'd was peculiar to Blacks … So soon as this Disease again appear'd, I thought, that perhaps this was proper to Blacks, and so might come from some peculiar indisposition of their Black skin … This was a very strange Disease not only in itself, but that it followed very regularly the Full and New Moon.[95]

Even here, however, one suspects that Sloane, who – generally, in this text – downplayed any physiological differences between Blacks, Indians, and Europeans, might well have placed this 'strange Disease' into the category of those 'singular disease[s]' that one encountered even in England.[96]

Overall, Sloane was greatly loath to ascribe any oddities in diseases to general climatic causes. Thus, discussing a fever that lasted less than a day, but caused a degree of weakness that one normally associated with illnesses that lasted months, he wrote: 'This was, I think, peculiar to this Fever, though at first I suspected it was to all diseases here, by reason of the hot climate, but I found all other diseases accompanied with the same symptoms as in Europe, and therefore look on this symptom as a thing particular to this fever, and such uncommon symptoms now and then attend Endemic diseases everywhere'.[97] Without mentioning him by name, Sloane rather pointedly refuted Trapham's claim that venereal diseases were more easily treated in the West Indies. 'It is generally believed in Europe', he claimed, 'that Gonorrhea and the Pox are with more ease and sooner, cured in Jamaica and hot countries than in Europe'. Sloane admitted that he himself 'was of the opinion of the

---

[95] Sloane, cvi–cvii.
[96] As Cristina Malcolmson has recently shown, Sloane's views on race were complex. While it is generally true, as Churchill has argued, that Sloane 'transgressed categories of gender and race' in the *Voyage*, the same was not true in material presented to the Royal Society. For the Society in the 1690s, Malcolmson shows, members were interested in skin colour generally and the skin of 'Negroes' particularly. In their discussions, Sloane spearheaded the drive to investigate the possibility of race-difference as he attacked the climate theory. At a meeting in March, 1690, Sloane argued that there was a 'Specifick Difference' between 'Negrow' and white skin, which made curing skin diseases and ulcers in the former more difficult than the latter. Sloane also claimed that 'woolly' hair was another characteristic of 'the Negro race of Mankind' and suggested that there were racial differences between skulls, although this latter point seems to have been met with little enthusiasm among the Society's members. Cristina Malcolmson, *Studies of Skin Color in the Early Royal Society: Boyle, Cavendish, Swift* (Farnham: Ashgate, 2013), 65, 76, 7. Sloane's complex and even contradictory positions are elegantly summarised on 189–90.
[97] Sloane, xcvii.

generality of the world when I went to Jamaica'. But he found himself mistaken: Gonorrheas 'have the same symptoms as in Europe … [I] found as the Disease was propagated there the same way and had the same symptoms and course among Europeans, Indians, and Negroes, so it requir'd the same remedies and time to be cur'd'.[98]

Yet, that one found almost no novel diseases in Jamaica did not mean that one found there all the diseases commonly treated in London, and certainly not that they were as prevalent in a warm climate as a cold one. Such a claim would, in fact, be very peculiar for a follower of Sydenham, who had insisted on the *seasonality* of diseases.[99] If Sloane argued with Trapham's claims about venereal diseases he was notably silent about Trapham's observations concerning the virtual absence of small pox, scurvy ('that almost universal contagion of our native country'), and plague. Small Pox is mentioned once amongst Sloane's cases (and not as the current affliction of the patient being treated);[100] scurvy and the plague not at all. All three of these were commonly associated with cold weather and, in general, winter afflictions are notably absent from Sloane's cases.[101] In a number of cases, in fact, where patients exhibited the symptoms of common cold-weather afflictions, Sloane made a point of explaining their occurrence. Thus, for example, the case of Sir Francis Watson, who suffered from asthma. Sloane pointed out that Watson lived in a location known as 'the Seven Plantations'. 'This place is cooler than the town of St Jago de la Vega and Sir Francis Watson, who lived here used to be more troubled with the *Asthma* than when in town. For this purpose, he had made a chimney in one of the rooms of his house, which was the only one I ever saw on this Island, except in Kitchens'.[102] Elsewhere, Sloane noted the oddity of having to treat patients for consumption in such a sultry climate: 'Although this Climate be very hot, some of these were troubled with true Consumptions, for which I ordered them some easie Opiates, and other Medicines. I have

[98] Ibid., cxxviii.

[99] 'Lastly, the seasons of the year that principally promote any particular kind of diseases, are to be carefully remarked. I own that some happen indiscriminately at any time, whilst many others, by a secret tendency of nature, follow the seasons of the year with as much certainty, as some birds and plants. And indeed, I have often wondered, that this tendency of some distempers, which is very obvious, has been hitherto observed but by a few … [C]ertain it is that knowledge of the seasons in which diseases ordinarily arise is of great use to a physician towards uncovering the species of the disease, as well as the method of curing it; and that the consequence of slighting this piece of knowledge is ill success in both'. 'The Author's Preface' in Thomas Sydenham and Benjamin Rush, *The Works of Thomas Sydenham, M.D., on Acute and Chronic Diseases with Their Histories and Modes of Cure: With Notes, Intended to Accommodate Them to the Present State of Medicine, and to the Climate and Diseases of the United States* (Philadelphia: B. & T. Kite, 1815), xxvi.

[100] A patient's mother notes that the ulcers and other symptoms with which her daughter was currently afflicted 'had come on after the small pox'. Sloane, cxx.

[101] Sloane notes the seasonality of small pox in ibid., 1.

[102] Ibid., lx.

observed the same disease about Montpelier, among the Inhabitants of that Place, though the air be esteemed a remedy for it'.[103]

This reference to the warm weather and concomitant diseases that one might experience in Europe was telling, for part of Sloane's overarching argument was that the climates of Jamaica and parts of Europe were not as different as might be imagined. Hence, presumably, the similarity of plant life between the West Indies and 'the South Parts of France'. Sloane took some pains to note that, although Jamaica lay in the 'torrid zone' between the tropics of Cancer and the Equator, 'yet the air of it may very well be affirm'd temperate, in that the heat of the days is qualified by the length of the nights'.[104] Indeed, 'I never found more heat here than as in some valleys near *Montpelier* where the situation of the Hills in their neighbourhood occasioned excessive heat'.[105] On this point one finds Sloane echoing Hickeringill once again. The self-styled 'Jolly Captain' could find little to criticise in Jamaica's weather, claiming that 'I have found the air as sulphurous and hot in *England*, in the months of *June, July, and August* ... as in the hottest seasons in *Jamaica*'.[106] Indeed, for Hickeringill, it was Jamaica that deserved the title 'temperate' more than any location in the Old World: 'Yet as the extremities of cold in these Regions betwixt the *Tropicks* are indisputably more remiss than in *England*, and the rest of *Europe*, so the Heat qualified with the benefit of Breezes, more justly styles them *Temperate*, than those *Climates* that have already falsly, (tho' with vulgar consent) *usurp'd* the title'.[107] Throughout his text, Sloane similarly sprinkled comments that, 'notwithstanding the heat', downplayed the environmental and atmospheric differences between Europe and the West Indies. Hence, for example, 'The Rainbow here is as frequent as any where in times of Rain';[108] 'Falling stars are as common as elsewhere', and thunder had the same effects as in Europe.[109]

It could not be gainsaid, however, that the island's heat had medically significant effects. Those who travelled there from colder climes needed to be seasoned to higher temperatures. It is worth noting, in fact, that while Trapham used neither the term nor the concept of seasoning, Sloane devoted no small amount of attention to it. One suspects that for Trapham, a discussion of the ill effects that might greet a newcomer's arrival would have gone against the boosterism that pervades most of his text. Thus, while he did acknowledge that

---

[103] Ibid., 14.
[104] Ibid., vii. Cf. Hickeringill.
[105] Ibid., ix. In making this point, Sloane was in agreement with Trapham, for both regarded the climate of Jamaica as a very salubrious one. 'The air here', Sloane wrote, 'notwithstanding the heat, is very healthy. I have known Blacks one hundred and twenty years of age, and one hundred years old is very common amongst temperate livers', ibid., ix.
[106] Hickeringill, 2.
[107] Ibid., 4.
[108] Sloane, xxxii.
[109] Ibid., xlv.

those who were newly come to Jamaica might wish to avoid the area around the port for some time, he also suggested that they regard the diarrhoea or flux that they were likely to experience as 'a friendly rather than injurious motion of Nature, caused either by a new sort of Drink & Diet, which falls out in most places more or less, the which ceaseth without prejudice or any other remedy than a little time; or else the same may arise from rejoicing intemperance, too often welcoming the new arrivers'.[110] Sloane had his own criticisms of the intemperate, but in describing the afflictions of newcomers to Jamaica, he tended to stress the direct effect of the action of a blazing sun.[111] Furthermore, whatever the discomfort felt, the body's response was a salutary one.[112]

I did not at all doubt that these eruptions were the effect of the Sun Beams, which throwing into our blood some fiery parts, put it into brisker motion, whereby it was purg'd of those *heterogenous* and unaccustom's Particles it had from the warm sun, and perhaps by that fermentation was likewise clear'd of some other parts might be hurtful to it ...[113]

The climate of Jamaica, then, was indeed different from that found in Europe – different enough that those coming from squally England needed to undergo an uncomfortable seasoning in order to inure them to a warmer part of the globe. One might expect – and indeed, found – that the winter diseases of cold climates were relatively or entirely absent. But it was not so bizarrely and extremely different that profoundly different disease environments might be expected. The key point for Sloane was that when diseases manifested themselves, they were to be identified and cured in precisely the same ways as they were in Europe. Intermittent fevers, to take merely one example, did not exhibit one variety in the temperate zone and another between the tropics and hence did not require different cures in each place. This was a claim at once ontological and social. Ontologically, one may note its similarity to doctrines espoused by Sydenham. 'Every specific disease', he wrote, 'arises from a specific exaltation, or peculiar quality of

---

[110] Trapham, 71. Trapham is one of the few authors I have come across who reverses the logic of seasoning, suggesting that new arrivals from chilly Europe might be *better off* than locals: 'It may not be improper to remark that those Brezes of the night do less injury to new comers from the colder Europe than to the more antient inhabitants, whose pores being as it were moulded into the bore of the Indian Air, are of larger size and more receptive of the chilling Brezes than such as come from the northern parts: hence also such as pass directly out of Europe hither are not so easily assaulted with fevorish attracts as those from the *Carib* Isles: for those little tracts of land of *Barbadoes, Nevis, Monserat &c* being well opened, and therefore affording nothing so much of night Brezes as the large woody mountains of Jamica do, hath not inured them thereto, while their greater diurnal heat hath sufficiently disposed them to a most ready reception of the night cold Invaders', ibid., 10–11.

[111] On the case of a 'Captain Nowel' and his excessive drinking, see James Delbourgo, 'Slavery in the Cabinet of Curiosities: Hans Sloane's Atlantic World', www.britishmuseum.org/research/news/hans_sloanes_atlantic_world.aspx (2007), last accessed 15 Jan. 2018.

[112] Sloane, xciv–xcv.

[113] Ibid., 25.

some humour contained in a living body'. Diseases were not, that is, merely the 'confused and irregular operations of disordered and debilitated nature'. Instead, they arose when humours were retained in the body too long, either because Nature could not remove them, because of atmospheric effects, or because they had been infected by some sort of poison. By these, or related causes:

these humours are worked up into a substantial form or species, that discovers itself by particular symptoms, agreeable to its peculiar essence; and these symptoms, notwithstanding they may, for want of attention, seem to arise either from the nature of the part in which the humour is lodged, or from the humour itself before it assumed this species, are in reality disorders that proceed from the essence of the species, newly raised to this pitch[.][114]

This specificity in the *cause* of diseases led to a specificity of both symptoms and methods of cure. Although Sydenham was willing to acknowledge that the age or constitution of a patient might cause some minor variations in the appearance of a given disease, he made no mention at all of differences that might be due to race or (perhaps more tellingly) geographic location. 'The same disease appears attended with the like symptoms in different subjects; so that those which were observed in Socrates, in his illness, may generally be applied to any other person afflicted with the same disease'.[115] Sloane appears to have had the same idea, for although he might often have mentioned the age or humoural constitution of a patient in his case notes, he rarely notes their location (even within the West Indies) except to suggest an environmental explanation for the manifestation of a disease seemingly out of season.

The social or professional significance of Sloane's arguments flows from this insistence on a common ontology for diseases in Jamaica and England. For if diseases differed due to climate, requiring distinct dosages according to place, as Trapham argued, then it would seem to follow that those, like Trapham, who possessed local knowledge, would be at an advantage in curing local manifestations of illnesses. Despite his connections, his training, and his experience in Europe, Sloane could be considered at a disadvantage, since he did not understand 'the country diseases having lived there several years'. Where diseases were identical in both places, however, Sloane's status could be deservedly transferred from England to the West Indies. Sloane's was not at all an argument that denied that Jamaica and Europe were different disease environments. It was an argument, rather, that insisted that the opinions of a high-status metropolitan doctor trumped the views of a Jamaican physician, however much the latter knew of local conditions.[116]

---

[114] Sydenham and Rush, xxx.
[115] Ibid., xxvii.
[116] One can see that this kind of argument would be particularly devastating to any knowledge claims made by local, non-European practitioners.

Again, despite Sloane's (rhetorically powerful) claims to the contrary, he was hardly alone in his views. The debate between those who claimed a kind of universal, or at least easily transferrable, medical knowledge and those claiming superior, locally-based empirical and experiential skills was one that shaped medical practice and socio-professional life throughout the growing empire. We have seen that the debate continued until at least 1750, when it culminated in a duel between two Jamaican physicians. One finds it in print, however, even before Sloane's *Voyage* was published, in a text with which he was probably familiar. In 1696, William Cockburn, a Baronet who would be elected a Fellow to the Royal Society the following year, published the first edition of his *An Account of the Nature, Causes, Symptoms, and Cure of the Distempers that are Incident to Seafaring People*. The work was based on his experiences, beginning in 1694, as one of the first physicians to an English naval fleet. Its aims were, in his words, 'to discover such sicknesses as may be peculiar to people that use our narrow Seas' and to distinguish these both from illnesses on land and those more common closer to the Equator.[117]

While such sicknesses might be peculiar, however, Cockburn concluded that the physician needed to know comparatively little that was new in order to practice in foreign climes: 'the reasoning will hold somewhere else'. After all, a sailor's diet was similar in most places, and diseases that followed from 'vict-ualling' might therefore be supposed to be familiar. The main difference would lie in the air 'which we know is more serene and warm in those places' near the equator. That said, the physician familiar with the mechanical philosophy could determine the effects of this air on the human frame without stirring from his chair. '[B]ecause of its gravity (which is always greatest in a serene Air)', Cockburn opined, 'the blood and all that's carried along in it, are more minutely broken and divided in the lungs ... and therefore is more apt to separate its small and fine parts, and so to have a greater motion and all the consequences that follow upon that'.[118] The second edition of the work appeared under an altered title in 1706, but Cockburn had not changed his views on the ease with which a suitably trained metropolitan physician might diagnose and treat trop-ical diseases from a distance.[119] So confident of his own analysis was he, that he declared himself 'convinced that this matter does admit of such certainty, as such Surgeons of an indifferent Education might be able to Practise in those

---

[117] Cockburn, 3.

[118] Ibid., 72–3. On Cockburn and his circle of 'Tory Newtonians', see Anita Guerrini, 'Archibald Pitcairne and Newtonian Medicine', *Medical History* 31 (1987); 'The Tory Newtonians: Gregory, Pitcairne, and Their Circle', *Journal of British Studies* 25 (1986); 'James Keill, George Cheyne, and Newtonian Physiology, 1690–1740', *Journal of the History of Biology* 8 (1985); Theodore M. Brown, 'Medicine in the Shadow of the Principia', *Journal of the History of Ideas* 48, no. 4 (1987).

[119] William Cockburn, *Sea Diseases: Or, a Treatise of Their Nature, Causes, and Cure. Also, an Essay on Bleeding in Fevers; Shewing, the Quantities of Blood to Be Let, in Any of Their Periods. The Second Edition Corrected and Much Improved* (London: Geo. Strahan, 1706).

Fevers, in the E. and W. Indies with as great success, as Physicians commonly have in *England* and other temperate Countries'.[120]

As Harold Cook has shown, arguments like Cockburn's were increasingly common within the British armed forces after the Glorious Revolution. In the larger army and navy after 1688, what was prized was a form of medicine that was 'more universalistic and empirical, less individualistic and learned'.[121] This contrasted with the more traditional and scholarly methods of the Royal College of Physicians, resulting in heated debates between the College and the Admiralty. 'A crucial difference in attitudes towards medicine itself divided the two groups', Cook writes. 'The military wanted quick and efficacious cures for specific diseases that would be good for any soldier or sailor in any circumstance, while the learned physicians wished to maintain the importance of learned physic, with its emphasis on the individual'.[122] Part of this latter emphasis, of course, involved knowledge about location. It was thus perhaps inevitable that Cockburn's attempts to operationalise his insights met with limited success, precisely because leading medical men in England found it difficult to accept that greater personal knowledge of the particulars of practice in the Indies might not be useful. Cockburn had conceived of a plan whereby surgeons overseas might produce a more easily standardised record, so that 'by their having a good number of Orderly Observations, it might be easy for any one to find the right method of these Fevers in the W. Indies'. Cockburn laid the scheme before the Admiralty, who were apparently enthusiastic, but proposed forwarding the matter for the approval of the College of Physicians. Protesting that this was unnecessary, Cockburn, somewhat disingenuously, sought to portray his proposal as one that had little to do with his own views: 'because I did not direct any particular Method to be followed, but only foretold the different success of each method in general use'. The College failed to come to a conclusion on the matter, but their reasons for doing so were illuminating. 'I perceive they were at a loss what Judgment to make of those Particularities which differ from our practice in these Parts of the World', wrote Thomas Millington, the College President, 'As being perfect Strangers to what does, or does not succeed in the *West Indies*'.[123]

One can see from Cockburn's failure to convince members of the College that Hippocratic arguments were a two-edged sword. What social work they might do depended upon location. In the metropole, elite physicians might insist on the applicability of the arguments of *Airs, Waters, and Places* in the

[120] Ibid., 105.
[121] Harold J. Cook, 'Practical Medicine and the British Armed Forces after the "Glorious Revolution"', *Medical History* 34 (1990): 26. See, similarly, Alsop, 30.
[122] Cook, 'Practical Medicine and the British Armed Forces after the "Glorious Revolution"', 14.
[123] All quotations, including that from Millington's letter in Cockburn, *Sea Diseases: Or, a Treatise of Their Nature, Causes, and Cure. Also, an Essay on Bleeding in Fevers; Shewing, the Quantities of Blood to Be Let, in Any of Their Periods. The Second Edition Corrected and Much Improved*, Preface.

face of claims that sidelined or rejected their scholarly expertise in favour of an emphasis on simplicity, universality, and efficacy. For Sloane in the West Indies, however, the practice that flowed from Hippocratic logics gave the advantage to those who were *not* metropolitan elites. Thus, in spite of the fact that Richard Towne dedicated *A Treatise of the Diseases Most Frequent in the West-Indies* to Sloane, one suspects that on this issue, at least, his sympathies were with Trapham. When the text appeared in 1726, one year after the publication of the second volume of Sloane's *Voyage*, Towne could boast of 'seven years practice' in Barbados.[124] The introduction to his short book was well crafted, showing Towne to be well-versed in current mechanical theories, but more committed to located empiricism. 'I have introduced no more Philosophy into this Treatise', he noted, 'than what was necessary to explain the Reasonableness of the Practice, and to guide those into a right Application of it, for whose Use it was principally calculated'.[125] And from the outset, although Towne did not acknowledge the point explicitly (indeed, he implicitly sought to play it down) the text was framed in opposition to Sloane's, arguing that the same diseases manifested differently in different places, and that illnesses existed in the West Indies that had never been seen in Europe.

It is no wonder then that the *Alterations* made in our *Constitutions* should be conformable to the Causes from whence they arise, and consequently that *Diseases* should be in some Places more or less frequent than they are in others, and attended with Symptoms as different as the *Qualities* of the *Countries* where they are produced. This Variety in the Degrees of *Violence*, and Diversity of *Types*, by which Distempers are distinguished from each other, must necessarily require the peculiar Attention of the Physician in his Management of them, and therefore no one *Methodus Medendi* can be framed so general and absolute as to tally with every *Climate*.[126]

Few of Towne's readers could have perused this last sentence without thinking of Sloane, who only the year before had defended his decision to publish the names of his patients when describing their case histories by suggesting that he only did so 'to prove that the Diseases there were the same as in *England*'. But Towne took some of the sting out of his implied criticism of Sloane's 'one method fits all' approach to the practice of medicine in warm climates by suggesting that Sloane himself had been interested, like Towne, in the particularities of place. Both men were, Towne claimed, part of a lineage of 'learned Physicians' that included Alpinus, William Piso, and Bontius, all of whom had 'employ[ed] their Pens upon such Diseases as are *endemic* or *popular*, in those Places where their Practice afforded them the greatest Opportunity for *Observation*'.[127]

[124] Towne, 3.
[125] Ibid.
[126] Ibid., 1–2.
[127] Ibid., 2–3.

In spite of this effort to construct a commonality with a powerful patron, it nonetheless seems clear that Towne, like Trapham and unlike Sloane, saw the diseases of the West Indies as entities different to those found in Europe and hence requiring treatment modified to local conditions.[128] Towne, in fact, even identified two illnesses 'to which the blacks are no strangers, but as far as I can be informed they are utterly unknown in Europe: I mean the Elefantiasis under the circumstances it occurs in the West Indies, and a distemper called there the *Joint-Evil'*.[129] For those whose careers were to be made in the colonies, an emphasis on geographical specificity played to their strengths. For the sojourning Sloane, lack of local knowledge was a potential liability, one to be removed by rejecting the putatively Hippocratic premise of his opponents.

Conclusion

In a now-classic article about the ways that the 'torrid zone' functioned within the European imaginary, Karen Kupperman offered a valuable periodisation. Whereas before the seventeenth century, English would-be travellers to the southern parts of North America 'expressed profound anxiety over the effect hot climates would have on them', from the 1630s, 'propagandists for southern colonies' began to argue that their regions provided an ideal middle zone between extremes of cold and heat.[130] A number of scholars have since nuanced the first part of this claim, pointing to both positive and negative responses to America, even in the earliest periods of its European exploration and settlement.[131] But most have tended to affirm the second part, stressing the strategic importance of promotional attitudes to imperial desires. Portraits of fecundity, verdancy, and the peacefulness of native inhabitants, Susan Parrish has noted, 'had everything to do with attracting settlement and investment in the face of negative reports of starvation, disease, hurricanes, intemperate weather, and Indian massacres'.[132] I believe we can assume a similar periodisation for the West Indies, although their later dates of English settlement (1627 for

---

[128] In terms of diagnosis, for example, one could not rely on an examination of the urine as one could in Europe. The warm weather changed the fluid too dramatically, so that 'Prognosticks taken from an examination of the urine are much more precarious here than in Europe'. 61–2. In terms of treatment, Towne called attention to the practice of Paracenthesis or 'tapping': 'How frightful soever this Undertaking may appear in Europe, yet it is practiced almost every day in Barbadoes with good success', 135.

[129] Towne, 184.

[130] Karen Kupperman, 'Fear of Hot Climates in the Anglo-American Experience', *William and Mary Quarterly* 41 (1984): 213–40, 213, 217.

[131] Chaplin, *Subject Matter: Technology, the Body, and Science on the Anglo-American Frontier, 1500–1676*. Parrish. Jan Golinski, 'American Climate and the Civilization of Nature', in *Science and Empire in the Atlantic World*, ed. James Delbourgo and Nicholas Dew (New York and London: Routledge, 2008).

[132] Parrish, 33.

Barbados; 1655 for Jamaica) suggest that periods in which attitudes about their climates were negative would have been short. Certainly, by 1679, Trapham was serving as a booster for a climate he and others were happy to portray as eminently suitable for British bodies. Eight years later, Richard Blome's *Present State of His Majesty's Isles and Territories in America*, declared that 'it is confirmed by a long experience, that there is no such antipathy betwixt our *Britanick* Temper and the Climate of Jamaica, as to necessitate them to any Distemper upon their arrival there, or occasion Diseases to prove mortal or contagious more than in other parts'.[133] It is possible, then, that Sloane – if he had been thinking of specific works when he claimed to have been led to believe that diseases were all different in Jamaica – had considerably older texts in mind. More up-to-date volumes, as we have seen, all tended to portray the West Indies as a summer version of England, and hence as a location that possessed many of the same diseases as England, and very few completely new ones. Where Trapham and Sloane disagreed – publicly – was not over diagnosis, but over therapeutics. And there, Sloane was indeed in a minority, at least among civilians, in insisting that what he had learned in Britain and France could be transferred directly to Jamaica.

In terms of the history of medicine, the stakes involved in not taking Sloane as simply a faithful barometer of medical opinion concerning the diseases of the New World are high. Among the tasks of this book is the attempt to explain how it came to be believed to be a fact that the latitudes between the tropics contained radically different disease environments compared to northern Europe. If Sloane accurately captured the tenor of the times, then the problem for the historian involves explaining how such attitudes spread from the West Indies to other imperial holdings where such understandings of fundamental difference were not common.[134] If Sloane's claims are to be nuanced in the ways I have suggested, the task is a different one. It amounts to asking about eighteenth-century events and processes that led to the *emergence* of conceptions both of similarity within the tropics and conceptions of difference between the tropics and the so-called temperate zones. It is to this latter question that we turn in subsequent chapters, beginning in the next with the emergence of a belief that we saw traces of in Trapham's writings: the notion that the movement of peoples via the slave trade was *producing* a disease environment in the West Indies resembling that in Africa, where no such commonality had existed before.

---

[133] Quoted in ibid., 87.
[134] As we shall see, geographical specification is required here. West Africa had a much poorer reputation as a disease environment than the East Indies in the early eighteenth century. Curtin, ' "The White Man's Grave": Image and Reality, 1780–1850'; 'Epidemiology and the Slave Trade'; *The Image of Africa: British Ideas and Action, 1780–1850*.

2 Changes in the Air: William Hillary and English Medicine in the West Indies, 1720–1760

In 1759, William Hillary, a physician who had kept a practice in the West Indies for the preceding dozen years, published a book on the diseases of Barbados.[1] Early reviews tended to be positive. Reviewers griped, not unreasonably, at the doctor's repetitive style and his often unnecessary displays of erudition, yet they lauded his judgement and attention to detail.[2] 'Reading his description', one claimed, 'is almost equivalent to seeing the patient, and differs only as a copy from the original ... [I]n this particular', the reviewer continued, offering perhaps the highest praise possible, 'he is little inferior to the *British Hippocrates, Sydenham*'.[3] In 1762, Solomon de Monchy, City Physician of Rotterdam and author of a prize-winning essay answering a question about the 'causes of the usual diseases among seamen in voyages to the West Indies', offered a list of British physicians upon whom he was relying.[4] The authors he cited were 'Mead, Pringle, Huxham, Lind, Watson, Bisset, Hillary', placing the last-mentioned author in illustrious company only three years after his text's first printing.[5] In 1766, Hillary's work appeared, unaltered, in a second edition. Benjamin Rush would be responsible for the publication of a third in 1811.[6] It would be a rare work on the diseases of the Caribbean in the last decades of the eighteenth century that did not cite Hillary's *Observations*.

In this chapter I aim to offer the first detailed intellectual history of Hillary's medical writings, a history that will simultaneously provide a description of

---

[1] William Hillary, *Observations on the Changes of the Air and the Concomitant Epidemical Diseases, in the Island of Barbados. To Which Is Added a Treatise on the Putrid Bilious Fever, Commonly Called the Yellow Fever; and Such Other Diseases as Are Indigenous or Endemial, in the West India Islands, or in the Torrid Zone* (London: C. Hitch and L. Hawes, 1759).

[2] *The Monthly Review, or Literary Journal* (November, 1759): 369–81; *The Critical Review, or Annals of Literature* 7 (1759): 520–29.

[3] *The Critical Review*, 521.

[4] de Monchy, iv.

[5] Ibid., v.

[6] William Hillary and Benjamin Rush, *Observations on the Changes of the Air, and the Concomitant Epidemical Diseases in the Island of Barbados: To Which Is Added, a Treatise on the Putrid Bilious Fever, Commonly Called the Yellow Fever; and Such Other Diseases As Are Indigenous or Endemial, in the West India Islands, or in the Torrid Zone* (Philadelphia: B. & T. Kite, 1811).

the medical landscape relevant to work on the diseases of warm climates from the 1720s to the 1760s.[7] Recovering the resources necessary for Hillary's theorising will allow us to track the complex interrelations between different forms of medicine informed by the mechanical philosophy, as well as the roles played by medical meteorology, theories of contagion, and notions of environmental causation in understanding the diseases of the 'torrid zone'. To this empirical or descriptive base, I add two further argumentative layers. Each relies on the structure of Hillary's text for its explication.

The volume was divided into two fairly distinct parts. The first – *Observations on the Changes of the Air and the Concomitant Epidemical Diseases, in the Island of Barbados* – was a diary of the weather on the island, correlated with descriptions of the diseases observed by Hillary in his practice over a period of several years in the 1750s. The second half – *A Treatise on the Putrid Bilious Fever, Commonly Called the Yellow Fever; and such Other Diseases as are Indigenous or Endemial, in the West India Islands, or in the Torrid Zone* – involved a description of diseases that were commonly found in the West Indies but would be unfamiliar to most physicians in England. In the terminology of the day, the first half of the book was concerned with *epidemical*, the second half with *endemial* diseases.

As we saw in the last chapter, by the seventeenth century the touchstone for works on diseases peculiar to a given part of the world was Hippocrates' *Airs, Waters, and Places*. Chapter 1 spent some time describing a 'Hippocratic revival' based around the text, as it was increasingly used to understand the distempers characteristic of lands between the Tropics. The study of epidemics and their relationship to the seasons also had a Hippocratic root. Those who produced a medico-meteorological diary in the early eighteenth century cited the Hippocratic works *Epidemics I* and *III* almost without fail.[8] Many of Hillary's contemporaries who vaunted Hippocrates for his empiricist method tended not to distinguish between these three texts, seeing in each examples of the author's attention to data rather than 'sterile' theory, as well as a common and characteristic emphasis on the relationship between human health and the weather. Historians, similarly, have often been more interested in the methodological differences between neo-Hippocratics and other medical sects (Galenists and chemists, for example) than the more seemingly narrow

---

[7] For shorter accounts, see Frederick Sargent, *Hippocratic Heritage: A History of Ideas About Weather and Human Health* (New York: Pergamon Press, 1982), 224–8; Sheridan, *Doctors and Slaves: A Medical and Demographic History of Slavery in the British West Indies, 1680–1834*, 22–4; Harrison, *Medicine in an Age of Commerce and Empire: Britain and its Tropical Colonies, 1660–1830*, 53–60.

[8] Hippocrates, 'Epidemics I', in *The Genuine Works of Hippocrates*, translated from the Greek by Francis Adams, with a Preliminary Discourse and Annotations. In Two Volumes, Vol. 1, 352–382 (London: Sydenham Society, 1849). Hippocrates, 'Epidemics III', Ibid., 388–420.

differences, in theory and practice, among neo-Hippocratics. In any case, if one is concerned with the *production* of the Hippocratic texts, treating the three texts together makes sense. It was assumed, in the eighteenth century, based on the language and logic of each work, that the same person authored both *Epidemics I* and *III* and *Airs, Waters, and Places*. And one might note that all three texts are quintessentially Hippocratic in that they examine collective diseases, rather than those of individual patients.

As can be seen from Hillary's volume, however, the *audiences* for new works based on each text were rather different. Hillary concluded his weather diary on 30 May 1758 when he returned to England. He published his observations, he claimed 'for the Benefit of the Inhabitants of that Island, and sincerely with that they may be of Service to them and all theirs'.[9] By contrast, in the preface to the part of the work on endemial diseases, Hillary declared that 'I principally write and publish these for the Good of the Inhabitants, and the Benefit of those who commonly practice in the West-India Islands'.[10] The two halves of the book were involved in two largely, if not completely, different conversations. In the first half, Hillary cited and engaged with metropolitan authors, such as Boerhaave and John Huxham. In the second, he argued with West Indian physicians – Towne and Warren, for example – and others who had treated diseases in the torrid zone.

My first argument, then, is that historians seeking to understand 'the' Hippocratic revival would do well to pay attention to the geographic location of those vaunting the physician from Cos. Speaking broadly, one might, indeed, be better off speaking of at least two, interacting, revivals – one more metropolitan and dealing with epidemic diseases, the other more colonial and dealing with endemic distempers. The point is an important one, given this book's emphasis on the history of 'difference-making', for *Epidemics* and *Airs, Waters, and Places*, in spite of many similarities, draw the attention to two rather different differences. *Airs, Waters, and Places*, of course, was concerned with the diseases characteristic of different regions and climates. *Epidemics*, on the other hand, opened with a discussion of the diseases found in a given year – broken down by seasons – in the town of Thasus. Subsequent sections described the 'constitutions' of successive years in the same place. If *Airs, Waters, and Places* was thus focused on spatial difference, *Epidemics* was concerned with temporal changes; the first compared climates, the second constitutions. A physician relying on *Epidemics* could, in fact, pay almost no attention to the question of how a different location might change their analysis. Sydenham's account of epidemic constitutions in London, for example, was resolutely local, a fact that drew criticisms from James Lind, a leading

---

[9] Hillary, 136.
[10] Ibid., Preface, unnumbered, 142.

naval physician and author of *An Essay on Diseases Incidental to Europeans in Hot Climates* (1768), a work solidly in the tradition of *Airs, Waters, and Places*. According to Lind, the reason that Sydenham found phlebotomy such a universal remedy for almost all fevers was because of his limited geographical experience. Had the 'eminent physician' practiced even a few miles from the metropolis, in the low marshy areas outside London, Lind opined, he would probably have changed his mind. Had he ventured even farther forth, yet more of his ideas would have been altered. Knowledge of the autumnal fever that one finds in Europe, or 'of the great mortality produced by its rage in hot climates' – precisely the information Lind supplied in his treatise – would have led Sydenham to retract the idea that a continual fever was 'the most constant and primary fever of nature'.[11]

Medical writers, like Sydenham, who used *Epidemics* as a model tended implicitly to downplay the differences made by geography and to emphasise those induced by seasonality. During a period in which Britain's imperial holdings and trading interests were growing, use of *Epidemics* to discuss the relationship between environment and health drew distant lands closer to the metropole, while use of *Airs, Waters, and Places* tended to stress the differences of foreign climes. As we shall see, Hillary's medico-meteorological diary made the West Indies seem familiar, his account of the diseases peculiar to Barbados made the entire torrid zone seem distinctive.

The second main argument I make in this chapter serves as part of an answer to the question posed at the end of the last. When and why did medical practitioners begin to conceive of the West Indies in particular and the tropics more generally as distinct disease environments, different from England and other northern countries not merely in degree, but in kind? Historians Kenneth Kiple and Kriemhild Ornelas have pointed to Hillary's text as 'the first to report a significantly different disease environment in the West Indies from that of Europe'.[12] In the next chapter, I suggest that naval medical texts served as a principal source for a new conception of tropical disease environments as *sui generis*, and point to British military engagements in the Caribbean in the late 1730s and 1740s as moments in which a broader English populace became aware of the dangers posed to 'unseasoned' soldiers in climates far from home. In the second half of the present chapter, however, my concern is with Hillary's

---

[11] James Lind, *An Essay on Diseases Incidental to Europeans in Hot Climates: With the Method of Preventing Their Fatal Consequences. To Which Is Added, an Appendix Concerning Intermittent Fevers* (London: T. Becket and P. A. de Hondt, 1768), 68.

[12] Kenneth F. Kiple and Kriemhild Coneé Ornelas, 'Race, War, and Tropical Medicine in the Eighteenth-Century Caribbean', in *Warm Climates and Western Medicine: The Emergence of Tropical Medicine, 1500–1900*, ed. David Arnold (Amsterdam and Atlanta: Rodopi, 1996). See also Kenneth F. Kiple, *The Caribbean Slave: A Biological History* (Cambridge: Cambridge University Press, 1984).

formulation of the medical distinctiveness of hot climates. His own explanation for this distinctiveness made almost no explicit use of military texts or mention of military campaigns.

As befits a figure writing in a transitional period – between the early eighteenth century when all climates were regarded as possessing both similarities and differences and the late eighteenth century, when disease environments had begun to harden into geographically determined zones – Hillary's arguments were both fascinating and complex. It is true that he described a good many diseases common to the 'torrid zone' and largely unknown in England, yet the reasons given for both similarities and differences varied. Yellow fever, for example, was a characteristic affliction in Barbados and one induced by the climate. For it, and perhaps it alone, Hillary associated its cause not merely with a warm climate, but with a specifically *tropical* one. Indeed, Hillary's yellow fever may be the first explicitly identified tropical disease. However, for other afflictions (yaws and elephantiasis, for example) he balked at equating geographical location and disease environment. The West Indies was not home to diseases common to countries with warm climates solely by virtue of its position between the tropics. It was not nature that connected the Guinea Coast to Barbados, but human action. The slave trade *made* the West Indies like parts of Africa and unlike England. The West Indian disease environment might have been distinctive to Hillary, but for the most part its difference was to be explained not by geography, but by history.

2.1   A Rational and Mechanical Essay

Born in 1698, Hillary began his medical career at 18, with an apprenticeship to an apothecary. His university training began roughly five years later, in Leiden, where his status as a religious dissenter did not prevent his attendance, as was the case at Oxford or Cambridge. There he studied under Hermann Boerhaave and completed his thesis, on intermittent fevers, towards the middle of 1722. Around a year later, he moved back to Yorkshire, establishing a practice in the town of Ripon, where he stayed for more than a decade before moving to Bath. The shift was a dramatic one. Ripon was a small country town, while Bath – famous since Roman times – had become not merely a site for water cures, but for aristocratic entertainment; where 'the cream of English Society ... divert[ed] itself with the waters, conversation, music, dancing, the theatre, and the pleasure of being seen in the company of the most distinguished people in the land'.[13] The rather dour Quaker clearly found that his relocation required some adjustment, as one can see from the two editions of his first publication,

---

[13] C. C. Booth, 'William Hillary: A Pupil of Boerhaave', *Medical History* 7, no. 4 (1963): 304; William Addison, *English Spas* (London: B. T. Batsford Ltd., 1951), 58–73. On medicine in spa towns, see Roy Porter, ed. *The Medical History of Waters and Spas, Medical History Supplement 10* (London: Wellcome Institute for the History of Medicine, 1990).

an essay on the smallpox. The first was completed at Ripon, its Preface dated May 1732, although it was not published until 1735. Hillary suggested that smallpox's frequency and mortality 'particularly to several Families of the first Rank' was the main impetus for his attempts to divine a better cure for the disease. That may have endeared him somewhat to leading local figures, yet his explanation for why it would be elites that seemed to suffer so much from the affliction nowadays cannot have been so appealing:

[Their] Educations and manner of living, do dispose their Constitutions to be more severely afflicted with this Disease, than those who are brought up with a more plain, simple Diet, and a hardier manner of Life; for I cannot but very much blame the Luxury of the present Age, for the fatal Advances which this, and some other Diseases, have of late Years made.[14]

The Preface to the second edition, completed in Bath and published in 1740, was shorter, with passages about several topics trimmed and omitted. Particularly striking, however, was the removal of his former criticisms of aristocratic lifestyles. Hillary now needed to make his living not from hardy farm folk, but from the coddled upper classes and if he still disapproved, he made efforts to hide it.[15]

In medical terms, the treatise on smallpox was thoroughly indebted, as Hillary noted, to the 'sagacious and learned Dr. Boerhaave', who was credited as the inventor of the cure for the disease promoted in the text (a cooling, 'antiphlogistic' regimen and repeated bloodletting).[16] In the early eighteenth century, Leiden was the centre for medical learning in Europe and Boerhaave was its leading light. More than 1900 students matriculated at Leiden between 1701 and 1738, with a third of these coming from England, Scotland, Ireland, and the British colonies. And more students studied directly with Boerhaave than any other medical professor at the university. In the 29 years he served as professor, he 'promoted' 178 students, of whom 43 came from English speaking countries.[17]

---

[14] William Hillary, *A Rational and Mechanical Essay on the Small-Pox: Wherein the Cause, Nature, and Diathesis of That Disease, Its Symptoms, Their Causes, and Manner of Production, Are Explained ... With the Diagnostic and Prognostic Symptoms ... To Which is Prefixed, a Short History of the First Rise and Progress of That Disease; and an Essay on a New Method of Curing It, as We Do Other Inflammatory Diseases* (London: G. Strahan, 1735), iv, v.

[15] '[O]nly those with sufficient leisure and capital could devote time to personal wellbeing', Guerrini has observed in her study of George Cheyne, another physician who sought to make a second career in Bath. 'The interface between the new culture of leisure and its relationship to health was especially evident in the new spa towns'. Anita Guerrini, *Obesity and Depression in the Enlightenment: The Life and Times of George Cheyne* (Norman: University of Oklahoma Press, 2000), 101.

[16] Hillary, 1735, xiv.

[17] G. A. Lindeboom, *Hermann Boerhaave: The Man and His Work* (London: Methuen, 1968), 356–7.

As one of these students Hillary imbibed his master's emphasis on the body as a machine, albeit more of a 'hydraulico-pneumatical engine' than the clockwork imagined by many earlier proponents of the mechanical philosophy.[18] One of Boerhaave's earliest orations at Leiden had been entitled 'On the Use of Rational Mechanics in Medicine' (1703). The first edition of Hillary's work bore the self-consciously similar title 'A Rational and Mechanical Essay on the Smallpox'. In his preface, Hillary declared that 'a human Body is (as much as it is the Object of Medicine) a Machine' and that 'Diseases are nothing but Defects and Irregularities of those actions, Motions, and Properties, produced in this wonderful Human Machine'.[19] Smallpox, he argued, was a disease that was both epidemical and contagious. Epidemical in that it proceeded from a common cause, afflicted the majority of people in a given region, and did so in a definite space of time; contagious in that it was passed from one patient to another via the air, which carried 'infectious Miasmata' from person to person.[20] The particles that made up this dangerous miasma were too minute to be directly perceived, but from their effects, Hillary concluded that they must affect both the solid and fluid parts of the body. By virtue of their sizes, either individually or through the production of larger molecules via mutual attraction, they must be able both to form obstructions in 'the ultimate minute subcuticular Arteries' – and hence allow the production and accumulation of putrid pus – and to stimulate the body's nervous solids to produce both stronger and more frequent contractions, driving fluids more rapidly and with more force throughout the body. The result, Hillary concluded, would be 'a violent Inflammatory Fever, with all its dangerous, and too often fatal, Consequences'.[21]

The focus of the essay would change substantially in the second edition, even if the contents would not. Gone were the encomiums to the wondrous human machine. In their place were blander materialist pronouncements: 'The *Agent* and *Patient* both being *Matter*, are subject to the same unalterable

---

[18] On Boerhaave as an iatrophysicist, see ibid., esp. 61–7, 272–4. The term 'hydraulico-pneumatical engine' was Robert Boyle's. See Barbara Orland, 'The Fluid Mechanics of Nutrition: Herman Boerhaave's Synthesis of Seventeenth-Century Circulation Physiology', *Studies in History and Philosophy of Biological and Biomedical Sciences* 43 (2012): 365. Orland offers a superb summary of Boerhaave's model on 364. For a helpful overview of medicine in this period, see Lester S. King, *The Philosophy of Medicine: The Early Eighteenth Century* (Cambridge, MA: Harvard University Press, 1978).

[19] Hillary, *A Rational and Mechanical Essay on the Small-Pox: Wherein the Cause, Nature, and Diathesis of That Disease, Its Symptoms, Their Causes, and Manner of Production, Are Explained ... With the Diagnostic and Prognostic Symptoms ... To Which Is Prefixed, a Short History of the First Rise and Progress of That Disease; and an Essay on a New Method of Curing It, as We Do Other Inflammatory Diseases*, vii.

[20] Ibid., 32.

[21] Ibid., 38.

Laws which *Matter* in general is'.[22] The title changed, so that it was now a
'Practical Essay' rather than a 'Rational and Mechanical' one. The mechanical explanation for the effect of the smallpox contagion on the human system
remained, but it was now moved from the first section following the historical introduction to chapter five of eight. Perhaps the decision to emphasise
more his novel treatment was occasioned by criticisms of some of the more
theoretical elements of Hillary's arguments. That, at least, would explain the
somewhat petulant tone the author adopted in his new preface, as he defended
theory against its detractors. 'It would be highly obliging to Mankind in general', he wrote sarcastically, 'if those Gentlemen who declaim so much against
Theories, would shew us some more effectual Methods (if such there are) of
improving our Knowledge in Physic and Diseases'.[23] Whatever he thought of
theory, however, Hillary downplayed it in his revisions. The subtitle of the first
edition emphasised the causes of the disease, that of the second its prevention
and cure.

The timing for the publication of the rational and mechanical essay was
perhaps not optimal. The last decade of the seventeenth and the first three
decades of the eighteenth centuries saw the rise of several mechanical theories of human health and disease, put forward by 'Newton-struck' British
physicians.[24] Hillary cited two of these 'Tory Newtonians' – Archibald Pitcairn
and John Freind – as 'Ornaments of the Faculty' of medicine, adding Boerhaave
to them to complete the triumvirate of those who so supported his therapeutic
venesection for those afflicted by the disease.[25] In fact, Boerhaave had attended
Pitcairn's lectures when the latter had served as professor at Leiden in the
early 1690s. Newton himself loaned his credibility and gave his patronage to
these followers, so that to be a Newtonian physician (though this could mean
many things) in the 1710s was to be almost assured of professional success.[26]

---

[22] *A Practical Essay on the Small-Pox: Wherein a Method of Preparing the Body before the
Disease Comes on, and of Deriving the Variolous Matter from the Vital to the Remote Parts of
the Body after the Accession …; to Which Is Added, an Account of the Principal Variations of
the Weather, and the Concomitant Epidemic Diseases, as They Appeared at Rippon … From the
Year 1726, to the End of 1734*, 2nd ed. (London: C. Hitch and J. Leake, 1740), vi.

[23] Ibid., v, vi–vii.

[24] Theodore M. Brown, 'Medicine in the Shadow of the Principia', *Journal of the History of
Ideas* 48, no. 4 (1987). Brown uses the term 'Newton-struck' on 630.

[25] Hillary, *A Practical Essay on the Small-Pox: Wherein a Method of Preparing the Body before
the Disease Comes on, and of Deriving the Variolous Matter from the Vital to the Remote Parts
of the Body after the Accession … to Which Is Added, an Account of the Principal Variations of
the Weather, and the Concomitant Epidemic Diseases, as They Appeared at Rippon … From the
Year 1726, to the End of 1734*, 24. On Tory Newtonianism, see Guerrini, 'James Keill, George
Cheyne, and Newtonian Physiology, 1690–1740'; 'The Tory Newtonians: Gregory, Pitcairne,
and Their Circle'.

[26] 'The Tory Newtonians: Gregory, Pitcairne, and Their Circle', 310. On the many meanings
of Newtonianism, see *Obesity and Depression in the Enlightenment: The Life and Times of
George Cheyne*, 38.

Hillary's model for the effect of the smallpox contagion on the body was solidly 'Newtonian', with its focus on attracting particles that blocked the body's tiniest arteries, causing obstructions that led to increased pressure through the remaining vessels.[27]

By the 1740s, it has been argued, Newtonian physiology was under threat on multiple fronts,[28] strict mechanism increasingly being supplemented by an attention to Hippocratic environmentalism. Where Pitcairne in 1688 had been critical of Hippocrates for lacking knowledge of science's true method – geometry – John Arburthnot captured the tenor of the new combination in 1733, while describing the logic of his *Essay Concerning the Effects of Air*.[29] 'I have ventur'd to explain the Philosophy of this Sagacious old Man [Hippocrates], by mechanical Causes arising from the properties and Qualities of the Air'.[30] Where an earlier mechanical medicine had focused on the body as a machine, the newer form turned increasingly towards a mechanical understanding of the environment around the body. In his essay on the smallpox, as in his later work, Hillary was something of a bell-weather, for the same text that saw him change his focus away from theory to therapy also saw his turn towards the systematic study of diseases, air, and seasonality.

2.2   Weathering Epidemics

Hillary opened his account of the smallpox by arguing that the disease had not always troubled humanity. Variations across both time and space mattered. Human bodies had not changed over time, but the distempers that afflicted those bodies had.[31] Hillary seemed conflicted over whether the disease, once

---

[27] Hillary, *A Rational and Mechanical Essay on the Small-Pox: Wherein the Cause, Nature, and Diathesis of That Disease, Its Symptoms, Their Causes, and Manner of Production, Are Explained ... With the Diagnostic and Prognostic Symptoms ... To Which Is Prefixed, a Short History of the First Rise and Progress of That Disease; and an Essay on a New Method of Curing It, as We Do Other Inflammatory Diseases*, 36. In common with other Newtonians, like Pitcairne, largely Hillary eschewed a Cartesian concern with the shape of the corpuscles involved. For Pitcairne's model and his critiques of Cartesianism, see Andrew Cunningham, 'Sydenham Versus Newton: The Edinburgh Fever Dispute of the 1690s between Andrew Brown and Archibald Pitcairn', *Medical History, Supplement* 1 (1981): 88–90.

[28] Anita Guerrini, 'Isaac Newton, George Cheyne, and the "Principia Medicinae"', in *The Medical Revolution of the Seventeenth Century*, ed. Roger French and Andrew Wear (Cambridge: Cambridge University Press, 1989), 222–3.

[29] 'Archibald Pitcairne and Newtonian Medicine', 72; John Arbuthnot, *An Essay Concerning the Effects of Air on Human Bodies* (London: Printed for J. Tonson, 1733).

[30] Quoted in Andrea A. Rusnock, 'Hippocrates, Bacon, and Medical Meteorology at the Royal Society, 1700–1750', in *Reinventing Hippocrates*, ed. David Cantor (Burlington: Ashgate, 2001), 146.

[31] Cf. the Preface: 'not only new Species of Disease, but new Symptoms attending the same ancient known Diseases, do frequently arise, either from the different Constitutions of Years, changes of Air, the variety of Men's Constitutions, their Inventions of Luxury, and Errors in the six Non-Naturals, or from some other accidental Causes', Hillary, *A Rational and*

it had appeared in Arabia, as he claimed, and moved from thence to the rest of the world, manifested in the same way. On the one hand, he observed that in the Islamic world of the eighth century, smallpox 'appeared with much the same symptoms then in their warm Climate, as it does now in ours'.[32] On the other, the disease seemed both 'more violent and fatal' in Britain than its neighbours, 'probably from our different manner of living, and different Qualities of the Air of our Island'. Yet whatever might be said of its symptomatology, there was no denying that *treatments* needed to be altered according to climate. The English physician had been informed of the successes of inoculation against smallpox by a native of Constantinople, but he remained unconvinced of its efficacy closer to home.[33] Hillary had little doubt over whether to closely follow Arabian physicians in their cures. Avicenna's advice, for example, to treat measles by submerging the patient in cold water was not to be followed. The practice might work in the climate in which the prince of physicians had worked, but it would be 'dangerous and imprudent' in Britain.[34]

If his historical survey led Hillary to attend to the effects of geography on the manifestation and treatment of disease, so too did the nature of smallpox itself. Smallpox was, for Hillary, an epidemic disease and as a result the physician needed to approach its aetiology in a way radically different to that of a distemper that afflicted only individuals. He would make the point explicit in an addendum to the second edition of his *Essay*. To understand epidemics, one needed to turn away from Galenic medicine, with its focus on the missteps of a single patient, towards Hippocratic medicine, with its attention to the shared environments in which many lived at once.

'Tis well known that many Diseases owe their Rise to Intemperance, and the irregular Use of the Non-naturals; but as these only affect particular Persons, they can't be the Cause of epidemic Diseases, these affecting People in general, whose Ages, Constitutions, and Way of Life is sometimes very different, and they must therefore proceed from more general Causes.[35]

Mechanical Essay on the Small-Pox: Wherein the Cause, Nature, and Diathesis of That Disease, Its Symptoms, Their Causes, and Manner of Production, Are Explained ... With the Diagnostic and Prognostic Symptoms ... To Which Is Prefixed, a Short History of the First Rise and Progress of That Disease; and an Essay on a New Method of Curing It, as We Do Other Inflammatory Diseases, vi, 1.

[32] Ibid., 12.

[33] Ibid., xviii.

[34] Ibid., 16. The problem, it should be noted, was not with the medical theories and practices of Arabian physicians *per se*. Hillary was hardly parochial in these matters, and tended to have more sympathy with the medical writers of the Islamic Middle Ages than with many of their Christian successors: 'it would have been a great Happiness to their Patients, if the *European* Physicians, their Successors, had more strictly followed them therein, (with some small Allowance for the change of Climate)'. Ibid., 19.

[35] 'An Account of the Principal Variations of the Weather, and the Concomitant Epidemic Diseases, as They Appeared in Rippon, and the Circumjacent Parts of Yorkshire, from the

The most likely general cause was the air, which could itself be malign and filled with harmful effluvia, or could be the vehicle by which miasmatic exhalations were carried from patient to patient. Thus the logic of the weather diary, which one might use to track the relationships between the emergence of particular diseases and the 'Changes of the Air and Weather' that preceded, accompanied, and followed them.[36]

Although he bemoaned the fact that 'so few beside the great Hippocrates, have thought such Inquiries worth their Notice', Hillary was not the first to produce such a medico-meteorological diary.[37] To his chagrin, he was not even the first to do so in Yorkshire.[38] By the 1720s and 1730s, such diaries had become something of a fad, but forms of them had a longer history. In 1663, Robert Hooke had called for a 'History of the Weather', one to be constructed using a variety of the new instruments then available (the thermometer and barometer chief among them), as well as observations of the diseases most rife in particular seasons and meteorological conditions. The latter, medical part of the call was not taken up to any great extent, but weather diaries were being published already by the end of the seventeenth century, when one could find preprinted forms circulating among observers.[39]

The weather diary became genuinely popular after 1723, when the physician and secretary of the Royal Society, James Jurin, published an invitation to observers around the world, asking for their participation in a global project to produce a 'compleat Theory of the Weather'.[40] Jurin offered explicit instructions for how to both make and record observations, supplying a sample table to encourage the production of more standardised results. Andrea Rusnock has noted, however, that standardisation remained a serious problem in a period where even different cities might use different measures. To avoid the difficulties posed by uncalibrated instruments, Jurin convinced the Royal Society Council to send thermometers built by the renowned instrument maker Francis Hauksbee to specific observers, particularly those 'in more distant

---

Year 1726 to the End of 1734', in *A Practical Essay on the Small-Pox* (London: C. Hitch and J. Leake, 1740), viii. The 'Account' begins on page 162 of Hillary's *Practical Essay*, but is separately paginated.

[36] Ibid., vii.

[37] Ibid., iv.

[38] Ibid., viii.

[39] Jan Golinski, *British Weather and the Climate of Enlightenment* (Chicago: University of Chicago Press, 2007), 54–5. The barometer quickly became a symbol of Enlightenment and a luxury object: 'few gentlemen [are] without one', noted Richard Neve, author of the *Baroscopologia*, in 1708. Ibid., 108–36, Neve quoted on 21. Sloane travelled to Jamaica with one in the 1680s, though he seems not to have used it in producing his 'Journal of the Weather' for St Jago de la Vega. Sloane, Vol. 1, ix, xxxiii–xlii.

[40] Quoted in Andrea A. Rusnock, *Vital Accounts: Quantifying Health and Population in Eighteenth-Century England and France* (Cambridge: Cambridge University Press, 2002), 113.

Regions'.[41] Results poured in from throughout Great Britain, Europe, and even America. In 1726, Jurin published a second edition of his Invitation, which added a call for information about the relationships between diseases and the weather, in the hope, as Jurin noted in a letter, that this 'may give us some light into ye obscure Theory of Epidemical Distempers'.[42] Hillary began his medico-meteorological diary that year.

He kept the diary in Ripon from the summer of 1726 to the fall of 1734, when he heard of the death of a leading physician in Bath and decided to leave behind both the 'fatigue' of a country practice and his daily record-keeping. Of course, a diary might be kept anywhere: the issue had more to do with the details of Hillary's practice than its location. He suggested that 'acute epidemical Diseases so seldom appear, that I could not pursue these Observations', but the point was surely less that Ripon was more sickly than Bath, and more that upper class visitors were more likely to suffer from chronic illnesses – hence their journey to partake of the waters – than epidemic outbreaks.[43] It has been argued that it was Sydenham's practice among the poor of London that led him to the study of epidemics that so many after him emulated. 'Without an extensive practice amongst the poor', Andrew Cunningham has written, 'such a topic would have been impossible and indeed unthinkable'.[44] One begins to see from this why so many medico-meteorological diaries were produced in peripheral locations – both outside England and within it – for it was there that even successful physicians treated a number and variety of patients unlikely in elite metropolitan settings.

2.3   From Bath to Barbados

One cannot imagine that Hillary had originally intended to practise medicine in the West Indies. When he travelled to Barbados in 1747, he was nearly 50 years old, and had uprooted himself once already in the move away from Yorkshire. The shift to Bath had originally seemed promising. As recently as 1744, John Fothergill, a prominent English physician and, like Hillary a Quaker, had written to his brother Alexander reporting that 'Dr. Hillary was well; he has pretty good business'.[45] But only two years later, matters were considerably worse. Hillary was contemplating a trip to Jamaica when news arrived of 'the

---

[41] Ibid., 114.

[42] Quoted in ibid., 122.

[43] Hillary, 'An Account of the Principal Variations of the Weather, and the Concomitant Epidemic Diseases, as They Appeared in Rippon, and the Circumjacent Parts of Yorkshire, from the Year 1726 to the End of 1734', 62.

[44] Andrew Cunningham, 'Thomas Sydenham: Epidemics, Experiment, and the "Good Old Cause"', in The Medical Revolution of the Seventeenth Century, ed. Roger French and Andrew Wear (Cambridge: Cambridge University Press, 1989), 176.

[45] Booth, 305.

Death of the only Physician at Barbados'.[46] Fothergill had recommended the position. 'His relations I doubt not will be averse to him leaving England at any rate', he acknowledged, yet 'his situation at Bath is not the most agreeable nor the prospect very pleasing'. Fothergill evinced no great enthusiasm for Jamaica, but Barbados was another question:

at Barbados there are several meetings, the Island pleasant and healthy: the people much more humane and polite than any where else with a prospect of good employ: I have been far from urging him to go to either, yet was I in the like situation, I own I should be strongly drawn to the last place ... The galling situation he is in at present, I see renders life a burthen to him, but this betwixt ourselves.[47]

Hillary's 'galling situation' had apparently arisen as a result of speculation. In 1737, a cooper named Milsom had discovered two springs just outside Bath. Hillary analysed the spring water and declared it to possess salutary properties, publishing a short book in 1742 entitled *An Inquiry into the Contents and Medicinal Virtues of Lincomb Spaw Water*.[48] Seeing the opportunity to dramatically expand his practice, Hillary partnered with Milsom to quickly construct a building suitable for the reception of patients with chronic conditions. Yet preparing the ground for construction appears to have destroyed the spa, leaving the investors without any return for the 1,500 pounds they had spent.[49] No doubt one of the appeals of a sojourn in Barbados was the fact that he could leave the Lindcomb debacle well behind him.[50]

Although there were fairly few medical practitioners in the West Indies for much of the eighteenth century, the medical marketplace could still be difficult to negotiate. A clear hierarchy existed, one that distinguished, for example, between surgeons who might tend to slaves on plantations and those who served whites in towns or military settings.[51] Above these surgeons were ranked doctors, 'generally one or two eminent Men', Charles Leslie claimed in *A New History of Jamaica* (1740), 'who have the Employment, and soon get to be rich'.[52] Wealth was indeed a possibility, if less of a certainty than Leslie made it

[46] Ibid., 306. The word eminent is missing in the letter published in Fothergill's letters.
[47] Ibid.
[48] William Hillary, *An Inquiry into the Contents and Medicinal Virtues of Lincomb Spaw Water, near Bath. By William Hillary, M.D* (London: Printed for J. Leake, in Bath; and sold by C. Hitch [London], 1742).
[49] The failure of a spa was not unusual. Addison notes that this was the likely outcome of at least 99 per cent of such ventures. Addison, 121. See also Hamlin on the cut-throat world of spa promotion: Christopher Hamlin, 'Chemistry, Medicine, and the Legitimization of English Spas, 1740–1840', *Medical History. Supplement* 10 (1990): 69.
[50] William Tyte, *Bath in the Eighteenth Century: Its Progress and Life Described*. Bath: 'Chronicle' Office, 1903. 47–8.
[51] Chakrabarti, 155.
[52] Cited in ibid. Charles Leslie, *A New History of Jamaica: From the Earliest Accounts, to the Taking of Porto Bello by Vice-Admiral Vernon. In Thirteen Letters from a Gentleman to His Friend.* (London: Printed for J. Hodges, 1740), 50.

seem. Having established a medical practice in Kingston in the seventeen teens, Dr John Cochrane had enough money on hand to be able to send his brother, Dr William Cochrane £500 in 1735.[53] Dr John Lettsom claimed to have made £2,000 in six months on Tortola and neighbouring islands in the 1760s.[54] Not all were so fortunate. Outfitting costs were higher for private practitioners than those serving in the army or navy.[55] At least Hillary, with his prestigious degree and links to the local Quaker community, would have had an easier entrée than those with fewer qualifications and connections. As in Britain, looking and sounding the part helped matters considerably. 'No body, and especially Surgeons in Jamaica are respected', wrote Cochrane in 1714, 'unless they go handsome in their Cloaths – this is not vanity but meer Necessity'.[56] It has been suggested that it was Hans Sloane's confident bedside manner, as much as his medical talents, that helped convince wary Jamaican patients. 'One wrote that Sloane's presence "was very much wanted", while commenting of a rival that "I never much beleave much of his Doctorin"'.[57] Hillary's long career in Barbados would seem to make clear that he had possessed similar capacities.

Given the paucity of physicians in the British Caribbean in this period, we can make a well-informed guess as to the identity of the unnamed physician whose death opened the space that Hillary would soon fill.[58] Of the elite doctors on the island, the best known outside the West Indies was probably Henry Warren, whose short book on the yellow fever became one of the standard references on the disease soon after its publication.[59] Warren had studied at Dublin and Leiden, where he had received his degree. We remain unsure about the date of his demise, but he would have been 57 in 1746 and while one finds occasional mention of him in various sources before that date, I can find none afterward.[60]

---

[53] Sheridan, *Doctors and Slaves: A Medical and Demographic History of Slavery in the British West Indies, 1680–1834*, 46.

[54] Ibid., 63.

[55] Ibid., 43.

[56] Quoted in ibid.

[57] Miles Ogborn, 'Talking Plants: Botany and Speech in Eighteenth-Century Jamaica', *History of Science* 51 (2013): 268.

[58] Numbers were usually low, but could rise sharply during, and just after, wartime. 'Doctors who were difficult to recruit for private practice in the colonies in wartime were generally in surplus at the conclusion of a European war ... Several years after Dr. Wright came to Jamaica [after Seven Years War], the widow of a doctor who had practiced in the island wrote concerning her son who wished to follow in his father's footsteps. She warned that if he intended to settle in Jamaica the medical profession would "not afford him bread"'. Sheridan, *Doctors and Slaves: A Medical and Demographic History of Slavery in the British West Indies, 1680–1834*, 44–5.

[59] Henry Warren, *A Treatise Concerning the Malignant Fever in Barbados: And the Neighbouring Islands: with an Account of the Seasons There, from the Year 1734 to 1738. in a Letter to Dr. Mead. by Henry Warren* (London: Printed for Fletcher Gyles, 1740).

[60] P. J. Wallis and R. V. Wallis, *Eighteenth Century Medics (Subscriptions, Licences, Apprenticeships)*, 2nd ed. (Newcastle Upon Tyne: Project for Historical Bibliography,

Were it indeed Warren who Hillary succeeded, the symmetry would be elegant. The author of the most-cited account of yellow fever in the West Indies for the 1740s and 1750s would be replaced by the author of the definitive account of the disease for at least the next two decades.

One advantage of Hillary's removal from Bath was that he could once again take up his habit of maintaining a medico-meteorological diary. This he did, and in spite of the fact that the publication dates of the two diaries were separated by almost two decades, the main bodies of the texts were remarkably similar, being largely concerned with descriptive correlations between weather and disease. 'The Season continuing very wet', Hillary noted toward the end of 1729, for example, 'and the Wind generally in the Southern Points; about the Middle of November an Epidemical Cough seiz'd almost every body'. In broad strokes, this is not markedly different from the following comments from October, 1752: 'The Weather continuing to be wet and cool, several were seized with an irregular, ingeminated, intermitting, quotidian Fever'.[61] The later diary had both more – and more numerical – meteorological information, exemplifying the growth of what has been termed the 'quantifying spirit' of the eighteenth century.[62] Hillary now owned a hygrometer, though he ceased recording its results, finding 'its Variations to be so immaterial ... as to not be worth recording'. He had waited to begin his observations until he possessed a barometer, the last having been lost through an accident. After making regular observations with the replacement, however, he lamented the delay, for much the same reason he had abandoned measuring the air's humidity: 'the greatest Variation in [the air pressure], in six Years time, was never more than four Tenths of an Inch'. His diary in Ripon had only noted the heaviness of precipitation in general terms. In Barbados a friend nearby supplied him with rainfall data, precise to the tenth of an inch, at least until the instrument broke in January 1757. And in the West Indies he now possessed a 'Fahrenheit's Mercurial Thermometer, made at Amsterdam', with which he could make numerical measures of the temperature, replacing the relative measures – 'cold', 'very cold' – used in his earlier diary.

In both texts etiological understandings were offered in addenda. In the Ripon diary, a collection of 'aphorisms' and 'remarks' – written by an

1988), 629. Wallis and Wallis list Warren's dates as 1689–a1740. He was, however, presumably still alive when Dale Ingram dedicated a book to him in 1744. Dale Ingram, *Essay on the Nature, Cause, and Seat of Dysentery's, in a Letter to Dr. Henry Warren of Barbados* (Barbados: William Beeby, 1744).

[61] Hillary, *Observations on the Changes of the Air and the Concomitant Epidemical Diseases, in the Island of Barbados. To Which Is Added a Treatise on the Putrid Bilious Fever, Commonly Called the Yellow Fever; and Such Other Diseases as are Indigenous or Endemial, in the West India Islands, or in the Torrid Zone*, 22.

[62] Tore Frängsmyr, J. L. Heilbron, and Robin E. Rider, *The Quantifying Spirit in the Eighteenth Century* (Berkeley: University of California Press, 1990).

'ingenious Acquaintance' – were supplied at the end. The author of these provided mechanical, but not, it should be noted, Newtonian explanations for various afflictions. The body was composed of fluids and fibres, but no mention was made of attracting particles or molecules. According to Hillary's 'acquaintance', to take one example, warm and dry seasons induce inflammatory diseases affecting the head because heat causes the thinner parts of the body's fluids to be lost, leaving behind a thicker portion that flows less easily through the body, with obstructions, inflammations and fevers as the result. The 'delicate Texture of the Blood Vessels of the Head', it was argued, are even more greatly affected by such obstruction than other parts of the body, hence the onset of melancholia and hypochondriac disorders.[63] In the Barbados diary, the explanations were Hillary's, proffered in footnotes phrased as numbered queries and thus styled after Newton's *Opticks*. None of the etiological claims made in these queries were specific to the climate of Barbados. Like Newton's queries, they made general causal claims (phrased as questions) and most followed the same logics invoked in Hillary's earlier work. The first query thus sought to explain why, when the summer of 1752 turned from hot and dry at the beginning of June to hot and wet for the rest of the summer, 'Dysenteries became very frequent and epidemical', and '[m]any Children were seized with an Aphthous Fever'.

Query. Was not both the Dysentery and this Aphthous Fever, caused by the falling of so much Rain, and rendering the Air cooler, by which the great Perspiration and Sweating, caused and continued by the long continued Driness and Heat before being suddenly abated and stopped; were they not now turned upon the Bowels, and the Humours being rendered acrid by that Heat, so produced these Diseases?[64]

Befitting the part of the text Hillary intended to contribute to metropolitan discussions, the conclusions were thus not phrased as being about West Indian weather and West Indian diseases, but rather about universal relationships between weather and disease, as informed by observations made in the West Indies.

Aetiology, of course, is not the entirety of medicine, and where climate made a difference in the diary (albeit a fairly small one) was in Hillary's medical practice. The introduction to his text noted his intention to describe those

---

[63] Hillary, *A Practical Essay on the Small-Pox: Wherein a Method of Preparing the Body before the Disease Comes on, and of Deriving the Variolous Matter from the Vital to the Remote Parts of the Body after the Accession ... to Which Is Added, an Account of the Principal Variations of the Weather, and the Concomitant Epidemic Diseases, as They Appeared at Rippon ... From the Year 1726, to the End of 1734*, 64.

[64] Hillary, *Observations on the Changes of the Air and the Concomitant Epidemical Diseases, in the Island of Barbados. To Which Is Added a Treatise on the Putrid Bilious Fever, Commonly Called the Yellow Fever; and Such Other Diseases as Are Indigenous or Endemial, in the West India Islands, or in the Torrid Zone*, Note, 18–19.

situations where the diseases he had observed differed from English afflictions due to the heat or other climatic variations, as well as the changes he had made to his methods or medicines.[65] Yet while a number of prescriptions were included (detailed, he suggested, for Barbadian residents), there were only a small handful of times where Hillary explicitly noted the ways in which diseases or cures changed substantially from the English norm. Intermitting fevers, he observed, were rarer on the island than they had been in the past, and it was difficult for the physician to induce a remitting fever to intermit, as was the practice and customary outcome in England.[66] The physician could learn little from studying the urine in the West Indies, despite its utility in England, and Hillary was forced to find a substitute for the usual cordial waters found in the shops. In Barbados these heated and inflamed the blood too much.[67] On the other hand, a number of diseases were completely unchanged – the climate having no effect at all. One October saw several afflicted with a continued remitting fever, but this changed soon to an 'ingeminated Quotidian, with all the Symptoms of that Fever, as usual in England'.[68] Inflammatory rheumatisms were common in Britain but not in the Indies, yet one year they appeared in Barbados just as they usually did in England.[69] In March 1754, an epidemic of slow nervous Fever broke out, but the physician aware of metropolitan discussions of the disease and its treatment required no new information:

And the Fever now put on and appeared in this warm Climate, with all the same Symptoms as it usually does in England; and as they are accurately described by that learned and able Physician Dr. Huxham in the cooler Climate of Plymouth, which therefore I need not here repeat.[70]

Almost all the diseases whose description fills page after page would be utterly familiar to an English audience: dropsies and dysentery; smallpox, catarrhs, and peripneumonies. The diseases of warm seasons in England predominated, but the overall sense is one of fundamental similarity. For the most part, only occasional mention was made of diseases specific to warm climates, like the prickly heat or one that seemed to have no name, but was characterised by the

---

[65] Ibid., xiii.

[66] Hillary associated the decline in the occurrence of intermitting fevers with the growing clearing and cultivation of land in Barbados. Ibid., 23, 125. On the difficulty in getting a remitting fever to intermit 'as it frequently uses to do in England', see ibid., 65, 126.

[67] Ibid., 92, 36. Towne made a similar argument about the problems involved in studying the urine in the warm climate. '*Prognosticks* taken from an Inspection of the *Urine* are much more precarious here than in *Europe*'. Towne, 61–2.

[68] Hillary, *Observations on the Changes of the Air and the Concomitant Epidemical Diseases, in the Island of Barbados. To Which Is Added a Treatise on the Putrid Bilious Fever, Commonly Called the Yellow Fever; and Such Other Diseases as Are Indigenous or Endemial, in the West India Islands, or in the Torrid Zone*, 22.

[69] Ibid., 41.

[70] Ibid., 56.

gangrenescent boils with which it afflicted children.[71] The only exception was an illness that recurred in almost every year and with which Hillary opened the second section of his book: the yellow fever.

2.4   Yellow Fever

We will take up Hillary's theory of yellow fever in a moment. First, however, we need to understand its predecessors, not least because Hillary himself framed his discussion as a response to Warren's *Treatise*, published two decades earlier. Warren, in turn, expressed his desire to correct Towne's comments on the affliction. Both earlier physicians had denied the disease the status of something entirely new. For Towne, yellow fever was simply a type of ardent fever, to be understood in clear parallel to other forms of the disease as they were familiar to European physicians. The Barbadian climate, with its humidity and the salinity of its air, contributed to the production of the disease, but Towne made no generalisation about 'tropical' climates and drew no analogies between this warm weather distemper and those found elsewhere at similar latitudes. For Warren, the yellow fever was not even originally produced in Barbados. It was a contagious disease bred in the Levant, which made its way to the otherwise healthy island through the movements of goods and people. It was thus precisely the same disease that afflicted others in Europe. Insofar as the West Indian climate mattered for the spread of yellow fever, then, its most important attribute was its difference to the climate in Palestine.

Born in 1690, Towne was probably the first person to publish a description of yellow fever in the West Indies. Like both Hillary and Warren (with the last of whom he may have overlapped), he was a graduate of Leiden and, like Hillary again, Towne's medical writing shows the marks of his training, with regular citations to Freind, Pitcairne, and Boerhaave, among others. The explanation he offered for the cause of many of Barbados' illnesses was largely mechanical. The moist warm air tended to relax the body's fibres and increase the viscidity of the blood while decreasing the air's capacity to expand the pulmonary vessels. The salt from the sea air stimulated the heart and organs, so that the blood pumped faster, but the thickened blood became less able to make its way through the secretory glands. The result was obstructions and stagnation. One particular outcome of such obstructions was fever, the heat arising from the 'unusually strong rubbing', according to Boerhaave, of the fluid Parts among each other, against the Vessels, and the Vessels against the liquid'.[72] Towne quoted the entirety of one of Boerhaave's aphorisms to

---

[71] Ibid., 129.

[72] Hermann Boerhaave, *Boerhaave's Aphorisms: Concerning the Knowledge and Cure of Diseases. Translated from the Last Edition Printed in Latin at Leyden, 1715. With Useful Observations and Explanations, by J. Delacoste, M.D.* (London: Printed for B. Cowse and W. Innys, 1725), Aphorism 675, 156.

describe the effect of the heating of the body that accompanied one particularly dangerous fever 'which so endemically rages in these *Parts*', and which he termed a *Febris Ardens Biliosa*, a particular kind of ardent fever.[73] That the fever was a *bilious* one seemed obvious to Towne, given that roughly three days after the first symptoms the surface of the body was suffused with that humour, giving the patient that 'Saffron Tincture' characteristic of the disease.[74] Drawing attention to his own local knowledge and expertise, Towne observed that those unfamiliar with the West Indies were sometimes confused. 'I have known some ingenious Practitioners', Towne wrote, 'upon their first coming strangely surprised at the Novelty of the *Appearances* they have met with, in this Island, even to so great a degree, that they have mistaken the *Yellowness* of the Skin in a Fever of no more than twenty four Hours standing, for a confirmed and inveterate Jaundice'.[75] Towne's book was aimed, in part, to help prevent the newcomer from making such dangerous errors. Once properly diagnosed, treatment followed along lines surely familiar to most physicians, whether newcomers or old hands, involving immediate and then repeated bloodletting to cool the body and relieve it of its surfeit of blood, followed by emetics to break up and remove the excess bile (blisters served this purpose, too), and cooling, subacid drinks.

Writing thirteen years later, Warren found this analysis preposterous. Without naming Towne, he sharply rebuked the author of a 'Treatise published a few years ago, concerning the Distempers of *Barbados*; which, I fear, has misled many unwary Practitioners into a false notion of the Distemper, and so into a wrong Method of Practice, full of Danger and pregnant of Errors'.[76] In the unlikely event that readers were unaware of Warren's precise target, all confusion would have been removed when he lambasted his unnamed opponent for introducing the term *Febris Ardens Biliosa* to describe the disease that he denoted as the 'malignant fever' of Barbados.

At the crux of Warren's disagreement with Towne was the question of yellow fever's aetiology. Warren believed it was contagious – and hence brought to the island from elsewhere – while Towne, of course, believed it to be a disease indigenous to the West Indies. Both men were loath to convey the impression

---

[73] Towne, 201. Boerhaave, 158. '689. Heat increased doth dissipate the most liquid parts out of our Blood, that is, the Water, Spirits, Salts, and subtilest Oils; it drieth the remaining Mass, thickens it; causes it to run together into an unmoveable and not resolvable Matter: it freeth the Salts and Oils, attenuates and makes 'em sharper, exhales and moves 'em; consequently it wears the smallest Vessels out and breaks 'em; dries the Fibres, makes 'em stiff and shrivell'd; hence produces suddenly many, quick, dangerous and mortal Diseases; which may easily be accounted for, and derived from the first effect of heat mention'd here'. 158. Quoted in Latin in Towne, Note, 24–5.

[74] · Towne, 23.

[75] Ibid., 4.

[76] Henry Warren, *A Treatise Concerning the Malignant Fever in Barbados and the Neighbouring Islands: With an Account of the Seasons There, from the Year 1734 to 1738. In a Letter to Dr. Mead.* (London: Printed for Fletcher Gyles against Grays-Inn in Holborn, 1740), 2.

that Barbados, in spite of the presence of dangerous diseases, was an unsalubrious spot. Towne assured his readers that the diseases he described in his book were not necessary consequences of travelling to the island from Europe. To insinuate such would be 'doing an unpardonable Act of Injustice to one of the most delightful *Countries* in the Creation'.[77] Yet Warren took this defence one step further, by arguing that there were 'no Malignant Distempers truly Indigenous, or Natives of this Island; and that such have always been brought in among us from some other infected places'.[78] The last time the disease made its appearance, Warren claimed, was 1733, when it had been introduced from Martinique. Yet it was no more a native of Martinique than Barbados, having made its way to the Americas on a ship from Marseilles, which was carrying goods from the Levant. The distemper, in its essence, was of an '*Asiatic Extract*'.[79]

One of Warren's best arguments in favour of his case turned on the problem of seasoning. Why did yellow fever disproportionately strike newcomers and not natives? Towne cited Sydenham's observation that fevers make up two-thirds of all chronic illnesses, suggesting that 'in the West Indies (especially with regard to strangers) the proportion runs much higher'.[80] Most people, he claimed, 'how wary soever they may be in their conduct, are obliged to undergo what the inhabitants call a *Seasoning*'.[81] Warren, similarly, noted that the fever the French called *La Maladie de Siam* or *La Fievre Matelotte* ('because Sea-Faring People and New-comers are chiefly obnoxious to it'),[82] upon its arrival in Barbados 'soon swept away a Multitude of People, especially New-comers, and Sea-faring persons, such as had purer Blood, and probably less adust than that of the Natives; or of those whose Constitutions had been for many Years fitted and habituated to the Climate'.[83] For Warren, however, the fact that the disease struck harder those who had cleaner fluids seemed to make a mockery of Towne's explanation, which relied on the effect of the climate on people's

---

[77] Towne, 15.
[78] Warren, 1.
[79] Ibid., 5.
[80] Towne, 19.
[81] Ibid., 19–20.
[82] Warren, 3–4. The connection to Siam seems to have been erroneous. 'In 1690', wrote Carter, 'began in Martinique an epidemic of which we have a full account by Père Labat (1722). It was brought quite certainly from Recife to Martinique by the *Oriflamme*, a French war vessel which had cleared from Bangkok, but had touched at Pernambuco. Because of this origin, the epidemic, which spread generally over the West Indies and the continental shores of the Caribbean, became known as the "epidemic of the *Oriflamme*", or the "*mal de Siam*". Indeed, it gave the latter name "*mal de Siam*" to the disease for a long time and over a wide area, much of which was infected from other sources and with a fever absolutely unknown to Siam'. Henry Rose Carter, *Yellow Fever: An Epidemiological and Historical Study of Its Place of Origin* (Baltimore: The Williams and Wilkins Company, 1931), 196.
[83] Warren, 5.

fluids and fibres, producing, in sickness, 'a *bilious*, adust, overfermented *Blood*'.[84] Why, Warren asked, should those who had spent the least time in the warm, saline, moist atmosphere be the most likely to suffer?

For how then comes it that Strangers and New-comers, whose blood is purest and least impregnated with exalted Oils and Salts, should be most liable to this Disease? How comes it that the Natives of the *Torrid Zone*, whose juices we may reasonably suppose to be more acrid and alcalescent, are however much less obnoxious to it, if the malignant Symptoms proceeded merely from a Suffusion of Bile? How comes it that all Sorts and Conditions of the People, who live in the same Island, nay, in the same Town and Air, shall never receive the Infection, provided they keep themselves a little out of its Reach, and at a sufficient Distance from infected Persons and Places?[85]

Warren claimed this critique was so salient that it even persuaded Towne. 'I had the Pleasure', he explained (with none to contradict him), 'of convincing him of those Mistakes and I must do him the Justice to declare that he frankly retracted his opinion before he died, and would willingly have called in the Copies, could he have found Means of doing it'.[86]

Whether Towne had been convinced or not, Hillary would have none of this in his *Observations*. Yet Warren was attempting to draw upon powerful allies. He had composed his treatise as a letter and dedicated it to Richard Mead, Fellow of the Royal Society and personal physician to George II. Warren's work relied heavily on the logic Mead had used in his enormously popular *Short Discourse Concerning Pestilential Contagion*.[87] First published in 1720, seven editions appeared within a year, with the ninth published in 1744. The work was inspired by the outbreak of plague in Marseilles in 1720 and the subsequent British panic about its spread.[88] Together with Sloane and John Arbuthnot, Mead played a significant role on producing the Quarantine Act of 1721. Quarantine made sense, Mead claimed, because the plague was not native to England: avoid contagious goods and people and the disease itself could be avoided.

If England were 'innocent' of inflicting this affliction on the world, however, from where did it spring? Mead pointed his finger firmly in the

---

[84] Towne, 33.

[85] 'How comes it that the *Negroes*', continued Warren, 'whose Food is mostly rancid Fish or Flesh, nay often the Flesh of Dogs, Cats, Asses, Horses, Rats &c, and who mostly lead very intemperate Lives, and who are always worse clad, and most exposed to Surfeits, Heats, Colds, and all the Injuries of the Air, are so little subject to this Danger?', Warren, 13–14.

[86] Ibid., 15.

[87] Richard Mead, *A Short Discourse Concerning Pestilential Contagion and the Methods to Be Used to Prevent It*. (London: Printed [by William Bowyer] for Sam Buckley, and Ralph Smith, 1720). The first seven editions would remain unchanged. Although the point is mentioned in the first edition, it is the eighth that offered a detailed discussion of the origin of the illness and the mode of its production in Africa.

[88] Arnold Zuckerman, 'Plague and Contagionism in Eighteenth-Century England', *Bulletin of the History of Medicine* 78, no. 2 (2004).

direction of Africa, guilty of breeding not only this disease but others as well. '[T]he *Plague* has always the same Original', he wrote, 'and is brought from *Africa*, the Country which has entail'd upon us two other infectious Distempers, the *Small-Pox* and *Measles*'. Epidemics might arise in any nation – particularly in spaces such as military camps or jails – and could spread like a pestilence. Yet the 'true' plague, claimed Mead, found its origin in Ethiopia or Egypt 'and the *Infection* of it carried by Trade into the other Parts of the World'.[89]

In essence, Warren would transfer Mead's arguments from England to the West Indies. Both men offered a dichotomous understanding of diseases across the globe. Many earlier authors, like Hoffmann, had avoided charging any one part of the world with producing worse afflictions than any other. Following the logic of *Airs, Waters, and Places,* each region simply had a number of diseases characteristic of it. For Warren and Mead, however, the globe could be divided in two: those regions responsible for the production of certain foul and pestilential afflictions and those who were the blameless victims of contagion. According to Mead, England was not only not the home of the plague, the measles, and smallpox, it was not even the origin for a disease known as the *Sudor Anglicus* (English Sweat) or *Febris Ephemera Britannica.* This was 'most probably of a foreign Original', and the English had in fact, 'by the salutary Influence of our Climate' reduced its malignity.[90] The habit of blaming foreign climes for the introduction of a given disease had a venerable history, but Mead and Warren had taken it one step further, by arguing that their locations were to be blamed for no particularly malign disorders at all. Warren would thus make a dual move, producing both difference and similarity, but it was an unusual coupling, one that joined the West Indies to England and opposed both to Asia and Africa.

Hillary was unimpressed. 'I cannot conceive', he wrote, 'what were the Motives which induced a late ingenious Author to think that this Fever was first brought from Palestine to Marseilles, and from thence to Martinique, and so to Barbadoes, about thirty seven Years since'. The disease, he argued, was rarely contagious and had, in any case, been observed on the island before the 1730s. Far from being a foreign import, it was 'indigenous to the West-India Islands, and the Continent of America which is situated between, or near to the Tropics, and most probably to all other Countries within the Torrid Zone'. If the disease was not new to the West Indies, however, it was new to European physicians. Hillary claimed to find no mention of it in any classical sources – 'none of them has ever mentioned, or probably ever seen this Disease' – or even those of

---

[89] Richard Mead, *A Short Discourse Concerning Pestilential Contagion and the Methods to Be Used to Prevent It.*, Eighth, with large Additions ed. (London: Sam. Buckley, 1722), 20–1.
[90] Ibid., 64.

the Arab world 'who lived and practiced in the hot climate'.[91] Word of it came from contemporary observers in the Spanish Americas, or from the French in Siam, a kingdom, Hillary informed the reader, 'which is situated between the Tropicks, near the same Latitude with the West India Islands'.[92] In Hillary's hands, yellow fever may have been the first tropical disease, an affliction native neither to only one particular country or place nor to warm climates in general, but rather to precisely the region between the Tropics of Cancer and Capricorn.

The disease's aetiology was also suitably tropical. Noting that the illness 'most commonly seizes Strangers' Hillary nonetheless ignored Warren's criticisms of a climatic explanation of seasoning.[93] The yellow fever, he argued – drawing upon and altering Towne's formulation – was a putrid bilious fever. Somewhat disingenuously, Hillary put forward two options for the fever's proximate cause: it was either occasioned by infectious miasmata, or else by the 'great Heat of the Air, and Water, and the Putrefaction of our Fluids etc. from thence'.[94] Since he had earlier spent a good deal of time dismissing the notion that the illness was infectious, this left the warm and humid Barbadian atmosphere as the remaining culprit. The body rotted from within.

As befitted a novel disease, Hillary's explanation was new as well. Almost all other afflictions described in his *Treatise* could be explained using a fairly mechanical and dyadic logic. The body in illness had consisted either of fibres too tense and rigid, accompanied by dense, viscid blood, or else fibres too lax and blood too weak and thin. Health was to be found in the balance. For the putrid bilious fever, however, Hillary closely followed John Huxham in his 1750 *Essay on Fevers* (the theoretical counterpart to his two volumes on *Observations of the Air*), in introducing a third state of the blood 'of more dangerous Consequence than either; I mean a state of it, that more immediately tends to *Dissolution* and *Putrefaction*'.[95] After the introduction to the blood of a 'bilious putrefying Diathesis', all the humours, but particularly the bile, became 'inquinated with a putrid bilious Acrimony', which broke the larger globules of blood that were characteristic of the body in health into smaller parts, allowing them then to pass through ducts intended for excretion. In time, even the brain was affected and 'all the Humours of the Body are almost

[91] Hillary, *Observations on the Changes of the Air and the Concomitant Epidemical Diseases, in the Island of Barbados. To Which Is Added a Treatise on the Putrid Bilious Fever, Commonly Called the Yellow Fever; and Such Other Diseases as Are Indigenous or Endemial, in the West India Islands, or in the Torrid Zone*, 144, 155.

[92] Ibid., 143.

[93] Ibid., 146.

[94] Ibid., 153.

[95] John Huxham, *An Essay on Fevers, and Their Various Kinds, as Depending on Different Constitutions of the Blood: With Dissertations on Slow Nervous Fevers; on Putrid, Pestilential, Spotted Fevers; on the Small-Pox; and on Pleurisies and Peripneumonies* (London: S. Austen, 1750), 41.

changed into a putrescent lethiferous Ichor'.[96] If not rapidly prevented, the inevitable result was death.

Huxham had discussed a number of means by which such a putrefactive state might be achieved, but for Hillary's analysis of yellow fever, they came down to only one: climate.[97] To be sure, climate had mattered for Towne's and Warren's accounts, too. For Warren, Barbados was warm enough to promote the spread of contagion once it reached the island, but the West Indies could not be the disease's original home. Like England, the West Indies was a victim, not a culprit. For Towne, the warmth, humidity, and salinity of the air affected the body's fluids and fibres, inducing an ardent fever. Yet where Towne and Warren both took time to defend the Barbadian climate against its detractors, Hillary made little such effort. For Hillary, yellow fever was a marker of the island's peculiarity, its commonality with the rest of the Torrid Zone and its difference from Europe. Putrefaction evoked not merely the relative differences of laxity and viscidity, but the fundamental difference of life and death.

2.5   Slavery, Nativity, and the Production of Similarity

Hillary's discussion of yellow fever came in a section concerned with *acute* endemial diseases, those 'not so frequently seen in most parts of Europe'.[98] It was, in fact, an outlier in its novelty for the European reader. Most of the other diseases considered alongside it were more or less familiar to metropolitan physicians.[99] The Dry Belly Ache, for example, frequently afflicted those in the West Indies, but it had been known to seize patients in England and parts of Europe; dysentery was all too common in England; tetany was a disease associated with warm but not necessarily tropical climates and was well known to the ancient Greeks; and rabies was 'neither new, nor endemial or epidemical to Mankind', though it might be endemic to dogs in hot countries.[100]

Quite different were the illnesses considered in the second part of the book – *chronic* endemial diseases – which Hillary declared to be 'unknown and never seen but in the hot climates, except when they are carried by the

---

[96] Hillary, *Observations on the Changes of the Air and the Concomitant Epidemical Diseases, in the Island of Barbados. To Which Is Added a Treatise on the Putrid Bilious Fever, Commonly Called the Yellow Fever; and Such Other Diseases as Are Indigenous or Endemial, in the West India Islands, or in the Torrid Zone*, 153–4.

[97] On Huxham and the 'putrefactive paradigm', see Chapter 4.

[98] Hillary, *Observations on the Changes of the Air and the Concomitant Epidemical Diseases, in the Island of Barbados. To Which Is Added a Treatise on the Putrid Bilious Fever, Commonly Called the Yellow Fever; and Such Other Diseases as Are Indigenous or Endemial, in the West India Islands, or in the Torrid Zone*, 276.

[99] The exception was a disease that had neither been seen nor described by earlier physicians, which Hillary termed *Apthoides Chronica*. See ibid., 277.

[100] Ibid., 182, 201, 20, 45.

Sick into the colder Countries'.[101] Nyctalopia, Elephantiasis, Guinea Worm, Yaws, and other illnesses joined the putrid bilious fever as distempers that made Barbados a disease environment very different from Europe's and much like that of warmer lands. According to Kiple and Ornelas, Hillary's medical perception of the West India islands as fundamentally dissimilar to England's arose due to important shifts in the demography of the West Indies since 1700. To that date, they point out, the number of imported slaves to Jamaica and Barbados had been relatively small, with 60 per cent of the 220, 000 slaves sent to Barbados. 'Indeed, 50 years earlier, Barbados was the only English Island importing slaves, and it was there, where the still mostly white populations had achieved a density of some 200 per square mile, that yellow fever made its first known epidemic appearance in the Western Hemisphere'.[102] Kiple and Ornelas plausibly suggest that Hillary's medical treatment of the huge numbers of those who suffered from the disease inspired his belief that he was working in a radically new disease environment.

One can certainly not deny the importance of demographic changes on the islands. Looking at Jamaica, it has been estimated that roughly 88,000 slaves were imported in the 46 years after British wrested control of the island from the Spanish in 1655. Almost three-and-a-half times this number (302,859) were imported in the period from 1702 to 1750, and more than five times the number (457,816) from 1751 to 1800.[103] Benjamin Moseley, writing in 1799, offered statistics on 'white' and 'black' populations on the same island across the eighteenth century. In 1698, he reported, the ratio of the black to the white population was 5.4 to 1 (40,000 blacks to 7,365 whites); in 1741, it was 10 to 1 (100,000 blacks to 10,000 whites); and in 1787, 11.1 to 1 (255,780 blacks to 23,000 whites).[104] Doctors on either Barbados or Jamaica thus saw a spectacular increase in the slave population in the middle of the eighteenth century, compared to the early 1700s.

This demographic explosion in the numbers of enslaved peoples was tied directly to the needs of the sugar trade. Sugar cultivation and production was both labour and capital intensive, considerably more so than cacao or indigo.[105] Between the 1680s and 1720, planters adopted an 'integrated' model for their plantations, one that combined both the growth of sugarcane and the transformation of the pressed juice into sugar crystals. To supply the necessary labour force, colonists imported increasing numbers of slaves, bought first

---

[101] Ibid., 276.
[102] Kiple and Ornelas, 68.
[103] Sheridan, *Doctors and Slaves: A Medical and Demographic History of Slavery in the British West Indies, 1680–1834*, 102.
[104] Benjamin Moseley, *A Treatise on Sugar* (London: Printed for G. G. and J. Robinson, 1799), 157.
[105] Dunn, 168.

from the Royal African Company, and then, after the Company lost its monopoly in 1698, from private slave traders. In the first years of the eighteenth century, Africans were being shipped to Jamaica at a rate of 4,500 a year, three times as fast as in the 1670s.[106] By the 1720s, most slaves worked in labour forces of one hundred or more people, arranged into gangs according to their stamina, with women in Jamaica and elsewhere making up the majority of field hands.[107] The economic success of such moves could not be gainsaid. Sugar output from Jamaica alone increased eightfold between 1700 and 1774, from 5,000 to 40,000 tons a year.[108] Barbadians who shifted from growing tobacco to growing sugar became rich almost overnight, so that they were already by 1680 the wealthiest men in British America.[109] The trend continued in the eighteenth century. Vincent Brown notes that the average net worth of a person in England or Wales in 1774 was £42, while that of free whites in the American colonies was roughly twice this (£89) and that of a free white person in the British West Indies was a staggering £1,042 sterling.[110]

Such financial success came at the expense of the lives of the enslaved, whose living and working conditions worsened with their rising numbers. 'Slavery had always been brutal in British America', observe Trevor Burnard and John Garrigus, 'but the violence exercised against Africans dramatically increased as the slave population grew'.[111] In 1740, Charles Leslie claimed of the Jamaican planters that 'No Country excels them in barbarous Treatment of Slaves, or in the cruel Methods they put them to death'.[112] Labour conditions were incredibly harsh, made even worse with shifts towards sugar monoculture.[113] Land that could have provided pasture for animals was instead turned to a more profitable crop. Ploughing that might have been performed by animals

---

[106] Ibid., 165.

[107] Trevor Burnard and John Garrigus, *The Plantation Machine: Atlantic Capitalism in French Saint-Domingue and British Jamaica* (Philadelphia: University of Pennsylvania Press, 2016), 41; Sheridan, *Doctors and Slaves: A Medical and Demographic History of Slavery in the British West Indies, 1680–1834*, 141–5; Richard S. Dunn, 'Sugar Production and Slave Women in Jamaica', in *Cultivation and Culture: Labor and the Shaping of Slave Life in the Americas*, ed. Ira Berlin and Philip D. Morgan (Charlottesville and London: University Press of Virginia, 1993); Barbara Bush, *Slave Women in Caribbean Society* (Bloomington: Indiana University Press, 1990); Barbara Bush-Slimani, 'Hard Labour: Women, Childbirth, and Resistance in British Caribbean Slave Societies', *History Workshop Journal* 36 (1993).

[108] Burnard and Garrigus, 38.

[109] Dunn, *Sugar and Slaves: The Rise of the Planter Class in the English West Indies, 1624–1713*, 85.

[110] Vincent Brown, *The Reaper's Garden: Death and Power in the World of Atlantic Slavery* (Cambridge, MA: Harvard University Press, 2008), 16.

[111] Burnard and Garrigus, 39.

[112] Leslie. Quoted in Burnard and Garrigus, 40.

[113] On labour conditions under slavery in the Americas, see in general Ira Berlin and Philip D. Morgan, eds., *Cultivation and Culture: Labor and the Shaping of Slave Life in the Americas* (Charlottesville and London: University Press of Virginia, 1993).

was instead carried out by slaves, who had the added burden of collecting grass after their work in the sugar fields was complete, in order to feed what cattle the islands could support.[114] Workdays lasted for twelve hours, although this number could increase during crop time, when the mill ran all night and planters feared the canes would spoil if they were not ground quickly enough.[115] Slaves were expected to supplement the rations supplied them by their masters by working on their own provision grounds when not in the fields.[116] As Sheridan notes, however, it seems likely that the typical Jamaican slave was 'underfed and overworked', with substantial dietetic deficiencies in protein and fat in particular.[117] As a point of comparison, it might be noted that slaves ate much less well than contemporary English agricultural labourers.[118] The effect of these conditions can be seen in the marked failure of slave populations in the Sugar Islands to reproduce themselves. Slave numbers may have risen dramatically across the eighteenth century, but this increase was due entirely to the importation of new enslaved peoples. By 1750, the enslaved population across the British Caribbean was somewhat less than 300,000 souls, despite the fact that, to that date, roughly 800,000 slaves had been imported.[119] The population density of slaves was rising, in other words, and slaves were 'highly stressed,

---

[114] Elsa V. Goveia, *Slave Society in the British Leeward Islands at the End of the Eighteenth Century* (New Haven and London: Yale University Press, 1965), 116–17.

[115] Ibid., 130.

[116] 'At Prospect Estate in the developing Parish of Portland, slaves worked 12 hours a day for an average of 272 days, with 60 days off. Illness or other problems stopped work for 33 days. During their days off, enslaved people produced their own food, constructed their own housing, and attended to the needs of themselves and their children'. Burnard and Garrigus, 42. On provision grounds, see also Sheridan, *Doctors and Slaves: A Medical and Demographic History of Slavery in the British West Indies, 1680–1834*, 164–9; Woodville K. Marshall, 'Provision Ground and Plantation Labor in Four Windward Islands: Competition for Resources During Slavery', in *Cultivation and Culture: Labor and the Shaping of Slave Life in the Americas*, eds. Ira Berlin and Philip D. Morgan (Charlottesville and London: University Press of Virginia, 1993).

[117] Sheridan, *Doctors and Slaves: A Medical and Demographic History of Slavery in the British West Indies, 1680–1834*, 171; Kiple; Jerome S. Handler, 'Diseases and Medical Disabilities of Enslaved Barbadians, from the Seventeenth Century to around 1838 (Part I)', *The Journal of Caribbean History* 40 (2006); 'Diseases and Medical Disabilities of Enslaved Barbadians, from the Seventeenth Century to around 1838 (Part II)', *The Journal of Caribbean History* 40 (2006).

[118] Dunn, *Sugar and Slaves: The Rise of the Planter Class in the English West Indies, 1624–1713*, 278.

[119] Philip D. Morgan, 'The Black Experience and the British Empire, 1680–1810', in *Black Experience and the Empire*, eds. Philip D. Morgan and Sean Hawkins (Oxford: Oxford University Press, 2006), 90. 'Sugar cultivation consumed enslaved labor', writes David Richardson, 'in most British sugar colonies deaths of slaves consistently exceeded births, some by as much as 4% a year'. David Richardson, 'Through a Looking Glass: Olaudah Equiano and African Experiences of the British Atlantic Slave Trade', ibid., 78. For contemporary debates over what Sheridan, *Doctors and Slaves: A Medical and Demographic History of Slavery in the British West Indies, 1680–1834*, 222–48. calls 'the problem of reproduction', see Chapter 7.

prone to disease, and likely to die'.[120] Hillary had clearly seen nothing like these conditions before his arrival in the New World.

One should be cautious nonetheless in seeing demography as a transparent explanation, for neither population increases nor the yellow fever outbreaks of the 1720s and 1730s are sufficient to explain Hillary's position. After all, Warren's arguments had been based on observations made on the island from 1734 to 1738, a period that saw striking demographic changes and outbreaks of the malignant fever.[121] Indeed, Warren claimed that in the six years after the most recent outbreak of the disease in 1733, the British crown had lost 'upwards of Twenty-Thousand very useful subjects, the much greatest part of whom were Sea-Faring People'.[122] Yet, unlike Hillary, Warren did not claim that Barbados constituted a novel disease environment, nor did he attempt to draw the West Indies into a larger complex of tropical countries.

To some extent, the seeming idiosyncrasy of West Indian diseases in the second half of Hillary's *Observations* was an artefact of the genre to which he was contributing. Writing about epidemic distempers in the first half of the text, as we have seen, Hillary had pointed to multiple similarities between the diseases in England and Barbados. Writing about endemial diseases, however, such similarities – while acknowledged – were then to be ignored. Inflammations of the bowels, various forms of colic, and multiple kinds of diarrhoea were all common to both parts of the world and were, 'with some Allowances for the Warmth of the Climate', to be managed in much the same manner. 'But as these last are all judiciously treated on by several learned and able Physicians in Europe, it is not necessary to say any thing on them here, since they should be treated here, much in the same manner as they are there'.[123] The effect, then, was to remove discussion of the illnesses that both affected the largest number of patients and were similar in both Europe and the West Indies and to focus discussions on those diseases that were 'indigenous and endemial in the West-India Islands, or peculiar to the Torrid Zone; and are seldom or never seen in the colder European Nations'.[124]

The very fact that Hillary's aim was to describe peculiar and endemic diseases thus tended to over-emphasise differences due to geographic location and under-emphasise the many similarities. That said, he was still able to list more than a dozen diseases likely to be unfamiliar (in practice, if not in theory)

[120] Burnard and Garrigus, 230.
[121] Warren.
[122] Ibid., 73–4.
[123] Hillary, *Observations on the Changes of the Air and the Concomitant Epidemical Diseases, in the Island of Barbados. To Which Is Added a Treatise on the Putrid Bilious Fever, Commonly Called the Yellow Fever; and Such Other Diseases as Are Indigenous or Endemial, in the West India Islands, or in the Torrid Zone*, 201–2.
[124] Ibid., 140.

to European physicians. From what causes did these illnesses arise? To a large extent, that question could be reduced to another: what was the geographical origin of each disease? Was the affliction *indigenous, endemial,* or both? Were the disease indigenous, the climate was the likely cause; were it endemial, but not indigenous, then it must have reached the West Indies by some set of movements.

For Hillary it was clear that many diseases – such as Elephantiasis, the *Lepra Arabum,* Leprosy of the Joints, and the Yaws – were not native to the West Indies, however much they might flourish on the islands now. Both Mead and Warren had pointed to trade as the cause for the increasing spread of contagious diseases. Hillary was rather more specific, pointing (like Kiple and Ornelas) to the slave trade in particular as the mechanism by which a once-healthy part of the New World had become a haven for disease.[125] In the past, Hillary claimed, 'we do not find that they had any of the before described diseases, which are indigenous to Africa, and have been imported with the African Negroes from thence, to these Western parts of the World; though these parts are as warm as Africa is'.[126] One can hear in the last part of this sentence an echo of Mead's arguments: a warm climate was necessary, but not sufficient for the first creation of many distempers. Hillary also clearly shared Mead's distaste for the African disease environment. Barbados was not as blessed as 'the happy Climate of England, which is totally a Stranger to this [the *Lepra Arabum*], and some other miserable diseases',[127] but it had been vastly more fortunate than Africa, where so many of the worst afflictions were native.

Adamant that Africa was and Barbados was not the origin for multiple distempers, Hillary was less clear on whether there was a rather more general climatic aetiology at work. Although he would argue that many diseases were common throughout the Torrid Zone, he hedged his bets on the reason for the commonality. Elephantiasis was 'a disease which is *either* indigenous or endemial to such countries as are within the Torrid Zone';[128] Nyctalopia, similarly 'may justly be deemed an indigenous or endemial disease in the Torrid Zone; though it is but very rarely seen in England, or in the other parts of Europe'.[129] His position was a complex one. A distinction of kind and not merely degree could be maintained between the disease environments of the temperate and torrid zones: disease environments defined by both geography

---

[125] Curtin, 'Epidemiology and the Slave Trade'. Sheridan, *Doctors and Slaves: A Medical and Demographic History of Slavery in the British West Indies, 1680–1834.*

[126] Hillary, *Observations on the Changes of the Air and the Concomitant Epidemical Diseases, in the Island of Barbados. To Which Is Added a Treatise on the Putrid Bilious Fever, Commonly Called the Yellow Fever; and Such Other Diseases as Are Indigenous or Endemial, in the West India Islands, or in the Torrid Zone*, 353.

[127] Ibid., 327.

[128] Ibid., 304. My emphasis.

[129] Ibid., 297–8.

and climate. But it was not obvious – despite the West Indies' geographical location within the tropics and its climatic similarity to Africa – that it had always belonged in the latter grouping. Medically speaking, Barbados had, in Hillary's eyes, become part of the Torrid Zone only recently and as a result of human action and human movements.

Conclusion

Although they were bound into a common volume, the two books that made up Hillary's *Observations* spoke to two fairly distinct audiences (one English, one West Indian) and two largely distinct medical traditions. The first, I have suggested, was written under the sign of Hippocrates' *Epidemics I* and *III*, at least as these books were reconceived by members of the Royal Society and other proponents of the new philosophy and mechanical studies of the air. The first book's aim and structure was demonstrably similar to that of an earlier medico-meteorological diary Hillary had produced in England and had appended to his first publication, a Newtonian account of smallpox and its treatment. Although the conceit of many weather diaries was that they detailed the air and diseases in a given location, Hillary's example makes clear that geographical specificity was, in fact, rather insignificant to the global project James Jurin envisioned, which aimed – as so many natural philosophical projects of the time did – to produce universality out of particularity.

It would not do, of course, to overstate the blindness to geographical diversity of works that drew upon *Epidemics*, but a broad pattern may nonetheless be discerned. One may see it most clearly in John Huxham's *Observations on the Air and Epidemical Diseases*, where *Epidemics* was cited on the first page for its description of 'the Constitution of the Air preceding the common Diseases'. Huxham turned to another Hippocratic text – *Airs, Waters, and Places* – to make a point about geographical difference, invoking presumably familiar arguments about the change of diseases across space to defend the mapping between seasonality (thus, temporality) and illness that characterised *Epidemics*.

But if the various Temperatures of the Air in different Climates produces Diseases altogether different, why should not different Tempers of the Air, even in the same Country, produce also different Affections for the Body? And so in Truth it happens, for Instance, in the Spring-Season, especially if dry, north-easterly Winds continue a long Time, inflammatory Fevers, Pleurisies, Peripneumonies, Squinsies most certainly prevail. – In Autumn on the contrary slow and putrid Fevers, Quartans, Cholerae, Dysenteries almost always rage. – Thus in like Manner humid, warm Weather brings on quite different Disorders from such as are found in cold and dry.[130]

---

[130] Orig. Latin is 1739. English trans, 1758. John Huxham, *The Works of John Huxham, M. D. F. R. S. In Two Volumes*, II vols., vol. I (London: W. Bent, 1788), xxvi–vii.

Using *Epidemics*, Hillary could produce a weather diary based on the climate and diseases of Barbados to contribute to universal (read: metropolitan) debates, repeatedly drawing attention to similarities between the West Indies and England. In his *Treatise on the Putrid Bilious Fever*, however, *Airs, Waters, and Places* formed the model for an account of the particularity and peculiarity – the differences – of the West Indian disease environment. The book's intended readers were not metropolitan physicians and natural philosophers collating material for a global project, but West Indian medics interested in the treatment and cure of the local afflictions with which they grappled every day. Huxham, or Boerhaave could be their guides for diseases known in Europe, Hillary's text was concerned with medicine as local knowledge.

Towne, also using *Airs, Waters, and Places* as a guide, had earlier discussed the island's endemial diseases, noting that most were also common in England. In Hillary's book, by contrast, commonalities between the diseases of the West Indies and Europe were ignored or at least underplayed. In the *Treatise* the Barbadian disease environment emerges as a profoundly foreign space. Yellow fever – thoroughly native and utterly novel – served as the most fundamental marker of this foreignness, the product of a distinctly tropical environment. As such, it was also something of an outlier among Barbados' other endemial diseases, a reminder of how complex are the answers as we try to track the emergence of conceptions of the diseases characteristic not of cities or countries, but of vast geographic regions, such as the Torrid and Temperate Zones. While the putrid bilious fever was indigenous, the majority of other endemial diseases were brought to the island via the movement of slaves. Medically speaking, West Indian difference for Hillary was made, not born.

Demography – the spectacular rise in the slave population of the sugar islands – surely had a large role to play in producing Hillary's vision of a distinct disease environment in Barbados. Just as important, however, were mid-century events in which the West Indian islands were only one among many players. It is to these events, and to the role played by military action and military medical genres in the production of difference, that we turn in the next chapter.

Part II

Empire

3   Seasoning Sickness and the Imaginative Geography of the British Empire

The hapless protagonist of Ebeneezer Cook's *The Sot-Weed Factor* (1708) suffered through a series of misadventures after his arrival in colonial Maryland. Battling poultry invaded his hostel room, making sleep impossible. After giving up on his lodgings and fleeing to an orchard, he encountered a rattlesnake; climbing a tree to make his escape, he then spent the evening tormented by 'curst muskitoes'. When, somewhat later, he finally managed a decent night's rest, he awakened to find his stockings, hat, and shoes had been stolen and thrown into a fire (a footnote informs us that this was common practice amongst planters). Most dangerous, perhaps, he soon found himself falling victim to disease: a local affliction known as 'the seasoning'.

> With Cockerouse as I was sitting,
> I felt a Feaver Intermitting:
> A fiery Pulse beat in my Veins,
> From Cold I felt resembling Pains:
> This cursed seasoning I remember
> Lasted from *March* to cold *December*:
> …
> And had my Doctress wanted skill,
> Or Kitchin Physick at her will,
> My Father's Son had lost his Lands,
> And never seen the *Goodwin-Sands*[1]

The idea of *seasoning* was a common one by the 1700s. The term dates back to at least the fifteenth century, when one finds the verb *to season* used in a sense very similar to the most common modern understanding: 'to render (a dish) more palatable by the addition of some savoury ingredient'. The word derives from the Old French *saisonner*, meaning 'to ripen, to render (fruit) palatable by the influence of the seasons'.[2] A second, somewhat different

---

[1] Ebenezer Cooke, *The Sot-Weed Factor, or, a Voyage to Maryland a Satyr: In Which Is Describ'd, the Laws, Government, Courts and Constitutions of the Country, and Also the Buildings, Feasts, Frolicks, Entertainments and Drunken Humours of the Inhabitants of That Part of America: In Burlesque Verse* (London: B. Bragg, 1708).

[2] Oxford English Dictionary Online, accessed 15 Aug. 2014. 'Season, *v*'.

and later English term flows from this original French usage, for one also speaks of seasoned timber, or seasoned metal. The analogous use of the term for people – to be inured to conditions by training and experience – appears already in the early seventeenth century.[3] 'Tis an unseasoned Courtier, Good my Lord', says the Countess of Rossillion to Lord Lafew in *All's Well that Ends Well* (1623), 'Advise him'. Then, as now, soldiers required considerable seasoning to adequately perform their tasks. Baker's *Chronicle* (1665) placed the blame for the Earl of Montross' defeat in battle to his reliance on 'unseason'd Orkney men'.[4]

Cook's usage, however, was rather different to these, for he was alluding to the notion of a 'seasoning sickness', an illness that helped habituate the sufferer to a foreign clime.[5] In 1707, Hans Sloane – then Secretary and later President of the Royal Society – offered the following explanation of 'what is call'd the Seasoning', derived from the time he spent in the West Indies:

that is to say, that every New-Comer before they be accustomed to the Climate and Constitution of the Air in *Jamaica* are to have an acute Disease, which is thought to be

---

[3] Joyce Chaplin has suggested that the term was already in usage in North America in the 1550s, although all the cited examples are from the seventeenth century and afterward. Chaplin, *Subject Matter: Technology, the Body, and Science on the Anglo-American Frontier, 1500–1676*, 151.

[4] Richard Baker, *A Chronicle of the Kings of England: From the Time of the Roman's Government Unto the Death of King James. Containing All Passages of State and Church, with All Other Observations Proper for a Chronicle. Faithfully Collected out of Authors Ancient and Modern; and Digested into a New Method* (London: Nathaniel Ranew and Jonathan Robinson, 1665), 647.

[5] We know a good deal about seasoning and 'acclimatisation' during the nineteenth century. We know a great deal less about the seventeenth and eighteenth centuries, although this situation has changed considerably with the publication of Harrison, *Medicine in an Age of Commerce and Empire: Britain and its Tropical Colonies, 1660–1830*. For early medical histories of the diseases of warm climates in the British Empire, see David Arnold, *Warm Climates and Western Medicine: The Emergence of Tropical Medicine, 1500–1900* (Amsterdam; and Atlanta: Rodopi, 1996); D. Arnold, 'India's Place in the Tropical World, 1770–1930', *Journal of Imperial and Commonwealth History* 26, no. 1 (1998). On Human acclimatisation in Britain, see David N. Livingstone, 'Human Acclimatization: Perspectives on a Contested Field of Inquiry in Science, Medicine, and Geography', *History of Science* 25 (1987); 'Tropical Climate and Moral Hygiene: The Anatomy of a Victorian Debate', *British Journal for the History of Science* 32, no. 1 (1999). For the specific case of Australia, see Anderson, *The Cultivation of Whiteness: Science, Health and Racial Destiny in Australia*. For French botanical and zoological acclimatisation, see Michael A. Osborne, *Nature, the Exotic and the Science of French Colonialism* (Bloomington: Indiana University Press, 1994); 'Acclimatizing the World: A History of the Paradigmatic Colonial Science', *Osiris* 15 (2000). The former contains excellent references to histories of acclimatisation societies around the world. For human acclimatisation in France, see Eric T. Jennings, *Curing the Colonizers: Hydrotherapy, Climatology, and French Colonialism* (Durham, NC: Duke University Press, 2006). For acclimatisation and anthropology in Germany, see Pascal Grosse, *Kolonialismus, Eugenik Und Bürgerliche Gesellschaft in Deutschland 1850–1918* (Frankfurt and New York: Campus, 2000); 'Turning Native? Anthropology, German Colonialism, and the Paradoxes of the "Acclimatization Question", 1885–1914', in *Worldly Provincialism: German Anthropology in the Age of Empire*, eds. H. Glenn Penny and Matti Bunzl (Ann Arbor: University of Michigan Press, 2003).

very dangerous, and that after this is over, their bodies are made more fit to live there, with less hazard than before: and this is not only thought so in that Island, but in *Guinea* and all over the remote Eastern parts of the world.[6]

Seventeenth and eighteenth-century travellers, doctors, soldiers, and sailors all paid a great deal of attention to an illness that seemed to be a disease of *place*. Seasoning affected neither 'natives' nor those who had spent a good deal of time in a specific locale. Only those habituated to one location who ventured to another in which they were strangers fell ill. If they survived their affliction, their bodies were then inured to the novelties of the environments in which they now found themselves.

Of particular interest in Sloane's definition is its geographical reach. The idea of seasoning, it would seem, was a commonplace of parts of the Americas, Africa, and Asia. Just as interesting as the locations included were those left out. Sloane was an English physician writing for a British and European audience that was presumably unfamiliar with the term. His phrasing – '*what is call'd* the Seasoning' – invoked distance. Seasoning was a distemper that plagued English bodies out of place: it made up a discourse of anti-nativity.

I offer in this chapter a history of seasoning in the eighteenth-century British Empire and through this a history of the medical construction of what Edward Said has termed an 'imaginative geography', a conceptual creation of a division of the world.[7] '[E]mpires', Mary Luise Pratt has noted, 'create in the imperial center of power an obsessive need to present and re-present its peripheries and its others continually to itself'.[8] My purpose is to examine the ways in which medicine and medical discourse functioned precisely as part of this far from static re-presentation (and representation) of peripheries to an imperial centre.

The chapter is divided chronologically into two halves. In the first (covering roughly the early seventeenth through the mid-eighteenth centuries) I examine seasoning discourse in its presence throughout the periphery and its relative absence at the centre. In part two I look first at the effect of the wars of the late 1730s and 1740s in bringing seasoning talk to the metropole, before concentrating on the role played by James Lind, author of the most important eighteenth-century medical treatise in English on the diseases of the periphery: *An Essay on Diseases Incidental to Europeans in Hot Climates* (1768). In Lind's work, as we will see, seasoning became a global discourse, as applicable to Britain as elsewhere. Seasoning remained a strangers' affliction, but in the newly and unsettlingly large empire that followed British victories in the Seven Years War, even familiar locations contained pockets of strangeness.

[6] Sloane, xcviii.
[7] Said, *Orientalism*.
[8] Mary Louise Pratt, *Imperial Eyes: Travel Writing and Transculturation*, 2nd ed. (London and New York: Routledge, 2008), 4.

3.1   Seasoning on the Periphery

My suspicion is that early military – particularly naval – deployments were the source for the earliest usages of the notion that one needed to endure illness in order to become seasoned to a place. It is in the writings of soldiers and sailors – or at least those discussing war – that I have found the first mention of the term. John Smith, in his accounts of the first European plantation in Virginia, for example, described a battle with local inhabitants in 1608. His company had been drastically reduced due to illness: 'were we but fiue (with our captaine) [that] could stand: [f]or within 2. daies after wee left *Kecoughtan*, the rest ... were sick almost to death (vntill they were seasoned to the country)'.[9] In 1640, John Pym addressed parliament and discussed a number of grievances. Among them was King Charles' failure to engage in war with Spain over the West Indies. In New England, Virginia, the Caribbean, and the Bermudas, Pym argued, there were now 'at least sixty thousand able persons of this nation, many of them well armed and their bodies seasoned to that climate' who could prosecute a conflict to the Crown's advantage.[10] After Charles' execution in 1649, Cromwell initiated a far more aggressive foreign policy. A year after the Protector's forces seized Jamaica in 1655, a letter from a ship lying in wait for the Spanish Fleet off the coast of Havannah noted that 'as many of us are left are in good health, being seasoned to the country'.[11]

One may multiply other naval examples of the use of the concept of seasoning in the seventeenth and early eighteenth centuries. Yet, at least within the New World, seasoning would soon also pass into common, civilian parlance. Daniel Denton, in 1670, alluded to the term's popularity, even as he denied its application to New York. The climate there, he argued, 'hath such an affinity with that of England, that it breeds ordinarily no alteration to those who remove thither; that the name of seasoning, which is common to some other Countreys hath never there been known'.[12] Colonists elsewhere had no such reservations in applying the term. 'My sister has had her seasoning ...

---

[9] Edward Arber, ed. *Capt. John Smith, of Willoughby by Alford, Lincolnshire; President of Virginia, and Admiral of New England: Works. 1608–1631* (Birmingham: The English Scholars Library, 1884), 117. Smith was fairly complimentary about the climate, however. 'The temperature of the Country doth agree well with *English* constitutions, being once seasoned to the Country'. See ibid., 47, 343.

[10] Charles Kendall Adams, *Representative British Orations* (New York: Putnam, 1884), 82.

[11] Thomas Birch, ed. *A Collection of the State Papers of John Thurloe, Esq; Secretary First to the Council of State and Afterwards to the Two Protectors Oliver and Richard Cromwell* (Burlington: TannerRitchie, 2005), 367.

[12] Daniel Denton, *A Brief Description of New-York, Formerly Called New-Netherlands: With the Places Thereunto Adjoyning: Together with the Manner of Its Scituation, Fertility of the Soyle, Healthfulness of the Climate, and the Commodities Thence Produced: Also Some Directions and Advice to Such as Shall Go Thither ... Likewise a Brief Relation of the Customs of the Indians There* (London: John Hancock and William Bradley, 1670), 59.

two or three fits of a feaver and ague', noted William Fitzhugh to a doctor in the Chesapeake in 1687. Two weeks later he wrote similarly to his brother: she has had 'two or three small fits of a feaver and ague, which now has left, and so consequently her seasoning [is] over'.[13] Despite clear differences in climate, seasoning discourse could be found in the North as well as the South. Christopher Merret, surveyor of the port of Boston, published a short 'Account of several Observables in Lincolnshire' in the Philosophical Transactions in 1696 in which he drew attention to 'Agues (here called *Holland Baylies*) [that] are very rife, few strangers escaping without a seasoning'.[14] In his treatise on the *British Empire in America* (1708), John Oldmixon treated the seasoning not as the affliction of a single colony, but of many of them: 'The *Seasoning* here, as in other parts of *America*, is a Fever or Ague, which the Change of Climate and Diet generally throws New Comers into'.[15] By the early years of the eighteenth century, Robert Beverley had already become critical of what he saw as the overuse of the term. His *History of the First Settlement of Virginia*, dedicated a section to the diseases of Virginia and a subsection to 'The Seasoning', yet he dismissively noted that 'The first sickness that any New-Comer happens to have there, he unfairly calls a Seasoning, be it Fever, ague, or any thing else, that his own Folly, or excesses bring upon him'.[16]

Fear of the illness kept the schoolmaster James Kirkwood in Scotland, after apparently being offered a position as professor of Greek and Latin at the College of Jamestown. 'Persons', claimed Kirkwood, had informed his wife that 'it was ten to one of the whole Family should go there alive; and when they are arrived, commonly they are seiz'd on with a Fever, call'd a Seasoning, of which as many die as escape'.[17] One wonders who Kirkwood's informants were, since it was more common to treat the seasoning as one might treat most other fevers: an annoyance that had the potential to become fatal, but was unlikely to. John Norris framed his *Profitable Advice for Rich and Poor* (1712) as a dialogue between James Freeman, a Carolina Planter, and Simon Question, a

---

[13] Darrett B. Rutman and Anita H. Rutman, 'Of Agues and Fevers: Malaria in the Early Chesapeake', *The William and Mary Quarterly* 33, no. 1 (1976): quoted on 43–4.

[14] Christopher Merret, 'An Account of Several Observables in Lincolnshire, Not Taken Notice of in Camden, or Any Other Author', *Philosophical Transactions* 19 (1695–97): 351.

[15] Rutman and Rutman, quoted on 45.

[16] Robert Beverley, *The History and Present State of Virginia, in Four Parts. I. The History of the First Settlement of Virginia, and the Government Thereof, to the Present Time. II. The Natural Productions and Conveniencies of the Country, Suited to Trade and Improvement. III. The Native Indians, Their Religion, Laws, and Customs, in War and Peace. IV. The Present State of the Country, as to the Polity of the Government, and the Improvements of the Land. By a Native and Inhabitant of the Place.*, 1st ed. (London: R. Parker, 1705), 69.

[17] James Kirkwood, *The History of the Twenty Seven Gods of Linlithgow Being an Exact and True Account of a Famous Plea Betwixt the Town-Council of the Said Burgh, and Mr. Kirkwood* (Edinburgh: 1711), 51.

West Country farmer, which included the following exchange, suggesting that the seasoning was unlikely to claim as many victims as Kirkwood had feared:

S. QUESTION: *Have you not some Distempers there peculiar to the Country which is not usual here in* England?

J. FREEMAN: There is, in the Spring of the Year, a Feaver and Ague seizes many that are settled on the lowest Marsh Land, especially when they are new Comers into the Country, which is commonly called a Seasoning to them; after which, if their Habitations is on dry, healthy Land, they are, generally, very healthful, if temperate.[18]

James Oglethorpe pursued a similar theme in 1732, putting the threat of dangerous illness down to intemperance rather than the climate. 'In this country', he wrote, 'as almost in every new Climate, strangers are apt to have a seasoning; an ague, or sort of a Fever, but then 'tis very slight: And for the rest, People very seldom want Health here but by Intemperance (which indeed is too common)'.[19]

In the West Indies, the term was both common enough and geographically specific enough that Edward Phillips, in his *The New World of Words* (1706) defined a plural noun, *seasonings* as 'An Aguish distemper, which strangers are subject to, in the West-Indies, upon their first coming'.[20] Not all, however, were willing to buy the claim that newcomers were disproportionately afflicted by disease. Barbados had its own Denton in the physician Thomas Trapham, who insisted in 1679 that the island possessed fewer diseases than England and that it was those who had become habituated to the warm air who were most likely to be afflicted by distempers caused by cool night time breezes. Trapham granted that the area around the Port of Jamaica and other places near the water were better suited to the 'well inured *Jamaica* Man than any later arrived persons', but for the most part he ascribed the diarrhoeas and fluxes that greeted the stranger to the isle either to new drinks and diet or to 'rejoicing intemperance', rather than any insalubrious quality of his 'Summer Country'.[21]

As one might tell from Sloane's remarks, Trapham was probably in a minority, at least by the last decade of the seventeenth century. For Sloane and his informants, the question was not whether a seasoning sickness existed, but

---

[18] John Norris, *Profitable Advice for Rich and Poor: In a Dialogue, or Discourse between James Freeman, a Carolina Planter, and Simon Question, a West Country Farmer. Containing a Description ... Of South Carolina* (London: J. How, 1712), 28.

[19] J. Edward Oglethorpe, *A New and Accurate Account of the Provinces of South-Carolina and Georgia: With Many Curious and Useful Observations on the Trade, Navigation and Plantations of Great-Britain* (London: J. Worrall, 1732), 24.

[20] Edward Phillips, *The New World of Words: Or, Universal English Dictionary*, 6th ed. (London: J. Phillips, 1706). The word is not to be found in the first edition (1658). However, too much should not be made of this, since no meanings of the word 'season' are to be found in the earliest edition.

[21] Trapham, 23, 3.

rather the specific nature of the disease. Sloane dismissed the idea that jaundice seasoned strangers, on the grounds that it afflicted old hands and often spared newcomers. Instead, he argued that the true seasoning was marked by the eruption of small red boils all over the body. Positing that the pustules were caused by the body's attempt to remove from the blood the 'heterogenous and unaccustom'd Particles it had from the warm Sun', Sloane insisted that the illness was a salutary one, and was not to be checked:

therefore instead of prescribing a Remedy for its Cure I told those who importun'd me, that I thought this Distemper was the greatest advantage they could have, and that this was the effect of the change of Climate, and a proper seasoning, and what might secure them from future sickness by purging the blood from hot and sharp parts, and rather than check it, wish'd them to help the expulsion with a little *Flos Sulphuris*.[22]

What Sloane termed jaundice, however, was likely what later authors described as yellow fever, and it was that disease, more than any other, that became associated with the seasoning in the West Indies. Indeed, as we saw in the last chapter, the fact of seasoning soon became a point of contention in a dispute between Towne and Warren over aetiology. Warren's text would be instrumental in disseminating the connection between yellow fever and seasoning and, relatedly, the idea that a bout of the seasoning protected one from later virulent illness. Agues and generic fevers might recur: only a small number of diseases struck only once. As John Lining noted in *A Description of the American Yellow Fever* – a work heavily indebted to Warren's: 'it is a great happiness that our constitutions undergo such alterations in the small-pox, measles, and yellow fever, as for ever afterwards secure us from a second attack of those diseases'.[23] By the early nineteenth century, the yellow fever was literally synonymous, at least in the New World, with the seasoning.[24]

One tends to find the concept more than the language of seasoning in those parts of the periphery with more impermanent British settlement. Harrison has pointed to the existence of seasoning discourse about India in the late seventeenth and early eighteenth centuries, although the examples given seem only to indicate an awareness that European bodies were out of place in warmer climes. Thus Ovington's description from *A Voyage to Suratt in the Year 1689*: the English in India, he claimed, are 'as Exotick Plants brought home to us, not agreeable to the soil'.[25] The Italian Gernelli Caveri, travelling in India around

[22] Sloane, Vol. 1, 25.
[23] John Lining, *A Description of the American Yellow Fever* (Edinburgh: G. Hamilton and J. Balfour, 1756), 7.
[24] George Pinckard and Andrew Dickson White, *Notes On the West Indies, Including Observations Relative to the Creoles and Slaves of the Western Colonies, and the Indians of South America: Interspersed with Remarks Upon the Seasoning Or Yellow Fever of Hot Climates.* 2d ed. (London: Baldwin, Cradock and Joy [etc.], 1816).
[25] Quoted in Harrison, *Climates* 39.

the same time as Ovington, noted a similar, but general, discomfort: 'Generally throughout all Indostan the heat is excessive, except near the mountains. We Europeans fare ill there because of the seasons differing from ours; because their winter begins in June and ends in September'.[26] Sloane's remarks would indicate that a discourse concerning seasoning *sickness* probably existed in the late seventeenth and early eighteenth centuries, yet examples are fairly rare. In 1711, Charles Lockyer wrote of a 'Seasoning Sickness, that we commonly meet, soon after our arrival in *India*', yet it is worth noting his insistence that the cause was diet rather than climate.[27] We find little mention of diseases that particularly strike strangers in Bontius' *Account of the Diseases, Natural History, and Medicines of the East Indies* (1629), but William Dampier's *A New Voyage Round the World* (1699) contains an account of the gold mines of Achin in Sumatra and the miners who are seasoned to the illnesses that arise there:

That at the mines it was so sickly that not the half of those that went thither did ever return again; tho they went thither only to Traffick with the Miners, who live there, being seasoned ... that some there made it their constant imployment to visit the Miners once every year; for after they are once seasoned, and have found the profit of that trade, no thoughts of danger can deter them from it.[28]

If the ideal climate required no seasoning, one might also find climates where habituation seemed virtually impossible. James Houston, physician for the Royal African Company and Chief Surgeon at Cape Coast Castle, mentioned the seasoning as the first disease to strike newcomers, but without the sense that, as Sloane had phrased it, 'after this is over, their bodies are made more fit to live there, with less hazard than before'. 'There is but one other Disease epidemically fatal to your Servants, which they call the *Seasoning*, known to all *Europeans* that come under the *Torrid Zone*, which is nothing but a Fever, caus'd by the change of the Climate'.[29] None were as scathing about

---

[26] Quoted in Harrison, *Climates*, 45.

[27] Charles Lockyer, *An Account of the Trade in India Containing Rules for Good Government in Trade ... With Descriptions of Fort St. George ... Calicut ... To Which Is Added, an Account of the Management of the Dutch in Their Affairs in India.* (London: Samuel Crouch, 1711), 177.

[28] William Dampier, *A New Voyage Round the World: Describing Particularly the Isthmus of America, Several Coasts and Islands in the West Indies, the Isles of Cape Verd, the Passage by Terra Del Fuego, the South Sea Coasts of Chili, Peru and Mexico, the Isle of Guam One of the Ladrones, Mindanao, and Other Philippine and East-India Islands near Cambodia, China, Formosa, Luconia, Celebes, &C., New Holland, Sumatra, Nicobar Isles, the Cape of Good Hope, and Santa Hellena: Their Soil, Rivers, Harbours, Plants, Fruits, Animals, and Inhabitants: Their Customs, Religion, Government, Trade, &C.* (London: James Knapton, 1697–1703), 133. On Dampier's debts to the questions raised in Robert Boyle's 'General Heads for a Natural History of a Countrey', see Malcolmson, 182.

[29] James Houstoun, *Some New and Accurate Observations Geographical, Natural and Historical. Containing a True and Impartial Account of the Situation, Product, and Natural History of the Coast of Guinea* (London: J. Peele, 1725), 56.

the disease environment as Willem Bosman, whose writings we encountered in Chapter 1. As Bosman made clear, not only were newcomers liable to illness in Guinea, even those 'who have long continued here' remained under threat. Only those born to what he referred to as 'the Stench' were immune.

However inured they may have been to their own climate, African bodies suffered just as those of Europeans did in the move to the New World. In an age before the rise of theories of racial fixity, the key questions concerned nativity and habituation. Slaves newly arrived to the Caribbean suffered enormously from the seasoning, a fact commonly described by slavers in economic terms. Some planters in the Antilles, we are informed in Volume V of the *Atlas Geographus* (1717), possessed 20000 pounds worth of slaves 'and many Planters are undone in a time of Mortality for want of Money to renew their Stock, which must be filled up every Year, because a 4th part die in Seasoning'.[30] James Grainger combined economic and moral reasoning in 1764 in what he claimed to be the first medical tract 'purposely written on the method of seasoning new Negroes'. It was not sufficient, Grainger insisted, to care for slaves when they were ill:

they should also be well clothed and regularly fed. Neglecting either of these important precepts is not only inhuman, it is the worst species of prodigality. One Negroe saved in this manner more than pays the additional expences which owners of slaves by this means incur. But, supposing it did not, it ought seriously to be considered by all masters, that they must answer before the Almighty for their conduct towards their Negroes.[31]

'New Negroes', Grainger argued, needed to be gradually accustomed to labour and no new slave could be said to be seasoned before they had been in the West Indies for at least a year. Nor were those newly arrived from Africa the only labourers in peril. Creoles who moved from one island to another also underwent a seasoning. Once seasoned, however, a slave commanded a higher price than a 'salt-water' Negroe. And those born in the region were the most valuable of all, hence the admonition that 'too great care cannot be taken either of Negresses when pregnant, and in the month, or of infants when born'.[32] Seasoning, it becomes clear, was central to the language – economic, moral, and medical – of both settlement and slavery.

While examples certainly exist, one finds comparatively little said about seasoning closer to the British Isles. Where seasoning is mentioned, it tends to be in the context of what, to British authors, were intra-European peripheries.

---

[30] Herman Moll, *Atlas Geographus: Or, a Compleat System of Geography, Ancient and Modern*, vol. V (London: J. Nutt, 1717), 492.

[31] James Grainger, 'An Essay on the More Common West-India Diseases, James Grainger, MD (1764), with Additional Notes by William Wright, MD, FRD (1802)', in *On the Treatment and Management of the More Common West-India Diseases (1750–1802)*, ed. J. Edward Hutson (Kingston, Jamaica: University of the West Indies Press, 2005), 51.

[32] Ibid., 13.

In 1708, for example, John Polus Lecaan – who had been employed as a physician in the service of King William – offered *Advice to the Gentlemen of the Army of her Majesty's Forces in Spain and Portugal*, which advice he proposed would be useful in all hot climates, including 'our Plantations in the West-Indies, &c'.

As in other Countries the Differences of Seasons produce different Effects in our Bodies; for by the more or less Heat the Pores of our Bodies are more or less open, the Air more or less pure, Food more or less spirituous; so without doubt great Difference of Climate, or of Heat and Cold, is very prejudicial to all Strangers, and the cause of numerous Distempers, especially to the *English*, who are very Irregular and Careless in their way of Living.[33]

Were the English instead to adapt their habits to mirror that of locals, such distempers could likely be avoided: 'This way of Living Strangers should observe, especially in the beginning, by which they will season themselves to the Country, and be able to bear the Climate almost as well as the Natives, who are the most abstemious People in the World'.[34]

I have found fairly few examples of the term seasoning applied to an English affliction before mid-century, although each is telling in its own way. Closest to the meanings explored here are comments found in John Graunt's *Natural and Political Observations ... Upon the Bills of Mortality* (1676). Graunt was attempting to explain why London's rate of burials outstripped its number of christenings in the period from 1603 to 1644. The reason he gave was that London's air was, for artificial reasons, particularly harmful. The problem was not intrinsic climate, but the effects of what moderns would call urbanisation. As William Cowper would phrase it: 'God made the country, and men made the town'.[35] London had been *made* a place where visitors from other parts of England required a new habituation.

As for unhealthiness, it may well be supposed, that although seasoned Bodies may, and do live near as long in *London*, as elsewhere, yet new-comers and Children do not: for the *Smoaks, stinks*, and close *Air*, are less healthful than that of the Country; otherwise why do sickly Persons remove into the Country-Air?[36]

London, it would seem, was like a foreign country to those brought up in the purer environs of the English countryside. A quirkier example may be found in Defoe's *Tour Thro' the Whole Island of Great Britain*, where the marital

---

[33] Lecaan, 4.
[34] Ibid., 9.
[35] On similar visions of London in this period, see Roy Porter, 'Cleaning up the Great Wen: Public Health in Eighteenth-Century London', *Medical History. Supplement* 11 (1991).
[36] Quoted in Andrew Wear, 'Health and the Environment in Early Modern England', in *Medicine in Society: Historical Essays*, ed. Andrew Wear (Cambridge: Cambridge University Press, 1992), 130.

habits of the inhabitants of the marshlands of Essex are described. '[A]ll along this Country', Defoe explains, 'it is very frequent to meet with Men that have had from Five or Six, to Fourteen or Fifteen Wives'. The reason had to do with location, the men of the region seeking wives in regions with healthier air. Their brides, brought back, soon fell sick and died, while the men, being 'seasoned to the Place, did pretty well', soon returning to the Uplands to 'fetch another' to replace their unfortunate spouse.[37] But such examples tend to be the exception rather than the rule. While writers in the New World (at least those assuming a local audience) spoke of seasoning with the expectation of being easily understood, those in England often glossed or explained the term, indicating its relative unfamiliarity.[38] This, as we will see, would begin to change after mid-century, in the aftermath of multiple imperial conflicts.

3.2   Seasoning an Empire

The Mid-Century Wars

The Spring of 1738 saw an intensification of the usual hostility between England and Spain over trade and piracy. And just as conflict between the two nations had inspired talk of the need for soldiers seasoned to the West Indian climate a century before, so too it reoccurred now. Parliamentary debates concerned both the question of whether war was advisable and also – should conflict be engaged – whether troops should be raised at home or in the Antilles. In arguing for war, Lord Bathurst rejected the idea that troops be raised from

---

[37] Daniel Defoe, *A Tour Thro' the Whole Island of Great Britain: Divided into Circuits or Journeys. Giving a Particular and Entertaining Account of Whatever Is Curious, and Worth Observation ... By a Gentleman*, 4 vols., vol. I (London: J. Osborn, S. Birt, D. Browne, J. Hodges, A. Millar, J. Whiston, and J. Robinson, 1742), 8–9.

[38] In 1696, for example, Gideon Harvey seemed unaware that the term was not a neologism in the medical context, drawing an analogy with a fired clay pot. 'The suffering of that Distemper [smallpox], I look upon as a seasoning to the demipestiferous Air; for as a new earthen Pot is seasoned, by letting the particles of the Fire gradually enter its pores, whereby they are by little and little widened, and then the Fire entering with a full force and finding no straitness or resistance, passeth through without any injury to the Pot; whereas should it at first be committed to a vigorous Fire, it would soon be crackt by the Fiery particles forcing the pores asunder, and this is called a Seasoning'. Gideon Harvey, *A Treatise of the Small-Pox and Measles: Describing Their Nature, Causes, and Signs, Diagnostick and Prognostick, in a Different Way to What Hath Hitherto Been Known: Together, with the Method of Curing the Said Distempers, and All, or Most, of the Best Remedies: Also, a Particular Discourse of Opium, Diacodium, and Other Sleeping Medicines: With a Reference to a Very Great Case* (London: W. Freeman, 1696), 31–2. Close to a century later, and in the same context as Graunt, Price inserted a parenthetical analogy to aid the reader: 'after that age, the inhabitants consisting chiefly of persons, who (like men *used* to drink) have been *seasoned* to *London*', Richard Price, *Observations on Reversionary Payments; on Schemes for Providing Annuities for Widows, and for Persons in Old Age; on the Method of Calculating the Values of Assurances on Lives; and on the National Debt* (London: T. Cadell, 1771), 266.

the 'few spare hands' working on the West Indian plantations as well as the suggestion that the difference in climates between the two regions would prove an insurmountable obstacle to the deployment of British soldiers and seamen:

It would have been much better to have sent eight or ten thousand of the idle Fellows we have at Home, to some of our most healthful Plantations, in order to have been there ready at a Call; for the Difference of the Climate is so far from being an Argument against, that it is a strong Argument for sending them thither some Months before we have Use for them, that they may have Time to be seasoned to the Climate, and to recover from the Fatigues of a long Voyage, before they are sent upon any Expedition against an Enemy.[39]

By contrast, Lord Hervey was considerably less sanguine about the capacities of men habituated to northern European climes.

[I]f we should strike a blow in the West Indies, it must be struck with the forces that our own settlements furnish. These are the most proper, and our ships will never want abundance of people there, who will be glad to enroll for any expedition of that nature; they are seasoned to the climate, and they know how to deal with the Spaniards. Whereas, if we send forces from this kingdom, one half will probably die in the passage, and the other half will be so sickly and weak when they land, that they can be sent upon no service.[40]

Those agitating in favour of open hostilities soon gained the upper hand. War was declared in October 1739, and British forces scored a first and easy victory at the end of the year in their attack on Porto Bello. The English public responded with enormous enthusiasm (naming the London road for the victory) and – so at least one story goes – singing *Rule Britannia* for the first time in celebration.[41] The country's happy mood would not last, for this would essentially be the last good bit of news for some time. Fired up, English forces decided to attack the much more heavily fortified city of Carthagena. Aiming for their fleet to leave during the summer of 1740, they did not sail until November, by which time scurvy had already broken out on a number of ships. Before they even reached Jamaica, from whence they planned to make the final leg of their journey to Carthagena, their commanding officer, Lord Cathcart, was dead of dysentery. Betrayed by their guides during their assault on the town's fortifications, they were butchered by Spanish troops.[42] But the

---

[39] Ebenezer Timberland, *The History and Proceedings of the House of Lords from the Restoration in 1660 to the Present Time: Containing the Most Remarkable Motions, Speeches, Debates, Orders and Resolutions* (London: Printed for Ebenezer Timberland in Ship-Yard, Temple Bar, 1742), vol. 6, 1738–40, 152.

[40] Great Britain. Parliament., *A Collection of the Parliamentary Debates in England, from the Year MDCLXVIII. To the Present Time*, vol. 17 (London: John Torbuck, 1739–42), 450.

[41] Kathleen Wilson, 'Empire, Trade and Popular Politics in Mid-Hanoverian Britain: The Case of Admiral Vernon', *Past and Present* 121 (1988).

[42] J. W. Fortescue, *A History of the British Army*, 2nd ed., vol. II (London: Macmillan, 1910), 55–79.

battle was the least of their worries. It has been estimated that of the 10,000 troops sent to the West Indies, more than 80 per cent died. The Spanish, by contrast, lost only 200–600 men in the defence of Carthegena.[43] And it was from disease, rather than their wounds, that the vast majority of soldiers and sailors perished. As Lord Elibank noted in 1740: 'We lost above a 3d of our people as well officers as soldiers, in 3 weeks that we remained in Carthagena Harbour. Everybody was taken alike; they call the distemper a bilious fever, it kills in five days; if the patient lives longer it's only to die of greater agonies of what they then call Black Vomit'.[44] About 74 per cent of the troops sent to the West Indies were dead by October, 1742, only 6 per cent of them from their wounds; a large proportion, probably a majority, died in Jamaica. In July and August, troops died on the island at the rate of 100 per week. The dramatic difference between mortality rates on the Carthagenian expedition and most European wars was not lost on either military or civilian observers. Many would soon note that in the contemporaneous War of the Austrian Succession, the death rate was about 8 per cent (disease and wounds together); in the Jacobite Uprising a few years later (1745–6) it was about 2 per cent.[45]

It is hard to overestimate the significance of the mid-century wars on broader British culture.[46] According to Stephen Conway, around one in fifteen available men served in the military during the War of the Austrian Succession (1740–8). One in nine served during the Seven Years War (1756–63), with soldiers and sailors coming from a wide variety of social backgrounds. The costs as well as the promises of empire became very tangible to a broad swathe of the population in this period. Kathleen Wilson has pointed to the celebration of Admiral Vernon, victor of Porto Bello and the face of the opposition to Walpole's Eurocentrism, as evidence for 'the existence of a vibrant, national extra-parliamentary political culture'.[47] Vernon was supported by a growing middle and merchant class and the 'Vernon agitation', Wilson has argued, 'revealed both the readiness and propensity of urban middling groups in London and the provinces to engage in a "commercialized" politics, and their capacity for disciplined political action. Even further, it demonstrates the growing importance of Britain's empire in the nascent political and national consciousness of ordinary citizens'.[48] Just as important as the changes wrought on military

[43] John Robert McNeill, *Mosquito Empires: Ecology and War in the Greater Caribbean, 1620–1914* (New York: Cambridge University Press, 2010), 162–3.

[44] Elibank quoted in ibid., 163.

[45] Ibid., 166–8.

[46] Erica Charters, *Disease, War, and the Imperial State: The Welfare of the British Armed Forces During the Seven Years War* (Chicago and London: University of Chicago Press, 2014).

[47] Wilson, 'Empire, Trade and Popular Politics in Mid-Hanoverian Britain: The Case of Admiral Vernon', 108.

[48] Ibid., 77.

and political culture were those induced in medical attitudes towards the outer reaches of the empire. It was hard for English observers not to suspect that something radically different was happening in the disease environment of the torrid zone.

One of the ways to track this sentiment is by the striking increase in the number of texts published on shipboard diseases and on the diseases of warm climates as they affected soldiers and sailors. Henry Warren's *Treatise on the Malignant Fever of Barbados,* published in 1740, suggested that the King had lost 'upwards of Twenty-Thousand very useful subjects, the much greatest part of whom were Sea-Faring People' to the yellow fever between 1733 and 1739. John Tennent, writing in 1741, described 'that Epidemic Fever so mortal among Northern Foreigners, soon after they arrive in *Jamaica,* and other Parts of the *West-Indies*' and suggested that 'Many Instances prove that Armies suffer as much by marching into hot Climates, from their natural temperate ones, as from a Rencounter with an Enemy; whence appears the Importance of proper Methods, to prevent or cure their mortal epidemic Distempers'.[49] James Lind's *Treatise on Scurvy* was written largely in response to events in the European theatre, in the aftermath of the war of Austrian succession.[50] Charles Bisset's – which treated the West Indian Scurvy – was written while Bisset served in the West Indies during the war with Spain.[51] As J. D. Alsop has argued, 'From 1740, the publications in the medical topography of empire reflected the needs of state and, in particular, the priorities of war'.[52]

The Works of James Lind

Perhaps no works better exemplify Alsop's claim than the medical texts of James Lind. Born in Edinburgh in 1716, Lind began an apprenticeship with a local physician at the age of fifteen. He joined the navy in 1739 as a surgeon's mate and became a full surgeon in 1747, serving in multiple locations throughout the empire, including the Guinea Coast, the West Indies, and Minorca. In 1748 he completed his medical degree at Edinburgh and the following year resigned his military position. The *Treatise on Scurvy* appeared in 1753, with a second edition in 1757, the same year that he published *An Essay on the most Effectual Means of Preserving the Health of Seamen in the*

---

[49] John Tennent, *A Reprieve from Death: In Two Physical Chapters ... With an Appendix. Dedicated to the Right Honourable Sir Robert Walpole.* (London: Printed for John Clarke, 1741), vi. Cf. Alsop, 35.

[50] Lind, *A Treatise of the Scurvy. In Three Parts. Containing an Inquiry into the Nature, Causes, and Cure of That Disease. Together with a Critical and Chronological View of What Has Been Published on the Subject.*

[51] Charles Bisset, *A Treatise on the Scurvy. Design'd Chiefly for the Use of the British Navy.* (London: R. and J. Dodsley, in Pall-Mall, 1755).

[52] Alsop, 35.

Royal Navy. In 1758 he was appointed Physician-in-charge of the Royal Naval Hospital at Haslar. The second edition of Lind's *Health of Seamen* appeared in 1762. The first edition of the work deemed most important at the time, *An Essay On Diseases Incidental to Europeans in Hot Climates*, was published in 1768. A fifth edition appeared in 1792, two years before Lind's death, with a sixth published posthumously in 1808.[53] For the entirety of the second half of the eighteenth century, Lind was the leading figure in British naval medicine. It is in Lind's writings, I argue, that one may best track radically shifting attitudes towards both medicine and empire. In the early texts, written soon after 1748, Lind maintained differences between Europe and its distant holdings, with his gaze largely on the former. After the end of the Seven Years War, however – which concluded with the dramatic expansion of British imperial holdings – one finds a much more complex attitude toward the familiar and the foreign: an attitude expressed in the language of seasoning.

Today, it may be the *Treatise on Scurvy* that remains most famous, for it was there that Lind offered his description of the first 'controlled trial' of the efficacy of different supposed cures for the maritime disease that had destroyed so many lives, concluding that 'oranges and lemons were the most effectual remedies for this distemper at sea'.[54] For our purposes, however, interest in the text is more limited. As one might expect for a work dedicated to the understanding and cure of a disease whose 'native seat' was to be found 'in the cold northern climates', Lind said little about seasoning. The disease may have been foreign to the ancients, who had lived in warmer, Mediterranean climes and had confined their naval journeys to short coastal voyages, but it was all too familiar to the British.[55] John Pringle's *Observations on the Diseases of the Army* (1752), similarly concerned with afflictions in Northern Europe (particularly the low countries), says nothing about becoming seasoned to the climate. 'By well-seasoned troops are commonly understood', Pringle wrote, 'such as having gone through much fatigue, are therefore supposed best qualified to bear more'.[56] One was to be seasoned, that is, to the service, not to a geographical region.

---

[53] For biographical details, see Louis H. Roddis, *James Lind: Founder of Nautical Medicine* (New York: Henry Schuman, 1950).

[54] Lind, *A Treatise of the Scurvy. In Three Parts. Containing an Inquiry into the Nature, Causes, and Cure of That Disease. Together with a Critical and Chronological View of What Has Been Published on the Subject*, 196.

[55] It had become even more so after the publication of a description of Lord Anson's disastrous circumnavigation of the globe. John Philips, *An Authentic Account of Commodore Anson's Expedition: Containing All That Was Remarkable, Curious and Entertaining, During That Long and Dangerous Voyage: ... Taken from a Private Journal* (London: J. Robinson, 1744). Anson lost half his crew to scurvy in rounding Cape Horn and returned to England with less than 200 of an initial complement of more than 1800 men. Lind dedicated his *Treatise* to Anson.

[56] John Pringle, *Observations on the Diseases of the Army: In Camp and Garrison. In Three Parts. With an Appendix* (London: A. Millar, and D. Wilson; and T. Payne, 1752), 147–8.

Strikingly different was Charles Bisset's *A Treatise on the Scurvy*, published in 1755, two years after Lind's. Bisset, too, was born in Scotland and studied medicine at Edinburgh before joining the service and becoming second surgeon of the military hospital in Jamaica in 1740. He spent five years in the West Indies and America before returning to Britain in 1745 and his book drew heavily on his medical experiences in the New World. Seasoning was central to the published work, which Bisset claimed was only part of a larger tract, concerned with 'the natural constitution of the atmosphere, and the diseases incident to new-comers, seasoned Europeans, and natives of the West Indies'.[57] Bisset paired scurvy with what he termed (combining Warren and Towne's terminology) the 'malignant bilious fever', arguing that one could become seasoned to both. One rarely found scurvy in the West Indies during the winter months, he argued, 'and Negroes, Creols, and seasoned Europeans are not obnoxious to the malignant Bilious Fever, and are seldom much afflicted with the Scurvy'.[58] In the course of a year, Bisset claimed, European bodily fibres gradually became drier, more rigid and more elastic, thus approximating those of 'Creoles and Negroes'. It was this change in the fibres, and concomitant alterations in bodily 'juices' that constituted seasoning. Comparing his analysis to Lind's, Bisset noted that scurvy might strike the European in either hot or cold climes, but in the Torrid Zone it was unseasoned strangers who were most at risk.

It is observed by Dr. Lind, that the principal predisposing cause to the Scurvy, in climates where the winters are cold, is a cold and moist air; and we have shewn, that the chief predisposing cause in the West Indies, consists in an unseasoned constitution to the Torrid Zone, joined with the sultry heat of the hot sun.[59]

Lind would summarise Bisset's main conclusions in the second edition of his *Treatise* and one finds talk of seasoning in Lind's *Essay on ... the Health of Seamen*, also published in 1757. The first edition of *The Health of Seamen*, Lind noted, was published soon after the beginning of what we now term the Seven Years War and what Lind called 'the present war with France'.[60] It was thus largely concerned with the illnesses of sailors, since many more died from disease than from 'shipwreck, capture, famine, fire, or sword'.[61] The second edition was published in 1762 and Lind claimed that he had revised the work so that it could serve not only those on ships, but could also prove useful to those in British colonies and factories.[62]

[57] Bisset, 1–2.
[58] Ibid., 10.
[59] Ibid., 41.
[60] James Lind, *An Essay of the Most Effectual Means of Preserving the Health of Seamen in the Royal Navy*, 2nd ed. (London: D. Wilson, 1762), xvii.
[61] Ibid.
[62] Ibid., xviii.

Perhaps because his book was aimed at two rather different audiences – one at sea, one on land – one finds two rather different usages of 'seasoning talk' in Lind's text. Like Pringle and earlier military authors, Lind spoke of the need to use men seasoned to the armed services, particularly the navy. In times of peace, Lind claimed, it was common to find smaller ships of war manned with 'sound and seasoned sailors'.[63] In times of war, however, one often found newer men serving on larger ships, which led to higher incidences of shipboard illnesses, for 'raw sailors and unseasoned marines are often the Occasion of great Sickness in Fleets'.[64] But the only problem was not that one had too many newly raised men and not enough veterans, as was often the complaint in the army. An even more important distinction was that between landmen and those used to a marine life. Larger warships should be made up, Lind urged, of 'seasoned healthy Men from other Ships, and of such Landmen who have been somewhat inured to the Sea'.[65]

Just as the Crown needed men seasoned to the service and to maritime life, it also needed men seasoned to certain climates. It may seem intuitively obvious that one should favour strong young men for a crew, rather than more grizzled, older sailors, but this might well prove to be a mistake. '[M]any hardened veteran Sailors are sometimes to be met with', wrote Lind, 'who enjoy a better State of Health in the *West-Indies* than in *Europe*, having been long seasoned and inured to that Climate, either in the King's, or in the Merchant's service'.[66]

It was fairly rare, in the mid-eighteenth century, to find an author deploying both meanings of seasoning in the same text. Military authors, like Pringle, tended to write of seasoned soldiers; medical writers concerned with the diseases of warm climates tended to emphasise the need to become habituated to a given part of the globe, and often stressed, as we have seen, the promises and perils of a seasoning sickness. Interested in the diseases of both sailors and colonists in Europe as well as the Indies and the Guinea coast, however, Lind was a likely first candidate to bring the two discourses together. That said, in doing so, some of the particularity of the discourse about seasoning in the Torrid Zone dropped away. One became sick because of 'a quick Transition to a new way of life' or because of 'sudden Changes of Climates'.[67] For sailor or settler, the problem was rapid change. Effects were largely the same as well: Lind credited no particular illness with being a seasoning sickness. Indeed, while he acknowledged that yellow fever struck those who had newly arrived to the West Indies, he also argued that the disease was much rarer than earlier authors had claimed.[68] As a result, he could advocate the same prophylactic treatment

63 Ibid., vii.
64 Ibid., 9.
65 Ibid., 10.
66 Ibid., 11.
67 Ibid., x.
68 Ibid., 50.

for the unseasoned. Those unaccustomed to life at sea should be gradually habituated to marine life by first serving on smaller warships and merchant vessels; those travelling to the West Indies from England should leave Britain in the Autumn (when the weather was most like that in the Tropics) and become gradually used to increased temperatures, finally arriving at Jamaica at a relatively healthy time of year.[69] In Pringle's treatment of the diseases of the army, the ideal soldier was one who had avoided illnesses best: 'those troops will be best seasoned to go through the difficulties of a second campaign, whose health has been most preserved in the first'.[70] For Lind, similarly, newcomers became seasoned to a climate by assiduously avoiding what others might see as an evil necessary for eventual habituation:

It has been a received opinion, that the first fever or fit of sickness alters the constitution of the body, so as to season it to a new climate: but I am of opinion, that the sudden changes of climates are greatly the cause of sickness, and that a seasoned constitution in any part of the world is chiefly to be acquired by remaining there for some length of time.[71]

Lind's most extensive account of seasoning came in his most widely cited work, *On Diseases Incidental to Europeans in Hot Climates.* He himself pitched the text as a 'sequel' to his earlier studies. Having formerly been concerned with those aboard ships, he now took up the problem of the health of those arrived at their destination in a foreign land. One might also regard the text as the longest and most detailed meditation on the problem of seasoning published in the eighteenth century. That fact is not obvious from its superficial structure, for in many ways the book fits into an established mode. Emulating Hippocrates' *Airs, Waters, and Places,* a number of works had been written that treated of the diseases of regions far from home. Some – perhaps the larger number – considered the afflictions of a given location. A smaller number imitated Hippocrates more directly, and offered a scholarly appraisal of the diseases endemic or native to all places in the known world.[72] Lind's *Hot Climates* would seem to fit into this latter mould, for it discusses diseases found, successively, in Europe and North America, Africa, the East Indies, and the West Indies. And yet, whereas earlier works had taken as their implicit patient a *native* of a given region of the world, almost two-thirds of Lind's work was explicitly concerned with the diseases that attacked *strangers* to a given climate. That is, Lind's was a work concerned with anti-nativity, with diseases that plagued those who were not seasoned to a climate. And the number of the unseasoned, as he noted, was increasing.

---

[69] Ibid., 9, 48.
[70] Pringle, 150.
[71] Lind, *An Essay on Diseases Incidental to Europeans in Hot Climates: With the Method of Preventing Their Fatal Consequences. To Which Is Added, an Appendix Concerning Intermittent Fevers*, 188.
[72] See, for example, Hoffmann and Ramazzini.

Few persons visit the East or the West Indies for their pleasure, but thousands leave England every year, with the design of settling in some of our colonies. Numbers have lately gone to people those parts of America and the West Indies ceded to us by the last treaty of peace. Regiments are often sent out from England, to relieve others stationed in the most distant parts of the globe; and recruits for those regiments are still more frequently ordered abroad.[73]

The traveller, Lind suggested, was like a plant in foreign soil, requiring care to ensure its survival. And while many soils could be salutary, those that were far beyond Europe and in which Europeans now had particular interests were unhealthy, even possibly fatal.[74] Jamaica's climate was deadly to the point that it strained belief. Lind cited a 'common computation' suggesting that a number equivalent to the entire white population died every five years.[75] In many factories on the Guinea Coast, one-third of Europeans might die in a year.[76] It was on these grounds that Lind used the idea of seasoning not – as abolitionists had and would – against slavery, but in slavery's defence. Europeans, especially those newly arrived, were safest on board ship, away from the unhealthy effluvia of the shore. Of particular danger were uncultivated lands, precisely the kinds of places where unseasoned men were often sent to collect wood. 'If the purchasing of negroes on the coast of Guinea can be justified', he wrote, 'it must be from the absolute necessity of employing them in such services as this. It does not seem consistent with British humanity to assign such employments to a regiment of gallant soldiers, or to a company of brave seamen'.[77] 'British humanity', of course, seemed only to apply to the British and their near neighbours. Lind clearly saw no irony in a defence of enslavement that sought to incite the reader's pity for the poor treatment of others. '[N]othing can be more inhuman', he opined, 'that sending unseasoned Europeans high up from the mouths of the rivers, into an uncultivated country, especially during the rainy season, and where there is no shelter from the pestiferous noctural air'.[78]

One should be clear, however, that the issue at hand was one of nativity and seasoning, rather than race, as we might understand that term from the nineteenth century onwards. The capacity to survive in a dangerous climate was not innate. In Africa, Lind twinned 'natives, and such others as are perfectly seasoned to the country'.[79] In the West Indies he paired 'Negroes and Creoles', both of whom could apparently sleep outside on dewy ground – an act against which he strongly counseled European strangers. That this could

---

[73] Lind, *An Essay on Diseases Incidental to Europeans in Hot Climates: With the Method of Preventing Their Fatal Consequences. To Which Is Added, an Appendix Concerning Intermittent Fevers*, 2.

[74] Ibid., 2–3.

[75] Ibid., 9.

[76] Ibid., 151.

[77] Ibid., 134.

[78] Ibid., 139.

[79] Ibid., 141.

be done by some without hurt was 'a proof how far the Constitution may be framed and accustomed to bear what otherwise is so highly prejudicial'.[80] This anti-essentialist logic had a political corollary. Native factors could be highly useful for British trade – as they were for the Portuguese – and such utility should be rewarded with all the privileges of British subjecthood. Europeans might, over time, become habituated to the climate of the Guinea coast, and Africans could become naturalised servants of the crown.[81]

Although his status may have added medical legitimacy to such claims, Lind was hardly unusual either for views that defended the slave trade or those that advocated for the promotion of useful 'natives'. Where Lind was unlike many of his contemporaries, however, was in refusing to regard extended regions of the globe as inherently dangerous to Europeans. The concluding summary of his remarks on the diseases that afflicted strangers across the earth pointed to peculiar similarities and differences. Hippocratic and neo-Hippocratic texts on *Airs, Waters, and Places* tended to emphasise differences in native diseases due to location: Lind effaced these differences in his focus on newly arrived foreigners. '[T]he diseases of strangers in different climates', he wrote, 'bear everywhere a great similitude to one another'. Difference could be found elsewhere, however, for no country could be regarded in monolithic terms. Seemingly deadly regions had their 'healthy and pleasant seasons' during which strangers could visit with impunity. And insalubrity was archipelagic:

The most unhealthy spots in the world have in their neighbourhood, and often at no great distance from them, places which afford a secure retreat and protection from diseases and death ... In a word, the diseases most fatal to strangers in every country, seem not only to be confined to particular seasons, but even during those seasons to certain places only.

The corollary, then, was that one could be safe or unsafe almost anywhere, depending on whether one was habituated to a given climate. Seasoning had earlier been a discourse that had divided the world into a (northern) European centre and an extra-European periphery. In Lind's hands, the dichotomy ceased, fundamentally, to be explicable in purely geographic terms. What mattered now was only strangeness and habituation. Hence the fact that Lind's survey of the globe's illnesses began at home, with an account of the diseases that afflicted those unseasoned to England's more dangerous regions. Strangers in this context included not only those born outside the country, but even English soldiers unused to the diseases of places like the Hilsea Barracks in Portsea. But strangeness could, with care, be overcome. Lind counselled newcomers to stay on board ship as much as possible, to arrive at the right time

---

[80] Ibid., note 69.
[81] Ibid., 224–5.

and disembark at the right place, and to avoid diseases until one was inured to the new environment. A merchant, sailor, or factor who did so, Lind claimed, was then worth 'ten newly arrived unseasoned Europeans'. Yet the protections of nativity might also be lost. Lind suggested that 'many persons, dreading what they may again be exposed to suffer from a change of climate, choose rather to spend the remainder of their lives abroad, than to return to their native country'.[82] Imperial power came with a medical price.

Conclusion

In this chapter, I have attempted to trace the changing nature of seasoning discourse across the first two-thirds of the eighteenth century, following the ways in which medical logics shifted along with dramatically new conceptions of the relationships between a British centre and its hinterlands. In the earlier eighteenth century, as we have seen, the foreign and the familiar had possessed fairly fixed referents. The metropole was treated as an unmarked category: one needed to be seasoned only to lands in the periphery. By the late 1760s, in medical discourse, centres and peripheries lived cheek by jowl. England had its sites of foreignness, Jamaica could become so familiar that a Briton could fear returning home. Seasoning discourse changed fundamentally in Lind's hands and across his publications, and did so in ways that mirrored equally fundamental changes in the nature and scope of Britain's imperial holdings. The British Empire was dramatically larger after the victories of the Seven Years War than it had been before. With the rapid growth in size came, according to Linda Colley, an uncertainty about the very question of what it was to be British. Before the war, she has suggested, 'Britain's empire had been small enough and homogeneous enough to seem reasonably compatible with the values that the British, and above all the English, believed they uniquely epitomized'.[83] After 1763 and until at least the American Revolution, however, the British found themselves in a state of 'collective agoraphobia', unsettled by new territories that were 'at once too vast and too alien'.[84] Seasoning would appear to play the role of medical counterpart in this shift in an imperial sense of self. In the first half of the century, seasoning had served to define regions of potentially dangerous climatic difference. Such certainty would seem to have eroded by the time of Lind's publication of *Hot Climates* in 1768. Now difference was temporally specific and spatially archipelagic. England was no haven, the imperial periphery contained multiple sanctuaries, and one might be a stranger anywhere.

---

[82] Ibid., 146–7.
[83] Colley, *Britons: Forging the Nation, 1707–1837*, 103.
[84] Ibid., 105, 02.

4   Imperial Medicine and the Putrefactive Paradigm, 1720–1800

Introduction

James Lind, younger and less famous cousin to the author of a *Treatise on Scurvy*, with whom he shared a name, spent the first half of the 1760s in service as surgeon on the *Drake* Indiaman. In 1762 he found himself in North-Eastern India. Four years later he visited China and in 1768 he graduated with a medical degree from Edinburgh, with a thesis (translated from the Latin in 1776) on a fever he had observed while in Bengal.[1] Concise and straightforwardly written, with clear invocations of the intellectual resources upon which it was drawing, the dissertation provides a fine exemplar of thinking about the diseases of warm climates in the third quarter of the eighteenth century. The cause of the illness, a 'putrid and remitting marsh fever', was the putrescency of a sufferer's bodily fluids.[2] European seamen arriving at Bengal in the autumn were particularly subject to it. 'They are predisposed to it from the nature of their food, their confinement on board ship, the very great heats they are exposed to during the voyage, and their lying, for hours together, exposed to the night colds'.[3] The heat they endured on their voyage was less than that experienced once they arrived in India, but was still 'too much for a European constitution to bear', for it brought on the body's relaxation and promoted the corruption of its humours. The meat that made up a substantial part of their diet possessed a 'putrescent disposition', which the small amount of wine and spirits allowed them could not sufficiently correct, and the cold night air to which they were exposed when sleeping outdoors checked their perspiration, meaning that the 'excrementitious fluid' produced by the body could not be expelled through the pores.[4]

---

[1] T. C., 'Lind, James, M. D. (1736–1812)', in *Dictionary of National Biography*, ed. Sidney Lee (London: Smith, Elder, and Co., 1893).

[2] James Lind, *A Treatise on the Putrid and Remitting Marsh Fever, Which Raged at Bengal in the Year 1762* (Edinburgh: C. Elliot, 1776).

[3] Ibid., 30.

[4] Ibid., 31–3.

The body in warm climates thus possessed a 'putrid diathesis [tendency]'. In such a state, it was particularly susceptible to the environmental dangers posed by Bengal's swampy and insalubrious terrain. 'This part of the country', Lind wrote with obvious distaste, was 'infected with the putrid parts of dead animals, insects and rotten vegetables. The Ganges, besides, is the common receptacle of all the filth and nastiness of the inhabitants; they never ease nature anywhere else; and are constantly washing themselves and their cloaths in it'. Citing John Pringle, whose *Observations on the Diseases of the Army* had almost instantly become the standard reference for surgeons and physicians throughout Britain's armed forces after its publication in 1752, Lind argued that the 'most powerful' of the remote causes of the fever were 'the effluvia of marshes replete with putrid animal substances'. Rising from swampland and encountering bodies already inclined to internal putrefaction, air containing putrid particles induced a potentially deadly illness, one spread as easily by dead as by living victims. Water from old graves flowed into new ones, infecting grave-diggers and mourners alike. Once the disease was present it could be spread contagiously, although it was far more likely to effect newcomers than natives. Just as one could become habituated to quantities of poison that could kill those unused to the substance, so those who lived in 'countries replete with fenny miasmata' could find the air less dangerous than those newly come to the Calcutta garrison.[5]

Lind's was a fairly straightforward application of medical ideas that had become familiar since mid-century. His critiques were mild, tending to affirm general logics while questioning particulars. Pringle had correctly pointed to the rot of animal substances as the cause of putrid diseases, Lind opined, but his theory lacked specificity. After all, every kind of putrefaction did not have the same effect. Tanners and butchers were not more often afflicted by putrid diseases than others; nor were ship-stewards, 'who spend most of their time amongst the putrid and rancid effluvia' of the places where provisions were kept more at risk than their ship-mates. But such objections did not shake his overall faith. '[W]e are well assured', he claimed, 'by the testimony of Sir John Pringle, and other practical writers, that some putrid fermentations produce noxious vapours, which, united with those marshes, render them pernicious.[6]

Lind's position was orthodox, but it had not been so for long. Both his terminology and his stress on putrefaction as a cause of contagious disease tended to mask the novelty of what had rapidly become a widely accepted medical view. 'Putrid fevers', as a category of illness, dated back to antiquity, although

---

[5] Ibid., 67, 12–13, 33, 38–9.
[6] Ibid., 33–4.

there was considerable flexibility in the meaning of the term.[7] As the older Lind would note in 1768, 'the antients do not seem to have understood by the term putrid, when applied to a fever, that kind of putrefaction which a dead body naturally undergoes'. He suggested that the term derived from Aristotle's dictum 'Omnia quae putrescunt calidiora siunt', because the fever's distinguishing characteristic was a remarkable and disagreeable heat felt on the patient's skin.[8] This is perhaps too minimalist a definition, for it was common to associate putrid fevers with the corruption of humours (rather than, for example, their imbalance).[9] In the middle ages, putrid fevers were categorised according to which of the four humours was affected.[10] Putrefaction was also, as Andrew Wear has demonstrated, 'a crucial component in most accounts of disease' in the early modern period, providing a rare area of agreement among adherents to the old and new philosophies in the seventeenth century.[11] Surgeons, of course, encountered gangrene and sepsis in their daily work, but rot was, more generally, omnipresent in an age before the massive public health programs of the nineteenth and twentieth centuries. As a result, '[t]he corruption and putrefaction of the humours, of parts of the body and of food in the body were especially potent and widespread images of physical disorder and disease'.[12]

And yet, just as with the word putrid, 'putrescency' and 'putrefaction' were rather imprecise terms until the eighteenth century. Putrefaction was largely synonymous with corruption, and corruption could come in many forms.[13] As

---

[7] On the longer history of the term, I have found very useful Christopher Hamlin, 'What Is Putrid About Putrid Fever?', in *History of Science Society Annual Meeting* (Chicago: 2014). 'Putrescence was a vague concept', writes Harrison, 'but its vagueness accounts for its longevity'. Harrison, *Climates & Constitutions: Health, Race, Environment and British Imperialism in India, 1600–1850*, 38.

[8] Lind, *An Essay on Diseases Incidental to Europeans in Hot Climates: With the Method of Preventing Their Fatal Consequences. To Which Is Added, an Appendix Concerning Intermittent Fevers*, 13.

[9] Christopher Hamlin, *More Than Hot: A Short History of Fever* (Baltimore: Johns Hopkins University Press, 2014), 48.

[10] Faith Wallis, 'Medicine, Theoretical', in *Medieval Science, Technology, and Medicine: An Encyclopedia*, ed. Thomas F. Glick, Stephen Livesy, and Faith Wallis (New York: Routledge, 2005), 339.

[11] A. Wear, *Knowledge and Practice in English Medicine, 1550–1680* (Cambridge: Cambridge University Press, 2000), 136. For its use in explaining the fourteenth century plague, see J Arrizabalaga, 'Facing the Black Death: Perceptions and Reactions of University Medical Practitioners', in *Practical Medicine from Salerno to the Black Death*, ed. Luis Garcia-Ballester et al. (Cambridge: Cambridge University Press, 1994).

[12] Wear, 136. On surgeons and putrefaction, see 255.

[13] The most obvious classical reference was Aristotle's work 'On Generation and Corruption', but one finds little discussion of the material nature of corruption there. More specific detail may be found in 'On Meteorology', where putrefaction is delineated as 'the strictest general opposite of true becoming'. Everything, according to Aristotle, can putrefy, except fire: 'for earth, water and air putrefy, being all of them matter relatively to fire. The definition of putrefaction is: the destruction of the peculiar and natural heat in any moist subject by external heat,

Stephen Bradwell noted in a tract on the plague in 1625: 'For noisome vapours arising from filthy sincks, stincking sewers, channels, gutters, privies, sluttish corners, dunghills and uncast ditches; as also the mists and fogs that commonly arise out of fens, moores, mines and standing lakes; doe greatly corrupt the Aire; and in like manner the lying of dead rotten carrions in channels, ditches and dunghills; cause a *contagious* Aire'.[14] Lind's theory, by contrast, limited the cause of his putrid fever to – in his cousin's words – 'that kind of putrefaction which a dead body naturally undergoes'. This narrower understanding, and the suggestion that 'fens, moores, mines, and standing lakes' were dangerous because they contained 'putrid animal substances' was a very recent development, to be traced directly, in many cases, to the arguments laid out in Pringle's hugely important mid-century text on the diseases of the army. In Pringle's work, in fact, one can find the earliest and clearest articulation of what I term the 'putrefactive paradigm', a set of ideas and practices that dominated understandings of the diseases of warm climates for more than three decades.[15] Encompassing a theory of disease, a method of cure and prevention, and an investigative methodology, the paradigm consisted of five elements. The first was nosological: in the new understanding of mid-century, putrid fevers became a much larger and more significant class of illnesses than they had been before. In earlier taxonomies of disease, putrid fevers made up a smaller subclass of a larger grouping, often determined by the periodicity of the affliction's remittance. Thus, in Boerhaave's *Aphorisms,* the putrid fever is a kind of continual fever, with continual fevers differing from other fevers by the fact that they occur 'without any distinct paroxysms or remissions'.[16] In Pringle's hands, however, putrid fevers encompassed a good deal more: all fevers could be divided into two kinds: inflammatory and putrid, which in turn

that is, by the heat of the environment'. Putrefaction was thus an entirely general process, rather than (for example) one specific to living things.

[14] Quoted in Wear, 301.

[15] I use the term here in a rather loose Kuhnian sense. On the one hand, clear continuities to both earlier and later ideas make it clear that there can be no talk of incommensurability or, really, of revolutions. I have, elsewhere, been sceptical of any use of the term 'crisis' except where the word is explicitly used by one's historical actors. On the other hand, it seems clear that many, if not most, writers about the diseases of warm climates from the 1750s to the 1780s shared certain assumptions about cause and cure of fevers and that a good deal of work looked like 'normal science' as Kuhn defined it, involving the extension of the paradigm to encompass new disorders in the field and to discover new antiseptic curatives in the laboratory. Thomas S. Kuhn, 'The Structure of Scientific Revolutions', (Chicago: University of Chicago Press, 1962); Suman Seth, 'Crisis and the Construction of Modern Theoretical Physics', *British Journal for the History of Science* 40, no. 144 (2007). Hamlin also takes Pringle as one of the prime expositors of ideas about putrid diseases. See Hamlin, 114–24.

[16] Herman Boerhaave, *Boerhaave's Aphorisms: Concerning the Knowledge and Cure of Diseases. Translated from the Last Edition Printed in Latin at Leyden, 1715.,* trans. J. Delacoste (London: B. Cowse, and W. Innys, 1725), 168.

corresponded to the characteristic illnesses of the army in barracks and in the field. For John Huxham, whose *Essay on Fevers* appeared in 1750 and was very widely cited thereafter, there were three kinds of fevers, corresponding to different internal bodily conditions. To the two main states of the fluids and solids in illness (either over-elastic and rigid fibres, and very dense, viscid blood or too lax a state of the solids and weak, thin blood), Huxham added a third: 'But, besides these, there is moreover a third State of Blood, *of more dangerous Consequence than either; I mean a State of it, that more immedi-ately tends to Dissolution* and *Putrefaction*'.[17] This description brings us to the second element of the paradigm: putrid diseases were characterised by the putrefaction (or tendency to putrefaction) of the bodily solids or fluids – most commonly blood or bile – that they induced. As noted above, this putres-cence was a literal decay, not merely a corruption of the humours. The body was understood to be rotting (or having a diathesis to rot) from within. Such putrefaction was taken, thirdly, to have two possible causes. Either conditions (such as heat and/or humidity) promoted a spontaneous decay or else external matter (often described as effluvia and associated particularly with marsh- and swampland) made its way into the body and sponsored putrefactive decay. In the latter case, it was assumed that marshes were themselves sites of putre-faction, moist and muddy ground being a promoter of the rot of vegetable and (especially) animal matter. External putrefaction, taken into the body (most likely through the breath) produced internal putrefaction. The nature of the proposed cure for such afflictions, fourthly, re-affirmed the etiological reasoning of the paradigm. Since the cause of the disease was sepsis within the body, the cure should involve antiseptics taken internally. That substances known to retard putrefaction (such as citrus juices) seemed to work so well against putrid afflictions such as scurvy provided indirect but strong confirm-ation of the theory's assumptions. Lind explained the efficacy of the Peruvian bark against the putrid fever of Bengal – and the reason that it did not work against other afflictions – on precisely these grounds, deploying Pringle's two-fold taxonomy as he did so.

The bark, when too hastily administered in the fevers of cold climates, is so far from checking them, that it greatly endangers the life of the patient. This is owing to the inflammatory diathesis which accompanies these fevers. But we may give it sooner in fevers of warm climates; for here there is a putrid diathesis, the reverse of the inflamma-tory, to which the antiseptic virtue of the bark cannot be too soon opposed.[18]

---

[17] Huxham, *An Essay on Fevers, and Their Various Kinds, as Depending on Different Constitutions of the Blood: With Dissertations on Slow Nervous Fevers; on Putrid, Pestilential, Spotted Fevers; on the Small-Pox; and on Pleurisies and Peripneumonies*, 41.
[18] Lind, *A Treatise on the Putrid and Remitting Marsh Fever, Which Raged at Bengal in the Year 1762*, 67–8.

Fifth and finally, evidential support for the paradigm came not only from medical observations and practice, but from experimental analysis in the chemical laboratory. The internal state of the living body was essentially unobservable for the physician. In its place, Pringle made observations on meat and bodily fluids, demonstrating that a variety of substances could function as effective antiseptics and then arguing that such substances could function to the same end within the body. Experimental natural philosophy thus worked in the service of medicine, but it did not do so uncontested. As we shall see, many would find the idea that one might use dead flesh as a model for the workings of the living body a deeply problematic assumption.

This chapter offers a history of the rise and fall of the putrefactive paradigm, extending the analysis offered in the previous three chapters, which have tracked theories concerning the diseases of warm climates from the sixteenth century to the mid-1700s. The main part of the narrative here begins with the publication of John Pringle's *Observations on the Nature and Cure of Hospital and Jayl-Fevers* in 1750 and ends in the late 1790s, after two major texts on the diseases of the West Indies (published by Benjamin Moseley in 1787 and John Hunter in 1788) made it clear that putrefactive theories no longer had the salience they had once possessed. I should make clear from the outset that what is novel about the analysis here is not the observation that putrefaction was central to understandings of the diseases of warm climates around the middle of the eighteenth century. That point was made at least as early as 1837, as H. H. Goodeve offered a Sketch of Medical Progress in the East, which characterised the period under discussion here as one in which 'the fear of putrescency preserved its full sway', with the bark prescribed as an antiseptic to check the body's 'putrid tendency'.[19] In recent scholarship, Mark Harrison has been responsible for detailing the fundamentality of Pringle's putrefactive theory to medicine in the British Empire and particularly in the colonies.[20] 'Putrefaction', Harrison notes, 'loomed large in works issuing from the pens of most East India Company surgeons', and he has tracked the changes in medical therapeutics that accompanied the rise of putrefactive theories, as bleeding declined in favour of the administration of the antiseptic Bark.[21] Although he uses the term more loosely than do I, it is from Harrison that I draw the term the 'putrefactive paradigm'.

---

[19] H. H. Goodeve, 'Sketch of Medical Progress in the East', *The Quarterly Journal of the Calcutta Medical and Physical Society* (1837): 128.

[20] Harrison, *Medicine in an Age of Commerce and Empire: Britain and its Tropical Colonies, 1660–1830*, 64–88.

[21] Ibid., 69. 'The rapid and almost complete abandonment of bloodletting in the East Indies reflected the dominance of putrefactive notions of illness, and in particular, of the bilious theory of fevers', ibid., 127.

What this chapter offers is an intellectual history of the putrefactive paradigm, one that allows a specification of precisely what was novel about it. To understand what distinguished Pringle's ideas from earlier conceptions of putrid diseases or miasmatic theories requires detailing, as I do in Section 4.2, the roots of these ideas. Pringle's debts to his teacher, the famed Leiden professor Herman Boerhaave whom he referred to as his 'master', have long been acknowledged, if rarely spelled out. Just as important, however, were the writings of his effective patron, the physician Richard Mead. As we shall see, despite the fact that Mead has been overshadowed by other eighteenth-century figures, his works on poison and the plague would provide an essential resource for articulating the putrefactive paradigm. In Section 4.3 I explicate Pringle's own arguments before turning, in Section 4.4, to the application of these and similar (if not identical) claims by Huxham and the older Lind to work on scurvy and the diseases of warm climates. Section 4.5 then turns to the critiques of the paradigm that one begins to find in the early 1770s. These would grow across the decade, as former proponents turned against putrefactive theories and, somewhat ironically, as the kinds of laboratory experiments suggested by the paradigm's logics seemed to undercut its claims. The end result would be the rejection of the paradigm's theoretical claims but the retention of many of its practices.

Before turning to a discussion of the roots and fruits of Pringle's ideas, however, one further point should be made. While it is true that putrefactive theories characterised discussions of the diseases of warm climates after mid-century, it is also true that such discussions were not limited to the colonies. Pringle was almost certainly the most important figure in British medicine generally in the two decades after 1750, providing the bridge between the earlier period dominated by Boerhaave's teachings and a later one similarly dominated by William Cullen's. With this in mind, we might re-evaluate the significance and meaning of the characterisation of this period by Charles Creighton in his classic *History of Epidemics in Britain*. For Creighton, the middle third of the eighteenth century could be described, in Sydenhamian terms, as possessing a 'putrid constitution', coinciding 'within the great outburst of putrid or gangrenous sore-throat ... and it included an extensive prevalence of fevers which were also called putrid or nervous, and sometimes called miliary'.[22] In that period, medical authors in multiple locations – including Rouen, London, Worcestershire, Ireland, and Barbados – described their attempts to grapple with putrid disorders. For Creighton, the cause of such 'putridity-talk' was the rise and spread of a new disease. 'It was certainly not a mere fashion in medicine',

[22] Charles Creighton, *A History of Epidemics in Britain, vol. II. From the Extinction of Plague to the Present Time* (Cambridge: Cambridge University Press, 1894), 120.

he wrote, 'which produced these accounts of a similar fever, for these accounts came from places far apart and were independent of one another'.[23] Even if one accepts the realist logic of such an argument, however, there is no reason to assume that multiple observers were compelled to regard the new affliction as specifically putrid. The disease's *label* might surely be considered a matter of 'fashion' and in accounting for its spread it does not seem unreasonable to point both to Pringle's work and to an inversion of the kinds of spatial logics that have long been assumed to govern the dispersal of scientific and medical ideas. It seems necessary to distinguish between those metropolitan writers concerned with what Fothergill in 1748 termed a 'sore throat attended with ulcers' and what Huxham, almost a decade later called a 'malignant, ulcerous sore throat' and those more broadly concerned with putrid diseases. Most of these latter cited Pringle and Lind quite explicitly, several of them drawing on their experiences in warm climates while doing so. Some, like Pringle himself, sought to study putrid diseases (as he understood them) while acknowledging that they were fairly uncommon afflictions at home. What was quotidian in many of Britain's colonies was seen by many as unusual in Britain itself (at least outside heterotopic spaces like army camps, prisons, and hospitals).[24] One might thus explain part of the spread of putrid theories of disease in Britain as an example of the military-imperial tail wagging the metropolitan dog and a case of the incorporation of empire within a previously more geographically limited orthodox medicine. If the last chapter was concerned with medical articulations of imperial imaginaries, then, this chapter describes the rise of imperial articulations of medical logics, a rise that pre-dated Pringle's work. To provide a background for this aspect of the putrefactive paradigm, then, we turn first to a discussion of the ways in which warm climates were entering the medicine of the British Isles in the early 1700s.

4.1   Tropical Climates in Metropolitan Medicine

By the 1720s and 1730s, the periphery had begun to make its mark on metropolitan medicine. Medicinal products had already profoundly shaped medical practice before then, of course, with tea, coffee, cinchona, and many other substances native to warmer climates being added to traditional *materia medica* in the sixteenth and seventeenth centuries. From the eighteenth century, however, one finds mention not only of products *from* warm climates, but also of bodies *in* warm climates. Medical meteorological reflections seemed to

---

[23] Ibid., 121–2.
[24] Michel Foucault, 'Of Other Spaces: Utopias and Heterotopias', *Architecture/Mouvement/ Continuité*, no. October (1984).

lead writers almost unerringly to considerations of the climates and illnesses of foreign locations. Arguing that physicians should pay attention to seasonality, Huxham made the case by assuming that his readers would agree that attention to geographical differences mattered: 'What Celsus says of Difference of Places is equally true of Difference of Seasons'.[25] John Arbuthnot's *Essay Concerning the Effects of Air on Human Bodies* (1733) abounded with references to countries between the tropics, helping to make the general case that 'The Effects of Air on Human Bodies are as various as the Diversity of the Weather, Climates, and Countries'.[26] Thus, we are informed that barometers registered less variation in the Tropics, 'The Cold in the Parallel of *London* is much greater in the *West-Indies*', there are hot African winds that can kill elephants, and mountains in Ceylon where one might find snow.[27]

The point may seem obvious: were one interested in the effect of the aerial environment on distempers it would seem to make sense to compare spatially – and hence climatically – distinct areas. Yet, however obvious it might appear, this was not the approach taken fifty or sixty years earlier, when Britain's empire was less developed and had intruded less into the medical imagination. Sydenham's comparisons of epidemic constitutions in the 1660s, for example, were temporal, not spatial. Diseases had a yearly rhythm, corresponding to the seasons, but seasons in different years might lead to different diseases. There is, in fact, something surely telling about the structure of Huxham's argument in his *Observations on the Air and Epidemical Diseases*. Rather than letting the authority of Sydenham (or, indeed, of Hippocrates in his *Epidemics*) make the case for seasonal analyses, Huxham instead relied on classical arguments which proved the importance of geographic difference, and then analogised climates to seasons.[28] Asserting the need for a flexibility of practice, for example, Huxham suggested that 'the Physicians of different Countries abundantly testify by using different Methods, all which however very happily succeed. Is it not necessary therefore to have due Regard to the different Constitutions of the Atmosphere even in the same Country?'[29] Sydenham appeared to assume a readership interested in the diseases of London. Huxham assumed that his audience would accept claims about practice in Britain derived from evidence gleaned around the world. A global sensibility was to inform even the most local treatment.

[25] Huxham, *The Works of John Huxham, M. D. F. R. S. In Two Volumes*, I, xxvii.
[26] Arbuthnot, 119.
[27] Ibid., 75, 77, 81, 84.
[28] Not all Huxham's evidence, however, was derived from familiar classical sources. He cited both Boerhaave and the naturalist Joseph d'Acosta, for instance, for their views on the appropriate temperature for respirable air. Huxham, *The Works of John Huxham, M. D. F. R. S. In Two Volumes*, I, v, ix.
[29] Ibid., xxvii.

Huxham was hardly alone in this new global medical sensibility. Indeed, as a Fellow of the Royal Society, he was in good company.[30] The Reverend Stephen Hales, for example, was elected a Fellow in 1718 and was cited by all those working on the effects of airs on health. Of particular interest to many was how improving air might benefit the lives of those expanding Britain's trading empire and colonial holdings. Noxious effluvia were particularly dangerous in confined spaces such as that found on ships. Hence Hales' efforts to invent a ventilating system that could pump unhealthy air out of a ship's hold.[31] Preserving the lives of the sailors who made up 'by far the most numerous and Powerful Fleet in the World' also led Hales to a series of 'philosophical experiments' intended for those undertaking long sea voyages.[32] The question of how to preserve drinking water fresh had bedevilled fleets throughout Europe, as had the problem of producing sweet water from salt. Past failures, however, were not reason enough for Hales to give up the task, for the issue was now more pressing than ever. The numbers of those who plied their trade on the oceans, he wrote, 'have within little more than a Century, greatly increased, by a more enlarged Commerce through the World; so are they like to increase more and more in future Generations; and That especially on the vast *Atlantick Ocean*, in proportion as the *European* Colonies in *America*, may more and more increase in number of Inhabitants'.[33] Herman Boerhaave weighed in on the question of how to improve drinking water for sailors and those in warm climates in his *Elements of Chemistry*, a text one would not necessarily assume had a good deal to do with the torrid zone. He suggested that water that had grown putrid could be rendered wholesome by boiling it and then adding an

---

[30] On the Royal Society as part of 'a nascent British imperial complex' see Mark Govier, 'The Royal Society, Slavery, and the Island of Jamaica, 1660–1700', *Notes and Records of the Royal Society of London* 53 (1999).

[31] Stephen Hales, *A Description of Ventilators: Whereby Great Quantities of Fresh Air May with Ease Be Conveyed into Mines, Goals, Hospitals, Work-Houses and Ships, in Exchange for Their Noxious Air. An Account Also of Their Great Usefulness in Many Other Respects: As in Preserving All Sorts of Grain Dry, Sweet, and Free from Being Destroyed by Weevels, Both in Grainaries and Ships: And in Preserving Many Other Sorts of Goods. As Also in Drying Corn, Malt, Hops, Gun-Powder, &C. And for Many Other Useful Purposes* (London: W. Innys and R. Manby; T. Woodward, 1743).

[32] *Philosophical Experiments Containing Useful, and Necessary Instructions for Such as Undertake Long Voyages at Sea. Shewing How Sea-Water May Be Made Fresh and Wholsome: And How Fresh-Water May Be Preserv'd Sweet* (London: W. Innys and R. Manby; T Woodward, 1739), ii.

[33] Stephen Hales, *Philosophical Experiments: Containing Useful, and Necessary Instructions for Such As Undertake Long Voyages at Sea: Shewing How Sea-Water May Be Made Fresh and Wholsome: and How Fresh Water May Be Preserv'd Sweet. How Biscuit, Corn, &c. May Be Secured from the Weevel, Meggots, and Other Insects. and Flesh Preserv'd in Hot Climates, by Salting Animals Whole. to Which Is Added, an Account of Several Experiments and Observations on Chalybeate or Steel-Waters ... Which Were Read Before the Royal-Society, at Several of Their Meetings* (London: W. Innys and R. Manby [etc.], 1739), 3

acid. 'This is found to be of excellent service under the Equator, and between the Tropics', he noted.[34] Also of excellent service 'both to the *English* and *Dutch*' were jellies made from fruits, which would counteract the diseases suffered by sailors on long journeys, forced to subsist on salted, dried, and smoked provisions.[35]

Increasing commerce led to more cases of disease at sea, but it also brought diseases home. Contagion followed trade routes. Historians are familiar with the involvement of leading Fellows in the battle against contagious disease in the 1720s.[36] The plague appeared across the Channel in 1719, leading to the passage of the Quarantine Act in 1721, designed with the aid of Arbuthnot, Sloane, and Mead. In his *Short Discourse Concerning Pestilential Contagion*, Mead laid the blame for the spread of infectious diseases firmly at the feet of commercial interests. The plague, he claimed, was not indigenous to England, but was 'an *African* Fever, bred in *Aethiopia* or *Aegypt*, and the *Infection* of it carried by Trade into the other Parts of the World'.[37] Severe smallpox epidemics had swept England in 1710, 1714, 1719, and 1721, 1722, and 1723. Jurin produced tables comparing mortality rates with and without inoculation while Sloane advised King George I on a proposed experiment on six condemned prisoners at Newgate before turning to the inoculation of two of the Princess of Wales' children. This was Society medicine in the service of the state and the state extended far beyond the British Isles. According to Larry Stewart, Sloane's interest in smallpox 'was part of a general interest in contagion and especially the relationship between the British trade routes and epidemiology. This interest grew out of a network of communication which Sloane assiduously cultivated through his influence with the South Sea Company and the African Company in particular'.[38] Sloane substantially added to his natural historical collections through his correspondences with agents working for the South Sea Company in the Caribbean.[39] Meanwhile, the Duke of Chandos, elected a Fellow in 1694, played a prominent role in the affairs of the Royal African Company, seeking to leverage his connections with the Royal Society (Sloane among them) to improve the company's financial prospects as profits from the slave trade faltered.[40] Chandos and other members of the Company's

---

[34] Hermann Boerhaave, *Elements of Chemistry: Being the Annual Lectures of Herman Boerhaave, M. D.*, trans. Timothy Dallowe, 2 vols., vol. I (London: J. and J. Pemberton, 1735), 348.

[35] Ibid., II: 18.

[36] Larry Stewart, 'The Edge of Utility: Slaves and Smallpox in the Early Eighteenth Century', *Medical History* 29 (1985).

[37] Mead, *A Short Discourse Concerning Pestilential Contagion and the Methods to Be Used to Prevent It*, 20–21.

[38] Stewart, 60.

[39] On Sloane, see Malcolmson., Delbourgo, 'Slavery in the Cabinet of Curiosities: Hans Sloane's Atlantic World'; *Collecting the World: Hans Sloane and the Origins of the British Museum*.

[40] On the Royal Society's direct financial involvement in the African slave trade, see Govier.

Court of Assistants saw smallpox as one of the reasons for their financial woes. Inoculation, they suggested 'would be of great Advantage to Us, could it be put into practice by saving the Lives of great Numbers of Slaves, among whom the Small Pox is very fatall, especially, when it seizes them on their Voyage'.[41] Where smallpox and other epidemic diseases, then, were often a matter of local importance for metropolitan practitioners in the last third of the seventeenth century, they were increasingly a matter of global significance for their successors in the first third of the eighteenth.

4.2 Towards a New Putrescent Medicine

Boerhaave: Fahrenheit's Dog and the Power of Heat

We have already seen that Boerhaave had an interest in the health of sailors and those living and serving outside Europe. His work would also provide a key resource in articulating a new paradigm for understanding the diseases of warm climates. In the context of a detailed survey of theories of fever, Christopher Hamlin has identified three ways in which 'Boerhaave foreshadowed distinct approaches that would dominate the understanding of fever in the centuries to come'.[42] He focused on the nerves and the nervous system as 'the ulterior locus of explanation'; he recognised toxins as remote causes of illness, even where the precise nature or action of the toxin remained unknown; and he was profoundly interested in the body's temperature and the relationship of this to the environment, drawing regularly on the insights of his friend, Daniel Fahrenheit.[43] One might add a fourth element, which often connected the other three: an interest in putrefaction as a cause of particularly dangerous illnesses and – methodologically – the experimental study of putrefaction as a means of understanding disease.

This last element came to the fore in Boerhaave's published work after 1718, when he took up a chair in chemistry at Leiden (adding to his chairs in botany and medicine).[44] He had offered private lectures on chemistry since

---

[41] Quoted in Stewart, 65.

[42] The language of foreshadowing is useful here. If Boerhaave was not the sole inventor of such approaches (and he was not), he nonetheless synthesised and packaged them for his near-innumerable students. Hamlin, 83–6, quote on 83.

[43] Ibid., 83. 'Of what infinite use therefore are *Fahrenheit's* mercurial thermometers?' he would write: 'How certainly do they point out to us the danger that arises from the Heat in acute Diseases?' Boerhaave, *Elements of Chemistry: Being the Annual Lectures of Herman Boerhaave, M. D.*, II, 245.

[44] On the centrality of chemistry to Boerhaave's medical theory across his career, however, see John C. Powers, *Inventing Chemistry: Herman Boerhaave and the Reform of the Chemical Arts* (Chicago: University of Chicago Press, 2012).

1702, drawing a large paying audience. With the chair came public lectures and access to the university laboratory. An unauthorised edition of the lectures appeared in 1724, spurring Boerhaave to produce an official version, *The Elements of Chemistry*, which was published in two volumes in Latin in 1731 and in English translation in 1735.[45] The first volume examined the theory of chemistry, the second described a series of detailed experiments.[46] Putrefaction was a theme throughout. Boerhaave worked to carefully distinguish putrefaction from fermentation, a distinction that was crucial for his medical analyses. Many of those who had previously combined chemistry and medicine, he claimed, had assumed that fermentative processes governed the body in sickness and health. For example, Jean Baptiste van Helmont (the particular focus of Boerhaave's critique) had explained digestion by suggesting that a series of specific ferments worked with stomach acid to break down and transform food into the nourishment the body required.[47] Van Helmont and his many followers also assumed that the body's humours fermented in illness.[48] On the basis of his experiments, Boerhaave was willing to declare that one could now remove from medicine 'those idle notions of Ferments … introduc'd into it by some Dablers in Chemistry'.[49] At multiple points throughout the body, Boerhaave replaced fermentation with putrefaction.[50]

Boerhaave's logic was chemical. The results of fermentation were acidic, those of putrefaction were alkaline, and Boerhaave's experiments appeared to show that the humours did not tend towards acidity.[51] His object of analysis was urine, which he used as a marker of the body's internal state. Urine, he

---

[45] G. A. Lindeboom, *Herman Boerhaave: The Man and His Work* (London: Methuen, 1968), 109–207.

[46] Boerhaave, *Elements of Chemistry: Being the Annual Lectures of Herman Boerhaave, M. D.*, I; ibid., II.

[47] Boerhaave singled van Helmont out by name. *Elements of Chemistry: Being the Annual Lectures of Herman Boerhaave, M. D.*, II, 115. Other Iatrochemists were also roundly mocked, particularly for Sylvius' acid-alkali theory, in 'Discourse on Chemistry Purging Itself of Its Own Errors', in *Boerhaave's Orations: Translated with Introductions and Notes by E. Kegel-Brinkgreve and A. M. Luyendijk-Elshout*, ed. E. Kegel-Brinkgreve and A. M. Luyendijk-Elshout (Leiden: Brill, 1983). On van Helmont's theory of digestions, see, briefly, Allen G. Debus, *The Chemical Philosophy* (Mineola, NY: Dover, 2002), 368–71. In more detail, see Walter Pagel, 'Van Helmont's Ideas on Gastric Digestion and the Gastric Acid', *Bulletin of the History of Medicine* 30 (1956).

[48] On van Helmont's theory of disease, see 'Van Helmont's Concept of Disease – to Be or Not to Be? The Influence of Paracelsus', *Bulletin of the History of Medicine* XLVI, no. 5 (1972). Van Helmont used the term 'ferment' very generally, deploying it to describe any vital agent that facilitated the transformation of one chemical substance to another. Powers, 85.

[49] Boerhaave, *Elements of Chemistry: Being the Annual Lectures of Herman Boerhaave, M. D.*, II, 132.

[50] Thus, for example, on digestion: 'Of all Operations therfore, both artificial, and natural, Putrefaction best explains the first Action of the Mouth, Stomach, and Intestines', ibid., 202.

[51] For a clear statement of the difference between fermentation and putrefaction, see ibid., 116.

claimed, 'exhibits to us those Humours, that of all are by far the most changed by the powers of our Nature, and indeed too much to be of any farther advantage to the Body'.[52] In a healthy body the humours were neutral – neither acid nor alkaline – a fact that could be determined by noting that healthy, fresh urine was also neutral, regardless of diet. If one allowed urine to sit somewhere warm, however, it rapidly putrefied and became more alcalescent, and from this observation Boerhaave drew conclusions about the body in sickness. For urine contained 'those Salts and Oils which are the nearest to a state of Putrefaction', discharged from the body before injury could result. If diseases caused such 'putrid particles' to be retained, on the other hand, the results could be fatal.[53]

Even the healthy body, then, was constantly *inclined* towards putrefaction. At temperatures lower than that of the living body, after all, humours and dead flesh corrupted very quickly. What prevented the entire frame from being 'dissolved by Putrefaction' (as would certainly otherwise happen in a burning fever) was air, food, drink, and medicine, which could work to resist, retard, and reverse putridity. Those in most danger were those whose bodies were warmest. 'How necessary, therefore, are Water, Acids, acescent Substances, and Saline ones, to those Persons who live in hot Climates, or are daily exercised with hard Labour?'[54] In Boerhaave's hands, the processes most commonly at work in the human body were to be analogised not to those of the kitchen – in the making, for example, of beer or bread – but to those of the charnel house.

One suspects that one of the appeals of an explanation involving putrefaction rather than fermentation, for Boerhaave, was its simplicity and universality. Fermentation often required specific ferments, which were multiplied in complex processes. Putrefaction, however, required only heat and moisture, and all animal and vegetable substances could be made to rot. In terms of etiological understandings of disease, putrefaction also allowed a movement from individual afflictions to those spread through contagion. In Volume I, Boerhaave described an experiment carried out on his behalf by his 'friend and kinsman' Jodocus Provost and 'that industrious Gentleman Mr. Fahrenheit'. Having noticed that the air in rooms where sugar was dried was hot to the point of near-suffocation, Boerhaave asked his colleagues to test the effect of such high heats on an animal.[55] '[T]here is scarce any Experiment to be met with',

---

[52] Ibid., 215.

[53] 'As Urine now acquires these new qualities so easily, so soon, in a moderate degree of Heat, and in a close Vessel, hence we learn, that the human Nature does not generate Vinegars ... and consequently does not act by Fermentation, but causes the same alterations that Putrefaction does, and therefore in its effects, comes nearest to that'. Ibid., 224.

[54] Ibid., 225, 24.

[55] The letter in which Fahrenheit described his results to Boerhaave was undated. In an earlier letter, dated 12 December 1718, Fahrenheit alluded to the request, but noted that 'the people there are unwilling to have such an experiment done in their building, although I still propose

Boerhaave declared, 'that will help us better to understand the effects of this heat of Air upon the Bodies, Humours, and parts of Animals. Nor perhaps, is there any other, that is of greater service in the Art of Chemistry'.[56] The room, it was determined, was heated to 146 degrees. A Sparrow introduced into it perished, struggling and panting, after seven minutes; the cat lasted longer and died drenched in sweat. The most striking result, however, came from observations made as the dog expired. It, too, struggled and panted, but it also salivated continuously, exuding a liquid 'which was perfectly reddish, and stank so intolerably, that no body present was able to bear it'.[57] So noxious was the smell that one of the experimenters fainted and had to be revived. For Boerhaave, the conclusion was straightforward: heat so extreme (almost 50 degrees higher than that measured in the mouth of a child in health) could produce a fatal disease in an instant.

But how surprizingly, must all of the humours of the Body here be changed, as they gave such evident signs of a most fetid putrefaction? Certainly there is not in nature a more abominable stench than this terrible rancid one, more loathsome than that of a dead carcase, which was so soon produced, and exhaled from this Animal which was perfectly well just before?[58]

One should note the stress placed on the putrefaction of the *humours*. Heat had effected an internal alteration: Boerhaave noted that the flesh of the dead animal hung in the stove did not putrefy, but merely dried out. That the body's juices had changed utterly could be seen from the change in the colour and smell of the dog's saliva. And the smell that emanated from the poor canine's frame – another sign of putrefaction within – was dangerous to all around. Heat had induced a state deadly to the dog, but the product of that heat on a living animal was now capable of harming others: that 'abominable stench ... purely by its contagious quality, brought a strong man ... into imminent danger of present death'.[59] John Arbuthnot was only among the very many that would cite this experiment, but his summary of its significance was pithy: 'it is possible for pestilential Distempers to begin from excessive Heats'.[60] In

---

to try it at some time with a small bird'. Peter Van der Star, ed. *Fahrenheit's Letters to Leibniz and Boerhaave* (Leiden: Rodopi, 1983), 73, 181–3.

[56] Boerhaave, *Elements of Chemistry: Being the Annual Lectures of Herman Boerhaave, M. D.*, I, 163.

[57] Ibid.

[58] Ibid., 164.

[59] Ibid.

[60] The entire set of remarks is worth quoting: 'in A Sugar-Baker's Drying Room, where the Air was heated 146, or 54 beyond that of a Human Body, a Sparrow died in two Minutes, a Dog in 28 Minutes; but the most remarkable thing of all was that the Dog voided a red *Saliva*, foetid and putrid. We owe this luciferous experiment to the industrious *Boerhaave*, from which many important Inferences may be drawn; for why may not this putrid *Saliva* of

warm climates, then, one had to be concerned not only about the effect of high ambient temperatures on an individual body, but on the contagion that might spread to many once it was produced.

Mead: Poisons and Putrefaction

That putrefaction could cause pestilence was, of course, hardly a new claim.[61] One might regard Boerhaave's experiment as proving an assumption that had been made since at least the classical age.[62] There was, however, a particular timeliness to his observations, for the connection between putrefaction and pestilence had very recently been re-emphasised, in the work of Richard Mead, one of Boerhaave's oldest friends.[63] Mead, as we have seen, was interested in explaining the origin and cause of the plague that had recently struck Marseille and threatened England. The disease arose in Africa, where 'animal putrefaction' in the warm, humid climate conspired with some 'ill state of the air', peculiar to that part of the world. In northern climates, where one found the first element, but not the second, distempers also arose, which could prove very fatal, but they did not rise to the level of the true plague. 'For such fevers are often bred', he observed, 'where a large Number of People are closely confined together; as in *Gaols, Sieges*, and *Camps*'.[64] In the work by Boerhaave that Pringle borrowed from most explicitly, putrescence *inside* the body could produce contagious disease; in the key works by Mead, putrescence *outside* the body produced potentially fatal contagion.

Mead's explanation of the origin and spread of the plague drew heavily on his earlier work, particularly a series of essays on poisons, first published

the Dog be infectious? Consequently, it is possible for pestilential Distempers to begin from excessive Heats; no Human Creature can live long in an Air hotter than their own Bodies'. Arbuthnot, 49–50. For other citations to the experiment, see, for example, ibid., 159. John Huxham, *Observations on the Air and Epidemical Diseases, Made at Plymouth from the Year MDCCXXVIII [1728] to the End of the Year MDCCXXXVII [1737], to Which Is Added a Short Treatise on the Devonshire Colic*, 2 vols., vol. I (London: J. Coote; J. Staples, 1758), v. de Monchy, 66.

[61] On putrefaction and early modern medicine, see Wear. See the two chapters on plague (275–349) in particular.

[62] Boerhaave noted the antiquity of the connection himself. 'Physicians long ago asserted, that the plague itself is generated among animals, from an Air that has been both very moist and warm, for a considerable time'. Boerhaave, *Elements of Chemistry: Being the Annual Lectures of Herman Boerhaave, M. D.*, I, 282.

[63] Mead and Boerhaave lived together while attending Leiden University. Their friendship lasted through their lives. In 1731, Boerhaave sent three copies of his *Elementa Chemiae* to England: two for Hans Sloane, one for Mead. Lindeboom, *Herman Boerhaave: The Man and His Work*, 182. For details on Mead's life, see Arnold Zuckerman, 'Dr. Richard Mead (1673–1754): A Biographical Study', PhD Thesis (Urbana-Champaign: University of Illinois, 1965).

[64] Mead, *A Short Discourse Concerning Pestilential Contagion and the Methods to Be Used to Prevent It*, 33–4.

in 1702.[65] Explaining how the tiny amount of venom injected into the body by a viper or tarantula could kill so swiftly was no easy task. Mead's theory, like Boerhaave's, was chemical and mechanical. The 'fiery drop' communicated via the spider's bite, like that of other poisonous animals, 'put the nervous liquor into a ferment'. We might say that venom acted as a catalyst, inducing fermentation or effervescence in the fluids that flowed through the nerves. In other cases, such as the poison communicated by the bite of a mad dog, this effervescence allowed the disease to be passed from one animal to another, less like a catalyst and more strictly like the kinds of fermentation commonly found in the kitchen.

Now as we every day observe, that what is thrown out from liquors in a ferment, is capable of inducing the like motion in another liquor of the same kind, when duly mixed with it; so we may very well suppose in the present case, that the saliva, which is itself one of the most fermentative juices in nature ... when it comes by means of a wound to be mixed with the nervous liquor in another animal, must necessarily put it into violent agitations, in the nature of a ferment.[66]

Poison, in other words, could be contagious: fermentation inducing fermentation. But what of its original cause? In animals, one might simply assume that venom was produced as part of their nature. But what of poisons that were not characteristic of all of the same kind of animal; poisons, for example, that were incidental to its nature (such as that of the mad dog) or those communicated via the air, rather than animal to animal? After all, the air itself could be dangerous. That found in caves or grottos might be deadly for those who breathed it too long. Other 'venomous exhalations' might produce contagious afflictions, such as those produced from bodies putrefying on a battlefield.

All Authors do agree, one great Cause of Pestilential Distempers, especially in Armies and Camps, to be dead Bodies, lying exposed and rotting in the open Air: the Reason of which is plain from what we have been advancing; for Battles being generally fought in the Summer Time, it is no wonder if the Heat acting upon the unbury'd *Carcasses* and *Fermenting* the Juices, draws forth those above Particles, which in great quantities filling the Atmosphere, when they are inspired and let into the Stomach, do affect It after the manner already described.[67]

One can see here almost precisely the logic behind Mead's theory of the plague, which laid the blame at the feet of putrefactive animal material, breathed in by those who found their humours corrupting in ways both contagious and (often) fatal. One difference existed, however, and it was important.

[65] *A Mechanical Account of Poisons: In Several Essays* (London: Printed by J.R. for Ralph South, 1702).

[66] Ibid., 81.

[67] Ibid., 164.

The plague was no ordinary pestilential distemper and Mead insisted that only Africa could be considered its home, however easily the disease might be passed from person to person in other climates. As a result, he made a distinction between the first production of the poison and the means of the communication of the disease to which it gave rise. 'It must indeed be owned', he wrote, 'that some malignant fevers are contagious, and that contagion is a real Poison: but the original Cause of a disease and the Communication of it, are very different things. Of this I have largely discoursed on another occasion'.[68] That other occasion was, of course, his essay on the plague, which was divided into two sections that described, in turn, the origin and then the spread of the disease. To be honest, however, Mead was rather vague on the mechanism by which the plague's first cause was produced.

All that we know, is this, that the Cause of the *Plague*, whatever it be, is of such a Nature, that when taken into the Body, it works such Changes in the Blood and Juices, as to produce this Disease, by suddenly giving some Parts of the Humours such corrosive Qualities, that they excite *Inflammations* and *Gangrenes*, wherever they fall. But we are acquainted too little with the Laws, by which the small Parts of Matter act upon each other, to be able precisely to determine the Qualities requisite to change animal Juices into such acrimonious Humours, or to explain how all the distinguishing Symptoms attending this Disease are produced.[69]

Once produced, the disease spread from person to person by familiar mechanisms. In a later edition of the collected essays on poisons, Mead explicitly drew a comparison between the means of passing along the poison in a dog bite and that in a malignant fever like the plague. Putrefaction produced a poison, which induced a fermentation in the blood, which allowed the communication of the disease through the transfer of ferments from person to person. But putrefaction without did not breed putrefaction within. For that step, one required Pringle and the notion of a 'putrid ferment'.

4.3   John Pringle: The Putrefactive Turn

Given his training, Pringle was perfectly poised to bring Boerhaave's and Mead's logics together. Born in 1707, Pringle began his medical studies at Edinburgh at age 20.[70] After only a year he moved to Holland and in 1730 he

---

[68] In the 1702 edition of his essay on poisons, he had briefly flagged this distinction, noting a 'Difference of Contagion from the first Invasion of Malignant Distempers; the Effects of the *One* are the Cause and Beginning of the *Other*'. 'A Mechanical Account of Poisons: In Several Essays (4th Ed.)', in *The Medical Works of Richard Mead* (Dublin: Thomas Ewing, 1767), 106.

[69] Mead, *A Short Discourse Concerning Pestilential Contagion and the Methods to Be Used to Prevent It.*, 37–8.

[70] The biographical material below is derived from Dorothea Singer, 'Sir John Pringle and His Circle. Part I. Life', *Annals of Science* 6, no. 2 (1949).

completed his dissertation, on senile decay, under Boerhaave in Leiden. In 1734 he was appointed to the faculty at the University of Edinburgh, as Professor of Pneumatics and Moral Philosophy and also received his license to practice from the Royal College.[71] He became a Fellow of the College the following year. In 1742 he published a long essay on a specific remedy for dysentery and the same year became physician to the Earl of Stair, then commanding the British Army fighting against the French in Flanders. In 1745 the Duke of Cumberland promoted him to Physician General and physician to the Royal Hospitals in the low countries and overseas. It was that year that he became a Fellow of the Royal Society (his name likely first put forward by Mead). In 1749 he was appointed physician to the Duke of Cumberland. His most famous publication, *Observations on the Diseases of the Army in Camp and in Garrison,* appeared in 1752, following upon a short work on hospital and jail fevers (1750) and a series of papers which also appeared in 1750, on 'Septic and Antiseptic Substances', for which Pringle was awarded the Copley medal.

All of these last three works were connected. Pringle argued (following Mead) that external putrefaction led to internal putrefaction and (following Boerhaave) that one might cure putrid diseases by the internal application of substances that resisted sepsis. In doing so, he would need to make literal a connection that had been less direct in the past. Pringle first addressed the relationship between putrescence and disease in an epistolary essay, addressed to Mead, on hospital and jail fevers. The latter had broken out 'in such a manner as to alarm the town' as Pringle was revising the notes he had gathered for his work on the diseases of the army.[72] Both distempers were essentially the same, Pringle argued, brought about in situations where men were crowded together in poorly ventilated, dirty spaces, 'or what is the same, wherever there is a collection of putrid animal steams, from dead or even diseased bodies'.[73] Jails were filthy; hospitals filled with the 'effluvia' of wounds and excrement. The distemper also found a home on ships, where men had little space and breathed in the air that rose from bilge water, and in the less salubrious areas of cities. Addressing Mead directly, Pringle summarised:

In general, whenever in the less airy and cleanly parts of large and populous cities, a slow and low fever prevails ... we may conclude it belongs to this class of diseases; whereof the first and most exquisite, is the true plague, which YOU have shewn to arise from a high degree of putrefaction of animal substances in a sultry climate.[74]

---

[71] Pneumatics, or pneumatology, was the study of spirits or spiritual beings. One might thus best regard the position, as Singer notes, as a joint professorship in religion and moral philosophy.

[72] John Pringle, *Observations on the Nature and Cure of Hospital and Jayl-Fevers, in a Letter to Doctor Mead, Physician to His Majesty, &C.* (London: A. Millar and D. Wilson, 1750), 1.

[73] Ibid., 8.

[74] Ibid., 9–10.

Dissections gave a sense of the changes the fever wrought in the body. The putrefactive cause had a putrefactive effect. In life, the body gave off 'putrid sweats' and smelled offensive; in death one could observe the mortification of a part of the body or the production of an abscess in the brain. This 'tendency to putrefaction', Pringle declared, allowed the physician to reduce this disease to a class of other afflictions, which included the malignant smallpox, certain hectic fevers and 'the ardent and bilious fevers of moist and hot countries'. All were caused by putridity, either external or internal to the body. That the body was rendered rotten as a result could be determined from the cures for the affliction. The successful remedies were all, Pringle noted (in one of the earliest uses of the term) 'of the anti-septic kind'.[75]

These arguments were substantially elaborated upon in Pringle's most famous work, *Observations on the Diseases of the Army*, based on material he had gathered between 1742 and 1748, serving the British armed forces in Flanders in the War of the Austrian Succession.[76] The main text was divided into three parts, the first two intended for both officers and physicians, the last more technical and intended for the latter alone. An appendix then reproduced the papers that had gained Pringle the Copley medal, his experiments making clear the range of substances that could be used to retard putrefaction in meat and vegetable matter and hence the substances that could be taken internally to halt and even reverse the putrefactive tendency of the body's humours in illness. Part one supplied a medical meteorological journal of the years spent with the troops in Germany, Flanders, Britain, and Dutch Brabant. Absorbing a lesson from the Italian, Giovanni Lancisi, who had described the illnesses due to the stagnant and filthy waters around Rome in 1717, Pringle declared Zealand to possess the worst air, since it was low and watery and surrounded with 'oozy and slimy beaches'.[77] If the lower reaches of Flanders and the Netherlands produced summer and autumnal diseases of an 'extreme' kind, however, nowhere could be considered safe if it possessed swampy soil. In the summer the heat inclined the humours towards putrescence within, while warmth and moisture encouraged rot in the bodies of animals without.[78]

---

[75] Ibid., 30, 31, 32.

[76] Such a work was needed, Pringle argued, because no medical writers of the classical age had composed a text on the diseases of the army. Nor had any modern authors: none, at least, that one could trust. Works existed, but they had been written, Pringle sniffed, by those who had never (or hardly ever) been in the service. His *Observations*, then, ostensibly combined the expertise of the physician and the soldier. *Observations on the Diseases of the Army: In Camp and Garrison. In Three Parts. With an Appendix*, iii, v.

[77] A translation may be found in Giovanni Maria Lancisi, 'Of Marshes and Their Effluvia', in *The Medical Repository*, ed. Samuel Latham Mitchill and Edward Miller (New York: Collins & Perkins, 1810). Pringle cites Lancisi (the first citation of the main part of the book) on 4.

[78] Pringle, *Observations on the Diseases of the Army: In Camp and Garrison. In Three Parts. With an Appendix*, 2, 12, 5.

Having considered diseases peculiar to a given geographical region, Pringle next turned, in Part Two, to diseases peculiar to armed service. These could be divided into two kinds: those due to the weather and those due to infection. In each, putrefaction played a key role. Distempers related to the weather could be further divided according either to whether one considered the state of the season (summer or winter) or the state of the body (inflammatory or bilious diseases). The taxonomic outcome was equivalent, for inflammatory diseases were those of the winter, bilious diseases those of the summer. Seasons in turn corresponded to military sites. In summer, troops were in camp; in winter they were quartered. The long-standing analogy between seasons and climates then allowed a seemingly simple connection to be made between the diseases of the army at particular kinds of locations and those of warm climates at all times. Both could be termed 'bilious', following a tradition dating back to antiquity that had ascribed the cause of distempers such as cholera or dysentery to either an excess of bile or the corruption of that humour. 'In effect', wrote Pringle, 'in all hot countries, and in camps, where men are so much exposed to the sun, the gall, if not more abundant, is at this time more corrupted than usual'. What was true of seasons, then, was true of sites: '[W]e shall find the antient maxim, that held "the summer and autumn to be the most sickly seasons", not only verified with respect to the warmer climates, but also to a camp, where men are so much exposed to heat and moisture, the cause of putrid and contagious diseases'. Warm weather relaxed the body's solids and 'dispos[ed] the humours to putrefaction'.[79] When heat was coupled with moisture and humidity, the body could no longer effectively remove these corrupting humours through perspiration. Putrid diseases resulted.

But high temperatures had another role to play in producing illnesses, for warm, humid weather also promoted putrefaction in the body's surroundings. The 'most fatal, and the least understood' cause of sickness, asserted Pringle, was air 'corrupted by putrefaction'. Breathed in by bodies already inclined to rot, such air could produce deadly results. Proceeding taxonomically again, Pringle divided 'bad air' into four kinds, according to its source: stagnant marshes; human excrement; rotten straw; and crowded spaces, such as hospitals, barracks, and transport ships. Preventing illness in camps then boiled down to removing or controlling sources of dangerous effluvia. Camps should be situated away from swampland, straw should be changed regularly, a 'slight penalty, but strictly inflicted' should be imposed 'upon every man that shall ease himself any where about the camp, but on the privies', and confined spaces should be regularly ventilated, using Hales' invention.[80]

---

[79] Ibid., 91, 96–7.
[80] Ibid., 103, 24.

As striking as Pringle's obsession with putrefaction in and around the body was the fact that his focus on this single cause of illness led him to dramatically downplay the etiological logics deployed by previous authors of works on military diseases. Most had tended to point to problems in the diet of soldiers and sailors, emphasising their reliance on salted and hard to digest food. Many also adopted a moralistic tone, faulting men in service for their intemperance and lax behaviour, thereby effectively blaming soldiers and seamen for their own afflictions. Pringle would have none of it, on either account. Whoever chose to look at the seasonal periodicity of diseases and the state of the air would be convinced, he claimed 'that neither the abuse of spirits, or of fruit, or of drinking bad water, could have any considerable share in producing them'.[81] To those who would chastise soldiers for their drinking, Pringle was unsympathetic. They seemed not to understand precisely what life in campaigns was like. 'Let us not confound the necessary use of spirits in a camp', he insisted, 'with the vice of indulging them at home; but consider that soldiers are often to struggle with the extreams of hot and cold, with moist and bad air, long marches, wet cloaths and scanty provisions'.[82] That said, if Pringle placed relatively little blame on the average man in service, he also accorded him little agency. In preserving men from sickness, one could not rely on medicine or 'depend upon any thing a soldier shall have in his power to neglect'.[83] The solution was to regulate camp life, with orders that appeared reasonable and that men were compelled to obey. In Pringle's vision of the army, health and hygiene were matters of collective, rather than individual action.

The third part of the text then considered the cause and cure of specific illnesses. Inflammatory afflictions were given comparatively short shrift. Cold-weather distempers were well known and well treated elsewhere. The lion's share of the section (close to 80 per cent) was given over to discussions of putrid diseases: bilious fevers, the dysentery, and the hospital fever. Pringle was clear on the inapplicability of much of his analysis to ordinary, civilian life in Britain.

[W]e are not to confound the ordinary checks given to perspiration in Britain (where the weather is seldom close, moist, and hot for any considerable time) with what happens in other climates, subject to such intemperature, and where the inhabitants having in summer and autumn humours of a more putrescent nature, require a more constant evacuation of what is corrupted.[84]

---

[81] Ibid., 111.
[82] Ibid., 107.
[83] Ibid., ix.
[84] Ibid., 216–7. The difference, however, was as much of degree as kind. 'It may be proper to take notice, that we have also fevers of a bilious kind in this island; and that both our remitting and intermitting fevers and dysentery, seem no less the effects of a putrid cause than those of other countries. But I must add, that such is the driness of the soil, and its freedom from marshes,

The Low Countries were dangerous; Hungary, where cold and damp nights followed sultry days, was even more so; but the deadliest parts of the world were 'the marshy countries of the south', where heats were most intense and protracted. Pringle, of course, had not served in the latter, and he turned to literature both classical and modern to make his case. Celsus, Galen, and Livy offered evidence on Italy, Hippocrates on Greece, Prosper Alpinus on Egypt, Bontius on Java, 'an experienced surgeon, who lived some years in that country' on Guinea, and Warren on the West Indies. In all, heat and humidity rendered the body's solids relaxed, disposed the fluids to putrefaction, and encouraged the rot of 'plants, insects, and fishes' in marshland, producing effluvia that would reach blood primed for corruption.[85]

To understand the precise mechanism by which marsh effluvia caused putrid diseases, one needs to turn to Pringle's experiments on septic and antiseptic substances, and to read them as a direct response, correction, and elaboration of Boerhaave's.[86] The first order of business in Pringle's experiments was to demonstrate both that all putrid substances were not alkaline and that alkaline salts did not promote putrefaction. The method was simple, although it cannot have thrilled any neighbours within smelling distance.[87] Most commonly, Pringle took pieces of beef and set them somewhere warm, comparing the state of the flesh alone or in water to that of it combined with another substance. Thus, for example, in Experiment III he compared a phial of lean beef in water and salt of hartshorn (baker's ammonia) to one containing beef, water, and table salt, with a third containing meat and water alone 'to serve by way of index'. All were placed in a lamp-furnace, where the temperature stayed between 94 and 100 degrees Fahrenheit. In less than a day, the contents of the 'index' phial were rank; a few hours later, that containing sea salt was also putrid; but the

---

the constant perflation, and the moderate and interrupted heats of our summers, that, unless in extraordinary hot and close seasons, and in the fenny tracts, these distempers are always gentle, and seldom epidemic'. Ibid., 237.

[85] Ibid., 201–2, 20.

[86] Certainly Pringle noted the relation, commending the man he termed his 'celebrated master' for combining mechanics with chemistry in an understanding of medicine. Pringle also saw himself as continuing in research begun by Bacon and Hoffman. 'Ld. Bacon calls, "the inducing or accelerating putrefaction a subject of very universal inquiry"; and says, "that it is of excellent use to enquire into the means of preventing or staying putrefaction: which makes a great part of physic and surgery"'. Ibid., 367. See Gottlieb Benjamin Bergerus and Friedrich Hoffmann, *Dissertatio Physicomedica Inauguralis de Putredinis Doctrina Amplissimi in Medicina Usus. Praes. F. Hoffmann* (Halle: 1722).

[87] Pringle himself made mention of the distasteful elements of his research. 'Altho' an enquiry into the manner how bodies are resolved by putrefaction, with the means of accelerating or preventing that process, has been reckoned not only curious, but useful; yet we find it little prosecuted in an experimental way: nor is it to be wondered at, considering how offensive such operations are', Pringle, *Observations on the Diseases of the Army: In Camp and Garrison. In Three Parts. With an Appendix*, 367.

phial containing salt of hartshorn (considered in the past a promoter of putrefaction) still smelled sweet.

The range of substances that retarded putrefaction, Pringle discovered, was
vast: 'besides salts, fermented spirits, spices, and acids, commonly known to
have this property, many resins, astringents and refrigerants are of the number;
and even those plants called anti-acids, and supposed hasteners of putrefaction: of which class horse-radish is particularly antiseptic'. Later experiments
then turned to the question of whether antiseptics might not only resist, but
reverse putrefaction. In the case of the Bark, the answer was an unequivocal
yes. The famed specific against certain fevers could not only remove the putrid
smell from tainted meat, it could stiffen the fibres rendered lax by rot. Pringle
immediately connected these two properties of the Bark, arguing that the substance worked against gangrene and various fevers precisely because such
afflictions involved putrefaction. Without marking it, then, Pringle introduced
what would prove to be the most controversial element of his analysis, the
suggestion that sepsis in dead flesh was identical to – and could cause – rot
within a living body. Marsh effluvia, rendered putrid by the rotting animal
and vegetable substances within it, were a 'ferment', a term, he quickly clari-
fied (in order to avoid association with the fermentational theories of earlier
chemists) he meant only 'to express the assimilating power of all putrid animal
substances over the fresh'. Pringle put forward the results of simple experiment to demonstrate the point. A small amount of material taken from the yolk
of a putrid egg, when added to water and the yolk of half a fresh egg caused
more putrefaction than occurred in the other half, in water alone. This 'putrid
fermentation', Pringle asserted, offered a close 'connection' with the action of
contagion.[88]

Pringle claimed in the Preface to his *Observations on the Diseases of the
Army* that little of the etiological reasoning to be found in the text was properly his. 'The corruption of the humours is hinted at by Hippocrates', he noted,
and had been further developed by later authors well into the seventeenth century, before being lost by 'mechanical writers' and then revived by his teacher,
Boerhaave.[89] But we should be somewhat wary of accepting his history at face
value. Corruption and putrefaction were not necessarily the same thing. His
explanation was new – radically so – as one can learn by comparing it to that
of one of his own key sources. As we have seen, for Mead, the dead bodies of
animals could, in the hot and humid climate of Africa, become 'fit to breed'

---

[88] Ibid., 379, 68–9, 81–2, 87. Pringle cited Bacon as the first to make the connection between
contagion and 'putrid fermentation'. Hoffman, who Pringle cited as another key reference, also
pursued the analogy between putrescence and ferments in Bergerus and Hoffmann.

[89] Pringle, *Observations on the Diseases of the Army: In Camp and Garrison. In Three Parts.
With an Appendix*, xiii.

plague. The effluvia rising from carcasses could corrupt the humours until they were corrosive enough to damage the body's solids, and the disease could then be spread as ferments hopped from body to body via the air.[90] But Mead's was not an explanation in which putrescence bred putrescence. Literal putrefaction, by contrast – not merely a generalised 'corruption' – was placed at the centre of Pringle's theory of diseases in crowded hospitals, jails, and ships, as well as in warm and humid climes. In the colonies, as we will see, his ideas about sources of sepsis suggested a medical geography, one based on avoiding marshes (and their miasmas) at all costs. On ships, his theory of the effect of putrid disorders on the body's humours suggested a cure: the ingestion of antiseptic substances. Medical men at sea and on land would soon be locked in a battle with rot.

4.4   Putrefaction in the Periphery

Putridity at Sea

Perhaps no single voyage changed medical writing so dramatically as the journey of Lord Anson's fleet. In 1739, tensions were high between Spain and Britain. That year, Vernon would capture Portobello, and the following year George Anson, then Captain of the *Centurion*, was given command of a squadron of six warships and two merchant vessels, with orders to attack and capture the port that serviced Lima and, if possible, the city itself. After losing contact with three of the warships, the remaining ships encountered storms and high seas as they rounded Cape Horn. It was then that scurvy broke out, killing a staggering number of men. In the time since it had left England, the crew of the *Centurion* had been reduced by almost 60 per cent, and that of the *Gloucester* by even more. After eventually completing a circumnavigation of the globe, the squadron returned home in June 1744 to a heroes' welcome. Despite the tremendous loss of life – and the failure to achieve any of their main objectives – the ships had managed some very successful piracy, capturing several smaller ships and one Spanish Galleon. The seized treasure was paraded through the streets of London, Anson's share of the prize money made him a very wealthy man, and in 1751 he was promoted to First Lord of the Admiralty. The official account of the voyage was published in 1748 and was read voraciously, four editions appearing for the same London publishers that year and at least two more in 1749.[91]

---

[90] Mead, *A Short Discourse Concerning Pestilential Contagion and the Methods to Be Used to Prevent It*, 32.

[91] George Anson, *A Voyage Round the World: In the Years MDCCXL, I, II, III, IV. By George Anson ... Compiled from Papers and Other Materials Of ... George Lord Anson, and*

Leading physicians published tracts on the scurvy within only a few years of the squadron's return.[92] In 1747, Huxham described *A Method for Preserving the Health of Seamen in Long Cruises and Voyages*, which he then appended to his 1750 book on fevers.[93] Mead weighed in two years later, with an explanation that should now seem familiar: While a bad diet played a role, for Mead, scurvy was caused by bad air.[94] Mead proposed improving the seamen's food, adding wine vinegar to their provisions, and improving the air by using a ventilator, based on Sutton's design. By far the best known of the scurvy-tracts written in response to the appalling death rates during Anson's voyage was that by James Lind.[95] The book remains famous today, because in it Lind described the results of a trial made to determine which anti-scorbutics worked best. Twelve patients, kept on a common diet, were divided into six pairs. The first was given a quart of cider per day; the second an amount of *elixir vitriol* thrice daily; the third two spoonfuls of vinegar as often as the second; the fourth half a pint of sea water per day; the fifth two oranges and one lemon; and the

Published under His Direction, by Richard Walter ... Illustrated with Forty-Two Copper-Plates (London: John and Paul Knapton, 1748). The book remained enormously popular, in spite of the fact that it had considerable competition from various unofficial accounts of the journey. A fourteenth London edition appeared in 1769.

92 Kenneth J. Carpenter, *The History of Scurvy and Vitamin C* (Cambridge: Cambridge University Press, 1986).

93 Huxham, *An Essay on Fevers, and Their Various Kinds, as Depending on Different Constitutions of the Blood: With Dissertations on Slow Nervous Fevers; on Putrid, Pestilential, Spotted Fevers; on the Small-Pox; and on Pleurisies and Peripneumonies*, 259–65. Much like Pringle, Huxham combined his Boerhaavian training with readings of Mead to offer an account of putrid fevers as a class unto themselves (see Introduction). Huxham analogised the cause of this dissolution to the action of poisons, citing Mead, and paid particular attention to the putrefaction of the Bile: 'truly putrid Bile is little less pernicious than an actual Poison', he wrote. Ibid., 41, 114. Huxham argued that the cause of the scurvy was 'bad Provisions, bad Water, bad Beer &c', coupled with a moist, salty aerial atmosphere and foul air between decks. This led to a putrefaction of the blood, which – since in Huxham's view, putrefaction was alcalescent – could be corrected using acidic substances, like apple cider. Huxham prescribed at least a pint per day, in addition to the daily allowances of beer and water. Ibid., 259, 60–1.

94 Moisture weakened the air's spring; it was full of 'foul particles' breathed out by men crowded together, some of whom were no doubt diseased; filthy bilge-water stagnated and gave off effluvia; and salts were inhaled, some of which may have originated from animals putrefying in the water. When the latter made their way into the blood, they could, 'in the nature of a ferment, corrupt its whole mass'. Richard Mead, 'Discourse on the Scurvy', in *An Historical Account of a New Method for Extracting the Foul Air out of Ships, &C with the Description and Draught of the Machines, by Which It Is Performed: In Two Letters to a Friend, by Samuel Sutton, the Inventor*, ed. Samuel Sutton (London: J. Brindley, 1749), 102. Mead also related the comments made to him by Admiral Charles Wagner, who had supplied his men with oranges and lemons daily. The men ate them and added the juice to their beer. 'It was also their constant diversion to pelt one another with the rinds; so that the deck was always strewed and wet with the fragrant liquor. The happy effect was, that he brought his sailors home in good health'. Ibid., 112.

95 Lind, *A Treatise of the Scurvy. In Three Parts. Containing an Inquiry into the Nature, Causes, and Cure of That Disease. Together with a Critical and Chronological View of What Has Been Published on the Subject.* The text was dedicated to Anson.

sixth medicine recommended by a hospital surgeon. The citrus fruit won hands down, with one of the two previously scorbutic patients ready for duty only six days later, and the other well enough after some time to serve as nurse for the rest.[96] Cider – recommended by Huxham – did second best.

Nowadays, we regard the scurvy as a disease brought on by a vitamin deficiency. Oranges and lemons provide the requisite Vitamin C. Lind, of course, had no conception of such an explanation. *'The principal and main predisposing cause'* of the disease 'is a manifest and obvious quality of the air, *viz.* its *moisture'*, he wrote, systematically rejecting previous theories that pointed to the harmful effects of sea salt in the diet, the absence of fresh vegetables, or bad and vitiated air. Running sores and stinking gums clearly indicated rot within the body, but Lind rejected both Mead and Pringle's suggestions for the origins of putridity. Putrefaction required no unusual explanation, Lind argued, because it was the body's natural action to tend towards a putrescent state: 'the scorbutic putrefaction … is purely the natural effect of animal heat and motion caused by the action of the body'. Heat and motion produced two effects. The body's fluids tended to degenerate and become corrupted because of their constant mutual actions on each other; the body's solids tended to be abraded by the motion of the fluids, parts of them washed into the channels along which the fluids flowed. An animal body, Lind claimed was 'of all substances, the most liable to corruption and putrefaction'.[97] In a healthy body, the worst of the putrescent particles were removed either by urination or perspiration (particularly insensible perspiration), and the material lost from the solids was replaced by food that had been transformed into a nutritious chyle. Problems arose when insensible perspiration was impeded (when the weather was cold – particularly when it was also damp – and when men failed to exercise sufficiently), and when poor food made the production of useful chyle difficult.

Diet thus mattered, but the key question had less to do with 'freshness' and more to do with the ability of the body to use food to replace what had been lost. The fluids given off in perspiration were the thinnest and the most 'subtilised', thus those most able to pass through miniscule pores. The body also required a thin liquor to repair the abraded solids, since it had to pass through the 'most minute canals' to reach the sites of wear. The staples of sea-life, however – salty, dried food and unleavened bread – were notoriously difficult to break down. Green vegetables worked in their stead because they contained less oil than animal matter and because they were less solidly held together in the first place. 'There is no other particular virtue', Lind noted, 'in which they all agree'. Green vegetables shared with ripe fruits a

---

[96] Ibid., 192–3.
[97] Ibid., 107, 277, 73.

'fermentative quality'. From the fact that such substances seemed valuable remedies for the scurvy, Lind concluded that a fermentative operation, and foods that promoted it, was necessary for digestion and for preventing 'scorbutic corruption'. Vegetables also produced a chyle that tended towards the acidic, which could 'correct the continual putrescent tendency of the animal humours'.[98] Yet Lind was clear on the fact that acidity was not to be taken as the sole reason that oranges and lemons worked so well. Putrid bodies were not always alkaline and alcalescent vegetables, like the famed 'Scurvy-grass' or cresses, worked against the scurvy, the water they contained diluting and thinning the chyle; their viscid parts dulling the acrimony due to putrefaction; and the salts within them acting as a fine antiseptic. Nonetheless, he acknowledged, alcalescent plants did not seem as efficacious as acidic fruits. The ideal solution, Lind advised, was to use a mixture of different ingredients, each of which possessed one or more anti-scorbutic virtue to a high degree and which, when combined, produced a 'vegetable, saponaceous, fermentable acid'. Precisely such an acid was to be found 'in a certain degree' in oranges, which made them very effective as a means of preventing and remedying scurvy, even if they were not to be understood as, in our contemporary language, a magic bullet against the disease.[99]

Putridity on (Warm) Land

The Preface to the third edition of Pringle's *Diseases of the Army* (1761) contains a line not found in the first or second, or in any that followed. 'In reasoning upon the nature of the bilious fevers, the hospital-fever, and the dysentery, I have so much recourse to the *septic principle,* that the Reader may imagine I have considered it as a more universal cause than I really think it; for except in these distempers, and in a few more … I have hitherto referred no other disorder to that origin'.[100] Pringle had, in fact, been clear about the limitations of his analysis. He had focused on bilious diseases because they were less well treated in the medical literature, since Britons were far more likely to be afflicted by cold weather, inflammatory distempers. Putrid diseases were the illnesses of elsewhere, although some of the elsewheres – hospitals and jails – could be found in the heart of the metropole. If the 'septic principle' was of limited applicability in Britain, however, it would soon become ubiquitous – whether precisely in Pringle's terms or not – in the colonies, where

---

[98] Ibid., 290, 301, 8, 3. Green vegetables could thus produce the ideal chyle, one that could 'dilute and sweeten the acrimonious animal juices, to correct the putrescent tendency of the humours, and to repair the decay of the body'. Ibid., 296.

[99] Ibid., 306, 10.

[100] Quoted in Dorothea Singer, 'Sir John Pringle and His Circle, II', *Annals of Science* 6, no. 3 (1950): 245.

warmth and humidity seemed to make the centrality of rot to medical discourse seem almost natural. For perhaps a quarter of a century after 1750, distempers in the warm climates of the British Empire became putrefactive. Putrescence, one might say, was in the tropical air.

The change wrought in theories of medicine in warm climates around mid-century might be seen by returning to examples from Chapter 2. What Towne called an 'ardent bilious fever' in 1726, what Warren named a 'malignant' one in 1740, what Dale Ingram referred to merely as the 'yellow fever' in 1755, Hillary termed a *'putrid* bilious fever' in 1759.[101] There was no talk of putridity or rot in Towne's text at all. Warren, as we saw earlier, modelled his account after Mead's, and presented his fever as a contagious one, brought from the East. But he said little of its original (possibly putrefactive) cause. He followed Mead in arguing that contagious distempers acted like poisons on the body, the particles making them up mixing with the body's fluids and changing them 'into their own Likeness and Nature, and these again infect others in a sort of proliferous Manner, until the whole Mass becomes contaminated'.[102] Like the bites of venomous animals, gangrene could be a result of infection by the contagious poison and Warren described a possible 'gangrenous *Diathesis* of the sanguineous Mass' and labelled the third stage of the distemper the 'Gangrenous State'.[103] Necrotic decay thus seemed to play a role in Warren's theory, but he did not label the fever putrid, nor turn to chemistry as a means of healing. Ingram offered an alternative explanation, which pointed to external putrefaction as a cause of the fever and suggesting that it was 'brought on by a poison, that is, a *poisonous state of the air'* but denied that it was contagious and said little about the internal putrefaction of the body's fluids.[104]

---

[101] Putrefaction played no central explanatory role in Cleghorn's account of the Diseases of Minorca (1751) or in the debate between Williams and Bennet (1750). George Cleghorn, *Observations on the Epidemical Diseases in Minorca. From the Year 1744 to 1749* (London: Printed for D. Wilson, 1751). Williams and Bennet.

[102] Warren, 21.

[103] Ibid., 12, 16.

[104] Dale Ingram, *An Historical Account of the Several Plagues That Have Appeared in the World since the Year 1346. With an Enquiry into the Present Prevailing Opinion, That the Plague Is a Contagious Distemper ... In Which the Absurdity of Such Notions Is Exposed ... To Which Are Added a Particular Account of the Yellow Fever ... Also Observations on Dr Mackenzie's Letters; ... And an Abstract of Capt. Isaac Clemens's Voyage in the Sloop Fawey* (London: R. Baldwin and J. Clark, 1755), 133. The book received a scathing commentary in *The Monthly Review*, which described it as 'this worse than worthless piece'. Anonymous, 'Review of Dale Ingram, "A Historical Account of Several Plagues That Have Appeared in the World since the Year 1346"', *The Monthly Review* (1755): 139. The anonymous author of a 1776 tract on West Indian diseases offered yet another take on the yellow fever's aetiology. It was caused by either excessive heats, which induced putrefaction of the body's juices, or through the action of putrid effluvia, but it was not contagious. All those who shared the same air might become ill, but they did not infect one another. *Practical Remarks on West India Diseases* (London: F. Newbery; F. Blyth, 1776), 72–3.

By contrast, the 'septic principle' was front and centre in Hillary's explanation at the end of the 1750s.

From an attentive Consideration of all the Symptoms which attend this Disease, and a strict Examination of the putrid State, and dissolved gangrenescent Condition in which we find the Blood of those who labour under it; as well as the half putrefied and mortified State in which the Body is found immediately after their Death ... it evidently appears from all the Symptoms which attend it, as well as from their putrid Effects, that a bilious putrefying Diathesis, is actually introduced into the Blood and all the circulating Fluids of the Body.[105]

To effect a cure, one needed first to slow the excessively rapid motion of the fluids and to reduce the fever, second to remove as much of the putrid bile and other humours as possible, and third, to use 'suitable Antiscepticks' to 'put a Stop to the putrescent Disposition of the Fluids, and prevent the Gangrenes from coming on'.[106] Such antiseptics included the Peruvian bark (although it could be hard for a patient to stomach) or a julep made from serpent's root.[107] Hillary rejected so-called alkaline antiseptics, however. He did not mention Pringle by name, but there would seem to be little doubt whom he had in mind when he critiqued experiments 'made on Pieces of dead Flesh, or dead stagnating animal Fluids'. Trials made on the living, he asserted, had made it clear that alkaline salts and spirits brought on putrescence, rather than hindering it. On this point, as on many others, Hillary followed Huxham.[108]

By the early 1760s, one can see the emergence of a new orthodoxy, one that paired internal and external putrefaction and located both, in their most extreme forms, outside Northern Europe. '[A]lmost all Diseases in hot Climates', wrote Lind in his essay on the *Health of Seamen*, 'are thought to be of a putrid Nature'. Citing Pringle's 'excellent Observations' with enthusiasm, Lind also noted the dangers of marshy effluvia: 'The Fens, even in different Counties of *England*, are known to be very dangerous to the Health of those who live near them, and still more so to Strangers; but the woody and marshy lands in

---

[105] Hillary, *Observations on the Changes of the Air and the Concomitant Epidemical Diseases, in the Island of Barbados. To Which Is Added a Treatise on the Putrid Bilious Fever, Commonly Called the Yellow Fever; and Such Other Diseases as Are Indigenous or Endemial, in the West India Islands, or in the Torrid Zone*, 163.

[106] Ibid., 164.

[107] Hillary's treatments were subsequently used throughout the empire. Richard Huck, physician to the general hospital at Havaan noted that many of the medical men he met with recommended Hillary's work on the yellow fever as 'the best upon that distemper'. Quoted in Charters, 60.

[108] See Chapter 2. On Huxham's theory of putrid fevers, see above. Although they differed somewhat on how to cure such afflictions, Pringle was very enthusiastic about Huxham's text, noting that it appeared immediately after his short essay on jail and hospital fevers. Pringle, *Observations on the Diseases of the Army: In Camp and Garrison. In Three Parts. With an Appendix*, xii.

hot Countries are exceedingly more pernicious to the Health of *Europeans*'.[109] Solomon de Monchy drew heavily on 'Mead, Pringle, Huxham, Lind, Watson, Bisset, Hillary' in his prize-winning essay in answer to a question on the usual causes of illnesses among seamen in journeys to the West Indies. We should thus not be surprised to find putridity given a starring role in his explanations. The putrid fever, malignant fever, and the scurvy, he claimed, all flowed from the same cause: putrefaction. Pairing the ship and the colony, he argued that the source of the putrefaction was 'fetid vapours', found equally in ships' holds and the 'marshy coasts of the West Indies'. 'This retained putrescent vapour, or matter', he wrote, 'acting like yeast on the juices ... dangerous, putrid diseases must necessarily be the result in hot countries'.[110] It is difficult to date the 'Account of the True Bilious, or Yellow Fever', written by John Hume, who had served as Surgeon at the Naval Hospital at New Greenwich in Jamaica between 1739 and 1749, since it was only published after his death in 1777.[111] My suspicion, however, is that it was composed in the 1760s or early 1770s, since Hume describes as common the position that Hillary had first advocated in 1759: 'All practitioners in the West-Indies now agree', he stated, 'that the principal intentions in the cure of this fever must be, to correct the too-great tendency of the blood to putrefaction, and to carry off the putrid bile as expeditiously and safely as possible'.[112] In writing to Donald Monro in 1773, John Quier – who had practiced almost six years in Jamaica – was almost certainly right to suspect that Monro would find it surprising to be told that his correspondent had not 'met with a single case of what might properly be called an acute putrid disease, except the small-pox'. Of diseases arising from the corruption of fluids, particularly the bile, there were plenty, but of 'real putrefaction', none. Quier was well aware of his exceptionality, however. Among the endemial diseases of warm countries, he observed, those disorders which 'arise from, or are accompanied with putrefaction', were held to be the most common.[113] Andrew Wilson, Fellow of the Royal College of Physicians in Edinburgh was critical of the label, but nonetheless noted in 1780 'that tendency to putridity which so remarkably stigmatizes the diseases of hot climates'.[114]

---

[109] Lind, 25, 66, 64.

[110] de Monchy, 67, 88.

[111] The dates for Hume's tenure as surgeon are those given in Donald Monro et al., *Letters and Essays on the Small-Pox and Inoculation, the Measles, the Dry Belly-Ache, the Yellow, and Remitting, an Intermitting Fevers of the West Indies* (London: J. Murray, 1778), 195–6. Chakrabarti notes, however, that Hume resigned his position in 1746. Chakrabarti, 69. The editor of the volume in which Hume's essay appeared noted that a copy of the original text was made 'some years before his death'. Monro et al., xv.

[112] Monro et al., 197–249, 10.

[113] Letter sent from Jamaica, dated 23 March 1773. Ibid., 151.

[114] Andrew Wilson, *Rational Advice to the Military, When Exposed to the Inclemency of Hot Climates and Seasons* (London: W. Richardson, 1780), 33.

The importance of Pringle to medicine in the armed forces may be seen by the fact that two of the most well-cited texts of the mid-1760s function as essential paraphrases of his main arguments.[115] Richard Brocklesby published his *Oeconomical and Medical Observations* in 1764, having succeeded Pringle as Surgeon-General of the British Army in 1758. Brocklesby referred to Pringle as 'my most philosophical and ingenious immediate predecessor', but noted that Pringle's 'Verulamian' style may have been off-putting for officers reading his text. Hence this 'more popular treatise', describing 'the tender frame of man ... whose body is every instant pervious to all the minute seeds of putrefaction and dissolution'.[116] Donald Monro published his *Account of the Diseases Which were most Frequent in the British Military Hospitals in Germany* the same year. There he noted that, after time, diseases in warm climates 'tend to the putrid kind, and must be treated as such'. To effect a cure, the diet had to be made up of vegetable antiseptics, which could correct the tendency of the blood to putrefy.[117]

By the late 1760s, as can be seen from the text by the younger Lind, one finds Pringle's septic principle being applied to explain diseases in India. In 1773, John Clark, who had previously served as surgeon on the Talbot Indiaman also pointed to noxious exhalations from marshy ground as the cause of many illnesses in the East Indies. All the dangerous diseases of warm climates, he

---

[115] Erica Charters makes a more general argument for the crucial importance of the work of Pringle and Lind to medical practice during the Seven Years' War in Charters.

[116] Richard Brocklesby, *Oeconomical and Medical Observations, in Two Parts. From the Year 1758 to the Year 1763, Inclusive* (London: T. Becket, and P. A. De Hondt, 1764), 27, 167. The cause of decay within the body was decay without: 'Heat and moisture conspire to resolve the dead bodies of reptile and other animals, and the dying parts of vegetables; and the waters, the earth, and the air we breathe, abound with volatile putrescent effluvia, which are at this season scattered around in great abundance, as is fatally experienced by those who are obliged to live in marshy warm countries, near stagnant waters, or on lands annually laid under water by the inundations of great rivers, &c'. Ibid., 167.

[117] Donald Monro, *An Account of the Diseases Which Were Most Frequent in the British Military Hospitals in Germany, from January 1761 to the Return of the Troops to England in March 1763. To Which Is Added, an Essay on the Means of Preserving the Health of Soldiers, and Conducting Military Hospitals* (London: A. Millar, D. Wilson, and T. Durham, 1764), 239. A second and much revised edition appeared in 1780. In it, Monro drew heavily on the work of those in the West Indies, particularly John Hume. *Observations on the Means of Preserving the Health of Soldiers and of Conducting Military Hospitals. And on the Diseases Incident to Soldiers in the Time of Service, and on the Same Diseases as They Have Appeared in London. In Two Volumes. By Donald Monro, M.D,* 2nd ed. (London: J. Murray; and G. Robinson, 1780). 1764 also saw the original Latin publication of Lewis Rouppe, *Observations on Diseases Incidental to Seamen,* Translated from the Latin Edition [1764], Printed at Leyden ed. (London: T. Carnan and F. Newbery, 1772), 81., which continues the theme. Rouppe cited some of his key sources on 82: 'With respect to the effect which such a foul air must produce in the body, consult the histories of epidemical disorders published by *Hoffman, Huxham,* and *Pringle,* as well as *de Monchy'*.

claimed, 'depend upon a putrescent disposition in the fluids'.[118] The same year Edward Ives, whose thoughts on the diseases of Europeans in the East Indies had already appeared in print in Lind's book on Scurvy (and whose book was well known enough to end up on the desk of Immanuel Kant), described a practice in India about which there was 'nothing uncommon' and where 'antiseptic medicines' were regularly administered.[119] A decade later Stephen Mathews noted the 'pernicious' effect of the Indian climate on European constitutions, suggesting that the constant heat produced a relaxation of the body and a sluggish motion of the fluids, leading to obstructions and putrescency. In such a state, the body was particularly vulnerable to 'septic miasmata' with a putrefaction of the fluids a potentially deadly result.[120]

Tracking the spread of putrefactive theories of disease in the British Isles is a task rendered complex by the existence of two distinct (at least initially) conceptions of putrid disorders around 1750: one building upon John Fothergill's 1748 report on the deadly spread of cases of a sore throat attended with ulcers and the other drawing upon the work of figures such as Pringle, Lind, and Huxham on putrid disorders.[121] The disease described by Fothergill killed rapidly, after producing, among other symptoms, a 'Disposition to Putrefaction' of the body in general, and the back of the throat leading to the pharynx in particular. Fothergill ascribed the cause of this disposition to a 'putrid *Virus*, or *Miasma sui generis*', passed contagiously via the breath from person to person.[122] In 1755, Claude-Nicolas Le Cat, Professor of Anatomy and Chirurgery at Rouen, described a number of 'malignant fevers' that raged in the previous few years. Le Cat did not use the term 'putrid' to describe any of

---

[118] John Clark, *Observations on the Diseases in Long Voyages to Hot Countries, and Particularly on Those Which Prevail in the East Indies.* (London: Printed for D. Wilson and G. Nicol, 1773), 149.

[119] Edward Ives, *A Voyage from England to India, in the Year MDCCLIV: And an Historical Narrative of the Operations of the Squadron and Army in India, Under ... Watson And ... Clive ... Also, a Journey from Persia to England, by an Unusual Route. With an Appendix, Containing an Account of the Diseases Prevalent in Admiral Watson's Squadron: A Description of Most of the Trees, Shrubs, and Plants, of India ... Illustrated with a Chart, Maps, and Other Copper-Plates* (London: Edward and Charles Dilly, 1773), 444.

[120] Stephen Mathews, *Observations on Hepatic Diseases Incidental to Europeans in the East-Indies* (London: T. Cadell, 1783), 7, 19.

[121] Almost all of the texts cited by Creighton fall into one of these two camps. The exceptions are those that are too short or too vague for one to determine what, precisely, is meant by a 'putrid disease'. For example, the few lines penned in Latin by 'S' in the *Gentleman's Magazine* in 1755 or the multiple mentions of putrid fevers (with little, if any, discussion of their causes) in Thomas Short, *A Comparative History of the Increase and Decrease of Mankind in England, and Several Countries Abroad ... To Which Is Added, a Syllabus of the General States of Health, Air, Seasons, and Food for the Last Three Hundred Years: And Also a Meteorological Discourse* (London: W. Nicoll, 1767).

[122] John Fothergill, *An Account of the Sore Throat Attended with Ulcers; a Disease Which Hath of Late Years Appeared in This City, and the Parts Adjacent* (London: C. Davis, 1747), 60, 61.

these, but he did make mention of a number of 'gangrenous sore throats'.[123] Two years later, Huxham offered his own account of the disease, citing Fothergill as the first to provide an accurate depiction of it in England.[124]

If these three cases – drawn from Creighton's analysis – point to a metropolitan origin for part of the talk of putrid diseases in Britain at mid-century, many of the other examples Creighton used point towards imperial and colonial resources for this discourse. James Johnstone appears to have been the first to construct a lineage of authors writing about the malignant sore throat that included Fothergill, Le Cat, and Huxham. His work of 1758 was also one of the first (together with Huxham's) to link these studies of a singular disease with a more general discourse concerning putrid afflictions.[125] James Sims drew upon the experiences gained in his practice in Tyrone, Ireland in the mid-1760s and early-1770s in writing his *Observations on Epidemic Disorders*. But his remarks on nervous and malignant fevers in that volume are all offered in dialogue with the writings of Huxham and Pringle.[126] Creighton cited Charles Bisset's *Essay on the Medical Constitution of Great Britain* (1762), but did so without noting that Bisset came to his understanding of putrid disorders during time served as second surgeon to the hospital at Jamaica, beginning in 1740. This experience was reflected in his *Treatise on the Scurvy* (1755), a text which drew heavily on Lind's *Treatise* on the same topic, as well as Pringle's *Diseases of the Army*.[127] Citing Hillary's book on the diseases of the West Indies, Creighton suggested that 'Perhaps the most surprising testimony to the existence of an "epidemic constitution" of slow, continued, nervous fever comes from the Island of Barbados'.[128] Certainly, if one imagines the spread of a specific disease agent, it may be surprising to find it in Barbados as well as Rouen, England, and Ireland. However, if one imagines that what is spreading is a way of understanding disease, and that it spread via imperial networks,

---

[123] Mons. Le Cat, 'An Account of Those Malignant Fevers, That Raged at Rouen, at the End of the Year 1753, and the Beginning of 1754', *Philosophical Transactions* 49 (1755–6).

[124] John Huxham, *A Dissertation on the Malignant, Ulcerous Sore-Throat* (London: J. Hinton, 1757). That said, Fothergill's and Huxham's accounts of the disease – and the role played by putrefaction – were quite different. The former located the specific site of putrefaction (or a disposition to putrefaction) in the throat. For Huxham, however, in keeping with his earlier work on fevers, putrescence was located in the blood.

[125] James Johnstone, *An Historical Dissertation Concerning the Malignant Epidemical Fever of 1756* (London: W. Johnstone, 1758), 7. Johnstone makes explicit reference to Pringle's work on antiseptics on 57.

[126] James Sims, *Observations on Epidemic Disorders, with Remarks on Nervous and Malignant Fevers* (London: J. Johnson; G. Robinson, 1773).

[127] Bisset; *An Essay on the Medical Constitution of Great Britain, to Which Are Added Observations on the Weather, and the Diseases Which Appeared in the Period Included Betwixt the First of January 1758, and the Summer Solstice in 1760.* (London: A. Millar and D. Wilson, 1762). Bisset dedicated the *Medical Constitution* to Pringle.

[128] Creighton, II. *From the Extinction of Plague to the Present Time*, 127.

carried with particularly urgency after the outbreak of the Seven Years War, and travelling not from centre to periphery, but in all directions, the surprise tends to evaporate.[129]

4.5   The End of the Putrefactive Paradigm

Scurvy as Anomaly and the Problem of Method

Putrefactive theories of disease had become standards in texts produced in and about warm climates by the last quarter of the eighteenth century. The idea that marshes produced putrid effluvia that induced decay in the human frame provided a rationale for the placement of residences and soldiers' quarters and pointed towards at least some elements of a regimen of both prevention and treatment by means of the ingestion of antiseptics. In terms of practical medicine, then, views broadly similar to Pringle's had gained a great deal of traction, particularly – and unsurprisingly – within the military. No doubt, part of the appeal was the fact that the new set of explanations in fact recapitulated many older ideas, such as the dangers of marshlands and rotting corpses, and the value of curatives such as fresh produce and the Peruvian bark. Many of these notions would remain, even after the putrefactive paradigm was replaced, the Bark, for example, now employed for its properties as a nervous tonic, rather than an antiseptic.

In 1768, when the younger Lind published his Latin dissertation on the putrid fever of Bengal, the paradigm was orthodoxy. By the time the text was translated into English in 1776, a growing chorus of criticisms could be heard. Some of these criticisms – one suspects they were among the most damaging – came from earlier proponents of putrefactive theories and involved what had been one of the paradigm's earliest extensions and successes. Scurvy had become, after Lind's tract on the subject appeared in 1753, the quintessential putrid disease. With other illnesses one had to hazard guesses about the putrid inner state of the body. In the case of scurvy, the classic symptoms – rotting, stinking gums, running sores, wounds that could not heal or that freshly opened again – seemed obviously to point to decay within. Lind, as we have seen, called into question the classical pedigree of contemporary understandings of 'putrid' fevers in his 1768 text on *Diseases Incidental to Europeans in Hot*

---

[129] As Erica Charters has noted, the circulation between metropole and imperial periphery began before the publication of Lind's and Pringle's works. Both men 'relied on the network of British military medicine in order to empirically inform their theories of disease and treatment, As a result, the first-hand experience of even lowly military surgeons was solicited and assiduously collected, meaning that military medical men in the colonies were considered experts, providing reliable observations and informed medical judgments'. Charters, 35.

Climates. In the third edition of his book on Scurvy, however, he would go much further.[130] In the book's *Postscript*, Lind asked a fundamental question about the blood taken from scorbutic patients: did this substance in fact tend to corruption more than the blood of those in health? 'This is the opinion of most authors', he noted, 'and what I had formerly adopted from them, as the foundation of my reasoning on the theory of this disease'.[131] Now, however, he was not so sure. Blood taken from many different patients suffering from the disease seemed to possess few common traits other than an insipidity to the taste. It corrupted no more quickly than the blood of the healthy and could induce corruption in other substances no more readily.[132] The rottenness of the gums and their smell, Lind argued, was not to be taken as a sign of internal putrefaction, but proceeded 'solely from the corrupt state of the gums. For in their dead bodies, I never perceived any unusual marks of putrefaction'. On the other hand, he acknowledged, other physicians had observed clear signs of putrefaction in the bowels of scorbutics after death and one could note the tenderness and laxity of the body's fibres in dissections, which might indicate that the body was 'inclined to corruption'. Certainly, too, the gums were putrid, as, oftentimes, were scorbutic ulcers.[133] The jury was out, but Lind was doubtful enough to suggest that the terminology being used was too vague to be of service and had, in fact, misled those who had followed the logics implied by it in recommending specific treatments:

The term *putrid*, respecting animal and vegetable substances, is not indeed, in my opinion, sufficiently defined and restricted, so as to serve as a solid basis or foundation for explaining the symptoms of the scurvy. The idea of the scurvy proceeding from animal putrefaction, may, and hath misled physicians to propose and administer medicines for it, altogether ineffectual.[134]

Lind was not alone in his apostasy. In the early 1770s, Francis Milman was on the cusp of an illustrious establishment career. In 1776 he received his M. D. from Oxford; two years later he was elected Fellow of the College of Surgeons in London. In 1806 he would become physician to the King. In 1772

---

[130] James Lind, *A Treatise on the Scurvy. In Three Parts. Containing an Inquiry into the Nature, Causes, and Cure, of That Disease. Together with a Critical and Chronological View of What Has Been Published on the Subject*, 3rd ed. (London: S. Crowder, D. Wilson and G. Nicholls, T. Cadell, T. Becket and Co. G. Pearch, and W. Woodfall, 1772). Carpenter, 69–74; Charters, 34.

[131] Lind, *A Treatise on the Scurvy. In Three Parts. Containing an Inquiry into the Nature, Causes, and Cure, of That Disease. Together with a Critical and Chronological View of What Has Been Published on the Subject*, 511.

[132] On this point, Lind deployed Pringle's methods, steeping thin slices of mutton in the blood's serum and comparing the rate of its decay to that of blood drawn from the healthy. Ibid., 513.

[133] Ibid., 513, 14.

[134] Ibid., 514–5. Cited in Charters, 34.

he published a curious account of two cases of scurvy, not at sea (where the cold, moist air or salted provisions might be invoked as contributing factors), but on land. The case involved two old women who had survived for months on bread and tea alone. 'They pleaded, that the small pittance, allowed them by the parish, would not enable them to procure any better nourishment, during the winter season'.[135] As explanation, Milman invoked a 'gradually accumulated putrefaction', brought on by lack of food.[136] A decade later, however, Milman exchanged the old orthodoxy for a newer one, marking the change explicitly. 'In a paper which I had many years since the honour of transmitting to the College', he wrote, 'I adopted Sir J. Pringle's idea of a gradually accumulated putrefaction; but a reference to those who have examined the actual state of the blood in the scurvy, has taught me the groundlessness of such a notion'. Drawing on Lind and others, Milman now lambasted those who argued that putrid diseases were caused by the putridity of the blood and mocked those who sought recourse in antiseptics. With so many having been discovered in recent years, 'It must surely strike every unprejudiced mind with surprize, that ... the idea of a putrid disease should still be matter of so much alarm'.[137] Putridity, he argued, was not the cause of illness, but its effect. It was not that marsh miasma, for example, was not dangerous, or that exposure to noxious effluvia could not lead to a 'disposition to putridity'. It was rather that the direct impact of such effluvia was on the body's solids, not its fluids. Milman's was a nervous theory, which supposed that poison induced debility in the body's vital power.

I have no objection to suppose that these noxious contagious matters, which we will for the present call putrid matters, make their way into the circulation. But the question is, whether, having thus got admittance into the vital stream, they there act as ferments, and assimilate the blood to their own corrupt natures, or whether they produce their mischief by an action on the vital power, without affecting the sensible qualities of that fluid.[138]

Milman's answer – at least in 1782 – was clearly the second of the two options.

[135] Francis Milman, 'An Account of Two Instances of the True Scurvy, Seemingly Occasioned by the Want of Due Nourishment; Being an Extract of a Letter Addressed to Dr. Baker, by Francis Milman', *Medical Transactions, Published by the College of Physicians in London* 2 (1772): 476.

[136] Ibid., 477 Milman differed from standard accounts by arguing that the body required not antiseptic substances, but merely sufficient food. 'It is not then the antiseptic nature of the food taken in, which preserves our fluids from putrefaction, but the constant change of them, by which those parts, which are corrupting, and which, if retained would not fail to produce morbid effects, are expelled'. Ibid., 478, 79–80.

[137] *An Enquiry into the Source from Whence the Symptoms of the Scurvy and of Putrid Fevers Arise* (London: J. Dodsley, 1782), Note on 108, 211.

[138] Ibid., 134.

The critiques that both Lind and Milman levelled at putrefactive theories were not merely empirical, having to do with the question of whether the body and its fluids were really in a state of decay. They were also at once epistemological and ontological. Was dead flesh enough like the living body that experiments done on the former could reliably inform practice on the latter? I noted above that Hillary had little time for Pringle's assertion that alkaline substances could be used to treat putrefaction, whatever their abilities to retard the decay of beef may have been. And already, in the first edition of his text on his text on *Scurvy*, Lind offered similar objections to Pringle's method, although, like Hillary, he did not name his antagonist. Noting that salted and dried meat and fish did not putrefy in the air nearly as quickly as fresh flesh did, Lind suggested that one might conclude that salt meat was less likely to produce scorbutic putridity. Yet such a conclusion would be an obvious error:

This only proves how little we can learn of the effects of food and medicines in the body, by experiments made out of it. In a deep scurvy, there is the highest degree of putrefaction which a living animal can well subsist under: yet if we were so lucky as to find out the most powerful antiseptic in nature, it is not probable the scurvy could thereby be cured; although the body, after death, might be preserved by it as long as an *Aegyptian* mummy. On the contrary, the most putrid scurvies are daily cured by what quickly becomes putrescent out of the body, *viz.* broth made of coleworts and cabbage. However contradictory to some modern theories these facts may be, the truth of them is undeniable.[139]

There were clearly limits to the analogy between the dead and living body, however fruitful that analogy might be at times. Huxham was generally sympathetic to Pringle's approach, but he, too, observed that while volatile, alkaline salts might work to 'retard the Putrefaction of the Flesh of animals, and even in some Measure of the Blood, out of the Body ... yet mixed with the Blood, whilst actually under the Power of Circulation and the *Vis* Vitae, they certainly hasten its Dissolution, and consequent Putrefaction'.[140] Characteristically, Milman put the point even more bluntly: 'Many things', he wrote, 'which in the furnace or elaboratory of the chymist resist putrefaction powerfully, have no such action in the animal machine'.[141] He continued in a similarly vitalist vein a few pages later: 'The means of preserving dead substances from putrefaction, are no way applicable to the living moving fibre, a law peculiar to itself'.[142] In 1787, Benjamin Moseley denied that bile had any 'septical properties ... as

---

[139] Lind, *A Treatise of the Scurvy. In Three Parts. Containing an Inquiry into the Nature, Causes, and Cure of That Disease. Together with a Critical and Chronological View of What Has Been Published on the Subject*, note, 295–6.

[140] Huxham, *A Dissertation on the Malignant, Ulcerous Sore-Throat*, 54–5.

[141] Milman, *An Enquiry into the Source from Whence the Symptoms of the Scurvy and of Putrid Fevers Arise*, 225.

[142] Ibid., 228.

has been suggested from fallacious experiments, unconnected with life'.[143] By the 1770s, however, Pringle's theories were coming under fire even from those who agreed with his methods completely.

Problems in Pneumatic Medicine

Pringle was not, of course, alone in arguing for an analogy between what had happened in his experiments and what afflicted the body in sickness. Boerhaave's work provided a robust model for such studies, as had Robert Boyle's experiments on blood in the seventeenth century. Others quickly followed Pringle's lead, with some drawing upon the new pneumatic chemistry to do so. In 1754, Joseph Black had announced the discovery of a new kind of air, different from common atmospheric air. The air released when a given salt (magnesia alba) was heated or treated with acid had peculiar properties, being denser than common air, unable to support respiration or a flame, and turning lime water milky when bubbled through it. Black used the term 'fixed air', used by Hales to describe the air given off by various substances when they were decomposed by heat. In 1764, the surgeon David Macbride published a series of *Experimental Essays*, which he claimed to have designed as a sequel to the work of Hales, Black, and Pringle. In Macbride's account, dead bodies became putrid by losing fixed air. Replace the air artificially, and one could retard or even reverse putrefaction. In 1773, Pringle cited MacBride and others as the sources for Joseph Priestley's idea that water impregnated with antiseptic fixed air might work as a means for combating scurvy on long sea voyages.[144]

The next year, Priestley found himself defending Pringle's theories against a somewhat unlikely antagonist. In two books, one written in 1768, the other in 1771, the surgeon (and then doctor) William Alexander[145] proceeded to dismantle most of the central claims of the putrefactive paradigm, doing so by using Pringle's own tools.[146] In his first book, Alexander made it clear that

---

[143] Moseley, *A Treatise on Tropical Diseases; And on the Climate of the West-Indies*, 126.

[144] John Pringle, *A Discourse on the Different Kinds of Air, Delivered at the Anniversary Meeting of the Royal Society, November 30, 1773* (London: Royal Society, 1774), 15–16.

[145] Helping to make the point that putrid diseases were seen as afflictions more properly belonging to sites beyond the ken of the average metropolitan practitioner, Alexander noted that he had not personally encountered many cases of such distempers, though he had seen a number of putrid malignant fevers among French soldiers during the Seven Years War. William Alexander, *Experimental Essays on the Following Subjects: I. On the External Application of Antiseptics in Putrid Diseases. Ii. On the Doses and Effects of Medicines. Iii. On Diuretics and Sudorifics* (London: Edward and Charles Dilly, 1768), ii–iii, 6.

[146] In fact, Alexander made it a point to defend the use of experiments on dead flesh as a means of understanding the living body, while noting that 'it has been much litigated whether putrefaction be the same in the living and the dead animal'. It had been shown, he claimed, that a

he was in good company among those who found preposterous Boerhaave's suggestion – on the basis of his experiment on the dog in the sugar-baker's stove – that high heats alone could cause putrefaction within the living animal.[147] Putrid distempers required 'putrid particles' in the air, either due to 'putrid miasmata' or 'septic particles' flying from the breath of the diseased.[148] Alexander also advocated a change in treatment. Tests made on both dead rats and live patients made it clear that the best way to administer antiseptics was externally, by bathing or washing the patient in the substance. By this means, a much greater quantity of antiseptic could be introduced than would be possible were the treatment swallowed; the antiseptic would enter immediately into the blood, rather than travelling via the stomach; the stomach could not alter the substance by its action; and there was no danger of the patient's stomach rejecting (and ejecting) the cure.[149] The last point seemed to particularly recommend this method to the anonymous author of some *Practical Remarks on West India Diseases*. When vomiting was incessant in the yellow fever, the practitioner recommended a warm bath in which vinegar and nitre had been added, which by their 'antiseptic virtue' could resist the body's putrefaction.[150]

Alexander dedicated his second book to Pringle – as Priestley noted with some justifiable incredulity – even as it threatened Pringle's single most original argument: the claim that marsh miasmata caused putrid illnesses. Wherever else they may have disagreed, most previous medical writers (including Alexander only a few years earlier) seem to have found unproblematic the suggestion that effluvia arising from putrefying matter encouraged putrefaction in dead flesh. When he tested this supposition, however, Alexander found it wanting. Dangling pieces of meat above 'necessary houses' and swamps, he determined that such pieces lasted longer without putrefying than those kept in common air. Marshy vapours and the airs from human excrement (such

---

putrefying dead animal could communicate a putrid disease to a living one, which suggested that living and dead putrefaction were 'pretty nearly allied to each other'. This 'alliance' worked in both directions, since the breath of a diseased person could make meat rot faster than the breath of a healthy one. He also observed that the best modern physicians treated putrid disorders with substances proven to be antiseptic when applied to dead flesh. William Alexander, *An Experimental Enquiry Concerning the Causes Which Have Generally Been Said to Produce Putrid Diseases* (London: T. Becket and P. A. de Hondt, and T. Cadell, 1771), 47–8.

[147] Alexander cited a Dr Shebbeare who 'exclaims bitterly against Boerhaave, for inferring from an experiment he made, that a very great degree of heat is the cause of animal putrefaction', and noted that he had been told that a dissertation entitled *De Colore* had recently been published in Germany 'which asserts the same thing, and intirely overturns the Boerhaavian doctrine, of heat being the cause of putrefaction'. Alexander, 50–1.

[148] Ibid., 55–7.

[149] Ibid., 75.

[150] Anonymous, *Practical Remarks on West India Diseases*, 77.

as those in privies in camps) not only failed to encourage rot, they actively hindered it.[151]

The conclusion to be drawn from this experimental result seemed obvious and inescapable: however dangerous marshes might be, they could not be blamed for putrid diseases, for neither marsh water, nor the effluvia rising from it promoted putrefaction. Precisely the connection that Pringle had made central to the arguments of *Diseases of the Army* did not hold. Alexander went on, however, to make a second and even more radical claim. That he was aware of how radical it was may be seen from his hedging:

I do not mean here to plead the innocence of marsh miasmata, or to assume that marshes are salutary, because I have found the water of them to be antiseptic. I am not ignorant that almost all of the authors who have treated on this subject, and especially Lancisis, have agreed that it was hurtful, and adduced many instances of cities and armies having been attacked with putrid malignant diseases when exposed to it.[152]

Yet Alexander argued precisely not only that the noxious qualities of marshes might be 'a little doubtful', but that military observers may, in fact, have been systematically mistaken in associating swampy ground with illness. After all, it seemed likely that those in the army only paid attention to their marshy surroundings when sickness began to rage. Quizzed on the point, 'several military gentlemen' remembered that they had camped near putatively dangerous grounds with no ill effects, while suffering outbreaks of illnesses when nowhere near a marsh. In civilian life, it did not seem credible that boggy terrain proved uniquely deadly when those employed to drain such land did not seem adversely affected by their occupation. Perhaps, Alexander suggested, the problem was not putridity, but moisture alone. Humidity reduced perspiration, which could lead to many illnesses. Yet that explanation suggested that marsh water was no more dangerous than the water of the purest, clearest lake on a warm day. '[A]lmost all the authors who have treated on this subject' had indeed argued for the insalubrity of the putrid effluvia of marshes: Alexander was disagreeing with them all.[153]

In his 'Letter from the Rev. Dr. Priestley to Sir John Pringle', published in the *Philosophical* Transactions, Priestley could find little to dispute in Alexander's findings, but he firmly rejected the author's conclusions. 'I was particularly surprised, to meet with such an opinion as this', Priestley remarked to Pringle, making the stakes of the dispute clear, 'in a book inscribed to yourself, who have so clearly explained the great mischief of such a situation, in

---

[151] Alexander, 41.
[152] Ibid., 77–8.
[153] Ibid., 65, 80, 78.

your excellent treatise on the diseases of the army'.[154] Priestley offered his own explanation for the seemingly antiseptic properties of marsh air, relying on an unstated analogy with the role accorded common air in the phlogistic theory of combustion. Just as the flame of a candle burning under a glass would eventually die out because the phlogiston being released could no longer be absorbed by the saturated air, Priestley argued that putrid marsh air was already saturated, could absorb no more putrid effluvia from rotting substances, and hence worked to preserve them from further putrefactive processes. This did not mean, however, that such putrid effluvia were not enormously harmful when breathed into the lungs. That air remained 'very unfit for respiration'.[155]

Priestley portrayed Alexander as frankly irresponsible for suggesting that it might be safe to sleep, camp, or live near swampy terrain. He was not alone in this. In 1781, Thomas Dancer, who had served as physician for the expedition against Fort San Juan that had left Jamaica in 1780, made his objections clear. 'Alexander is of opinion', he declared, 'that marsh miasmata are not putrescent, but antiseptic; and he infers, therefore they are not hurtful: but the conclusion is both against reason and fact'.[156] Alexander Wilson, a physician trained by William Cullen, acknowledged in 1780 that it was hard to reconcile the antiseptic properties of marshes with 'their known effects in bringing on a putrescent tendency on living bodies', but proffered an explanation that echoed Priestley's nonetheless.[157] Marsh air, he argued, citing Priestley on the point, contained an 'overabundance' of phlogiston. In such air, lungs could not emit their own phlogiston-laden air, so that putrid diseases arose less because of what was taken *in* to the lungs and more because of what could not be expelled.

Although many of those with allegiances to Pringle and his ideas did not walk through it, Alexander's results opened a door towards the destruction of the putrefactive paradigm. Indeed, in saving Pringle's recommendations, Priestley had sacrificed the former's theoretical assumptions. In the seventh edition of *Diseases of the Army*, which appeared in 1775, even Pringle himself drew back from his earlier claims. He was careful, he noted, 'to avoid all denominations of fevers, communicating either no clear idea of their nature,

---

[154] J. Priestley, 'On the Noxious Quality of the Effluvia of Putrid Marshes. A Letter from the Rev. Dr. Priestley to Sir John Pringle', *Philosophical Transactions* 64 (1774): 91; Christopher Lawrence, 'Priestley in Tahiti: The Medical Interests of a Dissenting Chemist', in *Science, Medicine, and Dissent: Joseph Priestley*, ed. C. J. Lawrence and R. Anderson (London: Wellcome Trust/Science Museum, 1987).

[155] Priestley, 92.

[156] Thomas Dancer, *A Brief History of the Late Expedition against Fort San Juan, So Far as It Relates to the Diseases of the Troops; Together with Some Observations on Climate, Infection, and Contagion* (Kingston: D. Douglass & W. Aikman, 1781), 34.

[157] Alexander Wilson, *Some Observations Relative to the Influence of Climate on Vegetable and Animal Bodies* (London: T. Cadell, 1780), 154.

or a false one. The terms therefore of *nervous, bilious, putrid,* and *malignant,* applied so commonly to fevers, will either not occur at all, or be so defined as to occasion no ambiguity'.[158] To say that the air that arose from stagnant ponds was dangerous was not to say that it induced putrid diseases. And both Priestley and Wilson's explanations rested – either implicitly or explicitly – on a denial of the similarity between results on the living human body and those found in the laboratory based on dead flesh. More hostile readers, like Milman, cited Alexander's work with more enthusiasm, invoking it to critique the value of antiseptic treatments. Clearly, without following Alexander fully, one could hold on to a view that held marsh miasmas to be potentially deadly – a position that could not be countered with impunity – while rejecting the underlying logic of putrefactive explanations. External putridity did not lead directly to internal rot.

A New Paradigm

Of course, paradigms do not fall merely because they are criticised. One needs an alternative mode of explanation. Such alternatives were, particularly in the 1780s, both many and various. For some, a resource was the work of William Cullen, the Edinburgh professor who was, for the second half of the eighteenth century what Boerhaave had been for the first.[159] Indeed, one may note that most of the main proponents of the putrefactive paradigm (such as Huxham, Hillary and Pringle himself) were all students of Boerhaave's, Pringle being among the last to work with the Leiden professor.[160] A number of those most critical of the paradigm tended to be students of Cullen, who so denied the utility of the category of 'putrid fever', that he did not include it in his nosology.[161] He noted that both ancients and moderns ('who are in general much disposed to follow the former') had distinguished between putrid and non-putrid fevers,

---

[158] John Pringle, *Observations on the Diseases of the Army,* 7th ed. (London: W. Strahan, J. and F. Rivington, W. Johnston, T. Payne, T. Longman, Wilson and Nicoll, T. Durham, and T. Cadell, 1775), xv.

[159] For brief and elegant summaries of Cullen's ideas, see Lester S. King, *The Medical World of the Eighteenth Century* (Chicago: University of Chicago Press, 1958), 139–43; W. F. Bynum, 'Cullen and the Study of Fevers in Britain, 1760–1820', *Medical History (Supplement)* 1 (1981). See also A. Doig et al., eds., *William Cullen and the Eighteenth Century Medical World: A Bicentenary Exhibition and Symposium Arranged by the Royal College of Physicians of Edinburgh in 1990* (Edinburgh: Edinburgh University Press, 1993).

[160] Huxham began his medical degree at Leiden under Boerhaave in 1715. Due to financial reasons, he was forced to complete the degree at Rheims. R. M. McConaghey, 'John Huxham', *Medical History* 13, no. 3 (1969): 280.

[161] Dale C. Smith, 'Medical Science, Medical Practice, and the Emerging Concept of Typhus in Mid-Eighteenth-Century Britain', *Medical History (Supplement)* 1 (1981): 132.

but Cullen could not see the utility of the distinction.[162] It was not, he made clear, that he denied that putrescency was possible. In the 1784 edition of his *First Lines of the Practice of Physic* (but not in the first, 1777 edition) he alluded to the debates discussed above. 'I have no doubt', he wrote, 'how much soever it has been disputed by some ingenious men, that a putrescency of the fluids, to a certain degree, does really take place in many cases of fever'.[163] The problem, however, was that such putrescency attended many different kinds of fevers, and to varying different degrees. Putrefaction might be present, but it was not characteristic and hence was not usefully diagnostic. Putrescency was an effect and not a cause of fever, he argued (presumably this was the source of Milman's similar claims). Hence, the expulsion of putrid fluids could not effect a cure.

Where putrefaction retained an important role in Cullen's work was in his discussion of the remote causes of epidemic fevers. These Cullen limited to two: contagions and miasmata.[164] Contagions were effluvia deriving from the bodies of people in illness; miasmata derived from non-human substances. Each had similar causes and effects: 'They arise from a putrescent matter; their production is favoured, and their power increased, by circumstances which favour putrefaction, and they often prove putrefactive ferments with respect to the animal fluids'.[165] They caused fevers, however, not by the induction of putrefaction, but by the fact that putrid matter was a powerful sedative. In Cullen's scheme, this sedative power, when applied to the nervous system, diminished the brain's energy and induced debility. The body then reacted in such a way as to obviate these negative effects, entering a cold state as a means of stimulating the increased action of the heart and larger arteries (experienced as a fever), which would in turn raise the energy levels of the brain. Fevers, then, 'do not arise from changes in the state of the fluids', but rather 'chiefly depend upon changes in the state of the moving powers of the animal'.[166] Internal putridity

---

[162] William Cullen, 'First Lines of the Practice of Physic (1784)', in *The Works of William Cullen*, ed. John Thomson (Edinburgh and London: William Blackwood; T. & G. Underwood, 1827), 526.

[163] Ibid. Compare *First Lines of the Practice of Physic. For the Use of Students in the University of Edinburgh*, vol. 1 (London and Edinburgh: J. Murray; William Creech, 1777), 63. The mid-1780s seems to have been the high point for this debate. Another author noted in 1785 that '[t]he influence of putrid effluvia on the human system, has of late been the subject of much controversy'. M. de Lassone, 'Histoire de divers Accidens graves, occasionnés par les miasmes d'animaux en putrefaction, et de la nouvelle methode de traitment qui a été employé avec succés dans cette circonstance', *Medical Commentaries* 9 (1785).

[164] In discussing marsh effluvia or miasmata, Cullen drew heavily on 'Dr Lind's ingenious work on the preservation of health of Europeans in warm climates'. Cullen, 'First Lines of the Practice of Physic (1784)', 506. The quoted lines are from Cullen's notes on the manuscript for his text, added by Thomson.

[165] Ibid., 546.

[166] Ibid., 506.

might accompany a fever, but the seat of the illness was in the nervous system, not in the blood or bile.

One finds a related, although not identical, argument in the work of Benjamin Moseley, who studied medicine in London, Paris, and Leiden before establishing a practice in Jamaica in 1768. There he was appointed surgeon-general, returning to England after roughly a dozen years. He received his M. D. in 1784 and in 1787 published *A Treatise on Tropical Diseases; And on the Climate of the West-Indies*, a work that was the first to use the term 'tropical diseases' and that self-consciously set itself the task of supplanting Towne's and Hillary's works as the standard references on the illnesses of the West Indies. 'Worthy of imitation as the laudable efforts of Towne, and respectable as Hillary's accuracy is describing what he had actually seen, were, much improvement in the treatment of diseases has since their time taken place in that part of the world'.[167] There was no more reason, Moseley added, 'why all progress should stop with Towne and Hillary, than that it should have ceased with Hippocrates'.[168] The *Treatise* largely succeeded in its aims. A second edition appeared in 1789 under a slightly altered title, a German translation in 1790, and a fourth edition in 1803. One finds it cited throughout the literature on the diseases of warm climates at the end of the eighteenth and the beginning of the nineteenth centuries.

Hillary had declared the yellow fever to be a putrid distemper. Moseley rejected the general applicability of the category to the diseases of the West Indies.

Much has been said by writers concerning putrid fevers, and the tendency of all fevers to putrefaction, in hot climates. But such opinions are not founded on practice, however much they may seem to agree with theory. The great endemic there is the *Nervous Remittent Fever*, which is unattended with any putrid symptoms, and which has its seat in the nervous system; or, as I have often thought, in the brain itself.[169]

He was particularly scathing about those who took the antiseptic properties of wine, punch, and spirits as an excuse for revelry, arguing that this faulty prophylactic practice had resulted in the 'death of thousands'.[170] As can be

---

[167] Moseley, *A Treatise on Tropical Diseases; And on the Climate of the West-Indies*, 382.

[168] Ibid., 383.

[169] Ibid. That said, elsewhere Moseley seemed to use the term unproblematically, suggesting that it was perhaps the totalising element of putrefactive explanations to which he was opposed, rather than their specific deployment: 'Stagnant waters and swamps load the air with pernicious vapours, that are productive of obstinate intermittent fevers, diseases of the liver, and putrid diseases'. Or, later in the text, where he accepted Pringle's terminology as well: 'Dysenteries, as well as other disorders, in hot climates, in Autumn, have more of the putrid, than of the inflammatory diathesis'. Ibid., 36, 196.

[170] Ibid., 48.

seen, Moseley subscribed to something like Cullen's nervous theory of disease, although he regarded tropical heat as the cause of the body's debility, rather than miasmatic effluvia. Indeed, in Moseley's explanation, marshes were not at fault at all in producing the characteristic diseases of the climate. Nor was heat alone a problem. Moseley followed a long tradition in noting that he had experienced equally warm temperatures in Europe (in Naples, Rome and Montpellier).[171] As long as heat and humidity promoted perspiration, in fact, climatic conditions carried their own remedy with them. 'The mischief they produce is, that they dispose the body to the slightest impressions from cold', for even a slight change in the temperature was experienced as considerable by the debilitated tropical body. Drawing on a sub-element in Cullen's theorising, Moseley declared that it was this experience of sudden cooling that inspired the onset of fever.[172] '[H]owever paradoxical it may appear', he wrote, 'cold is the cause of almost all the diseases in hot climates, to which climate alone is accessory'.[173]

John Hunter was just as critical of putrefactive theories as Moseley, but he found less inspiration in Cullen, despite having been a student at Edinburgh from 1770 to 1775. After completing his thesis, Hunter was admitted as a licentiate to the Royal College of Physicians in 1777 and was then appointed physician to the army.[174] He served as Superintendent of the military hospitals in Jamaica from the beginning of 1781 to May 1783, after which he returned to London and began private practice. His *Observations on the Diseases of the Army in Jamaica* appeared in 1788.[175] Like Moseley's, Hunter's text became a standard reference for medical men in the West Indies and throughout the Tropics. Among its most oft-cited sections was that which supplied a long disquisition on Jamaica's remitting fevers, of which the most severe was probably the disease known as the yellow fever or black vomit. Previous authors, Hunter noted in a very fine summary of the logics of the putrefactive paradigm, had

---

[171] Ibid., 41–2.
[172] Although Cullen regarded human and marsh effluvia as the main cause of fevers, he also looked at other causes, cold included. In doing so, he stressed the historicity, so to speak, of the bodily experience of temperature, just as Moseley would: 'The *relative* power of cold with respect to the living human body, is that power by which it produces a sensation of cold in it; and with respect to this, it is agreeable to the general principle of sensation, that the sensation produced is not in proportion to the absolute force of impression, but according as the new impression is stronger or weaker than that which had been applied immediately before'. Cullen, 'First Lines of the Practice of Physic (1784)', 547.
[173] Moseley, *A Treatise on Tropical Diseases; And on the Climate of the West-Indies*, 47.
[174] It may well be this thesis – an early contribution to race-science – that remains Hunter's most famous work today. John Hunter, *Disputatio Inauguralis, Quaedam De Hominum Varietatibus, Et Harum Causis, Exponens* (Edinburgh: Balfour and Smellie, 1775).
[175] Hunter, *Observations on the Diseases of the Army in Jamaica; and on the Best Means of Preserving the Health of Europeans, in That Climate.*

laid blame for the distemper at the feet of a corrupted bile or a putrid state of the blood.

Next to the opinion that the fever proceeds from bile, none is more prevalent than that it is of a putrid nature; and that the whole mass of humours are running violently into putrefaction. If it be asked what is meant by the term *putrefaction*, it will doubtless be answered, that species of fermentation or change, which dead animal matter in a certain degree of heat and moisture, joined to an admission of air, spontaneously undergoes. That such is the acceptation of the term cannot be doubted, when it is observed that in reasoning on this subject, whatever is found to check putrefaction out of the body, is supposed to have the same effect taken internally, and is therefore recommended in diseases believed to be putrid; and whatever promotes putrefaction out of the body, is supposed to be noxious, and is therefore avoided.[176]

Hunter, however, found little to support in this account. It was true, he acknowledged, that putrefaction led to the dissolution of flesh and fluids and was often accompanied by a noxious smell and that, in fevers, the blood was sometimes found to be in a dissolved state and the patient's body emitted an 'extremely disagreeable' odour.[177] But there the similarity ended. In dead bodies the skin turned a greenish colour: no such change was observed in the living. The phenomena might be saved by arguing that putrefaction proceeded differently in the living and the dead, but then one could no longer make inferences (as Pringle had) from one to the other. In any case, Hunter argued, 'the opinion of the putrid nature of the disease is founded on a vague analogy, which will not stand the test of experiment, or observation'.[178] The dissolution of the blood was often observed in scorbutic cases, but (here he cited Lind) such blood did not putrefy any faster than the blood of anyone else. 'If the dissolved state of the blood in scurvy do not depend on putrefaction', he stated, making clear the once-paradigmatic stature of scurvy as a putrid disease, 'there is little reason to suppose, that in fevers it is owing to that cause'.[179]

What, then, was the cause? Hunter rejected several of Cullen's arguments, seeing no evidence that the fever arose as a reaction to a 'cold fit' and denying that symptoms all flowed from an 'affection of the brain and nervous system'.[180] He did, however, cite Cullen in support of the notion that marshy effluvia produced the illness by acting as a poison on the human frame, and Priestley for the fact that part of the air breathed in by the lungs made its way to the blood and hence might carry the poison with it.[181] Precisely how

---

[176] Ibid., 172–3.
[177] Ibid., 173.
[178] Ibid., 175.
[179] Ibid., 175–6.
[180] Ibid., 179, 82–3.
[181] Ibid., 184, 85.

such a poison produced a fever, Hunter professed not to know: 'Our ignorance of the animal economy absolutely precludes us, from giving any adequate answer to this question'. The operation of other poisons on the body provided an analogy, however. The symptoms of poisoning could be much like those of a febrile disease: vomiting, convulsions, a dissolution of the blood (in the case of the viper's bite), jaundice, weakness, fainting, and even death. Yet, however apt the analogy might be, it could only be of limited utility: no one properly understood how any other poisons, even the most common, actually worked. At the beginning of the eighteenth century, Mead had drawn on iatrochemical theories of ferments to explain the action of poisons and had then transferred that explanation to his theory of the plague. Almost at the end of the century, in an ironic twist, Hunter turned to more recent work on poisons, but eschewed any explanations for their action, seeming similarly agnostic about the cause of what had once been known as putrid fevers. Common ground, of course, remained across the paradigmatic divide, but it was marshy, perilous, and to be avoided as much as possible.

Conclusion

For Creighton, Britain's 'putrid constitution' ended around 1765, at roughly the time that the industrial revolution can be said to have begun. Christopher Hamlin has suggested that putrid theories reigned until the mid-1770s, at which point nervous theories of fever began to supplant them.[182] Looking at the colonies, Harrison has argued that it is from the 1790s that one begins to see the emergence of a new orthodoxy about the diseases of warm climates, one rooted in Cullenian notions of nervous debility.[183] Certainly one sees Cullen's mark very clearly in the work of William Lempriere, although even here the differences from Cullen's schema are as striking as the similarities. Lempriere served as 'Apothecary to his Majesty's Forces' and published his *Practical Observations on the Diseases of the Army in Jamaica* in 1799, there laying out a step-wise process by which the newly arrived to a warm climate could be afflicted by a 'tropical continued fever'. Those coming from cold climates arrived with tense fibres and a plethoric habit, but their bodies soon began to undergo a relaxation, with the energy of nervous systems declining somewhat. Initially, this loss of energy was counterbalanced by the stimulus provided by the high environmental heat, so that the blood tended to circulate with its usual force. Were this state now changed by the dimunition of the capacity

---

[182] Hamlin, 'What Is Putrid About Putrid Fever?'.
[183] Harrison, *Medicine in an Age of Commerce and Empire: Britain and its Tropical Colonies, 1660–1830*, 85.

of the voluntary muscles (due to fatigue, excessive heat, or intemperance, for example), the action of the involuntary muscles would increase to make up the balance. Blood would then be forced from the arteries into the veins, with a 'plethoric state of the venous system' as a necessary result. 'Look at the newly-arrived European after common exercise', Lempriere suggested, 'and see how his countenance is flushed, mark the turgescence of his veins, and take the whole of his countenance into your consideration, and you will find it to denote a very unequal circulation. Observe with what facility the robust and the athletic are fatigued, it will prove to you in what degree the voluntary nervous energy is impaired'.[184] And it was now, while a considerable venous plethora existed, that marsh miasmas had their most dire effect on the body, acting as a 'poison, or stimulus, or spasm-forming cause',[185] producing an even greater plethora in the veins and – even worse – congestions within the liver and the brain, where pressure could build to the point of fatality. Marsh miasmata is dangerous here, as in Cullen's *First Lines*, but the effluvia would appear to be a stimulant, rather than a sedative. And it is the heat of the climate that induces a nervous debility in the bodies described by Lempriere, not the poison of putrefactive matter.

For others writing in the 1790s, it seems harder to locate an end of the putrefactive paradigm. In 1793, Thomas Dickson Reide was still dividing fevers into three types: inflammatory, putrid, and those that were both.[186] In offering *Medical Advice to the Inhabitants of Warm Climates,* Robert Thomas seems simply to have ignored the notion that nervous and putrefactive theories might be opposed to one another, discussing nervous fevers and putrid fevers in succession.[187] John Bell denied that the climate – whether it acted on the nerves or the fluids – was much to blame for the suffering of soldiers: the real problem was the soldiers themselves and their near-constant intemperance.[188] It may not be wrong, however, to regard cases like these as hold-outs, for the trend would seem to be clear. Apart from anything else, one might compare the social status

---

[184] William Lempriere, *Practical Observations on the Diseases of the Army in Jamaica, as They Occurred between the Years 1792 and 1797,* 2 vols. (London: T. N. Longham and O. Rees, 1799), 95.

[185] Ibid., 97.

[186] Thomas Dickson Reide, *A View of the Diseases of the Army in Great Britain, America, the West Indies, and on Board of King's Ships and Transports, from the Beginning of the Late War to the Present Time* (London: J. Johnson, 1793), 39.

[187] Robert Thomas, *Medical Advice to the Inhabitants of Warm Climates, on the Domestic Treatment of All the Diseases Incidental Therein: With a Few Useful Hints to New Settlers, for the Preservation of Health, and the Prevention of Sickness* (London: J. Strahan and W. Richardson, 1790).

[188] John Bell, *An Inquiry into the Causes Which Produce, and the Means of Preventing Diseases among British Officers, Soldiers, and Others in the West Indies* (London: J. Murray, 1791).

of critics of the putrefactive paradigm in the late 1780s and 1790s with those who still made use of it. Hunter, Moseley, and Lempriere all held fairly prestigious positions within the British armed forces, while Reide, Thomas, and Bell did not.

As it held sway for roughly four decades after mid-century, the effect of the putrefactive paradigm in shaping attitudes towards the diseases of warm climates was profound. This was not, I think – although the connection seems tempting – because the paradigm aided in making the diseases of the tropics seem distinctive, the heat and humidity of the region encouraging the kinds of rot upon which the theories of putridity were built. For, in many ways, the putrefactive paradigm made it obvious that putrid diseases were not merely products of warm weather. Scurvy, which became the emblematic putrid disease after Lind's work, had long been associated with cold European winters. The putrefactive paradigm, in fact, paired the characteristic diseases of warm climates with the most distinctive disease of shipboard life, suggesting that we might best see the entire theoretical schema as one that encompassed the British Empire outside the metropole: the colonies it held and the fleets that allowed it to rule the waves. The putrefactive paradigm was imperial medicine.

We should also not ignore the significance of the paradigm within the medicine of the British Isles. What Boerhaave's *Aphorisms* had been for almost four decades after their first publication in 1709, and what Cullen's *First Lines of the Practice of Physic* was for several decades after 1777, Pringle's *Observations of the Diseases of the Army* was for the intervening period: a common and standard reference for medical men both civilian and military, both in Britain and throughout the empire. And in dividing fevers into two kinds, the inflammatory and the putrid, the first associated with the diseases of Pringle's home and the second with armies in camp and with warm climates, Pringle made a rather remarkable point. To understand fevers in general, one needed to understand them as they appeared throughout the Empire. It became the physician who wished to master his craft to understand not merely the afflictions of London, but also those of army, navy, and colonial life. There was what we might call an openness to empire about Pringle's vision, one that recalls Lind's archipelagic imaginary of the last chapter and seems characteristic of the period immediately after the victories of the Seven Years War.

That said, the putrefactive paradigm would indeed be partially responsible for later constructions of the diseases of warm climates as distinctive and requiring not a broad and imperial medicine, but one that could grapple with the specific pathologies of the tropics. For, precisely by associating putridity not solely with climate but with locations (jails, hospitals, ships, and warm countries),

Pringle weakened the analogy that had shaped earlier understandings of the illnesses of India, Africa, and the Americas. No longer could one simply associate the diseases of Britain's summer with those of warm climates, for they might as easily come in the cold and damp (as with scurvy) or at any season (as with jail and hospital fevers). The diseases of warm climates may have been seen by practitioners in the tropics as near-universally putrid, but all putrid diseases were not those of warm climates.

The climate/season analogy had, for a long time, worked against the idea that there was something truly distinctive about the diseases of warm countries. In troubling it, the putrefactive paradigm offered in its stead an even larger similitude, one that saw the empire as a whole as the space for British medicine. With the replacement of putrefactive theories by those that located the seat of disease in the nerves, authors like Moseley articulated a different vision of empire, one that saw the colonies as strikingly distinct from – and decidedly subordinate to – the metropole. Colley has noted the irony in conceptions of empire in the second half of the eighteenth century. The victories of the Seven Years War induced a kind of collective angst and thoughtful reflections about the relationship between the British Isles and the large swathe of the Earth that they now commanded. After the loss of the American colonies, however, one finds a counter-intuitive confidence about the imperial mission. 'Instead of being sated with conquests, alarmed at their own presumptuous grandeur as they had been after 1763, the British could now unite in feeling hard done by. Their backs were once more well and truly to the wall, filling many of them with grim relish and renewed strength'.[189] Where 'some leading Britons', she notes, 'had been embarrassed by the weight of empire, even questioning its morality', by the 1780s such scruples had evaporated and London passed a series of reforms (the India Act in 1784, the Canada Act in 1791) aimed at strengthening control of its remaining holdings.[190] In medicine, one finds a similar transition. In the work of Pringle and Lind there is a sense, medically speaking, that we are all in this together. From the 1780s, the colonies increasingly became portrayed as dangerous foreign zones, to be mastered, rather than incorporated. The introduction to Moseley's text addressed the book to those 'impelled by necessity, or induced by interest, to visit the torrid zone' thereby leaving behind 'the delightful climates of the earth ... for such as no care, or art, can ever make agreeable'.[191] Later, he simple declared England's climate to be 'the best on the habitable globe – For by what comparison is a climate to be estimated, which produces such a race of people as the English, and in

[189] Colley, *Britons: Forging the Nation, 1707–1837*, 146.
[190] Ibid., 147.
[191] Moseley, *A Treatise on Tropical Diseases; And on the Climate of the West-Indies*, 1–2.

which almost every species of animal arrives to their utmost perfection?'.[192] If others were less jingoistic, by 1800 they nonetheless portrayed the relationship between Britain and its tropical holdings as an oppositional one.[193] Among the categories that helped frame this opposition was race and it is to this different kind of difference as formulated in medical discourse that we now turn.

[192] Ibid., 44–5.
[193] Harrison, ' "The Tender Frame of Man": Disease, Climate and Racial Difference in India and the West Indies, 1760–1860'.

Part III

Race

5 Race-Medicine in the Colonies, 1679–1750

Introduction

In 1735, the former naval surgeon John Atkins penned what must be considered one of the more striking understatements of his age. In *A Voyage to Guinea, Brasil, and the West-Indies*, he described the differences between the physical appearance of the inhabitants of Guinea and that of 'the rest of Mankind'. These differences were so profound, he claimed, that 'tho' it be a little Heterodox, I am persuaded the black and white Race have, *ab origine*, sprung from different-coloured first parents'.[1] To suggest that Adam was not the original father of all humankind was, of course, considerably more than a little heterodox. This position, known as polygenism, was very uncommon in the eighteenth century. Yet Atkins was unusual even in his polygenism, for – unlike most polygenists of whom I am aware prior to the middle of the century – he spent very little time in relating his heterodoxy to Biblical views and he proffered his most detailed remarks within a medical text, as opposed to one concerned with theology, natural philosophy, or history.

The fact that Atkins espoused polygenism in the same volume in which he described diseases peculiar to native Africans led one of the few scholars to have considered his texts in any detail to suggest that one might therein find 'connections between concepts of race and concepts of disease'.[2] That Atkins gave up on his polygenism in a later edition of his best known work without significantly changing his etiological understanding leads me to the opposite conclusion. By the 1730s, I suggest, environmentalist understandings of human physical difference were beginning to change. Environmentalist

---

[1] John Atkins, *A Voyage to Guinea, Brasil, and the West-Indies; in His Majesty's Ships, the Swallow and Weymouth* (London: Caesar Ward and Richard Chandler, 1735), 39.

[2] Norris Saakwa-Mante, 'Western Medicine and Racial Constitutions: Surgeon John Atkins Theory of Polygenism and Sleepy Distemper in the 1730s', in *Race, Science, and Medicine, 1700–1960*, eds. Waltraud Ernst and Bernard Harris (London and New York: Routledge, 1999), 34. See also Curtin, *The Image of Africa: British Ideas and Action, 1780–1850*, 41, 83; Jennifer L. Morgan, '"Some Could Suckle over Their Shoulder": Male Travelers, Female Bodies, and the Gendering of Racial Ideology, 1500–1770', *The William and Mary Quarterly* 54 (1997).

understandings of disease, however, particularly with regard to the diseases of warm climates, were not. Atkins provides us with a fine example of a trend that would continue for the majority of the century: the widening gap between 'race-science' with its anatomical focus and what I am here terming 'race-medicine', with its emphasis on racial physiology and pathology.

This chapter and Chapter 7, divided chronologically, are dedicated to a history of race-medicine across the eighteenth century. Section 5.1 in this chapter provides an overview of the main arguments concerning the origins of racial difference from the discovery of the New World to the mid-1700s. Section 5.2 draws on literature that has insisted on reading discourses concerning race together with those concerning gender and sexuality, offering an analysis of the relationships connecting women's diseases, climate, race, and locality. Section 5.3 concentrates on the role played (or not) by racial thinking in medical texts from the late seventeenth century to roughly 1750. Section 5.4 is then dedicated to a close reading of Atkins' several publications from 1729 to 1742, situating his claims in the intellectual contexts previously described. As we shall see, Atkins may best be understood as being pulled in two opposite directions, as the doors to an increasingly anti-climatic racial thinking began to open, while the medicine of warm climates became increasingly Hippocratic and environmentalist.[3]

Before proceeding, however, some comments about terminology. Race-medicine is a neologism: like 'race-science', the term after which it is modelled, it was not an actors' category.[4] One does not find those who called themselves 'race-physicians' or 'race-surgeons', any more than one found, in the nineteenth century, scientists who called themselves 'race-biologists'. Both terms are, moreover, particularly fraught when applied to the eighteenth century, when the word race was only beginning to acquire the meanings we associate with it today. Indeed, those who study race have tended to divide themselves, according to the question of whether it is legitimate to use the term prior to (roughly) 1750 or not. Those who offer an expansivist definition note that observations concerning traits we now regard as quintessentially racialised (skin colour, for example, or hair type) have been made in almost every culture through history, and that one can find xenophobic remarks made against outsiders, who were at least partly distinguished by appearance, in works from the classical age onwards.[5] Those who offer a more restrictive

---

[3] On growing critiques of the climate theory in Britain in the seventeenth century, see Malcolmson.

[4] Stepan.

[5] See, for example, Thomas Gossett, *Race: The History of an Idea in America* (Oxford: Oxford University Press, 1997). The first edition of the text appeared in 1963. Gossett acknowledged that one finds very few examples of statements about the importance of racial differences before the eighteenth century. Nonetheless, he argued that one can find 'racism' and 'race-prejudice' in cultures at least 5,000 years old. Ibid., 3–4. As his title suggest, Benjamin Isaac finds the

reading argue, by contrast, that observations about physical difference carried little weight compared to observations about social or cultural differences. Physical differences made little difference. The real issue was whether one spoke Greek, for example, or (later) whether one was a Christian or pagan, not skin colour or the presence or absence of facial hair. Nancy Stepan, who coined the term, restricted her study of 'race-science' to the years from 1800–1960, a period in which, as Hannah Augstein has lucidly noted, one may identify three rather novel and agreed upon tenets undergirding the science of race: first, that mankind could be divided into 'races', the characteristics of which were fixed (or essentially fixed);[6] second, that all human races did not possess the same intellectual and moral qualities; and third, that intellect and character were determined (at least in large part) by physical characteristics – a position we can term racial determinism.[7] Clearly, nineteenth-century race theory did not closely resemble earlier claims about race, so that the debate over when a historian might begin a history of race comes to resemble that over the history of sexuality. One might identify forms of behaviour that we would regard as 'homosexual' in the classical era (just as we may identify statements that sound 'racist'), but these behaviours (and these statements) did not carry the meanings that we associate with them today. In particular, before a period we might roughly call the 'modern' age, neither sexuality nor race was seen as an essential category.[8]

case that racism has always existed less compelling, but locates its origin in the classical age. Benjamin H. Isaac, *The Invention of Racism in Classical Antiquity* (Princeton: Princeton University Press, 2004). One finds the middle ages posited as the origin for the concept in several of the essays in Miriam Eliav-Feldon, Benjamin H. Isaac, and Joseph Ziegler, eds., *The Origin of Racism in the West* (Cambridge: Cambridge University Press, 2009). Francisco Bethencourt, *Racisms: From the Crusades to the Twentieth Century* (Princeton: Princeton University Press, 2013). George Mosse is perhaps the most famous proponent of the view that, as he phrased it: 'Eighteenth-century Europe was the cradle of modern racism'. George L. Mosse, *Toward the Final Solution: A History of European Racism* (New York: H. Fertig, 1978). For a good overview of the literature that has seen racism as part of the 'dark side of the Enlightenment', see Colin Kidd, *The Forging of Races: Race and Scripture in the Protestant Atlantic World, 1600–2000* (Cambridge: Cambridge University Press, 2006), 79–120. See also Justin E. H. Smith, *Nature, Human Nature, and Human Difference: Race in Early Modern Philosophy* (Princeton: Princeton University Press, 2015).

[6] Nicholas Hudson makes an important addition to this criterion, by noting that the number of races in the late eighteenth and early nineteenth century are small, with concomitant populations within them then very large. Where once observers noted considerable differences between the inhabitants of a given region (such as the Americas), such differences were subordinated to a larger similitude imposed by the logic of race. Hudson.

[7] Stepan; Hannah Franziska Augstein, *Race: The Origins of an Idea, 1760–1850* (Bristol: Thoemmes Press, 1996), x.

[8] Michel Foucault, *The History of Sexuality*, 3 vols., vol. I (London: Allen Lane, 1978). Arnold I. Davidson, *The Emergence of Sexuality: Historical Epistemology and the Formation of Concepts* (Cambridge, MA: Harvard University Press, 2001). One of the central loci for this debate concerned the so-called 'Boswell thesis' about attitudes toward homosexuality in early Christianity. John Boswell, *Christianity, Social Tolerance, and Homosexuality: Gay*

My sympathies tend to lie with those offering more restrictive understandings of the terms involved, but there is no need to take understandings of race in the period in which race science became 'normal science' as entirely definitional of the concept. For the eighteenth century, I would suggest, the question should be rather broader: when did race become understood not as an effect, but as itself a cause?[9] A comparison between classical and nineteenth-century examples should make the distinction clear. In Hippocratic thought, physical differences were caused by climate and diet – by the 'Airs, Waters, and Places' in which people lived. Also produced by such environmental causes were forms of government, styles of behaviour, and systems of culture. 'Race' in other words did not cause differences in intellect or morality; it was itself an effect of environmental differences. In the nineteenth century, however, race became, as Robert Knox would infamously phrase it, 'destiny'.[10] Physical differences – understood racially – were taken to be the *cause* of mental differences. Africans had smaller brains, it was argued, and hence lower intellects.[11]

In attempting to identify when race moved from effect to cause, one should note that the debate between polygenists and monogenists may at times be something of a red herring. Darwinian monogenists happily used race as a causal mechanism and polygenism did not necessarily accord physical difference an explanatory role. As we shall see, some adopted the doctrine of special creations as a way of dealing with theological concerns that had little to do with questions of racialised difference, while other early polygenists took such differences as *explanandum*, without then turning to the question of whether they could then be used as *explanans*. It should also be noted that causal explanations in medicine differed from those in natural history or natural philosophy, not least because the questions being asked were different. Thus, while it might be suggested that race science was already, in many ways, race-medicine, since so many of those who have been identified as early prominent race-scientists were trained in medicine, anatomy, or surgery, my target here is rather different. The question is simple: when does one begin to find arguments that related racialised physical differences to the presence (or inclination) to

People in Western Europe from the Beginning of the Christian Era to the Fourteenth Century (Chicago: University of Chicago Press, 1980). For contemporary re-examinations, see Mathew Kuefler, ed. *The Boswell Thesis: Essays on Christianity, Social Tolerance, and Homosexuality* (Chicago: University of Chicago Press, 2006).

9 I am using the word 'cause' here in its contemporary sense. For excellent discussions of causes in eighteenth-century medicine, see Christopher Hamlin, 'Predisposing Causes and Public Health in Early Nineteenth-Century Medical Thought', *Social History of Medicine* 5 (1992). Margaret DeLacy, 'The Conceptualization of Influenza in Eighteenth-Century Britain: Specificity and Contagion', *Bulletin of the History of Medicine* 67 (1993); 'Nosology, Mortality, and Disease Theory in the Eighteenth Century', *Journal of the History of Medicine* 54 (1999).

10 Robert Knox, *The Races of Men: A Fragment* (London: H. Renshaw, 1850).

11 See, e.g. Stephen Jay Gould, *The Mismeasure of Man* (New York: Norton, 1981).

particular diseases in ways that saw them not as sharing a common cause (the environment, for example), but rather in ways that saw race as the *cause* of the affliction? The answer, at least in this chapter, is also fairly simple: with some few possible exceptions, not until at least after the mid-eighteenth century, even as race began to acquire a (limited) causal role in other realms.

Having laid out my question and hinted at my answer, let me lay out what I see as the stakes behind this study. My intention is to offer a contribution towards and correction of much of the work done on the intellectual history of naturalistic understandings of race.[12] The seminal work on the subject was Stepan's *The Idea of Race in Science: Great Britain, 1800–1960*. In retrospect, it seems easy to situate it at the centre of two complementary trends in early science studies. One sought to demonstrate the social, cultural, and political roots of seemingly 'objective' ideas in contemporary science. This brings to mind a number of studies of Darwinian thought, the Forman thesis, and an array of works within feminist history and philosophy of science. The other trend sought to problematise demarcation criteria, pointing out the difficulties in differentiating, methodologically, between 'good' science and so-called pseudo-science. This was the province of some early work in the sociology of scientific knowledge (on 'spoon-bending', and parapsychology, for example) and also work by historians on subjects such as magic, alchemy, phrenology, and eugenics. Science that was judged 'cranky' and objectionable by today's standards was clearly not always regarded as such. Stepan's book combined both of these arguments. On the one hand, she asserted: 'The scientists who gave scientific racism its credibility and respectability were often first-rate scientists struggling to understand what appeared to them to be deeply puzzling problems of biology and human society. To dismiss their work as merely "pseudoscientific" would mean missing an opportunity to explore something important about the nature of scientific inquiry itself'.[13] However troubling it may appear today, race science was good science done by scientists of excellent repute. On the other hand, even the casual reader could not help but notice that Stepan placed Darwin at the centre of her work on 'dubious', culturally-ridden science. 'Good science' (by then-contemporary standards) had produced ideas about racial fixity and racial limits; discourses about fixity and inequality had helped shape 'good science' (by standards that we continue to accept).

It is also in retrospect that we can identify some of the problems induced by the historiographical (and political) aims of Stepan's study. *The Idea of Race in*

---

[12] For my fruitless attempt to introduce the term 'the new intellectual history', see Suman Seth, 'The History of Physics after the Cultural Turn', *Historical Studies in the Natural Sciences* 41 (2011).

[13] Stepan, xvi.

Science joined a growing body of scholarship interested in challenging current norms and ideals and hence tended to emphasise the roots of those elements in the past. Stepan's was a study, for example, of race *science* (largely, biology and ethnology), not of race-medicine, in spite of the fact that many early 'race-scientists' were trained as doctors. James Cowles Prichard, for example, was a Bristol physician; Robert Knox an anatomist who left Edinburgh several years after his involvement in the Burke and Hare body-snatching scandal. The medical grounding of much race science is particularly clear if one looks (as Stepan would in her next monograph) beyond the European metropole.[14] The majority of those with scientific training in the colonies were medical men.

The metropolitan focus of *The Idea of Race in Science* was, of course, a conscious choice. The 'best' men of science were likely to be found in European capitals. Yet this meant that the study of race in science often concentrated on places with little contact between different 'races'. These 'races' were often represented by skulls and skeletons (immutable mobiles if ever such existed). We know too little about the ways in which daily contact between 'races' shaped taxonomic understanding. Beyond questions of 'collecting', our histories of the practices of race science often seem to avoid discussions of slavery and colonialism as quotidian experience.[15]

Finally, Stepan was most interested in race science as 'normal science' during the period in which biology came of age as a discipline in its own right. If seemingly misguided, the questions of race science are demonstrably part of the heritage of 'modern science'. The methods are naturalistic; physical features are assumed to provide adequate guides to mental characteristics. Yet the origins of race science lie (at least) in the eighteenth century and race as a category of analysis has grown dramatically in importance in our genomic age.[16]

My aim in this work is to re-locate race along three axes: discipline, geography, period. This chapter and Chapter 7 offer a history of eighteenth-century ideas about medicine and race largely drawn from texts either written (or drawing upon experiences) in places far beyond European metropoles. Of course, I am hardly the first to suggest that such relocations are necessary, although this book may be unique in arguing that all three should be considered simultaneously. Arguments rejecting the privileging of nineteenth-century understandings of race have already been noted. The eighteenth century has been paid particular attention by Roxanne Wheeler, Colin Kidd and Andrew

[14] Nancy Stepan, *The Hour of Eugenics: Race, Gender, and Nation in Latin America* (Ithaca: Cornell University Press, 1991).

[15] See, however, James Delbourgo, 'The Newtonian Slave Body: Racial Enlightenment in the Atlantic World', *Atlantic Studies* 9 (2012).

[16] Suman Seth, ed., 'Focus: Re-Locating Race'. *Isis* 105, no 4 (2014): 759–814.

Curran.[17] The last few decades have also seen compelling arguments made by students of race in the Spanish and Portuguese empires that have convincingly problematised the normalisation of racial views in Northern and Western Europe.[18] The relationship between medicine and race has continued, however, to be under-considered, with Warwick Anderson's study of nineteenth-century Australian medical attitudes towards 'whiteness' remaining a conspicuous exception.[19] At times, the absence can seem striking, as in Wheeler's excellent *The Complexion of Race*, where particular attention is paid to what is termed the 'humoral body', precisely because this body and its relationship to climate 'have been strangely omitted in recent eighteenth-century studies'.[20] Despite tracing the classical roots of such thinking to the works of (among others) Plato, Hippocrates, and Galen (the two latter of whom were, of course, physicians) and despite acknowledging that this was also the occupation of many of those working within a 'humoural' tradition in the eighteenth century, Wheeler nonetheless associates the mode of thought with natural history rather than medicine.[21] Although it would not do to over-emphasise the distinction between medicine and natural history (the two fields shared clear and obvious connections), collapsing one onto the other is equally problematic and speaks more to a persistent failure of communication between the history of science and the history of medicine than it does to the historical facts on the ground. Nor is the point simply a matter of boundary work. Insofar, I would argue, as we are interested in the ways that naturalistic understandings of race did *work* – not just intellectual work, but social and political work – then I think we have been looking in the wrong places. The right place – the place that we can see race in action – is medicine in the colonies.[22]

---

[17] Wheeler. Kidd, 79–120. Curran.

[18] The literature is vast. As a starting point, see Thomas E. Skidmore, *Black into White: Race and Nationality in Brazilian Thought* (New York: Oxford University Press, 1974); Francisco Bethencourt and A. J. Pearce, eds., *Racism and Ethnic Relations in the Portuguese Speaking World* (New York: Oxford University Press, 2012). Richard Graham, ed. *The Idea of Race in Latin America, 1870–1940* (Austin: University of Texas Press, 1990). Jorge Cañizares-Esguerra, 'New Worlds, New Stars: Patriotic Astrology and the Invention of Indian and Creole Bodies in Colonial Spanish America, 1600–1650', *American Historical Review* 104 (1999). In 2011, the *Hispanic American Historical Review* dedicated a special issue (Volume 91, number 3) to examining the significance of Stepan's work on science and medicine in Latin America. Warwick Anderson has very recently surveyed material on 'Racial Conceptions in the Global South' in *Isis* 105 (2014): 782–92.

[19] Anderson, *The Cultivation of Whiteness: Science, Health and Racial Destiny in Australia*. See also Stephen Snelders, 'Leprosy and Slavery in Suriname: Godfried Schilling and the Framing of a Racial Pathology in the Eighteenth Century', *Social History of Medicine* 26 (2013).

[20] Wheeler, 28.

[21] Ibid., 22, 28.

[22] This fact would suggest that scholars may need to reconsider several criteria by which we judge the significance or import of given texts. Some of these texts (Atkins', for example) went through multiple editions, providing some indication of their popularity. Many did not.

5.1   Race: The Terms of the Debate in the Early Enlightenment

By the mid-eighteenth century, the question of the origin of human physical differences had become a familiar one within European philosophy. The
orthodox view was known as monogenism and posited a single act of creation
for all humankind. At some point in the past, humanity had looked similar: if
Biblical narratives were taken literally, the resemblance was a familial one.
Human groups had spread from a common centre through different climatic
zones until their physical and intellectual features displayed the myriad diversity of the human species today.[23] This environmentalist explanation had roots
going back to antiquity, where even the differences between the inhabitants
of nearby city-states were explained by describing their various 'airs, waters,
and places'. But challenges to what might be termed naïve monogenism were
already to be found by the late seventeenth century. In 1665 the anatomist,
Marcello Malpighi, had seemed to identify the difference between black and
white skin by finding, in an African subject, a layer of skin that contained a
dark mucus or fluid.[24] Andrew Curran has termed this 'the most important skin-
related discovery of the early-modern era'.[25] In 1684, the traveller François
Bernier put forward 'A New Division of the Earth According to the Different
Species or Races of Men'. While willing to acknowledge that a myriad of
differences distinguished the nations of men, Bernier insisted that larger

Many (particularly with regard to their views on race) were not cited in subsequent writings.
Understanding their 'reception', then, is difficult and, beyond their published works, the historical record concerning a number of the authors I examine is fairly meagre. On the other
hand, by reading their published material, it becomes clear that many, if not most, of those that
I discuss had substantial medical interactions with populations both 'white' and 'black', free
and enslaved. It seems obvious that medical views on race – on the putative difference, if any,
between the afflictions of 'whites' and 'blacks' – could *make* a difference in both diagnosis and
treatment. By studying these authors, then, we can get a sense of the immediate effect of racial
ideas on the bodies of those who were the subject of discourse concerning race.

[23] It was apparently common, by the seventeenth century, to argue that black skin was a mark of
the curse laid on the descendants of Noah's son, Ham. John Josselyn, in his *Account of Two
Voyages to New England* (1674) noted that: 'It is the opinion of many men, that the blackness of
the *Negroes* proceeded from the curse upon *Cham's* posterity'. Quoted in Winthrop D. Jordan,
White over Black: American Attitudes toward the Negro, 1550–1812 (Chapel Hill: University
of North Carolina Press, 1968), 245. This, however, was a fairly late development. One finds
very little evidence that suggests that Ham or his children were seen as black or were unam-
biguously associated with Africa until around the Renaissance. On the changing understanding
of the curse, see Benjamin Braude, 'The Sons of Noah and the Construction of Ethnic and
Geographical Identities in the Medieval and Early Modern Periods', *The William and Mary
Quarterly* 54, no. 1 (1997).

[24] On Malpighi, see Domenico Bertoloni Meli, ed. *Marcello Malpighi: Anatomist and Physician*
(Firenze: Leo. S. Olschki, 1997). On studies of human skin colour in the early modern period
more generally, see Renato G. Mazzolini, 'Skin Color and the Origin of Physical Anthropology
(1640–1850)', in *Reproduction, Race, and Gender in Philosophy and the Early Life Sciences*,
ed. Susanne Lettow (New York: SUNY Press, 2014); Malcolmson.

[25] Curran, 121.

similarities grouped them into only four or five races, 'whose difference is so remarkable that it may be properly made use of as the foundation for a new division of the earth'. In some, skin colour was a relatively insignificant feature, to be explained by the 'accident' of their location in sunny climes. For others, however, skin colour seemed a more profound mark. The slave trade had produced data that appeared to trouble environmentalism, for new climates seemed to have but little effect on some races. '[I]f a black African pair be transported to a cold country', wrote Bernier, 'their children are just as black, and so are all their descendants ... The cause must be sought for in the peculiar texture of their bodies, or in the seed, or in the blood'.[26] Winthrop Jordan has suggested that some kind of 'fluid theory' was the most common explanation to be found in the early eighteenth century and one finds versions of it in the work of Alexis Littré in 1702 and Pierre Barrère in 1741, with each connecting the black layer to increased levels of black bile in African bodies.[27]

Not all were so impressed, however. The Virginian physician John Mitchell deployed Newtonian optics in arguing that Negro skin was only somewhat thicker than that of whites, so that differences existed 'only in the Degree of one and the same Colour'.[28] The Comte de Buffon did not deny the facts involved in the fluid theory, but he did question their significance. '[I]f one asserts that it is the blackness of the blood or the bile that gives this colour to the skin', he noted logically, 'then instead of asking why the *nègres* have black skin, one will ask why they have black bile or black blood; this is thus to dismiss the question, rather than resolving it'.[29] Buffon's environmentalist arguments, as laid out in 'On the Varieties in the Human Species', published in 1749, played down any notion of intrinsic differences, but they also tried to nuance earlier climatic claims. Most previous commentators had assumed that there was a reasonable correlation between latitude and complexion. Warmer climates produced people of darker skin and those from diverse nations in common latitudinal regions should look reasonably similar. It was becoming clear, however, that

---

[26] François Bernier, 'A New Division of the Earth', in *The Idea of Race*, ed. Robert Bernasconi and Tommy L. Lott (Indianapolis: Hackett, 2000), 2. Siep Stuurman, 'François Bernier and the Invention of Racial Classification', *History Workshop Journal* 50 (2000). Malcolmson suggests that it may have been the publication of Bernier's essay that inspired debates over the origin of human skin colour in the Royal Society in the 1690s. Malcolmson, 69–70.

[27] Jordan, 246; Curran, 121–2; Pierre Barrère, *Dissertation sur la Cause physique de la couleur des nègres, de la qualité de leurs cheveux, et de la dégénération de l'un et de l'autre* (Paris: Pierre-Guillaume Simon, 1741). On responses to Barrère's theories, see Sean Quinlan, 'Colonial Bodies, Hygiene, and Abolitionist Politics in Eighteenth-Century France', *History Workshop Journal* 42 (1996): 112.

[28] Mitchell quoted in Jordan, 247; John Mitchell, 'An Essay Upon the Causes of the Different Colours of People in Different Climates', *Philosophical Transaction* 43 (1744–45); Delbourgo, 'The Newtonian Slave Body: Racial Enlightenment in the Atlantic World'.

[29] Buffon quoted in Curran, 124.

neither of these assumptions properly held. If darker skin was produced by the action of the sun, why were peoples in the tropics and the polar zones both swarthy, while those in temperate climes were pale? According to Buffon, it was because one needed to take into account the effect not only of heat, but also of moisture. Both very cold and very hot environments, he argued, could produce a darkening of the skin because both were also dry.[30] Moreover, physical features could be altered indirectly by the climate. Different regions of the earth, for example, contained characteristically different flora and fauna. Humans who moved into such regions gradually developed different manners of living, ate different diets, and suffered from different diseases, all of which changed their physiognomy and intellectual characteristics in permanent, heritable ways.[31]

Buffon's explanations re-affirmed the brotherhood of man. Humans might come in different varieties, but – since crossings between different human groups produced fertile offspring – we were all one species.[32] Not all varieties were equal, however. The original human type was white, in Buffon's formulation, and all deviation from this original was to be understood as a form and sign of degeneracy. The animals of the New World were, for example, degenerate versions of those in the Old. Why else was there nothing to compare to the lion or elephant? So too were the human inhabitants and if one wished to restore them to their first and higher state they must be removed and transplanted. Given time, French food and a temperate climate could reverse their decline.[33]

Buffon's hierarchical monogenism provided the orthodox naturalistic position for the rest of the century. Much more unorthodox was polygenism, which held that different races had been made in separate acts of creation. This was an old heresy, given much greater weight after the European discovery of the Americas. Monogenetic theories that sought to explain how people had travelled from the Old World to the New abounded. One finds them still in the nineteenth century, as scholars argued, for example, that Native Americans might be descended from 'descendants of the Welsh emigrants of Prince Madog'.[34] Some few iconoclasts, however, found such notions impossible. Paracelsus

---

[30] Georges Louis Leclerc Buffon, 'Of the Varieties in the Human Species', in *Barr's Buffon. Buffon's Natural History Containing a Theory of the Earth, a General History of Man, of the Brute Creation, and of Vegetables, Minerals &C. &C.* (London: H. D. Symonds, 1807), 349.

[31] Ibid., 270.

[32] Phillip R. Sloan, 'Buffon, German Biology, and the Historical Interpretation of Biological Species', *The British Journal for the History of Science* 12, no. 2 (1979).

[33] Phillip R. Sloan, 'The Idea of Racial Degeneracy in Buffon's *Histoire Naturelle*', *Studies in Eighteenth-Century Culture* 3 (1973).

[34] D. W. Nash, 'The Welsh Indians: To the Editor of the Cambrian Journal', *The Cambrian Journal* (1860).

declared in 1520 that 'these people are from a different Adam', while Giordano Bruno – soon to be burned at the stake for related views – claimed that Adam was only one of three Patriarchs.[35] The first sustained polygenetic work, Isaac La Peyrère's *Prae-Adamitae* (*Men Before Adam*) appeared in 1655 to wide condemnation. In February of the following year he was jailed; in June he agreed to repent, apologise to the Pope, and convert from Calvinism to Catholicism.

In La Peyrère's account, the Bible was a description of history and destiny that applied only to the Jews. To them alone had the word of God been revealed. This meant that one need not consider the history of other peoples, for they were not part of the divine plan. Nor did one need any longer to worry about how to square the narrative of creation or the story of the Deluge with new discoveries of men in far-flung locations. Ancient pagans had not derived from the same stock as the chosen people; inhabitants of the New World had not descended from the sons of Noah. On the other hand, as Popkin has noted, La Peyrère was a universal humanist. If only Jews were the subject of a divine history, their Messianic salvation would include all others, pre- and post-Adamic alike.[36]

La Peyrère was a believer. Many of those who would follow in his polygenetic footsteps, however, would see the doctrine of separate creations as a means of mocking – rather than salvaging – Biblical exposition.[37] Thus, one finds 'L. P'. (presumably a nod to La Peyrère) offering a defence of rationalism in the face of biblical literalism in 1695. The work combined two essays, the first of which ridiculed the notion that the Noachic flood, if it had occurred, had spanned the globe. Why drown the earth and all its innocent creations, L. P. asked, when most of the world was uninhabited? Why destroy all on account of 'a few Wanton and Luxurious *Asiaticks*, who might have been drown'd by a *Topical Flood*, or by a particular Deluge, without involving all the Bowels of the whole Mass, and the remote Creatures upon the face of

---

[35] Quoted in David N. Livingstone, *Adam's Ancestors: Race, Religion, and the Politics of Human Origins* (Baltimore: Johns Hopkins University Press, 2008), 23. On Pre-Adamism before the seventeenth century, see Richard H. Popkin, *Isaac La Peyrère (1596–1676): His Life, Work, and Influence* (Leiden: Brill, 1987), 26–41; Livingstone, *Adam's Ancestors: Race, Religion, and the Politics of Human Origins*, 1–25. On whether it is entirely correct to call Paracelsus a polygenist (on the grounds that he did not necessarily treat non-Adamic peoples as fully human), see Popkin, 34.

[36] Popkin, 69–79.

[37] As Colin Kidd has argued: 'The subversion of scripture was not in most cases a strategy designed consciously to provide new polygenetic supports for white domination of non-European peoples; rather Enlightened critics used the fact of racial diversity as a weapon to undermine the authority of scripture'. Colin Kidd, 'Ethnicity in the British Atlantic World, 1688–1830', in *A New Imperial History: Culture, Identity, and Modernity in Britain and the Empire, 1660–1840*, ed. Kathleen Wilson (Cambridge: Cambridge University Press, 2004), 263.

the Earth, in the Ruin'?[38] The second essay then heaped scorn on the idea that the world had been populated from a single spot, with animals and men travelling vast distances across many different climes to reach the locations in which they were now found. '[H]ow the Animals, that cannot endure the extremity of Cold', he scoffed, 'should climb over inaccessible Mountains or Ice and Snow for many Thousands of Miles together, is hardly explicable to any thinking man'.[39] Nor could one imagine that they had been carried by men. Why would one do this with dangerous creatures and leave behind so many 'mild and useful ones'?[40] The logics that applied to animals would seem to apply to men, as well. In any case, however, there was reason beyond this to doubt that all men were related. As others had, L. P. noted the problems with climatic explanations for differences in skin colour between whites and blacks. One found different coloured people in similar climates; whites did not seem to darken appreciably in warm countries, blacks did not lighten in cooler ones. He declared of Negroes, then, that 'their Colour and Wool are Innate, or Seminal from their first beginning, and seems to be a Specifick Character, which neither the Sun, nor any curse from *Cham* could imprint upon them'.[41] Arguments derived from '*Eastern* Rubbish, or Rabbinical Weeds' could supply no reasonable answer to the questions raised by natural history.[42]

The tone in which Atkins expressed his musings about the several origins of mankind – matter-of-fact, if somewhat apologetic – would be the exception among polygenists in the first half of the eighteenth century. One might, indeed, say that the doctrine of special creations was a sarcastic position in this period. It was nowhere more so than in the writings of Voltaire, who turned La Peyrère's philosemitism on its head. Europeans, in Voltaire's view, had preceded Jews on the Earth. The Jewish patriarch was merely a pale imitation of the original, and Jews would remain a race apart, however long they lived in Western lands.[43] Writing of blacks in *The Philosophy of History,* Voltaire noted that it had now become common practice for the 'curious traveler' passing through Leiden to make a stop to view the *reticulum mucosum* (now known as the Malpighian layer) of a dissected negro.[44] This membrane, he added, is itself black and 'communicates to negroes that inherent blackness, which they do not lose'. The philosopher declared that 'none but the blind' could make of whites, negroes, Albinoes, Hottentots, Laplanders, the Chinese, and

---

[38] L. P., *Two Essays Sent in a Letter from Oxford to a Nobleman in London.* (London: R. Baldwin, 1695), 14.
[39] Ibid., 20.
[40] Ibid., 22.
[41] Ibid., 27.
[42] Ibid., 23.
[43] Popkin, 133–4.
[44] Voltaire, *The Philosophy of History* (London: I. Allcock, 1766), 6.

Americans anything but distinct races, and if one were to ask about the origins of such races, the answer was equally obvious: 'the same providence which placed men in Norway, planted some also in America and under the Antarctic circle, in the same manner as it planted trees and made grass to grow there'.[45] David Hume concurred in 1753, arguing that all races other than whites were inferior, and that the differences among such races were innate, nature having made an 'original distinction betwixt these breeds of men'. His tone might be captured by reproducing his comments on a counter-example to his claim that no negro had or would ever distinguish themselves through their intelligence. There were those in Jamaica, he noted, who spoke of one as a man of considerable learning. Hume dismissed the thought: "'tis likely', he wrote, 'he is admired for very slender accomplishments like a parrot, who speaks a few words plainly'.[46] Heterodox and uncommon, polygenism had nonetheless become a viable philosophical position by the mid-eighteenth century, even if one might regard it – in the main – as a view more reactive and antagonistic than deeply held in its own right.[47]

5.2   Gender, Medicine, and Climate

If the Bible appeared to license a unitary view of human races, it offered a binary conception of human sexes, with Eve produced in a special and derivative creation. Depending on what kinds of elements medical men discussed, this binary was more or less stark. Although scholars have identified cases

---

[45] Ibid., 6, 9. Material on the races of men first appeared in 1734.

[46] The remarks appeared originally in a footnote to the 1753 edition of a work published originally in 1748. David Hume, 'Of National Characters', in *Hume: Essays, Moral, Political, and Literary*, ed. E. F. Miller (Indianapolis: Liberty Fund, 1987), 197–215, footnote on 8. For a discussion of variant readings see 629–30. On the relation of this footnote to the remainder of the essay see Kidd, *The Forging of Races: Race and Scripture in the Protestant Atlantic World, 1600–2000*, 93–4.

[47] As Popkin has noted, one finds a number of thinkers whose views would seem to lead them almost inexorably to polygenism, but who were orthodox enough to draw back from the precipice. Popkin, 132. To offer merely one concrete example, one finds in Ovington's account of his voyage to Suratt and other locations in 1689 a discussion of the difference in skin colour of various peoples. Ovington rejected the idea that climate alone could produce such variation, arguing that diet was of crucial importance. An Indian of very dark colour who was taken into the English service, he claimed, had become noticeably paler by 'tasting wine and eating flesh'. J. Ovington, 'A Voyage to Suratt in the Year 1689', in *India in the Seventeenth Century: Being an Account of the Two Voyages to India by Ovington and Thevenot. To Which Is Added the Indian Travels of Careri*, ed. J. P. Guha (New Delhi: Associated Publishing House, 1976), 219. Differences between peoples, then, were not essential. Ovington, however, was scathing about the people he called 'Hotantots', whom he claimed to be 'the very reverse of human kind'. Were there a middle position 'between a rational animal and a beast', he asserted, 'the Hotantot lays the fairest claim to that species'. Ibid., 218. Yet Ovington remained silent on the question of the cause or origin of this bestial nature.

where even this boundary was blurred, the sources I have examined associated specifically reproductive elements solely with women.[48] The key questions for many physicians and surgeons writing about pregnancy, childbirth, menstruation, and menopause were about the ways in which such processes varied with the climate.[49] On other medical issues, concerning distempers that afflicted both sexes, differences were perceived as a matter of degree and not kind. Effeminate men, like women, were less liable to a fatal bout of yellow fever in climates that favoured the relatively emasculated. The relationships between sex and race were similarly complex, depending on the afflictions involved. As we shall see, one area where sex and race became particularly mutually imbricated concerned the putative threat posed by Afro-Caribbean women accused of prostitution and the spread of venereal disease.

Many of the observations found in medical texts concerning the diseases of warm climates are perhaps best understood as cultural tropes, rather than material aimed at diagnosis or treatment, with numerous authors, for example, discussing the relative ease of childbirth in foreign climes. This was a claim of considerable antiquity, with parts of Hippocrates' *Airs, Waters, and Places* dedicated to the difficulties attending parturition according to location, diet, and environment.[50] At the beginning of the sixteenth century, Amerigo Vespucci made sure that a claim about the Old World was also part of the understanding of the New. The women he observed in his voyage were 'very fruiteful, and refuse no laboure al the whyle they are with childe. They travayle in maner without payne, so that the nexte day they are cherefull and able to walk'.[51] As part of his *Travels*, published in 1687, Jean de Thevenot claimed of Indian women that they 'are easily delivered of their children' and, in common

---

[48] See Thomas Laqueur, *Making Sex: Body and Gender from the Greeks to Freud* (Cambridge, MA: Harvard University Press, 1990); Barbara Duden, *The Woman beneath the Skin: A Doctor's Patients in Eighteenth-Century Germany* (Cambridge, MA: Harvard University Press, 1991).

[49] All doctors did not take up the question of specifically female complaints in any detail. Neither Towne nor Hillary listed any specifically female illnesses among those they deemed characteristic of the West Indian climate. Thomas, in 1790, was one of the few to include a section on 'Women's diseases'. Towne. Hillary, *Observations on the Changes of the Air and the Concomitant Epidemical Diseases, in the Island of Barbados. To Which Is Added a Treatise on the Putrid Bilious Fever, Commonly Called the Yellow Fever; and Such Other Diseases as Are Indigenous or Endemial, in the West India Islands, or in the Torrid Zone*. Thomas. Those primarily treating soldiers and sailors made up a class of practitioners with understandably little dealing with female patients. For concrete descriptions of cases involving women – and hence more material useful for a history of *practice*, see for example, Sloane. On whom, Churchill. Of the twenty-four cases discussed by James Hendy, ten involved women and one a female child of eleven years. James Hendy, *A Treatise on the Glandular Disease of Barbadoes: Proving It to Be Seated in the Lymphatic System* (London: C. Dilly, 1784).

[50] Hippocrates, 'Airs, Waters, and Places'.

[51] Quoted in Jennifer L. Morgan, *Laboring Women: Reproduction and Gender in New World Slavery* (Philadelphia: University of Pennsylvania Press, 2004), 17.

with women all over the Indies, could 'walk about' the day after giving birth.[52] By the early eighteenth century, the topic was standard enough that Friedrich Hoffman, in his neo-Hippocratic survey of *Endemial Diseases*, considered it a common axis upon which to compare the various peoples of the world:

> In *Aethiopia* the Women are blessed with peculiarly easy and happy Labours, and are generally delivered on their Knees ... *Borlaeus* ... mentions the like Hardiness and Strength in the *Brasilian* Women, who, as he informs us, 'do not keep themselves up for five or six Weeks after Labour, like the *European* Women, but set about their ordinary Business next Day after their Delivery, though their Bodies, however firm and healthy, are yet very small'. I have often heard and read that in *Batavia*, the women immediately after their Delivery go into running Water, and wash both themselves and their Children, without any Danger to either.[53]

Less painful childbirth might seem to have been a positive characteristic, but it was not necessarily taken to be so. Since the agony of parturition was part of the punishment inflicted upon Eve, the suggestion that some women were spared could carry with it a whiff of polygenism. Edward Long, who espoused polygenist beliefs, and who – as we will see in the next chapter – would raise the status of Orangutans to that of men in order to lower the status of Africans to those of beasts, was characteristically offensive and distasteful in discussing African women, who 'are delivered with little or no labour; they have therefore no more occasion for midwives, than the female Oran-Outang, or any other wild animal. A woman brings forth her child in a quarter of an hour, goes the same day to the sea, and washes herself'.[54] Consistent with Long's belief that the transportation of Africans to the West Indies improved them, he also argued that 'Child-birth is not as easy here as in Afric'.[55] Increased pain in parturition, in other words, could be read as civilisational improvement. And, of course, in less abstract terms, asserting that Afro-Caribbean women could labour even in the last months of pregnancy and return to work within days afterward served to license a gruelling slave regime.[56] Benjamin Moseley declared that 'hot climates', in general 'are indeed very favourable to gestation and parturition', that difficult labours were uncommon, and that the lying in period was short. 'Indians and Negroes', he claimed, 'sometimes make it an affair of a few days, and sometimes of a few hours only, and then pursue their occupation'.[57] That

---

[52] Jean de Thevenot, 'The Third Part of the Travels of Mr. De Thevenot, Containing the Relation of Indostan, the New Moguls and of Other People and Countries of the Indies', in *India in the Seventeenth Century: Being an Account of the Two Voyages to India by Ovington and Thevenot. To Which Is Added the Indian Travels of Careri*, ed. J. P. Guha (New Delhi: Associated Publishing House, 1976 [1687]), 80, 143.

[53] Hoffmann and Ramazzini, 30.

[54] Edward Long, *The History of Jamaica*, 3 vols., vol. II (London: T. Lowndes, 1774), 380.

[55] Ibid., 436.

[56] Bush; Dunn, 'Sugar Production and Slave Women in Jamaica'.

[57] Moseley, *A Treatise on Tropical Diseases; And on the Climate of the West-Indies*, 61.

said, as we shall see in Chapter 7, abolitionists would focus upon the appalling treatment of pregnant and nursing women in propaganda that successfully turned public opinion against slave owners. One wonders whether this might have been an impetus behind the Jamaican doctor, John Quier's correction of Donald Monro's comments on this point.[58] Monro had read a letter from Quier on inoculation to the Royal College of Physicians in London in 1771 and had inserted a note concerning the propriety of inoculating pregnant women. Since the women involved were African, Monro insisted, one need not worry too much: 'Negro women and others of hardy constitutions', he opined, 'who are much exposed to the open air, often bear children, and go about their daily labour in a day or two afterwards, and undergo many other things without the least inconvenience, which would be in danger of destroying those of delicate habits, who have been educated in European luxury'.[59] Perhaps aware that such comments could be regarded as callousness, Quier rejected them in a second letter. '[W]hatever hardiness negroes may possess', he noted, 'I do not find that the females enjoy that immunity from the evils of child-bearing, at least in this country, that you seem to imagine'. As a result, Quier claimed, such women were 'carefully nursed for a fortnight; and excused from all kinds of labour', sometimes not emerging from her house for a month.[60] Whatever the truth of this claim – and there were many who suggested that slave women received no such careful nursing – its timing is worth noting. In 1773, a year after the Somerset case appeared to outlaw slavery on English soil, the plight of slaves was a matter of newly-urgent public discussion. Quier may well have seen the value in not adding fuel to the fire with talk of the physiological differences that putatively justified the comparative neglect of enslaved mothers.[61]

As common as the trope that related warm climates and easy parturition was one that pointed, within the same regions, to sexual precocity and a concomitantly early decline. 'Girls soon arrive at Maturity', wrote George Cleghorn in his *Observations on the Endemical Diseases in Minorca* (1751), 'and soon grow old'. The menses usually appeared before fourteen, frequently as early as eleven, and could sometimes 'return twice a month'.[62] No others reported a

---

[58] Cf. Schiebinger, 'Human Experimentation in the Eighteenth Century: Natural Boundaries and Valid Testing', 402–4. Schiebinger associates comments concerning the hardiness of Negroes with Quier and then suggests that he 'backtracked' on these in a subsequent letter. Quier, however, refers to '[t]he note, you have inserted concerning gravid women' in his letter of 28 March 1773 to Monro. The letters are reproduced in Monro et al., 1–104, the quotation is to be found on 54. See also Schiebinger, *Secret Cures of Slaves: People, Plants, and Medicine in the Eighteenth-Century Atlantic World*, 104–9.

[59] Monro et al., 12.

[60] Ibid., 55.

[61] I discuss the Somerset case in detail in the next chapter.

[62] Cleghorn, 53.

fortnightly period, but it was not uncommon to report that those living in warm climates might enter puberty at ten or eleven when, as Thomas observed, it seldom appeared before fifteen in colder regions.[63] Long imagined a speeding up of existence in general for creole white women in Jamaica, who 'attain earlier to maturity, and sooner decline' than their northern counterparts, and who were not unseldom mothers at twelve. 'They console themselves, however, that they can enjoy more of real existence here in one hour, than the fair inhabitants of the frozen, foggy regions do in two'.[64] Such a positive spin on precocity and early senescence was not granted to mulatto women, who arrived at puberty quickly, but then declined dramatically after the age of twenty-five 'till at length they grow horribly ugly'.[65] By 1787, Moseley seemed to be aware of how familiar observations of this kind were, for he both confirmed the fact of early menstruation, while rejecting the applicability of the wilder tales that filled travel narratives. 'Though females do arrive at early maturity in hot climates, there are none of those wonderful instances of early pregnancy in the West-Indies, that travellers speak of, and such as are said to have happened in other parts of the world'.[66]

Perhaps more interesting than the repetition of this familiar refrain concerning menstruation were observations about the benefits it conferred on women with regard to susceptibility to diseases otherwise unconnected to reproduction.[67] A sizeable portion of the authors who wrote about certain kinds of fevers (usually including the yellow fever) noted a peculiarity about those most badly afflicted by it. The disease laid low the strongest and most robust of men. In his *Description of the American Yellow Fever*, John Lining observed that while the disease was almost always fatal to 'valetudinarians', and often deadly to the intemperate, and those not habituated to the climate, it also seemed to particularly afflict 'those of an athletic and full habit'.[68] Lewis Rouppe, in a tract in the diseases of sailors, similarly pointed to 'young robust men' as those likely to die the soonest from bilious fevers, as did John Hume who noted that 'strong muscular men' were most liable to the 'true bilious, or yellow fever' while 'those of a lax habit are least liable to it, and most likely to recover'.[69] A 'lax

[63] Thomas, 279.
[64] Long, II, 285.
[65] Ibid., 335.
[66] Moseley, *A Treatise on Tropical Diseases; And on the Climate of the West-Indies*, 60.
[67] This was not, in general, uncommon. It had been believed since antiquity that some diseases – often precisely those that could be aided or cured through venesection – were less likely to afflict women, who lost blood naturally on a monthly basis.
[68] John Lining, *A Description of the American Yellow Fever, Which Prevailed at Charleston, in South Carolina, in the Year 1748* (Philadelphia: Thomas Dobson, 1799), 25–6.
[69] Rouppe, 413–4; John Hume, 'An Account of the True Bilious, or Yellow Fever; and of the Remitting Fevers of the West Indies', in *Letters and Essays on the Small-Pox and Inoculation,*

habit' could be acquired in many ways, from dissolution to simple aging, but it was also an effect of heat or humidity. Moisture and warmth could cause the strings of a well-tuned instrument to sag; so, too, could the tense and rigid fibres of a strong male body. The body best suited to the tropics, then, was the diametric opposite of that which was the perfect symbol of British manliness at home. As a reviewer of Charles Bisset's *Essay on the Medical Constitution of Great Britain* (1762) phrased it in rejecting the author's (unusual) assertion that northern Europeans were *less* likely to suffer from inflammatory diseases in warm climates: 'we imagined that the world was persuaded, that the very reverse of this assertion was true; that northern constitutions are the most subject to fevers when transplanted into hot climates'. The reason being:

that all bodies are the best adapted, by nature, for that climate in which they are produced and have been resident: that the inhabitants of warm climates are remarkable for a lax fibre, hence their weakness, sloth, and effeminacy; and the women, and such as lead the most sedentary and inactive lives, are the most exempt from all feverish and inflammatory complaints.[70]

A new climate would exact a price for the discrepancy between the bodily constitution native to it and that of a stranger; a price particularly high for robust masculinity in a land suited for the effeminate and inactive.

Gendered weakness, then, provided a kind of strength, or at least protection. The young and robust, with the tensest fibres were the 'most obnoxious' to the bilious fever, wrote John Williams, while 'women and men of lax habits are seldom seized with it; or, when they are, come through with much less danger and difficulty'.[71] In 1783, Stephen Mathews added children to women and those of a 'lax and delicate texture' on his list of those 'seldom harassed' by bilious fevers, arguing that by the time of his writing the idea that the 'strength of the disease is par with the vigour of the afflicted' was an observation of such long standing and general acknowledgement that it would be a 'presumption' to disagree. Although some authors were more inclined to point to social and behavioural differences to explain relative susceptibility to the disease, most thus appeared to point to gendered anatomies.[72] Those who advocated bleeding as

the Measles, the Dry Belly-Ache, the Yellow, and Remitting, and Intermitting Fevers of the West Indies (London: J. Murray, 1778), 237.

[70] Reviewer, 'Essay on the Medical Constitution of Great Britain', *The Critical Review, or Annals of Literature* (1763): 188–9.

[71] Williams and Bennet, 29. See also Lind, who noted that European women were more subject to fatal fevers on the Guinea coast, but were 'not so subject' to the yellow fever of Jamaica. Lind, *An Essay on Diseases Incidental to Europeans in Hot Climates: With the Method of Preventing Their Fatal Consequences. To Which Is Added, an Appendix Concerning Intermittent Fevers*, 54, 117.

[72] Gilbert Blane, for example, blamed exercise in the sun and intemperance for bringing on fevers. 'It is in favour of this position', he stated, 'that women are not subject to the same violent fevers as the other sex, which is probably owing to their not being exposed to the same

a treatment for the illness often also added a physiological reason to their anatomical explanations. The problem, as John Williams noted, was that Northern European bodies contained too much blood for their new climates, which then exerted an excessive pressure on the body's vessels as the fluid warmed.[73] This plethora had to be removed, a problem that nature took care of for women on a monthly basis. In noting that European women in the East Indies seemed less subject to hepatitis, Stephen Mathews could not quite determine whether the cause was the 'delicacy of their formation' or the menses, but he did observe that the greater the menstrual flow, the more relief the patient experienced. John Tennent was more sure of himself. 'Women are seldom invaded with [the yellow fever]', he asserted, 'which is owing to two reasons, 1. They have naturally a lax fibre. 2. They have the benefit of menstrual Discharges'.[74] Effeminate men – like the women they resembled in their fibrous anatomical structure – might be spared the most intense ravages of the illness, but they did not gain the benefit of women's physiological distinction.

Women in these texts were not always, however, the sufferers of disease. On many occasions they were deemed to be the cause. Willem Bosman devoted a sizeable portion – he himself called it a 'tedious while' – of his twelfth letter describing the Guinea Coast to the marital practices of the inhabitants, as well as to revealing to his correspondent 'all our Venereal Ware-houses and their contain'd Stores'. Bosman evinced some sympathy for the 'whores' that made up the subject of part of his narrative, noting that their deaths were 'wretched and miserable', being soon infected and dying young.[75] John Atkins had no such sympathy in *The Navy-Surgeon*, laying the original cause of venereal disease at the feet of 'common women' (and women alone).

When the Venereal Appetite is jaded with the too intemperate Efforts of several Men, it will be next to impossible for those Parts to suffer the continued frictions made there,

causes of illness'. Gilbert Blane, *Observations on the Diseases of Seamen* (London: Joseph Cooper, 1785), 226–7. Hunter also pointed to 'the regularity and temperance of their living', the avoidance of exertions in the open air, and the fact that they stayed indoors more, going out only in the cool of the morning or evening 'and even then in a carriage' for women's longer life expectancies. Hunter, *Observations on the Diseases of the Army in Jamaica; and on the Best Means of Preserving the Health of Europeans, in That Climate*, 25.

73 Williams and Bennet, 30. Similar arguments were made in the French colony of Saint Domingue. See Weaver, 20–1.

74 John Tennent, *Physical Enquiries Discovering the Mode of Translation in the Constitutions of Northern Inhabitants, on Going to, and for Some Time after Arriving in Southern Climates ... An Error ... In Recommending Vinegar to His Majesty's Fleet in the West Indies, to Prevent the Epidemic Fever ... And the Barren State of Useful Physical Knowledge, as Well as the Mercenary Practice of Physicians, by an Impartial State of Dr. Ward's Qualifications for the Practice of Physic ... Illustrated with Remarks Upon a Printed Letter to a Member of Parliament, Signed Philanthropos* (London: T. Gardner, 1742), 34. Tennent made a similar argument in Tennent, 13–14.

75 Bosman, 215.

(as common Women do) without excoriating and fretting the Membranes of the *Vagina*; and such Excoriations, how small soever in the Beginning, meeting with an ill habit of Body ... will soon degenerate to an Ulcer; which Ulcer will be the Distemper.[76]

This was a not uncommon etiological explanation and it was one that served to largely absolve men of guilt in the spread of diseases connected to the sexual act.[77] However promiscuous men might be, the fault lay with prostitutes that served as reservoirs of illness.

Racialised elements then entered this common discourse via claims that African women and their descendants were essentially all prostitutes. Thomas, for example, warned European ladies against using a 'negro, or mulatto woman' as a wet-nurse, for 'it is a great chance if she does not harbor in her blood the relics of many dreadful disorders, such as the yaws, leprosy, or a venereal taint; as all this race of people give themselves up to an unlimited prostitution'.[78] Long pointed to the excessive consumption of meat as one reason that Englishmen were more liable to bad fevers in the West Indies than the natives of other European countries, but he also emphasised their 'excessive indulgence in a promiscuous commerce, on their first arrival, with the black and mulatto women'. Ignoring the violence and compulsion involved in almost all instances of sexual contact between whites and blacks in a slave society. Long argued that black women, whether free or enslaved 'are few of them exempt from this *virus*'. But they kept their affliction secret 'by every artifice in their power, that no delay may happen in their business; for a hindrance in this respect would be a certain loss of profit to them'.[79] In this way, black women with venereal diseases became part of the trope of the 'scheming black

---

[76] John Atkins, *The Navy-Surgeon: Or, a Practical System of Surgery. Illustrated with Observations on Such Remarkable Cases, as Have Occurred to the Author's Practice in the Service of the Royal Navy. To Which Is Added, a Treatise on the Venereal Disease, the Causes, Symptoms, and Method of Cure by Mercury: An Enquiry into the Origin of That Distemper; in Which the Dispute between Dr Dover and Dr Turner, Concerning Crude Mercury, Is Fully Consider'd; with Useful Remarks Thereon. Also an Appendix, Containing Physical Observations on the Heat, Moisture and Density of the Air on the Coast of Guiney; the Colour of the Natives; the Sicknesses Which They and the Europeans Trading Thither Are Subject to; with a Method of Cure*, 2nd ed. (London: W. Warner, 1737), 208.

[77] Burnard and Follett argue that there was little social or even medical stigma, for men, associated with sexually transmitted diseases, for 'venereal infection was thoroughly embedded within the prevailing discourse of masculinity and empire'. Trevor Burnard and Richard Follett, 'Caribbean Slavery, British Anti-Slavery, and the Cultural Politics of Venereal Disease', *The Historical Journal* 55 (2012): 430.

[78] Thomas, 315. Contradictorily, however, slave-owners who forced females slaves into prostitution, 'did not accept that prostitution had adverse effects upon slaves' domestic relationships or their fertility'. Hilary McD. Beckles, 'Property Rights in Pleasure: The Marketing of Slave Women's Sexuality in the West Indies', in *West Indies Accounts: Essays on the History of the British Caribbean and the Atlantic Economy, in Honour of Richard Sheridan*, ed. Roderick A. McDonald (Kingston, Jamaica: University of the West Indies Press, 1996), 175.

[79] Long, II, 535, 36.

Jezebel', a bondswoman generally understood to be a prostitute who initiated a relationship with a white man 'solely to obtain material favours' and who then 'did everything possible to hurt her white partner immediately after he gave her money or gifts'.[80] Perhaps the most striking (if bizarre) version of this trope may be found in Robert Robertson's *Physical Journal Kept on Board his Majesty's Ship Rainbow, During Three Voyages to the Coast of Africa and West Indies, in the Years 1772, 1773, and 1774*. Robertson related the story of Charles Duplassey, a butcher, who presented himself to Robertson in pain and with a penis and scrotum considerably enlarged. Duplassey would die a few days later and after his death, Robertson was informed – although he had 'no great faith' in the information – that the butcher had been drunk the day before he had been taken ill and had lain 'with a black woman that night, who had *blown* him'. Robertson professed to being ignorant 'of what was meant by his having been *blown* by the woman' but called in another man from the ship who, apparently, 'had formerly sustained a like injury from a whore'. The informant claimed to have noticed nothing unusual in the act of coition, but felt certain that the woman was at fault, since she ran away as soon as she left the bed and never approached him again. As motive, he noted that both he and Duplassey, with whom he had conversed, had beaten the women before having sex with them, and that the butcher's partner had also fled afterwards. Radically playing down the violence committed against the women, Robertson treated the case as one almost supernatural, crediting the prostitutes (if such they were) with powers positively diabolic and used against men who had done little to earn their ire. '[I]t would appear', he noted with some relief, 'that only some prostitutes have this infernal act of *blowing* a man in the act of coition'. He confessed himself still 'perfectly ignorant of it; but if it really is in the power of a prostitute to commit so hellish a trick, I think it very providential that so few of them know the art, otherwise I may venture to say, that they would treat men in that abominable manner for every slight offence'.[81] The Jezebel would seem to merge here with the figure of the witch, able to

---

[80] Henrice Altink, 'Deviant and Dangerous: Pro-Slavery Representation of Jamaican Slave Women's Sexuality, C. 1780–1834', *Slavery and Abolition* 26 (2005): 274. See, more generally, *Representations of Slave Women in Discourses on Slavery and Abolition, 1780–1838* (New York and London: Routledge, 2007). Bush notes that opponents of slavery, on the other hand, 'saw the black woman not as a scheming black Jezebel, but as an innocent victim of the unholy lust of callous and brutal white men … Abolitionists did not deny that black women were promiscuous, or that slaves in general lacked a moral code, they merely represented the latter as corrupted innocents'. Thus, contemporaries 'presented two conflicting images of the black woman, the abject creatures subjected to harsh patriarchal rule and the wanton woman who flouted all codes of accepted morality, neither of which was accurate'. Bush, 18, 21.

[81] Robert Robertson, *A Physical Journal Kept on Board His Majesty's Ship Rainbow, During Three Voyages to the Coast of Africa, and West Indies, in the Years 1772, 1773, and 1774* (London: E. & C. Dilly, J. Robson, T. Cadell, and T. Evans, 1777), 122–3.

cause harm not only by the transmission of infection, but also via practices that seemed to elude rational explanation.

As with the relationship between race and climate, that between sex and climate was complex. One might observe claims of the radical difference between the sexes, the pain of childbirth introduced as a punishment for Eve at the Fall, yet that proved to be modifiable according to whether one was in temperate or tropical climes. There were also more relative differences, where climate exacted a price from those whose British masculinity differed too much from the requisite effeminacy of their surrounds, and where specifically female processes, such as menstruation, could provide a kind of doubled protection. And there were cases where climate seemed to matter little against tropes that portrayed black women as collectively emblematising the worst of all feminine subversions, with elements that allowed their transposition from realms of natural affliction – perhaps worthy of sympathy, perhaps worthy of condemnation – to realms of supernatural and vindictive maleficence.

5.3   Race and Medicine, 1679–1740

The number of texts that discussed both medical matters and the physical variety to be found among different peoples was small in the late seventeenth and early eighteenth centuries. The most detailed comments, unsurprisingly, are to be found in location-specific medical tracts, such as those by Trapham, Sloane, and Towne on the West Indies, or Aubrey and Atkins on the Guinea Coast. One finds some material, but considerably less, in what might be considered travel narratives, such as Bosman's account of the time he spent in Africa, or Ovington's *A Voyage to Suratt*. A final set of sources is comprised of metropolitan works of medicine and natural philosophy, such as those by Arbuthnot and Huxham, which took the relationship between place, disease, and appearance as a central question. With such small numbers, trends are difficult to identify, but one can point to a change over time. Particularly from the 1720s onward, we shall see, one finds an increasing Hippocratic bent, with *Airs, Waters, and Places* taken as a paradigmatic text in framing a problematic that related location, diet, physical features, behaviour, and forms of governance.

We should begin by indicating what a racialist approach to medicine in this period might look like. Based on the materials, two kinds of arguments seem to have been plausible. The first looked at diseases that might be caused by, or (more weakly) related to, physical differences between the races. The second studied diseases that could be passed from generation to generation and that were particularly associated with the inhabitants of a specific part of the world. Arguments of the first type gained a certain degree of plausibility with Malpighi's studies. The difference between white and black could be seen as a (relatively) fixed one – at least one inherited by the next generation – and was a physically identifiable trait. Sloane explored the possibility that one particularly unfortunate affliction was caused by a physical difference in black bodies. In his account of the diseases of Jamaica he included the case of a female slave, brought to him by her owner, with many ulcers on her fingers and toes and 'several Bladders fill'd with *Serum* on several of her Joints'. Most peculiarly, these bladders appeared to fill with a periodicity tied to the cycle of the moon. Sloane was informed that the disease could be fatal and 'was peculiar to Blacks'. The doctor's treatment secured relief for a little time, but the disease returned quickly. Sloane mused over its possible cause: 'So soon as this Disease again appear'd, I thought, that perhaps, this was proper to Blacks, and so might come from some peculiar indisposition of their black skin'. Not only a disease peculiar to one race, then, this affliction was regarded as possibly the result of specific elements of a racial make-up.[82]

Sloane's tentative (and rather vague) suggestion is the only example of the first kind of racialist argument that I have been able to find. More common (if still rare) were arguments of the second type. Perhaps unsurprisingly, all of these hereditarian aetiologies concerned venereal disease, particularly syphilis. Unknown in Europe until the late fifteenth century, the new venereal disease quickly became associated with the inhabitants of the New World. And as Anna Foa has noted, associating a dread novel affliction with Indians was 'clearly not an innocent act'.

It meant searching for the origin of a sickness/evil of this kind, a sickness/evil tied to sexual excess and located as far from oneself as possible in the absolute Other, the person who had never known Christianity. This was an extreme projection: the disease was thrown back onto the 'nonhuman', onto the totally alien. To attribute it to a people outside the Revelation of Christ served to attenuate the impact of the debates on blame and divine punishment which had been encouraged by endogamous theories of the origin as the result of lasciviousness.[83]

One finds precisely this logic played out in Trapham's (bizarre) account of the origin of the disease known as Yaws, although he extended the argument to include not only 'the animal Indians' but also Africans, or, as he phrased it, 'the cursed posterity of the naked *Cham*'.[84] All venereal diseases, however various, Trapham argued, found their origin in the Yaws. And the cause was the same as that which produced 'strange, monstrous mixtures of animal shapes, more than ordinarily imitating the actions as well as the shapes of mankind'.[85] Baboons,

---

[82] Sloane, cvi. On Sloane's interest in the causes of blackness, see Malcolmson.

[83] Foa, 33.

[84] Trapham, 113. See also Londa Schiebinger, 'Scientific Exchange in the Eighteenth-Century Atlantic World', in *Soundings in Atlantic History: Latent Structures and Intellectual Currents, 1500–1830*, ed. Bernard Bailyn and Patricia L. Denault (Cambridge, MA: Harvard University Press, 2009), 309.

[85] Trapham, 114.

drills, pongoes, monkeys, and malmasets all arose, Trapham claimed, from unnatural and sinful acts of bestiality. Human semen was corrupted within the animal that received it. The progeny that resulted was of an 'anomalous Breed' and the tainted matter made its way back to the 'spermatick vessels of the more noble unlading Animal'.[86] For this 'sin against the principles of our Being', offenders were therefore punished with the Yaws.[87] Indians and Africans, by this logic, were inclined to such forbidden acts and had populated their native lands with new (quasi-human) beasts. They had also passed on the loathsome disease they had acquired to Europeans. Yet non-Europeans had been punished twice, in Trapham's account.

Whereas should he descend to an unsutable communication, and such but generally obtain, he must quickly quit his Royalty, if not to the beastly herd itself, yet to whose retains entire Humanity. Hence the Black may well become naturally Slaves, and the vast Territories of the Indians be easily invaded, and kept in subjection by inconsiderable force of the Spanish Tyranny. And even those Conquerors through mixture with these animal people, reap their infirmity of body and mind.[88]

As one can see, monogenism hardly stood as a bulwark against hateful depictions of non-European peoples. Certain races had, in Trapham's account, acquired bestial natures after the first and common creation. Indians and Africans had produced people-like animals, but they had become animal-like people, and had thus contributed to their own oppression.

Syphilis' modes of spread could do double duty in connecting the disease to certain peoples. As a venereal illness, it was associated with the lascivious – Indians, Africans, Jews and others.[89] Gabriel Dellon, for example, noted in his *A Voyage to the East Indies* that venereal disease 'is as common, and appears with the same Symptoms among the *Frenchmen* living in those Parts, as among the *Negro's*, they being equally given to Debauchery'.[90] The affliction was also, however, regarded as one that could be passed to future generations.[91] It could thus be imagined as both proper to a certain people, and also dangerous to those who associated with them. Yet such people did not need to be racialised, for one might also regard the distemper as proper to a certain *place*.

[86] Ibid., 115–16.
[87] Ibid., 115.
[88] Ibid., 117.
[89] Foa.
[90] Gabriel Dellon, *A Voyage to the East-Indies: Giving an Account of the Isles of Madagascar, and Mascareigne, of Suratte, the Coast of Malabar, of Goa, Gameron, Ormus: As Also a Treatise of the Distempers Peculiar to the Eastern Countries: To Which Is Annexed an Abstract of Monsieur De Rennefort's History of the East-Indies, with His Propositions for the Improvement of the East-India Company* (London: D. Browne, A. Roper, D. Leigh, 1698), 231.
[91] Sydenham, 248.

Sydenham, more critical than Trapham of 'that barbarous Custom of changing Men for Ware', also associated the disease with lands outside Europe, but argued against those who claimed that its native seat lay in the Americas, suggesting that the disease was born in Africa, and had been spread through the slave trade.[92] The fact that it had declined in virulence over the years, however, seemed to suggest an environmental cause. '[L]ike vegetables, being as it were transplanted from its own Country into another', he wrote, 'it does not so much flourish in Europe, but languishes daily, and the *Phenomena* grow milder'.[93] Although communicated by people, then, the disease seemed produced or shaped not by the characteristics of a race, as Trapham had claimed, but by the characteristics of a climate.

The majority of authors tended to follow Sydenham in ascribing the cause of illnesses to climate, environment, or diet, rather than innate racial difference. Sloane, Sydenham's protégé, observed only one disease out of scores that seemed related to the physical peculiarities of black bodies. Otherwise, his emphasis was on similarities. Venereal diseases, for example, 'had the same symptoms and course among Europeans, Indians, and Negroes'.[94] Indeed, the similarity of bodies led to an uncharacteristic rebuke of white Creole custom. Black wet-nurses, he noted, were used as often as white ones, being much more common, but were 'not coveted by Planters, for fear of infecting their children with some of their ill customs, as Thieving &c'. Sloane remarked that he had never observed such a consequence 'and am sure a Black's milk comes much nearer the Mother's than that of a Cow'.[95]

Few other authors had much good to say about the natives they encountered, yet they did not phrase their hostility in racialist terms. Bosman, for example, claimed that the inhabitants of Africa were 'all without exception, Crafty, Villanous, and Fraudulent, and very seldom to be trusted', but he did not ascribe this character to a physical cause.[96] Medically, he noted that the characteristic diseases of the region were the small pox and worms. The former, of

---

[92] Ibid., 247.

[93] Ibid., 248.

[94] Sloane, cxxviii.

[95] Nonetheless, he acknowledged that 'yet in Jamaica some Children are bred up by the Hand very well'. Ibid., cxlviii.

[96] Bosman, 117. The only other group of people who seem to come close to Negroes in baseness for Bosman were Muscovites. See, for similar levels of disdain, James Houston, who wrote of the natives of the Guinea Coast: 'I shall say only in one Word, that their natural Temper is barbarously cruel, selfish, and deceitful, and their Government equally barbarous and uncivil; and consequently, the Men of greatest Eminency amongst them, are those that are most capable of being the greatest Rogues; Vice, being left without any Check on it, becomes a Virtue. As for their Customs, they exactly resemble their fellow Creatures and Natives, the Monkeys'. Houstoun, 33–4.

course, was the scourge of Europe, the latter afflicted Negroes most, but not exclusively. In terms of their afflictions, then, Negroes and Europeans were not remarkably different.[97] Towne made the same point even more explicitly in discussing a disease apparently unknown in Europe yet common among blacks, namely 'Elefantiasis under the circumstances it occurs in the West Indies'.[98] Towne made clear that the predisposing causes of the illness were not specific to any one group. It struck those who had suffered through tedious illnesses and were then 'constrained to subsist upon bad diet and undigestible unwholesome food' or exposed to inclement weather.[99] 'Sometimes', he noted, 'white people, whose unhappy circumstances have reduced them to hardships but little inferior to what the Blacks are obliged to undergo, have given us proof that this disease is not limited to one colour'.[100]

Other than Atkins, the most detailed account of racial difference in a medical text before 1740 is to be found in T. Aubrey's *The Sea-Surgeon, or the Guinea Man's Vade Mecum*.[101] A subtitle of the work noted that it was intended 'for the Use of young Sea Surgeons', and Aubrey offered particular advice for those given the charge of maintaining the health of slaves bought on the coast of Guinea. Reasons of both economy and morality, Aubrey suggested, should lead to better treatment of Negroes, which better treatment could be supplied by limiting the number of ignorant surgeons and curbing the abuses of sailors, 'who beat and kick them to that Degree, that sometimes they never recover, and then the Surgeon is blamed for letting the Slaves dye, when they are murthered, partly by Strokes, and partly famished'.[102] One of the surgeon's roles, Aubrey argued, was to convince captains that slaves be better treated, if only out of the latter's financial self-interest. Such cynicism might well work on captains who cursed slaves for dying, but Aubrey himself put forward a remarkable position that promoted equality of medical treatment on theological grounds while simultaneously advocating for a more profitable form of slavery.[103]

[O]ne ought to please and flatter them as much as one can, because the more you preserve of them for the Plantations, the more Profit you will have, and also the greater Reputation and Wages another Voyage; besides it's a Case of Conscience to be as carefull of them, as the white Men; for altho' they are Heathens, yet have they a rational

---

[97]   Bosman was, however, scathing about Mulattoes: 'This Bastard Strain is made up of a parcel of profligate Villains, neither true to the Negroes nor us ... [w]hatever is in its own Nature worst in the *Europeans* and *Negroes* is united in them'. Bosman, 141.

[98]   Towne, 184.

[99]   Ibid., 185.

[100]   Ibid., 188.

[101]   T. Aubrey, *The Sea-Surgeon, or the Guinea Man's Vade Mecum* (London: John Clarke, 1729). A *Vade Mecum* is, essentially, a handbook.

[102]   Ibid., 128.

[103]   Aubrey noted that his captain had asked 'what a Devil makes these plaguey Devils dye so fast?', ibid., 132.

Soul, as well as us; and God knows whether it may not be more tolerable for them in the latter Day, than for many, who profess themselves Christians.[104]

It was in the context of a discussion of improved care for the property of slavers that Aubrey introduced his comments on the physical and medical differences of different inhabitants of the African coast. 'It is highly necessary for you to endeavour to be acquainted with the Nature and Constitution of these People', he wrote in a chapter entitled 'Of the Negroes', 'together with their accustomed manner of Living, which will the better qualify you for preserving their Health, and also restoring them when afflicted'.[105] Aubrey divided Negroes into four groups, organised by colour, relative presence of 'aerial Spirit', and characteristic afflictions. The first were of 'a kind of Chocolate Colour; their Hair is commonly very short, crisped, and of a dark Russet'. Such people were, in terms of temperament, 'most commonly surly, proud, haughty, vain-glorious, quarrelsome, revengeful, implacable, yet commonly very valiant, and much given to Venery'. Possessed of the greatest amount of aerial spirit, the blood in such bodies was greatly inclined to inflammation and common illnesses included erysipelas and ardent fevers. The second group were 'natural Black, and are commonly lusty, strong, vigorous, cheerful, merry, affable, amorous, kind, docile, faithful, and easily diverted from Wrath, their Hair is very black, and may be drawn out to a great Length'. With less aerial fluid than the first group, their bodily fluids circulated less rapidly. Their characteristic illness was the pleurisy. With an eye to a key element of his occupation, Aubrey noted that these people, of all he would discuss, were the best tempered and made the best slaves. The third group he described as 'yellow, and for the most Part dull, heavy, sluggish, lazy, idle, stupid, timorous, and easily impos'd on; their Hair is of a dark brown, and may be drawn out to a great Length'. Their fluids moved even more slowly than the first two peoples', containing still less aerial fluid, and their characteristic afflictions were diarrhoea and, among women, the Fluor Albus or the Whites. The fourth group were those for whom Aubrey had the greatest distaste and 'are of a dark russet Colour, their Hair black and crisped, and very thin, which never grows to any great Length; they are naturally sad, sluggish, sullen, peevish, forward, spiteful, fantastical, envious, self-conceited, proper at nothing, naturally Cowards, very indecent, and nasty in all their Transactions'. Their appalling character was matched by the diseases with which they were most commonly afflicted. With the least amount of aerial spirit in their fluids their humours circulated slowly and were inclined to corruption, leading to leprosy, scurvy and 'schirrhous Tumours'. They were, moreover, 'the worst of Slaves, and very few of them

---

[104] Ibid., 121.
[105] Ibid., 102.

can be brought to Decency, or any tolerable Subjection, either by Flattery, or Austerity'.[106]

That we should not understand these divisions in racial terms is fairly obvious. There was a common cause of both physical differences and the body's tendency to be afflicted by certain diseases: the relative presence or absence of aerial fluid. Such a presence or absence was not a racial trait so much as a constitutional one. Europeans could be divided into four groups as well, and those groupings precisely mirrored those of Aubrey's 'Negroes'. Where one found the most aerial spirit, skin was swarthy, the hair brown or black, the inclination to venery high, and the intellect witty; where there was less, the skin was florid and hair usually brown, and 'the Disposition cheerful'; less still and the complexion was pale, the hair whitish or yellow-brown, 'the Sleep sound and long in Duration'. Once again, the last group was the least appealing: the complexion 'duskish livid', the temperament 'peevish and sullen'.[107] Aubrey made the obvious connection: 'These are the several Constitutions which the Ancients call Choleric, Sanguine, Phlegmatic and Melancholy'.[108] Unlike the ancients, however, Aubrey denied that one could find any of these humours in the blood, pointing to air as the elemental difference. One can thus see that rather than describing four African races, he had merely described choleric, sanguine, phlegmatic, and melancholic constitutions in Africa. Of the reason that natives of the Guinea coast were, in general, darker than whites, Aubrey said nothing, although given the emphasis throughout the text on climate and diet, one suspects that he would offer a fairly conventional environmentalist explanation.[109]

One can see in both Aubrey and Towne evidence of the neo-Hippocratism described in some detail in Chapter 2. Hippocrates was the first source cited in either man's work and one might see each of them as exemplars, in the periphery, of a movement also occurring in the metropole, which wedded the questions and approaches of *Epidemics*, and *Airs, Waters, and Places* with natural philosophical investigations of the weather and air more generally. Of the metropolitan works, the most systematically Hippocratic was almost certainly John Arbuthnot's *Essay Concerning the Effects of Air on Human Bodies*.[110] The sixth chapter, 'Concerning the Influence of Air on Human Constitutions and Diseases' began with a five page summary of *Airs, Waters, and Places,* noting

---

[106] Ibid., 104–5.
[107] Ibid., 10.
[108] Ibid., 11.
[109] 'I am persuaded', he declared, for example, 'that there is no Disease of whatsoever kind it be, but is either generated from a Deficiency of insensible Transpiration, or vitious Food; or inquinated Air'. Ibid., 22.
[110] Arbuthnot.

that 'this great Man' explained not only the relationship between diseases and the weather, but also ascribed the various complexions, temperaments, and governments of mankind to the different constitutions of the air in which such people lived.[111] Climate generally, and the air specifically, was thus responsible for geographically specific distempers and the physical appearance of the natives of given lands. 'There are Faces not only individual', Arbuthnot wrote, 'but gentilitious and national; *European, Asiatick, Chinese, African, Grecian* Faces, are characteris'd'.[112] And while he acknowledged that part of this commonality of features within nations was due to 'propagation' from the same stock, he also argued, again following Hippocrates, that air had a role to play: 'That the Complexion depends much upon the Air, is plain from Experience; the Complexion of the Inhabitants of several Countries being fair, swarthy, black, and adust, according to the Degrees of Heat, Drought, Moisture, or Coolness of the Air'.[113] Perhaps most telling, however, Arbuthnot insisted that climate would trump race when it came to 'Temper and Genius', given only a few years. Those who lived in the same countries at different times, he claimed, would come to possess the same character, 'even tho' the Race has been changed'.[114] Today's Frenchmen were largely the same as the Gauls in the time of Caesar, he asserted, adding his belief that 'if a Race of *Laplanders*' were today transported to Paris, they would rapidly become much like the men in that location described by the Emperor Julian in the fourth century.[115] John Huxham would make similar claims about the common cause of racialised physical differences and disease, in his *Observationes de aëre et morbis epidemicis*, suggesting that a Hippocratic orthodoxy had taken hold on the issue by the 1730s.[116]

To summarise, then, it might be suggested that medicine and 'science' (meaning natural philosophy and natural history) were in a rather similar

---

[111] Ibid., 123.
[112] Ibid., 146–7.
[113] Ibid., 148.
[114] Ibid., 149.
[115] Ibid., 149–50.
[116] John Huxham, *Observationes de Aere et Morbis Epidemicis: Ab Anno MDCCXXVIII Ad Finem Anni MDCCXXXVII, Plymuthi Fact. His Accedit Opusculum de Morbo Colico Damnoniensi* (London: S. Austen, 1739). Huxham thus writes: 'The great Dictator in Medicine, *Hippocrates*, asserts that not only the Diseases, but also the Temperaments and very Manners of Men, depend greatly on the various Constitutions of the Air, in his most elegant Book on Air, Water, and Situations'. On the relationship between physical difference and endemic diseases, he wrote: 'The Heat of the torrid Zone so exhausts the Liquids of the Inhabitants, and so crisps up their Fibres, that they look as if quite burnt up. – From the Relation of Physicians, who have practised in these Parts, their Blood is found much more thick and black than that of the *Europeans*; hence most ardent and pestilential Fevers are endemic in such Climates, the Humours growing putrid on the slightest Occasion'. *The Works of John Huxham, M. D. F. R. S. In Two Volumes*, I, xxvi, xxv.

position at the beginning of the eighteenth century. One finds a few isolated flirtations with racial logics in each realm. Such flirtations would continue in race-science, with Voltaire and Hume's polygenism (from the 1730s and in the 1750s, respectively) suggesting that race was beginning to function as causal explanation and not merely a climatic or special creative effect. The same was not true in medicine, where an environmentalist Hippocratic orthodoxy after the 1720s twinned race and disease together, as common effects of a much more important set of causes: location, diet, and – most importantly – air. It is with this growing separation between 'science' and medicine on the subject of race in mind that we turn to John Atkins: polygenist surgeon.

5.4   A Little Heterodox: John Atkins, Polygenism, and African Diseases

Born in 1685, Atkins began his medical training as a surgeon's apprentice and then joined the navy, serving in multiple locations. In 1721, he sailed for the Guinea Coast, with two ships sent to suppress piracy there. After meeting with moderate success, but suffering significant casualties, the ships sailed to Brazil and the West Indies before returning to England in 1723. Failing to find another position at sea, Atkins turned to writing. In 1724, he published *A Treatise on the Following Chirurgical Subjects*, the fifth chapter of which was concerned with 'some *African* Distempers'.[117] The *Treatise* was restructured and republished in 1734, as *The Navy-Surgeon*, with the section on African diseases moved to an Appendix. Atkins expanded on this material the following year, in an account of his journeys in the early 1720s, *A Voyage to Guinea, Brasil, and the West-Indies; in His Majesty's Ships, the Swallow and Weymouth*. Second, unaltered editions of both texts appeared in 1737, and a substantially modified third edition of *The Navy-Surgeon* was published in 1742.[118]

The *Treatise* began with a defence of surgery against the pretensions of the modern physician. Before the present degenerate age, Mankind had lived longer, healthier lives. Physic had largely been limited to the preservation of health through attention to the six non-naturals, particularly diet, rather than 'the various and inexplicable Prescriptions of Physick as it now stands'.[119]

[117] There is no date given on the text. The *Daily Journal* of 21 December 1724, however, lists the text as 'To Morrow will be publish'd'. The copy located in the Beinecke library at Yale appears to have been given to Yale College by the author in 1729. My thanks to the research librarian, Elizabeth Frengel, for confirming this for me.

[118] For biographical materials, see N. M., 'Atkins, John (1685–1757)', *Dictionary of National Biography* 2 (1885); F. Tubbs, 'John Atkins: An Eighteenth-Century Naval Surgeon', *British Medical Bulletin* 5 (1947–8).

[119] John Atkins, *A Treatise on the Following Chirurgical Subjects* ... (London: T. Warner, 1729), Preface, i.

Surgery, Atkins claimed – citing the wounding of Abel – had preceded physic in the cure of maladies, and it was Chiron the centaur, skilled in the surgical treatment of ulcers, who had taught medicine to Aesculapius. Followers of Aesculapius in the present, however, had vastly and unnecessarily multiplied diseases, hypotheses, and prescriptions 'that the Age of Man is scarce sufficient to make a Disquisition into'. The surgeon, on the other hand, required relatively little theoretical knowledge to practice his craft: anatomy; 'the different secretions of the Body'; the use of a small number of basic *materia medica*; and knowledge of the non-naturals supplied almost everything that could be necessary, beyond extensive practical study. It was the fruits of such practice that Atkins offered the reader, with chapters on ruptures, fractures, amputations, dislocations, and (with separate pagination) that scourge of the military man: venereal diseases.[120]

All of the above topics can be considered basic knowledge for the naval surgeon at any location, so one may understand why, in the next version of his text, Atkins should move the section on venereal disease within the main body of the work and remove his 'Journal of the Sick on the Coast of Guiney' to an appendix. Where all military surgeons should be familiar with the treatment of ruptures and gunshot wounds, for example, Atkins recommended his diary to 'those whose Fortune may carry them in the same Tract'.[121] Beginning with a characterisation of the climate – very warm (but with cooling breezes) and with thick, moist air that could 'rust your Pocket Instruments, Swords, or any Kind of Steel Implements in a Day's Time' – Atkins soon turned to a discussion of the cause and treatment of the illnesses suffered by his crew in 1722. The death rate, as he would note in *A Voyage to Guinea*, was almost unimaginable. The *Weymouth*, for example, left England with a complement of 240 men: by the time the ship returned – having picked up more men along her journey – she had lost a total of 280.[122] At one point in his travels, Atkins was made purser, since everybody else who might take up the position had died.[123]

Atkins blamed the climate and the dubious morality of the men. The heat of the sun was near overpowering, vastly worse on land than at sea, and when the

---

[120] Discussing the last, Atkins denied that the disease was a new one, brought back from the Siege of Naples. The affliction arose, he argued, first in women who had received too many partners. Excessive friction, coupled with an 'ill habit of body' produced ulcers, 'which Ulcer will be the Distemper'. Since this vice had existed long before the Siege, Atkins argued, so too had the disease, 'as Antient as corrupted Nature, it being irrational, either to suppose a World drowned for their Sins, Strangers to the Vice that contracts it, or that their Wickedness any more than ours deserved Exemption'. Ibid., Appendix, 4, 1.

[121] Ibid., 177.

[122] *A Voyage to Guinea, Brasil, and the West-Indies; in His Majesty's Ships, the Swallow and Weymouth*, 139.

[123] Ibid., 196.

sun set the air cooled and was filled with vapours, leading to dews that soaked beds through. Drunk on palm wine by the end of the day, men would fall asleep in the open air, their perspiration suddenly checked by the chill, which led almost inexorably, in Atkins' telling, to fevers 'more or less Malignant'. Even when sober, however, the men were not to be trusted. Sent on shore, where they were harder to manage than within the confines of the ship, they were 'ungovernable in their Actions and Appetites', stealing from the locals 'and debauching their wives' while eating and drinking whatever they pleased 'without any Enquiry how proper or wholesome for Food, or having any Regard to Custom and Manner of Living'.[124] Medical treatment availed of little and the crew eventually pushed out to sea, hoping (rightly, as it turned out) that a change of location and concomitant alterations of behaviour might halt the 'epidemical rage'.[125]

Having explained the diseases of European sailors in terms of their environment and behaviour, Atkins turned finally to the diseases that afflicted Africans, dividing these into two groups: 'Coast Negroes' and 'Inland Negroes', the latter of whom made up the bulk of those taken for the slave trade. Coastal Negroes, he asserted, were untroubled by many of the chronic and acute European illnesses because they were spared a luxurious way of life, subsisting largely on vegetable matter, bathing occasionally, and exercising enough to expel the recrements of their food. These coastal dwellers, he claimed, 'were abundantly more sprightly and active than the Inland Natives' who had not been 'mended' by their interactions with Europeans and 'are to appearance but a few Degrees in Knowledge above Beasts'. Some distempers – smallpox and sore eyes, for example – were clearly common to Europeans and Africans alike, but Atkins focused his discussion on four that were distinctive to Negroes: the sleepy distemper, the croakra, the yaws, and the chicoes.

Although he declared all four diseases 'more properly their own', the latter three were barely peculiar to a given people, let alone to be explained in racialist terms.[126] The yaws was the local term for venereal disease and was so similar to 'our Pox and Clap' that Atkins deferred further discussion to a subsequent chapter, where he would treat the subject in its generality. Chicoes were what had been known for a long time as 'Guinea' worms and were 'common with them, tho' not so properly said to be peculiar', since one also found them in the West Indies. If they afflicted Africans more often than Europeans, it was presumably because locals more often walked barefoot in the waters where the eggs of the 'insects' were found. The croakra, Atkins explained, was a skin

---

[124] *A Treatise on the Following Chirurgical Subjects*, 185–6.
[125] Ibid., 192.
[126] Ibid., 197.

disease, brought on by a change of diet and possibly by carelessness in drying the skin when it had been wet by salt water.

It is worth emphasising the dietetic and behavioural aetiology for croakra that Atkins supplied because it was in the context of his discussion of 'the distempered skins of *Africans*' that he turned to a consideration of the cause of their skin's colour. His polygenetic views would follow, but he did not adopt a racialist explanation of the disease: black skin might be peculiar to Africans, who had been created separately to all other humans, but the diseases of that skin were to be explained not by originary physical difference, but by the fact that – on slave ships – they were constantly in contact with sea water and were forced into 'a sudden Change to an unusual and coarse, if not a salt, Diet'.[127]

The natural cause for the dark skin and woolly hair of the inhabitants of much of Africa, Atkins declared, 'must ever perplex Philosophers to assign'.[128] Malpighi, it was true, had located the cause in the colour of a subcuticular mucus, but that had merely pushed the question back a step: why was the mucus differently coloured in different peoples? One could explain tanning under a hot sun by suggesting that the lightly coloured mucus of fine European skin was warmed until its thinner parts were eliminated, leaving 'the Remainer dark, as the clearest Liquors, they say, will leave some sediment'.[129] But Atkins doubted that the darkness of Africans could be explained through this mechanism, offering five reasons for thinking that such mechanical explanations would be inadequate. First came the argument by analogy with animals. Atkins noted that the sun did not seem to have the same effects on other animals in Guinea as it was assumed to have on humans. If the sun were responsible for producing the woolly hair characteristic of Africans, why did local sheep 'have hair contrary to that closer Contexture of the Skin, which is supposed to contribute to the Production of Wool in the humane Species'? The second argument involved a comparison with Europeans. Why did white skin never turn black and why did the skin of Mulattoes remain intermediary in colour between the two extremes? Third, Atkins observed that one could not explain African skin colour entirely by pointing to the tint of a sub-cuticular mucus, for the colour of black skin changed as the higher layers of skin altered. Black feet and hands gradually whitened, Atkins claimed 'by Friction and constant use' and the cuticle paled after the skin was burnt or scalded. Fourth, one might compare Africans to Americans, the latter of whom lived under an equally burning sun, but were not as black. Fifth and finally, not all Africans – despite their residence under the same sun – were the same colour. 'I saw

---

[127] Ibid., 202.
[128] Ibid., 203.
[129] Ibid., 204.

one ... who was woolly and, in every Respect else, a Negro ... but in Colour', he reported. A conclusion seemed to follow by necessity. 'From the whole', he asserted, without seeming awareness of the radicalism of the claim, 'I imagine that White and Black must have descended of different Protoplasts [i.e. progenitors], and that there is no other Way of accounting for it'.[130] No more was said on the issue, and the discussion turned back to the diseases 'peculiar' to the Guinea Coast.

Despite the brevity of Atkins' polygenetic remarks, it seems a reasonable question to ask, as Norris Saakwa-Mante has, about possible connections between Atkins' racial theories and his understandings of African diseases.[131] Did the surgeon regard the distempers suffered by Negroes as a result of the originary difference between their physical frames and those of Europeans? For three of the four distempers he analysed, including the seemingly most obvious case, involving an affliction of the skin, the answer would appear to be no. The fourth case – the sleepy distemper – is more complex. Though the affliction was apparently common, the symptoms were unusual. It came on suddenly, prefaced only with a few days of reduced appetite. Most character-istically, it induced deep slumbers and reduced sensation. '[P]ulling, drubbing, or whipping', Atkins observed with a disturbing dispassion, 'will scarce stir up Sense and Power enough to move, and the Moment you cease beating, the Smart is forgot, and down they fall again into a State of Insensibility, drivling constantly from the Mouth as if in a deep Salivation'.[132] The immediate cause seemed obvious to Atkins. The sufferer's brains were filled with a surfeit of phlegm or serum, which obstructed the nerves. One found somewhat similar conditions in Europe, he noted, among the elderly. Those who, during a long lifetime had indulged too much in food and drink, found themselves eventually with a brain the tone of which was significantly weakened, which could lead to habitual sleepiness. And yet, Africans were largely strangers to luxury and the Sleepy Distemper in Africa seemed to afflict the young and those 'destitute of the Means of Surfeiting'.[133] Whatever the cause of excessive drowsiness might be in Europe, the same causes seemed not to be in operation in this disease.

Atkins, in fact, pointed to three causes for the Sleepy Distemper: 'Cold and Immaturity'; 'Diet and Way of Living'; and 'the natural Weakness of the Brain'. In this edition of the text, neither the first nor the second were racialised.

---

[130] Ibid., 204–5. Atkins would seem here to be explicitly referencing Giordano Bruno, who had written in his own polygenetic musings, that: 'Aethiopum/genus ad illum protoplasten nemo sani iudicii referet [No one of sound judgment will trace the nation of the Ethiopians to that first man.] Quoted in Malcolmson, 192.

[131] Saakwa-Mante.

[132] Atkins, *A Treatise on the Following Chirurgical Subjects*, 197–8.

[133] Ibid., 199.

That the young seemed to suffer disproportionately from the disease made some sense, for in youth, Atkins noted, the elements of the body 'have not yet attained their due Spring and Perfection' and the body produced more phlegm and other drossy matter. In the 1734 version of his remarks, Atkins added a single half sentence to this discussion: 'and it is only supposing the *Africans* continue longer Children than the Europeans'.[134] Whether this extended youth was a result of the climate or was inherited from a different protoplast, Atkins did not say. The inadequacies of the local diet meant that the blood produced from such nutriment declined in quality while the indolence characteristic of native Africans meant that waste matter that resulted from the concoction of food into blood was not adequately disposed of during exercise. As a result, this waste matter found its way to the brain, which Atkins declared to be the weakest part to be found among Negro slaves.

It was this 'natural Weakness' of the African brain that Atkins thought was 'the principal Cause' of the sleepy distemper.[135] And where neither youth, diet, nor way of life seemed to point to any fundamental or original difference between the bodies of Negroes and Europeans, Atkins did suggest that Africans were 'hereditarily ignorant'. Brains, he argued, were like muscles, which gained in strength through exercise. Africans were 'destitute of all Art and Science, or any mechanical Knowledge to exercise the Brain'.[136] In consequence, that organ became ever weaker over time and from this weakness flowed the disease: 'the Brain must grow weak, and such a State of Thoughtlessness and Inactivity, dispose it for the Reception of Serosities'.[137] Saakwa-Mante has argued that this claim about the weakness of African brains 'is clearly intended as a racial characteristic'.[138] I remain unsure. The muscular metaphor is unclear, for it seems to suggest that Black and White brains begin in similar states and that – over a lifetime – the brains of Africans atrophy for lack of significant use. Weakness would appear to be acquired rather than innate. Moreover, the language of hereditarianism, which would in most cases be the most convincing evidence for racialist thought, here applies not to physical characteristics, but to knowledge (or its lack). Two factors would seem, in fact, to speak against a racialist reading, both concerning the distinction Atkins drew between Coastal and Inland Negroes. While both groups, one assumed, derived from the same co-Adamic original, each was not equally afflicted by the sleepy distemper, which seemed particularly to strike slaves, who were drawn from 'Country

[134] *The Navy-Surgeon: Or, a Practical System of Surgery*, 1st ed. (London: Caesar Ward and Richard Chandler, 1734), 20.
[135] *A Treatise on the Following Chirurgical Subjects*, 201.
[136] Ibid.
[137] Ibid., 202.
[138] Saakwa-Mante, 44.

People', rather than those from the coast.[139] Coastal people were less ignorant (thus overcoming their heredity?) and exercised more, allowing the expulsion of recrementitious humours. Were the sleepy distemper a racial trait, derived from structures of the brain passed down from a protoplast, one would expect that the disease – like skin colour or hair type – was essentially fixed. Fixity, after all, was one of Atkins' strongest arguments against a climatic explanation of the hue of African skin. Yet susceptibility to the sleepy distemper was anything but fixed: contact with Europeans had apparently produced African peoples who were not habitually plagued by the affliction, even if their Country brethren remained so.

Later texts only seem to emphasise the disconnect between Atkins' polygenetic theories and his medical explanations.[140] With few changes, *The Navy-Surgeon* reproduced the claims of *The Treatise*. The *Voyage to Guinea*, however, considerably expanded upon them. The 'colour, language, and manners' of Africans, Atkins observed, was as different 'as we may imagine we should find in the planetary Subjects above, could we get there'.[141] And the difference in physical features led one, again, to an assumption concerning separate creations:

> The black Colour, and woolly Tegument of these *Guineans*, is what first obtrudes itself on our Observation, and distinguishes them from the rest of Mankind, who no where else, in the warmest Latitudes, are seen thus totally changed; nor removing, will they ever alter, without mixing in Generation. I have taken notice in my *Navy-Surgeon*, how difficultly the Colour is accounted for; and tho' it be a little Heterodox, I am persuaded the black and white Race have, *ab origine*, sprung from different-coloured first Parents.[142]

As in the earlier works, however, fixity seemed limited only to the skin and hair. Even other physical features were deemed changeable. 'Their flattish noses', for example, came about 'owing to a continued grubbing in their Infancy against their Mother's Backs'.[143] And levels of intelligence or civilisation were eminently improvable: ignorance may have been inherited, but it was not a permanent condition. 'That these people could arrive to better Knowledge by the use of proper Means and Instruction, there is no manner of doubt', Atkins declared. 'They give proof enough that their natural Endowments are

---

[139] Atkins, *A Treatise on the Following Chirurgical Subjects*, 198.
[140] The first edition of *The Navy-Surgeon* (1734) added only an ambiguous half line to the arguments offered in the section on the Guinea Coast in the 1724 *Treatise*, even as it restructured the latter text and made additions to the Preface.
[141] Atkins, *A Voyage to Guinea, Brasil, and the West-Indies; in His Majesty's Ships, the Swallow and Weymouth*, 34.
[142] Ibid., 39.
[143] Ibid., 180.

capable of following any pattern'. Although incapable of advance on their own, they could be led: 'when the Seeds and principles are laid by letter'd Nations, it is not then nigh so difficult to improve'.[144] The 'muscle' of the brain was capable of further exercise, in other words. What was now weak could become stronger.

It is hard, in general, to determine what drew Atkins to his polygenetic ruminations, or why he should have felt the need to publish views so heterodox. Cristina Malcolmson has placed Atkins toward the end of a lineage of authors responding to the set of questions posed in Robert Boyle's 'General Heads for a Natural History of a Counterey', published in the first volume of the *Philosophical Transactions* in 1666.[145] A paragraph of Boyle's queries asked after the inhabitants of new lands:

And in particular their Stature, Shape, Colour, Features, Strength, Agility, Beauty (or the want of it) Complexions, Hair, Dyet, Inclinations, and Customs that seem not due to Education. As to their Women (besides the other things) may be observed their Fruitfulness or Barrenness; their hard or easy Labour, &c. And both in Women and Men must be taken notice of what diseases they are subject to, and in these whether there be any symptom, or any other Circumstance, that is unusual and remarkable.[146]

The similarities to the issues discussed by Atkins seem self-evident. Yet both Boyle himself and the vast majority of those who took up his queries were committed to monogenism. It has sometimes been suggested that polygenism could function as a defence of slavery, but Atkins was deeply critical of that institution; considerably more so, indeed, than Boyle.[147] A theme running through *A Voyage* involves the debunking of the idea that Africans were cannibals. Tales about anthropophagy, he suggested, proceeded from the attempt 'to magnify the Miracle of escaping an inhospitable and strange Country' and also by design, in order 'to justify Dispossession … Conquest and Cruelty' from those who convinced themselves that they were 'only subduing of brutish Nature'.[148] Hardly enthusiastic about Africans, who he described as cowardly, thievish, and lazy, Atkins was nonetheless near absolute in his hostility to the slave trade. Highly critical of the natives of the Guinea Coast, then, Atkins was well aware that much harsher positions than his own existed, and a proportion of his text sought to push back against this harshness. In fact, one of

[144] Ibid., 82–3.
[145] Atkins, Malcolmson argues, 'writes for the Royal Society, since he constructs his narrative in terms of the "General Heads", comments on Boyle's experiments on the air, and mentions a wealth of articles from the *Philosophical Transactions*'. Malcolmson, 191. See also 62.
[146] Robert Boyle, 'General Heads for a Natural History of a Countrey, Great or Small, Imparted Likewise by Mr. Boyle', *Philosophical Transactions* 1 (1666): 188.
[147] On Boyle's support for slavery and defence of monogenism, see Malcolmson, e.g. 15.
[148] Atkins, *A Voyage to Guinea, Brasil, and the West-Indies; in His Majesty's Ships, the Swallow and Weymouth*, xxiii.

the most remarkable parts of *A Voyage* – and one of the few where polygenism was explicitly invoked in support of another contention, rather than simply for its own sake – involved the deployment of the doctrine of separate creations as a *defence* of Africans against those who would criticise their lack of true religion. Having never received the benefit of revelation, how could they be judged for their heathenism?

> They are set down as from the Clouds, without Guide, Letters, or any means of Cultivation to their better Part, but what immediately strike their Senses from beholding this Universe and the Beings contained in it; their Deductions from whence, as to a Deity devoid of Matter, is next to impossible, therefore we say mean and pitiful.[149]

Atkins polygenetic remarks remained unchanged in the second edition of *The Navy-Surgeon* and *A Voyage to Guinea*, both of which appeared in 1737. *A Voyage* would not be published again, but *The Navy-Surgeon* appeared in a third edition in 1742 and (posthumously) in 1758. And in these two last, Atkins completely retracted his polygenism while keeping unaltered his descriptions of diseases 'peculiar' to Africans. We shall get to Atkins' new racial views in a moment, but it is worth noting that the third edition of *The Navy-Surgeon* was, most generally, a very different book from its earlier versions. All of those had pitched themselves as practical works; guides to the day to day tasks of a surgeon at sea and in foreign lands. The 1742 edition, by contrast was considerably more scholarly. Loaded with many more quotations and references to classical and modern works, the book now opened not by getting straight into a discussion of fractures, but by considering the general question of the nature of sensation. Atkins added a 'dissertation' on cold and hot mineral springs and the introduction now included a disquisition on the life and changing fortunes of medical men in the Navy, covering many of the same issues that would reach a much larger audience with the publication of Tobias Smollett's *The Adventures of Roderick Random* in 1748. It was once easy to gain a berth as a naval surgeon, Atkins noted ruefully, 'when the Sea and the Gallows were said to refuse none'. Now, however, competition was fierce and seemed to turn not on the question of qualifications, but on personal wealth and powerful patronage.[150]

One finds multiple additions, small and large, even within the Appendix on Guinea.[151] In part, presumably, because the *Voyage* had covered not only Africa, but the West Indies and Brazil, and partly also because British troops had recently suffered such losses due to disease in the New World, Atkins now

---

[149] Ibid., 82.

[150] *The Navy-Surgeon; or, Practical System of Surgery with a Dissertation on Cold and Hot Mineral Springs; and Physical Observations on the Coast of Guiney* (London: J. Hodges, 1742), 1.

[151] Among the more minor, but still intriguing, is the addition of a name for the people living in Africa near the Southern latitude of 34 degrees: 'Hotmentotts'. Ibid., 367.

added several remarks about the West Indies. In the brief discussion of the Yaws, for example, he now noted that the word was used commonly in both places and that the disease might be more prevalent in the New World, 'where the Sexes not being balanced, may give greater Occasion for Infection'. In spite of a long tradition that sought to portray Africans and their descendants as promiscuous and immoral, Atkins argued that the opposite was true. The Yaws was uncommon on both the Guinea Coast and Inland, he observed. 'Nature perhaps repays their Ignorance of Means to cure, by a stronger Love and Inclination to Continency'. It was true that their women were almost always naked, but Atkins took this as a positive development. As a result, their 'Lust is glutted', and when they married, their friendships were stronger and more lasting, 'as not founded so much in Concupiscence'.[152] The section on Chicos, or worms, was also expanded, in this case dramatically. Natural Historical questions about the origin of Guinea worms segued into Natural Philosophical questions about the origin of life, the cause of the earth's rotation, and the nature of the soul and consciousness. In the previous two editions the text had concluded with remarks on removing worms from the skin. Now the final paragraph was pious and elegiac, Atkins 'advising all ... who wish for Immortality, to cast their Sheat-Anchor on Revelation', and commending 'one Faith, one Baptism, and one Lord Jesus Christ'.[153]

One must suspect that such seemingly new-found piety lay behind Atkins' decision to abandon views that were more than 'a little heterodox'.[154] In considering the differences between black and white bodies, the surgeon did not back off his criticisms of explanations that relied on the action of the Sun. All five objections to climatic causality were reproduced verbatim. But Atkins now excised his conclusion: there was no mention of different protoplasts. Instead, he offered a different explanation, and an environmental one at that. His 'Guess on this abstruse question' was now that differences in skin colour and hair type were due to differences in the soil in which generations had been bred.[155] Expanding his geographical perspective, Atkins acknowledged that it was not only blacks and whites who seemed utterly different. Brazilians were

---

[152] Ibid., 370.
[153] Ibid., 378.
[154] Another textual addition now offered an argument by design to explain the difficulties involved in navigating the Guinea Coast. 'If it be lawful to investigate the final Cause of such Obstacles as above to Navigation; one would think they had been set as a Guard to the Inability and Ignorance of the Natives, to protect them from the Cheat, Insult, and Slavery of Trading Nations'. Ibid., 351. The critique of slavery continued later: 'The Company mark [slaves] still *D. Y.* Duke of *York*, to perpetuate the Ignominy of his Headship to that Trade'. Ibid., 364.
[155] Ibid., 368. On seventeenth-century attempts to explain racial difference by pointing to differences in the soil of various locations, see Malcolmson, 58.

a different hue to Northern American natives, East Indians were different from each of these again, 'and all as distinct as black and white, which happens I imagine chiefly, on account of the Soil each is bred and nurtured in'. The soil changed the taste of plants when they were transplanted to different countries and 'Men by a like Analogy, change considerably by removing, even in their own Lives, and were they to marry and abide there'. Imagining earlier humans spreading across the globe, Atkins seemed to suggest that environs differing from that of their homelands could eventually turn even the whitest men as black as the African natives among whom they now found themselves and could make the English – a mixture of many peoples – into a single nation, physically distinguishable from its neighbours:

Particularly in those great Transmigrations of *Goths* and *Vandals*, quite to *Africa*, who are now without any Distinction from the ancienter Natives; so are the Moors in *Spain*. Ourselves are a Mixture of different Nations and *Complexions*, and 'tis the Soil has united them *English*, so as by that alone almost, to be distinguished from our nearest transmarine Neighbours.[156]

Having treated of plants and men, Atkins turned lastly to the animal kingdom, finding evidence there as well for the effects of transplantation. He had personally observed, he noted, that dogs, cocks, and sheep changed in both their 'Nature and Looks', and some animals simply could not be bred in regions of the earth far removed from their original.[157] Man was not so limited, but the price of his mobility was the alteration of his frame, not by the action of the sun in the heavens, but by the soil of the earth.

Atkins' case is a fascinating and revealing one, although it tends to trouble easy classification. For David Livingstone, Atkins' polygenetic utterances are evidence that '[p]lainly, the idea of multiple Adams was now receiving a more widespread airing'.[158] Yet Atkins published considerably earlier than all the other examples to whom Livingstone points and his 'airing' of co-Adamite ideas lasted only thirteen years before it was rejected in favour of a more orthodox environmentalism. If there was an opening for polygenetic views in the 1730s – Voltaire's comments suggest that this might have been so – it was narrow and, for Atkins at least, rapidly closed, opening again in the 1750s in the work of men such as the Reverend Hughes and David Hume. Perhaps the most interesting thing about Atkins' polygenism while it lasted, however, was its limitations. Co-Adamitism did virtually no *work* for Atkins. Unlike L. P., Voltaire or Hume, Atkins was seemingly uninterested in a critique of

---

[156] Atkins, *The Navy-Surgeon; or, Practical System of Surgery with a Dissertation on Cold and Hot Mineral Springs; and Physical Observations on the Coast of Guiney*, 368–9.
[157] Ibid., 369.
[158] Livingstone, *Adam's Ancestors: Race, Religion, and the Politics of Human Origins*, 61.

the Church or intellectual orthodoxies more generally. Polygenism was not part of a larger iconoclastic project. Nor, as we have seen, did Atkins' views on race inform his medical theories. If there is some little ambiguity about the connection between Atkins' posited aetiology for African sleepy distemper and his theories of originary physical differences, any supposed connection evaporates in later editions, which retain the former and abandon the latter.

Yet the conclusions that we may draw from a close reading of Atkins are not all negative. Indeed, the opposite is true, particularly when we compare his case to that of later polygenists (see Chapter 6). Virtually the sole target for ruminations about separate creations until the 1770s was the Church (Hume is an interesting exception). Apparently uninterested in an argument with clergy, Atkins' naturalistic heterodoxy went nowhere. In the latter part of the century, however, a second target emerged: the abolitionist movement. And one increasingly finds naturalistic arguments that apparently saw little value in a critique of literalist readings of biblical narratives turning their guns, instead, on a more secular vision of the brotherhood of Man and natural rights. Reading Atkins' earlier texts, then, helps us remember a time when medical environmentalism persisted, even while anti-climatic physical fixity was being posited, and when polygenism could, indeed, be only a 'little heterodox' (although even that little would prove too much), in the hands of a surgeon with seemingly no axe to grind against established theology.

6   Race, Slavery, and Polygenism: Edward Long and *The History of Jamaica*

Of all the Enlightenment figures to take up the question of race, there is perhaps none so infamous today as Edward Long, the Jamaican planter whose three-volume *History of Jamaica* appeared in 1774.[1] The notoriety is not undeserved. Long's racial calumnies stand out in a period where even those committed to monogenesis – the idea of the fundamental, original unity of humankind – stressed the bodily stench of 'Negroes' as an important, hereditary racial characteristic.[2] Hottentots, Long claimed, were 'a people certainly very stupid and brutal'.[3] So similar were they to orangutans that a Hottentot woman should regard it as no dishonour to be wedded to a simian husband. He suggested that the African slaves who worked sugar plantations in the West Indies were a different species from their white masters and denied that, in most cases, the offspring of white and black coupling could be fertile. Mulattoes were further analogised to mules.

Polygenism – the belief in separate creations for different human races – was, in the eighteenth century, a position both heterodox and unpopular.[4] Yet even among the radical racialist minority that adopted and promoted the position, Long's arguments were the most detailed and, frankly, the most odious. Hume's claim that nature had made an 'original distinction' between the various 'breeds of men', while oft quoted by pro-slavery advocates, was only to be found in a footnote to the second edition (1753) of his 1748 essay on 'National

---

[1] Edward Long, *The History of Jamaica, or, General Survey of the Antient and Modern State of the Island: With Reflections on Its Situation Settlements, Inhabitants, Climate, Products, Commerce, Laws, and Government: Illustrated with Copper Plates.*, 3 vols. (London: T. Lowndes, 1774).

[2] See, for example, Immanuel Kant, 'Von Den Verschiedenen Racen Der Menschen', in *Der Philosoph Für Die Welt*, ed. J. J. Engel (Liepzig: Dr Stintzings Bibl.,1777); Buffon.

[3] Long, *The History of Jamaica*, II, 364–5.

[4] That said, national distinctions mattered. Polygenism was more popular in France than Britain, where 'coy monogenism' dominated. Kidd refers to polygenism as a 'controversial fringe viewpoint in the British world'. Kidd, *The Forging of Races: Race and Scripture in the Protestant Atlantic World, 1600–2000*, 85. As Stepan has noted, polygenism 'remained a minority strand of British racial thought' into the 1860s. Stepan, 3.

Characters'.[5] Lord Kames, whose polygenist views appeared the same year as Long's, found himself unable to commit completely to contradicting Biblical testimony on the unity of man, even as he denied that any natural cause could produce current racial diversity from the supposition of a single creation.[6] Voltaire, of course, had no such qualms in refuting Biblical claims, yet his heresies seem rather tame compared to Long's vicious racialism. 'Few eighteenth-century writers', David Brion Davis noted in 1966, 'could equal Edward Long in gross racial prejudice'.[7]

Even Long's contemporaries found his racialist views reprehensible, or at least (when they felt some sympathy towards them) requiring public repudiation. The polygenist portions of his *History* were overwhelmingly more likely to be cited by abolitionists – who must have been delighted to find a straw man come to life – than by the pro-slavery advocates among whom Long numbered himself.[8] Among the reasons it proved easy to dismiss Long's arguments was the fact that they reeked of special pleading. As a Jamaican planter and owner of slaves, Long could not pretend to any objectivity on the questions of Negro inferiority or the permissibility of the slave trade. Presumably, this is why we possess no detailed account of Long's arguments across the three volumes of his *History of Jamaica*, nor even an answer to what would appear to be the most basic question: What is the relationship between Long's defence of slavery and his advocacy of polygenism?

We do not have such an answer, I would suggest, because we believe that we already know it. Yet if Long's motives appear transparent, his arguments are not.[9] One might, for example, imagine that, since Long advocated the idea of special creations, he was free to claim that Africans (and their descendants in

---

[5] David Hume, 'Of National Characters', in *Hume: Essays, Moral, Political, and Literary*, ed. E. F. Miller (Indianapolis: Online Library of Liberty, 1987), 197–215, on 8, discussion of variant readings on 629–30. On the relation of this footnote to the remainder of the essay, see Kidd, *The Forging of Races: Race and Scripture in the Protestant Atlantic World, 1600–2000*, 93–4.

[6] *The Forging of Races: Race and Scripture in the Protestant Atlantic World, 1600–2000*, 95–9.

[7] David Brion Davis, *The Problem of Slavery in Western Culture* (Ithaca: Cornell University Press, 1966), 459.

[8] Seymour Drescher, *The Mighty Experiment: Free Labor Versus Slavery in British Emancipation* (Oxford: Oxford University Press, 2002), 76–7. The situation may have been different in the United States. Curtin argues that 'Long's greatest importance was in giving an "empirical" and "scientific" base that would lead on to pseudo-scientific racism. The part of the *History of Jamaica* dealing with race was reprinted in America in the *Columbia Magazine* of 1788, where it became support for later American racism'. Curtin, *The Image of Africa: British Ideas and Action, 1780–1850*, 45.

[9] On this point, and on Long more generally, see Anthony J. Barker, *The African Link: British Attitudes to the Negro in the Era of the Atlantic Slave Trade, 1550–1807* (London: Frank Cass and Company, 1978). Barker notes: 'Long's ulterior motives seem obvious. And yet there is just enough about the man and his work to raise doubts as to whether his racism meant something more', 41–2. For an excellent and sophisticated take on Long, one that is also attuned to the complexities of his positioning, see Wheeler.

the West Indies) were subhuman: essentially a kind of animal. Since it was perfectly legal to own animals, human chattel slavery would be justified. Yet, this is precisely *not* what Long argued. Rather than reducing Negros to the level of beasts, Long raised the Orang-Outang to the level of men, offering a three-level ranking of human species within *genus Homo*. His claim naturalised Negro inferiority, of course, but it did not do so by literalising the claim that Negroes were beasts of burden.[10]

The aim of this chapter is both to explicate and situate Long's arguments, in order to answer the question posed above. Or, rather, to explain why Long himself never quite answered it. For there is no point in the more than 1500 pages of his *History* where Long explicitly invoked his racial theories to justify or excuse his anti-abolitionism. I am thus focused here on Long's understanding of racial anatomies, leaving, for the most part, his claims about racial pathologies for Chapter 7. Of the three axes on which Part III seeks to re-locate race, this chapter emphasises two: period and location. In terms of the former, it is useful to contrast Long's Enlightenment racialism with forms more familiar from the nineteenth century. Heterodox as he was, there were still limits to iconoclasm. Yet Long was idiosyncratic even compared to many of his contemporaries, for reasons related to his geographical position. As previously noted, many if not most intellectual histories of race have (for a variety of reasons) focused upon metropolitan figures.[11] By contrast, my own attention has largely been on men who lived or worked in locations far from Britain. Long was one such figure. By re-locating race discourse to the colonies, by situating Long in the context of West Indian debates over slavery and meanings of physical difference, and by contrasting his forms of racialism to ostensibly similar figures in Britain and Europe, this chapter aims to provide a nuanced account of the relationships between slavery, race, and place.

That such relationships must be understood as nuanced and complex should be stressed. I noted in Chapter 5 that there was no necessary connection between Atkins' polygenism and his understandings of diseases he deemed to be characteristic of Africans. A close study of Long's writings makes clear that we should be equally cognisant of the subtleties connecting race and slavery. The intellectual history of the former, of course, cannot be written independently

---

[10] *Contra* Barker, who has claimed that both Estwick and Long 'suddenly declared the Negro sub-human'. Barker, 58. The views described in this chapter are closer to the majority position. See Philip D. Curtin, *The Image of Africa; British Ideas and Action, 1780–1850* (Madison: University of Wisconsin Press, 1973), 44. Even earlier was Jordan, who notes: 'Long did *not* imply that the Negro was actually a beast … It is of the utmost significance that the most virulent traducers of the Negro were forced to wildly strenuous and preposterous attempts at proving that the orang-outang was nearly human'. Jordan, 493.

[11] An important exception is Delbourgo's study of the 'imperial creole', John Mitchell: Delbourgo, 'The Newtonian Slave Body: Racial Enlightenment in the Atlantic World'.

of the intellectual history of defences of the latter. Beliefs in racial fixity (and concomitant assertions of unchangeable racial inferiority) first became fully viable elements of public discourse in the 1760s and 1770s in response to strident criticisms of the slave system. Natural equality had been an easier position to hold when the slave system was largely unthreatened and anti-equality arguments followed quickly and reactively in the face of abolitionist critiques and – eventually – victories. Long's case provides a clear example of this reactive racialism, as he enunciated his positions, in 1772 and 1774, in direct response to a court ruling (the Somerset Case of 1772) which was read as negating the legitimacy of slavery on British soil. Yet Long's example also makes clear that the connection between defences of racial fixity and defences of slavery were not straightforward. Indeed, Long's arguments on these issues tended to point in opposite directions: legal arguments in defence of slavery posited a kind of equivalence between Africans and Britons; polygenism denied such equivalence outright. Forms of racialism and anti-abolitionism were related, then, but they were not necessarily connected in simplistic, instrumentalist ways.

The chapter is divided into four sections. The first two consider the justifications Long *did* offer for the necessity of the slave trade in the Americas. Almost all of these were presented in a legal register and need to be read as a response to the judgement delivered by Lord Mansfield in the Somerset case (1772), a decision that appeared to outlaw slavery on British soil. Section 6.1 discusses Long's criticisms of Mansfield's decision in 1772. The arguments in Long's *History* two years later must be read as a continuation, refinement, and elaboration of these criticisms. Many of these arguments, I show in Section 6.2, require the assumption not only of a bare humanity for Africans, but for the legitimacy of their legal systems, so that contracts entered into on African soil must be honoured.

Section 6.3 examines Long's articulation and defence of polygenism. Having done so, however, I point to the fundamental ambivalence of Long's position. It is an ambivalence that provides one of the major reasons – despite contemporary refutations – that we should pay attention to Long's claims. For Long was one of very few eighteenth-century writers on 'race science' with an extensive lived experience in and with political sympathies toward a part of the world that was both outside the bounds of the European metropole and which also contained a majority black population.[12] This ambivalence in Long's writings

---

[12] Long was born in England, but his family had strong connections to Jamaica. His great grandfather had served with Cromwell's army in 1655, his wife descended from an officer in the Penn and Venables expedition of the same year, and his family owned a large estate in Clarendon, Jamaica, known as Longville. It has been noted that the publication of his *History* 'marked the first occasion on which an extended historical narrative was undertaken by an author with a prolonged association with the island'. Howard Johnson, 'Introduction', in *The History of Jamaica* (Montreal: McGill-Queens University Press, 2002), 1. For other examples

on race, I show, stemmed directly from his desire to manage social relations and political systems in a slave society. Metropolitan figures who believed in the fixity of race (regardless of the question of origin) made a cornerstone of their position the essential identity of newly arrived African slaves and their descendants. If race were truly fixed, then the new environment of the New World could have little effect on the mental endowment, moral character, or physical features of the offspring of slaves born in Africa. For Long, however, the difference between 'salt-water' and 'creole' Negroes was to be the solution to the most pressing social problem of the sugar islands: slave insurrection. Where newly arrived slaves were believed to be the most likely protagonists in a future uprising, Long hoped that a selectively gentler slavery might win mulattoes and creoles to the side of plantation owners. This understanding of the (potential) political and social differences between generations of slaves, I argue, required a physical corollary: Long's polygenism presumed less fixity than the monogenism of a figure like Immanuel Kant.

If the realities of the Jamaican slave system provide one reason that Long's racialism is somewhat 'softer' than one might expect from a polygenist slave owner, Long's theology provides another. Long's, I argue in Section 6.4, was a physical rather than a mental racialism. Physical traits – skin colour foremost among them – were fixed; mental traits were far more subject to climatic and social influence. That this was a permissible distinction flowed from Long's dualism, for he refused to accept that the physical structures of the brain were responsible for human reason. Unlike Voltaire or Hume, then, Long was a polygenist who was not a materialist, willing to buck Biblical orthodoxy on one position while firmly rejecting heterodoxy on another.

In the conclusion, I reflect on two rather broader lessons to be drawn from Long's case. First, the need to pay more attention to the disjunction between the colonial practice of race science and its metropolitan theory; and second the need to distinguish, from Long's work onwards, between the registers in which proponents and opponents of polygenism spoke. Long's was the first major text, I would suggest, where polygenism was put forward, not as a minority position in theology, but rather as a minority position in natural history and physiology. It marks the point at which polygenism, and race theory more generally, became a claim about the racial present, rather than the biblical past.

---

of authors writing in a scientific register about race outside of Europe see, most famously, Thomas Jefferson, *Notes on the State of Virginia* (1781). See also Mitchell. On Mitchell, see Delbourgo, 'The Newtonian Slave Body: Racial Enlightenment in the Atlantic World'. Stepan's classic work is almost exclusively devoted to major metropolitan figures. This was, no doubt, part of a conscious choice to emphasise 'the main figures in science rather than the minor ones'. Stepan, xix.

6.1   Anti-Abolitionism and The Somerset Case

Candid Reflections

In March, 1749, James Somerset was purchased as a slave in Africa and transported to Virginia, where he was sold to Charles Steuart on 1 August. Twenty years later, in 1769, Steuart made a business trip to England and took Somerset with him, planning to stay for as long as necessary and then return to America. In 1771, Somerset fled Steuart's service, at which point Steuart tasked James Knowles, the Captain of a ship bound for Jamaica, to seize and imprison Somerset before taking him to the West Indies for sale. When news of Somerset's capture reached several prominent abolitionists, including the lawyer Granville Sharp, they brought a writ of *habeas corpus*, which Lord Mansfield, Chief Justice of the Court of King's Bench, granted. On 9 December, Knowles gave Somerset over to the custody of the court.[13] Mansfield delivered his judgement, in favour of Somerset, in June the next year

'Perhaps no 200 words', Dana Rabin has noted, 'have been subject to closer scrutiny'.[14] Mansfield's reported language left his ruling open to both narrow and expansive readings:

The state of slavery is of such a nature, that it is incapable of being now introduced by Courts of Justice upon mere reasoning, or inferences from any principles natural or political; it *must* take its rise from *positive* law; ... and in a case so odious as the condition of slaves must be taken strictly: the power claimed by this return was never in use here: no master ever was allowed here to take a slave by force to be sold abroad because he had deserted from his service, or for any other reason whatever.[15]

---

[13] This description of events derives from Captain John Knowles' testimony, quoted in Francis Hargrave, *An Argument in the Case of James Sommersett, a Negro, Lately Determined by the Court of King's Bench: Wherein It Is Attempted to Demonstrate the Present Unlawfulness of Domestic Slavery in England. To Which Is Prefixed a State of the Case* (London: W. Ostridge, 1772), 4–8. The classic discussions of the case are William M. Wiecek, 'Somerset: Lord Mansfield and the Legitimacy of Slavery in the Anglo-American World', *The University of Chicago Law Review* 42, no. 1 (1974); David Brion Davis, *The Problem of Slavery in the Age of Revolution, 1770–1823* (Ithaca: Cornell University Press, 1975), 469–522.

[14] Dana Rabin, ' "In a Country of Liberty?"': Slavery, Villeinage, and the Making of Whiteness in the Somerset Case (1772)', *History Workshop Journal* 72 (2011): 19. For an excellent discussion of the relationship between the Somerset case and that of Mary Hylas in Hylas v. Newton, see Katherine Paugh, 'The Curious Case of Mary Hylas: Wives, Slaves, and the Limits of British Abolitionism', *Slavery and Abolition* 35 (2014). *The Politics of Reproduction: Race, Medicine, and Fertility in the Age of Abolition* (Oxford: Oxford University Press, 2017).

[15] Taken from the report of the case given in *The Scots Magazine* 34 (1772): 297–9. There is considerable disagreement today over the precise wording of Mansfield's decision. The *Scots Magazine* version has been described as 'probably the most accurate account of the judgment' by George van Cleve, 'Somerset's Case Revisited: Somerset's Case and Its Antecedents in Imperial Perspective', *Law and History Review* 24, no. 3 (2006): 632. It is also the version reproduced by Samuel Estwick, although Estwick altered the punctuation in ways that slightly alter its meaning.

Today, most scholars tend to support the notion that Mansfield intended something quite narrow in his ruling. His decision did not outlaw slavery in England, although it did forbid the forced removal of slaves from England and granted that a writ of *habeas corpus* applied to such cases of removal. Yet, as Seymour Drescher has shown, many slaves and masters at the time read Somerset's case as the end of English slavery.[16] Certainly Long, claiming to speak for West Indian planters, read Mansfield's ruling broadly, as asserting 'That the laws of *Great Britain* do not authorize a master to reclaim his fugitive slave, confine, or transport him out of the kingdom. In other words; that a Negroe slave, coming from the colonies into *Great Britain*, becomes *ipso facto*, Free'. Lawyers, Long noted, had succeeded in 'washing the black-a-moor white'.[17]

If they were unhappy with Mansfield's decision, it was nonetheless clear that the specific ruling in Somerset would have little effect on the day to day life of West Indian planters. It would surely be no more than an inconvenience to be unaccompanied by a slave while spending time in England. Far more ominous for slave holders in the Americas were the implications of the ruling, for almost every colonial constitution included a clause that forbade local legislatures from enacting a law deemed 'repugnant' to the laws of England. If slavery was unlawful and even 'odious' in the mother country, what could its status be at the reaches of the Empire?[18] One can thus understand both why Long should think it worthwhile to publish a tract debating Mansfield's decision and also why his pamphlet on the 'Negroe cause' was structured as it was. Only the latter part of Long's text dealt with the perceived injustice and potential consequences of the Somerset ruling. The first half offered a more general legal defence of slavery within the British Empire. Long's arguments were threefold. First, there was nothing new about African slavery. In the language of Mansfield's decision, 'immemorial usage' condoned the practice, which Long likened to an earlier form of unfreedom: villeinage. Villeinage, Long acknowledged, no longer existed. Not because it had been abolished, but because it had grown into 'desuetude' on English soil. 'On the decline of

---

[16] Seymour Drescher, *Capitalism and Antislavery: British Mobilization in Comparative Perspective* (Oxford: Oxford University Press, 1987), 36ff.

[17] Edward Long, *Candid Reflections Upon the Judgement Lately Awarded by the Court of King's Bench in Westminster Hall, on What Is Commonly Called the Negroe-Cause, by a Planter* (London: T. Lowndes, 1772), 56, iii.

[18] As Long phrased it, the doctrine in Somerset's case 'maintains, that Negroe slave-holding is inconsistent with the laws of *England*; and if it be so, this plain conclusion follows, *viz.* that every colony law which has been enacted touching this supposed property, whether by securing it to the planter, by making it deviseable in last wills, inheritable by his heirs, liable as assets for payment of his debts, subject to mortgage or other grants and alienations, are entirely void and null in themselves, to every intent and purpose, *as being repugnant to the laws of England*'. Ibid., 58–9.

villeinage within the realm', however, 'a species of it sprang up in the remoter parts of the English dominion, the *American plantations*'. The vision of the torch of unfreedom being passed from metropole to periphery was powerful both in its general argument, which suggested a continuity of laws, and in its specifics. For an English villein, while enjoying the rights of a free man in relation to others, was essentially the property of his lord, who owned the rights to his labour and that of his posterity. Among the very few rights of the villein with respect to his master was that to *Habeas Corpus* – a right that protected against imprisonment without trial and hence unlawful incarceration. According to Long, however, villeinage laws deemed the mere refusal to serve one's master sufficient cause for imprisonment. By analogy, then, the only rights available to a Negroe slave were those available to 'a similar class of inhabitants', namely villeins. Hence 'a right to his *Habeas Corpus cum causa*, yet neither bailable nor deliverable, if the cause returned should be, *his refusal to serve his Planter-master*, in any lawful employment'.[19]

Long's second argument was perhaps less legal than it was political and economic. The West India colonies, he claimed, were simply not viable if they were not worked by those born in and inured to hot climates. The argument was not necessarily a racialist one, for Long acknowledged that white creoles made up a potential workforce. But, he claimed, few white workers would agree to take on the laborious tasks of clearing land and planting crops unless compelled to do so by indigence. Under such circumstances, slavery was a necessity.[20]

Long's third and perhaps most convincing argument charged the English state with hypocrisy for a ruling that outlawed slavery in England while passing legislation that regulated the slave trade in Africa so as to maximise English profits. Numerous statutes could be found that had decreed Negroes, in the colonies, to be a form of property, liable to be seized, for example, for the payment of debts. With some justice, Long pronounced it 'preposterous' that the same state that had passed laws declaring Negroes to be commodities could then say that 'Negroe slaves emigrating from our plantations into this kingdom are to be deemed *free subjects of the realm*'.[21]

To these three general defences of the legitimacy of West Indian slavery, Long next appended two arguments that ostensibly treated the Somerset case alone. One of these amounted to little more than racialist scare-mongering, raising the prospect that the promise of emancipation would bring thousands of former slaves to British shores. The ruling, he asserted, was 'a direct invitation

---

[19] Ibid., 13.
[20] Ibid., 21.
[21] Ibid., 29, 33.

to *three hundred thousand blacks*' who could only make worse the dreadful situation in which 'the nation already begins to be embronzed with the African tint'. Sounding somewhat hysterical, he alluded to the possibilities of miscegenation, made possible by the fact that 'The lower class of women in *England* are remarkably fond of the blacks, for reasons too brutal to mention; they would connect themselves with horses and asses, if the laws permitted them'. Negroes, Long suggested darkly, might even be able to exploit a system of rotten boroughs and buy their way into a parliamentary seat.[22]

Rather more intellectually serious were Long's arguments about the question of compensation for the loss of property represented by slaves emancipated by English courts. The imperial state had allowed a situation where its laws were 'inconsistent with itself; there appears a direct collision between one part and another'. The planter who legally purchased a slave as a form of property in the colonies could then be deprived of that property in England. The responsibility for ameliorating this seemingly obvious injustice, Long argued, lay firmly at the feet of the English state, who 'should make him some requital, and by a fair purchase ... redeem his Negroe from bondage'.[23] An apparently reasonable response to the specificities of the Somerset case, this argument must surely also have functioned as a shot across the bow for those who might hope, post-Somerset, to convince the English state to suddenly outlaw slavery in its colonies. Were slavery indeed to be deemed 'repugnant' to English law, the English state would be responsible, Long implied, for the losses experienced by colonial planters. Abolition was unlikely to harm planters alone.

Race Theory and Slavery: Samuel Estwick and Considerations on the Negroe Cause

I have spent some time in elaborating Long's multiple arguments against Mansfield's ruling and the possibility of abolition for three reasons. First, as we shall see, because we find in them the germs of several of the claims made in *The History of Jamaica* two years later. Second, because the differences between the arguments made in the *Candid Reflections* and the *History* are then revelatory of the specific effects of Long's responses to reading other tracts dealing with the Somerset case. We can assume, for example, that by 1774 Long had read Francis Hargrave's *An Argument in the Case of James Sommersett* (1772).[24] Hargrave had delivered what were among the most convincing arguments in favour of Somerset during the trial, and published a

---

[22] Ibid., 59, 54–5.
[23] Ibid., 44.
[24] Hargrave.

version of those arguments soon afterward. Chief among them was his rejection of the analogy between villeinage and slavery with which Long had opened his *Candid Reflections*.[25] Whether Long accepted Hargrave's arguments or not, his own claims concerning the analogy between slavery and villeinage – although they did not disappear – nonetheless declined in importance in his *History*.

The third reason for paying close attention to the arguments in Long's *Candid Reflections* is the most important for this chapter. In spite of the clear bigotry on display in the tract from 1772, Long made no use there of theories of polygenism or even racial fixity. Indeed, the opposite was true. Although 'unseasoned' whites were incapable of labouring in Jamaica's climate, the same was not true of white creoles. The most important issue with regard to the question of whether an individual could withstand the rigours of plantation labour was not race but nativity. White or black, the only way to withstand the West Indian climate was to be born in it, or one very like it.

The source for many of Long's initial ideas on polygenesis appears to have been another pamphlet written in opposition to Mansfield's judgement, penned by the assistant colonial agent for Barbados, Samuel Estwick. Long read Estwick's text while his own was in proofs.[26] Long claimed to identify a number of similarities between the two documents, but the central arguments were, in fact, strikingly different. Estwick began by agreeing with Somerset's allies that African slavery bore little connection to villeinage.[27] In Estwick's view, however, slavery – novel or not – was not the point. For Negroes, according to English law, were not slaves: they were property. The argument was counter-intuitive, but in a sense it needed to be. Like Long, Estwick emphasised the apparent contradiction in English laws that regulated slavery in Africa and the colonies while declaring it illegal on English soil. Like Long, too, he noted that no law could be allowed in the colonies that contradicted fundamental tenets of the legal system of the mother country. Unlike Long, however, he did not conclude that the contradiction in metropolitan and peripheral laws was simply a matter of hypocrisy. Instead, he sought to resolve the contradiction by arguing

---

[25] Cf. Granville Sharp, *A Representation of the Injustice and Dangerous Tendency of Tolerating Slavery; or of Admitting the Least Claim of Private Property in the Persons of Men, in England* (London: Printed for Benjamin White, (no. 63) in Fleet-Street, and Robert Horsfield, (no. 22) in Ludgate Street, 1769). To my mind, Davis overemphasises the intrinsic implausibility – in the 1770s – of the analogy between villeinage and slavery. See Davis, *The Problem of Slavery in Western Culture*, 483.

[26] Long, *Candid Reflections Upon the Judgement Lately Awarded by the Court of King's Bench in Westminster Hall, on What Is Commonly Called the Negroe-Cause, by a Planter*, 75–6. Estwick had intended to submit his remarks to Mansfield prior to the decision, but the text had been held up, and was published a month after the ruling. Samuel Estwick, *Considerations on the Negroe Cause, Commonly So Called, Addressed to the Right Honourable Lord Mansfield, Lord Chief Justice of King's Bench, &C. By a West Indian* (London: J. Dodsley, 1772), 45–6.

[27] Estwick, *Considerations on the Negroe Cause, Commonly So Called, Addressed to the Right Honourable Lord Mansfield, Lord Chief Justice of King's Bench, &C. By a West Indian*, 5.

that the objects of legislation in each place were different. In regulating the sale of Negroes, Estwick argued, Parliament had declared them non-human property, like any other goods. If they were not human under the law, they could not be slaves.

The case is this, my Lord: seeing that Negroes are human creatures, it would follow that they should be allowed the privileges of their nature; which, in this country particularly, are in part the enjoyment of person and property. Now, my Lord, from hence a relation is inferred, that has not the least colour of existence in law. A Negroe is looked upon to be the servant of his master; but by what authority is the relation of *servant* and *master* created? Not by the authority of law, however it may be by the evidence of reason. By the law, the relation is, as *Negroe* and *Owner*: he is made matter of trade; he is said to be property; he is goods, chattel, and effects, vestable and vested in his owner.[28]

If Somerset was property, Estwick concluded, then the writ of *Habeas Corpus* could not apply, and Steuart should have his property returned to him.

Estwick's argument thus turned on the non-humanity of Negroes under English law. The second edition of his text – much extended and offered at a price sixpence higher than the first – elaborated on this claim. What was largely implicit in the first edition now became explicit, as in the following definition of slavery:

Slavery, my Lord, is that state of subjection, which mankind, by force or otherwise, acquire *the one over the other*. In every society therefore where this state of subjection prevails, the object and subject of those laws necessary for the regulation thereof are, what? *Human nature itself*. Let it be considered then whether *human nature* is either the object or subject of the laws of England, respecting the state and condition of Negroes.[29]

Answering his own question, Estwick claimed that it was both the will and the effect of 'the wisdom of parliament, that Negroes under the law should not be considered as human beings'. Rhetorically distancing himself from such an odious supposition, he then set himself the task of ascertaining why Parliament should have believed such a thing, dividing the putative arguments into two types: physical and political. 'Now the physical motive supposes a difference of species among men, and an inferiority of that species in Negroes: whereas the political consideration, on the other hand, infers a universal sameness in human nature; that is to say, in fact, that Englishmen are Negroes, and Negroes are Englishmen, to all *natural* intents and purposes'. Such a division, it will be noted, renders the political argument purely cynical, since it amounts to the following question: Given that Parliament believed that Negroes were fellow

---

[28] Ibid., 34–5.
[29] Samuel Estwick, *Considerations on the Negroe Cause, Commonly So Called, Addressed to the Right Honourable Lord Mansfield, Lord Chief Justice of the Court of King's Bench, &C.*, 2nd ed. (London: J. Dodsley, 1773), 69–70.

human beings, why did it pass legislation that declared them not to be so? Estwick's answer charged the Government with explicit duplicity. Wishing to legislate to its own advantage, but fearing a public backlash to the legalisation of slavery, the state masked its real designs. 'Instead then of that Demon Slavery being called in to preside over Negroes, Trade, the guardian angel of England, was made the ruler of them'.[30]

Since the political argument accused the English state of intentionally misleading the public, Estwick's physical argument seems more palatable. This is no mean feat, given it was while explicating the latter that he came to posit polygenism. The differences between whites and Negroes, he claimed, were both corporeal and intellectual. Of the corporeal, he cited complexion and 'the wooly covering of their heads so similar to the fleece of sheep'. Of intellectual differences, Estwick pointed to what he described as savage forms of justice and other customs, and a 'barbarity' in their treatment of children which 'debases their nature even below that of beasts'.[31] The gulf between Africans and other humans, he suggested, was too large to be one merely of degree. Within the human *genus* one found not merely different races, but different species.

Like Long, who would follow him in this argument, Estwick made no explicit mention of the religious heterodoxy of his position. He made no reference to the Biblical passages usually cited by monogenists and their opponents: neither Adam nor Noah entered the discussion. Instead, he proffered a different kind of theological explanation, eschewing Biblical literalism in favour of an invocation of God's design in nature. In the vegetable and mineral kingdoms, as well as the animal kingdom excluding Man, one found 'these grand divisions of nature arranged in classes, orders, kinds, and sorts: we shall contemplate systems morally perfect'. Humanity – composed, it had been assumed, of a single, unified kind – stood alone in disrupting this ordered perfection. The assumption that Mankind was composed of multiple species, Estwick suggested, was one that exchanged the unity of a human brotherhood for a unity in God's design.[32]

Invoking the idea of a 'great chain of Heaven, which in due gradation joins and unites the whole with its parts', Estwick could then transform an originary difference into a natural inferiority.[33] Negroes were lower on the chain than

---

[30] Ibid., 88.
[31] Ibid., 80.
[32] Ibid., 72–3, 74.
[33] Estwick, *Considerations on the Negroe Cause, Commonly So Called, Addressed to the Right Honourable Lord Mansfield, Lord Chief Justice of King's Bench, &C. By a West Indian*, 74. The classic work on the chain is Arthur O. Lovejoy, *The Great Chain of Being: A Study of the History of an Idea* (Cambridge, MA: Harvard University Press, 1936). On its use in race-theory, see Stepan, 1–19.

whites, even if each could be considered 'wisely fitted' to its station.[34] And they would stay that way, for the boundary between species was fixed. From his own conclusions he inferred the logic of English lawmakers:

From this then, my Lord, I infer, that the measure of these beings may be as compleat, as that of any other race or mortals; filling up that space in life beyond the bounds of which they are not capable of passing; differing from other men, not in *kind*, but in *species*; and verifying that unerring truth of Mr. Pope, that
Order is Heaven's first law; and this confest,
Some are, and must be, greater than the rest:
The application of what has been said, is, that the Legislature, perceiving the *corporeal* as well as *intellectual* differences of Negroes from other people, knowing the irreclaimable savageness of their manners, and of course supposing that they were an inferior race of people, the conclusion was, to follow the commercial genius of this country, in enacting that they should be considered and distinguished (as they are) as articles of its trade and commerce only.[35]

Long's arguments on race in his *History* would borrow heavily – to the point of plagiarism – from Estwick's. But, as we will see below, his arguments concerning the legitimacy of West Indian slavery did not. The point is a crucial one. Estwick's polygenism and his defence of slavery were intimately and logically connected. The legal justification for slavery was that Negroes were non-human property. His polygenist arguments from natural history then buttressed that argument. Long, however, largely based his defence of slavery on notions of contract theory, which pre-supposed that both sides of the contract were human actors, even if one was inferior to the other. Taking part of Estwick's argument, but not its entirety, Long was left with contradictions that his own text was never quite able to resolve.

6.2   Slavery and *The History of Jamaica*

The History of Jamaica is a frustrating work. Lengthy, detailed, and – as Long himself admitted – digressive, it can read more like a series of discrete arguments than a coherent, single book. Long was magpie-like in his reading and would often crib and copy pages at a time from other texts, sometimes without fully digesting the arguments of his sources. This could lead to seemingly obvious contradictions, even within the same general set of claims. In a section of Volume II devoted to a description of the African slave trade, for example, the reader is told both that 'the slaves of a family are considered no mean part of it … The owners are full as careful of bringing them up

---

[34] Estwick, *Considerations on the Negroe Cause, Commonly So Called, Addressed to the Right Honourable Lord Mansfield, Lord Chief Justice of the Court of King's Bench, &C.*, 74, 76.
[35] Ibid., 81–2.

as their own children' and also that Africans 'consider their slaves merely as their necessary beasts'.[36] More common, however, were contradictions between distinct sections, since Long clearly had different axes to grind in each. Discussing the culture of 'Guiney Negroes', Long was scathing about their legal systems. Their laws were 'irrational and ridiculous'.[37] On the other hand, part of Long's defence of slavery required him to argue that Europeans should respect the right of African states to endorse and encourage slavery, framing that right not with ridicule, but in impressive eighteenth-century legalese: 'Africans having the right power of dispensing life or death; they are likewise empowered to regulate the conditions upon which life is granted, where it has been adjudged by their forms of proceeding to be forfeited to their laws, or customary usages'.[38]

It would be wrong, however, to dismiss the *History* entirely as a collection of incoherent, *ad hoc* arguments devoted to Long's particular interests. In most cases it is better, I would argue, to read the text as being in an almost inevitable tension with itself, brought about by Long's situatedness in several different contexts. One can see this by comparing arguments made in his *Candid Reflections* – addressed primarily to an English metropolitan audience – and those in the *History*, which was intended both to 'obviate slanders' from 'enemies of the West India Islands' and itself to criticise elements of Jamaican culture.[39] The argument Long made in 1772 for the necessity of slavery for the survival and economic prosperity of the sugar islands was straightforward: the climate was deadly for unseasoned whites. In his later and larger text, however, Long had much less interest in encouraging the vision of the West Indies as a death trap for new settlers. Both works cited James Lind's to buttress an argument for the necessity of using Negroes for the laborious and dangerous tasks of felling trees and clearing land. The *History* also cited Lind, however, for his claim that the West Indies was not the graveyard that many thought it was: 'The truth is, as Dr Lind has well observed, that every island in the West Indies, and other parts of the world, has its healthy and unhealthy spots'.[40]

The effort to de-emphasise the perils of the West Indian climate played into one of the *History's* largest themes: the stress on greater colonial self-sufficiency. Jamaican planter society was characterised by absenteeism. One-third of Jamaican planters were absentees in 1740; two-thirds in 1800.[41] Deeply critical of those who saw themselves as sojourners rather than settlers, Long

---

[36] Long, *The History of Jamaica*, II, 384, 89.
[37] Ibid., 378.
[38] Ibid., 391.
[39] Ibid., I: 6.
[40] This point would be oft-repeated. See, e.g. ibid., II: 506, 508.
[41] Andrew Jackson O'Shaugnessy, *An Empire Divided: The American Revolution and the British Caribbean* (Philadelphia: University of Pennsylvania Press, 2000), 4, 5.

wanted to encourage the establishment of local institutions – schools, medical colleges, local militia – and to promote white immigration. Obviously, claims that suggested that Jamaica's climate was deadly to whites were anathema to such aims and to efforts to keep British subjects in the West Indies for generations. At the same time, Long suggested that English illnesses in the colony were due, not to the climate itself (which was perfectly salubrious), but to the fact that settlers refused to adjust to their new living conditions. As a social practice, sojourning could lead to sickness. Englishmen sweltered in the hot tropical sun, dressed in tightly fitting coats and waistcoats, when they would be better off adjusting to the fashions of the East, and donning a 'Chinese Banyan'.[42] Most Europeans refused to adjust their diet, indulging in 'vast quantities of animal food' when a diet more appropriate to the climate would combine meat and vegetables, even 'inclining to the vegetable'.[43]

For much of the *History*, then, behaviour and custom trumped race or climate as an explanation for the health and well-being of the West Indian population. And even when there appeared to be racial differences in susceptibility to disease, Long was far more willing to incorporate social and cultural reasoning into the naturalistic explanations that had characterised his *Candid Reflections*. Making reference to the practices of slavery, for example, Long drew on the writings of the Revered Hughes, who had recommended that newly imported slaves be given only the 'gentlest' work during the first few years of their labour in the West Indies. They did not, that is, arrive 'seasoned' by virtue of their birth in the tropics. Like whites, they too required a period of adjustment.[44] And it was possible that race made no difference at all:

Their bodies and constitutions seem peculiarly adapted to a hot climate; yet, perhaps, they owe their health not more to this adaptation, than to their mode of living: since it is certain that the native Whites on this island, I mean such of them as are not addicted to drunkenness, nor have any hereditary distemper, are equally healthy and long-lived.[45]

Understanding Long's arguments, then, requires the realisation that there were often (at least) two distinct audiences for a given discussion: one in England, the other in the West Indies. This is certainly the case for Long's

---

[42] Long's discussion of the appropriateness of 'Eastern' dress was drawn from Hillary, *Observations on the Changes of the Air and the Concomitant Epidemical Diseases, in the Island of Barbados. To Which Is Added a Treatise on the Putrid Bilious Fever, Commonly Called the Yellow Fever; and Such Other Diseases as Are Indigenous or Endemial, in the West India Islands, or in the Torrid Zone*.

[43] Long, *The History of Jamaica*, II, 526.

[44] Ibid., 433, 28.Cf. Griffith Hughes, 'The Natural History of the Island of Barbados, Book II (1750)', in *On the Treatment and Management of the More Common West-India Diseases (1750–1802)*, ed. J. Edward Hutson (Kingston, Jamaica: University of the West Indies Press, 2005).

[45] Long, *The History of Jamaica*, II, 29.

defence of slavery, which is effectively divided into two parts. One deals with the trade in slaves in Africa, the other with the treatment and management of slaves in the West Indies. The former is legalistic and uncompromising – clearly written in opposition to abolitionists – the latter contains anti-abolitionist elements (refuting claims about the ill-treatment of slaves, for example), but is also, as we shall see, rather nuanced, offering prescriptions to ameliorate the practice of slavery on the island. In the end, *The History of Jamaica* would staunchly defend the legitimacy of the slave trade on legal grounds while criticising Parliamentary laws governing the trade on grounds that were at once moral and locally particular.

Long's opening salvo in defence of African slavery took on the question of its antiquity. Writing against prominent abolitionists like the 'Father of Atlantic Abolitionism', Anthony Benezet, Long asserted that a trade in slaves had been carried on by Africans for 'some thousand years'.[46] Although Europeans obviously profited by a trade in slaves, they could hardly be held responsible for creating the trade in the first place. Moreover, Long argued, European participation, far from ruining African lives, had improved them. Portuguese slavers, he suggested (while relying on the most critical accounts of African societies), may have thought it a 'meritorious act' to send slaves to work in their mines, thus saving them from the death, torture, cannibalism, and human sacrifice that characterised day to day life on the Guiney coast, 'thus mak[ing] their private gain compatible with the suggestions of humanity or religion'.[47] Regardless of motive, however, economics alone had lessened the savagery of African customs. Criminals and those captured in war were now worth far more alive than dead. It was those who sought to abolish the trade, Long argued with cynical cunning, who were without sufficient humanity, for to do so 'is therefore no other than to resign them up to those diabolical butcheries, cruelty, and carnage, which ravaged their provinces before the European commerce with them began'.[48]

Long's humanitarian defence of slavery stemmed from more than the desire not to immediately cede the moral register to his opponents. His moralising also drew the reader's attention to a more significant part of his argument: the character of those sold as slaves and, more particularly, the idea of slavery as punishment for legal infraction. Long suggested that those slaves sold to Europeans came from four distinct groups: war-captives; those sold 'by brutal parents, or husbands'; native slaves sold for some crime; and the free born, punished with slavery for a particularly egregious offence.[49] Ignoring the second category

---

[46] Ibid., 386; Maurice Jackson, *Let This Voice Be Heard: Anthony Benezet, Father of Atlantic Abolitionism* (Philadelphia: University of Pennsylvania Press, 2009).
[47] Long, *The History of Jamaica*, II, 387.
[48] Ibid., 391–2.
[49] Ibid., 388.

and minimising the impact of the first, he concentrated his attention on the two kinds of criminals. Citing a figure he had only recently read, Long claimed that it was 'well-known' that 99 per cent of slaves shipped from Africa were felons, their sentences commuted from death to exile and servitude.[50] Accepting this fact as true licensed a comparison both easy and powerful, for the British state had few qualms about the use of transportation as a punishment for criminals; fewer still about using such criminals as an indentured work force. Long had only to forget that he had recently condemned African laws as 'ridiculous' and to argue instead for an equivalence between the rights of African and European states to dispose of their unwanted as they saw fit.

It may be said of our English transported felons, as of the Negroe criminals, that neither of them go into a voluntary banishment; but it must be allowed, that the Africans may with equal justice sell their convicts, as the English sell theirs; and equally well vest a legal right to their service in the purchasers.[51]

Of course, Long was well aware of the limits of his analogy. African states may well have had the right to sell both criminals and their labour to Europeans in Africa. But by what right could one keep an individual convicted of no crime by British law in servitude in Britain or its colonies? The right, Long answered, of an implicit contract. Those captured in war, he argued, submitted voluntarily to slavery, for they had known the consequences of their actions in going to war, and had sought to reduce their opponent to the same state. Other slaves accepted the right of their owner to sell them 'as part of the law or usage of his society' and that right, Long asserted, was transferred across the seas. 'Surely a voyage from Afric to any other country, where this claim of property is continued, cannot dissolve the bargain'.[52]

Long's 'surely' in the sentence above was disingenuous. Abolitionists argued precisely that the claim of property over another human being – whatever its presumed legality in other nations – was anathema in Britain. Here Long must have felt the force of the Somerset ruling keenly. If a claim over property could dissolve in moving from Britain's periphery to its centre, how could one argue that contracts had to be maintained in moving between nations? But Long thought Mansfield had made a poor ruling, and he believed more generally that abolitionists overstated what was often portrayed as an innate English opposition to any loss of liberty. The fact of the matter was that unfreedom was a basic part of social life. It was hardly restricted to Africans

---

[50] Ibid., 391. The figure is given in An African Merchant, *A Treatise Upon the Trade from Great-Britain to Africa. Humbly Recommended to the Attention of Government* (London: R. Baldwin, 1772), 12.

[51] Long, *The History of Jamaica*, II, 390.

[52] Ibid., 394.

and their progeny and could only be defended by the exertion of force. It was force alone that kept the convict transported to America from evading his sentence, the inhabitants of debtor's prisons in confinement, the sailor and soldier in service, and the labourer in his place.

A labourer in England never consented to the laws which impose restrictions upon him; but there is in every government a certain supreme controuling power, included in the social compact, having the energy of law, or published and declared as the law of the land; by which every member of the community, high and low, rich and poor, is respectively bound: it is in truth an association of the opulent and the good, for better preserving their acquisitions, against the poor and the wicked. For want, complicated with misery and vice, generally seeks relief by plundering from those who are better provided. An African is as much bound by this supreme power, as the English labourer.[53]

In Jamaica and the other West Indian colonies, this broad social compact was supplemented by a set of formal laws that constrained the liberty of slaves in particular ways. In turning to an examination of such laws, Long also turned away from a discussion of the African slave trade and toward the management of slaves on British colonial soil. In general, his arguments now took a particularist turn. No longer concerned with the general right of another nation to make its own laws, or the transfer of property rights between nations, Long focused instead on the specific legal framework for enslavement on the sugar islands.

The Jamaica *Code Noir*, Long claimed, had been based on the model used in Barbados, itself drawn from English villeinage laws. As he had in his *Candid Reflections*, Long sought to establish a temporal and legal continuity between metropolitan and colonial forms of unfreedom. 'At the time we first entered on the settlement of Barbadoes', he noted, 'the idea of slavery could hardly be extinguished in England'. However, villeinage also had another role to play in the argument of the *History*. Here it was a potent symbol of the savagery of English laws, compared to the leniency of West Indian practice. Villeinage laws were characterised by 'severity', which was the source for the inclemency of the original laws governing slaves in the West Indies. Nor was legislative barbarity limited to those formally denoted as slaves. Long had compared Africans to English labourers on the grounds of their shared subordination to a 'social compact'. Now he did so on the basis of the punishments incurred for infractions. 'The penal laws in England', he wrote, 'were always sanguinary, and still retain this savage complexion'.[54]

If English laws thus provided clear models for harsh treatment, the characters of African slaves, claimed Long, appeared to require it. '[W]ild and savage to

---

[53] Ibid., 392–3.
[54] Ibid., 495, 96.

an extreme: their intractable and ferocious tempers naturally provoked their masters to rule them with a rod of iron; and the earliest laws enacted to affect them are therefore rigid and inclement, even to a degree of inhumanity'. Long equivocated over whether the cause for African depravity was due to nature or custom. Whatever its cause, however, it resulted in the treatment of slaves as 'brute beasts' rather than men. Now taking up Estwick's major theme, Long suggested that this attitude on the part of the early settlers in the West Indies – the attitude of a harder and less enlightened age – had been shared by Parliament, who 'fell in with the general idea and considered Negroes, purchased from that continent, as a lawful commercial property'.[55]

At this point in his argument, Long sprang a trap, one that had been some time in the making, and which deflected one of the most stinging criticisms of planters and slave owners back onto the law makers of the mother country. Long had spent some time, in a discussion of the character of white creoles, defending them from the charge that they sorely mistreated their slaves. Citing Granville Sharp by name, Long noted that abolitionists had compared the overworking of slaves to the 'merciless usage practiced in England over post-horses, sand-asses, &c'.[56] Long's response was both to deny the veracity of such a charge and to indulge in his now familiar ploy of invoking the treatment of British labourers and prisoners.[57] The careful reader of the entire text, however, could note that Long did not deny that some people *did* treat African slaves as mere beasts. Their fellow Africans did so, which was why transportation to the West Indies was, by comparison, 'perfect freedom'.[58] The original white settlers had also done so, a century earlier. This placed the English parliament, which had legislated to create an equivalency between Negroes and other property, in unpleasant company. And where neither Africans nor long-dead settlers could have any effect on the contemporary practices of slavery in Jamaica, Parliament's decisions, Long claimed, made it legally impossible for planters to do as they wished and to improve the lot of many of their slaves. '[T]he greatest oppression, under which our Negroes in the islands at present labour, arises materially from that statute, which declares them as houses, lands, hereditaments, assets, and personal estate, transferrable, and amenable to payment of debts due to the king and his subjects'.[59]

The problem, as Long saw it, was that Parliamentary statutes made no distinction between Creole slaves and those who had arrived directly from Africa.

[55] Ibid., 497.
[56] Ibid., 268.
[57] Ibid., 269–70, 400.
[58] Ibid., 399.
[59] Ibid., 497.

New slaves probably still required the draconian laws on the books. But Long asserted that the majority of Negroes, particularly on the older islands, were now Creoles and bore a more 'humanized' aspect than their ancestors. As a result, in practice at least, laws now wore a 'milder aspect'. Long suggested that this distinction between kinds of slaves be formalised in law, to make the servitude of Creoles 'approach near to a well-regulated liberty' and to 'make them forget the very idea of slavery'.[60]

Some *medium*, it is said, might be struck, between liberty, and that absolute slavery which now prevails; in this *medium* might be placed *all Mulattos*, after a certain temporary servitude to their owner; and such *native Blacks*, as their owners, for their faithful services, should think proper to enfranchise.[61]

For Long, the only barrier in the way of striking this medium between liberty and slavery was Parliamentary law. It was Parliament that treated Negroes as chattel and Parliament that must newly model its laws to raise the status of black Creoles 'some degrees above sheep and oxen'.[62]

In spite of their shared condemnation of Parliament, Long and Estwick's arguments on legal questions were significantly different. Estwick had set himself the task of explaining and justifying what he represented as the logic behind the English State's legislation; Long found himself deeply critical of that logic. Estwick's defence of slavery relied on the presumed inhumanity of slaves; Long's – with its emphasis on contract law and his constant comparisons between Negro slaves and members of the English lower classes – presumed that Africans (however 'depraved' their customs) were men. The differences between the two strident critics of Lord Mansfield's Somerset decision are perhaps nowhere clearer than in their treatment of the fixity of race. Long suggested that the savage manners of newly arrived African slaves may have led early settlers and then Parliament to see them as subhuman. Unlike Estwick, however, Long met every such suggestion with equivocation. Above all, whatever customs were carried from Africa, these were not racial traits. Estwick made no distinction between African and native slaves. For Long, it was of the essence and important enough to require a modification of the Negro Code to reflect it. African 'savagery' was a product of Africa and was not transmitted to African progeny born and raised in the West Indies. Racial fixity, put simply, was not part of Long's defence of slavery. What role(s), then, did it play in the *History of Jamaica*?

[60] Ibid., 498–502.
[61] Ibid., 503.
[62] Ibid., 500.

6.3   Special Creation and the Problem of Race

Fixity

The central issue in Long's discussion of race – as for those of his contemporaries interested in the question – was the relative effect of climate and innate, heritable racial characteristics. Which aspects of physique and behaviour were malleable under different skies (given enough time), and which were not to be changed? For most monogenists – Kant was a rare but important exception – climate (understood broadly) explained everything. At some point in the past, humanity had looked similar. If Biblical narratives were taken literally, the resemblance was a familial one. Human groups spread from a common centre through different climatic zones until their physical and intellectual features displayed the myriad diversity of the human species today.

As we saw in the last chapter, Buffon had enriched this rather simplistic explanation by expanding upon the ways in which climate could affect the body. Kant's theory of the origins of human racial difference was a response to another criticism of what we might call naïve monogenism. By the late 1700s both the slave trade and settler colonialism had encouraged the conviction that skin colour and other features did not change nearly as quickly as had once been imagined. Neither black slaves in the Americas, nor white settlers in the tropics had altered their skin tone perceptibly over the course of several generations. Kant sought to reconcile the contradiction between monogenism and this apparent racial fixity in a manner directly opposed to Buffon's and played down the possible effects of climate, direct or otherwise. Human races, he claimed, did indeed share a common origin and Mankind had spread to the various regions of the earth, changing by small amounts in direct response to their new environments. Members of that original common race, however, carried with them seeds of change.[63] In the right climate, those seeds had come to fruition and the four major races were born. Further dramatic change was now no longer possible. New races could only be born from the original stock and that was now largely extinct. Kant thus replaced a mechanical explanation with a teleological principle, while at the same time defending monogenism from one of its most pertinent critiques.

No polygenist, of course, denied the effect of climate (most, in fact, granted it more agency than did Kant). They argued merely for its limits. Thus, Long

---

[63] 'Human beings', he argued, 'were created in such a way that they might live in every climate and endure each and every condition of the land. Consequently, numerous seeds and natural predispositions must lie ready in human beings either to be developed or held back in such a way that we might become fitted to a particular place in the world'. Immanuel Kant, 'Of the Different Human Races', in *The Idea of Race*, eds. Robert Bernasconi and Tommy L. Lott (Indianapolis: Hackett, 2000), 8–22, 14.

noted of white Jamaican Creoles that the shape of their eye sockets had changed to protect them in the strong sunlight of the West Indies. 'Although descended from British ancestors, they are stamped with these characteristic deviations'.[64] Invoking a common trope, Long suggested that native women, like tropical plants and animals, 'attain earlier to maturity' in the West Indies. They married young, and bore children at age twelve. Like hothouse flowers, they also faded fast, but 'console[d] themselves, however, that they can enjoy more of real existence here in one hour than the fair inhabitants of the frozen, foggy regions do in two'.[65] Climate had its effects on behaviour and intellect, too. The warm weather 'rouzed the passions', so that chastity was to be all the more admired. And nativity could even trump race. Creole blacks and whites, Long noted, shared a common fondness for music and an 'exceedingly correct' ear for melody.[66]

If climate could change much, however, it could not change all. Those in England who believed that birth in Jamaica had turned the children of English parents tawny-skinned had been deceived. Encountering planters' children in the most expensive public schools of the mother country, they had assumed that the progeny were legitimate. Instead, Long asserted, the swarthy West Indian offspring were, in fact, the product of English men indulging in 'goatish embraces' with black women.[67] Generalising from his Jamaican experiences to the broadest question of human malleability, Long denied that any external effects could explain the most pertinent differences between black and whites.

Climate, perhaps, has had some share in producing the variety of feature which we behold among the different societies of mankind, scattered over the globe: so that, were an Englishman and woman to remove to China, and there abide, it may be questioned, whether their descendants, in the course of a few generations, constantly residing there, would not acquire somewhat of the Chinese cast of countenance and person? I do not indeed suppose, that, by living in Guiney, they would exchange hair for wool, or a white cuticle for a black: change of complexion must be referred to some other cause.[68]

To skin colour and hair, Long proceeded to add a raft of physical and intellectual differences that characterised blacks: the shapes of the features of their face; the colour of the lice on their bodies; their 'bestial or fetid smell'; the failure of Africans to make 'any progress in civility or science'; and the miserable state of their houses and roads. They were, as a people, 'brutish, ignorant, idle, crafty, treacherous, bloody, thievish, mistrustful and superstitious': characteristics

---

[64] Long, *The History of Jamaica*, II, 262.
[65] Ibid., 285.
[66] Ibid., 283, 63.
[67] Ibid., 328. Trevor Burnard, ' "Rioting in Goatish Embraces": Marriage and Improvement in Early British Jamaica', *The History of the Family* 11 (2006).
[68] Long, *The History of Jamaica*, II, 262.

that were not the effect of climate.[69] Common climates, then, failed to eradicate essential differences between whites and blacks. And diverse climates, such as those found across Africa or the Americas, failed to produce racial diversity. America, for example, lay between 65 degrees North of the equator and 55 degrees South, with climates that encompassed those of all the known continents. Yet the complexion of its inhabitants was everywhere the same, 'only with more or less of a metalline luster'.[70] Distinctions between Whites and Negroes would appear, then, to be innate and permanent. To these anti-climatological arguments, which spoke to *racial* difference, Long then added one from his observations – such as they were – of interracial coupling, which suggested that the difference was even more profound. Mulattoes, he argued, were infertile with each other, but not necessarily with individuals from the races of their parents.[71] 'The subject', Long concluded, 'is really curious, and deserves a further and very attentive enquiry'.

[I]t tends, among other evidences, to establish an opinion, which several have entertained, that the White and the Negroe had not one common origin ... For my own part, I think there are extremely potent reasons for believing, that the White and the Negroe are two distinct species.[72]

Marshalling a great deal more evidence – however questionable it may have been – Long had arrived at a position much like Estwick's. And, like Estwick, Long next proceeded from a natural historical to a natural theological defence of polygenesis. Diversity within *genus Homo* would bring Man within the compass of the great system God had produced, which divided and subdivided every other class of animal. Long's invocation of the racialised chain of being amounted to rank plagiarism of Estwick's language.[73] Yet, differences existed between Long and Estwick, and important ones at that. Long's chain included Mulattoes, placed between Whites and Blacks. More significantly, Long's argument was ultimately more consistent. Both men had argued that Mankind needed to be divided into a number of distinct species. Neither argued that whites were the only humans. Both established a system where Africans were lesser men, but men nonetheless. Estwick, however, ostensibly speaking for

---

[69] Ibid., 352–3, 54.

[70] Ibid., 375.

[71] Even by Long's standards, this was a weak claim. He claimed not to know of any counter-examples to his claims about Mulatto sterility, but quickly sought to deflect any produced by others by suggesting that any such were, in fact, likely the secret product of 'intrigue' with one of the parent races. Even more problematic for his case was his acceptance that, in some cases, Mulatto men and women did produce offspring. In such situations, he asserted, their young did not survive to maturity. This was not a case discussed by Buffon or other naturalists and would seem to significantly detract from the argument regarding distinct specieshood.

[72] Long, *The History of Jamaica*, II, 336.

[73] Ibid., 375.

Parliament in its defence of slavery, had argued that Negroes – being less than Whites – were therefore beasts, and hence property. Long's defence of slavery, on the other hand, required the assumption that Africans were capable of making and assenting to contracts and were hence men. And in Long's taxonomy, Negroes were indeed men, as were Whites, Mulattoes, and – most peculiarly – Orangutans.

The amount of space devoted to demonstrating the humanity of Orangutans in the *History* is at first baffling. One is tempted to read it as little more than a shallow attempt to be scandalous, and to allow Long to titillate and appal his readers with his obsessively repeated stories of 'amorous intercourse' between the male animal and Negroe women.[74] Closer attention to the text does not rid one of this impression entirely, but it becomes clear that the dozen pages Long dedicated to the topic are not without significance as part of his overall argument. His central aims in discussing the tripartite division of humankind were, first, to establish a ranking and, second, to insist that essential differences existed without physical causes. That is, the physical differences between Orangutans and 'other' men were minor; intellectual differences were merely of degree; and these intellectual differences could not be explained by differences in the structure of the body. Orangutans, wrote Long, 'have some trivial resemblance to the ape-kind, but the strongest similitude to mankind, in countenance, figure, stature, organs, erect posture, actions or movements, food, temper, and manner of living'.[75]

If Polygenism was a heterodox position, arguing that Orangutans were men might be called ultra-heterodox. Long had drawn the idea from James Burnet, Lord Monboddo, who had offered reams of evidence suggesting that certain apes were humans in a primitive state of development. Rousseau had also flirted with the notion.[76] Many naturalists, of course, had noted striking similarities between the physical structure of apes and men. Buffon and Long both cited Edward's Tyson's careful dissection of an Orangutan in 1699. Tyson had marvelled at the familiarity of the ape's anatomy, but refused utterly (as did Buffon later) to see this as evidence for the creature's humanity. 'Physical similarities', he wrote, 'merely emphasized the intellectual and spiritual gulf between man and chimpanzee'.[77]

For Long, on the other hand, the 'gulf' was not as wide as naturalists had imagined. Gathering as many travellers' accounts as possible, he provided

---

[74] Ibid., 370.
[75] Ibid., 358.
[76] Barker, 54. On Monboddo, see Alan J. Barnard, '*Orang Outang* and the Definition of *Man*: The Legacy of Lord Monboddo', in *Fieldwork and Footnotes: Studies in the History of European Anthropology*, ed. Han F. Vermeulen and Arturo Alvarez Roldán (London: Routledge, 1995).
[77] Quoted in Barker, 49.

a wealth of examples of Orangutans wearing clothes, building huts, making noises like children, being taught to drink wine, handling cutlery at the dining table, and understanding enough of the medical treatment given one during an illness to request the same again. Like Monboddo, Long compared Orangutans to children, and suggested that the only true test of the creature's natural inferiority (including the capacity for speech) would be to educate a specimen as a man, through school and university, up to the age of 20 or 25.[78] The example might seem farcical, yet it possessed rhetorical power. Few would imagine that such an education would produce a thinking, speaking man – white or black. Orangutans, most would be happy to conclude, were naturally inferior. But what, then, was the *cause* of such inferiority if the animal was, with regard to its physical structure and organisation, largely identical to the other species within *genus Homo*? It could only be an originary difference in mental faculties, created by the Deity:

[I]f we admit with Mr. Buffon, that with all this analogy of organization, the oranoutang's brain is a senseless *icon* of the human; that it is meer matter, unanimated with a thinking principle, in any, or at least in a very minute and imperfect degree, we must then infer the strongest conclusion to establish our belief of a natural diversity of the human intellect, in general, *ab origine* ... the supposition, then, is well-founded, that the brain, and intellectual organs, so far as they are dependent upon meer matter, though similar in texture and modification to those of other men, may in some of the Negroe race be so constituted, as *not to result to the same effects*; for we cannot but allow, that the Deity might, if it was his pleasure, diversify his works in this manner, and either withhold the *superior principle* entirely, or in part only, or infuse it into the different classes and races of human creatures in such portions, as to form the same gradual climax towards perfection in this human system, which is so evidently designed in every other.[79]

What Buffon regarded as a gulf, in other words, Long portrayed as a graduated progression.

To this point in his argument, Long had attempted to demonstrate that enough differences existed to declare blacks and whites different species, while enough similarities existed to insist upon them being common members of the same genus. He had also, with his argument involving Orangutans, sought to make plausible the case that profound mental distinctions between the species might exist, even if their physical structure was essentially similar. To prove that point, however – and to establish the intellectual inferiority of Negroes *ab origine* – Long had also to show that a change in external circumstances could not efface the apparent mental failings of the darker races. This, after all,

[78] Long, *The History of Jamaica*, II, 359–61, 70.
[79] Ibid., 371.

was the claim of many abolitionists. Long had to envision an experiment for a Negroe that had a form like that earlier proposed for the Orangutan.

Long believed that such an experiment had already been tried. It was surely what he'd had in mind (and intended to mock) when he conjured for his readers the image of an ape at university. In the late eighteenth century, a story commonly told concerned Francis Williams, born in Jamaica the son of two freed slaves.[80] The Duke of Montagu, so the tale went (Long reproduced it) had sought to test the proposition that climate and external circumstances were vastly more important than any innate racial capacity, and had sent the young man to university in England. He returned to the West Indies and opened a school where he taught reading, writing, Latin, and mathematics. Williams' case would seem, on its face, to refute the claim that the difference in intellectual capacity between whites and blacks was due to race, rather than upbringing. As a result, those committed to the reality and permanency of race tended to try to dismiss the force of his example. Hume, for one, had mocked him in his infamous footnote. 'In Jamaica indeed', the Scottish philosopher had written, 'they talk of one Negroe as a man of parts and learning, but 'tis likely he is admired for very slender accomplishments, like a parrot, who speaks but a few words plainly'.[81] Long reproduced, translated, and annotated one of Williams' Latin poems in the *History*, so that his readers might judge its merits. He insisted, however, that appropriate criteria be used for that judgement. Critics were not to be impressed merely by the fact that a black man had produced a Latin poem at all. Instead, Long maintained, one had to determine the quality of the poem, given that Williams had the advantage of 'an academic education, under every advantage that able preceptors, and munificent patrons, could furnish'. In Long's judgement, the poem was 'a piece highly laboured; designed modeled and perfected, to the utmost stretch of his invention, imagination, and skill'. It was the kind of production one might expect from any 'middling scholar' who had attended one of England's elite institutions.[82] The implication, then, was that the best a Negroe could produce was equal only to (elite) white mediocrity. Long's conclusion, cribbed from Estwick and jumbling together two couplets from Pope, affirmed the humanity of all races – *contra* Estwick – while insisting upon rankings in the quality of men.

The Spaniards have a proverbial saying, '*Aunque Négros somos génte*' 'though we are Blacks, we are men'. The truth of which no one will dispute; but if we allow the system

---

[80] On Williams, see Vincent Carretta, 'Who Was Francis Williams?', *Early American Literature* 38 (2003).

[81] Hume, 'Of National Characters', 208, 629–30.

[82] Long, *The History of Jamaica*, II, 484.

of created beings to be perfect and consistent, and that this perfection arises from an exact scale of gradation, from the lowest to the highest, combining and connecting every part into a regular and beautiful harmony, reasoning them from the visible plan and operation of infinite wisdom in respect to the human race, as well as every other series in the scale, we must, I think, conclude, that,

'The general *order*, since the whole began,
Is kept in *nature*, and is kept in *man*.
Order is heaven's first law; and, this confest,
Some are, and *must be, greater* than the rest.[83]

Malleability

One might think that this was rather weak tea for a man who had been adamant about the radical inferiority of another race. Where Estwick had made Negroes beasts, Long was ultimately reduced, by Williams' example, to the anaemic insistence that the bounds of the race limited them to rising no higher than the average level of the best educated sons of England's elites. Long, however, had already called attention to what he portrayed as the deficiencies of the Duke of Montagu's experiment.

Considering the difference which climate may occasion, and which Montesquieu has learnedly examined, the noble duke would have made the experiment more fairly on a native African; perhaps, too, the Northern air imparted a tone and vigour to his organs, of which they never could have been susceptible in a hot climate.[84]

The objection seems peculiar: the point of the (thought) experiment had been to determine how much of the difference between whites and blacks was permanent and how much due to climate, education, and other factors. If Long and Estwick were right, and the Deity had imposed natural limits on the intelligence of Negroes, then no change in external circumstance could raise them beyond their pre-determined bounds. As Long noted, in his own version of Hume's remarks, changes in climate and training might produce the semblance of true intelligence, but not the reality.[85] In his contestation of the significance of Montagu's results, however, Long would seem to be admitting a far more important role for climate – and hence malleability, as opposed to racial fixity – in determining the intelligence and mental capacities of non-white

---

[83] Ibid., 484–5.
[84] Ibid., 476–7.
[85] 'The examples which have been given of Negroes born and trained up in other climates, detract not from the general idea of a narrow, humble intellect, which we affix to the inhabitants of Guiney. We have seen *learned horses, learned* even *talking dogs*, in England; who by dint of much pains and tuition, were brought to exhibit the signs of a capacity far exceeding what is ordinarily allowed to be possessed by those animals'. Ibid., 375.

races. As he noted explicitly, 'The climate of Jamaica is temperate, and even cool, compared to many parts of Guiney; and the Creole Blacks have undeniably more acuteness and better understandings than the natives of Guiney'.[86]

In his objection to Montagu's results, Long revealed not only the fundamental ambivalence of his arguments about racial fixity, but also the source of this ambivalence: the necessary difference between Creole and African Blacks. We have noted the stress placed on this difference earlier, when discussing Long's plans to produce distinct legal codes for Mulattoes and Creoles on the one hand, and newly arrived African slaves on the other. It is worth dwelling on this contradiction for a moment. Remember that within a framework that insisted upon the fixity of race, a key point of evidence (perhaps *the* key point) was that races did not change in significant ways as they moved from one climate to another. A great deal of Long's description of the native black inhabitants of Jamaica, however, concerns their radical differences from their African brethren. In terms of behaviour, where Africans were dirty, violent, and inclined to cruelty, even to their own children, Creoles were fastidious; could, with Christian instruction, 'be kept in good order without the whip'; and were good, if somewhat stern parents. Physically, Long noted that Black Creole women had more trouble during childbirth than those in Africa. Most generally, 'the Creole Blacks differ much from the Africans, not only in manners, but in beauty of shape, feature, and complexion'.[87] The last point is well worth emphasising, since it will be remembered that Long had been adamant that complexion could *not* change in different climates. Why, then, when the best argument in favour of racial fixity and separate creations was the essential sameness of Blacks born in Africa and Jamaica, did Long keep asserting the importance of their differences?

The simplest answer is fear. Long was quite explicit about his anxieties. The decade before the publication of the *History* had seen a large number of slave insurrections on Jamaica and other West Indian Islands. Barbara Bush puts the average at one significant revolt every two years between 1731 and 1823.[88] Vincent Brown estimates that rebellions and conspiracies occurred on average once a decade on Jamaica alone in the century after 1740.[89] A description of the most significant of these took up a sizeable number of pages in Long's *History*. What became known as Tacky's Revolt began on 7 April 1760, when

---

[86] Long, *The History of Jamaica*, II, 476–7.
[87] Ibid., 411, 10.
[88] Bush, 68.
[89] Brown, 3. 'Slave conspiracies and revolts were especially frequent during the "most troubled decade in Jamaica's long history as a slave society" – the 1760s'. O'Shaugnessy, 38.

ninety slaves (led by two Coromantees named Tacky and Jamaica) killed several whites and burned and looted a number of plantations.[90] By the time the Rebellion was quelled – in a particularly brutal fashion – an estimated 400 slaves, sixty whites, and sixty free blacks had been killed or committed suicide. One hundred slaves were executed and a further five hundred were exiled.[91] As savage as the response by white authorities was, rebellions by Coromantees and their allies occurred again in 1765, 1766, and 1767.[92]

As with so many of the problems of the slave system, Long laid part of the blame at the feet of absent landlords.[93] Solving the problem of sojourning planters might help reduce the risk of rebellions, but Long also had another solution: winning part of the slave population to the side of white residents. In his mind, the population was already divided, although those who lived outside of the colonies could not see it and insisted (as a true racialist might) that there was little difference between groups of slaves. 'The vulgar opinion in England', wrote Long dismissively, 'confounds all the Blacks in one class, and supposes them equally prompt for rebellion; an opinion that is grossly erroneous'.[94] It was 'imported Africans', he insisted, 'who are the most to be feared'.[95]

Long's suggestion that two legal codes be adopted instead of a single, draconian *Code Noir* was thus part of an overall argument that sought, for political and social reasons, to divide into disparate groups what a dedicated polygenist should have seen as an essentially indiscriminate whole. Long was utterly blunt in his logic: Whites could not withstand a fully coordinated rebellion from a population seasoned to its environs and outnumbering them ten to one. 'We are obliged to it, both from reason and self-interest; bodily strength and their adaptation to the climate, would enable them to pass from the lowest to the highest stations, and give the law to their masters, if they were willing unanimously to accept it'. Creoles and Mulattoes needed to be made use of as 'instruments … to restrain one another within the bounds of their allotted condition'.[96] Complete consistency on the question of racial fixity, Long might have argued, was a luxury that West Indian planters could not afford. Whatever the arguments might be in favour of the identity of native-born and imported Negroes, social and political exigencies required that they be treated very differently. Facts and fears on colonial soil tended to trouble the simpler boundary-making of the metropole.

---

[90] Burnard and Garrigus, 125–6.
[91] Ibid., 122–3.
[92] Brown, 149.
[93] Long, *The History of Jamaica*, I, 389.
[94] Ibid., II: 444.
[95] Ibid., 309–10.
[96] Ibid., 503–4.

6.4   Polygenism, Theology, Materialism

Among the many striking aspects of Long's heterodoxy in espousing polygenism was his refusal to acknowledge it as such. The pages of the *History of
Jamaica* are more likely to vaunt Long's radicalism in Natural Philosophy –
comparing his racial theories, for example, with Copernican astronomy – than
in theology.[97] References to Genesis, or other relevant biblical passages are, at
best, oblique. One should probably read the following as a swipe at the story
given in Genesis, but it is to be noted that neither the book, nor the name of
God's first human creation is given.

Without puzzling our wits, to discover the occult causes of this diversity of colour
among mankind, let us be content with acknowledging that it was just as easy for
Omnipotence to create black-skinned, as white-skinned men; or to create five millions
of human beings, as to create one such being.[98]

Long's text does not mention the Fall, although that may well be what he
had in mind when he noted that childbirth was easy in Africa. If Negroes were
part of a separate creation, then it would follow that African women were not
punished for the sin of eating of the Tree of Knowledge. On the other hand,
Long noted that slaves in Jamaica had a harder time with delivery, implying
that climate, not divine justice, was the cause of labour pains.[99]

The few explicit Biblical references in the *History* show that Long had little
sympathy for literal readings of the Holy book, particularly when literalists
used their readings as a basis for contemporary policy. In general, the theological arguments of the *History* were based far more on the book of nature than
the book of God. The design involved in the Great Chain of Being was only
one instance of Long's natural theological leanings. Providence, he suggested,
had designed the vegetable products of the West Indian Islands to counteract
the potential ill effects of heat, humidity, and a poorly adapted diet. The local
succession of morning and evening breezes appeared, to Long as 'gracious
dispensations of the Ruler of the universe' and a prime reason that the plague
had never been known on the island.[100] Even seemingly negative aspects of
nature in the tropics, like hurricanes and earthquakes, were 'doubtless ...
destined to answer some wise and perhaps salutary purpose in the oeconomy of
nature'.[101] What may have happened in the Garden of Eden seemed to pale in
comparison to the evidence for God's beneficent plan through time and across
the globe.

---

[97] Ibid., 337.
[98] Ibid., 352.
[99] See Chapter 7.
[100] Long, *The History of Jamaica*, I, 372.
[101] Ibid., III: 619.

Keeping this in mind suggests that Long's seemingly radical polygenist heterodoxy may have flowed from (or at least been supported by) a rather more commonly unorthodox anti-literalism, one shared with many Enlightenment figures. It seems necessary to downplay Long's religious iconoclasm somewhat, since on other theological issues he was far from espousing any form of heresy. Compared to Voltaire, for example, who Long cited as a supporter of polygenism, Long was decidedly conservative, most clearly so in his rejection of even the hint of materialism. The brains, physical structure, and organisation of the three species in the human *genus*, Long had argued, were essentially identical. Not even the most skilful dissector could locate the source of the intellectual differences between orangutans and men in their material make-up. 'The sole distinction between [an orangutan] and man, must consist in the measure of intellectual faculties; those faculties which the most skilful anatomist is incapable of tracing the source of, and which exist *independent of the structure of the brain*'.[102] The difference was a spiritual one: the graded amounts of the 'superior principle' that God had allowed each species.

Long did not make the point himself, but it is worth noting that decoupling the connection between intellect and the physical body provides a way of reconciling his insistence on the reality and fixity of race with his equally adamant arguments concerning the important differences between Negroes born in Africa and Jamaica. One need only assume that he was willing to grant that the range of intellectual capabilities susceptible to climatic change (and other changes in external circumstances) was larger than the concomitant range for physical characteristics. Williams' case would seem to make this point immediately. Long knew of no black man who had – over any period of time, let alone a single generation – come to physically resemble the members of the British elite attending Westminster or Eton. Complexion, facial features, and the texture of hair appeared fixed enough for Long to think of them as largely incapable of variation, and hence evidence for separate creations in and of themselves. Training and a new environment, however, could change the behaviour, morals, and even intellectual level of slaves brought to Jamaica, and in that possibility for change stood also the hope that Whites could build alliances with their non-brothers to defend their mastery in the West Indies.

Conclusion

Long was willing to offer indirect criticisms of narratives given in Genesis. Materialism, however, was a bridge too far. His espousal of polygenesis was

---

[102] Ibid., II: 368–9.

heterodoxy, but Long was an orthodox enlightened Christian.[103] The best way to resolve this apparent contradiction, I would suggest, is by seeing the radicalism of Long's support of the notion of special creations as lying within the domain of politics or social theory, rather than theology. Such a claim requires us to read Long's polygenesis as written in a somewhat different register to that of Lord Kames, who published in the same year and fretted much more openly about the conflict between his position and that given in the Bible. It requires us to realise that all of those who argued against that brotherhood of man – whether they did so in a religious vein or not – risked social opprobrium. This was particularly true, of course, when their position appeared self-serving, as in Long's case. But even Georg Forster, who put forward the notion of special creations in the course of a debate with Kant in the late 1780s, acknowledged that opponents of his position had accused him of removing one of the few barriers still holding Europeans back from perpetrating horrors against Africans. (With some justice, Forster retorted that a belief in monogenesis had hardly stayed the whip in a slave owner's hand thus far.)[104] In the age of empire and slavery, polygenesis was no longer (if it had ever been) a purely theological heresy. It was, as Long's text showed, a question of profound scientific and political significance.

That said, nineteenth-century British polygenists and racial theorists found Long a problematic source. I have noted already that those who cited his work on race tended to be abolitionists, who mined the *History* for its viler comments, as evidence of the moral failings of their opponents. Those wishing to make serious scientific points on the nature of humanity probably shied away from an author who spoke credulously of Orangutans as part of the human species, capable of dressing and dining like Men, and indulging in illicit sexual relations with human women. Even beyond this, one suspects that Long would have seemed old-fashioned, with his refusal to accept that differences in the organisation and make-up of the brain caused differences in intellect. This supposition, drawn from phrenological research, formed the bedrock of nineteenth-century race science. Long's refusal to see significant differences in the brain structures of the races placed his ideas outside the realm of normal race science.

I began this chapter by asking about the connection between Long's polygenism and his defence of slavery. We can now see that the answer is that there wasn't really one, but that this absence was no mere oversight. Where Estwick was content to see Negroes as beasts and hence property, Long refused

---

[103] On enlightened Christianity in this context, see Kidd, *The Forging of Races: Race and Scripture in the Protestant Atlantic World, 1600–2000*, 79–120.

[104] Georg Forster, 'Noch etwas über die Menschenraßen. An Herrn Dr. Biester', *Teutsche Merkur* October and November (1786).

to deny slaves humanity, even as he maintained their natural inferiority. The assumption of humanity was central to a legal argument based on contract law, but it was also essential for a socio-political argument that saw a certain part of the slave population as potential allies against the insurrectionary remainder.

For the intellectual historian of race, it is the polygenist planter's insistence on these differences between Creole and newly arrived slaves that remains one of the most striking aspects of the *History of Jamaica*. In part, this surely flows from the logical oddity of the position. Yet is also derives from the fact that Long was one of the few racial theorists writing with a deep experience in a plantation colony. I am certainly not the first person to point to the ways that the colonial context shifted the terms of seemingly familiar debates about the nature of race. In a study of the medical construction of 'whiteness' in nineteenth-century Australia, Warwick Anderson noted that the very categories of race science seemed irrelevant to the concerns of most of his actors. Terms like monogenesis, polygenism and social Darwinism, he suggested 'may be malapropisms that distract us from working out how racial theory ... was produced and transacted among colonial scientists and ordinary doctors. In my experience, terms of this sort are at best blunt tools that tend to mutilate the racial thought of out-of-the-way intellectuals'.[105]

I have tried to show here, at least for the eighteenth-century Jamaican case, that terms like poly- and monogenesis *do* make sense, whether they were actors' categories or not. But we must also note – in agreement with Anderson's larger point – that the fact that race relations were lived on a daily basis, that race was more than mere theory for Long, that the survival of whites in close propinquity to an enslaved, majority black population appeared to require making alliances and accommodations, made his polygenesis seem convoluted, even contradictory. Ultimately, if we still regard Long's polygenism as the product of a rather transparent self-interest, we must nonetheless understand that the interests of those in the colonies were not always those of the metropole. Seemingly familiar structures of racial difference were made differently in the centre and periphery.

---

[105] Anderson, *The Cultivation of Whiteness: Science, Health and Racial Destiny in Australia*, 3.

7 Pathologies of Blackness: Race-Medicine, Slavery, and Abolitionism

In 1773, when he penned a brief and anonymous pamphlet entitled *An Address to the Inhabitants in America upon Slave-Keeping*, Benjamin Rush was twenty-seven years old and three years away from adding his name to the Declaration of Independence.[1] He had completed his MD in Edinburgh under William Cullen in 1768 and had returned to Philadelphia the following year to begin his own practice, soon thereafter taking up the professorship for chemistry at the University of Pennsylvania. A figure of no mean importance, then, in spite of his relative youth, it seems no surprise that Rush should have been approached, according to his own account, to write something in support of a petition to the Pennsylvania Assembly arguing for a higher duty to be imposed on the importation of slaves, and thus providing an economic impetus for the eventual eradication of what abolitionists called the 'man-trade'.

Less than thirty pages long, Rush's *Address* offered a crisp and scathing summary of the arguments put forward to defend slavery, rejecting each as only so much self-serving or simply wicked rhetoric. Proponents of slavery had declared Negroes to be the natural inferiors of Europeans in intelligence or morality: Rush denied it outright. Were slaves idle, treacherous, or inclined to thievery then this was a result of their enslaved condition and would end when they were free. 'The vulgar notion' that the colour of their skin was a mark of the curse on Cain, their forefather, Rush rejected as 'too absurd to need refutation'.[2] Indeed, black skin was no curse, but rather a blessing, for it 'qualifies them for that part of the Globe in which Providence has placed them. The ravages of heat, diseases, and time, appear less in their faces than in a white

---

[1] Benjamin Rush, *An Address to the Inhabitants of the British Settlements in America Upon Slave-Keeping (the Second Edition). To Which Are Added, Observations on a Pamphlet, Entitled, 'Slavery Not Forbidden by Scripture; or, a Defence of the West-India Planters'. By a Pennsylvanian* (Philadelphia: John Dunlap, 1773). On the local context for the debate that ensued, see W. Caleb McDaniel, 'Philadelphia Abolitionists and Antislavery Cosmopolitanism', in *Antislavery and Abolition in Philadelphia: Emancipation and the Long Struggle for Racial Justice in the City of Brotherly Love*, ed. Richard Newman and James Mueller (Baton Rouge: Louisiana State University Press, 2011).

[2] Rush, 3.

one'.[3] To the common economic defence of the trade – that one could not produce sugar, indigo, or rice without slave labour – Rush offered three retorts. First, were the claim true, economic necessity could hardly justify the violation of 'the Laws of justice or humanity'.[4] Second, the economic premise of the claim was, in fact, false: free labour in Cochin China produced sugar at prices lower than those gained from the use of slaves in the West Indies.[5] Third, and perhaps most interesting, there was something wrong with the assumption that only those born in climates like those of the West Indies could labour there.

I know it has been said by some, that none but the natives of warm climates could undergo the excessive heat and labour of the West-India islands. But this argument is founded upon an error; for the reverse of this is true. I have been informed by good authority, that one European who escapes the first or second year, will do twice the work, and live twice the number of years that an ordinary Negro man will do.[6]

Rush's argument was unusual, for he was suggesting that those born in Africa, where the soil supplied all that the human frame required with minimal effort, were not used to hard labour, however accustomed they might be to warm environs. A European, by contrast, could become seasoned to the climate in a year or so, and could then use their native capacity for labour to their advantage under a different sky.

More familiar were Rush's rejections of moralist and religious pro-slavery arguments. Claiming that the trade in men served a moral purpose by introducing pagan Africans to Christianity, for example, was 'like justifying highway robbery because part of the money acquired in this manner was appropriated to some religious use'.[7] Rush had no more time for positions holding that slavery had saved Africans from death (their lives forfeit as captives of war) or who found support for slavery in the Old Testament. There was nothing decent about slavery and much that was degrading and terrible. Taking a page from the book of his fellow Philadelphian, Anthony Benezet, Rush detailed the horrors of the torture inflicted upon slaves by brutish masters: 'Behold one covered with stripes, into which melted wax is poured – another tied down to a block or a stake – a third suspended in the air by his thumbs – a fourth – I cannot relate it'.[8] Magistrates and legislators, 'men of sense and virtue' and – above

---

[3] Ibid., 3–4.
[4] Ibid., 4.
[5] On the debate over the economic value of free v. enslaved labour, see Drescher, *The Mighty Experiment: Free Labor Versus Slavery in British Emancipation*. On the question of how 'free' some free labour was, see Andrea Major, *Slavery, Abolitionism, and Empire in India, 1772–1843* (Liverpool: Liverpool University Press, 2012).
[6] Rush, 8.
[7] Ibid., 14–15.
[8] Ibid., 23.

all – ministers all had to speak out to end a trade that violated every sense of justice, economic logic, and Christian benevolence.

The rejoinder from the pro-slavery camp was rapid.[9] Writing as 'A West-Indian', Richard Nesbit sought in *his Defence of the West-India Planters* to cast stories of horrific brutality as either outright falsifications – 'I never knew a single instance of such shocking barbarities' – or else the actions not of all planters, but of exceptional villains within their number.[10] Nisbet followed what would become the general trend of pro-slavery tracts in many of his other attacks and defences. He invoked 'self-interest' as a reason to deny that slave owners regularly damaged or destroyed their valuable human property. He cited the existence of slavery in the Old Testament to defend the practice today, suggesting also that one could not – as Rush had – use either the absence of such approval in the Gospels or Christ's 'general maxims of charity and benevolence' to condemn the trade.[11] And Nisbet pointed to the plight of others, closer to home, whom abolitionists should seek to protect before they pled the cause of Negroes in other lands. If the exigencies and necessities of states required a kind of slavery for soldiers and sailors, why could the same arguments not be made for labourers in sugar fields? Were Britain to give up on the sugar trade, the kingdom would soon be beggared and left defenceless, easy prey for the French or other powerful adversaries.[12]

As in Rush's case, however, the most unusual of Nisbet's arguments turned on the question of African physiology. Rush had attempted to turn two pro-slavery arguments against themselves, arguing that black skin was no curse, but rather an advantage in the warm climates of Africa, and also that African slaves were not the best labourers in the similarly warm climate of the West Indies. Nisbet was having none of it. 'The writer confesses, that hard labour within the tropics shortens human life, and that the colour of the negroes qualifies them for hot countries, yet he is desirous, that our white fellow subjects should toil in these sultry climates, that the Africans might indulge their natural laziness in their own country. The former are, no doubt, much obliged to him for his kind intentions'.[13] And Nisbet rejected completely Rush's claims for

---

[9] Rush's pamphlet in fact inspired three different rejoinders, which Tise has characterised as 'constitute[ing] the most acute formulations of traditional proslavery thought prior to the nineteenth century'. Larry E. Tise, *Proslavery: A History of the Defense of Slavery in America, 1701–1840* (Athens and London: University of Georgia Press, 1987), 28.

[10] Richard Nisbet, *Slavery Not Forbidden by Scripture. Or a Defence of the West-India Planters* (Philadelphia: 1773), 15.

[11] 'If the custom had been held in abhorrence by Christ and his disciples, they would, no doubt, have preached against it in direct terms'. Ibid., 8.

[12] By freeing Africans, Nisbet intoned, 'Britons, themselves, must become abject slaves to despotick power'. Ibid., 13–14.

[13] Ibid., 10.

African equality. Although he acknowledged that it was 'impossible to determine, with accuracy' whether European or African intellects were superior, since Africans 'have not the same opportunities of improving as we have', Nisbet determined the matter in favour of Europeans in any case. With a reference to Hume's infamous footnote as support, Nisbet declared that 'it seems probable, that they are a much inferior race of men to the whites, in every respect'.[14] Importing slaves to the New World appeared to improve both their work ethic and intellect, but Nisbet was wary of geographic explanations for what he suggested was African inferiority to all other peoples, both past and present. 'The stupidity of the native cannot be attributed to *climate*', he opined, for the nearby Moors and Egyptians were not so inferior.[15] Without advocating for polygenism explicitly, Nisbet opened the door to the position and similarly left it as merely implied that natural inferiority should serve as justification for African enslavement.

Rush would have the last word. To the planters' invocation of self-interest as a reason to doubt stories of brutality, he replied by questioning the applicability of such economic rationalities: 'It is to no purpose to urge here that Self Interest leads the Planters to treat their Slaves well. There are many things which appear true in Speculation, which are false in Practice. The Head is apt to mistake its real Interest as the Heart its real Happiness'.[16] He gave ground on the question of African inferiority even as he suggested that physical causes (i.e. climate) could explain the discrepancy. Yet, he questioned the import of this argument in the current debate. Let it be allowed, he suggested, that his opponent had made his case: 'Would it avail a man to plead in a Court of Justice that he defrauded his neighbor, because he was inferior to him in Genius or Knowledge?'.[17] Rush listed his extant allies ('Montesquieu, Franklin, Wallis, Hutchinson, Sharp, Hargrave, Warburton, and Forster') and sought to win more, by analogising the fight for African freedom to the fight against British tyranny in America.[18] 'Where is the difference', Rush asked, 'between the British Senator who attempts to enslave his fellow subjects in America, by imposing Taxes upon them contrary to Law and Justice; and the American Patriot, who

---

[14] Ibid., 20–1.
[15] Ibid., 23–4.
[16] Rush, 13. The British public would, in any case, increasingly fault slave-owners for their exclusively economic rationalities. The turning point may have been the infamous *Zong* incident in 1781, when 133 African slaves – insured as cargo – were thrown overboard as supplies of potable water ran low. 'The *Zong* affair', note Burnard and Garrigus, 'played a central role in making the abolition of the slave trade a matter of intense public interest in Britain. It served as a supreme example of the callous financial calculations on which the slave trade was based'. Burnard and Garrigus, 216.
[17] Rush, 33.
[18] Ibid., 18.

thoroughly imbricated within the slave system. From the 1760s one begins to find medical texts written on ways to handle the initial seasoning and later care of slaves. From the 1780s, the writings of men who claimed to administer to the medical needs of thousands of slaves per year were cited, critiqued, and debated in parliamentary sessions devoted to the question of the continuation of the trade within the British Empire. Abolitionists excoriated planters for the death and suffering – from disease, neglect, and harsh treatment – of the slaves they owned, while some West Indian doctors used their experiences to offer *apologia* and negations of precisely these charges.

Before turning to the structure of this chapter, let me be clear about why the history of race-medicine should matter for the broader intellectual history of race, by looking at two forms of boundary-making that have helped to shape our understandings of that history. The first comes from one of the foremost analysts of Kant's theories on race. 'The fact that the scientific concept of race was developed initially in Germany rather than in Britain or America', Robert Bernasconi has written, 'suggests that it was not specifically the interests of the slaveowners that led to its introduction, but rather, as Kant's essays themselves confirm, an interest in classification and above all the attempt to provide a theoretical defence of monogenism'.[25] On the one hand, I share Bernasconi's scepticism with what are common lay beliefs, which suggest that scientific racism was invented largely as a justification for slavery and a rapacious colonialism.[26] If abolitionist debates are an important place for locating the rise of racial conceptions, such simple instrumentalism – as I noted in Chapter 6 – is nonetheless not adequate as a means of understanding the complexity of the issues involved. On the other hand, Bernasconi appears to leave as unconsidered the question of why, in 1775, monogenism should need such vigorous defence? Attention only to elite discourse – and hence to the provocations of Kames – ignores the fact that the Scottish jurist was only one of several polygenist authors in the second half of the century and that most others were directly responding to Benezet and his allies in the 1760s and the threat posed by the Somerset decision in 1772. Monogenism did, indeed, require defence, but it did so in part because of the attacks levelled by slave owners.

The second attempt at boundary-making comes from Blumenbach, whose history of previous thinkers on race has tended to shape the boundaries of many subsequent reconstructions. It was with some chagrin that Blumenbach

---

[25] Robert Bernasconi, 'Who Invented the Concept of Race? Kant's Role in the Enlightenment Construction of Race', in *Race*, ed. Robert Bernasconi (Malden, MA and Oxford: Blackwell, 2001), 21.

[26] This is, for example, the first answer my undergraduate students proffer when asked about the origin of scientific racism. Of course, from the end of the eighteenth century, scientific racism worked as a powerful defence of an already-established slave-trade.

lamented, in 1775, that some should try to allow pathology to 'obtrude' into the natural history of the varieties of mankind.[27] His aim, he suggested, was to restore each area to its natural place, assuming that separation was the original state. Like Bernasconi, Blumenbach's aim here was to offer a purified understanding of what the 'real' question of race was. For both, however, refusing the act of purification – rejecting it as poor history – pays dividends, for it insists on keeping power and politics in the story. Of course, it is not difficult to see power and politics in Kant's claim that 'all Negroes stink' or Blumenbach's studious examination of the skulls of peoples sent him by Europeans in far-flung lands. Yet attention to the history of medicine brings to the fore the immediate power-relations between, for example, a West Indian physician and the thousands of slaves nominally under his care, or the forms of authority that treated the melioration of pain and suffering as an issue requiring race as a category of analysis. A dual denial of boundaries is necessary, for we need to understand race in the later eighteenth century – even seemingly abstract, taxonomic and naturalistic understandings of race – as intimately related to the theories and practices of slavery. One way to do so is to broaden our understanding of what such naturalistic understandings were, and to insist, as I have throughout this part of the book, on seeing the pathologies and physiologies of race together with its anatomies.[28]

The chapter is divided into three sections. Section 7.1 explores the role of medicine in abolitionist debates. West Indian doctors and other men who claimed to possess medical understanding offered critiques or defences of slavery that relied on their own expertise and experience; they put forward their own practice as examples of the ways in which slavery might be meliorated or reformed; and some, as we shall see, even penned manuals that served simultaneously as propagandistic tracts that sought to demonstrate the existence of a humane slavery and also offered descriptions of the kinds of practices that would keep slaves healthy through the seasoning and beyond.

Section 7.2 continues and develops the arguments of Chapter 5, noting that climatic, cultural, and dietetic explanations of 'racial' disparities remained the orthodox position throughout the century.[29] While many writers noted that

---

[27] Johann Blumenbach, 'De Generis Humani Varietate Nativa (1775)', in *The Anthropological Treatises of Johann Friedrich Blumenbach*, ed. Thomas Bendyshe (London: Longman, Green, Longman, Roberts, and Green, 1865), 101.

[28] For the literature's near-exclusive focus on anatomy, rather than pathology, see, e.g. Curran. See also Wheeler. An exception, in spite of its title, is Hogarth.

[29] Much has been written about ongoing tensions between universalistic and racially particular medical theory and practice into the nineteenth century. See, for example, John S. Haller, 'The Negro and the Southern Physician: A Study of Medical and Racial Attitudes, 1800–1860', *Medical History* 16 (1972); Savitt; 'The Use of Blacks for Medical Experimentation and Demonstration in the Old South', *The Journal of Southern History* 48 (1982); 'Slave Health and Southern Distinctiveness', in *Disease and Distinctiveness in the American South*, ed. Todd

Africans, Europeans, and Creoles seemed to suffer from different afflictions, fixed physical attributes were rarely invoked as an explanation within medicine. Hippocratism, broadly construed, remained the standard paradigm for etiological claims. It is, however, useful to note a division *within* these Hippocratic causes that may be discerned in writings about the diseases of warm climates. Where the objects of comparison were different parts of the globe – and the different distempers characteristic of these parts – climate was invoked as the standard and primary explanation. Different diseases (or different manifestations of the same disease) were found in different climates. Where medical men were interested in understanding the cause of varying susceptibilities within the *same* geographic region, on the other hand, climate unsurprisingly played much less of a role.[30] As specific attention to the diseases of slaves rose in response to the pressures of abolitionist critiques, medical texts increasingly emphasised the diet, clothing, housing, and behaviour of slaves (and other members of non-white populations), rather than the impact of a common climate. Thus, if one does not find 'race' in these orthodox medical tracts, one does find increasing attention to the social and cultural differences between whites and others.

Section 7.3 continues the arguments of Chapter 6, in that it explores a number of the heterodox and racialist positions that were increasingly defining a real and significant minority in European conversations. Edward Long would not be alone in his polygenism in the last decades of the 1700s. Hard versions of racial thinking would play particular roles in a debate over whether free labour was a possible alternative to slave labour in the West Indies.[31] As we have seen in the exchange between Rush and Nisbet, this issue contained mine fields for both sides. Abolitionists tended to play down the intrinsic dangers of the warm climate in favour of trenchant critiques of the backbreaking and relentless labour slaves were forced to undergo. Pro-slavery advocates who were unwilling to simply describe Africans as animals, on the other hand, needed to portray the West Indian climate as deadly to whites, but seemingly innocuous to slaves, else they be charged with murder by forced labour. Medical and anatomical claims thus abounded in a discourse about an innate, physically-rooted capacity (or not) for those of African descent to endure that which could not be tolerated by Europeans. Just as significantly, by 1780 one can begin to locate precisely the sorts of arguments that had been absent in the first half of

L. Savitt and James Harvey Young (Knoxville: University of Tennessee Press, 1988); Martin S. Pernick, *A Calculus of Suffering: Pain, Professionalism, and Anesthesia in Nineteenth-Century America* (New York: Columbia University Press, 1985); Fett.

[30] This is in spite of a close attention to what today would be called 'micro-climates'. See Johnston.

[31] Drescher, *The Mighty Experiment: Free Labor Versus Slavery in British Emancipation*.

the eighteenth century, arguments where medical logics and racial logics were combined and where racialised physical differences were described as causing characteristically racial medical differences. At the end of the century, race-medicine was beginning to emerge.

7.1   Medicine and Abolitionism

In 1789, when the Jamaica House of Assembly published two reports on the slave trade, the abolitionist debate was coming to a head.[32] The year before, William Wilberforce had introduced a parliamentary resolution that would have committed the British House of Commons to a discussion of the trade in its next session. Petitions were already flooding in, from both sides. An investigatory report on the matter by the Privy Council was published in April 1789 and in May Wilberforce delivered an immediately famous speech describing the horrors of the middle passage and arguing that abolition would lead to a near-certain improvement of the situation of slaves in the West Indies.[33] The Committee of the Jamaican House responded in October and November, dividing the criticisms levelled in the many petitions before Parliament into those that concerned the African slave trade and those that concerned the treatment of slaves in the West Indies. On the first matter, they (disingenuously) suggested that 'the inhabitants of the West-India islands have no concern in the ships trading to Africa'. The African trade was a British interest. Jamaican planters were involved in the trade only as the buyers 'of what British acts of Parliament have declared to be legal objects of purchase'.[34] The crucial accusations, then, were those regarding the treatment of the enslaved within the island, which they divided into four charges: that the laws governing negroes were harsh; that the laws were executed with inhumanity and without mercy; that negroes were grossly overworked and were not granted sufficient days of rest; and that the decline in the numbers of slaves on the island was due to their poor treatment.[35] It is this last charge and the attempts at defences against it that should most

---

[32] Jamaica.

[33] '[H]is *speech* is circulated everywhere', wrote one pro-slavery writer with chagrin in 1792, 'and the cruelties recorded in it are becomes as familiar to *children* as the story of *Blue Beard* or *Jack the Giant Killer*'. Jesse Foot, *A Defence of the Planters in the West Indies; Comprised in Four Arguments* (London: J. Debrett, 1792), 75.

[34] Jamaica, 2–3. On medicine and the middle passage, see Sheridan, 'The Guinea Surgeons on the Middle Passage: The Provision of Medical Services in the British Slave Trade'. Latest estimates suggest that roughly one in seven of the 3.4 million African slaves taken by the British Empire died in the middle passage. The proportion changed over time, however, with losses averaging roughly 20 per cent before 1600 and dropping to 12 per cent in the second half of the eighteenth century. David Northrup, *Africa's Discovery of Europe, 1450–1850* (Oxford: Oxford University Press, 2002), 118.

[35] Jamaica, 3.

capture our attention here, for it was on this issue that the Committee invoked the evidence of medical men.

Beginning with deeply suspicious exculpatory calculations that still indicated that there had been a net loss of more than 26, 000 lives among slaves on the island since 1655,[36] the report then listed the two main causes of slave mortality: 'The great proportion of deaths that happen among negroes newly imported' (that is, the seasoning), and 'The loss which prevails among the negro infants that are born in the country'.[37] The three medical men called to provide evidence to the committee (whose interviews were then published as appendices) came to the same broad conclusions on the question of the seasoning. Deaths were not to be laid at the doors of planters, they averred. Losses among newly arrived slaves were due to diseases from which they were suffering prior to landing, acquired either in Africa or on board ship. They differed more on the causes of the deaths of infants. James Chisholme and Adam Anderson both agreed that roughly one-quarter of all negro children died within two weeks of their birth. Chisholme ascribed this to the lack of cleanliness and care with which they were treated and dressed, a point that Anderson denied.[38] Neither, however, seemed to regard the issue as one that was easily solvable in practice. John Quier reported that the affliction was not common in the area of his practice and placed the blame for the island's declining slave population on the promiscuity of negro women, which led both to frequent abortions and to a lack of care for children, who were 'lost through neglect and the want of maternal affection, which the mothers seldom retain for their offspring by a former husband'.[39] Rehearsing standard tropes about the wickedness, ignorance, and wantonness of slaves, then, physicians lent their expertise to the apologist cause.

We shall return to some of these claims soon, but for us the most basic point to be drawn from the report of the Jamaican Assembly is the centrality of medical arguments to the abolitionist debate.[40] Reading abolitionist tracts,

---

[36] Burnard and Garrigus also call this figure 'highly improbable'. Burnard and Garrigus, 233.

[37] Jamaica., 15.

[38] Chisholme argued that paying greater attention to the sanitary conditions of newborns would thus, in principle, solve the problem quite easily. 'But, simple as this may appear in theory, those who are much conversant with negroes', he asserted, 'will be aware of the difficulty, if not impossibility, of putting it in practice, in a degree sufficient to answer the purpose. For, such is the ignorance, obstinacy, and inattention of negroes: so little regard have they for each other, and so averse are they to executing the directions of white people, when repugnant to their own prejudices', ibid., Chisholme, Appendix 6, 26–8, Anderson, Appendix 7, 28–30.

[39] Ibid., Quier, Appendix 8, 30–3.

[40] Beyond the specific elements cited below, I want to cite here my more general debts to Sheridan's coverage of the relationships between medicine and slavery in Sheridan, *Doctors and Slaves: A Medical and Demographic History of Slavery in the British West Indies, 1680–1834.*

the public was horrified by stories of torture and punishment and moved by descriptions of the backbreaking labour slaves were forced to undergo. Almost every island passed laws in response to such critiques, but it was hard to deny charges that such laws were mere unenforceable (and certainly unenforced) window dressing when faced with the brute fact of a decline in population. Claims like Rush's, which held the slave system responsible for a prodigious loss of life, required expert responses, which blamed not planters or their laws, but shipboard conditions and the practices of slaves themselves. Among the most trenchant critics of slavery were medical men – Rush and James Ramsay perhaps the most famous. As we can see, however, physicians and surgeons also argued for the other side. It was not slavery *per se,* that was to blame, they argued, for matters were complex. But the situation could be improved and, practiced properly, medicine could aid in melioration.

If we accept that medicine played a role in abolitionist debates, we should also acknowledge the role played by abolitionist debates in pushing certain medical issues to the fore. The Jamaican Assembly seemed to make it obvious that the profound losses due to the seasoning should be discussed in explicitly medical terms, but this had not always been so. Charles Leslie's *New History of Jamaica* (1740) did not shy away from describing some of the worst elements of life on the island: 'trivial errors' punished with brutal whippings, slaves treated cruelly simply for the pleasure of the overseer, and 'their Bodies all in a Gore of Blood, the skin torn off their Backs with the cruel Whip, beaten Pepper, and Salt, rubbed in the Wounds, and a large Stick of Sealing-wax dropped leisurely upon them'.[41] And yet, only a half-dozen pages after this horrific depiction, Leslie described the stunning number of deaths due to the seasoning without any of this emotion or empathy.[42] An Owner, he noted, must replenish 'his Stock ... every Year, or he would soon want Hands for his Work. Almost half of the new imported Negroes die in the Seasoning'.[43] One should compare this invocation of a numerical claim to that of Anthony Benezet, the French-born Quaker who has been called the 'father of Atlantic abolitionism'.[44] In 1762, Benezet, too, noted that roughly half of the slaves imported to Jamaica died of the seasoning, while a quarter perished in Barbados, bringing the total number

[41] Leslie, 305.
[42] As Delbourgo observes, discussions of the appalling treatment of slaves were not necessarily understood, in the first half of the eighteenth century, as 'self-evident horrors', but rather (as in the case of Sloane's descriptions, which were endlessly cited and reproduced by later abolitionists) as 'morally and politically indeterminate curiosities'. Delbourgo, 'Slavery in the Cabinet of Curiosities: Hans Sloane's Atlantic World'. 15.
[43] Leslie, 312.
[44] Jackson. David L. Crosby, ed. *The Complete Antislavery Writings of Anthony Benezet, 1754–1783* (Baton Rouge: Louisiana State University Press, 2013).

of deaths, including the passage, for a single year of British trading to the West Indies and colonies in North America to twelve thousand souls.

What a sad dreadful Affair then is this Man-Trade, whereby so many Thousands of our Fellow rational Creatures lose their lives, are, truly and properly speaking, murdered every Year; I do not think there is an Instance of so great Barbarity and Cruelty carried on in any Part of the World, as is this, Year after Year. It is enough to make one tremble, to think what a Load of Guilt lies upon this Nation, on this Account, and that the Blood of Thousands of poor innocent Creatures, murdered every Year, in carrying on this cursed Trade, cry aloud to Heaven for Vengeance.[45]

It is surely no coincidence that the first tract on how to properly season slaves to avoid such losses appeared two years later. James Grainger was born in Scotland around 1721 and graduated with a medical degree from Edinburgh in 1753, then moving in 1759 to St Kitts. In publishing his 'Essay on the More Common West-India Diseases' in 1764, Grainger registered his 'astonishment, that among the many valuable medical tracts which of late years have been offered to the public, none has been purposely written on the method of seasoning new negroes'.[46] This 'method' was fairly straightforward, involving gradual habituation to the work of the fields. Or, as he phrased it in his poem, 'The Sugar Cane': 'Let gentle work,/Or rather playful exercise, amuse/The novel gang: and far be angry words;/Far ponderous chains: and far disheartening blows'.[47] This was valuable counter-propaganda and signalled the beginning of medicine's involvement in a discourse about the development of a more benevolent slavery. The seasoning, in Grainger's work, was not a brutal statistical fact that underscored the fundamental inhumanity of the man-trade. It was, rather, a problem to be resolved by better and more medically informed management. Urging better medical treatment for the enslaved, the planter could be economically rational and take back the moral high-ground ceded to the abolitionist:[48]

But it is not enough to take care of Negroes when they are sick; they should also be well clothed and regularly fed. Neglecting either of these important precepts is not only

---

[45] Anthony Benezet, *A Short Account of That Part of Africa, Inhabited by the Negroes* (Philadelphia: William Dunlap, 1762), 39–40.

[46] Grainger, 6.

[47] 'The Sugar-Cane (1764). Book IV'., in *On the Treatment and Management of the More Common West-India Diseases (1750–1802)*, ed. J. Edward Hutson (Kingston, Jamaica: University of the West Indies Press, 2005), 62–3. On the poem, see Kelly Wisecup, *Medical Encounters: Knowledge and Identity in Early American Literatures* (Amherst: University of Massachusetts Press, 2013), 127–60. See also Smith.

[48] 'The antislavery movement, particularly in its evangelical Christian incarnation, drew strength from a new rhetoric about slave mortality; what had earlier been described principally in economic terms became a moral problems of vital importance to the "soul" of the British nation'. Brown, 157.

inhuman, it is the worst species of prodigality. One Negroe saved in this manner more than pays the additional expences which owners of slaves by this means incur. But, supposing it did not, it ought seriously to be considered by all masters, that they must answer before the Almighty for their conduct towards their Negroes.[49]

As Larry Tise has noted, pro-slavery writings tended to be reactive: a number appearing in response to the criticisms levelled by Benezet and others in the 1760s, another grouping, including those written against Rush, emerging after the Somerset case in 1772, and a third in response to a book written by the former surgeon, Reverend James Ramsay in 1784. *An Essay on the Treatment and Conversion of African Slaves in the British Sugar Colonies* excoriated planters for their treatment of the enslaved and drew bitter and often *ad hominem* replies. Ramsay covered some of the same ground as abolitionists before him, building before the reader's eye an image of the grossly excessive labour and brutal punishments to which slaves were subjected. He also added comparatively new elements, drawing on surgical knowledge gained first in his training under Dr George Macaulay, physician at the British Lying-in Hospital in London, and then his practice in the Navy and – even after his ordination – on the island of St Christopher.[50] Ramsay may have been the first major abolitionist writer to detail the system for caring for sick slaves. A poorly paid surgeon, he noted, was employed to care for sick slaves, with his income set at a certain amount per head per year. Some 'frugal planters' eschewed the services of medical men, dosing their slaves with commercially available powders and pills, calling in a practitioner only to 'pronounce them past recovery'.[51] Where the plantation manager was a steady, stable and married man, Ramsay suggested, one could count on better diets and treatment for the sick, with the manager's wife taking on a supervisory role. Yet the practice of hiring married men was becoming less common, and when such a figure was a 'gadding, gossiping reveller (a character sometimes to be met with)', the sick were very poorly served. 'Often, while the manager is feasting abroad, careless and ignorant of what has happened, some hapless wretch among the slaves is taken ill, and unnoticed, unpitied, dies, without even the poor comfort of a surgeon, in his last moments, to say, "It is now too late"'.[52] And it was not unusual for as many as one in eight (presumably seasoned) negroes to die of 'fevers, fluxes, dropsies' in a year as a result of excessive labour and minimal food and

---

[49] Grainger, 'An Essay on the More Common West-India Diseases, James Grainger, Md (1764), with Additional Notes by William Wright, MD, FRS (1802)', 51.

[50] James Watt, 'Surgeon James Ramsay, 1733–1789: The Navy and the Slave Trade', *Journal of the Royal Society of Medicine* 87 (1994).

[51] James Ramsay, *An Essay on the Treatment and Conversion of African Slaves in the British Sugar Colonies* (Dublin: T. Walker, C. Jenkin, R. Marchbank, L. White, R. Burton, P. Byrne, 1784), 70–1.

[52] Ibid., Note, 71–2.

care.[53] Even more disturbing than this portrayal of callous neglect may have been Ramsay's description of the treatment of pregnant and nursing women.[54] Plantation owners forced all who were deemed capable to work in the field gang, so that 'hardly any remonstrance from the surgeon can, in many cases, save a poor diseased wretch from the labour'. To this work were assigned even pregnant women in the last months of their term: 'and hence suffer many an abortion; which some managers are unfeeling enough to express joy at, because the woman, on recovery, having no child to care for, will have no pretence for indulgence'.[55] Were she to carry the child to term, Ramsay continued, the infant would be born in a 'dark, damp, smoky hut', which explained the loss of such infants to cramps and convulsions.[56]

Philip Gibbes published his *Instructions for the Treatment of Negroes* two years after Ramsay's *Essay*, although he was at pains in a later edition to stress that his 'sentiments were entertained and these instructions given, long before Ramsay wrote or Wilberforce spoke'.[57] His positive recommendations were fairly basic and involved allowing sufficient time for new slaves to become seasoned to the climate before they were put to strenuous labour and providing them with sufficient amounts of nutritious food, after the recommendations of Count Rumford.[58] Turning to the question of whether pregnant women should work in the fields, Gibbes agreed with Ramsay (albeit for somewhat different reasons): 'A small degree of the knowledge of the human frame', he asserted, 'will inform you, that laborious exercise obstructs procreation: for which reason it is extremely improper and ill-judged to make females carry

---

[53] Ibid., 83.

[54] Ramsay's interest in this topic no doubt derived from his time spent training at the British lying-in hospital. See Watt; Paugh, 'The Politics of Childbearing in the British Caribbean and the Atlantic World During the Age of Abolition, 1776–1838', 128.

[55] Ramsay, 75. Such critiques had some effect. 'Under the Leeward Islands Act of 1798, for instance, female slaves "five months gone" were to be employed only on light work and were to be punished by confinement only "under penalty of five pounds". Ameliorative legislation passed in the Leewards in 1798 and Jamaica in 1809 included provisions that female slaves "having six children living" should be "exempt from hard labour" and the owner "exempt from taxes" for such female slaves'. Bush, 29.

[56] Ramsay, 76.

[57] Philip Gibbes, *Instruction for the Treatment of Negroes &C. &C. &C.*, 2nd ed. (London: Shepperson and Reynolds, 1797), 132. That said, he did confess that his hope in originally publishing lay in 'repelling the illiberal attacks of dangerous and mistaken zealots'. Ibid., 68.

[58] Gibbes' *Instructions* are perhaps most remarkable for the execrable poetry they contain. Gibbes reproduced songs intended to be sung by slaves and written by 'a very ingenious Lady'. For example, this one, on labour: 'How useful is labour, how healthful and good!/It keeps us from mischief, procures wholesome food;/ It saves from much sickness and loathsome disease/ That fall on the idle and pamper'd with ease'. Or this one, on the curse of Ham: 'We're children of Cham! He his father offended,/ Who gave him the curse which to us is descended./ "A servant of servants" alas! is our curse;/ And bad as it is, it has sav'd us from worse'. Ibid., 107, 33.

canes to the mill or in uneven fields'.[59] Robert Thomas, writing in 1790, concurred, suggesting that benevolence was already a part of the care provided by several proprietors, who did not assign women to the field gang after their first three or four months of pregnancy, demanded lighter work until the seventh or eighth month, when no further duty was required, and 'annually send out baby-clothes for the use of their breeding women'.[60] That position marked a difference from John Quier's, in his testimony to the Assembly. Quier had insisted that he had not known any cases of abortions to follow – as Ramsay had claimed – from excessive labour or 'ill usage', and averred instead that 'moderate labour is beneficial to pregnant women, as being the best means of preserving general health'.[61]

Where Gibbes, Quier, Thomas and other defenders of slavery were all in apparent agreement, however, was on the necessity to move the debate on the declining slave population away from the question of death rates and towards those concerning birth rates. For on the latter they could dwell on questions of the promiscuity of enslaved women and avoid many of the ugly questions about infant mortality that abolitionist authors were raising. Deploying a trope explored in Chapter 5, Gibbes thus claimed that 'Early prostitution is the certain obstruction to population', offering a frankly graphic farming analogy (derived from a 'very sensible friend') to explain his logic:

When the earth is prepared and ploughed, and the seed, at the proper season, is cast into the furrows, if it be ploughed over and over again, would the seed thus, disturbed in its germination strike root deeply, or would it vegetate at all? If sowed with different seeds, inimical to each other, how weak and mingled would be the produce! Let the divine command be carefully observed as well in your care of the women as of the soil, *Sow not thy land with divers seeds.*[62]

More standard explanation connected Afro-Caribbean hyper-sexuality with a resultant venereal infection, leading to infertility, or else tied 'prostitution' to the procuring of abortions, which then led to medical difficulties.[63] Long, for example, stated simply that 'the women here are, in general, common

---

[59] Ibid., 86.
[60] Thomas, xi–xii.
[61] Jamaica., Appendix 8, 32.
[62] Gibbes, note, 125–6.
[63] 'Put simply', writes Katherine Paugh, 'many British authors believed that racially characteristic sexual promiscuity led to venereal disease and infertility, while they believed that Christian monogamy encouraged fertility'. Paugh, 'The Politics of Childbearing in the British Caribbean and the Atlantic World During the Age of Abolition, 1776–1838', 129. On hyper-sexuality, see Morgan, '"Some Could Suckle over Their Shoulder": Male Travelers, Female Bodies, and the Gendering of Racial Ideology, 1500–1770'. Altink, *Representations of Slave Women in Discourses on Slavery and Abolition, 1780–1838*; 'Deviant and Dangerous: Pro-Slavery Representation of Jamaican Slave Women's Sexuality, C. 1780–1834'.

prostitutes; and many take specifics to cause abortion'.[64] The Governor, Edward Trelawney, invoked abortions as the direct cause of low populations: 'what chiefly contributes to their being so few Children among the *English* Negroes', he asserted, 'is the Practice of the Wenches in procuring Abortions. As they lie with both Colours, and do not know which the Child may prove of, to disoblige neither, they stifle it at birth'.[65] Thomas insisted that the frequency, amongst Afro-Caribbean women, of cases of 'the whites' [probably Leucorrhea] was due to 'the frequent abortions they designedly bring upon themselves, in order to prevent their having the trouble of rearing their offspring, to which they are seldom bound by the same ties of maternal tenderness and affection that white women are'.[66] Thomas, in fact, offered a litany of reasons for the fact that 'not one estate in fifty can keep up its original number, even although the greatest humanity and lenity have been practice, and all possible pains have been taken for rearing the children that have been born', ranging from early promiscuity, prostitution, abortions, early loss of infant life, and diseases to which women in warm climates were more subject than in colder ones.[67] How powerful was this discourse may be gleaned from the fact that even an author profoundly critical of the Report of the Jamaican Assembly and of Quier's testimony in particular found himself in agreement with the doctor's claim that many abortions on the island were the result of 'promiscuous intercourse'.[68] Negative judgements about black female sexuality made unlikely bedfellows.[69]

Like many of the owners of plantations in the West Indies, Gibbes was an absentee landlord, living in Britain. Such owners were, as Sheridan noted, 'highly vulnerable to antislavery propaganda', and many pushed for measures to improve, although not abolish, slavery.[70] Where general problems with the treatment of slaves were acknowledged by this group, blame was placed largely on the backs of managers and overseers, who became the public face of the atrocities and neglect abolitionists had identified. Coupled with rising prices for slaves in the last decades of the century, the weight of public opinion pushed colonial legislatures to institute new laws and codes to protect slaves from the most brutal treatment and, eventually, to encourage an increase

---

[64] Long, *The History of Jamaica*, II, 436.
[65] Quoted in Sheridan, *Doctors and Slaves: A Medical and Demographic History of Slavery in the British West Indies, 1680–1834*, 224.
[66] Thomas, 279.
[67] Ibid., xix–xx, xvi.
[68] A. Jamaica Planter, *Notes on the Two Reports from the Committee of the Honourable House of Assembly of Jamaica* (London: James Phillips, 1789), 61.
[69] For more on this point, see Paugh, 'The Politics of Childbearing in the British Caribbean and the Atlantic World During the Age of Abolition, 1776–1838'.
[70] Sheridan, *Doctors and Slaves: A Medical and Demographic History of Slavery in the British West Indies, 1680–1834*, 230.

in their population.[71] In Jamaica, the Consolidated Slave Act of 1781, for example, introduced clauses requiring adequate clothing, the allocation of provision grounds and 'sufficient time to work the same', and prescribing the punishment for a master who mutilated or dismembered slaves. The Act of 1787 added further clauses, with medical elements that seem to have been a direct response to Ramsay's criticisms, allowing towns and parishes to levy taxes to provide 'food, medical care, and attendance' for slaves – too old or sick to care for themselves – who had been abandoned by their owners and requiring that a surgeon provide, under oath, an account of the increase or decrease of numbers on every plantation, with a description of the cause of each decrease, in order to 'prevent the destruction of negroes, by excessive labour and unreasonable punishments'. Critics noted, however, that many such laws were essentially toothless. As one writer identifying himself as a 'Jamaica Planter' put it: 'I have for many years been conversant with Jamaica, and know of but one instance of the law against mutilation being inforced, and that instance occurred since the people in Britain have interested themselves in favour of the poor negroes'.[72] The editor for that work put his finger on one of the most obvious intrinsic problems with legislation that pitted masters against slaves in the realm of the law: the testimony of slaves was not admissible against owners.[73]

Laws that mandated that medical men, dependent upon owners for their livelihoods, testify in cases of excessive neglect or unlawful deaths also seem impossibly naïve (assuming that they were intended to have real effects in the first place).[74] Indeed, the testimony of such practitioners seems to have largely served the opposite cause. Thus, Jesse Foot, who had served as a surgeon for three years in the West Indies, with the 'care of two thousand negroes annually' invoked his own experiences as part of his *Defence of the Planters in the West Indies*.[75] Foot declared that he had not seen 'any other treatment than that which humanity dictates', adding that 'during my practice I never was called

---

[71] Ramsay noted that 'slaves be now raised to a price that few old settled plantations can afford to give'. Ramsay, 76. On the new slave laws, see Goveia, 152–202. 'The West Indian Slave Laws of the Eighteenth Century', *Chapters in Caribbean History* 2 (1970). Similar logics applied in the French West-Indies. Weaver, 29.

[72] Jamaica Planter, 20.

[73] Ibid., i–ii.

[74] As Goveia notes, the position of a doctor 'was a difficult one, since he was himself an employee of the planter on whom he would be forced to inform if he took his responsibilities for his slaves more seriously than his loyalty to an employer and fellow inhabitant'. Goveia, *Slave Society in the British Leeward Islands at the End of the Eighteenth Century*, 198. 'Only with the Coroner's Act of 1817 did an actual law establish a clear and unambiguous requirement that coroners perform inquests into the deaths of slaves, also stipulating that slaveholders could not be jurors at inquests concerning their own slaves. A belated response to antislavery pressure, the act established that, in principle, the deaths of black people merited serious investigation'. Brown, 80.

[75] Foot, 31.

to give *surgical relief* to any negroes who had suffered from the severity of chastisement'.[76] Robert Thomas drew on nine years of medical care for three thousand negroes a year to make a similar point: 'I never was called upon', he asserted, 'to administer assistance to a negro in consequence of any violence or cruelty exercised over him, either by the master, manager, or overseer'.[77] It is possible that one outcome of the new laws – coupled with the need to be seen to be responding to anti-slavery critiques and the economic incentives introduced by the increasing value of slaves – may have been a reduction in the number of planters who relied on their own judgement alone in treating sick or injured slaves. And yet, even though the number of practitioners rose, it should be clear from the sheer number of slaves under their yearly care the minimal attention each patient could receive. Foot and Thomas were hardly alone in having thousands of slaves under their charge.[78] In their testimony before the Jamaica Assembly, Chisholme, Anderson, and Quier detailed the size of their practices – around 4000 slaves a year – as part of their credentials. The 'Jamaica Planter' placed this number in some perspective by noting that a regiment or a ship of war of five hundred men was accorded a surgeon and perhaps several surgeon's mates. 'Once, twice, or thrice in a week, to gallop to a plantation, to take a peep into the hospital, or hot-house, as it is called, write in a book, "bleed this", "purge that", "blister another", "here give an opiate", "there the bark", is not, in my opinion, taking care of, though it may be called taking charge of, the healths of 4000 or 5000 negroes'.[79]

The abolitionist debate – spearheaded, in some cases, by those with medical training – managed to place the medical care of slaves near the forefront of public concern. As a measure of this, one might note that in 1789, the Privy Council Committee systematically asked witnesses about the care of slaves in sickness, the laws that existed to regulate such care, and the provision for slaves when they were old and infirm.[80] Colonial legislatures acted to place such laws on the books from the 1780s onwards. Yet much of the attention in the colonies had been reactive. Tracts about such medical care for the enslaved tended to dissipate after Wilberforce's bill – delayed until 1791 – sputtered in the House, the country's political mood swinging against radical reform in the aftermath of the French Revolution. In 1792 all Wilberforce was able to extract from his fellow parliamentarians was the agreement on a 'gradual abolition' of

---

[76] Ibid., 75–6.
[77] Thomas, xv.
[78] For average number of slaves per practitioner on different islands, see Sheridan, *Doctors and Slaves: A Medical and Demographic History of Slavery in the British West Indies, 1680–1834*, 302 ff.
[79] Jamaica Planter, 60.
[80] Sheridan, *Doctors and Slaves: A Medical and Demographic History of Slavery in the British West Indies, 1680–1834*, 271.

the slave trade. An Act to that effect would wait until 1807. Beyond legislation, it should be clear that medical logics were a key part of the discourse around abolitionism, with practitioners arrayed on either side of the debate. For every Rush or Ramsay who drew attention to the tremendous losses of life due to the seasoning or infant tetanus, or to the appalling treatment of pregnant and nursing women and sick or aged slaves, there was a Quier, a Foot, or a Thomas willing to testify to the exceptionality of horrific punishments, when they were meted out, or to the culpability of slaves in their own declining population. Medical expertise was a valuable commodity in a battle between melioration and abolition. It was no less so in the debates over relationships between disease and 'race'.

7.2   Race, Climate, Disease

It was not at all uncommon for medical men writing about the diseases of warm climates to discuss differences in susceptibilities and outcomes between the peoples native to different places. It was, however, very rare (at least until the 1780s) for anyone to explain these differences by invoking fixed physical characteristics as a cause. For roughly the first half of the eighteenth century, as I argued in Chapter 5, the standard element – with some striking exceptions – invoked to explain both seemingly geographically particular diseases and 'racial', political, and cultural variance was environment, broadly construed. The touchstone was Hippocrates' *Airs, Waters, and Places*, which had been the model for location-specific medical texts since the early 1700s. Neo-Hippocratism as 'anthropological' method reached new heights around mid-century, with the publication of Montesquieu's *Spirit of the Laws* in 1748.[81] Drawing on John Arbuthnot's equally Hippocratic *Essay Concerning the Effects of Air on Human Bodies* (1733), Montesquieu argued that cold air caused the body's fibres to contract, which increased their 'spring' and strength, while warmth relaxed and lengthened them.[82] 'Therefore', he wrote, 'men are more vigorous in cold climates'.[83] Indeed, 'The people in hot countries are timid like old men; those in cold countries are courageous like young men'.[84] More broadly, both large-scale modes of governance and smaller-scale social mores were rooted in climatic conditions.[85] The text was

---

[81] Anne M. Cohler, Basia C. Miller, and Harold S. Stone, eds., *Montesquieu: The Spirit of the Laws* (Cambridge: Cambridge University Press, 2010).

[82] Arbuthnot. Curran, 134.

[83] Cohler, Miller, and Stone, 231.

[84] Ibid., 232.

[85] We find it claimed in Book 17, on the relationship between climate and political servitude, for example, that '[P]ower should always be despotic in Asia', while Book 14, on the laws and the

to prove enormously influential in abolitionist discourse as well as many other sites. Rush was far from the only anti-slavery writer to invoke the authority of the French *philosophe* to bolster his claims about the non-essential, climatically variable differences between peoples, even as he avoided Montesquieu's more troubling suggestion that warm climates might provide the only locations where natural slavery could be countenanced.[86]

Within medicine, as within political writings, climate served to explain both differences and similarities. Where climates were distinct, one found people of different appearance and political systems, as well as different diseases. Where seemingly different peoples inhabited the same region, however, one would expect, over time, the emergence of common political and social orders as well as afflictions. Climatic similarity, that is, overpowered other forms of difference. It was climate that produced the unity that was England, for example, despite the variety of human stocks that made up the population. In an age that saw the emergence of European national states, such unities mattered, but they were far more fraught in the colonies, particularly those built on the binary distinction between the enslaved and the free. Montesquieu's equivocation over whether slavery could ever be tolerated was telling. I have found at least two medical texts from the 1750s and 1760s, however, that take climatic reasoning to its logical conclusion. In them, one finds whites and blacks, Europeans and Africans, the free and the enslaved, grouped together by a discourse about nativity and habituation. In Charles Bisset's *Treatise on the Scurvy* 'Negroes, Creoles, and seasoned Europeans' are grouped together by the fact that they rarely suffer from either the 'malignant Bilious Fever' or the scurvy.[87] What the three kinds of peoples have in common is a relative rigidity of the fibres internal to the body. To become seasoned to the climate is to acquire such rigidity and in such a way to have one's body 'become nearly assimilated to those of Creoles and Negroes'.[88] James Lind's essay on the health of seamen

---

climate argues that Mohammed's prohibition on the drinking of wine 'is a law of the climate of Arabia'. Ibid., 283, 39.

[86] Montesquieu vacillated on this point: 'But as all men are created equal, one must say that slavery is against nature, although in certain countries it may be founded on natural reason, and these countries must be distinguished from those in which even natural reason rejects it, as in the countries of Europe where it has so fortunately been abolished ... Therefore, natural slavery must be limited to certain particular countries of the world ... I do not know if my spirit or my heart dictates this point. Perhaps there is no climate on earth where one could not engage freemen to work'. Ibid., 251–3. Cf. Curran, 137. 'While Montesquieu clearly found the enslavement of any human to be antithetical to his overall philosophical project, his understanding of climate and the *nègre's* physiology produced a significant exception to this rule: although unfortunate, under certain conditions, enslaving the black Africa was a *reasonable* decision'.

[87] Bisset, *A Treatise on the Scurvy. Design'd Chiefly for the Use of the British Navy.*, 10.

[88] Ibid., 41.

similarly paired whites and blacks on the grounds of their shared habituation. 'The *Negroes* and *Creoles*, sleeping without Hurt in the Dews,' he wrote, 'is a proof how far the Constitution may be framed and accustomed to bear what otherwise is so highly prejudicial'.[89]

Climatic explanations applied *within* a given region thus tended to produce (perhaps unnerving) similarities. We should therefore not be surprised to find that, within a slave society like the West Indies or colonial settings like those in India, climate alone was more rarely invoked to explicate medical distinctions between blacks/Africans and whites/Europeans than other elements. Far more common were invocations of particularistic diets and behaviours, which served to re-affirm important differences without making such differences either essential or unchangeable. J. Z. Holwell, for example, offered a sympathetic *Account of the Manner of Inoculating for the Small-Pox in the East Indies* (1767), one that extensively praised and recommended the practices deployed by Bengali Brahmins. He was somewhat less enthusiastic, however, about the dietary habits of the natives of the Island of St Helena, whose overuse of yam, in particular, seemed to incline them to death when afflicted with the smallpox.[90] Writing about the dysentery as it appeared on the Bite of Benin on the Guinea Coast in the mid-1780s, Robert Atchison also pointed an accusatory finger at the use of yams or fish as a 'chief food' instead of grains. Coupled with a climate where labour was largely unnecessary to supply human wants, the result were slaves who were of a 'very weak habit of body, subjected to disorders in a most remarkable degree', in stark contrast to those found on the Windward Coast, where grain was plentiful and the enslaved were strong, hardy, and 'consequently less subject to disorders than any others'.[91] James Hendy paired the putrid dysentery with leprosy in 1784 in a discussion of the effects a change of diet had effected on Barbados in the last quarter century. Earlier, he suggested, Negroes had eaten a great deal of flying fish and salted fish. Now that their diet consisted largely of vegetables, both diseases were considerably less common.[92]

Perhaps as part of an indirect criticism of what was increasingly being cast as the gluttony and intemperance of white West Indian Creoles, some authors

---

[89] Lind, note, 69.

[90] 'African Coffries', he noted, appeared to have the same mortal susceptibility, 'altho' I know not what to ascribe it to, unless we suppose one similar to that above mentioned, to wit, some fundamental aggravating principle in their chief diet'. J. Z. Holwell, *An Account of the Manner of Inoculating for the Small Pox in the East Indies* (London: T. Becket and P.A. De Hondt, 1767), 6.

[91] Robert Atchison, 'Observations on the Dysentery, as it Appears among the Negroes on the Coast of Guinea', *Medical Commentaries* 9 (1785): 268–9.

[92] Hendy, note, 43–4.

saw fit to praise the sparse and limited diet forced upon slaves.[93] John Quier, in a letter written to Donald Monro in 1770, suggested that the small amount of meat available to the enslaved was probably partly responsible for the relative absence of bilious complaints among them.[94] The anonymous author of a 1776 text providing *Practical Remarks on West India Diseases* similarly lauded the food customarily eaten by slaves in the context of a broader social taxonomy of West Indian life based on diet. People living in warm climates, the author claimed, could be divided according to whether they ate mostly animal food, a mixture of animal and vegetable food, or mostly vegetable food. This tripartite division mapped onto social distinctions between European men of all classes, women and Creoles, and Negroes. Upper class Europeans in the tropics, it was argued, indulged in plentiful quantities of meat and strong liquor, while lower class Europeans ate animal food of lower quality, such as salted provisions, and drank substantial quantities of new rum. As a result, both fell victim to bilious complaints. Women and creoles moderated their consumption of meat with 'various salads, fruits and vegetable compounds of the country' and displayed an admirable temperance with regard to drink.[95] Negroes, finally, had meals that were largely vegetable, with some small portion of salted animal food. The medical outcome of this diet was, according to the author, straightforward. 'To their food alone it is they are indebted for an exemption from the variety of diseases arising rather from a superabundance or acrimony of the bilious fluid; insomuch that acute bilious disorders are to be met with in no negroes'. The only exceptions to this rule allowed by the author – and that with a more than somewhat moralising edge – were when slaves were, though their connections with white people, allowed to 'indulge in luxury and idleness, and that kind of living which more properly place them in the first class'.[96] That said, a vegetable diet had its own problems, leading to worms, jaundice, and stomach-complaints, such as pains, diarrhoea, and constipation.

Other authors were thankfully either more equivocal or straightforwardly critical of the limitations of slave diets. In his *Essay on the More Common West-India Diseases,* James Grainger argued that the excessive consumption of 'new fiery spirits' by slaves resulted in more cases of the distemper known as the 'dry belly-ache'.[97] One might expect blacks to suffer more from

---

[93] Christer Petley, 'Gluttony, Excess, and the Fall of the Planter Class in the British Caribbean', *Atlantic Studies* 9 (2012).

[94] Monro et al., 192–3.

[95] Anonymous, *Practical Remarks on West India Diseases*, 8.

[96] Ibid., 9.

[97] Grainger, 'An Essay on the More Common West-India Diseases, James Grainger, MD (1764), with Additional Notes by William Wright, MD, FRS (1802)', 27–8. The intemperance of slaves was a complaint made by several authors. See also Anonymous, *Practical Remarks on West India Diseases*, 10.

heartburn as well, given that they ate far more vegetable matter than whites. That they were spared this discomfort, Grainger put down to well-salted and – seasoned greens and the fact they 'drink little punch and no wine'.[98] William Chamberlaine also pointed to the downsides of a mainly vegetable diet, in an account of the efficacy of cowhage as a treatment for worms. 'Very little animal food comes to the share of a negro slave', he noted, and what was available was 'of the most indigestible kind', such as salted fish and cured meat. Almost sole reliance on vegetable food meant that it was rare to see a negro child, Chamberlaine claimed, without a swollen belly or other symptoms due to worms.[99] Writing from Demerary almost at the end of the century, William Macbeth pointed not to food as the cause of 'a singular affection of the urinary organs', but to drink. Negroes, he claimed, had to drink 'bush-water', while whites did not, which led to the discrepancy in susceptibility to the affliction. Macbeth strengthened his case by noting that the two cases of whites suffering from the illness came about when rain-water was scarce, and that there were very few cases among black 'domestics', who drank the same cistern water as white plantation owners.

Of course, not all afflictions seemed to have dietetic causes. While the author of *Practical Remarks on West-India Diseases* argued that a want of luxury in diet meant that blacks were spared some diseases, he noted that they were plagued by many due to their occupations, 'which expose them to every change and inclemency of the weather'.[100] In this way, he suggested, they were like European sailors and soldiers, although their disorders were probably even more acute. Lewis Rouppe, who had practiced both medicine and surgery in the French army and Dutch navy, made a similar observation in his doctoral thesis, completed in Leiden in 1764, on the diseases of seamen. Rouppe seemed astonished by the fact that West Indian slaves did not suffer from scurvy, while European sailors did.[101] Rouppe's best guess was that slaves did better from the fact that they ate fruit unavailable to men at sea. It was, in fact, a commonplace to point to slaves' exposure to the elements and environment – either through poor housing or clothing – as the cause of multiple distempers. C. Chisholm reported on a West Indian liver disease to which all 'people of

---

[98] Grainger, 'An Essay on the More Common West-India Diseases, James Grainger, MD (1764), with Additional Notes by William Wright, MD, FRS (1802)', 37–8.

[99] William Chamberlaine, *A Practical Treatise on the Efficacy of Stizolobium, or Cowhage, Internally Administered, in Diseases Occasioned by Worms. To Which Are Added, Observations on Other Anthelmintic Medicines of the West Indies* (London: J. Murray, 1784), 3–4.

[100] Anonymous, *Practical Remarks on West India Diseases*, 10.

[101] 'But whosoever considers the situation of the negroes, who are slaves to the Europeans in the West-Indies, and compares their food with that of the sailors; the huts in which they dwell, their want of cloaths and covering, and the miserable life which they lead, will wonder that these unhappy creatures can escape the scurvy'. Rouppe, 133–4.

all colours, sexes, and ages' were subject, but to which blacks and the young were particularly liable. 'The distinction', he argued, 'appears to have chiefly arisen from the greater exposure of the negroes to the cold dews of the night, and their habitations more readily admitting the cold northerly winds which generally blow at that time'.[102] Quier blamed the frequency of stomach and bowel disorders among negroes to their greater exposure to the 'vicissitudes of the weather than white people', while Hendy argued that negroes in Barbados suffered from a glandular disease there because of their poor clothing, although wealthy white inhabitants were also victims, because of their foolish insistence on sleeping with their windows open to the night air.[103] Lack of adequate shoe-wear led to chigoes and sores.[104]

In amongst all of these differences between the kinds of illnesses that troubled blacks and whites, the degrees of their severity, and the capacity to recover, one finds – for most of the eighteenth century – little talk of innate, *racial* distinctions. Chamberlaine may have observed that the blood of negroes was different to that of white people – thinner, for example, and 'less disposed to coagulate' – but this was due to hard labour in a hot climate, to a lack of time to rest, and a vegetable diet.[105] Quier similarly argued that negro constitutions were 'more robust' than that of whites, and hence less inclined to bilious diseases, but this robustness was not given from birth, but gained 'on account of the labour and hardships they go though'.[106] The broadest statement of the inessentiality of the differences that divided white and black patients came from the author of the *Practical Remarks*. Variety in food and forms of labour, he argued, led to different diseases, but if one held all such changeable causes equal, then all peoples were equally liable to the same afflictions: 'for though these various circumstances have most undoubtedly an effect on the consti-tution, so as to make it more susceptible of certain diseases, yet that can by no means imply the impossibility of the like symptoms, and being, *caeteris paribus*, equally contingent to the whole race of mankind in these climates'.[107]

7.3   Racial Pathologies

It was the central contention of Chapter 5 that 'race-medicine' as I have defined the term did not really exist prior to at least the 1750s. Even a polygenist such

---

[102] C. Chisholm, 'The History of a Singular Affection of the Liver, Which Prevailed Epidemically in Some Parts of the West Indies', *Medical Commentaries* Second Decade, Vol. 1 (1787): 357.
[103] Monro et al., 192–3. Hendy, 31–2.
[104] Hendy, 32.
[105] Chamberlaine, 7.
[106] Monro et al., 193.
[107] Anonymous, *Practical Remarks on West India Diseases*, 30.

as John Atkins did not make use of conceptions of intrinsic racial difference in his explanations of the causes of diseases common among the inhabitants of the Guinea Coast. I show here that matters would be different in the last decades of the century, with at least half a dozen writers from the mid-1770s to 1820 putting forward medical theories of the difference between black and white bodies. Such theories, I show, can be divided according to the dominant medical logics of the day. Those up until the mid-1780s tended to work within what I have called the 'putrefactive paradigm', stressing the ability of African skin to throw out the putrid matter that was so easily produced in warm climes. Dark skin was thus an advantage, but one that was put to work in defending the use of black enslaved labour in the colonies against the charges of abolitionists. From the late 1780s, putrefactive theories were increasingly replaced by the nervous theories most commonly associated with Haller and Cullen. Within the nervous paradigm, more emphasis was placed on the differential 'sensibility' of black and white bodies. Moving inward, physicians found race to be more than skin deep, and black bodies were less able to feel pain or discomfort, for putatively physiological reasons. What would be deemed poor treatment or neglect if endured by whites, then, could be deemed appropriate for slaves and the sharp critiques of abolitionists might be blunted. For a group of writers committed to claims about the essential differences between black and white bodies, paradigms might change, but medicine remained in the service of slavery.

'So Far From Suffering an Inconvenience': Medicine, Climate, and Labour

The sixth chapter of the second volume of Edward Long's massive *History of Jamaica* was concerned with 'Regulations for Preserving Health' on the island. Long had worked through the major authors on the diseases of warm climates, citing Pringle, Huxham, Bisset, Hillary, Rouppe, and De Monchy (among others), and at times resorting to near-plagiarism of the various works of James Lind. Long recommended gradual habituation to the new climate and the avoidance of swampy areas, 'infested with muskeetos, which seem as if placed there by the hand of Providence, to assault with their stings, and drive away every human being, who may ignorantly venture to fix his abode among them'.[108] Long also advocated wearing the loose garb of the 'Mandarin', rather than the heavy clothing favoured by Europeans, and the consumption of sugar – 'so welcome and necessary a substance' – as well as the 'mild vegetable acids' and peppers that grew locally, in order to combat the body's

---

[108] Long, *The History of Jamaica*, I, 506.

putrefactive tendencies.[109] When it came to the diseases customary among slaves, Long pointed to the standard causes: climate, diet, and behaviour. Negroes, for example, were the first to be afflicted with epidemic distempers because they indulged 'too liberally' in fruits and roots after the heavy rains that followed a long drought.[110] On the positive side, however, the 'custom of the negroes' to light fires in their dwellings in order to drive away mosquitoes 'has another good effect, the correcting of the night air, and disarming it of its damp and chill, which might be prejudicial to their healths'.[111] And, erasing putative racial distinctions, Long contrasted the diseases characteristic of those born on Jamaica – regardless of colour – to those of newly arrived Europeans.

The natives, black and white, are not subject, like Europeans, to bilious, putrid, and malignant fevers: they are not only habituated to the climate, but to a difference in respect to diet and manners; which works no small change in men's constitutions. A Creole, if he was to addict himself to that kind of diet which is known to have a tendency to produce disorders, or an acrid, corrupt bile, would no more be exempt from them, than an European.[112]

In most cases, then, broadly Hippocratic conceptions, coupled with an emphasis on nativity, served to explain the diseases of all groups on the island. I can, in fact, find only one part of this chapter in which Long emphasised intrinsic physical differences between black and white bodies. It came, tellingly, in a discussion about the relative capacity to labour in tropical climates and invoked Benjamin Franklin as its authority. 'Dr Franklin very properly concludes', he noted, 'that the quicker evaporation of perspirable matter from the skin and lungs of Negroes, by cooling them more, enables them to bear the sun's heat so much better than the Whites can do; though, abstracted from this, the colour of their skins would, otherwise, make them more sensible of that heat'. Franklin, who had made these observations in a letter to the South Carolinian physician John Lining in 1758 had made clear his awareness of the stakes of this question: 'if this is a fact, as it is said to be', he noted parenthetically, 'for the alledg'd necessity of having negroes rather than whites, to work in the West-India fields, is founded upon it'.[113] Long had, in fact, invoked a more explicitly medicalised version of this argument earlier in his text, precisely to defend black slavery (and simultaneously taking the opportunity to critique

---

[109] Ibid., 549–50, 28.
[110] Ibid., II: 614.
[111] Ibid., I: 510.
[112] Ibid., 534.
[113] In Benjamin Franklin, *Experiments and Observations on Electricity* (London: Printed for David Henry, 1769), 363–8. The same claims were made in the United States, of course. Curtin notes that 'some believed that whites could not even do hard labour as far north as South Carolina'. Curtin, *The Image of Africa: British Ideas and Action, 1780–1850*, 85.

slaves for their promiscuity). 'Negroes', he asserted, so far from suffering an inconvenience, are found to labour with most alacrity and ease to themselves in the very hottest part of the day ... The openness of their pores gives a free transpiration to bad humours; and they would enjoy robust health, under the hardest toils expedient here, if they were less prone to debauch, and venereal excess'.[114]

As Jordan observed in *White over Black,* the trope that held that black skin conferred advantages when labouring in warm climates was very common in the eighteenth century, but also usually 'formless and imprecise'.[115] One can see, however, that medical discussions formed one site for a general claim to acquire form and precision. In 1780, the physician Johann Peter Schotte had his weather diary for a year spent on the island of St Lewis, in the river Senegal, communicated to the Royal Society by Joseph Banks.[116] In 1782, he reproduced that letter in a larger book dedicated to the analysis of a fever that had broken out in Senegal at the beginning of August 1778 and had raged until the middle of September.[117] Counting those who survived the initial onslaught, but relapsed later, 59 of 92 white people were dead at the end of January the next year.[118] Schotte offered no precise count of native deaths, but he did note that 'Europeans suffered much more by it, in proportion, than the mulattoes, and those much more, than the blacks'.[119] Increasing darkness of skin (or at least decreasing admixture of 'European' characteristics), in other words, seemed to offer some protection, but only once the disease struck. 'The blacks are almost as subject to it as white people', Schotte observed, 'but in them it is not so violent'.[120] Interestingly, he did not put this differential mortality down to diet, although he noted that brackish water and a diet consisting overwhelmingly of animal food, as well as excessive sweating seemed to produce a disposition to the disease, which then required only the addition of 'human contagion' to become manifest. Nor did Schotte suggest that blacks were proportionately spared because of their nativity or seasoning. Indeed, Schotte argued that those

[114] Long, *The History of Jamaica*, II, 412.

[115] Jordan, 261. See also 526–7.

[116] J. P. Schotte, 'Journal of the Weather at Senegambia, During the Prevalence of a Very Fatal Putrid Disorder, with Remarks on That Country', *Philosophical Transactions* 70 (1780). Schotte communicated a second letter, via Banks, three years later. 'A Description of a Species of Sarcocele of a Most Astonishing Size in a Black Man in the Island of Senegal: With Some Account of Its Being an Endemial Disease in the Country of Galam', *Philosophical Transactions* 73 (1783).

[117] *A Treatise on the Synochus Atrabiliosa, a Contagious Fever, Which Raged at Senegal in the Year 1778, and Proved Fatal to the Greatest Part of the Europeans, and to a Number of the Natives.* (London: M. Scott, 1782).

[118] Ibid., 40.

[119] Ibid.

[120] Ibid., 108.

who had been in the country longer were 'more subject to some disorders, and have less chance of recovering from them, than fresh people from Europe'.[121] Instead, just as Long had, the physician pointed to the ability of black skin to allow an easier passage of matter that would prove dangerous if retained in the body.

[This] induces me to believe, that their bodies are constitutionally better adapted to throw off this rank and noxious matter, formed in the fluids, by the outlets of the skin, than the Europeans, and that it is for this reason, that they are less subject to those putrid diseases, which originate from its retention within the body; for it cannot be supposed, that this noxious matter should be more copiously generated in their bodies, than in those of Europeans, as they seem to be intended by Nature to inhabit that country.[122]

This explanation also supplied a cause for another 'fact' invoked casually but consistently in discussions of race from at least mid-century onwards: the claim, as Kant would put it, that 'all Negroes stink [*stinken*]'.[123] Schotte argued that the smell derived from sweat containing 'rancid and putrid particles', and that European perspiration also smelled bad in the humid months, 'though its fetor is not to be compared to that of the blacks'.[124] The latter bathed regularly, he observed, so the odour could not be due 'any nastiness harbouring on the surface of the skin'.[125] Instead, it must derive from the sweat itself, which did a better job in their bodies than in those of mulattoes or whites in removing toxic elements from their bodies.

Schotte would seem to have been flirting with polygenism with his suggestion that 'Nature' had intended blacks to live in warm climates and hence had purposefully adapted their skin to aid them there. Alexander Wilson, who had studied under Cullen at Edinburgh, was not so coy. In *Some Observations Relative to the Influence of Climate on Vegetable and Animal Bodies* (1780), he made arguments that combined phlogiston theory with claims about the cause of the blackness of skin, the capacity of such skin to keep its possessors healthier under the tropical sun, and the concomitant smell of 'phlogisticated' sweat:

---

[121] Ibid., 115–16.

[122] Ibid., 105.

[123] Kant, 151. The essay is reproduced, with the same pagination, in Robert Bernasconi, ed. *Concepts of Race in the Eighteenth Century. Volume 3: Kant and Forster* (Bristol: Thoemmes Press, 2001). See also Long, who listed the 'bestial or fetid smell' of negroes as one of five physical differences between them and whites. 'This rancid exhalation', he noted somewhat later, 'for which so many of the Negroes are remarkable, does not seem to proceed from uncleanliness, nor the quality of their diet'. Long, *The History of Jamaica*, I, 352, 425.

[124] Schotte, *A Treatise on the Synochus Atrabiliosa, a Contagious Fever, Which Raged at Senegal in the Year 1778, and Proved Fatal to the Greatest Part of the Europeans, and to a Number of the Natives.*, 105. Cf. Curtin, *The Image of Africa: British Ideas and Action, 1780–1850*, 85.

[125] Schotte, *A Treatise on the Synochus Atrabiliosa, a Contagious Fever, Which Raged at Senegal in the Year 1778, and Proved Fatal to the Greatest Part of the Europeans, and to a Number of the Natives.*, 104.

The perspiration of negroes is of a strong pungent alkaline odour, which seems to arise from some peculiar property or power in the reticular covering which gives colour to the skin. This extraordinary reticulated perspiration, so remarkable in blacks, we suppose, depends on the powers of secretion in the *rete mucosum*, by which the putrescent matter is more copiously discharged from the surface of the body; and undoubtedly a more free discharge of the putrescent effluvium by the skin, may not only liberate the constitution in a certain degree, but tend to produce the very blackness in the *rete mucosum* itself.[126]

We see in Wilson's text perhaps the best example of the close interlocking of polygenist and medical arguments in the later eighteenth century. 'From these very distinguishing marks', he concluded, 'negroes seem a peculiar variety of the human species, better fitted by nature than those of fair complexions to discharge by the pores of the skin the phlogiston evolved from their bodies, and consequently much better adapted to the warm climates'.[127] What is perhaps most striking about Wilson's claims, however, is that they made explicit the profound limitations of medical polygenist arguments in this period. His polygenist contentions only concerned black people, while his arguments about medicalised racial characteristics were limited to assertions about the *benefits* of black skin in warm climes. Otherwise, as the title of his book might have suggested, almost all of his arguments dealt with the role played by climate in producing (neither fixed nor racialised) differences in animal and vegetable bodies.

On the matter of skin colour, for example, Wilson argued that it was caused by the discharge of phlogiston through the skin, and that phlogiston was released when bodies putrefied. Putrefaction was greater in warmer climates, hence the darker skin of those living nearer the equator. The darker skin of those near the poles, on the other hand, was due to their great consumption of animal food, particularly fish (which putrefied easily), coupled with the fact that cold weather hindered perspiration and the carrying off of putrid matter, thus allowing it to remain and build up in the body.[128] Much less phlogiston passed through the skin in temperate climates, 'and in consequence the colour and appearances of body, and faculties of mind, of the nations of the middle regions, are as widely different from those of the torrid and frigid zones, as the climates which produce and nourish them'.[129] Brownness of skin was thus 'acquirable ... by a long continued habitual putrescency' but it could also be reversed: within even a few generations 'a better colour, form, and understanding' could be brought to Indians, for example, if they were brought to the temperate latitudes

---

[126] Wilson, Andrew, 270.

[127] Ibid., 270–1.

[128] . 'A putrescent tendency is the only point in which the inhabitants of the torrid and frigid zones are necessarily alike from circumstances of climate, and this cause alone', he opined, 'seems capable of regulating their external appearance, as well as mental faculties'. Ibid., 261–2.

[129] Ibid., 263.

of the globe.[130] Blackness, however, could be neither gained nor lost. Negroes, and negroes alone, were the result of a creation separate to that of the rest of humanity.

And yet, in spite of this original difference, black bodies *ceteris paribus* largely suffered from the same diseases and for the same reasons, as whites. Unusually for the time, Wilson claimed that a diet largely made up of animal food was a positive thing in warm climates. In the heat, such food was broken down more easily and provided strength to the entire bodily frame. If it was strong in health, however, it was also more prone to putrid illnesses. Thus it was that negroes – deprived of meat, for the most part – were seldom afflicted by such distempers. It was therefore diet and not race that made the difference in medical terms, as Wilson would state explicitly: 'what proves this in a still stronger manner is, that negro domestics, who live on animal food, are as subject to putrid epidemics as the white inhabitants'.[131] If whites and 'negro domestics' were thus more inclined to some diseases by their shared mode of life, they were also spared in common. Neither were often struck down by tetanus, unless (in the case of whites) they were 'reduced to a low and very relaxed state by long sickness or excessive debauchery', while the disease was common among labourers.[132] Once again, diseases were, for the most part, caused by climate, diet, and behaviour.

We have looked here at three texts, published within less than a decade of one another. The authors of each were very different. Long had no formal medical training while Schotte and Wilson were both physicians. Long was drawing on his experiences in the West Indies, Schotte from Senegal, and Wilson from unspecified 'warm climates'.[133] Yet, in terms of their claims, the similarities are abundant. All either explicitly or implicitly denied monogenist orthodoxy; all pointed to the black skin of those from Africa as a racial peculiarity; but all also seemed to suggest that the truly significant medical characteristic of black skin was not primarily its colour, but rather the protection it afforded its possessor in warm climates. And they identified that protection in the same way. Franklin had argued natural philosophically, so to speak, positing that dark skin allowed the easier passage of perspiration, which then evaporated on the outer surface of the skin. Long, Schotte, and Wilson on the other hand, argued medically, stressing not the perspiration alone, but rather what it carried with it: black skin allowed dangerous matter (bad humours for Long, rancid and putrid particles for Schotte, phlogiston for Wilson) to be expelled from the body more easily than white skin, one side effect being the racialised smell supposedly typical

---

[130] Ibid., 271, 72.
[131] Ibid., 173.
[132] Ibid., 182.
[133] Ibid., v.

of negroes. The three also held in common what they did *not* argue. Race did not make much of a difference in susceptibility to the vast majority of diseases. And where blacks might be *afflicted* disproportionately, rather than protected, the cause was never innate. Of course, we should not be misled or confused by claims that suggested black superiority on any issue, particularly not when such arguments were made by those arguing that all humans were not of the same species. The ability to function better than whites meant, fundamentally, the ability to labour better than whites. One does not find here anything like Rush's attempts to assert the suitability of Africans for their own climates, but their fundamental unsuitability to work as slaves in the new world. This was a medicine either explicitly or implicitly in defence of unfreedom.

Black Beneath the Skin

In Chapter 4 I discussed Benjamin Moseley as one of the first writers on the diseases of warm climates to turn against the putrefactive paradigm. In its place, he proffered a nervous theory of tropical diseases, relying particularly on the work of Albrecht von Haller and William Cullen. It was Haller's distinction between the 'sensible' and 'irritable' parts of animals that Moseley would draw upon in attempting to elucidate the differences between black and white bodies.[134] In Moseley's hands, the distinction between the irritable and the sensible became a racial trait. His *Treatise on Tropical Diseases* (1787) tended not to discuss the afflictions of the enslaved population in any detail, but in considering tetanus, he drew a number of observations together. The locked jaw, he asserted, was a disease 'entirely of irritability' and not of sensibility, meaning it affected only the muscles and not the nerves. Negroes, he observed (as had many medical men before him, citing various different reasons) were particularly subject to the disease. And Negroes, he continued:

whatever the cause may be, are void of sensibility to a surprising degree. They are not subject to nervous diseases. They sleep sound in every disease; nor does any mental disturbance ever keep them awake. They bear chirurgical operations much better than white people; and what would be the cause of insupportable pain to a white man, a Negro would almost disregard.[135]

---

[134] 'I call that part of the human body irritable', Haller had written, 'which becomes shorter upon being touched ... I call that a sensible part of the human body, which upon being touched transmits the impression of it to the soul; and in brutes, in whom the existence of a soul is not so clear, I call those parts sensible, the irritation of which occasions evident signs of pain and disquiet in the animal'. Only those parts of the body that possessed nerves, Haller discovered, were sensible, while irritability was a property of muscle fibres. Albrecht von Haller, *A Dissertation on the Sensible and Irritable Parts of Animals [London, J. Nourse, 1755]* (Baltimore: Johns Hopkins Press, 1936), 8–9.

[135] Moseley, *A Treatise on Tropical Diseases; And on the Climate of the West-Indies*, 472–3.

It does not take a cynical reader to suspect that Moseley's interest in reporting his beliefs on black insensitivity to pain and suffering (however firmly believed) might be related to criticisms levelled by abolitionists against planters and their harsh treatment of the enslaved. That suspicion seems confirmed when one notes that, having made so much of essential differences between the two main racial groups on the island, and having suggested that there might be some connection between a given, apparently racial, characteristic and a specific disease, Moseley did little with this racial difference in his further analysis of the disease. He noted, as had many others, that black children were 'chiefly the victims of this disease in the West-Indies', that the numbers of those who perished by it annually 'are scarcely to be credited', and 'This drain of native inhabitants is far more detrimental to estates in the course of time, than all other casualties put together'.[136] But in adducing the causes, neither irritability nor sensibility was mentioned. Moseley rejected a range of previous explanations, from the intemperance or even wickedness of the mother, to irritation of the navel after birth, to the impact of damp, cold, or smoke upon the newborn. Instead, he suggested simply that the ignorance of the mother and the lack of necessities in keeping the child dry and clean were to blame.

If Moseley was somewhat vague about the precise connections between race and susceptibility to disease, Dr Collins was clearer. In 1811, under the pseudonym 'A Professional Planter', Collins published his *Practical Rules for the Management and Medical Treatment of Negro Slaves in the Sugar Colonies*. In it, he was critical of earlier authors on the diseases of the climate (Moseley included) who had not 'devoted their pens very particularly to the subject of negro disorders', effectively generalising from their treatment of whites. Yet whites, Collins noted, 'have all the advantages of good nursing, lodging, and medical attendance' that were usually denied slaves.[137] Thus far, Collins was following the dietetic and environmentalist orthodoxy I described in Section 7.1, but he proceeded to add a further, seemingly fixed and innatist distinction: 'Besides, there are many striking variations between the temperaments of the whites, and those of the negroes, sufficient almost to induce a belief of a different organization, which the knife of the anatomist, however, has never been able to detect'. The first was one with which the reader is now familiar: levels of heat that were 'intolerable' to whites were 'pleasant' and 'even necessary' to the negro.[138] The import of such a claim should be equally familiar. Collins rejected utterly the claims of abolitionists that the fields of

---

[136] Ibid., 508, 12.
[137] A Professional Planter (Dr Collins), *Practical Rules for the Management and Medical Treatment of Negro Slaves in the Sugar Colonies* (New York: Books for Libraries Press, 1971), 199–200.
[138] Ibid., 200.

the West Indies could be worked by free men, whether white or black. For all races, heat 'not only extinguishes the power, but the will, for exertion', and for Europeans who were under a 'corporeal disability', the effect was even greater.[139] Not only slavery, but specifically black slavery, was an economic and physical necessity.

The other medical differences of 'temperament' between whites and blacks were somewhat more novel. Europeans were vastly more susceptible to fevers, Collins claimed. More than nineteen out of twenty Europeans were killed by them, while barely one in a hundred negroes were. On the other hand, negroes were more subject to bowel complaints than whites, a fact that Collins put down not to any intrinsic variation, but to food, clothing, housing, and exposure to the elements. Most significantly for our purposes, Collins insisted that in terms of treatments, neither nauseous drugs nor blisters had the effects of black bodies that they did on whites. '[T]here is reason to think', Collins concluded, 'that the sensibilities, both of their minds and bodies, are much less exquisite than our own'. Travelling the same road as Moseley, he added: 'they are able to endure, with few expressions of pain, the accidents of nature, which agonize white people'. Yet where Moseley left the matter there, Collins offered an explanation. 'It is difficult to account for this otherwise than by supposing (which probably is the case) that animal sufferings derive a great part of their activity from the operations of the intellect'.[140] The power of such a set of claims should be clear. On the one hand, Collins could stand with the orthodox when discussing disease causation, relating it to dietetic, behavioural, and environmental factors. There were no diseases, he acknowledged, 'peculiar to either constitution, which may not be entertained by both'.[141] Differences were a matter of degree and not kind. On the other hand, he could still deploy racialist and essentialist arguments that denigrated the intellectual and emotional capacities of black people. Such arguments required no concrete anatomical evidence, since they were apparently undetectable by the 'knife of the anatomist', but they had palpable effects in terms of the day to day practice of medicine. 'It will be observed', he wrote, 'that in the treatment of negro disorders, I have frequently departed from the rules laid down by European practitioners; and that has been done, as well from a regard to the peculiarities of their constitutions, as to their general habits of life, which neither require, nor admit of the refinement practiced with respect to white patients'.[142] Many physicians had simply taken it for granted that black and white patients would be treated differently.[143]

---

[139] Ibid., 31.
[140] Ibid., 201. On race, gender, class, and assumed sensitivity to pain, see Pernick.
[141] A Professional Planter, 202.
[142] Ibid., 215–16.
[143] For example, Chamberlaine: '[T]he very small annual sum allowed to surgeons, for the care of negroes in the country parts, will not admit of the exhibition of very expensive medicines'.

With Collins, one finds an attempt at a justification for this rooted not in the brute social and economic realities of a slave system, but in the seemingly intangible but essential physiological peculiarities of the races.

Conclusion

I will leave for the concluding chapter a more comprehensive discussion of the multiple relationships between theories of the diseases of warm climates and theories of race. Here, I want to end by pointing to the specific stakes for the history of race and 'race science' in this chapter. In general, as Chapter 5 also showed, conceptions of the causes for the distempers of the tropics were environmentalist and variable, working almost precisely against any notion that the illnesses of any given 'race' might be innate or fixed. For most of the century, that was true, too, of the majority of theories of the origins of racial differences, which were usually ascribed to climatic causes acting on a single human species. Yet, as we have seen, even those committed to monogenism were, by the 1770s, beginning to question the extent to which climate, diet, or behaviour could explain all of the characteristic features of the peoples of the world. The doctrine of special creations remained heterodoxy – although less heterodox than earlier – but race was hardening as a concept. Medicine, I would suggest, played a not insubstantial role in this hardening, but it did so in ways that were not straightforward.

Authors trying to understand the reification of racial conceptions at the end of the eighteenth century have long pointed to the abolitionist debate as one somewhat counter-intuitive locus for discussions. Black slavery required little explicit justification prior to the 1750s – no more, that is, than the other forms of slavery common to the West from at least the classical age. In response to the strident humanitarian critiques of men like Benezet, however, one finds both explicit forms of polygenism being floated – blunting humanitarianism by weakening the African's claim to humanity – and more subtle and unexpected reactions. One of these was the attempt to pay attention to the diseases of slaves, thereby rebutting the charges of neglect and lack of care made by Ramsay and others. In tracts like Grainger's, however, what emerges is a narrow focus on those afflictions that differentiated Europeans from Afro-Caribbeans – else why produce a work separate to the extant treatises on the

Chamberlaine, 20. Or Makittrick-Adair: 'White children generally used the warm pediluvium for some nights before the period of eruption; but the number of negro patients was so great as to render it impracticable, at least very inconvenient'. James Makittrick-Adair, 'Observations on Regimen and Preparation under Inoculation, and on the Treatment of the Natural Small-Pox, in the West Indies. To Which Are Added, Strictures on the Suttonian Practice; in a Letter to Dr Andrew Duncan' *Medical Commentaries* 8 (1784): 240.

diseases of the climate? Such works remained Hippocratic, for the most part, in the sense that they looked at 'airs, waters, and places', yet their focus was always on difference – in diet, in customs, in housing – rather than the broader similitudes that climatic arguments might suggest. This was not a reification of race, but it did contribute to a kind of boundary-making that stressed nativity or creolisation (regardless of colour) less than it did cultural differences inscribed onto differently coloured bodies.

In more heterodox accounts, which were becoming more common, one finds a blending of anatomical conceptions of race (rooted in the skin, for example) with medical paradigms, the combination working to affirm the interests of planters and those who participated in the man-trade. General assertions about the capacity of Africans and their descendants to labour in conditions deadly to Europeans were given a medical extension. Black skin not only cooled when it should have warmed, but it also encouraged the removal of the putrefactive elements that built up within the body in hot and humid conditions. As putrefactive theories waned in the last decades of the century, medical apologists argued for other innate physical differences between blacks and whites, rooting these in the nervous system, and arguing that withholding from slaves the kind of careful and sensitive treatment that would be standard for Europeans was not merely an economic decision, but one based on physiological differences.

Whether heterodox or not, medicine and racialised forms of difference were clearly, if complexly intertwined. That complexity is part of the value of the topic. I have long been struck by a sentence in Blumenbach's dissertation at the moment where he turned away from a focus on skin towards skulls: 'I intend to treat now a little more at length upon that part of the argument which has to do with skulls', he wrote, 'since things very nearly allied may be conveniently embraced and handled at the same time'.[144] The 'things' of the sentence here would seem to include not only conceptual matters, but the objects themselves. In the quiet of a study, the natural historian might handle and compare solid representations of racial variety. Precisely this was denied to the student of race-medicine. Skulls might be considered immutable mobiles: diseases most certainly were not. Moreover, for the historian trying to reconstruct the logics behind the study of diseases *in situ*, the contexts of colonialism and slavery are unavoidable. Racial difference, whether rooted in a nominally changeable set of dietetic or cultural practices, or bred in the skin, bone, and nerves increasingly shaped the interactions between medical men and their patients. In turn, forms of medical knowledge increasingly shaped the course of colonialism and abolition.

[144] Blumenbach, 114.

Conclusion: Place, Race, and Empire

In the introduction I noted that this work was conceived as an example of the postcolonial history of colonial science and medicine: 'postcolonial' because it takes as its subject the emergence and maintenance in colonial settings of categories that structured colonial relations and modes of life (and that continue to function as categories in a world after formal de-colonisation). In its three parts, this book has tracked changing understandings of place, race, and empire. To end, then, let me lay out both the state of such understandings at the end of the eighteenth century and the ways in which the three were conjugated with one another.[1] How, to put it simply, were ideas about locatedness, racial pathologies, and imperial power thought together in medical texts?

Locality and Expertise

It was a common refrain, in the first part of the eighteenth century, for medical men to bemoan the paucity of texts that might guide them in their practices beyond British or even European lands. In *Sea Diseases* (1706), William Cockburn evocatively spoke of the methods used by former 'Sea-Physicians', which had left no more trace than 'the Furrows a Ship makes in the Sea'.[2] Three years later, Thomas Bates similarly lamented 'the want of Books treating of Distempers incident to Seafaring People'.[3] As late as 1751, George Cleghorn

---

[1] On the 'conjugation' of forms of discourse, see Gabrielle Hecht, 'Rupture-Talk in the Nuclear Age: Conjugating Colonial Power in Africa', *Social Studies of Science* 32 (2002).

[2] Cockburn, *Sea Diseases: Or, a Treatise of Their Nature, Causes, and Cure. Also, an Essay on Bleeding in Fevers; Shewing, the Quantities of Blood to Be Let, in Any of Their Periods. The Second Edition Corrected and Much Improved*, 3. A similar sentiment is to be found in Cockburn's 1696 work: 'the paths of former Curers are as little perceptible, as the furrows made on the face of the Angry Abyss, by our lofty floating Forts', *An Account of the Nature, Causes, Symptoms, and Cure of the Distempers That Are Incident to Seafaring People with Observations on the Diet of the Sea-Men in His Majesty's Navy: Illustrated with Some Remarkable Instances of the Sickness of the Fleet During the Last Summer, Historically Related*.

[3] Thomas Bates, *An Enchiridion of Fevers Incident to Sea-Men (During the Summer) in the Mediterranean; ... The Second Edition, Corrected and Amended. With Several Medicinal Observations ...* (London: Printed for John Barns and sold by B. Bragg, 1709), ix.

confessed that he had not been long on the island of Minorca before he began to wish that those who had tried to treat distempers there and 'who must have seen' how much they differed from those in England 'had been at Pains to furnish their Successors with some Hints, some Observations, by which the fatal Consequences frequently attending those Diseases, might have been timely foreseen, or happily prevented'.[4] By the end of the century, however, many noted that the opposite was now true. William Lempriere spent some time at the beginning of his *Practical Observations on the Diseases of the Army in Jamaica* explaining why any further publications were necessary, given that the 'public are already in possession of so many valuable observations on the diseases of tropical climates, made by several authors, and at various periods'.[5] A few years earlier Thomas Reide had described what he called 'perhaps a matter of the greatest surprise to the medical world, that within these last few years more has been written on diseases between the tropics than had been before that period from the earliest discoveries in that part of the globe'.[6] Alas, for Reide, all of that production amounted to little useful, for no two authors could seem to agree on even the most basic points.

For some, the existence of works on topics related to their own concerns was a positive. Edward Ives noted in 1773 that he had once planned to write about the diseases to which Europeans were subject in the East Indies, but found no need to do so after Lind had published on similar matters.[7] But most saw the sheer number of new essays and books to be a problem: works abounded, but still left sizeable omissions and errors. Benjamin Moseley seemed to identify the root cause of the problem in the kinds of people who were writing the new studies. They were 'transient practitioners', men who 'make a few months voyage to the West Indies and bring home materials for a book, or a method of treating diseases', rather than acquiring the kind of knowledge that came only through a long residence.[8] In a twist on a debate that we have examined in several forms, Moseley was insisting that knowledge *in situ* was not itself sufficient. It was not enough to make observations on the spot, for these needed to be repeated over much time. The point might seem obvious, but he had particular targets in mind, namely those military men who used their (brief) time stationed in a country within the tropics to gather material for a publication. 'A transient practitioner', he wrote, 'more zealous to distinguish himself, than to benefit mankind, no sooner meets with a disease which he has never seen before, and perhaps does not remain long enough in a situation

---

[4] Cleghorn, vi.
[5] Lempriere, ix.
[6] Reide, xi.
[7] Ives, 447.
[8] Moseley, *A Treatise on Tropical Diseases; And on the Climate of the West-Indies*, 384.

to see again, than he transmits an account of it to his agent, who transmits it to his literary friend'.[9] Hence his specific warning, to 'inexperienced and transient practitioners; and such in the navy and army, whose residence may not be long enough to acquire a thorough and competent knowledge of the endemics of those countries'.[10] Those who had noticed a proliferation of works on the diseases of warm climates in the last decades of the century were not wrong, and the majority of the authors of such works were military men, seeing a market that they (and perhaps their 'agents' and 'literary friends') could exploit. Claiming 'twelve years extensive practice' in the West Indies, Moseley was unwilling to grant them the claimed expertise that they believed their time in the tropics had bought them.[11]

By the time of Moseley's writing, the most basic part of the debate over whether knowledge gained solely in the metropole could suffice in the colonies had been settled. Conditions were different enough in warm climates that a practitioner needed *some* local experience to have the authority to speak and be heard. One cannot imagine, in the late eighteenth century, a text like Cockburn's, which confessed openly to its author's complete lack of direct knowledge of climates far from Europe. Gilbert Blane's *Observations of the Diseases of Seamen* may stand as the polar opposite of Cockburn's, for Blane's confession in 1785 was that he *only* had experience of the diseases at sea in warm climates.[12] The question left was not *whether* local expertise was necessary, but rather, as Moseley made clear, how much was sufficient.

Moseley's text is remembered today in part because it was the first book to use the term 'tropical diseases' in its title. One must be wary of reading too much into this singular fact, but it is true that, by the beginning of the nineteenth century, there was a growing sense *both* that the diseases of the tropics were similar across widely divergent longitudes *and* that they were fundamentally different from those in more temperate latitudes, and particularly Britain. That is, it had come to be accepted (where, as we have seen, it had not been before) that there existed what might be called fundamental intra-zonal similitudes and inter-zonal differences when it came to disease environments.[13] Thus, for example, in 1788 John Hunter claimed generally, that there 'is much similarity among the diseases of warm climates', and more specifically, that the remittent fever 'described on the Coast of Africa and the banks of the Ganges would

---

[9] Ibid., 389–90.
[10] Ibid., 393.
[11] Ibid., xvii.
[12] Blane, 227.
[13] As I argued in Chapter 1, this is one of the issues on which I disagree with Harrison's similar attempts to explain how it came to be that the tropics were understood as a distinct disease zone. One cannot assume that such conceptions of difference were already extant in the West Indies in the late seventeenth century.

seem to be nearly the same as in Jamaica'.[14] Blane, similarly, was willing to admit that 'most of the diseases of one hot climate resemble those of another, so far as I know', although inflammation of the liver seemed to be an exception, being common in the East Indies and not often met with in the West.[15] Several authors explicitly paired similitude and difference. When troops were sent on an expedition into warm climates, Donald Monro advised, 'particular care should be taken to guard them against the diseases peculiar to such climates, which are different from those common to our more northern latitudes'.[16] For Moseley, there was a fundamental difference between 'the delightful climates of the earth, in temperate regions' and those, in the torrid zone, 'such as no care, nor art, can ever make agreeable'.[17] Lempriere shared Moseley's dismay, noting that 'the climate between the tropics, on so many occasions, has proved destructive to our fleets and armies' so that many now deemed extensive casualties to be unavoidable, with even the best regulations and discipline still involving the sacrifice of troops to the climate. Lempriere held out some hope, however. It was true 'that a tropical climate is unfavourable to the European constitution', but rational and judicious practices offered the possibility, at least, of alleviating its effects.[18]

Race and Place

It is not only in analyses of disease environments that this doubled move – the elision of 'smaller' differences in some areas and the expansion and elaboration of 'larger' ones – can be observed at the end of the eighteenth century. One finds it also in studies of the variation of human physical differences, or the races of humankind. Nineteenth-century racial thinking was characterised by three main tenets: first, that humankind could be divided into a comparatively small number of races, the characteristics of which were not easily modified (if at all) by cultural or physical causes; second, that races were not equal in terms of their intellectual and moral capacities; and third, that these intellectual and moral capacities bore measurable relationships to physical characteristics

---

[14] Hunter, *Observations on the Diseases of the Army in Jamaica; and on the Best Means of Preserving the Health of Europeans, in That Climate*, viii, ix.

[15] Blane, 91.

[16] Monro, *An Account of the Diseases Which Were Most Frequent in the British Military Hospitals in Germany, from January 1761 to the Return of the Troops to England in March 1763. To Which Is Added, an Essay on the Means of Preserving the Health of Soldiers, and Conducting Military Hospitals*, 331. The sentence is reproduced in the second edition, *Observations on the Means of Preserving the Health of Soldiers and of Conducting Military Hospitals. And on the Diseases Incident to Soldiers in the Time of Service, and on the Same Diseases as They Have Appeared in London. In Two Volumes. By Donald Monro, M.D*, 44.

[17] Moseley, *A Treatise on Tropical Diseases: And on the Climate of the West-Indies*, 1–2.

[18] Lempriere, 240–1.

of the body.[19] Unsurprisingly, most of the literature on the history of racial thinking has been concerned with uncovering the roots and fruits of the latter two ideas, reasoning (probably rightly) that the horrors of the nineteenth and twentieth centuries were more properly laid at the feet of biological determinism than the mere idea of racial division. One may note, at the very least, that of the three tenets listed, the only one that has remained continuously scientifically viable since the 1950 UNESCO Statement on Race is the first.[20]

That the first tenet feels familiar to a twenty-first century reader who still thinks (however informally) of five major races, each located on their own continent, should not blind us to its historical oddity. As Nicholas Hudson has shown in a now-classic essay, the word 'race' was originally used to designate a common bloodline or origin and was commonly used synonymously with the Latin term *gens*, often translated to mean 'peoples'.[21] Medieval and classical authors often identified as many peoples as there were cities or kingdoms. And, for the most part, such peoples were distinguished by what we would term cultural, rather than physical characteristics. Differences in language, custom, and religion thus trumped putative similarities in physical features – like skin colour or hair type – even when these could be found. It was far from natural, for example, for visitors to the New World to regard all the peoples they met as belonging to a single group. The Baron de Lahontan, travelling through Canada in the late seventeenth century, identified what he understood as eighty-five different 'nations'.[22] By contrast, for Immanuel Kant, in 1777, one needed only to speak of a single 'copper-red' American race, one of only four major divisions of humanity.[23] At some point during the eighteenth century, eyes that saw near-innumerable cultural differences among non-European peoples began only to see physical commonality.

To conclude this study of race, medicine, and empire, then, I wish to offer some reasons to explain the emergence of each pairing of inter-zonal difference and intra-zonal similarity and – however incompletely – to point to ways in which each is related to the other. Many authors have tried to explain why race should have emerged as an essentialist category at the end of the Enlightenment. Fewer have identified the same period as one in which the

---

[19] In Augstein's words, 'that mental endowments are bound up with certain physiognomical specificities which, being defined as racial characteristics, are considered to reveal the inward nature of the individual or the population in question'. Augstein, x.

[20] As Reardon has shown, the UNESCO statement actually enshrined this idea as scientific or expert orthodoxy, even as it advocated removing talk of race from popular or lay discourse. Jenny Reardon, *Race to the Finish: Identity and Governance in an Age of Genomics* (Princeton: Princeton University Press, 2005), 17–44.

[21] Hudson.

[22] Ibid., 250.

[23] Kant.

major opposition between 'tropical diseases' and those of Northern latitudes first emerged. I would contend that the two are not unconnected, for medicine was essential to the making of difference, and racial differences became integral to the theories and practices of medicine in the last decades of the eighteenth century.

I have pointed to some of these reasons already. The most obvious may be the slave trade. I noted in Chapter 2 that scholars have suggested that major demographic shifts can explain the *production* of a similar disease environment in the West Indies and the Guinea Coast where one had not existed before. The number of slaves brought from Africa to Jamaica increased dramatically across the eighteenth century. Insofar as diseases could be transmitted by the movement of people and goods, one would expect the introduction of distempers with a new population. William Hillary was in good company in claiming that many diseases had been 'imported with the African Negroes'. That said, many also disagreed with Hillary on some of his specific arguments. In 1784, for example, James Hendy wrote that he had asked 'many of the most intelligent *negroes* who have come from *Africa*' whether the yellow fever had been known in their country. They answered in the negative. Hendy claimed that it was not his intention to argue that a similar distemper did not exist in Africa, but rather that the disorder suffered in Barbados had not been brought from there. Agreeing with Hillary about the fact that the same disease could be found in two very different locations, Hendy was arguing over its aetiology. The point is worth stressing, for in explaining why actors *believed* that disease environments were similar (or had become so) in widely separated geographical regions, we must be careful not to impute modern beliefs and suppositions to them. Particularly in the case of yellow fever, we should be wary in awarding the laurel to either side of an eighteenth-century debate.[24]

The slave trade also, of course, played a role in the emergence of the concept of race, although not in the naïve way that some imagine. Race was not invented, in an instrumentalist fashion, in order to justify black slavery. Slavery had long pre-dated the use of Africans as slaves, and had long traditions of justifications within the West that did not rely on essentialist physical differences. As Hudson argued, however, the practices of slavery certainly provided the conditions of possibility for the elision of differences between

---

[24] It would not be until the twentieth century that it was generally accepted that the mosquito was the vector responsible for spreading the disease. Eighteenth-century contagionists were partly right, by our standards, for they had noted that the disease spread when large populations of the infected were located together, but they were not correct in imagining that the distemper was passed from person to person. Miasmatists may have been incorrect in imagining that the air around swamps was responsible for the illness, but of course such environments are prime breeding grounds for mosquitos.

slaves from widely different parts of the African continent: 'the process of shipping and marketing slaves literally stripped the signs of national difference from the bodies of Africans' as they were deprived of clothing, jewellery, and other cultural markers, while also being forced to learn a new and common language.[25] Evidence from slave holders also came to question the once-assumed obviousness of climatic explanations of physical difference. Black slaves seemed not to change colour over several generations; nor did white children born in the tropics. Observations made in locations in which black slaves were common seemed to point to a greater 'stickiness' of racial characteristics than had previously been imagined.

However, a more likely cause of the emergence of rigid racial conceptions, as I have argued, was not the beginning, but rather debates over the end of slavery. The practices of the trade in humans tended to produced similarities between diverse locations and similarities among diverse peoples. The abolitionist debate focused attention on differences. Proponents of slavery were more likely than others to invoke radical racial differences to justify their stance, but they too trod carefully. Even Edward Long balked, in his *History of Jamaica* (1774) at the straightforward association of human slaves with beasts of burden, managing to defend the trade and polygenism in the most odious terms without making this final step. Within medicine, particularly in the last decades of the century, one finds some examples of physicians ready to argue that racial difference was the cause of variations in physiology and pathology between whites and blacks. I have identified two foci for such arguments. First, attempts to evidence and defend the claim that black skin protected against the harsh sun, so that Negroes could labour without inconvenience in conditions potentially fatal to whites. And, second, arguments that deployed the new nervous theories of physiology and disease to provide reasons for the putative lesser sensitivity of black bodies to pain. This latter, in turn, served as a kind of license for precisely the kinds of neglect and poor medical treatment with which slave owners had been charged in anti-slavery propaganda.

More common and more orthodox medical arguments – across the century – tended not to invoke essentialist physical differences to explain diseases peculiar to given locations, following instead the broad logic of Hippocrates' *Airs, Waters, and Places*. Yet even these changed in response to abolitionist critiques, as plantation owners were forced to pay attention – or be seen to pay attention – to the tremendous losses of life among Afro-Caribbeans, both during the passage and the 'seasoning' and throughout the life cycle in the West Indies. Where climatic arguments worked well to explain why inhabitants of the Gold Coast, for example, suffered from different ailments to the English

---

[25] Hudson, 251.

(because the climate of each location was distinct), such arguments clearly seemed to do less work in explaining why black slaves and white Europeans in similar locations should be afflicted differently. In most texts that grappled with this problem, one does not find an emphasis on race, but one does find increasing attention to the medical differences that variations in culture and custom could make. For the most part, as well, differences in susceptibility to diseases were not given hard racialist explanations. Lind was only one of the first to argue that negroes should be used instead of white soldiers and sailors in tasks deemed dangerous. Yet he, like others, did not rely on differences in physical characteristics as justification, arguing instead that assigning such work to 'brave seamen' and 'gallant soldiers' did 'not seem consistent with British humanity'.[26] When Hunter offered a medical justification for a similar position, it was not on the grounds of essential difference, but rather because 'negroes afford a striking example of the power acquired by habit of resisting the causes of fevers'.[27] This emphasis on habituation should not surprise, given the discussion of the relative gendering of susceptibility offered in Chapter 5. The inhabitants of warm climates were deemed more immune to attacks of yellow fever, for example, because the climate rendered their bodily fibres more lax. Robust and masculine Englishmen would pay a price for their strength in such climates, but if they survived the seasoning they, too, would become more effeminate. Susceptibility was due to differences of degree, not kind.

New and newly focused forms of difference thus emerged over the bodies of slaves. They also emerged over the bodies of sailors and soldiers. I pointed in Chapter 3 to the effect of catastrophic losses at Cartagena in the 1740s as a particular turning point in the British public's understandings of the West Indies and the Americas as peculiarly dangerous locations for military men in service of the Empire. Cartagena cast a long shadow.[28] In 1787, Moseley observed that the debacle was unfortunately now better remembered for the 'flagrant enmity and jealousy between the commanders' than from the illnesses that 'made the crimes of individuals so expensive to the nation'.[29] A year later, Hunter made a somewhat different claim about the ways the venture were now recalled, but one that nonetheless emphasised losses due to disease: 'The unfortunate expedition against Carthagena is still remembered, more from the mortality

---

[26] See Chapter 3.
[27] Hunter, *Observations on the Diseases of the Army in Jamaica; and on the Best Means of Preserving the Health of Europeans, in That Climate*, 24.
[28] Harrison makes a related argument in Harrison, *Medicine in an Age of Commerce and Empire: Britain and its Tropical Colonies, 1660–1830*, pointing in particular to the significance of the Seven Years War for spreading the belief that the diseases of warm climates were quite radically distinct from those in colder regions. See also Charters.
[29] Moseley, *A Treatise on Tropical Diseases; And on the Climate of the West-Indies*, 75.

that attended it, than the want of success'.[30] The Seven Years War and subsequent campaigns provided further evidence for the differences between battles fought in the Old World and the New. 'The late dreadful mortality of the troops at *Lucia*, as well as at other parts of *America*', wrote Thomas Dancer, who had served in the campaign against Fort San Juan, 'serve to evince the insalubrity of these climates, and the difficulty attending all military operations in this part of the world'.[31] Lempriere, writing at the end of the century, concurred. 'Since Great Britain has been in possession of West India colonies', he wrote, 'every succeeding war in which they have been concerned, has afforded additional proofs of the dreadful mortality with which all our expeditions have been attended and which our troops ... must ever experience in a tropical climate'.[32] John Bell, in his *Inquiry into the Causes which Produce, and the Means of Preventing Diseases among British Officers, Soldiers and Others in the West Indies* (1791), was not alone in noting that many more soldiers died in the West Indies from disease than the sword, but Hunter made the point most clearly by claiming that in one period, of less than four years, 3, 500 men died in Jamaica, with half that number again discharged because of 'the climate and other causes of mortality, without a man dying by the hands of the enemy'.[33] Bell, on the other hand, made the argument explicitly comparative, emphasising not only the danger of the West Indies, but the relative mildness of Northern Europe. Fighting in Germany, British forces had outnumbered those in Jamaica by a factor of ten. Yet in comparable periods, close to the same absolute number of men were lost to disease in each location.[34]

Africa, as Philip Curtin has shown, had long been seen as 'the White Man's Grave' because of its hostile climate, but that popular image was not widely publicised until after the loss of the American War of Independence. In part due to failed attempts to replace the lost thirteen American colonies with new settlements in West Africa, in the half century after 1780 'the "deadly climate" of the African coast became gradually more common knowledge'.[35] India may have occupied a somewhat more ambiguous role within a discourse about the peculiar deadliness of hot climates. On the one hand, as we have seen, it was often included within claims about the diseases common to the tropics. And

---

[30] Hunter, *Observations on the Diseases of the Army in Jamaica; and on the Best Means of Preserving the Health of Europeans, in That Climate*, 12–13.

[31] Dancer, Note, 20.

[32] Lempriere, 1.

[33] Bell. Hunter, *Observations on the Diseases of the Army in Jamaica; and on the Best Means of Preserving the Health of Europeans, in That Climate*, 70–71.

[34] 'In the last war, British forces in Germany outnumbered those in Jamaica 10 to 1. Yet in 4.5 years, only 6500 men were lost to disease, which in four years 5250 were lost to disease in Jamaica alone'. Bell, 38–9.

[35] Curtin, ' "The White Man's Grave": Image and Reality, 1780–1850', 102.

it was increasingly cast as utterly different from Britain in terms of its characteristic afflictions. In Stephen Mathews' eyes, the diseases of each Indian settlement were similar to one another and different to those found in Europe. They were, moreover more similar to one another – despite their geographical distance from each other – than one would expect in other regions. Reflecting a trope that went back to Hippocrates' *Airs, Waters, and Places*, then, Asia was cast as a realm of remarkable sameness, compared to the more vibrant changeability of Europe. '[T]he diseases peculiar to [each settlement]', Mathews wrote, 'are similar in their fundamental origin; and by a just comparison of the air, soil, and situation of the different presidencies, we do not find such an essential difference arise as is common to places describing similar parallels which are suited without the tropics'.[36] Charles Curtis in 1807 was even more emphatic about the peculiarity of medicine in the East, insisting that 'European nosology and definitions would, in India, prove but uncertain or fallacious guides', and that the newly arrived physician would need to unlearn a good deal in 'a country, where scarce a single production, whether of the animal or vegetable kingdom, is to be met with, bearing a true resemblance to its prototype in Europe'.[37] On the other hand, by the end of the eighteenth century, it could also be seen as a relative success story, compared to the perils of the West Indies and, particularly, the West African Coast. 'Forty years ago', Bell wrote in 1791, 'we could not send a ship to the East Indies, without often being deprived of one half of the crew, either by death, or by diseases which rendered the men unfit for service'.[38] But now the situation had changed and India might teach by its example. 'The West Indies has been emphatically and often too justly, stiled the grave of the British army', Bell insisted. 'To what causes is it owing, that the same mortality does not happen among our troops on the continent of Asia?'. Answering his own question, Bell implicitly played down climatic differences between eastern and western colonies. Soldiers suffered more in the West Indies not because of 'any particularly noxious power in the climate', but because of 'irregularity and inattention', as well as diet, matters that could be altered with more care and a more rational approach to victualling. The tropics would remain dangerous, but there was no reason that one part should be more deadly than another

---

[36] Mathews, 37–8.
[37] Charles Curtis, *An Account of the Diseases of India: As They Appeared in the English Fleet, and in the Naval Hospital at Madras, in 1782 and 1783, with Observations on Ulcers, and the Hospital Sores of That Country &C. &C., to Which Is Prefixed a View of the Diseases of an Expedition, and Passage of a Fleet and Armament to India in 1781* (Edinburgh: W. Laing, 1807), xvi–vii. Cf Harrison, ' "The Tender Frame of Man": Disease, Climate and Racial Difference in India and the West Indies, 1760–1860', 71.
[38] Bell, 122.

Medicine and the Making of Empire

Forms of distinctness and similarity in ideas about disease environments and race have been two major pre-occupations of this book. A third has been relationships between theories of medicine and conceptions of empire. Let me end, then, by discussing the ways in which imperial medicine helped to bring about 'tropical diseases' and distinct races of humankind. I noted, in the introduction, my unwillingness to follow those who have declared military texts to be the most valuable and important in understanding diseases outside Britain in the eighteenth century. The problem with such an assumption can be revealed quickly by noting that the five most important works on the distempers of the West Indies from the late 1670s to the late 1760s were all written by – and largely for – civilians.[39] But matters would change as an effect of the dramatic expansion of the British Empire after the end of the Seven Years' War in 1763. Lind's *Essay on Diseases Incidental to Europeans in Hot Climates* (1768) marked the beginning of a new era, one in which 'location-specific' texts diminished in importance compared to works intended for use by military men throughout the empire.

It is the characteristics of such works – as a *genre* – upon which I wish to focus, for those characteristics are quite strikingly different from those found in works devoted to the diseases of a specific place, written by practitioners living there for a sizeable period.[40] Both works, at least after the first decades of the eighteenth century, tended to emphasise personal experience *in situ*. A local practitioner-author like Towne, or Warren, however tended to invoke their experiences to position themselves as local experts, aiming to help those who laboured with them in Jamaica or Barbados. Hillary, too, cast that part of his 1759 work on diseases 'indigenous or endemial, in the West India Islands, or in the Torrid Zone' as being for the 'Good of the Inhabitants, and the Benefit of those who commonly practice in the West-India Islands'.[41] The authors of military texts, however, had broader ambitions, seeing their audience in terms of the network of medical men practicing their craft in multiple geographically distinct locations. Thus, for example, Cleghorn's treatise on the afflictions common to Minorca was not addressed solely to physicians and surgeons there.

---

[39] Trapham. Sloane. Towne. Warren. Hillary, *Observations on the Changes of the Air and the Concomitant Epidemical Diseases, in the Island of Barbados. To Which Is Added a Treatise on the Putrid Bilious Fever, Commonly Called the Yellow Fever; and Such Other Diseases as Are Indigenous or Endemial, in the West India Islands, or in the Torrid Zone.*

[40] On military texts as a genre, see Alsop.

[41] Hillary, *Observations on the Changes of the Air and the Concomitant Epidemical Diseases, in the Island of Barbados. To Which Is Added a Treatise on the Putrid Bilious Fever, Commonly Called the Yellow Fever; and Such Other Diseases as Are Indigenous or Endemial, in the West India Islands, or in the Torrid Zone*, Preface, unnumbered, 142.

Minorca, Cleghorn confessed, was only 'a small, remote Part of the *British Dominions*', albeit one in which a large number of British subjects could be found, both in times of peace and war. To make the case for the more general utility of a close study of Minorca's illnesses in other British dominions, Cleghorn needed to play down the peculiarity of the island's climate. Since 'the Qualities of the Air, and the Course of the Seasons in *Minorca* correspond nearly with those in several other Parts of the World, to which our Fleets frequently repair, it is probable the Diseases may likewise be similar'.[42] Texts written for the benefit of local readers tended to emphasise local particularity, often emphasising how far from homogenous a given location could be. Those aiming to be used in multiple sites within the empire stressed the difference between the site in which experience had been gained and the metropole – hence the need for the book for men trained within Europe – but tended to gloss differences between the author's site and those in other peripheral locations. The number of military medical texts – and their share of the global market – expanded with the number of troops stationed overseas. Thus, increasingly, emphases on the particularity of any given island or country faded compared to stress on the similarities between the countries of a given region.[43] Towne's text was essential for those working in Barbados: Lind's was carried throughout the empire.

The attempt to reach a broader market was not the only reason that military texts did not dwell on the geographical quirks or specificities of given places. In many, if not most, cases practitioners did not have time enough in the places they were to practice. Those in his Majesty's service, Cleghorn noted, 'are often obliged to take Care of Numbers of their Fellow Subjects, in Climates exposed to such Disorders; whilst at the same Time their quick Transition from one Place to another, prevents their acquiring a competent Knowledge of the various Epidemicks from their own Observation'.[44] Blane confessed of himself that 'the fleets I belonged to seldom remained more than six weeks or two months at any one place, so that any series of observation that might have been instituted was interrupted'.[45] Moseley, in other words, may have been right about the limitations of some forms of military service compared to a long residence in a given locale.

Naval service, in particular, may have led to a distorted vision of the countries men served in. Curtis acknowledged openly what few others did. In his *Account of the Diseases of India: as they appeared in the English Fleet, and*

---

[42] Cleghorn, iv.
[43] On the character of British military medicine after 1688, see Cook, 'Practical Medicine and the British Armed Forces after the "Glorious Revolution"'.
[44] Cleghorn, xii.
[45] Blane, xi.

in the Naval Hospital in Madras, he noted the limitations of his own experience: 'Let it be observed, however, that what is here stated, applies properly to *maritime* India only, and not to all the variety of inland country comprehended within that vast peninsula'. Curtis was thus honest about an aspect that strikes the reader familiar with civilian works as well as those written by military men: accounts of the diseases that strike sailors throughout the British Empire tend to treat ports as synecdoches for entire countries. Flattening, or simply ignoring, local differences of place also made it easier to connect ports at considerable geographical distance within a single discourse of tropical climates.

One might note, finally, that the bodies that inhabit military medical texts are not as varied as those found in civilian works. '[T]his was a peculiar body', J. D. Alsop has written, 'gendered male, identified as a young adult, characterized as temperamentally childlike and in need of firm guidance'.[46] To be sure, observations drawn from experience both with women and with non-Europeans are to be found in such texts, for not all practitioners were as limited as Hunter professed himself to be.[47] Lempriere served as regimental-surgeon and then superintendent of the military hospitals in Jamaica, but he also drew on a 'very extensive line of private practice in Spanish Town', which no doubt explains, for example, how he was able to observe that tetanus was much more common among the black than the white population.[48] On the other hand, those involved in extensive military practice could not have the same depth of experience as local practitioners in the West Indies, who purported to treat thousands of slaves, of all ages and both sexes, every year. And there is certainly some element of truth in the observation that, in military texts, both women and those of African descent appear more as counter-examples to the male experience than fully-fledged figures in their own right.[49] Differences of both race and sex tended to be amplified in texts that took young white males as largely uncontested exemplars of what it was to be British.

The causes were multiple, but the effect was striking. It was an outcome that was far from inevitable and produced by forces far from constant. A Briton looking back nearly a century in 1800 would not recognise a good deal that was familiar in the Britain of 1707. A Briton looking back in 1900, however, could see at least the frame of the empire shared across a century. Above all, I think, they would recognise the divisions that were as essential to empire as its unities. By 1800, the fissures that ran throughout a network of imperial control could be seen. The differences – by place and by race – that would characterise the British Empire for the next century and a half, had emerged.

---

[46] Alsop, 37.
[47] See Introduction, page x.
[48] Lempriere, 47–8.
[49] Alsop, 37–8.

Bibliography

Adams, Charles Kendall. *Representative British Orations*. New York: Putnam, 1884.

Adams, Vincenne and Warwick Anderson. 'Pramoedya's Chickens: Postcolonial Studies of Technoscience'. In *The Handbook of Science and Technology Studies*, edited by Edward J. Hackett, Olga Amsterdamska, Michael Lynch and Judy Wajcman, 181–207. Cambridge, MA: MIT Press, 2007.

Addison, William. *English Spas*. London: B. T. Batsford Ltd., 1951.

African Merchant, An. *A Treatise Upon the Trade from Great-Britain to Africa. Humbly Recommended to the Attention of Government*. London: R. Baldwin, 1772.

Alexander, William. *An Experimental Enquiry Concerning the Causes Which Have Generally Been Said to Produce Putrid Diseases*. London: T. Becket and P. A. de Hondt and T. Cadell, 1771.

Experimental Essays on the Following Subjects: I. On the External Application of Antiseptics in Putrid Diseases. II. On the Doses and Effects of Medicines. III. On Diuretics and Sudorifics. London: Edward and Charles Dilly, 1768.

Alpini, Prosper. *La Médicine des Egyptiens*. Translated by R. de Fenoyl. Paris: Institut français d'archéologie orientale, 1980.

Alpinus, Prosper and Jacobus Bontius. *P. Alpini, de Medicina Aegyptiorum & Jacobus Bontii, de Medicina Indorum*. Paris: Nicalaus Redelichuysen, 1645.

Prosperi Alpini, Medicina Aegyptiorum ... Ut et Jacobi Bontii, Medicina Indorum. Lugduni Batavorum: Apud Gerardum Potvliet, 1745.

Alsop, J. D. 'Warfare and the Creation of British Imperial Medicine, 1600–1800'. In *British Military and Naval Medicine, 1600–1830*, edited by Geoffrey L. Hudson, 23–50. Amsterdam: Rodopi, 2007.

Altink, Henrice. 'Deviant and Dangerous: Pro-Slavery Representation of Jamaican Slave Women's Sexuality, c. 1780–1834'. *Slavery and Abolition* 26 (2005): 271–88.

Representations of Slave Women in Discourses on Slavery and Abolition, 1780–1838. New York and London: Routledge, 2007.

Anderson, Warwick. *Colonial Pathologies: American Tropical Medicine, Race, and Hygiene in the Philippines*. Durham, NC and London: Duke University Press, 2006.

The Cultivation of Whiteness: Science, Health and Racial Destiny in Australia. New York: Basic Books, 2003.

Anonymous. *Practical Remarks on West India Diseases*. London: F. Newbery; F. Blyth, 1776.

'Review of Dale Ingram, "A Historical Account of Several Plagues that Have Appeared in the World since the Year 1346"'. *The Monthly Review* (1755): 129–40.

Anson, George. *A Voyage Round the World: In the Years MDCCXL, I, II, III, IV. By George Anson ... Compiled from Papers and Other Materials Of ... George Lord Anson, and Published under His Direction, by Richard Walter ... Illustrated with Forty-Two Copper-Plates.* London: John and Paul Knapton, 1748.

Aranda, Marcelo, Katherine Arner, Lina Del Castillo, Helen Cowie, Matthew Crawford, Joseph Cullon, Marcelo Figueroa, et al. 'The History of Atlantic Science: Collective Reflections from the 2009 Harvard Seminar on Atlantic History'. *Atlantic Studies* 7 (2010): 493–509.

Arber, Edward, ed. *Capt. John Smith, of Willoughby by Alford, Lincolnshire; President of Virginia, and Admiral of New England: Works. 1608–1631.* Birmingham: The English Scholars Library, 1884.

Arbuthnot, John. *An Essay Concerning the Effects of Air on Human Bodies.* London: Printed for J. Tonson, 1733.

Arnold, David. *Colonizing the Body: State Medicine and Epidemic Disease in Nineteenth-Century India.* Berkeley: University of California Press, 1993.

'India's Place in the Tropical World, 1770–1930'. *Journal of Imperial and Commonwealth History* 26, no. 1 (1998): 1–21.

Warm Climates and Western Medicine: The Emergence of Tropical Medicine, 1500–1900. Amsterdam and Atlanta: Rodopi, 1996.

Arrizabalaga, Jon. 'Facing the Black Death: Perceptions and Reactions of University Medical Practitioners'. In *Practical Medicine from Salerno to the Black Death*, edited by Luis Garcia-Ballester, Roger French, Jon Arrizabalaga and Andrew Cunningham, 237–88. Cambridge: Cambridge University Press, 1994.

Ashcroft, M. T. 'Tercentenary of the First English Book on Tropical Medicine, by Thomas Trapham of Jamaica'. *British Medical Journal* 2 (1979): 475–7.

Atchison, Robert. 'Observations on the Dysentery, as it Appears among the Negroes on the Coast of Guinea'. *Medical Commentaries* 9 (1785): 268–71.

Atkins, John. *The Navy-Surgeon; Or, Practical System of Surgery with a Dissertation on Cold and Hot Mineral Springs; and Physical Observations on the Coast of Guiney.* London: J. Hodges, 1742.

The Navy-Surgeon: Or, a Practical System of Surgery. 1st ed. London: Caesar Ward and Richard Chandler, 1734.

The Navy-Surgeon: Or, a Practical System of Surgery. Illustrated with Observations on Such Remarkable Cases, as Have Occurred to the Author's Practice in the Service of the Royal Navy. To Which Is Added, a Treatise on the Venereal Disease, the Causes, Symptoms, and Method of Cure by Mercury: An Enquiry into the Origin of That Distemper; in Which the Dispute between Dr Dover and Dr Turner, Concerning Crude Mercury, Is Fully Consider'd; with Useful Remarks Thereon. Also an Appendix, Containing Physical Observations on the Heat, Moisture and Density of the Air on the Coast of Guiney; the Colour of the Natives; the Sicknesses Which They and the Europeans Trading Thither Are Subject to; with a Method of Cure. 2nd ed. London: W. Warner, 1737.

A Treatise on the Following Chirurgical Subjects ... London: T. Warner, 1724.

A Voyage to Guinea, Brasil, and the West-Indies; in His Majesty's Ships, the Swallow and Weymouth. London: Caesar Ward and Richard Chandler, 1735.

Aubrey, T. *The Sea-Surgeon, or the Guinea Man's Vade Mecum.* London: John Clarke, 1729.

Augstein, Hannah Franziska. *Race: The Origins of an Idea, 1760–1850*. Bristol: Thoemmes Press, 1996.

Baker, Richard. *A Chronicle of the Kings of England: From the Time of the Roman's Government Unto the Death of King James. Containing All Passages of State and Church, with All Other Observations Proper for a Chronicle. Faithfully Collected out of Authors Ancient and Modern; and Digested into a New Method*. London: Nathaniel Ranew and Jonathan Robinson, 1665.

Barker, Anthony J. *The African Link: British Attitudes to the Negro in the Era of the Atlantic Slave Trade, 1550–1807*. London: Frank Cass and Company, Ltd., 1978.

Barnard, Alan J. 'Orang Outang and the Definition of *Man*: The Legacy of Lord Monboddo'. In *Fieldwork and Footnotes: Studies in the History of European Anthropology*, edited by Han F. Vermeulen and Arturo Alvarez Roldán. London: Routledge, 1995.

Barrère, Pierre. *Dissertation sur la Cause physique de la couleur des nègres, de la qualité de leurs cheveux, et de la dégénération de l'un et de l'autre*. Paris: Pierre-Guillaume Simon, 1741.

Bates, Thomas. *An Enchiridion of Fevers Incident to Sea-Men (During the Summer) in the Mediterranean; … The Second Edition, Corrected and Amended. With Several Medicinal Observations …* London: Printed for John Barns and sold by B. Bragg, 1709.

Bayly, C. A. *Imperial Meridian: The British Empire and the World, 1780–1830*. London and New York: Routledge, 1989.

Beckles, Hilary McD. 'Property Rights in Pleasure: The Marketing of Slave Women's Sexuality in the West Indies'. In *West Indies Accounts: Essays on the History of the British Caribbean and the Atlantic Economy, in Honour of Richard Sheridan*, edited by Roderick A. McDonald, 169–87. Kingston, Jamaica: University of the West Indies Press, 1996.

Bell, John. *An Inquiry into the Causes Which Produce, and the Means of Preventing Diseases among British Officers, Soldiers, and Others in the West Indies*. London: J. Murray, 1791.

Benezet, Anthony. *A Short Account of That Part of Africa, Inhabited by the Negroes*. Philadelphia: William Dunlap, 1762.

Bergerus, Gottlieb Benjamin and Friedrich Hoffmann. *Dissertatio Physicomedica Inauguralis de Putredinis Doctrina Amplissimi in Medicina Usus*. Halle: 1722.

Berlin, Ira and Philip D. Morgan, eds. *Cultivation and Culture: Labor and the Shaping of Slave Life in the Americas*. Charlottesville and London: University Press of Virginia, 1993.

Bernasconi, Robert, ed. *Concepts of Race in the Eighteenth Century. Volume 3: Kant and Forster*. Bristol: Thoemmes Press, 2001.

'Who Invented the Concept of Race? Kant's Role in the Enlightenment Construction of Race'. In *Race*, edited by Robert Bernasconi, 11–36. Malden, MA and Oxford: Blackwell, 2001.

Bernier, François. 'A New Division of the Earth'. In *The Idea of Race*, edited by Robert Bernasconi and Tommy L. Lott, 1–4. Indianapolis: Hackett, 2000.

Bethencourt, Francisco. *Racisms: From the Crusades to the Twentieth Century*. Princeton: Princeton University Press, 2013.

Bethencourt, Francisco and A. J. Pearce, eds. *Racism and Ethnic Relations in the Portuguese Speaking World*. New York: Oxford University Press, 2012.

Beverley, Robert. *The History and Present State of Virginia, in Four Parts. I. The History of the First Settlement of Virginia, and the Government Thereof, to the Present Time. II. The Natural Productions and Conveniencies of the Country, Suited to Trade and Improvement. III. The Native Indians, Their Religion, Laws, and Customs, in War and Peace. IV. The Present State of the Country, as to the Polity of the Government, and the Improvements of the Land. By a Native and Inhabitant of the Place*. 1st ed. London: R. Parker, 1705.

Bewell, Alan. *Romanticism and Colonial Disease*. Baltimore: Johns Hopkins University Press, 1999.

Birch, Thomas, ed. *A Collection of the State Papers of John Thurloe, Esq; Secretary First to the Council of State and Afterwards to the Two Protectors Oliver and Richard Cromwell*. Burlington: TannerRitchie, 2005.

Bisset, Charles. *An Essay on the Medical Constitution of Great Britain, to Which Are Added Observations on the Weather, and the Diseases Which Appeared in the Period Included Betwixt the First of January 1758, and the Summer Solstice in 1760*. London: A. Millar and D. Wilson, 1762.

A Treatise on the Scurvy. Design'd Chiefly for the Use of the British Navy. London: R. and J. Dodsley, in Pall-Mall, 1755.

Blane, Gilbert. *Observations on the Diseases of Seamen*. London: Joseph Cooper, 1785.

Bleichmar, Daniela. 'Books, Bodies, and Fields: Sixteenth-Century Transatlantic Encounters with New World Materia Medica'. In *Colonial Botany: Science, Commerce, and Politics in the Early Modern World*, edited by Londa Schiebinger and Claudia Swan, 83–99. Philadelphia: University of Pennsylvania Press, 2005.

Blumenbach, Johann. 'De Generis Humani Varietate Nativa (1775)'. In *The Anthropological Treatises of Johann Friedrich Blumenbach*, edited by Thomas Bendyshe, 65–143. London: Longman, Green, Longman, Roberts, & Green, 1865.

Boerhaave, Hermann. *Boerhaave's Aphorisms: Concerning the Knowledge and Cure of Diseases. Translated from the Last Edition Printed in Latin at Leyden, 1715. With Useful Observations and Explanations, by J. Delacoste, M.D.* London: Printed for B. Cowse, and W. Innys, 1725.

'Discourse on Chemistry Purging Itself of Its Own Errors'. In *Boerhaave's Orations: Translated with Introductions and Notes by E. Kegel-Brinkgreve and A. M. Luyendijk-Elshout*, edited by E. Kegel-Brinkgreve and A. M. Luyendijk-Elshout, 180–213. Leiden: Brill, 1983.

Elements of Chemistry: Being the Annual Lectures of Herman Boerhaave, M. D. Translated by Timothy Dallowe. 2 vols. Vol. I. London: J. and J. Pemberton, 1735. Latin ed. (1731).

Elements of Chemistry: Being the Annual Lectures of Herman Boerhaave, M. D. Translated by Timothy Dallowe. 2 vols. Vol. II. London: J. and J. Pemberton, 1735. Latin ed. (1731).

Bontius, James. *An Account of the Diseases, Natural History, and Medicines of the East Indies*. London: John Donaldson, 1776.

Booth, C. C. 'William Hillary: A Pupil of Boerhaave'. *Medical History* 7, no. 4 (1963): 297–316.

Bosman, Willem. *A New and Accurate Description of the Coast of Guinea, Divided into the Gold, the Slave, and the Ivory Coasts ... Illustrated with Several Cutts. Written Originally in Dutch by William Bosman ... To Which Is Prefix'd, an Exact Map of the Whole Coast of Guinea.* London: Printed for James Knapton and Dan. Midwinter, 1705.

Boswell, John. *Christianity, Social Tolerance, and Homosexuality: Gay People in Western Europe from the Beginning of the Christian Era to the Fourteenth Century.* Chicago: Chicago University Press, 1980.

Boyle, Robert. 'General Heads for a Natural History of a Countrey, Great or Small, Imparted Likewise by Mr. Boyle'. *Philosophical Transactions* 1 (1666): 186–9.

Braude, Benjamin. 'The Sons of Noah and the Construction of Ethnic and Geographical Identities in the Medieval and Early Modern Periods'. *The William and Mary Quarterly* 54, no. 1 (1997): 103–42.

Brocklesby, Richard. *Oeconomical and Medical Observations, in Two Parts. From the Year 1758 to the Year 1763, Inclusive.* London: T. Becket and P. A. de Hondt, 1764.

Brown, Theodore M. 'Medicine in the Shadow of the Principia'. *Journal of the History of Ideas* 48, no. 4 (1987): 629–48.

Brown, Vincent. *The Reaper's Garden: Death and Power in the World of Atlantic Slavery.* Cambridge, MA: Harvard University Press, 2008.

Buffon, Georges Louis Leclerc. 'Of the Varieties in the Human Species'. In *Barr's Buffon. Buffon's Natural History Containing a Theory of the Earth, a General History of Man, of the Brute Creation, and of Vegetables, Minerals &C. &C.*, 190–352. London: H. D. Symonds, 1807.

Burnard, Trevor. ' "Rioting in Goatish Embraces": Marriage and Improvement in Early British Jamaica'. *The History of the Family* 11 (2006): 185–97.

Burnard, Trevor and Richard Follett. 'Caribbean Slavery, British Anti-Slavery, and the Cultural Politics of Venereal Disease'. *The Historical Journal* 55 (2012): 427–51.

Burnard, Trevor and John Garrigus. *The Plantation Machine: Atlantic Capitalism in French Saint-Domingue and British Jamaica.* Philadelphia: University of Pennsylvania Press, 2016.

Bush, Barbara. *Slave Women in Caribbean Society.* Bloomington: Indiana University Press, 1990.

Bush-Slimani, Barbara. 'Hard Labour: Women, Childbirth, and Resistance in British Caribbean Slave Societies'. *History Workshop Journal* 36 (1993): 83–99.

Bynum, W. F. 'Cullen and the Study of Fevers in Britain, 1760–1820'. *Medical History (Supplement)* 1 (1981): 135–47.

C., T. 'Lind, James, M. D. (1736–1812)'. In *Dictionary of National Biography*, edited by Sidney Lee, 272–3. London: Smith, Elder, and Co., 1893.

Cañizares-Esguerra, Jorge. *How to Write the History of the New World: Histories, Epistemologies, and Identities in the Eighteenth-Century Atlantic World.* Stanford: Stanford University Press, 2001.

'New Worlds, New Stars: Patriotic Astrology and the Invention of Indian and Creole Bodies in Colonial Spanish America, 1600–1650'. *American Historical Review* 104 (1999): 33–68.

Carpenter, Kenneth J. *The History of Scurvy and Vitamin C.* Cambridge: Cambridge University Press, 1986.

Carretta, Vincent. 'Who Was Francis Williams?'. *Early American Literature* 38 (2003): 213–37.

Carter, Henry Rose. *Yellow Fever: An Epidemiological and Historical Study of Its Place of Origin*. Baltimore: The Williams and Wilkins Company, 1931.

Chakrabarti, Pratik. *Materials and Medicine: Trade, Conquest and Therapeutics in the Eighteenth Century*. Manchester: Manchester University Press, 2011.

Chakrabarty, Dipesh. *Provincializing Europe: Postcolonial Thought and Historical Difference*. Princeton: Princeton University Press, 2000.

Chamberlaine, William. *A Practical Treatise on the Efficacy of Stizolobium, or Cowhage, Internally Administered, in Diseases Occasioned by Worms. To Which Are Added, Observations on Other Anthelmintic Medicines of the West Indies*. London: J. Murray, 1784.

Chaplin, Joyce E. 'Earthsickness: Circumnavigation and the Terrestrial Human Body, 1520–1800'. *Bulletin of the History of Medicine* 86, no. 4 (2012): 515–42.

Subject Matter: Technology, the Body, and Science on the Anglo-American Frontier, 1500–1676. Cambridge, MA: Harvard University Press, 2001.

Charters, Erica. *Disease, War, and the Imperial State: The Welfare of the British Armed Forces During the Seven Years War*. Chicago and London: University of Chicago Press, 2014.

Chisholm, C. 'The History of a Singular Affection of the Liver, Which Prevailed Epidemically in Some Parts of the West Indies'. *Medical Commentaries* Second Decade, 1 (1787): 353–72.

Christie, J. *An Abstract of Some Years Observations Concerning Such General and Unperceived Occasions of Sickliness in Fleets and Ships of War*. 1709.

Churchill, Wendy D. 'Bodily Differences?: Gender, Race, and Class in Hans Sloane's Jamaican Medical Practice, 1687–1688'. *Journal of the History of Medicine and Allied Sciences* 60, no. 4 (2005): 391–444.

Clark, John. *Observations on the Diseases in Long Voyages to Hot Countries, and Particularly on Those Which Prevail in the East Indies*. London: Printed for D. Wilson and G. Nicol, 1773.

Cleghorn, George. *Observations on the Epidemical Diseases in Minorca. From the Year 1744 to 1749*. London: Printed for D. Wilson, 1751.

Cleve, George van. 'Somerset's Case Revisited: Somerset's Case and its Antecedents in Imperial Perspective'. *Law and History Review* 24, no. 3 (2006): 601–45.

Cockburn, William. *An Account of the Nature, Causes, Symptoms, and Cure of the Distempers that are Incident to Seafaring People with Observations on the Diet of the Sea-Men in His Majesty's Navy: Illustrated with Some Remarkable Instances of the Sickness of the Fleet During the Last Summer, Historically Related*. London: Hugh Newman, 1696.

Sea Diseases: Or, a Treatise of Their Nature, Causes, and Cure. Also, an Essay on Bleeding in Fevers; Shewing, the Quantities of Blood to Be Let, in Any of Their Periods. The Second Edition Corrected and Much Improved. London: Geo. Strahan, 1706.

Cohler, Anne M., Basia C. Miller, and Harold S. Stone, eds. *Montesquieu: The Spirit of the Laws*. Cambridge: Cambridge University Press, 2010.

Colley, Linda. 'Britishness and Otherness: An Argument'. *Journal of British Studies* 31 (1992): 309–29.

Britons: Forging the Nation, 1707–1837. New Haven and London: Yale University Press, 2009.

Cook, Harold J. 'Global Economies and Local Knowledge in the East Indies: Jacobus Bontius Learns the Facts of Nature'. In *Colonial Botany: Science, Commerce, and Politics in the Early Modern World*, edited by Londa Schiebinger and Claudia Swan, 100–18. Philadelphia: University of Pennsylvania Press, 2005.

Matters of Exchange: Commerce, Medicine, and Science in the Dutch Golden Age. New Haven and London: Yale University Press, 2007.

'Practical Medicine and the British Armed Forces after the "Glorious Revolution"'. *Medical History* 34 (1990): 1–26.

Cooke, Ebenezer. *The Sot-Weed Factor, or, a Voyage to Maryland a Satyr: In Which Is Describ'd, the Laws, Government, Courts and Constitutions of the Country, and Also the Buildings, Feasts, Frolicks, Entertainments and Drunken Humours of the Inhabitants of That Part of America: In Burlesque Verse.* London: B. Bragg, 1708.

Cowley, Abraham. *The Poetical Works of Abraham Cowley in Four Volumes.* Edinburgh: Apollo Press, 1784.

Crawford, Matthew. *The Andean Wonder Drug: Cinchona Bark and Imperial Science in the Spanish Atlantic, 1630–1800.* Pittsburgh: University of Pittsburgh Press, 2016.

Creighton, Charles. *A History of Epidemics in Britain. Vol. II. From the Extinction of Plague to the Present Time.* Cambridge: Cambridge University Press, 1894.

Crosby, David L., ed. *The Complete Antislavery Writings of Anthony Benezet, 1754–1783.* Baton Rouge: Louisiana State University Press, 2013.

Cullen, William. 'First Lines of the Practice of Physic (1784)'. In *The Works of William Cullen*, edited by John Thomson, 465–676. Edinburgh and London: William Blackwood; T. & G. Underwood, 1827.

First Lines of the Practice of Physic. For the Use of Students in the University of Edinburgh. Vol. 1, London and Edinburgh: J. Murray; William Creech, 1777.

Cunningham, Andrew. 'Sydenham Versus Newton: The Edinburgh Fever Dispute of the 1690s between Andrew Brown and Archibald Pitcairne'. *Medical History, Supplement* 1 (1981): 71–98.

'Thomas Sydenham: Epidemics, Experiment, and the "Good Old Cause"'. In *The Medical Revolution of the Seventeenth Century*, edited by Roger French and Andrew Wear, 164–91. Cambridge: Cambridge University Press, 1989.

Curran, Andrew S. *The Anatomy of Blackness: Science & Slavery in an Age of Enlightenment.* Baltimore: Johns Hopkins University Press, 2011.

Curtin, Philip D. 'Epidemiology and the Slave Trade'. *Political Science Quarterly* 83, no. 2 (1968): 190–216.

The Image of Africa: British Ideas and Action, 1780–1850. Madison: University of Wisconsin Press, 1964.

'"The White Man's Grave": Image and Reality, 1780–1850'. *Journal of British Studies* 1 (1961): 94–110.

Curtis, Charles. *An Account of the Diseases of India: As They Appeared in the English Fleet, and in the Naval Hospital at Madras, in 1782 and 1783, with Observations on Ulcers, and the Hospital Sores of That Country &C. &C., to Which Is Prefixed a View of the Diseases of an Expedition, and Passage of a Fleet and Armament to India in 1781.* Edinburgh: W. Laing, 1807.

Dampier, William. *A New Voyage Round the World: Describing Particularly the Isthmus of America, Several Coasts and Islands in the West Indies, the Isles of Cape Verd, the Passage by Terra Del Fuego, the South Sea Coasts of Chili, Peru and Mexico, the Isle of Guam One of the Ladrones, Mindanao, and Other Philippine and East-India Islands near Cambodia, China, Formosa, Luconia, Celebes, &C., New Holland, Sumatra, Nicobar Isles, the Cape of Good Hope, and Santa Hellena: Their Soil, Rivers, Harbours, Plants, Fruits, Animals, and Inhabitants: Their Customs, Religion, Government, Trade, &C.* London: James Knapton, 1697–1703.

Dancer, Thomas. *A Brief History of the Late Expedition against Fort San Juan, So Far as it Relates to the Diseases of the Troops; Together with Some Observations on Climate, Infection, and Contagion.* Kingston: D. Douglass & W. Aikman, 1781.

Davidson, Arnold I. *The Emergence of Sexuality: Historical Epistemology and the Formation of Concepts.* Cambridge, MA: Harvard University Press, 2001.

Davis, David Brion. *The Problem of Slavery in the Age of Revolution, 1770–1823.* Ithaca: Cornell University Press, 1975.

The Problem of Slavery in Western Culture. Ithaca: Cornell University Press, 1966.

Debus, Allen G. *The Chemical Philosophy.* Mineola: Dover, 2002.

Defoe, Daniel. *A Tour Thro' the Whole Island of Great Britain: Divided into Circuits or Journeys. Giving a Particular and Entertaining Account of Whatever Is Curious, and Worth Observation; ... By a Gentleman.* 4 vols. vol. I. London: J. Osborn, S. Birt, D. Browne, J. Hodges, A. Millar, J. Whiston, and J. Robinson, 1742.

DeLacy, Margaret. 'The Conceptualization of Influenza in Eighteenth-Century Britain: Specificity and Contagion'. *Bulletin of the History of Medicine* 67 (1993): 74–118.

'Nosology, Mortality, and Disease Theory in the Eighteenth Century'. *Journal of the History of Medicine* 54 (1999): 261–84.

Delbourgo, James. *Collecting the World: Hans Sloane and the Origins of the British Museum.* Cambridge, MA: Belknap Press, 2017.

A Most Amazing Scene of Wonders: Electricity and Enlightenment in Early America. Cambridge, MA: Harvard University Press, 2006.

'The Newtonian Slave Body: Racial Enlightenment in the Atlantic World'. *Atlantic Studies* 9 (2012): 185–207.

'Slavery in the Cabinet of Curiosities: Hans Sloane's Atlantic World'. www.britishmuseum.org/research/news/hans_sloanes_atlantic_world.aspx (2007).

Dellon, Gabriel. *A Voyage to the East-Indies: Giving an Account of the Isles of Madagascar, and Mascareigne, of Suratte, the Coast of Malabar, of Goa, Gameron, Ormus: As Also a Treatise of the Distempers Peculiar to the Eastern Countries: to Which is Annexed an Abstract of Monsieur de Rennefort's History of the East-Indies, with His Propositions for the Improvement of the East-India Company.* London: D. Browne, A. Roper, D. Leigh, 1698.

Denton, Daniel. *A Brief Description of New-York, Formerly Called New-Netherlands: With the Places Thereunto Adjoyning: Together with the Manner of Its Situation, Fertility of the Soyle, Healthfulness of the Climate, and the Commodities Thence Produced: Also Some Directions and Advice to Such as Shall Go Thither ... Likewise a Brief Relation of the Customs of the Indians There.* London: John Hancock and William Bradley, 1670.

Doig, A., J. P. S. Ferguson, I. A. Milne, and R. Passmore, eds. *William Cullen and the Eighteenth Century Medical World: A Bicentenary Exhibition and Symposium Arranged by the Royal College of Physicians of Edinburgh in 1990.* Edinburgh: Edinburgh University Press, 1993.

Drescher, Seymour. *Capitalism and Antislavery: British Mobilization in Comparative Perspective.* Oxford: Oxford University Press, 1987.

'The Ending of the Slave Trade and the Evolution of European Scientific Racism'. *Social Science History* 14 (1990): 415–50.

The Mighty Experiment: Free Labor Versus Slavery in British Emancipation. Oxford: Oxford University Press, 2002.

Duden, Barbara. *The Woman beneath the Skin: A Doctor's Patients in Eighteenth-Century Germany.* Cambridge, MA: Harvard University Press, 1991.

Dunn, Richard S. *Sugar and Slaves: The Rise of the Planter Class in the English West Indies, 1624–1713.* Chapel Hill and London: University of North Carolina Press, 2000.

'Sugar Production and Slave Women in Jamaica'. In *Cultivation and Culture: Labor and the Shaping of Slave Life in the Americas*, edited by Ira Berlin and Philip D. Morgan, 49–72. Charlottesville and London: University Press of Virginia, 1993.

Eliav-Feldon, Miriam, Benjamin H. Isaac, and Joseph Ziegler, eds. *The Origin of Racism in the West.* Cambridge: Cambridge University Press, 2009.

Estwick, Samuel. *Considerations on the Negroe Cause, Commonly So Called, Addressed to the Right Honourable Lord Mansfield, Lord Chief Justice of King's Bench, &C. By a West Indian.* London: J. Dodsley, 1772.

Considerations on the Negroe Cause, Commonly So Called, Addressed to the Right Honourable Lord Mansfield, Lord Chief Justice of the Court of King's Bench, &C. 2nd ed. London: J. Dodsley, 1773.

Fabian, Johannes. *Time and the Other: How Anthropology Makes Its Object.* New York: Columbia University Press, 1983.

Fett, Sharla M. *Working Cures: Healing, Health, and Power on Southern Slave Plantations.* Chapel Hill and London: The University of North Carolina Press, 2002.

Findlay, G. M. 'John Williams and the Early History of Yellow Fever'. *The British Medical Journal* 2, no. 4574 (1948): 474–6.

Foa, Anna. 'The New and the Old: The Spread of Syphilis (1494–1530)'. Translated by Carole C. Gallucci. In *Sex and Gender in Historical Perspective*, edited by Edward Muir and Guido Ruggiero, 26–45. Baltimore: Johns Hopkins University Press, 1990.

Foot, Jesse. *A Defence of the Planters in the West Indies; Comprised in Four Arguments.* London: J. Debrett, 1792.

Forster, Georg. 'Noch etwas über die Menschenraßen. An Herrn Dr. Biester'. *Teutsche Merkur* October and November (1786): 57–86, 150–66.

Fortescue, J. W. *A History of the British Army.* 2nd ed. Vol. II. London: Macmillan, 1910.

Fothergill, John. *An Account of the Sore Throat Attended with Ulcers; a Disease Which Hath of Late Years Appeared in This City, and the Parts Adjacent.* London: C. Davis, 1747.

Foucault, Michel. *The History of Sexuality*. 3 vols. Vol. I. London: Allen Lane, 1978.
'Of Other Spaces: Utopias and Heterotopias'. *Architecture/Mouvement/Continuité*, no. October (1984).
Frängsmyr, Tore, J L. Heilbron, and Robin E. Rider. *The Quantifying Spirit in the Eighteenth Century*. Berkeley: University of California Press, 1990.
Franklin, Benjamin. *Experiments and Observations on Electricity*. London: Printed for David Henry, 1769.
Gibbes, Philip. *Instruction for the Treatment of Negroes &C. &C. &C.* 2nd ed. London: Shepperson and Reynolds, 1797. 1786.
Golinski, Jan. 'American Climate and the Civilization of Nature'. In *Science and Empire in the Atlantic World*, edited by James Delbourgo and Nicholas Dew, 153–74. New York and London: Routledge, 2008.
British Weather and the Climate of Enlightenment. Chicago: University of Chicago Press, 2007.
Gómez, Pablo F. 'The Circulation of Bodily Knowledge in the Seventeenth-Century Black Spanish Caribbean'. *Social History of Medicine* 26 (2013): 383–402.
The Experiential Caribbean: Creating Knowledge and Healing in the Early Modern Atlantic. Chapel Hill: University of North Carolina Press, 2017.
'Incommensurable Epistemologies?: The Atlantic Geography of Healing in the Early Modern Caribbean'. *Small Axe* 18 (2014): 95–107.
Goodeve, H. H. 'Sketch of Medical Progress in the East'. *The Quarterly Journal of the Calcutta Medical and Physical Society* (1837): 124–56.
Gossett, Thomas. *Race: The History of an Idea in America*. Oxford: Oxford University Press, 1997.
Gould, Stephen Jay. *The Mismeasure of Man*. New York: Norton, 1981.
Goveia, Elsa V. *Slave Society in the British Leeward Islands at the End of the Eighteenth Century*. New Haven and London: Yale University Press, 1965.
'The West Indian Slave Laws of the Eighteenth Century'. *Chapters in Caribbean History* 2 (1970): 7–53.
Govier, Mark. 'The Royal Society, Slavery, and the Island of Jamaica, 1660–1700'. *Notes and Records of the Royal Society of London* 53 (1999): 203–17.
Graham, Richard, ed. *The Idea of Race in Latin America, 1870–1940*. Austin: University of Texas Press, 1990.
Grainger, James. 'An Essay on the More Common West-India Diseases, James Grainger, MD (1764), with Additional Notes by William Wright, MD, FRS (1802)'. In *On the Treatment and Management of the More Common West-India Diseases (1750–1802)*, edited by J. Edward Hutson, 1–56. Kingston, Jamaica: University of the West Indies Press, 2005.
'The Sugar-Cane (1764). Book IV'. In *On the Treatment and Management of the More Common West-India Diseases (1750–1802)*, edited by J. Edward Hutson, 57–84. Kingston, Jamaica: University of the West Indies Press, 2005.
Grosse, Pascal. *Kolonialismus, Eugenik und Bürgerliche Gesellschaft in Deutschland 1850–1918*. Frankfurt and New York: Campus, 2000.
'Turning Native? Anthropology, German Colonialism, and the Paradoxes of the "Acclimatization Question", 1885–1914'. In *Worldly Provincialism: German Anthropology in the Age of Empire*, edited by H. Glenn Penny and Matti Bunzl, 179–96. Ann Arbor: University of Michigan Press, 2003.

Guerrini, Anita. 'Archibald Pitcairne and Newtonian Medicine'. *Medical History* 31 (1987): 70–83.

'Isaac Newton, George Cheyne, and the "Principia Medicinae"'. In *The Medical Revolution of the Seventeenth Century*, edited by Roger French and Andrew Wear, 222–45. Cambridge: Cambridge University Press, 1989.

'James Keill, George Cheyne, and Newtonian Physiology, 1690–1740'. *Journal of the History of Biology* 8 (1985): 247–66.

Obesity and Depression in the Enlightenment: The Life and Times of George Cheyne. Norman: University of Oklahoma Press, 2000.

'The Tory Newtonians: Gregory, Pitcairne, and Their Circle'. *Journal of British Studies* 25 (1986): 288–311.

Hales, Stephen. *A Description of Ventilators: Whereby Great Quantities of Fresh Air May with Ease Be Conveyed into Mines, Goals, Hospitals, Work-Houses and Ships, in Exchange for Their Noxious Air. An Account Also of Their Great Usefulness in Many Other Respects: As in Preserving All Sorts of Grain Dry, Sweet, and Free from Being Destroyed by Weevels, Both in Grainaries and Ships: And in Preserving Many Other Sorts of Goods. As Also in Drying Corn, Malt, Hops, Gun-Powder, &C. And for Many Other Useful Purposes.* London: W. Innys and R. Manby; T. Woodward, 1743.

Philosophical Experiments Containing Useful, and Necessary Instructions for Such as Undertake Long Voyages at Sea. Shewing How Sea-Water May Be Made Fresh and Wholsome: And How Fresh-Water May Be Preserv'd Sweet. London: W. Innys and R. Manby; T Woodward, 1739.

Hall, Catherine. *Civilising Subjects: Colony and Metropole in the English Imagination, 1830–1867.* Chicago: Chicago University Press, 2002.

Haller, Albrecht von. *A Dissertation on the Sensible and Irritable Parts of Animals [London, J. Nourse, 1755].* Baltimore: Johns Hopkins Press, 1936.

Haller, John S. 'The Negro and the Southern Physician: A Study of Medical and Racial Attitudes, 1800–1860'. *Medical History* 16 (1972): 238–53.

Hamlin, Christopher. 'Chemistry, Medicine, and the Legitimization of English Spas, 1740–1840'. *Medical History. Supplement* 10 (1990): 67–81.

More Than Hot: A Short History of Fever. Baltimore: Johns Hopkins University Press, 2014.

'Predisposing Causes and Public Health in Early Nineteenth-Century Medical Thought'. *Social History of Medicine* 5 (1992): 43–70.

'What Is Putrid About Putrid Fever?' In *History of Science Society Annual Meeting*, Chicago, 2014.

Handler, Jerome S. 'Diseases and Medical Disabilities of Enslaved Barbadians, from the Seventeenth Century to around 1838 (Part I)'. *The Journal of Caribbean History* 40 (2006): 1–38.

'Diseases and Medical Disabilities of Enslaved Barbadians, from the Seventeenth Century to around 1838 (Part II)'. *The Journal of Caribbean History* 40 (2006): 177–214.

Hargrave, Francis. *An Argument in the Case of James Sommersett, a Negro, Lately Determined by the Court of King's Bench: Wherein It Is Attempted to Demonstrate the Present Unlawfulness of Domestic Slavery in England. To Which Is Prefixed a State of the Case.* London: W. Ostridge, 1772.

Harrison, Mark. *Climates & Constitutions: Health, Race, Environment and British Imperialism in India, 1600–1850*. New Delhi and New York: Oxford University Press, 1999.

Medicine in an Age of Commerce and Empire: Britain and Its Tropical Colonies, 1660–1830. Oxford: Oxford University Press, 2010.

'"The Tender Frame of Man": Disease, Climate and Racial Difference in India and the West Indies, 1760–1860'. *Bulletin of the History of Medicine* 70, no. 1 (1996): 68–93.

Harvey, Gideon. *A Treatise of the Small-Pox and Measles: Describing Their Nature, Causes, and Signs, Diagnostick and Prognostick, in a Different Way to What Hath Hitherto Been Known: Together, with the Method of Curing the Said Distempers, and All, or Most, of the Best Remedies: Also, a Particular Discourse of Opium, Diacodium, and Other Sleeping Medicines: With a Reference to a Very Great Case*. London: W. Freeman, 1696.

Headley, John M. 'The Sixteenth-Century Venetian Celebration of the Earth's Total Habitability: The Issue of the Fully Habitable World for Renaissance Europe'. *Journal of World History* 8, no. 1 (1997): 1–27.

Hecht, Gabrielle. 'Rupture-Talk in the Nuclear Age: Conjugating Colonial Power in Africa'. *Social Studies of Science* 32 (2002): 691–727.

Hendy, James. *A Treatise on the Glandular Disease of Barbadoes: Proving It to Be Seated in the Lymphatic System*. London: C. Dilly, 1784.

Hickeringill, Edmund. *Jamaica Viewed with All the Ports, Harbours, and Their Several Soundings, Towns, and Settlements Thereunto Belonging*. 3rd ed. London: Printed and sold by B. Bragg, 1705.

Hillary, William. 'An Account of the Principal Variations of the Weather, and the Concomitant Epidemic Diseases, as They Appeared in Rippon, and the Circumjacent Parts of Yorkshire, from the Year 1726 to the End of 1734'. In *A Practical Essay on the Small-Pox*. London: C. Hitch and J. Leake, 1740.

An Inquiry into the Contents and Medicinal Virtues of Lincomb Spaw Water, near Bath. By William Hillary, M.D [in English]. London: Printed for J. Leake, in Bath; and sold by C. Hitch [London], 1742.

Observations on the Changes of the Air and the Concomitant Epidemical Diseases, in the Island of Barbados. To Which Is Added a Treatise on the Putrid Bilious Fever, Commonly Called the Yellow Fever; and Such Other Diseases as Are Indigenous or Endemial, in the West India Islands, or in the Torrid Zone. London: C. Hitch and L. Hawes, 1759.

A Practical Essay on the Small-Pox: Wherein a Method of Preparing the Body before the Disease Comes on, and of Deriving the Variolous Matter from the Vital to the Remote Parts of the Body after the Accession ...; to Which is Added, an Account of the Principal Variations of the Weather, and the Concomitant Epidemic Diseases, as They Appeared at Rippon ... From the Year 1726, to the End of 1734. 2nd ed. London: C. Hitch and J. Leake, 1740.

A Rational and Mechanical Essay on the Small-Pox: Wherein the Cause, Nature, and Diathesis of That Disease, Its Symptoms, Their Causes, and Manner of Production, Are Explained ... With the Diagnostic and Prognostic Symptoms ... To Which Is Prefixed, a Short History of the First Rise and Progress of That Disease; and an

Essay on a New Method of Curing It, as We Do Other Inflammatory Diseases. London: G. Strahan, 1735.

Hippocrates. 'On Airs, Waters, and Places', *The Genuine Works of Hippocrates*, Translated from the Greek by Francis Adams, with a preliminary discourse and annotations. In two volumes, vol. 1, 190–222. London: Sydenham Society, 1849.

'Epidemics I', *The Genuine Works of Hippocrates*, Translated from the Greek by Francis Adams, with a preliminary discourse and annotations. In two volumes, vol. 1, 352–382. London: Sydenham Society, 1849.

'Epidemics III', *The Genuine Works of Hippocrates*, Translated from the Greek by Francis Adams, with a preliminary discourse and annotations. In two volumes, vol. 1, 388–420. London: Sydenham Society, 1849.

Hoffmann, Friedrich and Bernardino Ramazzini. *A Dissertation on Endemial Diseases or, Those Disorders Which Arise from Particular Climates, Situations, and Methods of Living; Together with a Treatise on the Diseases of Tradesmen ... The First by the Celebrated Frederick Hoffman ... The Second by Bern. Ramazini ... Newly Translated with a Preface and an Appendix by Dr. James.* London: Printed for Thomas Osborne, and J. Hildyard at York, 1746.

Hogarth, Rana Asali. 'Comparing Anatomies, Constructing Races: Medicine and Slavery in the Atlantic World, 1787–1838'. PhD Thesis. New Haven: Yale University, 2012.

Holwell, J. Z. *An Account of the Manner of Inoculating for the Small Pox in the East Indies.* London: T. Becket and P. A. De Hondt, 1767.

Houstoun, James. *Some New and Accurate Observations Geographical, Natural and Historical. Containing a True and Impartial Account of the Situation, Product, and Natural History of the Coast of Guinea.* London: J. Peele, 1725.

Hudson, Nicholas. 'From "Nation" to "Race": The Origin of Racial Classification in Eighteenth-Century Thought'. *Eighteenth-Century Studies* 29, no. 3 (1996): 246–64.

Hughes, Griffith. 'The Natural History of the Island of Barbados, Book II (1750)'. In *On the Treatment and Management of the More Common West-India Diseases (1750–1802)*, edited by J. Edward Hutson, 85–99. Kingston, Jamaica: University of the West Indies Press, 2005.

Hume, David. 'Of National Characters'. In *Hume: Essays, Moral, Political, and Literary*, edited by E. F. Miller. Indianapolis: Online Library of Liberty, 1987.

Hume, John. 'An Account of the True Bilious, or Yellow Fever; and of the Remitting Fevers of the West Indies'. In *Letters and Essays on the Small-Pox and Inoculation, the Measles, the Dry Belly-Ache, the Yellow, and Remitting, and Intermitting Fevers of the West Indies*, 195–248. London: J. Murray, 1778.

Hunter, John. *Disputatio Inauguralis, Quaedam de Hominum Varietatibus, et Harum Causis, Exponens.* Edinburgh: Balfour and Smellie, 1775.

Observations on the Diseases of the Army in Jamaica; and on the Best Means of Preserving the Health of Europeans, in That Climate. London: G. Nicol, 1788.

Huxham, John. *A Dissertation on the Malignant, Ulcerous Sore-Throat.* London: J. Hinton, 1757.

An Essay on Fevers, and Their Various Kinds, as Depending on Different Constitutions of the Blood: With Dissertations on Slow Nervous Fevers; on Putrid, Pestilential,

Spotted Fevers; on the Small-Pox; and on Pleurisies and Peripneumonies. London: S. Austen, 1750.

Observationes de Aëre et Morbis Epidemicis: Ab Anno MDCCXXVIII ad Finem Anni MDCCXXXVII, Plymuthi Fact. His Accedit Opusculum de Morbo Colico Damnoniensi. London: S. Austen, 1739.

Observations on the Air and Epidemical Diseases, Made at Plymouth from the Year MDCCXXVIII [1728] to the End of the Year MDCCXXXVII [1737], to Which Is Added a Short Treatise on the Devonshire Colic. 2 vols. Vol. I, London: J. Coote; J. Staples, 1758.

The Works of John Huxham, M. D. F. R. S. In Two Volumes. II vols. Vol. I, London: W. Bent, 1788.

Ince, Joseph. 'Prosper Alpinus, de Medicina Aegyptiorum Libri Quatuor. A. D. 1591'. *Pharmaceutical Journal and Transactions* II (1860): 367–72.

Ingram, Dale. *Essay on the Nature, Cause, and Seat of Dysentery's, in a Letter to Dr. Henry Warren of Barbados.* Barbados: William Beeby, 1744.

An Historical Account of the Several Plagues That Have Appeared in the World since the Year 1346. With an Enquiry into the Present Prevailing Opinion, That the Plague Is a Contagious Distemper ... In Which the Absurdity of Such Notions Is Exposed ... To Which Are Added a Particular Account of the Yellow Fever ... Also Observations on Dr Mackenzie's Letters; ... And an Abstract of Capt. Isaac Clemens's Voyage in the Sloop Fawey. London: R. Baldwin and J. Clark, 1755.

Isaac, Benjamin H. *The Invention of Racism in Classical Antiquity.* Princeton: Princeton University Press, 2004.

Ives, Edward. *A Voyage from England to India, in the Year MDCCLIV: And an Historical Narrative of the Operations of the Squadron and Army in India, Under ... Watson And ... Clive ... Also, a Journey from Persia to England, by an Unusual Route. With an Appendix, Containing an Account of the Diseases Prevalent in Admiral Watson's Squadron: A Description of Most of the Trees, Shrubs, and Plants, of India ... Illustrated with a Chart, Maps, and Other Copper-Plates.* London: Edward and Charles Dilly, 1773.

Jackson, Maurice. *Let This Voice Be Heard: Anthony Benezet, Father of Atlantic Abolitionism.* Philadelphia: University of Pennsylvania Press, 2009.

Jamaica, Assembly. *Two Reports (One Presented the 16th of October, the Other on the 12th of November, 1788) from the Committee of the Honourable House of Assembly of Jamaica, Appointed to Examine into ... The Slave-Trade ... Published, by Order of the House of Assembly, by Stephen Fuller ... Agent for Jamaica.* London: B. White and Son; J. Sewell; R. Faulder; and J. Debrett, and J. Stockdale, 1789.

Jamaica Planter, A. *Notes on the Two Reports from the Committee of the Honourable House of Assembly of Jamaica.* London: James Phillips, 1789.

Jennings, Eric T. *Curing the Colonizers: Hydrotherapy, Climatology, and French Colonialism.* Durham, NC: Duke University Press, 2006.

Johnson, Howard. 'Introduction'. In *The History of Jamaica.* Montreal: McGill-Queens University Press, 2002.

Johnston, Katherine. 'The Constitution of Empire: Place and Bodily Health in the Eighteenth-Century Atlantic'. *Atlantic Studies* 10 (2013): 443–66.

Johnstone, James. *An Historical Dissertation Concerning the Malignant Epidemical Fever of 1756.* London: W. Johnstone, 1758.

Jordan, Winthrop D. *White over Black: American Attitudes toward the Negro, 1550–1812*. Chapel Hill: University of North Carolina Press, 1968.

Jordanova, L. J. 'Earth Science and Environmental Medicine: The Synthesis of the Late Enlightenment'. In *Images of the Earth: Essays in the History of the Environmental Sciences*, edited by L. J. Jordanova and Roy S. Porter, 119–46. London: The British Society for the History of Science, 1979.

Kant, Immanuel. 'Of the Different Human Races'. In *The Idea of Race*, edited by Robert Bernasconi and Tommy L. Lott, 8–22. Indianapolis: Hackett, 2000.

'Von den Verschiedenen Racen der Menschen'. In *Der Philosoph Für Die Welt*, edited by J. J. Engel, 125–64, Liepzig: Dr Stintzings Bibl.,1777

Kidd, Colin. 'Ethnicity in the British Atlantic World, 1688–1830'. In *A New Imperial History: Culture, Identity, and Modernity in Britain and the Empire, 1660–1840*, edited by Kathleen Wilson, 260–77. Cambridge: Cambridge University Press, 2004.

The Forging of Races: Race and Scripture in the Protestant Atlantic World, 1600–2000. Cambridge: Cambridge University Press, 2006.

King, Lester S. *The Medical World of the Eighteenth Century*. Chicago: University of Chicago Press, 1958.

The Philosophy of Medicine: The Early Eighteenth Century. Cambridge, MA: Harvard University Press, 1978.

Kiple, Kenneth F. *The Caribbean Slave: A Biological History*. Cambridge: Cambridge University Press, 1984.

Kiple, Kenneth F. and Kriemhild Coneé Ornelas. 'Race, War, and Tropical Medicine in the Eighteenth-Century Caribbean'. In *Warm Climates and Western Medicine: The Emergence of Tropical Medicine, 1500–1900*, edited by David Arnold, 65–79. Amsterdam and Atlanta: Rodopi, 1996.

Kirkwood, James. *The History of the Twenty Seven Gods of Linlithgow Being an Exact and True Account of a Famous Plea Betwixt the Town-Council of the Said Burgh, and Mr. Kirkwood*. Edinburgh: 1711.

Knox, Robert. *The Races of Men: A Fragment*. London: H. Renshaw, 1850.

Kuefler, Mathew, ed. *The Boswell Thesis: Essays on Christianity, Social Tolerance, and Homosexuality*. Chicago: University of Chicago Press, 2006.

Kuhn, Thomas S. *'The Structure of Scientific Revolutions'*. Chicago: University of Chicago Press, 1962.

Kupperman, Karen. "Fear of Hot Climates in the Anglo-American Experience". *William and Mary Quarterly* 41 (1984): 213–40.

'The Puzzle of the American Climate in the Early Colonial Period'. *The American Historical Review* 87 (1982): 1262–89.

Lancisi, Giovanni Maria. 'Of Marshes and Their Effluvia'. Translated by Samuel Latham Mitchill. In *The Medical Repository*, edited by Samuel Latham Mitchill and Edward Miller, 9–18, 126–35, 237–45, 326–30. New York: Collins & Perkins, 1810.

Laqueur, Thomas. *Making Sex: Body and Gender from the Greeks to Freud*. Cambridge, MA: Harvard University Press, 1990.

Lassone, M. de. 'Histoire de divers Accidens graves, occasionnés par les miasmes d'animaux en putrefaction, et de la nouvelle methode de traitment qui a été employé avec succés dans cette circonstance'. *Medical Commentaries* 9 (1785): 57–63.

Lawrence, Christopher. 'Priestley in Tahiti: The Medical Interests of a Dissenting Chemist'. In *Science, Medicine, and Dissent: Joseph Priestley*, edited by C. J. Lawrence and R. Anderson. London: Wellcome Trust/Science Museum, 1987.

Le Cat, Mons. 'An Account of Those Malignant Fevers, That Raged at Rouen, at the End of the Year 1753, and the Beginning of 1754'. *Philosophical Transactions* 49 (1755–6): 49–61.

Lecaan, John Polus. *Advice to the Gentlemen of the Army of Her Majesty's Forces in Spain and Portugal: With a Short Method How to Preserve Their Health; and Some Observations Upon Several Distempers Incident to Those Countries, and All Other Hot Climates, as Our Plantations in the West-Indies, &C. To Which Are Added the Medicinal Virtues of Many Peculiar Plants Growing Naturally in Those Parts, and Not Wild in England.* London: P. Varenne, 1708.

Lempriere, William. *Practical Observations on the Diseases of the Army in Jamaica, as They Occurred between the Years 1792 and 1797.* 2 vols. London: T. N. Longham and O. Rees, 1799.

Leslie, Charles. *A New History of Jamaica: From the Earliest Accounts, to the Taking of Porto Bello by Vice-Admiral Vernon. In Thirteen Letters from a Gentleman to His Friend.* London: Printed for J. Hodges, 1740.

Ligon, Richard. *A True and Exact History of the Island of Barbados.* London: Humphrey Moseley, 1657.

Lind, James. *An Essay on Diseases Incidental to Europeans in Hot Climates: With the Method of Preventing Their Fatal Consequences. To Which Is Added, an Appendix Concerning Intermittent Fevers.* London: T. Becket and P. A. de Hondt, 1768.

An Essay of the Most Effectual Means of Preserving the Health of Seamen in the Royal Navy. 2nd ed. London: D. Wilson, 1762.

A Treatise of the Scurvy. In Three Parts. Containing an Inquiry into the Nature, Causes, and Cure of That Disease. Together with a Critical and Chronological View of What Has Been Published on the Subject. London: A. Millar, 1753.

A Treatise on the Scurvy. In Three Parts. Containing an Inquiry into the Nature, Causes, and Cure, of That Disease. Together with a Critical and Chronological View of What Has Been Published on the Subject. 3rd ed. London: S. Crowder, D. Wilson and G. Nicholls, T. Cadell, T. Becket and Co. G. Pearch, and W. Woodfall, 1772.

Lind, James. *A Treatise on the Putrid and Remitting Marsh Fever, Which Raged at Bengal in the Year 1762.* Edinburgh: C. Elliot, 1776.

Lindeboom, G. A. *Herman Boerhaave: The Man and His Work.* London: Methuen, 1968.

Lining, John. *A Description of the American Yellow Fever.* Edinburgh: G. Hamilton and J. Balfour, 1756.

A Description of the American Yellow Fever, Which Prevailed at Charleston, in South Carolina, in the Year 1748. Philadelphia: Thomas Dobson, 1799.

Livingstone, David N. *Adam's Ancestors: Race, Religion, and the Politics of Human Origins.* Baltimore: Johns Hopkins University Press, 2008.

'Human Acclimatization: Perspectives on a Contested Field of Inquiry in Science, Medicine, and Geography'. *History of Science* 25 (1987): 359–94.

'Tropical Climate and Moral Hygiene: The Anatomy of a Victorian Debate'. *British Journal for the History of Science* 32, no. 1 (1999): 93–110.

Lockyer, Charles. *An Account of the Trade in India Containing Rules for Good Government in Trade ... With Descriptions of Fort St. George ... Calicut ... To Which Is Added, an Account of the Management of the Dutch in Their Affairs in India.* London: Samuel Crouch, 1711.

Long, Edward. *Candid Reflections Upon the Judgement Lately Awarded by the Court of King's Bench in Westminster Hall, on What Is Commonly Called the Negroe-Cause, by a Planter.* London: T. Lowndes, 1772.

The History of Jamaica, or, General Survey of the Antient and Modern State of the Island: With Reflections on Its Situation Settlements, Inhabitants, Climate, Products, Commerce, Laws, and Government: Illustrated with Copper Plates. 3 vols. London: T. Lowndes, 1774.

Lovejoy, Arthur O. *The Great Chain of Being: A Study of the History of an Idea.* Cambridge, MA: Harvard University Press, 1936.

M., N. 'Atkins, John (1685–1757)'. *Dictionary of National Biography* 2 (1885): 220.

Major, Andrea. *Slavery, Abolitionism, and Empire in India, 1772–1843.* Liverpool: Liverpool University Press, 2012.

Makittrick-Adair, James. 'Observations on Regimen and Preparation under Inoculation, and on the Treatment of the Natural Small-Pox, in the West Indies. To Which Are Added, Strictures on the Suttonian Practice; in a Letter to Dr Andrew Duncan'. *Medical Commentaries* 8 (1784): 211–47.

Malcolmson, Cristina. *Studies of Skin Color in the Early Royal Society: Boyle, Cavendish, Swift.* Farnham: Ashgate, 2013.

Marshall, Woodville K. 'Provision Ground and Plantation Labor in Four Windward Islands: Competition for Resources During Slavery'. In *Cultivation and Culture: Labor and the Shaping of Slave Life in the Americas*, edited by Ira Berlin and Philip D. Morgan, 203–20. Charlottesville and London: University Press of Virginia, 1993.

Mathews, Stephen. *Observations on Hepatic Diseases Incidental to Europeans in the East-Indies.* London: T. Cadell, 1783.

Mazzolini, Renato G. 'Skin Color and the Origin of Physical Anthropology (1640–1850)'. In *Reproduction, Race, and Gender in Philosophy and the Early Life Sciences*, edited by Susanne Lettow, 131–61: New York: SUNY Press, 2014.

McClellan III, James 'Science & Empire Studies and Postcolonial Studies: A Report from the Contact Zone'. In *Entangled Knowledge: Scientific Discourses and Cultural Difference*, edited by Klaus Hock and Gesa Mackenthun, 51–74. Münster: Waxmann, 2012.

McConaghey, R. M. 'John Huxham'. *Medical History* 13, no. 3 (1969): 280–7.

McCoskey, Denise Eileen. 'On Black Athena, Hippocratic Medicine, and Roman Imperial Edicts: Egyptians and the Problem of Race in Classical Antiquity'. In *Race and Ethnicity: Across Time, Space, and Discipline*, edited by Rodney D. Coates, 297–330. Leiden: Brill, 2004.

McDaniel, W. Caleb. 'Philadelphia Abolitionists and Antislavery Cosmopolitanism'. In *Antislavery and Abolition in Philadelphia: Emancipation and the Long Struggle for Racial Justice in the City of Brotherly Love*, edited by Richard Newman and James Mueller, 149–73. Baton Rouge: Louisiana State University Press, 2011.

McNeill, John Robert. *Mosquito Empires: Ecology and War in the Greater Caribbean, 1620–1914.* New York: Cambridge University Press, 2010.

Mead, Richard. 'Discourse on the Scurvy'. In *An Historical Account of a New Method for Extracting the Foul Air out of Ships, &C with the Description and Draught of the Machines, by Which It Is Performed: In Two Letters to a Friend, by Samuel Sutton, the Inventor*, edited by Samuel Sutton, 93–120. London: J. Brindley, 1749.

A Mechanical Account of Poisons: In Several Essays. London: Printed by J.R. for Ralph South, 1702.

'A Mechanical Account of Poisons: In Several Essays (4th Ed.)'. In *The Medical Works of Richard Mead*, iii-111. Dublin: Thomas Ewing, 1767.

A Short Discourse Concerning Pestilential Contagion and the Methods to Be Used to Prevent It. London: Printed [by William Bowyer] for Sam. Buckley, and Ralph Smith, 1720.

A Short Discourse Concerning Pestilential Contagion and the Methods to Be Used to Prevent It. Eighth, with large Additions ed. London: Sam. Buckley, 1722.

Meli, Domenico Bertoloni, ed. *Marcello Malpighi: Anatomist and Physician*. Firenze: Leo. S. Olschki, 1997.

Merret, Christopher. 'An Account of Several Observables in Lincolnshire, Not Taken Notice of in Camden, or Any Other Author'. *Philosophical Transactions* 19 (1695-7): 343–53.

Miller, G. '"Airs, Waters, and Places" in History'. *Journal of the History of Medicine* 17 (1962): 129–40.

Milman, Francis. 'An Account of Two Instances of the True Scurvy, Seemingly Occasioned by the Want of Due Nourishment; Being an Extract of a Letter Addressed to Dr. Baker, by Francis Milman'. *Medical Transactions, Published by the College of Physicians in London* 2 (1772): 471–85.

An Enquiry into the Source from Whence the Symptoms of the Scurvy and of Putrid Fevers Arise. London: J. Dodsley, 1782.

Mitchell, John. 'An Essay Upon the Causes of the Different Colours of People in Different Climates'. *Philosophical Transaction* 43 (1744–5): 102–50.

Moll, Herman. *Atlas Geographus: Or, a Compleat System of Geography, Ancient and Modern*. Vol. V, London: J. Nutt, 1717.

Monchy, Solomon de. *An Essay on the Causes and Cure of the Usual Diseases in Voyages to the West Indies*. London: T. Becket and P. A. De Hondt, 1762.

Monro, Donald. *An Account of the Diseases Which Were Most Frequent in the British Military Hospitals in Germany, from January 1761 to the Return of the Troops to England in March 1763. To Which Is Added, an Essay on the Means of Preserving the Health of Soldiers, and Conducting Military Hospitals*. London: A. Millar, D. Wilson, and T. Durham, 1764.

Observations on the Means of Preserving the Health of Soldiers and of Conducting Military Hospitals. And on the Diseases Incident to Soldiers in the Time of Service, and on the Same Diseases as They Have Appeared in London. In Two Volumes. By Donald Monro, M.D. 2nd ed. London: J. Murray; and G. Robinson, 1780.

John Quier, Thomas Fraser, John Hume, George Monro, and Ambrose Dawson. *Letters and Essays on the Small-Pox and Inoculation, the Measles, the Dry Belly-Ache, the Yellow, and Remitting, an Intermitting Fevers of the West Indies*. London: J. Murray, 1778.

Montagu, Ashley. *Man's Most Dangerous Myth: The Fallacy of Race*. 2nd ed. New York: Columbia University Press, 1945.

Morgan, Jennifer L. *Laboring Women: Reproduction and Gender in New World Slavery*. Philadelphia: University of Pennsylvania Press, 2004.

' "Some Could Suckle over Their Shoulder": Male Travelers, Female Bodies, and the Gendering of Racial Ideology, 1500–1770'. *The William and Mary Quarterly* 54 (1997): 167–92.

Morgan, Philip D. 'The Black Experience and the British Empire, 1680–1810'. In *Black Experience and the Empire*, edited by Philip D. Morgan and Sean Hawkins, 86–110. Oxford: Oxford University Press, 2006.

Moseley, Benjamin. *A Treatise on Sugar*. London: Printed for G.G. and J. Robinson, 1799.

A Treatise on Tropical Diseases; And on the Climate of the West-Indies. London: T. Cadell, 1787.

Mosse, George L. *Toward the Final Solution: A History of European Racism*. New York: H. Fertig, 1978.

Nash, D. W. 'The Welsh Indians: To the Editor of the Cambrian Journal'. *The Cambrian Journal* (1860): 142.

Nisbet, Richard. *Slavery Not Forbidden by Scripture. Or a Defence of the West-India Planters*. Philadelphia: 1773.

Norris, John. *Profitable Advice for Rich and Poor: In a Dialogue, or Discourse between James Freeman, a Carolina Planter, and Simon Question, a West Country Farmer. Containing a Description ... Of South Carolina*. London: J. How, 1712.

Northrup, David. *Africa's Discovery of Europe, 1450–1850*. Oxford: Oxford University Press, 2002.

Numbers, Ronald and Todd L. Savitt, eds. *Science and Medicine in the Old South*: Baton Rouge: Louisiana State University Press, 1999.

Nutton, Vivian. 'Hippocrates in the Renaissance'. *Sudhoffs Archiv* 27 (1989): 420–39.

Ogborn, Miles. 'Talking Plants: Botany and Speech in Eighteenth-Century Jamaica'. *History of Science* 51 (2013): 251–82.

Oglethorpe, J. Edward. *A New and Accurate Account of the Provinces of South-Carolina and Georgia: With Many Curious and Useful Observations on the Trade, Navigation and Plantations of Great-Britain*. London: J. Worrall, 1732.

Orland, Barbara. 'The Fluid Mechanics of Nutrition: Herman Boerhaave's Synthesis of Seventeenth-Century Circulation Physiology'. *Studies in History and Philosophy of Biological and Biomedical Sciences* 43 (2012): 357–69.

Orta, Garcia de, Francisco Manuel de Melo Ficalho, and Clements R. Markham. *Colloquies on the Simples and Drugs of India*. London: H. Sotheran, 1913.

Osborne, Michael A. 'Acclimatizing the World: A History of the Paradigmatic Colonial Science'. *Osiris* 15 (2000): 135–51.

Nature, the Exotic and the Science of French Colonialism. Bloomington: Indiana University Press, 1994.

O'Shaugnessy, Andrew Jackson. *An Empire Divided: The American Revolution and the British Caribbean*. Philadelphia: University of Pennsylvania Press, 2000.

Ovington, John. 'A Voyage to Suratt in the Year 1689'. In *India in the Seventeenth Century: Being an Account of the Two Voyages to India by Ovington and Thevenot. To Which Is Added the Indian Travels of Careri*, edited by J. P. Guha. New Delhi: Associated Publishing House, 1976.

P., L. *Two Essays Sent in a Letter from Oxford to a Nobleman in London*. London: R. Baldwin, 1695.

Pagel, Walter. 'Van Helmont's Concept of Disease – to Be or Not to Be? The Influence of Paracelsus'. *Bulletin of the History of Medicine* XLVI, no. 5 (1972): 419–54.

'Van Helmont's Ideas on Gastric Digestion and the Gastric Acid'. *Bulletin of the History of Medicine* 30 (1956): 524–36.

Parliament., Great Britain. *A Collection of the Parliamentary Debates in England, from the Year MDCLXVIII. To the Present Time*. Vol. 17, London: John Torbuck, 1739–42.

Parrish, Susan Scott. *American Curiosity: Cultures of Natural History in the Colonial British Atlantic World*. Chapel Hill: University of North Carolina Press, 2006.

Paugh, Katherine. 'The Curious Case of Mary Hylas: Wives, Slaves, and the Limits of British Abolitionism'. *Slavery and Abolition* 35 (2014): 629–51.

'The Politics of Childbearing in the British Caribbean and the Atlantic World During the Age of Abolition, 1776–1838'. *Past and Present*, no. 221 (2013): 119–60.

The Politics of Reproduction: Race, Medicine, and Fertility in the Age of Abolition. Oxford: Oxford University Press, 2017.

Pernick, Martin S. *A Calculus of Suffering: Pain, Professionalism, and Anesthesia in Nineteenth-Century America*. New York: Columbia University Press, 1985.

Petley, Christer. 'Gluttony, Excess, and the Fall of the Planter Class in the British Caribbean'. *Atlantic Studies* 9 (2012): 85–106.

Philips, John. *An Authentic Account of Commodore Anson's Expedition: Containing All That Was Remarkable, Curious and Entertaining, During That Long and Dangerous Voyage: ... Taken from a Private Journal*. London: J. Robinson, 1744.

Phillips, Edward. *The New World of Words: Or, Universal English Dictionary*. 6th ed. London: J. Phillips, 1706.

Pinckard, George and Andrew Dickson White, *Notes On the West Indies, Including Observations Relative to the Creoles and Slaves of the Western Colonies, and the Indians of South America: Interspersed with Remarks Upon the Seasoning Or Yellow Fever of Hot Climates*. 2d ed. London: Baldwin, Cradock and Joy [etc.], 1816.

Popkin, Richard H. *Isaac La Peyrère (1596–1676): His Life, Work, and Influence*. Leiden: E. J. Brill, 1987.

Pormann, Peter E. and Emilie Savage-Smith. *Medieval Islamic Medicine*. Washington, DC: Georgetown University Press, 2007.

Porter, Roy. 'Cleaning up the Great Wen: Public Health in Eighteenth-Century London'. *Medical History. Supplement* 11 (1991): 61–75.

ed. *The Medical History of Waters and Spas, Medical History Supplement 10*. London: Wellcome Institute for the History of Medicine, 1990.

Powers, John C. *Inventing Chemistry: Herman Boerhaave and the Reform of the Chemical Arts*. Chicago: University of Chicago Press, 2012.

Prakash, Gyan. *Another Reason: Science and the Imagination of Modern India*. Princeton: Princeton University Press, 1999.

Pratt, Mary Louise. *Imperial Eyes: Travel Writing and Transculturation*. 2nd ed. London and New York: Routledge, 2008.

Price, Richard. *Observations on Reversionary Payments; on Schemes for Providing Annuities for Widows, and for Persons in Old Age; on the Method of Calculating the Values of Assurances on Lives; and on the National Debt*. London: T. Cadell, 1771.

Priestley, J. 'On the Noxious Quality of the Effluvia of Putrid Marshes. A Letter from the Rev. Dr. Priestley to Sir John Pringle'. *Philosophical Transactions* 64 (1774): 90–5.

Pringle, John. *A Discourse on the Different Kinds of Air, Delivered at the Anniversary Meeting of the Royal Society, November 30, 1773*. London: Royal Society, 1774.

———. *Observations on the Diseases of the Army*. 7th ed. London: W. Strahan, J. and F. Rivington, W. Johnston, T. Payne, T. Longman, Wilson and Nicoll, T. Durham, and T. Cadell, 1775.

———. *Observations on the Diseases of the Army: In Camp and Garrison. In Three Parts. With an Appendix*. London: A. Millar, and D. Wilson; and T. Payne, 1752.

———. *Observations on the Nature and Cure of Hospital and Jayl-Fevers, in a Letter to Doctor Mead, Physician to His Majesty, &C*. London: A. Millar and D. Wilson, 1750.

Professional Planter, A (Dr Collins). *Practical Rules for the Management and Medical Treatment of Negro Slaves in the Sugar Colonies*. New York: Books for Libraries Press, 1971. 1811.

Quinlan, Sean. 'Colonial Bodies, Hygiene, and Abolitionist Politics in Eighteenth-Century France'. *History Workshop Journal* 42 (1996): 106–25.

Rabin, Dana. '"In a Country of Liberty?": Slavery, Villeinage, and the Making of Whiteness in the Somerset Case (1772)'. *History Workshop Journal* 72 (2011): 5–29.

Raj, Kapil. 'Beyond Postcolonialism ... And Postpositivism: Circulation and the Global History of Science'. *Isis* 104 (2013): 337–47.

———. *Relocating Modern Science: Circulation and the Construction of Knowledge in South Asia and Europe, 1650–1900*. Basingstoke: Palgrave Macmillan, 2007.

Ramsay, James. *An Essay on the Treatment and Conversion of African Slaves in the British Sugar Colonies*. Dublin: T. Walker, C. Jenkin, R. Marchbank, L. White, R. Burton, P. Byrne, 1784.

Ray, John. *The Correspondence of John Ray: Consisting of Selections from the Philosophical Letters Published by Dr. Derham: And Original Letters of John Ray in the Collection of the British Museum / Edited by Edwin Lankester*. London: Printed for the Ray Society, 1848.

Reardon, Jenny. *Race to the Finish: Identity and Governance in an Age of Genomics*. Princeton: Princeton University Press, 2005.

Reide, Thomas Dickson. *A View of the Diseases of the Army in Great Britain, America, the West Indies, and on Board of King's Ships and Transports, from the Beginning of the Late War to the Present Time*. London: J. Johnson, 1793.

Reviewer. 'Essay on the Medical Constitution of Great Britain'. *The Critical Review, or Annals of Literature* (1763): 186–9.

Richardson, David. 'Through a Looking Glass: Olaudah Equiano and African Experiences of the British Atlantic Slave Trade'. In *Black Experience and the Empire*, edited by Philip D. Morgan and Sean Hawkins, 58–85. Oxford: Oxford University Press, 2006.

Robertson, Robert. *A Physical Journal Kept on Board His Majesty's Ship Rainbow, During Three Voyages to the Coast of Africa, and West Indies, in the Years 1772, 1773, and 1774*. London: E. & C. Dilly, J. Robson, T. Cadell, and T. Evans, 1777.

Roddis, Louis H. *James Lind: Founder of Nautical Medicine*. New York: Henry Schuman, 1950.

Rouppe, Lewis. *Observations on Diseases Incidental to Seamen*. Translated from the Latin Edition [1764], Printed at Leyden ed. London: T. Carnan and F. Newbery, 1772.

Rush, Benjamin. *An Address to the Inhabitants of the British Settlements in America Upon Slave-Keeping (the Second Edition). To Which Are Added, Observations on a Pamphlet, Entitled, 'Slavery Not Forbidden by Scripture; or, a Defence of the West-India Planters'. By a Pennsylvanian*. Philadelphia: John Dunlap, 1773.

Rusnock, Andrea A. 'Hippocrates, Bacon, and Medical Meteorology at the Royal Society, 1700–1750'. In *Reinventing Hippocrates*, edited by David Cantor. Burlington: Ashgate, 2001.

    Vital Accounts: Quantifying Health and Population in Eighteenth-Century England and France. Cambridge: Cambridge University Press, 2002.

Rutman, Darrett B. and Anita H. Rutman. 'Of Agues and Fevers: Malaria in the Early Chesapeake'. *The William and Mary Quarterly* 33, no. 1 (1976): 31–60.

Saakwa-Mante, Norris. 'Western Medicine and Racial Constitutions: Surgeon John Atkins Theory of Polygenism and Sleepy Distemper in the 1730s'. In *Race, Science, and Medicine, 1700–1960*, edited by Waltraud Ernst and Bernard Harris, 28–57. London and New York: Routledge, 1999.

Said, Edward W. *Orientalism*. New York: Vintage, 2003.

Sargent, Frederick. *Hippocratic Heritage: A History of Ideas About Weather and Human Health*. New York: Pergamon Press, 1982.

Savitt, Todd L. *Medicine and Slavery: The Diseases and Health Care of Blacks in Antebellum Virginia*. Champaign: University of Illinois Press, 1978.

    'Slave Health and Southern Distinctiveness'. In *Disease and Distinctiveness in the American South*, edited by Todd L. Savitt and James Harvey Young, 120–53. Knoxville: University of Tennessee Press, 1988.

    'The Use of Blacks for Medical Experimentation and Demonstration in the Old South'. *The Journal of Southern History* 48 (1982): 331–48.

Schaffer, Simon, Lissa Roberts, Kapil Raj, and James Delbourgo, eds. *The Brokered World: Go-Betweens and Global Intelligence, 1770–1820*. Sagamore Beach: Science History Publications, 2009.

Schiebinger, Londa. 'Human Experimentation in the Eighteenth Century: Natural Boundaries and Valid Testing'. In *The Moral Authority of Nature*, edited by Lorraine Daston and Fernando Vidal, 384–408. Chicago: University of Chicago Press, 2004.

    'Scientific Exchange in the Eighteenth-Century Atlantic World'. In *Soundings in Atlantic History: Latent Structures and Intellectual Currents, 1500–1830*, edited by Bernard Bailyn and Patricia L. Denault, 294–328. Cambridge, MA: Harvard University Press, 2009.

    Secret Cures of Slaves: People, Plants, and Medicine in the Eighteenth-Century Atlantic World. Stanford: Stanford University Press, 2017.

Schotte, J. P. 'A Description of a Species of Sarcocele of a Most Astonishing Size in a Black Man in the Island of Senegal: With Some Account of Its Being an Endemial Disease in the Country of Galam'. *Philosophical Transactions* 73 (1783): 85–93.

    'Journal of the Weather at Senegambia, During the Prevalence of a Very Fatal Putrid Disorder, with Remarks on That Country'. *Philosophical Transactions* 70 (1780): 478–506.

A Treatise on the Synochus Atrabiliosa, a Contagious Fever, Which Raged at Senegal in the Year 1778, and Proved Fatal to the Greatest Part of the Europeans, and to a Number of the Natives. London: M. Scott, 1782.

Seth, Suman. 'Colonial History and Postcolonial Science Studies'. *Radical History Review* 127 (2017): 63–85.

'Crisis and the Construction of Modern Theoretical Physics'. *British Journal for the History of Science* 40, no. 144 (2007): 25–51.

ed. 'Focus: Re-Locating Race'. *Isis* 105, no 4 (2014): 759–814.

'The History of Physics after the Cultural Turn'. *Historical Studies in the Natural Sciences* 41 (2011): 112–22.

Sharp, Granville. *A Representation of the Injustice and Dangerous Tendency of Tolerating Slavery; or of Admitting the Least Claim of Private Property in the Persons of Men, in England.* London: Printed for Benjamin White, (no. 63) in Fleet-Street, and Robert Horsfield, (no. 22) in Ludgate Street, 1769.

Sheridan, Richard B. 'Africa and the Caribbean in the Atlantic Slave Trade'. *The American Historical Review* 77, no. 1 (1972): 15–35.

'The Doctor and the Buccaneer: Sir Hans Sloane's Case History of Sir Henry Morgan, Jamaica, 1688'. *Journal of the History of Medicine and Allied Sciences* 41 (1986): 76–87.

Doctors and Slaves: A Medical and Demographic History of Slavery in the British West Indies, 1680–1834. Cambridge: Cambridge University Press, 1985.

'The Guinea Surgeons on the Middle Passage: The Provision of Medical Services in the British Slave Trade'. *The International Journal of African Historical Studies* 14, no. 4 (1981): 601–25.

Short, Thomas. *A Comparative History of the Increase and Decrease of Mankind in England, and Several Countries Abroad ... To Which Is Added, a Syllabus of the General States of Health, Air, Seasons, and Food for the Last Three Hundred Years: And Also a Meteorological Discourse.* London: W. Nicoll, 1767.

Sims, James. *Observations on Epidemic Disorders, with Remarks on Nervous and Malignant Fevers.* London: J. Johnson; G. Robinson, 1773.

Singer, Dorothea. 'Sir John Pringle and His Circle. Part I. Life'. *Annals of Science* 6, no. 2 (1949): 127–80.

'Sir John Pringle and His Circle, II'. *Annals of Science* 6, no. 3 (1950): 229–47.

Siraisi, Nancy. *History, Medicine, and the Traditions of Renaissance Learning.* Ann Arbor: University of Michigan Press, 2007.

Sivasundaram, Sujit. 'Sciences and the Global: On Methods, Questions, and Theory'. *Isis* 101 (2010): 146–58.

Skidmore, Thomas E. *Black into White: Race and Nationality in Brazilian Thought.* New York: Oxford University Press, 1974.

Sloan, Phillip R. 'Buffon, German Biology, and the Historical Interpretation of Biological Species'. *The British Journal for the History of Science* 12, no. 2 (1979): 109.

'The Idea of Racial Degeneracy in Buffon's *Histoire Naturelle'. Studies in Eighteenth-Century Culture* 3 (1973): 293–321.

Sloane, Hans. *A Voyage to the Islands Madera, Barbados, Nieves, S. Christophers and Jamaica, with the Natural History of the Herbs and Trees, Four-Footed Beasts, Fishes, Birds, Insects, Reptiles, &C. Of the Last of Those Islands; to Which Is*

Prefix'd an Introduction, Wherein is an Account of the Inhabitants, Air, Waters, Diseases, Trade, &C. of That Place, with Some Relations Concerning the Neighbouring Continent, and Islands of America. 2 vols. London: printed by B. M. for the author, 1707 & 1725.

Sloane, Hans and Christoph L. Becker. *Johann Sloane ... Von den Krankheiten, Welche er in Jamaika Beobachtet und Behandelt hat: aus dem Englischen Übersetzt und mit Einigen Zusätzen Begleitet.* Augsburg: Klett, 1784.

Smith, Dale C. 'Medical Science, Medical Practice, and the Emerging Concept of Typhus in Mid-Eighteenth-Century Britain'. *Medical History (Supplement)* 1 (1981): 121–34.

Smith, Justin E. H. *Nature, Human Nature, and Human Difference: Race in Early Modern Philosophy.* Princeton: Princeton University Press, 2015.

Smith, Sean Morey. 'Seasoning and Abolition: Humoural Medicine in the Eighteenth-Century British Atlantic'. *Slavery and Abolition* 36 (2015): 684–703.

Snelders, Stephen. 'Leprosy and Slavery in Suriname: Godfried Schilling and the Framing of a Racial Pathology in the Eighteenth Century'. *Social History of Medicine* 26 (2013): 432–50.

Stannard, Jerry. 'Alpini, Prospero'. In *Complete Dictionary of Scientific Biography*, 124–5. Detroit: Charles Scribner's Sons, 2008.

Stepan, Nancy. *The Idea of Race in Science: Great Britain, 1800–1960.* Hamden: Archon, 1982.

Stewart, Larry. 'The Edge of Utility: Slaves and Smallpox in the Early Eighteenth Century'. *Medical History* 29 (1985): 54–70.

Stubbes, Henry. 'An Enlargement of the Observations, Formerly Publisht Numb. 27, Made and Generously Imparted by That Learn'd and Inquisitive Physician, Dr. Stubbes'. *Philosophical Transactions* 3 (1668): 699–709.

'Observations Made by a Curious and Learned Person, Sailing from England, to the Caribe-Islands'. *Philosophical Transactions* 2 (1666): 493–502.

Stuurman, Siep. 'François Bernier and the Invention of Racial Classification'. *History Workshop Journal* 50 (2000): 1–21.

Sweet, James H. *Domingo Álvares, African Healing, and the Intellectual History of the Atlantic World.* Chapel Hill: University of North Carolina Press, 2011.

Sweet, John Wood. *Bodies Politic: Negotiating Race in the American North, 1730–1830.* Baltimore: Johns Hopkins University Press, 2003.

Sydenham, Thomas. *The Whole Works of That Excellent Practical Physician, Dr. Thomas Sydenham Wherein Not Only the History and Cures of Acute Diseases Are Treated Of ... But Also the Shortest and Fastest Way of Curing Most Chronical Diseases.* 9th ed. London: Printed for J. Darby, A. Bettesworth, and F. Clay, in trust for Richard, James, and Bethel Wellington, 1729.

Sydenham, Thomas and Benjamin Rush. *The Works of Thomas Sydenham, M.D., on Acute and Chronic Diseases with Their Histories and Modes of Cure: With Notes, Intended to Accommodate Them to the Present State of Medicine, and to the Climate and Diseases of the United States.* Philadelphia: B. & T. Kite, 1815.

Tadman, Michael. 'The Demographic Cost of Sugar: Debates on Slave Societies and Natural Increase in the Americas'. *The American Historical Review* 105 (2000): 1534–75.

Tennent, John. *A Reprieve from Death: In Two Physical Chapters ... With an Appendix. Dedicated to the Right Honourable Sir Robert Walpole.* London: Printed for John Clarke, 1741.

Physical Enquiries Discovering the Mode of Translation in the Constitutions of Northern Inhabitants, on Going to, and for Some Time after Arriving in Southern Climates ... An Error ... In Recommending Vinegar to His Majesty's Fleet in the West Indies, to Prevent the Epidemic Fever ... And the Barren State of Useful Physical Knowledge, as Well as the Mercenary Practice of Physicians, by an Impartial State of Dr. Ward's Qualifications for the Practice of Physic ... Illustrated with Remarks Upon a Printed Letter to a Member of Parliament, Signed Philanthropos. London: T. Gardner, 1742.

Thevenot, Jean de. 'The Third Part of the Travels of Mr. De Thevenot, Containing the Relation of Indostan, the New Moguls and of Other People and Countries of the Indies'. In *India in the Seventeenth Century: Being an Account of the Two Voyages to India by Ovington and Thevenot. To Which Is Added the Indian Travels of Careri*, edited by J. P. Guha, 1–186. New Delhi: Associated Publishing House, 1976 [1687].

Thomas, Robert. *Medical Advice to the Inhabitants of Warm Climates, on the Domestic Treatment of All the Diseases Incidental Therein: With a Few Useful Hints to New Settlers, for the Preservation of Health, and the Prevention of Sickness.* London: J. Strahan and W. Richardson, 1790.

Tilley, Helen. 'Global Histories, Vernacular Science, and African Genealogies: Or, Is the History of Science Ready for the World?'. *Isis* 101 (2010): 110–19.

Timberland, Ebenezer. *The History and Proceedings of the House of Lords from the Restoration in 1660 to the Present Time: Containing the Most Remarkable Motions, Speeches, Debates, Orders and Resolutions.* London: Printed for Ebenezer Timberland in Ship-Yard, Temple Bar, 1742.

Tise, Larry E. *Proslavery: A History of the Defense of Slavery in America, 1701–1840.* Athens and London: University of Georgia Press, 1987.

Towne, Richard. *A Treatise of the Diseases Most Frequent in the West-Indies, and Herein More Particularly of Those Which Occur in Barbadoes.* London: J. Clarke, 1726.

Trapham, Thomas. *A Discourse of the State of Health in the Island of Jamaica with a Provision Therefore Calculated from the Air, the Place, and the Water, the Customs and Manner of Living &C.* London: Printed for R. Boulter, 1679.

Tubbs, F. 'John Atkins: An Eighteenth-Century Naval Surgeon'. *British Medical Bulletin* 5 (1947–8): 83–4.

Turner, Daniel. *Syphilis. A Practical Dissertation on the Venereal Disease ... In Two Parts.* London: Printed for R. Bonwicke, Tim. Goodwin, J. Walthoe, M. Wotton, S. Manship, Richard Wilkin, Benj. Tooke, R. Smith and Tho. Ward, 1717.

Turner, Sasha. 'Home-Grown Slaves: Women, Reproduction, and the Abolition of the Slave Trade, Jamaica 1788–1807'. *Journal of Women's History* 23 (2011): 39–62.

Van Dantzig, Albert. 'English Bosman and Dutch Bosman: A Comparison of Texts'. *History in Africa* 2 (1975): 185–216.

'Willem Bosman's "New and Accurate Description of the Coast of Guinea": How Accurate Is It?'. *History in Africa* 1 (1974): 101–8.

Van der Star, Peter, ed. *Fahrenheit's Letters to Leibniz and Boerhaave.* Leiden: Rodopi, 1983.

Vaughan, Megan. *Curing Their Ills: Colonial Power and African Illness*. Stanford: Stanford University Press, 1991.

Voltaire. *The Philosophy of History*. London: I. Allcock, 1766.

W., G. 'The Cures of the Diseased in Forraine Attempts of the English Nation, London, 1598. Reproduced in Facsimile', edited by Charles Joseph Singer. Oxford: Clarendon Press, 1915.

Walker, Timothy. 'Acquisition and Circulation of Medical Knowledge within the Early Modern Portuguese Colonial Empire'. In *Science in the Spanish and Portuguese Empires, 1500–1800*, edited by Daniela Bleichmar, Paula De Vos and Kristin Huffine, 247–70. Stanford: Stanford University Press, 2008.

Waller, Edmund. *The Works of Edmund Waller, Esq., in Verse and Prose: Published by Mr. Fenton*. London: J. and R. Tonton and S. Draper, 1744.

Wallis, Faith. 'Medicine, Theoretical'. In *Medieval Science, Technology, and Medicine: An Encyclopedia*, edited by Thomas F. Glick, Stephen Livesy and Faith Wallis, 336–40. New York: Routledge, 2005.

Wallis, P. J. and R. V. Wallis. *Eighteenth Century Medics (Subscriptions, Licences, Apprenticeships)*. 2nd ed. Newcastle Upon Tyne: Project for Historical Bibliography, 1988.

Ward, Estelle Frances. *Christopher Monck, Duke of Albemarle*. London: J. Murray, 1915.

Warren, Henry. *A Treatise Concerning the Malignant Fever in Barbados and the Neighbouring Islands: With an Account of the Seasons There, from the Year 1734 to 1738. In a Letter to Dr. Mead*. London: Printed for Fletcher Gyles against Grays-Inn in Holborn, 1740.

Watt, James. 'Surgeon James Ramsay, 1733–1789: The Navy and the Slave Trade'. *Journal of the Royal Society of Medicine* 87 (1994): 773–6.

Wear, Andrew. 'Health and the Environment in Early Modern England'. In *Medicine in Society: Historical Essays*, edited by Andrew Wear. Cambridge: Cambridge University Press, 1992.

Knowledge and Practice in English Medicine, 1550–1680. Cambridge: Cambridge University Press, 2000.

'Place, Health, and Disease: The Airs, Waters, Places Tradition in Early Modern England and North America'. *Journal of Medieval and Early Modern Studies* 38, no. 3 (2008): 443–65.

Weaver, Karol. *Medical Revolutionaries: The Enslaved Healers of Eighteenth-Century Saint Domingue*. Urbana and Chicago: University of Illinois Press, 2006.

Wey Gómez, Nicolás. *The Tropics of Empire: Why Columbus Sailed South to the Indies*. Cambridge, MA: MIT Press, 2008.

Wheeler, Roxann. *The Complexion of Race: Categories of Difference in Eighteenth-Century British Culture*. Philadelphia: University of Pennsylvania Press, 2000.

Wiecek, William M. 'Somerset: Lord Mansfield and the Legitimacy of Slavery in the Anglo-American World'. *The University of Chicago Law Review* 42, no. 1 (1974): 86–146.

Williams, John. *[an] Essay on the Bilious, or Yellow Fever of Jamaica*. Kingston, Jamaica: William Daniell, 1750.

Williams, John and Parker Bennet. *Essays on the Bilious Fever: Containing the Different Opinions of Those Eminent Physicians John Williams and Parker Bennet, of Jamaica: Which Was the Cause of a Duel, and Terminated in the Death of Both*. Jamaica and London: T. Waller, 1752.

Wilson, Alexander. *Some Observations Relative to the Influence of Climate on Vegetable and Animal Bodies*. London: T. Cadell, 1780.

Wilson, Andrew. *Rational Advice to the Military, When Exposed to the Inclemency of Hot Climates and Seasons*. London: W. Richardson, 1780.

Wilson, Kathleen. 'Empire, Trade and Popular Politics in Mid-Hanoverian Britain: The Case of Admiral Vernon'. *Past and Present* 121 (1988): 74–109.

'Introduction: Histories, Empires, Modernities'. In *A New Imperial History: Culture, Identity, and Modernity in Britain and the Empire, 1660–1840*, edited by Kathleen Wilson, 1–26. Cambridge: Cambridge University Press, 2004.

The Island Race: Englishness, Empire and Gender in the Eighteenth Century. London: Routledge, 2003.

ed. *A New Imperial History: Culture, Identity, and Modernity in Britain and the Empire, 1660–1840*. Cambridge: Cambridge University Press, 2004.

Wisecup, Kelly. *Medical Encounters: Knowledge and Identity in Early American Literatures*. Amherst: University of Massachusetts Press, 2013.

Zuckerman, Arnold. 'Dr. Richard Mead (1673–1754): A Biographical Study'. PhD Thesis. Urbana-Champaign: University of Illinois, 1965.

'Plague and Contagionism in Eighteenth-Century England'. *Bulletin of the History of Medicine* 78, no. 2 (2004): 273–308.

Index

Admiral Vernon, 103
Albemarle, Duke of, 25
Alexander, William, 18
  critique of Joseph Priestley, 151
  and the decline of the putrefactive
    paradigm, 152
  on putrefactive paradigm, 150
  on treatment of putrefaction, 151
Alpini, Prosper, 38
  Medicina Aegyptiorum, De (1591), 29, 33–4
Anderson, Adam, 251
Arbuthnot, John, 77, 126, 260
  *Essay Concerning the Effects of Air on
    Human Bodies* (1733), 65, 194
  on medical meteorology, 120
  on racial difference, 194
Atchison, Robert, 262
Atkins, John, 19, 266
  biography of, 196
  on the diseases of Africans, 198–9
  on human racial difference, 205
  on the origins of human racial
    difference, 200
  polygenism of, 202–4, 206–7
    and disease, 200
    and medical theories, 202
  on sleepy distemper, 200, 201
    and race, 202
  *Treatise on the Following Chirurgical
    Subjects, A* (1724), 196
    and polygenism, 167
  on women as origins of disease, 185
Aubrey, T
  on racial difference
  *The Sea Surgeon, or the Guinea Man's
    Vade Mecum* (1740), 192–4
Avicenna, 66

Bancroft, Dr, 245
Banks, Joseph, 268
Barbados, 70
barometer, 71

Barrère, Pierre
  on race
  skin colour, 175
Bates, Thomas, 277
Bath
  Hillary, William at, 71
Bell, John, 286
  *Inquiry into the Causes which Produce,
    and the Means of Preventing Diseases
    among British Officers, Soldiers
    and Others in the West Indies, An*
    (1791), 285
Bernier, François, 174
Bisset, Charles, 184
  biography of, 106
  on seasoning, 106
  on race, 261
Black, Joseph
  on pneumatic chemistry, 150
Blane, Gilbert
  Observations on the Diseases of Seamen
    (1785), 279
Blumenbach, Johann, 276
Boerhaave, Hermann, 18, 61, 74, 135,
    150, 161
  on drinking water for sailors, 121
  Elements of Chemistry (1735), 124–7
  as influence on John Pringle, 118
  on medicine and mechanical
    philosophy, 63
  on putrefaction, 115
    and pestilence, 126
Bontius, Jacobus, 39, 42
  biography of, 38
  Medicina Indorum, De (1645), 29, 37
  on seasoning, 98
Bosman, Willem, 40–1
  on the diseases of Africans, 192
  on seasoning, 99
  on women as origins of disease, 185
Boyle, Robert, 150, 203
Bradwell, Stephen, 115

Brocklesby, Richard
  as a paraphrase of John Pringle, 143
Buffon, Comte de
  on race, 228
    skin colour, 175

Caveri, Gernelli, 97
Chamberlaine, William, 264
Chandos, Duke of, 122
childbirth
  and disease, 183
  in the New World, 180–1
  and sexual maturity, 182–3
Chisholm, C., 264
Chisholme, James, 251
Christie, J., 44
Clark, John
  on putrefaction, 143
Cleghorn, George, 277, 288
  on gender, 182
climate
  and racial difference, 261
Cochrane, John, 70
Cochrane, William, 70
Cockburn, William, 43, 53, 277, 279
  Account of the Nature, Causes, Symptoms,
    and Cure of the Distempers that are
    Incident to Seafaring People, An, 52–3
  Sea Diseases (1696), 8
Collins, William, 274
Consolidated Slave Act of 1781, 258
contagion, 122
  miasmatic theory, 63
  theories of, 58
controlled medical trial
  Lind, James, 105
Cook, Ebeneezer
  Sot Weed Factor, The (1708), 91
Cook, James, 37
  on seasoning, 92
Cowley, Abraham, 43
Cullen, William, 118, 154, 159, 161, 272
  on epidemic fevers, 156
  on putrid fever
    First Lines of the Practice of Physic
      (1777), 155
Curtis, Charles, 286, 288

Dancer, Thomas, 153, 285
de Monchy, Solomon, 12–13, 57, 142
Dellon, Gabriel
  on race and venereal disease, 190
disease
  dry belly ache, 80
  dysentery, 39, 80

elephantiasis, 55, 61, 85
endemial vs epidemic, 84
English sweat, 78
epidemic disease vs endemic distemper, 59
joint-evil, 55
leprosy, 85
neonatal tetanus, 246
nyctalopia, 85
plague, 122
scurvy, 37, 136, 146, 161
smallpox
  inoculation, 122–3
syphilis, 41, 189
tetanus, 80
theories of, 16
treatment of, 44, 50
Tymorenses, 38
yaws, 61, 85
yellow fever, 4, 61, 70
zones of, 11, 42
d'Orta, Garcia
  Colloquies on the Simples and Drugs of
    India (1563), 33–4
Dutch West India Company, 40

empire
  and Britishness, 6
  and the history of medicine, 6
  medicine and the imaginative
    geography of, 93
  medical mapping of, 11
Estwick, Samuel
  defence of slavery, 227
  polygenism
    influence on Edward Long, 217–20

Foot, Jesse
  defence of slavery
    Defence of the Planters in the West
      Indies, A (1792), 258
Fothergill, John, 68
  on putrefaction, 144
Franklin, Benjamin, 267
Freind, John, 64

Galen/Galenic medicine, 32, 66
gender, 179
  and susceptibility to disease, 183–4
  and women as racialised origins of
    disease, 185–8
Gibbes, Philip, 257
  Instructions for the Treatment of Negroes
    (1786, 1797), 255–6
  on race and sexuality, 256
Giunti, Tomaso, 42

Grainger, James, 275
  *Essay on the More Common West-India
    Diseases* (1759), 253, 263
  on the seasoning of newly arrived slaves,
    99, 253–4
Guinea Coast, 40

Hales, Stephen, 121
  on ventilation, 121–2
Hargrave, Francis
  *Argument in the Case of James Sommerset,
    An* (1772), 216
Hauksbee, Francis, 67
Havart, Dr, 40, 41
Hendy, James, 262
Hickeringill, Edmund, 49
  Jamaica Viewed, 45
Higginson, Francis, 40
Hillary, William, 13, 57, 282, 287
  biography of, 62, 68–9
  *Inquiry into the Contents and Medicinal
    Virtues of Lincomb Spaw Water, An*
    (1742), 69
  on medicine and mechanical
    philosophy, 63
  *Observations on the Changes of the Air
    and Concomitant Epidemical Diseases
    in the Island of Barbados* (1759),
    15, 84, 86
  on the origins of disease, 78–9, 84–6
  on the septic principle, 141
  on smallpox, 65
  on treatment, 66
  weather diary of, 58, 59, 68, 71, 72, 86
  on yellow fever, 74, 79–80
Hippocrates/Hippocratic Medicine, 14,
    33, 135
  Airs, Waters, and Places, 15, 29, 36, 39, 40,
    43, 53, 58, 78, 108, 110, 180, 194, 260,
    283, 286
  and geography of disease, 59
  eighteenth-century revival of, 15, 33, 59
  Epidemics I and *III*, 58, 86, 194
  and seasonality of disease, 59
  medical environmentalism, 19, 58, 65
  and race, 194–5, 249
Hoffman, Friedrich
  on childbirth in the New World, 181
  Dissertation on Endemial Diseases, A
    (1705), 30
Holwell, J. Z., 262
Hooke, Robert, 67
Hume, David
  on race
    polygenism, 208

Hume, John, 142
  on gender and disease, 183
Hunter, John, 117, 279
  biography of, 157
  on putrid fevers
    *Observations on the Diseases of the Army
      in Jamaica*, 157
  and race, 8
Huxham, John, 118, 145
  Essay on Fevers, An (1750), 79
  on medical meteorology, 120
  *Method for Preserving the Health of Seamen in
    Long Cruises and Voyages, A* (1750), 137
  *Observations on the Air and Epidemical
    Diseases* (1758), 86, 120
  on putrefaction, 116
  on scurvy, 137n91
  hygrometer, 71

inoculation
  of enslaved women, 182
Ives, Edward, 278
  and anti-septic medicines, 144

Jamaica House of Assembly
  reports on the slave trade, 250
  response to critiques of slavery, 250
Java, 39
Jesuit's bark, 25
Johnstone, James, 145
Jurin, James, 68
  theory of the weather, 67

Kames, Lord
  on race
    polygenism, 209
Kant, Immanuel, 144, 228, 281
  on race, 247, 269
knowledge
  circulation of, 6
  local vs metropolitan, 279
  non-European, 13

Lahontan, Baron de, 281
Le Cat, Claude Nicolas
  on putrefaction, 144
Lecaan, John Polus, 43
  on seasoning, 100
Leiden, 264
  Boerhaave at, 62, 123
  Warren, Henry at, 70
Lempriere, William, 278
  on putrid fevers
    *Practical Observations on the Diseases
      of the Army in Jamaica* (1799), 159

Leslie, Charles, 82
  New History of Jamaica, A (1740), 69, 252
Lettsom, John, 70
Ligon, Richard, 44
Lind, James, 118, 161, 278, 284
  anti-scorbutic trials, 138
  biography of, 105, 112
  on decline of putrefactive theory, 146–7
  *Essay on Diseases Incidental to Europeans
    in Hot Climates, An* (1768), 93,
    108–11, 287
  on putrefaction, 112, 113–14, 138,
    141, 146
  on seasoning, 93, 106–8
  seasoning and defence of slavery, 109
Lining, John, 267
Littré, Alexis
  on race
    skin colour, 175
local knowledge
  of disease, 29
  and medical practice, 2
  and treatment of disease, 51
Lockyer, Charles, 98
Long, Edward, 19, 208, 228
  on African women as origins of
    disease, 186
  Candid Reflections (1772), 216, 221, 225
  on childbirth and race, 181
  defence of slavery, 227, 268
  History of Jamaica, The (1774), 216,
    220–7, 237, 266–7, 283
  biblical references in, 237
  and the defence of slavery, 227
  and disease, 222
  materialism in, 238
  on the necessity of slavery, 221
  on polygenism, 212
  on race, 20
    fixity of, 229–30
    hierarchies of, 231–4
    and Montagu's experiment, 235
    polygenism, 209
  on race and sexual maturity, 229
  rejection of materialism, 212
  on salt water vs creole slaves, 212
  on sexual maturity in women, 183
  on the Somerset Case (1772), 214–16
Lord Anson's fleet (1739)
  and loss of life due to scurvy, 136

Macaulay, George Dr, 254
Macbride, David
  on pneumatic chemistry, 150
Malpighi, Marcello, 174, 188
Mansfield, Lord, 213

Mathews, Stephen, 144, 185, 286
  on gender and disease, 185
Mead, Richard, 77, 159
  on the origins of disease, 78, 85
  on the origins of the plague, 122,
    127–9
  as patron for John Pringle, 118
  on putrefaction and pestilence, 127
  on scurvy, 137
  *Short Discourse Concerning Pestilential
    Contagion, A* (1720), 77
mechanical philosophy, 58
  and the body, 63, 72
  and disease, 64, 72, 74
  Newtonian physicians, 64
  Newtonian physiology, 65
medical marketplace
  structure of, 69
medical meteorology, 58, 68, 119
medicine
  empirical medicine, 7, 53, 54, 58
  naval medicine, 60
Milman, Francis
  on the decline of putrefactive theory, 147
Mitchell, John
  on race
    skin colour, 175
Monro, Donald, 182, 263, 280
  on putrefaction, 143
Montagu, Duke of, 234
  race experiment of, 233
Montesquieu, 261
  Spirit of the Laws, 260
Moryson, Fynes, 35
Moseley, Benjamin, 81, 117, 162, 272, 278,
    280, 284
  on childbirth and race, 181
  on putrefactive fevers
    *Treatise on Tropical Diseases; And on
      the Climate of the West-Indies, A*
      (1787), 156–7
  on race, 272–4
  on sexual maturity in women, 183

Nisbet, Richard
  on race
    and skin colour, 243
  *Slavery Not Forbidden by Scripture. Or a
    Defence of the West-India Planters*
    (1773), 243

Oldmixon, John
  British Empire in America (1708), 95

Paracelsus
  on race, 176

Parker, Bennet
  dual with Williams, 1–3
Peckham, George, 40
Peruvian bark, 116, 141
Peyrère, Isaac La
  on race
    polygenism, 177–8
Pitcairn, Archibald, 64, 65
pneumatic chemistry, 150
Priestley, Joseph, 18
  on pneumatic chemistry, 150
  on putrefaction
    response to William Alexander, 153
Pringle, John, 161
  biography of, 129–30
  Observations on the Diseases of the Army
    (1752), 17, 105, 131–6
  Observations on the Nature and Cure of
    Hospital and Jayl-Fevers (1750), 117
  on putrefaction, 113, 115
    and disease, 130
    and pestilence, 127
putrefaction
  conceptual origins of, 114, 115
  decline of theory of, 146–50
putrefactive paradigm, 161, 266
  critiques of, 118
  destruction of, 153
  five elements of, 115–17

Quier, John, 9, 142, 182, 251, 256, 263, 265

race
  and anatomy, 18, 210, 276
  conceptual origins of, 170–1
  and disease categories, 167n2
  fixity of, 265
  historiography of, 173, 247–8
  influence of climate on, 228
  and medicine
    relationship between, 188
  and medical practice, 5
  monogenism, 176, 208
  pathologies of, 18
  polygenism, 19, 106–8, 176
    limited influence of climate on, 231
  race medicine, 265, 276
    definition of, 168
    and race science, 6
  race science vs race medicine, 168
  role of colonies in defining, 210, 212
  role of slavery in defining, 210
  and seasoning, 109
  and skin colour, 174–6
    labour in the tropics, 266
  and venereal disease, 189–91

Ramsay, James, 252
  Essay on the Treatment and Conversion
    of African Slaves in the British
    Sugar Colonies, An (1784), 254–5
Ray, John, 25
Reide, Thomas Dickson, 278
  on putrid fevers, 160n186
Robertson, Robert
  on African women as origins of disease, 187
Rotterdam, 12
Rouppe, Lewis, 264
  on gender and disease, 183
Royal African Company, 82, 122
Royal College of Physicians, 53
Royal Society, 15, 122, 268
Rush, Benjamin, 57, 252, 261
  Address to the Inhabitants in America upon
    Slave Keeping, An (1773), 241
  anti-slavery arguments in, 241–3
  biography of, 241
  on race
    and skin colour, 243

Schotte, Johann
  on disease and skin colour, 268–70
seasoning, 49, 60, 217, 246, 247
  colonial vs metropolitan discourses, 93
  conceptual origins of, 94
  early accounts of
    Beverley, Robert, 95
    Dampier, William, 98
    Denton, Daniel, 94n12
    Fitzhugh, William, 95
    Merret, Christopher, 95
    Norris, John, 95
    Oglethorpe, James, 96
    Phillips, Edward, 96
    Pym, John, 94
    Smith, John, 94
  etymology of, 5, 91–3
  impossibility of, 98
  in the metropole, 100
  of newly arrived slaves, 253
  opposition to, 96
  sickness, 5, 11, 76, 93
Seven Years War, 162
  impact on British culture, 102–3
Sharp, Granville, 213
slave trade, 40, 61
  and Barbados, 81
  and disease, 81
  and Jamaica, 81
  and sugar production, 81
slavery
  abolitionism, 19
  and gender, 182

slavery (*cont.*)
  and medical men, 246
  polygenism, 209
  role of medical texts, 247, 251
  and abortion, 257
  defence of by medical men, 258
  and diet of slaves, 262–5
  medical care of slaves, 253–6
  medical defences and critiques of, 20
  and reproduction, 83–4, 255–7
  role of medical texts in maintaining, 247
  slave insurrections, 235
  working conditions, 81–3
Sloane, Hans, 15, 21, 25–8, 43, 45, 46, 49, 54,
    56, 70, 77, 191
  History of Plants (1686–1704), 25
  Newgate experiment, 122
  on race, 51
  and disease, 189
  on seasoning, 92, 96–7
  Voyage to the Islands Madera, Barbados,
    Nieves, S. Christophers and Jamaica,
    A, (1707 & 1725), 27
Smollett, Tobias
  Adventures of Roderick Random, The
    (1748), 204
Somerset Case (1772), 211
  ruling in, 213–14
  impact on West Indian planters, 214
Somerset, James
  biography of, 213
Sydenham, Thomas, 42, 46, 48, 50, 59, 68,
    76, 120
  on race, 51
  on slave trade and origins of disease, 191

Taylor, George, 245
Thevenot, Jean de
  on childbirth in the New World, 180
Thomas, Robert
  on African women as origins of disease, 186
  defence of slavery, 259
  on putrid fevers, 160
Towne, Richard, 74, 87, 287
  biography of, 74
  on the diseases of Africans, 192
  local knowledge of, 75
  Treatise of the Diseases Most Frequent in
    the West Indies, A (1726), 30, 54
  on yellow fever, 74, 80, 87
Trapham, Thomas, 26, 43, 46, 48, 49,
    54, 56
  Discourse on the State of Health the Island
    of Jamaica (1679), 26

  on race and origins of disease, 189–90
  on seasoning, 96
  on venereal disease, 47
Trelawney, Edward Governor, 257
tropical diseases, 287
tropical medicine, 4
Turner, Daniel, 42

UNESCO Statement on Race (1950), 281

Van Helmont, Jean Baptiste, 124
Vespucci, Amerigo, 41
  on childbirth in the New World, 180
von Haller, Albrecht, 272

Waller, Edmund, 43
War of Austrian Succession
  impact on British culture, 102–3
  and works on disease, 104
War of Jenkins' Ear, 102–3
  impact on British culture, 104
  origins of, 101
  and seasoning of troops
    Bathurst, Lord, 101
    Hervey, Lord, 102
  and works on disease
    Tennent, John, 104
    Warren, Henry, 104
Warren, Henry, 70, 74, 287
  on the origins of disease, 78, 85
  on yellow fever, 75–7, 84
weather diary, 34–5
West Indies, 44
  Barbados, 68
  and disease, 8, 12, 58
  Jamaica, 49, 153, 235
  climate of, 50
  Code Noir, 225
Whetstone, George, 36
Wilberforce, William, 250
Williams, Francis
  and Montagu's experiment, 233
Williams, John
  dual with Bennet, 1–3
  Essay on the Bilious, or Yellow Fever of
    Jamaica, An (1750), 1
  on gender and disease, 185
Wilson, Alexander
  on putrefaction, 153
  Some Observations Relative to the Influence
    of Climate on Vegetable and Animal
    Bodies (1780), 269–71
Wilson, Andrew
  on putrefaction, 142